Today's most **popular authors** have collaborated on this exciting new series, which combines **great literature** with remarkably **effective instruction,** bringing real writers and real tools together for real results.

Give your students

Real writers unprecedented access to award-winning authors (see page T2)

Real tools remarkably effective tools for differentiated instruction (see page T4)

Real results built-in benchmarking to guarantee standards mastery and learning success (see page T6)

> **This project is what I wish I'd had when I was in school . . . a resource where I could not only read really good writing, but also get a sense about how the authors actually felt!**
>
> **—Cornelius Eady**
> featured unit author

TEACHER'S EDITION CONTENTS

TEACHER'S EDITION

PRENTICE HALL LITERATURE

PENGUIN  EDITION

THE AMERICAN EXPERIENCE

VOLUME I

Upper Saddle River, New Jersey
Boston, Massachusetts

ISBN 0-13-131758-X
2 3 4 5 6 7 8 9 10   09 08 07 06 05

Real writers

Fifty-three of today's most popular writers have collaborated on this extraordinary new program.

Now your students can learn about reading, writing, and literature from the authors themselves as they share their personal experiences, insights, and expertise while presenting key instructional concepts.

"It's a little bit like having you, the students, come backstage with Tim O'Brien, a writer."

—**Tim O'Brien**
Grade 11, Unit 5 author

JUDITH ORTIZ COFER INTRODUCES
"Ithaka" by Constantine Cavafy

An Interview with Judith Ortiz Cofer
Conducted by Prentice Hall

What aspect of the ancient Greek epic the *Odyssey* would most help someone reading Cavafy's "Ithaka"? The *Odyssey* contains worlds. It's a love story. It's a story of a man trying to get back home to his wife after fighting and suffering in a long war. It's a story of a king and a story of loyalty. But to Cavafy, I think it was especially a story of the journey in between here and there. He shows you how the journey becomes a symbolic journey, standing for your life and goals

…poem is so often recited at graduations …nies? Yes, the theme is that, when you go

Judith Ortiz Cofer has won numerous awards for her work as a poet, an essayist, and a novelist. In 1994, she won the O. Henry Prize for short story. Ort…

Each **unit** in *Prentice Hall Literature* is hosted by one of the featured **authors**. Each author serves as a **guide** for your students, taking them on an unforgettable journey through the writer's world, and introducing them to a universe of great literature.

Give your students unprecedented access to award-winning authors!

JAMAICA KINCAID INTRODUCES

from Annie John: A Walk to the Jetty

Jamaica Kincaid

Jamaica Kincaid won the Morton Dauwen Zabek Award for *At the Bottom of the River* (1983) and she was a finalist for the PEN Faulkner Award for *The Autobiography of My Mother* (1995). Kincaid's stories often focus on the development of relationships between women, especially between mothers and daughters.

Making Memories and Stories

I come from a small island in the Caribbean that was part of the British Empire until the early 1970s when it gained political independence. Everyone I knew was literate and everyone I knew told stories.

My mother, in particular, not only knew how to read, she did so for sheer pleasure. At the time, she was the only person I ever saw do this, sit and read just for the sake of reading.

She also told me stories but these stories were not folk tales or stories about revered ancestors; they were stories about what she was like as a child, what her mother and father did, what had happened to her before I was born, what the world into which I was born was like before I was born, what the day was like when I took my first steps, the first words I said, the things I liked to eat. I was too young then to make proper memories for myself and so the memory I have of that time are the memories she created for me.

It was at that time, the time before I could make my own memories, that she taught me to read. I believe now that this set of circumstances, my mother telling me stories and teaching me to read, led to my own obsession with literature and writing and especially writing about her.

The Influence of Autobiography

Walk to the Jetty
novel traces th

Each author

- hosts a unit in *Prentice Hall Literature*
- introduces a literary genre or historical period
- provides insight into the "story behind the story"
- answers questions about writing and literature from real students
- shares their expertise as scholars or translators of great works of literature

From the Author's Desk DVD

A corresponding video program brings your students into the writer's world as the authors explain how their personal experiences shaped their writing, and how they use the world around them to create the stories that inform, engage, and entertain readers around the world.

Real tools

Presenting: QuickTake™
instant progress monitoring as easy as 1, 2, 3!

1. Pose questions to the entire class
2. Students answer via response pads
3. Results are recorded and displayed instantly

Deliver differentiated instruction easily and seamlessly.

For every selection:

- **Leveled Reading Warmups**
  Brief reading passages comprising high-interest text and low-level Lexile™ vocabulary pre-teach essential reading skills.
- **Leveled Vocabulary Warmups**
  Lexiled™ word lists and activities prepare students for reading selections.
- **Leveled Assessment**
  Two levels of selection tests allow you to provide assessment targeted for different ability levels.
- **Reader's Notebook series**
  3 levels of interactive readers support every selection.

Technology to help you Plan, Teach, and Assess:

- **TeacherEXPRESS™**
  Powerful lesson planning, resource management, and standards-aligned assessment tools all in one place make class preparation quick and easy!
- **StudentEXPRESS™**
  An interactive textbook, electronic worksheets, and links to online activities make this the perfect student tool for studying or test review.
- **Exam*View*™ Test Generator**
  Create standards-aligned tests in seconds or customize tests to suit individual students' needs.

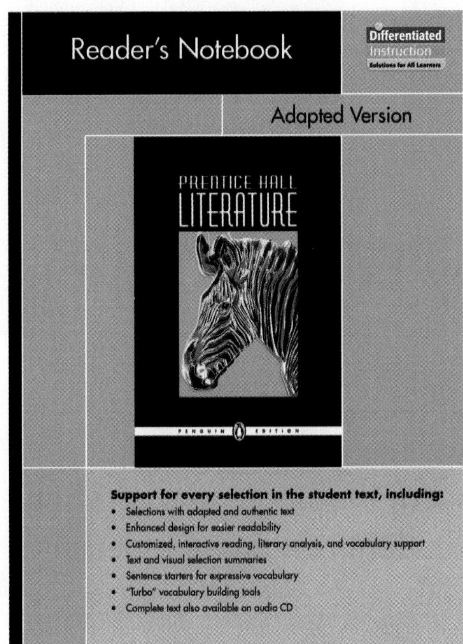

Reader's Notebook
Differentiated
Instruction
Adapted Version
PRENTICE HALL
LITERATURE
PENGUIN EDITION
Support for every selection in the student text, including:
• Selections with adapted and authentic text
• Enhanced design for easier readability
• Customized, interactive reading, literary analysis, and vocabulary support
• Text and visual selection summaries
• Sentence starters for expressive vocabulary
• "Turbo" vocabulary building tools
• Complete text also available on audio CD

Three levels of Reader's Notebooks ensure all students get the help they need.

The Reader's Notebook is an interactive companion to the student text that provides additional support for the skills presented. The Adapted version provides additional scaffolding through the use of modified text summaries and partially filled-in graphic organizers, while the English Learner's version provides additional language and vocabulary support.

Accessibility at a Glance charts help you find the best fit for your students.

These charts, at the beginning of each selection grouping, provide a quick way to determine which selections will be more accessible—and more challenging—for your students.

Differentiated Instruction Solutions for All Learners

Accessibility at a Glance

	Creation Hymn	Night
Context	Hindu speculations about the world's origin	Hindu belief in nature's protective forces
Language	Abstract nouns and several series of short questions	Concrete nouns and different personal pronouns referring to a goddess
Concept Level	Accessible (The origin of the world is mysterious.)	Accessible (Think of night as a protective goddess.)
Literary Merit	Vedic hymn from the *Rig Veda*	Vedic hymn from the *Rig Veda*
Lexile	590	590
Overall Rating	Average	Average

Differentiated Instruction Solutions for All Learners

Strategy for Less Proficient Readers
Have students identify three of the four short story elements—main characters, setting, and main events of the plot. Have them use these three elements to try to establish the story's theme or themes.

Strategy for English Learners
Have students diagram the story's plot. Remind them that plot consists of exposition, rising action, climax, falling action, and resolution. Can students find all five stages in this story, or do they think it is missing one or more stages? Which ones?

Strategy for Advanced Readers
Have students discuss which narrative element—plot, character, setting, or theme—is most important to this story. Have them explain their answers in brief essays.

Differentiated instruction for every selection.

These notes provide specific strategies you can use to tailor instruction for all students, including English-language learners, gifted students, and less-proficient readers.

Real results

Catch small learning problems before they become big ones!

Diagnose Readiness

Brief assessments at the beginning of each part determine student readiness to learn new skills.

Monitor Progress

Assessment Practice features after each selection set check skills proficiency and make sure students are on track.

Benchmark Mastery

Frequent benchmark tests gauge standards mastery and determine whether intervention is needed.

Online Reading Intervention

Introducing: Prentice Hall Success Tracker™
Help your students make real progress!

This fully automated, interactive online diagnostic and remediation system provides:

- Diagnosis and benchmarking of skills
- Customized skills practice
- At-a-glance standards reporting

See page T80 for more information.

Built-in benchmarking ensures success

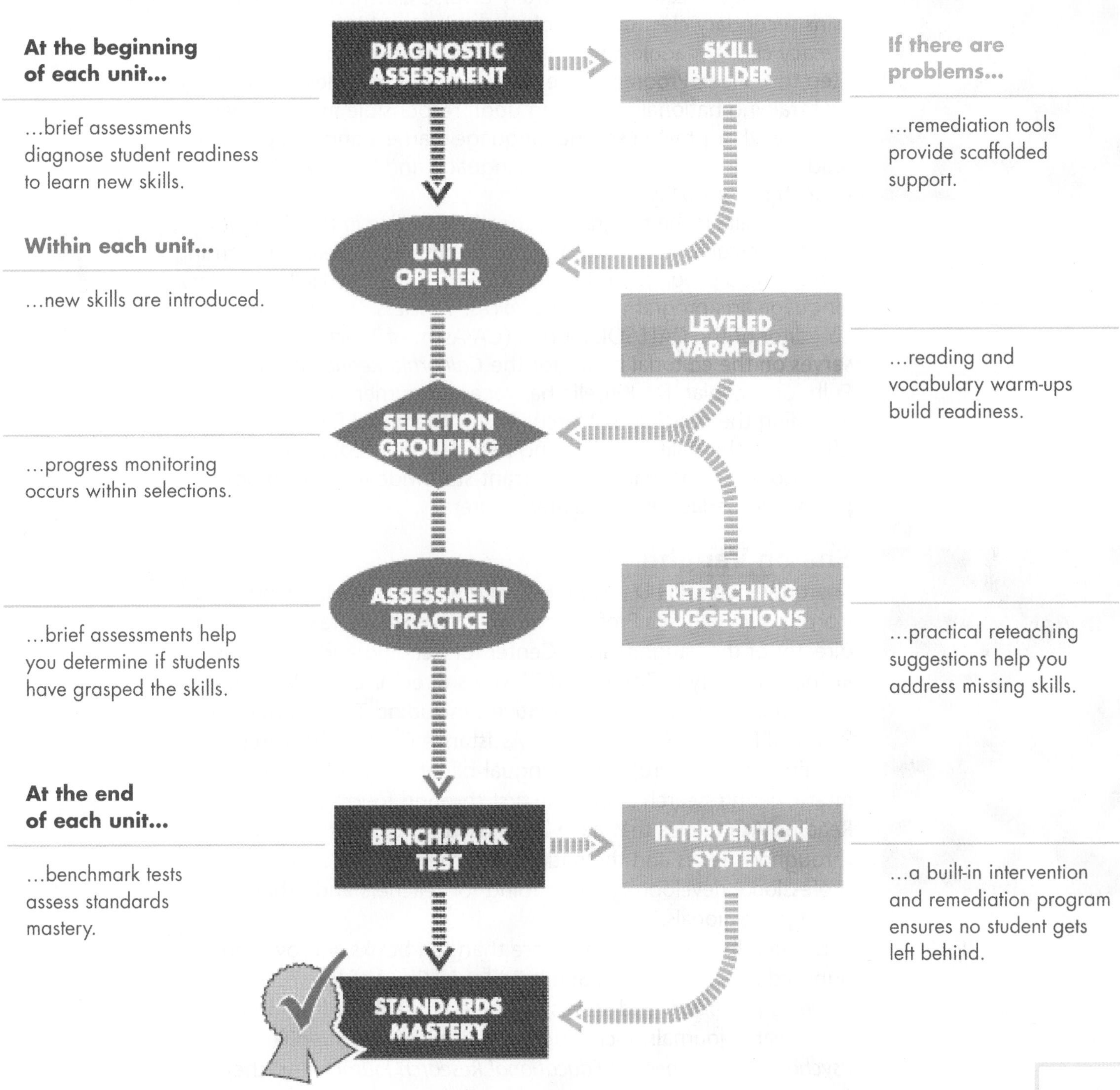

At the beginning of each unit...
...brief assessments diagnose student readiness to learn new skills.
DIAGNOSTIC ASSESSMENT
SKILL BUILDER
If there are problems...
...remediation tools provide scaffolded support.
Within each unit...
...new skills are introduced.
UNIT OPENER
LEVELED WARM-UPS
...reading and vocabulary warm-ups build readiness.
SELECTION GROUPING
...progress monitoring occurs within selections.
ASSESSMENT PRACTICE
RETEACHING SUGGESTIONS
...brief assessments help you determine if students have grasped the skills.
...practical reteaching suggestions help you address missing skills.
At the end of each unit...
...benchmark tests assess standards mastery.
BENCHMARK TEST
INTERVENTION SYSTEM
...a built-in intervention and remediation program ensures no student gets left behind.
STANDARDS MASTERY

CONTRIBUTING AUTHORS

The contributing authors guided the direction and philosophy of Prentice Hall Literature: Penguin Edition. Working with the development team, they helped to build the pedagogical integrity of the program and to ensure its relevance for today's teachers and students.

Kate **Kinsella**

Kate Kinsella, Ed.D., is a teacher educator in the Department of Secondary Education at San Francisco State University. She teaches coursework addressing academic language and literacy development in linguistically and culturally diverse classrooms. She maintains secondary classroom involvement by teaching an academic literacy class for adolescent English learners through the University's Step to College Program. She publishes and provides consultancy and training nationally, focusing upon responsible instructional practices that provide second language learners and less proficient readers in grades 4–12 with the language and literacy skills vital to educational mobility.

Dr. Kinsella is the program author for *Reading in the Content Areas: Strategies for Reading Success,* published by Pearson Learning and the lead program author for the 2002 Prentice Hall secondary language arts program *Timeless Voices: Timeless Themes.* She is the co-editor of the CATESOL Journal (CA Assn. of Teachers of ESL) and serves on the editorial board for the *California Reader.* A former Fulbright scholar, Dr. Kinsella has received numerous awards, including the prestigious Marcus Foster Memorial Reading Award, offered by the California Reading Association in 2002 to a California educator who has made a significant statewide impact on both policy and pedagogy in the area of literacy.

Sharon **Vaughn**

Sharon Vaughn, PH.D., is the H.E. Hartfelder/The Southland Corporation Regents Professor at the University of Texas and also director of the Vaughn Gross Center for Reading and Language Arts at the University of Texas (VGCRLA). As director of the VGCRLA, she leads more than five major initiatives, including The Central Regional Reading First Technical Assistance Center; the Three-Tier Reading Research Project; a bilingual-biliteracy (English/Spanish) intervention research study; the first through fourth grade Teacher Reading Academies that have been used for teacher education throughout Texas and the nation; and the creation of online professional development in reading for teachers and other interested professionals.

Dr. Vaughn has published more than ten books and over one hundred research articles. She is Editor in Chief of the *Journal of Learning Disabilities* and serves on the editorial board of more than ten research journals, including the *Journal of Educational Psychology,* the *American Educational Research Journal,* and the *Journal of Special Education.*

Kevin **Feldman**

Kevin Feldman, Ed.D., is the Director of Reading and Intervention for the Sonoma County Office of Education and an independent educational consultant. He publishes and provides consultancy and training nationally, focusing upon improving school-wide literacy skills as well as targeted interventions for struggling readers, special-needs students, and second language learners. Dr. Feldman is the co-author of the California Special Education Reading Task Force report and the lead program author for the 2002 Prentice Hall secondary language arts program *Timeless Voices: Timeless Themes.* He serves as technical consultant to the California Reading and Literature Project and the CalSTAT State Special Education Improvement Project. Dr. Feldman has taught for nineteen years at the university level in Special Education and Masters' level programs for University of California, Riverside and Sonoma State University.

Dr. Feldman earned his undergraduate degree in Psychology from Washington State University and has a Master's Degree from UC Riverside in Special Education, Learning Disabilities, and Instructional Design. He has an Ed.D. from the University of San Francisco in Curriculum and Instruction.

Differentiated Instruction Advisor

Don **Deshler**

Don Deshler, Ph.D, is the Director of the Center for Research on Learning (CRL) at the University of Kansas. Dr. Deshler's expertise centers on adolescent literacy, learning strategic instruction, and instructional strategies for teaching content-area classes to academically diverse classes. He is the author of *Teaching Content to All: Evidence-Based Inclusive Practices in Middle and Secondary Schools,* a text which presents the instructional practices that have been tested and validated through his research at CRL.

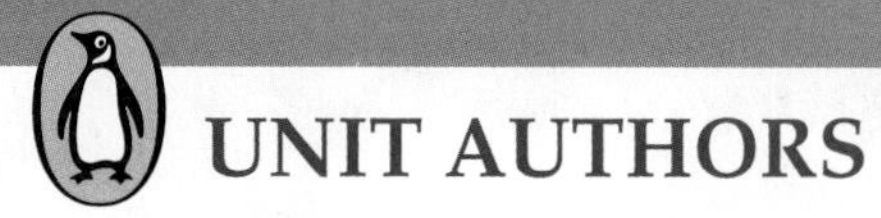

UNIT AUTHORS

An award-winning contemporary author hosts each unit in each level of *Prentice Hall Literature: Penguin Edition.* In the upper-level courses, some of these authors are renowned scholars or translators, while others are famous for their own contributions to literature. All of these authors serve as guides for your students, helping to introduce the period or culture covered in a unit, discussing the work of a traditional author or their own work or translation, and revealing their own writing processes. Following are the featured unit authors who guide students for The American Experience.

Susan **Power (b. 1961)**

Unit 1: Beginnings–1750

Native American novelist Susan Powers is the ideal guide for this unit. She discusses the oral tradition and introduces her own work in relation to traditional Native American selections. Of Dakota Sioux heritage, Ms. Power won the PEN/Hemingway Award for First Novel for *The Grass Dancer.*

William L. **Andrews (b. 1946)**

Unit 2: A Nation Is Born (1750–1800)

Professor William L. Andrews, who studies the links between white and black writers in the formation of American literature, is well suited to introduce this unit and the work of Olaudah Equiano. Holder of a named chair at the University of North Carolina, Professor Andrews is a co-editor of *The Norton Anthology of African American Literature.*

Gretel **Ehrlich (b. 1946)**

Unit 3: A Growing Nation (1800–1870)

Gretel Ehrlich, one of the best essayists writing on nature today, is the perfect choice to introduce this unit and the work of Thoreau. Ehrlich's books have received many prizes, including the Harold D. Vursell Award from the American Academy of Arts and Letters. Newsday called her essays in *The Solace of Open Spaces* "stunning."

Charles **Johnson (b. 1948)**

Unit 3: A Growing Nation (1800–1870)

Charles Johnson's versatility and individualism would have delighted Emerson, the author whom he introduces. Johnson, who in high school was influenced by Emerson's essays, is the author of the novel *Middle Passage,* a National Book Award winner, as well as screenplays and works of philosophy.

Nell Irvin **Painter (b. 1942)**

Unit 4: Division, Reconciliation, and Expansion (1850–1914)

Nell Irvin Painter introduces this unit and the work of Sojourner Truth. Her qualifications include her award-winning books *Standing at Armageddon,* which focuses on the time period covered by this unit, and *Sojourner Truth, a Life, a Symbol.* Currently the Edwards Professor of American History at Princeton University, Ms. Painter was the Director of Princeton's Program in African-American Studies from 1997 to 2000.

Tim **O'Brien (b. 1946)**

Unit 5: Disillusion, Defiance, and Discontent (1914–1946)

One of the best novelists writing today, Tim O'Brien pays homage to authors from this unit that he first read in high school. He also introduces his story "Ambush," which builds on the work of early twentieth-century writers as it explores themes arising from wartime experience. Mr. O'Brien's novel *Going After Cacciato* won the National Book Award, and *The Things They Carried,* from which *"Ambush"* comes, was a Pulitzer Prize finalist.

Arthur **Miller (1915–2005)**

Unit 6: Prosperity and Protest (1946–Present)

Arthur Miller, whose play *The Crucible* is a major selection in the unit, introduces both the unit and the play. Widely regarded as a great American playwright, Miller discusses theater's contribution to society and provides personal and historical background on the writing of *The Crucible.* Among other honors, Miller received a Pulitzer Prize for *Death of a Salesman,* a Tony Award for lifetime achievement, and a National Medal of the Arts.

PROGRAM ADVISORS

The program advisors provided ongoing input throughout the development of *Prentice Hall Literature: Penguin Edition.* Their valuable insights ensure that the perspectives of the teachers throughout the country are represented within this literature series.

Sherice Alford
Language Arts Instructor
Cape Fear Senior High School
Fayetteville, North Carolina

Leslie Ballard
State Director
North Central Association CASI
Indiana State University
Terre Haute, Indiana

Heather Barnes
Language Arts Instructor
Central Crossing High School
Grove City, Ohio

Kathryn Shelley-Barnes
District Support Specialist
Traverse City Central High School
Traverse City, Michigan

Karen C. Lilly-Bowyer
Instructional Services Assessment Team
Winston-Salem Forsyth County Schools
Winston-Salem, North Carolina

Lee Bromberger
English Department Chairperson
Mukwonago High School
Mukwonago, Wisconsin

Shawn L. Brumfield
Literacy Coach
Horace Mann Middle School
Los Angeles Unified School District
Local 3
Los Angeles, California

Susanne Buttrey
Librarian
Sycamore Middle School
Pleasant View, Tennessee

Denise Campbell
K-12 Literacy Content Coordinator
Cherry Creek School District
Centennial, Colorado

Patricia A. Cantrowitz
Language Arts Instructor (Retired)
Union-Endicott High School

Holly Carr
Language Arts Instructor
Central Crossing High School
Grove City, Ohio

Melody Renee Chalmers
Language Arts Instructor
E. E. Smith High School
Fayetteville, North Carolina

Susan Cisna
Language Arts Instructor
East Prairie Junior High School
Tuscola, Illinois

Barbra Evans-Thompson
English Department Chairperson
Westover High School
Fayetteville, North Carolina

Ebony Forte
Language Arts Instructor
Pine Forest Senior High School
Fayetteville, North Carolina

Linda Fund
Reading Specialist
Ezra L. Nolan Middle School #40
Jersey City, New Jersey

Karen Gibson, Ph.D.
Communication Arts Program Leader
Appleton Area School District
Appleton, Wisconsin

Gail Hacker
Language Arts Instructor, Retired
North Charleston High School
North Charleston, South Carolina

Kimberly Hartman
Language Arts Instructor
Franklin Heights High School
Columbus, Ohio

Doris Sue Hawkins
Language Arts Instructor
C. W. Otto Middle School
Lansing, Michigan

Darby Holley
Language Arts Instructor
Henry L. Sneed Middle School
Florence, South Carolina

Helen Hudson
Language Arts Instructor
Crawfordsville High School
Crawfordsville, Indiana

Kathleen Keane
English Department Chairperson
Foxborough High School
Foxborough, Massachusetts

John Kiser
English Curriculum Specialist (Retired)
Charlotte-Mecklenburg Schools
Charlotte, North Carolina

Cheryl W. Lee
Language Arts Instructor
Douglas Byrd High School
Fayetteville, North Carolina

Carrie Lichtenberg
Language Arts Instructor
Highlands High School
Ft. Thomas, Kentucky

Catherine Linn
Language Arts Instructor
Palm Springs High School
Palm Desert, California

Agathaniki Locklear
District Technology Resource Teacher
Kenton County Schools
Ft. Wright, Kentucky

John Ludy
Language Arts Instructor
Fremont High School
Fremont, Indiana

Louise R. Matthewson
Language Arts Instructor
Albuquerque Public Schools
Albuquerque, New Mexico

Sherrie McDowell
Language Arts Instructor
Central High School
Cheyenne, Wyoming

Suzanne Mitoraj
English/Language Arts Consultant
Berlin, Connecticut

Nancy Monroe
Language Arts Instructor
Bolton High School
Alexandria, Louisiana

Gail Phelps
Language Arts Instructor
Northwood Middle School
North Little Rock, Arkansas

Matthew Scanlon
K-12 Humanities Supervisor
Hackettstown Public Schools
Hackettstown, New Jersey

John Scott
Language Arts Instructor (Retired)
Hampton City Schools
Hampton City, Virginia

Jean Shope
Language Arts Instructor
Grant Middle School
Albuquerque, New Mexico

Margaret St. Sauver
Staff Development-English/Language Arts
St. Paul Public Schools
St. Paul, Minnesota

Steve Thalheimer
Language Arts Instructor
Lawrenceburg High School
Lawrenceburg, Indiana

Cathy Robbs Turner
Director of Academies
Chattanooga Central High School
Harrison, Tennessee

Sandra VanBelois
Language Arts Instructor
Jack Britt High School
Fayetteville, North Carolina

Martha Lee Wildman
Language Arts Instructor
Lynn Middle School
Las Cruces, New Mexico

Melissa Williams
Language Arts Instructor
Delsea Regional High School
Franklinville, New Jersey

Charles Youngs
HS Language Arts Curriculum Facilitator
Bethel Park High School
Bethel Park, Pennsylvania

CONTENTS IN BRIEF

Unit 1

A Gathering of Voices:
Literature of Early America (Beginnings to 1750)

Unit 2

A Nation Is Born

Early National Literature (1750–1800)

From the Scholar's Desk

William L. Andrews

Part One Voices for Freedom

Unit 3

A Growing Nation

Nineteenth-Century Literature (1800–1870)

From the Scholar's Desk

Gretel Ehrlich

Part One Fireside and Campfire

Part Two Shadows of the Imagination

Unit 4

Division, Reconciliation, and Expansion: The Age of Realism (1850–1914)

Unit 5

Disillusion, Defiance, and Discontent:
The Modern Age (1914–1946)

Unit 6

Prosperity and Protest

The Contemporary Period (1946–Present)

From the Author's Desk

Arthur Miller

Part One Literature Confronts the Everyday

INFORMATIONAL TEXTS AND OTHER NONFICTION

Reading Informational Materials—Instructional Workshops

Additional Nonfiction—Selections by Type

Primary Sources: Political Texts and Speeches

Primary Sources: Diaries, Journals, and Letters

Essays:

Narrative Accounts

Autobiography

Historical and Literary Background

INFORMATIONAL TEXTS AND OTHER NONFICTION
(continued)

The American Experience—Reading in the Humanities

Literature in Context—Reading in the Content Areas

A Closer Look

Focus on Literary Forms

SKILLS WORKSHOPS

Writing Workshops

SAT® PREP ACT

Vocabulary Workshops

SAT® PREP ACT

Assessment Workshops

SAT® PREP ACT

Communications Workshops

Connections to Literature

Literature Around the World

British Literature

PRENTICE HALL LITERATURE: A RICH TRADITION OF LEARNING SUCCESS

The Research Process

Since 1988, *Prentice Hall Literature* has been at the forefront of language arts instruction, providing teachers and their students with quality instruction and assessment tools to ensure success. Each successive edition builds on the strong heritage of *Prentice Hall Literature*.

To develop the current edition of *Prentice Hall Literature*, we conducted a variety of research studies, yielding three key elements of an effective language arts program: clean, clear, non-distracting design with considerate text; systematic, consistent skills instruction; and built-in benchmarking to ensure learning success. Our research comprised these three design stages:

1 EXPLORATORY NEEDS ASSESSMENT

In conjunction with Prentice Hall authors, we conducted research proven to explore educational reading methodologies. This research was incorporated into our instructional strategy and pedagogy to create a more effective literature program. This stage included:

- Reading research
- Review of state standards
- Teacher interviews

2 FORMATIVE RESEARCH, DEVELOPMENT AND FIELD TESTING

During this phase of the research, we developed and field-tested prototype material with students and teachers. Results informed revisions to the final design and pedagogy. Formative research included:

- Field testing of prototypes in classroom pilots
- Classroom observations
- Teacher reviews
- Supervisor reviews
- Educator advisory panels

3 SUMMATIVE RESEARCH, VALIDATION RESEARCH

Finally, we have conducted and will continue to conduct longer-term research under actual classroom conditions. Research at this phase includes:

- Pilot-testing
- Prepublication learner verification research
- Postpublication validation studies, including validation of test questions
- Evaluation of results on standardized tests

RESEARCH BIBLIOGRAPHY

Reading

Alexander, Patricia A., and Tamara Jetton. "Learning from Text: A Multidimensional and Developmental Perspective." In *Handbook of Reading Research*, vol. 3, ed. M. L. Kamil, P. B. Mosenthal, P. D. Pearson, and R. Barr, 285–310. Mahwah, NJ: Lawrence Erlbaum Associates, 2000.

Finders, Margaret J. and Susan Hynds. *Literacy Lessons: Teaching and Learning with Middle School Students.* Upper Saddle River, NJ: Merrill, 2003.

Guthrie, John T. and Allan Wigfield. "Engagement and Motivation in Reading." In *Handbook of Reading Research,* vol. 3, ed. M. L. Kamil, P. B. Mosenthal, P. D. Pearson, and R. Barr, 403–422. Mahwah, NJ: Lawrence Erlbaum Associates, 2000.

Harvey, Stephanie, and Anne Goudvis. "Determining Importance in Text: The Nonfiction Connection." In *Strategies That Work: Teaching Comprehension to Enhance Understanding.* Portland, ME.: Stenhouse Publishers, 2000.

Langer, Judith. "Beating the Odds: Teaching Middle and High School Students to Read and Write Well," 1999. Center on English Learning and Achievement. May 2003. <http://cela.albany.edu/eie2/main.html>

National Reading Panel. *Teaching Children to Read: An Evidence-Based Assessment of the Scientific Research on Reading and Its Implications for Reading Instruction.* NIH Publication 00-4769. Bethesda, MD: U.S. Department of Health and Human Services, 2000.

Pressley, Michael. "What Should Comprehension Instruction Be the Instruction Of?" In *Handbook of Reading Research*, vol. 3, ed. M. L. Kamil, P. B. Mosenthal, P. D. Pearson, and R. Barr, 545–562. Mahwah, NJ: Lawrence Erlbaum Associates, 2000.

Vocabulary

Baumann, J.F. and E.J. Kame'enui. *Vocabulary Instruction: From Research to Practice.* New York: Guilford Press, 2004.

Blachowicz, Camille, and Peter Fisher. *Teaching Vocabulary in All Classrooms*, Second Edition. Upper Saddle River, NJ: Merrill, 2002.

Coxhead, Averil. "A New Academic Word List." *TESOL Quarterly*, 2000.

Kinsella, Kate. "Strategies to Teach Academic Vocabulary." Strategies to Promote Academic Literacy for Second Language Learners Within the English Language Arts Classroom, 2005.

Kinsella, Kate and Kevin Feldman. *Narrowing the Language Gap: The Case for Explicit Vocabulary Instruction.* New York: Scholastic, Inc., 2005.

Marzano, Robert J. "The Developing Vision of Vocabulary Instruction." *Vocabulary Instruction: From Research to Practice.* New York: Guilford Press, 2004

Differentiated Instruction

Allington, Richard L. *What Really Matters for Struggling Readers: Designing Research-Based Programs.* New York: Longman, 2001.

Armbruster, Bonnie, and Thomas H. Anderson. "On Selecting 'Considerate' Content Area Textbooks." *Remedial and Special Education*, vol. 9 (1): 47–52.

Carnine, Douglas, Jerry Silbert, and Edward J. Kameenui. *Direct Instruction Reading. 3rd ed.* Upper Saddle River, NJ: Prentice Hall, 1997.

Deshler, Donald D., Keith B. Lenz, and Brenda R. Kissam. *Teaching Content to All: Evidence-Based Inclusive Practices in Middle and Secondary Schools.* Boston: Allyn and Bacon, 2004.

Moore, David. W. and Kathleen A. Hinchman. *Starting Out: A Guide to Teaching Adolescents Who Struggle with Reading.* Boston: Allyn and Bacon, 2003.

Vaughn, Sharon, Candace S. Bos, and Jeanne Shay Schumm. *Teaching Exceptional, Diverse, and At-Risk Students in the General Education Classroom.* Boston: Allyn and Bacon, 2002.

FIELD-TESTING OF PRENTICE HALL LITERATURE, PENGUIN EDITION

Background In May of 2004, six Language Arts teachers and 133 students field-tested grade 7 and grade 9 prototypes. Each teacher taught the prototype with one or more classes for three weeks. The students involved in the study represented a wide range of backgrounds and ability levels.

Prentice Hall researchers and editors used a variety of tools to gather information, including classroom observation and weekly debriefings with teachers who kept weekly lesson logs to note their experiences and observations about the prototype. In addition, we reviewed the results of pre-tests and post-tests to assess students' knowledge of the skills addressed in the prototypes.

Key Findings Reaction to the prototype from both teachers and students was highly favorable. The most highly-praised features of the program included the following:

Paired Selections: Teachers liked choosing which selection to teach. They agreed that this organization was useful for differentiated instruction.

Skills Instruction: Teachers praised the systematic skills instruction in the prototype. Classroom observation, teacher lesson logs, and student post-test results confirmed student mastery of the skills taught in the prototype.

Literature Selections: Students praised the selections as "interesting" and "fun-to-read," while teachers also noted that the content of the prototype was appropriate for their students' grade and ability levels.

Unit Authors: Teachers felt the featured unit authors added value by providing the writers' insights into their works.

Program Design and Organization: Both students and teachers enjoyed the bright, vibrant pictures. Teachers also commended the ratio of text to visuals, consistent organization, and the ease of navigation.

How Field Testing Informed Development

Finding	Response
Pacing The prototype included more material than could be taught in a three-week cycle.	The final product includes fewer part-level features and provides suggestions for revised pacing.
Reading Informational Materials Students and teachers commented that the prototype selection was not age-appropriate.	Editors identified selections for the feature that would be more relevant to students' everyday lives, such as articles, recipes, applications, and schedules.
Practice & Assess Questions Students and teachers told us some questions were too complicated.	Questions in the final product are direct, clear, and concise.
Vocabulary Instruction Teachers told us they wanted to see more vocabulary development.	We expanded the part vocabulary preview and review. For each selection, we developed Vocabulary Warm ups to increase the number of words taught per selection.

PRENTICE HALL LITERATURE: PROVEN TO GET RESULTS

National Effect-Size Study: Student Performance of Prentice Hall Literature, Users vs. Non-Users

This quasi-experimental study design examined longitudinal test results of 976 closely matched user and non-user districts as a point of comparison across the same time periods and achievement tests.

Prentice Hall users performed as well or better than their counterparts, achieving approximately a 56% gain in the percentage of students meeting or exceeding state reading/ELA standards and a 62% gain in national percentile ranking after one or more years of program implementation. A sustained gain was noted in districts that have implemented the program for two or more years.

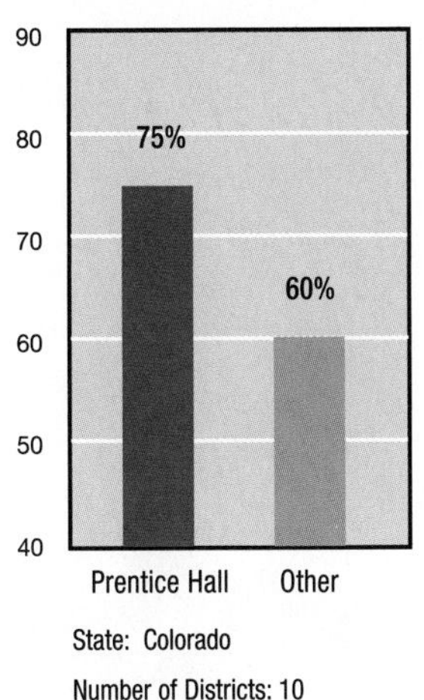

State: Colorado
Number of Districts: 10
Assessment: CSAP

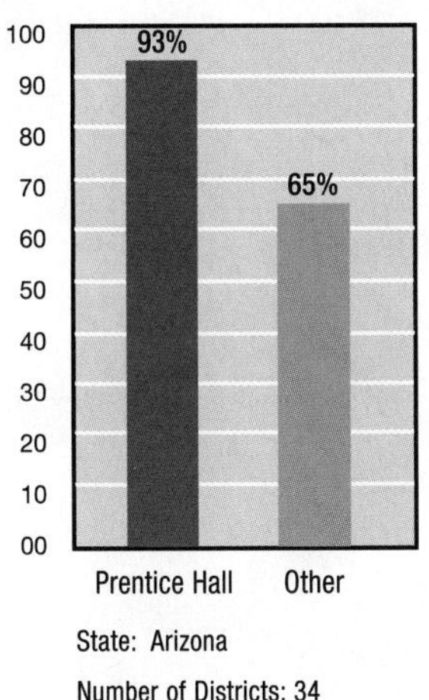

State: Arizona
Number of Districts: 34
Assessment: Stanford

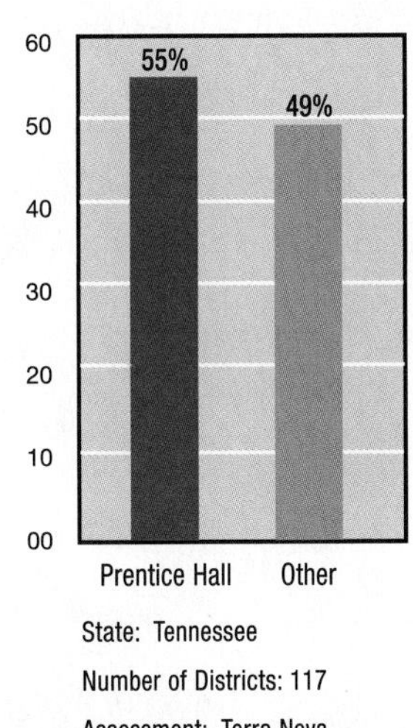

State: Tennessee
Number of Districts: 117
Assessment: Terra Nova

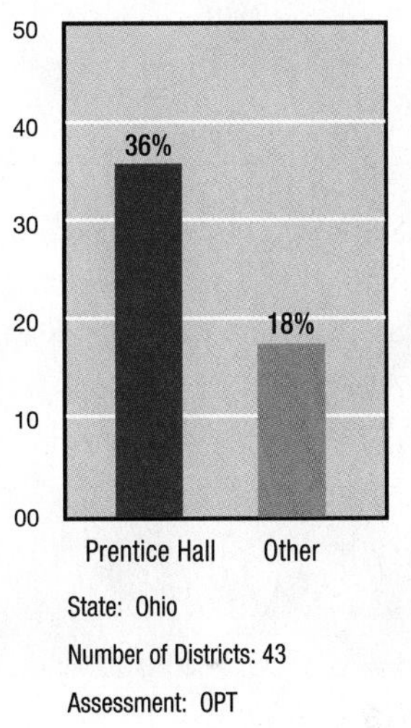

State: Ohio
Number of Districts: 43
Assessment: OPT

Learner Verification Research

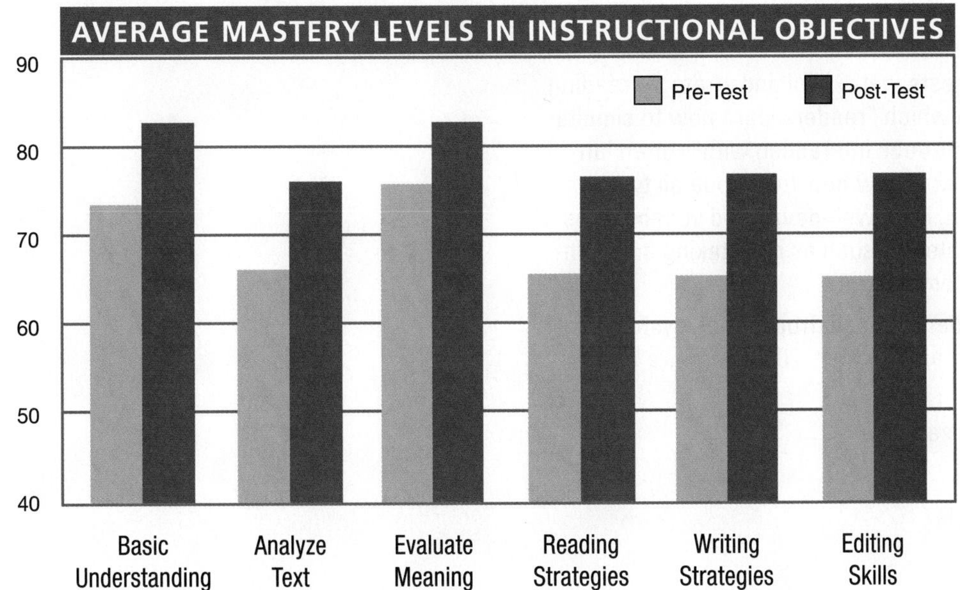

In a yearlong learner verification study, students using Prentice Hall Literature increased their mastery levels in several diagnostic skill areas for reading/ language arts.

All students were tested at the start of the year with a nationally normed standardized test, the TerraNova™ Complete Battery Plus exam. At the end of the treatment period, students were retested with the same standardized test. Only students who completed both the pre- and post-tests were included in this analysis. All tests were scored by CTB/McGraw Hill, publisher of the TerraNova™.

PROFESSIONAL DEVELOPMENT GUIDEBOOK

The Prentice Hall contributing authors and advisors guided the pedagogical design and content of Prentice Hall Literature Penguin Edition. Their expertise informed the development of instruction and support. In these pages, we share the authors' expertise on some of the key issues in language arts education.

BECOMING A STRATEGIC READING TEACHER

> *It's not what you say or do that ultimately matters. It is what you get the students to do as a result of what you said and did that counts.*
>
> **Kate Kinsella Ed.D.**

Strategic Reading

Recent research (Snow et al. 2002) suggests that skillful and strategic reading is a long-term developmental process in which "readers learn how to simultaneously extract and construct meaning through interaction with written language." In other words, successful readers know how to decode all types of words, read with fluency, and expression, have well-developed vocabularies and possess various comprehension strategies such as note-taking and summarizing to employ as the reading task demands.

Research illustrates that virtually all students benefit from direct, systematic, and explicit instruction in reading (Baker and Gersten, 200) There are three stages to the instructional process:

- **Instructional Frontloading** (before reading)
- **Guided Instruction** (during reading)
- **Reflection and Study** (after reading)

Instructional Frontloading

If teachers emphasize preteaching or frontloading instruction , they will help structure learning to ensure student success. Frontloading instruction is especially critical in mixed ability classrooms with English language learners, students with special needs and other students performing below grade level in terms of literacy. Before reading, prepare students with the following prereading activities and instruction.

- Introduce the big concepts.
- Provide direct teaching of vocabulary necessary to comprehend key ideas.
- Build academic vocabulary.
- Build, activate, and elaborate on background knowledge
- Pique curiosity and guide students to generate questions.
- Use launch activities the incorporate key vocabulary.

Guided Instruction

In guided instruction, the teacher models approaches for how to actively engage with the text to gain meaning. The teacher guides the students through the text using reading strategies and then guides discussion about the content using participation strategies.

Structured Accountable Responses

During the prereading phase and the guided instruction, it is important to ensure participation by all students in a nonthreatening environment. The following strategies are ways to structure your instruction so that all students are accountable and prepared to participate.

Use partners Partner response increases active language use, attention, and higher order thinking during instruction.

- Choose partners, alternating ranking based on literacy/social skills.
- Assign roles—such as A and B. *"A's tell B's two things we have learned about. . . "*
- Give a specific topic. *"What do you predict. . . ?" "What are two things we have learned about. . . . ?"*
- Allow a brief time of exchange: *"A's tell B's two things we have learned about. . . "*
- Call on students to share with the class after they have practiced with a partner.

Write first. Writing first increases thinking, accountability, and focus. It provides you as the teacher with concrete formative feedback. Having students write before responding connects written language to oral language, and it provides an opportunity for students to target academic language. F

Nominated Volunteers. Choosing volunteers based on your observations during partner work or written work allows you to ensure that all students participate and succeed. Circulate and observe as students discuss or write about the topic. Ask students to share with you their responses. Then, "nominate" the students you will ask to share with the class—that is, alert the student that he or she will be sharing with the class, so that the student the student can practice with a partner or with you before sharing with the larger group.

PRENTICE HALL LITERATURE

Putting Research into Practice

You can introduce the big concepts for each selection using the **Connecting to the Selection** feature in the **Student Edition.**

You will find teaching plans for instructional frontloaing in the **General Resources** including plans and student pages for the following activities

- Anticipation Guide
- KWL Chart
- Idea Wave

PRENTICE HALL LITERATURE

Putting Research into Practice

You can use questions and prompts provided in the **Student Edition** and the **Teacher's Edition** as prompts for structured accountable responses.

Language for Active Classroom Participation

Explicitly teach students ways to express themselves in class discussions. Model the use of these phrases, and encourage students to use them in responding.

Expressing an Opinion
I think that ________
I believe that ________
In my opinion________

Asking for Clarification
What do you mean?
Will you explain that again?
I have a question about that.

Soliciting a Response
What do you think?
Do you agree?

Individual Reporting
I discovered from________that_____
I found out that________
________pointed out that

Disagreeing
I don't agree with you because
I got a different answer than you.
I see it a different way.

Affirming
That's an interesting idea.
I hadn't thought of that.
I see what you mean.

Predicting
I predict that ________
I imagine that ________
Based on________I predict that_____

Paraphrasing and Clarifying
So you are saying that________
In other words, you think that_____
What I hear you saying is________

Acknowledging Ideas
My idea is related to________'s idea.
My idea is similar to ________'s idea.
My idea builds on ________'s idea.

Partner and Group Reporting
We agreed that ________
We decided that ________
We had a different approach.
We had a similar idea.

Offering a Suggestion
Maybe we could________
What if we________
Here's something we might try.

Holding the Floor
As I was saying ________
What I was trying to say was_____

PRENTICE HALL LITERATURE

Putting Research into Practice

- Questions and notes in the **Student Edition** provide frequent, regular opportunity for applying the strategies.
- In the Reading and Vocabulary Preview in the **Student Edition**, students learn the academic vocabulary needed to write and talk about the concepts taught in the part.
- The **Teachers' Edition** provides strategies for ensuring student participation.
- You will find teaching plans and student pages in the **General Resources** for participation strategies, including
  - Oral Cloze
  - Choral Reading
  - ReQuest

ENERGIZING VOCABULARY INSTRUCTION

Educators need to make robust intentional vocabulary instruction a high priority. . . We must keep in mind, however that teaching vocabulary robustly is not an end in itself but only a means to an end. The critical outcome is how well we equip students to thrive in academic contexts.

Kevin Feldman Ed.D.

Vocabulary Instruction

There is a clear consensus among literacy researchers that accelerating vocabulary growth is a vital and often neglected component of comprehensive language arts instruction. (Baumann and Kameenui, 2004). Numerous studies have documented the strong and recipricol relationship between vocabulary knowledge and reading comprehension. Research focused on school age second language learners similarly concludes that vocabulary knowledge is the single best predictor of there academic achievement across subject matter domains. Therefore, educators need to make robust intentional vocabulary instructional a high priority. Intensive instruction should focus on words related to central lesson concepts and high-use academic words. Academic word lists developed by researchers can help educators determine appropriate high-use academic words. (Coxhead, 2000; Xu and Nation, 1984).

Big Ideas in Vocabulary Teaching

Connect
Assess students' current knowledge of the target lesson vocabulary. Give explanations before definitions. Use student friendly explanations. Use language students already know. Use examples from students' experiential realm. Use synonyms.
Process
Have students give examples and images. Have students use "Show you know" sentences. Have students generate synonyms and antonyms.
Practice
Have students use graphic organizers and webs. Have students use the words in new contexts.

PRENTICE HALL LITERATURE

Putting Research into Practice

- You can preteach academic vocabulary in the **Reading and Vocabulary Preview** at the beginning of each part of the **Student Edition.**
- All vocabulary activities in the **Student Edition** are structured to be generative, "show you know" types of activities.
- You can develop students' expressive vocabulary for talking about the big concepts and themes of the literature with the **Connecting to the Selection** feature that precedes every selection in the **Student Edition.**
- The **Teachers' Edition** provides consistent support for introducing vocabulary at the beginning of every selection.
- The **Unit Resources** provides generative activities for all vocabulary instruction and activities.

Rationale for Direct Vocabulary Instruction

Over the past two decades, mounting research has challenged traditional views regarding the role of direct teaching in vocabulary development. Numerous studies have documented the positive impact of direct, explicit, vocabulary instruction on both immediate word learning and longer-term reading comprehension. (Baker, Kameenui, and Simmons, 1995; Beck, McKeown, and Kucan, 2002; Bielmiller, 2004, Marzano, 2004).

A Powerful Teaching Routine

The following steps can be elaborate and adapted, depending on the relative importance of the word sin question and the students' background knowledge. However, students benefit greatly from a consistent and recognizable approach that incorporates the following step:

1) **Pronounce** The first step in teaching a new term is guiding students in correctly pronouncing the word. This will support learners in decoding the word confidently, while also supporting both auditory and muscle memory. (Shaywitz, 2003). Engage all students in saying the word together two or three times.
2) **Explain** Understanding the meaning of a new term requires a clear explanation of the meaning, using language familiar to the students (Beck et al., 2002; Stahl, 1999). If possible, provide a synonym or known phrase to solidify the connection between the new vocabulary term and the students' prior knowledge.
3) **Provide examples** Student will usually need at least two or three examples of a new term to firmly grasp the meaning of it. Moreover, these examples should be drawn form a variety of contexts, not only the one used in the reading or lesson. It is helpful to phrase the examples such that students repeat the target word in completing the example.
4) **Elaborate** Research in cognitive psychology consistently indicates that learners understand and remember information better when they elaborate on it themselves (Marzano et al. 2001). Thus students understanding of new vocabulary terms is strengthened when they are given opportunities to elaborate word meanings by generating their own additional examples and visual representations.
5) **Assess** Research such as Baker et al.(1995) and Marzano (2004) have documented the importance of incorporating regular informal assessment into the instructional process, especially with academically diverse learners. Assessment of vocabulary involves both formative, quick informal checking for understanding during the lesson, and summative evaluation as students subsequently take a formal quiz or test.

PRENTICE HALL LITERATURE

Putting Research into Practice

- Use the Vocabulary notes in the **Teacher's Edition** for consistent, predictable vocabulary instruction structure.
- Use the **Vocabulary Knowledge Rating Sheet** in **General Resources** to assess students' current knowledge.
- Use the **Academic Vocabulary** lessons in the **Vocabulary Preview and Review** to introduce high-frequency words.
- Use the sample sentences in the **Vocabulary Builder** feature with each selection in the **Student Edition** to preteach words.

GIVING HOPE TO STRUGGLING READERS

Although students are cognizant of their deficiencies in reading and are motivated to improve their reading, they feel hopeless to do so in their current school situations.

Sharon Vaughn Ph.D.

Middle and high school students are expected to read at proficient levels and possess vocabularies and comprehension skills for understanding complex reading material. However, despite reading intervention programs during the primary grades, most students continue to experience learning problems well into their adolescent years (Ackerman, Dykman, and Peters, 1977; Ackerman, Wir, Metzler, and Dykman, 1996). Many of these students experience difficulty in phonological awareness and word recognition skills, decoding, and reading fluency (Greene, 1999; Wilson, 1999). Moreover, besides their scant word recognition skills and poor reading fluency, students with low reading skills may demonstrate significant deficits in reading comprehension. Unfortunately, findings from previous research indicate that adolescents with reading related learning disabilities become further behind in reading each year in school and risk losing the skills they acquired during elementary school.

Older students with reading disabilities need explicit and systematic instruction in reading. In addition , their instruction in reading is enhanced by experiences that are designed explicitly to foster vocabulary development, background knowledge, the ability to detect and comprehend relationships among verbal concepts and the ability to actively use strategies to ensure understanding and retention of material.

PRENTICE HALL LITERATURE

Putting Research into Practice

- **The Vocabulary and Reading Warmups** in the **Unit Resources** are explicitly designed to foster vocabulary development and build background knowledge.
- Use the **Reader's Notebook** series to enhance students' ability to actively use reading strategies taught in the **Student Edition**.

Attitudes Toward Reading

In general, students with low reading skills perceive reading as a difficult unsuccessful, and unappealing activity. (McKenna, Kear, and Ellsworth, 1995).Increasingly, researchers have used qualitative studies to describe middle and high school students' reading opportunities and reader characteristics. Kos (1991) for example, explores the reasons why middle school students reading problems persist. Using a case study approach, Kos identified three reasons why middle school students make limited progress in reading.

- First, although students are cognizant of their deficiencies in reading and in the instruction they have received and are motivated to improve their reading, they feel hopeless to do so in their current school situations.
- Second, reading problems may manifest themselves in stress-related behaviors and distraction from instruction.
- Third, even when students attempt to use reading strategies, they often fail to use them efficiently.

Bintz (1993) examined reasons for declining interest in reading during middle and high school years. According to Bintz, although students interest in school reading declines, they do not necessarily lose interest in pleasure reading and informational reading outside of school. Second, students are not nonstrategic in their approach to reading, nor do they use dysfunctional strategies. Rather, Bintz maintained, middle and high school students use different strategies for in school and out of school reading. For instance, in school students were observed using shortcut strategies to assist them in completing assignments. Outside of school, however, these students were more iinclined to use higher level strategies because the material was personally interesting. Third, students do no fit into developmental categories such as avid, passive, or reluctant readers, but instead demonstrate different literate behaviors depending on the task they perform, the texts they read, and the interpretive stances they have toward them.

Likewise, Worthy and McKool (1996), through analysis off students interview of sixth grade students who were good readers but who also had negative attitudes toward reading, suggested that students' negative attitudes toward reading may be related to their limited opportunities in reading instruction. Students who indicated negative attitudes toward reading also indicated that they had limited opportunities to read independently, select reading materials or read personally interesting materials in school. Moreover, their feelings about reading instruction and materials used in school might have distorted their opinion about reading in general and thus their willingness to read.

PRENTICE HALL LITERATURE

Putting Research into Practice

Use the **On Your Own** feature and the **For Further Reading** page in the **Student Edition** to encourage independent reading.

MAKING THE DIFFERENCE MATTER

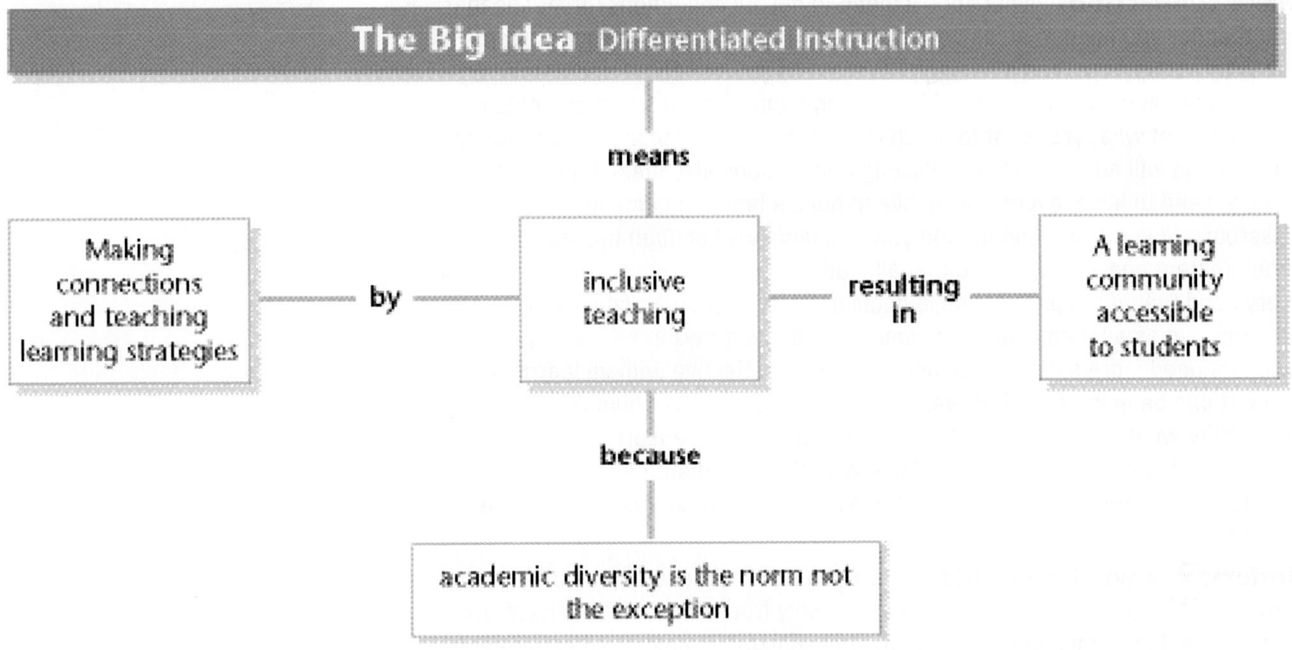
The Big Idea Differentiated Instruction
means
Making connections and teaching learning strategies
by
inclusive teaching
resulting in
A learning community accessible to students
because
academic diversity is the norm not the exception

Why do we need differentiated instruction?

The wide range of academic diversity present in schools today presents both a challenge and an opportunity to all teachers. Because the challenge is so great and the need to accommodate all students so urgent, we need to think about the problem of planning and teaching to include all learners in a new way.

Diversity is the norm. Thinking about diversity among students as the norm rather than as something out of the ordinary is important as a first step in building inclusive teaching practices. Diane Ferguson (1995) has noted that "Meaningful change will require nothing less than a joint effort to reinvent schools to be more accommodating to all dimensions of human diversity" (p. 282). She argues that we must change our view of the school's role from one of providing educational services, to one of providing educational support for learning:

> Valuing diversity and difference, rather than trying to change or diminish it so that everyone fits some ideal of similarity, leads to the realization that we can support students in their efforts to become active members of their communities….Perhaps the most important feature of support as a concept for schooling is that is it grounded in the perspective of the person receiving it, not the person providing it.

This is not to say, however, that differences should be ignored. It is important to respect differences and acknowledge them by incorporating them into the life of the classroom, as well as the curriculum, so that learning is grounded in what is familiar to students.

Don Deshler Ph.D.

How do we provide inclusive instruction?

Make connections. What does it mean to make connections? It means that as a teacher you need to be as concerned about understanding your students and what is important and meaningful to them as you are about understanding your content and how to teach it. Making connections means that students need to believe that what you want to teach is important and relevant to them and that you can and will help them learn. Making connections also means that you as the teacher need to believe it is worthwhile to build a learning community in your classroom, to know and understand your students well enough to make choices about content and instruction so that all students have an opportunity to learn. Every good teacher aspires to these goals and many teachers successfully realize them. But as academic diversity among students grows in secondary schools, teachers need more support and more tools to be effective with all learners. Support can be gained, we believe, by thinking about a classroom as a learning community where teacher and students work together to ensure that everyone is learning. More tools become available with the implementation of teaching routines and learning strategies that make learning more accessible to more learners.

Understand what students already know. What students already know, or their "prior knowledge," comes not only from what students have previously learned in school, but also from their lived experiences. Lived experience includes all the differences that students bring with them into the schools, such as culture, language, ethnic backgrounds, as well as previous learning successes or failures. Valuing and using the prior knowledge of students allows teachers to link new knowledge to what students already know, thereby making learning more meaningful for students. It also allows students to construct new knowledge for themselves.

Teach learning strategies. Finally, students are more likely to make connections in learning the content in your class if they know how to learn. All good listeners use strategies to learn new things. Some students are better than others at developing strategies to learn. Inclusive teaching means that you have to take into account whether all your students are good strategic learners, and the only way to do this is to teach them—explicitly—how to use and develop learning strategies.

What is the result of differentiated instruction?

A learning community. Making connections and building a learning community in your classroom will establish an environment where learning, cooperation, and respect for differences are all valued. The "work" of this community is learning. Everyday practices and routines are based on cooperation in accomplishing this work, and the interests and learning needs of everyone in the community are taken seriously.

PROGRAM CONSULTANTS

The Prentice Hall national language arts consultants advised on many aspects of this program, particularly the professional development strand. The professional development notes in this textbook represent successful strategies acquired and applied during their many years of experience in classrooms.

Yvonne R. Cadiz
Language Arts, ESOL and Spanish teacher
Curriculum Specialist for ESOL
Hillsborough County, Tampa, Florida
Director of the MERIT Program (Multilingual Educational Resource Information and Training Program), University of South Florida

Anita Clay
District Coordinator, Gateway Institute of Technology
St. Louis, MO

Nancy McDonald
K-12 Reading Specialist Waterloo School District, Waterloo, WI Belleville School District, Belleville, WI
Title I Language Arts Teacher, 6-8
Beloit Turner Middle School, Beloit, WI
Grade 8 Language Arts Teacher
Olson Junior High School, Woodstock, IL

Jean Ripple
Language Arts Teacher, 1-10
Model Classroom for Inclusion
Pennsylvania

John R. Scannell
Teacher, 9-12 English, Writing, Acting and Drama, Debate and Public Address
Newport HS, Bellevue, WA
Lykens Jr. HS, Lykens, PA
Nazareth HS, Nazareth, PA

Kathryne Lewis Stewart
Director of Humanities Instruction
Tomball Independent School District
Tomball, Texas
Teacher/ GT Specialist
Burleson High School
Burleson Independent School District
Burleson, Texas

Joseph A. Wieczorek, PhD
Instructor, Georgetown University
College of Notre Dame
University of Maryland, Baltimore County
Howard County Public Schools, Maryland
Language Specialist, FBI

LITERATURE REVIEW PANEL

These teachers helped develop the Penguin Edition of Prentice Hall Literature by testing new selections by contemporary authors and gathering student questions for these authors to answer. The work of these teachers helped ensure that the program would be truly interactive, with a built-in dialogue between authors and students.

Sherry Abner
Two Rivers Middle School
Covington, KY

Heather Barnes
Central Crossing High School
Grove City, OH

Bonnie Bellows
Humboldt Senior High School
St. Paul, MN

Shawn L. Brumfield
Los Angeles Unified School District
Los Angeles, CA

Donna Burch
Southern Middle School
Somerset, KY

Susanne Buttrey
Sycamore Middle School
Pleasant View, TN

Denise Campbell
Cherry Creek School District
Centennial, CO

Holly Carr
Central Crossing High School
Grove City, OH

Vanessa Carroll
LBJ High School
Austin, TX

Joanne Chambers
Swiftwater Intermediate School
Swiftwater, PA

Susan Cisna
East Prairie Junior High School
Tuscola, IL

Nancy DiGasso
Pine Bush High School
Pine Bush, New York

Karen Gibson
Appleton North High School
Appleton, WI

Margaret Jan Graham
Cobb Middle School
Tallahassee, FL

Doris Sue Hawkins
C. W. Otto Middle School
Lansing, MI

Deanna Hilliard
Soddy Daisy Middle School
Soddy Daisy, TN

Helen Hudson
Crawfordsville High School
Crawfordsville, IN

Gisele Le Duc
East Lyme Middle School
Niantic, CT

Greg MacAvoy
Pine Bush High School
Pine Bush, New York

Deb Madej
Norris Middle School
Omaha, NE

Nancy Mast
Hobart Middle School
Hobart, Indiana

Nancy Monroe
Bolton High School
Alexandria, LA

Suzanne Moore
Sunrise Middle School
Clackamas, OR

Paul Putnoki
Torrington Middle School
Torrington, CT

Herb Ranlose
Zion Benton High School
Zion, IL

Robert Rarrick
Union Endicott Senior High
Endicott, NY

Margaret St. Sauver
St. Paul Public Schools
St. Paul, MN

Denise Greer Wallace
Western Valley Middle School
Phoenix, AZ

Debbie Watts
Jacobs Fork Middle School
Newton, NC

Melissa Williams
Delsea Regional High School
Franklinville, NJ 08322

Charles Youngs
Bethel Park High School
Bethel Park, PA

1 WHERE DO I START?

Right here! These pages will guide you through the program's organization and describe the resources you have available to enrich your teaching. *Prentice Hall Literature, Penguin Edition* is carefully designed to make pacing, lesson planning, teaching, and assessment easier.

2 HOW DO I INTRODUCE THE UNIT?

Each unit in this book presents the literature of a specific time period. The unit is hosted by a featured contemporary author, scholar, or translator who introduces a literary trend or theme in the **Setting the Scene** essay.

The *From the Author's Desk* orange banner appears throughout the unit when the featured author appears.

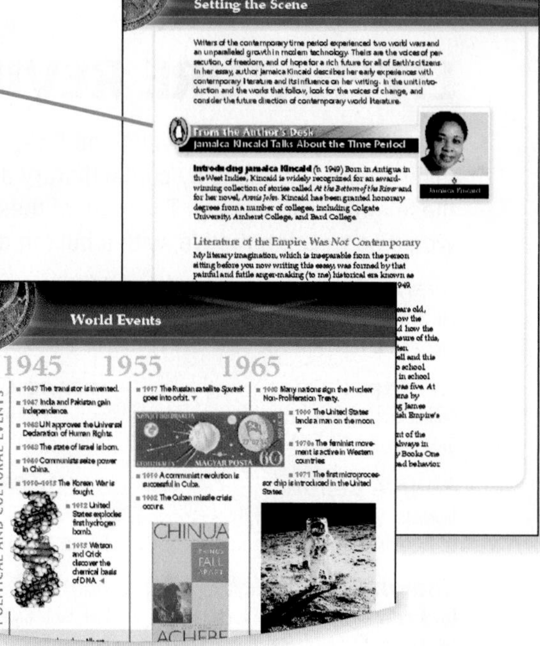

Use the unit **Introduction** to develop students' understanding and appreciation for literature in its broader context.

The timeline shows the literature in the context of key world events and other literary milestones.

Technology

From the Author's Desk

Stimulate students' interest with this engaging DVD featuring in-depth interviews with unit authors discussing unit concepts, literature, history, reading, and writing.

Use the **History of the Period** and the **Literature of the Period** essays to introduce the major events, influential people, critical themes, and important trends of the time period. This background information will build a strong foundation for the literary exploration to follow in the unit selections.

3 WHAT SHOULD I USE TO PLAN AND PREPARE?

Start your planning with the **Time and Resource Manager** before every selection or selection grouping. This guide provides these tools:

- a detailed lesson plan
- suggestions for incorporating program resources into your instruction
- recommended for pacing each element of your lesson
- information about lesson objectives

Meeting Your Standards
Standards coverage information

Step-by-Step Teaching Guide
A systematic approach to teaching the literature

Pacing Column
Suggested pacing information

Resources Column
Suggested resources for differentiated instruction

TIME AND RESOURCE MANAGER *from the Rig Veda*

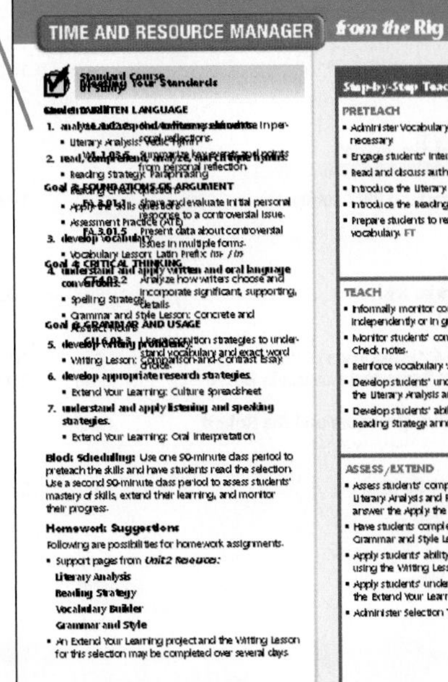

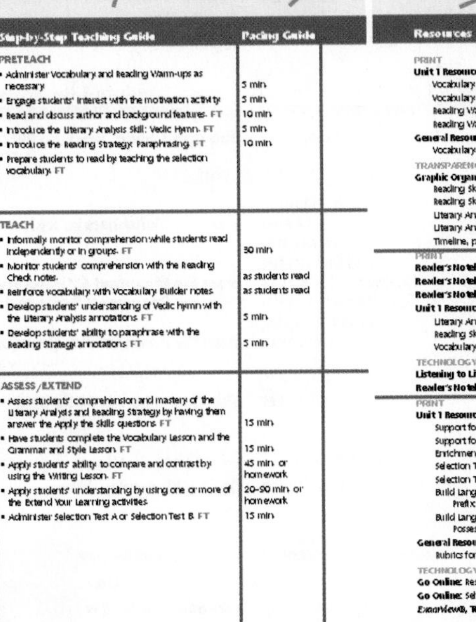

Step-by-Step Teaching Guide	Pacing Guide
PRETEACH	
• Administer Vocabulary and Reading Warm-ups as necessary.	5 min.
• Engage students' interest with the motivation activity.	5 min.
• Read and discuss author and background features. FT	10 min.
• Introduce the Literary Analysis Skill: Vedic Hymn. FT	5 min.
• Introduce the Reading Strategy: Paraphrasing. FT	5 min.
• Prepare students to read by teaching the selection vocabulary. FT	10 min.
TEACH	
• Informally monitor comprehension while students read independently or in groups. FT	30 min.
• Monitor students' comprehension with the Reading Check notes.	as students read
• Reinforce vocabulary with Vocabulary Builder notes.	as students read
• Develop students' understanding of Vedic hymn with the Literary Analysis annotations. FT	5 min.
• Develop students' ability to paraphrase with the Reading Strategy annotations. FT	5 min.
ASSESS/EXTEND	
• Assess students' comprehension and mastery of the Literary Analysis and Reading Strategy by having them answer the Apply the Skills questions. FT	15 min.
• Have students complete the Vocabulary Lesson and the Grammar and Style Lesson. FT	15 min.
• Apply students' ability to compare and contrast by using the Writing Lesson. FT	45 min. or homework
• Apply students' understanding by using one or more of the Extend Your Learning activities.	20–90 min. or homework
• Administer Selection Test A or Selection Test B. FT	15 min.

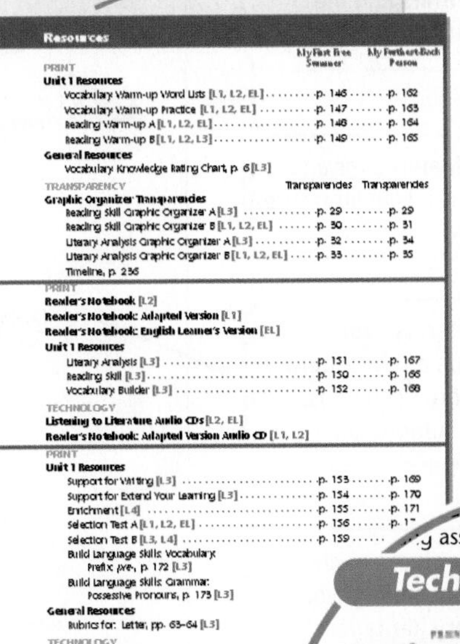

Technology

PRENTICE HALL **TeacherEXPRESS™** Plan · Teach · Assess Use this complete suite of powerful teaching tools to make lesson planning and testing quicker and easier.

PRENTICE HALL **StudentEXPRESS™** Learn · Study · Succeed Use the Interactive Textbook (online and on CD-ROM) to make selections and activities come alive with audio and video support and interactive questions.

4 HOW DOES THE PROGRAM HELP ME WITH PACING?

The **Diagnostic and Benchmark Tests** divide the program into three-week instructional blocks, with each segment focusing on core skills and standards. This consistent organization ensures thorough skills coverage presented in manageable chunks. A benchmark test is provided for each part, allowing you to administer assessment at 3-, 6-, or 9-week intervals. This systematic, logical organization with built-in progress monitoring allows you to make sound instructional choices for your class without missing any skills or standards.

5 HOW DO I TEACH EACH UNIT?

A Start each unit with the **Introduction** featuring the unit author and providing key literary and historical background.

B Teach literary analysis with representative literature of the period. (See p. T53 for more information.)

C Develop student mastery of literary elements with the instruction in **Focus on Literary Forms** and the selections that follow.

D Use **A Closer Look** features for an in-depth exploration of trends in literature.

E Teach **Comparing Literary Works** groupings to help students analyze literary elements in two or more selections. (See p. T53 for more information.)

F Present **Connections** features to show the thematic relationship among works from different literary heritages.

G Show your students how to apply reading skills to real-life reading situations with the **Reading Informational Materials** feature.

H Use the workshops to provide opportunities for skills practice and high-stakes test preparation.

Unit 2

Sacred Texts and Epic Tales

Indian Literature (c. 1400 B.C. – c. A.D. 500)

Every selection is supported by these resources:

- Skills Development Workbook
- Graphic Organizers on Transparency
- Selection Tests
- Reader's Notebook series
- Listening to Literature audio program
- Student Express
- Teacher Express

6 HOW DO I TEACH A SELECTION?

Each selection or selection grouping follows a consistent pattern. This allows you and your students to appreciate significant works of literature by developing essential literary analysis and critical reading skills.

Check the **Accessibility at a Glance** chart in the Teacher's Edition for an analysis of the factors influencing accessibility, and choose the most appropriate literature for your students.

Use the **Build Skills** pages to present a full author biography and instruction on literary analysis, reading strategy, and vocabulary. Build context with the **Background** notes that appear at the beginning of each selection.

After completing the selection, use the **Critical Reading** and **Apply the Skills** pages to assess students' understanding. For grammar, vocabulary skills, and writing practice, use the **Build Language Skills** pages.

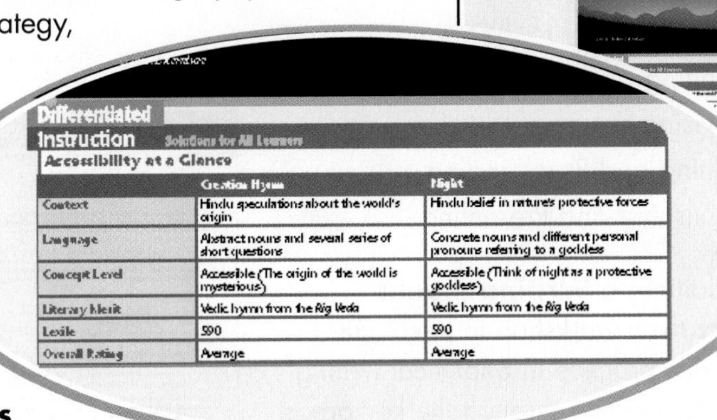

Differentiated Instruction Solutions for All Learners

Accessibility at a Glance

	Creation Hymn	Night
Context	Hindu speculations about the world's origin	Hindu belief in nature's protective forces
Language	Abstract nouns and several series of short questions	Concrete nouns and different personal pronouns referring to a goddess
Concept Level	Accessible (The origin of the world is mysterious)	Accessible (Think of night as a protective goddess)
Literary Merit	Vedic hymn from the *Rig Veda*	Vedic hymn from the *Rig Veda*
Lexile	590	590
Overall Rating	Average	Average

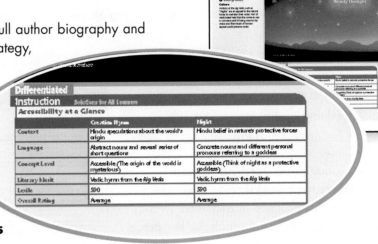

7 HOW DO I DIFFERENTIATE INSTRUCTION?

Prentice Hall Literature provides unprecedented opportunities for differentiated instruction:

- **Teacher's Edition:** Use the strategies and techniques geared toward different reading levels and learning styles.
- **Reader's Notebooks:** Customize instruction for every selection with reading support for struggling readers and English learners.
- **Leveled Vocabulary and Reading Warm-ups:** For each selection, build background, fluency, and vocabulary.
- **Leveled Selection Tests:** Choose from two tests for each selection according to students' ability levels.
- **Graphic Organizers:** Give struggling readers additional support with completed versions of all organizers in the Student Edition.

Differentiated Instruction Solutions for All Learners

Support for Special Needs Students
Students may have difficulty understanding that the dialogue between Jean and Priscilla is imaginary. Make certain that they understand the purpose of the note at the bottom of the previous page. Then remind students that the Pilgrims were the first people from Europe to move to America and that some of them arrived on the *Mayflower*. Explain that when Jean opens the book, she imagines the Pilgrims are with her and on their way to America just as she will be one day soon.

Enrichment for Gifted/Talented Students
Ask students to consider why Jean probably relates to Priscilla. Have them think of story characters with whom they identify or admire. Have them create an imaginary discussion with the character of their choice. Their discussion should consider an issue or solve a problem. Encourage students to choose their individual tone (e.g., serious, formal, humorous) and perform the dialogue for the class.

8 WHEN DO I TEACH WRITING?

This program incorporates opportunities for both process writing and writing for assessment in every unit.

Writing Workshop

Persuasion: Persuasive Essay

English Renaissance writers such as Sir Thomas Moore and Queen Elizabeth I argued vigorously for their humanistic ideals and objectives in **persuasive essays.** A persuasive essay is a prose work that presents a case for or against a position using supporting evidence and clear, convincing language. Follow the steps outlined in this workshop to write your own persuasive essay.

Assignment Write a persuasive essay focusing on an issue of concern or importance to you.

What to Include To succeed, your persuasive essay must feature the following elements:

- a clear thesis statement that identifies your position and the action you want readers to take
- details, facts, reasons, examples, and descriptions that support your position
- an understanding of the knowledge, experience, needs, and concerns of your intended audience
- language and arguments that are fair but convincing

To preview the criteria on which your persuasive essay may be judged, see the rubric on page 413.

Using the Form You may use elements of a persuasive essay in these writing situations:
- speeches
- letters to the editor
- advertisements
- cover letters
- newspaper articles

Reading Writing Connection: To get a feel for persuasive writing, read from *Utopia* by Sir Thomas More, page 272.

406 ■ *Celebrating Humanity (1485–1625)*

Process Writing In each unit, a **Writing Workshop** with step-by-step instruction guides students to develop their ideas into full-length compositions, addressing these key stages in the writing process:

- Prewriting
- Drafting
- Revising
- Editing and Proofreading
- Publishing and Presenting

In addition, a **Writing About Literature** workshop in each unit provides practice in analytical writing, guiding students through the key areas of writing a thesis statement, gathering evidence, and drafting a response to a specific literature-based prompt.

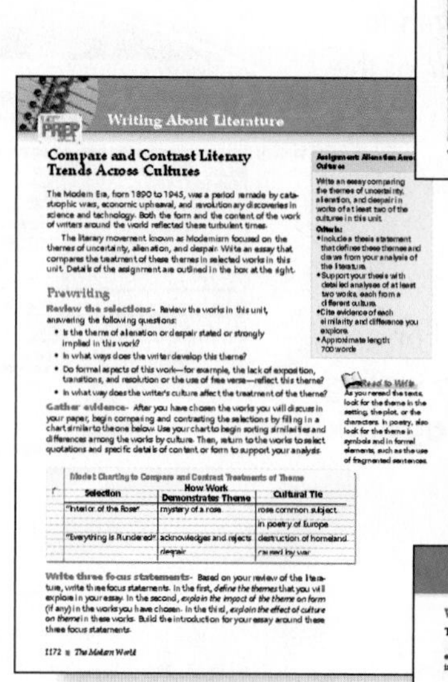

Writing About Literature

Compare and Contrast Literary Trends Across Cultures

The Modern Era, from 1890 to 1945, was a period remade by catastrophic wars, economic upheaval, and revolutionary discoveries in science and technology. Both the form and the content of the work of writers around the world reflected these turbulent times.

The literary movement known as Modernism focused on the themes of uncertainty, alienation, and despair. Write an essay that compares the treatment of these themes in selected works in this unit. Details of the assignment are outlined in the box at the right.

Assignment: Alienation Across Cultures
Write an essay comparing the themes of uncertainty, alienation, and despair in works of at least two of the cultures in this unit.
Criteria:
- Include a thesis statement that defines these themes and draws from your analysis of the literature.
- Support your thesis with detailed analyses of at least two works, each from a different culture.
- Cite evidence of each similarity and difference you explore.
- Approximate length: 700 words

Prewriting

Review the selections- Review the works in this unit, answering the following questions:
- Is the theme of alienation or despair stated or strongly implied in this work?
- In what ways does the writer develop this theme?
- Do formal aspects of this work—for example, the lack of exposition, transitions, and resolution or the use of free verse—reflect this theme?
- In what way does the writer's culture affect the treatment of the theme?

Gather evidence- After you have chosen the works you will discuss in your paper, begin comparing and contrasting the selections by filling in a chart similar to the one below. Use your chart to begin sorting similarities and differences among the works by culture. Then, return to the works to select quotations and specific details of content or form to support your analysis.

Read to Write As you reread the texts, look for the theme in the setting, the plot, or the characters. In poetry, also look for the theme in symbols and in formal elements, such as the use of fragmented sentences.

Model: Charting to Compare and Contrast Treatments of Theme

Selection	How Work Demonstrates Theme	Cultural Tie
"Interior of the Rose"	mystery of a rose	rose common subject in poetry of Europe
"Everything Is Plundered"	acknowledges and rejects despair	destruction of homeland caused by war

Write three focus statements- Based on your review of the literature, write three focus statements. In the first, *define the themes* that you will explore in your essay. In the second, *explain the impact of the theme on form* (if any) in the works you have chosen. In the third, *explain the effect of culture on theme* in these works. Build the introduction for your essay around these three focus statements.

1172 ■ *The Modern World*

Timed Writing To address the growing call for on-demand writing and to prepare students for college entrance exams, the program provides many opportunities in each unit to help students practice writing for assessment. Timed Writing prompts ask students to produce brief expository or persuasive writing relating to the literature they have read.

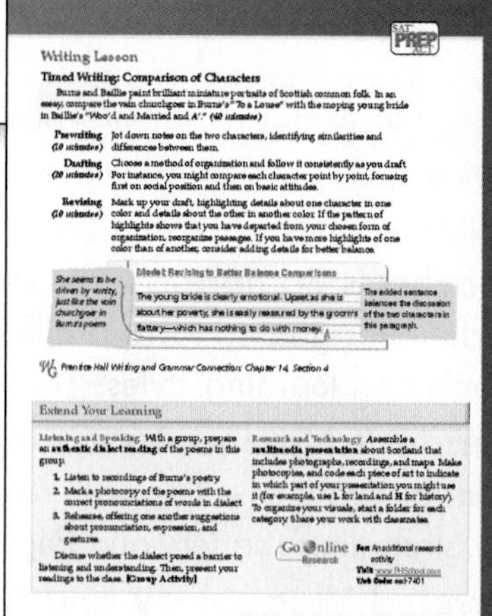

Writing Lesson

Timed Writing: Comparison of Characters

Burns and Baillie paint brilliant miniature portraits of Scottish common folk. In an essay, compare the vain churchgoer in Burns's "To a Louse" with the moping young bride in Baillie's "Woo'd and Married and A'." *(40 minutes)*

Prewriting *(10 minutes)* Jot down notes on the two characters, identifying similarities and differences between them.

Drafting *(20 minutes)* Choose a method of organization and follow it consistently as you draft. For instance, you might compare each character point by point, focusing first on social position and then on basic attitudes.

Revising *(10 minutes)* Mark up your draft, highlighting details about one character in one color and details about the other in another color. If the pattern of highlights shows that you have departed from your chosen form of organization, reorganize passages. If you have more highlights of one color than of another, consider adding details for better balance.

Model: Revising to Better Balance Comparisons

The young bride is clearly emotional. Upset as she is about her poverty, she is easily reassured by the groom's flattery—which has nothing to do with money. *She seems to be driven by vanity, just like the vain churchgoer in Burns's poem.*

The added sentence balances the discussion of the two characters in this paragraph.

Prentice Hall Writing and Grammar Connection: Chapter 14, Section 4

Extend Your Learning

Listening and Speaking With a group, prepare **an authentic dialect reading** of the poems in this group.
1. Listen to recordings of Burns's poetry.
2. Mark a photocopy of the poems with the correct pronunciations of words in dialect.
3. Rehearse, offering one another suggestions about pronunciation, expression, and gestures.

Discuss whether the dialect posed a barrier to listening and understanding. Then, present your readings to the class. **[Group Activity]**

Research and Technology Assemble a **multimedia presentation** about Scotland that includes photographs, recordings, and maps. Make photocopies, and code each piece of art to indicate in which part of your presentation you might use it (for example, use L for land and H for history). To organize your visuals, start a folder for each category. Share your work with classmates.

Go Online Research — **For:** An additional research activity **Visit:** www.PHSchool.com **Web Code:** esd-7401

To a Mouse / To a Louse / Woo'd and Married and A' ■ 677

Technology

Score student essays in seconds.

Finally, to facilitate your teaching of writing, the Prentice Hall **Online Essay Scorer** provides instant scoring and feedback, plus tips for revision. You save time and your students become better writers!

9 HOW DO I MONITOR STUDENT PROGRESS?

Prentice Hall makes progress monitoring easy with frequent opportunities to evaluate student progress and reteach material.

- Use the **Diagnostic Tests** as indicated at the beginning of each unit or part to determine readiness. You will find frequent reading checks and suggestions in the Teacher's Edition for monitoring student progress during reading.
- After reading the selections, use the **Selection Tests** to assess compre-hen-sion and mastery of the reading and literary analysis skills.
- As you teach the unit, use the **Monitor Your Progress** pages in standardized-test format. These appear after the Reading Informational Materials section and in unit workshops to give students practice in applying specific skills under test-taking conditions.
- Use the **Benchmark Tests** to monitor progress at regular, frequent intervals. For your convenience, tests are provided at 3-week intervals.

Technology

Monitor student progress instantly in an interactive format.

Access companion Web sites for self-tests.

Use the electronic test generator to customize assessment.

10 HOW DOES PRENTICE HALL LITERATURE HELP ME DEVELOP AS A TEACHER?

The Teacher's Edition provides built-in professional development. Look for these special features:

- **Step-by-Step Teaching:** Margin notes provide strategies, tips, and examples for teaching skills.
- **Differentiated Instruction:** Notes provide support, strategies, and enrichment for learners of varied abilities.
- **Professional Development:** Pedagogical explanations of specific techniques enhance your effectiveness as a teacher.

GRADE 11

Units 1–6

	Unit	From the Author's Desk	Focus on Literary Forms	A Closer Look	Connections	Reading Informational Materials
1	**A Gathering of Voices** Beginnings–1750	Susan Power, **Museum Indians** pp. 32–39	Narrative Accounts pp. 56–57	Captivity Narratives pp. 66–67	*from* **the Rig Veda** pp. 52–54	Websites: Locating Appropriate Information pp. 87–90
2	**A Nation is Born** 1750–1800	William Andrews pp. 156–157	Speeches pp. 198–199	News pp. 154–155	**African Proverbs** pp. 194–196	Press Releases: Distinguishing Between Fact and Opinion pp. 190–193
3	**A Growing Nation** 1800–1870	Gretel Ehrlich pp. 402–403; Charles Johnson pp. 386–387	Poetry pp. 422–423	Transcendentalism pp. 384–385	Introduction to **Frankenstein,** Mary Shelley pp. 378–382	Memorandums: Analyzing Text Structures pp. 292–295
4	**Division, Reconciliation, and Expansion** 1850–1914	Nell Irvin Painter pp. 546–547	Diaries, Journals, and Letters pp. 544–545	Mark Twain: The American Bard pp. 572–573	**War,** Luigi Pirandello pp. 566–570	Public Documents: Analyzing an Author's Beliefs pp. 540–542
5	**Disillusion, Defiance, and Discontent** 1914–1946	Tim O'Brien, **Ambush** pp. 832–833	Short Story pp. 804–805	The Harlem Renaissance pp. 910–911	**"Fern Hill"** Dylan Thomas pp. 948–949	Public Relations Documents: Making Inferences pp. 944–947
6	**Prosperity and Protest** 1946–Present	Arthur Miller, **The Crucible** pp. 1252–1253	Essay pp. 1142–1143	Twentieth Century Drama pp. 1250–1251	**"I Wandered Lonely as a Cloud,"** William Wordsworth pp. 1058–1059	Critical Commentaries: Interpreting an Author's Arguments pp. 1362–1363

Technology

Go Online PHSchool.com	From the Author's Desk DVD				ExamView® QuickTake
• Author Biography • Self-tests • Research Activities	Bring real Writers into your classroom				Monitor student progress instantly

Prentice Hall StudentEXPRESS™ Learn · Study · Succeed — Prentice Hall TeacherEXPRESS™ Plan · Teach · Assess — Instant access to all program resources with the click of a mouse

Skills Navigator Overview

Writing About Literature	Writing Workshop	Vocabulary Workshop	Assessment Workshop	Communications Workshop
Analyze Literary Periods pp. 110–111	Autobiographical Narrative pp. 112–119	Define, Identify, Label p. 120	Sequential Order p. 121	Delivering Autobiographical Presentations p. 122
Evaluate Literary Themes pp. 226–227	Persuasion pp. 228–235	Recall, Predict, Summarize p. 236	Forms of Propaganda p. 237	Analyzing Advertising p.238
Compare and Contrast Literary Trends pp. 454–455	Reflective Essay pp. 456–463	Differentiate, Analyze, Infer p. 464	Writer's Point of View p. 465	Analyzing Persuasive Techniques p. 466
Compare and Contrast Literary Themes pp. 682–683	Research Paper pp. 684–695	Illustrate, Apply, Demonstrate p. 694	Critical Reasoning p. 695	Critiquing Persuasive Devices p. 696
Evaluate Literary Trends pp. 950–951	Multimedia Presentation pp. 952–959	Compare and Contrast, Conclude, Deduce p. 960	Paired Passages p. 961	Delivering a Persuasive Speech p. 962
Analyze Literary Trends pp. 1366–1367	Job Portfolio pp. 1368–1375	Evaluate, Judge, Interpret p. 1376	Strategy, Organization, and Style p. 1377	Analyzing Bias in News p. 1378
	Online Essay Scorer PH Online Essay Scorer: electronic essay grader	ExamView® QuickTake Monitor student progress instantly.	ExamView® QuickTake Monitor student progress instantly.	ExamView® QuickTake Monitor student progress instantly.

Interactive Textbook — ExamView test generator — Instant access to all program resources with the click of a mouse

UNIT 1 A Gathering of Voices (Beginnings to 1750)

	Selection	Reading Strategy	Literary Analysis	Vocabulary
PART 1	**"The Earth on Turtle's Back"** (MA), SE, p. 18; **"When Grizzlies Walked Upright"** (MA), SE, p. 21; **from *The Navajo Origin Legend*** (MA), SE, p. 28; **from *The Iroquois Constitution*** (A), SE, p. 26	**Recognizing Cultural Details,** SE, p. 17; *UR1,* p. 12; **Reading Warm-ups A and B,** *UR1,* pp. 9–10; **Reading Strategy Graphic Organizers A and B,** *GOT,* pp. 1–2	**Origin Myth,** SE, p. 17; *UR1,* p. 11; **Literary Analysis Graphic Organizers A and B,** *GOT,* pp. 3–4	**Vocabulary Builder,** SE, p. 17: *ablutions, protruded, confederate, disposition, deliberations* **Latin Suffix** *-tion,* SE, p. 30; *UR1,* p. 13
	"A Journey Through Texas" (A), Alvar Núñez Cabeza de Vaca, SE, p. 42; **"Boulders Taller Than the Great Tower of Seville"** (A), García López Cárdenas, SE, p. 47	**Recognizing Signal Words,** SE, p. 41; *UR1,* p. 31; **Reading Warm-ups A and B,** *UR1,* pp. 28–29; **Reading Strategy Graphic Organizers A and B,** *GOT,* pp. 5–6	**Exploration Narratives,** SE, p. 41; *UR1,* p. 30; **Literary Analysis Graphic Organizers A and B,** *GOT,* pp. 7–8	**Vocabulary Builder,** SE, p. 41: *entreated, feigned, mortality, subsisted, traversed, dispatched* **Latin Root** *-mort-,* SE, p. 56; *UR1,* p. 32
PART 2 FOCUS ON NARRATIVE ACCOUNTS	**from *Journal of the First Voyage to America*** (A), Christopher Columbus, SE, p. 60	**Recognizing Author's Purpose,** SE, p. 59; *UR1,* p. 48; **Reading Warm-ups A and B,** *UR1,* pp. 45–46; **Reading Strategy Graphic Organizers A and B,** *GOT,* pp. 9–10	**Journal,** SE, p. 59; *UR1,* p. 47; **Literary Analysis Graphic Organizers A and B,** *GOT,* pp. 11–12	**Vocabulary Builder,** SE, p. 59: *exquisite, affliction, indications, abundance* **Latin Root** *-flict-,* SE, p. 64; *UR1,* p. 49
	from *The General History of Virginia* (MC), John Smith, SE, p. 70; **from *Of Plymouth Plantation*** (A), William Bradford, SE, p. 76	**Breaking down Sentences,** SE, p. 69; *UR1,* p. 65; **Reading Warm-ups A and B,** *UR1,* pp. 62–63; **Reading Strategy Graphic Organizers A and B,** *GOT,* pp. 13–14	**Narrative Accounts,** SE, p. 69; *UR1,* p. 64; **Literary Analysis Graphic Organizers A and B,** *GOT,* pp. 15–16	**Vocabulary Builder,** SE, p. 69: *pilfer, palisades, conceits, mollified, peril, loath, sundry, recompense* **Related Forms** *peril,* SE, p. 85; *UR1,* p. 66
PART 3	**"Huswifery"** (MA) Edward Taylor, SE, p. 94; **"To My Dear and Loving Husband"** (MA), Anne Bradstreet, SE, p. 96	**Paraphrasing,** SE, p. 93; *UR1,* p. 82; **Reading Warm-ups A and B,** *UR1,* pp. 77–80; **Reading Strategy Graphic Organizers A and B,** *GOT,* pp. 17–18	**The Puritan Plain Style,** SE, p. 93; *UR1,* p. 81; **Literary Analysis Graphic Organizers A and B,** *GOT,* pp. 19–20	**Vocabulary Builder,** SE, p. 93: *recompense, manifold, persevere* **Anglo-Saxon Suffix** *-fold,* SE, p. 98; *UR1,* p. 83
	from *Sinners in the Hands of an Angry God* (MC), Jonathan Edwards, SE, p. 102	**Using Context Clues,** SE, p. 101; *UR1,* p. 99; **Reading Warm-ups A and B,** *UR1,* pp. 96–97; **Reading Strategy Graphic Organizers A and B,** *GOT,* pp. 21–22	**Sermon,** SE, p. 101; *UR1,* p. 98; **Literary Analysis Graphic Organizers A and B,** *GOT,* pp. 23–24	**Vocabulary Builder,** SE, p. 101: *omnipotent, ineffable, dolorous* **Latin Prefix** *omni-,* SE, p. 108; *UR1,* p. 100

UNIT 2 A Nation Is Born (1750–1800)

	Selection	Reading Strategy	Literary Analysis	Vocabulary
PART 1	**from *The Autobiography*** (MC), Benjamin Franklin, SE, p. 142; **from *Poor Richard's Almanack*** (MC), Benjamin Franklin, SE, p. 148	**Drawing Conclusions,** SE, p. 141; *UR2,* p. 12; **Reading Warm-ups A and B,** *UR2,* pp. 9–10	**Autobiography,** SE, p. 141; *UR2,* p. 11; **Literary Analysis Graphic Organizers A and B,** *GOT,* pp. 26–29	**Vocabulary Builder,** SE, p. 141: *arduous, avarice, vigilance, disposition, foppery, felicity, squander, fasting* **Latin Root** *-vigil-,* SE, 152; *UR2,* p. 13

Key to Program References:
SE: Student Edition **UR:** Unit Resources **GOT:** Graphic Organizer Transparencies **GR:** General Resources **WG:** Writing and Grammar
MA: More accessible **A:** Average **MC:** More Challenging. See Accessibility at a Glance chart on selection pages.

Skills Navigator

Grammar	Writing	Extend Your Learning	Assessment
Compound Sentences, SE, p. 30; *UR1,* p. 14; *WG,* Ch. 19, Section 4	**Writing Lesson:** Retelling of a Story, SE, p. 31; *UR1,* p. 15; *WG,* Ch. 5, Section 3	**Listening and Speaking:** Dramatic Reenactment, SE, p. 31 **Research and Technology:** Logo, SE, p. 31, *UR1,* p. 16	**Selection Tests A and B,** *UR1,* pp. 20–25; **Rubric for Narration:** Short Story, *GR,* pp. 57–58
Past and Perfect Verb Tenses, SE, p. 56; *UR1,* 33; *WG,* Ch. 21, Section 2	**Writing Lesson:** Explorer's Journal, SE, p. 57; *UR1,* p. 34; *WG,* Ch. 6, Section 4	**Listening and Speaking:** Persuasive Speech, SE, p. 57 **Research and Technology:** Exploration Booklet, SE, p. 57, *UR1,* p. 35	**Selection Tests A and B,** *UR1,* pp. 37–42; **Rubrics for Narration:** Short Story, *GR,* pp. 57–58; **Rubric for Peer Assessment:** Speech, *GR,* p. 129
Action and Linking Verbs, SE, p. 64; *UR1,* p. 50; *WG,* Ch. 17, Section 2	**Writing Lesson:** Oral Report on the Voyage, SE, p. 65; *UR1,* p. 51; *WG,* Ch. 8, Section 2	**Listening and Speaking:** Presentation, SE, p. 65 **Research and Technology:** Chart, SE, p. 65, *UR1,* p. 52	**Selection Tests A and B,** *UR1,* pp. 54–59; **Rubrics for Descriptive Essay,** *GR,* pp. 63–64
Singular and Plural Possessive Nouns, SE, p. 85; *UR1,* p. 67; *WG,* Ch. 27, Section 6	**Writing Lesson:** Comparison of Narratives, SE, p. 86; *UR1,* p. 68; *WG,* Ch. 9, Section 3	**Listening and Speaking:** Persuasive Speech, SE, p. 86 **Research and Technology:** Historic Menu, SE, p. 86, *UR1,* p. 69	**Selection Tests A and B,** UR1, pp. 71–76; **Rubrics for Exposition:** Comparison-and-Contrast Essay, *GR,* pp. 69–70
Direct Address, SE, p. 98; *UR1,* p. 84; *WG,* Ch. 27, Section 2	**Writing Lesson:** Reflective Essay, SE, p. 99; *UR1,* p. 85; *WG,* Ch. 6, Section 2	**Listening and Speaking:** Informal Debate, SE, p. 99 **Research and Technology:** Graphic Display, SE, p. 99; *UR1,* p. 86	**Selection Tests A and B,** *UR1,* pp. 88–93; **Rubrics for Reflective Essay,** *GR,* pp. 47–48; **Rubric for Speaking:** Presenting Pros and Cons, *GR,* p. 92
Forms of Adjectives and Adverbs, SE, p. 108; *UR1,* p. 101; *WG,* Ch. 25, Section 1	**Writing Lesson:** Evaluation of Persuasion, SE, p. 109; *UR1,* p. 102; *WG,* Ch. 14, Section 3	**Listening and Speaking:** Oral Report, SE, p. 109 **Research and Technology:** Puritan Handbook, SE, p. 109; *UR1,* p. 103	**Selection Tests A and B,** *UR1,* pp. 105–110; **Rubrics for Critique,** *GR,* pp. 75–76; **Rubric for Speaking:** Delivering a Research Presentation, *GR,* p. 91

Grammar	Writing	Extend Your Learning	Assessment
Pronoun Case, SE, p. 152; *UR2,* p. 14; *WG* Ch. 22, Section 1	**Writing Lesson:** Autobiographical Account, SE, p. 153; *UR2,* p. 15; *WG,* Ch. 4, Section 4	**Listening and Speaking:** Class Improvement Plan, SE, p. 153 **Research and Technology:** Travel Brochure, SE, p. 153; *UR2,* p. 16	**Selection Tests A and B,** *UR2,* pp. 18–23; **Rubrics for Narration:** Autobiographical Narrative, *GR,* pp. 43–44

All selections are supported in the Reader's Notebooks.

UNIT 2 A Nation Is Born (1750–1800) *(continued)*

	Selection	Reading Strategy	Literary Analysis	Vocabulary
PART 1 (continued)	**from *The Interesting Narrative of the Life of Olaudah Equiano*** (A), Olaudah Equiano, SE, p. 160	**Summarizing,** SE, p. 159; *UR2,* p. 31; **Reading Warm-ups A and B,** *UR2,* pp. 28–29; **Reading Strategy Graphic Organizers A and B,** *GOT,* pp. 30–31	**Slave Narratives,** SE, p. 159; *UR2,* p. 30; **Literary Analysis Graphic Organizers A and B,** *GOT,* pp. 32–33	**Vocabulary Builder,** SE, p. 159: *loathsome, pestilential, copious, improvident, avarice, pacify* **Latin Root** *-vid-,* SE, p. 166; *UR2,* p. 32
	The Declaration of Independence (MC), Thomas Jefferson, SE, p. 170; **from *The Crisis, Number 1*** (A), Thomas Paine, SE, p. 174	**Recognizing Charged Words,** SE, p. 169; *UR2,* p. 48; **Reading Warm-ups A and B,** *UR2,* pp. 45–46; **Reading Strategy Graphic Organizers A and B,** *GOT,* pp. 34–35	**Persuasion,** SE, p. 169; *UR2,* p. 47; **Literary Analysis Graphic Organizers A and B,** *GOT,* pp. 36–37	**Vocabulary Builder,** SE, p. 169: *unalienable, usurpations, perfidy, redress, magnanimity, acquiesce, consanguinity, impious, infidel* **Latin Root** *-fid-,* SE, p. 178; *UR2,* p. 49
	"An Hymn to the Evening" (MC), Phillis Wheatley, SE, p. 183; **"To His Excellency, General Washington"** (A), Phillis Wheatley, SE, p. 184	**Clarifying Meaning,** SE, p. 181; *UR2,* p. 65; **Reading Warm-ups A and B,** *UR2,* pp. 62–63; **Reading Strategy Graphic Organizers A and B,** *GOT,* pp. 38–39	**Personification,** SE, p. 181; *UR2,* p. 64; **Literary Analysis Graphic Organizers A and B,** *GOT,* pp. 40–41	**Vocabulary Builder,** SE, p. 181: *placid, scepter, celestial, refulgent, propitious, refluent, pensive* **Latin Prefix** *re-,* SE, p. 188; *UR2,* p. 66
PART 2 FOCUS ON SPEECHES	**"Speech in the Virginia Convention"** (MC), Patrick Henry, SE, p. 202; **"Speech in the Convention"** (MC), SE, p. 207	**Evaluating Persuasive Appeals,** SE, p. 201; *UR2,* p. 82; **Reading Warm-ups A and B,** *UR2,* pp. 79–80; **Reading Strategy Graphic Organizers A and B,** *GOT,* pp. 42–43	**Speeches,** SE, p. 201; *UR2,* p. 81; **Literary Analysis Graphic Organizers A and B,** *GOT,* pp. 44–45	**Vocabulary Builder,** SE, p. 201: *arduous, insidious, subjugation, vigilant, infallibility, despotism, salutary, unanimity, posterity, manifest* **Latin suffix** *-ity,* SE, p. 211; *UR2,* p. 83
PART 3	**"Letter to Her Daughter From the New White House"** (A), Abigail Adams, SE, p. 216; **from *Letters From an American Farmer*** (MC), Michel-Guillaume Jean de Crèvecoeur, SE, p. 220	**Distinguishing Between Fact and Opinion,** SE, p. 215; *UR2,* p. 99; **Reading Warm-ups A and B,** *UR2,* pp. 96–97; **Reading Strategy Graphic Organizers A and B,** *GOT,* pp. 46–47	**Private and Public Letters (Epistles),** SE, p. 215; *UR2,* p. 98; **Literary Analysis Graphic Organizers A and B,** *GOT,* pp. 48–49	**Vocabulary Builder,** SE, p. 215: *extricate, agues, asylum, penury, despotic, subsistence* **Etymologies,** SE, p. 224; *UR2,* p. 100

UNIT 3 A Growing Nation (1800–1870)

	Selection	Reading Strategy	Literary Analysis	Vocabulary
PART 1	**"The Devil and Tom Walker"** (A), Washington Irving, SE, p. 258	**Inferring Cultural Attitudes,** SE, p. 257; *UR3,* p. 12; **Reading Warm-ups A and B,** *UR3,* pp. 9–10; **Reading Strategy Graphic Organizers A and B,** *GOT,* pp. 51–52	**Third-Person Omniscient Point of View,** SE, p. 257; *UR3,* p. 11; **Literary Analysis Graphic Organizers A and B,** *GOT,* pp. 53–54	**Vocabulary Builder,** SE, p. 257: *avarice, usurers, extort, ostentation, parsimony* **Latin Prefix** *ex-,* SE, p. 270; *UR3,* p. 13

Key to Program References:
SE: Student Edition **UR:** Unit Resources **GOT:** Graphic Organizer Transparencies **GR:** General Resources **WG:** Writing and Grammar
MA: More accessible **A:** Average **MC:** More Challenging. See Accessibility at a Glance chart on selection pages.

Skills Navigator

Grammar	Writing	Extend Your Learning	Assessment
Active and Passive Voice, SE, p. 166; *UR2,* p. 33; *WG*, Ch. 21, Section 4	**Writing Lesson:** Museum Placard, SE, p. 167; *UR2,* p. 34; *WG*, Ch. 10, Section 3	**Listening and Speaking:** Debate, SE, p. 167 **Research and Technology:** Research Presentation, SE, p. 167; *UR2*, p. 35	**Selection Tests A and B,** *UR2,* pp. 37–42; **Rubrics for Research: Research Report,** *GR,* pp. 49–50; **Rubric for Speaking:** Delivering a Research Presentation, *GR,* p. 91
Parallelism, SE, p. 178; *UR2,* p. 50; *WG*, Ch. 20, Section 6	**Writing Lesson:** A Proposal to the Principal, SE, p. 179; *UR2,* p. 51; *WG*, Ch. 7, Section 4	**Listening and Speaking:** News Reports, SE, p. 179 **Research and Technology:** Write a Précis, SE, p. 179; *UR2,* p. 52	**Selection Tests A and B,** *UR2,* pp. 54–59; **Rubrics for Exposition:** Problem-Solution Essay, *GR,* pp. 59–60; **Rubric for Listening:** Evaluating a Media Presentation, *GR,* p. 86
Subject and Verb Agreement, SE, p. 188; *UR2,* p. 67; *WG*, Ch. 23, Section 1	**Writing Lesson:** Inscription for a Monument, SE, p. 189; *UR2,* p. 68; *WG*, Ch. 7, Section 4	**Listening and Speaking:** Dramatic Reading, SE, p. 189 **Research and Technology:** Graphic Display, SE, p. 189; *UR2,* p. 69	**Selection Tests A and B,** *UR2,* pp. 71–76; **Rubrics for Descriptive Essay,** *GR,* pp. 63–64
Double Negatives, SE, p. 211; *UR2,* p. 84; *WG*, Ch. 25, Section 1	**Writing Lesson:** Commentary on a Speech, SE, p. 212; *UR2,* p. 85; *WG*, Ch. 28, Section 1	**Listening and Speaking:** Debate, SE, p. 212 **Research and Technology:** Display, SE, p. 212; *UR2,* p. 86	**Selection Tests A and B,** *UR2,* pp. 88–93; **Rubrics for Critique,** *GR,* pp. 75–76
Semicolons, SE, p. 224; *UR2,* p. 101; *WG*, Ch. 27, Section 3	**Writing Lesson:** Personal Letter, SE, p. 225; *UR2,* p. 102; *WG*, Ch. 9, Section 2	**Listening and Speaking:** Interview, SE, p. 225 **Research and Technology:** Advertisements, SE, p. 225; *UR2,* p. 103	**Selection Tests A and B,** *UR2,* pp. 105–110; **Rubrics for Business Letter,** *GR,* pp. 61–62

Grammar	Writing	Extend Your Learning	Assessment
Adjective Clauses, SE, p. 270; *UR3,* p. 14; *WG*, Ch. 19, Section 3	**Writing Lesson:** Updating a Story, SE, p. 271; *UR3,* p. 15; *WG*, Ch. 5, Section 2	**Listening and Speaking:** Enactment, SE, p. 271 **Research and Technology:** Exhibition, SE, p. 271; *UR3,* p. 16	**Selection Tests A and B,** *UR3,* pp. 18–23; **Rubrics for Narration:** Short Story, *GR,* pp. 57–58; **Rubrics for Research Report,** *GR,* pp. 49–50

All selections are supported in the Reader's Notebooks.

UNIT 3

A Growing Nation (1800–1870) *(continued)*

	Selection	Reading Strategy	Literary Analysis	Vocabulary
PART 1 *(continued)*	**"The Tide Rises, The Tide Falls"** (MA), Henry Wadsworth Longfellow, SE, p. 275; **"Thanatopsis"** (MC), William Cullen Bryant, SE, p. 277; **"Old Ironsides"** (A), Oliver Wendell Holmes, SE, p. 280; **from *Snowbound*** (A), John Greenleaf Whittier, SE, p. 282	**Summarizing,** SE, p. 273; *UR3,* p. 29; **Reading Warm-ups A and B,** *UR3,* pp. 26–27; **Reading Strategy Graphic Organizers A and B,** *GOT,* pp. 57–58	**Meter,** SE, p. 273; *UR3,* p. 28; **Literary Analysis Graphic Organizers A and B,** *GOT,* pp. 55–56	**Vocabulary Builder,** SE, p. 273: *bivouac, sublime, efface, sepulcher, pensive, venerable, gloaming, ominous, querulous, patriarch* **Latin Root** *-patr-,* SE, p. 290; *UR3,* p. 30
	"Crossing the Great Divide" (A), Meriweather Lewis, SE, p. 298; **"The Most Sublime Spectacle on Earth"** (A), John Wesley Powell, SE, p. 301	**Noting Spatial Relationships,** SE, p. 297; *UR3,* p. 46; **Reading Warm-ups A and B,** *UR3,* pp. 43–44; **Reading Strategy Graphic Organizers A and B,** *GOT,* pp. 61–62	**Description,** SE, p. 297; *UR3,* p. 45; **Literary Analysis Graphic Organizers A and B,** *GOT,* pp. 59–60	**Vocabulary Builder,** SE, p. 297: *conspicuous, sublime, labyrinth, excavated, demarcation, multifarious, multitudinous* **Latin Prefix** *multi-,* SE, p. 307; *UR3,* p. 47
PART 2	**"The Fall of the House, of Usher"** (MC), Edgar Allen Poe, SE, p. 312; **"The Raven"** (A), Edgar Allen Poe, SE, p. 330	**Breaking Down Long Sentences,** SE, p. 311; *UR3,* p. 63; **Reading Warm-ups A and B,** *UR3,* pp. 60–61; **Reading Strategy Graphic Organizers A and B,** *GOT,* pp. 63–64	**Single Effect,** SE, p. 311; *UR3,* p. 62; **Literary Analysis Graphic Organizers A and B,** *GOT,* pp. 65–66	**Vocabulary Builder,** SE, p. 311: *importunate, munificent, equivocal, appellation, specious, anomalous, sentience, obeisance, craven* **Latin Root** *-voc-,* SE, p. 336; *UR3,* p. 64
	"The Minister's Black Veil" (MC), Nathaniel Hawthorne, SE, p. 340	**Drawing Inferences About Meaning,** SE, p. 339; *UR3,* p. 80; **Reading Warm-ups A and B,** *UR3,* pp. 77–78; **Reading Strategy Graphic Organizers A and B,** *GOT,* pp. 67–68	**Parable,** SE, p. 339; *UR3,* p. 79; **Literary Analysis Graphic Organizers A and B,** *GOT,* pp. 69–70	**Vocabulary Builder,** SE, p. 339: *venerable, iniquity, indecorous, ostentatious, sagacious, vagary, tremulous, waggery, impertinent, obstinacy* **Latin Root** *equi-,* SE, p. 354; *UR3,* p. 81
	from *Moby Dick* (MC), Herman Melville, SE, p. 358	**Recognizing Symbols,** SE, p. 357; *UR3,* p. 106; **Reading Warm-ups A and B,** *UR3,* pp. 103–104; **Reading Strategy Graphic Organizers A and B,** *GOT,* pp. 71–72	**Symbol,** SE, p. 357; *UR3,* p. 105; **Literary Analysis Graphic Organizers A and B,** *GOT,* pp. 73–74	**Vocabulary Builder,** SE, p. 357: *inscrutable, maledictions, prescient, pertinaciously* **Latin Prefix** *mal-,* SE, p. 376; *UR3,* p. 107
PART 3	**from *Nature*** (A), Ralph Waldo Emerson, SE, p. 430; **from *Self-Reliance*** (A), Ralph Waldo Emerson, SE, p. 393; **from "Concord Hymn"** (A), Ralph Waldo Emerson, SE, p. 395; **from "The Snowstorm"** (A), Ralph Waldo Emerson, SE, p. 396	**Challenging the Text,** SE, p. 389; *UR3,* p. 125; **Reading Warm-ups A and B,** *UR3,* pp. 122–123; **Reading Strategy Graphic Organizers A and B,** *GOT,* pp. 75–76	**Transcendentalism,** SE, p. 389; *UR3,* p. 124; **Literary Analysis Graphic Organizers A and B,** *GOT,* pp. 77–78	**Vocabulary Builder,** SE, p. 389: *blithe, connate, chaos, aversion, suffrage, divines, radiant, tumultuous, bastions* **Latin Root** *-radi-,* SE, p. 400; *UR3,* p. 126
	from *Walden* (MC), Henry David Thoreau, SE, p. 406; **from *Civil Disobedience*** (A), Henry David Thoreau, SE, p. 416	**Evaluating the Writer's Statement of Philosophy,** SE, p. 405; *UR3,* p. 144; **Reading Warm-ups A and B,** *UR3,* pp. 141–142; **Reading Strategy Graphic Organizers A and B,** *GOT,* pp. 79–80	**Style,** SE, p. 405; *UR3,* p. 143; **Literary Analysis Graphic Organizers A and B,** *GOT,* pp. 81–82	**Vocabulary Builder,** SE, p. 405: *dilapidated, sublime, superfluous, evitable, magnanimity, expedient, posterity, alacrity* **Latin Root** *-flu-,* SE, p. 419; *UR3,* p. 145

Key to Program References:
SE: Student Edition **UR:** Unit Resources **GOT:** Graphic Organizer Transparencies **GR:** General Resources **WG:** Writing and Grammar
MA: More accessible **A:** Average **MC:** More Challenging. See Accessibility at a Glance chart on selection pages.

Skills Navigator

Grammar	Writing	Extend Your Learning	Assessment
Participles as Adjectives, SE, p. 290; *UR3,* p. 31; *WG,* Ch. 19, Section 2	**Writing Lesson:** Précis, SE, p. 291; *UR3,* p. 32; *WG,* Ch. 31, Section 1	**Listening and Speaking:** Dramatic Reading, SE, p. 291 **Research and Technology:** Oral Presentation, SE, p. 291; *UR3,* p. 33	**Selection Tests A and B,** *UR3,* pp. 35–40; **Rubrics for Summary,** *GR,* pp. 71–72
Participial Phrases, SE, p. 307; *UR3,* p. 48; *WG,* Ch. 19, Section 2	**Writing Lesson:** Description of a Natural Wonder, SE, p. 308; *UR3,* p. 49; *WG,* Ch. 6, Section 2	**Listening and Speaking:** Tourism Presentation, SE, p. 308 **Research and Technology:** Expedition Map, SE, p. 308; *UR3,* p. 50	**Selection Tests A and B,** *UR3,* pp. 52–57; **Rubrics for Descriptive Essay,** *GR,* pp. 63–64
Coordinate Adjectives, SE, p. 336; *UR3,* p. 65; *WG,* Ch. 27, Section 2	**Writing Lesson:** Literary Criticism, SE, p. 337; *UR3,* p. 66; *WG,* Ch. 14, Section 2	**Listening and Speaking:** Dramatic Reading, SE, p. 337 **Research and Technology:** Movie Analysis, SE, p. 337; *UR3,* p. 67	**Selection Tests A and B,** *UR3,* pp. 69–74; **Rubrics for Response to Literature,** *GR,* pp. 65–66; **Rubric for Peer Assessment:** Dramatic Performance, *GR,* p. 131
Varying Sentence Openers, SE, p. 354; *UR3,* p. 82; *WG,* Ch. 20, Section 3	**Writing Lesson:** Response to a Short Story, SE, p. 355; *UR3,* p. 83; *WG,* Ch. 14, Section 2	**Listening and Speaking:** Monologue, SE, p. 355 **Research and Technology:** Oral Presentation, SE, p. 355; *UR3,* p. 84	**Selection Tests A and B,** *UR3,* pp. 86–91; **Rubrics for Respons to Literature,** *GR,* pp. 65–66; **Rubric for Peer Assessment:** Dramatic Performance, *GR,* p. 131
Agreement with Collective Nouns, SE, p. 376; *UR3,* p. 108; *WG,* Ch. 23, Section 1	**Writing Lesson:** A Character Study, SE, p. 377; *UR3,* p. 109; *WG,* Ch. 14, Section 2	**Listening and Speaking:** Monologue, SE, p. 377 **Research and Technology:** Report, SE, p. 377; *UR3,* p. 110	**Selection Tests A and B,** *UR3,* pp. 112–117; **Rubrics for Response to Literature,** *GR,* pp. 65–66; **Rubric for Peer Assessment:** Dramatic Performance, *GR,* p. 131
Vary Sentence Length, SE, p. 400; *UR3,* p. 127; *WG,* Ch. 20, Section 3	**Writing Lesson:** Critical Evaluation of a Philosophical Essay, SE, p. 401; *UR3,* p. 128; *WG,* Ch. 14, Section 3	**Listening and Speaking:** Public Service Announcement, SE, p. 401 **Research and Technology:** Profile, SE, p. 401: *UR3,* p. 129	**Selection Tests A and B,** *UR3,* pp. 131–136; **Rubrics for Response, to Literature,** *GR,* pp. 65–66; **Rubrics for Research: Research Report,** *GR,* pp. 49–50
Infinitives and Infinitive Phrases, SE, p. 419; *UR3,* p. 146; *WG,* Ch. 19, Section 2	**Writing Lesson:** Editorial, SE, p. 420; *UR3,* p. 147; *WG,* Ch. 7, Section 2	**Listening and Speaking:** Debate, SE, p. 420 **Research and Technology:** Oral Presentation, SE, p. 420: *UR3,* p. 148	**Selection Tests A and B,** *UR3,* pp. 150–155; **Rubrics for Persuasion:** Persuasive Essay, *GR,* pp. 45–46; **Rubric for Speaking:** Presenting Pros and Cons, *GR,* p. 92

All selections are supported in the Reader's Notebooks.

UNIT 3 A Growing Nation (1800–1870) *(continued)*

PART 4 FOCUS ON POETRY

Selection	Reading Strategy	Literary Analysis	Vocabulary
Emily Dickinson's Poetry (MC, A, MC, MC, MC, A, A), Emily Dickinson, SE, p. 426	**Analyzing Images,** SE, p. 425; *UR3,* p. 161; **Reading Warm-ups A and B,** *UR3,* pp. 158–159; **Reading Strategy Graphic Organizers A and B,** *GOT,* pp. 83–84	**Slant Rhyme,** SE, p. 425; *UR3,* p. 160; **Literary Analysis Graphic Organizers A and B,** *GOT,* pp. 85–86	**Vocabulary Builder,** SE, p. 425: *cornice, surmised, oppresses, finite, infinity* **Latin Root** *-finis-,* SE, p. 436; *UR3,* p. 162
Walt Whitman's Poetry (MC, A, MA, A, A, MA), Walt Whitman, SE, p. 440	**Inferring the Poet's Attitude,** SE, p. 439; *UR3,* p. 178; **Reading Warm-ups A and B,** *UR3,* pp. 175–176; **Reading Strategy Graphic Organizers A and B,** *GOT,* pp. 87–88	**Free Verse,** SE, p. 439; *UR3,* p. 177; **Literary Analysis Graphic Organizers A and B,** *GOT,* pp.89–90	**Vocabulary Builder,** SE, p. 439: *abeyance, effuse* **Latin Root** *-fus-,* SE, p. 452; *UR3,* p. 179

UNIT 4 Division, Reconciliation, and Expansion (1850–1914)

PART 1

Selection	Reading Strategy	Literary Analysis	Vocabulary
"An Episode of War" (A), Stephen Crane, SE p. 486; **"Willie Has Gone to War"** (A), Stephen Foster, SE p. 491	**Recognizing Historical Details,** SE, p. 485; *UR1,* p. 9; **Reading Warm-ups A and B,** *UR1,* pp. 6–7	**Realism and Naturalism,** SE, p. 485; *UR1,* p. 8, *GOT,* pp. 149–152	**Vocabulary Builder,** SE, p. 485: *precipitate, aggregation, inscrutable, disdainfully, glade* **Latin Root** *-greg-,* SE, p. 488; *UR1,* p. 13
"Swing Low, Sweet Chariot" (MA), SE p. 498; **"Go Down, Moses"** (A), SE p. 500	**Listening,** SE p. 497; *UR1,* p. 29; **Reading Warm-ups A and B,** *UR1,* pp. 26–27, *GOT,* pp. 96–99	**Refrain,** SE, p. 497; *UR1,* p. 28	**Vocabulary Builder,** SE, p. 497: *oppressed, smite* **Latin Root** *-press-* SE, p. 500; *UR1,* p. 30
from *My Bondage and My Freedom* (MC), Frederick Douglass, SE, p. 506	**Establishing a Purpose,** SE, p. 505; *UR1,* p. 46; **Reading Warm-ups A and B,** *UR1,* pp. 43–44; **Reading Strategy Graphic Organizers A and B,** *GOT,* pp. 100–103	**Autobiography,** SE, p. 505; *UR1,* p. 45	**Vocabulary Builder,** SE, p. 97: *congenial, benevolent, stringency, depravity, consternation, redolent* **Latin Root:** *-bene-,* SE, p. 507; *UR1,* p. 47
"An Occurrence at Owl Creek Bridge" (A), Ambrose Bierce, SE, p. 518	**Identifying Chronological Order,** SE, p.517; *UR1,* p. 63; **Reading Warm-ups A and B,** *UR1,* pp. 60–61; **Reading Strategy Graphic Organizers A and B,** *GOT,* pp. 104–105	**Point of View,** SE, p. 517; *UR1,* p. 62; **Literary Analysis Graphic Organizers A and B,** *GOT,* pp. 106–107	**Vocabulary Builder,** SE, p. 517: *etiquette, deference, imperious, dictum, summarily, effaced, oscillation, apprised, malign, ineffable* **Latin Root:** *-summa-,* SE, p. 521; *UR1,* p. 64
"The Gettysburg Address" (A), Abraham Lincoln, SE, p. 532; **"Second Inaugural Address"** (MC), Abraham Lincoln, SE, p. 533; **"Letter to His Son"** (MC), Robert E Lee, SE, p. 535	**Using Background Knowledge,** SE, p. 531; *UR1,* p. 80; **Reading Warm-ups A and B,** *UR1,* pp. 77–78; **Reading Strategy Graphic Organizers A and B,** *GOT,* pp. 108–109	**Diction,** SE, p. 531; *UR1,* p. 79; **Literary Analysis Graphic Organizers A and B,** *GOT,* pp. 110–111	**Vocabulary Builder,** SE, p. 531: *consecrate, hallow, deprecated, insurgents, discern, scourge, malice, anarchy, redress* **Greek Root** *-archy-,* SE, p. 535; *UR1,* p. 81

Key to Program References:
SE: Student Edition **UR:** Unit Resources **GOT:** Graphic Organizer Transparencies **GR:** General Resources **WG:** Writing and Grammar
MA: More accessible **A:** Average **MC:** More Challenging. See Accessibility at a Glance chart on selection pages.

Skills Navigator

Grammar	Writing	Extend Your Learning	Assessment
Gerunds, SE, p. 436; *UR3,* p. 163; *WG*, Ch. 19, Section 2	**Writing Lesson:** Letter to an Author, SE, p. 437; *UR3,* p. 164; *WG*, Ch. 14, Section 3	**Listening and Speaking:** Poetry Reading, SE, p. 437 **Research and Technology:** Report, SE, p. 437; *UR3,* p. 165	**Selection Tests A and B,** *UR3,* pp. 167–172; **Rubrics for a Business Letter,** *GR,* pp. 61–62; **Rubrics for Research:** Research Report, *GR,* pp. 49–50
Pronoun and Antecedent Agreement, SE, p. 452; *UR3,* p. 180; *WG*, Ch. 23, Section 2	**Writing Lesson:** Imitation of an Author's Style, SE, p. 453; *UR3,* p. 181; *WG*, Ch. 3, Section 3	**Listening and Speaking:** Collage, SE, p. 453 **Research and Technology:** Research Poetry, SE, p. 453; *UR3,* p. 182	**Selection Tests A and B,** *UR3,* pp. 184–189; **Rubrics for Poem (Rhyming),** *GR,* pp. 73–74; **Rubric for Speaking:** Delivering a Research Presentation, *GR,* p. 91

Grammar	Writing	Extend Your Learning	Assessment
Usage: *Like* and *As,* SE, p. 494; *UR1,* p. 11, *WG*, Ch. 19, Sections 1–3	**Writing Lesson:** Field Report on Hospital Conditions, SE, p. 495; *UR1*, p. 15, *WG*, Ch. 6, Section 3	**Listening and Speaking:** Role-play, SE, p. 495 **Research and Technology:** Definition Essay, p. 495, *UR1*, p. 16	**Selection Tests A and B,** UR1, pp. 18–23; **Rubrics for Descriptive Essay,** *GR,* pp. 63–64; **Rubric for Listening:** Evaluating a Media Presentation, *GR,* p. 86
Direct Address, SE, p. 502; *UR1,* p. 31, *WG*, Ch. 27, Section 2	**Writing Lesson:** Reflective Essay, SE, p. 503; *UR1*, p. 32, *WG*, Ch. 4, Section 2	**Listening and Speaking:** Choral Reading, SE p. 503 **Research and Technology:** Anthology, SE, p. 503, *UR1*, p. 33	**Selection Tests A and B,** UR1, pp. 35–40; **Rubric for Reflective Essay,** *GR*, pp. 47–48
Correlative Conjunctions, SE, p. 514; *UR1,* p. 48; *WG*, Ch. 17, Section 4	**Writing Lesson:** College Admission Essay, SE, p. 515; *UR1*, p. 49; *WG*, Ch. 4, Section 3	**Listening and Speaking:** Oral Presentation, SE, p. 515 **Research and Technology:** Multimedia Presentation, SE, p. 515; *UR1*, p. 50	**Selection Tests A and B,** *UR1*, pp. 52–57; **Rubrics for Reflective Essay,** *GR*, pp. 47–48, **Rubrics for Media Presentation,** *GR*, pp. 51–52
Semicolons in Compound Sentences, SE, p. 528; *UR1,* p. 65; *WG*, Ch. 27, Section 3	**Writing Lesson:** Critical Essay, SE, p. 529; *UR1*, p. 66; *WG*, Ch. 14, Section 3	**Listening and Speaking:** Summary, SE, p. 529 **Research and Technology:** Visual Model, SE, p. 529; *UR1*, p. 67	**Selection Tests A and B,** *UR1*, pp. 69–74 **Rubrics for Response to Literature,** *GR*, pp. 65–66
Parallel Structure, SE, p. 538; *UR1,* p. 82; *WG*, Ch. 8, Section 4	**Writing Lesson:** Diary Entry, SE, p. 539; *UR1*, p. 83; *WG*, Ch. 7, Section 3	**Listening and Speaking:** mock Supreme Court Hearing, SE, p. 539 **Research and Technology:** Poster, SE, p. 539; *UR1*, p. 84	**Selection Tests A and B,** *UR1*, pp. 86–91; **Rubrics for Response to Literature,** *GR*, pp. 65–66; **Rubric for Speaking:** Presenting Pros and Cons, *GR*, p. 92

All selections are supported in the Reader's Notebooks.

UNIT 4 Division, Reconciliation, and Expansion (1850–1914) *(continued)*

Part	Selection	Reading Strategy	Literary Analysis	Vocabulary
PART 2 FOCUS ON JOURNALS/LETTERS	**Civil War Diaries, Journals, and Letters** (A, A, A, MA, MA, MA), SE, pp. 550–561	**Distinguishing Fact from Opinion**, SE, p. 549; *UR1*, p. 99; **Reading Warm-ups A and B**, *UR1*, pp. 96–97; **Reading Strategy Graphic Organizers A and B**, *GOT*, pp. 114–115	**Diaries, Journals, and Letters**, SE, p. 549; *UR1*, p. 98; **Literary Analysis Graphic Organizers A and B**, *GOT*, pp. 112–113	**Vocabulary Builder**, SE, p. 549: *capitulate, audaciously, foreboding, obstinate, imprecations, serenity* **Latin Prefix** *ob-*, SE, p. 555; *UR1*, p. 100
PART 3	**"The Boys' Ambition" from *Life on the Mississippi*** (A), Mark Twain, SE, p. 576; **"The Notorious Jumping Frog of Calaveras County"** (MA), Mark Twain, SE, p. 581	**Understanding Regional Dialect**, SE, p. 575; *UR1*, p. 125; **Reading Warm-ups A and B**, *UR1*, pp. 122–123; **Reading Strategy Graphic Organizers A and B**, *GOT*, pp. 116–119	**Humor**, SE, p. 575; *UR1*, p. 125	**Vocabulary Builder**, SE, p. 575: *transient, prodigious, eminence, garrulous, conjectured, monotonous, interminable, ornery* **Greek Prefix** *mono-*, SE, p. 581; *UR1*, p. 126
	"The Outcasts of Poker Flat" (A), Bret Harte, SE, p. 592	**Questioning the Text**, SE, p. 591; *UR1*, p. 142; **Reading Warm-ups A and B**, *UR1*, pp. 139–140; **Reading Strategy Graphic Organizers A and B**, *GOT*, pp. 122–123	**Regionalism**, SE, p. 591; *UR1*, p. 141; **Literary Analysis Graphic Organizers A and B**, *GOT*, pp. 120–121	**Vocabulary Builder**, SE, p. 549: *expatriated, anathema, bellicose, recumbent, equanimity, vociferation, vituperative, querulous* **Latin Word Part** *-bel-*, SE, p. 595; *UR1*, p. 143
	"Heading West" (MA), Miriam Davis Colt, SE, p. 608; **"I Will Fight No More Forever"** (MA), Chief Joseph, SE, p. 614	**Responding**, SE, p. 607; *UR1*, p. 159; **Reading Warm-ups A and B**, *UR1*, pp. 156–157	**Tone**, SE, p. 607; *UR1*, p. 158; **Literary Analysis Graphic Organizers A and B**, *GOT*, pp. 124–127	**Vocabulary Builder**, SE, p. 549: *genial, pervading, terra firma, emigrants, profusion, depredations, nonplused* **Latin Term** *terra firma*, SE, p. 609; *UR1*, p. 160
	"To Build a Fire" (A), Jack London, SE, p. 620	**Predicting**, SE, p. 619; *UR1*, p. 176; **Reading Warm-ups A and B**, *UR1*, pp. 173–174; **Reading Strategy Graphic Organizers A and B**, *GOT*, pp. 128–129	**Conflict**, SE, p. 619; *UR1*, p. 175; **Literary Analysis Graphic Organizers A and B**, *GOT*, pp. 130–131	**Vocabulary Builder**, SE, p. 619: *conjectural, unwonted, conflagration, peremptorily,* **Latin Root** *-ject-*, SE, p. 621; *UR1*, p. 177
PART 4	**"The Story of an Hour"** (A), Kate Chopin, SE, p. 642	**Recognizing Ironic Details**, SE, p. 641; *UR1*, p. 193; **Reading Warm-ups A and B**, *UR1*, pp. 190–191; **Reading Strategy Graphic Organizers A and B**, *GOT*, pp. 132–133	**Irony**, SE, p. 641; *UR1*, p. 192; **Literary Analysis Graphic Organizers A and B**, *GOT*, pp. 134–135	**Vocabulary Builder**, SE, p. 641: *forestall, repression, elusive, tumultuously, importunities* **Anglo-Saxon Prefix** *fore-*, SE, p. 644; *UR1*, p. 194
	"Douglass" (A), Paul Laurence Dunbar, SE, p. 652; **"We Wear the Mask"** (A), Paul Laurence Dunbar, SE, p. 654	**Interpreting**, SE, p. 651; *UR1*, p. 210; **Reading Warm-ups A and B**, *UR1*, pp. 207–208; **Reading Strategy Graphic Organizers A and B**, *GOT*, pp. 136–139	**Rhyme**, SE, p. 651; *UR1*, p. 209	**Vocabulary Builder**, SE, p. 549: *salient, tempest, stark, guile, myriad*

Key to Program References:
SE: Student Edition **UR:** Unit Resources **GOT:** Graphic Organizer Transparencies **GR:** General Resources **WG:** Writing and Grammar
MA: More accessible **A:** Average **MC:** More Challenging. See Accessibility at a Glance chart on selection pages.

Skills Navigator

Grammar	Writing	Extend Your Learning	Assessment
Capitalization of Proper Nouns, SE, p. 564; *UR1,* p. 101; *WG,* Ch. 26	**Writing Lesson:** Problem-and-Solution Essay, SE, p. 565; *UR1,* p. 102; *WG,* Ch. 4, Section 2	**Listening and Speaking:** Multimedia Presentation, SE, p. 565 **Research and Technology:** Model or Map, SE, p. 565; *UR1,* p. 103	**Selection Tests A and B,** *UR1,* pp. 105–110; **Rubrics for Problem-and-Solution Essay,** *GR,* pp. 59–60; **Rubric for Peer Assessment:** Oral Interpretation, *GR,* p. 130
Double Negatives, SE, p. 588; *UR1,* p. 127; *WG,* Ch. 25, Section 1	**Writing Lesson:** Analytic Essay, SE, p. 589; *UR1,* p. 128; *WG,* Ch. 14, Section 3	**Listening and Speaking:** Interview, SE, p. 589 **Research and Technology:** Multimedia Report, SE, p. 589; *UR1,* p. 129	**Selection Tests A and B,** *UR1,* pp. 132–136; **Rubrics for Response to Literature,** *GR,* pp. 65–66; **Rubrics for Multimedia Presentation,** *GR,* pp. 51–52
Coordinating Conjunctions in Compound Sentences, SE, p. 604; *UR1,* p. 144; *WG,* Ch. 17, Section 4	**Writing Lesson:** Critical Review, SE, p. 605; *UR1,* p. 145; *WG,* Ch. 14, Section 4	**Listening and Speaking:** Eulogy, SE, p. 605 **Research and Technology:** Prospecting and Mining Report, SE, p. 605; *UR1,* p. 146	**Selection Tests A and B,** *UR1,* pp. 148–153; **Rubrics for Response to Literature,** *GR,* pp. 65–66
Sentence Fragments, SE, p. 616; *UR1,* p. 161; *WG,* Ch. 20, Section 4	**Writing Lesson:** Position Paper on Development, SE, p. 617; *UR1,* p. 162; *WG,* Ch. 7, Section 4	**Listening and Speaking:** Oral Interpretation, SE, p. 617 **Research and Technology:** Marketing Brochure, SE, p. 617; *UR1,* p. 163	**Selection Tests A and B,** *UR1,* pp. 165–170; **Rubrics for Persuasion:** Persuasive Essay, *GR,* pp. 45–46; **Rubric for Peer Assessment:** Oral Interpretation, *GR,* p. 130
Adverb Clauses, SE, p. 637; *UR1,* p. 178; *WG,* Ch. 19, Section 3	**Writing Lesson:** Literary Analysis, SE, p. 638; *UR1,* p. 179; *WG,* Ch. 14, Section 4	**Listening and Speaking:** Enactment, SE, p. 638 **Research and Technology:** Booklet, SE, p. 638; *UR1,* p. 180	**Selection Tests A and B,** *UR1,* pp. 182–187; **Rubrics for Response to Literature,** *GR,* pp. 65–66
Appositives and Appositive Phrases, SE, p. 648; *UR1,* p. 195; *WG,* Ch. 19, Section 1	**Writing Lesson:** Reflective Essay, SE, p. 649; *UR1,* p. 196; *WG,* Ch. 4, Section 2	**Listening and Speaking:** Soliloquy, SE, p. 649 **Research and Technology:** Oral Report, SE, p. 649; *UR1,* p. 197	**Selection Tests A and B,** *UR1,* pp. 199–204; **Rubrics for Reflective Essay,** *GR,* pp. 47–48; **Rubric for Peer Assessment:** Dramatic Performance, *GR,* p. 131
Punctuation of Interjections, SE, p. 656; *UR1,* p. 212; *WG,* Ch. 17, Section 1	**Writing Lesson:** Poem to Honor a Hero, SE, p. 657; *UR1,* p. 213; *WG,* Ch. 7, Section 3	**Listening and Speaking:** Oral Interpretation, SE, p. 657 **Research and Technology:** Report, SE, p. 657; *UR1,* p. 214	**Selection Tests A and B,** *UR1,* pp. 216–221; **Rubrics for Poem (Rhyming),** *GR,* pp. 73–74; **Rubric for Peer Assessment:** Oral Interpretation, *GR,* p. 130

All selections are supported in the Reader's Notebooks.

UNIT 4 Division, Reconciliation, and Expansion (1850–1914) *(continued)*

	Selection	Reading Strategy	Literary Analysis	Vocabulary
PART 4	**"Luke Havergal"** (A), Edwin Arlington Robinson, SE, p. 660; **"Richard Cory"** (A), Edwin Arlington Robinson, SE, p. 662; **"Lucinda Matlock"** (A), Edgar Lee Masters, SE, p. 663; **"Richard Bone"** (A), Edgar Lee Masters, SE, p. 664	**Recognizing Attitudes,** SE, p. 659; *UR1*, p. 236; **Reading Warm-ups A and B,** *UR1*, pp. 233–234; **Reading Strategy Graphic Organizers A and B,** *GOT*, pp. 140–143	**Speaker,** SE, p. 659; *UR1*, p. 235	**Vocabulary Builder,** SE, p. 659: *imperially, repose, degenerate, epitaph*
	"A Wagner Matinee" (MC), Willa Cather, SE, p. 670	**Clarifying,** SE, p. 669; *UR1*, p. 253; **Reading Warm-ups A and B,** *UR1*, pp. 250–251; **Reading Strategy Graphic Organizers A and B,** *GOT*, pp. 144–145	**Characterization,** SE, p. 669; *UR1*, p. 252; **Literary Analysis Graphic Organizers A and B,** *GOT*, pp. 146–147	**Vocabulary Builder,** SE, p. 641: *reverential, tremulously, semisomnambulant, inert, prelude, jocularity* **Word Origins,** SE, p. 674; *UR1*, p. 254

UNIT 5 Disillusion, Defiance, and Discontent (1914–1946)

	Selection	Reading Strategy	Literary Analysis	Vocabulary
PART 1	**"The Love Song of J. Alfred Prufrock"** (MC), T. S. Eliot, SE, p. 716	**Listening,** SE, p. 715; *UR1*, p. 9; **Reading Warm-ups A and B,** *UR1*, pp. 6–7	**Dramatic Monologue,** SE, p. 715; *UR1*, p. 8; *GOT*, pp. 149–152	**Vocabulary Builder,** SE, p. 715: *insidious, digress, malingers, meticulous, obtuse* **Greek Prefix** *di-*, SE, p. 718; *UR1*, p. 10
	Poetry by Ezra Pound, William Carlos Williams, and H.D. (MC, A, MA, A, A, A, A, A) SE, pp. 727–736	**Engaging Your Senses,** SE, p. 726; *UR1*, p. 26; **Reading Warm-ups A and B,** *UR1*, pp. 23–24; *GOT*, pp. 153–154	**Imagist Poetry,** SE, p. 726; *UR1*, p. 25; *GOT*, pp. 155–156	**Vocabulary Builder,** SE, p. 497: *voluminous, dogma, apparition* **Forms of** *appear* SE, p. 732; *UR1*, p. 30
	"Winter Dreams" (MC), F. Scott Fitzgerald, SE, p. 742	**Drawing Conclusions About Characters,** SE, p. 741; *UR1*, p. 43; **Reading Warm-ups A and B,** *UR1*, pp. 40–41; **Reading Strategy Graphic Organizers A and B,** *GOT*, pp. 157–158	**Characterization,** SE, p. 741; *UR1*, p. 42; *GOT*, pp. 159–160	**Vocabulary Builder,** SE, p. 741: *fallowness, fortuitous, sinuous, mundane, poignant, pugilistic, somnolent* **Latin Root** *-somn-*, SE, p. 757; *UR1*, p. 44
	"The Turtle" from *The Grapes of Wrath* (A), John Steinbeck, SE, p. 766	**Finding Clues to Theme,** SE, p. 765; *UR1*, p. 60; **Reading Warm-ups A and B,** *UR1*, pp. 57–58; **Reading Strategy Graphic Organizers A and B,** *GOT*, pp. 161–162	**Theme,** SE, p. 765; *UR1*, p. 59; **Literary Analysis Graphic Organizers A and B,** *GOT*, pp. 163–164	**Vocabulary Builder,** SE, p. 765: *embankment, protrude* **Latin Prefix** *pro-*, SE, p. 767; *UR1*, p. 61
	"old age sticks" (MC), E. E. Cummings, SE, p. 774; **"anyone lived in a pretty how town"** (MC), E. E. Cummings, SE, p. 775; **"The Unknown Citizen "**(A), W. H. Auden, SE, p. 777	**Relating Structure to Meaning,** SE, p. 773; *UR1*, p. 77; **Reading Warm-ups A and B,** *UR1*, pp. 74–75; **Reading Strategy Graphic Organizers A and B,** *GOT*, pp. 165–166	**Satire,** SE, p. 773; *UR1*, p. 76; **Literary Analysis Graphic Organizers A and B,** *GOT*, pp. 167–168	**Vocabulary Builder,** SE, p. 531: *statistics, psychology* **Greek Root** *-psych-*, SE, p. 780; *UR1*, p. 78

Key to Program References:
SE: Student Edition **UR:** Unit Resources **GOT:** Graphic Organizer Transparencies **GR:** General Resources **WG:** Writing and Grammar
MA: More accessible **A:** Average **MC:** More Challenging. See Accessibility at a Glance chart on selection pages.

Skills Navigator

Grammar	Writing	Extend Your Learning	Assessment
Noun Clauses, SE, p. 666; *UR1,* p. 238; *WG*, Ch. 19, Section 3	**Writing Lesson:** Firsthand Biography, SE, p. 667; *UR1*, p. 239; *WG*, Ch. 4, Connected Assignment	**Listening and Speaking:** Class Discussion, SE, p. 667; **Research and Technology:** Illustrated Booklet, SE, p. 667; *UR1*, p. 240	**Selection Tests A and B,** *UR1*, pp. 242–247; **Rubrics for Biography,** *GR*, pp. 77–78
Reflexive and Intensive Pronouns, SE, p. 680; *UR1,* p. 255; *WG*, Ch. 17, Section 1	**Writing Lesson:** Editorial, SE, p. 681; *UR1*, p. 256; *WG*, Ch. 15, Section 2	**Listening and Speaking:** Monologues, SE, p. 681; **Research and Technology:** Musical Presentation, SE, p. 681; *UR1*, p. 257	**Selection Tests A and B,** *UR1*, pp. 259–264; **Rubrics for Persuasion:** Persuasive Essay, *GR*, pp. 45–46; **Rubric for Peer Assessment:** Dramatic Performance, *GR*, p. 131

Grammar	Writing	Extend Your Learning	Assessment
Adjectival Modifiers, SE, p. 722; *UR1*, p. 11, *WG*, Ch. 19, Sections 1–3	**Writing Lesson:** Character Analysis, SE, p. 723; *UR1*, p. 12; *WG*, Ch. 14, Section 2	**Listening and Speaking:** Role-play, SE, p. 723; **Research and Technology:** Report, p. 723; *UR1*, p. 13	**Selection Tests A and B,** *UR1*, pp. 15–20; **Rubrics for Response to Literature,** *GR*, pp. 65–66; **Rubric for Peer Assessment:** Dramatic Performance, *GR*, p. 131
Concrete and Abstract Nouns, SE, p. 738; *UR1*, p. 28; *WG*, Ch. 17, Section 1	**Writing Lesson:** An Editor's Review of Manuscript, SE, p. 739; *UR1*, p. 29; *WG*, Ch. 16, Section 1	**Listening and Speaking:** Informal Debate, SE, p. 739; **Research and Technology:** Anthology, SE, p. 739; *UR1*, p. 30	**Selection Tests A and B,** UR1, pp. 32–37; **Rubric for a Critique,** *GR*, pp. 75–76
Dashes, SE, p. 762; *UR1,* p. 45; *WG*, Ch. 27, Section 5	**Writing Lesson:** Character Analysis, SE, p. 763; *UR1*, p. 46; *WG*, Ch. 4, Section 3	**Listening and Speaking:** Presentation, SE, p. 763; **Research and Technology:** Report, SE, p. 763; *UR1*, p. 47	**Selection Tests A and B,** *UR1*, pp. 49–54; **Rubrics for Response to Literature,** *GR*, pp. 65–66
Parallel Structure, SE, p. 770; *UR1*, p. 62; *WG*, Ch. 20, Section 6	**Writing Lesson:** Essay About Historical Context, SE, p. 771; *UR1*, p. 63; *WG*, Ch. 12, Section 6	**Listening and Speaking:** Interview, SE, p. 771; **Research and Technology:** Cartoon Strip, SE, p. 771; *UR1*, p. 64	**Selection Tests A and B,** *UR1*, pp. 66–71; **Rubrics for Research: Research Report,** *GR*, pp. 49–50
Parentheses, SE, p. 780; *UR1,* p. 79; *WG*, Ch. 27, Section 5	**Writing Lesson:** Introduction to a Poetry Reading, SE, p. 781; *UR1*, p. 80; *WG*, Ch. 7, Section 3	**Listening and Speaking:** Group Discussion, SE, p. 781; **Research and Technology:** Written Report, SE, p. 781; *UR1*, p. 81	**Selection Tests A and B,** *UR1*, pp. 83–88; **Rubrics for Comparison-and-Contrast Essay,** *GR*, pp. 69–70

All selections are supported in the Reader's Notebooks.

UNIT 5

Disillusion, Defiance, and Discontent (1914–1946) *(continued)*

Part	Selection	Reading Strategy	Literary Analysis	Vocabulary
PART 1 (continued)	**"The Far and the Near"** (MC), Thomas Wolfe, SE, p. 784	**Predicting,** SE, p. 783; *UR1*, p. 103; **Reading Warm-ups A and B,** *UR1*, pp. 100–101; **Reading Strategy Graphic Organizers A and B,** *GOT*, pp. 169–170	**Climax and Anticlimax,** SE, p. 783; *UR1*, p. 102; **Literary Analysis Graphic Organizers A and B,** *GOT*, pp. 171–172	**Vocabulary Builder,** SE, p. 549: *tempo, sallow, sullen, timorous, visage* **Latin Root** *-temp-*, SE, p. 786; *UR1*, p. 100
	"Of Modern Poetry" (MC), Wallace Stevens, SE, p. 794; **"Anecdote of the Jar"** (MC), Wallace Stevens, SE, p. 795; **"Ars Poetica"** (MC), Archibald MacLeish, SE, p. 796; **"Poetry"** (MA), Marianne Moore, SE, p. 798	**Paraphrasing,** SE, p. 793; *UR1*, p. 120; **Reading Warm-ups A and B,** *UR1*, pp. 117–118; **Reading Strategy Graphic Organizers A and B,** *GOT*, pp. 173–174	**Simile,** SE, p. 793; *UR1*, p. 119; **Literary Analysis Graphic Organizers A and B,** *GOT*, pp. 175–176	**Vocabulary Builder,** SE, p. 793: *suffice, insatiable, slovenly, dominion, palpable, derivative, literalists* **Latin Root** *-satis-*, SE, p. 794; *UR1*, p. 121
PART 2 FOCUS ON SHORT STORY	**"In Another Country"** (A), Ernest Hemingway, SE, p. 809; **"The Corn Planting"** (MA), Sherwood Anderson, SE, p. 815; **"A Worn Path"** (MC), Eudora Welty, SE, p. 821	**Identifying with Characters,** SE, p. 808; *UR1*, p. 137; **Reading Warm-ups A and B,** *UR1*, pp. 134–135; **Reading Strategy Graphic Organizers A and B,** *GOT*, pp. 179–180	**Point of View,** SE, p. 808; *UR1*, p. 136; **Literary Analysis Graphic Organizers A and B,** *GOT*, pp. 177–178	**Vocabulary Builder,** SE, p. 808: *invalided, grave, limber, obstinate* **Latin Root** *-val-*, SE, p. 814; *UR1*, p. 138
PART 3	**"Chicago"** (MA), Carl Sandburg, SE, p. 840; **"Grass"** (A), Carl Sandburg, SE, p. 842	**Responding,** SE, p. 839; *UR1*, p. 156; **Reading Warm-ups A and B,** *UR1*, pp. 153–154	**Apostrophe,** SE, p. 839; *UR1*, p. 155; **Literary Analysis Graphic Organizers A and B,** *GOT*, pp. 181–184	**Vocabulary Builder,** SE, p. 839: *brutal, wanton, cunning* **Related Words** *brutal*, SE, p. 841; *UR1*, p. 157
	"The Jilting of Granny Weatherall" (A), Katherine Anne Porter, SE, p. 848	**Clarifying Sequence of Events,** SE, p. 847; *UR1*, p. 173; **Reading Warm-ups A and B,** *UR1*, pp. 170–171	**Stream of Consciousness,** SE, p. 847; *UR1*, p. 172; **Literary Analysis Graphic Organizers A and B,** *GOT*, pp. 185–188	**Vocabulary Builder,** SE, p. 847: *piety, frippery, dyspepsia* **Greek Prefix** *dys-*, SE, p. 856; *UR1*, p. 174
	"A Rose for Emily" (A), William Faulkner, SE, p. 862; **"Nobel Prize Acceptance Speech"** (A), William Faulkner, SE, p. 875	**Clarifying Ambiguities,** SE, p. 861; *UR1*, p. 193; **Reading Warm-ups A and B,** *UR1*, pp. 190–191; **Reading Strategy Graphic Organizers A and B,** *GOT*, pp. 189–190	**Conflict and Resolution,** SE, p. 861; *UR1*, p. 192; **Literary Analysis Graphic Organizers A and B,** *GOT*, pp. 191–192	**Vocabulary Builder,** SE, p. 861: *encroached, obliterated, vanquished, vindicated, imperviousness, divulge, circumvent, thwarted, virulent, inextricable* **Latin Prefix** *in-*, SE, p. 869; *UR1*, p. 194
	Robert Frost's Poetry (A, A, A, MA, A, MC), SE, pp. 882	**Reading Blank Verse,** SE, p. 881; *UR1*, p. 207; **Reading Warm-ups A and B,** *UR1*, pp. 204–205;	**Blank Verse,** SE, p. 881; *UR1*, p. 206 **Literary Analysis Graphic Organizers A and B,** *GOT*, pp. 193–196	**Vocabulary Builder,** SE, p. 881: *poise, rueful, luminary* **Latin Root** *-lum-*, SE, p. 892; *UR1*, p. 208
	"The Night the Ghost Got In" (A), James Thurber, SE, p. 898 ***from* "Here Is New York"** (A), E. B. White, SE, p. 903	**Recognizing Hyperbole,** SE, p. 897; *UR1*, p. 224; **Reading Warm-ups A and B,** *UR1*, pp. 221–222;	**Informal Essay,** SE, p. 897; *UR1*, p. 223 **Literary Analysis Graphic Organizers A and B,** *GOT*, pp. 197–200	**Vocabulary Builder,** SE, p. 897: *intuitively, blaspheming, aspiration, subterranean, claustrophobia, cosmopolitan* **Latin Prefix** *sub-* and **Latin Root** *-terr-* SE, p. 904; *UR1*, p. 225

Key to Program References:
SE: Student Edition **UR:** Unit Resources **GOT:** Graphic Organizer Transparencies **GR:** General Resources **WG:** Writing and Grammar
MA: More accessible **A:** Average **MC:** More Challenging. See Accessibility at a Glance chart on selection pages.

Skills Navigator

Grammar	Writing	Extend Your Learning	Assessment
Restrictive and Nonrestrictive Participial Phrases, SE, p. 790; *UR1*, p. 105; *WG*, Ch. 19, Section 2	**Writing Lesson:** Comparison-and-Contrast Essay, SE, p. 791; *UR1*, p. 106; *WG*, Ch. 9, Section 2	**Listening and Speaking:** Interview, SE, p. 791; **Research and Technology:** Written Report, SE, p. 791; *UR1*, p. 107	**Selection Tests A and B,** *UR1*, pp. 132–136; **Rubrics for Comparison-and-Contrast,** *GR*, pp. 69–70; **Rubrics for Research: Research Report,** *GR*, pp. 49–50
Subject Complements, SE, p. 801; *UR1*, p. 122; *WG*, Ch. 18, Section 3	**Writing Lesson:** Definition, SE, p. 802; *UR1*, p. 123; *WG*, Ch. 9, Section 3	**Listening and Speaking:** Round-table Discussion, SE, p. 802; **Research and Technology:** Collection of Poems, SE, p. 802; *UR1*, p. 124	**Selection Tests A and B,** *UR1*, pp. 126–131; **Rubrics for Comparison-and-Contrast,** *GR*, pp. 69–70; **Rubric for Listening:** Evaluating a Persuasive Presentation, *GR*, p. 83
Punctuating Dialogue, SE, p. 830; *UR1*, p. 139; *WG*, Ch. 5, Section 4	**Writing Lesson:** Memorial Speech, SE, p. 831; *UR1*, p. 140; *WG*, Ch. 14, Section 4	**Listening and Speaking:** Sequel, SE, p. 831; **Research and Technology:** Research Report, SE, p. 831; *UR1*, p. 141	**Selection Tests A and B,** *UR1*, pp. 145–150; **Rubric for Response to Literature,** *GR*, pp. 65–66; **Rubric for Research: Research Report,** *GR*, pp. 49–50
Sentence Types, SE, p. 844; *UR1*, p. 158; *WG*, Ch. 20, Section 1	**Writing Lesson:** Essay Analyzing the Use of Repetition, SE, p. 845; *UR1*, p. 159; *WG*, Ch. 8, Section 2	**Listening and Speaking:** Stand-up Comedy Routine, SE, p. 845; **Research and Technology:** Report, SE, p. 845; *UR1*, p. 160	**Selection Tests A and B,** *UR1*, pp. 162–167; **Rubrics for Cause-and-Effect,** *GR*, pp. 55–56
Imperative Sentences, SE, p. 858; *UR1*, p. 175; *WG*, Ch. 20, Section 1	**Writing Lesson:** Stream of Consciousness Monologue, SE, p. 859; *UR1*, p. 176; *WG*, Ch. 5, Section 4	**Listening and Speaking:** Conversation, SE, p. 859; **Research and Technology:** Oral Report, SE, p. 859; *UR1*, p. 177	**Selection Tests A and B,** *UR1*, pp. 179–184; **Rubrics for Short Story,** *GR*, pp. 57–58; **Rubric for Narrative Account,** *GR*, p. 88
Appositives and Appositive Phrases, SE, p. 878; *UR1*, p. 192; *WG*, Ch. 27, Section 3	**Writing Lesson:** Critical Review, SE, p. 879; *UR1*, p. 196; *WG*, Ch. 14, Section 3	**Listening and Speaking:** Broadcast, SE, p. 879; **Research and Technology:** Debate, SE, p. 879; *UR1*, p. 194	**Selection Tests A and B,** *UR1*, pp. 196–201; **Rubrics for Response to Literature,** *GR*, pp. 65–66
Use of Infinitives, SE, p. 894; *UR1*, p. 209; *WG*, Ch. 19, Section 2	**Writing Lesson:** Introduction to an Anthology, SE, p. 895; *UR1*, p. 210; *WG*, Ch. 3, Section 2	**Listening and Speaking:** Eulogy, SE, p. 895; **Research and Technology:** Interpretive Presentation, SE, p. 895; *UR1*, p. 211	**Selection Tests A and B,** *UR1*, pp. 213–218; **Rubrics for Response to Literature,** *GR*, pp. 65–66; **Rubric for Narrative Account,** *GR*, p. 88
Commas in Series, SE, p. 908; *UR1*, p. 226; *WG*, Ch. 27, Section 2	**Writing Lesson:** Critical Response, SE, p. 909; *UR1*, p. 227; *WG*, Ch. 14, Section 3	**Listening and Speaking:** Role Play, SE, p. 909; **Research and Technology:** Written Report, SE, p. 909; *UR1*, p. 228	**Selection Tests A and B,** *UR1*, pp. 230–235; **Rubrics for Response to Literature,** *GR*, pp. 65–66

All selections are supported in the Reader's Notebooks.

UNIT 5 Disillusion, Defiance, and Discontent (1914–1946) *(continued)*

PART 3

Selection	Reading Strategy	Literary Analysis	Vocabulary
from *Dust Tracks on a Road* (A), Zora Neale Hurston, SE, p. 914	**Analyzing How a Writer Achieves Purpose,** SE, p. 913; *UR1*, p. 250; **Reading Warm-ups A and B,** *UR1*, pp. 247–248; **Reading Strategy Graphic Organizers A and B,** *GOT*, pp. 203–204	**Social Context in Autobiography,** SE, p. 913; *UR1*, p. 249; **Literary Analysis Graphic Organizers A and B,** *GOT*, pp. 201–202	**Vocabulary Builder,** SE, p. 913: *foreknowledge, brazenness, caper, exalted, geography, avarice* **Greek Root** *-graph-*, SE, p. 917; *UR1*, p. 251
Poetry by Langston Hughes and Claude McKay (MC, A, A, A), SE, pp. 926–932	**Drawing Inferences About the Speaker,** SE, p. 925; *UR1*, p. 267; **Reading Warm-ups A and B,** *UR1*, pp. 281–282; **Reading Strategy Graphic Organizers A and B,** *GOT*, pp. 207–208	**Speaker,** SE, p. 925; *UR1*, p. 266; **Literary Analysis Graphic Organizers A and B,** *GOT*, pp. 205–206	**Vocabulary Builder,** SE, p. 925: *lulled, dusky, liberty* **Latin Root** *-lib-*, SE, p. 931; *UR1*, p. 268
"From the Dark Tower" (A), Countee Cullen, SE, p. 938; **"A Black Man Talks of Reaping"** (MC), Arna Bontemps, SE, p. 939; **"Storm Ending"** (A), Jean Toomer, SE, p. 940	**Metaphor,** SE, p. 937; *UR1*, p. 284; **Reading Warm-ups A and B,** *UR1*, pp. 281–282	**Connecting to Historical Context,** SE, p. 937; *UR1*, p. 283; **Literary Analysis Graphic Organizers A and B,** *GOT*, pp. 209–212	**Vocabulary Builder,** SE, p. 937: *increment, countenance, beguile, stark, reaping, glean* **Latin Root** *-cre-*, SE, p. 938; *UR1*, p. 285

UNIT 6 Prosperity and Protest (1946–Present)

PART 1

Selection	Reading Strategy	Literary Analysis	Vocabulary
"The Life You Save May Be Your Own" (A), Flannery O'Connor, SE, p. 982	**Making Predictions,** SE, p. 981; *UR1*, p. 9; **Reading Warm-ups A and B,** *UR1*, pp. 6–7	**Grotesque Characters,** SE, p. 981; *UR1*, p. 8; **Literary Analysis Graphic Organizers A and B,** *GOT*, pp. 214–215, 216–217	**Vocabulary Builder,** SE, p. 981: *desolate, listed, ominous, ravenous, morose, guffawing* **Latin Root** *-sol-*, SE, p. 994; *UR1*, p. 10
"The First Seven Years" (A), Bernard Malamud, SE, p. 998	**Identifying with Characters,** SE, p. 997; *UR1*, p. 26; **Reading Warm-ups A and B,** *UR1*, pp. 23–24	**Epiphany,** SE, p. 997; *UR1*, p. 25; **Literary Analysis Graphic Organizers A and B,** *GOT*, pp. 218–219, 220–221	**Vocabulary Builder,** SE, p. 997: *diligence, connivance, illiterate, unscrupulous, repugnant, discern* **Latin Root** *-litera-*, SE, p. 1008; *UR1*, p. 27
"The Writer in the Family" (A), E. L. Doctorow, SE, p. 1012	**Judging Characters' Actions,** SE, p. 1011; *UR1*, p. 43; **Reading Warm-ups A and B,** *UR1*, pp. 40–41; **Reading Strategy Graphic Organizers A and B,** *GOT*, pp. 224–225	**Static and Dynamic Characters,** SE, p. 1011; *UR1*, p. 42; **Literary Analysis Graphic Organizers A and B,** *GOT*, pp. 222–223	**Vocabulary Builder,** SE, p. 1011: *bronchitis, cronies, barometer, anthology* **Greek Suffix** *-itis*, SE, p. 1026; *UR1*, p. 44
"Aliceville" (A), Tony Earley, SE, p. 1030	**Visualizing,** SE, p. 1029; *UR1*, p. 60; **Reading Warm-ups A and B,** *UR1*, pp. 57–58	**Tone,** SE, p. 1029; *UR1*, p. 59; **Literary Analysis Graphic Organizers A and B,** *GOT*, pp. 226–227, 228–229	**Vocabulary Builder,** SE, p. 1029: *revelation, excluded, allegiances, disdain, stealthy, gingerly* **Word Analysis** The meanings of *dis-*, SE, p. 1046; *UR1*, p. 61

Key to Program References:
SE: Student Edition **UR:** Unit Resources **GOT:** Graphic Organizer Transparencies **GR:** General Resources **WG:** Writing and Grammar
MA: More accessible **A:** Average **MC:** More Challenging. See Accessibility at a Glance chart on selection pages.

Grammar	Writing	Extend Your Learning	Assessment
Parallelism in Coordinate Elements, SE, p. 922; *UR1,* p. 252; *WG*, Ch. 20, Section 6	**Writing Lesson:** Moment of Inspiration, SE, p.923; *UR1*, p. 253; *WG*, Ch. 4, Section 2	**Campaign Speech,** SE, p. 923; **Research and Technology:** Folk Tale Collection, SE, p. 923; *UR1*, p. 254	**Selection Tests A and B,** *UR1*, pp. 256–261; **Rubrics for Autobiographical Narrative,** *GR*, pp. 43–44
Verb Tenses: Past and Present Perfect, SE, p. 934; *UR1*, p. 286; *WG*, Ch. 21, Section 2	**Writing Lesson:** Poetry Comparison, SE, p. 935; *UR1*, p. 287; *WG*, Ch. 9, Section 2	**Listening and Speaking:** Presentation, SE, p. 935; **Research and Technology:** Posters, SE, p. 935; *UR1*, p. 288	**Selection Tests A and B,** *UR1*, pp. 290–295; **Rubrics for Response to Literature,** *GR*, pp. 65–66
Placement of Adjectives, SE, p. 942; *UR1*, p. 286; *WG*, Ch. 27, Section 2	**Writing Lesson:** Comparison-and-Contrast Essay, SE, p. 943; *UR1*, p. 287; *WG*, Ch. 9, Section 2	**Listening and Speaking:** Dramatic Reading, SE, p. 943; **Research and Technology:** Research Report, SE, p. 943; *UR1*, p. 288	**Selection Tests A and B,** *UR1*, pp. 290–295; **Rubrics for Comparison-and-Contrast Essay,** *GR*, pp. 69–70; **Rubric for Delivering a research Presentation,** *GR*, p. 91

Grammar	Writing	Extend Your Learning	Assessment
Subjunctive Mood, SE, p. 994; *UR1*, p. 11; *WG*, Ch. 21, Section 3	**Writing Lesson:** Deposition, SE, p. 995; *UR1*, p. 12; *WG*, Ch. 10, Section 4	**Listening and Speaking:** Readers Theatre, SE, p. 995; *UR1*, p. 13; **Research and Technology:** Body Language Presentation, SE, p. 995	**Selection Tests A and B,** *UR1*, pp. 15–20; **Rubrics for Response to Literature,** *GR*, pp. 65–66; **Rubric for Peer Assessment:** Oral Interpretation, *GR*, p. 130
Usage: *who* and *whom*, SE, p. 1008; *UR1*, p. 28; *WG*, Ch. 22, Section 2	**Writing Lesson:** Personality Profile, SE, p. 1009; *UR1*, p. 29; *WG*, Ch. 6, Section 2	**Listening and Speaking:** Presentation, SE, p. 1009; *UR1*, p. 30; **Research and Technology:** Cultural Research, SE, p. 1009	**Selection Tests A and B,** *UR1*, pp. 32–37; **Rubrics for Descriptive Essay,** *GR*, pp. 63–64; **Rubric for Speaking:** Narrative Account, *GR*, p. 88
Commonly Confused Words: *affect* and *effect*, SE, p. 1026; *UR1*, p. 45; *WG*, Ch. 25, Section 2	**Writing Lesson:** Advice Column, SE, p. 1027; *UR1*, p. 46; *WG*, Ch. 11, Connected Assignment	**Listening and Speaking:** Eulogy, SE, p. 1027; *UR1*, p. 47; **Research and Technology:** Costume Proposal, SE, p. 1027	**Selection Tests A and B,** *UR1*, pp. 49–54; **Rubrics for Exposition:** Problem-and-Solution Essay, *GR*, pp. 59–60; **Rubric for Peer Assessment:** Speech, *GR*, p. 129
Using *Like*, *As*, and *As If*, SE, p. 1046; *UR1*, p. 62; *WG*, Ch. 25, Section 2	**Writing Lesson:** Critical Response, SE, p. 1047; *UR1*, p. 63; *WG*, Ch. 14, Section 3	**Listening and Speaking:** Monologue, SE, p. 1047; **Research and Technology:** Debate, SE, p. 1047; *UR1*, p. 64	**Selection Tests A and B,** *UR1*, pp. 66–71; **Rubrics for Response to Literature,** *GR*, pp. 65–66; **Rubric for Speaking:** Presenting Pros and Cons, *GR*, p. 92

All selections are supported in the Reader's Notebooks.

Prosperity and Protest (1946–Present) *(continued)*

PART 1 *(continued)*

Selection	Reading Strategy	Literary Analysis	Vocabulary
"Gold Glade" (MC), Robert Penn Warren, SE, p. 1050; **"The Light Comes Brighter"** (MC), Theodore Roethke, SE, p. 1052; **"Traveling Through the Dark"** (A), William Stafford, SE, p. 1053	**Paraphrasing,** SE, p. 1049; *UR1*, p. 77; **Reading Warm-ups A and B,** *UR1*, pp. 74–75; **Reading Strategy Graphic Organizers A and B,** *GOT*, pp. 230–231	**Style and Diction,** SE, p. 1049; *UR1*, p. 76; **Literary Analysis Graphic Organizers A and B,** *GOT*, pp. 232–233	**Vocabulary Builder,** SE, p. 1049: *declivity, domain, vestiges, exhaust* **Related Words** *exhaust*, SE, p. 1056; *UR1*, p. 78
"Average Waves in Unprotected Waters" (A), Anne Tyler, SE, p. 1062	**Putting Events in Order,** SE, p. 1061; *UR1*, p. 94; **Reading Warm-ups A and B,** *UR1*, pp. 91–92; **Reading Strategy Graphic Organizers A and B,** *GOT*, pp. 234–235	**Foreshadowing,** SE, p. 1061; *UR1*, p. 93; **Literary Analysis Graphic Organizers A and B,** *GOT*, pp. 236–237	**Vocabulary Builder,** SE, p. 1061: *orthopedic, transparent, stocky, staunch, viper* **Latin Prefix** *trans-*, SE, p. 1072; *UR1*, p. 95
from *The Names* (MA), N. Scott Momaday, SE, p. 1076; **"Mint Snowball"** (MA), Naomi, Shihab Nye, SE, p. 1081; **"Suspended"** (MA), Joy Harjo, SE, p. 1083	**Relating to Your Own Experiences,** SE, p. 1075; *UR1*, p. 111; **Reading Warm-ups A and B,** *UR1*, pp. 108–109; **Reading Strategy Graphic Organizers A and B,** *GOT*, pp. 240–241	**Anecdote,** SE, p. 1075; *UR1*, p. 110; **Literary Analysis Graphic Organizers A and B,** *GOT*, pp. 238–239	**Vocabulary Builder,** SE, p. 1075: *supple, concocted, flamboyant, elixir, permeated, replicate, revelatory, confluence* **Latin Prefix** *con-*, SE, p. 1086; *UR1*, p. 112
"Everyday Use" (A), Alice Walker, SE, p. 1090	**Contrasting Characters,** SE, p. 1089; *UR1*, p. 137; **Reading Warm-ups A and B,** *UR1*, pp. 134–135; **Reading Strategy Graphic Organizers A and B,** *GOT*, pp. 242–243	**Character's Motivation,** SE, p. 1089; *UR1*, p. 136; **Literary Analysis Graphic Organizers A and B,** *GOT*, pp. 244–245	**Vocabulary Builder,** SE, p. 1089: *furtive, lye, oppress, doctrines* **Latin Root** *-doc-, -doct-*, SE, p. 1100; *UR1*, p. 138
from *The Woman Warrior* (A), Maxine Hong Kingston, SE, p. 1104	**Applying Background Information,** SE, p. 1103; *UR1*, p. 154; **Reading Warm-ups A and B,** *UR1*, pp. 151–152; **Reading Strategy Graphic Organizers A and B,** *GOT*, pp. 246–247	**Memoirs,** SE, p. 1103; *UR1*, p. 153; **Literary Analysis Graphic Organizers A and B,** *GOT*, pp. 248–249	**Vocabulary Builder,** SE, p. 1103: *hysterically, encampment, inaudibly, gravity, oblivious* **Latin Root** *-aud-*, SE, p. 1112; *UR1*, p. 155
"Antojos" (MA), Julia Alvarez, SE, p. 1116	**Identifying with a Character,** SE, p. 1115; *UR1*, p. 171; **Reading Warm-ups A and B,** *UR1*, pp. 168–169; **Reading Strategy Graphic Organizers A and B,** *GOT*, pp. 250–251	**Plot,** SE, p. 1115; *UR1*, p. 170; **Literary Analysis Graphic Organizers A and B,** *GOT*, pp. 252–253	**Vocabulary Builder,** SE, p. 1115: *dissuade, loath, appease, machetes, collusion, docile, enunciated* **Words from Spanish,** SE, p. 1128; *UR1*, p. 172
"Who Burns for the Perfection of Paper" (MA), Martín Espada, SE, p. 1132; **"Most Satisfied by Snow"** (A), Diana Chang, SE, p. 1133; **"Hunger in New York City"** (A), Simon J. Ortiz, SE, p. 1134; **"What For"** (MC), Garret Hongo, SE, p. 1135	**Summarizing,** SE, p. 1131; *UR1*, p. 188; **Reading Warm-ups A and B,** *UR1*, pp. 185–186; **Reading Strategy Graphic Organizers A and B,** *GOT*, pp. 254–255	**Voice,** SE, p. 1131; *UR1*, p. 187; **Literary Analysis Graphic Organizers A and B,** *GOT*, pp. 256–257	**Vocabulary Builder,** SE, p. 1131: *crevices, pervade, automation, liturgy, conjure, calligraphy, trough* **Greek Prefix** *auto-*, SE, p. 1139; *UR1*, p. 189

Key to Program References:
SE: Student Edition **UR:** Unit Resources **GOT:** Graphic Organizer Transparencies **GR:** General Resources **WG:** Writing and Grammar
MA: More accessible **A:** Average **MC:** More Challenging. See Accessibility at a Glance chart on selection pages.

Skills Navigator

Grammar	Writing	Extend Your Learning	Assessment
Subject and Verb Agreement, SE, p. 1056; *UR1*, p. 79; *WG*, Ch. 23, Section 1	**Writing Lesson:** Critical Response, SE, p. 1057; *UR1*, p. 80; *WG*, Ch. 14, Section 3	**Listening and Speaking:** Evaluation, SE, p. 1057; *UR1*, p. 81; **Research and Technology:** Oral Presentation, SE, p. 1057	**Selection Tests A and B,** *UR1*, pp. 83–88; **Rubrics for Response to Literature,** *GR*, pp. 65–66; **Rubrics for Critique,** *GR*, pp. 75–76
Correct Use of Adjectives and Adverbs, SE, p. 1072; *UR1*, p. 96; *WG*, Ch. 17, Section 3	**Writing Lesson:** Social Worker's Report, SE, p. 1073; *UR1*, p. 97; *WG*, Ch. 10, Section 4	**Listening and Speaking:** Political Speech, SE, p. 1073; **Research and Technology:** Fact-Finding Research Report, SE, p. 1073; *UR1*, p. 98	**Selection Tests A and B,** *UR1*, pp. 100–105; **Rubrics for Cause-and-Effect Essay,** *GR*, pp. 55–56; **Rubrics for Research:** Research Report, *GR*, pp. 49–50
Elliptical Clauses, SE, p. 1086; *UR1*, p. 113; *WG*, Ch. 22, Section 2	**Writing Lesson:** Reflective Essay, SE, p. 1087; *UR1*, p. 114; *WG*, Ch. 4, Section 3	**Listening and Speaking:** Musical Analysis, SE, p. 1087; **Research and Technology:** Class Anthology, SE, p. 1087; *UR1*, p. 115	**Selection Tests A and B,** *UR1*, pp. 117–122; **Rubrics for Reflective Essay,** *GR*, pp. 47–48
Sentence Fragments, SE, p. 1100; *UR1*, p. 139; *WG*, Ch. 20, Section 4	**Writing Lesson:** Review of a Short Story, SE, p. 1101; *UR1*, p. 140; *WG*, Ch. 14, Section 3	**Listening and Speaking:** Television Talk Show, SE, p. 1101; **Research and Technology:** African Languages Presentation, SE, p. 1101; *UR1*, p. 141	**Selection Tests A and B,** *UR1*, pp. 143–148; **Rubrics for Critique,** *GR*, pp. 75–76; **Rubric for Listening:** Evaluating a Media Presentation, *GR*, p. 86
Punctuating a Quotation Within a Quotation, SE, p. 1112; *UR1*, p. 156; *WG*, Ch. 27, Section 4	**Writing Lesson:** Character Analysis, SE, p. 1113; *UR1*, p. 157; *WG*, Ch. 28, Section 3	**Listening and Speaking:** Panel Discussion, SE, p. 1113; **Research and Technology:** Immigration Report, SE, p. 1113; *UR1*, p. 158	**Selection Tests A and B,** *UR1*, pp. 160–165; **Rubrics for Response to Literature,** *GR*, pp. 65–66; **Rubric for Speaking:** Delivering a Research Presentation, *GR*, p. 91
Absolute Phrases, SE, p. 1128; *UR1*, p. 173; *WG*, Ch. 19, Section 2	**Writing Lesson:** New Version of the Story, SE, p. 1129; *UR1*, p. 174; *WG*, Ch. 5, Section 4	**Listening and Speaking:** Cause-and-Effect Flowchart, SE, p. 1129; **Research and Technology:** Multimedia Report, SE, p. 1129; *UR1*, p. 175	**Selection Tests A and B,** *UR1*, pp. 177–182; **Rubrics for Narration:** Short Story, *GR*, pp. 57–58; **Rubrics for Multimedia Presentation,** *GR*, pp. 51–52
Participial Phrases, SE, p. 1139; *UR1*, p. 190; *WG*, Ch. 19, Section 2	**Writing Lesson:** Comparison-and-Contrast Essay, SE, p. 1140; *UR1*, p. 191; *WG*, Ch. 14, Section 4	**Listening and Speaking:** Interview, SE, p. 1140; *UR1*, p. 192; **Research and Technology:** Anthology, SE, p. 1140	**Selection Tests A and B,** *UR1*, pp. 194–199; **Rubrics for Comparison-and-Contrast Essay,** *GR*, pp. 69–70

All selections are supported in the Reader's Notebooks.

Prosperity and Protest (1946–Present) *(continued)*

PART 2

FOCUS ON Essay

Selection	Reading Strategy	Literary Analysis	Vocabulary
"Onomatopoeia" (MA), William Safire, SE, p. 1146; **"Coyote v. Acme"** (A), Ian Frazier, SE, p. 1148; **"Loneliness . . . An American Malady"** (MC), Carson McCullers, SE, p. 1153; **"One Day, Now Broken in Two"** (A), Anna Quindlen, SE, p. 1156	**Identifying Line of Reasoning,** SE, p. 1145; *UR1*, p. 205; **Reading Warm-ups A and B,** *UR1*, pp. 202–203; **Reading Strategy Graphic Organizers A and B,** *GOT*, pp. 258–259	**Essay,** SE, p. 1145; *UR1*, p. 204; **Literary Analysis Graphic Organizers A and B,** *GOT*, pp. 260–261	**Vocabulary Builder,** SE, p. 1145: *contiguous, precipitate, caveat, tensile, pristine, corollary, aesthetic, maverick* **Latin Root** *-ten-*, SE, p. 1160; *UR1*, p. 206
"Straw Into Gold: The Metamorphosis of Everyday" (A), Sandra Cisneros, SE, p. 1164; **"For the Love of Books"** (MA), Rita Dove, SE, p. 1169; **"Mother Tongue"** (A), Amy Tan, SE, p. 1172	**Evaluating a Writer's Message,** SE, p. 1163; *UR1*, p. 222; **Reading Warm-ups A and B,** *UR1*, pp. 219– 220; **Reading Strategy Graphic Organizers A and B,** *GOT*, pp. 264–265	**Reflective Essay,** SE, p. 1163; *UR1*, p. 221; **Literary Analysis Graphic Organizers A and B,** *GOT*, pp. 262–263	**Vocabulary Builder,** SE, p. 1163: *transcribed, empirical, benign, semantic, quandary, nascent* **Latin Root** *-scrib-, -script-*, SE, p. 1179; *UR1*, p. 223
"The Rockpile" (A), James Baldwin, SE, p. 1184	**Identifying Cause and Effect,** SE, p. 1183; *UR1*, p. 248; **Reading Warm-ups A and B,** *UR1*, pp. 245–246; **Reading Strategy Graphic Organizers A and B,** *GOT*, pp. 266–267	**Setting,** SE, p. 1183; *UR1*, p. 247; **Literary Analysis Graphic Organizers A and B,** *GOT*, pp. 268–269	**Vocabulary Builder,** SE, p. 1183: *intriguing, benevolent, decorously, latent, engrossed, jubilant, arrested, malevolence, perdition* **Latin Prefix** *mal-*, SE, p. 1194; *UR1*, p. 249
from *Hiroshima* (MC), John Hershey, SE, p. 1198; **"Losses"** (MA), Randall Jarrell, SE, p. 1209; **"The Death of the Ball Turret Gunner"** (MA), Randall Jarrell, SE, p. 1210	**Drawing Inferences about Theme,** SE, p. 1197; *UR1*, p. 265; **Reading Warm-ups A and B,** *UR1*, pp. 262–263; **Reading Strategy Graphic Organizers A and B,** *GOT*, pp. 270–271	**Implied Theme,** SE, p. 1197; *UR1*, p. 264; **Literary Analysis Graphic Organizers A and B,** *GOT*, pp. 272–273	**Vocabulary Builder,** SE, p. 1197: *evacuated, volition, rendezvous, philanthropies, incessant, convivial* **Latin Root** *-vol-*, SE, p. 1212; *UR1*, p. 266
"Mirror" (A), Sylvia Plath, SE, p. 1216; **"In a Classroom"** (MC), Adrienne Rich, SE, p. 1217; **"The Explorer"** (MC), Gwendolyn Brooks, SE, p. 1218; **"Frederick Douglass"** (MA), Robert Hayden, SE, p. 1219; **"Runagate Runagate"** (MA), Robert Hayden, SE, p. 1220	**Interpreting,** SE, p. 1215; *UR1*, p. 282; **Reading Warm-ups A and B,** *UR1*, pp. 279–280; **Reading Strategy Graphic Organizers A and B,** *GOT*, pp. 274–275	**Theme,** SE, p. 1215; *UR1*, p. 281; **Literary Analysis Graphic Organizers A and B,** *GOT*, pp. 276–277	**Vocabulary Builder,** SE, p. 1215: *preconceptions, meditate, din, wily* **Latin Root** *-cep-/-cept-*, SE, p. 1224; *UR1*, p. 283
Inaugural Address (A), John F. Kennedy, SE, p. 1228; **from "*Letter from Birmingham City Jail*"** (A), Martin Luther King, Jr., SE, p. 1232	**Identifying the Main Idea and Supporting Details,** SE, p. 1227; *UR1*, p. 299; **Reading Warm-ups A and B,** *UR1*, pp. 296–297; **Reading Strategy Graphic Organizers A and B,** *GOT*, pp. 278–279	**Parallelism,** SE, p. 1227; *UR1*, p. 298; **Literary Analysis Graphic Organizers A and B,** *GOT*, pp. 280–281	**Vocabulary Builder,** SE, p. 1227: *heirs, tyranny, alliance, invective, adversary, eradicate, impelled, flagrant, profundity* **Latin Root** *vert-* or *-vers-*, SE, p. 1236; *UR1*, p. 300
"For My Children" (A), Colleen McElroy, SE, p. 1240; **"Bidwell Ghost"** (A), Louise Erdrich, SE, p. 1243; **"Camouflaging the Chimera"** (MC), Yusef Komunyakaa, SE, p. 1245	**Reading in Sentences,** SE, p. 1239; *UR1*, p. 316; **Reading Warm-ups A and B,** *UR1*, pp. 313–314; **Reading Strategy Graphic Organizers A and B,** *GOT*, pp. 284–285	**Lyric Poetry,** SE, p. 1239; *UR1*, p. 315; **Literary Analysis Graphic Organizers A and B,** *GOT*, pp. 282–283	**Vocabulary Builder,** SE, p. 1239: *shackles, heritage, effigies, refuge* **Related Words** *heritage*, SE, p. 1248; *UR1*, p. 317
The Crucible, Act I (A), Arthur Miller, SE, p. 1257	**Questioning the Characters' Motives,** SE, p. 1256; *UR1*, p. 344; **Reading Warm-ups A and B,** *UR1*, pp. 341–342; **Reading Strategy Graphic Organizers A and B,** *GOT*, pp. 286–287	**Dialogue and Stage Directions,** SE, p. 1256; *UR1*, p. 343; **Literary Analysis Graphic Organizers A and B,** *GOT*, pp. 288–289	**Vocabulary Builder,** SE, p. 1256: *predilection, ingratiating, dissembling, calumny, inculcation, propitiation, licentious* **Latin Root** *-grat-*, SE, p. 1289; *UR1*, p. 345
The Crucible, Act II (A), Arthur Miller, SE, p. 1291	**Reading Drama,** SE, p. 1290; *UR1*, p. 360; **Reading Warm-ups A and B,** *UR1*, pp. 357–358; **Reading Strategy Graphic Organizers A and B,** *GOT*, pp. 292–293	**Allusion,** SE, p. 1290; *UR1*, p. 359; **Literary Analysis Graphic Organizers A and B,** *GOT*, pp. 290–291	**Vocabulary Builder,** SE, p. 1290: *pallor, ameliorate, avidly, base, deference, theology, quail, gingerly, abomination, blasphemy* **Greek Suffix** *-logy*, SE, p. 1313; *UR1*, p. 361
The Crucible, Act III (A), Arthur Miller, SE, p. 1315	**Characterizing Characters by Role,** SE, p. 1314; *UR1*, p. 376; **Reading Warm-ups A and B,** *UR1*, pp. 373–374; **Reading Strategy Graphic Organizers A and B,** *GOT*, pp. 294–295	**Dramatic and Verbal Irony,** SE, p. 1314; *UR1*, p. 375; **Literary Analysis Graphic Organizers A and B,** *GOT*, pp. 296–297	**Vocabulary Builder,** SE, p. 1314: *contentious, deposition, imperceptible, deferentially, anonymity, prodigious, effrontery, confounded, incredulously, blanched* **Concept Development:** Legal Terms, SE, p. 1341; *UR1*, p. 345
The Crucible, Act IV (A), Arthur Miller, SE, p. 1343	**Applying Themes to Contemporary Events,** SE, p. 1342; *UR1*, p. 392; **Reading Warm-ups A and B,** *UR1*, pp. 389–390	**Theme,** SE, p. 1342; *UR1*, p. 391; **Literary Analysis Graphic Organizers A and B,** *GOT*, pp. 298–299, 300–301	**Vocabulary Builder,** SE, p. 1342: *agape, conciliatory, beguile, floundering, retaliation, adamant, cleave, sibilance, tantalized, purged* **Concept Development:** Words from Myths, SE, p. 1360; *UR1*, p. 393

SE: Student Edition **UR:** Unit Resources **GOT:** Graphic Organizer Transparencies **GR:** General Resources **WG:** Writing and Grammar
MA: More accessible **A:** Average **MC:** More Challenging. See Accessibility at a Glance chart on selection pages.

Grammar	Writing	Extend Your Learning	Assessment
Pronouns with Appositives, SE, p. 1160; *UR1*, p. 207; *WG*, Ch. 19, Section 1	**Writing Lesson:** Parody, SE, p. 1161; *UR1*, p. 208; *WG*, Ch. 3, Section 2	**Listening and Speaking:** Opening Statement, SE, p. 1161; *UR1*, p. 209; **Research and Technology:** Essay, SE, p. 1161	**Selection Tests A and B,** *UR1*, pp. 211–216; **Rubrics for Response to Literature,** *GR*, pp. 65–66; **Rubric for Listening:** Evaluating a Persuasive Presentation, *GR*, p. 83
Varying Sentence Structure, SE, p. 1179; *UR1*, p. 224; *WG*, Ch. 20, Section 3	**Writing Lesson:** Letter to the Author, SE, p. 1180; *UR1*, p. 225; *WG*, Ch. 14, Section 4	**Listening and Speaking:** Speech, SE, p. 1180; *UR1*, p. 226; **Research and Technology:** Team Report, SE, p. 1180	**Selection Tests A and B,** *UR1*, pp. 228–233; **Rubrics for Critique,** *GR*, pp. 75–76; **Rubric for Peer Assessment:** Speech, *GR*, p. 129
Restrictive and Nonrestrictive Adjective Clauses, SE, p. 1194; *UR1*, p. 250; *WG*, Ch. 19, Section 3	**Writing Lesson:** Roy's Journal, SE, p. 1195; *UR1*, p. 251; *WG*, Ch. 14, Section 3	**Listening and Speaking:** Radio Play, SE, p. 1195; **Research and Technology:** Illustrated Report, SE, p. 1195; *UR1*, p. 252	**Selection Tests A and B,** *UR1*, pp. 254–259; **Rubrics for Response to Literature,** *GR*, pp. 65–66; **Rubrics for Research: Research Report,** *GR*, pp. 49–50
Transitions and Transitional Phrases, SE, p. 1212; *UR1*, p. 267; *WG*, Ch. 3, Section 2	**Writing Lesson:** Book Review, SE, p. 1213; *UR1*, p. 268; *WG*, Ch. 13, Section 2	**Listening and Speaking:** Dramatic Reading, SE, p. 1213; *UR1*, p. 269; **Research and Technology:** Written Report, SE, p. 1213	**Selection Tests A and B,** *UR1*, pp. 271–276; **Rubrics for Critique,** *GR*, pp. 75–76; **Rubric for Peer Assessment:** Oral Interpretation, *GR*, p. 130
Parallel Structure, SE, p. 1224; *UR1*, p. 284; *WG*, Ch. 8, Section 4	**Writing Lesson:** Literary Analysis, SE, p. 1225; *UR1*, p. 285; *WG*, Ch. 14, Section 4	**Listening and Speaking:** Debate, SE, p. 1225; *UR1*, p. 286; **Research and Technology:** Multimedia Presentation, SE, p. 1225	**Selection Tests A and B,** *UR1*, pp. 288–293; **Rubrics for Response to Literature,** *GR*, pp. 65–66; **Rubric for Speaking:** Presenting Pros and Cons, *GR*, p. 92
Parallel Structure, SE, p. 1236; *UR1*, p. 301; *WG*, Ch. 20, Section 6	**Writing Lesson:** Public Letter, SE, p. 1237; *UR1*, p. 302; *WG*, Ch. 7, Section 4	**Listening and Speaking:** Speech, SE, p. 1237; *UR1*, p. 303; **Research and Technology:** Multimedia Presentation, SE, p. 1237	**Selection Tests A and B,** *UR1*, pp. 305–310; **Rubrics for Persuasion:** Persuasive Essay, *GR*, pp. 45–46; **Rubric for Peer Assessment:** Speech, *GR*, p. 129
Sequence of Terms, SE, p. 1248; *UR1*, p. 318; *WG*, Ch. 21, Section 2	**Writing Lesson:** Ghost Story, SE, p. 1249; *UR1*, p. 319; *WG*, Ch. 5, Section 3	**Listening and Speaking:** Dramatic Presentation, SE, p. 1249; **Research and Technology:** Multimedia Cultural Presentation, SE, p. 1249; *UR1*, p. 320	**Selection Tests A and B,** *UR1*, pp. 322–327; **Rubrics for Narration:** Short Story, *GR*, pp. 57–58; **Rubric for Speaking:** Delivering a Research Presentation, *GR*, p. 91
Pronoun Case in Incomplete Construction, SE, p. 1289; *UR1*, p. 346; *WG*, Ch. 22, Section 2		**Listening and Speaking:** Oral Report, SE, p. 1289; **Research and Technology:** News Account, SE, p. 1289; *UR1*, p. 347	**Selection Tests A and B,** *UR1*, pp. 349–354
Commas After Introductory Words, SE, p. 1313; *UR1*, p. 362; *WG*, Ch. 21, Section 2		**Listening and Speaking:** Scene, SE, p. 1313; **Writing:** Wanted Poster, SE, p. 1313; *UR1*, p. 363	**Selection Tests A and B,** *UR1*, pp. 365–370
Subject and Verb Agreement in Inverted Sentences, SE, p. 1341; *UR1*, p. 346; *WG*, Ch. 23, Section 2		**Listening and Speaking:** Monologue, SE, p. 1341; **Writing:** Character Sketch, SE, p. 1341; *UR1*, p. 347	**Selection Tests A and B,** *UR1*, pp. 381–386
Commonly Confused Words, SE, p. 1360; *UR1*, p. 394; *WG*, Ch. 21, Section 2	**Writing Lesson:** Defense of a Character's Actions, SE, p. 1361; *UR1*, p. 395; *WG*, Ch. 5, Section 3	**Listening and Speaking:** Mock Trial, SE, p. 1361; **Research and Technology:** Compare and Contrast Chart, SE, p. 1361; *UR1*, p. 396	**Selection Tests A and B,** *UR1*, pp. 398–403; **Rubrics for Persuasion:** Persuasive Essay, *GR*, pp. 45–46; **Rubric for Speaking:** Delivering a Research Presentation, *GR*, p. 91

All selections are supported in the Reader's Notebooks.

Language Arts Standards-at-a-Glance

This chart provides an overview of where you will find the general Language Arts standards addressed in ***Prentice Hall Literature, The Penguin Edition.*** Prentice Hall developed this list of standards based on a review of state standards across the country. For more detailed information regarding skills coverage, see the **Skills Navigator**, found on page T56, which provides an overview of the skills by selection. The **Time and Resource Manager** will show the skills breakdown for each unit of study.

Standard Course of Study for Language Arts																			
UNIT	1			2			3				4				5			6		
PART	1	2	3	1	2	3	1	2	3	4	1	2	3	4	1	2	3	1	2	3
Reading—Reflection and Response: Students will reflect upon and respond to print and non-print text.																			
Create memoirs that elaborate upon a significant past episode.					●					●					●		●			
Create memoirs that project student voice.			●		●	●				●				●	●	●	●	●		●
Write memoirs for a specific audience and purpose.	●		●	●						●	●			●			●		●	●
Respond to texts to discover multiple perspectives.								●									●			●
Respond to text to investigate connections between life and literature.								●									●			
Explore how life experiences influence response to the selection.							●						●					●	●	
Recognize how responses to text of others may be different.	●			●									●					●		●
Articulate connections between life and literature through response.	●		●			●				●	●	●	●					●		●
Consider cultural or historical significance in response.	●	●															●			
Select, monitor, and modify reading strategies appropriate to purpose.	●										●							●		●
Identify and analyze text components and evaluate their impact on the text.							●									●	●	●		●
Provide textual evidence to support understanding of response to text.			●					●					●							
Demonstrate comprehension of main idea and supporting details.																		●	●	●
Summarize key events and/or points from text.						●												●		
Make inferences, predict, and draw conclusions based on text.		●						●		●					●		●	●		●

● *Supports standard mastery*

Standard Course of Study for Language Arts

UNIT	1			2			3				4				5			6		
PART	1	2	3	1	2	3	1	2	3	4	1	2	3	4	1	2	3	1	2	3
Identify and analyze influences, contexts, or biases.	●	●				●				●							●	●		
Make connections between works, self, and related topics.		●								●		●	●	●			●			
Analyze and evaluate the effects of author's craft and style.			●				●				●							●		●
Analyze and evaluate the connections between ideas, concepts, characters, and/or experiences.		●	●					●					●	●						●
Identify and analyze elements of expressive environment found in text.			●			●								●				●		
Research—Multimedia: Students will use a variety of media to conduct research.																				
Locate facts and details related to U.S. culture for elaboration.				●		●	●					●								
Organize information related to U.S. culture.		●	●												●			●	●	●
Exclude extraneous information about U.S. culture.		●																●		●
Provide accurate documentation about U.S. culture.		●									●									
Show the evolution of forms of communication in the United States.				●								●								
Trace the development of technology to show how culture influences language.																	●			●
Demonstrate proficiency in accessing and sending information electronically.					●													●		●
Select, monitor, and modify reading strategies to provide cultural insight.							●								●					
Identify and analyze text components and evaluate their impact on understanding of culture.			●						●	●	●									
Provide textual evidence to support understanding and cultural insight in response to text.				●																
Demonstrate comprehension of main idea and supporting details to show cultural insight.		●		●			●			●				●	●		●			●
Identify and analyze cultural influences, contexts, or biases.		●								●	●	●						●		
Make cultural connections between works, self, and related topics.		●					●			●				●			●			
Analyze the effects of author's craft and style on cultural understanding.			●				●										●	●		

Standard Course of Study for Language Arts

UNIT	1			2			3				4				5			6		
PART	1	2	3	1	2	3	1	2	3	4	1	2	3	4	1	2	3	1	2	3
Analyze cultural connections between ideas, concepts, characters, and experiences.						●		●	●						●					
Analyze elements of cultural informational environment in text.		●									●		●							
Summarize key events and/or points from text.			●		●					●										
Make inferences, predict, and draw conclusions based on text.		●					●							●						
Critical Reading—Evaluation: Students will use critical thinking skills to analyze and evaluate text structures and develop and support arguments.																				
Find and interpret information effectively.														●			●			●
Recognize propaganda as a purposeful technique.				●				●						●			●			●
Establish and defend a point of view in argument.				●		●								●		●				●
Respond respectfully to viewpoints and biases.					●			●									●			
Reflect viewpoint(s) of Americans of different times and places in argument.				●		●				●				●						
Show sensitivity or empathy for the culture represented in argument.											●				●					
Support argument with specific reasons.								●												●
Interpret researched information for argument.													●	●			●			●
Establish and defend a point of view in argument.	●						●													
Address concerns of the opposition in argument.				●		●														
Use logical strategies and sophisticated techniques in argument.	●										●			●						●
Develop a sense of completion in argument.					●															
Select, monitor, and modify reading strategies.						●		●									●			●
Analyze text components and evaluate their impact on argument in the text.			●						●		●									
Provide evidence to support understanding.						●					●			●				●		
Demonstrate comprehension of main argument.								●							●					
Summarize key events and points from argument.							●										●			●
Make inferences, predict, and draw conclusions.										●			●		●		●	●		
Analyze influences, contexts, or biases.						●												●		
Make connections between works and self.													●			●	●			
Analyze the effects of author's craft and style.					●				●											●
Analyze connections between ideas, concepts, characters, and experiences in argument.						●	●								●		●			

Standard Course of Study for Language Arts

UNIT	1			2			3				4				5			6		
PART	1	2	3	1	2	3	1	2	3	4	1	2	3	4	1	2	3	1	2	3
Identify and analyze elements of argumentative environment found in text.																	●			
Critical Reading—Analysis: Students will analyze text to gain meaning and synthesize ideas.																				
Examine the functions and the effects of narrative strategies.	●	●		●									●	●	●	●	●	●		●
Interpret the effects of figures of speech and the effects of devices of sound.	●	●							●	●										●
Analyze stylistic features, such as word choice and links between sense and sound.	●	●								●				●				●		●
Identify ambiguity, contradiction, irony, parody, and satire.		●		●		●		●									●	●		●
Demonstrate how literary works reflect the culture that shaped them.									●					●			●	●		
Connect themes that occur across genres or works from different time periods.											●			●	●					●
Use specific references to validate connections between themes.											●			●			●	●		●
Examine how representative elements impact the development of a theme.								●	●	●			●					●		●
Identify the intent and message of the author or artist in argument.		●												●	●	●				
Recognize how the author addresses opposing viewpoints in public documents.	●			●			●				●									
Articulate a personal response to the message of the author of public documents.		●		●						●						●	●			
Evaluate the historical significance of public documents.					●				●						●		●			
Select, monitor, and modify reading strategies appropriate to purpose of critical analysis.				●				●						●			●			
Identify and analyze text components and evaluate their impact on critical analysis.								●							●			●	●	
Provide evidence to support understanding of and response to critical analysis.								●							●		●		●	
Demonstrate comprehension of main idea and supporting details in critical analysis.													●	●	●		●			●
Summarize key events and points from critical analysis.															●	●				●
Make inferences and draw conclusions based on critical analysis.									●	●					●		●			

Standard Course of Study for Language Arts

UNIT	1			2			3				4				5			6		
PART	**1**	**2**	**3**	**1**	**2**	**3**	**1**	**2**	**3**	**4**	**1**	**2**	**3**	**4**	**1**	**2**	**3**	**1**	**2**	**3**
Identify and analyze influences, contexts, or biases in critical analysis.											●	●					●			●
Make connections between works, self, and related topics in critical analysis.														●	●			●		
Analyze the effects of author's craft and style.					●															
Analyze connections between ideas, concepts, characters, and experiences in critical analysis.													●				●			
Analyze elements of critical environment found in text in light of purpose, audience, and context.						●											●			
Literary Analysis: Students will analyze and interpret U.S. literature.																				
Analyze characteristics of literary genres in the U.S. and how the selection of genre shapes meaning.										●					●		●		●	●
Relate ideas, styles, and themes within literary movements of the United States.	●		●								●			●				●		●
Understand influences that progress through the literary movements of the U.S.	●			●	●								●				●	●		●
Evaluate the literary merit and historical significance of American works.									●		●		●		●	●	●	●		●
Support valid responses about U.S. texts through references to other works.	●		●	●	●				●	●	●			●			●		●	
Compare American texts to show similarities or differences.				●				●					●	●	●			●		●
Select, monitor, and modify reading strategies.				●				●				●	●				●	●		●
Identify and analyze text components and evaluate their impact on U.S. literature.	●		●				●					●	●	●				●		●
Provide textual evidence to support understanding of and response to U.S. literature.		●					●										●		●	
Demonstrate comprehension of main idea and supporting details in U.S. literature.							●						●		●					
Summarize key events and points from U.S. literature.			●	●													●		●	●
Make inferences and draw conclusions.						●				●							●			

Standard Course of Study for Language Arts

UNIT	1			2			3				4				5			6		
PART	1	2	3	1	2	3	1	2	3	4	1	2	3	4	1	2	3	1	2	3
Analyze influences, contexts, or biases in U.S. literature.				●										●					●	
Make connections between works, self, and related topics in U.S. literature.							●						●					●		
Analyze the effects of author's craft and style in U.S. literature.												●		●	●					
Analyze connections between ideas, concepts, characters, and experiences in U.S. literature.					●							●								
Identify and analyze elements of literary environment found in text in light of purpose, audience, and context.								●							●			●		
Language—Vocabulary, Grammar, Usage, and Mechanics: Students will apply conventions of grammar and language usage.																				
Decode vocabulary using knowledge of bases and affixes.			●				●	●		●	●		●	●	●	●	●	●		●
Use vocabulary strategies to determine meaning.			●	●		●	●			●		●	●	●	●		●	●	●	●
Discern the relationship of meanings between pairs of words in analogies.		●		●		●			●		●			●	●		●	●	●	●
Revise writing to enhance voice and style in accord with purpose.							●									●		●		
Contrast use of language conventions of authors in different time periods of United States literature.							●							●	●					
Analyze the power of standard usage over nonstandard usage in formal settings.													●				●		●	
Review and refine varying sentence types with correct punctuation.							●				●	●					●			●
Review and refine correct pronoun usage, antecedents, and case.				●									●					●		
Refine subject/verb agreement and choice of tense.				●						●			●				●	●		
Extend effective use of phrases and clauses.				●											●		●	●		
Discuss parts of speech as they relate to writing.			●	●	●										●		●	●		●
Edit for correct spelling and mechanics.			●	●	●	●							●					●		●

Instant intervention, tailored for each student!

Catch small problems *before* they become big ones.

How it works:
Success Tracker diagnoses student readiness to learn new skills and benchmarks their progress towards standards mastery.

1 AT THE BEGINNING OF EACH UNIT OR PART:

- Students take Diagnostic Tests online.
- Tests measure skills necessary to successfully complete the unit.
- Tests are scored instantly and results trigger one of three levels of remediation:

High Score	=	no remediation required
Medium Score	=	Level B remediation
Low Score	=	Level A remediation

- Success Tracker provides a list of recommended remediation assignments students automatically.

DIAGNOSE READINESS

2 AT THE END OF EACH UNIT OR PART:

- Students take Benchmark Tests online.
- Tests measure mastery of skills covered in the unit.
- Tests are scored instantly, and a list of "mastered" and "unmastered" skills are reported to the teacher.
- Remediation activities are automatically assigned, based on "unmastered" skills.
- Benchmark re-tests can be assigned online to students by the teacher, if needed.

BENCHMARK MASTERY

3 AS YOU DOCUMENT ADEQUATE YEARLY PROGRESS (AYP):

Success Tracker's easy-to-use reporting system lets you see at a glance where students may be having trouble mastering standards. These reports give you the kind of data you need make decisions that will positively affect student performance on high-stakes tests.

AYP DOCUMENTATION

Welcome to your new classroom.

PRENTICE HALL LITERATURE

THE AMERICAN EXPERIENCE

Flag on Orange Field by Jasper Johns (b. 1930) is an example of Johns's use of familiar objects as subject matter. It is this focus that made Johns the "Father of Pop Art and Minimalism," movements that became popular in the 1960s. In this work, painter, sculptor, and printmaker Johns uses *encaustic* paint, paint pigments mixed with hot wax. The material gave his work a sculpture-like appearance. Johns's style has been called "art of assemblage," for its use of ordinary and familiar objects and integration of three-dimensional objects.

PENGUIN  EDITION

Upper Saddle River, New Jersey

Boston, Massachusetts

ISBN 0-13-131719-9

1 2 3 4 5 6 7 8 9 10   09 08 07 06 05

Cover: *Flag on Orange Field*, 1957, oil on canvas, Jasper Johns (b. 1930) / Ludwig Museum, Cologne, Germany, Lauros / Giraudon/www.bridgeman.co.uk. Cover art © Jasper Johns/Licensed by VAGA, New York, NY

Acknowledgments

Grateful acknowledgment is made to the following for copyrighted material:

The James Baldwin Estate "The Rockpile" is collected in *Going to Meet the Man*, (c) 1965 by James Baldwin. Copyright renewed. Published by Vintage Books. Used by arrangement with the James Baldwin Estate.

Peter Basch, Literary Agent "When Grizzlies Walked Upright" by Modoc Indians from *American History Customized Reader*.

Susan Bergholz Literary Services "Antojos" by Julia Alvarez, copyright © 1991 by Julia Alvarez. Later published in slightly different from in *How the Garcia Girls Lost Their Accents*, copyright © 1991 by Julia Alvarez. Published by Plume, an imprint of Dutton Signet, a division of Penguin USA, Inc., and originally in hardcover by Algonquin Books of Chapel Hill. Reprinted by permission of Susan Bergholz Literary Services, New York. All rights reserved. "Straw into Gold: The Metamorphosis of the Everyday" by Sandra Cisneros From *The Texas Observer*. Copyright © 1987 by Sandra Cisneros. First published in The Texas Observer, September 1987. Reprinted by permission of Susan Bergholz Literary Services, New York. All rights reserved.

Brooks Permissions "The Explorer" from *Blacks* by Gwendolyn Brooks, published by The David Company, Chicago, IL. Copyright © 1987, renewed by Third World Press, Chicago, IL, 1991. Used by permission of The Estate of Gwendolyn Brooks.

Sandra Dijkstra Literary Agency "Mother Tongue" by Amy Tan. Copyright © 1990 by Amy Tan. First appeared in *The Threepenny Review*. Used by permission of the author and the Sandra Dijkstra Literary Agency.

Doubleday "Light Comes Brighter", copyright 1938 from *The Collected Poems of Theodore Roethke* by Theodore Roethke. Used by permission of Doubleday, a division of Random House, Inc. "Adamant", copyright 1938 from *The Collected Poems of Theodore Roethke* by Theodore Roethke. Used by permission of Doubleday, a division of Random House, Inc.

Rita Dove "For the Love of Books (Introduction pp xix-xxi)" by Rita Dove from *Selected Poems*.

The Echo Foundation "The Echo Foundation Brings Henry Gates, Jr. to Charlotte" by Staff from *The Echo Foundation*.

Faber and Faber Limited "Folding Chairs" by Gunter Grass from *Modern European Poetry*. Copyright © 1966 by Bantam Books, Inc. All rights reserved.

Farrar, Straus & Giroux, LLC "When in early summer" by Nelly Sachs translated by Matthew & Ruth Mead From *The Seeker And Other Poems*. "Coyote v. Acme" by Ian Frazier *from Coyote Vs. Acme*. "The Death of the Ball Turret Gunner" by Randall Jarrell From *The Complete Poems Of Randall Jarrell*. "Losses" by Randall Jarrell from *The Complete Poems Of Randall Jarrell*. "The First Seven Years" by Bernard Malamud from *The Magic Barrel*. Copyright © 1950, 1958 and copyright renewed © 1977, 1986 by Bernard Malamud. "Hawthorne" by Robert Lowell from *For The Union Dead*. Copyright © 1964 by Robert Lowell.

Fulcrum Publishing, Inc. "The Earth on Turtle's Back" by Joseph Bruchac and Michael. J. Caduto from *Keepers of the Earth: Native American Stories and Environmental Activities*.

Graywolf Press "Traveling through the Dark" copyright 1962, 1998 by the Estate of William Stafford. Used from *The Way It Is: New and Selected Poems* with the permission of Graywolf Press, Saint Paul, Minnesota.

Harcourt, Inc. "The Life You Save May Be Your Own" by Flannery O'Connor from *A Good Man Is Hard To Find And Other Stories*. "Everyday Use" by Alice Walker from *In Love And Trouble: Stories Of Black Women*.

Joy Harjo "Suspended" by Joy Harjo from *In Short: A Collection of Brief Nonfiction*.

HarperCollins Publishers, Inc. "Bidwell Ghost" from *Baptism of Desire* by Louise Erdrich. Copyright © 1990 by Louise Erdrich. Used by permission of Harper Collins Publishers, Inc. "Mirror" from *Crossing the Water* by Sylvia Plath. Copyright © 1963 by Ted Hughes. Originally appeared in The New Yorker. Used by permission of HarperCollins Publishers, Inc.
(Continued on page R60, which is hereby considered an extension of this copyright page.)

PRENTICE HALL LITERATURE

PENGUIN EDITION

THE AMERICAN EXPERIENCE

VOLUME I

Meeting Your Standards

Students will

1. read selections from the beginnings of the American literary tradition through 1750.
2. apply literal comprehension strategies appropriate for reading these selections.
3. analyze literary elements.
4. use a variety of strategies to read unfamiliar words and to build vocabulary.
5. learn elements of grammar, usage, and style.
6. use recursive writing processes to write in a variety of forms.
7. develop listening and speaking skills.
8. express and support responses to various types of texts.
9. prepare, organize, and present literary interpretation.

Unit Instructional Resources

In **Unit 1 Resources,** you will find materials to support students in developing and mastering the unit skills and to help you assess their progress.

Vocabulary and Reading

- **Vocabulary Warm-up Word Lists A and B** identify selection words for students who read at one or two grades below level.
- **Vocabulary Warm-up Practice (A and B)** provides practice on the Word List words.
- **Reading Warm-ups A and B** provide reading passages containing the Word List words, along with questions and activities for students working at one or two grades below level.

Selection Support

- Reading Strategy
- Literary Analysis
- Vocabulary Builder
- Grammar and Style
- Support for Writing
- Support for Extend Your Learning
- Enrichment

You may also access these resources on TeacherExpress.

Unit 1 A Gathering of Voices

Beginnings to 1750

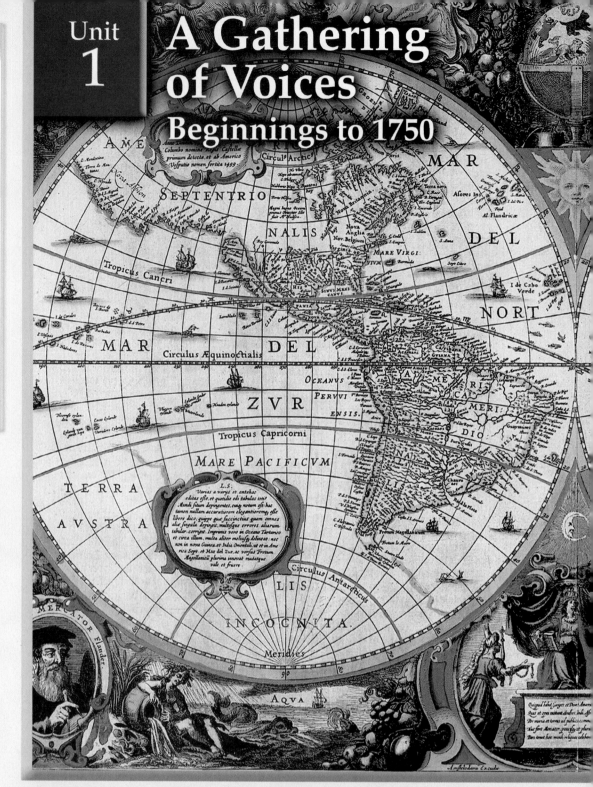

Assessment Resources

Listed below are the resources available to assess and measure students' progress in meeting the unit objectives and your state standards.

Skills Assessment

Unit 1 Resources
- Selection Tests A and B

TeacherExpress™
- *ExamView*® Test Bank Software

Adequate Yearly Progress Assessment

Unit 1 Resources
- Diagnostic Tests
- Benchmark Tests

Standardized Assessment

Standardized Test Preparation Workbook

World Map, 1630, Jan Jansson, The Huntington Library, Art Collections and Botanical Gardens, San Marino, CA

Literature of Early America

“We shall be as a City upon a Hill, the eyes of all people are upon us; so that if we shall deal falsely with our God in this work we have undertaken and so cause him to withdraw his present help from us, we shall be made a story and a by-word through the world.”

—John Winthrop,
Governor of the Massachusetts
Bay Colony

◀ This map shows what was known about the geography and oceanography of the world in 1630.

Introduce Unit 1

- Direct students' attention to the title and time period of this unit. Have a student read the quotation. **Ask** them: What does the quotation suggest about Americans at this point in their history? **Possible response:** The quotation suggests that these new settlers will create a model society for the world to see.
- Have students look at the art. Read the Humanities note to them, and ask the discussion question.
- Then **ask:** What kinds of literature or themes in literature do you think might come out of this period in American history?
  Possible response: Students probably will suggest themes concerning settlement and exploration.

Humanities

World Map, 1630

This map of the world in 1630 contains much detail. The Latin legend written across the top reads “New Geographic and Hydrologic Map of All the Lands of the Globe.” The four elements—fire (Ignis), air (Aer), water (Aqua), and earth (Terra)—are depicted above and below the two large hemispheres. The portraits in the four corners (clockwise from top left) are of Julius Caesar, Ptolemy, Mercator, and Hondius.

1. How much of the new world had been explored by 1630?
   Answer: The outlines of South America and the Atlantic coastline of Central and North America are roughly accurate.
2. What name was given to the northeastern area of what is now the United States?
   Answer: Nova Britannia

Unit Features

Susan Power
Each unit features commentary by a contemporary writer or scholar under the heading “From the Author's Desk. Author Susan Power introduces Unit 1 in Setting the Scene, in which he discusses the oral tradition. Later in the unit she introduces her own selection, “Museum Indians.” She also contributes her insights in the Writing Workshop.

Connections
Every unit contains a feature that connects the American literature of the period to British or World literature. In this unit, students will connect the sacred Indian text known as the *Rig Veda* to Native American texts.

Use the information and questions on the Connections pages to help students enrich their understanding of the selections in this unit.

Reading Informational Materials
These selections will help students learn to analyze and evaluate informational materials, such as workplace documents, technical directions, and consumer materials. Students will learn the organization and features unique to nonnarrative text.

In this unit, students will read a site on the World Wide Web.

From the Author's Desk

Introduce Susan Power

- Susan Power introduces the unit and explains how the oral tradition helps Native Americans maintain cultural continuity in the modern world. Later in this unit, on pages 32–33, Power provides context and background information that introduces readers to her essay "Museum Indians."
- Have students read the introductory paragraph about Susan Power. Tell students that Power is noted for her writing about Native American cultural and social issues and about the connections between Native Americans and mainstream American culture.
- Use the *From the Author's Desk* DVD to introduce Susan Power. Show Segment 1 to provide insight into her career as a writer. After students have watched the segment, **ask:** What community traditions observed during Susan Power's youth might have contributed to her interest in writing about Native American culture?
Possible responses: Her Native American community in Chicago exposed her to a blend of Native American traditions; her mother shared stories from her own childhood.

The Oral Tradition

- Have students read Power's comments about the way history is passed down in stories and the ways in which her family preserved these stories.
- Power discusses the importance of spoken stories in Native American literature and explains how stories help preserve Native American history.
- **Ask:** In what way is Chief Two Bear's winter count an example of the use of stories to preserve history?
Answer: The winter count functions as a history book; people use its pictures as an index of spoken stories.

Critical Viewing

Possible answer: The winter count tells a story about the lives of Power's ancestors.

Setting the Scene

Unit 1 features writing from many cultures that began the American experience. The following essay by Susan Power introduces you to American stories and history from a Native American perspective. As you read her essay, the unit introduction that follows, and the literature in Unit 1, let yourself participate in the richness and diversity of the early American experience.

From the Author's Desk
Susan Power Talks About the Time Period

Susan Power

Introducing Susan Power (b. 1961) Born in Chicago, Susan Power was greatly influenced by parents representing two distinct cultures. Her mother helped found the American Indian Center in Chicago, and her father was a descendent of the New Hampshire governor during the Civil War.

The Oral Tradition Links the Past With the Present

History in Stories I was raised in the oral tradition and from earliest memory was gifted with stories that surrounded me like my family, like air. The **oral tradition** is America's earliest form of literature—stories spoken aloud rather than committed to paper. In my Native American community of Chicago, consisting of members of at least a dozen tribes, history wasn't found in books, but in the stories elders told us. We had television and schoolbooks and radio, like everyone else in America, but we also had storytellers who kept us up late at night with ghost stories, tales of doomed romance, or comic yarns involving trickster characters—creatures who were part animal or insect, part human, who were always getting into scrapes.

Critical Viewing What kind of story do you think this winter count is telling? **[Speculate]**

Sacred Symbols on Tanned Hides For those of us who practiced a Native spirituality rather than Christianity, Judaism, or Islam, there were no religious texts like the Bible or the Koran—literary scriptures handed down on stone tablets or paper. Instead, we had sacred symbols drawn on tanned hides, embroidered with beadwork, spelled out in complicated designs woven into rugs or wampum belts.

Teaching Resources

The following resources can be used to enrich or extend the instruction for the Unit 1 introduction.

Unit 1 Resources
- **Names and Terms to Know,** p. 5
- **Focus Questions,** p. 6
- **Listening and Viewing,** p. 19

From the Author's Desk DVD
- **Susan Power, Segment 1**

The Death of Sitting Bull My Yanktonnai Dakota grandmother was born in 1888 in Fort Yates, North Dakota, and was three years old when our Chief, Sitting Bull, died. She told me stories of his death so vivid I felt that I remembered the tragic event myself, though it occurred nearly a century before I was born. She told me that when his body was brought into town on a wagon, Dakota mourners walked behind him, singing and crying, spontaneously composing the story of his life and accomplishments in a poetry of grief. When I think of those mourning singers, I'm reminded of the quick-witted verbal skills of many rap music artists of today—constructing their own stories without benefit of pen, paper, or computer.

Finding Two Bear's Winter Count My grandmother also told me stories about her own grandfather, Chief Two Bear, who had been a council chief known for his eloquence and fairness. She said that she hoped we would find his winter count one day, and when I asked her what that was, she explained that it was something like our version of a history book. The winter count was a tanned buffalo hide painted with symbols, one picture chosen for each year to represent the most significant event our band had experienced that year. Two Bear and his community could look at the hide and read it like a book, telling the story of earlier years, keeping a historical record.

Our Lives Are Stories I was taught that our lives are stories: our adventures and achievements, losses and goals, plans, our beliefs and fears, our dreams. The oral tradition was, and continues to be, a way of documenting our human experience, our interactions with the world around us. We tell each other stories of creation and God, of family and friends, love and combat, death, birth. Our stories are spoken, sung, or drawn, rather than written on paper, but their spirit is the same as any culture's: the saga of what it is to be a human being.

For: An online video
Visit: www.PHSchool.com
Web Code: ere-8101

For: More about Susan Power
Visit: www.PHSchool.com
Web Code: ete-9102

Reading the Unit Introduction

Reading for Information and Insight Use the following terms and questions to guide your reading of the unit introduction on pages 6–13.

Names and Terms to Know
Christopher Columbus
Massachusetts Bay Colony
Anne Bradstreet
Native Americans
The Great Awakening
Edward Taylor
Puritans and Pilgrims
Explorers' Accounts
John Smith

Focus Questions As you read this introduction, use what you learn to answer these questions:

- What were the similarities and differences between Northern and Southern colonies?
- What evidence of Puritan attitudes still exists today?
- What role did religion play in the settlement of North America by Europeans? How was this influence reflected in the literature of the period?

Tell students that the terms and questions listed here are the key points in this introductory materials. This information provides a context for the selections in the unit. Students should use the terms and questions as a guide to focus their reading of the unit introduction. When students have completed the unit introduction, they should be able to identify or explain each of these terms and answer the Focus Questions.

Concept Connector

After students have read the unit introduction, return to the Focus Questions to review the main points. For key points, see p. 13.

Go Online — Author Link Typing in the Web Code when prompted will bring students to a video clip of Susan Power.

Using the Timeline

The timeline can serve a number of instructional purposes, as follows:

Getting an Overview

Use the timeline to help students get a quick overview of themes and events of the period. This approach will benefit all students but may be especially helpful for visually oriented students, English-language learners, and those less proficient in reading. (For strategies in using the timeline as an overview, see the bottom of this page.)

Thinking Critically

Have students answer critical-thinking questions about the timeline to help them establish the "so what" behind the "what happened." (For Critical Thinking and Critical Viewing questions, see the bottom and side columns of the facing page.)

Connecting to Selections

Have students refer back to the timeline when beginning to read individual selections. By consulting the timeline regularly, they will gain a better sense of the period's chronology. In addition, they will appreciate what was occurring in the world that gave rise to these works of literature.

Projects

Students can use the timeline as a launching pad for projects like these:

- **Customized Timeline** Have students create period timelines in their notebooks, adding key details as they read new selections. They can use dates from this timeline as a starting framework.
- **Special Report** Have students scan the timeline for items that interest them, research these further, and report on them to the class.

American and World Events

1490 1540 1590

AMERICAN EVENTS

- 1492 Christopher Columbus lands in the Bahamas. ▼

- 1513 Juan Ponce de Léon lands on the Florida peninsula.
- 1515 Vasco Núñez de Balboa reaches the Pacific Ocean.
- 1540 Francisco Vázquez de Coronado explores the Southwest.
- 1565 St. Augustine, Florida: First permanent settlement in U.S., founded by Pedro Menendez.
- 1586 English colony at Roanoke Island disappears; known as the Lost Colony.
- 1590 Iroquois Confederacy established to stop warfare among the Five Nations.
- 1607 First permanent English settlement at Jamestown, Virginia.
- 1608 Captain John Smith writes *A True Relation . . . of Virginia.* ◀
- 1620 Pilgrims land at Plymouth, Massachusetts. ▼

- 1636 Harvard College founded in Massachusetts.
- 1639 First printing press in English-speaking North America arrives in Massachusetts.
- 1640 *Bay Psalm Book* published; first book printed in the colonies.

WORLD EVENTS

- 1499 England: 20,000 die in London plague.
- 1503 Italy: Leonardo da Vinci paints the *Mona Lisa.*
- 1508 Italy: Michelangelo paints ceiling of Sistine Chapel.
- 1518 Africa: Barbarossa drives the Spanish from most of Algeria.
- 1519 Spain: Chocolate introduced to Europe.
- 1520 Magellan sails around the world.
- 1520 Mexico: Cortez conquers Aztecs.
- 1531 Peru: Pizarro conquers Incas.
- 1558 England: Elizabeth I inherits throne. ▶

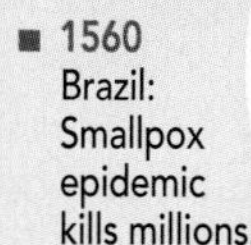

- 1560 Brazil: Smallpox epidemic kills millions.
- 1566 Belgium: Bruegel paints *The Wedding Dance.*
- 1580 France: Montaigne's *Essays* published.
- 1595 England: Shakespeare completes *A Midsummer Night's Dream.*
- 1605 Spain: Cervantes publishes Part I of *Don Quixote.*
- 1609 Italy: Galileo builds first telescope.
- 1630 Japan: All Europeans expelled.
- 1639 India: English establish settlement at Madras.
- 1642 Holland: Rembrandt paints *The Nightwatch.*
- 1642 England: Civil War begins.
- 1644 China: Ming Dynasty ends.

4 ■ *Beginnings–1750*

Getting an Overview of the Period

Introduction To give students an overview of the period, indicate the span of dates along the top of the timeline. Point out the division of the timeline into American and World Events, and have students practice scanning the timeline to look at both categories. Finally, tell them that the events in the timeline represent beginnings, turning points, and endings. For example, European explorers first encountered Native Americans in 1492.

Key Events One story this timeline tells is that of the European discovery and colonization of the North American continent. Have students select items in the American Events section that help tell this story.

Possible answers: 1607, first permanent English settlement at Jamestown; 1647, Massachusetts establishes free public schools.

Have students look at American Events from 1698 to 1741 and identify trends.

Answer: The colonies were in the midst of a religious revival.

1640 1695 1750

- 1647 Massachusetts establishes free public schools.
- 1650 Publication (in London) of Anne Bradstreet's *The Tenth Muse . . .* , a collection of poems.

- 1675 King Philip, chief of the Wampanoags, begins raiding New England frontier towns. ▲
- 1692 Salem witchcraft trials result in the execution of twenty people.

- 1735 John Peter Zenger acquitted of libel, furthering freedom of the press.
- 1741 Great Awakening, a series of religious revivals, begins to sweep the colonies. ▼

- 1741 Jonathan Edwards first delivers his sermon *Sinners in the Hands of an Angry God.*

- 1652 South Africa: First Dutch settlers arrive.
- 1664 France: Molière's *Tartuffe* first performed.
- 1667 England: Milton publishes *Paradise Lost.*
- 1683 China: All ports opened to foreign trade.
- 1690 India: Calcutta founded by British.

- 1702 England: First daily newspaper begins publication.
- 1719 England: Daniel Defoe publishes *Robinson Crusoe.*
- 1721 Germany: Bach composes *Brandenburg Concertos.*
- 1726 England: Jonathan Swift publishes *Gulliver's Travels.*
- 1727 Brazil: First coffee plants cultivated. ◀
- 1748 France: Montesquieu publishes *The Spirit of Laws.*

Answers continued

Answer: It suggests that colonists had violent conflicts with Native Americans.

4. What does the picture of the minister suggest about the Puritan style of preaching?
Answer: The minister's gesture indicates a dramatic style of preaching.

helped open the North American continent to Europeans.
(b) Judging by these names, which country took an especially active role in exploration?
Answer: (a) Juan Ponce de Léon, Vasco Núñez de Balboa, Francisco Vásquez de Coronado (b) Spain

2. (a) How many years elapsed between the first European encounter with Native Americans and the first permanent European settlement? (b) What might account for this length of time?
Answer: (a) 73 years
(b) **Possible answers:** fear of the unknown; difficulty of journey across the ocean
3. (a) Name three key developments in colonial life. (b) Show how each indicates that life in the colonies improved steadily.
Answer: (a) founding of Harvard University, first printing press, free public schools (b) These developments point to the spread of information and learning.
4. (a) What was the cause of the executions of 1692? (b) What does this event suggest about colonial life?
Answer: (a) People were convicted of witchcraft. (b) The executions suggest that religious law superseded any other.
5. (a) What happened in the field of publishing in 1735? (b) What does this reveal?
Answer: (a) John Peter Zenger was acquitted of libel charges.
(b) Colonists had begun to recognize freedom of speech as valuable.

Critical Viewing

1. What does Columbus's pose indicate?
Answer: He seems triumphant. The flag shows that he is claiming the land for his country.
2. What does the picture of the Pilgrims' ship suggest about the voyage across the Atlantic?
Answer: It was probably difficult and dangerous. The ship is small and appears to be tossing in rough water.
3. What does the picture of King Philip's raid suggest about life in the colonies?

Literature of the Period

- Students will encounter Native American works from several of the areas shown on the map on page 6. These works include an Onondaga origin myth "The Earth on Turtle's Back," p. 18, "When Grizzlies Walked Upright," p. 21, and an excerpt *from The Navajo Origin Legend,* p. 24 (Southwest).
- Students will gain greater insight into Puritan values and style as they read Anne Bradstreet's "To My Dear and Loving Husband," p. 96, and the excerpt from Jonathan Edwards's "Sinners in the Hands of an Angry God," p. 102.

Critical Viewing

Answer: (a) any two of the following: Hopi, Pueblo, Navajo, Apache (b) Presence or absence of bodies of water, forests, and mountains would lead to different ways of adapting to the natural world and thus to different ways of life.

Literature of Early America

More than a century after European explorers first landed in North America, there were still no permanent settlements in the Western Hemisphere north of St. Augustine, Florida. By 1607, however, a small group of English settlers was struggling to survive on a marshy island in the James River in the present state of Virginia. In 1611, Thomas Dale, governor of the colony, wrote a report to the king expressing the colonists' determination to succeed. Despite disease and starvation, Jamestown did survive.

The first settlers were entranced by the native inhabitants they met. They did not at first realize that these earlier Americans, like Europeans, had cultural values and literary traditions of their own. Their literature was entirely oral, for the tribes of North America had not yet developed writing systems. This extensive oral literature, along with the first written works of the colonists, forms the beginning of the American literary heritage.

Native American Culture Areas

▲ Critical Viewing As Native Americans spread out to populate North America, they developed varied cultures.
(a) Name two tribes in the Southwest culture area.
(b) What geographic features might have led to the development of different ways of life? **[Interpret]**

Historical Background

When Christopher Columbus reached North America in 1492, the continent was already populated, though sparsely, by several hundred Native American tribes. Europeans did not encounter these tribes all at one time. Explorers from different nations came into contact with them at different times. As we now know, these widely dispersed tribes of Native Americans differed greatly from one another in language, government, social organization, customs, housing, and methods of survival.

The Native Americans No one knows for certain when or how the first Americans arrived in what is now the United States. It may have been as recently as 12,000 years ago or as long ago as 70,000 years. Even if the shorter estimate is correct, Native Americans have been on the continent thirty times longer than the Europeans. Colonists from Europe did not begin arriving on the east coast of North America until the late 1500s.

What were the earliest Americans doing for those many centuries? To a great extent, the answer is shrouded in mystery. No written story of the Native Americans exists. Archaeologists have deduced a great deal from artifacts, however, and folklorists have recorded a rich variety of songs, legends, and myths.

Enrichment

Social Studies Connection

Scholars now believe that "Native American" may be a misleading term, because these peoples actually originated in Asia. They came to this continent by way of a land bridge across the Bering Strait, migrating southward and eastward and eventually spreading over the entire continents of North South, and Central America. The different phases of this migration account for the different linguistic and cultural groups indicated on the map on this page. Remind students that Native Americans had probably been living in the Americas for thousands of years before Europeans arrived.

What we do know is that the Native Americans usually, but by no means always, greeted the earliest European settlers as friends. They instructed the newcomers in their agriculture and woodcraft and introduced them to maize, beans, squash, maple sugar, snowshoes, toboggans, and birch bark canoes. Indeed, many more of the European settlers would have succumbed to the bitter northeastern winters had it not been for the help of these first Americans.

▲ **Critical Viewing**
What Puritan values does this painting illustrate? **[Interpret]**

Pilgrims and Puritans A small group of Europeans sailed from England on the *Mayflower* in 1620. The passengers were religious reformers—Puritans who were critical of the Church of England. Having given up hope of "purifying" the Church from within, they chose instead to withdraw from the Church. This action earned them the name Separatists; we know them as the Pilgrims. They landed in North America and established a settlement at what is now Plymouth, Massachusetts. With help from friendly tribes of Native Americans, the Plymouth settlement managed to survive the rigors of North America. The colony never grew very large, however. Eventually, it was engulfed by the Massachusetts Bay Colony, the much larger settlement to the north.

Like the Plymouth Colony, the Massachusetts Bay Colony was founded by religious reformers. These reformers, however, did not withdraw from the Church of England. Unlike the Separatists, they were Puritans who intended instead to reform the Church from within. In America, the Puritans hoped to establish what John Winthrop, governor of the Colony, called a "city upon a hill," a model community guided in all aspects by the Bible. Their form of government would be a theocracy, a state under the immediate guidance of God.

Among the Puritans' central beliefs were the ideas that human beings exist for the glory of God and that the Bible is the sole expression of God's will. They also believed in predestination—John Calvin's doctrine that God has already decided who will achieve salvation and who will not. Nevertheless, these who are to be saved cannot take their salvation for granted. For that reason, all devout Puritans searched their souls with great rigor and frequency for signs of grace. The Puritans felt that they could accomplish good only through continual hard work and self-discipline, a principle known today as the "Puritan ethic."

Puritanism was in decline throughout New England by the early 1700s, as more liberal Protestant congregations attracted followers. A reaction against

History

Religion affected every aspect of Puritan life, although the Puritans were not always as stern and otherworldly as they are sometimes pictured. Their writings occasionally revealed a sense of humor, and the hardships of daily life forced them to be practical. In one sense, the Puritans were radical, since they demanded fundamental changes in the Church of England. In another sense, however, they were conservative. They interpreted the Bible literally and insisted on rigid standards for full church membership.

Critical Viewing

Answer: The painting illustrates the values of hard work, family and children, religion, and community.

Differentiated Instruction Solutions for All Learners

Strategy for Less Proficient Readers
Have students preview the art and illustrations for this period before reading "Historical Background." Have them write one or two questions about the illustrations and read the text to find the answers.

Strategy for English Learners
Have students use the art and illustrations on these pages to speculate about the era. Have them read the boldfaced heads and formulate questions based on these heads.

Strategy for Advanced Readers
Have students use the evidence from "Historical Background" and the accompanying illustrations to draw conclusions about the daily life of colonial teenagers.

Background
Science

Europeans coming to North America for the first time encountered many plants and animals that were previously unknown to them. Among the new types of trees were the locust, the live oak, and the hickory. Fruits, vegetables, and nuts included eggplant, persimmons, pecans, sweet potatoes, and squash.

The colonists adopted the Indians' names for some animals, such as the skunk, the opossum, the chipmunk, the moose, and the raccoon. They made up their own names for others, such as the bullfrog, the garter snake, the mud hen, the potato bug, the groundhog, and the red bird.

Literature of the Period

- In reading Native American selections like "When Grizzlies Walked Upright," p. 21, students should try to "hear" them as if they are being told aloud. This technique will help students remember that Native American literature was part of an oral tradition.
- In Jonathan Edwards's "Sinners in the Hands of an Angry God," p. 102, students will encounter the sermon, a type of literature that is characteristically Puritan.

Critical Viewing

Answer: (a) They both include chairs, tables, and utensils and dishes. (b) The landowner's living quarters are luxurious; the slave quarters are simple. The slave house is made of logs. The landowner's house includes ornaments such as pictures on the walls.

▲ Critical Viewing These exhibition rooms in Colonial Williamsburg illustrate the living quarters of African slaves and white landowners. (a) What do these rooms have in common? (b) What are the major differences? **[Compare and Contrast]**

this new freedom, however, set in around 1720. The Great Awakening, a series of religious revivals led by such eloquent ministers as Jonathan Edwards and George Whitefield, swept through the colonies. The Great Awakening attracted thousands of converts to many Protestant groups, but it did little to revive old-fashioned Puritanism. Nevertheless, Puritan ideals of hard work, frugality, self-improvement, and self-reliance are still regarded as basic American virtues.

The Southern Planters The Southern Colonies differed from New England in climate, crops, social organization, and religion. Prosperous coastal cities grew up in the South, just as in the North, but beyond the southern cities lay large plantations, not small farms. Despite its romantic image, the plantation was in fact a large scale agricultural enterprise and a center of commerce. Up to a thousand people, many of them enslaved, might live and work on a single plantation.

The first black slaves were brought to Virginia in 1619, a year before the Pilgrims landed at Plymouth. The plantation system and the institution of slavery were closely connected from the very beginning, although slavery existed in every colony, including Massachusetts.

Most of the plantation owners were Church of England members who regarded themselves as aristocrats. The first generation of owners, the men who established the great plantations, were ambitious, energetic, self-disciplined, and resourceful, just as the Puritans were. The way of life on most plantations, however, was more sociable and elegant than that of any Puritan. By 1750, Puritanism was in decline everywhere, and the plantation system in the South was just reaching its peak.

Literature of the Period

It was an oddly assorted group that established the foundations of American literature: the Native Americans with their oral traditions, the Puritans with their preoccupation with sin and salvation, enslaved and free African Americans, and the southern planters with their busy social lives. Indeed, much of the literature that the colonists read was not produced in the colonies—it came from England. Yet, by 1750, there were the clear beginnings of a native literature that would one day be honored throughout the English-speaking world.

Native American Tradition For a long time, Native American literature was viewed mainly as folklore. The consequence was that song lyrics, hero tales, migration legends, and accounts of the creation were studied more for their content than for their literary qualities. In an oral tradition, the telling of a tale may change with each speaker, and the words are almost sure to change over time. Thus, no fixed versions of such literary works exist. Still, in cases where the words of Native American lyrics or narratives have been captured in writing, the language is often poetic and moving. As might be expected in an oral setting, oratory was much prized among Native Americans. The names of certain orators, such as Logan and Red Jacket, were widely known.

The varied Native American cultures produced a diverse body of literature. However, while the myths, legends, and folk tales vary greatly, one common characteristic is the deep respect that Native American literature generally shows for nature. Tales and chants celebrate the wonders of the natural world and its interconnectedness with the world of the spirit.

The samples of Native American literature in this unit reveal the depth and power of those original American voices.

Explorers' Accounts No one knows when the first Europeans came to the Americas. However, archaeological evidence suggests that the seafaring northern Europeans known as Vikings set up small encampments on the islands of northeastern Canada beginning some time around A.D. 1000. Still, our knowledge about Viking settlements is largely speculative. Not until the late fifteenth century did Europe inaugurate an Age of Exploration in which its journeys to the Americas were well documented.

Christopher Columbus, an Italian living in Portugal, was convinced that he could reach Asia by sailing west. After receiving financial backing from Spain's Queen Isabella, he set sail in August of 1492 and landed on October 12 on an island in what is now the Bahamas. He wrote about his experience in his Journal of the First Voyage to America, in which he stressed the rich potential of the new lands that he still regarded as part of Asia.

Other explorers who wrote accounts of their voyages were the Spaniards Alvar Núñez Cabeza de Vaca and García López de Cárdenas. Cabeza de Vaca was one of four survivors of a 400-man expedition to Texas. In his narrative,

guage are closer to us than students usually realize. Tell them that they can find one-word examples of various tribal languages simply by looking at maps or road signs. A great number of American place names come from Native American words.

Critical Thinking

1. What motives might have prompted the earliest European explorers to sail to North America?
   Answer: greed, curiosity, sense of adventure
2. What aspect of Native American literature might have caused the Europeans to overlook it?
   Answer: It wasn't written down; it wasn't in a language they could understand.
3. Were Puritan ideals especially suited to the task of colonizing New England? Explain.
   Answer: The Puritan commitment to hard work, frugality, and self-reliance is compatible with establishing a colony in a harsh wilderness.
4. In what way were the roots of the American Civil War planted during colonial times?
   Answer: Southern plantation owners relied more heavily on the labor of enslaved Africans than northerners did.

Cambridge in 1640. Its full title was *The Whole Book of Psalms Faithfully Translated into English Metre.*

Critical Viewing

Possible answer: The stern preacher standing above the congregation suggests the importance of religion in the lives of the pilgrims. The people are standing and following along in their books obediently. The structure of the scene reflects their way of life.

he describes a wilderness that is sometimes bountiful and sometimes very harsh. López de Cárdenas was the first European to see and describe the Grand Canyon, as we learn from Pedro de Castañeda's retelling.

"In Adam's Fall/We Sinned All" Just as religion dominated the lives of the Puritans, it also dominated their writings—most of which would not be considered literary works by modern standards. Typically, the Puritans wrote theological studies, hymns, histories, biographies, and autobiographies. The purpose of such writing was to provide spiritual insight and instruction. When Puritans wrote for themselves in journals or diaries, their aim was the serious kind of self-examination they practiced in other aspects of their lives. The Puritans produced neither fiction nor drama because they regarded both as sinful.

The Puritans did write poetry, however, as a vehicle of spiritual enlightenment. Although they were less concerned with a poem's literary form than with its message, some writers were more naturally gifted than others. A few excellent Puritan poets emerged in the 1600s, among them Anne Bradstreet and Edward Taylor. Anne Bradstreet's moving, personal voice and Edward Taylor's devotional intensity shine through the conventional Puritanism of their themes.

▼ **Critical Viewing** What details in this print of Puritans attending church reveal what life was like in seventeenth-century New England? **[Interpret]**

Enrichment

African-American Culture

African Americans made up the majority of the population of South Carolina and Georgia. They generally had contact with only a handful of European colonists. As a result, they were able to exercise greater control over their day-to-day existence than those enslaved in other colonies and to preserve many of their cultural traditions. Many had come to South Carolina and Georgia straight from Africa. They still practiced the crafts of their homeland, such as basket weaving and pottery, and they continued singing their music and telling the old stories from home. In some cases they maintained aspects of their native languages. The best-known example of this is Gullah, a combination of English and African. As late as the 1940s, speakers of Gullah were using 4,000 words from the languages of more than 21 separate West African languages. African Americans even preserved the African manner of burial.

The Puritans had a strong belief in education for both men and women. In 1636, they founded Harvard College to ensure a well-educated ministry. Three years later, they set up the first printing press in the colonies. In 1647, free public schools were established in Massachusetts. *The New England Primer*, first published around 1690, combined instruction in spelling and reading with moralistic teachings, such as "In Adam's fall/ We sinned all."

One of the first books printed in the colonies was the *Bay Psalm Book*, the standard hymnal of the time. Richard Mather, one of the book's three authors, was the father of Increase Mather, who served for many years as pastor of the North Church in Boston. Increase Mather was also the author of more than 130 books.*Cases of Conscience Concerning Evil Spirits*, published in 1693, was a discourse on the Salem witchcraft trials of the previous year. The trials, conducted in an atmosphere of hysteria, resulted in the hanging of twenty people as witches.

▲ Critical Viewing The Puritans founded Harvard College at Newtowne in 1636. Three years later, they renamed the city Cambridge to honor the British city where many of the colonists had studied. What does this fact reveal about the group who fled England? **[Draw Conclusions]**

Increase's eldest son, Cotton Mather, far exceeded his father's literary output, publishing at least 400 works in his lifetime. Cotton Mather, like his father, is remembered in part because of his connection with the Salem witchcraft trials. Although he did not actually take part in the trials, his works on witchcraft had helped to stir up some of the hysteria. Still, Cotton Mather was one of the most learned men of his time, a power in the state and a notable author. Although his writing was multifaceted, his theory of writing was simple: The more information a work contains, the better its style.

In fact, the Puritans in general had a theory about literary style. They believed in a plain style of writing, one in which clear statement is the highest goal. An ornate or clever style would be a sign of vanity and, as such, would not be in accordance with God's will. Despite the restrictions built into their life and literature, the Puritans succeeded in producing a small body of excellent writing.

Southern Writers Considering the number of brilliantly literate statesmen who would later emerge in the South, especially in Virginia, it seems surprising that only a few notable southern writers appeared prior to 1750.

and more Indian lands, the Indians began attacking and burning colonial villages and kidnapping women and children for ransom. When Cotton Mather learned that settlers had captured the wife and son of a Native American leader and sold them into slavery, he declared, "It must be bitter as death to him to lose his wife and only son, for the Indians are marvelously fond and affectionate toward their children."

Critical Viewing

Possible answer: The colonists valued education and sought to re-create important educational institutions in their new country.

Background
Literature

Complied by Benjamin Harris, the *New England Primer* might have sold up to two million copies in the 1700s. It was the standard text from which most colonial children learned to read. Moral instruction was interwoven throughout the text, and letters of the alphabet were taught through inspirational couplets.

The American Experience
A Living Tradition

- Point out that John Berryman, a 20th century poet, identifies with Anne Bradstreet. He sympathizes with the difficulty of her physical life in New England and her emotional life with her husband, Simon.
- **Ask** students to identify which lines in the poem show Berryman's sympathy for Bradstreet's physical and emotional life. What key words helped them reach their conclusions?
  Possible answers: Lines 1–4 indicate Berryman's sympathy for Bradstreet's physical life. Key words: *winters, lashing, sigh, stunned.* Lines 5–8 indicate his sympathy for her emotional life. Key words: *doubt, blast, rigor, unhanded.*

As in Puritan New England, those who were educated produced a substantial amount of writing, but it was mostly of a practical nature. For example, John Smith, the leader of the settlement at Jamestown, Virginia, wrote *The General History of Virginia* to describe his experiences for Europeans. In addition to accounts like Smith's, letters written by southern planters also provide insight into this time period. Unlike the Puritans, southerners did not oppose fiction or drama, and the first theater in America opened in Williamsburg, Virginia, in 1716.

The Planter From Westover The important literature of the pre-Revolutionary South can be summed up in one name: William Byrd. Byrd lived at Westover, a magnificent plantation on the James River bequeathed to him by his wealthy father. Commissioned in 1728 to survey the boundary line between Virginia and North Carolina, Byrd kept a journal

A Living Tradition

John Berryman and Anne Bradstreet

In the 1950s, the American poet John Berryman responded powerfully to the life and work of Puritan poet Anne Bradstreet, who had lived 300 years earlier. He wrote her a long poem of praise entitled "Homage to Mistress Bradstreet." In this adventurous poem, Berryman speaks both in his own voice and in the voice of Bradstreet herself. He also uses unusual sentence structures that seem to suggest both the difficulty in contacting Bradstreet and the difficulty of life in the New World.

Speaking as himself in the beginning of the poem, he imagines the terrible "New World winters" that must have "stunned" Bradstreet and her Puritan companions. Berryman also addresses Bradstreet directly, indicating that he is more sympathetic to her poetry than was her busy husband, Simon Bradstreet.

from "Homage to Mistress Bradstreet" by John Berryman

Outside the New World winters in grand dark
white air lashing high thro' the virgin stands°   °unexplored forests

foxes down foxholes sigh,
surely the English heart quails, stunned.
I doubt if Simon than this blast, that sea,
spares from his rigor for your poetry
more. We are on each other's hands
who care. Both of our worlds unhanded us.
 Lie stark,

thy eyes look to me mild. Out of maize° & air   °corn
your body's made, and moves. I summon, see,
from the centuries it. . . .

paper, creating a printed page.

Critical Thinking

1. Why do you think Puritans regarded fiction and drama as sinful?
   Answer: They may have viewed fiction and drama as forms of entertainment rather than of spiritual enlightenment.
2. Why do you think early Americans read so much work produced in England?
   Answer: They relied on what was familiar. Books from England were written in English, which was the language of many of the immigrants.

The American Experience

A Writer's Voice

- Emphasize that both the Puritans in the North and the planters in the South faced the hardships of settling unfamiliar territory. While the Puritans were stern and serious, Southerners were less restricted, and some, like Byrd, met their challenges with humor. Byrd's writing highlights one of the differences between these two cultures.
- **Ask** students to read the passage and to identify what makes Byrd's writing humorous.
  Possible answers: The following aspects of Byrd's writing contribute to its humor: The way Byrd constructs the anecdote as a type of fairy tale; the way Byrd describes the poor insect; the description of how terrified the man was at the end of the story.

of his experiences. That journal served as the basis for his book, *The History of the Dividing Line,* which was circulated in manuscript form among Byrd's friends in England. Published nearly a century after Byrd's death, the book was immediately recognized as a minor humorous masterpiece. More of Byrd's papers were published later, establishing his reputation as the finest writer in the pre-Revolutionary South.

The writers whose work appears in this unit are not the great names in American literature. They are the founders, the men and women who laid the groundwork for the towering achievements that followed. The modest awakening of American literature seen in this unit had repercussions that echoed down the years.

▲ Critical Viewing
This is a picture of the first printing press in English-speaking North America. Judging by its appearance, how do you think it worked? **[Infer]**

A Writer's Voice

William Byrd, Writer with a Sense of Humor

Byrd's humor comes through in this anecdote he passes on to readers. It tells about a man from the north of England who out of curiosity explored the Dismal swamp, where Byrd later did his surveying.

from *The History of the Dividing Line* by William Byrd

. . . he, having no compass nor seeing the sun for several days together, wandered about till he was almost famished: but at last he bethought himself of a secret his countrymen make use of to pilot themselves in a dark day. He took a fat louse out of his collar and exposed it to the open day on a piece of white paper which he brought along with him for his journal. The poor insect, having no eyelids, turned himself about till he found the darkest part of the heavens and so made the best of his way toward the north. By this direction he steered himself safe out and gave such a frightful account of the monsters he saw and the distresses he underwent that no mortal since has been hardy enough to go upon the like dangerous discovery.

Concept Connector

Have students discuss the Focus Questions on p. 3. Students' discussions should include the following points:

Role of religion in the settlement of North America:
- The early American settlers were religious reformers.
- The Pilgrims left the Church of England; Puritans wanted to reform it from within.
- Literature of the period often focused on morality, sin, and redemption.

Similarities and differences between Northern and Southern colonies:
- Slavery existed in each colony.
- Prosperous coastal cities developed in both regions.
- Both plantation owners and Puritans were ambitious and resourceful.
- Farming took place on large plantations in the South. Farms were small in the North.
- Most Southern plantation owners were Church of England members. Northern Puritans rejected the established church.

Evidence of Puritan attitudes today:

Puritan values—hard work, self-reliance, practicality and frugality—are part of American culture today.

Critical Thinking

1. If the animal and plant species that settlers encountered in North America had been the same as those in Europe, how might American English have developed differently?
   Possible answer: The settlers probably wouldn't have adopted Indian names for the plants and animals.
2. What does the anglicizing of Native American names suggest about what happens when one language adopts terms from another?
   Possible answer: Adopted terms are usually altered to make them conform to the adopting language's rules of spelling and pronunciation.

Answers to Activity

1. The following states have Native American names:
   Alabama, Alaska, Arkansas, Arizona, Connecticut, Illinois, Hawaii, Iowa, Kansas, Kentucky, Massachusetts, Michigan, Minnesota, Mississippi, Missouri, Nebraska, North Dakota, Ohio, Oklahoma, South Dakota, Tennessee, Texas, Utah, Wisconsin, Wyoming.
   Different sources give different translations for some of these names. If students have trouble finding sources, suggest that they use an almanac.
2. Answers will vary depending on the area where students live. You might suggest that students use road maps to pick out names of local places. In searching out the origin of names, try consulting local historical societies or Native American organizations.

The Development of American English

Our Native American Heritage

BY RICHARD LEDERER

If you had been one of the early explorers or settlers of North America, you would have found many things in your new environment unknown to you. The handiest way of filling voids in your vocabulary would have been to ask local Native Americans what words they used. The early colonists began borrowing words from friendly Native Americans almost from the moment of their first contact, and many of those shared words have remained in our everyday language.

ANGLICIZING

Pronouncing many of the Native American words was difficult for the early explorers and settlers. In many instances, they shortened and simplified the names. For example, *otchock* became "woodchuck," *rahaugcum* turned to "raccoon," and the smelly *seganku* transformed into a "skunk." The North American menagerie brought more new words into the English language, including caribou (Micmac), chipmunk (Ojibwa), moose (Algonquian), muskrat (Abenaki), and porgy (Algonquian).

THE POETRY OF PLACE NAMES

William Penn said he did not know "a language spoken in Europe that hath words of more sweetness and greatness." To Walt Whitman, *Monongahela* "rolls with venison richness upon the palate." Some of our loveliest place names—*Susquehanna, Shenandoah, Rappahannock*—began life as Native American words. Such names are the stuff of poetry.

If you look at a map of the United States, you will realize how freely settlers used words of Indian origin to name our states, cities, towns, mountains, lakes, rivers, and ponds. Five of our six Great Lakes and exactly half of our states have names that were borrowed from Native American words. Many other bodies of water and land have taken on names we have come to know as part of the American language.

Food	
squash (Natick)	pecan (Algonquian)
hominy (Algonquian)	pone (Algonquian)
pemmican (Cree)	succotash (Narraganset)
People	
sachem (Narraganset)	papoose (Narraganset)
squaw (Massachuset)	mugwump (Natick)
Native American life	
moccasin (Chippewa)	toboggan (Algonquian)
tomahawk (Algonquian)	wigwam (Abenaki)
tepee (Dakota)	caucus (Algonquian)
pow-wow (Narraganset)	wampum (Massachuset)
bayou (Choctaw)	potlatch (Chinook)
hogan (Navajo)	hickory (Algonquian)
kayak (Inuit)	totem (Ojibwa)

Activity

1. Brainstorm for a list of the states that have Native American names. Research the origin of each name.
2. With help from an encyclopedia or other source, find out which Native American tribes live—or once lived—in your part of the country. Do their languages survive in many place names? Pick out ten names of places in your state—cities, towns, mountains, or bodies of water—that have Native American names. Try to find their exact origins. What can you find out about the history of your state that will help explain why these names were chosen?

Enrichment

Linguistic Contributions of Immigrants

In addition to borrowing words from Native Americans, English colonists borrowed terms from the languages of various immigrant groups.

The Dutch, who colonized New York and the surrounding area before the English, contributed *cookie, cruller, boss, stoop, and scow.*

The French colonists in and around Canada, northern New York, the Ohio River, and New Orleans contributed *levee, cache, caribou, bayou, chowder,* and *portage.*

The Spaniards who first explored the Southwest, Florida, Texas, and the southeast contributed *alligator, armadillo, canoe,* and *maize.*

Unit 1 Part 1

Meeting of Cultures

Oneida Chieftan Shikellamy, Unknown American Artist, Philadelphia Museum of Art

Selection Planning Guide

This section introduces students to the cultural groups that claimed a place in the early American wilderness. The origin myths and Iroquois constitution offer a closer look at the culture of several Native American nations. The focus shifts to the Southwest with two accounts of Spanish quests to explore the New World. Part 1 closes with a connection between Native American texts and a sacred Indian text known as the Rig Veda.

Humanities

Oneida Chieftain Shikellamy

Like other Iroquois tribes, the Oneida, who lived in what is now New York State, raised corn and formed permanent settlements. They lived together in longhouses that sheltered extended families. By the nineteenth century, most Oneida were living in either Oneida County, New York; Ontario, Canada; or Green Bay, Wisconsin. About 3,000 Oneida live in these three areas today.

1. What do you think the artist thought of Shikellamy? Why?
   Answer: The artist respected Shikellamy. He is shown full-length, which makes him look impressive and powerful. His posture makes him look commanding. There is nothing in the background to distract the viewer's attention from the chieftain.
2. What does this painting suggest about relations between Indians and Europeans?
   Answer: Shikellamy has a gun, which suggests that they traded with each other. The Europeans would have had to be interested in the Indians in order to paint their portraits. Enemies would not agree to pose for or paint each other; the existence of the portrait suggests that relations were cordial.

Differentiated Instruction Solutions for All Learners

Accessibility at a Glance

More Accessible
The Earth on Turtle's Back
When Grizzlies Walked Upright
from The Navajo Origin Legend

Average
from The Iroquois Constitution
A Journey Through Texas
Boulders Taller Than the Great Towers of Seville

Meeting Your Standards

Students will

1. **analyze and respond to literary elements.**
   - Literary Analysis: Origin Myths
2. **read, comprehend, analyze, and critique myths.**
   - Reading Strategy: Recognizing Cultural Details
   - Reading Check questions
   - Apply the Skills questions
   - Assessment Practice (ATE)
3. **develop vocabulary.**
   - Vocabulary Lesson: Latin suffix: *-tion*
4. **understand and apply written and oral language conventions.**
   - Spelling Strategy
   - Grammar and Style Lesson: Compound Sentences
5. **develop writing proficiency.**
   - Writing Lesson: Retelling of a Story
6. **develop appropriate research strategies.**
   - Extend Your Learning: Logo
7. **understand and apply listening and speaking strategies.**
   - Extend Your Learning: Dramatic Reenactment

Block Scheduling: Use one 90-minute class period to preteach the skills and have students read the selection. Use a second 90-minute class period to assess students' mastery of skills, extend their learning, and monitor their progress.

Homework Suggestions

Following are possibilities for homework assignments.

- Support pages from ***Unit 1 Resources:***
  Literary Analysis
  Reading Strategy
  Vocabulary Builder
  Grammar and Style
- An Extend Your Learning project and the Writing Lesson for this selection group may be completed over several days.

Step-by-Step Teaching Guide	Pacing Guide
PRETEACH	
• Administer Vocabulary and Reading Warm-ups as necessary.	5 min.
• Engage students' interest with the motivation activity.	5 min.
• Read and discuss author, background, and From the Author's Desk features. **FT**	10 min.
• Introduce the Literary Analysis Skill: Origin Myths. **FT**	5 min.
• Introduce the Reading Strategy: Recognizing Cultural Details. **FT**	10 min.
• Prepare students to read by teaching the selection vocabulary. **FT**	
TEACH	
• Informally monitor comprehension while students read independently or in groups. **FT**	30 min.
• Monitor students' comprehension with the Reading Check notes.	as students read
• Reinforce vocabulary with Vocabulary Builder notes.	as students read
• Develop students' understanding of origin myths with the Literary Analysis annotations. **FT**	5 min.
• Develop students' ability to recognize cultural details with the Reading Strategy annotations. **FT**	5 min.
ASSESS/EXTEND	
• Assess students' comprehension and mastery of the Literary Analysis and Reading Strategy by having them answer the Apply the Skills questions. **FT**	15 min.
• Have students complete the Vocabulary Lesson and the Grammar and Style Lesson. **FT**	15 min.
• Apply students' ability to use effective repetition by using the Writing Lesson. **FT**	45 min. or homework
• Apply students' understanding by using one or more of the Extend Your Learning activities.	20–90 min. or homework
• Administer Selection Test A or Selection Test B. **FT**	15 min.

Resources

PRINT

Unit 1 Resources

TRANSPARENCY

Graphic Organizer Transparencies

TECHNOLOGY

From the Author's Desk DVD Susan Power, Segment 2

PRINT

Reader's Notebook [**L2**]
Reader's Notebook: Adapted Version [**L1**]
Reader's Notebook: English Learner's Version [**EL**]

Unit 1 Resources

TECHNOLOGY

Listening to Literature Audio CDs [**L2, EL**]
Reader's Notebook: Adapted Version Audio CD [**L1, L2**]

PRINT

Unit 2 Resources

General Resources

TECHNOLOGY

Go Online: Research [**L3**]
Go Online: Self-test [**L3**]
***ExamView®* Test Bank** [**L3**]

Choosing Resources for Differentiated Instruction

[**L1**] Special Needs Students
[**L2**] Below-Level Students
[**L3**] All Students
[**L4**] Advanced Students
[**EL**] English Learners

FT Fast Track Instruction: To move the lesson more quickly, use the strategies and activities identified with **FT**.

Scaffolding for Less Proficient and Advanced Students

The leveled Critical Thinking questions after selections progress in the levels of thinking required to answer them. To address the needs of your different students, you may use the (a) level questions for your less proficient students and the (b) level questions with your on-level and advanced students. The occasional (c) level questions are appropriate for your advanced students.

PRENTICE HALL **TeacherEXPRESS™** Plan · Teach · Assess Use this complete suite of powerful teaching tools to make lesson planning and testing quicker and easier.

PRENTICE HALL **StudentEXPRESS™** Learn · Study · Succeed Use the interactive textbook (online and on CD-ROM) to make selections and activities come alive with audio and video support and interactive questions.

PRETEACH

Motivation

Ask students to imagine a time before people had developed much scientific knowledge about the world. Remind students that human beings asked the same questions—"Why am I here?" and "How did Earth come to be?"—that they ask today. Form small groups in which students can share any folklore they may know that seeks to explain natural phenomena such as the changing moon, the shifting ocean tides, and the beginnings of various life forms.

Let students know that this series of Native American myths provides insight into early peoples' thinking about the origins of life on Earth.

❶ Background

More About the Authors

Joseph Bruchac is a novelist, poet, and storyteller of Abenaki descent. He lives in the foothills of New York's Adirondack Mountains, where his ancestors also lived.

The Modoc tale "When Grizzlies Walked Upright" was selected by Richard Erdoes and Alfonso Ortiz along with 165 other tales to appear in their anthology, *American Indian Myths and Legends.*

The Navajo migrated from northwestern Canada to the Southwest around 1300.

The Iroquois—who call themselves People of the Long House—are an alliance of North American tribes whose homelands range from the Atlantic coast westward to Lake Erie and from Ontario southward to North Carolina.

Build Skills Myths • Legend • Primary Source

❶ The Earth on Turtle's Back • When Grizzlies Walked Upright • *from* The Navajo Origin Legend • *from* The Iroquois Constitution

Onondaga

As one of the original five member nations, the Onondaga were an influential force in the Iroquois Confederation, a league of Iroquoian-speaking Native Americans in what is now the northeastern United States. The Onondaga lived in what is now central New York State, in villages of wood-and-bark long houses occupied by related families. The Onondaga were originally from Canada, where they acquired the French language. They practiced hospitality toward all people and did not believe in fighting. Following the breakup of the Iroquois Confederation after the American Revolution, factions of Onondaga scattered to various parts of the country, but the majority returned to their ancestral valley in New York where the Onondaga reservation now exists.

Modoc

The Modoc once lived in villages in the area of Oregon and Northern California, where they farmed, fished, and hunted. They also had a highly developed method of weaving. Though each village was independent and had its own leaders, in times of war they would band together. In the mid-nineteenth century, the Modoc were forced onto a reservation in Oregon. A band of Modoc, under the leadership of a subchief known as Captain Jack, later fled the reservation. The result was several years of hostilities with United States troops and the eventual relocation of Captain Jack's followers to Oklahoma. They were later allowed to return to the Oregon reservation, since dissolved.

Navajo

Today, the Navajo nation is the largest Native American nation in the United States and has more than 100,000 members. Many live on the Navajo reservation, which covers 24,000 square miles of Arizona, Utah, and New Mexico. Fierce warriors and hunters, the ancient Navajo settled in the Southwest about 1,000 years ago and eventually intermarried with the peaceful Pueblo people, who taught them to weave and raise crops. In 1864, after decades of fighting off encroaching American settlers, the Navajo were driven from their territory by the United States Army. They were eventually allowed to return to a reservation on Navajo land. Many Navajo still carry on native customs, living in earth-and-log structures and practicing the tribal religion.

Iroquois

The powerful Iroquois nation lived in what is now central New York State in the northeastern United States. During the sixteenth century, an Iroquoian mystic and prophet named Dekanawidah traveled from village to village urging the Iroquois-speaking people to stop fighting and band together in peace and brotherhood. Dekanawidah's efforts led to the formation of the Iroquois Confederation of the Five Nations, a league of five Iroquois tribes: Mohawk, Oneida, Seneca, Cayuga, and Onondaga. These tribes were democratic in process and composition, with leaders elected by their own people. The Iroquois tribes still exist today as self-governing bodies.

Preview

Connecting to the Literature

Just as you collect stories of your family history, cultures create stories to explain their world and place themselves in it. We share a fundamental desire to understand our origins—where we came from and our place in the world. In these stories, different cultures explain the world as they know it.

2 Literary Analysis

Origin Myths

The need to explain how life began gave birth to myths and traditional stories that were passed down from generation to generation. These stories are called **origin myths.** Myths explain phenomena, including:

- customs, institutions, or religious rites;
- natural landmarks such as a great mountain;
- events beyond people's control.

Look for the roles that nature and animals play in Native American life, and note who or what is responsible for the start of life on Earth.

Comparing Literary Works

In cultures without a written language, the **oral tradition** captures a group's ideals. Stories, poems, and songs convey a people's values, concerns, and history by word of mouth. As you read these selections, compare the worlds they describe. Note what each culture values, fears, or determines important to pass on to its next generation.

3 Reading Strategy

Recognizing Cultural Details

The Navajo Origin Legend excerpt opens with an image of the spirit men and women drying themselves with cornmeal. They call upon the gods, who appear carrying ears of corn. The references to corn reflect corn's importance to Navajo life.

Literature mirrors the culture that produces it. As you read, **recognize cultural details** by noticing references to objects, animals, or practices that signal how the people of a culture live, think, or worship. Use a chart like the one shown to record the details you find.

Details that signal how each group lives, thinks, or worships	
Onondaga	
Modoc	
Navajo	
Iroquois	

Vocabulary Builder

ablutions (ab lo͞o′ shənz) *n.* cleansing the body as part of a religious rite (p. 24)

protruded (prō tro͞od′ id) *v.* jutted out (p. 25)

confederate (kən fed′ ər it) *adj.* united with others for a common purpose (p. 26)

disposition (dis′ pə zish′ ən) *n.* an inclination or tendency (p. 26)

deliberation (di lib′ ər ā′ shən) *n.* careful consideration (p. 28)

2 Literary Analysis

Origin Myths

- Tell students that as they read the four selections in this lesson, they will focus on origin myths—traditional stories that recount the origins of life on Earth.
- Remind students that each selection is an example of one culture's origin myth.
- As students follow the narrative of each myth, have them try to recognize which ideas, landmarks, or events the narrative was designed to explain.
- Prepare students to read the selection by telling them that many characters in the narratives are gods, animals, or personified aspects of nature.
- You may wish to review personification with students; ask them to note the capitalization that is used to signify the names of such characters as the Duck.

3 Reading Strategy

Recognizing Cultural Details

- Origin myths contain cultural details—such as references to objects, animals, or practices—that illuminate how the people of the culture live, think, and worship.
- Give students a copy of **Reading Strategy Graphic Organizer A,** p. 1 in ***Graphic Organizer Transparencies.*** Remind students that noting the cultural details that appear in each group's origin myth can help them gain insight into the Native American cultures to which these myths belong.
- Encourage students to think about the cultural details that may be evident in a traditional story from their own cultures.

Vocabulary Builder

- Pronounce each vocabulary word for students, and read the definitions as a class. Have students identify any words with which they are already familiar.

Differentiated Instruction Solutions for All Learners

Support for Special Needs Students
Have students read the adapted version of the excerpt from *The Iroquois Constitution* in the ***Reader's Notebook: Adapted Version.*** This version provides basic-level instruction in an interactive format with questions and write-on lines. Completing these pages will prepare students to read the selection in the Student Edition.

Support for Less Proficient Readers
Have students read the excerpt from *The Iroquois Constitution* in the ***Reader's Notebook.*** This version provides basic-level instruction in an interactive format with questions and write-on lines. After students finish the selection in the ***Reader's Notebook,*** have them complete the questions and activities in the Student Edition.

Support for English Learners
Have students read the excerpt from *The Iroquois Constitution* in the ***Reader's Notebook: English Learner's Version.*** This version provides basic-level instruction in an interactive format with questions and write-on lines. Completing these pages will prepare students to read the selection in the Student Edition.

Learning Modalities
Logical/Mathematical Learners
When they read the excerpt from "The Navajo Origin Legend," have students look for number patterns and offer logical explanations for them. For instance, students may notice that the ceremony in this myth begins on the *twelfth* day. Twelve is a number often used in literature to indicate a year, a complete life cycle, or an indeterminate period of long waiting. Ask students to speculate about what the use of such number patterns meant to the myth's creators.

❶ About the Selection

This myth from the Onondaga people relates a story about the creation of the world. In this version, the Earth forms as an offshoot of a celestial place called Skyland.

❷ Critical Viewing

Answer: The marks on the turtle's shell are explained as muddy paw prints left by Muskrat.

❶ The Earth on Turtle's Back

(Onondaga-Northeast Woodlands)

Retold by Michael J. Caduto and Joseph Bruchac

Background Native Americans have great respect for the natural world. They believe that each creature has its own power by which it maintains itself and affects others. Each Native American culture has its own name for this power, but many Native American cultures recognize a Great Spirit—an invisible power that is the source of life and good for humans. Many of the animals that helped feed and clothe the early Native Americans are also highly revered. Native American folklore, much of which portrays animals, reflects this great respect.

Differentiated Instruction Solutions for All Learners

Accessibility at a Glance

	The Earth on Turtle's Back	When Grizzlies Walked	Navajo Origin Legend	Iroquois Constitution
Context	Creation Myth	Creation Myth	Creation Myth	Government document
Language	Accessible vocabulary; some dialogue	Accessible vocabulary	Some difficult vocabulary; complicated sentences	Formal, complicated sentences
Concept Level	Accessible (simple plot)	Challenging (complicated plot)	Abstract (religious ceremony)	Abstract (organization of government)
Literary Merit	Cross-cultural experience	Cross-cultural experience	Cross-cultural experience	Cross-curricular: government
Lexile	740	1070	900	1510
Overall Rating	More accessible	More accessible	More accessible	Average

3 Before this Earth existed, there was only water. It stretched as far as one could see, and in that water there were birds and animals swimming around. Far above, in the clouds, there was a Skyland. In that Skyland there was a great and beautiful tree. It had four white roots which stretched to each of the sacred directions,[1] and from its branches all kinds of fruits and flowers grew.

There was an ancient chief in the Skyland. His young wife was expecting a child, and one night she dreamed that she saw the Great Tree uprooted. The next day she told her husband the story.

4 He nodded as she finished telling her dream. "My wife," he said, "I am sad that you had this dream. It is clearly a dream of great power and, as is our way, when one has such a powerful dream we must do all we can to make it true. The Great Tree must be uprooted."

Then the Ancient Chief called the young men together and told them that they must pull up the tree. But the roots of the tree were so deep, so strong, that they could not budge it. At last the Ancient Chief himself came to the tree. He wrapped his arms around it, bent his knees and strained. At last, with one great effort, he uprooted the tree and placed it on its side. Where the tree's roots had gone deep into the Skyland there was now a big hole. The wife of the chief came close and leaned over to look down, grasping the tip of one of the Great Tree's branches to steady her. It seemed as if she saw something down there, far below, glittering like water. She leaned out further to look and, as she leaned, she lost her balance and fell into the hole. Her grasp slipped off the tip of the branch, leaving her with only a handful of seeds as she fell, down, down, down, down.

Far below, in the waters, some of the birds and animals looked up.

"Someone is falling toward us from the sky," said one of the birds.

"We must do something to help her," said another. Then two Swans flew up. They caught the Woman From The Sky between their wide wings. Slowly, they began to bring her down toward the water, where the birds and animals were watching.

"She is not like us," said one of the animals. "Look, she doesn't have webbed feet. I don't think she can live in the water."

"What shall we do, then?" said another of the water animals.

"I know," said one of the water birds. "I have heard that there is Earth far below the waters. If we dive down and bring up Earth, then she will have a place to stand."

So the birds and animals decided that someone would have to bring up Earth. One by one they tried.

The Duck dove first, some say. He swam down and down, far beneath the surface, but could not reach the bottom and floated back up. Then the Beaver tried. He went even deeper, so deep that it all was

1. **the sacred directions** North, South, East, and West.

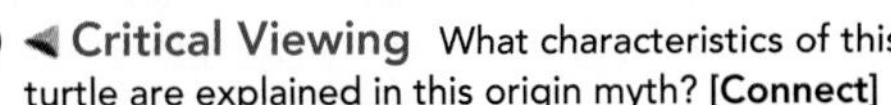
2 ◄ Critical Viewing What characteristics of this turtle are explained in this origin myth? **[Connect]**

Literary Analysis
Origin Myths How do the opening words of this story identify it as an origin myth?

Reading Strategy
Recognizing Cultural Details What do the chief's words to his wife tell you about the beliefs of the Onondaga?

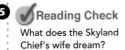

5 **Reading Check**
What does the Skyland Chief's wife dream?

3 Literary Analysis
Origin Myths

- Explain to students that origin myths can be seen as a mixture of science and religion—they explain how the world and the things in it came to be.
- Read the story's first sentence aloud with students.
- Then, **ask** them the Literary Analysis question: How do the opening words of this story identify it as an origin myth?
  Answer: The first sentence describes what existed before the creation of the earth.

4 Reading Strategy
Recognizing Cultural Details

- Read the second and third paragraphs aloud with students.
- Then, write a list on the chalkboard as students identify cultural details or topics that appear in this passage. Encourage students to note the references to marriage, childbirth, respect for age, and the role of dreams.
- Then, **ask** students the Reading Strategy question: What do the chief's words to his wife tell you about the beliefs of the Onondaga?
  Answer: The Onondaga believe that dreams are powerful, influential messages and that the dreams must be obeyed.

5 Reading Check

Answer: She dreams that she sees the Great Tree uprooted.

Differentiated Instruction
Solutions for All Learners

Strategy for Less Proficient Readers
Have students participate in a choral reading of this origin myth. Then, invite them to form groups in order to discuss what the myth reveals about the people who created it. How do students think the Onondaga viewed their environment?

Enrichment for Advanced Readers
Ask students to note details about how the Onondaga pictured the time before the creation of Earth. Have students discuss whether they know of any other origin stories that seem similar, such as that in the Bible's book of Genesis. Can students find further parallels between these narratives and scientific thinking about the formation of life on earth?

6 Literary Analysis
Origin Myths and Oral Tradition

- Read aloud with students the paragraphs in which various animals dive down in the ocean.
- Invite students to identify the unusual aspect of the animals' names. If necessary, draw students' attention to the "generic" quality of each name.

Monitor Progress: Ask students the Literary Analysis question: In oral literature, why might characters have generic names like "Loon" or "Muskrat"?
Answer: Often, characters in oral literature are symbolic or archetypal figures that embody important cultural ideas rather than complex personalities.

ASSESS
Answers

1. Students may say that they would be obliged to take the dream seriously and follow tradition, as the chief did; others may say that they would not have let a dream persuade them to alter or remove a sacred tree.
2. (a) In trying to look down the hole left by the uprooted tree, she leans too far and falls into the hole. (b) After the animals rescue her, they realize that she cannot live in the water, as they do.
3. (a) Each animal attempts (and fails) to dive deep enough to retrieve some earth. (b) As they take these actions, the animals exhibit concern, kindness, generosity, and heroism. None of the animals is fearful or selfish.
4. (a) They credit the animals of the waters, as well as the Sky Woman. (b) The myth suggests that the Onondaga felt respect and even affection for nature. They recognize that the world belonged to the animals first.
5. Often substantive achievements require bold action. Society benefits by enjoying the results of such brave efforts.

dark, but he could not reach the bottom, either. The Loon tried, swimming with his strong wings. He was gone a long long time, but he, too, failed to bring up Earth. Soon it seemed that all had tried and all had failed. Then a small voice spoke.

"I will bring up Earth or die trying."

6 They looked to see who it was. It was the tiny Muskrat. She dove down and swam and swam. She was not as strong or as swift as the others, but she was determined. She went so deep that it was all dark, and still she swam deeper. She swam so deep that her lungs felt ready to burst, but she swam deeper still. At last, just as she was becoming unconscious, she reached out one small paw and grasped at the bottom, barely touching it before she floated up, almost dead.

When the other animals saw her break the surface they thought she had failed. Then they saw her right paw was held tightly shut.

"She has the Earth," they said. "Now where can we put it?"

"Place it on my back," said a deep voice. It was the Great Turtle, who had come up from the depths.

They brought the Muskrat over to the Great Turtle and placed her paw against his back. To this day there are marks at the back of the Turtle's shell which were made by the Muskrat's paw. The tiny bit of Earth fell on the back of the Turtle. Almost immediately, it began to grow larger and larger and larger until it became the whole world.

Then the two Swans brought the Sky Woman down. She stepped onto the new Earth and opened her hand, letting the seeds fall onto the bare soil. From those seeds the trees and the grass sprang up. Life on Earth had begun.

Literary Analysis
Origin Myths and the Oral Tradition In oral literature, why might characters have generic names like "Loon" or "Muskrat"?

Critical Reading

1. **Respond:** If you had been the Great Chief, would you have pulled up the Great Tree? Explain your answer.
2. **(a) Recall:** Explain what happened to the wife of the chief when the young men uprooted the Great Tree. **(b) Interpret:** Why did this action generate concern among the animals?
3. **(a) Recall:** Describe the actions of the swans, the beaver, and the duck. **(b) Analyze:** How do these actions exhibit the best aspects of human nature?
4. **(a) Infer:** Whom do the Onondaga credit with bringing Earth into existence? **(b) Analyze:** From this myth, what can you conclude about the relationship between the Onondaga and their natural environment? Explain your answer.
5. **Generalize:** Muskrat makes a risky and desperate swim. How does society benefit from brave actions like this?

Go Online — Author Link
For: More about the Onondaga
Visit: www.PHSchool.com
Web Code: ere-9101

Go Online — Author Link For additional information about the Onondaga, have students type in the Web Code, then select O from the alphabet, and then select Onondaga.

7 When Grizzlies Walked Upright

Modoc

Retold by Richard Erdoes and Alfonso Ortiz

8 Before there were people on earth, the Chief of the Sky Spirits grew tired of his home in the Above World, because the air was always brittle with an icy cold. So he carved a hole in the sky with a stone and pushed all the snow and ice down below until he made a great mound that reached from the earth almost to the sky. Today it is known as Mount Shasta.

Literary Analysis
Origin Myths What natural phenomenon is explained here?

Then the Sky Spirit took his walking stick, stepped from a cloud to the peak, and walked down to the mountain. When he was about halfway to the valley below, he began to put his finger to the ground here and there, here and there. Wherever his finger touched, a tree grew. The snow melted in his footsteps, and the water ran down in rivers.

The Sky Spirit broke off the small end of his giant stick and threw the pieces into the rivers. The longer pieces turned into beaver and otter; the smaller pieces became fish. When the leaves dropped from the trees, he picked them up, blew upon them, and so made the birds. Then he took the big end of his giant stick and made all the animals that walked on the earth, the biggest of which were the grizzly bears.

Now when they were first made, the bears were covered with hair and had sharp claws, just as they do today, but they walked on two feet and could talk like people. They looked so fierce that the Sky Spirit sent them away from him to live in the forest at the base of the mountain.

Pleased with what he'd done, the Chief of the Sky Spirits decided to bring his family down and live on earth himself. The mountains of snow and ice became their lodge. He made a big fire in the center of the mountain and a hole in the top so that the smoke and sparks could fly out. When he put a big log on the fire, sparks would fly up and the earth would tremble.

Late one spring while the Sky Spirit and his family were sitting round the fire, the Wind Spirit sent a great storm that shook the top of 9 the mountain. It blew and blew and roared and roared. Smoke blown back into the lodge hurt their eyes, and finally the Sky Spirit said to his

What is the biggest animal made by the Sky Spirit?

7 About the Selection

This Modoc legend tells the story of the origin of all Native American people. After creating the world, the Chief of the Sky Spirits makes his home inside a mountain, where his daughter disobeys him and is stranded on the mountainside. Adopted and brought up by the grizzly bear people, who walk and talk, the spirit girl eventually marries a grizzly bear. When her father discovers her whereabouts, he curses the bears to walk on all fours and takes away their power of speech. The daughter's children with her grizzly husband are the ancestors of the Native American people.

8 Literary Analysis
Origin Myths

- Explain to students that origin myths not only provided explanations for the formation of the natural world, but also provided entertainment.
- Read aloud with students the story's opening paragraph.
- **Ask** students the Literary Analysis question: What natural phenomenon is explained here?
  Answer: This passage explains the origin of the volcano. Mount Shasta is a volcanic peak about fifty miles south of the Oregon border in present-day California.

Reteach: If students have difficulty understanding the explanation of natural phenomena in origin myths, have them reread the explanation of origin myths on page 17. Help students to recognize that Mt. Shasta was so much a part of the Modoc people's everyday lives that the story arose to explain its origin.

9 Reading Check

Answer: The grizzly bear is the largest animal made by the Sky Spirit.

Differentiated Instruction Solutions for All Learners

Strategy for Special Needs Students

Use the Venn Diagram in the ***Graphic Organizer Transparencies,*** p. 316 to help students contrast the way creation is presented in the Modoc myth and in the Onondaga myth. Help students understand that the Onondaga believe that existing animals were instrumental in creating Earth, whereas the Modoc believe that the Sky Spirit created both Earth and its creatures.

Enrichment for Gifted/Talented Students

Ask students to relate this story to others in which people are rescued or raised by caring animals. Urge students to do research in order to collect two or three other examples of this narrative detail (such as those in the stories of Tarzan, Mowgli, and various other folktales). Students might make brief oral presentations in which they compare and contrast these tales and hypothesize about why this theme appears so often in literature.

⑩ Critical Viewing

Answer: The bear, feathers, paw print, and hides are part of the natural world; the shield and spear are the work of humans. The artwork reflects the Native Americans' sense of harmony with the natural world.

⑪ Humanities

Dreamwalker by Nancy Wood Taber

Taber lives in the Manzano Mountains outside Albuquerque, New Mexico, where she creates detailed, lifelike paintings and colored pencil drawings of the birds and animals living in the wilderness near her home. She infuses her work with images relating to Native American lore.

This colored-pencil drawing—one in a series of works the artist calls "Spirit Shield"—shows a bear who has chosen "to take the earth walk among the two-leggeds." The bear's hibernation represents introspection and the quest for inner knowledge and strength. Use these questions for discussion:

1. In what way does the artist blend the natural and human worlds?
   Answer: Some of the objects, such as the shield and spear, are made by people using parts of animals.
2. What might the artist suggest about the bear by portraying it in the upright position?
   Answer: The artist is making a connection between this animal and humans, since humans also walk in an upright position.

⑪

Dreamwalker, Nancy Wood Taber

◀ **Critical Viewing** ⑩
Which elements of the natural world are included in this image? Which elements represent the human world? What is the effect of the presentation of both together? **[Assess]**

youngest daughter, "Climb up to the smoke hole and ask the Wind Spirit to blow more gently. Tell him I'm afraid he will blow the mountain over."

As his daughter started up, her father said, "But be careful not to stick your head out at the top. If you do, the wind may catch you by the hair and blow you away."

⑫ The girl hurried to the top of the mountain and stayed well inside the smoke hole as she spoke to the Wind Spirit. As she was about to climb back down, she remembered that her father had once said you could see the ocean from the top of their lodge. His daughter wondered what the ocean looked like, and her curiosity got the better of her. She poked her head out of the hole and turned toward the west, but before she could see anything, the Wind Spirit caught her long hair,

12 pulled her out of the mountain, and blew her down over the snow and ice. She landed among the scrubby fir trees at the edge of the timber and snow line, her long red hair trailing over the snow.

There a grizzly bear found the little girl when he was out hunting food for his family. He carried her home with him, and his wife brought her up with their family of cubs. The little red-haired girl and the cubs ate together, played together, and grew up together.

When she became a young woman, she and the eldest son of the grizzly bears were married. In the years that followed they had many children, who were not as hairy as the grizzlies, yet did not look exactly like their spirit mother, either.

All the grizzly bears throughout the forests were so proud of these new creatures that they made a lodge for the red-haired mother and her children. They placed the lodge near Mount Shasta—it is called Little Mount Shasta today.

13 After many years had passed, the mother grizzly bear knew that she would soon die. Fearing that she should ask of the Chief of the Sky Spirits to forgive her for keeping his daughter, she gathered all the grizzlies at the lodge they had built. Then she sent her eldest grandson in a cloud to the top of Mount Shasta, to tell the Spirit Chief where he could find his long-lost daughter.

When the father got this news he was so glad that he came down the mountainside in giant strides, melting the snow and tearing up the land under his feet. Even today his tracks can be seen in the rocky path on the south side of Mount Shasta.

As he neared the lodge, he called out, "Is this where my little daughter lives?"

He expected his child to look exactly as she had when he saw her last. When he found a grown woman instead, and learned that the strange creatures she was taking care of were his grandchildren, he became very angry. A new race had been created that was not of his making! He frowned on the old grandmother so sternly that she promptly fell dead. Then he cursed all the grizzlies:

"Get down on your hands and knees. You have wronged me, and from this moment all of you will walk on four feet and never talk again."

He drove his grandchildren out of the lodge, put his daughter over his shoulder, and climbed back up the mountain. Never again did he come to the forest. Some say that he put out the fire in the center of his lodge and took his daughter back up to the sky to live.

Those strange creatures, his grandchildren, scattered and wandered over the earth. They were the first Indians, the ancestors of all the Indian tribes.

That's why the Indians living around Mount Shasta would never kill 14 a grizzly bear. Whenever a grizzly killed an Indian, his body was burned on the spot. And for many years all who passed that way cast a stone there until a great pile of stones marked the place of his death.

Reading Strategy
Recognizing Cultural Details What detail about the way Native American women wear their hair is revealed here?

Reading Strategy
Recognizing Cultural Details What does the mother grizzly bear's decision reveal about the culture's view of responsibility or guilt?

Reading Check
What is the Spirit Chief's reaction to the mother grizzly bear's confession?

12 Reading Strategy
Recognizing Cultural Details

- Make sure that students don't overlook the significance of what they may think are minor details. Even a small detail can provide information about a particular culture.
- Have a student volunteer read aloud the paragraph in which the girl falls off the mountain.
- **Ask** students the first Reading Strategy question: What detail about the way some Native American women wear their hair is revealed here?
  Answer: Some Native American women wear their hair long.

13 Reading Strategy
Recognizing Cultural Details

- **Ask** students the second Reading Strategy question: What does the mother grizzly bear's decision reveal about the culture's view of responsibility or guilt?
  Answer: Her decision shows that the culture prizes a sense of personal responsibility.

14 Reading Check

Answer: He is filled with gladness when he first hears the news of his daughter's whereabouts.

Differentiated Instruction
Solutions for All Learners

Strategy for Less Proficient Readers
Have students brainstorm a list of natural landmarks in their geographical region, such as lakes, valleys, cliffs, rivers, mesas, forests, plains, springs, or rock formations. Invite students to choose one and write (or narrate) a short myth that explains how this natural feature was created.

Vocabulary for English Learners
Invite students to share origin myths with which they may be familiar. First, have students compile English vocabulary lists for words that appear in their stories. Then, as they tell the stories, have them consult the lists to help them remember the vocabulary. Finally, have them add the vocabulary lists to their portfolios.

Enrichment for Gifted/Talented Students
To illustrate how these stories functioned for Native Americans, have students recreate a tale-telling session. Invite them to perform this story for classmates, speaking expressively, making eye contact, and adding gestures. Have other students retell other origin myths from this collection or from other sources.

⓯ About the Selection

This creation story tells how the first Navajo man and woman were created from wind and ears of corn. The wind comes to represent life, an idea reflected in the fact that human beings breathe to survive. The legend illuminates the Navajo belief in the wind's sacredness, as well as other cultural details such as the importance of corn and deer as sources of sustenance.

⓰ Reading Strategy

Recognizing Cultural Details

- Remind students that myths often reflect important elements of a society's fundamental beliefs.
- Have a student volunteer read the opening paragraph and the first sentence of the second paragraph.
- **Ask** students the Reading Strategy question: What does this description suggest about the role of deer in Navajo life?
  Answer: The use of "sacred" buckskins in the ceremony suggests that deer are extremely important in Navajo life.

⓱ Critical Thinking

Hypothesize

- Have students read to the second sentence of the second paragraph.
- Then, **ask** students why, if the myth recounts the creation of the first people, the first sentence alludes to unnamed people washing and drying themselves with cornmeal?
  Answer: Students will observe that in addition to these, the story's first paragraphs also refer to the Mirage People. Students should hypothesize that the Navajo creation myths regard many kinds of beings as "people," but that the story specifically refers to the creation of human beings.

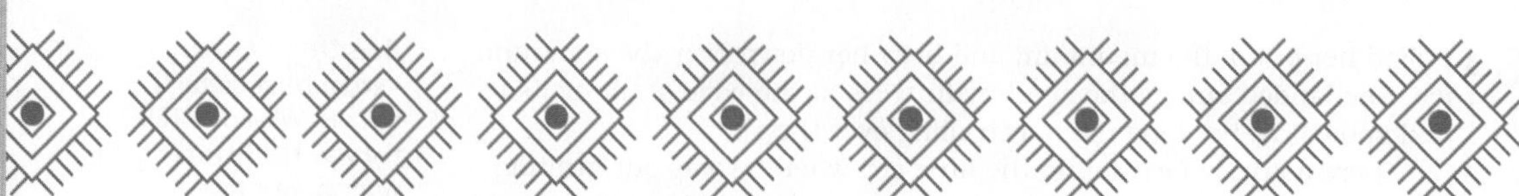

⓯ from The Navajo Origin Legend

Navajo

Retold by Washington Matthews

⓰ On the morning of the twelfth day the people washed themselves well. The women dried themselves with yellow cornmeal; the men with white cornmeal. Soon after the ablutions were completed they heard the distant call of the approaching gods.[1] It was shouted, as before, four times—nearer and louder at each repetition—and, after the fourth call, the gods appeared. Blue Body and Black Body each carried a sacred buckskin. White Body carried two ears of corn, one yellow, one white, each covered at the end completely with grains.

The gods laid one buckskin on the ground with the head to the west: on this they placed the two ears of corn, with their tips to the east, and over the corn they spread the other buckskin with its head to ⓱ the east; under the white ear they put the feather of a white eagle, under the yellow ear the feather of a yellow eagle. Then they told the people to stand at a distance and allow the wind to enter. The white wind blew from the east, and the yellow wind blew from the west, between the skins. While the wind was blowing, eight of the Mirage People[2] came and walked around the objects on the ground four

1. **the approaching gods** the four Navajo gods: White Body, Blue Body, Yellow Body, and Black Body.
2. **Mirage People** mirages personified.

Vocabulary Builder
ablutions (ab lo͞o′ shən*z*) *n.* cleansing the body as part of a religious rite

Reading Strategy
Recognizing Cultural Details What does this description suggest about the role of deer in Navajo life?

    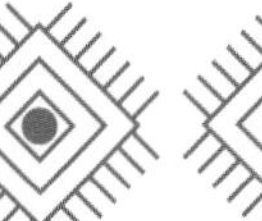   

times, and as they walked the eagle feathers, whose tips protruded from between the buckskins, were seen to move. When the Mirage People had finished their walk the upper buckskin was lifted; the ears of corn had disappeared, a man and a woman lay there in their stead.

18 The white ear of corn had been changed into a man, the yellow ear into a woman. It was the wind that gave them life. It is the wind that comes out of our mouths now that gives us life. When this ceases to blow we die. In the skin at the tips of our fingers we see the trail of the wind; it shows us where the wind blew when our ancestors were created.

The pair thus created were First Man and First Woman (Atsé Hastin and Atsé Estsán). The gods directed the people to build an enclosure of brushwood for the pair. When the enclosure was finished, First Man and First Woman entered it, and the gods said to them: "Live together now as husband and wife."

Vocabulary Builder
protruded (prō tro͞od′ id) *v.* jutted out

Literary Analysis
Origin Myths Why might the Navajo have viewed the wind as the source of life?

Critical Reading

1. **Respond:** What words would you use to describe the images in these tales and the impression they made on you?
2. **(a) Recall:** What do the grizzly bears do that angers the Chief of the Sky Spirit? **(b) Analyze:** What does his reaction tell you about him?
3. **(a) Recall:** What punishment does the Chief of the Sky Spirits levy against the grizzlies? **(b) Analyze Cause and Effect:** How does this action affect his grandchildren, the people of the Earth?
4. **(a) Recall:** Identify the stages of the Navajo creation ceremony. **(b) Analyze:** What do the order and ritual of the ceremony tell you about the Navajo people?
5. **(a) Recall:** What is the wind's role in the ceremony? **(b) Contrast:** How does the wind's role contrast with the order and ritual of the ceremony?
6. **(a) Compare and Contrast:** In what ways do the two tales differ in their attitude toward nature? **(b) Evaluate:** With which attitude do you most identify? Why?

Go Online Author Link

For: More about the Modoc and Navajo
Visit: www.PHSchool.com
Web Code: ere-9111

18 Literary Analysis
Origin Myths

- Read aloud with students the story's next-to-last paragraph.
- **Ask** students the Literary Analysis question: Why might the Navajo have viewed the wind as the source of life?
  Answer: The wind is a major climatic force, so the Navajo may have come to ascribe many powers to the wind. Also, since breath and wind are both movements of air, and since breath sustains human and animal life, it makes sense to compare wind to breath.

ASSESS
Answers

1. The impressions created by the works will vary from tale to tale and student to student.
2. (a) They take in his daughter and marry her to their oldest son. (b) It reveals that he is proud as creator of the Earth and does not want to share his powers of creation.
3. (a) He forbids them to talk or to walk upright. (b) His action causes his grandchildren, the first Indians, to scatter and wander over the Earth.
4. (a) First stage—the spirit people cleanse and dry themselves and call forth the gods; second—gods appear and place corn and feathers on buckskin; third—Mirage People circle buckskins, wind blows and transforms ears into people. (b) The Navajo people value and rely on a sense of order and ritual in life.
5. (a) The wind transforms the ears of corn into human beings. (b) The wind's work is "magical," in contrast to the logical and precise actions taken by the spirit people in anticipation of the wind's arrival.
6. (a) The Navajo legend does not explain the formation of the Earth. Although animals play a key role in bringing human life to Earth in the first two myths, vegetation (corn) is the key to life in the Navajo tale. (b) Students' responses will vary and should be supported with references to one or more texts.

Differentiated Instruction
Solutions for All Learners

Strategy for English Learners
Draw students' attention to the items in the story that function as symbols. Encourage students to list the items—buckskins, ears of corn, and eagle feathers, as well as the colors white, yellow, blue, and black. On the lists, have students jot suggested explanations of the significance of these items to the Navajo.

Enrichment for Gifted/Talented Students
Encourage students to research Native Americans' use of symbolism in other arts. For example, interested students might study the meanings of totems—carved and painted images on vertically mounted logs—that are constructed by the Indians of the Northwest Coast of the United States and Canada.

Go Online Author Link For additional information about the Modoc and the Navajo, have students type in the Web Code, then select M or N from the alphabet, and then select Modoc or Navajo.

19 About the Selection

The Iroquois Constitution tells how and why representatives of the Iroquois nation should hold formal councils to discuss and decide issues of concern to all. When Dekanawidah presented his *Kaianerekowa,* or Great Law of Peace, much of the Iroquois world was beset by persecution, disease, and power struggles. His plan led to the most far-reaching and notable political unit north of the Aztec civilization. The Constitution's sense of mutual respect, cooperation, and ritual among the Iroquois nations may have served as a model for what became the Constitution of the United States of America.

20 Literary Analysis

Origin Myths and the Oral Tradition

- Explain to students that stories in an oral tradition are not only important for the values and ideas they contain, but also for their style and form. For example, word choice and descriptive language are very important features, as they can help the speaker to remember the text and the listener to visualize the text.
- **Ask** students the Literary Analysis question: How would this visual description facilitate the oral transmission of this constitution?
  Answer: The description of a majestic tree vividly conveys the unity and good will enjoyed by the members of the Five Nations.

21 Vocabulary Builder

The Latin Suffix *-tion*

- Draw students' attention to the word *disposition* and its definition.
- Let students know that the suffix *-tion* forms a noun when added to a modified form of the verb.
- To show students how verbs may be made into nouns by using *-tion,* write the following on the chalkboard:

  Anyone outside the Five Nations who *is disposed* to do so, may join.
- Then, show students how to form the noun using *-tion:*

  Anyone outside the Five Nations who has the *disposition* to do so, may join.

19 *from*

The Iroquois Constitution

Iroquois

Translated by Arthur C. Parker

I am Dekanawidah and with the Five Nations[1] confederate lords I plant the Tree of the Great Peace. I name the tree the Tree of the Great Long Leaves. Under the shade of this Tree of the Great Peace we spread the soft white feathery down of the globe thistle as seats for you, Adodarhoh, and your cousin lords.

20 We place you upon those seats, spread soft with the feathery down of the globe thistle, there beneath the shade of the spreading branches of the Tree of Peace. There shall you sit and watch the council fire of the confederacy of the Five Nations, and all the affairs of the Five Nations shall be transacted at this place before you.

Roots have spread out from the Tree of the Great Peace, one to the north, one to the east, one to the south and one to the west. The name of these roots is the Great White Roots and their nature is peace and strength.

21 If any man or any nation outside the Five Nations shall obey the laws of the Great Peace and make known their disposition to the lords of the confederacy, they may trace the roots to the tree and if their minds are clean and they are obedient and promise to obey the wishes of the confederate council, they shall be welcomed to take shelter beneath the Tree of the Long Leaves.

We place at the top of the Tree of the Long Leaves an eagle who is able to see afar. If he sees in the distance any evil approaching or any

1. **Five Nations** the Mohawk, Oneida, Onondaga, Cayuga, and Seneca tribes. Together, these tribes formed the Iroquois Confederation.

Vocabulary Builder
confederate (kən fed′ ər it) *adj.* united with others for a common purpose

Literary Analysis
Origin Myths and the Oral Tradition How would this visual description facilitate the oral transmission of this constitution?

Vocabulary Builder
disposition (dis′ pə zish′ ən) *n.* an inclination or tendency

danger threatening he will at once warn the people of the confederacy.

The smoke of the confederate council fire shall ever ascend and pierce the sky so that other nations who may be allies may see the council fire of the Great Peace . . .

Whenever the confederate lords shall assemble for the purpose of holding a council, the Onondaga lords shall open it by expressing their gratitude to their cousin lords and greeting them, and they shall make an address and offer thanks to the earth where men dwell, to the streams of water, the pools, the springs and the lakes, to the maize and the fruits, to the medicinal herbs and trees, to the forest trees for their usefulness, to the animals that serve as food and give their pelts for clothing, to the great winds and the lesser winds, to the thunderers, to the sun, the mighty warrior, to the moon, to the messengers of the Creator who reveal his wishes and to the Great Creator who dwells in the heavens above, who gives all the things useful to men, and who is the source and the ruler of health and life.

Then shall the Onondaga lords declare the council open . . .

All lords of the Five Nations' Confederacy must be honest in all things . . . It shall be a serious wrong for anyone to lead a lord into trivial affairs, for the people must ever hold their lords high in estimation out of respect to their honorable positions.

When a candidate lord is to be installed he shall furnish four strings of shells (or wampum)[2] one span in length bound together at one end. Such will constitute the evidence of his pledge to the confederate lords that he will live according to the constitution of the Great Peace and exercise justice in all affairs.

When the pledge is furnished the speaker of the council must hold the shell strings in his hand and address the opposite side of the council fire and he shall commence his address saying: "Now behold him. He has now become a confederate lord. See how splendid he looks." An address may then follow. At the end of it he shall send the bunch of shell strings to the opposite side and they

22

Red Jacket, George Catlin, The Thomas Gilcrease Institute of American History and Art, Tulsa, Oklahoma

23 **▲ Critical Viewing**

What details or features of this portrait reflect a belief in the dignity and nobility of the Native Americans? **[Analyze]**

24  **Reading Check**

What does the speaker say is the nature of the Great White Roots?

2. **wampum** (wäm′ pəm) *n.* small beads made of shells.

22 Humanities

Red Jacket, by George Catlin

George Catlin was born in Wilkes-Barre, Pennsylvania. To please his father, he practiced law until 1823, at which time he became intrigued by "the dignity and nobility of the Native Americans." It was then that Catlin decided to devote himself to art and to becoming a historian of Native American peoples.

This portrait depicts fiery Seneca orator Sagoyewatha, who reluctantly followed his people into an alliance with the British. He received a red coat from the British as a ritual gift. Although in this portrait he is not wearing the red coat that led to his English nickname, the viewer can see the large medal given to him by George Washington after the American Revolution. Use these questions for discussion:

1. What personality traits has the artist tried to capture in this portrait?
   Possible answer: Strength, determination, and pride
2. How are these traits related to the values and ideas set forth in the Iroquois Constitution?
   Answer: The Constitution says a leader needs wisdom, patience, and a sense of duty—all of which require the inner strength and determination captured in the portrait.

23 Critical Viewing

Answer: The artist's portrayal of Red Jacket's serious, penetrating stare, defiant stance, face paint, and ceremonial objects—a tomahawk, a peace pipe, and a beaded belt—reflect the dignity and nobility of his subject.

24 Reading Check

Answer: The speaker says that the nature of the Great White Roots is "peace and strength."

Differentiated Instruction

Solutions for All Learners

Enrichment for Gifted/Talented Students

Point out that the Iroquois Constitution began as an oral "document," and as such it needed to hold the attention of multiple listeners. Ask students to deliver the speech orally to classmates to demonstrate how this literary work uses imagery and phrasing to create a memorable impression.

Enrichment for Advanced Readers

Assign students to compare and contrast the Iroquois Constitution and the Constitution of the United States of America. Have students read each text more than once before they begin to analyze the documents' similarities and differences. Encourage them to prepare a short presentation on the topic for the class.

25 Reading Strategy
Recognizing Cultural Details

- **Ask** students why they think the antlers of a deer are used to crown the lords of the Five Nations Confederacy.
  Answer: Students may say it is because the deer live in peace, as the Iroquois do.
- **Ask** students the Reading Strategy question: What can you learn about the Iroquois culture from the items mentioned here?
  Answer: The Iroquois show deep respect for the principles of just leadership.

ASSESS
Answers

1. Students are likely to say yes, that peace and strength in unity under a Constitution is very appealing.
2. (a) They plant the Tree of the Great Peace. (b) The roots symbolize strength and peace.
3. (a) They should thank one another and then "offer thanks to the earth where men dwell." (b) They respect each other and their environment and are conscious of their dependence on the earth.
4. (a) He uses the image of the Tree of the Long Leaves and its roots, the eagle, and the council fire. (b) They show that the Iroquois are conscious of creating a strongly rooted union that would shelter its members, be vigilant against threats from without, and welcome new members.
5. (a) A lord must be honest in all things, slow to anger, and full of peace, good will, and a desire for the welfare of his people. A lord's actions should always exhibit farsightedness, deliberation, and compassion. (b) Students' responses should include examples and supporting details.
6. Students should support their responses with clear reasoning.

shall be received as evidence of the pledge. Then shall the opposite side say:

"We now do crown you with the sacred emblem of the deer's antlers, the emblem of your lordship. You shall now become a mentor of the people of the Five Nations. The thickness of your skin shall be seven spans—which is to say that you shall be proof against anger, offensive actions and criticism. Your heart shall be filled with peace and good will and your mind filled with a yearning for the welfare of the people of the confederacy. With endless patience you shall carry out your duty and your firmness shall be tempered with tenderness for your people. Neither anger nor fury shall find lodgement in your mind and all your
25 words and actions shall be marked with calm deliberation. In all of your deliberations in the confederate council, in your efforts at law making, in all your official acts, self-interest shall be cast into oblivion. Cast not over your shoulder behind you the warnings of the nephews and nieces should they chide you for any error or wrong you may do, but return to the way of the Great Law which is just and right. Look and listen for the welfare of the whole people and have always in view not only the present but also the coming generations, even those whose faces are yet beneath the surface of the ground—the unborn of the future nation."

Reading Strategy
Recognizing Cultural Details What can you learn about the Iroquois culture from the items mentioned here?

Vocabulary Builder
deliberation (di lib′ ər ā′ shən) *n.* careful consideration

Critical Reading

1. **Respond:** If you were the chief of a Native American nation, would this speech persuade you to join the Confederation? Explain.
2. **(a) Recall:** What do the lords plant to commemorate their meeting? **(b) Analyze:** What do the roots of this plant symbolize?
3. **(a) Recall:** According to the Constitution, what must confederate lords do to open a council meeting? **(b) Infer:** What does this decree suggest about the Iroquois?
4. **(a) Analyze:** What three images from nature does Dekanawidah use in the Iroquois Constitution? **(b) Infer:** What do these references tell you about the Iroquois?
5. **(a) Summarize:** Summarize the qualities and conduct required of council lords by the Iroquois Constitution. **(b) Synthesize:** How well do these qualities apply to leaders in the modern world?
6. **Take a Position:** Do you agree with and support the ideas presented in *The Iroquois Constitution*? Why or Why not?

For: More about the Iroquois
Visit: www.PHSchool.com
Web Code: ere-9113

Apply the Skills

The Earth on Turtle's Back • *When Grizzlies Walked Upright* • from *The Navajo Origin Legend* • from *The Iroquois Constitution*

Literary Analysis

Origin Myths

1. According to the Modoc **origin myth,** who formed the landscape and the creatures of the Earth?
2. **(a)** Review the selections and use a chart like the one shown here to record the roles nature plays in explaining and maintaining Native American life.

Aspect of Nature	Connection to Native American Life

   (b) What can you conclude from the details you have collected?
3. How do animals and natural objects portray aspects of human nature in these origin myths?
4. Origin myths explain natural phenomena, customs, and specific characteristics of animals. Cite examples from the myths.

Comparing Literary Works

5. In cultures with **oral traditions** such as these, in what ways do myths and stories instruct or share important values?
6. **(a)** Which culture sees the spirits as generous and kind? Explain. **(b)** Which culture sees them as vengeful? Explain.
7. **(a)** In what way does the language of the Iroquois Constitution differ from that of the other selections? **(b)** How does this contrast reflect the Constitution's purpose?

Reading Strategy

Recognizing Cultural Details

8. Identify two **cultural details** you learned from each selection. Then, describe what each selection reveals about the culture that created it.
9. What do the prevalent attitudes in the Iroquois Constitution reveal about the culture behind the literature?

Extend Understanding

10. **Social Studies Connection:** In what ways is the United States Constitution similar to the Iroquois Constitution? In what ways is it different?

QuickReview

Origin myths are stories passed from generation to generation to explain the creation of the world and all it holds.

In an **oral tradition,** people share their values, concerns, and history through verbal literature such as storytelling.

Cultural details are references to objects, animals, or practices that reflect aspects of daily life or prevalent attitudes.

For: Self-test
Visit: www.PHSchool.com
Web Code: era-6101

Answers

1. The Chief of the Sky Spirits formed the landscape and the creatures of Earth.
2. (a) **Possible answers:** Marks on turtle's back explain cooperation and toil necessary to form the world; grizzlies' muteness and need to walk on four legs explains ancestry of Indians; ears of corn becoming men and women explains centrality of this crop in Native American culture (b) The environment plays a central role in the traditions and beliefs of Native Americans.
3. **Possible response:** Animals in the Onondaga myth persevere, cooperate, and show compassion.The strings of shells in the Iroquois Constitution represent human loyalty.
4. Examples include the marks on a turtle's back ("The Earth on Turtle's Back"), the walking posture of grizzly bears ("When Grizzlies Walked Upright"), and the importance of deer ("The Navajo Origin Legend").
5. Elders instruct young people about their culture by passing along its myths and stories orally. The oral tradition allows sharing of traditions and cultural details.
6. (a) The spirits in the Navajo culture generously transform corn into human beings. (b) The Modoc culture sees the Sky Spirit as vengeful, as evidenced by his punishment of the grizzlies.
7. (a) The language of the Iroquois Constitution is more formal than the language in the other selections. (b) This formality reflects the serious purpose that the work describes.
8. **Possible answers:** Onondaga: Dreams are important; water and water animals are also central to their culture; Modoc: The Modoc live among mountains, valleys, rivers, and volcanoes; Mount Shasta is an important place to them; Navajo: Corn is central to Navajo life; the culture associates the wind with life; Iroquois: Trees and fire symbolize strength and community to the Iroquois; the Iroquois prize peace, obedience, honesty, patience, and goodwill.

continued

Answers continued

9. The prevalent attitudes reveal that the culture prizes integrity, cooperation, peacefulness, compassion, thoughtfulness, and wisdom.
10. Students should make comparisons and contrasts about both the content and style of the two documents.

Go Online Assessment — Students may use the **Self-test** to prepare for **Selection Test A** or **Selection Test B.**

Answers

❶ Vocabulary Lesson

Word Analysis

1. constitution; People's rights are presented in the Constitution.
2. estimation; The lords held Dekanawidah high in their estimation.
3. disposition; Only those with a peaceful disposition could remain in the group.
4. hesitation; The lord's hesitation to join almost cost him his place on the council.
3. inoculation; To prevent tetanus, doctors give an inoculation.

Vocabulary Builder

1. b
2. c
3. b
4. c
5. a

Spelling Strategy

1. location; We could not identify the location of the treasure.
2. insulation; Thick insulation between the walls kept the cold air outside the house.
3. excavation; The excavation uncovered an old burial site.

❷ Grammar and Style Lesson

Sample rewrite: Then the Beaver tried. He went even deeper into the darkness, but he could not reach the bottom, either. The loon dove next, swimming deep into the water. Even with his strong wings, he could not reach the bottom, and he floated back up. Then a voice spoke. "I will bring up Earth, or I will die trying."

Writing Application

Students' paragraphs should contain at least two compound sentences.

Build Language Skills

❶ Vocabulary Lesson

Word Analysis: Latin Suffix *-tion*

The word *deliberation* contains the Latin suffix *-tion,* which forms a noun when added to a verb. The literal meaning of *deliberation* is "the act of deliberating." Change the following verbs to nouns by adding the suffix *-tion.* Then, use each new word in a sentence.

1. constitute: to set up in a legal or official form; establish
2. estimate: to form an opinion or judgment based on preliminary information
3. dispose: to tend or incline; to place in a certain order
4. hesitate: to stop because of indecision; pause or delay
5. inoculate: to provide a vaccine that creates immunity

Vocabulary Builder: Synonyms

For each grouping, identify the word whose meaning does not match the other two.

1. **(a)** cleansings, **(b)** imaginings, **(c)** ablutions
2. **(a)** deliberation, **(b)** consideration, **(c)** commotion
3. **(a)** protruded, **(b)** dangled, **(c)** jutted
4. **(a)** disposition, **(b)** inclination, **(c)** assumption
5. **(a)** varied, **(b)** confederate, **(c)** united

Spelling Strategy

When you add the suffix *-tion* to a verb that ends in *te,* drop the *te*: deliberate + *-tion* = *deliberation*. Add *-tion* to the following verbs. Use the resulting nouns in sentences.

1. locate **2.** insulate **3.** excavate

❷ Grammar and Style Lesson

Compound Sentences

A main clause is a complete thought that contains a subject that tells who or what the sentence is about and a predicate that tells what the subject is or does.

In oral and written language, compound sentences provide a natural way to link ideas. A **compound sentence** has two or more main clauses linked by a semicolon or a comma and a coordinating conjunction such as *and, or,* or *but.* In the example, subjects are underlined and predicates are italicized.

Example: Muskrat *dove down and brought up Earth,* and Earth *was placed on Turtle's back.*

Practice Rewrite the following paragraph so that it contains at least three compound sentences. You may need to add or change some words. Then, underline the subject and predicate in each clause.

> Then the Beaver tried. He went deeper into the darkness. He could not reach the bottom. Next, the loon dove into the water. Even he could not reach the bottom. He floated back up. Then a voice spoke, "I will bring up Earth or die trying."

Writing Application Write a paragraph about a natural landmark such as a river, cliff, or mountain in your state. In your writing, use at least two compound sentences.

WG *Prentice Hall Writing and Grammar Connection: Chapter 19, Section 4*

Assessment Practice

Summarizing Written Texts

Students will need to recognize accurate summaries on tests. Use this sample test item to help students practice:

> The need to explain the origins of life and other great mysteries gave birth to myths, traditional stories, often about immortal beings, that are passed down from generation to generation. Myths often explain other phenomena, including customs, institutions, or religious rites.

(For more practice, see *Standardized Test Preparation Workbook*, p.1.)

Which of the following is the best summary of the passage?

A Myths are created to help explain things that can't be otherwise understood.
B Myths are created to explain religious rites.
C Myths explain how life begins.
D Myths are passed through the generations.

Choices *B, C,* and *D* offer accurate but incomplete information. Choice *A* is the best summary.

Writing Lesson

Retelling of a Story

Storytellers add something of their own when repeating stories. Select one of the myths presented here and retell it. Keep the structure and sequence of events, but rewrite the tale to appeal to your audience. For example, you might update the setting.

Prewriting Create a rough story outline based on the myth. Then, using a chart like the one shown, list elements of the myth that you will retain and elements that you will adapt.

Model: Gathering Details from the Original

Food	Clothing	Beliefs	Environment

Drafting Following your outline, create a rough draft. Consider using repetition of actions, phrases, or words to create drama and to heighten suspense.

Revising Read your tale aloud, listening carefully to your repetition. Make sure it includes vibrant words and dynamic actions that create dramatic and memorable effects.

WG *Prentice Hall Writing and Grammar Connection: Chapter 5, Section 3*

Extend Your Learning

Listening and Speaking With a group, develop a **dramatic reenactment** of a council meeting called to install a new Iroquois lord.

- Create the roles outlined in *The Iroquois Constitution.*
- Plan the staging to determine the physical movement of the reenactment.
- Rehearse your reenactment several times to learn your roles.

When you are ready, present your reenactment to the class. Then answer audience questions about the Constitution or reenactment. **[Group Activity]**

Research and Technology Using the images in *The Iroquois Constitution* for inspiration, design a **logo** that represents or symbolizes the Iroquois Confederation. Be sure to include details in your design that relate to the culture and history of the Iroquois. Produce your logo by hand or using graphic design software. Then, write a brief explanation of it, and share your work with classmates.

For: An additional research activity
Visit: www.PHSchool.com
Web Code: erd-7101

❸ Writing Lesson

- To guide students in writing their retellings, give them the **Support for Writing Lesson** page (***Unit 1 Resources,*** p. 15).
- Students' retellings should retain the major narrative elements of the original, though they may feature contemporary settings or characters. The basic motives of characters and the fundamental qualities of settings, however, should not change.
- Tell students that their retellings should be adapted to a particular contemporary audience. Encourage them to identify which existing elements will interest their audience and which will benefit from modification.
- Use the rubrics for Narration: Short Story, pp. 57–58 in ***General Resources,*** to evaluate students' retellings.

❹ Research and Technology

- Have students reread the text carefully before planning and designing their logos. Encourage them to think about interesting, effective logos they have seen. Let students know that often an effective logo conveys a single central feature of its subject.
- Ask students to select images that communicate the fundamental ideas of the Iroquois Constitution.
- Urge students to refine these images by making more than one version of their logos.
- The **Support for Extend Your Learning** page (***Unit 1 Resources,*** p. 16) provides guided note-taking opportunities to help students complete the Extend Your Learning activities.

Go Online Research Have students type in the Web Code for another research activity.

Assessment Resources

The following resources can be used to assess students' knowledge and skills.

Unit 1 Resources
- **Selection Test A,** pp. 20–22
- **Selection Test B,** pp. 23–25

General Resources
- **Rubrics for Narration: Short Story,** pp. 57–58

Go Online Assessment Students may use the **Self-test** to prepare for **Selection Test A** or **Selection Test B.**

From the Author's Desk

Susan Power

- Point out the brief biography of Susan Power. Explain that Power, the daughter of a Native American activist, is a graduate of Harvard Law School. Power was editor of the University of Chicago Law Review before leaving to write full time. Have students reread Power's introduction to Unit 1 on pp. 4–5 if necessary.
- Show students Segment 2 on Susan Power on the *From the Author's Desk DVD* to provide insight into the sources of "Museum Indians."
- **Ask:** How does "Museum Indians," an essay, differ from a story?
  Possible response: "Museum Indians" differs from a story because it is about the author's actual experiences. However, writing an essay involves the kind of shaping readers might associate more closely with fiction.

Bringing the Spark of Your Own Imagination

- Explain to students Power's point that the origin myths they have read in Unit 1 have been transmitted orally from generation to generation. **Ask:** How, according to Power, does being a part of the oral tradition shape these stories?
  Possible response: Power says that the stories are meant to be flexible, as they change and evolve with each telling. The listener plays an active role in bringing the stories to life.

Exposed to Two Cultures

- Point out to students that to a large extent, Power characterizes the differing worlds of traditional Native American culture and mainstream American culture in terms of their literary expression.
- **Ask** students to describe the connections Power suggests between her two cultures.
  Possible response: Power's memorization and reciting of Shakespearean dialogue recalls the storytelling of her Native culture.

Critical Viewing

Answer: The lively expression on her face and the gesture of her hands suggest that the storyteller is acting out her story.

From the Author's Desk

SUSAN POWER INTRODUCES
"Museum Indians"

Susan Power's novel *The Grass Dancer* won the PEN/Hemingway Award for First Fiction. She has also written a book of stories and autobiographical essays entitled *Roofwalker.*

Bringing the Spark of Your Own Imagination

The origin myths of the Onondaga, Modoc, and Navajo tribes, recounted on pages 18–25 of this textbook, are examples of the oral tradition, stories repeated within a community, passed down from one generation to the next, keeping them alive. These spoken stories are meant to be performed, acted out with great drama before a circle of avid listeners of all ages. Each retelling of the story changes it a little, the performer emphasizing one episode over another, choosing slightly different words each time. These stories are meant to be flexible, interactive—modified according to the present audience's mood and tastes.

So as you read these tales, try to imagine them being acted out. Try to hear the storyteller's voice changing as different characters speak, rising with excitement, falling to a whisper. Your imaginative spark is needed to bring these stories fully to life.

Exposed to Two Cultures

I am a grateful listener, eager to hear a gripping yarn, but I myself am not a traditional storyteller. I was very shy as a child and found it difficult to stand before people and speak aloud either a story or an idea. I was silent in my classes, unless called upon, and preferred committing my words to quiet paper rather than the storm of conversation. I was raised to be both Native (Yanktonnai Dakota) and American, and so I was exposed not only to traditional Native American stories, songs, ceremonies, and dances, but also to the culture of mainstream America and the wider world.

I loved reading and graduated from pop-up books and comics to the Nancy Drew mystery series and the *Chronicles of Narnia.* When I was about twelve, I began listening to recordings made of the plays

▶ **Critical Viewing** What details in this photograph suggest that the storyteller is acting out her story, rather than simply reciting it? **[Analyze]**

Teaching Resources

The following resources can be used to enrich or extend the instructions for From the Author's Desk.

Unit 1 Resources
- **From the Author's Desk,** p. 18
- **Listening and Viewing,** p. 19

From the Author's Desk DVD
- **Susan Power,** Segment 2

of William Shakespeare and would memorize long passages that I delighted in performing privately, with no one but my mother and our cats to overhear. I didn't understand much of what was being spoken in the famous plays, but I was fascinated with the rhythmic poetry of the words, the dramatic plot lines, and thought to myself that Shakespeare would have felt at home in the Native world, dramatic as our oral literature can be.

Two Literary Traditions

The Oral Tradition	The Written Tradition
Begins earlier in time	Begins later in time
Requires language but not a system of writing	Requires language and a system of writing
Based on memory and oral transmission	Based on texts that can be written down, read, and copied
Includes folklore, proverbs, chants, and ballads	Includes novels, short stories, history books
Uses strong rhythms and repetition to help memory	Use less repetition because memory is not as essential
Performer can vary presentation in response to audience	Writer cannot vary text in response to a reader's reaction
Material can change with each presentation, resulting in different versions	Material tends to be fixed in a single version

Looking for My Own Experience

I began writing my own poems, stories, essays, and political songs when I was very young—five or six years old. Perhaps I needed to write because, although I heard traditional stories of the people who came before me and inhabited this continent prior to European contact, and although I read dozens of books that taught me what it was like to live everywhere else in the world, I never found myself, my own experience, in either of these literatures: the oral tradition or the novels of the world. Where were the stories of little girls who attended church as well as a Native ceremony in the deep Wisconsin woods? Where were the books that told of a child who could perform a variety of traditional dances at an intertribal powwow and also excel in her ballet classes? I could not find myself on the literary map, and so I had to develop my own literature, plot my own place in this world.

But is my writing more Native than American? In my fiction and essays, Native American themes are emphasized—my characters believe, as I do, that everything is potentially alive, a creature of spirit, whether it be a person, an animal, a family car, a stone. But the language I use is English, the paintbrush of words I wield to draw you a picture of what I see with my eyes.

▲ Critical Viewing
According to this chart, what are two differences between the oral tradition and the written tradition in literature? **[Read Chart]**

Two Literary Traditions

- Review the chart with the class. Be sure they recognize that Power associates the oral tradition with Native American culture and the written tradition with mainstream American and world cultures.
- **Ask:** Which similarities and differences between the two traditions do you find most striking? **Possible response:** Both traditions are based in language and are concerned with transmitting stories and ideas. The most striking difference is that the oral tradition is very flexible, while the written tradition is very fixed, even rigid.
- Explain to students that in her comments, Power seems to be drawn to elements of each tradition. While she loves the quiet comfort of reading and writing, she is also enamored of the powerful rhythms of oral literature.

Looking for My Own Experience

- Be sure students understand that in the first paragraph of this section, Power is searching for the reason she began to write. **Ask:** How did her relationship to her two cultures influence her as a writer? **Possible response:** Power suggests that in being part of two cultures, her experience belonged to neither. She felt a need to create her own literary tradition using elements of both Native and mainstream American cultures.
- Call students' attention to the question Power asks of her work: "But is my writing more Native than American?" Encourage them to keep this question in mind as they read "Museum Indians."

Critical Viewing

Possible response: The oral tradition begins early in time and the written tradition begins later in time. Only one version is used in the written tradition, but the oral tradition can have multiple versions of a story.

"Museum Indians": Oral Literature and Print

- Explain to students that Power is describing one way she tries to unite the oral tradition of Native American literature and the written tradition of mainstream American culture: by including her mother's storytelling in this written essay.
- Instruct students to watch for moments of storytelling as they read "Museum Indians."

Critical Viewing

Answer: One can infer that the written language of the Sioux is poetic and reads like a ballad or song, rather than prose.

ASSESS

Answers

1. (a) She says that as a child, she was too shy to stand before people and tell stories. (b) Her experiences of Native American culture, of storytelling, dances, and other rituals, may have led her to become a writer. Also, her experience of being a part of two cultures at once may have contributed.
2. (a) Because she could not find her own experience in literature, she became a writer and tried to create a tradition that could include her experience. (b) Students may identify any number of categories of young adult literature as speaking to their own experience. Some students will point to a broader range of literature.
3. Students are likely to point to her mother's old and new hair, as well as the contrast between the ways Native culture is displayed in the museum and the way Power and her mother experience it.
4. Students are likely to note that Power seems both more conscious of her Native heritage and less fully a part of Native culture than her mother, who is so fully Native that she can cut her hair short without affecting her identity. Students may also point to images of the mother's strength and stature in Power's young eyes.

From the Author's Desk

"Museum Indians": Oral Literature and Print

The essay that follows, "Museum Indians," is a brief examination of my childhood in cultural terms—specifically, what it was like to be Native American in the city of Chicago. Notice that even though I have *written* several scenes describing adventures I shared with my mother, employing narrative strategies familiar to any reader of books, my mother is constantly *telling* me stories within the piece—instances of our own family oral tradition still in practice today. So I have captured the oral literature with my printed words.

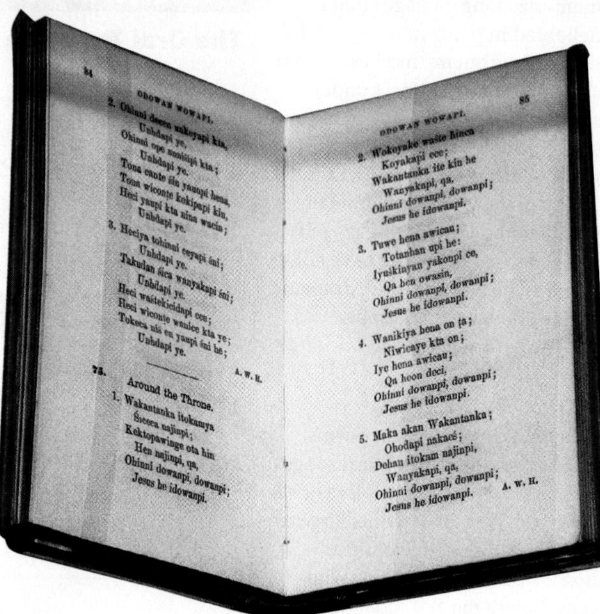

84

ODOWAN WOWAPI.

2. Ohinni deeca unkoyapi kta,
Unhdapi ye.
Ohinni ope unniŝapi kta;
Unhdapi ye.
Tona cante ŝin yaunpi hena,
Tona wiconte kokipapi kin,
Heci yaupi kta nina wacin;
Unhdapi ye.

3. Heciya tohinni ceyapi ŝni;
Unhdapi ye.
Takudan ŝica wanyakapi ŝni;
Unhdapi ye.
Heci waŝtekicidapi ece;
Heci wiconte wanice kta ye;
Tokeca niŝ eu yaupi ŝni he;
Unhdapi ye.

A. W. H.

75. Around the Throne.

1. Wakantanka itokamya
Ŝiceca najinpi;
Kektopawinge ota hin
Hen najinpi, qa,
Ohinni dowanpi, dowanpi;
Jesus he idowanpi.

ODOWAN WOWAPI. 85

2. Wokoyake waŝte hinca
Koyakapi ece;
Wakantanka ite kin he
Wanyakapi, qa,
Ohinni dowanpi, dowanpi;
Jesus he idowanpi.

3. Tuwe hena awicau;
Totanhan upi he:
Iyuŝkinyan yakonpi ce,
Qa hen owasin,
Ohinni dowanpi, dowanpi;
Jesus he idowanpi.

4. Wanikiya hena on ta;
Niwicaye kta on;
Iye hena awicau;
Qa heon deci,
Ohinni dowanpi, dowanpi;
Jesus he idowanpi.

5. Maka akan Wakantanka;
Ohodapi nakaeŝ;
Dehan itokam najinpi,
Wanyakapi, qa,
Ohinni dowanpi, dowanpi;
Jesus he idowanpi.

A. W. H.

▶ **Critical Viewing** What can you infer about the Sioux written language from these pages? **[Infer]**

Thinking About the Commentary

1. **(a) Recall:** What reason does Susan Power give to explain why she is not a traditional storyteller? **(b) Connect:** What life experiences do you think contributed to Power's decision to become a writer?
2. **(a) Recall:** What is Power's solution to not finding her own experience in the literature she read as a child? **(b) Assess:** What kind of literature speaks to your own lived experience?

As You Read "Museum Indians" . . .

3. **Analyze:** Look for details in the essay that show the contrast between the "Native" and the "American" that Power describes here.
4. **Compare and Contrast:** Consider the ways that Power is like her mother, and the ways she is different.

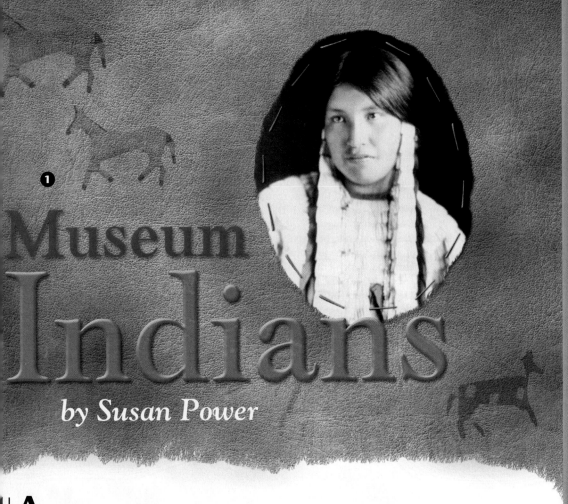

1

Museum Indians

by Susan Power

A snake coils in my mother's dresser drawer; it is thick and black, 3 glossy as sequins. My mother cut her hair several years ago, before I was born, but she kept one heavy braid. It is the three-foot snake I lift from its nest and handle as if it were alive.

"Mom, why did you cut your hair?" I ask. I am a little girl lifting a sleek black river into the light that streams through the kitchen window. Mom turns to me.

"It gave me headaches. Now put that away and wash your hands for lunch."

"You won't cut my hair, will you?" I'm sure this is a whine.

"No, just a little trim now and then to even the ends."

I return the dark snake to its nest among my mother's slips, arranging it so that its thin tail hides beneath the wide mouth sheared by scissors. My mother keeps her promise and lets my hair grow long,

▲ Critical Viewing
What might motivate someone—like the young Sioux woman in this photograph or the author's' mother— to cut her hair or change some other traditional aspect of her appearance? **[Speculate]**

TEACH

Learning Modalities
Visual/Spatial Learners Much of "Museum Indians" unfolds in various museums in Chicago where the exhibits inspire revealing discussions between Susan Power and her mother. Encourage students to design their own museum exhibits: one based on an exhibit Power describes in her essay and one of their own that captures something similar. Students should illustrate or make models of their exhibits, using reproductions of pieces of art.

1 About the Selection

In this personal essay, Susan Power describes aspects of the relationship she and her mother had when Power was a child. Her mother, a Dakota woman, is an inspiring figure—tall, fearless, and outspoken. She brings Power all over Chicago, giving her daughter a sense of owning the city. Power focuses on the museums they visited together and on the stories the exhibits inspired her mother to tell. Through bits of her stories, we learn that Power's mother is so connected to her Native American heritage that she can never be as at home as her daughter is in the Chicago her daughter loves.

2 Critical Thinking

Interpret

- Have students read the marked passage. Explain that the snake Power describes is a long braid of her mother's hair.
- **Ask:** Why does Power describe her mother's braid as a snake?
  Possible response: Power uses this metaphor to show that her mother's hair still has life in her mind. It also shows how powerful a figure Power's mother is.

3 Critical Viewing

Answer: In traditional Native American culture, to cut one's hair is a symbol of death and mourning. The woman in the photograph might cut her hair because she mourns the loss of her traditional lifestyle.

❹ Author's Insight

- Discuss the first five paragraphs of "Museum Indians" and point out that Power is establishing a sense of the relationship she and her mother had when she was a young girl.
- **Ask:** Why does Power describe her hair as "tiny garden snakes?"
  Possible response: She is comparing it to her mother's old braid, which she has described as "the three-foot snake."
- Call students' attention to the Author's Insight note next to the marked passage. Explain that Power describes her hair as she does to emphasize how much bigger and stronger than herself her mother seemed to be.
- Have students **identify** other instances in the essay's first five paragraphs in which Power compares herself to her mother.
- **Possible response:** Her mother tells stories, but when Power tries to repeat the stories, she only "chatters like a monkey." Furthermore, her mother is outspoken and politically active, but Power can "rage only on paper."

❺ Author's Insight

- Have students read the marked passage. **Ask** them to describe the image of Power's mother the passage creates.
  Possible response: Power presents her mother as a woman of enormous scale and power and capable of virtually anything.
- Call students' attention to the Author's Insight note next to the marked passage.
- **Ask:** Does Power's use of this simile achieve the purpose she has in mind?
  Possible answer: The simile makes Power's mother seem huge because, like a skyscraper, she fills up her daughter's range of vision entirely.

❻ Critical Viewing

Possible answer: Cultural institutions might place statues of lions at the entrance to instill a sense of awe and respect in visitors.

❹ but I am only half of her; my thin brown braids will reach the middle of my back, and in maturity will look like tiny garden snakes.

My mother tells me stories every day: while she cleans, while she cooks, on our way to the library, standing in the checkout line at the supermarket. I like to share her stories with other people, and chatter like a monkey when I am able to command adult attention.

"She left the reservation when she was sixteen years old," I tell my audience. Sixteen sounds very old to me, but I always state the number because it seems integral to my recitation. "She had never been on a train before, or used a telephone. She left Standing Rock to take a job in Chicago so she could help out the family during the war. She was petrified of all the strange people and new surroundings; she stayed in her seat all the way from McLaughlin, South Dakota, to Chicago, Illinois, and didn't move once."

❺ I usually laugh after saying this, because I cannot imagine my mother being afraid of anything. She is so tall, a true Dakota woman; she rises against the sun like a skyscraper, and when I draw her picture in my notebook, she takes up the entire page. She talks politics and attends sit-ins, wrestles with the Chicago police and says what's on her mind.

I am her small shadow and witness. I am the timid daughter who can rage only on paper.

Susan Power
Author's Insight
I compare my mother's braid to my own—hers is a "sleek black river," mine are "two tiny garden snakes"—to underscore my childhood impression that I was so much smaller and weaker, a diluted version.

Vocabulary Builder
integral (in′tə grəl) *adj.* essential

petrified (pe′trə fīd′) *adj.* *paralyzed* as with fear

Susan Power
Author's Insight
I describe my mother as a "skyscraper" so the reader will have a visual image of my child's-eye view of her as a towering force.

❻ **Critical Viewing**
Why do you think cultural institutions such as the Art Institute of Chicago might choose to place statues of lions at the entrance? **[Speculate]**

Enrichment

Chicago's Museums

Chicago is known for its many fine museums. The Chicago Historical Society, where Power's mother complains about the negative representation of Native Americans, has a highly regarded collection focusing on Abraham Lincoln and the American Civil War.

The Art Institute of Chicago is one of the largest museums in the United States, housing art from all over the world. The museum is especially famous for its collections of nineteenth-century Impressionist paintings and of modern art. Picasso's *The Old Guitarist* is only one of the many masterworks whose home is in Chicago.

The Field Museum is also among America's largest museums. One of the world's most important natural history museums, the Field has a collection of more than 19 million items, and also conducts scientific research and education.

We don't have much money, but Mom takes me from one end of the city to the other on foot, on buses. I will grow up believing that Chicago belongs to me, because it was given to me by my mother. Nearly every week we tour the Historical Society, and Mom makes a point of complaining about the statue that depicts an Indian man about to kill a white woman and her children: "This is the only monument to the history of Indians in this area that you have on exhibit. It's a shame because it is completely one-sided. Children who see this will think this is what Indians are all about."

My mother lectures the guides and their bosses, until eventually that statue disappears.

Some days we haunt the Art Institute, and my mother pauses before a Picasso.

"He did this during his blue period," she tells me.

I squint at the blue man holding a blue guitar. "Was he very sad?" I ask.

"Yes, I think he was." My mother takes my hand and looks away from the painting. I can see a story developing behind her eyes, and I tug on her arm to release the words. She will tell me why Picasso was blue, what his thoughts were as he painted this canvas. She relates anecdotes I will never find in books, never see footnoted in a biography of the master artist. I don't even bother to check these references because I like my mother's version best.

When Mom is down, we go to see the mummies at the Field Museum of Natural History. The Egyptian dead sleep in the basement, most of them still shrouded in their wrappings.

"These were people like us," my mother whispers. She pulls me into her waist. "They had dreams and intrigues and problems with their teeth. They thought their one particular life was of the utmost significance. And now, just look at them." My mother never fails to brighten. "So what's the use of worrying too hard or too long? Might as well be cheerful."

7

The Old Guitarist, 1903, Pablo Picasso, The Art Institute of Chicago, © 2004 Estate of Pablo Picasso/Artists Rights Society (ARS), New York

8 ▲ **Critical Viewing** Do you think that the color blue evokes a sad mood in this painting? Explain. **[Respond]**

Vocabulary Builder

shrouded (shroud′ əd) *v.* wrapped

intrigues (in′ trēgz′) *n.* secrets

7 Humanities

***The Old Guitarist*, 1903, by Pablo Picasso**

Pablo Picasso (1881–1973) was among the most important and famous artists of the twentieth century. Picasso was born in Spain and studied art in La Coruña and Barcelona. By the time he was a teenager, he was producing exceptionally advanced work.

Picasso emerged as a truly original artist in 1901, when he entered what is known as his "blue period." For a few years, his palette was dominated by shades of blue. The paintings from this period focused on poor and downtrodden people. *The Old Guitarist* is among the best-known painting from this stage of Picasso's career. The sorrow and misery radiating from the elderly guitar player epitomizes the mood of the period.

Picasso's blue period ended in 1904. The artist remained incredibly prolific for almost his entire life. He pioneered numerous movements within modern art, including cubism and construction or assemblage sculpture. Use these questions for discussion:

1. What details in this painting suggest that Picasso was "very sad," as Power imagines, when he painted it?
   Possible response: The old guitar player is emaciated, and his clothes are ragged and torn, suggesting poverty. His head is bowed, and his face carries an expression almost beyond sorrow. All of these details suggest sadness.
2. Why do you think this painting would attract Power and her mother?
   Possible response: It is a famous image of exceptional beauty, and its sorrowful mood might attract their attention when Power's mother is feeling sad.

8 Critical Viewing

Possible response: The color blue does evoke a sad mood in this painting because the color blue often refers to sadness or a state of depression.

Differentiated Instruction Solutions for All Learners

Support for Less Proficient Readers

These students may need extra help to understand what Susan Power is trying to convey in her descriptions of her mother. Review the Author's Insight notes on page 36 with students. Point out that as a writer, Power wants to show that her mother was a "towering force" to her "diluted version." Then, have students find and write down the details Power uses to describe her mother. Discuss these details with students, guiding them to recognize that they depict a great, powerful woman through the eyes of an awestruck young girl.

Enrichment for English Learners

These students might feel a personal connection to Power's description of simultaneously being part of two different cultures. In discussion, encourage students to compare their own connections to their native cultures and American culture to those of Power. Students who were born in the United States to immigrant parents, or who moved here while very young, may have the most in common with Power. Encourage students to write their own essays about experiences they have had where their two cultures come together.

9 Author's Insight

- Have students pause before reading the marked passage. Explain that Power and her mother are gazing at a beaded Native dress—apparently made by Power's great-grandmother—in a display case.
- Call students' attention to the image of the beaded dress on this page. **Ask** them to describe the dress in their own words. What similarities and differences do they see between this dress and the one Power describes? **Possible response:** Although it does not have the geometric patterns of the dress Power describes, it has the same azure blue and heaviness.
- Have students read the marked passage. Then, call their attention to the Author's Insight note. Explain that Power is linking the Native art represented by the dress and the art of Picasso.
- **Ask** students what the connection Power makes between the dress and the Picasso painting suggests about the cultural traditions from which each comes.
  Possible response: Power feels that she belongs to two cultures, her mother's Native culture and the mainstream culture of America and the world. By connecting the Native dress to the Picasso painting, she shows that she values both cultures equally, and sees both from the same perspective—her own.

10 Critical Viewing

Answer: As opposed to Picasso's painting, the blue in this Sioux dress creates a very cheerful mood, celebrating life and paying homage to the horses on which the Sioux relied heavily to support their lifestyle.

11 Critical Thinking
Make a Judgment

- Discuss the marked passage. Be sure students recognize that Power's mother thinks that neither she nor the buffalo belong in a city like Chicago.
- **Ask** students if the mother's tears make her less of the brave, towering figure her daughter describes.
  Possible response: Her tears show us that even the bravest of people have their own sorrows.

Before we leave this place, we always visit my great-grandmother's buckskin dress. We mount the stairs and walk through the museum's main hall—past the dinosaur bones all strung together, and the stuffed elephants lifting their trunks in a mute trumpet.

Vocabulary Builder
disconcerting (dis′ kən surt′ iŋ) *adj.* upsetting

The clothed figures are disconcerting because they have no heads. I think of them as dead Indians. We reach the traditional outfits of the Sioux in the Plains Indian section, and there is the dress, as magnificent as I remembered. The yoke is completely beaded—I know the garment must be heavy to wear. My great-grandmother used
9 blue beads as a background for the geometrical design, and I point to the azure[1] expanse.

"Was this her blue period?" I ask my mother. She hushes me unexpectedly, she will not play the game. I come to understand that this is a solemn call, and we stand before the glass case as we would before a grave.

"I don't know how this got out of the family," Mom murmurs. I feel helpless beside her, wishing I could reach through the glass to disrobe the headless mannequin. My mother belongs in a grand buckskin dress such as this, even though her hair is now too short to braid and has been trained to curl at the edges in a saucy flip.

We leave our fingerprints on the glass, two sets of hands at different heights pressing against the barrier. Mom is sad to leave.

"I hope she knows we visit her dress," my mother says.

There is a little buffalo across the hall, stuffed and staring. Mom doesn't always have the heart to greet him. Some days we slip out of the museum without finding his stall.

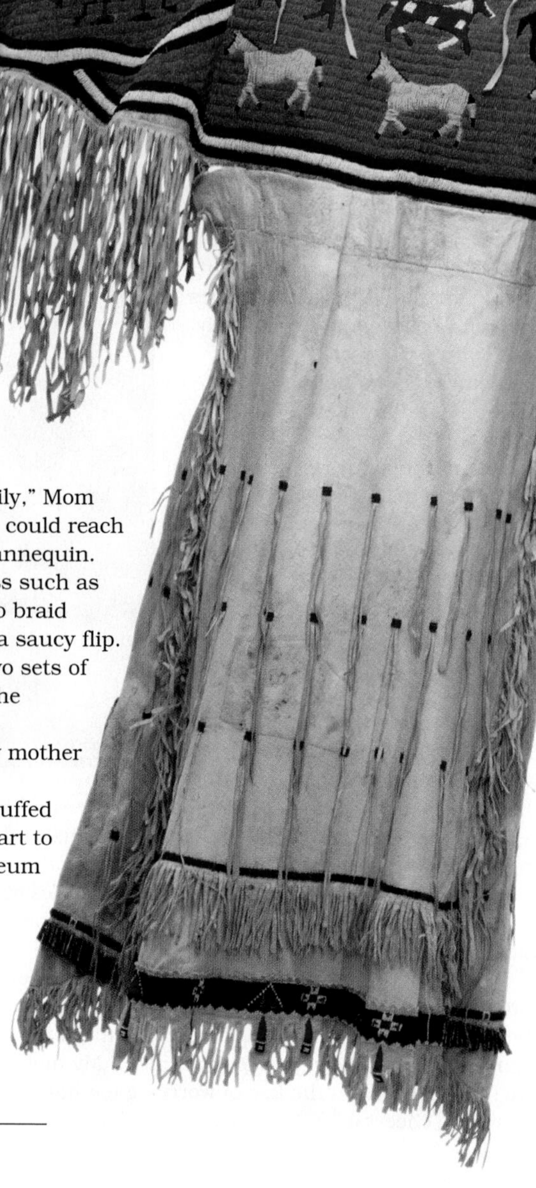

10 ▶ Critical Viewing
Does the blue in this Sioux dress create the same mood as the blue in the Picasso painting on page 37? Explain your response. **[Respond]**

1. **azure** (azh′ ər) *adj.* sky blue

Enrichment

The Sioux People

In "Museum Indians," Susan Power's great-grandmother's buckskin dress is housed in an exhibit on the Sioux people of America's Great Plains. The Sioux were an alliance of several tribes that dominated the plains from the mid-1700s until well into the nineteenth century. The Sioux resisted the encroachment of the United States, ultimately losing their battles and most of their territory in the late 1800s.

Sioux culture was centered on the buffalo herds that once populated the plains. They hunted the buffalo, using them for food and to make tools, the tents or *tipis* they used for housing, and clothing. Sioux and other Native peoples of the plains made much of their clothing from animal hides. They decorated their clothing with dyes and beadwork, often using geometric designs, as well as fringes. Power's great-grandmother's dress is an example of this kind of clothing.

"You don't belong here," Mom tells him on those rare occasions when she feels she must pay her respects. "We honor you," she continues, "because you are a creature of great endurance and great generosity. You provided us with so many things that helped us to survive. It makes me angry to see you like this."

Few things can make my mother cry; the buffalo is one of them. "I am just like you," she whispers. "I don't belong here either. We should be in the Dakotas, somewhere a little bit east of the Missouri River. This crazy city is not a fit home for buffalo or Dakotas."

I take my mother's hand to hold her in place. I am a city child, nervous around livestock and lonely on the plains. I am afraid of a sky without light pollution—I never knew there could be so many stars. I lead my mother from the museum so she will forget the sense of loss. From the marble steps we can see Lake Shore Drive spill ahead of us, and I sweep my arm to the side as if I were responsible for this view. I introduce my mother to the city she gave me. I call her home.

Susan Power
Author's Insight
"Was this her blue period?" my character asks, to draw a connection between Picasso's art (one phase of Picasso's painting is called his "blue period") and the exquisite beadwork of Native American women.

Critical Reading

1. **(a) Recall:** What is the snake in Power's mother's dresser drawer? **(b) Interpret:** Why does she keep it there?
2. **(a) Recall:** What is her mother's complaint about the statue at the Historical Society? **(b) Analyze:** What is the effect of her complaints? **(c) Contrast:** How does the statue contrast with the exhibit at the Art Institute?
3. **(a) Recall:** What is unique about Power's relationship to the buckskin dress at the Art Institute? **(b) Interpret:** What is her mother's attitude toward seeing the dress there?
4. **(a) Interpret:** In what ways does her mother identify with the buffalo? **(b) Contrast:** How is Power different from her mother? **(c) Generalize:** What does the final paragraph tell you about the relationship between the writer and her mother, and their relationship with the city? Explain.
5. **Speculate:** In what ways do you think her mother influenced Power to become a writer? Base your answer on this essay.

For: Self-test
Visit: www.PHSchool.com
Web Code: era-6102

ASSESS

Answers

1. (a) The snake in the dresser drawer is a long, heavy braid of Susan's mother's hair. (b) Susan's mother no longer wears her hair long. She may keep the braid as a reminder of her roots or as a memento of her more traditional past.
2. (a) She complains that the statue presents a one-sided and very negative picture of Native Americans. (b) Because she makes clear, well-reasoned complaints over and over, the statue is eventually removed. (c) The statue is very negative, representing an inflammatory stereotype of Native Americans. The exhibit at the Art Institute is much more respectful, paying honor to the beauty of Native culture.
3. (a) The buckskin dress was made by her great-grandmother. (b) She is moved to see the dress but deeply saddened that it is no longer in the possession of her family.
4. (a) She feels that she and the buffalo are out of place, and that they should both be in the open land of the Dakotas. (b) Unlike her mother, Power feels she is a part of the city. (c) Although she lives in Chicago, Susan's mother is fully a part of Native culture. Susan, however, feels that Chicago is her city. She loves her mother and feels connection to her Native culture, but is also fully a part of the mainstream world Chicago represents.
5. Power's mother is a storyteller, and her stories move Power and inspire her imagination. By becoming a writer, perhaps she found a way to tell her mother's stories, and her own as well.

Go Online Assessment Students may use the **Self-test** to prepare for **Selection Test A** or **Selection Test B.**

Meeting Your Standards

Students will

1. **analyze and respond to literary elements.**
   - Literary Analysis: Exploration Narratives
2. **read, comprehend, analyze, and critique nonfiction.**
   - Reading Strategy: Recognizing Signal Words
   - Reading Check questions
   - Apply the Skills questions
   - Assessment Practice (ATE)
3. **develop vocabulary.**
   - Vocabulary Lesson: Latin Root: *-mort-*
4. **understand and apply written and oral language conventions.**
   - Spelling Strategy
   - Grammar and Style Lesson: Past and Perfect Verb Tenses
5. **develop writing proficiency.**
   - Writing Lesson: Explorer's Journal
6. **develop appropriate research strategies.**
   - Extend Your Learning: Exploration Booklet
7. **understand and apply listening and speaking strategies.**
   - Extend Your Learning: Speech

Block Scheduling: Use one 90-minute class period to preteach the skills and have students read the selection. Use a second 90-minute class period to assess students' mastery of skills, extend their learning, and monitor their progress.

Homework Suggestions

Following are possibilities for homework assignments.

- Support pages from ***Unit 1 Resources:***
  Literary Analysis
  Reading Strategy
  Vocabulary Builder
  Grammar and Style
- An Extend Your Learning project and the Writing Lesson for this selection group may be completed over several days.

Step-by-Step Teaching Guide	Pacing Guide
PRETEACH	
• Administer Vocabulary and Reading Warm-ups as necessary.	5 min.
• Engage students' interest with the motivation activity.	5 min.
• Read and discuss author and background features. **FT**	10 min.
• Introduce the Literary Analysis Skill: Exploration Narratives. **FT**	5 min.
• Introduce the Reading Strategy: Recognizing Signal Words. **FT**	10 min.
• Prepare students to read by teaching the selection vocabulary. **FT**	
TEACH	
• Informally monitor comprehension while students read independently or in groups. **FT**	30 min.
• Monitor students' comprehension with the Reading Check notes.	as students read
• Reinforce vocabulary with Vocabulary Builder notes.	as students read
• Develop students' understanding of exploration narratives with the Literary Analysis annotations. **FT**	5 min.
• Develop students' ability to recognize signal words with the Reading Strategy annotations. **FT**	5 min.
ASSESS/EXTEND	
• Assess students' comprehension and mastery of the Literary Analysis and Reading Strategy by having them answer the Apply the Skills questions. **FT**	15 min.
• Have students complete the Vocabulary Lesson and the Grammar and Style Lesson. **FT**	15 min.
• Apply students' ability to use precise details by using the Writing Lesson. **FT**	45 min. or homework
• Apply students' understanding by using one or more of the Extend Your Learning activities.	20–90 min. or homework
• Administer Selection Test A or Selection Test B. **FT**	15 min.

Resources

TECHNOLOGY

Go Online: Research [**L3**]
Go Online: Self-test [**L3**]
***ExamView*® Test Bank** [**L3**]

Choosing Resources for Differentiated Instruction

[**L1**] Special Needs Students
[**L2**] Below-Level Students
[**L3**] All Students
[**L4**] Advanced Students
[**EL**] English Learners

FT Fast Track Instruction: To move the lesson more quickly, use the strategies and activities identified with **FT**.

Scaffolding for Less Proficient and Advanced Students

The leveled Critical Thinking questions after selections progress in the levels of thinking required to answer them. To address the needs of your different students, you may use the (a) level questions for your less proficient students and the (b) level questions with your on-level and advanced students. The occasional (c) level questions are appropriate for your advanced students.

Use this complete suite of powerful teaching tools to make lesson planning and testing quicker and easier.

Use the interactive textbook (online and on CD-ROM) to make selections and activities come alive with audio and video support and interactive questions.

PRETEACH

Motivation

Invite students to imagine finding themselves in a strange land among people whose language and customs were unknown to them. What if they had no way of sending for help and no way of knowing exactly how to get back home? How would it feel to spend several years in this land with no apparent hope of returning home? On whom could they depend for help? Emphasize that Cabeza de Vaca and his followers spent eight years—many of them in enforced captivity—in just such a situation.

❶ Background

More About the Author

Alvar Núñez Cabeza de Vaca came to North America as treasurer of the Narváez expedition, the goal of which was to colonize lands north of Mexico. Cabeza de Vaca was shipwrecked on an island in the Gulf of Mexico with two other Spaniards and a slave. In a unique role reversal, the four became servants to the Cahoques Indians for about eight years. During this time, Cabeza de Vaca grew to understand the Native Americans as no other Spaniard had done before him.

Build Skills *Narrative Accounts*

❶ A Journey Through Texas • Boulders Taller Than the Great Tower of Seville

Alvar Núñez Cabeza de Vaca (1490?–1557?)

In 1528, Pánfilo de Narváez and 400 Spanish soldiers landed near Tampa Bay and set out to explore Florida's west coast. Alvar Núñez Cabeza de Vaca (äl′ bär no͞on′ yes kä bā′ sä dā bā′ kä) was second in command. Beset by hostile natives, illness, and the prospect of starvation, Narváez and his men then set sail for Mexico in five flimsy boats, but he and most of the men drowned. Cabeza de Vaca and a party of about sixty survived and reached the Texas shore near present-day Galveston.

Shipwrecked without supplies, only fifteen of the group lived through the winter. In the end, Cabeza de Vaca and three others survived. They were captured by natives and spent the next several years in captivity. During that time, Cabeza de Vaca gained a reputation as a medicine man and trader. The four Spaniards finally escaped and wandered for eighteen months across the Texas plains. In 1536, the survivors finally reached Mexico City.

Invitation to Others Cabeza de Vaca's adventures and his reports on the richness of Texas sparked exploration of the region. In "A Journey Through Texas," he speaks of Estevanico, the first African to set foot in Texas.

In 1541, Cabeza de Vaca also led a 1,000-mile expedition through the south of present day Brazil to Asunción, the capital of Río de la Plata. He was appointed governor of the Río de la Plata region (now Paraguay), but he was ousted two years later as a result of revolt.

Through his journals, Cabeza de Vaca encouraged others, including Francisco Vásquez de Coronado, to explore America.

García López de Cárdenas (c. 1540)

García López de Cárdenas (gär sē′ ä lō′ pes dā kär′ dā näs) is best remembered as the first European to visit the Grand Canyon. As a leader of Francisco Vásquez de Coronado's expedition to New Mexico (1540–1542), Cárdenas was dispatched from Cibola (Zuni) in western New Mexico to see a river that the Moqui Native Americans of northeastern Arizona had described to one of Coronado's captains. The river was the Colorado. López de Cárdenas departed on August 25, 1540, reaching the Grand Canyon after a westward journey of about twenty days. He became the first explorer to view the canyon and its river, which from the vantage of the canyon's rim appeared to be a stream merely six feet wide! Unable to descend to the river, they took back to Europe descriptions that attempted to record the magnitude of the sight. López de Cárdenas reported that boulders in the Grand Canyon were taller than the 300-foot high Great Tower of Seville, one of the world's tallest cathedrals.

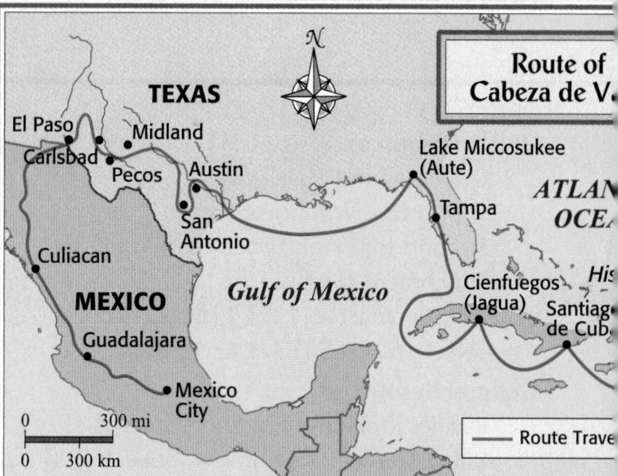

Preview

Connecting to the Literature

The writers of these historical accounts describe places their readers could barely imagine. Think of the tales you would have told had you been among the first Europeans to travel to the southwest region of North America to meet the natives.

2 Literary Analysis

Exploration Narratives

The Europeans who trailblazed the Americas recounted their experiences in **exploration narratives**—firsthand accounts of their travels. These accounts provided information to the people back home in Europe, so the explorers were careful to record in detail what they observed. For example, López de Cárdenas gives these details about the region.

> This region was high and covered with low and twisted pine trees; it was extremely cold, being open to the north . . .

As you read, look for details that provide descriptive images and insights about the regions these men explored.

Comparing Literary Works

These exploration narratives reflect two distinctly different authors' **styles,** or choices of words, details, and focus. Cabeza de Vaca uses descriptive details in his narrative. In contrast, López de Cárdenas avoids description and instead provides a detailed explanation of events. Create a Venn diagram like the one shown to compare and contrast the authors' styles.

Cabeza de Vaca's Style

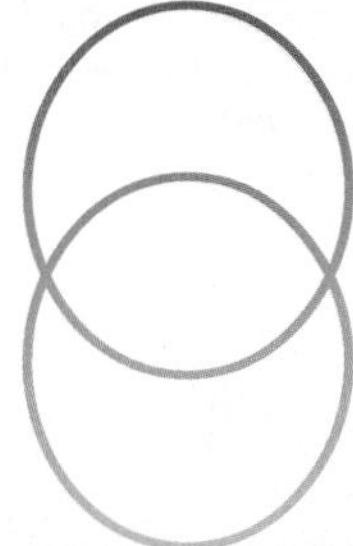

López de Cárdenas's Style

3 Reading Strategy

Recognizing Signal Words

To follow the order of events, pay close attention to **signal words**—words that highlight the relationships among ideas. Look at these examples:

- **time:** *After five days,* they had not *yet* returned.
- **contrast:** . . . *although* this was the warm season, no one could live in this canyon because of the cold.

As you read, take note of signal words and the relationships they indicate.

Vocabulary Builder

entreated (en trēt′ id) *v.* begged; pleaded (p. 43)

feigned (fānd) *v.* pretended; faked (p. 43)

mortality (môr tal′ ə tē) *n.* death on a large scale (p. 44)

subsisted (səb sist′ id) *v.* remained alive; were sustained (p. 45)

traversed (trə vurst′) *v.* moved over, across, or through (p. 46)

dispatched (di spacht′) *v.* sent off on a specific assignment (p. 47)

2 Literary Analysis

Exploration Narratives

- Let students know that many early explorers kept detailed records of their travels. Many of these records were composed for kings or other powerful people who had financed the journeys.
- As they read each exploration narrative, have students note general insights and descriptive details that the explorer includes in his account.
- Encourage students to relate to the explorers' experiences by using their own prior knowledge about the thoughts and feelings that arise when people, things, and places are utterly new and strange.
- Give students a copy of **Literary Analysis Graphic Organizer A,** p. 5 in ***Graphic Organizer Transparencies***. Tell them to fill it in with details about each author's style as they read.

3 Reading Strategy

Recognizing Signal Words

- Remind students that signal words tip off a reader about the relationships among ideas.
- Explain that there are several different types of relationships that signal words help readers to recognize: time order, cause-and-effect, level of importance, and contrast, for example.
- Encourage students to identify some of the signal words they know and the type of relationships expressed by these words.
- Point out to students that recognizing signal words is especially important in narratives.

Vocabulary Builder

- Pronounce each vocabulary word for students, and read the definitions as a class. Have students identify any words with which they are already familiar.

Differentiated Instruction Solutions for All Learners

Support for Special Needs Students
Have students complete the **Preview** and **Build Skills** pages for the selections in the ***Reader's Notebook: Adapted Version***. These pages provide a selection summary, an abbreviated presentation of the reading and literary skills, and the graphic organizer on the **Build Skills** page in the student book.

Support for Less Proficient Readers
Have students complete the **Preview** and **Build Skills** pages for the selections in the ***Reader's Notebook***. These pages provide a selection summary, an abbreviated presentation of the reading and literary skills, and the graphic organizer on the **Build Skills** page in the student book.

Support for English Learners
Have students complete the **Preview** and **Build Skills** pages for the selections in the ***Reader's Notebook: English Learner's Version***. These pages provide a selection summary, an abbreviated presentation of the skills, additional contextual vocabulary, and the graphic organizer on the **Build Skills** page in the student book.

Learning Modalities
Visual/Spatial Learners Students may enjoy and benefit from referring to the map on p. 40, as well as to a contemporary map of the region in which the authors traveled. Have them use either map to orient themselves and try to trace Cabeza de Vaca's route from Cuba all the way to Mexico City.

❶ About the Selection

Cabeza de Vaca was a Spanish adventurer whose views and beliefs were dramatically altered by his extraordinary experiences living with Native Americans. This narrative describes his journey into what is now the state of Texas as he attempts to reach the Spanish settlements in Mexico City. Cabeza de Vaca came (albeit reluctantly) to understand and appreciate something of the people whose land he traveled through.

❷ Critical Viewing

Answer: Students may note that the landscape appears to be hot, sunny, and very dry. Such terrain would probably supply little food or water, and travelers might easily starve, dehydrate, or suffer heatstroke.

❶ A Journey Through Texas

Alvar Núñez Cabeza de Vaca

Background Alvar Núñez Cabeza de Vaca and three countrymen wandered for months through Texas as they journeyed toward the Spanish settlement in Mexico City. In the course of his travels, Cabeza de Vaca healed a Native American by permforming the first recorded surgery in Texas. His resulting fame attracted so many followers that Cabeza de Vaca noted in his journal, "The number of our companions became so large that we could no longer control them." As they continued traveling westward, the group was well received by the Native Americans they encountered.

❷ ▼ **Critical Viewing** What details of a landscape like this one might pose difficulty for the expeditions that explored it? **[Speculate]**

Differentiated Instruction Solutions for All Learners

Accessibility at a Glance

	A Journey Through Texas	Boulders Taller . . .
Context	Travel Journal	Travel Journal
Language	Long, sentences; some archaic vocabulary	Long, sentences; some archaic vocabulary
Concept Level	Accessible (cultural perspective)	Accessible (geographical description)
Literary Merit	Primary Source	Primary Source
Lexile	1400	1220
Overall Rating	Average	Average

The same Indians led us to a plain beyond the chain of mountains, where people came to meet us from a long distance. By those we were treated in the same manner as before, and they made so many presents to the Indians who came with us that, unable to carry all, they left half of it. . . . We told these people our route was towards sunset, and they replied that in that direction people lived very far away. So we ordered them to send there and inform the inhabitants that we were coming and how. From this they begged to be excused, because the others were their enemies, and they did not want us to go to them. Yet they did not venture to disobey in the end, and sent two women, one of their own and the other a captive. They selected women because these can trade everywhere, even if there be war.

We followed the women to a place where it had been agreed we should wait for them. After five days they had not yet returned, and the Indians explained that it might be because they had not found anybody. So we told them to take us north, and they repeated that there were no people, except very far away, and neither food nor water. Nevertheless we insisted, saying that we wanted to go there, and they still excused themselves as best they could, until at last we became angry.

One night I went away to sleep out in the field apart from them; but they soon came to where I was, and remained awake all night in great alarm, talking to me, saying how frightened they were. They entreated us not to be angry any longer, because, even if it was their death, they would take us where we chose. We feigned to be angry still, so as to keep them in suspense, and then a singular[1] thing happened.

On that same day many fell sick, and on the next day eight of them died! All over the country, where it was known, they became so afraid that it seemed as if the mere sight of us would kill them. They besought[2] us not to be angry nor to procure the death of any

1. **singular** *adj.* strange.
2. **besought** (be sôt′) *v.* pleaded with.

Literary Analysis
Exploration Narratives
Why does Cabeza de Vaca include such detail about the conversation with the Indians in his narrative?

Vocabulary Builder
entreated (en trēt′ id) *v.* begged; pleaded

feigned (fānd) *v.* pretended; faked

5 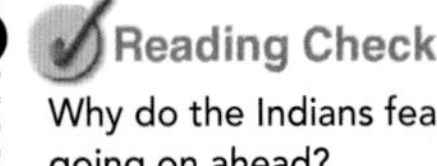
Reading Check
Why do the Indians fear going on ahead?

3 Literary Analysis
Exploration Narratives

- Draw students' attention to the way Cabeza de Vaca indirectly paraphrases, rather than reports word-for-word, the Native Americans' speech.
- **Ask** students what effect this has on the reader.
  Possible response: Students may say the effect is to emphasize the distance between the Spanish explorers and the Native Americans. They may note that no Native American emerges as an individual and none is named.
- **Ask** students the Literary Analysis question: Why does Cabeza de Vaca include such details about the conversation with the Indians in his narrative?
  Answer: With these details the author is able to heighten the drama of the apparent fearsomeness of the distant tribe.

4 Critical Thinking
Making Inferences

- Explain to students that exploration narratives not only provide information about explorers' experiences, but also reveal information about the explorers themselves and the cultures from which they came.
- **Ask** students to describe the character of the Spanish explorers as shown by their interaction with the Native Americans.
  Answer: Students may call the Spaniards single-minded, uncompromising, or manipulative.

5 Reading Check

Answer: Their enemies live there.

Differentiated Instruction
Solutions for All Learners

Background for Less Proficient Readers
Help students recognize that the Spanish explorers probably infected the Native Americans with the illness of which eight of them died. Let students know that Europeans and Native Americans had no immunity to one another's diseases. Tragedies of this kind happened often, and contributed to distrust and hostility between the two groups.

Strategy for English Learners
Take advantage of this opportunity to invite English learners to share some of their insights about strategies people use to surmount language differences. Students might mention sign language, gestures, drawings, and so on, as techniques for communicating in the absence of a common spoken language.

Enrichment for Advanced Readers
Remind students to keep in mind the chronicler's purpose as they read. Have them consider whether the narrator knows he's making history. Though he must observe and record events carefully, he may also want to present his efforts and results in the best possible light. Do students see any evidence to this effect?

6 Critical Viewing

Answer: Students may respond that the Native Americans seem respectful or even slightly in awe of the Spaniards. They bring their sick to the Spaniards, then give them room to work their healing.

7 Vocabulary Builder

The Latin Word Root *-mort-*

- Draw students' attention to the word *mortality* and its definition. Let students know that the Latin word root *-mort-* means "death."
- Have students **volunteer** words containing this word root, and list them on the chalkboard.

  Possibilities include: *mortal, immortal, mortuary, mortician.*
- Have students identify how the meaning of the word root *-mort-* contributes to the meanings of the words they volunteered.

8 Reading Strategy

Recognizing Signal Words

- **Ask** students to explain the function of signal words.
- Then, **ask** students the Reading Strategy question: What words signal time or other relationships in this paragraph?

  Answer: *when, already, as, So, and*

9

Painting of Cabeza de Vaca, Esteban, and their companions among various

6 ▲ **Critical Viewing** What does this painting suggest about the relationship between Cabeza de Vaca and the Native Americans? Why? **[Infer]**

more of their number, for they were convinced that we killed them by merely thinking of it. In truth, we were very much concerned about it,
7 for, seeing the great mortality, we dreaded that all of them might die or forsake us in their terror, while those further on, upon learning of it, would get out of our way hereafter. We prayed to God our Lord to assist us, and the sick began to get well. Then we saw something that astonished us very much, and it was that, while the parents, brothers and wives of the dead had shown deep grief at their illness, from the moment they died the survivors made no demonstration whatsoever, and showed not the slightest feeling; nor did they dare to go near the bodies until we ordered their burial. . . .

Vocabulary Builder
mortality (môr tal′ ə tē) *n.* death on a large scale

The sick being on the way of recovery, when we had been there already three days, the women whom we had sent out returned, saying that they had met very few people, nearly all having gone after the cows, as it was the season. So we ordered those who had been sick to remain, and those who were well to accompany us, and that,
8 two days' travel from there, the same women should go with us and get people to come to meet us on the trail for our reception.

Reading Strategy
Recognizing Signal Words What words signal time or other relationships in this paragraph?

Enrichment

Herbal Medicine

Native Americans at the time of the arrival of the Europeans would have been little helped by the meager healing powers of the conquistadors. Many Native American groups knew how to use wild plants to restore health; some knew of the healing properties of more than 200 plants. They knew, for instance, that boiled sagebrush leaves cured headaches, simmered rabbit brush stems and leaves made an effective cough medicine, and boiled willow leaves rubbed into the scalp could cure dandruff. Furthermore, some Native Americans discovered the natural source of digitalis and of salicylic acid, the active ingredient in aspirin.

Did Native Americans have a knowledge of herbal medicine that equaled or surpassed ours today, as some pharmacologists have claimed? Invite interested students to look into the matter and see what they can find out about Native American folk medicine.

The next morning all those who were strong enough came along, and at the end of three journeys we halted. Alonso del Castillo and Estevanico,[3] the negro, left with the women as guides, and the woman who was a captive took them to a river that flows between mountains, where there was a village, in which her father lived, and these were the first abodes we saw that were like unto real houses. Castillo and Estevanico went to these and, after holding parley[4] with the Indians, at the end of three days Castillo returned to where he had left us, bringing with him five or six of the Indians. He told how he had found permanent houses, inhabited, the people of which ate beans and squashes, and that he had also seen maize.

Of all things upon earth this caused us the greatest pleasure, and we gave endless thanks to our Lord for this news. Castillo also said that the negro was coming to meet us on the way, near by, with all the people of the houses. For that reason we started, and after going a league and a half met the negro and the people that came to receive us, who gave us beans and many squashes to eat, gourds to carry water in, robes of cowhide, and other things. As those people and the Indians of our company were enemies, and did not understand each other, we took leave of the latter, leaving them all that had been given to us, while we went on with the former and, six leagues beyond, when night was already approaching, reached their houses, where they received us with great ceremonies. Here we remained one day, and left on the next, taking them with us to other permanent houses, where they subsisted on the same food also, and thence on we found a new custom.

The people who heard of our approach did not, as before, come out to meet us on the way, but we found them at their homes, and they had other houses ready for us. . . . There was nothing they would not give us. They are the best formed people we have seen, the liveliest and most capable; who best understood us and answered our questions. We called them "of the cows," because most of the cows die near there, and because for more than fifty leagues up that stream they go to kill many of them. Those people go completely naked, after the manner of the first we met. The women are covered with deerskins, also some men, especially the old ones, who are of no use any more in war.

The country is well settled. We asked them why they did not raise maize, and they replied that they were afraid of losing the crops, since for two successive years it had not rained, and the seasons were so dry that the moles had eaten the corn, so that they did not dare to plant any more until it should have rained very hard. And they also begged us to ask Heaven for rain, which we promised to do. We also wanted to know from where they brought their maize, and they said it came from where the sun sets, and that it was found all over that

3. **Estevanico** (es´ tä vä nē´ kō) Of Moorish extraction, Estevanico was the first African man to set foot in Texas.

4. **holding parley** (pär´ lē) conferring.

Literary Analysis
Exploration Narratives
What specific details about the region does the writer provide here?

Vocabulary Builder
subsisted (səb sist´ id) *v.* remained alive; were sustained

11  **Reading Check**
What prevents some of the expedition group from completing the planned trip?

9 Humanities

Painting of Cabeza de Vaca, Esteban, and their companions, by Tom Mirrat

This work portrays the encounter between the Spanish explorers and the sick Native Americans, as described in Cabeza de Vaca's journal. Use these questions for discussion:

1. How can you distinguish the Spaniards from the Native Americans?
   Answer: Students may say that the Spaniards are the ones with beards. Three Spaniards kneel beside sick Native Americans, and Esteban is the African man standing to the left.
2. What are the people in the picture doing?
   Answer: Students may say that the Spaniards are praying over the victims or offering sympathy or medical help, while some frightened and worried Native Americans stand aside looking on.

10 Literary Analysis
Exploration Narratives

- Have students reread silently the first paragraph on this page.
- Then, **ask** them the Literary Analysis question: What specific details about the region does the writer provide here?
  Answer: He provides details about the housing and diet of the Native Americans who inhabit the region.

➤ **Monitor Progress: Ask** students to explain the primary purpose of Europeans' exploration narratives.
Answer: Students should specify that these exploration narratives were intended to provide detailed information about places and experiences to the people back home.

11 Reading Check

Answer: Some of the group were beset by illness.

Differentiated Instruction
Solutions for All Learners

Strategy for Special Needs Students
Encourage students to create a graphic organizer that helps them distinguish among the various Native American peoples mentioned by Cabeza de Vaca. Students might create a cluster diagram for each group, using words and phrases from the text to characterize each. The author alludes to five groups. Ensure that students record details about each group and their relationships with other groups and with the explorers.

Enrichment for Advanced Readers
Between 1492 and 1540, exploration and expansion fever spread through western Europe. By the time Cabeza de Vaca landed in Texas, the Spanish had gained a solid foothold in the Caribbean basin and in Mexico; Ponce de León had explored the coasts of what is now Florida; Verrazano had been up the Atlantic coast to Newfoundland; and Magellan's ships had rounded South America and crossed the Pacific Ocean. Invite interested students to prepare a research report on one or more of these explorers.

⓬ Literary Analysis
Exploration Narratives and Author's Style

- Have students take turns reading the selection's final eight paragraphs aloud. Ask students to be alert for references to maize.
- **Ask** students the Literary Analysis question: What might readers in Europe have thought about the group's determination to find maize?
  Answer: Students may say that readers would have believed the explorers thought maize was a valuable crop.

 country, and the shortest way to it was in that direction. We asked them to tell us how to go, as they did not want to go themselves, to tell us about the way.

They said we should travel up the river towards the north, on which trail for seventeen days we would not find a thing to eat, except a fruit called *chacan,* which they grind between stones; but even then it cannot be eaten, being so coarse and dry; and so it was, for they showed it to us and we could not eat it. But they also said that, going upstream, we could always travel among people who were their enemies, although speaking the same language, and who could give us no food, but would receive us very willingly, and give us many cotton blankets, hides and other things; but that it seemed to them that we ought not to take that road.

In doubt as to what should be done, and which was the best and most advantageous road to take, we remained with them for two days. They gave us beans, squashes, and calabashes.[5] Their way of cooking them is so new and strange that I felt like describing it here, in order to show how different and queer are the devices and industries of human beings. They have no pots. In order to cook their food they fill a middle-sized gourd with water, and place into a fire such stones as easily become heated, and when they are hot to scorch they take them out with wooden tongs, thrusting them into the water of the gourd, until it boils. As soon as it boils they put into it what they want to cook, always taking out the stones as they cool off and throwing in hot ones to keep the water steadily boiling. This is their way of cooking.

After two days were past we determined to go in search of maize, and not to follow the road to the cows, since the latter carried us to the north, which meant a very great circuit, as we held it always certain that by going towards sunset we should reach the goal of our wishes.

So we went on our way and traversed the whole country to the South Sea,[6] and our resolution was not shaken by the fear of great starvation, which the Indians said we should suffer (and indeed suffered) during the first seventeen days of travel. All along the river, and in the course of these seventeen days we received plenty of cowhides, and did not eat of their famous fruit (*chacan*), but our food consisted (for each day) of a handful of deer-tallow, which for that purpose we always sought to keep, and so endured these seventeen days, at the end of which we crossed the river and marched for seventeen days more. At sunset, on a plain between very high mountains, we met people who, for one-third of the year, eat but powdered straw, and as we went by just at that time, had to eat it also, until, at the end of that journey we found some permanent houses, with plenty of harvested maize, of which and of its meal they gave us great quantities, also squashes and beans, and blankets of cotton. . . .

Literary Analysis
Exploration Narratives and Style What might readers in Europe have thought about the group's determination to find maize?

Vocabulary Builder
traversed (trə vurst′) *v.* moved over, across, or through

5. **calabashes** (kal′ ə bash′ əz) *n.* dried, hollow shells of gourds used to hold food or beverages.
6. **the South Sea** the Gulf of Mexico.

13 Boulders Taller Than the Great Tower of Seville

From an account by García López de Cárdenas
Retold by Pedro de Castañeda

Information was obtained of a large river and that several days down the river there were people with very large bodies. As Don Pedro de Tovar had no other commission, he returned from Tusayán and gave his report to the general. The latter at once dispatched Don García López de Cárdenas there with about twelve men to explore this river. When he reached Tusayán he was well received and lodged by the natives. They provided him with guides to proceed on his journey. They set out from there laden with provisions, because they had to travel over some uninhabited land before coming to settlements, which the Indians said were more than twenty days away. Accordingly when they had marched for twenty days they came to gorges of the river, from the edge of which it looked as if the opposite side must have been more than three or four leagues[1] away by air. This region was high and covered with low and twisted pine trees; it was extremely cold, being open to the north, so that, although this was the warm season, no one could live in this canyon because of the cold. 14

The men spent three days looking for a way down to the river; from the top it looked as if the water were a fathom[2] across. But, according to the information supplied by the Indians, it must have been half a league wide. The descent was almost impossible, but, after these three days, at a place which seemed less difficult, Captain Melgosa, a certain Juan Galeras, and another companion, being the most agile, began to go down. They continued descending within view of those on top until they lost sight of them, as they could not be seen from the top. They returned about four o'clock in the afternoon, as they could not reach the bottom because of the many obstacles they met, for what from the 15

Vocabulary Builder
dispatched (di spacht′) *v.* sent off on a specific assignment

Literary Analysis
Exploration Narratives
What impression of the group's efforts is López de Cárdenas trying to convey in his narrative?

Reading Check
Who is dispatched to explore the river?

1. **leagues** (lēgz) *n.* units of measurement of approximately three miles.
2. **fathom** (fath′ əm) *n.* a unit of measurement of six feet.

13 About the Selection

By the time of Coronado's expedition in 1540, the Spanish knew there was gold and silver in the Americas. Although Coronado's search for the Seven Cities of Cibola led only to impoverished villages in present-day New Mexico, the group he dispatched northward led to European discovery of the Grand Canyon. García López de Cárdenas, with the help of Hopi guides from nearby mesas, became the first European to see this natural wonder. Unable to find water or to cross the canyon, Cárdenas eventually left in frustration.

14 Literary Analysis
Exploration Narratives

- Review with students the purpose a writer brings to an exploration narrative: to convey information about a travel expedition to an audience.
- Point out to students that some exploration narratives may be thought of as reports to an employer.
- **Ask** students the Literary Analysis question: What impression of the group's efforts is Lopez de Cárdenas trying to convey in his narrative?
  Answer: By including details relating to the harsh landscape and the Spaniards' sober determination to explore it, the writer seems to wish to convey an impression of the group's physical and mental hardiness.

15 Reading Check

Answer: Don García López de Cárdenas and approximately twelve other men are dispatched to explore the river.

Differentiated Instruction
Solutions for All Learners

Strategy for Less Proficient Readers

Cultural anthropologists observe peoples of the world: recording what they eat, how they dress, the roles of the young and elderly, relationships with neighbors and outsiders, their values and beliefs, and so on. Ask students to imagine that a cultural anthropologist from another culture is visiting your community. Challenge pairs of students to prepare a list of features of public and private life that would help that social scientist better understand your culture.

Enrichment for Gifted/Talented Students

Within the boundaries of Grand Canyon National Park are about 2,000 sites once inhabited by the Anasazi—the name given to the Native American peoples who lived in settlements throughout the plateau country of the Southwest. Encourage students to read further in the library or on the Internet about the Anasazi people. Have students write a poem or a drama about the Anasazi, focusing on what they might have thought upon seeing the European explorers gazing across the Grand Canyon.

16 Reading Strategy
Recognizing Signal Words

- **Ask** students the Reading Strategy question: What change do the words "up to that time" signal?
  Answer: This phrase signals a change in the course of the journey.

▶ **Monitor Progress: Ask** a student volunteer to explain the three most common types of relationships between ideas that are indicated by signal words.
Answer: Signal words most commonly indicate time relationships, connections of causality, and contrasts.

ASSESS

Answers

1. Students who have never visited the canyon may be surprised that the Spaniards were unable to descend.
2. (a) They wanted them to serve as guides. (b) The Native Americans may have been afraid of the Spaniards.
3. (a) They are afraid that the Native Americans will flee in terror and leave them stranded—and that other Native Americans will then avoid them. (b) They believe the Spaniards have the power to wish them dead.
4. (a) They are expecting to explore the Colorado River. (b) Possible reasons include meeting and learning about the people reputed to live near the river or exploring the river's possible use as a means of travel.
5. (a) It appears to be about six feet wide. (b) They are viewing the river from an extraordinary height.
6. The account might contain detailed descriptions of the canyon's impressive size and beauty in order to convince financial backers that exploration of the canyon could bring them fame, glory, and riches.

Go Online Author Link For additional information about Alvar Núñez Cabeza de Vaca or García López de Cardenas, have students type in the Web Code, then select C or L from the alphabet, and then select Alvar Núñez Cabeza de Vaca or García López de Cardenas.

top seemed easy, was not so, on the contrary, it was rough and difficult. They said that they had gone down one-third of the distance and that, from the point they had reached, the river seemed very large, and that, from what they saw, the width given by the Indians was correct. From the top they could make out, apart from the canyon, some small boulders which seemed to be as high as a man. Those who went down and who reached them swore that they were taller than the great tower of Seville.[3]

16 The party did not continue farther up the canyon of the river because of the lack of water. Up to that time they had gone one or two leagues inland in search of water every afternoon. When they had traveled four additional days the guides said that it was impossible to go on because no water would be found for three or four days, that when they themselves traveled through that land they took along women who brought water in gourds, that in those trips they buried the gourds of water for the return trip, and that they traveled in one day a distance that took us two days.

This was the Tizón river, much closer to its source than where Melchior Díaz and his men had crossed it. These Indians were of the same type, as it appeared later. From there Cárdenas and his men turned back, as that trip brought no other results.

3. **great tower of Seville** The Giralda, the tower on the Cathedral of Seville in Spain, rises above the cathedral more than twice its height.

Reading Strategy
Recognizing Signal Words What change do the words "up to that time" signal?

Critical Reading

1. **Respond:** How does López de Cárdenas's description compare with your knowledge of the Grand Canyon?
2. **(a) Recall:** Why do the Spaniards in "A Journey Through Texas" order the Native Americans to travel with them? **(b) Infer:** Why do the Native Americans obey the orders?
3. **(a) Recall:** In "A Journey Through Texas," why do the Spaniards become fearful when the Native Americans in their company die? **(b) Draw Conclusions:** What do the Native Americans believe is the cause of the sickness?
4. **(a) Recall:** What are López de Cárdenas and his men expecting to explore? **(b) Infer:** Why does Coronado send the group on this mission?
5. **(a) Recall:** How wide does the river appear from the edge? **(b) Hypothesize:** Why does the river seem narrow from above?
6. **Extend:** How might these accounts have been different if they had been written to secure further funding?

For: More about Alvar Núñez Cabeza de Vaca and García López de Cárdenas
Visit: www.PHSchool.com
Web Code: ere-9103

Apply the Skills

A Journey Through Texas • Boulders Taller Than the Great Tower of Seville

Literary Analysis

Exploration Narratives

1. Why is the image of the great tower of Seville used to convey the size of the boulders?
2. How do López de Cárdenas's experiences with the rough Grand Canyon terrain affect which details he includes in his **narrative**?

Comparing Literary Works

3. Compare and contrast the reactions of Cabeza de Vaca and López de Cárdenas to the Native American culture they encounter in their explorations. Record them in a chart like the one shown here.

Writer	Landscape and Cultural Details	Writer's Reaction
Cabeza de Vaca		
López de Cárdenas		

4. **(a)** How are the authors' **styles** similar? **(b)** How do they differ?
5. Which narrative do you think is more effective? Explain.

Reading Strategy

Recognizing Signal Words

6. Determine the type of relationship (time, reason, or contrast) in each of the italicized **signal words** in these passages.
   a. *Nevertheless* we insisted, saying that we wanted to go there, and they still excused themselves as best they could, *until* at last we became angry.
   b. We feigned to be angry still, *so as* to keep them in suspense, and *then* a singular thing happened.
   c. The party did not continue farther up the canyon of the river *because* of a lack of water.

Extend Understanding

7. **Social Studies Connection:** What other searches have led to settlement of specific areas of what is now the United States?

QuickReview

Exploration narratives recount the firsthand expedition experiences of their authors.

An author's **style** reflects his choice and arrangement of words and details.

Signal words indicate relationships of time, reason, or contrast among ideas or events in a narrative.

For: Self-test
Visit: www.PHSchool.com
Web Code: era-6103

Answers

1. The awe-inspiring height of the great tower would have been well known to López de Cárdenas's contemporaries.
2. Because he cannot reach the Colorado River, Cárdenas must describe its appearance from above and the ruggedness of the surrounding terrain.
3. Though both writers seem to find the Native Americans friendly and cooperative, neither appears to consider them as equals. Cabeza de Vaca, however, interacts freely with the Native Americans and describes their diets, customs, and practices in greater detail than López de Cárdenas, who does not record his reactions to his Native American guides.

   Another sample answer can be found on **Literary Analysis Graphic Organizer B,** p. 8 in ***Graphic Organizer Transparencies.***
4. The authors' styles are similar in their straightforward, earnest tone. Of the two writers, Cabeza de Vaca seems to write from a more personal vantage point.
5. Students' responses should be supported with reasons and with examples from the texts.
6. (a) contrast; time (b) causality; time (c) causality
7. Suggested responses include: Ponce de León explored the land he named Florida. Cortés came upon the lower peninsula of California. Lewis and Clark explored westward from the Louisiana territory to the Oregon territory. Each of these explorations foretold European development of a part of North America.

Go Online Assessment Students may use the **Self-test** to prepare for **Selection Test A** or **Selection Test B.**

EXTEND/ASSESS

Answers

1 Vocabulary Lesson

Word Analysis

Paragraphs should present a coherent narrative and use the four words correctly.

Spelling Strategy

1. indirect
2. improper
3. independent
4. dishonest

Vocabulary Builder

1. dispatched
2. entreated
3. feigned
4. traversed
5. subsisted
6. mortality

2 Grammar and Style Lesson

1. past; past perfect
2. past
3. past
4. past perfect
5. past perfect

Writing Application

Students' descriptions should make proper use of both past and past perfect tenses in order to show time relationships among the various steps or processes involved in the activity.

Writing and Grammar, Ruby Level

Students will find further instruction and practice on past and perfect verb tenses in Chapter 21, Section 2.

Build Language Skills

1 Vocabulary Lesson

Word Analysis: Latin Root *-mort-*

The word *mortality* includes the Latin root *-mort-*, meaning "death." With a small group, develop a paragraph about a modern-day space explorer who dies during the landing of a dangerous mission. Use the following words in your description.

mortally	mortuary
mortician	immortalized

Spelling Strategy

Prefixes do not change spellings. When you add a prefix to a word, keep all the letters of the original word: *im-* + mortality = immortality.

Add a prefix such as *in-*, *im-*, or *dis-* to each of the words listed below to create a new word.

1. ___ direct
2. ___ proper
3. ___ dependent
4. ___ honest

Vocabulary Builder: Context

Choose the word from the vocabulary list on page 41 that best completes each sentence.

1. The soldiers were __?__ by the expedition leader to find the river.
2. The Spaniards __?__ their guides to continue leading the way.
3. When pleading didn't work, they __?__ anger in order to intimidate their guides.
4. In the course of their seventeen-day march, they __?__ a barren stretch of land.
5. The starving travelers __?__ on mouthfuls of deer tallow.
6. The conquistadors were alarmed by the __?__ that befell the natives.

2 Grammar and Style Lesson

Past and Perfect Verb Tenses

The **past tense** of a verb shows an action that began and ended at a given time in the past. The **past perfect tense** indicates an action that ended before another past action began. Verbs in the past perfect consist of *had*, followed by the past participle. In this example, the past tense verbs are in italicized text and the past perfect verbs are underlined.

After five days they had not returned and the Indians *explained* that it might be because they had not found anybody.

(The explorers *had not returned* and *had not found* before the Indians *explained*.)

Practice Identify the tense of the italicized verb where appropriate, and then indicate the sequence of the action.

1. We *followed* the woman to a place where it *had been agreed* we should wait for them.
2. Many *fell* sick.
3. On the next day, eight of them *died*!
4. They *had gone* down one third of the distance.
5. Until then, they *had gone* one or two leagues inland in search of water.

Writing Application Write a description of an activity that you had worked on for some time. Use both the past and past perfect tenses.

Prentice Hall Writing and Grammar Connection: Chapter 21, Section 2

Assessment Practice

Grammar and Language

(For more practice, see *Standardized Test Preparation Workbook*, p. 2.)

Some tests ask students to make revision suggestions to fix erroneous sentences. A working knowledge of the sequence of verb tenses will help students spot verb tense errors, as in this example:

The chart listed those who were still lost and those that have been found.

A NO CHANGE
B those who had been found
C those who are found
D the saved

A correct answer must use the past perfect tense. The correct answer is Choice *B*.

Writing Lesson

Explorer's Journal

Imagine that like Cabeza de Vaca and López de Cárdenas, you have begun to explore a territory where no one has gone before. Write a journal entry that provides precise details about your discoveries.

Prewriting Choose a location to explore. Gather specific details, through research if necessary, so that your description will help others follow in your footsteps.

Drafting Use precise details, identifying items as clearly and exactly as you can. Remember, your audience may be unfamiliar with these objects.

Revising Ask a friend to read your draft. If your reader cannot "see" your description, highlight vague words and replace them with more precise details.

Model: Revising to Add Precise Details

The narrow valley ^stretched out^ ~~was~~ nearly a mile from end to end. ^Evergreen^ Trees dotted the upper mountain slopes, giving way first to ^laurel^ bushes and then to grassy areas pierced by ^granite^ outcroppings.

Words like *evergreen, laurel,* and *granite* identify with more precision.

Prentice Hall Writing and Grammar Connection: Chapter 6, Section 4

Extend Your Learning

Listening and Speaking As a member of the party that explored the Grand Canyon with López de Cárdenas, give a **speech** to convince Coronado that the entire expedition should travel to view the canyon. Use these tips:

- Incorporate your personal experiences.
- Blend vivid description with well-supported persuasion.

Present your speech to the class.

Research and Technology In a group, create an **exploration booklet** covering either the Grand Canyon or the area between Austin and El Paso, Texas. Gather information from the selections and Internet sources. Use a desktop publishing program to blend these with your text. **[Group Activity]**

For: An additional research activity
Visit: www.PHSchool.com
Web Code: erd-7102

Assessment Resources

The following resources can be used to assess students' knowledge and skills.

Unit 1 Resources
- **Selection Test A,** pp. 37–39
- **Selection Test B,** pp. 40–42

General Resources
- **Rubrics for Narration: Short Story** p. 57–58
- **Rubric for Peer Assessment: Speech** p. 129

Go Online Assessment — Students may use the **Self-test** to prepare for **Selection Test A** or **Selection Test B.**

3 Writing Lesson

- To guide students in writing an autobiographical narrative, give them the **Support for Writing Lesson** page (***Unit 1 Resources,*** p. 34).
- Students' journal entries should contain a wealth of details that make the descriptions of places, things, and people as vivid and specific as possible.
- Remind students to consider their audience as they gather details and then begin to draft their journal entries. Urge them to ask themselves the question, "How will I make this clear and interesting to my readers?"
- Use the Narration: Short Story rubrics in ***General Resources,*** pp. 57–58, to evaluate students' journal entries.

4 Listening and Speaking

- Ask students to recall López de Cárdenas's goal: to explore the river we know now as the Colorado. Then have students reread the entire narrative to sharpen their understanding of what the expedition did and did not accomplish.
- Encourage students to plan their speeches by brainstorming a list of items and ideas to include. Remind them that their audience is their superior officer, Coronado. Their speeches should contain concise and vivid descriptions and explanations of student explorers' ideas.
- Urge students to deliver their speeches to the class from outlines rather than from completely composed scripts.
- The **Support for Extend Your Learning** page (***Unit 1 Resources,*** p. 35) provides guided note-taking opportunities to help students complete the Extend Your Learning activities.
- Use the rubric for Peer Assessment: Speech, p. 129 in ***General Resources,*** to evaluate student speeches.

Go Online Research — Have students type in the Web Code for another research activity.

ancient Hindu text.

2. understand the connection between origin myths of different cultures (Native American and ancient Indian).

Connections

Literature Around the World

Students might reread "Earth on Turtle's Back," "When Grizzlies Walked Upright," and the excerpt from *The Navajo Origin Legend.* Like these selections, the hymns from the *Rig Veda* seek to explain the mysterious phenomena of life. Have students compare the explanations different cultures offer for the origin of the universe. Students may also reread "Museum Indians" and consider the common tone of oral traditions.

Mysteries of Nature

- In earlier cultures, natural phenomena was often mysterious. Have students discuss the phenomena the Native American origin myths sought to explain. What phenomena most concerned the Onondaga, Modoc, and Navajo peoples? How are their explanations similar to or different from those in the *Rig Veda*?
- Point out that even in modern times, many of the questions at the heart of these origin myths still concern us. Have students identify timeless themes in "Earth on Turtle's Back," "When Grizzlies Walked Upright," and *The Navajo Origin Legend.* Students should look for similar themes in the "Creation Hymn" and "Night."

Literature Around the World

India

Mysteries of Nature

Native American origin myths, like the ones in this unit, are enormously varied, but they have one element in common: they attempt to explain important phenomena, including features of the natural world, religious rites, and events beyond people's control. Most of all, origin myths contain stories about beginnings. Because most Native American cultures lacked a written language, such stories were passed down orally from one generation to the next.

Many other cultures have produced origin or creation myths, as well as other stories and poems about natural phenomena. In ancient India around 1400 B.C., the Aryans, an Indo-European people, compiled a collection of such texts. This collection, which formed the basis for the Hindu religion, is known as the *Rig Veda.* Like Native American origin myths, the hymns of the *Rig Veda* were passed down through the ages by word of mouth long before they were preserved in written form. Two of these hymns are presented here.

Timeless Concerns Native American origin myths and the hymns of the *Rig Veda* (known as *Vedic hymns*) offer clues to ancient cultures, yet they also reflect timeless concerns. Like the speaker in "Creation Hymn," you, too, may wonder about the origin of the universe. Like the speaker in "Night," you may have nighttime fears, despite all modern protections. As you read, notice that both hymns address the mysteries of nature, but they approach these mysteries from different angles. "Creation Hymn" confronts the unknown on an abstract level, speaking of concepts such as existence and immortality, yet deliberately leaving many questions unanswered. In contrast, "Night" uses concrete language, familiar terms, and personification to make the unknown easier to comprehend.

from the Rig Veda

translated by Wendy Doniger

Creation Hymn

1 There was neither non-existence nor existence then; there was
neither the realm of space nor the sky which is beyond. What
stirred? Where? In whose protection? Was there water, bottomlessly
deep?
2 There was neither death nor immortality then. There was no
distinguishing sign of night nor of day. That one breathed, windless,
by its own impulse. Other than that there was nothing beyond.
3 Darkness was hidden by darkness in the beginning; with no distinguishing sign, all this was water. The life force that was covered
with emptiness, that one arose through the power of heat.
4 Desire came upon that one in the beginning; that was the first
seed of mind. Poets seeking in their heart with wisdom found the
bond of existence in nonexistence.
5 Their cord was extended across. Was there below? Was there
above? There were seed-placers; there were powers. There was
impulse beneath; there was giving-forth above.
6 Who really knows? Who will here proclaim it? Whence was it produced?
Whence is this creation? The gods came afterwards, with the creation
of this universe. Who then knows whence it has arisen?
7 Whence this creation has arisen—perhaps it formed itself, or perhaps it did not—the one who looks down on it, in the highest
heaven, only he knows—or perhaps he does not know.

Vocabulary Builder

immortality (im′ môr tal′ i tē) *n.* a quality or state of being exempt from death; unending existence

distinguishing (di stiŋ′ gwish iŋ) *adj.* serving to mark as separate or different

Thematic Connection

According to the speaker, why might the gods themselves not know how the universe was created?

Thematic Connection

- Explain to students that the "Creation Hymn" speculates on the origin of the universe. In this respect, it is an origin myth that can be compared to *The Navajo Origin Legend* from which students have read an excerpt.
- Point out that the "Creation Hymn" does not offer answers. Rather, the speaker chooses not to fill in gaps in knowledge with mythical explanations. Instead of searching for explanations, the speaker seems to be at peace with uncertainty.
- Be sure that students recognize the speaker's willingness to question all that the hymn has already suggested about the origins of the universe.
- **Ask** students the Thematic Connection question: According to the speaker, why might the gods themselves not know how the universe was created?
  Possible response: The speaker says that the gods came into being after the creation, and thus may not know the origin of the universe. Only "the one who looks down on it, in the highest heaven" may know how the universe was created—and even this entity might not know.
- Encourage students to discuss how this uncertainty sets the "Creation Hymn" apart from the Native American origin myths.

Differentiated Instruction Solutions for All Learners

Support for Less Proficient Readers

Students may find the "Creation Hymn" highly challenging. Guide students through the numbered verses, reading them one at a time with the group. Pause after each verse and ask students to explain what the speaker is saying. Students may recognize that the hymn describes the origins of the universe, but may have difficulty with the vagueness and uncertainty the speaker embraces. Explain that in verses 1 and 2, the speaker says all that existed before the universe was the breathing of one divine entity. In verse 4, the speaker suggests that desire and the seeking of poets may have caused the universe to take shape. But in verses 6 and 7, the speaker admits that no one can know for certain.

Thematic Connection

- Tell students that, like the "Creation Hymn," "Night" is an attempt to explain the unknown phenomena of the natural world.
- Point out that one of the speaker's strategies in "Night" is using personification—applying human traits to nonhuman objects. Then **ask** students the Thematic Connection question: How does the speaker personify Night and her sister in this verse?

  Possible response: The speaker describes Night as a goddess, with features such as eyes. Twilight is described as Night's sister, and the speaker describes them pushing one another aside.
- Have students discuss the use of personification and how this use of language makes natural phenomena easier to understand.

ASSESS

Answers

1. (a) The hymns from the *Rig Veda* are more formal and poetic than the Native American origin myths. The *Rig Veda* seems less like orally transmitted legends and more like written poems. (b) Because they are more poetic, the *Rig Veda* hymns are less explanatory and express less certainty about the origin of the universe.
2. In both "Night" and "When Grizzlies Walked Upright," natural forces such as night, sky, and wind are personified as gods and spirits that have families and human-like interactions.
3. (a) Both explanations are told by a third-person narrator. The details of creation in the "Creation Hymn" are presented as a list and are largely unknown; Creation is a mystery, and the speaker has unanswered questions. "The Earth on Turtle's Back" is told as a narrative of how animals help create Earth. (b) The Onondaga tale offers more precise and detailed descriptions of creation.
4. *Students may say that Native American origin myths are more successful because their central ideas seem to be easier to grasp. Some students, however, will say the Vedic hymns are more*

Answers continued

successful because their themes are not diluted by narrative.

Night

1 The goddess Night has drawn near, looking about on many sides with her eyes. She has put on all her glories.
2 The immortal goddess has filled the wide space, the depths and the heights. She stems the tide of darkness with her light.
3 The goddess has drawn near, pushing aside her sister the twilight. Darkness, too, will give way.
4 As you came near to us today, we turned homeward to rest, as birds go to their home in a tree.
5 People who live in villages have gone home to rest, and animals with feet, and animals with wings, even the ever-searching hawks.
6 Ward off the she-wolf and the wolf; ward off the thief. O night full of waves, be easy for us to cross over.
7 Darkness—palpable black, and painted—has come upon me. O Dawn, banish it like a debt.
8 I have driven this hymn to you as the herdsman drives cows. Choose and accept it, O Night, daughter of the sky, like a song of praise to a conqueror.

Thematic Connection
How does the speaker personify Night and her sister in this verse?

About the *Rig Veda* (compiled c. 1400 B.C.)

The *Rig Veda* is a collection of 1,028 hymns composed in Sanskrit by various authors at different times. Many of the hymns portray natural phenomena as godlike beings, but the poems do not set forth religious ideas in a systematic manner. The authors praise the gods for their power and beauty and for the benefits they bring to humankind. They also invoke the gods for protection and sustenance. Overall, however, the poems' homage to the gods of nature sets a tone of devotion and piety.

Connecting Literature Around the World

1. **(a)** How does the presentation style of the creation story in the *Rig Veda* differ from the Native American origin myths? **(b)** How does the contrast in narrative styles influence the feel of the works?
2. What key role does nature play in both "Night" and "When Grizzlies Walked Upright"?
3. **(a)** Compare and contrast the way creation is explained in "Creation Myth" and "The Earth on Turtle's Back. **(b)** Which origin myth expresses greater certainty about its subject?
4. Of the Native American myths and the Vedic hymns, which one do you feel is most successful at expressing its central idea? Explain.

Unit 1 Part 2

Focus on Literary Forms: Narrative Accounts

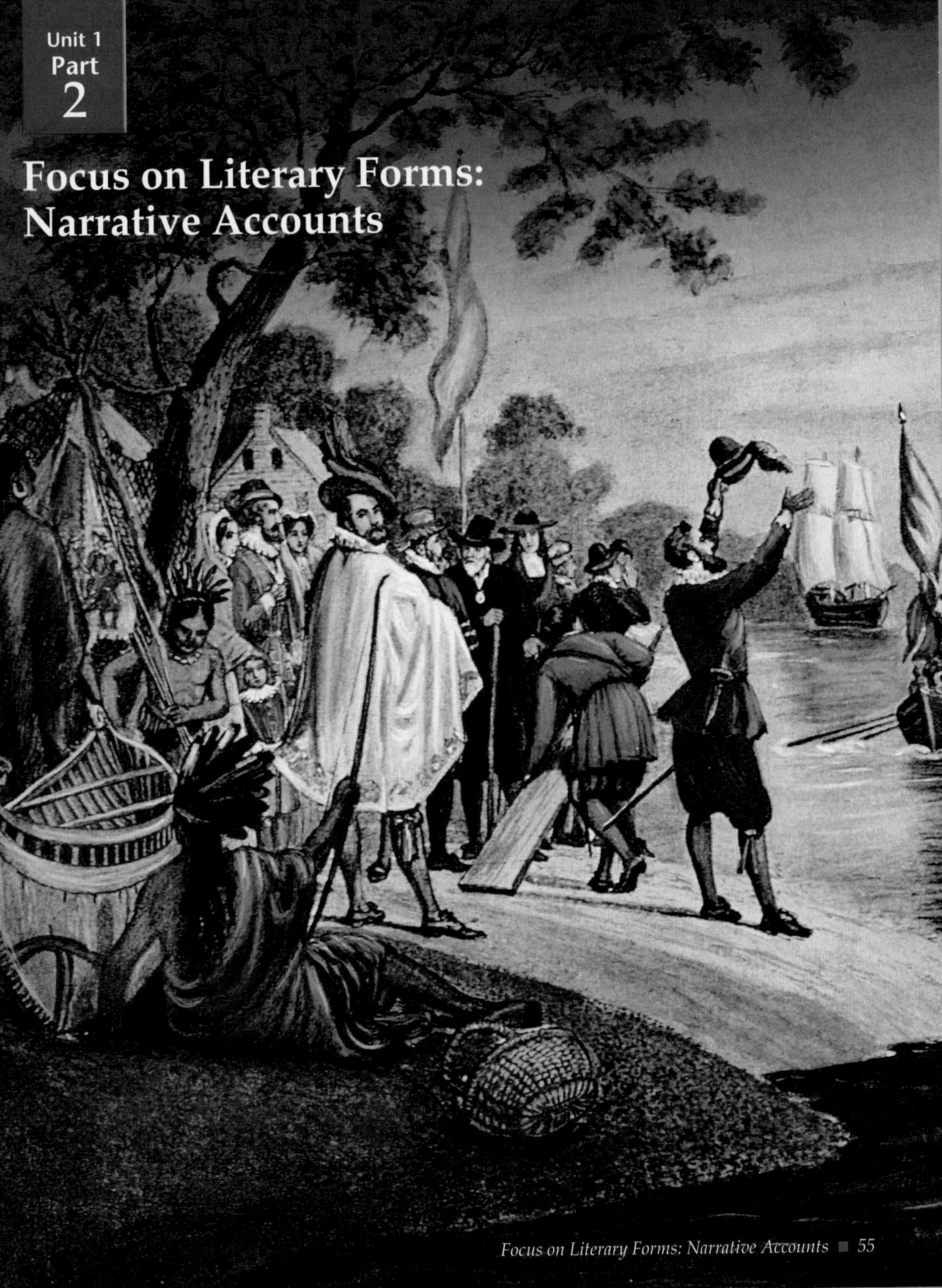

Selection Planning Guide

This section explores narrative accounts, both as a literary form and as a firsthand look at the lives of some of America's first European settlers. Columbus's *Journal of the First Voyage to America* describes the explorer's first encounters with local natives. John Smith's *The General History of Virginia* is a colorful and subjective account of the establishment of Jamestown Colony. Smith's account is paired with William Bradford's modest, straightforward retelling of the Pilgrims' plight in *Of Plymouth Plantation.* Though quite different in tone, all three accounts describe the Native Americans' important role in helping the settlers survive in the New World.

Humanities

Landing in Jamestown, the Founding of the Colony of Jamestown, Virginia by Captain Christopher Newport and 105 of His Followers, English School, 17th century

This painting depicts the first settlers arriving at what would become Jamestown, Virginia. In 1606, The Virginia Company of London provided financial backing for this journey to North America. Like other European powers at the time, England had hoped to find a western passage to Asia. They also had hoped to expand power, influence, and the royal coffers by investing resources into exploration and settlement.

Use the following question for discussion:

- Looking at the image, would you say that the painter's attitude toward the founding of the Jamestown settlement was positive or negative? Why?
  Possible response: Most students will say that the painter's attitude was positive, based on such details as the celebratory gestures of the people and that they all appear to be well-dressed, well-fed, and rested after such a long ocean voyage.

Differentiated Instruction Solutions for All Learners

Accessibility at a Glance

Average	More Challenging
from Journal of the First Voyage to America	*from* The General History of Virginia *from* Of Plymouth Plantation

Meeting Your Standards

Students will

1. recognize and appreciate the types and elements of narrative accounts.
2. apply strategies for reading narrative accounts.

❶ Firsthand and Secondhand Narrative Accounts

- Tell students that in Part 2 they will focus on narrative accounts.
- Explain that firsthand accounts are created by participants or observers. Add that not all accounts are connected to significant events; a letter or journal entry written during a certain time period might shed light on how people thought or what they did.
- Remind students that a narrative account can be fiction or nonfiction and that sometimes it is difficult to distinguish between the two. A reader cannot know whether the writer has added or omitted information.

❷ Narrative Nonfiction

- Review with students the types of narrative accounts. Clarify the information available on these pages, and suggest that students use these pages as a reference as they read Part 2.
- Mention that although people continue to write narrative accounts, television and film provide much of the information that narrative accounts did in the past.
- **Ask** students to give examples of situations or events that now would be photographed or filmed. **Possible answers:** A vacation, a wedding, and news events are often filmed or photographed rather than written about.

Defining Narrative Accounts

Narrative accounts tell the story of real-life events. Though these accounts have literary qualities, many are also useful to historians and other researchers as primary or secondary sources.

❶ Firsthand and Secondhand Narrative Accounts

Narrative accounts may be classified as either firsthand or secondhand.

- Some historical narratives are **firsthand accounts,** created by people who lived through significant historical events. These texts are considered **primary sources.** Although written by eyewitnesses or participants, firsthand accounts may be subjective or even **biased;** they may reflect the writer's personal "slant" or one-sided perspective.
- Other narratives are **secondhand accounts,** written by people who researched the events but did not directly witness or experience them. Such accounts are **secondary sources.** They are more likely to be objective than firsthand accounts. What they gain in objectivity, however, they may lose in immediacy and accuracy.
- Sometimes an author blurs the distinction between firsthand and secondhand accounts. For example, in *The General History of Virginia,* John Smith refers to himself in the third person as "Captain Smith."

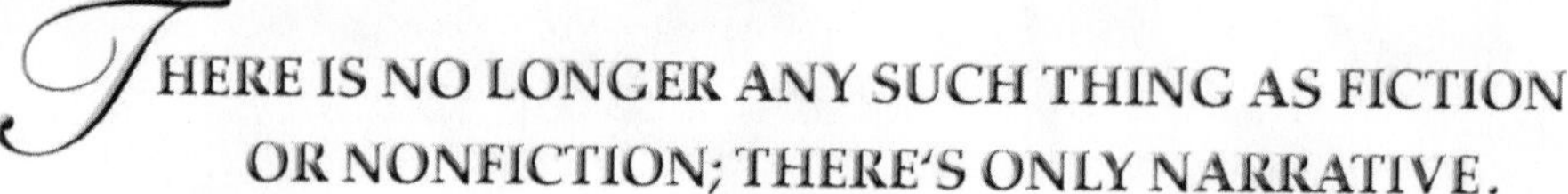

THERE IS NO LONGER ANY SUCH THING AS FICTION OR NONFICTION; THERE'S ONLY NARRATIVE.

—*E.L. Doctorow*

❷ Narrative Nonfiction

Narrative accounts may be classified as a type of **narrative nonfiction,** or prose writing, that tells about real people, places, objects, and events. A nonfiction work, by definition, must be true. Narrative accounts, therefore, have elements in common with autobiographies, biographies, journals, diaries, and news stories. They may even overlap with such forms; for example, a narrative account may be written in the form of a journal.

❸ Features of Narrative Accounts

Information The main purpose of most narrative accounts is to provide **information** about events and experiences. In his stories about his own adventures, for instance, John Smith provides vivid details about the early exploration of America. William Bradford presents a rich history of the founding of Plymouth Colony and the Pilgrims' encounters with Native Americans.

Distinctive Style In addition to providing information, narrative accounts often include the writer's personal observations and feelings. Many are written in a distinctive style and tone. **Style** is the writer's characteristic way of writing, and **tone** is the writer's attitude toward the audience and subject. For example, though William Bradford is typically sober and reserved, John Smith is often flamboyant and boastful.

Types of Narrative Accounts	Examples
An **exploration narrative** records information about the writer's own travels to an unfamiliar place.	Alvar Núñez Cabeza de Vaca, "A Journey Through Texas," p. 42 García López de Cárdenas, "Boulders Taller Than the Great Tower of Seville," p. 47
A **journal** records daily events and personal observations.	Christopher Columbus, *Journal of the First Voyage to America*, p. 60
A **historical narrative** records major historical events that the writer may or may not have experienced firsthand.	John Smith, *The General History of Virginia*, p. 70 William Bradford, *Of Plymouth Plantation*, p. 76
A **captivity narrative** records events and personal feelings during the writer's captivity.	Mary Rowlandson, *A Narrative of the Captivity, Sufferings, and Removes of Mrs. Mary Rowlandson*, p. 66
A **slave narrative** records the injustices of slavery and often tells how the writer escaped or was freed.	Olaudah Equiano, *The Interesting Narrative of the Life of Olaudah Equiano*, p. 160

4

Strategies for Reading Narrative Accounts

Use these strategies as you read narrative accounts.

Identify the Writer's Purpose Determine whether the writer wants to record information, to reveal personal thoughts and feelings, to persuade readers to believe or do something, or simply to entertain. Then, decide whether the writer achieves this purpose.

Check for Subjectivity or Bias Keep in mind that firsthand accounts may reflect the writer's bias. Even secondhand accounts may not be wholly objective, particularly if the writer is trying to present a historical figure as heroic, misguided, or villainous.

- Remind students that while narrative accounts do provide historical information, the accounts can often be biased. A writer's style and tone often indicates his or her bias.
- Review the definitions of style and tone with students. Tell students to keep these terms in mind while reading the selections in Part 2.

4 Strategies for Reading Narrative Accounts

- Remind students that the authors of narrative accounts write for different purposes.
- Remind them also that people reading historical narrative accounts, will read them from a different perspective. They will be interested in the time period as well as the content and purpose.
- Make sure students realize that a narrative account claiming objectivity may contain or reflect the writer's perspective or bias. Tell students that the writer's word choice, tone, and style may reveal bias, as might the selection of details.

Differentiated Instruction Solutions for All Learners

Support for Less Proficient Readers
Students may have difficulty identifying the style and tone of the selections. Give students a copy of the Three—column Chart, p. 312 in ***Graphic Organizer Transparencies.*** Have students write the title of the selection in the left column. In the center column, students should write the style of the selection and examples from the text that demonstrate the style. Ask students to use the right column to identify the tone and list their reasons for their choices. After reading a selection, have students compare their charts with a partner. Ask students to write their responses on the board. Explain any styles or tones that were not correctly identified.

Meeting Your Standards

Students will

1. **analyze and respond to literary elements.**
   - Literary Analysis: Journal
2. **read, comprehend, analyze, and critique a journal.**
   - Reading Strategy: Recognizing Author's Purpose
   - Reading Check questions
   - Apply the Skills questions
   - Assessment Practice (ATE)
3. **develop vocabulary.**
   - Vocabulary Lesson: Latin Root *-flict-*
4. **understand and apply written and oral language conventions.**
   - Spelling Strategy
   - Grammar and Style Lesson: Action and Linking Verbs
5. **develop writing proficiency.**
   - Writing Lesson: Oral Report on the Voyage
6. **develop appropriate research strategies.**
   - Extend Your Learning: Chart
7. **understand and apply listening and speaking strategies.**
   - Extend Your Learning: Humanities Presentation

Block Scheduling: Use one 90-minute class period to preteach the skills and have students read the selection. Use a second 90-minute class period to assess students' mastery of skills, extend their learning, and monitor their progress.

Homework Suggestions

Following are possibilities for homework assignments.

- Support pages from *Unit 1 Resources.*
  Literary Analysis
  Reading Strategy
  Vocabulary Builder
  Grammar and Style
- An Extend Your Learning project and the Writing Lesson for this selection group may be completed over several days.

Step-by-Step Teaching Guide	Pacing Guide
PRETEACH	
• Administer Vocabulary and Reading Warm-ups as necessary.	5 min.
• Engage students' interest with the motivation activity.	5 min.
• Read and discuss author and background features. **FT**	10 min.
• Introduce the Literary Analysis Skill: Journal. **FT**	5 min.
• Introduce the Reading Strategy: Recognizing Author's Purpose. **FT**	10 min.
• Prepare students to read by teaching the selection vocabulary. **FT**	
TEACH	
• Informally monitor comprehension while students read independently or in groups. **FT**	30 min.
• Monitor students' comprehension with the Reading Check notes.	as students read
• Reinforce vocabulary with Vocabulary Builder notes.	as students read
• Develop students' understanding of journals with the Literary Analysis annotations. **FT**	5 min.
• Develop students' ability to recognize author's purpose with the Reading Strategy annotations. **FT**	5 min.
ASSESS/EXTEND	
• Assess students' comprehension and mastery of the Literary Analysis and Reading Strategy by having them answer the Apply the Skills questions. **FT**	15 min.
• Have students complete the Vocabulary Lesson and the Grammar and Style Lesson. **FT**	15 min.
• Apply students' ability to use vivid elaboration by using the Writing Lesson. **FT**	45 min. or homework
• Apply students' understanding by using one or more of the Extend Your Learning activities.	20–90 min. or homework
• Administer Selection Test A or Selection Test B. **FT**	15 min.

Resources

PRINT

Unit 1 Resources

- Vocabulary Warm-up Word Lists [**L1, L2, EL**] .... p. 43
- Vocabulary Warm-up Practice [**L1, L2, EL**] .... p. 44
- Reading Warm-up A [**L1, L2, EL**] .... p. 45
- Reading Warm-up B [**L1, L2, L3**] .... p. 46

TRANSPARENCY

Graphic Organizer Transparencies

- Literary Analysis Graphic Organizer A [**L3**] .... p. 11
- Literary Analysis Graphic Organizer B [**L1, L2, EL**] .... p. 12
- Reading Strategy Graphic Organizer A [**L3**] .... p. 9
- Reading Strategy Graphic Organizer B [**L1, L2, EL**] .... p. 10

PRINT

Reader's Notebook [L2]
Reader's Notebook: Adapted Version [L1]
Reader's Notebook: English Learner's Version [EL]

Unit 1 Resources

- Literary Analysis [**L3**] .... p. 47
- Reading Strategy [**L3**] .... p. 48
- Vocabulary Builder [**L3**] .... p. 49

TECHNOLOGY

Listening to Literature Audio CDs [L2, EL]

PRINT

Unit 1 Resources

- Grammar and Style [**L3**] .... p. 50
- Support for Writing Lesson [**L3**] .... p. 51
- Support for Extend Your Learning [**L3**] .... p. 52
- Enrichment [**L4**] .... p. 53
- Selection Test A [**L1, L2, EL**] .... pp. 54–56
- Selection Test B [**L3, L4**] .... pp. 57–59

General Resources

- Rubrics for Descriptive Essay [**L3**] .... pp. 63–64

TECHNOLOGY

Go Online: Research [**L3**]
Go Online: Self-test [**L3**]
***ExamView®* Test Bank** [**L3**]

Choosing Resources for Differentiated Instruction

[**L1**] Special Needs Students
[**L2**] Below-Level Students
[**L3**] All Students
[**L4**] Advanced Students
[**EL**] English Learners

FT Fast Track Instruction: To move the lesson more quickly, use the strategies and activities identified with **FT**.

Scaffolding for Less Proficient and Advanced Students

The leveled Critical Thinking questions after selections progress in the levels of thinking required to answer them. To address the needs of your different students, you may use the (a) level questions for your less proficient students and the (b) level questions with your on-level and advanced students. The occasional (c) level questions are appropriate for your advanced students.

PRENTICE HALL **TeacherEXPRESS™** Plan · Teach · Assess — Use this complete suite of powerful teaching tools to make lesson planning and testing quicker and easier.

Use the interactive textbook (online and on CD-ROM) to make selections and activities come alive with audio and video support and interactive questions.

ation

e students to read the selec- y asking them the following on: If someone agreed to ce a travel venture for them, re would they wish to go? Ask nteers to share their responses n the class. Then, explain that stu- nts are about to read an account ritten by a man whose dream of nding a faster shipping route to the iches of the Indies led him to make a voyage to a place where no Euro- pean had ever gone.

❶ Background

More About the Author

Christopher Columbus tried for years to finance his voyage. After rejections from the kings of Portugal, England, and France, he went to Spain in 1485. It took him two years even to get an audience with Ferdinand and Isabella and six more years to get their approval. In addition to assuring him ten percent of all valuables discovered, the deal between Columbus and the Spanish monarchs made him Governor General of any lands he discovered.

❶ *from* Journal of the First Voyage to America

Christopher Columbus (1451–1506)

Not much is known about the early life of Christopher Columbus, one of history's most famous explorers. In the late 1400s, Europeans had little knowledge about world geography, but Columbus left his home in Genoa, Italy, at a young age and went to sea. At age 25, he was shipwrecked off the coast of Portugal. Once back on land, Columbus studied mapmaking and navigation. He also learned Latin and read Marco Polo's account of the riches of Asia. Between 1480 and 1482, Columbus sailed to the Azores and to the Canary Islands off Africa. He then began to dream of more challenging voyages. Within ten years, he embraced the idea that led to his lifelong goal: reaching the fabled cities of Asia by sailing westward around the world.

First, Columbus tried to convince King John II of Portugal to fund a westward voyage. When his request was rejected there, he sought funding from other European rulers. After a series of unsuccessful attempts, Columbus won the support of Queen Isabella of Spain.

A Hard Bargain Queen Isabella and her husband, King Ferdinand, agreed to finance Columbus's first voyage in 1492. In forging the agreement, Columbus negotiated favorable terms. In addition to funding, he asked for and received the right to rule any lands he conquered. The agreement also noted that he would be entitled to 10 percent of all wealth from those lands.

The Famous Voyage On August 3, 1492, Columbus set sail from Palos, a small port in southwestern Spain, with his three ships—the *Niña*, the *Pinta*, and the *Santa Maria*. Although he knew how to measure latitude by using the North Star, Columbus had no navigational instruments. He used a compass to determine direction and an hourglass to estimate time. After more than a month at sea, his crews became disillusioned when they did not reach the islands Columbus had led them to expect. However, soon signs of life such as coastal seaweed and birds flying overhead indicated land was near, and the crew members' hopes were renewed. On October 12, Columbus reached one of the islands of Bahama, which he mistook for an island off India. He named the island San Salvador; he then continued to explore the Caribbean.

Linking East and West When Columbus reached these islands he had no idea there were millions of people living a short distance away in North and South America. He faced many challenges sailing the largely uncharted waters, but his voyages linked the Eastern and Western hemispheres. Over the next twelve years, he made three more transatlantic journeys, ever convinced that he had reached Asia and always hopeful of finding Marco Polo's fabled cities.

His Final Years Columbus was driven by his unrelenting desire to discover new territories, and he continued to sail until nearly the end of his life. His goal in his final voyage was to find a passage to the mainland of China. He set out from Cadiz, Spain, in 1502, traveling to Martinique and later east and south to the coasts of Honduras, Nicaragua, Costa Rica, Panama, and Jamaica. Suffering from exhaustion and malaria, he abandoned his search for China and returned to Spain in 1504. Although many scholars believe Columbus was poor at the time of his death, others say he died a wealthy man at the age of 54 in 1506. Today, he is recognized as one of the greatest mariners of all time.

Preview

Connecting to the Literature

Fulfilling the desire to circle the globe in a boat or discovering the cure for a deadly disease takes more than sheer will. A dreamer needs financial resources. To achieve his dream of circling the globe, Christopher Columbus had to persuade others to provide the funding. More often than not, people did not think it was worth the expense.

Literary Analysis

Journal

The European expeditions in the Americas are recorded in the journals of the explorers. A **journal** is an individual's day-by-day account of events. As the example below shows, a journal provides valuable details that only a participant or an eyewitness can supply.

> . . . the inhabitants on discovering us abandoned their houses, and took to flight, carrying off their goods to the mountains.

As a record of personal reactions, a journal reveals as much about the writer as it does about events. As you read, look for details that reveal Columbus's values, hopes, and reactions.

Connecting Literary Elements

A journal is not necessarily a reliable record of the facts. The author's **point of view,** or attitudes about the topic or audience, may color the telling of events, particularly when the writer is a participant. Journals written for publication rather than private use are even less likely to be objective. While reading Columbus's journal, look for evidence that he was writing for an audience.

Reading Strategy

Recognizing Author's Purpose

Columbus's purpose for writing his journal was to convince Queen Isabella and King Ferdinand to continue funding his explorations. **Recognizing the author's purpose** will help you to understand why a work was written, and it will also help you to understand Columbus's careful choice of words, details, and events to include in his journal. As you read, use a chart like this one to record Columbus's favorable descriptions and events. Then, explain his purpose for describing it that way.

Favorable Descriptions	Author's Purpose

Vocabulary Builder

exquisite (eks′ kwi zit) *adj.* very beautiful; delicate; carefully wrought (p. 60)

affliction (ə flik′ shən) *n.* something causing pain or suffering (p. 61)

indications (in′ di kā′ shənz) *n.* signs; things that point out or signify (p. 62)

abundance (ə bun′ dəns) *n.* a great supply; more than enough (p. 62)

Differentiated Instruction Solutions for All Learners

Support for Special Needs Students
Have students complete the **Preview** and **Build Skills** pages for the selection in the ***Reader's Notebook: Adapted Version.*** These pages provide a selection summary, an abbreviated presentation of the reading and literary skills, and the graphic organizer on the **Build Skills** page in the student book.

Support for Less Proficient Readers
Have students complete the **Preview** and **Build Skills** pages for the selection in the ***Reader's Notebook.*** These pages provide a selection summary, an abbreviated presentation of the reading and literary skills, and the graphic organizer on the **Build Skills** page in the student book.

Support for English Learners
Have students complete the **Preview** and **Build Skills** pages for the selection in the ***Reader's Notebook: English Learner's Version.*** These pages provide a selection summary, an abbreviated presentation of the reading and literary skills, additional contextual vocabulary, and the graphic organizer on the **Build Skills** page in the student book.

2 Literary Analysis

Journal

- Explain that students will focus on a journal—an individuals' day-by-day account of events—as they read this selection.
- **Ask** whether students have ever kept a journal or diary of events in their own lives. Invite student volunteers to share their reflections about the process of keeping a journal. What are its rewards? What are its challenges or frustrations?
- Point out that a journal not only records events, but also reveals the ideas, beliefs, and feelings of its author.
- Encourage students to look for details in Columbus's journal that reveal his motives.

3 Reading Strategy

Recognizing Author's Purpose

- Remind students that every writer has a purpose for writing, to entertain, inform, or persuade. Invite students to identify some common purposes for writing journal entries.
- Encourage students to reread details from the author biography about Columbus's efforts to secure funding for his explorations.
- Point out that in addition to a desire to record private impressions for his own personal use, Columbus also wanted to convince his benefactors that funding his explorations was money well spent.
- Give students a copy of **Reading Strategy Graphic Organizer A,** p. 9 in ***Graphic Organizer Transparencies.*** Urge students to look for passages in Columbus's journal in which this purpose is detectable.

Vocabulary Builder

- Pronounce each vocabulary word for students, and read the definitions as a class. Have students identify any words with which they are familiar.

TEACH

Learning Modalities
Verbal/Linguistic Learners
Columbus uses archaic measurement terms such as *span, league,* and *quintal.* Have students use encyclopedias and dictionaries to learn more about the origins of these and more current terms of measurement, such as *inch, mile,* and *meter.* Have students record the words, together with their origins, in a chart.

1 About the Selections

This excerpt from Christopher Columbus's journal conveys the explorer's observations and evaluations of San Salvador and its resources and states his plans for further exploration. Columbus appears to be taken with the natural beauty of the island and with the friendliness of its inhabitants. However, his choice of language and details make it clear that his purpose in writing is to impress Spain's king and queen, who were financing his expedition and expecting a return on their investment.

2 Critical Viewing

Answer: Students should note that the astrolabe has a needle and markings around its perimeter similar to those of a navigational compass.

1 *from* Journal of the First Voyage to America

Christopher Columbus

Background In the 1450s, the only way to India from Europe involved traveling through Turkey, but explorers in Portugal and Spain began to look at alternate sea routes. Columbus's search brought Europe into contact with North and South America. His voyages took him from Lisbon, Portugal, to Palos, Spain, and the Canary Islands before he crossed the Atlantic. He landed first on the island of San Salvador. This account begins nine days after Columbus landed there.

SUNDAY, OCT. 21ST [1492]. At 10 o'clock, we arrived at a cape of the island,[1] and anchored, the other vessels in company. After having dispatched a meal, I went ashore, and found no habitation save a single house, and that without an occupant; we had no doubt that the people had fled in terror at our approach, as the house was completely furnished. I suffered nothing to be touched, and went with my captains and some of the crew to view the country. This island even exceeds the others in beauty and fertility. Groves of lofty and flourishing trees are abundant, as also large lakes, surrounded and overhung by the foliage, in a most enchanting manner. Everything looked as green as in April in Andalusia.[2] The melody of the birds was so exquisite that one was never willing to part from the

1. **the island** San Salvador.
2. **Andalusia** (an′ də lo͞o′ zhə) a region of Spain.

2 **▲ Critical Viewing** The astrolabe was an invention that made the age of exploration possible. What features of this one suggest that it is an instrument of navigation? **[Support]**

Vocabulary Builder
exquisite (eks′ kwi zit) *adj.* very beautiful; delicate; carefully wrought

Differentiated Instruction Solutions for All Learners

Accessibility at a Glance

	from Journal of the First Voyage
Context	Travel Journal
Language	Difficult diction
Concept Level	Accessible (description of environment and encounter with natives)
Literary Merit	Primary Source
Lexile	1160
Overall Rating	Average

spot, and the flocks of parrots obscured the heavens. The diversity in the appearance of the feathered tribe from those of our country is extremely curious. A thousand different sorts of trees, with their fruit were to be met with, and of a wonderfully delicious odor. It was a great affliction to me to be ignorant of their natures, for I am very certain they are all valuable; specimens of them and of the plants I have preserved. Going round one of these lakes, I saw a snake, which we killed, and I have kept the skin for your Highnesses; upon being
3 discovered he took to the water, whither[3] we followed him, as it was not deep, and dispatched him with our lances; he was seven spans[4] in length; I think there are many more such about here. I discovered also the aloe tree, and am determined to take on board the ship tomorrow, ten quintals[5] of it, as I am told it is valuable. While we were in search of some good water we came upon a village of the natives about half a league from the place where the ships lay; the inhabitants on discovering us abandoned their houses, and took to flight, carrying off their goods to the mountain. I ordered that nothing which they had left should be taken, not even the value of a pin. Presently we saw several of the natives advancing towards our party, and one of them came up to us, to whom we gave some hawk's bells and glass beads, with which he was delighted. We asked him in return, for water, and after I had gone on board the ship, the natives 4

3. **whither** to which place.
4. **spans** *n.* units of measure, each equal to about nine inches.
5. **quintals** (kwin′ təlz) *n.* units of weight, each equal to 100 kilograms, or 220.46 pounds.

Vocabulary Builder
affliction (ə flik′ shən) *n.* something causing pain or suffering

Literary Analysis
Journal Why do you think Columbus relates the story of capturing and skinning the snake?

Reading Check
Does Columbus encounter any people when he lands? Explain.

5

◀ Critical Viewing 6
Evaluate the artist's interpretation of Columbus's landing in the Western Hemisphere. What aspects of the moment does he emphasize? **[Evaluate; Support]**

3 Literary Analysis
Journal

- Remind students that a journal is the product of an author with a particular point of view and a specific purpose for writing.
- **Ask** students the Literary Analysis question: Why do you think Columbus relates the story of capturing and skinning the snake?
  Answer: Students may suggest that Columbus wished to record any possible threats to subsequent explorers in the area.

4 Reading Check

Answer: Immediately upon landing, Columbus encounters a furnished, but empty, house; later he discovers a similarly abandoned village. Finally he meets a few inhabitants of the village.

5 Humanities
Columbus Landing in the New World

The lithograph was made by an unknown artist. The lithography process was invented in the late 1700s and was used as an alternative to engraving for reproducing paintings and drawings for books. Use these questions for discussion:

1. Does this lithograph present a romanticized view of Columbus's landing? If so, how?
   Answer: Students may say that the scene is romanticized because everyone is dressed in formal attire and the land seems beautiful and hospitable.
2. What can you learn about Columbus and his crew from this lithograph?
   Answer: Students may cite the crew's religious inclinations, their formal dress, their sense of pageantry, and their seriousness.

6 Critical Viewing

Answer: Students may say that the artist emphasizes Columbus's role as the "discoverer" of America.

Differentiated Instruction
Solutions for All Learners

Strategy for Special Needs Students
Point out to students that this part of Columbus's journal reads like a descriptive postcard sent home to Spain. Help students work through the selection a few sentences at a time. You might have students list sensory images of the New World in a five-column chart on the chalkboard as they encounter them.

Enrichment for Gifted/Talented Students
You may not need to remind students that Columbus and other European explorers did not "discover" the Americas, since at the time of their arrival, Native Americans had lived in the hemisphere for thousands of years. Encourage students to prepare a research report on the Native American civilizations that preceded European discovery.

ASSESS

Answers

1. Students may say they would feel proud, intrigued, surprised, or wary after reading of Columbus's successes.
2. (a) Details such as lofty and flourishing trees, wonderfully delicious *odor,* and *exquisite* . . . melody of the birds convey Columbus's attitude toward the island. (b) Columbus thinks that the landscape is beautiful and possibly contains things of great value.
3. (a) He trades glass beads and hawk's bells with the Native Americans. (b) The Native Americans are "delighted" with these items, and Columbus implies that this causes the Native Americans "great pleasure" in presenting the Europeans with water.
4. (a) Apparently Columbus respects the Native Americans. (b) He reveals his respect by ordering his men to touch nothing that belongs to the people and by trading honestly with them. (c) **Possible response:** Students may say that the clothing worn by Columbus and his men or the ships themselves may have frightened the island natives. In addition, Columbus and his men discover a house that is completely furnished, as though its inhabitant's had fled in haste without taking their belongings.
5. **Possible response:** (a) A Native American's account probably would include more details that reveal concern, worry, shock, or fear about the foreign visitors. (b) Although a crew member also might be impressed by the landscape, a sailor's account might include more details about the Native Americans he met.

came down to the shore with their calabashes[6] full, and showed great pleasure in presenting us with it. I ordered more glass beads to be given them, and they promised to return the next day. It is my wish to fill all the water casks of the ships at this place, which being executed, I shall depart immediately, if the weather serve, and sail round the island, till I succeed in meeting with the king, in order to see if I can acquire any of the gold, which I hear he possesses. Afterwards I shall set sail for another very large island which I believe to be *Cipango,*[7] according to the indications I receive from the Indians on board. They call the Island *Colba,*[8] and say there are many large ships, and sailors there. This other island they name *Bosio*[9] and inform me that it is very large; the others which lie in our course, I shall examine on the passage, and according as I find gold or spices in abundance, I shall determine what to do; at all events I am determined to proceed on to the continent, and visit the city of Guisay[10] where I shall deliver the letters of your Highnesses to the *Great Can,*[11] and demand an answer, with which I shall return.

Vocabulary Builder
indications (in′ di kā′ shənz) *n.* signs; things that point out or signify

abundance (ə bun′ dəns) *n.* a great supply; more than enough

6. **calabashes** (kal′ ə bash′ əz) *n.* dried, hollow shells of gourds used as cups or bowls.
7. **Cipango** (si paŋ′ gō) old name for a group of islands east of Asia, probably what is now Japan.
8. **Colba** (kôl′ bə) Cuba.
9. **Bosio** (bō′ sē ō) probably the island on which the Dominican Republic and Haiti are now located.
10. **Guisay** (gē sā′) the City of Heaven, the name given by Marco Polo to the residence of Kublai Khan (ko͞o′ blī kän), the ruler of China from A.D. 1260–1294.
11. **Great Can** (kän) Kublai Khan.

Critical Reading

1. **Respond:** If you had sponsored Columbus's voyage, how would you feel upon reading this account of his experience?
2. **(a) Recall:** What details convey Columbus's attitude toward the tropical island? **(b) Interpret:** What is Columbus's reaction to the landscape?
3. **(a) Recall:** What items does Columbus trade with the natives? **(b) Generalize:** According to Columbus, how does this trade influence the success of the first meeting with the natives?
4. **(a) Infer:** How do you think Columbus views the natives? **(b) Support:** How does he reveal those views? **(c) Infer:** Why does Columbus think the natives fear him and his men?
5. **(a) Hypothesize:** How might this account be different if it were written by a Native American observing Columbus and his crew? **(b)** What might an account written by a crew member reveal?

For: More about Christopher Columbus
Visit: www.PHSchool.com
Web Code: ere-9105

Go Online Author Link For additional information about Christopher Columbus, have students type in the Web Code, then select C from the alphabet, and then select Christopher Columbus.

Apply the Skills

from *Journal of the First Voyage to America*

Literary Analysis

Journal

1. Use a chart like the one shown here to list three details from the **journal** that only an eyewitness or participant could provide.

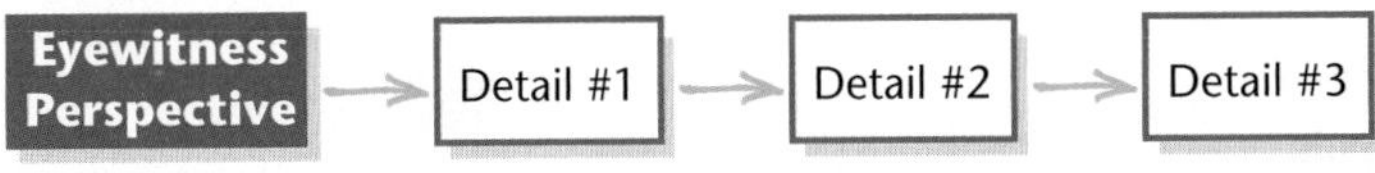

2. Explain Columbus's thoughts and feelings about each of the details you have listed.
3. **(a)** What appears to have been Columbus's primary consideration in choosing "specimens" to send back to Spain? **(b)** What does this consideration reveal about his priorities?

Connecting Literary Elements

4. What can you guess about the author's **point of view** that would cause Columbus to say he hopes to find "gold or spices in abundance"?
5. What is Columbus's level of confidence in his ability to lead the expedition?
6. In what ways does Columbus's role as leader of the expedition affect the way he narrates events?

Reading Strategy

Recognizing Author's Purpose

7. How does the journal reflect the **author's purpose**—chronicling the voyage for his investors, the king and queen of Spain?
8. **(a)** Why do you think Columbus often refers to the monetary value of things he has seen? **(b)** Find two examples of this in the journal.
9. **(a)** What impression of the Americas does Columbus seem to be trying to convey? **(b)** Find three examples from the journal to support your answers.

Extend Understanding

10. **Science Connection:** How would this account be different if it were written by a botanist or other natural scientist?

QuickReview

A **journal** is an individual's day-by-day account of events.

An author's **point of view**, or attitude toward the work's topic or audience, may influence the facts or details a writer includes.

Recognizing the author's purpose helps you to understand the specific choice of words, details, and events.

Go Online Assessment

For: Self-test
Visit: www.PHSchool.com
Web Code: era-6104

Go Online Assessment Students may use the **Self-test** to prepare for **Selection Test A** or **Selection Test B**.

Answers

1. **Possible response:** Students' charts should accurately list details that only an eyewitness can provide.
   Another sample answer can be found on **Literary Analysis Graphic Organizer B**, p. 12 in ***Graphic Organizer Transparencies.***
2. Students should report details from the text that reveal Columbus's views about the details they listed.
3. (a) Columbus's primary considerations are value and novelty. (b) It reveals that he wants the new world to be of value to Spain and a subject of curiosity.
4. Columbus may wish to portray this new land as being potentially valuable to Spain, so that it will continue to fund voyages.
5. Columbus seems confident in his ability to lead the expedition.
6. Because he is the leader of the expedition, Columbus is obliged to present not only details about the places and people he encounters, but also an overview of the prospects for European profit from this part of the world.
7. Columbus includes many details that are likely to interest investors.
8. (a) Columbus includes monetary references to keep his financial supporters interested. (b) Two examples are the fruit he believes to be "valuable" and his wish to acquire gold from the island's king.
9. (a) Columbus describes a paradise where the landscape is beautiful and the people are friendly and helpful. (b) Three examples include the following: Columbus describes the land as beautiful and fertile; the melody of the birds is exquisite; the natives are timid but delighted with the Europeans' trinkets.
10. A natural scientist's observations of the island's landscape would be more precise and detailed.

EXTEND/ASSESS

Answers

❶ Vocabulary Lesson

Word Analysis

1. Things that can be described as "conflicting" clash or strike against each other.
2. *Inflict* means to strike with something that causes pain.
3. Someone with an affliction is stricken with an illness or injury that causes suffering.

Spelling Strategy

1. acquaint
2. question, query, quiz
3. quench

Vocabulary Builder

1. b
2. a
3. b
4. c

❷ Grammar and Style Lesson

1. linking; linking
2. action
3. linking
4. action; action
5. action

Writing Application

Students should discover that action verbs make writing more lively and that linking verbs make it less so.

WG Writing and Grammar, Ruby Level

Students will find further instruction and practice on action and linking verbs in Chapter 17, Section 2.

Build Language Skills

❶ Vocabulary Lesson

Word Analysis: Latin Root *-flict-*

Words like *afflict, conflict,* and *inflict* build on the Latin root *-flict-*, meaning "to strike." The following words contain the root *-flict-*. Using the definitions, explain how the root contributes to the meaning of each word.

1. *conflicting:* fighting; battling
2. *inflict:* to give or cause pain
3. *affliction:* the condition of pain or suffering

Spelling Strategy

In some words, like *exquisite,* the *kw* sound is spelled with *qu*. Using the definitions below, write *qu* words that have the *kw* sound.

1. to familiarize yourself with
2. to ask
3. to satisfy thirst

Vocabulary Builder: Synonyms

Study the list of vocabulary words on page 59. Then, review each item below. In your notebook, write the letter of the synonym, or word that is closest in meaning, for the first word.

1. indication: **(a)** delight, **(b)** sign, **(c)** value, **(d)** contradiction, **(e)** pride
2. abundance: **(a)** overflow, **(b)** dearth, **(c)** preservation, **(d)** generosity, **(e)** anger
3. exquisite: **(a)** shocking, **(b)** beautiful, **(c)** sorrowful, **(d)** trustworthiness, **(e)** shoddy
4. affliction: **(a)** extension, **(b)** magnificence, **(c)** trouble, **(d)** institution, **(e)** perspective

❷ Grammar and Style Lesson

Action and Linking Verbs

Action verbs like *anchored, found,* and *saw* express physical or mental action.

Linking verbs such as *be, become,* and *look* express a state of being. Linking verbs are followed by a noun or pronoun that renames the subject or by an adjective that describes it.

Action Verbs: We *arrived* at a cape off the island.
The island *exceeds* the others in beauty.

Linking Verbs: Groves of trees *are* abundant.
Everything *looked* green.

Practice Indicate whether the italicized words are action or linking verbs.

1. I *am* very certain that they *are* all valuable.
2. Presently, we *saw* several of the natives. . .
3. This other island they *name* Bosio.
4. I *ordered* more glass beads to be given them and they *promised* to return the next day.
5. They *call* the island Colba.

Writing Application Write two descriptive paragraphs—one using only linking verbs and the other using only action verbs. Compare and contrast the different effects.

WG Prentice Hall Writing and Grammar Connection: Chapter 17, Section 2

Assessment Practice

Summarizing Written Texts

(For more practice, see *Standardized Test Preparation Workbook*, p. 1.)

Have students practice identifying the best summary of a passage.

In forging the agreement, Columbus had negotiated favorable terms. In addition to funding, he asked for and received the right to rule any lands he conquered. He would also be entitled to 10 percent of all wealth from those lands.

Which is the best summary of this passage?

A The agreement would make Columbus wealthy.
B Columbus expected to be a ruler.
C Columbus made an agreement that would bring him both wealth and the right to rule.
D Columbus was not only an explorer, but also was a shrewd politician.

Choice *C* is correct. Responses *A* and *B* contain accurate information but are incomplete. Choice *D* is an opinion.

Writing Lesson

Oral Report on the Voyage

Columbus's funding depended on his ability to sell his experiences to an audience of readers who had not seen the lands he explored. Imitating Columbus's writing style, write an oral report that you would give to the king and queen of Spain upon your return to Europe.

Prewriting Imagine the landscape of the island Columbus visited. List the tropical sights, sounds, textures, smells, and tastes that he may have encountered.

Drafting As you describe the island, elaborate by including as many sensory details as you can. Instead of telling how lovely the island is, describe what you see, hear, feel, touch, or smell. Strive to imitate Columbus's style by choosing ornate words.

Model: Elaborating for Vividness

As we sailed the ocean, the sun sparkled on the water like translucent prisms of color. Yonder, we could see the different shades of lush, green foliage on the beach surrounded by many flowers of every hue.

Sensory details such as *translucent prisms of color* and *different shades of lush, green foliage* help readers imagine what they have never experienced.

Revising Add details to strengthen your images. Add smells to descriptions that appeal only to sight and sound; consider adding details about texture or taste where appropriate.

WG *Prentice Hall Writing and Grammar Connection: Chapter 8, Section 2*

Extend Your Learning

Listening and Speaking Many Native American cultures have strong artistic traditions. For a **humanities presentation,** find pictures of Native American art forms, and compare them to European art from the same time period.

- Consider art, music, and dance.
- Determine the historical influences on the cultures.

Share your analysis with your class, including samples of the art you discuss.

Research and Technology With a group, use online newspapers and databases to research Columbus's presence in today's world. Create a **chart** of parks and public places named after him. Present your findings to the class. **[Group Activity]**

For: An additional research activity
Visit: www.PHSchool.com
Web Code: erd-7103

3 Writing L[...]

- To guide students i[...] descriptive essay for a[...] give them the **Support f[...] Lesson** page (*Unit 1 Resour[...]* p. 51).
- Students' oral reports should be written in Columbus's formal style and should contain a wealth of sensory details about the tropical landscape.
- Remind students to keep their audience and purpose in mind as they write. In other words, each sentence should appeal to their readers' interests and sensibilities about what is beautiful, interesting, beneficial, and profitable about this place.
- As they write and practice delivering their oral reports, students might find it helpful to imagine the king and queen of Spain sitting in the room and listening to their words.
- Use the Descriptive Essay rubrics in *General Resources*, pp. 63–64 to evaluate students' oral reports.

4 Research and Technology

- You might encourage various groups to focus attention on different geographical areas. For instance, one group might research Columbus's presence within a fifty-mile radius of your school. Another group could research a neighboring county, state, or large city.
- The **Support for Extend Your Learning** page (*Unit 1 Resources,* p. 52) provides guided note-taking opportunities to help students complete the Extend Your Learning activities.

Go Online Research Have students type in the Web Code for another research activity.

Assessment Resources

The following resources can be used to assess students' knowledge and skills.

Unit 1 Resources

Selection Test A, pp. 54–56
Selection Test B, pp. 57–59

General Resources

Rubrics for Descriptive Essay, pp. 63–64

Go Online Assessment Students may use the **Self-test** to prepare for **Selection Test A** or **Selection Test B.**

point of
l relations.
vely with
cussion.

Background

The fighting that Rowlandson mentions was part of the conflict known as King Phillip's War. King Philip's War was the most savage of any war in American history, in proportion to the population. One of every sixteen men of fighting age were killed, in addition to the many men, women and children who died of starvation or exposure as a result of being kidnapped. Such a tremendous loss of life was a threat to the continued survival of New England. The war also brought the economy to the edge of disaster, costing nearly a hundred thousand pounds and destroying half the towns in the colony.

Critical Viewing

Answer: It suggests that King Philip was of high status and well respected.

Captivity Narratives: Colonial Bestsellers

Tensions were high in the Massachusetts Bay Colony near the end of the seventeenth century. The once-friendly relations between the peaceful Wampanoag tribe and English settlers had broken down. By the 1670s, colonial troops were driving the Wampanoag from their land. As the winter of 1676 approached, the Wampanoag were in desperate need of food, and they were angered by an attack on Wampanoag Indians in Rhode Island the previous December.

The Town Falls On February 10, 1676, a group of Wampanoag Indians stormed the English frontier settlement of Lancaster, Massachusetts. Most of Lancaster's leaders were in Boston, seeking help in their struggle with the Indians from the royal governor. When gunshots rang out that morning, the settlement was virtually unguarded.

Mary Rowlandson, a minister's wife, huddled in her house and watched as friends and family were cut down by gunfire. "The attack was launched not by human contestants in a struggle for land and power but by wolves . . . ," Rowlandson later wrote. In all, twenty colonists were

> *"The attack was launched not by human contestants in a struggle for land and power but by wolves."*

killed and twenty-four were taken captive, including Rowlandson and her son and daughter.

Thus began Rowlandson's three-month odyssey among the Wampanoag Indians. In May, Rowlandson and her children were ransomed back to her husband. After their release, she wrote an account of her captivity. The book, which has come to be called *A Narrative of the Captivity,* was originally published with a much longer title: *The Soveraignty & Goodness of God, Together with the Faithfulness of His Promises Displayed; Being a Narrative of the Captivity and Restauration of Mrs. Mary Rowlandson.* It was the first American bestseller written by a woman.

Rowlandson's book was so successful it spawned dozens of imitations. These other captivity narratives were largely fictional, though they claimed to be true. Immensely popular, they portrayed Native Americans as brutal savages, contributing to a stereotype that persisted for hundreds of years.

A Different Culture Ironically, though Rowlandson's book offered a one-sided and often negative view of Native Americans, her observations helped explain Indian culture to colonists. Native Americans had a rich

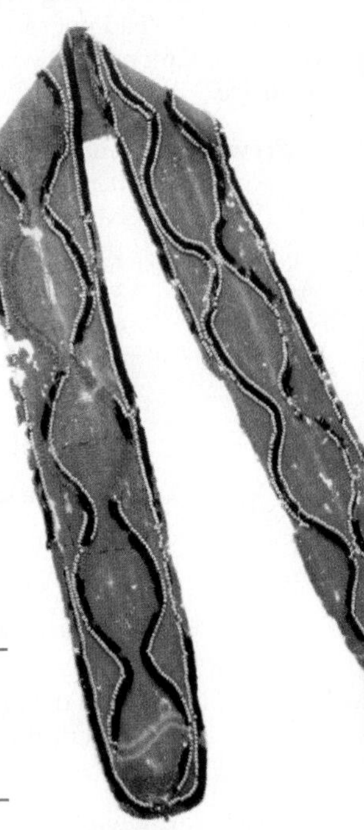

▲ **Critical Viewing**
What does the beautiful bead work and design of this sash belonging to Wampanoag leader King Philip suggest about his status in his society? **[Interpret]**

Enrichment

The Last of the Mohicans

The captivity narrative probably reached its literary high point in 1826 with the publication of *The Last of the Mohicans,* an adventure story by American novelist James Fenimore Cooper. Although it is a work of fiction, it includes all the ingredients that made Mary Rowlandson's narrative so popular—the clash between natural and civilized man, danger, battle, hairbreadth escapes, heroes, and villains.

The Last of the Mohicans is set in 1757, during the French and Indian wars. Two English girls, Alice and Cora Munro, are captured by Delaware and Huron tribes. Cora is eventually killed during the battle between the Indians and the rescue party.

Cooper portrays a variety of Indian personalities in his novel. Several of them are heroic, and even Magua, the Huron villain, wins the reader's sympathy as he speaks of the white man's greed and cruelty. Although all his characters seem clichéd to modern eyes, Cooper marks a turning point in the literary depiction of the Native American. Scholars consider Cooper America's first great social critic.

oral tradition, but they had no literary tradition. In most Native American communities, designated storytellers learned all the tales that served as a repository for their tribe's traditions, history, and religious beliefs. They also chose and trained their successors. One break in the cycle between generations, and these stories—and the worldview they depicted—could vanish completely.

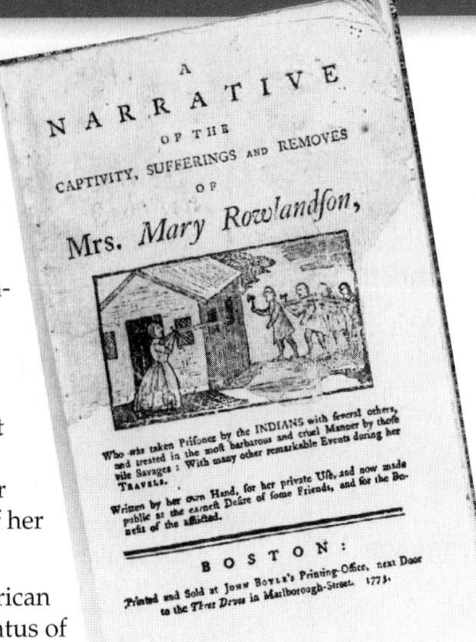

A NARRATIVE OF THE CAPTIVITY, SUFFERINGS AND REMOVES OF Mrs. *Mary Rowlandson*,

Who was taken Prisoner by the INDIANS with several others, and treated in the most barbarous and cruel Manner by those vile Savages: With many other remarkable Events during her TRAVELS.

Written by her own Hand, for her private Use, and now made public at the earnest Desire of some Friends, and for the Benefit of the afflicted.

BOSTON:

Printed and Sold at JOHN BOYLE's Printing-Office, next Door to the *Three Doves* in Marlborough-Street. 1773.

Rowlandson's narrative gave Europeans their first peek into Native American beliefs. She tells of the Indians' struggle for survival—how they ate beaver, foraged for wild foods, and built rafts to cross rivers. Rowlandson describes how she knitted and sewed in exchange for food and asserted herself to receive better treatment. Some of the Indians were kind to her. She calls one of her captors her "best friend." Another found a Bible to comfort her.

Eventually, Rowlandson came to respect aspects of Native American culture. She admired their reverence for their elders, the high status of their women, and their sense of community. She also noted details about Indian social hierarchy and government, reporting how the Indians credited their chief, or *sachem*, with great authority, but also used a "General Court to consult and determine."

Rowlandson died in 1711. The Wampanoag, meanwhile, came close to extinction. By the summer of 1676, most of their warriors had been killed and their families sold into slavery. By the nineteenth century, the U.S. government abolished the tribe as a legal entity. Still, efforts were made to maintain Wampanoag traditions. Today, Rhode Island's Native American community has managed to preserve much of the tribe's culture, history, and language.

▲ **Critical Viewing**
What details on this early edition of Mary Rowlandson's book would be regarded as one-sided or inflammatory today? **[Analyze]**

Activity

Popular Entertainment

The captivity narratives of colonial times have their counterpart in many of today's reality-based books, television shows, and movies. With a group, discuss the ways in which real people and events are transformed by television and other media into entertainment. Use these questions to guide your discussion:

- Do you think it is appropriate that real people and events are often turned into entertainment? Should certain people and situations be off-limits? Explain.
- How "real" do you think most reality-based entertainment is? Does everyone in your group agree? Why or why not?

Choose a point person to share your group's views with the class.

the subtitle, the illustration, and the phrases "barbarous and cruel" and "vile savages" below the illustration are all inflammatory.

Critical Thinking

1. Why do you think captivity narratives were so popular in early America?
   Answer: They were exciting stories. People enjoyed them for the adventure and suspense. The church approved their publication for their improving moral aspects, so people could buy and read them openly even if they weren't reading them for their instructive qualities.
2. Why do you think Mary Rowlandson chose to write about her experience?
   Possible answers: She was traumatized by the kidnapping and wrote the book as a form of therapy. She wanted to make some money. The book's original title suggests that she wanted to use her experience to preach to her readers.

Activity

Form students into groups. Be sure that the point person in each group takes notes from the discussion, writing down opinions and why each person feels the way he or she does. Students might also discuss why some reality-based programs are popular while others are not.

Meeting Your Standards

Students will

1. **analyze and respond to literary elements.**
   - Literary Analysis: Narrative Accounts
2. **read, comprehend, analyze, and critique nonfiction.**
   - Reading Strategy: Breaking Down Sentences
   - Reading Check questions
   - Apply the Skills questions
   - Assessment Practice (ATE)
3. **develop vocabulary.**
   - Vocabulary Lesson: Related Forms of *peril*
4. **understand and apply written and oral language conventions.**
   - Spelling Strategy
   - Grammar and Style Lesson: Singular and Plural Possessive Nouns
5. **develop writing proficiency.**
   - Writing Lesson: Comparison of Narratives
6. **develop appropriate research strategies.**
   - Extend Your Learning: Historic Menu
7. **understand and apply listening and speaking strategies.**
   - Extend Your Learning: Persuasive Speech

Block Scheduling: Use one 90-minute class period to preteach the skills and have students read the selection. Use a second 90-minute class period to assess students' mastery of skills, extend their learning, and monitor their progress.

Homework Suggestions

Following are possibilities for homework assignments.

- Support pages from *Unit 1 Resources.*
  Literary Analysis
  Reading Strategy
  Vocabulary Builder
  Grammar and Style
- An Extend Your Learning project and the Writing Lesson for this selection group may be completed over several days.

Step-by-Step Teaching Guide	Pacing Guide
PRETEACH	
• Administer Vocabulary and Reading Warm-ups as necessary.	5 min.
• Engage students' interest with the motivation activity.	5 min.
• Read and discuss author and background features. **FT**	10 min.
• Introduce the Literary Analysis Skill: Narrative Accounts. **FT**	5 min.
• Introduce the Reading Strategy: Breaking Down Sentences. **FT**	10 min.
• Prepare students to read by teaching the selection vocabulary. **FT**	
TEACH	
• Informally monitor comprehension while students read independently or in groups. **FT**	30 min.
• Monitor students' comprehension with the Reading Check notes.	as students read
• Reinforce vocabulary with Vocabulary Builder notes.	as students read
• Develop students' understanding of narrative accounts with the Literary Analysis annotations. **FT**	5 min.
• Develop students' ability to break down sentences with the Reading Strategy annotations. **FT**	5 min.
ASSESS/EXTEND	
• Assess students' comprehension and mastery of the Literary Analysis and Reading Strategy by having them answer the Apply the Skills questions. **FT**	15 min.
• Have students complete the Vocabulary Development Lesson and the Grammar and Style Lesson. **FT**	15 min.
• Apply students' ability to use clear organization by using the Writing Lesson. **FT**	45 min. or homework
• Apply students' understanding by using one or more of the Extend Your Learning activities.	20–90 min. or homework
• Administer Selection Test A or Selection Test B. **FT**	15 min.

Resources

PRINT

Unit 1 Resources

- Vocabulary Warm-up Word Lists [**L1, L2, EL**] .... p. 60
- Vocabulary Warm-up Practice [**L1, L2, EL**] .... p. 61
- Reading Warm-up A [**L1, L2, EL**] .... p. 62
- Reading Warm-up B [**L1, L2, L3**] .... p. 63

TRANSPARENCY

Graphic Organizer Transparencies

- Literary Analysis Graphic Organizer A [**L3**] .... p. 15
- Literary Analysis Graphic Organizer B [**L1, L2, EL**] .... p. 16
- Reading Strategy Graphic Organizer A [**L3**] .... p. 13
- Reading Strategy Graphic Organizer B [**L1, L2, EL**] .... p. 14

PRINT

Reader's Notebook [L2]
Reader's Notebook: Adapted Version [L1]
Reader's Notebook: English Learner's Version [EL]

Unit 1 Resources

- Literary Analysis [**L3**] .... p. 64
- Reading Strategy [**L3**] .... p. 65
- Vocabulary Builder [**L3**] .... p. 66

TECHNOLOGY

Listening to Literature Audio CDs [L2, EL]
Reader's Notebook: Adapted Version Audio CD [L2, EL]

PRINT

Unit 1 Resources

- Grammar and Style [**L3**] .... p. 67
- Support for Writing Lesson [**L3**] .... p. 68
- Support for Extend Your Learning [**L3**] .... p. 69
- Enrichment [**L4**] .... p. 70
- Selection Test A [**L1, L2, EL**] .... pp. 71–73
- Selection Test B [**L3, L4**] .... pp. 74–76

General Resources

- Rubrics for Comparison-and-Contrast Essay [**L3**] .... pp. 69–70

TECHNOLOGY

Go Online: Research [**L3**]
Go Online: Self-test [**L3**]
***ExamView*® Test Bank** [**L3**]

Choosing Resources for Differentiated Instruction

[**L1**] Special Needs Students
[**L2**] Below-Level Students
[**L3**] All Students
[**L4**] Advanced Students
[**EL**] English Learners

FT Fast Track Instruction: To move the lesson more quickly, use the strategies and activities identified with **FT**.

Scaffolding for Less Proficient and Advanced Students

The leveled Critical Thinking questions after selections progress in the levels of thinking required to answer them. To address the needs of your different students, you may use the (a) level questions for your less proficient students and the (b) level questions with your on-level and advanced students. The occasional (c) level questions are appropriate for your advanced students.

PRENTICE HALL **TeacherEXPRESS**™ Plan · Teach · Assess Use this complete suite of powerful teaching tools to make lesson planning and testing quicker and easier.

Use the interactive textbook (online and on CD-ROM) to make selections and activities come alive with audio and video support and interactive questions.

PRETEACH

Motivation

Write the following "Help Wanted" advertisement on the chalkboard:

> Wanted: Leader capable of governing people in life-threatening crisis. Ability to mediate disputes and maintain order in the face of chaos; good interpersonal and communication skills essential. Community outreach efforts require overcoming language and cultural barriers. Basic bookkeeping, homebuilding, farming, trading, and political skills a must. Salary cannot be guaranteed; no job security.

Ask students whether they would apply for this job and discuss their reactions to the description. Then, tell students that the two narratives they are about to read were written by men whose lives were the inspiration for this advertisement.

❶ Background

More About the Authors

John Smith's expedition to America in 1607 was financed by wealthy English people who expected to profit from whaling and gold. However, the only objects of value that Smith and his fellow explorers netted were furs and fish for trade. While the trip's sponsors may have been disappointed, Smith conceived of the newly charted land (from Maine to Cape Cod) as an English colony.

Orphaned in the first year of life, William Bradford was trained by relatives to be a farmer. Receiving little formal education, he was forced to educate himself. Although *Of Plymouth Plantation* was not published until more than two hundred years after it was written, the book was known to the public (and even quoted by colonial historians) long before 1856.

Build Skills | *Primary Sources*

❶ *from* The General History of Virginia • *from* Of Plymouth Plantation

John Smith (1580–1631)

If John Smith were alive today, he would probably be starring opposite Arnold Schwarzenegger in blockbuster adventure films—at least, that might be where he would see himself. Adventurer, poet, mapmaker, and egotist are just a few of the labels that apply to Smith, who earned a reputation as one of England's most famous explorers by helping to lead the first successful English colony in America. Stories of his adventures, often embellished by his own pen, fascinated readers of his day and continue to provide details about the early exploration of the Americas.

Smith and a group of colonists landed in Virginia in 1607 and founded Jamestown. As president of the colony from 1608 to 1609, Smith helped to obtain food, enforce discipline, and deal with the local Native Americans. Although Smith returned to England in 1609, he made two more voyages to America and, in 1614, explored what he called New England. Using his skills as a mapmaker to chart his course, Smith mapped out the coast from Penobscot Bay, Maine, to Cape Cod, Massachusetts.

On a second voyage to further carve out new and chartered lands, Smith found himself in the dangerous company of pirates who held him against his will. Although Smith managed to escape, he returned to England without any money. In 1617, he made one final colonizing effort, but his ship was held back by wind gusts that lasted three months. After that, he never had a chance to set sail. Smith published several works in the course of his life, including *The General History of Virginia, New England,* and the *Summer Isles* (1624).

William Bradford (1590–1657)

Survival in North America was a matter of endurance, intelligence, and courage. William Bradford had all three. Thirteen years after the first permanent English settlement was established in Jamestown, Virginia, Bradford helped lead the Pilgrims to what is now Massachusetts.

Seeking Freedom Bradford, who was born in Yorkshire, England, joined a group of Puritans who believed that the Church of England was corrupt. This group wished to separate from the church. In the face of stiff persecution, they eventually fled to Holland and from there sailed to North America. In *Of Plymouth Plantation,* Bradford provides an account of the experiences of these early settlers. Historians consider this account to be accurate.

A Long Leadership After the death of the colony's first leader, the Pilgrims elected William Bradford governor. He was reelected thirty times. During his tenure, he organized the repayment of debts to financial backers, encouraged new immigration, and established good relations with the Native Americans, without whose help the colony never would have survived. He also instituted the town meeting within the colonies, a democratic process that continues to take place in state government today. Bradford was largely responsible for leading the infant colony through many hardships to success.

In 1630, Bradford began writing *Of Plymouth Plantation,* a firsthand account of the Pilgrims' struggle to endure, sustained only by courage and unbending faith. The work, written in the simple language known as Puritan Plain Style, was not published until 1856.

Preview

Connecting to the Literature

You may remember a point in your life when you kept going even when everything seemed to be going against you. Consider the difficulties the early American colonists faced when they fought against all odds in their determination to cross the ocean and find a new homeland.

Literary Analysis

Narrative Accounts

Narrative accounts tell the story of real-life events. Some historical narratives, including these, are firsthand accounts by people who lived through significant historic events. Others are secondhand accounts, written by people who researched the events but did not experience them. In the following passage, John Smith provides a firsthand description.

> From May to September, those that escaped lived upon sturgeon and sea crabs. Fifty in this time we buried. . . .

Because of the writer's personal involvement, firsthand accounts are sometimes subjective, expressing the writer's opinions and perhaps even bias.

Comparing Literary Works

John Smith and the settlers at Jamestown came to the New World in search of wealth. In contrast, Bradford and the Pilgrims sought religious freedom. As you read, compare and contrast the experiences of the two groups, and note how their different purposes are reflected.

Reading Strategy

Breaking Down Sentences

You can analyze meaning by **breaking down sentences** and considering one section at a time. Look at a complex sentence, and separate its essential parts (the *who* and *what*) from the difficult language until you get to the main idea. As you read, use a diagram like the one shown to help you analyze and interpret the meaning of complex sentences.

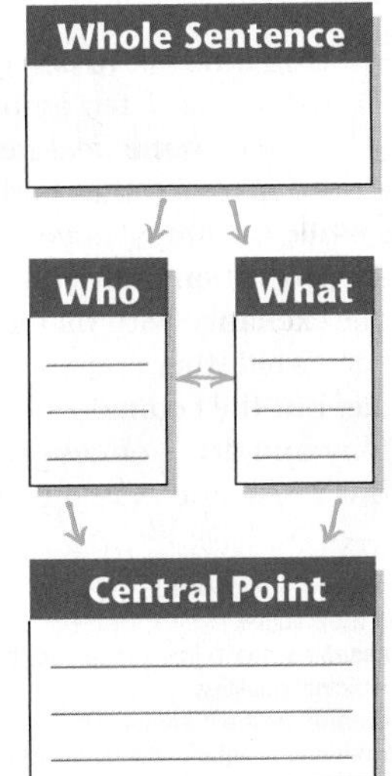

Vocabulary Builder

pilfer (pil′ fər) *v.* steal (p. 70)

palisades (pal′ ə sādz′) *n.* large, pointed stakes set in the ground to form a fence used for defense (p. 71)

conceits (kən sēts′) *n.* strange or fanciful ideas (p. 71)

mollified (mäl′ ə fīd′) *v.* soothed; calmed (p. 74)

peril (per′əl) *n.* danger (p. 76)

loath (lōth) *adj.* reluctant; unwilling (p. 76)

sundry (sun′ drē) *adj.* various; different (p. 77)

recompense (rek′ əm pens′) *n.* reward; repayment (p. 80)

feigned (fānd) *adj.* pretended; sham (p. 83)

2 Literary Analysis
Narrative Accounts

- Tell students that they will focus on narrative accounts as they read the two prose selections in this lesson.
- Read aloud together the instruction about narrative accounts.
- With students, review the differences between firsthand and secondhand accounts.
- Clarify for students that although Smith's is a firsthand account, he chooses to refer to himself in the third person, as "Captain Smith." Explain that this convention was commonly used by those keeping narrative records about explorations or other group ventures.
- Invite students to look for evidence of subjectivity in the works of John Smith and William Bradford.

3 Reading Strategy
Breaking Down Sentences

- Explain that most long or complicated sentences can be broken into sections or clauses. Analyzing each section individually can help readers distinguish the writer's main ideas from less crucial details.
- Point out that punctuation can guide students to logical places to break sentences for analysis.
- Remind students to look for signal words that indicate relationships among the ideas in various parts of a sentence.
- Give students a copy of **Reading Strategy Graphic Organizer A,** p. 13 in ***Graphic Organizer Transparencies.*** Tell them to fill in the graphic organizer with information from a complex sentence.

Vocabulary Builder

- Pronounce each vocabulary word for students, and read the definitions as a class. Have students identify any words with which they are already familiar.

Differentiated Instruction Solutions for All Learners

Support for Special Needs Students
Have students read the adapted version of the excerpt from *The General History of Virginia* in the ***Reader's Notebook: Adapted Version.*** This version provides basic-level instruction in an interactive format with questions and write-on lines. Completing these pages will prepare students to read the selection in the Student Edition.

Support for Less Proficient Readers
Have students read the excerpt from *The General History of Virginia* in the ***Reader's Notebook.*** This version provides basic-level instruction in an interactive format with questions and write-on lines. After students finish the selection in the ***Reader's Notebook,*** have them complete the questions and activities in the Student Edition.

Support for English Learners
Have students read the excerpt from *The General History of Virginia* in the ***Reader's Notebook: English Learner's Version.*** This version provides basic-level instruction in an interactive format with questions and write-on lines. Completing these pages will prepare students to read the selection in the Student Edition.

Learning Modalities
Interpersonal Learners As students begin to read William Bradford's narrative (which follows John Smith's), have them form pairs to discuss the issues potentially hostile neighbors must work out to survive when living in such close proximity. Encourage students to consider the difficulties each party will face in such asituation.

❶ About the Selection

In this excerpt from *The General History of Virginia,* John Smith describes the rough beginning of the founding of Jamestown Colony. He emphasizes the ordeal the Europeans experienced in crossing the ocean, the struggle to find nourishment, and the challenge of living side by side with the Native Americans. The narrative, which contains the romantic tale of Smith's rescue by Pocahontas, is not always historically accurate, as it strives to present the writer's deeds in a favorable light. It is, however, a firsthand account of a significant event and provides a rare look at the life of a historical figure written in his own words.

❷ Critical Viewing

Possible response: Both the image and the text suggest the extreme exhaustion and despair of the Jamestown settlers.

❶ *from* The General History of Virginia

John Smith

The First Day at Jamestown, 14th May 1607, from "The Romance and Tragedy of Pioneer Life" by Augustus L. Mason, 1883, William Ludlow Sheppard/Bridgeman Art Library, London/New York

What Happened Till the First Supply

Being thus left to our fortunes, it fortuned[1] that within ten days, scarce ten amongst us could either go[2] or well stand, such extreme weakness and sickness oppressed us. And thereat none need marvel if they consider the cause and reason, which was this: While the ships stayed, our allowance was somewhat bettered by a daily proportion of biscuit which the sailors would pilfer to sell, give, or exchange with us for money, sassafras,[3] or furs. But when they departed, there remained neither tavern, beer house, nor place of relief but the common kettle.[4] Had we been as free from all sins as gluttony and drunkenness we might have been canonized for saints, but our President[5] would never have been admitted for engrossing to

❷ ▲ **Critical Viewing**
Contrast the feeling this image evokes with the details of the first sentence of Smith's account. **[Connect]**

Vocabulary Builder
pilfer (pil′ fər) *v.* steal

1. **fortuned** *v.* happened.
2. **go** *v.* be active.
3. **sassafras** (sas′ ə fras′) *n.* a tree, the root of which was valued for its supposed medicinal qualities.
4. **common kettle** communal cooking pot.
5. **President** Wingfield, the leader of the colony.

Differentiated Instruction Solutions for All Learners

Accessibility at a Glance

	from The General History	*from* Of Plymouth Plantation
Context	Historical	Historical
Language	Difficult vocabulary; long sentences, complex syntax	Complex sentence structure; long sentences
Concept Level	Accessible (description of ocean voyage and founding of colony)	Accessible (description of settlement development)
Literary Merit	Primary Source	Primary Source
Lexile	1490	1400
Overall Rating	More challenging	More challenging

his private,[6] oatmeal, sack,[7] oil, aqua vitae,[8] beef, eggs, or what not but the kettle; that indeed he allowed equally to be distributed, and that was half a pint of wheat and as much barley boiled with water for a man a day, and this, having fried some twenty-six weeks in the ship's hold, contained as many worms as grains so that we might truly call it rather so much bran than corn; our drink was water, our lodgings castles in the air.

With this lodging and diet, our extreme toil in bearing and planting palisades so strained and bruised us and our continual labor in the extremity of the heat had so weakened us, as were cause sufficient to have made us as miserable in our native country or any other place in the world.

From May to September, those that escaped lived upon sturgeon and sea crabs. Fifty in this time we buried; the rest seeing the President's projects to escape these miseries in our pinnace[9] by flight (who all this time had neither felt want nor sickness) so moved our dead spirits as we deposed him and established Ratcliffe in his place . . .

But now was all our provision spent, the sturgeon gone, all helps abandoned, each hour expecting the fury of the savages; when God, the
3 patron of all good endeavors, in that desperate extremity so changed the hearts of the savages that they brought such plenty of their fruits and provision as no man wanted.

And now where some affirmed it was ill done of the Council[10] to send forth men so badly provided, this incontradictable reason will show them plainly they are too ill advised to nourish such ill conceits: First, the fault of our going was our own; what could be thought fitting or necessary we had, but what we should find, or want, or where we should be, we were all ignorant and supposing to make our passage in two months, with victual to live and the advantage of the spring to work; we were at sea five months where we both spent our victual and lost the opportunity of the time and season to plant, by the unskillful presumption of our ignorant transporters that understood not at all what they undertook.

Such actions have ever since the world's beginning been subject to such accidents, and everything of worth is found full of difficulties, but nothing so difficult as to establish a commonwealth so far remote from men and means and where men's minds are so untoward[11] as neither do well themselves nor suffer others. But to proceed.

The new President and Martin, being little beloved, of weak judgment in dangers, and less industry in peace, committed the managing of all things abroad[12] to Captain Smith, who, by his own example,

6. **engrossing to his private** taking for his own use.
7. **sack** *n.* type of white wine.
8. **aqua vitae** (ak′ wə vī′ tə) brandy.
9. **pinnace** (pin′ is) *n.* small sailing ship.
10. **Council** the seven persons in charge of the expedition.
11. **untoward** *adj.* stubborn.
12. **abroad** *adv.* outside the palisades.

Vocabulary Builder
palisades (pal′ ə sādz′) *n.* large, pointed stakes set in the ground to form a fence used for defense

Reading Strategy
Breaking Down Sentences
In the long sentence beginning "But now" there is an important turn of events. Break the sentence down to understand its meaning.

Vocabulary Builder
conceits (kən sētz′) *n.* strange or fanciful ideas

4 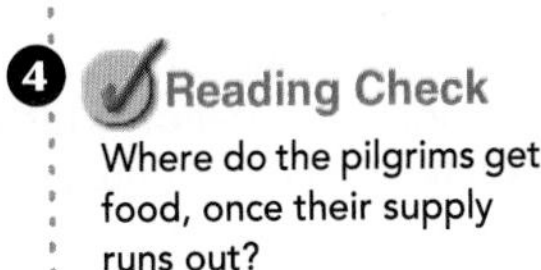

Where do the pilgrims get food, once their supply runs out?

3 Reading Strategy
Breaking Down Sentences

- Have two or three student volunteers take turns reading the sentence aloud.
- Write the entire sentence, with punctuation, on the chalkboard.
- Then, **ask** students the Reading Strategy feature: Break the sentence down to understand its meaning.
  Answer: If necessary, help students see that a natural break occurs after the semicolon, that *the patron of all good endeavors* is an appositive referring to *God,* that *in that desperate extremity* refers to the situation described in the first part of the sentence, and that the writer attributes the change in the hearts of the Native Americans to God. This change prompts them to bring food to the settlers.

4 Reading Check
Answer: The Pilgrims receive gifts of food from the Native Americans.

Differentiated Instruction
Solutions for All Learners

Support for Special Needs Students
Encourage students to follow the written text as they listen to a recording of Smith's narrative. Stop the recording after each paragraph, discuss the topics Smith covers, reread the paragraph aloud with students, and then analyze the text sentence by sentence, so that students can distinguish main ideas.

Enrichment for Gifted/Talented Students
The London Trading Company was the financial backer of the Jamestown expedition. It operated the settlement as a private venture from 1607 to 1624. The company expected to acquire land and eventually to export produce that could not be grown at home, such as tobacco. Unfortunately, the men who went to Jamestown were unfit for the task. Have students prepare a written or oral report on the fate of Jamestown, expanding on the history of the settlement.

5 Humanities

Founding of the First Permanent English Settlement in America, c. 19th century, by Asa Coolidge Warren

The engraving illustrates the moment when Pocahontas, Powhatan's daughter, came to the rescue of the English captive, John Smith.

1. Imagine that you were present at the scene depicted here. How would you describe it?
   Answer: Students' answers can include the looks of surprise and confusion many express, the eagerness of the young men to do Smith harm, and the body language of those in the scene.
2. The engraving describes Smith's account of the incident. Do you believe it happened this way? Did it happen at all?
   Answer: Students will have differing opinions about the accuracy of Smith's account; they should be prepared to explain the reasoning behind their answers.

6 Critical Viewing

Answer: Students may respond that the artist views Native Americans as dangerous because some are shown armed and hostile. Other students may point out that Pocahontas and the other women show compassion.

7 Literary Analysis

Narrative Accounts

- **Ask** a student volunteer to read aloud this paragraph, as other students listen carefully for loaded words that indicate the author's bias toward Native Americans.
- **Ask** students the Literary Analysis question: Which words in this paragraph alert you to the fact that Smith's account is not completely objective?
  Answer: Smith's use of the terms *barbarians* and *savages* indicates that his account is not completely objective. You may wish to engage students in a discussion of Europeans' general lack of understanding of Native American cultures.

5

Founding of the First Permanent English Settlement in America, A. C. Warren, New York Public Library

good words, and fair promises, set some to mow, others to bind thatch, 6 some to build houses, others to thatch them, himself always bearing the greatest task for his own share, so that in short time he provided most of them lodgings, neglecting any for himself. . . .

Leading an expedition on the Chickahominy River, Captain Smith and his men are attacked by Indians, and Smith is taken prisoner.

When this news came to Jamestown, much was their sorrow for his loss, few expecting what ensued.

7 Six or seven weeks those barbarians kept him prisoner, many strange triumphs and conjurations they made of him, yet he so demeaned himself amongst them, as he not only diverted them from surprising the fort, but procured his own liberty, and got himself and his company such estimation amongst them, that those savages admired him.

▲ Critical Viewing What can you infer about the artist's attitude toward Native Americans from the way he depicts them? **[Infer]**

Literary Analysis
Narrative Accounts Which words in this paragraph alert you to the fact that Smith's account is not completely objective?

Enrichment

North American Colonies

In the early settling of North America there were four frontiers, or boundaries of settlement: the Spanish, French, English, and Dutch. There were Spanish settlements in present-day Florida and in the Southwest. The French settled in Quebec and explored the interior by sailing down the Mississippi River. The English hugged a narrow strip along the East Coast. In addition to frontiers in Jamestown, Virginia, and in Plymouth, Massachusetts, the English established colonies in Pennsylvania and in South Carolina. The Dutch briefly had settlements in New York.

You may wish to have some students conduct independent research to find a firsthand historical narrative describing life in a settlement other than Jamestown or Plymouth. Have them compare that narrative, in style and content, to those by Smith and Bradford.

The manner how they used and delivered him is as followeth:

The savages having drawn from George Cassen whither Captain
Smith was gone, prosecuting that opportunity they followed him with
three hundred bowmen, conducted by the King of Pamunkee,[13] who in
8 divisions searching the turnings of the river found Robinson and Emry
by the fireside; those they shot full of arrows and slew. Then finding the
Captain, as is said, that used the savage that was his guide as his
shield (three of them being slain and divers[14] others so galled),[15] all the
rest would not come near him. Thinking thus to have returned to his
boat, regarding them, as he marched, more than his way, slipped up to
the middle in an oozy creek and his savage with him; yet dared they not
come to him till being near dead with cold he threw away his arms.
9 Then according to their compositions[16] they drew him forth and led
him to the fire where his men were slain. Diligently they chafed his
benumbed limbs.

He demanding for their captain, they showed him Opechancanough,
King of Pamunkee, to whom he gave a round ivory double compass
dial. Much they marveled at the playing of the fly and needle,[17] which
they could see so plainly and yet not touch it because of the glass
that covered them. But when he demonstrated by that globe-like
jewel the roundness of the earth and skies, the sphere of the sun,
moon, and stars, and how the sun did chase the night round about
10 the world continually, the greatness of the land and sea, the diversity
of nations, variety of complexions, and how we were to them
antipodes[18] and many other such like matters, they all stood as
amazed with admiration.

Nothwithstanding, within an hour after, they tied him to a tree, and as many as could stand about him prepared to shoot him, but the King holding up the compass in his hand, they all laid down their bows and arrows and in a triumphant manner led him to Orapaks where he was after their manner kindly feasted and well used. . . .

At last they brought him to Werowocomoco, where was Powhatan, their Emperor. Here more than two hundred of those grim courtiers stood wondering at him, as he had been a monster, till Powhatan and his train had put themselves in their greatest braveries. Before a fire upon a seat like a bedstead, he sat covered with a great robe made of raccoon skins and all the tails hanging by. On either hand did sit a young wench of sixteen or eighteen years and along on each side the house, two rows of men and behind them as many women, with all their heads and shoulders painted red, many of their heads bedecked

13. Pamunkee Pamunkee River.
14. divers (dī′ vərz) *adj.* several.
15. galled *v.* wounded.
16. compositions *n.* ways.
17. fly and needle *n.* parts of a compass.
18. antipodes (an tip′ ə dēz′) *n.* two places on opposite sides of the Earth.

Reading Strategy
Breaking Down Sentences
Analyze the first sentence in this paragraph to determine who was killed.

Literary Analysis
Narrative Accounts
How does Smith portray himself in this description?

11 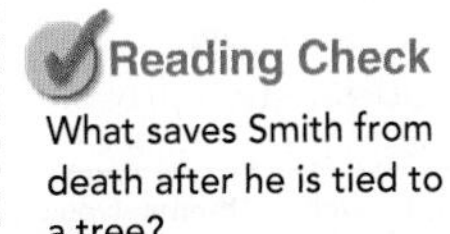
Reading Check
What saves Smith from death after he is tied to a tree?

8 Reading Strategy
Breaking Down Sentences

- Have students analyze this long sentence by distinguishing these individuals or groups: the "savages," Cassen, Smith, three hundred bowmen led by the King of Pamunkee, and the pair "Robinson and Emry."
- After students have clarified that the Native Americans have left Cassen in search of Smith and in the process discover Robinson and Emry, **ask** them who is killed.
  Answer: Robinson and Emry are killed.

9 Critical Thinking
Speculate

- Read aloud this passage with students. Invite a student volunteer to recall Smith's descriptions of the Native Americans during the first weeks of his captivity.
- Then, **ask** students to explain why the Native Americans let Smith live yet killed the others in his party.
  Answer: Students might respond that they respect Smith for being a leader or that they are impressed by the way he defends himself.

10 Literary Analysis
Narrative Accounts

- Focus students' attention on the long sentence that ends the paragraph. As you read it aloud, invite students to visualize the scene between Smith and the Native Americans.

Monitor Progress: Then, **ask** students the Literary Analysis question: How does Smith portray himself in this description?
Answer: Smith portrays himself as an intelligent, sophisticated authority in the process of dazzling the Native Americans with his knowledge.

11 Reading Check

Answer: The King of Pamunkee holds Smith's compass in the air, and this gesture causes the other Native Americans to put down their bows and arrows.

⓬ Literature in Context
Pocahontas

In 1609, after relations between the Virginian settlers and the Powhatan tribe had floundered, Pocahontas was kidnapped by the Virginian settlers under Captain Samuel Argall in the hope of using her to negotiate peace with the Powhatan. During her captivity Pocahontas not only converted to Christianity, but also fell in love with a settler named John Rolfe. Her father agreed to their marriage, and she was renamed and baptized Lady Rebecca. After returning to England with her husband and giving birth to a son, she died of smallpox in 1617.

Connect to the Literature Tell students that historians must question the validity of the information presented in a primary source.
Possible answers: What motivated Pocahontas to involve herself in the situation? What was the status of women and children within the tribe? What was the status of the King within the tribe? How did the tribe make decisions? Why would Pocahontas's wishes take precedence over the King's?

⓭ Literary Analysis
Narrative Accounts

- Encourage students to be alert for words naming or describing Native Americans (*Powhatan, more like a devil than a man, some two hundred more as black as himself*).
- **Ask** students the Literary Analysis question: What do you notice about the writer's attitudes toward people who are different from Europeans?
  Answer: When he is not mortally afraid of them, Smith seems to view Native Americans as curiosities.

with the white down of birds, but every one with something, and a great chain of white beads about their necks.

At his entrance before the King, all the people gave a great shout. The queen of Appomattoc was appointed to bring him water to wash his hands, and another brought him a bunch of feathers, instead of a towel, to dry them; having feasted him after their best barbarous manner they could, a long consultation was held, but the conclusion was, two great stones were brought before Powhatan: then as many as could, laid hands on him, dragged him to them, and thereon laid his head and being ready with their clubs to beat out his brains, Pocahontas,♦ the King's dearest daughter, when no entreaty could prevail, got his head in her arms and laid her own upon his to save him from death; whereat the Emperor was contented he should live to make him hatchets, and her bells, beads, and copper, for they thought him as well of all occupations as themselves.[19] For the King himself will make his own robes, shoes, bows, arrows, pots; plant, hunt, or do anything so well as the rest.

Two days after, Powhatan, having disguised himself in the most fearfulest manner he could, caused Captain Smith to be brought forth to a great house in the woods and there upon a mat by the fire to be left alone. Not long after, from behind a mat that divided the house, was made the most dolefulest noise he ever heard; then Powhatan more like a devil than a man, with some two hundred more as black as himself, came unto him and told him now they were friends, and presently he should go to Jamestown to send him two great guns and a grindstone for which he would give him the country of Capahowasic and forever esteem him as his son Nantaquond.

⓭ So to Jamestown with twelve guides Powhatan sent him. That night they quartered in the woods, he still expecting (as he had done all this long time of his imprisonment) every hour to be put to one death or other, for all their feasting. But almighty God (by His divine providence) had mollified the hearts of those stern barbarians with compassion. The next morning betimes they came to the fort, where Smith having used the savages with what kindness he could, he showed Rawhunt, Powhatan's trusty servant, two demiculverins[20] and a millstone to carry Powhatan; they found them somewhat too heavy, but when they did see him discharge them, being loaded with stones, among the boughs of a great tree loaded with icicles, the ice and branches came so tumbling down that the poor savages ran away half dead with fear. But at last we regained some conference with them and gave them such toys and sent to Powhatan, his women, and children such presents as gave them in general full content.

---

19. **as well . . . themselves** capable of making them just as well as they could themselves.
20. **demiculverins** (dem′ ē kul′ vər inz) large cannons.

⓬ Social Studies Connection

♦ ***Pocahontas***

There has been much speculation about Pocahontas and John Smith. Smith's story of Pocahontas raises questions because of his relationship with her and because there is no other documentation that substantiates his account.

In early accounts of his capture, Smith never mentions that Pocahontas is only twelve or thirteen years old. He was twenty-eight at the time. In addition, Smith also speaks of other similar adventures with admiring women, leading historians to question the accuracy of his account of Pocahontas.

Connect to the Literature

What questions would you ask to evaluate the accuracy of *The General History of Virginia?*

Vocabulary Builder

mollified (mäl′ ə fīd′) *v.* soothed; calmed

Literary Analysis

Narrative Accounts What do you notice about the writer's attitudes toward people who are different from Europeans?

14 Now in Jamestown they were all in combustion,[21] the strongest preparing once more to run away with the pinnace; which, with the hazard of his life, with saker falcon[22] and musket shot, Smith forced now the third time to stay or sink.

Some, no better than they should be, had plotted with the President the next day to have him put to death by the Levitical law,[23] for the lives of Robinson and Emry; pretending the fault was his that had led them to their ends: but he quickly took such order with such lawyers that he laid them by their heels till he sent some of them prisoners for England.

Now every once in four or five days, Pocahontas with her attendants brought him so much provision that saved many of their lives, that else for all this had starved with hunger.

His relation of the plenty he had seen, especially at Werowocomoco, and of the state and bounty of Powhatan (which till that time was unknown), so revived their dead spirits (especially the love of Pocahontas) as all men's fear was abandoned.

Thus you may see what difficulties still crossed any good endeavor; and the good success of the business being thus oft brought to the very period of destruction; yet you see by what strange means God hath still delivered it.

21. **combustion** (kəm bus′ chən) *n.* tumult.
22. **saker falcon** small cannon.
23. **Levitical law** "He that killeth man shall surely be put to death" (Leviticus 24:17).

Reading Strategy
Breaking Down Sentences Break down the long sentence beginning "Now in Jamestown" to interpret its meaning.

Critical Reading

1. **Respond:** If you faced a situation similar to Smith's, would you have returned to England at the earliest opportunity or stayed on at Jamestown? Why?
2. **(a) Recall:** Give one example of the way Smith praises his own good qualities. **(b) Infer:** What impression of Smith do you get from this account?
3. **(a) Recall:** What words does Smith use when he refers to himself? **(b) Draw Conclusions:** Why do you think he does this?
4. **(a) Interpret:** What is Smith's attitude toward the Native Americans? **(b) Analyze:** Do you think Smith's attitude changes after he gets to know them and they help him? Explain.
5. **Evaluate:** Do you think Smith's account is accurate? Why or why not?
6. **Take a Position:** Do you admire Smith? Why or why not?

For: More about John Smith
Visit: www.PHSchool.com
Web Code: ere-9106

14 Reading Strategy
Breaking Down Sentences

- Write the sentence on the chalkboard, and have several volunteers read it aloud as you divide it into sections.
- Mark natural division points with slashes after the words *combustion* and *pinnace.* Then, use parentheses to separate *with the hazard of his life, with saker falcon and musket shot* from surrounding words.

ASSESS

Answers

1. Some students may point out that the voyage back to England might well have been just as dangerous as staying in Jamestown.
2. (a) Examples include *Captain Smith, who, by his own good example, good words, and fair promises, set some to mow, others to bind thatch . . . himself always bearing the greatest task for his own share. . . .* (b) Smith seems to think very well of himself and to be a resourceful, capable, and influential man.
3. (a) Smith uses the third person and refers to himself with the proper noun *Captain Smith* and the pronouns *he, him,* and *his.* (b) Smith may do this to distance himself from the writing and to make it seem less subjective.
4. (a) He calls them barbarians and savages but also observes that they can be kind. (b) His attitude doesn't appear to change dramatically, though he acknowledges the charitable acts of Pocahontas.
5. Students may suspect that Smith embellished and exaggerated some of his adventures.
6. Students should support their positions with solid reasons, examples, and details from Smith's narrative.

Go Online Author Link For additional information about John Smith, have students type in the Web Code, then select S from the alphabet, and then select John Smith.

Differentiated Instruction Solutions for All Learners

Strategy for Special Needs Students
Help students clarify the purpose and implications of the trip to Jamestown by having them make a graphic representation of the deal suggested by Powhatan. Have students write the names Powhatan and Smith on opposite sides of a sheet of paper. Using images or words, they can then show that Powhatan wants "two great guns and a grindstone"; in return he will give Smith "the country of Capahowasic" and his everlasting "esteem."

Enrichment for Gifted/Talented Students
Encourage students to write short poems that capture the spirit of Smith's narrative using his language and tone. Prompt them to include descriptions and details that convey Smith's personality and the overall mood of his account. Have students share their poems when they finish. Do the poems reflect similar impressions of Smith?

15 About the Selection

William Bradford presents a firsthand description of the initial experiences of the Massachusetts settlers known to us as the Pilgrims. Historians consider this to be a factually accurate account. Bradford relates how this community of families, united in their goals and religious beliefs, begins the task of building a new settlement in the harsh wilderness. His account reflects religious faith, which he credits for the settlers' peaceful, beneficial relationship with their Native American neighbors.

16 Reading Strategy

Breaking Down Sentences

- Point out to students that Bradford's style is notable for its clarity. Despite the considerable length and apparent complexity of some sentences, students will probably find his prose easier to follow than John Smith's.
- Help students break down the sentence into sections. Draw students' attention to signal words (such as *after, and,* and *which*) that indicate relationships among ideas and events.

17 Vocabulary Builder

Word Analysis: Related Forms of *Peril*

- Point out the word *peril* in the text, and let students know the word means "danger."
- **Ask** students to volunteer forms of the word such as *perilous* and *imperiled,* and write sentences using the words on the chalkboard.
  Possible answers: *Had the Pilgrims known of the* perils *associated with their voyage, they might have planned differently.*

  The greatest peril *that Captain John Smith encountered was probably being imprisoned by angry Native Americans.*

  History shows that most perilous *element of settling the Americans was disease rather than violence.*

from

15 Of Plymouth Plantation

William Bradford

Background In 1620, the Pilgrims made the difficult voyage to America aboard the tiny *Mayflower.* After fierce storms and the loss of lives, the Pilgrims landed near Cape Cod, Massachusetts, not in Virginia as intended. It was mid-December before they could build shelters and move ashore. Once ashore, the Pilgrims found the hardships of settling in a strange land worsened by a harsh winter. They struggled to make a new life in America.

from Chapter 9

Of Their Voyage and How They Passed the Sea; and of Their Safe Arrival at Cape Cod

16 [1620] SEPTEMBER 6 . . . After they[1] had enjoyed fair winds and weather for a season, they were encountered many times with crosswinds, and met with many fierce storms, with which the ship was shrewdly[2] shaken, and her upper works made very leaky; and one of the main beams in the mid ships was bowed and cracked, which put them in some fear that the ship could not be able to perform the voyage. So some of the chief of the company, perceiving the mariners to fear the 17 sufficiency of the ship, as appeared by their mutterings, they entered into serious consultation with the master and other officers of the ship, to consider in time of the danger; and rather to return then to cast themselves into a desperate and inevitable peril. And truly there was great distraction and difference of opinion amongst the mariners themselves; fain[3] would they do what could be done for their wages' sake (being now half the seas over), and on the other hand they were loath to hazard their lives too desperately. But in examining of all opinions, the master and others affirmed they knew the ship to be strong and firm under water; and for the buckling of the main beam, there was a great

Reading Strategy
Breaking Down Sentences
To better comprehend its meaning, break down the first sentence of this account.

Vocabulary Builder
peril (per′ əl) *n.* danger

loath (lōth) *adj.* reluctant; unwilling

1. **they** Even though Bradford is one of the Pilgrims, he refers to them in the third person.
2. **shrewdly** (shro͞od′ lē) *adv.* severely.
3. **fain** (fān) *adv.* gladly.

Enrichment

Immigrants in America

The Pilgrims and the Jamestown colonists needed great fortitude to succeed in the New World. Discuss with students the idea that today's immigrants to the United States face their own (and different) kinds of hardships. Have groups discuss the opportunities and challenges that greet today's newcomers to America. These include overcoming language barriers, securing housing and jobs, dealing with different cultural traditions, facing discrimination, and adjusting to life in a new place.

Have students compare and contrast the obstacles described by Smith and Bradford with the obstacles immigrants face today. Ask students to suggest and list the skills and strengths people must possess to overcome these difficulties. Some students may have firsthand knowledge of such as challenge. Invite any willing students to share personal or family experiences with you and their classmates.

iron screw the passengers brought out of Holland, which would raise the beam into his place; the which being done, the carpenter and master affirmed that with a post under it, set firm in the lower deck, and other ways bound, he would make it sufficient. And as for the decks and upper works, they would caulk them as well as they could, and though with the working of the ship they would not long keep staunch,[4] yet there would otherwise be no great danger, if they did not over-press her with sails. So they committed themselves to the will of God, and resolved to proceed.

In sundry of these storms the winds were so fierce, and the seas so high, as they could not bear a knot of sail, but were forced to hull,[5] for diverse day together. And in one of them, as they thus lay at hull, in a mighty storm, a lusty[6] young man (called John Howland) coming upon some occasion above the gratings, was, with a seele[7] of the ship thrown into [the sea]; but it pleased God that he caught hold of the topsail halyards,[8] which hung overboard, and ran out at length; yet he held his hold (though he was sundry fathoms under water) till he was held

4. **staunch** (stônch) *adj.* watertight.
5. **hull** *v.* drift with the wind.
6. **lusty** *adj.* strong; hearty.
7. **seele** *n.* rolling; pitching to one side.
8. **halyards** (hal′ yərdz) *n.* ropes for raising or lowering sails.

Vocabulary Builder
sundry (sun′ drē) *adj.* various; different

20 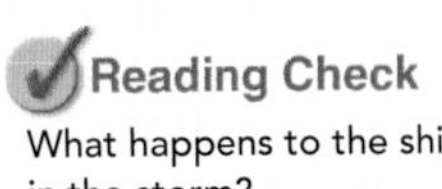 **Reading Check**
What happens to the ship in the storm?

19 **▼ Critical Viewing**
Is this an idealized or a realistic depiction of the *Mayflower's* Atlantic crossing? Explain your decision. **[Judge; Support]**

18

The Coming of the Mayflower, N. C. Wyeth, from the Collection of Metropolitan Life Insurance Company, New York City, photograph by Malcolm Varon

18 Humanities

The Coming of the Mayflower by N. C. Wyeth

Wyeth (1882–1945) was a prolific American illustrator. His work appeared with many popular and well-known works of literature, and he also took up the difficult art of mural painting. Wyeth's last mural commission was a series of eight huge pieces that express the spirit and heritage of New England. *The Coming of the Mayflower* is one of this series. Wyeth died before completing the project, but his son, the artist Andrew Wyeth, and his son-in-law, John McCoy, finished the work for him. Use these questions for discussion:

1. What viewpoint does Wyeth use to lend drama to the scene?
   Possible response: The view is from land—perhaps the famous Plymouth Rock—toward which the ship appears to be headed. There is a sense of excitement and expectation.
2. Wind plays a key role in the first part of Bradford's account. How does Wyeth demonstrate the power of wind in this mural?
   Answer: Responses might point to the billowing sails, the listing ship, and the whitecaps in the choppy seas.

19 Critical Viewing

Answer: Students may respond that the colorful painting serves to glorify or romanticize the crossing because it does not portray the hardships endured by the ship's passengers. Others might say that the painting depicts realistically the rough seas the *Mayflower* faced.

20 Reading Check

Answer: The ship is shaken and damaged by the wind and seas: in addition to leaks, the ship sustains a crack in a main beam amidships.

Differentiated Instruction Solutions for All Learners

Background for Special Needs Students
Seeing a visual representation of the *Mayflower* will help students picture the repairs made to the ship. If possible, display a photograph, painting, or drawing of the *Mayflower,* the *Mayflower II,* or another similar vessel.

Enrichment for Gifted/Talented Students
Challenge students to write a scene that dramatizes Bradford's decision to document his experiences in writing. Encourage students to depict Bradford discussing the Pilgrims' experiences with Myles Standish. Remind students to use what they have learned about writing dialogue, and encourage students to perform (or at least to read) their scenes to the class.

21 Literature in Context
The Mayflower

Unfortunately, historians have been unable to locate any detailed description of the original *Mayflower*. The ship was intended to make the journey accompanied by a smaller ship, the *Speedwell,* but this vessel was forced to return to port in Southampton twice before finally being judged unseaworthy. Eventually, the *Mayflower* set off from England alone carrying some of the smaller ship's passengers and supplies.

Connect to the Literature
Encourage students to envision a rough ocean voyage in a small ship with no engines and no modern conveniences.
Possible answer: Bradford mentions cross winds and fierce storms that threatened to destroy the ship and caused some passengers to be tossed overboard. On a ship this size, the travelers might have faced problems and disease or hunger.

22 Literary Analysis
Narrative Accounts

- Ask students to distinguish the characteristics of firsthand and secondhand narratives. Make sure they recognize that firsthand accounts are written by participants and that secondhand accounts are written by people who did not witness events directly.

➤ **Monitor Progress: Ask** students this question: How does Bradford blur the line between firsthand and secondhand historical narrative?
Answer: Students can respond that Bradford blurs the line by using not only the pronoun *I* but also *they* and *them;* the former pronoun suggests a firsthand telling, and the latter two suggest a secondhand telling. Students may also point out that Bradford includes observations about how the sailors feel and inserts his own first-person comments in parentheses.

up by the same rope to the brim of the water, and then with a boat hook and other means got into the ship again, and his life saved; and though he was something ill with it, yet he lived many years after, and became a profitable member both in church and commonwealth. In all this voyage there died but one of the passengers, which was William Butten, a youth, servant to Samuel Fuller, when they drew near the coast.

But to omit other things (that I may be brief), after long beating at sea they fell with that land which is called Cape Cod; the which being made and certainly known to be it, they were not a little joyful. After some deliberation had amongst themselves and with the master of the ship, they tacked about[9] and resolved to stand for the southward (the wind and weather being fair) to find some place about Hudson's River for their habitation. But after they
22 had sailed that course about half the day, they fell amongst dangerous shoals[10] and roaring breakers, and they were so far entangled therewith as they conceived themselves in great danger; and the wind shrinking upon them withal,[11] they resolved to bear up again for the Cape, and thought themselves happy to get out of those dangers before night overtook them, as by God's providence they did. And the next day they got into the Cape harbor,[12] where they rid in safety. . . .

Being thus arrived in a good harbor and brought safe to land, they fell upon their knees and blessed the God of heaven, who had brought them over the vast and furious ocean, and delivered them from all the perils and miseries thereof, again to set their feet on the firm and stable earth, their proper element. . . .

But here I cannot but stay and make a pause, and stand half amazed at this poor people's present condition; and so I think will the reader too, when he well considers the same. Being thus passed the vast ocean, and a sea of troubles before in their preparation (as may be remembered by that which went before), they had now no friends to welcome them, nor inns to entertain or refresh their weather-beaten bodies, no houses or much less towns to repair to, to seek for succor.[13] It is recorded in Scripture[14] as a mercy to the apostle and his shipwrecked company, that the barbarians showed them no small kindness

Literature in Context

21 History Connection

The Mayflower

The *Mayflower* was the British ship on which 102 Pilgrims sailed from Southampton, England, to North America during September, October, and November of 1620. In November, the Pilgrims disembarked at the tip of Cape Cod. Shortly before Christmas, they moved to the more protected site of Plymouth, Massachusetts. According to historians' estimates, the square-rigged *Mayflower* probably measured about 90 feet long and weighed 180 tons.

Connect to the Literature

What details in *Of Plymouth Plantation* suggest the kinds of challenges the travelers faced on the journey? What other challenges do you think travelers might face on a ship this size?

The Mayflower in Plymouth Harbor, William Halsall, Burstein Collection

9. **tacked about** sailed back and forth so that the wind would hit the sails at the best angles.
10. **shoals** (shōlz) *n.* sandbars or shallow areas that are dangerous to navigate.
11. **withal** (with ôl′) *adv.* also.
12. **Cape harbor** now called Provincetown Harbor.
13. **succor** (suk′ ər) *n.* help; relief.
14. **Scripture** In Acts 27–28, when the Apostle Paul and a group of other Christians are shipwrecked on the island of Malta, they are treated kindly by the "barbarians" who live there.

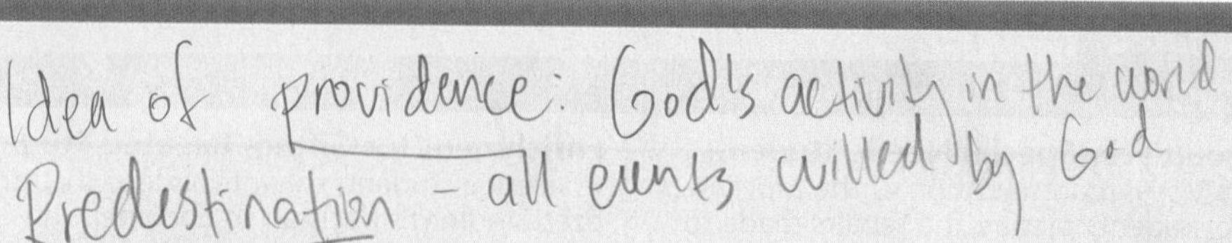
Idea of providence: God's activity in the world
Predestination - all events willed by God

in refreshing them, but these savage barbarians, when they met with them (as after will appear) were readier to fill their sides full of arrows then otherwise. And for the season it was winter, and they that know the winters of that country know them to be sharp and violent, and subject to cruel and fierce storms, dangerous to travel to known places, much more to search an unknown coast. Besides, what could they see but a hideous and desolate wilderness, full of wild beasts and wild men? And what multitudes there might be of them they knew not. . . . What could now sustain them but the spirit of God and his grace? May not and ought not the children of these fathers rightly say: *Our fathers were Englishmen which came over this great ocean, and were ready to perish in this wilderness;*[15] *but they cried unto the Lord, and He heard their voice, and looked on their adversity, etc.*[16] *Let them therefore praise the Lord, because He is good, and His mercies endure forever. . . .*

from Book 2[17]

[1620] In these hard and difficult beginnings, they found some discontents and murmurings arise amongst some, and mutinous speeches and carriages in others; but they were soon quelled and overcome by the wisdom, patience, and just and equal carriage of things by the Governor[18] and better part, which cleaved faithfully together in the main. But that which was most sad and lamentable was that in two or three months' time, half of their company died, especially in January and February, being the depth of winter, and wanting houses and other comforts; being infected with the scurvy[19] and other diseases, which this long voyage and their inaccommodate[20] condition had brought upon them; so as there died sometimes two or three of a day, in the foresaid time; that of one hundred and odd persons, scarce fifty remained.

23 And of these in the time of most distress, there was but six or seven sound persons, who, to their great commendations be it spoken, spared no pains, night nor day, but with abundance of toil and hazard of their own health, fetched them wood, made them fires, dressed them meat, made their beds, washed their loathsome clothes, clothed and unclothed them; in a word, did all the homely[21] and necessary offices for them which dainty and queasy stomachs cannot endure to hear named; and all this willingly and cheerfully, without any grudging in the least, showing herein their true love unto their friends and brethren. A rare example and worthy to be remembered. Two of these

15. **wilderness** Bradford is comparing the Pilgrims to the ancient Hebrews, who wandered in the desert after fleeing Egypt and before reaching the Promised Land.
16. **they cried . . . etc.** Bradford is paraphrasing a passage from the Hebrew Bible (Deuteronomy 26:7).
17. **Book 2** Here Bradford switches from chapter divisions to book divisions.
18. **Governor** John Carver (c. 1576–1621) was the first governor of Plymouth Colony but died during his first year of office. Bradford succeeded him as governor.
19. **scurvy** (skur′ vē) *n.* disease cause by a vitamin C deficiency.
20. **inaccommodate** (in′ ə käm′ ə dāt′) *adj.* unfit.
21. **homely** *adj.* domestic.

24 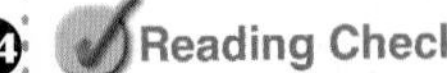
Reading Check
What did some of the pilgrims do to help those who become sick?

23 Critical Thinking
Synthesize

- **Ask** students how Bradford's description of the few who are not afflicted by disease reflects his moral values.
  Answer: Bradford admires the virtue of self-sacrifice that arises from their religious beliefs and sense of community.
- **Ask** students what Bradford wants his readers to think about these people. What does he hope his readers will gain from learning of this experience?
  Answer: Students may assert that the care and concern the Pilgrims exhibit is a function of their strong religious beliefs and of the powerful sense of community they share. Bradford wants his readers to understand how the settlers' faith influenced their behavior toward one another.

24 Reading Check

Answer: They fetched wood, made fires, prepared food, made beds, washed clothes, and cleaned.

Differentiated Instruction
Solutions for All Learners

Strategy for English Learners
Invite students to listen carefully as you read a sentence aloud in a way that accentuates its overall rhythms and structure. Then, work with students to break down the sentence into parts for better understanding. Seeing the sectioning of the sentence will help students. You might consider other visual aids, as well, such as color-coding a sentence's nouns and verbs or its subject and predicate.

Enrichment for Advanced Readers
Have students do research in order to create summaries of medical practices and other ways in which people cared for the sick in the early seventeenth century. Encourage students to share these summaries with the class in short oral presentations.

25 Literary Analysis
Narrative Accounts

- Have students identify the first sentence that indicates that the author was one of the Pilgrims struck down by illness.
- If necessary, draw students' attention to the sentence that begins, *Two of these seven.*
- **Ask** students the Literary Analysis question: Do you think Bradford's illness would have been included in a secondhand narrative account? Explain.
  Answer: Considering the many cases of extreme sickness in the colony, it is unlikely that a secondhand account would have included the minor incident Bradford describes.

26 Literary Analysis
Narrative Accounts

- Students may be surprised at the behavior described in this long paragraph. Tell students that less than half of the 102 passengers on the *Mayflower* were Pilgrims. Forty people were recruited in England without regard to religious beliefs; there were also eighteen servants and three hired workers. In all, there were fifty men, twenty women, and thirty-two children.
- **Ask** students the Literary Analysis question: What is revealed here about the Pilgrims' religious beliefs?
  Answer: Students will observe that Bradford's narrative reveals that the Pilgrims believed in showing compassion even to those who did not share their religious convictions.

seven were Mr. William Brewster,[22] their reverend Elder, and Myles Standish,[23] their Captain and military commander, unto whom myself, and many others were much beholden in our low and sick condition. And yet the Lord so upheld these persons, as in this general calamity they were not at all infected either with sickness, or lameness. And what I have said of these, I may say of many others who died in this general visitation,[24] and others yet living, that whilst they had health, yea, or any strength continuing, they were not wanting to any that had need of them. And I doubt not but their recompense is with the Lord.

25 But I may not here pass by another remarkable passage not to be forgotten. As this calamity fell among the passengers that were to be left here to plant, and were hasted ashore and made to drink water, that the seamen might have the more beer, and one[25] in his sickness desiring but a small can of beer, it was answered that if he were their own father he should have none; the disease began to fall amongst them also, so as almost half of their company died before they went away, and many of their officers and lustiest men, as the boatswain, gunner, three quartermasters, the cook, and others. At which the master was something stricken and sent to the sick ashore and told the Governor he should send for beer for them that had need of it, though he drunk water homeward bound.

But now amongst his company there was far another kind of carriage[26] in this misery then amongst the passengers; for they that had been boon[27] companions in drinking and jollity in the time of their health and welfare began now to desert one another in this calamity, saying they would not hazard their lives for them, they should be infected by coming to help them in their cabins, and so, after they came to die by it, would do little or nothing for them, but if they died let them die. But such of the passengers as were yet aboard showed them what mercy they could, which made some of their hearts relent, as the boatswain (and some others), who was a proud young man, and would often curse and scoff at the passengers; but when he grew weak, they had 26 compassion on him and helped him; then he confessed he did not deserve it at their hands, he had abused them in word and deed. O! saith he, you, I now see, show your love like Christians indeed one to another, but we let one another lie and die like dogs. . . .

All this while the Indians came skulking about them, and would sometimes show themselves aloof of, but when any approached near them, they would run away. And once they stole away their tools where they had been at work, and were gone to dinner. But about the 16th of

Vocabulary Builder
recompense (rek′ əm pens′) *n.* reward; repayment

Literary Analysis
Narrative Accounts
Do you think Bradford's illness would have been included in a secondhand narrative account? Explain.

Literary Analysis
Narrative Accounts
What is revealed here about the Pilgrims' religious beliefs?

22. **William Brewster** (1567–1644) one of the Pilgrim leaders.
23. **Myles Standish** (c. 1584–1656) professional soldier hired by the Pilgrims to be their military advisor. He was not originally a Puritan but later became a member of the congregation.
24. **visitation** *n.* affliction.
25. **one** Bradford is referring to himself.
26. **carriage** *n.* behavior.
27. **boon** *adj.* close.

Enrichment

Living Museums

Restoration villages are specific kinds of museums where people in period clothing attempt to recreate history for modern-day visitors. Plymouth Plantation in Massachusetts (pictured on p. 81) is one such place. In this reconstructed colonial village, costumed guides use period tools and materials to demonstrate seventeenth-century farming, homemaking, and survival skills. They even speak as the Pilgrims did. The *Mayflower II,* a full-size replica of the original 96-foot-long vessel, is moored nearby.

Encourage students to gather information about Plymouth Plantation and the Mayflower II by contacting the Plymouth Area Chamber of Commerce. They also can learn more about restoration villages closer to their area. In either case, students can request bibliographical material and information about summer jobs available to those interested in American history.

March a certain Indian came boldly amongst them, and spoke to them in broken English, which they could well understand, but marveled at it. At length they understood by discourse with him that he was not of these parts, but belonged to the eastern parts, where some English ships came to fish, with whom he was acquainted, and could name sundry of them by their names, amongst whom he had got his language. He became profitable to them in acquainting them with many things concerning the state of the country in the east parts where he lived, which was afterwards profitable unto them; as also of the people here, of their names, number, and strength; of their situation and distance from this place, and who was chief amongst them. His name was Samoset;[28] he told them also of another Indian whose name was Squanto,[29] a native of this place, who had been in England and could speak better
28 English then himself. Being, after some time of entertainment and gifts, dismissed, a while after he came again, and 5 more with him, and they brought again all the tools that were stolen away before, and made way for the coming of their great sachem,[30] called Massasoit,[31] who, about four or five days after, came with the chief of his friends, and other

27 ▲ **Critical Viewing**
What can you learn about the lifestyle at Plymouth Plantation from this photograph of an authentic re-creation of the settlement? **[Infer]**

---

28. **Samoset** (sam′ ə set′) (d. 1655) a Pemaquid tribal chief from Maine.
29. **Squanto** (skwän′ tō) (d. 1622) a member of the Pawtuxet tribe who in 1614 had been kidnapped by an English sea captain and taken to Spain to be sold as a slave. He escaped and eventually returned to Massachusetts in 1619, only to find that his home village had been destroyed by plague.
30. **sachem** (sā′ chəm) chief.
31. **Massasoit** (mas′ ə soit′) (c. 1580–1661) the supreme sachem (chief) of the Wampanoag peoples.

Reading Check
Who is Samoset, and how do the Pilgrims meet him?

27 Critical Viewing

Answer: Students may respond that the photo indicates that life at the stark seaside plantation was hard. There is nothing lush or prosperous about the plain, unadorned buildings. Student responses should reflect the idea that the Pilgrims struggled to create a settlement within a rugged, unforgiving environment.

28 Background

Hisotry

English-speaking Squanto had been kidnapped by an English slave trader in 1615. When he finally returned to his people, the Patuxets, in 1619, he found that everyone had died of disease.

Massasoit (c. 1580–1661), one of the most powerful Native American leaders in New England, was chief of the Wampanoag Indians. He faithfully observed the 1621 treaty with the Pilgrims.

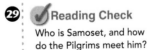

29 Reading Check

Answer: Samoset is an extraordinary Native American from lands east of Plymouth. He speaks basic English absorbed while living in the vicinity of European settlers. The Pilgrims meet Samoset after he approaches their settlement and addresses them.

Differentiated Instruction Solutions for All Learners

Vocabulary for English Learners

Pair students with more proficient English speakers to create picture cards for the key vocabulary words on these two pages. Students might illustrate and spell words such as *compassion, confess, companion, tools, gifts,* and *people.*

Enrichment for Gifted/Talented Students

Point out that readers of Bradford's text can gain a vivid sense of the time period and of the settlers' lives and can learn much about how they survived hardship and danger to start a new life in a new land. Encourage students as they read to put themselves in the place of a settler at Plymouth Plantation. After reading, have students write a diary page from the point of view of a settler.

30 Humanities

The First Thanksgiving at Plymouth, 1914 by Jennie A. Brownscombe

Jennie Brownscombe (1850–1936) was an American illustrator known for her detailed, nostalgic images. In fact, she has been called a kind of "Norman Rockwell" for her time. From a young age, Brownscombe earned a living creating illustrations for books, magazines, Christmas cards, and calendars. Her skillful presentation of images won her awards, and her work has been exhibited around the world.

- This famous, symbolic painting is known for providing an emotional image of what people across the United States have come to know as Thanksgiving. How does this painting echo Bradford's narrative? **Answer:** It shows the colonists at Plymouth as a community, and it portrays a peaceful gathering with Native Americans. The scene also appears to be very solemn, religious, and low-key—the same mood Bradford creates in his narrative.

31 Critical Viewing

Possible answer: Students may say that most of the items in the painting seem historically accurate, but the log cabin and the feather headdresses seem inaccurate.

32 Literary Analysis
Narrative Accounts

- Have a volunteer read aloud the excerpt's final paragraph.
- **Ask** students the Literary Analysis question: What does Bradford reveal about his religious beliefs in this description of Squanto as a "special instrument"? **Answer:** Students might note that Bradford's belief that God is an active, benevolent presence in the Pilgrim's daily lives.

30

attendance, with the aforesaid Squanto. With whom, after friendly entertainment, and some gifts given him, they made a peace with him (which hath now continued this 24 years)[32] in these terms:

1. That neither he nor any of his should injure or do hurt to any of their people.
2. That if any of his did any hurt to any of theirs, he should send the offender, that they might punish him.
3. That if anything were taken away from any of theirs, he should cause it to be restored; and they should do the like to his.
4. If any did unjustly war against him, they would aid him; if any did war against them, he should aid them.
5. He should send to his neighbors confederates, to certify them of this, that they might not wrong them, but might be likewise comprised in the conditions of peace.
6. That when their men came to them, they should leave their bows and arrows behind them.

32 After these things he returned to his place called Sowams,[33] some 40 mile from this place, but Squanto continued with them and was their interpreter, and was a special instrument sent of God for their good beyond their expectation. He directed them how to set their corn, where to take fish and to procure other commodities, and was also their pilot to bring them to unknown places for their profit, and never left them till he died. He was a native of this place, and scarce any left alive besides himself. He was carried away with diverse others by one

32. **now . . . 24 years** The treaty actually lasted until King Philip's War began in 1675.
33. **Sowams** (sō̆ ämz) present site of Warren, Rhode Island.

31 **Critical Viewing** Do you think this picture is an accurate representation of history? Why or Why not? **[Judge; Support]**

Literary Analysis
Narrative Accounts
What does Bradford reveal about his religious beliefs in this description of Squanto as a "special instrument"?

Hunt,[34] a master of a ship, who thought to sell them for slaves in Spain; but he got away for England and was entertained by a merchant in London and employed to Newfoundland and other parts, and lastly brought hither into these parts. . . .

[1621] . . . They began now to gather in the small harvest they had,[35] and to fit up their houses and dwellings against winter, being all well recovered in health and strength, and had all things in good plenty; for as some were thus employed in affairs abroad, others were exercised in fishing, about cod and bass and other fish, of which they took good store, of which every family had their portion. All the summer there was no want. And now began to come in store of fowl, as winter approached, of which this place did abound when they came first (but afterward decreased by degrees). And besides water fowl, there was great store of wild turkeys, of which they took many, besides venison, etc. Besides they had about a peck of meal a week to a person, or now since harvest, Indian corn to that proportion. Which made many afterwards write so largely of their plenty here to their friends in England, which were not feigned, but true reports.

Vocabulary Builder
feigned (fānd) *adj.* pretended; sham

34. **Hunt** Thomas Hunt was captain of one of the ships in John Smith's expedition (page 70).
35. **They . . . had** This section of Bradford's narrative is often titled "The First Thanksgiving."

Critical Reading

1. **Respond:** If you had been making the journey on the *Mayflower,* what would you have done to prepare for life in America?
2. **(a) Recall:** What were some of the hardships the Pilgrims faced during their trip across the Atlantic and their first winter at Plymouth? **(b) Interpret:** What do their troubles suggest about the climate and landscape of Plymouth?
3. **(a) Recall:** How do the Pilgrims explain Squanto's role in their experience? **(b) Interpret:** What does this explanation suggest about the Pilgrims' religious convictions?
4. **(a) Draw Conclusions:** What do you think is the message that Bradford tries to convey in this narrative? **(b) Apply:** How might the message have meaning for people today?
5. **Hypothesize:** In what ways might this account have been different if the Pilgrims had settled farther south?
6. **Evaluate:** How has this account changed your impression of the Pilgrims? Explain.

Go Online
Author Link
For: More about William Bradford
Visit: www.PHSchool.com
Web Code: ere-9107

ASSESS

Answers

1. Students' answers should show an understanding of the settlers' hardships.
2. (a) On the ocean, the Pilgrims encounter fierce storms and their ship falls into disrepair. During the first winter, they lack shelter, warmth, and food. Many Pilgrims suffer from scurvy or die of other illnesses. (b) These troubles suggest that Plymouth's climate is harsh and that its landscape is rugged and unyielding.
3. (a) Bradford suggests that Squanto was sent to the Pilgrims by God to help them survive and thrive in the new world. (b) It suggests that the Pilgrims believed they were being guided and protected by God.
4. (a) Students might say that Bradford wishes to convey the idea that the Pilgrims' perseverance, courage, and faith in God allowed them to surmount enormous odds and to make a new life in a new world. (b) The message is universal in its assertion that human beings' inner resources strongly affect what they are able to endure and accomplish.
5. Bradford might have been more able to focus on matters other than basic survival.
6. Students may not have realized how hard the Pilgrims had to struggle to establish themselves in the new world.

Go Online Author Link For additional information about William Bradford, have students type in the Web Code, then select B from the alphabet, and then select William Bradford.

Answers

1. Students should include specific textual references in their charts.
2. (a) Smith's purpose is to describe the settlement of Jamestown and to encourage others to join it. He also boasts about his own strength and cleverness. (b) Bradford wished to record a factual and modest account of the Pilgrims' experience. He wishes to credit God, rather than people, with the good things that happened to them.
3. Smith seems to find the Native Americans backward, ignorant, and dangerous. Bradford and the Pilgrims at first seem disapproving and curious about the Native Americans; later they befriend them and enjoy entertaining them.
4. Smith may have preferred that his financial backers see his deeds in the best possible light and shaped his account accordingly.
5. Students may say that Bradford may have seen the settler's hardships as a trial sent by God.
6. (a) Smith's account is in some ways the story of an individual because he repeatedly places himself in the foreground of the narrative; Bradford's sensibility seems more sober and wise, and his account has an authentic and authoritative ring. (b) Students may explain the difference by pointing to the authors' different motivations for writing: Smith seems interested in entertaining his readers and promoting his own heroism, and Bradford seems more interested in presenting the experience of the community.
7. Students should state opinions clearly and support ideas with examples from the texts.
8. Students should select appropriately complex or lengthy sentences and break them down into components that are more manageable or easily understood.
9. **Sample response:** Yes, at first strangers are usually apprehensive with one another. When they become familiar with one another, the fear and anxiety diminish.

Go Online Assessment Students may use the **Self-test** to prepare for **Selection Test A** or **Selection Test B**

Apply the Skills

from *The General History of Virginia* • from *Of Plymouth Plantation*

Literary Analysis

Narrative Accounts

1. Use a chart like the one shown to find examples of the key characteristics of **narrative accounts** in the selections.

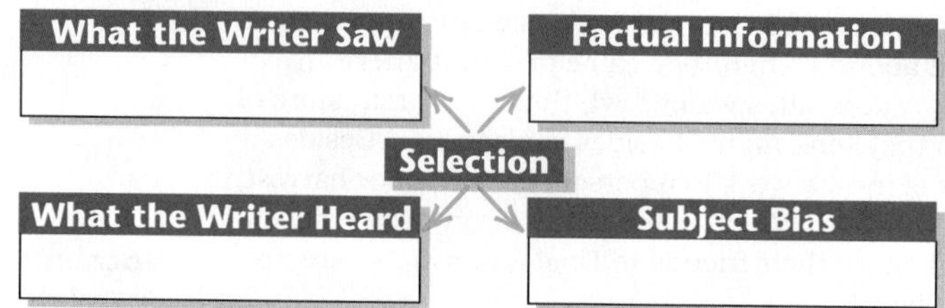

2. **(a)** What do you think Smith's purpose was in writing his narrative? **(b)** In what way was Bradford's purpose different?

Comparing Literary Works

3. Compare and contrast the relationship Smith and the Pilgrims had with the Native Americans.
4. In what way might political concerns have played a part in shaping John Smith's account of the Jamestown Colony's early days?
5. How might the Puritans' religious beliefs have influenced Bradford's account of the first experiences of the Massachusetts settlers?
6. **(a)** In what ways do the authors' presentations of events and the impressions they convey differ? **(b)** How do these differences reflect the purpose of each group's settlement?
7. Which account seems more reliable to you? Explain.

Reading Strategy

Breaking Down Sentences

8. Scan the narratives for three sentences that you found particularly challenging to interpret. Separating the complex language from the essential parts, analyze the sentences. Then, write the meaning of the sentences as you understand them.

Extend Understanding

9. **Social Studies Connection:** Do you feel that the changing attitudes of the settlers and the Native Americans reflect typical experiences with newcomers? Why or why not?

QuickReview

A **narrative account** is a story about real-life experiences.

Breaking down sentences into simpler parts helps to interpret the meaning of lengthy and difficult sentences.

For: Self-test
Visit: www.PHSchool.com
Web Code: era-6105

Build Language Skills

Vocabulary Lesson

Word Analysis: Related Forms of *Peril*

The word *peril* comes from the Latin word *periculum,* which means "danger." Using your knowledge of the base word, fill in each blank with the word that best completes the sentence.

a. perilous **b.** perilously **c.** imperiled

1. Undertaking the risky voyage ___?___ the Pilgrims' lives.
2. The ship tossed___?___ in the waves.
3. Building a new home in the wilderness was ___?___ as well.

Spelling Strategy

When you add *-ed* to a word that ends in the letters *-ify,* change the *y* to *i* before adding the suffix. For example, *mollify* becomes *mollified.* Write sentences using the past tense of each word.

1. pacify 2. modify 3. testify

Vocabulary Builder: Antonyms and Synonyms

Antonyms are words that have opposite meanings. **Synonyms** are words that have similar meanings. Decide whether the words in each of following pairs are antonyms or synonyms. Write *A* for *Antonym* or *S* for *Synonym.*

1. pilfer, donate
2. palisades, fences
3. conceits, fantasies
4. mollified, angered
5. peril, safety
6. loath, willing
7. sundry, single
8. recompense, reward
9. feigned, genuine

Grammar and Style Lesson

Singular and Plural Possessive Nouns

The **possessive** form of nouns indicates kinship and ownership. Add an apostrophe and *-s* to form the **possessive singular** of most nouns. Add an apostrophe to form the **possessive of plural** nouns that end in *-s* or *-es.*

Singular: The *passenger's* spirits were low.

Plural: The *passengers'* spirits were low.

Do not use an apostrophe for simple plurals that do not show possession. Do not add an extra *s* for the possessive of plural nouns ending in *-s.*

Practice Rewrite this paragraph, correcting any mistakes in italicized plurals or possessives.

> Much to *Bradfords* amazement, Samoset spoke to the *Pilgrims* in broken English. Samoset convinced his fellow *Indians'* to return the *settler's* tools. He persuaded Massasoit to pay his *respects* to the *Pilgrims* and introduced them to one of his *friend's,* Squanto.

Writing Application Write a paragraph about the Pilgrims' arrival in Plymouth, using at least five plural and possessive nouns.

WG Prentice Hall Writing and Grammar Connection: Chapter 27, Section 6

EXTEND

Answers

1 Vocabulary Lesson

Word Analysis

1. imperiled
2. perilously
3. perilous

Spelling Strategy

Possible responses:

1. Patting the baby's back pacified him.
2. The plan was modified so that my visiting sister could accompany us to dinner.
3. My friend testified in a criminal trial last week.

Vocabulary Builder

1. A
2. S
3. S
4. A
5. A
6. A
7. A
8. S
9. A

2 Grammar and Style Lesson

Much to Bradford's amazement, Samoset spoke to the Pilgrims in broken English. Samoset convinced his fellow Indians to return the settlers' tools. He persuaded Massasoit to pay his respects to the Pilgrims and introduced them to one of his friends, Squanto.

Writing Application

Students' paragraphs should convey a realistic sense of the Pilgrims' arrival and should correctly use at least five plural and possessive nouns.

WG Writing and Grammar, Ruby Level

Students will find further instruction and practice on singular and plural possessive nouns in Chapter 27, Section 6.

Assessment Practice

Supporting Details **(For more practice, see *Standardized Test Preparation Workbook*, p.5.)**

Many tests require students to recognize summaries by identifying main ideas and supporting details. Students should recognize which details are important to the main idea and which are not. Present the following sample test item:

> With this lodging and diet, our extreme toil in bearing and planting palisades so strained and bruised us and our continual labor in the extremity of the heat had so weakened us, as were cause sufficient to have made us so miserable in our native country or any other place in the world.

Which of the following does NOT support the main idea that early Virginians were miserable in their new country?

A They were weak from planting their crops.
B They had little food.
C The heat was extreme.
D They were in conflict with the local Native Americans.

All of these support the main idea EXCEPT choice *D*.

3 Writing Lesson

You may use this lesson as timed-writing practice, or you may allow students to develop it as a writing assignment over several days.

- To guide students in writing this comparison of narratives, give them the **Support for Writing Lesson** page (*Unit 1 Resources,* p. 68).
- Students' comparisons should analyze each narrative and discuss the similarities and differences between them.
- Regardless of which method of organization students choose to employ, their compositions should deal as thoroughly as possible with each writer's style, purpose, and level of objectivity.
- Use the Comparison-and-Contrast Essay rubrics in *General Resources,* pp. 69–70 to evaluate students' Comparisons of Narratives.

4 Research and Technology

- Encourage students to do research using traditional print sources (such as encyclopedias, biographies and journals, and social histories), as well as online resources.
- Students might also report on the ways in which the Pilgrims' dietary experiences in Virginia differed from those aboard the *Mayflower* and those in England.
- The **Support for Extend Your Learning** page (*Unit 1 Resources,* p. 69) provides guided note-taking opportunities to help students complete the Extend Your Learning activities.

Go Online Research Have students type in the Web Code for another research activity.

SAT® PREP ACT

3 Writing Lesson

Timed Writing: Comparison of Narratives

These narratives leave readers with the impression that Smith and Bradford held distinctly different outlooks on life. Compare these firsthand accounts. ***(40 minutes)***

Prewriting *(10 minutes)* Review the two narratives, noting each author's style, purpose, and objectivity. To help you gather and organize details, use a Venn diagram like the one shown.

Model: Gathering Details

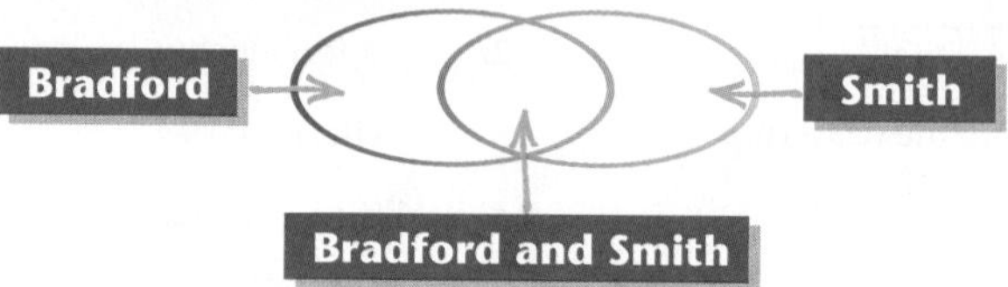

Drafting *(20 minutes)* To keep your ideas clear for readers, choose a method of organization. You might discuss each aspect of your subjects in turn. For example, you could discuss Smith's tone and immediately contrast it with Bradford's tone. Alternatively, you might discuss all the qualities of one subject and then all the qualities of the other.

Revising *(10 minutes)* To clarify your comparison and contrast, consider transitions, such as *similarly* and *equally, to compare* and *in contrast,* and *instead* and *to contrast.* Be sure your conclusion effectively reinforces your ideas.

WG *Prentice Hall Writing and Grammar Connection: Chapter 9, Section 3*

4 Extend Your Learning

Listening and Speaking As Samoset, deliver a **persuasive speech** to make the case for fostering peace between the settlers and your tribe. Make your speech dramatic and convincing. To prepare, consider these questions:

- What personal experiences can you relate?
- What events prove your point?
- What are your greatest concerns?

Organize and review your notes before presenting your speech to your class.

Research and Technology Many Pilgrims suffered from scurvy, a disease caused by a diet lacking in vitamin C. Research to learn about the foods the colonists ate and the crops they planted. Check the Internet or the library for colonial recipes. Then, plan a historically accurate **menu** for a typical day in the life of an early American colonist.

For: An additional research activity
Visit: www.PHSchool.com
Web Code: erd-7104

Assessment Resources

The following resources can be used to assess students' knowledge and skills.

Unit 1 Resources
- **Selection Test A,** pp. 71–73
- **Selection Test B,** pp. 74–76

General Resources
- **Rubrics for Exposition: Comparison-and-Contrast Essay,** pp. 69–70

Go Online Assessment Students may use the **Self-test** to prepare for **Selection Test A** or **Selection Test B.**

Reading Informational Materials

Web Sites

About Web Sites

A **Web site** is a collection of Web pages—text and graphics on a topic, accessible over the Internet through browser software. Each page has its own URL, or "address." Web sites feature underlined words and icons that serve as links to other sites or pages within that site. By clicking on these words, you can find more information.

The Web can be a wonderful tool. You can perform business transactions on the Web—for example, trading stocks or buying clothing. The Web also offers great ways to learn. Whether your interests are academic or recreational, you probably can locate several useful Web sites.

Reading Skill

Locating Appropriate Information

To get the most out of Internet research, learn how to locate appropriate information. Familiarize yourself with search engines on the Web. These services will list any page on the Web that contains text matching the search term that you type in. To use a search engine effectively, select search terms with care. For instance, if you are looking for information on the Puritans who settled in America, you might use the word *Pilgrim.* Too broad a term, such as *colony,* will produce a list that is unmanageably long and cluttered with irrelevant listings, such as pages on space colonies.

Even a focused search term may yield irrelevant results. To further narrow your search results, review the name of the sponsor that is listed on the search engine results page, along with the brief excerpt from the site. Before you search, you can eliminate sites in languages you do not speak and, depending on your requirements, personal home pages or commercial sites.

When you arrive at a Web site, you usually will find that it offers many features. The box at the right lists just a few. A home page is the "front door" of a Web site. It provides an overview of the site's information and features and allows a visitor to "navigate," or move to interior pages within the site. On the next page, you will find the home page of the Web site for Plimoth Plantation, a museum in Plymouth, Massachusetts, devoted to the colonial history of the town. On page 89 you will find an interior page that describes the re-created village at Plimoth Plantation.

Elements of Web Sites

- **Links, hotspotted text,** and other **navigation elements** help you move around the site quickly. Click on any area of the page over which your cursor changes to a hand, and you will be brought to a linked page.
- **A SEARCH function** helps you locate information anywhere on the site, using search terms.
- **Photos, videos, and audio clips** enrich many sites. You may need to download additional software to use these resources.
- **Links** connect you to other pages within the site and to other related Web sites.
- **Contact information** tells you who sponsored the site. An e-mail address to which you may send questions or comments may be included.

Meeting Your Standards

Students will

1. **locate appropriate information on a Web site.**
2. **learn how to read a home page.**

*See **Teacher Express™/Lesson View** for a detailed lesson plan for Reading Informational Materials.*

About Web Sites

- Write the term "Web sites" on the chalkboard. Have students share whatever they know about the different parts of a Web site. List specific terms such as "home page" and "URL" on the chalkboard as students mention them, and have students define these terms.
- **Ask** students to describe the kinds of information they find on specific Web sites they visit.
  Possible answers: Students might mention schedule information for sports teams or movies; historical information for research assignments; or the cost of an airline ticket.

Reading Strategy
Locating Appropriate Information

- Have students read and discuss the Reading Strategy information.
- **Ask** students to share strategies for locating Web sites. How do they narrow their searches?
- Make sure students understand the terms in the box labeled "Elements of Web Sites." If possible, demonstrate each term on an actual Web site in the classroom or the school library.

Differentiated Instruction Solutions for All Learners

Reading Support
Give students reading support with the appropriate version of the ***Reader's Notebooks:***

Reader's Notebook, **[L2, L3]**

Reader's Notebook, **[L1, L2]**

Reader's Notebook: English Learner's Version, **[EL]**

Reading Web Sites

- Before discussing home pages, you might have some students volunteer to print out a home page and bring it to class. Preview the home pages before using them as visual aids in class discussions.
- Make sure students understand what a home page is. Have them examine the model home page shown here, identifying icons or items about which they have questions. If students have brought in copies of more home pages, have students examine these as well.
- Challenge students to formulate questions about Plimoth Plantation and indicate which links on the home page might lead them to answers.
- **Ask** students to identify the type of information the links on the sample home page provide.
  Answer: Students should notice that the home page contains links to interior pages within the Web site, links to contact information about the site, photograph links to pages within the Web site, and other text links to informational pages.

continued on page 89

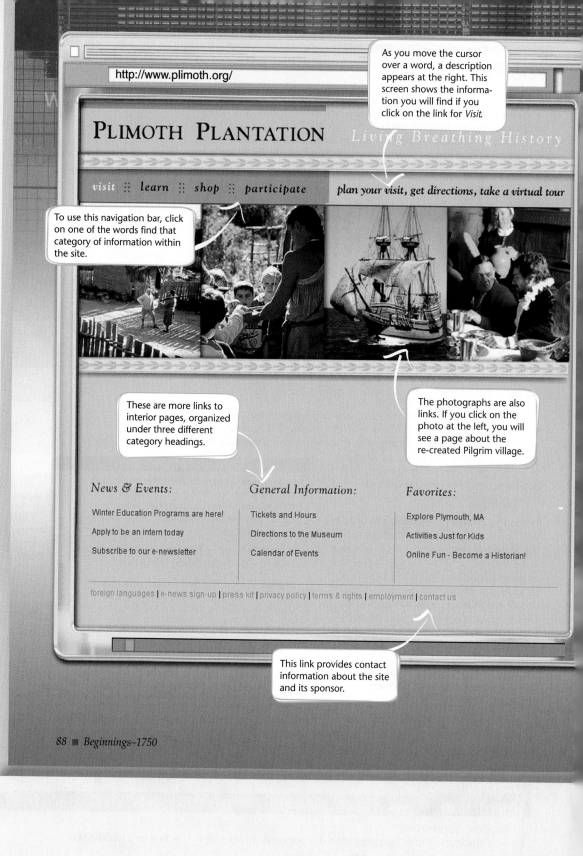

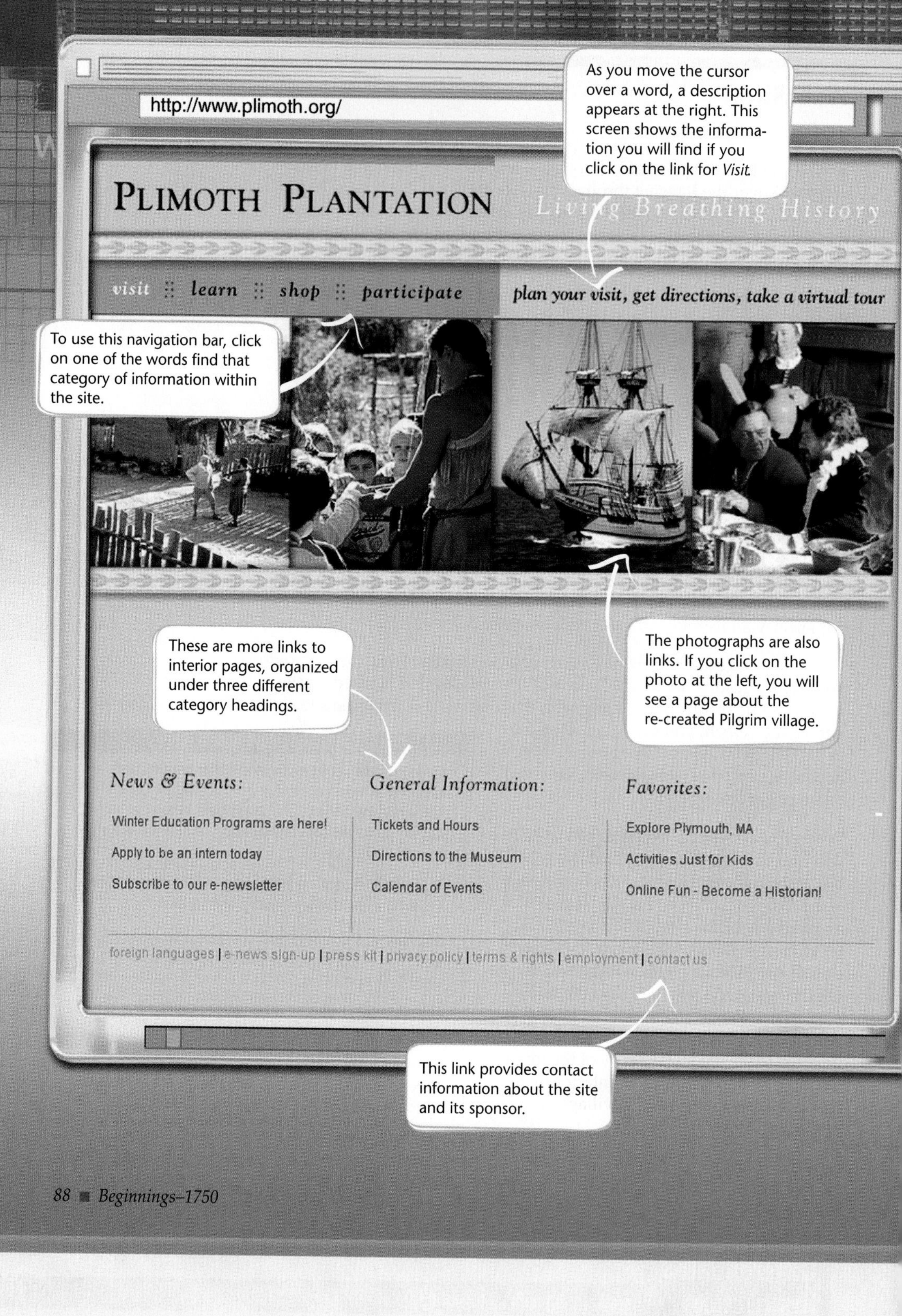

http://www.plimoth.org/
As you move the cursor over a word, a description appears at the right. This screen shows the information you will find if you click on the link for *Visit*.
PLIMOTH PLANTATION
Living Breathing History
visit :: learn :: shop :: participate
plan your visit, get directions, take a virtual tour
To use this navigation bar, click on one of the words find that category of information within the site.
These are more links to interior pages, organized under three different category headings.
The photographs are also links. If you click on the photo at the left, you will see a page about the re-created Pilgrim village.
News & Events:
Winter Education Programs are here!
Apply to be an intern today
Subscribe to our e-newsletter
General Information:
Tickets and Hours
Directions to the Museum
Calendar of Events
Favorites:
Explore Plymouth, MA
Activities Just for Kids
Online Fun - Become a Historian!
foreign languages | e-news sign-up | press kit | privacy policy | terms & rights | employment | contact us
This link provides contact information about the site and its sponsor.

http://www.plimoth.org/visit/what/1627.asp

The navigation bar on the home page is also available here.

PLIMOTH PLANTATION *Living Breathing History*

virtual tour :: what to see & do :: plan your visit :: explore plymouth, ma :: calendar of events :: group tours :: functions

READING INFORMATIONAL MATERIALS

what to see & do

- 1627 pilgrim village
- hobbamock's homesite
- mayflower II
- crafts center
- nye barn
- thanksgiving exhibit
- dining
- practical questions about visiting

"Welcome to the town! How do you fare? Are you just passing through, or mayhaps you are desiring to settle in this wilderness?"

These are links to the other pages under *What to See & Do*, under the broader category *Visit*.

1627 Pilgrim Village

This is one of the ways you may be greeted in the 1627 Pilgrim Village, a re-creation of the small farming town built by English colonists in the midst of the Wampanoag homeland. Find yourself immersed in the year 1627, just seven years after the voyage of the Mayflower. In the village you will be surrounded by the modest timber-framed houses, fragrant raised-bed gardens, well-tended livestock and fascinating townspeople of Plymouth Colony, the first permanent English settlement in New England.

The people you will meet are costumed role players who have taken on the names, viewpoints and life histories of the people who actually lived in the colony in 1627, popularly known as the "Pilgrims" today. Each one has a unique story to tell. Learn about the colony's difficult beginnings or discover the gossip of the day. Ask about religious beliefs, medical practices or relations with the local Wampanoag People. Talk to a housewife and learn what a "pottage" is, or see how a duck or bluefish is cooked on the hearth. Help a young colonist pull up a few weeds in a cornfield, mix daub with your feet for a house under construction, or just relax on a bench enjoying the unique atmosphere of 17th-century New Plymouth.

This screen shows the top of the page that describes the Pilgrim Village. As you scroll down, you can view the rest of the page.

Reading Web Sites (cont.)

- Point out that this interior page is called "1627 Pilgrim Village." It is highlighted in orange in the left margin because it has been opened. The other interior pages listed in the left margin have not.
- **Ask** students why they think the navigation bar on the home page is also listed on this interior page. **Answer:** This allows the user to move easily from any page in the site to any other page.
- **Ask** students what they would do if they wanted more information about Hobbarnock's homesite. **Answer:** Students would click on the link to the interior page titled "Hobbarnock's homesite" in the left margin.

Differentiated Instruction Solutions for All Learners

Support for Less Proficient Readers

Make enlarged photocopies of the home page for "Plimoth Plantation." Challenge students to mark up the photocopies, identifying each part of the home page and the purpose it serves. For instance, "Plimoth Plantation" is the title of the site, and "Take a virtual tour" allows you to do just that. The underline indicates that the phrase is a "hotlink"; clicking on it will lead the computer user to a new screen.

Enrichment for English Learners

Students may want to look for Web sites in languages other than English. Remind them that the World Wide Web is international, as its name suggests, and that it contains plenty of sites in many languages. The model on this page, for instance, offers its text in Dutch, German, Italian, Spanish, and French. Challenge each student to find a home page in a language of his or her choice, print it out, bring it to class, and explain his or her searching strategies.

ASSESS

Answers

Reading: Locating Appropriate Information

1. A
2. C
3. A
4. D

Reading: Comprehension and Interpretation

5. Select the "foreign languages" link at the bottom of the home page.
6. Using photographs is a good way to show a great deal of information, and this provides a quick reference for Web site visitors.
7. The links on the first page link to pages throughout the whole Web site. The links on the second page link to pages within the more specific category of that page.

Timed Writing

- Tell students that their evaluations must include examples of problems with the Web page, and recommendations must address those specific problems.
- Suggest that students plan their time to give 5 minutes to planning, 10 minutes to writing, and 5 minutes to reviewing and revising.

Monitor Your Progress

Assessment Practice

Reading: Locating Appropriate Information

Directions: *Choose the letter of the best answer to each question about the Web site.*

1. On the home page, under what category will you find a link to Plimoth Plantation's calendar of events?
   A News & Events
   B Favorites
   C Participate
   D General Information
2. Where might you find information about the costumed role players who portray the Pilgrims at Plimoth Plantation?
   A through the link to *Hobbamock's Homesite*
   B through the link to *Practical Questions About Visiting*
   C on the page titled *The 1627 Pilgrim Village*
   D on the *Upcoming Member Events* page
3. How can you use the Web site to buy books about seventeenth-century New England?
   A Click on the *Shop* link.
   B Click on the *Participate* link.
   C Click on the *Contact Us* link.
   D Click on the *Thanksgiving Exhibit* link.
4. What do you think is the **fastest** way to locate information about Plimoth Plantation's educational programs?
   A Take the virtual tour.
   B Read the discussion of the re-created Pilgrim village.
   C Click on one of the photographs on the home page.
   D Click on the *Learn* link.

Reading: Comprehension and Interpretation

Directions: *Write your answers on a separate sheet of paper.*

5. What can you do if you want to access the Web site's information in Spanish?
6. Why do you think the home page uses photographs as links?
7. Why do you think that most of the links on the home page are different from those on the interior page?

Timed Writing: Evaluation

Write a brief evaluation of this Web site, based on the two pages shown here. Consider what information and features the site offers and whether that information is easy to find and clearly organized. Include your recommendations for any improvements that could make this site more useful. ***(20 minutes)***

Extend the Lesson

Finding Reliable Sources of Information

Remind students that the first rule when using the Web for research is to look at who created the site. Because anyone can post any information he or she chooses on the Web, many sites are not reliable sources of information.

Give students practice identifying who creates or sponsors a particular Web site. Have students select three Web sites, and tell them to identify the creator or sponsor of the Web site. Then have them print a copy of each Home page, and mark the link that gives this information.

Unit 1
Part
3

The Puritan Influence

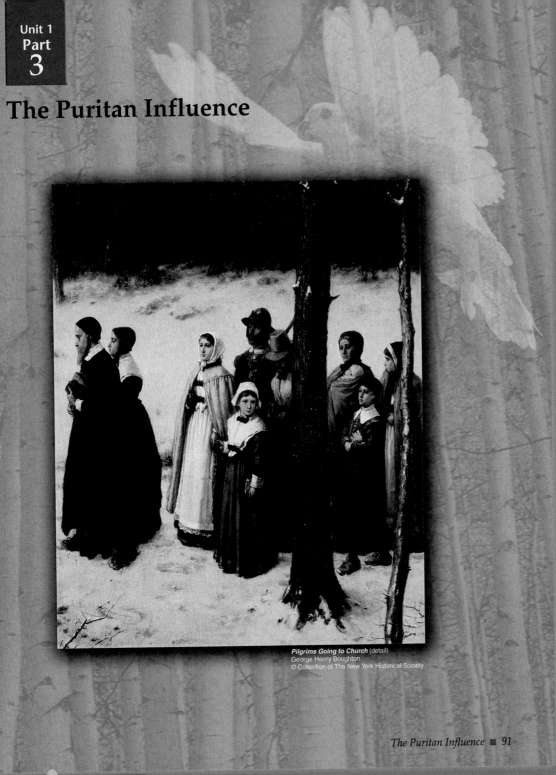

Pilgrims Going to Church (detail)
George Henry Boughton
© Collection of The New York Historical Society

Differentiated Instruction Solutions for All Learners

Accessibility at a Glance

Average
"To My Dear and Loving Husband"

More Challenging
"Huswifery"
from Sinners in the Hands of an Angry God

Selection Planning Guide

This section explores the Puritan influence on America's emerging literary identity. The poetry of Anne Bradstreet and Edward Taylor exemplifies the Puritan Plain Style, though Bradstreet's "To My Dear and Loving Husband" is unusual for its treatment of marital—rather than religious—love. Like the Puritans who first heard it, students are sure to find Jonathan Edwards's fiery sermon "Sinners in the Hands of an Angry God" to be an eye-opening look at Puritanism.

Humanities

Pilgrims Going to Church by George Henry Boughton

George Henry Boughton (1833–1905) was born in Norwich, England. From 1852 to 1858, he lived in Albany, New York, concentrating on landscape painting. After a year in New York City, he went to Europe and settled back in England in the 1860s. Throughout his career, Boughton's work was exhibited in both England and the United States. He became known primarily as a painter of "subject pictures" like *Pilgrims Going to Church.*

Use these questions for discussion:

1. What does the way people are looking around and holding their guns tell you about their state of mind as they go to church? Why might they feel this way?
   Possible responses: They seem to be wary of some kind of danger. Perhaps there have been incidents in which colonists have been ambushed or attacked by animals, or perhaps they are afraid because they are in an unknown land, where anything might happen.
2. What do the details of the painting—the weather, the setting, the colors, the posture of the people—reveal about life in the early days of the Puritan settlement?
   Possible responses: The frozen landscape, the darkness at the edges of the painting, the stark colors, the watchful posture of the people all suggest that life among the Puritans was harsh, joyless, and possibly filled with danger.

Meeting Your Standards

Students will

1. **analyze and respond to literary elements.**
   - Literary Analysis: The Puritan Plain Style
2. **read, comprehend, analyze, and critique two poems.**
   - Reading Strategy: Paraphrasing
   - Reading Check questions
   - Apply the Skills questions
   - Assessment Practice (ATE)
3. **develop vocabulary.**
   - Vocabulary Lesson: Anglo-Saxon Suffix: *-fold*
4. **understand and apply written and oral language conventions.**
   - Spelling Strategy
   - Grammar and Style Lesson: Direct Address
5. **develop writing proficiency.**
   - Writing Lesson: Reflective Essay
6. **develop appropriate research strategies.**
   - Extend Your Learning: Graphic Display
7. **understand and apply listening and speaking strategies.**
   - Extend Your Learning: Informal Debate

Block Scheduling: Use one 90-minute class period to preteach the skills and have students read the selection. Use a second 90-minute class period to assess students' mastery of skills, extend their learning, and monitor their progress.

Homework Suggestions

Following are possibilities for homework assignments.

- Support pages from *Unit 1 Resources:*
  Literary Analysis
  Reading Strategy
  Vocabulary Builder
  Grammar and Style
- An Extend Your Learning project and the Writing Lesson for this selection group may be completed over several days.

Step-by-Step Teaching Guide	Pacing Guide
PRETEACH	
• Administer Vocabulary and Reading Warm-ups as necessary.	5 min.
• Engage students' interest with the motivation activity.	5 min.
• Read and discuss author and background features. **FT**	10 min.
• Introduce the Literary Analysis Skill: The Puritan Plain Style. **FT**	5 min.
• Introduce the Reading Strategy: Paraphrasing. **FT**	10 min.
• Prepare students to read by teaching the selection vocabulary. **FT**	
TEACH	
• Informally monitor comprehension while students read independently or in groups. **FT**	30 min.
• Monitor students' comprehension with the Reading Check notes.	as students read
• Reinforce vocabulary with Vocabulary Builder notes.	as students read
• Develop students' understanding of the Puritan plain style with the Literary Analysis annotations. **FT**	5 min.
• Develop students' ability to paraphrase with the Reading Strategy annotations. **FT**	5 min.
ASSESS/EXTEND	
• Assess students' comprehension and mastery of the Literary Analysis and Reading Strategy by having them answer the Apply the Skills questions. **FT**	15 min.
• Have students complete the Vocabulary Development Lesson and the Grammar and Style Lesson. **FT**	15 min.
• Apply students' ability to provide descriptive details by using the Writing Lesson. **FT**	45 min. or homework
• Apply students' understanding by using one or more of the Extend Your Learning activities.	20–90 min. or homework
• Administer Selection Test A or Selection Test B. **FT**	15 min.

Resources

PRINT

Unit 1 Resources

TRANSPARENCY

Graphic Organizer Transparencies

PRINT

Reader's Notebook [L2]
Reader's Notebook: Adapted Version [L1]
Reader's Notebook: English Learner's Version [EL]

Unit 1 Resources

TECHNOLOGY

Listening to Literature Audio CDs [L2, EL]

PRINT

Unit 1 Resources

General Resources

TECHNOLOGY

Go Online: Research [**L3**]
Go Online: Self-test [**L3**]
***ExamView®* Test Bank** [**L3**]

Choosing Resources for Differentiated Instruction

[**L1**] Special Needs Students
[**L2**] Below-Level Students
[**L3**] All Students
[**L4**] Advanced Students
[**EL**] English Learners

FT Fast Track Instruction: To move the lesson more quickly, use the strategies and activities identified with **FT**.

Scaffolding for Less Proficient and Advanced Students

The leveled Critical Thinking questions after selections progress in the levels of thinking required to answer them. To address the needs of your different students, you may use the (a) level questions for your less proficient students and the (b) level questions with your on-level and advanced students. The occasional (c) level questions are appropriate for your advanced students.

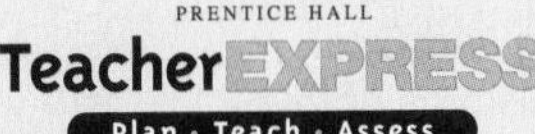

Use this complete suite of powerful teaching tools to make lesson planning and testing quicker and easier.

Use the interactive textbook (online and on CD-ROM) to make selections and activities come alive with audio and video support and interactive questions.

PRETEACH

Motivation

As an advance homework assignment, ask students to think of one or two love songs they know and enjoy. Have them jot down the lyrics and/or bring recordings of the songs to class. Invite student volunteers to read the song lyrics or to play excerpts from the recordings. Ask students to explain why they find the songs interesting or involving.

On the chalkboard, write "If ever two were one, then surely we." You might identify the quotation as a line from a love poem not yet set to music. Ask students to respond to it and to state their opinion of its relevance today. Then, explain to students that the line was written by a Puritan woman more than three hundred years ago in a poem expressing her deep love for her husband.

Finally, invite students to think about a wider definition of the term "love song." Point out that certain gospel songs might be described as love songs celebrating the divine bond between a human being and God. Tell students that it is this type of love that a Puritan poet celebrates in "Huswifery."

❶ Background

More About the Authors

Edward Taylor's poetry expresses intensity, lyricism, and a love of language that contradicts the joyless Puritan creed. Taylor asked his heirs to refrain from publishing his works during his life, and it was only in 1883 that one of his descendants presented Taylor's "Poetical Works" to Yale University. In 1939 Taylor's verse was published for the first time.

Anne Dudley was sixteen when she married Simon Bradstreet. The couple emigrated to America and lived in North Andover, Massachusetts. Anne Bradstreet's best poems are those inspired by the rhythms of daily New England life. Her later poems reveal her spiritual growth as she came to embrace Puritan beliefs.

Build Skills *Poems*

❶ Huswifery • To My Dear and Loving Husband

Edward Taylor (1642–1729)

Puritanism was a religious reform movement that began in England in the sixteenth century. The Puritans sought to reform the Church of England and to reshape English society according to their beliefs. These efforts led to both civil strife and government persecution of the Puritans. In response, many Puritans, including Edward Taylor, fled to the American colonies.

Before his emigration to America, Edward Taylor worked as a teacher in England. Upon arriving in Boston in 1668, Taylor entered Harvard College as a sophomore, graduating in 1671. After graduation, he accepted the position of minister and physician in the small frontier farming community of Westfield, Massachusetts, and then walked more than one hundred miles, much of it through snow, to his new home.

Harsh Life in a New World Life in the village of Westfield was filled with hardships. Fierce battles between the Native Americans and the colonists left the community in constant fear. In addition, Taylor experienced many personal tragedies. Five of his eight children died in infancy; then, his wife died while she was still a young woman. He remarried and had five or six more children. (Biographers differ on the exact number.)

Edward Taylor is now generally regarded as the best of the North American colonial poets. Yet, because Taylor thought of his poetry as a form of personal worship, he allowed only two stanzas to be published during his lifetime. In 1833, one of his descendants gave Taylor's writings to Yale University, and, in 1939, *The Poetical Works of Edward Taylor* was published. Most of Taylor's poetry, including "Huswifery," uses extravagant comparisons, intellectual wit, and subtle argument to explore religious faith and affection.

Anne Bradstreet (1612–1672)

Anne Bradstreet and her husband, Simon, arrived in the Massachusetts Bay Colony in 1630, when she was only eighteen. Armed with the convictions of her Puritan upbringing, she left behind her hometown of Northampton, England, to start afresh in America. It was not an easy life for Bradstreet, who raised eight children and faced many hardships.

A Private Writer Made Public Despite the difficulties she endured, Bradstreet was able to devote her spare moments to the very "unladylike" occupation of writing. She wrote for herself, not for publication. Nevertheless, in 1650, John Woodbridge, her brother-in-law, arranged for the publication in England of a collection of her scholarly poems, *The Tenth Muse Lately Sprung Up in America, By a Gentlewoman of Those Parts*. Generally considered to be the first collection of original poetry written in colonial America, the book examined the rights of women to learn and express themselves. Bradstreet's later poems, such as "To My Dear and Loving Husband," are more personal, expressing her feelings about the joys and difficulties of everyday Puritan life. In one, she wrote about her thoughts before giving birth. In another, she wrote about the death of a grandchild.

Bradstreet's poetry reflects the Puritans' knowledge of the stories and language of the Bible, as well as their concern for the relationship between earthly and heavenly life. Her work also exhibits some of the characteristics of the French and English poetry of her day.

In 1956, the poet John Berryman wrote "Homage to Mistress Bradstreet," a long poem that pays tribute to this first American poet.

Preview

Connecting to the Literature

Unlike most of us today, the Puritans had few possessions, dressed uniformly, and frowned on creative expression. Because they left so few personal belongings behind, they remain a mystery. These poems provide us with glimpses into the poets' inner lives and show the universal emotions individual Puritans experienced within the confines of their culture.

Literary Analysis

The Puritan Plain Style

The Puritans' writing style reflected the plain style of their lives—spare, simple, and straightforward. The **Puritan Plain Style** is characterized by short words, direct statements, and references to ordinary, everyday objects. Puritans believed that poetry should serve God by clearly expressing only useful or religious ideas. Poetry appealing to the senses or emotions was viewed as dangerous.

Comparing Literary Works

The poems by Taylor and Bradstreet are both expressions of devotion, but they are very different in the way they address the beloved. Taylor uses **apostrophe**—a figure of speech in which a speaker directly addresses a person who is dead or not physically present, a personified object or nonhuman thing, or an abstract quality or idea. For example:

Line 1: Make me, O Lord, Thy spinning wheel complete.

By contrast, the title of Bradstreet's poem indicates that the speaker is addressing her husband, but the poem contains no apostrophe. As you read, look for ways in which each poem reflects a distinct relationship between the speaker and his or her object of affection.

Reading Strategy

Paraphrasing

Although these poems capture the simplicity of Puritan life, they are not necessarily simple to understand. To help you better absorb the meaning of each poem, take time to **paraphrase,** or restate in your own words, the ideas expressed by each poet. Because it helps to clarify meaning, paraphrasing will allow you to make accurate statements about each poet's ideas. Use a chart like the one shown to organize your paraphrases.

Poet's Version

My love is such that rivers cannot quench, Nor ought but love from thee, give recompense.

Restatement

My love is so strong that rivers cannot relieve its thirst; only your love will satisfy me.

Vocabulary Builder

recompense (rek′ əm pens′) *n.* repayment; something given or done in return for something else (p. 96)

manifold (man′ ə fōld′) *adv.* in many ways (p. 96)

persevere (pʉr′ sə vir′) *v.* persist; be steadfast in purpose (p. 96)

❷ Literary Analysis
The Puritan Plain Style

- Tell students that as they read the two poems in this lesson, they will focus on the simple, spare, and straightforward writing of the Puritan Plain Style.
- Read the instruction about the Puritan Plain Style together as a class. Draw students' attention to the description of Puritan writers' use of short words, direct statements, and references to ordinary, everyday objects.
- As they read the poems, invite students to look for words and phrases that exemplify the Puritan Plain Style. Help them understand that the apparent "extravagance" of Taylor's extended metaphor is offset by the humble nature of the items he uses in his comparisons.

❸ Reading Strategy
Paraphrasing

- Make sure that students understand that paraphrasing means restating ideas or descriptions in one's own words.
- Point out that paraphrasing can be especially useful when students read literature from distant eras, since this type of writing often contains syntax and usage that is uncommon today.
- Give students a copy of **Reading Strategy Graphic Organizer A,** p. 17 in ***Graphic Organizer Transparencies.*** As they read the two poems, urge students to paraphrase whenever the underlying meaning of a line or idea is ambiguous to them.

Vocabulary Builder

- Pronounce each vocabulary word for students, and read the definitions as a class. Have students identify any words with which they are already familiar.

Differentiated Instruction Solutions for All Learners

Support for Special Needs Students
Have students complete the **Preview** and **Build Skills** pages for these selections in the ***Reader's Notebook: Adapted Version.*** These pages provide a selection summary, an abbreviated presentation of the reading and literary skills, and the graphic organizer on the **Build Skills** page in the student book.

Support for Less Proficient Readers
Have students complete the **Preview** and **Build Skills** pages for these selections in the ***Reader's Notebook.*** These pages provide a selection summary, an abbreviated presentation of the reading and literary skills, and the graphic organizer on the **Build Skills** page in the student book.

Support for English Learners
Have students complete the **Preview** and **Build Skills** pages for these selections in the ***Reader's Notebook: English Learner's Version.*** These pages provide a selection summary, an abbreviated presentation of the skills, additional contextual vocabulary, and the graphic organizer on the **Build Skills** page in the student book.

Learning Modalities
Intrapersonal Learners As students read, have them look for the ways in which the poems' speakers convey their strong feelings about their subjects. Challenge students to list other ways in which people can demonstrate devotion to others.

❶ About the Selection

"Huswifery" compares the household task of making cloth with the gift of God's salvation. This extended metaphor expresses Edward Taylor's deep belief in God and celebrates the divine presence in daily life. The poem is like a prayer imploring God to guide the speaker to do His bidding. By submitting to God's will, the speaker hopes to achieve eternal glory.

❷ Humanities

Crewel work chair seat cover

Although Puritan homes contained few works of art, Puritan women did produce artisanal crafts, such as embroidery and quilting, and men sometimes engaged in fine leather work, bookbinding, or metal smithing. Point out to students that the crewel work depicted on this page is attributed to Anne Bradstreet.

Use this question for discussion:

- How would you describe the subject of this image?
  Answer: In soft but definite colors, the work shows various forms of animal, insect, and plant life.

❸ Critical Viewing

Answer: The needlework was created around the same time as the poem. Moreover, it reflects the bright colors and "varnished flowers" of the needlework that Taylor describes in "Huswifery."

❶

Huswifery

Edward Taylor

❷

Crewel work chair seat cover, Gift of Samuel Bradstreet, Museum of Fine Arts, Boston

❸ ▲ Critical Viewing What makes this sampler an effective illustration to accompany Taylor's poem? **[Make a Judgment]**

Background Edward Taylor's work was generally unknown during his lifetime. Some believe that he chose not to publish his poems because their joyousness and delight in sensory experience ran counter to Puritan attitudes that poetry be for moral instruction only. The discovery in the 1930s of a stash of Taylor's poetry, including the poem that appears here, is considered one of the major literary finds of the twentieth century.

Although there were many writers of verse in Puritan times, few were women. Anne Bradstreet knew that writing was considered an unacceptable activity for women, but she persevered nonetheless, writing while children slept or in moments between household chores.

Differentiated Instruction Solutions for All Learners

Accessibility at a Glance

	Huswifery	To My Dear . . .
Context	Puritan Poem	Puritan Poem
Language	Simple language	Simple Language
Concept Level	Challenging (extended metaphor)	Accessible (wife's love for husband)
Literary Merit	Early work from the American colonies	Early work from the American colonies
Lexile	NP	NP
Overall Rating	More challenging	Average

Make me, O Lord, Thy spinning wheel complete.
Thy holy word my distaff[1] make for me.
Make mine affections[2] Thy swift flyers[3] neat
And make my soul Thy holy spoole to be.
My conversation make to be Thy reel
And reel the yarn thereon spun of Thy wheel.

4

Make me Thy loom then, knit therein this twine:
And make Thy holy spirit, Lord, wind quills:[4]
Then weave the web Thyself. The yarn is fine.
Thine ordinances[5] make my fulling mills.[6]
Then dye the same in heavenly colors choice.
All pinked[7] with varnished flowers of paradise.

Then clothe therewith mine understanding, will,
Affections, judgment, conscience, memory
My words, and actions, that their shine may fill
My ways with glory and Thee glorify.
Then mine apparel shall display before Ye
That I am clothed in holy robes for glory.

Literary Analysis
Puritan Plain Style In what sense are the words *spinning wheel, distaff, flyers, spoole, reel,* and *yarn* symbolic of the Puritan Plain Style?

1. **distaff** (dis′ taf′) *n.* staff on which flax or wool is wound for use in spinning.
2. **affections** (ə fek′ shənz) *n.* emotions.
3. **flyers** *n.* part of a spinning wheel that twists fibers into yarn.
4. **quills** *n.* weaver's spindles or bobbins.
5. **ordinances** (ôrd′ nəns əz) *n.* sacraments or religious rites.
6. **fulling mills** *n.* machines that shrink and thicken cloth to the texture of felt.
7. **pinked** *v.* decorated.

Critical Reading

1. **Respond:** *Huswifery* means "housekeeping." Given the title, were you surprised by the content of this poem? Explain.
2. **(a) Recall:** To what household objects and activities is the speaker compared in the first two stanzas? **(b) Analyze:** How do the images in the first two stanzas contribute to the idea of being "clothed in holy robes for glory," stated in the third stanza?
3. **(a) Interpret:** What images in this poem may have contradicted the Puritan requirement that clothing be dark and undecorated? **(b) Deduce:** What do these images suggest about the speaker's feelings about God?
4. **(a) Interpret:** What details in the final two lines convey Taylor's belief that religious grace comes as a gift from God? **(b) Analyze:** What seems to be the poem's overall purpose?
5. **Synthesize:** What household task or process might Taylor describe if he were writing this poem today?

For: More about Edward Taylor
Visit: www.PHSchool.com
Web Code: ere-9108

4 Literary Analysis
Puritan Plain Style

- **Ask** students to scour each stanza for nouns and verbs relating to cloth-making. Have a student volunteer make a list of these terms on the chalkboard.

Monitor Progress: Then, **ask** them the Literary Analysis question: In what sense are the words *spinning wheel, distaff, flyers, spoole, reel,* and *yarn* symbolic of the Puritan Plain Style?
Answer: Each word names a part of a device for making cloth.

- Point out that although this poem uses simple words to describe common household items, Taylor has created a rich, multi-layered metaphor. Increasingly complex connections—spinning wheel to yarn to loom to cloth to holy robes—represent steps the speaker hopes he can follow in life to glorify God and to achieve a state of grace.

ASSESS
Answers

1. Students should be specific.
2. (a) The speaker is compared to a spinning wheel, distaff, flyers, spoole, reel, yarn, loom, twine, quills, fulling mills, and dyeing. (b) All of these images relate the speaker to the objects and process of clothmaking. By thinking and behaving in ways that serve and glorify God, the speaker figuratively wears "holy robes" that reflect divinity.
3. (a) *dye the same in heavenly colors choice; pinked with varnished flowers of paradise; their shine* (b) These images suggest that the speaker's feelings about God are deep, intense, and vivid.
4. (a) The lines describe the speaker offering himself to God in the hope of sharing in His grace. (b) **Sample response:** The poem's overall purpose is to convey to God (as a prayer might) the speaker's utter devotion.
5. Students' might identify cleaning, cooking, or caring for children.

Go Online Author Link For additional information about Edward Taylor, have students type in the Web Code, then select T from the alphabet, and then select Edward Taylor.

Differentiated Instruction
Solutions for All Learners

Background for Special Needs Students
Draw students' attention to the differences between abstract ideas, such as patriotism, and concrete images, such as saluting an American flag. With students' help, list a handful of abstract ideas on the chalkboard. Then, invite students to brainstorm concrete images that illustrate each of these ideas. Finally, explain to students that Taylor's poem contains numerous concrete images that serve to illustrate aspects of the speaker's love for God.

Enrichment for Advanced Readers
This version of Taylor's poem uses modern spelling and capitalization. During Taylor's day, the rules for spelling and capitalization were extremely flexible. Most of the time, varied use of such conventions reflected a writer's preferences. In some cases, however, they may also have added meaning to a work. Encourage students to locate and read a copy of Taylor's poem in its original form. Then, have them write a paragraph analyzing Taylor's use of uppercase letters in the original version.

5 About the Selection

Simon Bradstreet was often away from home on business for months at a time, and Anne Bradstreet wrote this poem during one of his absences. In it, she expresses her deep love and admiration for her husband and her own spiritual conviction.

6 Reading Strategy
Paraphrasing

- **Ask** a volunteer to define the term *paraphrase* and to explain how this skill can be used in reading.
  Answer: To paraphrase is "to restate in one's own words." Paraphrasing helps readers clarify obscure or difficult syntax.
- Have students read the first stanza silently. Then, ask a volunteer to read aloud the first two lines.
- **Ask** students the Reading Strategy question: How would you paraphrase these first two lines?
  Possible response: We must be the ideal couple; you are the most beloved husband.

7 Vocabulary Builder
Anglo-Saxon Suffix *-fold*

- Draw students' attention to Bradstreet's use of the word *manifold,* and read its definition. Then, tell students that the suffix *-fold* means "a specific number of times or ways."
- Invite students to create three new words using the suffix *-fold,* and meaning *by ten times, by one hundred times,* and *by one thousand times.*
  Answer: tenfold; a hundredfold; a thousandfold.

ASSESS

Answers

1. Students may express surprise at Bradstreet's passion, given her Puritan pedigree.
2. (a) Bradstreet repeats the phrase *if ever* and the words *were* and *then.* (b) Repetition suggests the strength of the speaker's feelings.
3. (a) She prizes her husband's love. (b) Other images include *riches,* unquenchable rivers, *I can no way repay.*

5 To My Dear and Loving Husband

Anne Bradstreet

6
If ever two were one, then surely we.
If ever man were lov'd by wife, then thee;
If ever wife was happy in a man,
Compare with me ye women if you can.

I prize thy love more than whole mines of gold,
Or all the riches that the East doth hold.
My love is such that rivers cannot quench,
Nor ought[1] but love from thee, give recompense.
Thy love is such I can no way repay,

7
The heavens reward thee manifold, I pray.
Then while we live, in love let's so persevere,[2]
That when we live no more, we may live ever.

---

1. **ought** (ôt) *n.* anything whatever.
2. **persevere** pronounced *per se´ver* in the seventeenth century, and thus rhymed with the word *ever.*

Reading Strategy
Paraphrasing How would you paraphrase these first two lines?

Vocabulary Builder
recompense (rek′ əm pens′) *n.* repayment; something given or done in return for something else

manifold (man′ ə fōld′) *adv.* in many ways

persevere (pur′ sə vir′) *v.* persist; be steadfast in purpose

Critical Reading

1. **Respond:** What is your image of Anne Bradstreet after reading this poem? Does she fit your concept of a Puritan? Explain.
2. **(a) Recall:** Note where Bradstreet uses repetition in the first stanza. **(b) Analyze:** How does her use of repetition suggest a growing emotional intensity?
3. **(a) Recall:** What does the speaker value more than "whole mines of gold"? **(b) Distinguish:** What other images suggest the richness and abundance of the love the speaker and her husband share?
4. **(a) Analyze:** What is the apparent contradiction in the last two lines? **(b) Draw Conclusions:** What does the last stanza reveal about Puritan beliefs in the afterlife?
5. **Apply:** Do you think personal devotion is as much esteemed today as it was in Bradstreet's day? Support your answer.

For: More about Anne Bradstreet
Visit: www.PHSchool.com
Web Code: ere-9109

Answers continued

4. (a) The apparent contradiction is their "living" after their lives are over. (b) The last stanza indicates the Puritan belief in an afterlife.
5. Students should support their responses with clear reasoning and/or relevant personal observations and experiences.

Go Online Author Link For additional information about Anne Bradstreet, have students type in the Web Code, then select B from the alphabet, and then select Anne Bradstreet.

Apply the Skills

Huswifery • To My Dear and Loving Husband

Literary Analysis

Puritan Plain Style

1. Which words, phrases, and references in each poem reflect the plainness of the Puritans' lives? Use a chart like the one shown to organize your perceptions.

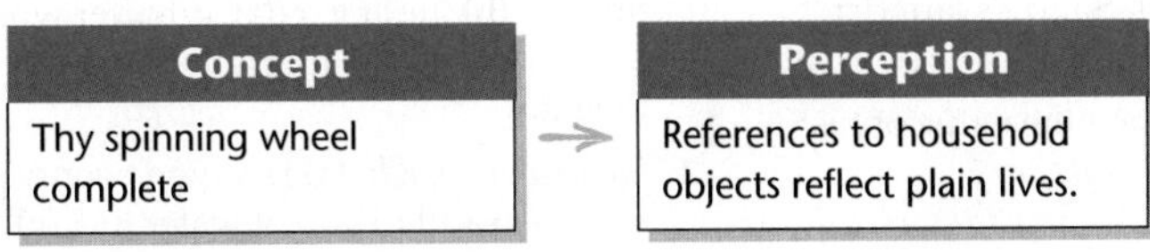

Concept
Thy spinning wheel complete
Perception
References to household objects reflect plain lives.

2. Which aspects of each poem are not typical of the **Puritan Plain Style**? Explain.
3. Compared to other poetry you know, how would you describe the effect of the Puritan Plain Style?

Comparing Literary Works

4. **(a)** Compare and contrast the emotions each of these speakers directs toward his or her subject. **(b)** What do these speakers want from the objects of their devotion? Explain.
5. **(a)** How does Taylor's use of **apostrophe** in lines 1 and 8 help convey the speaker's relationship with God? **(b)** In Bradstreet's poem, what connection does the speaker see between her love for her husband and God's grace?
6. A **conceit** is an elaborate comparison between two very different subjects. **(a)** How does Taylor's use of conceit help to structure his poem? **(b)** By contrast, how does Bradstreet build the ideas in her poem?

Reading Strategy

Paraphrasing

7. **Paraphrase** these passages from the poems as though you were explaining their meaning to a friend: **(a)** "To My Dear and Loving Husband," lines 9–12, **(b)** "Huswifery," lines 9–12.

Extend Understanding

8. **History Connection: (a)** What was the Puritan attitude toward material wealth and spirituality? **(b)** In our culture today, what is the general view of the relationship between the two?

QuickReview

The **Puritan Plain Style** is a simple, direct style of writing characterized by the use of short, easily understood words common to seventeenth-century conversation.

An **apostrophe** is a figure of speech in which a speaker directly addresses a person who is dead or not physically present, a personified object or nonhuman thing, or an abstract concept.

When you **paraphrase**, you restate important ideas in your own words.

For: Self-test
Visit: www.PHSchool.com
Web Code: era-6106

Answers continued

Go Online Assessment Students may use the **Self-test** to prepare for **Selection Test A** or **Selection Test B**.

Answers

1. **Taylor**—Concept: distaff, flyers, spoole, reel, yarn; Perceptions: ordinary objects. **Bradstreet**—Concept: I prize thy love more than. . . ; Perceptions: love is more precious than wealth.
2. **Taylor**—extended use of metaphors and vivid images; **Bradstreet**—personal, emotional subject of love for husband.
3. Students should clearly describe their understanding of the effect of the Puritan Plain Style, and they should explain how this effect compares with that of other poetry.
4. (a) Taylor's speaker directs spiritual love and devotion toward God; Bradstreet's speaker directs conjugal love and devotion toward her husband. (b) Taylor's speaker wants to achieve eternal glory by serving God; Bradstreet's speaker wants her husband to share her love even after death.
5. (a) The use of apostrophe makes the speaker's relationship with God seem more intimate. (b) The speaker believes that her love for her husband will translate into an afterlife for her husband and herself.
6. (a) Taylor establishes the metaphor in the poem's first line; he adds details (different aspects of the same metaphor) to fill out the conceit. (b) Bradstreet establishes her main idea about marital love in the first stanza, develops it with figurative language in the second stanza and extends it by addressing the idea of the afterlife in the last stanza.
7. **Possible responses:** (a) Your love is so strong I can't repay it, so I pray heaven will reward you in many ways. (b) Weave the web yourself. The yarn is delicate. Your sacraments clean and thicken it. Then, dye it in heavenly colors, decorated with flowers of paradise.
8. **Possible responses:** (a) The Puritans regarded material wealth with suspicion, since they believed their duty lay in striving to serve God. (b) Our culture today is more accepting of material wealth—in fact, it might be said to celebrate it.

EXTEND/ASSESS

Answers

1 Vocabulary Lesson

Word Analysis

1. fourfold
2. threefold

Spelling Strategy

Taylor—*clothe, therewith;* Bradstreet—*doth*

Vocabulary Builder

1. b
2. c
3. b

2 Grammar and Style

1. I beseech you, O Muse, to bring me inspiration!
2. And make Thy holy spirit, Lord, wind quills:/Then weave the web Thyself.
3. I could not love thee, dear, so much,/Loved I not honor more.
4. How can I repay, my love, the love you have given to me?
5. I see you in the holy work I strive to perform, Lord.

Writing Application

Students' letters should address a serious societal issue and should include at least one instance of direct address. For example, in the body of the letter, a student might write:

I hope you can focus the nation's attention on this problem, Senator Smith.

Writing and Grammar, Ruby Level

Students will find further instruction and practice and direct address in Chapter 27, Section 2.

Build Language Skills

1 Vocabulary Lesson

Word Analysis: Anglo-Saxon Suffix *-fold*

The Anglo-Saxon suffix *-fold,* meaning "a specific number of times or ways," is used to form both adjectives and adverbs. *Tenfold* means "ten times." Replace the italicized phrases with a word containing the suffix *-fold*.

1. Since having quadruplets, Sandy's laundry has grown *by four times.*
2. The savvy investor watched the value of his stock increase to *three times its size.*

Spelling Strategy

When the unvoiced *th* sound occurs at the end of a word, spell it with the letters *th.* When the voiced *th* sound occurs, include a final *e.* Find examples of each of these rules in these poems.

Vocabulary Builder: Word Meaning

Identify the letter of the situation that best demonstrates the meaning of the italicized word or phrase.

1. *well-deserved recompense:* **(a)** getting a flat tire while taking your grandmother to the doctor, **(b)** getting a day off after working overtime, **(c)** cleaning a messy room after a long day
2. *increase manifold:* **(a)** receive a twenty percent raise, **(b)** add a drop of water to a full bucket, **(c)** get a 300 percent return on an investment
3. *persevere:* **(a)** quit when you get tired, **(b)** practice until you improve, **(c)** argue with a referee

2 Grammar and Style Lesson

Direct Address

When the speaker in a poem talks directly to someone or something, the form of speech is called a **direct address.** Commas are used to separate the word or phrase of the direct address from the rest of the sentence, regardless of its position in the sentence.

Middle: Make me, *O Lord,* Thy spinning wheel complete.

End: May you be rewarded for your love, *dear husband.*

Practice Identify the word or phrase of direct address. Add punctuation where needed.

1. I beseech you O Muse to bring me inspiration!
2. And make Thy holy spirit Lord wind quills: / Then weave the web Thyself.
3. I could not love thee dear so much, / Loved I not honor more.
4. How can I repay my love the love you have given to me?
5. I see you in the holy work I strive to perform Lord.

Writing Application Write a letter to a political figure explaining your opinion about a subject of your choice. Use at least one direct address.

Prentice Hall Writing and Grammar Connection: Chapter 27, Section 2

Assessment Practice

Summarizing Written Texts

(For more practice, see *Standardized Test Preparation Workbook*, p. 6.)

Some tests measure students' ability to identify the best summary of a passage. Explain that summarizing is especially useful when reading poetry. After students reread the poem on p. 102, have them pick the best summary from the choices below.

A The author wants to live forever with her husband.
B The author's love for her husband, which she values more than gold and riches, will never die.
C The author owes her husband money.
D The author wants heaven to reward her husband.

Choices *A* and *D* make only partially complete claims; *C* presents incorrect information. *B* is the best summary.

Resources

PRINT

Unit 1 Resources

Vocabulary Warm-up Word Lists **[L1, L2, EL]** ....p. 94
Vocabulary Warm-up Practice **[L1, L2, EL]** ....p. 95
Reading Warm-up A **[L1, L2, EL]** ....p. 96
Reading Warm-up B **[L1, L2, L3]** ....p. 97

TRANSPARENCY

Graphic Organizer Transparencies

Literary Analysis Graphic Organizer A **[L3]** ....p. 23
Literary Analysis Graphic Organizer B **[L1, L2, EL]** ....p. 24
Reading Strategy Graphic Organizer A **[L3]** ....p. 21
Reading Strategy Graphic Organizer B **[L1, L2, EL]** ....p. 22

PRINT

Reader's Notebook [L2]
Reader's Notebook: Adapted Version [L1]
Reader's Notebook: English Learner's Version [EL]

Unit 1 Resources

Literary Analysis **[L3]** ....p. 98
Reading Strategy **[L3]** ....p. 99
Vocabulary Builder **[L3]** ....p. 100

TECHNOLOGY

Listening to Literature Audio CDs [L2, EL]
Reader's Notebook: Adapted Version Audio CD [L1, L2]

PRINT

Unit 1 Resources

Grammar and Style **[L3]** ....p. 101
Support for Writing Lesson **[L3]** ....p. 102
Support for Extend Your Learning **[L3]** ....p. 103
Enrichment **[L4]** ....p. 104
Selection Test A **[L1, L2, EL]** ....pp. 105–107
Selection Test B **[L3, L4]** ....pp. 108–116

General Resources

Rubrics for Critique **[L3]** ....pp. 75–76
Rubric for Delivering a Research Presentation **[L3]** ....p. 91

TECHNOLOGY

Go Online: Research **[L3]**
Go Online: Self-test **[L3]**
***ExamView®* Test Bank [L3]**

Choosing Resources for Differentiated Instruction

[L1] Special Needs Students
[L2] Below-Level Students
[L3] All Students
[L4] Advanced Students
[EL] English Learners

FT Fast Track Instruction: To move the lesson more quickly, use the strategies and activities identified with **FT**.

Scaffolding for Less Proficient and Advanced Students

The leveled Critical Thinking questions after selections progress in the levels of thinking required to answer them. To address the needs of your different students, you may use the (a) level questions for your less proficient students and the (b) level questions with your on-level and advanced students. The occasional (c) level questions are appropriate for your advanced students.

Use this complete suite of powerful teaching tools to make lesson planning and testing quicker and easier.

Use the interactive textbook (online and on CD-ROM) to make selections and activities come alive with audio and video support and interactive questions.

PREТEACH

Motivation

Most students are all too familiar with the persuasive power of advertising, of peer pressure, and of other methods people use to influence the actions or attitudes of others. Have small groups brainstorm for persuasive techniques that they find especially effective. Then, engage students' interest in Jonathan Edwards's persuasive sermon by reading the following passage to them:

"O, sinner! Consider the fearful danger you are in: it is a great furnace of wrath, a wide and bottomless pit, full of the fire of wrath, that you are held over in the hand of that God. . . "

Ask students to characterize Edwards's basic approach: is it emotional or intellectual? Invite other responses to this quotation, as well as speculation about how Edwards, a conservative Puritan preacher, might attempt to persuade a congregation to accept his message about their "wickedness."

❶ Background

More About the Author

As he toiled to strengthen Puritanism against what he saw as new waves of liberalism and rationalism, Jonathan Edwards deeply influenced American religious history. He wrestled continually with the theological issue of free will: if God determines all, how is human free will possible? Edwards concluded that since God gives people the power to choose, they hold responsibility for their acts and will earn God's praise or wrath accordingly. After Edwards left his preaching duties at Northampton, he ministered to the Housatonic Indians and to scattered frontier settlers in the area.

Build Skills Sermon

❶ *from* Sinners in the Hands of an Angry God

Jonathan Edwards (1703–1758)

The sermons of Jonathan Edwards were so filled with "fire and brimstone"—a phrase symbolizing the torments of hell endured by sinners—that his name alone was enough to make many eighteenth-century Puritans shake in their shoes. Yet, Edwards was not merely a stone-faced religious zealot. He was also a man who believed in science and reason and who saw in the physical world the proof of God's presence and will.

A Preacher Born and Raised This great American theologian and powerful Puritan preacher was born in East Windsor, Connecticut, where he grew up in an atmosphere of devout discipline. As a young boy, he is said to have demonstrated his religious devotion by preaching sermons to his playmates from a makeshift pulpit he built behind his home. Edwards also displayed academic brilliance at an early age. By the time he was twelve, he had learned to speak Latin, Greek, and Hebrew and had written numerous philosophical and scientific essays. These essays, which include "Of Insects," and "Of the Rainbow," display Edwards's remarkable powers of observation and analysis. Edwards entered the Collegiate School of Connecticut (now Yale University) at the age of thirteen and graduated four years later as the valedictorian of his class. He went on to earn his master's degree in theology.

The Great Awakening Edwards began his preaching career in 1727 as assistant to his grandfather, Solomon Stoddard, pastor of the church at Northampton, Massachusetts, one of the largest and wealthiest Puritan congregations. Edwards became the church pastor two years later when his grandfather died. He also began preaching throughout New England. Committed to a return to the orthodoxy and fervent faith of the Puritan past, Edwards became one of the leaders of the Great Awakening, a religious revival that swept the colonies in the 1730s and 1740s. His sermons stimulated religious zeal and sparked conversions, often in a frenzied atmosphere.

Changing Attitudes As pastor of the church at Northampton, Edwards had instituted disciplinary proceedings against members of his congregation for reading what he considered improper books. In his sermons he denounced by name those he considered sinners. Such actions, combined with the severity of his views, drew criticism. In 1750, a council representing ten congregations in the region dismissed Edwards as pastor.

Fall from Favor Edwards then moved to Stockbridge, Massachusetts, where he preached to the Native Americans. While in Stockbridge, Edwards wrote his most important theological works, including "A Careful and Strict Enquiry into . . . Notions of . . . Freedom of Will" (1754), in which he argued that human beings do not possess self-determination. The essay remains one of the most famous theological works ever written in America. Edwards continued to preach and write until his death in 1758, shortly after becoming president of the College of New Jersey (now Princeton University).

Although in most of his sermons, books, and essays Edwards appeals to reason and logic, his highly emotional sermon "Sinners in the Hands of an Angry God" is by far his most famous work. This sermon, which was delivered to a congregation in Enfield, Connecticut, in 1741 and is said to have caused listeners to rise from their seats in a state of hysteria, demonstrates Edwards's tremendous powers of persuasion and captures the religious fervor of the Great Awakening.

Preview

Connecting to the Literature

Suppose a friend is involved with the "wrong crowd" and you are concerned about his or her awful future. Jonathan Edwards had such concerns about his congregation. To turn his congregants toward repentance, Edwards filled his sermons with descriptions of the horrors that awaited those who did not mend their ways.

2 Literary Analysis

Sermon

A **sermon** is broadly defined as a speech given from a pulpit in a house of worship. Like its written counterpart, the essay, a sermon conveys to an audience the speaker's message or point of view. In colonial America's religious atmosphere, the sermon flourished as a popular literary form.

Connecting Literary Elements

Sermons are one example of **oratory,** or formal public speaking. The best oratory almost always displays the following elements:

- It is persuasive, inspiring listeners to take action.
- It appeals to the emotions.
- It addresses the needs and concerns of its audience.
- It includes expressive and rhythmic language.

Although oratory has become less common in American society, its lofty tones can still be heard in Senate chambers, courtrooms, and houses of worship. In Edwards's time, oratory played an important role in the lives of nearly all citizens of a community.

3 Reading Strategy

Using Context Clues

Searching the **context**—the surrounding words, phrases, and sentences—for clues can help you understand the meaning of unfamiliar words. For example, look at the word *abominable* in this passage:

You are ten thousand times more *abominable* in his [God's] eyes, than the most hateful venomous serpent is in ours. . . .

Edwards likens the way the sinner appears in God's eyes with our view of a snake. From this clue, you can determine that *abominable* must be close in meaning to *disgusting* or *horrible.* Use a chart like the one shown to define other difficult words by using context clues.

Difficult Words

↓

Context Clues

↓

Meaning

Vocabulary Builder

omnipotent (äm nip′ ə tənt) *adj.* all-powerful (p. 103)

ineffable (in ef′ ə bəl) *adj.* inexpressible (p. 104)

dolorous (dō′ lər əs) *adj.* sad; mournful (p. 105)

Differentiated Instruction Solutions for All Learners

Support for Special Needs Students
Have students read the adapted version from *Sinners in the Hands of an Angry God* in the ***Reader's Notebook: Adapted Version.*** This version provides basic-level instruction in an interactive format with questions and write-on lines. Completing these pages will prepare students to read the selection in the Student Edition.

Support for Less Proficient Readers
Have students read the excerpt from *Sinners in the Hands of an Angry God* in the ***Reader's Notebook.*** This version provides basic-level instruction in an interactive format with questions and write-on lines. After students finish the selection in the ***Reader's Notebook,*** have them complete the questions and activities in the Student Edition.

Support for English Learners
Have students read the excerpt from *Sinners in the Hands of an Angry God* in the ***Reader's Notebook: English Learner's Version.*** This version provides basic-level instruction in an interactive format with questions and write-on lines. Completing these pages will prepare students to read the selection in the Student Edition.

2 Literary Analysis

Sermon

- Tell students that they will focus on sermons as they read this excerpt from one of the most famous sermons in American history, delivered two and a half centuries ago by Jonathan Edwards.
- As they read the sermon, students should remember that Edwards conceived the work as a piece of oratory—*spoken* text. Have a volunteer read the list of elements often found in oratory in the Connecting Literary Elements passage.
- Encourage students to look for examples of colorful or rhythmic language, including the use of repetition, alliteration, and other sound devices.
- As they read, invite students to imagine being one of Edwards's parishioners. Do his fiery words affect them emotionally? Encourage students to discuss the idea that the concepts of guilt, redemption, and mercy do not become outdated.

3 Reading Strategy

Using Context Clues

- Remind students that every text that contains unfamiliar words also contains context clues. Readers can use these clues to unlock the meanings of difficult words.
- Point out that context clues can take several forms: a single word, a phrase, or a word group.
- Tell students that the use of context clues is not limited to literature. Point out that they can (and no doubt already do) use this skill in daily conversation. Encourage students to use context clues to determine the meanings of unfamiliar words every time they read.
- Give students a copy of **Reading Strategy Graphic Organizer A,** p. 21 in ***Graphic Organizer Transparencies.*** Tell them to use the chart to keep track of context clues for difficult words.

Vocabulary Builder

- Pronounce each vocabulary word for students, and read the definitions as a class. Have students identify any words with which they are already familiar.

TEACH

Learning Modalities
Verbal/Linguistic Learners
Invite volunteers to select a portion of this sermon to practice and deliver to classmates. After the presentations, encourage listeners to give constructive feedback about the effectiveness of the speakers' deliveries.

❶ About the Selection

The foundation of Edwards's sermon is the Puritan belief in a life of hard work, self-discipline, and religious devotion. The preacher intended to frighten his listeners into pursuing lives of humility and righteousness in the hope of achieving salvation. What Edwards's listeners probably found most dreadful was the idea of an omniscient God being indifferent to human misery. Moreover, the congregation was surely chilled by the realization that—though their only hope of salvation lay in observing divine laws to the letter—God might dole out mercy according to His whims.

❷ Humanities

The Puritan, 1898, by Frank E. Schoonover

Frank Schoonover (1877–1922) was an American illustrator for magazines and books, such as *LaFitte, the Pirate of the Gulf,* and the *Hopalong Cassidy* series of westerns. His paintings show great precision and detail. This accurately illustrates Puritan garb, and conveys the subject's austere Puritan attitude. Use this question for discussion:

- This is a formal portrait, one in which the subject was posed by the artist. How does this concept echo Edwards's sermon?
  Answer: The rigid pose suggests obedience to the will of the artist. Likewise, Edwards's sermon preaches a rigid obedience to the commands of God.

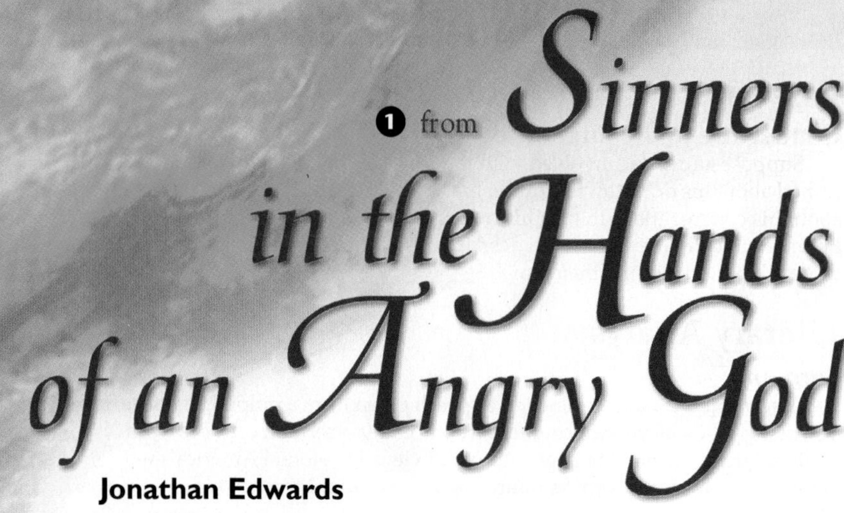

❶ from Sinners in the Hands of an Angry God

Jonathan Edwards

Background Surprisingly, Jonathan Edwards preached this famous fire-and-brimstone sermon in a quiet, restrained style. According to one account, he read the six-hour work in a level voice, staring over the heads of his congregation at the bell rope that hung against the back wall "as if he would stare it in two." Despite his calm demeanor, his listeners are said to have groaned and screamed in terror, and Edwards stopped several times to ask for silence.

This is the case of every one of you that are out of Christ:[1] That world of misery, that lake of burning brimstone, is extended abroad under you. There is the dreadful pit of the glowing flames of the wrath of God; there is Hell's wide gaping mouth open; and you have nothing to stand upon, nor anything to take hold of; there is nothing between you and Hell but the air; it is only the power and mere pleasure of God that holds you up.

You probably are not sensible of this; you find you are kept out of Hell, but do not see the hand of God in it; but look at other things, as the good state of your bodily constitution, your care of your own life, and the means you use for your own preservation. But indeed these things are nothing; if God should withdraw his hand, they would avail no more to keep you from falling than the thin air to hold up a person that is suspended in it.

1. **out of Christ** not in God's grace.

Differentiated Instruction Solutions for All Learners

Accessibility at a Glance

	from Sinners in the Hands . . .
Context	Puritan Sermon
Language	Challenging vocabulary; complicated sentences
Concept Level	Challenging (Puritan view of God)
Literary Merit	Primary Source
Lexile	1210
Other	Fire and brimstone language
Overall Rating	More challenging

Your wickedness makes you as it were heavy as lead, and to tend downwards with great weight and pressure towards Hell; and if God should let you go, you would immediately sink and swiftly descend and plunge into the bottomless gulf, and your healthy constitution, and your own care and prudence, and best contrivance, and all your righteousness, would have no more influence to uphold you and keep you out of Hell, than a spider's web would have to stop a fallen rock. Were it not for the
5 sovereign pleasure of God, the earth would not bear you one moment . . . The world would spew you out, were it not for the sovereign hand of Him who hath subjected it in hope. There are black clouds of God's wrath now hanging directly over your heads, full of the dreadful storm, and big with thunder; and were it not for the restraining hand of God, it would immediately burst forth upon you. The sovereign pleasure of God, for the present, stays[2] his rough wind; otherwise it would come with fury, and your destruction would come like a whirlwind, and you would be like the chaff of the summer threshing floor.

2

The Puritan, 1898, Frank E. Schoonover, Collection of the Brandywine River Museum

The wrath of God is like great waters that are dammed for the present; they increase more and more, and rise higher and higher, till an outlet is given; and the longer the stream is stopped, the more rapid and mighty is its course, when once it is let loose. It is true, that judgment against your evil works has not been executed hitherto; the floods of God's vengeance have been withheld; but your guilt in the meantime is constantly increasing, and you are every day treasuring up more wrath; the waters are constantly rising, and waxing more and more mighty; and there is nothing but the mere pleasure of God, that holds the waters back, that are unwilling to be stopped, and press hard to go forward. If God should only withdraw his hand from the floodgate, it would immediately fly open, and the fiery floods of the fierceness and wrath of God, would rush forth with
4 inconceivable fury, and would come upon you with omnipotent power; and if your strength were ten thousand times greater than it is, yea, ten thousand times greater than the strength of the stoutest, sturdiest devil in Hell, it would be nothing to withstand or endure it.

The bow of God's wrath is bent, and the arrow made ready on the string, and justice bends the arrow at your heart, and strains the bow, and it is nothing but the mere pleasure of God, and that of an angry God, without any promise or obligation at all, that keeps the arrow one moment from being made drunk with your blood. Thus all you that never passed under a great change of heart, by the mighty power of the

2. stays (stāz) *v.* restrains.

3 **Critical Viewing** What words from the text would you apply to describe the mood of this painting? [Analyze]

Literary Analysis
Sermon In what ways do these images of the fury of water help convey Edwards's message?

Vocabulary Builder
omnipotent (äm nip´ ə tənt) *adj.* all-powerful

6 **Reading Check**
What does Edwards say is the state of his congregation?

3 Critical Viewing

Answer: Citations may include "your own care and prudence," "infinite gloom," "fierceness," "moral and strict, sober and religious," and "miserable condition that you are in."

4 Vocabulary Builder

Latin prefix *omni-*

- Draw students' attention to Edwards's use of the word *omnipotent,* and read its definition. Then, tell students that the prefix *omni-* means "all" or "every."
- **Ask** students why they might expect to find words beginning with the prefix *omni-* in a sermon.
  Answer: The prefix *omni-* expresses the idea of encompassing all, a characteristic often attributed to God.
- Then, invite students to combine the prefix *omni-* with the word *present* to create another word Edwards might have used to describe God.

5 Literary Analysis

Sermon

- **Ask** a student volunteer to read aloud the first two paragraphs on this page. Have students raise their hands when they hear images involving water. List these images on the chalkboard.

Monitor Progress: Ask students the Literary Analysis question: In what ways do these images of the fury of water help convey Edwards's message?
Answer: The image of dammed water, rising in volume and power, serves as an effective metaphor for God's potential wrath. It is an image of the *possibility* of destruction. This is perfect for Edwards's purpose, as it checks his congregation's impulse to rationalize away the possibility of God's judgment.

6 Reading Check

Answer: Edwards indicates that his congregation is poised above a "world of misery" and that at any moment God could let go and consign them to Hell forever.

Differentiated Instruction
Solutions for All Learners

Strategy for Special Needs Students
Students may benefit from a demonstration of how to use context clues. Invite them to identify a paragraph that includes one or more unfamiliar words or phrases. Write the passage on the board, underlining the difficult words. Then, circle the surrounding context clues that can help students determine the meanings of the unknown words. By reading the challenging words in relationship to the context clues, students may be able to interpret the meaning of the unfamiliar terms.

Strategy for Gifted/Talented Students
Ask students to find details that distinguish this piece as a sermon. They may cite Edwards's use of religious references or his use of repetition to heighten the sense of the congregants' peril. Also, have students look for examples of figurative language (such as the personification of hell's "wide gaping mouth"), which add poetic and dramatic impact to the sermon.

7 Literature in Context
Biblical Imagery

The King James Version of the Bible was preceded in English by Wyclif's Bible (1380), Tyndale's Bible (1525), Coverdale's Bible (1535), Matthew's Bible (1537), Taverner's Bible (1539), the Geneva Bible (1560), and the Bishops' Bible (1568). Also known as the "Authorized Version," the King James Version was composed from 1604 to 1611 by a group of scholars working for King James I. It is widely considered to be the most beautifully written translation of the Hebrew scriptures, and it has had an incalculable effect on English and American literary history.

Connect to the Literature
Encourage students to reflect on contemporary views of God before responding to the question.
Possible responses: A contemporary audience would probably be turned off by Edwards's use of Biblical imagery. Today, it is more common for worshippers to view God as loving and benevolent rather than angry and capricious.

spirit of God upon your souls; all you that were never born again, and made new creatures, and raised from being dead in sin, to a state of new, and before altogether unexperienced light and life, are in the hands of an angry God. However you may have reformed your life in many things, and may have had religious affections, and may keep up a form of religion in your families and closets,[3] and in the house of God, it is nothing but His mere pleasure that keeps you from being this moment swallowed up in everlasting destruction. However unconvinced you may now be of the truth of what you hear, by and by you will be fully convinced of it.

Those that are gone from being in the like circumstances with you, see that it was so with them; for destruction came suddenly upon most of them; when they expected nothing of it, and while they were saying, peace and safety: now they see, that those things on which they depended for peace and safety, were nothing but thin air and empty shadows.

The God that holds you over the pit of Hell, much as one holds a spider, or some loathsome insect over the fire, abhors you, and is dreadfully provoked: his wrath towards you burns like fire; he looks upon you as worthy of nothing else, but to be cast into the fire; he is of purer eyes than to bear to have you in his sight; you are ten thousand times more abominable in his eyes, than the most hateful venomous serpent is in ours. . . .

O sinner! Consider the fearful danger you are in: it is a great furnace of wrath, a wide and bottomless pit, full of the fire of wrath, that you are held over in the hand of that God, whose wrath is provoked and incensed as much against you, as against many of the damned in Hell. You hang by a slender thread, with the flames of divine wrath flashing about it, and ready every moment to singe it, and burn it asunder; and you have no interest in any mediator, and nothing to lay hold of to save yourself, nothing to keep off the flames of wrath, nothing of your own, nothing that you ever have done, nothing that you can do, to induce God to spare you one moment. . . .

When God beholds the ineffable extremity of your case, and sees your torment to be so vastly disproportioned to your strength, and sees how your poor soul is crushed, and sinks down, as it were, into an infinite gloom; he will have no compassion upon you, he will not forbear the executions of his wrath, or in the least lighten his hand; there shall be no moderation or mercy, nor will God then at all stay his rough wind; he will have no regard to your welfare, nor be at all careful lest you should suffer too much in any other sense, than only that you shall *not suffer beyond what strict justice requires.* . . .

3. **closets** *n.* small, private rooms for meditation.

7 Literature in Context

History Connection
Biblical Imagery
Jonathan Edwards's frightening imagery of God's potential for wrath and destruction recalls stories of fires, floods, and divine retribution in the Old Testament of the King James Bible. While this imagery terrified Edwards's audience, they would have found it quite familiar. In fact, in 1741, when Edwards delivered this sermon, the King James Bible had been in wide circulation for 130 years. The first English version of the Bible to include both the Old and New Testaments, the King James Bible had been produced at the express request of the Puritans in England in 1611. This Bible, with its haunting language and powerful imagery, would have been common daily reading for most of Edwards's listeners.

Connect to the Literature
How do you think a contemporary audience of worshippers would react to this type of "fire and brimstone" biblical imagery?

Vocabulary Builder
ineffable (in ef′ ə bəl) *adj.* inexpressible

Enrichment
The Afterlife

Edwards's apparent belief in an afterlife is typical of the followers of most major religions. According to the ancient Greeks, people who led a good life were sent to Elysium, a paradise filled with fields of flowers and sunlight. Ancient Egyptians also believed in the afterlife as an agricultural land of plenty. In Norse mythology, heroes slain in battle went to Valhalla, a golden palace in the gods' homeland where they would battle every morning and feast every noon forever. In Buddhism and in Hinduism, the soul is reincarnated (reborn in another body or form) until it achieves a state of spiritual perfection.

Encourage students to choose a religion or culture and investigate its beliefs about life after death. Students may also elect to examine the religious beliefs of two different cultures and compare and contrast their views of the afterlife. Have students examine the ways in which different religious beliefs express human values and emotions. Students can then report their findings in a presentation to the class.

God stands ready to pity you; this is a day of mercy; you may cry now with some encouragement of obtaining mercy. But once the day of mercy is past, your most lamentable and dolorous cries and shrieks will be in vain; you will be wholly lost and thrown away of God, as to any regard to your welfare. God will have no other use to put you to, but to suffer misery; you shall be continued in being to no other end; for you will be a vessel of wrath fitted to destruction; and there will be no other use of this vessel, but to be filled full of wrath. . . .

Thus it will be with you that are in an unconverted state, if you continue in it; the infinite might, and majesty, and terribleness of the omnipotent God shall be magnified upon you, in the ineffable strength of your torments. You shall be tormented in the presence of the holy angels, and in the presence of the Lamb,[4] and when you shall be in this state of suffering, the glorious inhabitants of Heaven shall go forth and look on the awful spectacle, that they may see what the wrath and fierceness of the Almighty is; and when they have seen it, they will fall down and adore that great power and majesty. . . .

It would be dreadful to suffer this fierceness and wrath of Almighty God one moment; but you must suffer it to all eternity. There will be no end to this exquisite horrible misery. When you look forward, you shall see a long forever, a boundless duration before you, which will swallow up your thoughts and amaze your soul; and you will absolutely despair of ever having any deliverance, any end, any mitigation, any rest at all. . . .

How dreadful is the state of those that are daily and hourly in the danger of this great wrath and infinite misery! But this is the dismal
8 case of every soul in this congregation that has not been born again, however moral and strict, sober and religious, they may otherwise be. Oh that you would consider it, whether you be young or old! . . . Those of you that finally continue in a natural condition, that shall keep you out of Hell longest will be there in a little time! Your damnation does not slumber; it will come swiftly, and, in all probability, very suddenly upon many of you. You have reason to wonder that you are not already in Hell. It is doubtless the case of some whom you have seen and known, that never deserved Hell more than you, and that heretofore appeared as likely to have been now alive as you. Their case is past all hope; they are crying in extreme misery and perfect despair; but here you are in the land of the living and in the house of God, and have an opportunity to obtain salvation. What would not those poor damned hopeless souls give for one day's opportunity such as you now enjoy!

And now you have an extraordinary opportunity, a day wherein Christ has thrown the door of mercy wide open, and stands in calling and crying with a loud voice to poor sinners; a day wherein many are flocking to him, and pressing into the kingdom of God. Many are daily
coming from the east, west, north and south; many that were very lately in the same miserable condition that you are in, are now in a

4. **the Lamb** Jesus.

Vocabulary Builder
dolorous (dō′ lər əs) *adj.* sad; mournful

Literary Analysis
Sermon and Oratory
What action is this passage beginning "But this is the dismal case" designed to inspire?

9 **Reading Check**
What does Edwards say will happen when the day of mercy has passed?

8 Literary Analysis
Sermon and Oratory

- Invite students to explain the basic purpose of oratory.
  Answer: Oratory is intended to persuade listeners and to inspire them to take action.
- **Ask** a student volunteer to read the first three sentences of the third paragraph on this page.

Monitor Progress: Ask students the Literary Analysis question: What action is the passage beginning "But this is the dismal case" designed to inspire?
Answer: This passage is designed to inspire parishioners to repent for their sins and convert their hearts by becoming "born again."

9 Reading Check

Answer: He says that sinners "will be wholly lost and thrown away of God" and that "God will have no other use to put you to, but to suffer misery."

Differentiated Instruction
Solutions for All Learners

Strategy for Less Proficient Readers
Invite students to engage in choral readings of parts of Edwards's sermon. (You might wish to alternate students' choral readings with your own reading aloud.) Choose short passages for students to read together, and encourage discussion after each passage of important images, symbols, and ideas. Encourage students to listen for repetition of words, phrases, or ideas.

Strategy for Gifted/Talented Students
Invite students to prepare oral interpretations of passages from Edwards's sermon. Have them consider various ways to make the work accessible to an audience, such as gestures, correct pronunciation, appropriate speaking rate, volume, pitch, and tone. Remind students that all of these elements must be properly utilized to achieve just the right mood for the sermon.

10 Reading Strategy
Using Context Clues

- Read aloud with students the selection's penultimate paragraph. Have them listen for images suggesting abundance.
- Invite a student volunteer to explain what it means to *feast*.
- **Ask** students the Reading Strategy question: What clue does the reference to "feasting" provide to the meaning of *perishing*?
  Answer: Edwards sets up a series of opposites in this passage. Thus, knowing that *feasting* means "eating a rich and elaborate meal" suggests that *perishing* means "dying" as from lack of nourishment.

ASSESS

Answers

1. **Possible responses:** (a) fearful, humbled, and confused (b) shocked to learn of the Puritans' harsh religious beliefs (c) impressed by the power, and beauty of Edwards's oratory.
2. (a) the hand of God (b) His listeners mistakenly believe that their behavior keeps them from falling into Hell.
3. (a) The words *angry* and *sinners* suggest the emotional focus of Edwards's message. (b) He presents God as indifferent, contemptuous, and merciless, although capable of pity as well.
4. (a) mercy and salvation; (b) To obtain these things, sinners must repent.
5. (a) **Sample response:** black clouds hanging over the heads of sinners and dammed waters waiting to burst through the floodgate; (b) According to Edwards's creed, all of nature is controlled by God. Images of destructive and powerful nature thus become symbolic of God's own power.
6. **Sample answer:** Edwards's sermon was highly effective. Even contemporary readers can feel the sting of Edwards's threats.
7. (a) Students might mention subjects such as the perils of substance abuse. (b) Students should support their opinions with clearly stated reasons, examples, and details.

happy state, with their hearts filled with love to him who has loved
them, and washed them from their sins in his own blood, and rejoicing
10 in hope of the glory of God. How awful is it to be left behind at such a
day! To see so many others feasting, while you are pining and perishing! To see so many rejoicing and singing for joy of heart, while you
have cause to mourn for sorrow of heart, and howl for vexation of
spirit! . . .

Therefore, let everyone that is out of Christ now awake and fly from the wrath to come. The wrath of Almighty God is now undoubtedly hanging over a great part of this congregation: let everyone fly out of Sodom.[5] "Haste and escape for your lives, look not behind you, escape to the mountain, lest you be consumed."[6]

5. **Sodom** (säd′ əm) In the Bible, a city destroyed by fire because of the sinfulness of its people.
6. **"Haste . . . consumed"** from Genesis 19:17, the angels' warning to Lot, the only virtuous man in Sodom, to flee the city before they destroy it.

Reading Strategy
Using Context Clues
What clue does the reference to "feasting" provide to the meaning of *perishing*?

Critical Reading

1. **Respond:** How might you have reacted to this sermon if you had been **(a)** a "Puritan," **(b)** a Native American, **(c)** another leader of the Great Awakening? Explain.
2. **(a) Recall:** According to the opening paragraph, what keeps sinners from falling into hell? **(b) Interpret:** According to Edwards, what do his listeners mistakenly feel keeps them from falling into hell?
3. **(a) Recall:** What words in the sermon's title suggest the emotional focus of Edwards's message? **(b) Analyze:** What additional traits does Edwards attribute to God as the sermon progresses?
4. **(a) Recall:** Toward the end of the sermon, what does Edwards say sinners can obtain? **(b) Analyze Cause and Effect:** What must sinners do to obtain these things?
5. **(a) Classify:** Note at least two images of natural destruction that Edwards uses to depict the wrath of God. **(b) Evaluate:** Why would images of the power of nature be particularly appropriate to Edwards's message?
6. **Evaluate:** Given his purpose and the audience of worshipers to whom he spoke, do you think Edwards's sermon was effective? Why or why not?
7. **(a) Extend:** For what other types of subjects might an appeal to an audience's fears be an effective persuasive technique? **(b) Judge:** Do you think it is right for a speaker to appeal to an audience's fears? Why or why not?

Go Online
Author Link
For: More about Jonathan Edwards
Visit: www.PHSchool.com
Web Code: ere-9110

Go Online **Author Link** For additional information about Jonathan Edwards, have students type in the Web Code, then select E from the alphabet, and then select Jonathan Edwards.

Apply the Skills

from *Sinners in the Hands of an Angry God*

Literary Analysis

Sermon

1. What point of view or message is Edwards conveying in this **sermon**?
2. **(a)** To what emotion does Edwards primarily appeal in his effort to motivate his congregation? **(b)** Considering Edwards's purpose, why is this an appropriate choice? Explain your answer.
3. **(a)** Use the chart shown here to identify the many symbols and images Edwards uses to describe God's wrath. **(b)** How do these symbols and images add to the impact of Edwards's message?

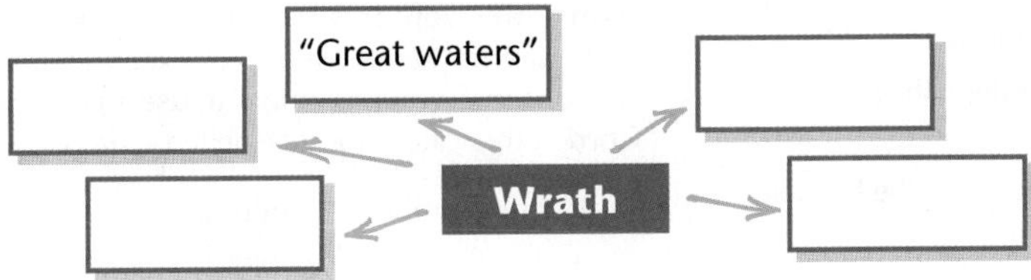

4. What does Edwards seem to feel about those who maintain a "form of religion" or who seem "moral and strict"?

Connecting Literary Elements

5. What statements does Edwards make that indicate an understanding of the people he is addressing?
6. Why might Edwards's **oratory** have been less effective if he had not had a reputation as a brilliant spiritual leader?

Reading Strategy

Using Context Clues

7. Use **context clues** to define the italicized words:
8. "you are every day treasuring up more wrath; the waters are constantly rising, and *waxing* more and more mighty. . . ."
9. "The God that holds you over the pit of Hell, much as one holds a spider, or some loathsome insect over the fire, *abhors* you, and is dreadfully provoked. . . ."

Extend Understanding

10. **Cultural Connection:** In which situations, if any, is it justifiable to use fear to get a person to improve his or her behavior? Explain.

QuickReview

A **sermon** is a speech that has a definite point of view and is delivered from the pulpit during a worship service.

Oratory is public speaking that is formal and persuasive and that appeals to the emotions.

Using the **context**—the surrounding words or sentences—can be an effective way to unlock the meaning of an unfamiliar word.

Go Online
Assessment

For: Self-test
Visit: www.PHSchool.com
Web Code: era-6107

Go Online Assessment Students may use the **Self-test** to prepare for **Selection Test A** or **Selection Test B**.

Answers

1. Edwards is trying to convince his audience of the need to repent in order to save themselves from damnation.
2. (a) He appeals to his listeners' sense of fear and uncertainty. (b) It is an appropriate choice because it taps into listeners' existing doubts about the strength of their faith and virtuousness of their behavior. Their fear of damnation might make them heed Edwards's message.
3. (a) Possible responses include bow and arrow, fire, and rough wind. (b) These symbols and familiar, concrete images reinforce the idea of God as a hostile force with a variety of means—both physical and psychological—to cause human suffering.

   Another sample answer can be found on **Literary Analysis Graphic Organizer B**, p. 24 in ***Graphic Organizer Transparencies***.
4. Edwards seems to feel that these individuals will nonetheless be viewed by God as contemptible.
5. **Possible response:** He appeals to their innate sense of fear and humility. He describes their religious beliefs accurately.
6. Edwards's reputation preceded him; it made people give greater credence to his message. Had he been less famous, the congregation might have doubted his motives or his techniques.
7. (a) *Waxing* means "growing or building." References to water that is "constantly increasing" and "constantly rising" and the words "more and more" indicate something that is getting larger in size. (b) *Abhors* means "detests or is disgusted by." If God feels towards the listener as he might toward a spider or "some loathsome insect," then abhor must be associated with feelings of hatred or disgust.
8. Students may say that scare tactics are justified in situations where someone's habits or actions endanger his or her health or well-being, or where attempts to reason with or educate the person are unsuccessful.

EXTEND/ASSESS

Answers

❶ Vocabulary Lesson

Word Analysis

1. b
2. a
3. c

Vocabulary Builder

dolorous; ineffable; omnipotent

Spelling Strategy

1. provocation
2. preferable
3. opposite

❷ Grammar and Style Lesson

Sample rewrite: When we think of great preachers, Edwards is the name that most quickly comes to mind. Of the many Puritan sermonizers who rose to fame during the Great Awakening, Edwards is considered the most influential. Most of his writing appealed to reason; "Sinners" is his most emotional and most famous work.

Looking at Style

Sample response: ". . . ten thousand times greater than the strength of the stoutest, sturdiest devil in Hell . . . " —Edwards uses "greater" to compare a sinner's strength to that of a devil; he uses the superlatives "stoutest" and "sturdiest" to distinguish the particular devil among all devils.

WG Writing and Grammar, Ruby Level

Students will find further instruction and practice on adjectives and adverbs in Chapter 24, Section 1.

Build Language Skills

❶ Vocabulary Lesson

Word Analysis: Latin Prefix *omni-*

The Latin prefix *omni-* means "all" or "every." *Omnipotent,* then, means "all-powerful." Each of the adjectives below contains the prefix *omni-*. Use the information in parentheses to match each adjective with the situation to which it best applies.

1. omniscient (*sciens* = knowing)
2. omnivorous (*vor* = to eat)
3. omnipotent (*potent* = powerful)

a. how a zoologist might describe an animal that eats both meat and plants

b. how a student might describe a brilliant teacher

c. how a prisoner might describe his jailer

Vocabulary Builder: Context

Fill each blank in the following sentence with the appropriate word from the vocabulary list on page 101.

The citizens of Oz sighed with a __?__ air, indicating their __?__ sadness at learning that the Wizard they considered __?__ was just an ordinary man, hiding behind a curtain.

Spelling Strategy

To decide how to spell the unstressed vowel sound represented by a schwa (ə), think of another form of the word in which the vowel is stressed. Then, use the same vowel. For example, think of *morality,* and you will know to use an *a* in *moral.* Correct the following misspelled words.

1. provacation **2.** prefarable **3.** oppasite

❷ Grammar and Style Lesson

Forms of Adjectives and Adverbs

The **comparative** form of adjectives and adverbs is used to compare two things or ideas; the **superlative** form is used to compare more than two things or ideas. Many words follow the pattern below to indicate comparative and superlative degrees:

Regular form: Ann is *tall.*

Comparative: Yvette is *taller.*

Superlative: Miku is the *tallest.*

Other adjectives and adverbs use the words *more* or *most,* as in "Ann is *more punctual* than Joe. Mina is the *most punctual* of all."

Finally, some forms such as "good, better, best" are irregular.

Practice Rewrite the following paragraph, correcting all errors in comparisons:

When we think of great preachers, Edwards is the name that quickliest comes to mind. Of the many Puritan sermonizers who rose to fame during the Great Awakening, Edwards is considered the more influential. Most of his writing appealed to reason; "Sinners" is his most emotional and more famous work.

Looking at Style Review the sermon, and find an adjective and an adverb in each form. Explain how Edwards uses each one to create a powerful image.

WG *Prentice Hall Writing and Grammar Connection: Chapter 24, Section 1*

Assessment Practice

Summarizing Written Texts (For more practice, see *Standardized Test Preparation Workbook*, p. 7.)

Many tests require students to identify the best summary of a written passage. Present the following sample, and ask students to choose the best summary.

> However you may have reformed your life in many things, and may have had religious affections, and may keep up a form of religion in your families and closets, and in the house of God, it is nothing but his mere pleasure that keeps you from being this moment swallowed up in everlasting destruction.

A God can still condemn you even if you live virtuously, pray privately, and go to church.

B God will pardon you if you go to church.

C People should pray and lead virtuous lives.

D People should be religious in order to win God's approval.

B is accurate, but incomplete. C and D are misleading: praying and being religious don't necessarily secure God's grace. *A* is the best summary.

Writing Lesson

Timed Writing: Evaluation of Persuasion

A speaker's choice of persuasive techniques should depend on the audience and the occasion. Write an evaluation of the persuasive techniques of imagery and theme that Edwards uses. Discuss the response he evokes and the ways he achieves it. Your evaluation will have greater clarity and strength if its elements work together to form a unified effect. ***(40 minutes)***

Prewriting ***(10 minutes)*** To help focus your writing, jot down examples of Edwards's uses of imagery and identify his specific themes. Then, evaluate their effectiveness in a clearly defined statement.

Drafting ***(20 minutes)*** Use the statement you wrote as the basis for a strong, focused opening paragraph. Support your main point in the paragraphs that follow.

Model: Building Unity

Jonathan Edwards appealed to his audience's vulnerability by using powerful, elemental images of nature run amok. His images of air, water, and fire terrified his audience by summoning up mental pictures of unlimited natural destruction.

A general statement followed by specific examples builds unity.

Revising ***(10 minutes)*** Read your evaluation as though you were seeing it for the first time. Eliminate any information that is unrelated to the main idea.

WG Prentice Hall Writing and Grammar Connection: Chapter 14, Section 3

Extend Your Learning

Listening and Speaking Sermons like those of Dr. Martin Luther King, Jr., still have the power to inspire us to take action in our own lives. With a group, research King's sermons and their role in the civil rights movement. Give a brief **oral report** on your findings. Be sure to include the following:

- direct quotes from Dr. King's sermons
- quotes from reports in the media

If possible, include a short video or audiotape of King as part of your report. **[Group Activity]**

Research and Technology Because of their religious beliefs, Puritans developed a strong sense of the importance of work. Gather information about Puritan doctrine and the famous "work ethic." Create a **handbook** that includes guidelines and rules for living and working as a proper Puritan.

For: An additional research activity
Visit: www.PHSchool.com
Web Code: erd-7106

Assessment Resources

The following resources can be used to assess students' knowledge and skills.

Unit 1 Resources

Selection Test A, pp. 105–107
Selection Test B, pp. 108–110

General Resources

Rubrics for Critique, pp. 75–76
Rubric for Delivering a Research Presentation, p. 91

Go Online Assessment — Students may use the **Self-test** to prepare for **Selection Test A** or **Selection Test B.**

3 Writing Lesson

- To guide students in writing this evaluation of persuasion, give them the **Support for Writing Lesson** page (***Unit 1 Resources,*** p. 102).
- Students' evaluations should express a clear and definite view of Edwards's achievement in this excerpt from *Sinners in the Hands of an Angry God.* Remind students that the effectiveness of the sermon is related directly to Edwards's Puritan audience, not to a contemporary American one.
- Students should not only identify Edwards's principal themes, but should also explain how these themes interrelate. Similarly, students should cite the sermon's key images and symbols and explain how they reinforce each other.
- Use the rubrics for Critique in ***General Resources,*** pp. 75–76 to evaluate students' writing.

4 Listening and Speaking

- Encourage students to use various types of research sources. Possible print sources include biographies of Dr. King, oral histories of the civil rights movement, encyclopedias, and newspaper and magazine articles. In addition, students may be able to locate audio recordings of King's sermons and speeches, as well as video documentaries such as *Eyes on the Prize.* Lastly, students might use the Internet to gather additional information.
- For their oral presentations, encourage students to provide written transcripts of certain passages of sermons so that their classmates might follow along with the text as they listen to Dr. King's speaking style.
- To evaluate students' oral reports, use the Rubric for Delivering a Research Presentation in ***General Resources,*** p. 91.
- The **Support for Extend Your Learning** page (***Unit 1 Resources,*** p. 103) provides guided note-taking opportunities to help students complete the Extend Your Learning activities.

Go Online Research — Have students type in the Web Code for another research activity.

Meeting Your Standards

Students will

1. **write an analytic essay on literary periods.**
2. **use writing strategies to generate ideas and to plan, organize, evaluate, and revise writing.**

Prewriting

- To give students guidance in developing this assignment, give them the **Writing About Literature** support pages, pp. 111–112 in ***Unit 1 Resources.***
- Have a class discussion on the ways in which the writers represented in this unit respond to their circumstances and their world. This discussion should help students find ideas for topics.
- Suggest that students take notes on the three selections they will explore in their essays.
- When constructing their thesis statements, students should focus on common threads they find in their notes.

Tips for Test Taking

A writing prompt on the SAT or ACT test may assess students' ability to analyze a topic, state a point of view regarding the topic, and support the point of view with evidence. When writing under timed circumstances, students will need to quickly clarify a point of view (their thesis statement) and the evidence that supports it. Since they won't be able to refer to a text, their evidence must be based on their own experiences, readings, or observations.

Writing About Literature

Analyze Literary Periods

Although the forms and context of earliest American literature are diverse, much of it deals with people's attempts to cope with the world around them. Strategies included everything from trying to overcome hunger and disease, to trying to set up a workable government, to trying to please an angry God. Writers' concerns reflected both their own belief systems and the circumstances in which they found themselves. Using the assignment outlined in the yellow box, write an analytical essay about this period in American literature.

Assignment: Living in This World

Write an analytical essay that explores the way the earliest Americans (both Native Americans and European immigrants) tried to cope with their world.

Criteria:

- Include a thesis statement that draws on information from at least three different selections in the unit.
- Support your thesis with details from specific selections.
- Approximate length: 700 words.

Prewriting

Review the selections. Look for ways in which the writers try to cope with the world. Use these questions as a guide:

- Does the writer focus on the physical world?
- Does the writer focus on other people?
- Does the writer discuss political and social systems?
- Does the writing explain how the world was created?

Use index cards to note details of people's efforts to cope. On each card, identify the title of the selection and the page number, details describing people's actions or reactions, and the conclusions you draw from these details.

Conclusion: The urge to explore was limited by obstacles within the environment. This account shows that some newcomers survived by following the advice of local inhabitants.

Model: Drawing Conclusions Based on Evidence

"Boulders Taller Than the Great Tower of Seville"

p. 34 Two of the explorers descend the canyon, determining that the terrain is rough and the river is as wide as was previously reported by Indians.

p. 34 The explorers do not travel farther up the canyon because of the lack of water reported by their Indian guides.

Find a focus. Review your notes to find a working thesis that expresses the main idea you want to explore. Write the idea in one sentence, and use this sentence as a working thesis.

Gather details. Once you have your working thesis, focus on the relevant selections. Return to your index cards to gather more details. Then, identify the ideas that will best support your thesis statement.

Read to Write

Reread the texts and focus on the motivation behind the individuals' questions, explanations, and struggles. Take notes to discover how those individuals attempted to cope in the world.

Teaching Resources

The following resources can be used to extend or enrich the instruction for Writing About Literature.

Unit Resources

Writing About Literature, pp. 111–112

General Resources

Rubrics for Comparison-and-Constrast Essay, pp. 69–70

Graphic Organizer Transparencies

Cause-and-Effect Flowchart, p. 305

Drafting

Organize into paragraphs. You might want to write a separate paragraph for each selection that illustrates your thesis, or you might choose to devote each paragraph to a unique concept that all the selections you have identified support.

Develop each paragraph. Develop each paragraph, supplying details from the selections that clearly support your ideas.

Two Approaches to Paragraph Organization

By Selection	Selection One	Selection Two
Survival required • getting food and shelter. • overcoming enemy attacks.	Discuss all the ways in which this selection supports your thesis.	Discuss all the ways in which this selection supports your thesis.

By Subject	Aspect One	Aspect Two
Survival was threatened by hostilities between old and new arrivals.	Analyze all of the selections that illustrate this idea.	Analyze all of the selections that illustrate this idea.

Write to Learn
Writing can help you transform vague ideas into a clear analysis.

Revising and Editing

Review content: Check the relevance of details. Review each paragraph, evaluating the connection between the main idea and the support. Confirm that details are relevant, and delete those that do not further your analysis.

Review style and format: Replace unclear pronouns. Improve your writing by checking for unclear pronouns. Review your essay, circling each pronoun and checking that the word to which it refers will be clear to your readers.

Vague Referent: The *guides* told the *Spaniards* that the terrain was dry and difficult, so they turned back.

Clarify the sentence above by replacing the pronoun with a noun that clearly refers to the Spaniards, such as *the European explorers.*

Write to Explain
Help your reader understand your reasoning by making clear connections between details from the selections and the conclusions you have drawn.

Publishing and Presenting

Hold a panel discussion. In today's world, we still have to figure out how to adapt to our environment and one another if we are to live successfully. Hold a panel discussion in which you and your classmates identify the selections that had the wisest lessons for today's reader.

WG *Prentice Hall Writing and Grammar Connection: Chapter 14*

Drafting

Make sure students understand the two methods of organization: by selection and by subject. Students should choose the method that helps to make their essay clear.

Revising and Editing

Students may want to exchange papers with partners. Partners can help identify irrelevant details and unclear pronoun references. Students' ideas may be clear to them, but may not be clear to their readers.

Publishing and Presenting

You may want to organize students so that each selection is represented in each group, rather than grouping students who wrote about the same selection.

WG **Writing and Grammar, Ruby Level**

Students will find additional instruction on writing an analytical essay in Chapter 14.

Writing and Grammar Interactive CD-ROM Students can use the following tools as they complete their analytical essays:

- Topic Bank
- Cause and Effect
- Unity and Coherence

Six Traits Focus

✓	Ideas		Word Choice
✓	Organization		Sentence Fluency
	Voice	✓	Conventions

Assessing the Essay

To evaluate students' essays, use the Comparison-and-Contrast Essay rubrics, pp. 69–70 in ***General Resources.***

Differentiated Instruction Solutions for All Learners

Strategy for Less Proficient Writers
Have students identify their main arguments and list the supporting details. Remind them to return to the text for quotations that support their arguments.

Strategy for English Learners
Encourage students to include quotations from the selections in their essays. Students should be careful to copy these quotations exactly. They should look up any unfamiliar words to be sure the quotations support their ideas.

Strategy for Advanced Writers
Encourage students to review their essays, making sure they have explained the relevance of each quotation, rather than simply including it in the text.

Meeting Your Standards

Students will

1. write an autobiographical narrative.
2. use writing strategies to generate ideas, organize, evaluate, and revise the composition.
3. apply grammar skills.

From the Author's Desk

Susan Power

Show students Segment 3 on Susan Power on *From the Author's Desk DVD.* Discuss Power's comments about how she grounds her fictional writing in real-life events (see Power's writing on p. 115).

Writing Genres

Using the Form Point out to students that autobiographical narration is often incorporated into other types of writing. Point out these examples:

- Speeches and persuasive essays frequently include autobiographical segments.
- Personal letters often contain descriptions of autobiographical events.
- Autobiographical writing is usually a core element in journals and other personal writing.

Online Essay Scorer

A writing prompt for this mode of writing can be found on the *PH Online Essay Scorer* at PHSuccessNet.com.

Writing Workshop

Narration: Autobiographical Narrative

An old saying tells writers to write about what they know. This advice has produced some of the finest stories in literature. Some of these stories are fiction, but others are true stories about what the writer knows best: his or her own life. Such writing is called **autobiographical narrative.** Follow the steps outlined in this workshop to write your own autobiographical narrative.

Assignment Write an autobiographical narrative about an important moment or a special relationship in your own life.

What to Include Your autobiographical narrative should feature the following elements:

- the writer as the main character and other clearly defined characters
- vivid details that bring events, settings, and people to life
- a logical organization that relates events
- a sequence of events that incorporates conflict or tension
- an insight that the writer has gained as a result of the experience

To preview the criteria on which your autobiographical narrative may be assessed, see the rubric on page 119.

Using the Form

You may use elements of autobiographical narrative in these writing situations:

- personal letters
- college-application essays
- journal entries
- anecdotes

To get the feel for autobiographical narrative, read "A Journey Through Texas" by Alvar Núñez Cabeza de Vaca on pages 42–46.

Teaching Resources

The following resources can be used to enrich or extend the instruction for the Writing Workshop.

Unit 1 Resources
Writing Workshop—Narration: Autobiographical Narrative, pp. 113–114

General Resources
Rubrics for Narration: Autobiographical Narrative, pp. 43–44

Graphic Organizer Transparencies
Cluster Diagram, p. 307

From the Author's Desk DVD
Susan Power, Segments 3 and 4

Prewriting

Choosing Your Topic

Choose an experience, a memory, or a relationship to write about in your autobiographical narrative. To find a topic, use one of the following strategies:

- **Timeline of Your Life** Beginning with your earliest memory, create a timeline that lists important events in your life in chronological order. Include significant people and places. Review your timeline, and choose one key event as your topic.
- **Idea Notebook** For an entire day, record your activities and thoughts in a notebook. Keep track of your daily experiences, but also jot down ideas about how you got to this point in your life. What events, relationships, accomplishments, or even failures have made you the person you are today? Isolate a few incidents from your past that were memorable turning points in your life, and then choose one as your topic.
- **Memory Notes** Sit down with a relative or friend, and go through a photo album or scrapbook. Jot down notes about what these moments were really like—how you actually felt back then. Talk to an older relative who might remember some of your big moments from a different perspective. Review your notes, and then choose one of these memories as your topic.

Narrowing Your Topic

Once you have chosen a basic topic, think about how you can sharpen your focus. For example, if you have decided to write about your family's move to California when you were in the sixth grade, you might focus on a specific event or episode that occurred as a result of your move—something that turned out to be a turning point in your life.

Gathering Details

Create an event chart. Once you have chosen your topic, gather details by creating an event chart like the one shown. In each box of the chart, list a key event or episode related to your topic. The chart should flow from one association to another and help you isolate the specific event that ultimately led to an important insight or a change in your life. In the chart shown, the writer has highlighted a key event in yellow.

EVENTS

Father got promotion
↓
Family moved to California from Ohio
↓
Loss of friends — fear of new
↓
Mom gave us surfboards and lessons
↓
Began to love the ocean
↓
Decided to study oceanography in college

Tips for Using Rubrics

- Before students begin work on this assignment, have them preview the **Rubric for Self-Assessment**, p. 25 in ***Graphic Organizer Transparencies*** to know what is expected.
- Review the Assessment criteria in class. Before students use the **Rubric for Self-Assessment**, work with them to rate the Student Model by applying one or two criteria to it.
- If you wish to assess students' autobiographical narratives with either a 4-point, 5-point, or a 6-point scoring rubric, see ***General Resources***, pp. 43 and 44.

TEACH

Prewriting

- Explain to students that the events of their narratives do not necessarily have to be told in chronological order, but putting these events on a timeline will help them to organize their thoughts.
- In narrowing their topic, suggest that students identify ideas related to their topics with the **Cluster Diagram** in ***Graphic Organizer Transparencies***, p. 307. Students may decide that one of the related ideas is a more focused topic for an essay.
- Explain that research may be needed if students refer to factual events with details they do not recall or if they need to clarify the context in which they are writing for their readers.
- Point out to students how differently they may describe an event to a friend their own age and to a teacher. Remind them that the style and many of the details they include should be determined by their audience.

Six Traits Focus

✔	Ideas		Word Choice
✔	Organization		Sentence Fluency
	Voice		Conventions

Writing and Grammar, Ruby Level

Students will find additional instruction on prewriting for an autobiographical narrative in Chapter 4, Section 2.

Writing and Grammar Interactive Textbook CD-ROM

Students can use the following tools as they complete their autobiographical narratives:

- Timeline
- Cluster Diagram
- Story Map
- Character Trait Word Bin
- Vague Adjectives Revising Tool

Drafting

- Instruct students to hint at the conflict in the opening of their drafts before telling how it began, developed, and was resolved. To conclude, students should reflect or comment on what they learned from the experience.
- Explain that because the climax is a story's most interesting and suspenseful moment, it is the most important point in a story. Therefore, all the details that come before the climax should clearly lead to it.
- Before students think about their lead, suggest that they identify the focal point of the narrative. For example, is it the setting, a person, or an event? Tell students to write their compelling lead around this central point.
- Discuss how dialogue can help the reader understand characters and how it can increase suspense and develop the conflict. Emphasize, however, that dialogue should not be included unless it contributes directly to the main idea and plot of the narrative.
- Remind students that each time a new character begins speaking, they should start a new paragraph. The paragraph might include just the words of the character, or it might also include a description of the character or a commentary on the words spoken.

Six Traits Focus

✔	Ideas		Word Choice
✔	Organization		Sentence Fluency
	Voice		Conventions

WG Writing and Grammar, Ruby Level

Students will find additional instruction on drafting an autobiographical narrative in Chapter 4, Section 3.

Writing Workshop

Drafting

Shaping Your Writing

Organize significant events. Like any good story, your narrative will need a beginning, a middle, and an end. You will also need to identify its central **conflict**—a problem that needs to be resolved. Organize the events of your story to build tension as the conflict develops and the reader begins to care about what is happening. Identify the **climax**, the moment when the conflict reaches its greatest intensity. Then, analyze how the tension will decrease as the conflict moves toward an ending, or resolution. Use a diagram like the one shown to organize your events.

Climax
The conflict is greatest.
The conflict intensifies.
Rising Action
Falling Action
The conflict winds down.
Exposition
The conflict is introduced.
Resolution
The conflict is resolved.

Begin with a compelling lead. Devise a simple but catchy sentence that provides just the right amount of information to hook the reader's curiosity. Then, let the rest of your narrative develop this lead.

Providing Elaboration

Use thought shots. As you draft, pause for a moment at the end of each paragraph. Then, follow these steps:

1. Scan the paragraph for uses of the word *I*. For each one, ask yourself how you reacted to what you described.
2. For each reaction, draw a circle, or thought shot, in the margin.
3. Inside the circle, jot down notes about your reaction.

Choose your best thought shots to include in your final draft.

Include dialogue. One of the best ways to make your writing more vivid is to include dialogue. Presenting people's actual words will bring them alive as characters and help reveal the story's conflict and climax.

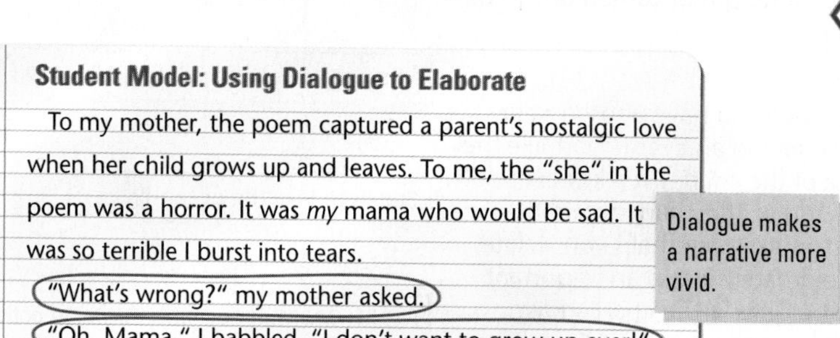
Student Model: Using Dialogue to Elaborate

To my mother, the poem captured a parent's nostalgic love when her child grows up and leaves. To me, the "she" in the poem was a horror. It was *my* mama who would be sad. It was so terrible I burst into tears.

"What's wrong?" my mother asked.

"Oh, Mama," I babbled. "I don't want to grow up ever!"

Dialogue makes a narrative more vivid.

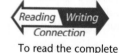

Reading Writing Connection

To read the complete student model, see page 118.

Tips for Using Technology in Writing

Encourage students to write their narratives on computers. Composing on a computer facilitates writing by allowing students to put down their thoughts quickly as they develop. Students can easily go forward and backward in the text to add, delete, or move around ideas.

Students can also take advantage of the reviewing feature on many word processing programs; this will enable them to enter comments that are not part of the text. (The reviewing feature is accessible as a tool bar option.) Students can use this feature to enter "Throughshots" or other ideas that they want to think more about before incorporating them into the text.

From the Author's Desk
Susan Power on Choosing the Right Word

Susan Power

Beginnings are always difficult for me. I'll have an idea for a story, or, as in this excerpt from a nonfiction essay, a memory from childhood, but I won't know where to start. Here I wanted to write about the body of water where I'd spent many happy hours—Lake Michigan. Should I begin with hard facts, its depth and circumference? No. After many drafts, I began with my mother's stories.

"Finding the precise word can be tricky."

—Susan Power

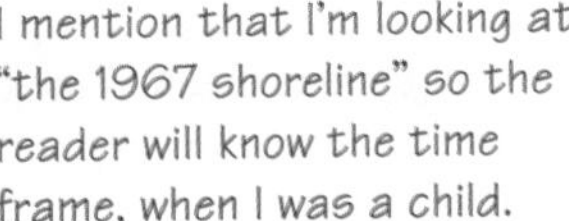

Professional Model:

from "Chicago Waters," from *Roofwalker*

My mother used to say that by the time I was an old woman, Lake Michigan would be the size of a silver dollar. She pinched her index finger with her thumb to show me the pitiful dimensions.

"People will gather around the tiny lake, what's left of it, and cluck over a spoonful of water," she told me.

I learned to squint at the 1967 shoreline until I had carved away the structures and roads built on landfill and could imagine the lake and its city as my mother found them in 1942 when she arrived in Chicago. I say *the lake and its city* rather than *the city and its lake,* because my mother taught me another secret: the city of Chicago belongs to Lake Michigan.

But which of my mother's pronouncements to believe? That Chicago would swallow the Midwestern sea, smother it in concrete, or that the lake wielded enough strength to outpolitick even Mayor Richard Daley?

Mayor Daley, Sr. is gone now, but the lake remains, alternately tranquil and riled, changing colors like a mood ring. I guess we know who won.

When my mother watches the water from her lakeside apartment building, she still sucks in her breath. "You have to respect the power of that lake," she tells me. And I do now. I do.

I mention that I'm looking at "the 1967 shoreline" so the reader will know the time frame, when I was a child.

I rely on a dictionary and thesaurus to help me find the precise, specific word. First I tried, *sayings,* but that didn't exhibit my mother's strength as much as *pronouncements.*

Wrestling with word choice again, I used *beat* initially but later selected *outpolitick*—more appropriate when describing a politician.

From the Author's Desk

- Show students Segment 4 on Susan Power on **From the Author's Desk DVD.** Discuss how incorporating autobiographical events into her writing has acted as a tool of self-discovery for Power.
- **Ask** students why *pronouncements* is a better word choice in Power's narrative than *sayings.*
  Possible response: *Pronouncements* is a more specific word, and it better conveys the mother's strength. *Sayings* is bland and imprecise.
- **Ask** students to explain why autobiographical writing could benefit from the kinds of adjustments Power made in the excerpt *from Roofwalker.*
  Possible response: An autobiographical narrative vividly describes a real-life event to readers. Specific, precise words that fit the context of the narrative help bring the event to life.
- Have students **identify** how Powers makes a connection between the past and the present.
  Answer: At the end of the excerpt, she says that she now "respects the power of the lake," as her mother once told her to do.

Revising

- If time permits, let students wait 24 hours before they begin to revise their drafts. Explain that time away from a piece of writing helps the writer see his or her work with fresh eyes and renewed attention and energy.
- Point out that the connection to the present does not have to appear at any particular point in the narrative. It can occur at the beginning, at the end, or in comments throughout the narrative.
- Point out that transitional words that show a shift in time and a connection of ideas help make connections between the past and the present. In the Student Model, explain that the word *since* tells that the writer has changed. The transition *because* shows a cause-and-effect connection between what happened in the past and what the writer now feels.
- Write these sentences on the board, and **ask** students to suggest fresh, powerful adjectives to replace vague, unimaginative ones.

  1. *My grandmother was a cheerful and happy woman.*
  2. *The loud thunder of the approaching storm sent cold shivers down my back.*
  3. *A big, noisy crowd gathered outside the school.*
  4. *A cold chill was in the air, but the good smell of the chili made me glad to be there.*

  Possible responses:

  1. *My grandmother was a merry and contented woman.*
  2. *The deafening thunder of the approaching storm sent icy shivers down my back.*
  3. *An immense, boisterous crowd gathered outside the school.*
  4. *An arctic chill was in the air, but the welcoming aroma of the chili made me glad to be there.*

Six Traits Focus

✔	Ideas	✔	Word Choice
✔	Organization		Sentence Fluency
	Voice		Conventions

Writing and Grammar, Ruby Level

Students will find additional instruction on revising an autobiographical narrative in Chapter 4, Section 4.

Writing Workshop

Revising

Revising Your Overall Structure

Connect to the present. The resolution, or ending, of your autobiographical narrative should make a connection between the experience you are writing about and the person you have become as a result of that experience. To strengthen that connection, follow these steps:

1. Think about how the experience has affected you—what you learned or how you changed as a result of what happened to you in the past.
2. Highlight passages that show exactly what brought about your insight or change.
3. Revise your draft by adding statements that show how the autobiographical experience you have written about in your narrative continues to affect you today.

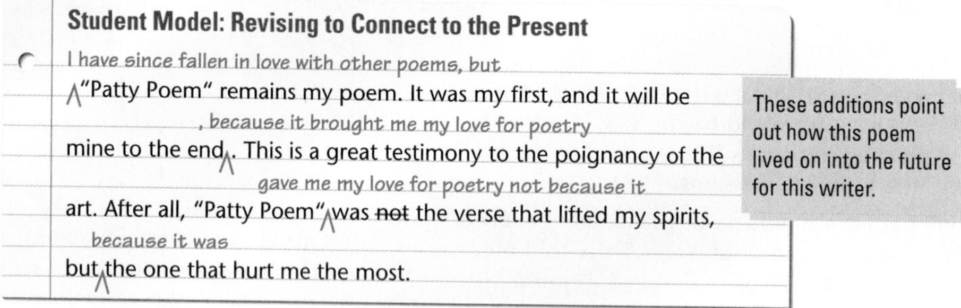

Student Model: Revising to Connect to the Present

I have since fallen in love with other poems, but
^"Patty Poem" remains my poem. It was my first, and it will be
, because it brought me my love for poetry
mine to the end^. This is a great testimony to the poignancy of the
gave me my love for poetry not because it
art. After all, "Patty Poem"^was ~~not~~ the verse that lifted my spirits,
because it was
but^the one that hurt me the most.

These additions point out how this poem lived on into the future for this writer.

Revising Your Word Choice

Use specific, precise adjectives. Some nouns always seem to wind up being modified by the same overused adjectives. All *efforts* are *noble*. Most *fears* seem to be *overwhelming*. In your writing, avoid these usual suspects by replacing general or vague adjectives with specific and precise ones.

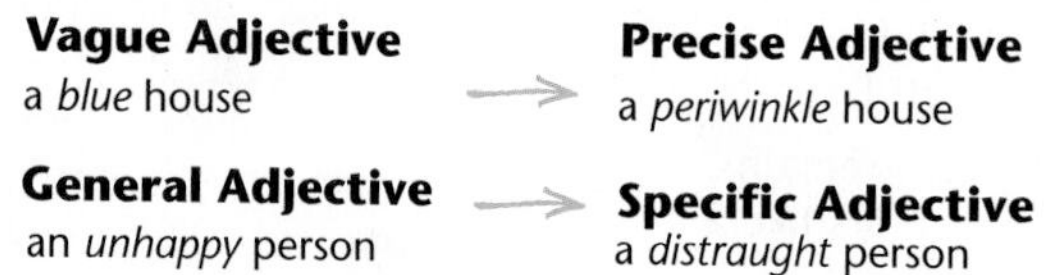

Vague Adjective		Precise Adjective
a *blue* house	→	a *periwinkle* house
General Adjective		**Specific Adjective**
an *unhappy* person	→	a *distraught* person

Peer Review: Have a partner review your draft, underlining adjectives and adjective-noun combinations that are vague or clichéd. Then, replace these words with more specific and surprising choices. Be prepared to justify your revision choices by explaining why your new adjectives and nouns are livelier, more specific, or less predictable.

Tips for Using Technology in Writing

When they reach the revision stage, students using word processing software may want to set their line spacing at double or even triple spacing before printing copies of their drafts. The extra spacing allows plenty of space to make changes between the lines, and the hard copy allows students to spread the pages out and look at the essay as a whole, rather than seeing only a few lines of it at once on a screen. Students should then transfer the changes to the electronic file.

Encourage students to save a version of their draft so that they can compare it to the revised version. Having a copy of previous versions will also allow them to go back to an earlier version if they decide some of the original passages were better before changes were made.

Developing Your Style

Vivid Word Choice

Word Choice Writers are constantly revising their words to make their writing clearer, sharper, and fresher. Adjectives are only one type of word that writers tweak to avoid generalities and clichés. You can also enliven your writing by making your nouns and verbs more precise and vivid. For example, use *convertible* instead of *car; bounded* instead of *ran; intoned* instead of *said*. Take the time to find the right word rather than a merely good-enough word.

Find It in Your Reading Read or review "Museum Indians," on page 35.

1. Identify three sentences that include specific nouns, active verbs, and vivid adjectives or adverbs. Make a list of these words, and identify their part of speech.
2. From the three sentences that you identified, choose the one you find most effective. In that sentence, point out two or more examples of Power's vivid word choice.

Apply It to Your Writing Review the draft of your autobiographical narrative. For each paragraph you have written, follow these steps:

1. Underline any nouns or verbs that strike you as vague or weak. Be sure to underline every use of the verb *to be* (*am, is, are, was,* and *were*). In the margin, jot down a few juicy alternatives for each word, and then choose the best replacement.
2. Highlight phrases that are wordy, and think about what you are really trying to say. Then, find one or two punchy words that mean the same thing or express your idea more forcefully than the highlighted phrase.
3. Check to see if there are any sentences with no underlining or highlighting. Take a look at these sentences more carefully. Challenge yourself to find any places where you could add vivid words to create a clearer picture or convey a stronger attitude.

Dull, Vague Words	Lively, Precise Words
The dog ran through the woods.	The terrier bounded through the underbrush.
I fell into the rough water.	I tumbled into the churning foam.
People yelled at the mayor.	Irate citizens harangued the mayor.

WG *Prentice Hall Writing and Grammar Connection: Chapter 1.*

Developing Your Style

- Ask volunteers to provide example sentences from their drafts. Have the class identify the nouns, verbs, adjectives, and adverbs.
- Guide the class in finding alternative word choices for the example sentences. Encourage students to debate alternative word choices. Ask them to explain why one word fits the context of the sentence better than another. Discuss why students should examine the reasons behind their word choices as they revise their own essays.
- As students apply the skill to their own writing, have them work in pairs to help each other in replacing vague words with more dynamic and precise ones.

WG **Writing and Grammar, Ruby Level**

Students will find additional instruction on making vivid word choices in Chapter 1.

Differentiated Instruction Solutions for All Learners

Strategy for English Learners

Students with more limited vocabularies should be advised to use a thesaurus for help in finding alternative word choices. Caution students against selecting words from a thesaurus without also evaluating their meaning in a dictionary; explain that the words listed may not be exact synonyms.

Strategy for Advanced Writers

Review with students how words with similar meanings can have different connotations; use the words *cheap, inexpensive, thrifty,* and *penny-pinching* to illustrate how different words appeal to a reader's emotions. Have students work in pairs to identify the connotations of key descriptive words and, if necessary, replace the words with those that better fit the tone and context of the narrative.

Student Model

- Explain that the Student Model is a sample and that narratives may be longer.
- Point out that Branden has centered her narrative around a crucial event that happened in her childhood. This may give students ideas for topics of their own.
- Have students discuss the details with which Branden sets the scene. Have them list specific details that they will use in their own essays.
- **Ask** students how the essay would have been affected if Branden had not quoted from the poem.
Possible response: Being able to read the poem themselves makes readers much more likely to identify with Branden's reaction to it.
- Ask three volunteers to take the roles of Branden, her mother, and the narrator and read the passage of dialogue that follows the poem.
- Emphasize that the dialogue is a much more powerful way of showing the scene than just telling the reader what happened. Point out that it gives insight into the feelings of the characters and makes the scene immediate—almost as though it is happening right now.
- Have a student read aloud the final paragraph of the narrative. Help students see that Branden states the reason she chose her topic and that she connects her experience to a broader statement about human life with a reference to "the poignancy of art."

Writing Genres
Autobiographical Writing

Explain to students that they will use autobiographical writing in many ways throughout their lives. They will find, for example, that many college applications require students to write essays on a given topic. Frequently, these essay topics are autobiographical. Likewise, cover letters for job applications are concise autobiographical essays that include only certain relevant details.

Writing Workshop

Student Model: Branden Boyer-White, Palm Springs, California

Discovering Poetry

My mother was a night owl. She worked nights as a nurse at the hospital. She liked it; the schedule suited her. The nights she was off, she maintained her nocturnal routine—active at night and asleep in the early part of the day.

One early morning, I went into the living room to find my mother reading a thick book called *Best Loved Poems to Read Again and Again*. My interest was piqued solely by the fact that the word *Poems* appeared in big, hot pink letters.

> Branden uses concrete details to set the scene.

"Is it good?" I asked her.

"Yeah, " she answered. "There's one you'll really like."

She began to thumb through the grainy white pages. She finally stopped and asked, "Ready?" I certainly was! I leaned forward.

"'Patty Poem,'" she read the title. *Who is Patty?* my mind buzzed. The poem began:

She never puts her toys away,
Just leaves them scattered where they lay, . . .

The poem was just three short stanzas. The final one came quickly:

> The inclusion of excerpts from the poem allows readers to understand the writer's emotional reaction.

When she grows and gathers poise,
I'll miss her harum-scarum noise,
And look in vain for scattered toys,
And I'll be sad.

A terrible sorrow washed over me. Whoever Patty was, she was a dreadful, mean girl. Then, the bombshell.

"It's you, honey," my mother sentimentalized.

To my mother, the poem captured a parent's nostalgic love when her child grows up and leaves. To me, the "she" in the poem was a horror. It was *my* mama who would be sad. It was so terrible I burst into tears.

"What's wrong?" my mother asked.

"Oh Mama," I babbled. "I don't want to grow up *ever*!"

> Dialogue makes the narrative more realistic and poignant.

She smiled. "Honey, it's okay. You're not growing up anytime soon. And when you do, I'll still love you, okay?"

"Okay," I hiccuped. My panic had subsided. But I could not stop thinking about that silly poem. After what seemed like a safe amount of time, I read the poem again and was mystified. It all fit so well together, like a puzzle. The language was simple, so simple I could plainly understand its meaning, yet it was still beautiful. I was now transfixed by the idea of poetry, words that had the power to make or break a person's world. . . .

I have since fallen in love with other poems, but "Patty Poem" remains my poem. It was my first, and it will be mine to the end, because it brought me my love for poetry. This is a great testimony to the poignancy of the art. After all, "Patty Poem" gave me my love for poetry not because it was the verse that lifted my spirits, but because it was the one that hurt me the most.

> Branden clearly demonstrates the importance of this experience.

Tips for Writing Dialogue

Have students work with partners when revising dialogue. Tell them to read the dialogue aloud and then discuss the following questions:

- Is the dialogue realistic?
- Do the quotes stand alone, or do you need to add an explanation to make the thought complete?
- Does the dialogue capture any dialect or speech mannerisms of the character?
- Have you described the speaker's hand gestures or facial expressions?
- Have you described the speaker's tone of voice or attitude?

Tell students to reproduce the quotations as accurately as they can recall. Caution them against making up dialogue. If they cannot remember the exact words, suggest that they paraphrase it.

Editing and Proofreading

Read your narrative, and correct errors in grammar, usage, punctuation, and spelling.

Focus on Spelling: As you review your draft, double-check words you tend to misspell. Because your narrative is autobiographical, be especially careful to spell the names of people and places correctly.

Publishing and Presenting

Consider one of the following ways to share your writing:

Deliver an oral presentation. Practice reading your autobiographical narrative aloud. Underline the most important passages so that you will remember to emphasize them. Also mark places where you want to change your tone of voice or pause briefly for dramatic effect.

Create an illustrated class anthology. With classmates, combine several narratives in a single binder. Include photographs or artwork that illustrate the narrative or capture its mood, setting, or time period. Also add a copy of your narrative to your own portfolio of written work.

Reflecting on Your Writing

Writer's Journal Jot down your thoughts on the experience of writing an autobiographical narrative. Begin by answering these questions:

- Which part of the writing process did you enjoy the most? Why?
- Did writing an autobiographical narrative make you look at your life differently? Explain.

 *Prentice Hall Writing and Grammar Connection: Chapter 4.*

Rubric for Self-Assessment

Evaluate your autobigraphical narrative *using the following criteria and rating scale, or, with your classmates, determine your own reasonable evaluation criteria.*

Criteria	Rating Scale not very				very
Focus: How well do you establish yourself as the main character?	1	2	3	4	5
Organization: How effectively organized is the sequence of events?	1	2	3	4	5
Support/Elaboration: How well do you use sensory details to describe events?	1	2	3	4	5
Style: How effectively do you use dialogue to bring characters alive?	1	2	3	4	5
Conventions: How accurate is your spelling?	1	2	3	4	5

Tips for Test Taking

When students encounter test prompts that ask them to write autobiographical essays, remind them not to waste too much time agonizing over a topic. Students should read the test prompt carefully to determine whether it sets any limits on the topic. Then, they should choose a topic that they know well, and move ahead to the prewriting phase. Remind students to leave enough time to reread their essays and to revise them with requirements given in the prompt in mind.

Editing and Proofreading

- If students have composed their narratives on a computer, tell them to print a hard copy to edit and proofread. They will overlook fewer errors by reading hard copy.
- Have students exchange papers and read for errors in spelling and grammar. Have them circle the names of people and places for their partners to double-check the spellings of.

Six Traits Focus

	Ideas		Word Choice
	Organization	✔	Sentence Fluency
	Voice	✔	Conventions

ASSESS

Publishing and Presenting

- Suggest that students planning an oral presentation try practice reading their narratives in front of a mirror so they can watch their performance. Better still, have them make a video so they can critique themselves.
- Encourage students to place their anthologies in a display in the classroom or in the library so other students can read their work. Have students work in small groups to find suitable images for the anthology cover.

Reflecting on Your Writing

- Ask students to brainstorm for additional questions that will explore their experience with writing an autobiographical narrative. (For example: What did I learn about myself while writing this narrative? Which part of the writing process did I find the most enjoyable?)
- After students complete their journal entries, have them meet in small groups to discuss and compare their answers to the questions.

WG Writing and Grammar, Ruby Level

Students will find additional instruction on editing, proofreading, publishing, and presenting an autobiographical narrative in Chapter 4, Sections 5 and 6.

Meeting Your Standards

Students will

1. **learn the terms *define, identify,* and *label.***
2. **apply knowledge of these terms in standardized-test situations.**

Knowing Your Terms: Recalling Information

Explain that the terms listed under Terms to Learn will be used in standardized-test situations when students are asked to recall information and extrapolate from it.

Terms to Learn

- Review *define.* Tell students that defining means naming the specific qualities or features that make something what it is. When defining a term, suggest that students ask themselves "What is...?" For example, "What is Puritanism?" Guide students to focus on stating the essential meaning, not the details.
- Review *identify.* Emphasize that identification is a process of selecting or pointing out. When students are asked to identify an error in usage, they are being asked to point out something specific.
- Review *label.* Remind students that a label is a name on something. To label the prepositions in a sentence, students will first identify the prepositions, then write "preposition" by the words that are prepositions.

Vocabulary Workshop

High-Frequency Academic Words

High-frequency academic words are words that appear often in textbooks and on standardized tests. Though you may already know the meaning of many of these words, they usually have a more specific meaning when they are used in textbooks and on tests.

Know Your Terms: Recalling Information

Each of the words listed is a verb that tells you to show that you know or remember details or information. Each of these words asks you to remember material that you have learned. The words indicate the kinds of details and information you should provide in your answer.

Terms to Learn

Define Tell the specific qualities or features that make something what it is.
Sample test item: ***Define*** Puritanism.

Identify Name or show that you recognize something.
Sample test item: In the following sentence, ***identify*** the error in usage.

Label Attach the correct name to something.
Sample test item: ***Label*** the parts of the microscope.

Practice

Directions: *Items 1–3 refer to the passage.*

Oral tradition is the process of handing down stories, poems, songs, and sayings from one generation to the next by word of mouth. Among the products of oral tradition are myths, legends, folk tales and songs, proverbs, ballads, nursery rhymes, and even jokes and riddles. The literature of some cultures is overwhelmingly oral. For example, most Native American narratives were transmitted by elder generations to younger ones.

1. *Define* oral tradition.
2. *Identify* three types of literature that belong to the oral tradition.
3. Copy the last sentence. *Label* each preposition.

Directions: *Identify the usage error in the following sentence.*

Writers often draw from the oral tradition by incorporating folkloric but mythological elements into their written literary works.

A but
B into
C draw
D incorporating

ASSESS

Answers

1. *Define:* Oral tradition is the process of handing down stories from one generation to the next by word of mouth.
2. *Identify:* Types of literature that belong to the oral tradition include myths, legends, folk tales and songs.
3. *Label: by* and *to.*
4. The correct answer is A.

Tips for Test Taking

- When students are asked to choose the best definition of a term on a multiple-choice test, they may find that the best definition synthesizes information. Students should examine the answer choices for the one that most clearly and concisely includes all the essential elements of the meaning. Also, tell students that the part of speech of the definition should correspond to the part of speech of the term being defined.
- If asked to identify an error in usage, students may want to read the sentences quietly to themselves to try to hear what sounds wrong.

Critical Reading:
Summaries of Written Texts

The reading sections of some tests often require you to identify the implied main idea in a passage. They may also require you to choose the best summary of a passage. Use these strategies to help you answer test questions on these skills.

- As you read, identify the sentence in the text that best expresses the main idea of the passage.
- If you are having difficulty identifying the implied main idea, ask yourself, "What general idea is the writer expressing?"

Practice

Directions: *Read the passage and then answer the questions that follow.*

Haiku are three-line poems in which the first and third lines contain five syllables and the second line contains seven syllables. This form of poetry, which originated in Japan, reflects Japanese views of simplicity and nature. Matsuo Bashō, a seventeenth-century Japanese poet, is credited with making haiku an important art form.

Born into a wealthy family, Bashō left home to study Zen Buddhism, history, and classical Chinese poetry. His nomadic life increased the popularity of haiku—a concise style of lyric poetry—as he shared his verse in the communities through which he passed. Most literary historians agree that he was influential in building the recognition of haiku as a poetic form.

1. Which of the following choices best identifies the main idea implied in the first paragraph?

   A Haiku originated in Japan.

   B Bashō was the first great writer of haiku.

   C Haiku is a unique and an important art form in Japan.

   D People have been writing haiku for 300 years.

2. Which of the following would you identify as the best summary of the second paragraph?

   A Uniquely Japanese, haiku is a concise poetic form popularized by the seventeenth-century poet Bashō.

   B Most literary historians agree that Bashō was an important poet.

   C Haiku would never have developed as a separate form were it not for wandering poets.

   D Bashō, a talented seventeenth-century poet who traveled widely throughout Japan, popularized haiku.

Test-Taking Strategies

- Look for the details in the passage that will help you identify the main idea.
- Taking notes as you read is an active way to organize and condense the material. Try giving each note a label to make it more specific.

Meeting Your Standards

Students will

1. **identify the implied main idea of a passage.**
2. **summarize written texts in standardized-test situations.**

Critical Reading

- Remind students that a summary expresses the main idea of a paragraph. When students are dealing with a brief text like a paragraph, the summary and the main idea are the same thing.
- Explain that the main idea of a reading is often implied rather than stated directly. Remind students that writers often use details to suggest a big idea.
- Have students read the Practice passage and answer the questions.
- Point out that in question 1, A, B, and D give specific details about haiku. C pulls the details together into a main idea.
- Point out that in question 2, B and C cite details, but A states a larger idea that covers the details.

ASSESS

Answers

1. C
2. B

Tips for Test Taking

In order to identify the best summary on a standardized test, students must compare a summary against the passage. Remind students that a good summary is concise; it includes only the main points or points of a passage. A good summary does not include most details but rather stays focused on the larger ideas.

Meeting Your Standards

Students will

1. **prepare, rehearse, and deliver a speech.**
2. **modify a speech to fit an audience.**
3. **perform and present a speech effectively.**

Organizing Content

- A speech's main idea is its most important point. Communicating this main idea to the audience is the goal of the speech. Students should state the main idea at least twice in the course of the speech, preferably at the beginning and at the end.
- Remind students to include necessary background information depending on their audience. If they speak to their classmates on an issue relating to the school, for instance, they need not include background information. If they give the same speech to a gathering of outside citizens, they might need to provide some background.
- Remind students to choose language appropriate for their audience.

Giving the Speech

- Students should rehearse their speeches frequently before delivering them, making sure that they are familiar with the main points and supporting details. They need not memorize the text, but they should be familiar enough with it so they can make eye contact with the audience rather than read the entire speech from their notes.
- Do not require students to use visuals or sound effects. These may not be appropriate to every speech. Remind them that Lincoln's *Gettysburg Address* and Martin Luther King's "I Have a Dream" speech were delivered with no special effects but have proved unforgettable nonetheless.

Assess the Activity

To evaluate students' speeches, use the Peer Assessment: Speech rubric, p. 129 in ***General Resources.***

Delivering a Speech

Whether you are recounting an autobiographical incident while accepting an award or explaining the new student-government rules, delivering speeches offers a unique opportunity to convey ideas. The following speaking strategies can help you master the components of **speech delivery.**

Organizing Content

Before you begin rehearsing your speech, spend time planning and refining the content you will present.

Focus on purpose. Determine whether your purpose is narrative or informative. Then, choose and develop main points and details that suit your purpose.

Modify to fit your audience. Keep the knowledge level and interest of your audience in mind when you organize content. With a general audience, for example, plan frequent pauses to refer to explanatory visual material. Choose examples and illustrations, such as personal anecdotes and common experiences, that will draw your audience in.

Craft the speech. Using numbered index cards like the ones shown here, outline your main ideas. Then, choose from techniques such as rhetorical questions, figurative language, and dialogue to convey your ideas. You can keep the interest level high by choosing and combining informal expressions, Standard English, and technical language as dictated by your topic, audience, and purpose.

I NEW STUDENT GOVERNMENT
Announce new government
A. Format and Rules
B. Offices

II GOALS FOR SCHOOL YEAR
A. Develop priorities and clear vision
B. Focus on 5 key projects
C. Raise necessary funds

III HOW TO GET INVOLVED
A. Come to meetings
B. Join project committees
C. Help raise funds

Giving the Speech

Effective speakers use appropriate rehearsal and delivery strategies to keep audiences engaged and control their own anxiety about public speaking.

- **Performance details** Memorize main ideas so that you can refer only briefly to notes, and maintain eye contact with the audience.
- **Special effects** Use sound or visual effects, graphics, and background music to enhance your presentation.
- **Artistic staging** Choose movements, gestures, and facial expressions that support the speech content and suit the occasion.

Activity *Prepare and Deliver a Speech* Choose a situation, audience, and purpose for which you might deliver a speech. Then, prepare, rehearse, and deliver a three-minute speech. Use index cards to highlight and sequence key ideas. Ask classmates for feedback so you can improve your public speaking skills. Be sure to modify your speech based on any audience confusion.

Differentiated Instruction Solutions for All Learners

Strategy for English Learners

Giving a speech is a good opportunity for these students to practice their spoken English. Give them plenty of time to rehearse their speeches. Suggest that, if possible, they deliver their speeches in advance before an audience, such as a friend or family member. Remind students that speaking clearly, intelligibly and deliberately is very important. If students are shy because they speak with strong foreign accents, reassure them that the United States is full of regional accents: Abraham Lincoln and Martin Luther King had very well-defined regional accents. Remind students that they will have their written speeches in front of them; they need not memorize the text.

Suggestions for Further Reading

Featured Titles:

American Colonies: The Settling of North America

Alan Taylor *Penguin Books, 2001*

Nonfiction The settling of the American colonies was not a simple, straightforward story but an interweaving of many narratives. Pulitzer Prize–winning author Alan Taylor does justice to this multifaceted history by explaining the roles that different peoples played in this process: enslaved Africans, Native American tribes, and European colonizers from England, the Netherlands, Spain, Russia, and France. In addition, Taylor expands his focus to include regions of the continent beyond the Eastern seaboard as well as ecological factors influencing colonial settlement.

Chronicle of the Narváez Expedition

Alvar Núñez Cabeza de Vaca, translated by Fanny Bandelier *Penguin Books, 2002*

Cultural Anthology In the early sixteenth century, Spain sent the Narváez expedition to the southern United States to claim vast territories for the Spanish empire. Cabeza de Vaca, who went on this journey, describes the fascinating but sad fate of this expedition. After being shipwrecked, members of the expedition traveled by foot all the way from Florida to California. Their numbers diminished until, by the end of the nine-year ordeal, only Cabeza de Vaca and three others remained.

Native American Literature

Prentice Hall *Pearson Prentice Hall, 2000*

Cultural Anthology The literature of Native Americans from the Northeast through Central America is a rich and varied collection of myths and legends, poems, tribal histories, personal experiences, dreams, and songs. More than fifty such selections are collected in this anthology. This collection of Native American literature offers several perspectives on history, nature, Native American heritage and culture, and the relationships between humans and the spirit world. Through this anthology, readers can experience a wealth of information and tradition as told by Native American writers of the past and present.

Work Presented in Unit One:

If sampling a portion of the following text has built your interest, treat yourself to the full work.

The Four Voyages

Christopher Columbus, edited and translated by J. M. Cohen *Penguin Books, 1969*

***Many of these titles are available in the* Prentice Hall/Penguin Literature Library.**
Consult your teacher before choosing one.

Planning Students' Further Reading

Discussions of literature can raise sensitive and often controversial issues. Before you recommend further reading to your students, consider the values and sensitivities of your community as well as the age, ability, and sophistication of your students. It is also good policy to preview literature before you recommend it to students. The notes below offer some guidance on specific titles.

Interesting Narrative and Other Writings by Olaudah Equiano

Any discussion of slavery needs to be handled sensitively. This book deals with the kidnapping of children who are then sold into slavery, the horrors of the trip across the ocean on the slave ship, the mistreatment of slaves, and the suicides of several slaves. There is a lot of Christian doctrine in this narrative.

Lexile: N/A

American Colonies by Alan Taylor

This book deals with many controversial topics, including Columbus's exploration, the conflicts between Europeans and Native Americans, and the enslavement of Native Americans and Africans.

Lexile: N/A

The Four Voyages by Christopher Columbus

In this book, the attitudes of the European explorers toward the natives of the islands may be offensive to some readers.

Lexile: N/A

Chronicle by Alvar Núñez Cabeza de Vaca Both the Spanish explorers and the Native Americans treat each other very poorly in this book. Harsh conditions, cannibalism, and the killing of girl babies may disturb readers.

Lexile: N/A

Native American Literature The selections depict violence, prejudice, and harsh living conditions and contain criticism of white Americans, missionaries, and the U.S. government.

Lexile: N/A

Meeting Your Standards

Students will

1. read selections from the American literary tradition written between 1750 and 1800.
2. apply a variety of reading strategies, particularly strategies for constructing meaning, to these selections.
3. analyze literary elements.
4. use a variety of strategies to build vocabulary.
5. learn elements of grammar, usage, and style.
6. use recursive writing processes to write in a variety of forms.
7. develop listening and speaking skills.
8. express and support responses to various types of texts.
9. prepare, organize, and present literary interpretations.

Unit Instructional Resources

In ***Unit 2 Resources,*** you will find materials to support students in developing and mastering the unit skills and to help you assess their progress.

Vocabulary and Reading

- **Vocabulary Warm-up Word Lists A and B** identify selection words for students who read at one or two grades below level.
- **Vocabulary Warm-up Practice (A and B)** provides practice on the Word List words.
- **Reading Warm-ups A and B** provide reading passages containing the Word List words, along with questions and activities for students working at one or two grades below level.

Selection Support

- **Reading Strategy**
- **Literary Analysis**
- **Vocabulary Builder**
- **Grammar and Style**
- **Support for Writing**
- **Support for Extend Your Learning**
- **Enrichment**

You may also access these resources on TeacherExpress.

Unit 2 A Nation Is Born

1750–1800

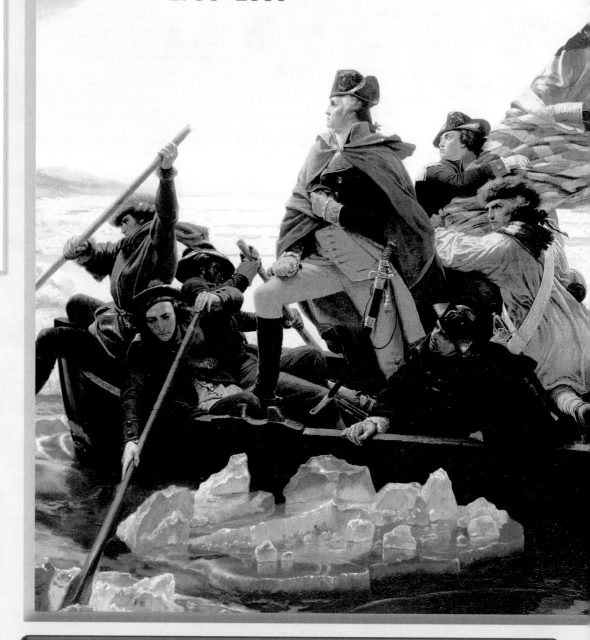

Assessment Resources

Listed below are the resources available to assess and measure students' progress in meeting the unit objectives and your state standards.

Skills Assessment

Unit 2 Resources
Selection Tests A and B

TeacherExpress™
ExamView® Test Bank Software

Adequate Yearly Progress Assessment

Unit 2 Resources
Diagnostic Tests
Benchmark Tests

Standardized Assessment

Standardized Test Preparation Workbook

Washington Crossing the Delaware, Emanuel Gottlieb Leutze, Metropolitan Museum of Art

Early National Literature

"The fate of unborn millions willl now depend, under God, on the courage and conduct of this army. Our cruel and unrelenting enemy leaves us only the choice of brave resistance, or the most abject submission. We have, therefore, to resolve to conquer or die."

—George Washington, addressing the Continental Army before the battle of Long Island, August 27, 1776

◄ This painting, *Washington Crossing the Delaware* by Emanuel Gottlieb, shows the Revolutionary War general and his men on Christmas Eve of 1776 as they crossed the Delaware River to surprise the British.

Introduce Unit 2

Direct students' attention to the title and time period of this unit. Have a student read the quotation. **Ask** them: What does the quotation suggest about Americans at this point in their history? **Possible response:** The quotation suggests that Americans are preparing for war.

Have students look at the art. Read the Humanities note to them, and **ask** the discussion question.

Then ask: What kinds of literature or themes in literature do you think might come out of this period in American history?

Possible response: Students probably will suggest themes concerning freedom and independence in the literature of this time period.

Humanities

Washington Crossing the Delaware, copy after Emanuel Gottlieb Leutze

On Christmas night, 1776, 2,400 American soldiers crossed the Delaware River from Pennsylvania to Trenton, New Jersey. George Washington commanded that campfires be left burning on the Pennsylvania side to fool the German-born Hessian mercenaries. The Hessians had celebrated the holiday and were asleep when the Americans attacked the next morning.

- Which figure in the painting is George Washington? How do you know?
  Answer: He is the man just to the left of the center, in the hat and red-lined cloak. Since his head is the highest in the painting, this is probably the commander.

Unit Features

William Andrews
Each unit features commentary by a contemporary writer or scholar under the heading "From the Author's Desk." Author William Andrews introduces Unit 2 in Setting the Scene, in which he discusses the paradox of new freedom and the acceptance of slavery. Later in the unit he introduces the selection from *The Interesting Narrative of the Life of Olaudah Equiano*. He also contributes his insights on p. 231 in the Writing Workshop.

Connections
Every unit contains a feature that connects the American literature of the period to British or World Literature. In this unit, students will connect African proverbs with Benjamin Franklin's *Poor Richard's Almanac.*

Use the information and questions on the Connections page to help students enrich their understanding of the selections in this unit.

Reading Informational Materials
These selections will help students learn to analyze and evaluate informational materials, such as workplace documents, technical directions, and consumer materials. They will expose students to the organization and features unique to nonnarrative texts.

In this unit, students will learn to read newspaper editorials.

- William L. Andrews, a well-known teacher and historian, introduces the unit by linking the popularity of the autobiography to the characteristically American talent for self-invention (and re-invention). Andrews introduces "The Interesting Narrative of the Life of Olaudah Equiano on pp. 156–157.
- Have students read the introductory paragraph about William L. Andrews. Raised in Virginia, he received a doctorate in history from the University of North Carolina at Chapel Hill and has taught at Texas Tech University, the University of Wisconsin, and the University of Kansas. He served as head of the English Department at the University of North Carolina from 1997 to 2001. Andrews has edited or co-edited more than twenty books. He says, "I continue to study the historical linkages between white and black writers in the formation of American literature, African American literature, and southern literature."
- Use the ***From the Author's Desk*** DVD to introduce William L. Andrews. Show Segment 1 to provide insights into Andrews's career as a historian and teacher. After the students have watched the segment, **ask** students how Andrews's writing in anthologies of slave narratives might make it easier for modern readers to fully appreciate the significance of those narratives. **Answer:** his scholarship allows him to offer insights that may help readers better understand the narratives.

A Promise and a Paradox

- Have students read Andrews's comments about the popularity of autobiography in early American literature.
- Andrews notes the disconnect between America's promise of freedom and the fact that many of the founding fathers espoused universal freedom but were also slaveholders. **Ask:** What paradox does Andrews see in the history of America's founders? **Answer:** The nation was founded on the promise of freedom and democracy, but a number of the men who defined this promise were themselves slaveholders.

Unit 2 contains works of literature based in the American struggle for independence. The following essay by the distinguished literary scholar William L. Andrews focuses on a paradox of this era: America's promise of a new birth of freedom existed side by side with the dehumanizing institution of slavery. As you read his essay, the unit introduction that follows, and the literature in Unit 2, consider the ways in which the authors of this period helped to forge our identity as Americans.

From the Scholar's Desk
William L. Andrews Talks About the Time Period

William L. Andrews

Introducing William L. Andrews (b. 1946) An award-winning scholar and teacher, William L. Andrews studies the historical links between white and black writers in the formation of American literature. In addition to his many scholarly publications, he has coedited three major literature anthologies: *The Norton Anthology of African American Literature, The Oxford Companion to African American Literature,* and *The Literature of the American South: A Norton Anthology.*

America Begins With a Promise and a Paradox

It's not just a coincidence that America's earliest literature is highly autobiographical. Nor is it by accident that autobiography emerged as a literary form about the same time that the United States became a new nation. Autobiography and America were made for each other.

The Promise: A New Person and a New Country The revolution in the United States created a new person, as well as a new country. At least that's what the great spokesmen and propagandists of the Revolution, especially Thomas Jefferson, Patrick Henry, and Benjamin Franklin, claimed. Franklin, who wore a coonskin cap to the royal courts of Europe, became famous for inventing everything from streetlights to eyeglasses. But we read him today because his greatest invention was himself. Franklin gave the new nation (which he also helped to invent) its first literary classic. *The Autobiography* of Benjamin Franklin is the first great American success story: a tale of a poor boy who made good.

The Paradox: Freedom and Slavery In 1789 Franklin, head of Pennsylvania's largest antislavery society, signed a petition to Congress advocating an end to slavery. In the same year, a pioneering African American autobiography, *The Interesting Narrative of the Life of Olaudah Equiano,* adapted the success story to antislavery purposes. Before the American Revolution got under way, Phillis Wheatley, an African-born slave in Boston, published a book of poetry, written in the learned and ornate style of the day to show that the enslaved were just as intelligent and

Teaching Resources

The following resources can be used to enrich or extend the instruction for the Unit 2 Introduction.

From the Author's Desk DVD
William L. Andrews, Segment 1

Unit 2 Resources
Names and Terms to Know, p. 5
Focus Questions, p. 6
Listing and Viewing, p. 25

capable as their so-called masters. Yet when the revolutionary orator Patrick Henry demanded in 1775, "Give me liberty or give me death!" no one asked whether the slaves he held on his Virginia plantation deserved the same freedom he so passionately proclaimed.

When I was in the sixth grade in a public school not far from Patrick Henry's plantation, I studied Virginia history, a mandatory subject at the time. I remember learning then that my home state was "the mother of presidents." My teacher didn't mention that all of Virginia's great heroes, including Washington and Jefferson, were slaveholders as well. No one, not even the framers of the U.S. Constitution in 1787, had found a way to justify the presence of slavery in a land supposedly dedicated to freedom. Eventually the only solution to America's political paradox was civil war.

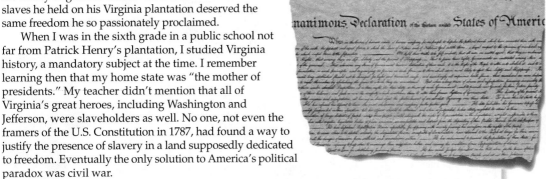

America's Destiny and a Persistent Question Ever since the founding of the United States, Americans have trumpeted the new country's special destiny: to create a new form of government, democracy, that would reform humankind itself. The transplanted Frenchman Jean de Crevecoeur believed that democracy would inspire in all who had immigrated to America an "original genius" that would bind them together in a shared national identity. America's dedication to human rights, particularly "life, liberty, and the pursuit of happiness," would give the new people of America a grand ideal and mission. The most important writers of the early Republic extolled the nation's founding ideals but often questioned the national commitment to them. Then as now we ask of ourselves: Has America become what Jefferson and Crevecoeur imagined?

Go Online
Author Link

For: An online video
Visit: www.PHSchool.com
Web Code: ere-8201

For: More about William L. Anderson
Visit: www.PHSchool.com
Web Code: ete-9205

Reading the Unit Introduction

Reading for Information and Insight Use the following terms and questions to guide your reading of the unit introduction on pages 130–137.

Names and Terms to Know
Enlightenment
The American Revolution
Constitution
Bill of Rights
Declaration of Independence
Thomas Jefferson
Thomas Paine
The Federalist
Phillis Wheatley

Focus Questions As you read this introduction, use what you learn to answer these questions:

- What series of events set the stage for war between the American colonies and the British?
- What challenges did the new country face in its quest for self-government?
- In what ways did politics influence literature during this period?

Tell students that the terms and questions listed here are the key points in this introductory materials. This information provides a context for the selections in the unit. Students should use the terms and questions as a guide to focus their reading of the unit introduction. When students have completed the unit introduction, they should be able to identify or explain each of these terms and answer the Focus Questions.

Concept Connector

After students have read the unit introduction, return to the Focus Questions to review the main points. For key points, see p. 137.

Go Online Author Link Typing in the Web Code when prompted will bring students to a video clip of William L. Andrews.

Using the Timeline

The timeline can serve a number of instructional purposes, as follows:

Getting an Overview

Use the timeline to help students get a quick overview of themes and events of the period. This approach will benefit all students but may be especially helpful for visually oriented students, English learners, and those less proficient in reading. (For strategies in using the timeline as an overview, see the bottom of this page.)

Thinking Critically

Questions are provided on the facing page. Use these questions to have students review the events, discuss their significance, and examine the *so what* behind the *what happened.*

Connecting to Selections

Have students refer to the timeline when beginning to read individual selections. By consulting the timeline regularly, they will gain a better sense of the period's chronology. In addition, they will appreciate world events that gave rise to these works of literature.

Projects

Students can use the timeline as a launching pad for projects like these:

- **Customized Timeline** Have students create period timelines in their notebooks, adding key details as they read new selections. They can use dates from this timeline as a starting framework.
- **Special Report** Have students scan the timeline for items that interest them, research these further, and report on them to the class.

American and World Events

1750 1760 1770

AMERICAN EVENTS

- 1748 Benjamin Franklin retires from the printing business after 26 years. ▶

- 1752 Benjamin Franklin conducts his kite-and-key experiment with lightning. ▲
- 1753 African American Benjamin Banneker constructs the first striking clock with all parts made in America.
- 1754 French and Indian War begins.

Poor Richard, 1733.
AN
Almanack
For the Year of Chrift
1733,
Being the Firft after LEAP YEAR:
And makes fince the Creation Years
By the Account of the Eaftern Greeks 7241
By the Latin Church, when ☉ ent. ♈ 6932
By the Computation of W.W. 5742
By the Roman Chronology 5682
By the Jewifh Rabbies 5494
Wherein is contained
The Lunations, Eclipfes, Judgment of the Weather, Spring Tides, Planets Motions & mutual Afpects, Sun and Moon's Rifing and Setting, Length of Days, Time of High Water, Fairs, Courts, and obfervable Days.
Fitted to the Latitude of Forty Degrees, and a Meridian of Five Hours Weft from London, but may without fenfible Error, ferve all the adjacent Places, even from Newfoundland to South-Carolina.
By RICHARD SAUNDERS, Philom.
PHILADELPHIA:
Printed and fold by B. FRANKLIN, at the New Printing-Office near the Market.

- 1759–63 France gives up claims to North American territory.
- 1765 Stamp Act passed by British Parliament; colonists protest bitterly
- 1767 Townshend Acts impose new taxes, angering colonists further.

- 1773 Parliament's Tea Act prompts Boston Tea Party.
- 1773 Phillis Wheatley's *Poems on Various Subjects* published in England. ▶
- 1774 First Continental Congress meets in Philadelphia.
- 1775 The American Revolution begins.
- 1776 Second Continental Congress adopts Declaration of Independence. ▼

WORLD EVENTS

- 1755 France: School for deaf opens in Paris.
- 1755 England: Samuel Johnson publishes *Dictionary of the English Language*.
- 1759 France: Voltaire publishes *Candide*, satirizing optimism of the philosopher Leibniz.

- 1762 France: Jean Jacques Rousseau states his political philosophy in *The Social Contract*.
- 1763 Seven Years' War ends.
- 1769 Scotland: James Watt invents an improved steam engine.
- 1769 England: Richard Arkwright invents a frame for spinning; helps bring about factory system.

- 1770 Germany: Ludwig von Beethoven is born.
- 1774 England: Joseph Priestley discovers oxygen, named later by Lavoisier.
- 1779 South Africa: First of Kaffir wars between blacks and whites breaks out.

Getting an Overview of the Period

Introduction To give students an overview of the period, indicate the span of dates along the top of the timeline. Point out the division of the timeline into American and World Events, and have students practice scanning the timeline to look at both categories. Finally, tell them that the events in the Timeline represent beginnings, turning points, and endings. For example, the American Revolution began in 1775.

Key Events One story this timeline tells is how America won its independence from Great Britain. Have students select items in the American Events section that help tell this story. **Possible answers:** Students might mention 1765, 1767, imposition of Stamp Acts and Townshend Acts; and 1774, meeting of First Continental Congress.

Ask students what events after the Revolution show how the nation's identity was developing. **Possible answer:** Students might mention the election of George Washington in 1789 and the first census in 1790.

1780 1790 1800

- 1781 General Cornwallis surrenders British army to George Washington at Yorktown. ▼

- 1783 Noah Webster's *Spelling Book* first appears; 60 million copies would be sold.
- 1783 Revolutionary War ends.
- 1787 Constitutional Convention meets in Philadelphia to draft Constitution.
- 1789 George Washington elected first President of United States.

- 1790 First federal U.S. census shows approximately 757,208 blacks in the U.S., nearly 20% of the total population. 59,557 are free.
- 1793 Eli Whitney invents cotton gin. ▶

- 1800 Second U.S. census shows a total population of 5,308,483.
- 1801 Thomas Jefferson, principal author of Declaration of Independence, elected President.
- 1804 Federalist leader Alexander Hamilton killed in a duel with Aaron Burr.

- 1781 England: William Herschel discovers planet Uranus.
- 1786 Scotland: Robert Burns is widely acclaimed for his first book of poems.
- 1786 Austria: Wolfgang Amadeus Mozart creates the comic opera *The Marriage of Figaro*.
- 1789 France: Storming of Bastille in Paris sets off French Revolution.

- 1791 England: James Boswell publishes *The Life of Samuel Johnson*.
- 1793 France: King Louis XVI and Marie Antoinette executed.
- 1796 France: Napoleon Bonaparte comes to power in France. ▶
- 1798 England: William Wordsworth and Samuel Taylor Coleridge publish *Lyrical Ballads*.

- 1800 Germany: Ludwig von Beethoven composes *First Symphony*.

Continued from right column

2. How do the writing implements shown with the entry on the Declaration of Independence help you imagine the writing of that document?
   Answer: The implements suggest that Jefferson wrote the Declaration with a quill pen. The pen appears to be dipped in an inkwell.
3. What does the picture indicate about the British surrender?
   Answer: It was conducted with a great deal of ceremony.

1730 and 1760 mention Benjamin Franklin? (b) What do these entries reveal about Franklin's interests?
Answer: (a) 1748, Franklin retires from the printing business. 1752, Franklin conducts kite-and-key experiment. (b) His interests were varied. Some were literary, and some were scientific.

2. (a) What did France give up between 1759 and 1763?
   (b) Suggest some causes for France's decision.
   Answer: (a) France gave up claims to territory in North America. (b) France may have engaged in a contest for it, probably with the British. France's giving up this territory suggests it lost the conflict.
3. (a) Which actions did Congress take between 1770 and 1780?
   (b) What ongoing story does this suggest?
   Answer: (a) Congress appointed Washington commander in chief of the American army and adopted the Declaration of Independence.
   (b) These events show America declaring her independence and preparing to fight for it.
4. (a) Name two technological developments that occurred in Great Britain in 1769. (b) How might these developments have affected people's lives?
   Answer: (a) An improved steam engine and the spinning jenny were invented. (b) These developments made possible mass-produced goods and the factory system. They probably drew people to work in cities.
5. (a) When was the first federal census taken? (b) What does it indicate about the status of blacks in the United States?
   Answer: (a) It was taken in 1790.
   (b) Blacks made up 20% of the total population. More than 90% of them were enslaved.

Critical Viewing

1. What does the picture reveal about Franklin's experiment with lightning?
   Answer: He used a kite to get a bolt of lightning to strike a key.

Literature of the Period

- In "Speech to the Virginia Convention," Patrick Henry demonstrates the fiery oratorical style that helped inspire Americans to revolutionary fervor.
- In selections such as "The Declaration of Independence," and the excerpt from *The Crisis,* students will find eloquent expression of the American wish for independence.

Critical Viewing

Answer: The thirteen colonies enjoyed the strategic advantage of a long coastline. With several major ports, such as New York and Philadelphia, they could easily receive shipments of goods and troop transports.

Historical Background

It is easy to forget how long the thirteen original states had been colonies. By 1750, there were fourth- and fifth-generation Americans of European descent living in Virginia and New England. These people were English subjects, and, on the whole, they were well satisfied with that status. In fact, as late as the early 1760s, few Americans had given much thought to the prospect of independence.

Between the mid-1760s and the mid-1770s, however, attitudes changed dramatically. King George III and Parliament imposed a number of regulations that threatened the liberties of the colonists. With each succeeding measure, the outrage in America grew, finally erupting into war.

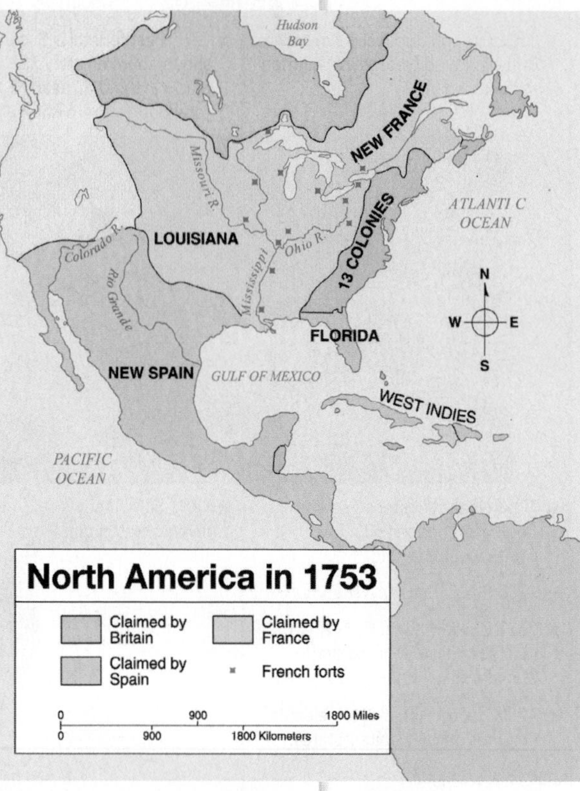

The Age of Reason Great upheavals in history occur when circumstances are ripe. The American Revolution was such an upheaval, and the groundwork for it had been laid by European writers and thinkers as well as by the English king and Parliament. The eighteenth century is often characterized as the Enlightenment, or the Age of Reason. Spurred by the work of many seventeenth-century thinkers—such as scientists Galileo and Sir Isaac Newton, philosophers Voltaire and Jean-Jacques Rousseau, and political theorist John Locke—the writers and thinkers of the Enlightenment valued reason over faith. Unlike the Puritans, they had little interest in the hereafter, believing instead in the power of reason and science to further human progress. They spoke of a social contract that forms the basis of government. Above all, they believed that people are by nature good, not evil. A perfect society seemed to them to be more than just an idle dream.

The American statesmen of the Revolutionary period were themselves figures of the Enlightenment. No history of the period would be complete without mention of the ideas and writings of Benjamin Franklin, Thomas Paine, and Thomas Jefferson. These Americans not only expressed the ideas of the Age of Reason but also helped to put them spectacularly into practice.

▲ Critical Viewing On the eve of the French and Indian War, France still had claim to a majority of the interior of North America. What strategic advantage did the thirteen colonies enjoy because of their geographic location? **[Interpret]**

Enrichment

The French and Indian War

The French and Indian War paved the way for the American Revolution. It strained the previously good relations between the colonies and the home country. The arrogance displayed by the British officers offended American military leaders such as Washington, and many New Englanders were shocked by what they regarded as the immorality of British soldiers.

During the years before the Revolution, the colonists began to develop their own identity—not English but American. They felt that though their manners were less formal than those of the British, their morals were superior. They began thinking of the British as corrupt people who had departed from the path of righteousness.

The Boston Massacre,
by Paul Revere

A group of Bostonians began taunting the British sentries and threw

Toward a Clash of Arms The American Revolution was preceded by the French and Indian War, a struggle between England and France for control of North America. The conflict broke out in 1754 and continued for nearly a decade. When the war officially ended in 1763, defeated France gave up its claims to North American territory. There was general jubilation in the thirteen English colonies.

The good feelings were short-lived, however. The British government, wanting to raise revenue in the colonies to pay its war debt, passed the Stamp Act in 1765. Colonial reaction to the Stamp Act, which required the buying and affixing of stamps to each of 54 ordinary items, was swift and bitter. Stamps were burned. Stamp distributors were beaten and their shops destroyed. Eventually, the Stamp Act was repealed.

Other acts and reactions followed. The Townshend Acts of 1767 taxed paper, paint, glass, lead, and tea. When the colonists organized a boycott, the British dissolved the Massachusetts legislature and sent two regiments of British troops to Boston. In 1770, these Redcoats fired into a taunting mob, causing five fatalities. This so-called Boston Massacre further inflamed colonial passions. Parliament repealed the Townshend duties except for the tax on tea, but a separate Tea Act giving an English company a virtual monopoly soon greeted the colonists. Furious, a group of Bostonians dressed as Mohawks dumped a shipment of tea into Boston harbor. As punishment for this Boston Tea Party, the English Parliament passed the Coercive Acts. Because these laws shut down the port of Boston, forbade meetings other than annual town meetings, and insisted that British troops could be housed in colonists' homes, colonists immediately dubbed them the Intolerable Acts.

In September 1774, colonial leaders, although not speaking openly of independence, met in Philadelphia for the First Continental Congress. The British, their authority slipping away, appointed General Thomas Gage governor of Massachusetts. The stage was set for war.

"The Shot Heard Round the World" On April 19, 1775, 700 British troops met some 70 colonial minutemen on the Lexington green. A musket shot was fired (from which side, no one knows), and before the shooting that followed was over, eight Americans lay dead. The British marched west to Concord, where another skirmish took place. The encounters at Lexington and Concord, a landmark in American history, have been referred to as "the shot heard round the world." The American Revolution had begun, and there would be no turning back.

▲ **Critical Viewi**
Paul Revere's engra
of the Boston Mass
played a major role
whipping up coloni
fury against the Brit
Revere purposefull
distorted the event
Which details sugg
the artist was
procolonist? **[Analy**

Background
Government

The British soldiers arrested after the Boston Massacre asked future president John Adams, then a young Boston lawyer, to defend them. Adams, a fierce patriot, knew that it might cost him friends and respect to appear on the side of England. He also believed that any accused person, no matter who, deserved a fair trial. He agreed to defend them. The case came to trial in October, and all the soldiers were acquitted. Adams had acted on an important principle of the future American government—that everyone was equal under the law.

Differentiated Instruction
Solutions for All Learners

Strategy for Less Proficient Readers
Have students preview the art and illustrations for this period before reading "A Nation Is Born." Have them make up questions based on the illustrations and then read the text to find the answers.

Strategy for English Learners
Have students use the art and illustrations on these pages to speculate about the era. Have them read the boldfaced heads and formulate questions based on these heads. Then, they can read the text to find the answers.

Enrichment for Advanced Readers
Have students consider this question: Did the political revolution in America have a counterpart in literature? Explain. Students can use selections from this unit and from Unit 1 to support their answers.

1775, two Americans fell, as did three redcoats. The British commander ordered a retreat to Boston. American snipers fired on the British troops all the way back, killing a total of 273 men.

In June, the Americans killed or wounded more than a thousand British soldiers at the Battle of Bunker Hill. Although all the fighting up to this point had occurred in Massachusetts, the revolt involved all of the colonies. Two days before Bunker Hill, the Second Continental Congress in Philadelphia had selected Virginian George Washington as commander in chief of the Continental Army.

The Battle of Saratoga in the fall of 1777 marked a turning point in the war. The British were surrounded and forced to surrender more than 5,000 men. When news of this victory reached Paris, the French government formally recognized the independence of the United States. Soon afterward, France began to commit troops to the American cause.

The American Experience
Close-up on History

- The story about Molly Pitcher, who loaded her husband's cannon, may actually belong to Margaret Corbin. Some scholars believe that history has confused the two stories. When Corbin's husband was killed during the attack on Fort Washington, she took over his cannon until she was seriously wounded. Corbin was the first woman to receive a government pension. There is a monument to her at West Point.
- **Ask** students to speculate about why African Americans and women were willing to participate in the revolution when they did not have the same civil rights as white men. **Possible response:** African Americans and women may have hoped to gain rights by demonstrating their dedication and value to the revolutionary cause.

In June, the Americans killed or wounded more than a thousand British soldiers at the Battle of Bunker Hill. Although the fighting up to this point had taken place in Massachusetts, the revolt involved all the colonies. Two days before Bunker Hill, the Second Continental Congress, meeting in Philadelphia, had named a commander in chief of the official American army. He was George Washington of Virginia.

More than a year would pass before the colonies declared their independence. More than six years would pass before the war ended, although the Battle of Saratoga, in the fall of 1777, marked a turning point. At Saratoga, in upstate New York, the British were surrounded and 5,700 of them were forced to surrender. When news of the American victory reached Paris, the government of France formally recognized the independence of the United States. Soon afterward, France began to commit troops to aid the American cause.

After six years of fighting, the war finally came to an end at Yorktown, Virginia, on October 19, 1781. Aided by the French army and navy, and enlisting the service of African American soldiers, General Washington's army bottled up the 8,000-man British force under General Cornwallis. Seeing that escape was impossible, General Cornwallis surrendered.

Close-up on History

African Americans and Women in the Revolution

In 1776, more than a half million African Americans lived in the colonies. At first, the Continental Congress did not permit enslaved or free African Americans to join the American army. However, when the British offered to free any male slave who fought for the king, George Washington changed American policy and allowed free African Americans to enlist.

About 5,000 African Americans fought against the British. As this eyewitness account demonstrates, they fought with great courage:

> Three times in succession, [African American soldiers] were attacked . . . by well-disciplined and veteran [British] troops, and three times did they successfully repel the assault, and thus preserve our army from capture.

Women also helped in the struggle for independence. When men went off to war, they took on added work. They planted and harvested the crops that fed the army. They also made shoes and wove cloth for blankets and uniforms. Many women joined their soldier-husbands at the front, where they washed, cooked, and cared for the wounded.

A few women actually took part in battle. In 1778, Mary Ludwig Hays carried water to her husband and other soldiers. The soldiers called her Moll of the Pitcher or Molly Pitcher. When her husband was wounded, she took his place, loading and firing a cannon. Another woman, Deborah Sampson of Massachusetts, dressed as a man and fought in several battles. Later, she wrote about her experiences in the army.

Enrichment

A People's War

About 200,000 fighters served at one time or another in the American cause. Most of them were young, relatively poor men. They and their officers were paid badly, if at all, and poorly fed and clothed.

Some 5,000 African American men took part in the war, on both sides. African American and white women served on both sides as well.

Many women followed husbands, lovers, or fathers into battle, cared for them, and nursed them. A few women actually fought in battles. Deborah Sampson, for example, disguised herself as a man, calling herself Robert Shurtleff, and served from May, 1782 to October, 1783. Her husband became the only man to receive a pension as a "widow" of a veteran!

The New Nation The path to self-government was not always smooth. After the Revolution, the Articles of Confederation established a "league of friendship" among the new states. This arrangement did not work well. The federal Constitution that replaced the Articles required many compromises and was ratified only after a long fight. Even then, a Bill of Rights had to be added to placate those who feared the centralized power that the Constitution conferred.

▲ **Critical Viewing** Patrick Henry criticized the Stamp Act in the Virginia House of Burgesses, and Virginia became the first colony officially to protest the new tax law. Based on this print, what type of citizen do you think was generally elected to serve in the Virginia House of Burgesses? **[Draw Conclusions]**

The old revolutionaries, by and large, remained true to their principles and continued their public duties. George Washington became the nation's first president. John Adams, a signer of the Declaration of Independence, succeeded him in that office. Then, in 1800, Americans elected as their president the brilliant statesman who had drafted the Declaration, one of the heroes of the Enlightenment, Thomas Jefferson.

Literature of the Period

A Time of Crisis In contrast to the private soul-searching of the Puritans of New England, much of what was produced during the Revolutionary period was public writing. By the time of the War for Independence, nearly thirty newspapers had been established in the coastal cities. At the time of Washington's inauguration, there were nearly forty magazines. Almanacs were popular from Massachusetts to Georgia.

The mind of the nation was on politics. Journalists and printers provided a forum for the expression of ideas. After 1763, those ideas were increasingly focused on relations with Great Britain and, more broadly, on the nature of government. As the literature presented in this unit testifies, the writing of permanent importance from the Revolutionary era is mostly political writing.

Politics as Literature The writing and speaking of American statesmen in two tumultuous decades, the 1770s and 1780s, helped to reshape not only the nation but also the world. James Otis of Massachusetts defended colonial rights vigorously in speeches and pamphlets. Otis is credited with giving Americans their rallying cry: "Taxation without representation is tyranny."

Patrick Henry was a spellbinding orator whose speech against the Stamp Act in the Virginia House of Burgesses brought cries of "Treason!" Ten years later, his electrifying speech to the Virginia Convention expressed the rising sentiment for independence.

Thomas Paine was perhaps more influential than any other in swaying public opinion in favor of independence. His 1776 pamphlet *Common Sense* swept the colonies, selling 100,000 copies in three months.

Critical Thinking

1. Why did the Enlightenment idea that people have a right to happiness prove a spur to revolution?
   Answer: If happiness is a natural right, then any form of government that makes people suffer must be wrong. People are therefore justified in changing their government.
2. In what way did the French and Indian War sow the seeds of the American Revolution?
   Answer: The British war debt was the immediate cause for raising colonial taxes.
3. How were the colonists able to defeat England, a great world power?
   Answer: The colonists were fighting on familiar ground; the British were in an unknown land. The colonists used effective guerrilla tactics to which the British were unaccustomed.

Sense, he was a recent immigrant from England. Nevertheless, he was able to capture the revolutionary mood in the colonies. His pamphlet sold about 500,000 copies, compared to the few hundred copies most political pamphlets averaged.

During the Revolution, Paine wrote 16 pamphlets that were collectively called *The Crisis*. These pamphlets also sold widely.

Shortly after the Revolution, Paine returned to England. There he wrote a tract called *The Rights of Man,* which was a defense of the French Revolution. In this work, Paine argued that people enjoy natural rights and that governments have an obligation to guarantee these rights.

The American Experience

A Writer's Voice

- Thomas Paine seems to have had revolution in his blood. During his time as an excise officer in England, he led to revolt for salary raises, causing him to be let go. After coming to America, he became involved in the fight for independence from England. After returning to England, he wrote essays defending the French Revolution and attacking English government.
- **Ask** students to speculate about whether reason can be divorced from passion during a revolution. **Possible answer:** Although one would hope that the reasons for revolt would be based on logic, if people did not feel passionately about the cause, they would be unlikely to participate.

A Writer's Voice

Thomas Paine and the Age of Reason

The Age of Reason was not necessarily reasonable or moderate. Indeed, a chief characteristic of reason during this era was that it led some writers very far past old customs and institutions. Questioning the way things were, these writers reasoned their way to revolution.

You can see this link between reason and revolution in Thomas Paine's *Common Sense.* Even the title is an appeal to everyday logic, and throughout this pamphlet, Paine uses what George Washington called "unanswerable reasoning" to make the case for dramatic political changes.

from *Common Sense* by Thomas Paine

In the following pages I offer nothing more than simple facts, plain arguments, and common sense; and have no other preliminaries to settle with the reader than that he will divest himself of prejudice and prepossession [preconceived ideas] and suffer [allow] his reason and his feelings to determine for themselves. . . .

. . . it is not in the power of Britain to do this continent justice: The business of it will soon be too weighty, and intricate, to be managed with any tolerable degree of convenience, by a power so distant from us, and so very ignorant of us; for if they cannot conquer us, they cannot govern us. To be always running 3000 or 4000 miles with a tale or a petition, waiting four or five months for an answer, which when obtained required five or six more to explain it in, will in a few years be looked upon as folly and childishness—there was a time when it was proper, and there is a proper time for it to cease. . . .

The Declaration of Independence was first drafted by Thomas Jefferson in June 1776. The finished document is largely his work, although a committee of five statesmen, including Benjamin Franklin, was involved in its creation. The Declaration, despite some exaggerated charges against King George III, is one of the most influential political statements ever made.

Another Revolutionary-period document written by committee that has stood the test of time is the Constitution of the United States, drafted in 1787. The framers, whose new nation boasted about four million people, hoped that the Constitution would last at least a generation. It still survives, amended only 27 times, as the political foundation of a superpower of 50 states and more than 250 million people. However, not everyone in 1787 was pleased with the Constitution. Alexander Hamilton called it a "weak and worthless fabric," and Benjamin Franklin supported it only because, as he said, "I expect no better."

The doubts of the framers were reflected in the controversy over ratification. Delaware ratified the Constitution within three months, thus becoming the first state in the Union. However, the ratification of nine states was necessary before the document could go into effect. The last few states proved difficult. The contest between supporters and opponents was especially

Enrichment

Planning a Capital City

At Congress's request, George Washington himself chose the site of the capital city that would bear his name—the banks of the Potomac and Anacostia rivers. French engineer and architect Pierre Charles L'Enfant designed the city plan, inspired by his beloved Paris. Broad boulevards radiate from the circular drives surrounding important sites like the Capitol building and the lawns of the presidential mansion. Quarrels over details resulted in L'Enfant's replacement by African-American engineer Benjamin Banneker, who in turn had to step down after three months owing to illness.

Many years passed before Washington became the gracious, majestic city today's tourists flock to visit. In 1842, Charles Dickens's reaction to Washington was, "Such as it is, it is likely to remain." In 1901, President Theodore Roosevelt appointed a commission that included landscaper Frederick Law Olmstead and architect Charles McKim to spruce up the city, make the Mall a permanent lawn, and build the monumental Union Station.

hard-fought in New York. Alexander Hamilton, who did not think highly of the Constitution, nevertheless wanted to see it pass in his home state. With James Madison and John Jay, he wrote a series of essays that were first published as letters to three New York newspapers. These essays, collected as *The Federalist,* served their immediate purpose. New York ratified the Constitution by a vote of 30 to 27. Over time, these essays have come to be recognized as authoritative statements on the principles of American government.

The Cultural Scene While politics dominated the literature of the Revolutionary period, not every writer of note was a statesman. Verse appeared in most of the newspapers, and numerous broadside ballads were published. (A broadside ballad is a single sheet of paper, printed on one or both sides, dealing with a current topic.) One of the most popular broadside ballads was called "The Dying Redcoat," supposedly written by a British sergeant mortally wounded in the Revolution. The sergeant in the ballad realizes too late that his sympathy lies with the American cause:

> Fight on, America's noble sons,
> Fear not Britannia's thundering guns:
> Maintain your cause from year to year,
> God 's on your side, you need not fear.

One poet of the time whose works were more sophisticated than the broadside ballads was Philip Freneau, a 1771 graduate of Princeton. A journalist and newspaper editor, Freneau wrote poetry throughout his life. Several of his poems, such as "The Indian Burying Ground," earned him a reputation as America's earliest important lyric poet.

Two other poets of the day were Joel Barlow and Phillis Wheatley. Barlow, a 1778 Yale graduate, is best remembered for "The Hasty Pudding," a mock-heroic tribute to cornmeal mush. Phillis Wheatley, born in Africa and brought to Boston in childhood as a slave, showed early signs of literary genius. A collection of her poems was published in England while she was still a young woman.

Another writer of the Revolutionary period recorded his impressions of everyday American life. Born into an aristocratic French family, Michel-Guillaume Crèvecoeur became a soldier of fortune, a world traveler, and a farmer. For fifteen years, he owned a plantation in Orange County, New York, and his impressions of life there were published in London in 1782 as *Letters From an American Farmer.*

▲ **Critical Viewing**
This painting captures the writing of the Declaration of Independence. What do the many papers on the floor of the room suggest about the writing of the document? **[Draw Conclusion]**

the painting. Benjamin Franklin is seated at the left, John Adams is in the center, and Jefferson stands at the right. These three men, along with Robert Livingston of New York and Roger Sherman of Connecticut, had been assigned to a congressional committee to write a declaration of independence. The committee members agreed that Jefferson, considered by Adams the best writer in Congress, would write the document.

Contrary to the suggestion made by the painting, Jefferson's fellow committee members were pleased with his work and suggested no changes. However, the full Congress debated Jefferson's wording for three days, making numerous minor changes and one major change—the deletion of Jefferson's reference to slavery as "cruel war against human nature." Dismayed at this reaction to what he considered a brilliant expression of the American mind, John Adams hotly contested every suggested change.

Critical Viewing

Answer: The numerous crumpled papers suggest that the document underwent many revisions and that writing it was very hard work.

$81,497,000.

Literature of the Period Comprehension Check

1. In what way was the writing produced during this period different from that produced by the Puritans?
Answer: The Puritans were concerned with private soul-searching, while writing of the Revolutionary era discussed political, public issues.
2. Name three important speakers and writers of this era.
Possible answers: Thomas Jefferson, John Adams, Benjamin Franklin, Patrick Henry, James Madison, Michel-Guillaume Crèvecoeur, and Thomas Paine were important speakers and writers of this era.
3. Name two political documents of the era whose final text was the result of committee debate.
Answer: The Declaration of Independence and the Constitution were the result of committee debate.
4. Outside the field of politics, which writer was most widely read?
Answer: Benjamin Franklin was most widely read.
5. As the eighteenth century came to a close, which types of literature were still largely untried by American writers?
Answer: Novels, short stories, and plays were largely untried.

Critical Viewing

Answer: Washington looks serious, focused, and determined. This might be a reflection of the colonists' determination to win independence from Britain.

Perhaps the best-known writing of the period outside the field of politics was done by Benjamin Franklin. His *Poor Richard's Almanack* became familiar to most households in the colonies. In addition to information on the calendar and the weather common to most almanacs, it contained such sayings as these:

> No man e'er was glorious, who was not laborious.
> Make haste slowly.
> Little Strokes, fell great Oaks.

A statesman, printer, author, inventor, and scientist, Franklin was a true son of the Enlightenment. His *Autobiography,* covering only his early years, is regarded as one of the finest autobiographies in any language.

Slave Narrative Olaudah Equiano came to America against his will as an enslaved African. However, he later purchased his freedom, settled in England, and worked to abolish slavery. As part of this effort, he wrote a two-volume autobiography entitled *The Interesting Narrative of the Life of Olaudah Equiano.* It contains a vivid and horrifying account of slaves journeying to America.

Culture and Art During the Revolutionary period, America began to establish a cultural identity of its own. Theaters were built from New York to Charleston. The first play written by an author born in America was Thomas Godfrey's tragedy *The Prince of Parthia* (1767). However, no truly American characters appeared in a play before Royall Tyler featured American types in his comedy *The Contrast* (1787). That play also dealt with a theme that would be popular in many early American dramas: the victory of honest Americans over deceitful foreigners.

A number of new colleges were established after the war, especially in the South. For example, what is today the University of Tennessee, Knoxville, was founded in 1794 as Blount College, and the University of North Carolina, Chapel Hill, opened its doors in 1795.

Several outstanding painters were at work in the colonies and the young republic. Among them were John Singleton Copley, Gilbert Stuart, John Trumbull, and Charles Willson Peale. Patience Wright, famous in the colonies as a sculptor of wax portraits, moved to London before the war. While there, she acted as a Revolutionary spy. In music, William Billings produced *The New England Psalm-Singer* and a number of patriotic hymns. Among his friends were such revolutionary activists as Samuel Adams and Paul Revere. This was a turbulent time—a time of action—and its legacy was cultural as well as political.

▼ Critical Viewing As the first secretary of the treasury, Alexander Hamilton had to develop a financial plan for the government. (a) What was the government's income in 1789? (b) How much did it owe? **[Analyze]**

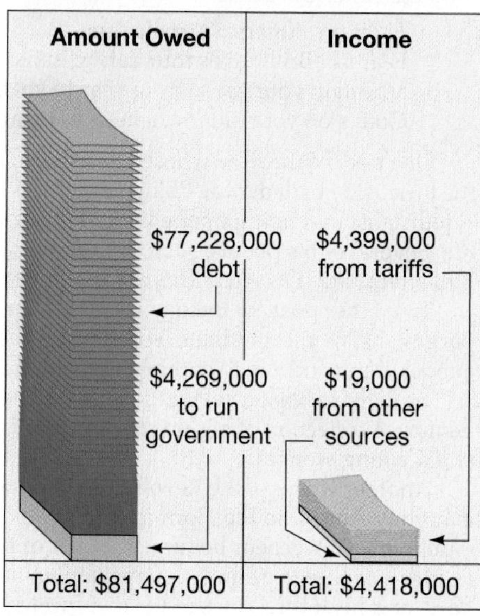

The American Experience: Art in the Historical Context

Gilbert Stuart, Portraitist

After Americans won the Revolution in 1781, one might have expected to see painters portray some of the most dramatic battle scenes—for example, the Battle of Bunker Hill or the surrender at Yorktown, Virginia. Most of the country's best-known painters, however, produced portraits.

Gilbert Stuart was among the most distinguished of these portraitists. He had studied with Benjamin West, a famous American painter who lived and worked in London. When Stuart did several paintings of the country's first citizen, George Washington, it was as if he were painting a portrait of the Revolution itself. Perhaps believing that the ideals of that struggle could be read in Washington's features and personality, Stuart focused on the upper part of Washington's body, especially his face, and he did not include any props or scenery.

George Washington (Vaughan portrait), Gilbert Stuart, Photograph © Board of Trustees, National Gallery of Art, Washington, D.C.

▶ **Critical Viewing** What impression of Washington—and, by extension, of the American Revolution—does this portrait convey? Explain. **[Infer]**

American Literature at Daybreak By the early 1800s, America could boast a small body of national literature. The Native Americans had contributed haunting poetry and legends through their oral traditions. The Puritans had written a number of powerful, inward-looking works. The statesmen of the Revolutionary period had produced political documents for the ages. A few poets and essayists had made a permanent mark on the literature of the young republic. There were, however, no American novels or plays of importance, and the modern short story had yet to be invented.

As the eighteenth century came to a close, however, the raw materials for a great national literature were at hand, waiting to be used. The nation stood on the threshold of a territorial and population explosion unique in the history of the world. It would take almost exactly a century to close the frontier of the vast and varied continent beyond the Appalachians. During that century, American literature would burst forth with a vitality that might have surprised even the farsighted founders of the nation. The colonial age ended with a narrow volume of memorable literature. The nineteenth century would close with a library of works that form a major part of America's literary heritage.

1795, by Gilbert Stuart

Born in Rhode Island in 1755, Gilbert Stuart became the most prominent American portrait painter of his era. Stuart painted three types of Washington portraits, named after the buyers of the first painted in each type. Stuart's full-length Washington portraits are known as Lansdowne portraits, his right-facing portraits as Athenaeum portraits, and left-facing portraits, as Vaughan portraits.

Use these questions for discussion.

1. What does this portrait reveal about President Washington?
   Possible Responses: Students may mention that it suggests his intelligence and his patience.
2. Point out that portraits painted at this time often depicted objects associated with accomplishments of the subjects of the portrait.
   Ask: Why did Gilbert Stuart paint the President without objects around him?
   Possible Responses: Students may mention that Washington's accomplishments were widely known and did not need to be shown.

Critical Thinking

1. Why do you think most of the important writing of the period was political?
   Answer: The colonists' minds were on political matters because the country was going through a momentous revolutionary struggle.

Concept Connector 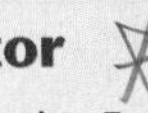

Have students return to the Focus Questions on p. 125. Ask them to use these questions to orally summarize the main points in the Unit Introduction. Student's summaries should include the following points:

Events that set the stage for the Revolution:

- The British government taxed the American colonies to pay for the French and Indian War. The Americans resented having to bear the cost of the war.
- The first of these taxes was the Stamp Act. Other Taxes and a British monopoly on tea soon followed.
- After the Boston Tea Party, the British imposed punitive laws that shut down the port of Boston, outlawed meetings, and forced colonists to house British troops.
- In 1774, colonial leaders formed the First Continental Congress.

Challenges in the quest for self-government faced by the new country:

- After declaring independence America had to win the war to expel British rule.
- After the war, the first government, The Articles of Confederation, did not work well.
- The new Constitution that was written to replace the Articles of Confederation required many compromises.
- The Bill of Rights was written to protect the people from excessive central authority.

The influence of politics on the literature of the period:
American literature of the Revolutionary period was greatly concerned with public and civic themes, unlike the literature of the Puritans, which had been personal and reflective.

Critical Thinking

1. Why do you think Washington called on Noah Webster?
   Answer: He wanted to meet the man who was struggling to "declare independence" for American English.
2. Why do you think Webster traveled across America?
   Answer: He knew that vocabulary, pronunciation, and definition varied by region, and he wanted his dictionary to represent everyone.
3. In what ways do Webster's efforts reflect a drive to standardize and innovate?
   Answer: He wanted to standardize American spellings, but he also wanted to change them from British spellings.
4. What can you deduce from the spelling changes Webster introduced?
   Answer: He wanted to spell words more simply. He deleted extra letters that don't affect pronunciation, such as the *u* in *honour.*

Answers to the Activity

1. Answers will vary depending on the words students choose. You might photocopy an entry from the OED and take students through it, showing them how it tells the history of a word in chronological order.
2. (a) suspenders (d) gasoline
   (b) elevator (e) TV
   (c) truck
   Additional words:

British	American
boot (of car)	trunk
mobile	cell phone
loo	bathroom
biscuit	cookie
tin	can

Noah Webster and the American Language

BY RICHARD LEDERER

Travel back in time to May 1787 to the city of Philadelphia. It is thronged with important visitors, including Benjamin Franklin, Alexander Hamilton, James Madison, and the brightest of these luminaries—George Washington. They have come to attend the Constitutional Convention "in order to form a more perfect Union" of states that have recently won a surprising military victory.

On the evening of May 26, 1787, General Washington pays a visit to talk about education with a 28-year-old New Englander who is teaching school in Philadelphia. His name is Noah Webster.

AMERICA'S SCHOOLMASTER

Why did Washington call on a young man scarcely half his age who was neither a Revolutionary War hero nor a Convention delegate? One reason was that Noah Webster was the author, publisher, and salesman of *The Blue-Backed Speller,* a book that was then more widely read in the United States than any other except the Bible.

WEBSTER AND THE AMERICAN DICTIONARY

On top of such an amazing achievement, Webster devoted thirty years to creating the first great American dictionaries. The fact that the name *Webster* and the word *dictionary* are practically synonymous indicates the enduring brightness of Webster's reputation.

Throughout his life, Noah Webster was afire with the conviction that the United States should have its own version of the English language. In 1789, he wrote:

As an independent nation, our honor requires us to have a system of our own, in language as well as government. Great Britain, whose children we are and whose language we speak, should no longer be our standard.

In putting this theory into practice, Noah Webster traveled throughout the East and South, listening to the speech of American people, and taking endless notes. He included in his dictionaries an array of shiny new American words, among them *applesauce, bullfrog, chowder, handy, hickory, succotash, tomahawk*—and *skunk:* "a quadruped remarkable for its smell."

In shaping the American language, Noah Webster also taught a new nation a new way to spell.

British	Webster's
honour	honor
humour	humor
musick	music
publick	public
centre	center
theatre	theater
plough	plow

Activity

1. Dictionary-makers are the biographers of words. Pick a word from the *Oxford English Dictionary* and write its "biography"—when the word was born and how it acquired new meanings over the course of its life.
2. Give the American equivalent of each of the following British words:
   (a) braces, (b) lift, (c) lorry, (d) petrol, (e) telly.
   Identify additional words that distinguish Americans from British citizens.

Enrichment

Noah Webster

It is difficult for us fully to appreciate the impact that Noah Webster had on American English, and especially on spelling. His *Blue-Backed Speller* sold about one million copies every year starting in 1850, when the population of the country was about 23 million.

Webster's schoolbooks sold so well that he was able to devote the latter part of his life to compiling dictionaries. *The American Dictionary of the English Language,* which appeared in 1828, achieved annual sales of about 300,000. In addition to providing definitions of some 70,000 words, it helped teach Americans how to pronounce these words in a uniform way.

Unit 2 Part 1

Voices for Freedom

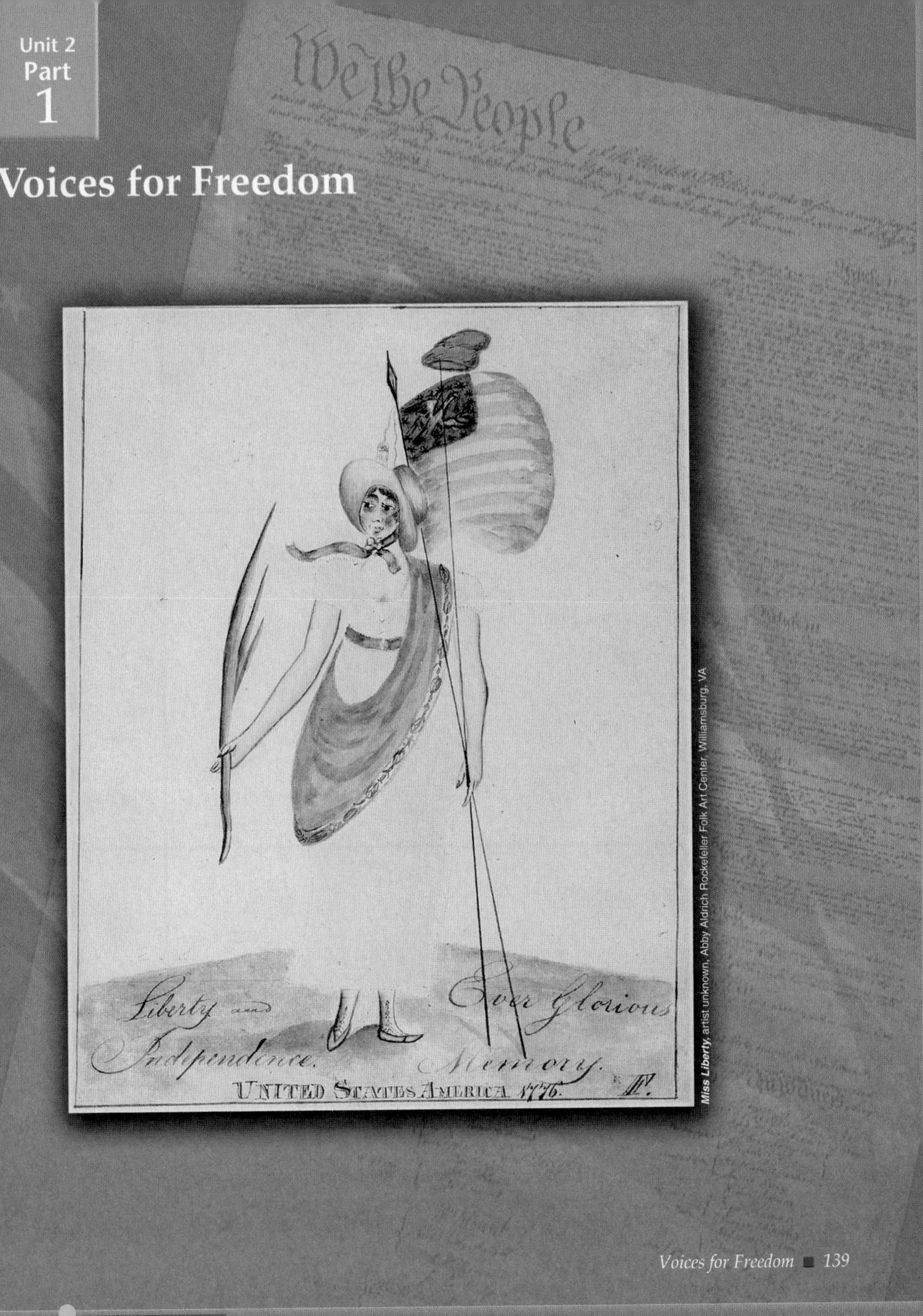

Miss Liberty, artist unknown, Abby Aldrich Rockefeller Folk Art Center, Williamsburg, VA

Selection Planning Guide

This section introduces students to some of colonial America's greatest revolutionary voices. The excerpts from *The Autobiography* and *Poor Richard's Almanack* present Franklin's self-disciplined, practical wisdom. In *The Crisis, Number 1*, the voice of Thomas Paine rings with a call to fight for freedom. Olaudah Equiano recounts the honours of the slave trading. The final text of Thomas Jefferson's Declaration of Independence as passed by Congress contains some of the most stirring prose ever written on the rights of man. Two poems by Phillis Wheatley, an African American, pay tribute to General Washington and reflect on the restorative powers of night and sleep.

Humanities

Miss Liberty, artist unknown

Folk art like *Miss Liberty* was produced by untrained artists. The stiff, doll-like appearance of the figure and the bright red spots on the cheeks are hallmarks of American folk art of the period. Abstract concepts like Truth and Justice had been personified in painting and sculpture for centuries, but they were usually shown as goddesses. *Miss Liberty* shows the new twist of portraying such a concept as an ordinary woman.

The red farmer's cap atop *Miss Liberty's* staff and the sheaf in her hand indicate the large role farmers played in the American Revolution.

1. Why do you think the artist personified Liberty as a young woman?
   Answer: The artist wanted to emphasize the naturalness and innocence of liberty.

Differentiated Instruction Solutions for All Learners

Accessibility at a Glance

Average
from The Interesting Narrative of the Life of Olaudah Equiano
from The Crisis, Number 1
An Hymn to the Evening

More Challenging
from The Autobiography
from Poor Richard's Almanac
The Declaration of Independence
To His Excellency, General Washington

Meeting Your Standards

Students will

1. **analyze and respond to literary elements.**
   - Literary Analysis: Autobiography
2. **read, comprehend, analyze, and critique nonfiction.**
   - Reading Strategy: Drawing Conclusions
   - Reading Check questions
   - Apply the Skills questions
   - Assessment Practice (ATE)
3. **develop vocabulary.**
   - Vocabulary Lesson: Word Root: *-vigil-*
4. **understand and apply written and oral language conventions.**
   - Spelling Strategy
   - Grammar and Style Lesson: Pronoun Case
5. **develop writing proficiency.**
   - Writing Lesson: Autobiographical Account
6. **develop appropriate research strategies.**
   - Extend Your Learning: Travel Brochure
7. **understand and apply listening and speaking strategies.**
   - Extend Your Learning: Class Improvement Plan

Block Scheduling: Use one 90-minute class period to preteach the skills and have students read the selection. Use a second 90-minute class period to assess students' mastery of skills, extend their learning, and monitor their progress.

Homework Suggestions

Following are possibilities for homework assignments.

- Support pages from *Unit 2 Resources:*
  Literary Analysis
  Reading Strategy
  Vocabulary Builder
  Grammar and Style
- An Extend Your Learning project and the Writing Lesson for this selection group may be completed over several days.

Step-by-Step Teaching Guide	Pacing Guide
PRETEACH	
• Administer Vocabulary and Reading Warm-ups as necessary.	5 min.
• Engage students' interest with the motivation activity.	5 min.
• Read and discuss author and background features. **FT**	10 min.
• Introduce the Literary Analysis Skill: Autobiography. **FT**	5 min.
• Introduce the Reading Strategy: Drawing Conclusions. **FT**	10 min
• Prepare students to read by teaching the selection vocabulary. **FT**	
TEACH	
• Informally monitor comprehension while students read independently or in groups. **FT**	30 min.
• Monitor students' comprehension with the Reading Check notes.	as students read
• Reinforce vocabulary with Vocabulary Builder notes.	as students read
• Develop students' understanding of autobiography with the Literary Analysis annotations. **FT**	5 min.
• Develop students' ability to draw conclusions with the Reading Strategy annotations. **FT**	5 min.
ASSESS/EXTEND	
• Assess students' comprehension and mastery of the Literary Analysis and Reading Strategy by having them answer the Apply the Skills questions. **FT**	15 min.
• Have students complete the Vocabulary Development Lesson and the Grammar and Style Lesson. **FT**	15 min.
• Apply students' ability to show cause and effect by using the Writing Lesson. **FT**	45 min. or homework
• Apply students' understanding by using one or more of the Extend Your Learning activities.	20–90 min. or homework
• Administer Selection Test A or Selection Test B. **FT**	15 min.

Resources

PRINT

Unit 2 Resources

Vocabulary Warm-up Word Lists **[L1, L2, EL]** .... p. 7
Vocabulary Warm-up Practice **[L1, L2, EL]** .... p. 8
Reading Warm-up A **[L1, L2, EL]** .... p. 9
Reading Warm-up B **[L1, L2, L3]** .... p. 10

TRANSPARENCY

Graphic Organizer Transparencies

Literary Analysis Graphic Organizer A **[L3]** .... pp. 26, 28
Literary Analysis Graphic Organizer B **[L1, L2, EL]** .... pp. 27, 29

PRINT

Reader's Notebook [L2]
Reader's Notebook: Adapted Version [L1]
Reader's Notebook: English Learner's Version [EL]

Unit 2 Resources

Literary Analysis **[L3]** .... p. 11
Reading Strategy **[L3]** .... p. 12
Vocabulary Builder **[L3]** .... p. 13

TECHNOLOGY

Listening to Literature Audio CDs [L2, EL]
Reader's Notebook: Adapted Version Audio CD [L1, L2]

PRINT

Unit 2 Resources

Grammar and Style **[L3]** .... p. 14
Support for Writing Lesson **[L3]** .... p. 15
Support for Extend Your Learning **[L3]** .... p. 16
Enrichment **[L4]** .... p. 17
Selection Test A **[L1, L2, EL]** .... pp. 18–20
Selection Test B **[L3, L4]** .... pp. 21–23

General Resources

Rubrics for Autobiographical Narrative **[L3]** .... pp. 43–44

TECHNOLOGY

Go Online: Research **[L3]**
Go Online: Self-test **[L3]**
***ExamView®*, Test Bank [L3]**

Choosing Resources for Differentiated Instruction

[L1] Special Needs Students
[L2] Below-Level Students
[L3] All Students
[L4] Advanced Students
[EL] English Learners

FT Fast Track Instruction: To move the lesson more quickly, use the strategies and activities identified with **FT**.

Scaffolding for Less Proficient and Advanced Students

The leveled Critical Thinking questions after selections progress in the levels of thinking required to answer them. To address the needs of your different students, you may use the (a) level questions for your less proficient students and the (b) level questions with your on-level and advanced students. The occasional (c) level questions are appropriate for your advanced students.

PRENTICE HALL **TeacherEXPRESS™** Plan · Teach · Assess Use this complete suite of powerful teaching tools to make lesson planning and testing quicker and easier.

PRENTICE HALL **StudentEXPRESS™** Learn · Study · Succeed Use the interactive textbook (online and on CD-ROM) to make selections and activities come alive with audio and video support and interactive questions.

PRETEACH

Motivation

Write the following quotation by Benjamin Franklin on the chalkboard: "I wished to live without committing any fault at any time." Ask students whether they believe they have committed any "faults" in the past twenty-four hours. Discuss reasons it would be difficult to live without committing any faults. Ask students to look for the difficulties Franklin may have faced in achieving this goal.

❶ Background

More About the Author

No other colonial American more closely embodied the promise of America than did Benjamin Franklin. Through hard work, dedication, and ingenuity, Franklin rose out of poverty to become a wealthy, famous, and influential person. Although he never received a formal education, Franklin made important contributions in science, literature, journalism, and education. In addition, as a statesman, he is the only American to sign the four documents that established the nation: the Declaration of Independence, the treaty of alliance with France, the peace treaty with England, and the Constitution.

Build Skills | *Autobiography • Aphorisms*

❶ *from* The Autobiography • *from* Poor Richard's Almanack

Benjamin Franklin (1706–1790)

From his teen years until his retirement at forty-two, Benjamin Franklin worked as a printer. Franklin got his start as an apprentice to his brother, James Franklin, a Boston printer. By the time he was sixteen, he was not only printing, but writing parts of his brother's newspaper. Using the name "Silence Dogood," Franklin satirized daily life and politics in Boston.

When he was seventeen, Franklin left Boston and traveled to Philadelphia, intending to open his own print shop. This move gave birth to one of Franklin's most popular and enduring contributions to American culture, *Poor Richard's Almanack.* This annual publication, which Franklin published from 1732 to 1757, contained information, observations, and advice and was very popular with readers of his day.

The "Write Reputation" Just as he had signed "Silence Dogood" to the letters he wrote for his brother's paper, Franklin created for the *Almanack* a fictitious author/editor, the chatty Richard Saunders (and his wife, Bridget). Although Poor Richard's early appearances in the *Almanack* present him as a dull and foolish astronomer, his character developed over the years, becoming more thoughtful, pious, and humorous. Despite the fact that Franklin published under a pseudonym, the *Almanack* earned him a reputation as a talented writer.

Secret to Success Like most almanacs, Franklin's contained practical information about the calendar, the sun and moon, and the weather. *Poor Richard's Almanack* also featured a wealth of homespun sayings and observations, many of which are still quoted today. It was these aphorisms, with their characteristic moral overtones, that made the *Almanack* a bestseller. Franklin put an aphorism at the top or bottom of most pages of his almanacs. The wit and brevity of these sayings allowed Franklin to include many moral messages in very little space, while also entertaining his readers.

Man of Science When Franklin was forty-two, he retired from the printing business to devote himself to science. He proved to be as successful a scientist as he had been a printer. Over the course of his lifetime, Franklin was responsible for inventing the lightning rod, bifocals, and a new type of stove; confirming the laws of electricity; and contributing to the scientific understanding of earthquakes and ocean currents. In spite of all these achievements, Franklin is best remembered for his career in politics.

Statesman and Diplomat Franklin played an important role in drafting the Declaration of Independence, enlisting French support during the Revolutionary War, negotiating a peace treaty with Britain, and drafting the United States Constitution. In his later years, he was ambassador first to England and then to France. Even before George Washington, Franklin was considered to be "the father of his country."

The Story Behind the Story Franklin wrote the first section of *The Autobiography* in 1771 at the age of sixty-five. At the urging of friends, he wrote three more sections—the last shortly before his death—but succeeded in bringing the account of his life only to the years 1757 to 1759. Though never completed, his *Autobiography,* filled with his opinions and suggestions, provides not only a record of his achievements but also an understanding of his character.

Preview

Connecting to the Literature

Autobiographies of historical figures such as Franklin allow us a closer look at world-shaping events and can be just as gripping as great fiction.

Literary Analysis

Autobiography

Benjamin Franklin's *Autobiography* set the standard for what was then a new genre. Usually written in the first person, **autobiographies** present life events as the writer sees them. They also provide a view of history that is more personal than accounts in history books. Use a chart like the one shown to record details from Franklin's *Autobiography* that paint a portrait of the man, his attitudes, and the world he inhabited.

Details of Franklin's life

Franklin's attitudes

Portrait of the times

Comparing Literary Works

Franklin's interest in self-improvement is evident both in this excerpt from *The Autobiography* and in the **aphorisms**—short sayings with a message—he wrote for the *Almanack:*

> If you would know the value of money, try to borrow some.

In *The Autobiography*, Franklin examines his own life and applies higher standards to his behavior. By contrast, the aphorisms offer witty advice to the general public. As you read these selections, examine how they each convey messages of moral self-improvement, but with very different effects.

Reading Strategy

Drawing Conclusions

Franklin vividly describes his life and goals, letting you form an impression of his character. To form an impression, **draw conclusions** based on evidence from the text and your own experience. For example:

Detail: Franklin makes lists to organize his plan.

Personal Experience: You make "to do" lists, too.

Conclusion: Franklin likes to plan ahead.

Draw conclusions about Franklin's character as you read these works.

Vocabulary Builder

arduous (är′ jo͞o əs) *adj.* difficult (p. 143)

avarice (av′ ə ris) *n.* greed (p. 143)

vigilance (vij′ ə ləns) *n.* watchfulness (p. 144)

disposition (dis′ pə zish′ ən) *n.* management (p. 146)

foppery (fäp′ ər ē) *n.* foolishness (p. 147)

felicity (fə lis′ i tē) *n.* happiness; bliss (p. 147)

squander (skwän′ dər) *v.* spend or use wastefully (p. 149)

fasting (fast′ iŋ) *v.* eating very little or nothing (p. 150)

2 Literary Analysis

Autobiography

- Tell students that as they read the excerpt from *The Autobiography,* they will focus on its literary genre, or form. *Autobiography* is a first-person account of the writer's own life.
- Have a volunteer read aloud the description of autobiography. Point out the special view of events that autobiographies offer readers.
- Emphasize that Benjamin Franklin's autobiography reveals up-close information about U.S. history that students might not know.
- Give students a copy of **Literary Analysis Graphic Organizer A,** p. 26 in ***Graphic Organizer Transparencies,*** to use as they read *The Autobiography*. Remind students that completing it as they read it will help them get to know Franklin better.

3 Reading Strategy

Drawing Conclusions

- Remind students that when they draw conclusions, they use both clues from the text and their own experiences to make reasonable statements about what they read.
- Then, tell students that drawing conclusions can help them paint more comprehensive picture of Franklin. As they read his autobiography, they can use hints from his style and language to help answer their questions.
- For example, point out that Franklin's detailed list of virtues might lead students to draw the conclusion that he is very serious about living without "fault."

Vocabulary Builder

- Pronounce each vocabulary word for students, and read the definitions as a class. Have students identify any words with which they are already familiar.

Differentiated Instruction Solutions for All Learners

Support for Special Needs Students
Have students read the adapted version of *The Autobiography* in the ***Reader's Notebook: Adapted Version.*** This version provides basic-level instruction in an interactive format with questions and write-on lines. Completing these pages will prepare students to read the selection in the Student Edition.

Support for Less Proficient Readers
Have students read *The Autobiography* in the ***Reader's Notebook.*** This version provides basic-level instruction in an interactive format with questions and write-on lines. After students finish the selection in the ***Reader's Notebook,*** have them complete the questions and activities in the Student Edition.

Support for English Learners
Have students read *The Autobiography* in the ***Reader's Notebook: English Learner's Version.*** This version provides basic-level instruction in an interactive format with questions and write-on lines. Completing these pages will prepare students to read the selection in the Student Edition.

TEACH

Learning Modalities
Verbal/Linguistic Learners

Tell students that this selection contains many words chosen by Franklin for their particular connotations. Remind students that a word's connotation is the set of ideas associated with it, in addition to its explicit meaning. For example, the noun *frugality* denotes a quality of thriftiness or economy, generally perceived as a positive quality. The word *stinginess,* which denotes the same thing, carries negative connotations. Have students note and discuss the positive, negative, or neutral connotation of other words as they read.

❶ About the Selection

This excerpt shows Franklin's struggle to reach moral perfection, a subject he writes about with the fervent hope that others will imitate the effort. Naming thirteen virtues, Franklin focuses on one at a time, the perfection of one leading to ease of perfecting the next. As years pass, he devotes more time to attaining each virtue before advancing to the next. In telling his story, Franklin displays his fastidious nature, detailed mind, logic in addressing the virtues, daily organization, and harsh self-evaluations. Finally, he claims the result of his lifelong struggle has been happiness.

❷ Critical Viewing

Answer: In the painting, students may note discipline in the worshippers' attention, their head coverings, the separation of sexes, and their row seats. Similarly, in *The Autobiography,* students may note that Franklin shows discipline in his use of the little book and of daily schedules.

❶ *from* The Autobiography

Benjamin Franklin

Background Benjamin Franklin arrived in the city of Philadelphia in 1723 at the age of 17. He knew no one, and he had little money and fewer possessions. However, his accomplishments shaped the city in ways that are still visible today. He helped establish Philadelphia's public library and fire department, as well as its first college. In addition, through his efforts, Philadelphia became the first city in the colonies to have street lights. While Franklin was a brilliant man, some of his success can be attributed to sheer self-discipline, which is evident in this excerpt from his *Autobiography.*

❸

Quaker Meeting, Unidentified Artist, Courtesy, Museum of Fine Arts, Boston

❷ ▲ Critical Viewing Relate this picture to *The Autobiography.* What does each suggest about discipline and order? **[Draw Conclusions]**

Differentiated Instruction Solutions for All Learners

Accessibility at a Glance

	Autobiography	Almanack
Context	Insight into colonial values	Aphorisms
Language	18th-century vocabulary and sentence structure	Simple vocabulary, familiar sayings
Concept Level	Challenging (ideas about achieving virtue)	Accessible (generalized sayings about life and human nature)
Literary Merit	Classic	Classic
Lexile	1400	500
Overall Rating	More challenging	More challenging

4 It was about this time I conceived the bold and arduous project of arriving at moral perfection. I wished to live without committing any fault at any time; I would conquer all that either natural inclination, custom, or company might lead me into. As I knew, or thought I knew, what was right and wrong, I did not see why I might not always do the one and avoid the other. But I soon found I had undertaken a task of more difficulty than I had imagined. While my care was employed in guarding against one fault, I was often surprised by another; habit took the advantage of inattention; inclination was sometimes too strong for reason. I concluded, at length, that the mere speculative conviction that it was our interest to be completely virtuous was not sufficient to prevent our slipping; and that the contrary habits must be broken, and good ones acquired and established, before we can have any dependence on a steady, uniform rectitude of conduct. For this purpose I therefore contrived the following method.

In the various enumerations of the moral virtues I had met with in my reading, I found the catalog more or less numerous, as different writers included more or fewer ideas under the same name. Temperance, for example, was by some confined to eating and drinking, while by others it was extended to mean the moderating every other pleasure, appetite, inclination, or passion, bodily or mental, even to our avarice and ambition. I proposed to myself, for the sake of clearness, to use rather more names, with fewer ideas annexed to each, than a few names with more ideas; and I included under thirteen names of virtues all that at that time occurred to me as necessary or desirable, and annexed to each a short precept, which fully expressed the extent I gave to its meaning.

These names of virtues, with their precepts, were:

1. TEMPERANCE Eat not to dullness; drink not to elevation.
2. SILENCE Speak not but what may benefit others or yourself; avoid trifling conversation.
3. ORDER Let all your things have their places; let each part of your business have its time.
4. RESOLUTION Resolve to perform what you ought; perform without fail what you resolve.
5. FRUGALITY Make no expense but to do good to others or yourself; i.e., waste nothing.
6. INDUSTRY Lose no time; be always employed in something useful; cut off all unnecessary actions.
7. SINCERITY Use no hurtful deceit; think innocently and justly, and, if you speak, speak accordingly.
8. JUSTICE Wrong none by doing injuries, or omitting the benefits that are your duty.
9. MODERATION Avoid extremes; forebear resenting injuries so much as you think they deserve.
10. CLEANLINESS Tolerate no uncleanliness in body, clothes, or habitation.

Vocabulary Builder
arduous (är′ jo͞o əs) *adj.* difficult

Literary Analysis
Autobiography What does Franklin's goal of moral "perfection" suggest about the values of the time period?

Vocabulary Builder
avarice (av′ ə ris) *n.* greed

5 **Reading Check**
What prompts Franklin to make his list?

3 Humanities

Quaker Meeting, artist unknown

Dating from the late 18th or early 19th century, this British painting is based on a print of a Quaker meeting by Egbert van Heemkirk of London (c. 1670). The painting, which now belongs to Haverford College's Quaker collection, depicts a sense of Quaker order and virtue. Use these questions for discussion.

1. What contributes to the severe mood of the painting?
   Answer: The lack of bright colors, the dark background, the parallel rows, and the worshippers' somber expressions and shaded eyes all contribute to the mood.
2. In what ways do the people shown in the painting seem to be following Benjamin Franklin's approach to life?
   Possible response: The worshippers are silent and orderly.

4 Literary Analysis
Autobiography

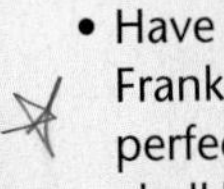

- Have students **paraphrase** Franklin's attitude toward moral perfection, and write it on the chalkboard.
  Possible response: Franklin believes that moral perfection is desirable and can be achieved through hard work.
- **Ask** students the Literary Analysis question: What does Franklin's goal of moral "perfection" suggest about the values of the time period?
  Answer: It suggests that people of the time period valued hard work and moral behavior very highly.

5 Reading Check

Answer: He makes a list to clarify his definitions of the virtues.

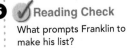

Differentiated Instruction
Solutions for All Learners

Strategy for Less Proficient Readers
To help students develop a rounded picture of Benjamin Franklin, have them create a character web. Using ***Graphic Organizer Transparencies,*** p. 317, demonstrate how to create such a web, placing Franklin's name in the center cell and creating outer cells labeled to describe Franklin's views, actions, and words.

Strategy for English Learners
Have students use dictionaries to define each of Franklin's listed virtues. Then, demonstrate the use of a word web to help students understand these concepts. Place the virtue in the center cell, and use outer cells for Franklin's examples and definitions. Help students to complete the outer cells with information from the text.

Strategy for Advanced Readers
Challenge students to explore the advantages and disadvantages of each virtue that Franklin describes. Demonstrate the use of a web in which the center cell contains the virtue and two outer rings of cells contain either advantages or disadvantages. Have students work in pairs to complete webs for each virtue.

❻ Literature in Context

Socrates Socrates wrote nothing of his own, so we are dependent on the writings of his contemporaries for information about his life. Some of the best sources of information are the early dialogues of his student Plato, who attempted to provide a full picture of Socrates' teaching methods. Socrates became well known for using a method of critical inquiry that explored and often undermined widely held beliefs.

Connect to Literature Encourage students to reflect on what they know about Jesus and Socrates before responding to the question. **Possible response:** There is some humor in Franklin's plan to achieve humility by imitating Jesus and Socrates in that Jesus and Socrates are almost perfect models. Very few people are able to hold themselves to such a standard.

❼ Vocabulary Builder
Latin Word Root: *-vigil-*

- Draw students' attention to the word *vigilance* and its definition, "watchfulness."
- Explain that the root *-vigil-* means "the act or period of remaining awake so as to guard or observe something."
- **Ask** students to name situations in which people might hold a vigil.

❽ Reading Strategy
Drawing Conclusions

- **Ask** students to give examples of goals they have worked hard to reach. Discuss how they developed systems or schedules for attaining intermediate goals or for keeping on track. Ask students why they developed these systems. **Possible answer:** When goals are important to us, we take great care to ensure we will reach them.
- **Invite** students to answer the question: What does Franklin's methodical approach, described in this passage, suggest about his dedication to his plan for self-improvement? **Answer:** He is dedicated to his plan and wants to do everything he can to ensure its success.

➤ **Monitor Progress:** As students continue to read, have them make a list of details that reveal Franklin's dedication to his plan.

11. TRANQUILLITY Be not disturbed at trifles, or at accidents common or unavoidable.
12. CHASTITY
13. HUMILITY Imitate Jesus and Socrates♦. ❻

My intention being to acquire the *habitude* of all these virtues, I judged it would be well not to distract my attention by attempting the whole at once but to fix it on one of them at a time; and, when I should be master of that, then to proceed to another, and so on, till I should have gone through the thirteen; and, as the previous acquisition of some might facilitate the acquisition of certain others, I arranged them with that view, as they stand above. *Temperance* first, as it tends to procure that coolness and clearness of head, which is so necessary where ❼ constant vigilance was to be kept up, and guard maintained against the unremitting attraction of ancient habits and the force of perpetual temptations. This being acquired and established, *Silence* would be more easy; and my desire being to gain knowledge at the same time that I improved in virtue, and considering that in conversation it was obtained rather by the use of the ears than of the tongue, and therefore wishing to break a habit I was getting into of prattling, punning, and joking, which only made me acceptable to trifling company, I gave *Silence* the second place. This and the next, *Order*, I expected would allow me more time for attending to my project and my studies. *Resolution*, once become habitual, would keep me firm in my endeavors to obtain all the subsequent virtues; *Frugality* and *Industry* freeing me from my remaining debt and producing affluence and independence, would make more easy the practice of *Sincerity* and *Justice*, etc., etc. Conceiving then, that, agreeably to the advice of Pythagoras[1] in his *Golden Verses*, daily examination would be necessary, I contrived the following method for conducting that examination.

❽ I made a little book, in which I allotted a page for each of the virtues. I ruled each page with red ink, so as to have seven columns, one for each day of the week, marking each column with a letter for the day. I crossed these columns with thirteen red lines, marking the beginning of each line with the first letter of one of the virtues, on which line and in its proper column I might mark, by a little black spot, every fault I found upon examination to have been committed respecting that virtue upon that day.

I determined to give a week's strict attention to each of the virtues successively. Thus, in the first week, my great guard was to avoid every[2] the least offense against *Temperance*, leaving the other virtues to

1. **Pythagoras** (pi *thag'* ə rəs) Greek philosopher and mathematician who lived in the sixth century B.C.
2. **every** even.

Literature in Context

History Connection

♦ ***Socrates***

A Greek philosopher and teacher who lived in the fifth century B.C., Socrates pioneered the kind of self-reflection that Benjamin Franklin undertakes with his moral improvement plan. Socrates believed that only through self-knowledge can people achieve virtue. Though he led many Athenians in searching for truth and defining rules for moral conduct, Socrates' criticism of the government resulted in his execution.

Connect to the Literature

Do you see any humor or irony in Franklin's plan for achieving humility—namely, by imitating Jesus and Socrates? Explain.

Vocabulary Builder

vigilance (vij' ə ləns) *n.* watchfulness

Reading Strategy

Drawing Conclusions What does Franklin's methodical approach, described in this passage, suggest about his dedication to his plan for self-improvement?

Enrichment

Franklin in Philadelphia

Benjamin Franklin greatly influenced daily life in colonial Philadelphia. He helped establish the city's public library and fire department, as well as its first college. In addition, through his efforts, Philadelphia became the first city in the colonies to have street lights.

Philadelphia was an important center of activity during the period leading up to the American Revolution. It was there that the Declaration of Independence, which established the United States as an independent nation, was written and signed.

In Philadelphia today, you can still walk down cobblestone streets and visit historic sites. Independence Hall (where the Declaration of Independence was signed), the Liberty Bell, and the home of Betsy Ross are within walking distance of one another for tourists and history enthusiasts.

their ordinary chance, only marking every evening the faults of the day. Thus, if in the first week I could keep my first line, marked *T.* clear of spots, I supposed the habit of that virtue so much strengthened, and its opposite weakened, that I might venture extending my attention to include the next, and for the following week keep both lines clear of spots. Proceeding thus to the last, I could go through a course complete in thirteen weeks, and four courses in a year. And like him who, having a garden to weed, does not attempt to eradicate all the bad herbs at once, which would exceed his reach and his strength, but works on one of the beds at a time, and, having accomplished the first, proceeds to a second, so I should have, I hoped, the encouraging pleasure of seeing on my pages the progress I made in virtue, by clearing successively my lines of their spots, till in the end, by a number of courses, I should be happy in viewing a clean book, after a thirteen weeks' daily examination. . . .

The precept of *Order* requiring that *every part of my business should have its allotted time,* one page in my little book contained the following scheme of employment for the twenty-four hours of a natural day.

9

THE MORNING. *Question.* What good shall I do this day?	5	Rise, wash, and
	6	address *Powerful Goodness!* Contrive day's business, and take the resolution of the day;
	7	prosecute the present study, and breakfast.
	8	
	9	Work.
	10	
	11	
NOON.	12	Read, or overlook
	1	my accounts, and dine.
	2	
	3	Work.
	4	
	5	
EVENING. *Question.* What good have I done today?	6	Put things in their places. Supper.
	7	Music or diversion, or conversation.
	8	Conversation. Examination of
	9	the day.
	10	
	11	
	12	
NIGHT.	1	Sleep.
	2	
	3	
	4	

Literary Analysis
Autobiography What insight into Franklin's character does this list provide?

10 **Reading Check**
Which virtue did Franklin hope to achieve by planning each day's activities?

9 Literary Analysis
Autobiography

- Read the bracketed passage. Confirm that students understand what it shows.
  Answer: It shows Franklin's daily schedule with guiding questions to organize his day.
- Focus students' attention on Franklin's guiding questions, pointing out that these highlight the author's desire to use his time for good deeds.
- Have volunteers read aloud the items under 6 a.m. and 6 p.m. Discuss ways that these are similar.
  Answer: Both reflect Franklin's desire for order and accomplishment.
- **Ask** students to answer the Literary Analysis question: What insight into Franklin's character does this list provide?
  Possible response: It suggests that he does not like to waste time and that he has a disciplined and purposeful way of living.

10 Reading Check

Answer: He hoped to achieve the virtue of *Order* by planning the day's activities.

Differentiated Instruction
Solutions for All Learners

Strategy for Special Needs Students
Have students add to the character webs they began on p. 143 using details from pp. 144–145. Encourage them to keep adding to their webs as they finish reading Franklin's autobiographical reflections.

Strategy for Less Proficient Readers
Focus students' attention on Franklin's two organizers: the list on p. 143 and the daily calendar on p. 145. Help students understand these two organizers by clarifying their structure and defining any unfamiliar terms.

Enrichment for Gifted/Talented Students
Have students read the additional excerpt from Franklin's *Autobiography,* found in **Authors In Depth,** *The American Experience,* p. 27. Discuss ways that the excerpt compares and contrasts with the excerpt included here.

⓫ Humanities

Benjamin Franklin as a Young Printer in Philadelphia

While most people are familiar with the grandfatherly, spectacled image of Franklin, this engraving provides a rare glimpse of Benjamin Franklin in his youth. Here we see the young Franklin carrying the tools of his trade, that of a printer. Discuss with students the calm confidence that radiates from Franklin's posture and expression. Use these questions for discussion:

1. What can we learn about Franklin from this picture?
   Answer: We can learn about Franklin's occupation, personality traits, and the era in which he lived.
2. How is this picture related to the selection?
   Answer: The picture shows a hard-working, self-disciplined Franklin, just the sort of person who might reach for moral perfection.

⓬ Critical Viewing

Answer: The expression suggests that Franklin is a calm, confident, and serious individual.

⓭ Literary Analysis

Autobiography

- With students, read aloud the bracketed passage.
- **Ask** the Literary Analysis question: What does this anecdote about the man with the axe reveal Franklin's sense of humor?
  Possible response: The anecdote reveals that Franklin understands that some of his goals are unrealistic.

Monitor Progress: Remind students that, as they read an autobiography, they can learn about the writer based on the details and anecdotes that he or she decides to include.

I entered upon the execution of this plan for self-examination, and continued it with occasional intermissions for some time. I was surprised to find myself so much fuller of faults than I had imagined; but I had the satisfaction of seeing them diminish. To avoid the trouble of renewing now and then my little book, which, by scraping out the marks on the paper of old faults to make room for new ones in a new course, became full of holes, I transferred my tables and precepts to the ivory leaves of a memorandum book, on which the lines were drawn with red ink that made a durable stain, and on those lines I marked my faults with a black-lead pencil, which marks I could easily wipe out with a wet sponge. After a while I went through one course only in a year, and afterward only one in several years, till at length I omitted them entirely, being employed in voyages and business abroad, with a multiplicity of affairs that interfered; but I always carried my little book with me.

⓫ *Benjamin Franklin as a Young Printer in Philadelphia,* The Granger Collection, New York

My scheme of *Order* gave me the most trouble; and I found that, though it might be practicable where a man's business was such as to leave him the disposition of his time, that of a journeyman printer, for instance, it was not possible to be exactly observed by a master, who must mix with the world and often receive people of business at their own hours. *Order,* too, with regard to places for things, papers, etc., I found extremely difficult to acquire. I had not been early accustomed to it, and, having an exceeding good memory, I was not so sensible of the
⓭ inconvenience attending want of method. This article, therefore, cost me so much painful attention, and my faults in it vexed me so much, and I made so little progress in amendment, and had such frequent relapses, that I was almost ready to give up the attempt, and content myself with a faulty character in that respect, like the man who, in

⓬ **▲ Critical Viewing** What does the expression on Franklin's face suggest about his personality? **[Infer]**

Vocabulary Builder
disposition (dis´ pə zish´ ən) *n.* management

Differentiated Instruction Solutions for All Learners

Enrichment for Advanced Readers

Suggest that students read additional works by Benjamin Franklin, such as *The Autobiography of Benjamin Franklin and Other Writings,* L. Jesse Lemisch, ed., *Benjamin Franklin's The Art of Virtue: His Formula for Successful Living,* George L. Rogers, ed., *Letters to the Press, 1758–1775,* Verner W. Crane, ed. You may also wish to use **Authors In Depth,** *The American Experience,* which contains the following selections:

- from *The Autobiography* (nonfiction, pp. 27–30)
- "Information to Those Who Would Remove to America" (nonfiction, pp. 31–32)
- "Speech in the Convention on the Subject of Salaries" (nonfiction, pp. 33–40)

After students have read these or other works by Franklin, ask them whether or not the body of his work conforms to an overall and consistent image of his character. Invite students to answer this question in a brief oral report containing quotations from the works.

buying an ax of a smith, my neighbor, desired to have the whole of its surface as bright as the edge. The smith consented to grind it bright for him if he would turn the wheel; he turned, while the smith pressed the broad face of the ax hard and heavily on the stone, which made the turning of it very fatiguing. The man came every now and then from the wheel to see how the work went on, and at length would take his ax as it was, without farther grinding. "No," said the smith, "turn on, turn on; we shall have it bright by and by; as yet, it is only speckled." "Yes," says the man, "*but I think I like a speckled ax best.*" And I believe this may have been the case with many, who, having, for want of some such means as I employed, found the difficulty of obtaining good and breaking bad habits in other points of vice and virtue, have given up the struggle, and concluded that "*a speckled ax was best*"; for something, that pretended to be reason, was every now and then suggesting to me that such extreme nicety as I exacted of myself might be a kind of foppery in morals, which, if it were known, would make me ridiculous; that a perfect character might be attended with the inconvenience of being envied and hated; and that a benevolent man should allow a few faults in himself, to keep his friends in countenance.

In truth, I found myself incorrigible with respect to *Order*; and now I am grown old, and my memory bad, I feel very sensibly the want of it. But, on the whole, though I never arrived at the perfection I had been so ambitious of obtaining, but fell far short of it, yet I was, by the endeavor, a better and a happier man than I otherwise should have been if I had not attempted it; as those who aim at perfect writing by imitating the engraved copies, though they never reached the wished-for excellence of those copies, their hand is mended by the endeavor, and is tolerable while it continues fair and legible.

It may be well my posterity should be informed that to this little artifice, with the blessing of God, their ancestor owed the constant felicity of his life, down to his seventy-ninth year in which this is written. What reverses may attend the remainder is in the hand of Providence; but, if they arrive, the reflection on past happiness enjoyed ought to help his bearing them with more resignation. To *Temperance* he ascribes his long-continued health, and what is still left to him of a good constitution; to *Industry* and *Frugality*, the early easiness of his circumstances and acquisition of his fortune, with all that knowledge that enabled him to be a useful citizen, and obtained for him some degree of reputation among the learned; to *Sincerity* and *Justice*, the confidence of his country, and the honorable employs it conferred upon him; and to the joint influence of the whole mass of the virtues, even in the imperfect state he was able to acquire them, all that evenness of temper, and that (15) cheerfulness in conversation, which makes his company still sought for, and agreeable even to his younger acquaintance. I hope, therefore, (14) that some of my descendants may follow the example and reap the benefit.

Literary Analysis
Autobiography What does this anecdote about the man with the axe reveal about Franklin's sense of humor?

Vocabulary Builder
foppery (fäp′ ər ē) *n.* foolishness

Vocabulary Builder
felicity (fə lis′ i tē) *n.* happiness; bliss

Reading Check
Did Franklin consider his moral improvement plan successful? Explain.

14 Critical Thinking
Analyze

- Have students read the bracketed passage. Point out that Franklin admits to the motivation of wanting to look good in the eyes of his descendents. He also wants to show that he produced some positive results in his life.
- **Ask** students to describe Franklin's final message to his readers.
Answer: He wants others to follow in his footsteps.

15 Reading Check
Possible response: Franklin considered his plan generally successful in that it led to moral improvements and to his overall happiness. He acknowledges, however, that it did not lead to moral perfection.

Differentiated Instruction Solutions for All Learners

Support for Less Proficient Readers
Review the selection with students, asking them to identify passages they found especially difficult. Using these passages to demonstrate, show students how to break long sentences into shorter units of thought by using punctuation—especially commas and semicolons—as a guide.

Strategy for English Learners
When they finish reading, have students write a summary of the selection. Then, have them compare their summary with the one in the **Readers Notebook: English Learners Version**. Discuss any discrepancies, making sure students understand the main ideas in the selection.

Enrichment for Gifted/Talented Students
Using the knowledge they've gained about Benjamin Franklin from his *Autobiography,* invite students to portray Franklin in a character study. Encourage students to return to the text and images for details about Franklin's character, mannerisms, and speech style.

⓰ About the Selection

By providing practical wisdom through aphorisms, Benjamin Franklin teaches valuable lessons in brief and easy-to-remember sayings.

⓱ Humanities

Cover, *Poor Richard's Almanack,* by Benjamin Franklin

Like most almanacs, Poor Richard's contained practical information about the calendar, the sun and moon, and the weather. It also contained a wealth of homespun sayings and observations, many of which are still used today. Use these questions for discussion:

1. What makes the original page more difficult to read than the reprinted excerpt?
   Answer: On the original page, the letter *s* is printed differently.
2. Would the information in this almanac have been accurate for the people where you live?
   Answer: The information is appropriate for areas near Philadelphia—from Newfoundland to South Carolina.

⓲ Critical Viewing

Answer: Students may speculate that *philomath* means "a love of learning," since the Greek prefix *philo* means "love" and *mathē* means "learning."

⓰ *from* Poor Richard's Almanack

Benjamin Franklin

⓱

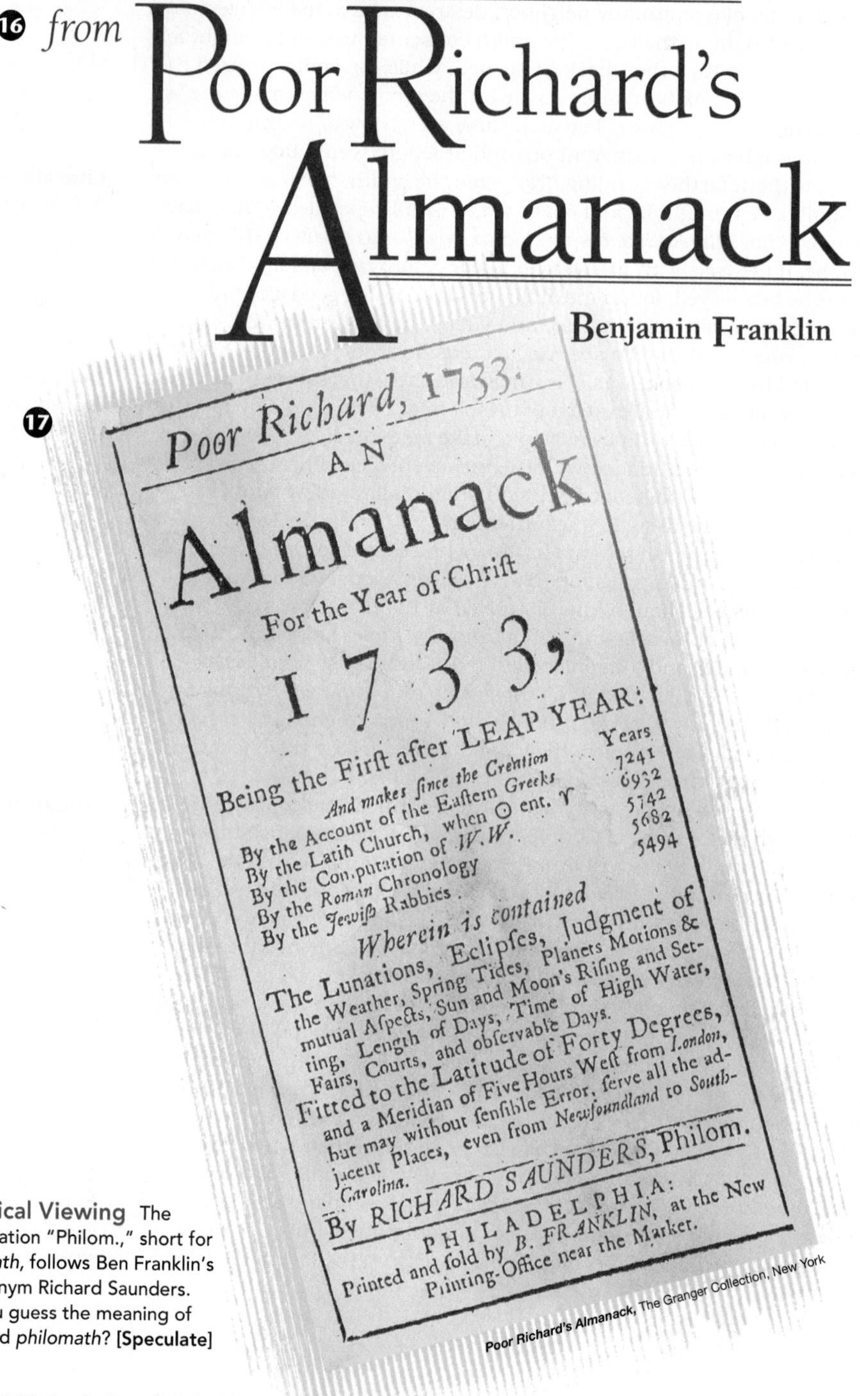

Poor Richard, 1733.

AN

Almanack

For the Year of Chriſt

1733,

Being the Firſt after LEAP YEAR:

	Years
And makes ſince the Creation	
By the Account of the Eaſtern Greeks	7241
By the Latin Church, when ☉ ent. ♈	6932
By the Computation of *W.W.*	5742
By the *Roman* Chronology	5682
By the *Jewiſh* Rabbies	5494

Wherein is contained

The Lunations, Eclipſes, Judgment of the Weather, Spring Tides, Planets Motions & mutual Aſpects, Sun and Moon's Riſing and Setting, Length of Days, Time of High Water, Fairs, Courts, and obſervable Days.

Fitted to the Latitude of Forty Degrees, and a Meridian of Five Hours Weſt from *London*, but may without ſenſible Error, ſerve all the adjacent Places, even from *Newfoundland* to *South-Carolina*.

By RICHARD SAUNDERS, Philom.

PHILADELPHIA:
Printed and ſold by *B. FRANKLIN*, at the New Printing-Office near the Market.

Poor Richard's Almanack, The Granger Collection, New York

⓲ ▶**Critical Viewing** The abbreviation "Philom.," short for *philomath*, follows Ben Franklin's pseudonym Richard Saunders. Can you guess the meaning of the word *philomath*? **[Speculate]**

Enrichment

Aphorisms

The aphorisms, or witty sayings, in *Poor Richard's Almanack* still circulate in modern conversation. An aphorism is a short, concise statement expressing a wise or clever observation or general truth. It usually reflects the setting and the time in which it was created. A variety of devices make aphorisms easy to remember. Some contain rhymes or repeated words or sounds; others use parallel structure to present contrasting ideas. The aphorism "no pain, no gain," for instance, uses rhyme, repetition, and parallel structure.

Ask students to name aphorisms they have heard. Discuss the language devices each uses to make a memorable impression on readers. Then, challenge students to check a dictionary of quotations to identify the source of each aphorism. Together, calculate how many come from Franklin's almanac.

Fools make feasts, and wise men eat them.

Be slow in choosing a friend, slower in changing.

Keep thy shop, and thy shop will keep thee.

Early to bed, early to rise, makes a man healthy, wealthy, and wise.

Three may keep a secret if two of them are dead.

God helps them that help themselves.

The rotten apple spoils his companions.

An open foe may prove a curse; but a pretended friend is worse.

Have you somewhat to do tomorrow, do it today.

A true friend is the best possession.

A small leak will sink a great ship.

No gains without pains.

Tis easier to prevent bad habits than to break them.

Well done is better than well said.

20 Dost thou love life? Then do not squander time; for that's the stuff life is made of.

Write injuries in dust, benefits in marble.

A slip of the foot you may soon recover, but a slip of the tongue you may never get over.

If your head is wax, don't walk in the sun.

A good example is the best sermon.

Hunger is the best pickle.

Genius without education is like silver in the mine.

19 **Literature in Context**

Cultural Connection

Proverbs

Most of Franklin's aphorisms are adapted from traditional or folk sayings, known as proverbs. Franklin, who believed that clarity and brevity were two of the most important characteristics of good prose, rewrote many proverbs, crafting short, witty sayings that taught a lesson.

Proverbs are nearly as old as language itself, and exist in all societies. They reflect each culture's view of the world, conveying feelings about fate, the seasons, the natural world, work and effort, love, death, and other universal experiences. These memorable bits of wisdom have survived for centuries, perhaps because they reflect unchanging truths about human nature.

Connect to the Literature

What familiar proverbs can you identify that are similar to Franklin's aphorisms?

Vocabulary Builder

squander (skwän′ dər) *v.* spend or use wastefully

21 **Reading Check**

Which aphorisms offer advice about using time wisely?

19 Literature in Context

Proverbs Share with students the following proverbs. Have them discuss their meanings and whether they think Franklin would agree or disagree with each one.

- "Brevity is the soul of wit." —William Shakespeare
- "Everything should be made as simple as possible, but not simpler." —Albert Einstein
- "Reading makes a full man, conference makes a ready man, and writing makes an exact man." —Francis Bacon

Connect to Literature Invite students to brainstorm popular proverbs. Record their ideas on the board. **Possible responses:** A good friend is hard to find. Don't put off until tomorrow what you can do today. Actions speak louder than words.

20 Critical Thinking

Apply

- Read aloud the bracketed aphorism. Then, **ask** students to paraphrase it.
  Answer: Time is precious and shouldn't be wasted.
- Invite volunteers to discuss how this aphorism relates to their own experiences.
  Possible response: Students should discuss how they handle the various demands on their time, and how they choose to spend their free time.

21 Reading Check

Answer: Students might mention these aphorisms: "Have you somewhat to do tomorrow, do it today"; "Dost thou love life? Then do not squander time; for that's the stuff life is made of"; and "Haste makes waste."

Differentiated Instruction Solutions for All Learners

Background for Less Proficient Readers
Because of their metaphoric quality, aphorisms may be difficult for less proficient readers to understand. Begin with a contemporary aphorism, such as "Life is like a box of chocolates." Discuss its metaphoric meaning so that students see how to draw their own comparisons as they read Franklin's aphorisms.

Vocabulary for English Learners
Have students concentrate on the multiple meanings of words in Franklin's aphorisms. For instance, "Fish and visitors smell in three days" includes a double meaning of "smell." As they read the aphorisms, encourage students to list and define words with multiple meanings.

Enrichment for Advanced Readers
Challenge students to distill the meaning from Franklin's aphorisms. Then, have them write their own aphorisms that convey the same message. Have volunteers compile their work and create a class booklet of aphorisms.

ASSESS

Answers

1. **Possible answer:** Temperance, or moderation, seems to be the most important virtue because it governs one's approach to all the other virtues.
2. (a) He makes a daily calendar with tasks and times outlined. (b) He does not succeed, finding that sometimes he must order tasks around others' and that he cannot change his own habit of relying on memory. (c) It illustrates the overwhelming effort involved in the struggle for order, as well as its likely impossibility.
3. (a) He probably felt very determined and optimistic. (b) As he gets older, Franklin learns the difficulty of attaining moral perfection, but he also realizes that the effort is more important than the goal.
(c) **Possible answer:** Perfection is probably unreasonable, but the desire to work hard to improve oneself is not.
4. (a) The following aphorisms concern friendship: "An open foe may prove a curse; but a pretended friend is worse"; "Be slow in choosing a friend, slower in changing"; and "A true friend is the best possession." (b) Yes, he says that friendship is precious and needs care.
5. (a) He will die of fasting. (b) If hope keeps people from taking action, it can be highly impractical and ultimately dangerous. (c) He might suggest effort or planning.
6. **Possible answer:** It can highlight counterproductive behavior for change.
7. (a) Most express timeless values. (b) Students should support their answers with reasons. (c) Students should support their answers with reasons.

Go Online Author Link For additional information about Benjamin Franklin, have students type in the Web Code, then select F from the alphabet, and then select Benjamin Franklin.

For want of a nail the shoe is lost; for want of a shoe
the horse is lost; for want of a horse the rider is lost.

Haste makes waste.

The doors of wisdom are never shut.

Love your neighbor; yet don't pull down your hedge.

He that lives upon hope will die fasting.

Vocabulary Builder
fasting (fast′ iŋ) *v.* eating very little or nothing

Critical Reading

1. **Respond:** Which virtue on Franklin's list strikes you as being the most important? Explain.
2. **(a) Recall:** According to his *Autobiography,* what efforts does Franklin make to become more orderly? **(b) Infer:** Is he successful? Explain. **(c) Analyze:** What aspect of his attempt to become more orderly is illustrated by the anecdote of the man with the speckled ax?
3. **(a) Interpret:** When Franklin began his project, he was a young man. How do you think he felt at the time about his chances of attaining moral "perfection"? **(b) Compare and Contrast:** What insights does Franklin gain about the importance of achieving moral perfection as he gets older? **(c) Take a Position:** Do you think the goal of achieving moral perfection is reasonable? Explain.
4. **(a) Recall:** Note three aphorisms that deal directly with friendship. **(b) Analyze:** Is Franklin's message about friendship consistent? Explain.
5. **(a) Recall:** According to the aphorisms from *Poor Richard's Almanack,* what happens to a person who "lives upon hope"? **(b) Infer:** Why might Franklin see hope as impractical or even dangerous? **(c) Speculate:** What more reliable value would Franklin say a person can successfully "live upon"?
6. **Generalize:** In what ways can analyzing one's own behavior contribute to personal growth?
7. **(a) Generalize:** Which of Franklin's aphorisms express values that are still widely held in America? Explain. **(b) Evaluate:** With which of Franklin's aphorisms do you most strongly agree? Why? **(c) Evaluate:** With which of Franklin's aphorisms do you disagree? Why?

For: More about Benjamin Franklin
Visit: www.PHSchool.com
Web Code: ere-9201

Apply the Skills

from *The Autobiography* • from *Poor Richard's Almanack*

Literary Analysis

Autobiography

1. What does Franklin's concern with moral virtue reveal about the period in which he lived?
2. **(a)** Do you think Franklin achieved the virtue of humility? **(b)** Do you find any evidence of pride—humility's opposite—in this account of his life?
3. How do you think the *Autobiography* would be different if it were written about Franklin rather than by him?

Comparing Literary Works

4. **(a)** Are Franklin's struggles to improve himself related to the advice he offers in the **aphorisms**? **(b)** Do these aphorisms seem to be written by the same person who wrote the *Autobiography*? Why, or why not?
5. Use a chart like the one below to match aphorisms with virtues from the *Autobiography*. Explain each choice.

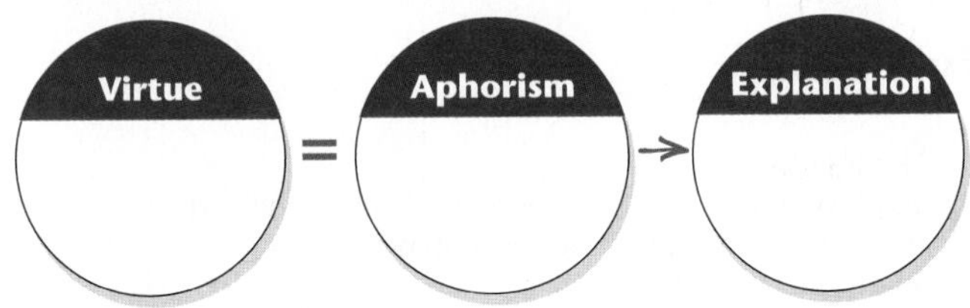

Reading Strategy

Drawing Conclusions

6. Franklin made adjustments to his record-keeping system as his plan progressed. What **conclusion** can you draw about his character from these adjustments? Explain.
7. **(a)** What conclusions can you draw from Franklin's statement that people dislike perfection in others? **(b)** Do you agree? Explain.

Extend Understanding

8. **Cultural Connection:** Franklin's aphorism, "If your head is wax, don't walk in the sun," is similar to a Russian proverb that advises, "One who sits between two chairs may easily fall down." **(a)** What do these proverbs mean? **(b)** How are they similar? **(c)** Why do different cultures preserve similar kinds of wisdom?

QuickReview

An **autobiography** is a person's account of his or her own life, usually written in the first person.

An **aphorism** is a short saying with a message.

A **conclusion** is a reasonable statement you develop from details in the text and your own life experience.

Go Online Assessment

For: Self-test
Visit: www.PHSchool.com
Web Code: era-6201

Students may use the **Self-test** to prepare for **Selection Test A** or **Selection Test B.**

Answers

1. His concern suggests that people of his time period cared a great deal about moral behavior.
2. (a) **Possible response:** He did not achieve this goal, because at the end of the selection he is still hoping to impress his descendants with his character. (b) Yes, he seems quite proud of his little book, lists, and daily calendar.
3. Another writer would not have been able to write as much about what Franklin was thinking at the time. Another writer might have pointed out contradictions between Franklin's aims and instances where he did not live up to these ideals. Another writer might have presented Franklin in a less positive light.
4. **Possible response:** (a) Yes, both reflect concerns for moral behavior and moral consequences. (b) Students' answers should be supported by the texts.
5. Students' charts should show insight into how Franklin's aphorisms teach the reader about moral virtues.

   Another sample answer can be found on **Literary Analysis Graphic Organizer B,** p. 29, in ***Graphic Organizer Transparencies.***
6. Franklin is willing to examine and change his behavior. He is capable of self-analysis and of growth.
7. (a) He understands people well and appreciates their human desire to avoid criticism.
   (b) Students should support their answers with evidence from personal experience.
8. **Possible responses:** (a) These proverbs mean that problems result when you don't pay attention to what you are doing. (b) Both describe inattentive behavior that can lead to injury. (c) People everywhere encounter many of the same problems.

Answers

❶ Vocabulary Lesson

Word Analysis

1. watchful
2. A group of people watching out for the public good; a volunteer who without authority assumes police powers such as pursuing and punishing criminal suspects.

Spelling Strategy

1. faddish
2. punning
3. snobbery
4. mapped

Vocabulary Builder

1. avarice
2. foppery
3. vigilance
4. felicity
5. arduous
6. disposition
7. squander
8. fasting

❷ Grammar and Style Lesson

1. me
2. us
3. they
4. We
5. he

Writing Application

When they finish, have students exchange papers and check each other's use of pronoun cases.

Writing and Grammar, Ruby Level

Students will find further instruction and practice on pronoun case in Chapter 22, Section 1.

Build Language Skills

❶ Vocabulary Lesson

Word Analysis: Word Root *-vigil-*

The word *vigilance*, meaning "watchfulness," contains the root *-vigil-*, which means "the act or period of remaining awake so as to guard or observe something." Write a definition of the italicized word in each sentence below.

1. He was *vigilant* in his efforts to reform.
2. To restore safety, members of a *vigilante* group patrolled the streets at night.

Spelling Strategy

When you add a suffix that begins with a vowel to a one-syllable word that ends with a consonant, double the consonant: *fop* + *-ery* = *foppery.* Add the indicated suffixes to the following words.

1. fad + *-ish*
2. pun + *-ing*
3. snob + *-ery*
4. map + *-ed*

Vocabulary Builder: Analogies

In each item, match the relationship between the first two words by selecting a word from the vocabulary list on page 141.

1. *Permission* is to *authorization* as __?__ is to *greed*.
2. *Danger* is to *peril* as __?__ is to *silliness*.
3. *Tragedy* is to *comedy* as __?__ is to *negligence*.
4. *Order* is to *chaos* as __?__ is to *sadness*.
5. *Rare* is to *common* as __?__ is to *easy*.
6. *Error* is to *mistake* as __?__ is to *arrangement*.
7. *Criticize* is to *praise* as __?__ is to *save*.
8. *Wasting* is to *conserving* as __?__ is to *feasting*.

❷ Grammar and Style Lesson

Pronoun Case

Pronouns are words that replace nouns. **Pronoun case** refers to the form that a pronoun takes to indicate its function in a sentence. Always use pronouns in the case reflecting their function.

Subjective case pronoun, also called **nominative** pronouns—*I, we, you, he, she, it, they,* are used when the pronoun is the subject of the sentence.

Objective case pronouns—*me, us, him, her, it, them*—are used when the pronoun receives the action of the verb or is the object of a preposition.

SUBJ. CASE / OBJ. CASE

I always carried my little book with *me.*

Practice Choose the correct pronoun to complete each sentence below.

1. At length a fresh difference arose between my brother and (I, me).
2. It was time for (we, us) to leave that place.
3. Though I did not give them any dissatisfaction, (they, them) dismissed me from my position.
4. (We, Us) two undertook to move to Boston.
5. Wilson and (he, him) took care to prevent my getting employment anywhere else.

Writing Application Write an account of a time when you made a conscious effort at self-improvement, using pronoun cases correctly.

Prentice Hall Writing and Grammar Connection: Chapter 22, Section 1

Assessment Practice

Cause and Effect (For more practice, see *Standardized Test Preparation Workbook*, p. 8.)

In many tests, students will have to identify causes and effects. Use the following sample test item to demonstrate.

> I proposed to myself, for the sake of clearness, to use rather more names [for virtues], with fewer ideas annexed to each, than a few names with more ideas; and I included under thirteen names of virtues all that at that time occurred to me as necessary or desirable . . . .

Why did Franklin name more virtues instead of fewer?

A He wanted to be clear.
B He wanted to measure the virtue of his friends.
C He thought thirteen was a lucky number.
D He decided there were only thirteen virtues.

Choices *B* and *C* do not contain any information from the passage. Students may be tempted by choice *D*, but should recognize that *A* is the best answer.

Writing Lesson

Autobiographical Account

With your activities, friendships, family and school events, successes and failures, you have a vast amount of material to build your autobiography. Choose an important experience and discuss it. Tell what made this experience memorable and describe what you have learned from it.

Prewriting Brainstorm for a list of details from the experience. Note what happened, what you felt, and what you learned. Include specific details that will help your readers understand your experience better.

Drafting As you draft, incorporate details that will make the event and its significance clear to readers. Remember to show the cause-and-effect relationship between the event or experience and your life.

Revising When you revise, pay attention to cause-and-effect relationships. Add transition words to make these relationships more obvious.

Model: Revising to Show Cause and Effect

I pivoted the wrong way. The ball bounced off Alec's back, and ricocheted into the goal. I had scored a goal for the other team! The buzzer sounded. The game was over. We had lost ^as a result of my mistake.

Transition words and phrases such as *as a result* highlight cause-and-effect relationships.

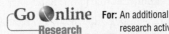

WG Prentice Hall Writing and Grammar Connection: Chapter 4, Section 4

Extend Your Learning

Listening and Speaking Think of a few areas in which the students in your class would like to improve. In small groups, generate a list of specific steps you might take, and write a **class improvement plan** based on your ideas. Be sure to identify the following elements of a plan:

- how you will define the steps to be taken
- how you will record your efforts
- what your time frame will be

Each group should then present its plan in brief oral reports. **[Group Activity]**

Research and Technology With a group, create a **travel brochure** for tourists visiting Philadelphia. Use the Internet and electronic reference sources to gather information and obtain appropriate pictures, maps, or lists. If possible, blend your text and images in one file using a desktop publishing program.

For: An additional research activity
Visit: www.PHSchool.com
Web Code: erd-7201

3 Writing Lesson

- To guide students in writing this autobiographical account, give them the Support for Writing Lesson, page 15 in ***General Resources.***
- Remind students of the features of an autobiography by rereading the definition on p. 141.
- Tell students that when they write autobiographies, they should try to develop a fully rounded picture of their experiences by including details that help readers envision both situations and emotions.
- Use the Autobiographical Narrative rubrics in ***General Resources,*** pp. 43–44, to evaluate students' autobiographies.

4 Research and Technology

- Encourage students to examine travel brochures in the school library to get a sense of the features they commonly include.
- Have students focus on three to five important historic sites, rather than trying to cover all of Philadelphia.
- As students research these sites, remind them to gather both text and images so they can create a brochure that is not only informative but also visually appealing.
- The **Support for Extend Your Learning** (***Unit 2 Resources,*** p. 16) provides guided note-taking opportunities to help students complete the Extend Your Learning.

Go Online Research — Have students type in the Web Code for another research activity.

Assessment Resources

The following resources can be used to assess students' knowledge and skills.

Unit 2 Resources

Selection Test A, pp. 18–20

Selection Test B, pp. 21–23

General Resources

Rubric for Autobiographical Narrative, pp. 43–44

Go Online Assessment — Students may use the **Self-test** prepare for **Selection Test A** or **Selection Test B.**

Students will

1. understand the development of the American free press.
2. communicate effectively with others in a cooperative environment.

Background
History

The quotation on this page expresses the political ideology of Benjamin Franklin and is often attributed to him, but it did not originate with Benjamin Franklin. The quotation was originally written in letter 15 ("Of Freedom of Speech: That the same is inseparable from publik Liberty") of John Trenchard and Thomas Gordon's *Cato's Letters,* or *Essays on Liberty, Civil, and Religious, and other Important Subjects.* These letters originally appeared in the London Journal between 1720 and 1723.

All the News That's Fit to Print

"EXTRA! EXTRA! Read all about it! Newspapers banned! Journalists Jailed! Americans Fight for a Free Press!" Those might have been the headlines blaring from your local newspaper if you had lived in eighteenth-century America. Might have been, that is, if colonial newspapers had used headlines. America's earliest newspapers bore little resemblance to those we know today. They were crudely printed on wooden presses and contained only a clumsy illustration or two. Most were one or two pages, and their stories were often just a list of ship arrivals. Despite their primitive character, these early newspapers laid the groundwork for a uniquely American phenomenon: a free press that could criticize the government.

> *"The American Revolution would not have happened when it did without the efforts of colonial newspapers."*

Trailblazers The first American newspaper, printed in Boston on September 25, 1690, was titled *Publick Occurrences, Both Foreign and Domestick.* The remarkable thing about *Publick Occurrences* was that it existed at all. England had no history of a free and independent press. If a newspaper criticized the crown, it could be shut down. Yet *Publick Occurrences* was published without British approval, and printed stories that the Massachusetts royal governor found offensive. As a result, it lasted exactly one issue.

Americans waited 14 years for another newspaper. In 1704, the Boston *News-Letter* appeared. Approved by the governor of Massachusetts, the *News-Letter* was little more than a British mouthpiece, careful not to offend colonial authorities.

▼ Critical Viewing
In this image portraying the trial of Peter Zenger, with what emotions does the audience seem to be reacting to the lawyer's argument? **[Interpret]**

The Franklin Brothers In contrast, other papers sought controversy. For example, the New England *Courant,* founded in 1721 by James Franklin, appeared without British approval. The paper jabbed mercilessly at the royal governor, and eventually landed Franklin in jail. He handed control of the paper to his 16-year-old brother, Benjamin—someone who would play his own significant role in our nation's history.

In 1729, Benjamin Franklin, now living in Philadelphia, founded the Pennsylvania *Gazette.* It was the first newspaper to carry weather reports, interviews, and cartoons, and it became the most successful paper in the colonies.

Freedom of the Press is Born A landmark legal case helped establish freedom of the press in America. In 1733, John Peter Zenger, a German immigrant, began publishing the *New York Weekly Journal.* The paper immediately ran afoul of the royal governor by publishing articles critical of his policies. One year later, Zenger was thrown in jail for libel.

In his 1735 trial, Zenger's lawyer, Andrew Hamilton, argued that while Zenger had indeed printed material offensive to the governor, the material was true and, therefore, not libelous. Under British law, even true statements against the government could be legally silenced. Hamilton made an impassioned plea to the jury to defend the "cause of liberty . . . both of exposing and opposing arbitrary power . . . by speaking and writing truth."

The jury found Zenger innocent. As a result of the case, the British stopped prosecuting American journalists, even when their criticisms of the government grew intense in the years leading up to the American Revolution.

Revolutionary Journalists Most historians agree that the American Revolution would not have happened when it did without the efforts of colonial newspapers. Newspapers stoked the flames of revolution, coining phrases like "taxation without representation" and influencing public perception of England as an enemy. When the British Stamp Act of 1765 imposed a heavy tax on all printed materials, the press denounced the legislation and refused to pay the tax. Even though the Stamp Act was repealed in 1766, it united editors and publishers in support of independence. Indeed, in 1776, most newspapers printed the Declaration of Independence on their front page.

During the Revolution, newspapers brought accounts of military developments to an eager readership. By the end of the war, newspapers had gained enormous strength. American newspapers represented something the world had never before seen: a press committed to telling the truth, not pleasing the government.

Activity

News Media Today

Today, reading a newspaper is just one of many ways to stay informed. Radio, television, and the Internet allow people to get news as it happens.

With a group, discuss your thoughts about the changing job of the American news media. Use these questions to guide your discussion:

- What is the role of new technology in twenty-first century news coverage?
- What do you think is the most effective way to stay informed? Why?
- What would you do to improve today's news media?

Choose a point person to share your ideas with the class.

were so popular in early America?
Answer: American newspapers were not censored. People liked reading about news and opinions, just as they do today. People who did not have time to catch up on news with their friends might have time to glance at a paper. Newspapers attacked unpopular politicians, and readers enjoyed these attacks.

2. What role did newspapers play in the Revolution?
Answers: They spread popular ideas and opinions. They informed readers about new Parliamentary edicts and taxes. They helped everyone keep abreast of the political situation. Their editorials urged people to rebel against the king and the royal governors. They helped to create and maintain a revolutionary mood and keep readers informed about events.

Activity

Form students into groups. Suggest that individuals take responsibility for different aspects of news coverage: newspapers, radio, television, online news. Once individuals have done their research, they can pool their information and create the timeline.

Meeting Your Standards

Students will

1. **analyze and respond to literary elements.**
   - Literary Analysis: Slave Narratives
2. **read, comprehend, analyze, and critique nonfiction.**
   - Reading Strategy: Summarizing
   - Reading Check questions
   - Apply the Skills questions
   - Assessment Practice (ATE)
3. **develop vocabulary.**
   - Vocabulary Lesson: Latin Word Root: *-vid-*
4. **understand and apply written and oral language conventions.**
   - Spelling Strategy
   - Grammar and Style Lesson: Active and Passive Voice
5. **develop writing proficiency.**
   - Writing Lesson: Museum Placard
6. **develop appropriate research strategies.**
   - Extend Your Learning: Research Presentation
7. **understand and apply listening and speaking strategies.**
   - Extend Your Learning: Round-table Discussion

Block Scheduling: Use one 90-minute class period to preteach the skills and have students read the selection. Use a second 90-minute class period to assess students' mastery of skills, extend their learning, and monitor their progress.

Homework Suggestions

Following are possibilities for homework assignments.

- Support pages from *Unit 2 Resources:*
  Literary Analysis
  Reading Strategy
  Vocabulary Builder
  Grammar and Style
- An Extend Your Learning project and the Writing Lesson for this selection group may be completed over several days.

Step-by-Step Teaching Guide	Pacing Guide
PRETEACH	
• Administer Vocabulary and Reading Warm-ups as necessary.	5 min.
• Engage students' interest with the motivation activity.	5 min.
• Read and discuss author and background features. **FT**	10 min.
• Introduce the Literary Analysis Skill: Slave Narratives. **FT**	5 min.
• Introduce the Reading Strategy: Summarizing. **FT**	10 min.
• Prepare students to read by teaching the selection vocabulary. **FT**	
TEACH	
• Informally monitor comprehension while students read independently or in groups. **FT**	30 min.
• Monitor students' comprehension with the Reading Check notes.	as students read
• Reinforce vocabulary with Vocabulary Builder notes.	as students read
• Develop students' understanding of slave narratives with the Literary Analysis annotations. **FT**	5 min.
• Develop students' ability to summarize with the Reading Strategy annotations. **FT**	5 min.
ASSESS/EXTEND	
• Assess students' comprehension and mastery of the Literary Analysis and Reading Strategy by having them answer the Apply the Skills questions. **FT**	15 min.
• Have students complete the Vocabulary Lesson and the Grammar and Style Lesson. **FT**	15 min.
• Apply students' ability to write using sequence of events by using the Writing Lesson. **FT**	45 min. or homework
• Apply students' understanding by using one or more of the Extend Your Learning activities.	20–90 min. or homework
• Administer Selection Test A or Selection Test B. **FT**	15 min.

Resources

PRINT

Unit 2 Resources

Vocabulary Warm-up Word Lists [**L1, L2, EL**] ....p. 26
Vocabulary Warm-up Practice [**L1, L2, EL**] ....p. 27
Reading Warm-up A [**L1, L2, EL**] ....p. 28
Reading Warm-up B [**L1, L2, L3**] ....p. 29

TRANSPARENCY

Graphic Organizer Transparencies

Literary Analysis Graphic Organizer A [**L3**] ....p. 32
Literary Analysis Graphic Organizer B [**L1, L2, EL**] ....p. 33
Reading Strategy Graphic Organizer A [**L3**] ....p. 30
Reading Strategy Graphic Organizer B [**L1, L2, EL**] ....p. 31

PRINT

Reader's Notebook [L2]
Reader's Notebook: Adapted Version [L1]
Reader's Notebook: English Learner's Version [EL]

Unit 2 Resources

Literary Analysis [**L3**] ....p. 30
Reading Strategy [**L3**] ....p. 31
Vocabulary Builder [**L3**] ....p. 32

TECHNOLOGY

Listening to Literature Audio CDs [L2, EL]
Reader's Notebook: Adapted Version Audio CD [L1, L2]

PRINT

Unit 2 Resources

Grammar and Style [**L3**] ....p. 33
Support for Writing Lesson [**L3**] ....p. 34
Support for Extend Your Learning [**L3**] ....p. 35
Enrichment [**L4**] ....p. 36
Selection Test A [**L1, L2, EL**] ....pp. 37–39
Selection Test B [**L3, L4**] ....pp. 40–42

General Resources

Rubrics for Research Report [**L3**] ....pp. 49–50
Rubrics for Speaking: Delivering a Research Presentation [**L3**] ....p. 91

TECHNOLOGY

Go Online: Research [**L3**]
Go Online: Self-test [**L3**]
***ExamView®*, Test Bank [L3]**

Choosing Resources for Differentiated Instruction

[**L1**] Special Needs Students
[**L2**] Below-Level Students
[**L3**] All Students
[**L4**] Advanced Students
[**EL**] English Learners

FT Fast Track Instruction: To move the lesson more quickly, use the strategies and activities identified with **FT**.

Scaffolding for Less Proficient and Advanced Students

The leveled Critical Thinking questions after selections progress in the levels of thinking required to answer them. To address the needs of your different students, you may use the (a) level questions for your less proficient students and the (b) level questions with your on-level and advanced students. The occasional (c) level questions are appropriate for your advanced students.

Use this complete suite of powerful teaching tools to make lesson planning and testing quicker and easier.

PRENTICE HALL
StudentEXPRESS™
Learn · Study · Succeed

Use the interactive textbook (online and on CD-ROM) to make selections and activities come alive with audio and video support and interactive questions.

From the Scholar's Desk

William L. Andrews

- William L. Andrews, a well-known historian, writes about Olaudah Equiano's harrowing description of the "Middle Passage"—the experience of Africans being transported from their native lands to the New World on slave ships (page 160).
- Have students read the introductory paragraph about William L. Andrews. He is a renowned scholar who has dedicated his career to the study of the historical linkages between white and black writers in the formation of American literature, African American literature, and southern literature.
- Use the ***From the Author's Desk*** DVD to introduce William L. Andrews. Show Segment 2 to provide insights into his study of Olaudah Equiano. After the students have watched the segment, **ask:** How does this video segment with Professor Andrews show the importance of diligence in historical scholarship?
  Answer: Professor Andrews mentions that recently there has been doubt about Equiano's claim to have been born in Africa. New versions of the account of Equiano's life must indicate this new doubt.

The Middle Passage

- Have students read Andrews's comments about how Equiano recreates the horrors of a slave ship for white readers.
- Andrews explains that the Middle Passage that Africans traveled across the Atlantic Ocean was a horrific experience in which hundreds of thousands perished. Andrews notes that hardly anyone who survived the trip wrote about it, so that Equiano's account is particularly valuable, opening the eyes of his white American and English readers to the suffering that one race inflicted on another.
  Ask: What point does Andrews make by suggesting that Equiano's readers must have identified more with the African narrator than with the whites on the ship?
  Answer: Andrews's comment about Equiano's reversal of expected racial identifications suggests that Equiano wanted his readers to see that humaneness rather than race is important when judging someone's value.

From the Scholar's Desk

WILLIAM L. ANDREWS INTRODUCES

The Interesting Narrative of the Life of Olaudah Equiano *by Olaudah Equiano*

William L. Andrews

William L. Andrews is the series editor of *North American Slave Narratives, Beginnings to 1920.* His book *To Tell a Free Story* is a history of African American autobiography up to 1865.

A Rare Firsthand Account of the Middle Passage

One of the most astonishing facts about the Middle Passage—the Atlantic crossing of enslaved Africans to the Americas—is that, although millions of Africans endured it, and as many as one in eight died from it, history has preserved almost no firsthand accounts of it. *The Interesting Narrative of the Life of Olaudah Equiano* contains one of the rare detailed reports of the catastrophic journey that survives in English. Imagine how hard it would be for someone who had been through such a horrifying experience to write about it. Writing about past trauma almost certainly requires a person to relive it.

A Virtual Tour of the Slave Ship Equiano's account of the Middle Passage directly thrusts his reader, who Equiano expected would be either English or American, into a terrifying situation. Whatever Equiano's white readers thought about slavery, we can be pretty sure that they didn't want to think about how the Africans got to the Americas. By taking his reader on a virtual tour of the slave ship above and below decks, Equiano seems determined to confront his reader with the hideous—and generally hidden—truth about life aboard a slave ship.

The first stop is the ship's suffocating hold, where its human cargo was stored for most of the transatlantic voyage. Here we can see, hear, feel, and, especially, smell how "loathsome" a place it really was. Hell on earth would not be too strong a term to describe the hold of a slave ship.

Equiano doesn't confine us long in the miserable hold before taking us up into the fresh air, where we might hope for some relief from the horrors we've experienced. However, we soon find ourselves accompanied by dying Africans who've been brought up to the deck to perish of the illnesses they've contracted in the hold. Meanwhile, the European ship hands merely watch and wait, supremely indifferent to the suffering they witness.

Identifying with the Abused Africans The cruelty of the whites aboard the slave ship must have shocked Equiano's readers, particularly since, as whites themselves, they would likely have felt more in common with the Europeans on the ship than the Africans. But Equiano's storytelling

Teaching Resources

The following resources can be used to enrich or extend the instruction for from the Scholar's Desk.

Unit 2 Resources
- **From the Scholar's Desk,** p. 24
- **Listening and Viewing,** p. 25

From the Author's Desk DVD
- **William L. Andrews,** Segment 2

◀ Critical Viewing
What details in this painting convey the inhuman conditions that Africans experience aboard slave ships? **[Analyze]**

gradually alienates his reader from the brutal whites while helping the reader to identify with the abused Africans. Through the point of view of the ten-year-old African narrator, we inevitably feel the same shock and dread that the innocent African boy felt. Our sympathy with the narrator goes beyond pitying him as a victim, however. We follow as the curious African boy steps forward to take a peek through the ship's quadrant. As an unimagined world opens up to him, we realize that no matter how unjustly that new world may treat him in the future, Equiano the inquisitive, resilient traveler, will survive.

Thinking About the Commentary

1. (a) **Recall:** What was the Middle Passage? **(b) Speculate:** Why do you think firsthand accounts of it are so rare?
2. (a) **Recall:** What does Equiano show readers in his virtual tour of a slave ship? **(b) Infer:** What do you think was his purpose in conducting such a "tour"?

As You Read *from* The Interesting Narrative of the Life of Olaudah Equiano . . .

3. Identify details that justify Andrews's description of Equiano as "inquisitive" and "resilient."

Critical Viewing

Possible response: The amount of people crowded into small spaces and the chains detail the inhuman conditions.

ASSESS

Answers

1. (a) The Middle Passage was the voyage on a slave ship of captive Africans being brought to the Americas to live in slavery.
(b) Firsthand accounts of the Middle Passage are rare because most the enslaved people who survived the voyage did not have the opportunity to learn to write English. Even for those who did learn to write English, the experience of recalling the passage would be a horribly traumatic one.
2. (a) Equiano showed people the dreadful sights, sounds, and smells of life below the deck, where many enslaved people were forced to spend weeks. He also portrayed the inhumanity of the white crew members on deck as they watched the suffering and death of many of their passengers.
(b) It is likely that Equiano's purpose is to make his white readers feel ashamed of what had been done to the enslaved people who suffered through the Middle Passage. Perhaps he hoped that this shame would eventually lead to the end of slavery, which he calls an "accursed trade."
3. Equiano did not succumb to the despair that led several of his fellow passengers to jump into the ocean. He also preserved his curiosity, which led him to relate his interest in the flying fish and the quadrant. The fact that he observed and remembered many of the details of his experience also testifies to his resilience and inquisitiveness.

Go Online **Author Link** Typing in the Web Code when prompted will bring students to a video clip of William L. Andrews.

PRETEACH

Motivation

Students are probably familiar with common expressions using the term *slave,* which inadvertently trivialize the horrors of slavery. You might ask students if they have ever heard—or used—expressions such as *to slave over homework* or *slave to fashion.*

Invite students to empathize with victims of slavery by imagining being forcibly captured and then hauled like cargo for many weeks in the dark and airless hold of a ship.

❶ Background

More About the Author

In the Ibo language, the author's name means "well-spoken leader," and after his years of slavery, Olaudah Equiano lived up to his name—not only publishing his acclaimed *Interesting Narrative,* but also playing a prominent role in the British abolitionist movement. Equiano lectured, protested, and personally petitioned the British Parliament to outlaw slavery.

Build Skills Autobiography

❶ *from* The Interesting Narrative of the Life of Olaudah Equiano

Olaudah Equiano (1745–1797)

When published in 1789, the autobiography of Olaudah Equiano (ō lä o͞o′ dā ek′ wē än′ ō) created a sensation. It was so widely acclaimed that by 1794 it had run through eight editions in England and one in the United States. *The Interesting Narrative of the Life of Olaudah Equiano* made society face the cruelties of slavery and contributed to the banning of the slave trade in both the United States and England.

Born to Leadership The son of a tribal elder in the powerful kingdom of Benin, Equiano might have followed in his father's footsteps had he not been sold into slavery. When Equiano was eleven years old, he and his sister were kidnapped from their home in West Africa and sold to British slave traders. Their circumstance was not unusual. About 15 million Africans were captured between 1500 and 1800 and shipped to the Western Hemisphere, where they became slaves. Historians estimate that nearly two million slaves died before reaching their destination.

The Middle Passage As Equiano reports, the conditions of the Atlantic voyage were atrocious. For six to ten weeks, the slaves were crammed below deck in spaces sometimes less than five feet high. Families were torn apart, with men and women placed in separate holds. The men were often shackled together in pairs. Because Equiano was so young at the time of his capture, however, he was allowed to remain on deck, unshackled. There, he observed the mariners using a compass-like instrument to determine the ship's heading. Seeing Equiano's fascination with the device, the mariners allowed him to get a closer look. It was on that deck, perhaps, that Equiano first gained an interest in the sea.

The ship first anchored in Bridgetown, the capital of Barbados in the West Indies. Separated from his sister, Equiano was taken to Virginia, where he was purchased by a British captain and employed at sea.

Saving to Buy Liberty Renamed Gustavus Vassa, Equiano was enslaved for nearly ten years. After managing his Philadelphia master's finances and making his own money in the process, Equiano amassed enough to buy his freedom. In later years, he settled in England and devoted himself to the abolition of slavery. In 1787, he was named commissary of the slave ship *Vernon,* which held more than five hundred freed slaves who were taken to Freetown, Sierra Leone, to establish a settlement there.

Telling the Tale To publicize the plight of slaves, Equiano wrote his two-volume autobiography, *The Interesting Narrative. . . .* Although his writing raised concerns about the inhumane conditions of slavery, the U.S. slave trade was not abolished by law until 1808, nearly twenty years after its publication. In addition to his writings on American slavery, Equiano also lectured and rallied against the cruelty of British slave owners in Jamaica.

Equiano's writing demonstrates the important influence slave narratives have in documenting historic events. Encouraged by abolitionists, many other freed or escaped slaves published narratives in the years before the Civil War. Others told their stories in the first part of the twentieth century. Henry Louis Gates, Jr., professor of English and African American studies, notes that "No other group of slaves anywhere, at any other period in history, has left such a large repository of testimony about the horror of becoming the legal property of another human being."

Preview

Connecting to the Literature

Imagine knowing that members of your family are valuable merchandise and could be shipped to a distant land to perform forced labor! If you lived in a world where slavery exists, you might develop a new attitude about the sweetness of freedom and the value of life.

Literary Analysis

Slave Narratives

A uniquely American literary genre, a **slave narrative** is an autobiographical account of life as a slave. Often written to expose the horrors of human bondage, it documents a slave's experiences from his or her own point of view. In this example, Equiano describes the conditions on the ship.

> The shrieks of the women, and the groans of the dying, rendered the whole a scene of horror almost inconceivable.

As you read, look for other details that describe the horrors of the voyage.

Connecting Literary Elements

Equiano's narrative speaks persuasively against the slave trade by using deliberate **emotional appeals** to strengthen its impact. Writers create emotional appeals with evocative words, such as *groans* and *shrieks*, and details that trigger feelings of sympathy or outrage. For example, when Equiano describes the Africans begging for food, readers who have experienced hunger can likely sympathize with their plight. Notice how Equiano appeals to readers' emotions.

Reading Strategy

Summarizing

As you read material published in another time period or written in an unfamiliar style, it is often helpful to **summarize** the main points. When you summarize, you state briefly in your own words the main ideas and key details of the text. Use a chart like the one shown which summarizes Equiano's first paragraph. As you read, write notes like these to help you summarize Equiano's ideas.

Main Point: The slaves were kept in unbearable conditions.

- **Detail**: People were chained.
- **Detail**: Disease ran rampant.
- **Detail**: People were hungry.

Vocabulary Builder

loathsome (lōth́ səm) *adj.* hateful; detestable (p. 161)

pestilential (pes′ tə len′ shəl) *adj.* likely to cause disease (p. 161)

copious (kō′ pē əs) *adj.* plentiful; abundant (p. 161)

improvident (im präv′ ə dənt) *adj.* shortsighted (p. 161)

avarice (av′ ə ris) *n.* greed for riches (p. 161)

pacify (pas′ ə fī′) *v.* calm; soothe (p. 164)

❷ Literary Analysis

Slave Narratives

- Tell students that they will focus on the characteristics of slave narratives as they read the following selection.
- As they read Olaudah Equiano's firsthand account of his experiences in slavery, have students consider his purpose for writing and reflect on how his tone affects their perceptions of the things he describes.
- Make sure to allow students sufficient time to discuss their personal responses to the selection.

❸ Reading Strategy

Summarizing

- Explain that summarizing can help students understand and remember a piece of writing.
- Give students a copy of **Reading Strategy Graphic Organizer B,** p. 30 in ***Graphic Organizer Transparencies,*** to use as they read the narrative. Remind students that summarizing requires that they identify and extract only the main ideas and most important details from their reading.
- Point out that summarizing can be especially useful in helping students master literary works that concern unfamiliar events, perspectives, and settings.

Vocabulary Builder

- Pronounce each vocabulary word for students, and read the definitions as a class. Have students identify any words with which they are already familiar.

Differentiated Instruction
Solutions for All Learners

Support for Special Needs Students
Have students read the adapted version of *The Interesting Narrative of the Life of Olaudah Equiano* in the ***Reader's Notebook: Adapted Version.*** This version provides basic-level instruction in an interactive format with questions and write-on lines. Completing these pages will prepare students to read the selection in the Student Edition.

Support for Less Proficient Readers
Have students read *The Interesting Narrative of the Life of Olaudah Equiano* in the ***Reader's Notebook.*** This version provides basic-level instruction in an interactive format with questions and write-on lines. After students finish the selection in the ***Reader's Notebook,*** have them complete the questions and activities in the Student Edition.

Support for English Learners
Have students read *The Interesting Narrative of the Life of Olaudah Equiano* in the ***Reader's Notebook: English Learner's Version.*** This version provides basic-level instruction in an interactive format with questions and write-on lines. Completing these pages will prepare students to read the selection in the Student Edition.

Learning Modalities
Visual/Spatial and Bodily/Kinesthetic Learners

To convey a modest approximation of the desperately crowded and deadly conditions on a slave ship, urge students to imagine the experience of being jammed tightly for weeks at a time into a rush-hour bus.

1 About the Selection

Like Harriet Beecher Stowe's explosive, best-selling novel *Uncle Tom's Cabin* (1853), Equiano's work had a significant effect on the institution of slavery. By exposing the cruelty of slavery, both works contributed to its eventual demise in the United States. Unlike Stowe's work, *The Interesting Narrative* is a firsthand account of an actual event. Equiano communicates heinous details of the slave trade vividly but simply.

2 Humanities

Slaves Below Deck (detail), by Lt. Francis Meynell

This picture depicts a scene aboard a Spanish slave ship on its way to the West Indies.

- Do you think Meynell or Equiano more vividly captures the horror of the voyage? Explain.
  Possible response: Students may say Equiano's description seems more horrible than the scene portrayed in the painting because it tells of the stench, the pain of the shackles, and the mistreatment that slaves endured—none of which are immediately evident in the painting.

3 Critical Viewing

Answer: Students may say that the painting is less dire than the scenes Equiano describes. Students may point to details such as the apparent lack of shackles and air and light reaching into the hold from the deck above.

1 *from* The Interesting Narrative of the Life of Olaudah Equiano

Olaudah Equiano

2

Slaves Below Deck (detail), Lt. Francis Meynell, National Maritime Museum, Greenwich

3 ▲ **Critical Viewing** The artist portrays conditions on a slave ship. Compare and contrast this image with the one that Equiano describes. **[Compare and Contrast]**

Differentiated Instruction Solutions for All Learners

Accessibility at a Glance

	from The Interesting Narrative of the Life of Olaudah Equiano
Context	Slave Narrative
Language	Challenging vocabulary; long sentences
Concept Level	Accessible (description of slave ship)
Literary Merit	Primary Source
Lexile	1240
Overall Rating	Average

Background

In the first several chapters of his narrative, Olaudah Equiano describes how he and his sister were kidnapped by slave traders from their home in West Africa and transported to the African coast. During this six- or seven-month journey, Equiano was separated from his sister and held at a series of way stations. After reaching the coast, Equiano was shipped with other slaves to North America. The following account describes this horrifying journey.

At last when the ship we were in, had got in all her cargo, they made ready with many fearful noises, and we were all put under deck, so that we could not see how they managed the vessel. But this disappointment was the least of my sorrow. The stench of the hold while we were on the coast was so intolerably loathsome, that it was dangerous to remain there for any time, and some of us had been permitted to stay on the deck for the fresh air; but now that the whole ship's cargo were confined together, it became absolutely pestilential. The closeness of the place, and the heat of the climate, added to the number in the ship, which was so crowded that each had scarcely room to turn himself, almost suffocated us. This produced copious perspirations, so that the air soon became unfit for respiration, from a variety of loathsome smells, and brought on a sickness among the slaves, of which many died—thus falling victims to the improvident avarice, as I may call it, of their purchasers. This wretched situation was again aggravated by the galling of the chains, now become insupportable, and the filth of the necessary tubs, into which the children often fell, and were almost suffocated. The shrieks of the women, and the groans of the dying, rendered the whole a scene of horror almost inconceivable. Happily perhaps, for myself, I was soon reduced so low here that it was thought necessary to keep me almost always on deck; and from my extreme youth I was not put in fetters.[1] In this situation I expected every hour to share the fate of my companions, some of whom were almost daily brought upon deck at the point of death, which I began to hope would soon put an end to my miseries. Often did I think many of the inhabitants of the deep much more happy than myself. I envied them the freedom they enjoyed, and as often wished I could change my condition for theirs. Every circumstance I met with, served only to render my state more painful, and heightened my apprehensions, and my opinion of the cruelty of the whites.

1. **fetters** (fet′ ərz) *n.* chains.

Vocabulary Builder

loathsome (lōth′ səm) *adj.* hateful; detestable

pestilential (pes′ tə len′ shəl) *adj.* likely to cause disease

copious (kō′ pē əs) *adj.* plentiful; abundant

improvident (im präv′ ə dənt) *adj.* shortsighted

avarice (av′ ə ris) *n.* greed for riches

William L. Andrews
Scholar's Insight

The wasteful greed of European slave traders makes them so callous that they don't even care about the profits they lose when slaves die in transit aboard their ships. The words *improvident avarice* help Equiano portray slavery as both inhuman and unprofitable.

6  **Reading Check**

What conditions on the ship caused many of the slaves to die?

4 Vocabulary Builder

The Latin Root *-vid-*

- Call students' attention to the word *improvident* and its definition. Tell students that the Latin root *-vid-* comes from the Latin word *videre,* meaning "to see."
- Remind students that the prefix *im-* reverses (or negates) the meaning of *provident,* "to have foresight."
- Invite students to brainstorm a list of English words that contain the Latin root *-vid-*. Such words include *video* and all related terms (*videocassette, videotape, videodisk*).

5 Scholar's Insight

- Direct students' attention to Andrews' remark about Equiano's word choice. Tell students that writers select words or phrases to produce a desired effect.
- Read the bracketed passage. **Ask** students how Equiano's word choice would affect his audience.
Possible response: Equiano's word choice would appeal to the readers' emotions, and it also helps point out the faults of the slave traders.

6 Reading Check

Answer: The author indicates that the foulness of the air causes respiratory problems that in turn cause some people to die.

Differentiated Instruction Solutions for All Learners

Support for Special Needs Students

Help students focus on the text as they read Equiano's descriptions by having them use a graphic organizer to list sensory words and phrases. Students might use multiple cluster diagrams, sunbursts, or a basic five-column vertical chart. Students in pairs might take turns reading aloud and listing sensory images such as *fearful noises, stench,* and *almost suffocated.*

Support for English Learners

Have small groups of students listen to the recording of the selection on the **Listening to Literature Audio CDs** as they follow along in their texts. Have students pause the recording after each paragraph in order to discuss what they have heard and read. Encourage groups to end each discussion with a summary of the paragraph's most important ideas and details.

7 Critical Viewing

Answer: Students' estimates will vary and may be obtained by estimating the number of slaves per row and then multiplying by the number of rows. Although it is impossible for students to know what the artist thought and felt about slavery, they may surmise from the overcrowding that the ship's captain, owner, designer, or builder had little regard for its human cargo.

8 Scholar's Insight

- Read the insight note to students. Have students share their ideas about how Christian readers would react to the bracketed passage.
- **Ask** if they feel this passage would change European stereotypes of the Africans.
  Possible response: Some students may feel the description of the Africans praying would erase prejudices. Others may feel that readers would only be momentarily swayed from their beliefs.

9 Literary Analysis

Slave Narratives and Emotional Appeal

- Read aloud with students the long sentence that starts the paragraph on this page. Encourage students to **identify** two distinct injustices that are presented in this passage.
  Answer: Injustices include the crew's throwing food overboard rather than allowing the slaves to eat it, and the crew's flogging some slaves for trying to get something to eat.
- **Ask** students the Literary Analysis question: What is the effect of these floggings on the reader's emotions?
  Answer: Most readers will feel disgust, anger, or sadness while reading the report of these floggings.

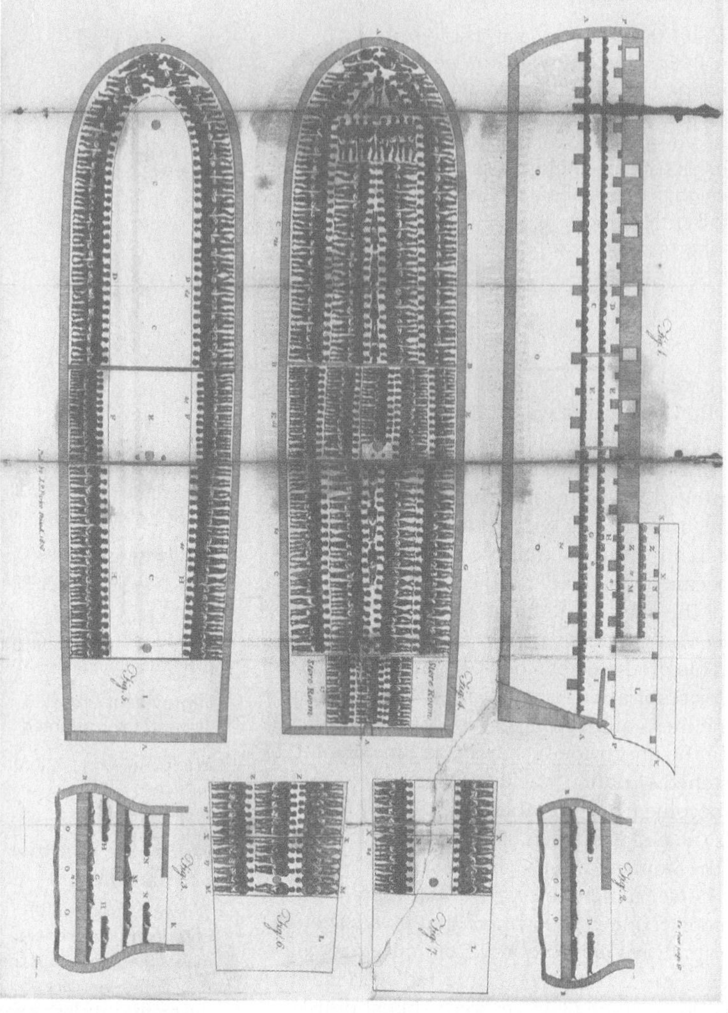

7 ◀ **Critical Viewing** Estimate the number of slaves that this ship can carry. What do the drawings suggest about the ship designer's attitude toward slavery? **[Draw Conclusions]**

8 One day they had taken a number of fishes; and when they had killed and satisfied themselves with as many as they thought fit, to our astonishment who were on deck, rather than give any of them to us to eat, as we expected, they tossed the remaining fish into the sea again, although we begged and prayed for some as well as we could, but in vain; and some of my countrymen, being pressed by hunger, took an opportunity, when they thought no one saw them, of trying to get a
9 little privately; but they were discovered, and the attempt procured them some very severe floggings. One day, when we had a smooth sea and moderate wind, two of my wearied countrymen who were chained together (I was near them at the time), preferring death to such a life of

William L. Andrews
Scholar's Insight
The inexplicable cruelty of the Europeans, contrasted with the pleading and praying of the Africans, is designed to challenge the prejudices of Equiano's readers. These readers would have expected the supposedly heathen Africans, not the Christian Europeans, to be indifferent to human need.

Literary Analysis
Slave Narratives What is the effect of these floggings on the reader's emotions?

Enrichment

Music

John Newton (1725–1807), a slave trader, experienced a total personal transformation after several voyages transporting slaves. He renounced what he now saw as his evil deeds and expressed his repentance in a musical composition, *Amazing Grace,* which was published in 1799. Reverend Newton dedicated his remaining years to the church. His inspiring song is still heard today at family gatherings and as a hymn sung in churches around the world.

You may wish to play a recording of this song or to invite a volunteer to sing it. Interested students can do research to learn more about the history and recordings of this song and of the unusual life of John Newton. In addition to library or Internet research, students may enjoy viewing the PBS video *Amazing Grace,* which presents background on Newton and explores the evolution and widespread social impact of his song.

misery, somehow made through the nettings and jumped into the sea; immediately, another quite dejected fellow, who, on account of his illness, was suffered to be out of irons, also followed their example; and I believe many more would very soon have done the same, if they had not been prevented by the ship's crew, who were instantly alarmed. Those of us that were the most active, were in a moment put down under the deck; and there was such a noise and confusion amongst the people of the ship as I never heard before, to stop her, and get the boat out to go after the slaves. However, two of the wretches were drowned, but they got the other, and afterwards flogged him unmercifully, for thus attempting to prefer death to slavery. In this manner we continued to undergo more hardships than I can now relate, hardships which are inseparable from this accursed trade. Many a time we were near suffocation from the want of fresh air, which we were often without for whole days together. This, and the stench of the necessary tubs, carried off many. ⑩

During our passage, I first saw flying fishes, which surprised me very much; they used frequently to fly across the ship, and many of them fell on the deck. I also now first saw the use of the quadrant;[2] I had often with astonishment seen the mariners make observations with it, and I could not think what it meant. They at last took notice of my surprise; and one of them, willing to increase it, as well as to gratify my curiosity, made me one day look through it. The clouds appeared to me to be land, which disappeared as they passed along. This heightened my wonder; and I was now more persuaded than ever, that I was in another world, and that every thing about me was magic. At last, we came in sight of the island of Barbados, at which the whites on board gave a great shout, and made many signs of joy to us. We did not know what to think of this; but as the vessel drew nearer, we plainly saw the harbor, and other ships of different kinds an sizes, and we soon anchored amongst them, off Bridgetown.[3] Many merchants and planters now came on board, though it was in the evening. They put us in separate ⑪

Literature in Context

Economics

The Slave Trade

While many people came to the Western Hemisphere in search of riches, many others were brought against their will to be sold as slaves. The map below indicates the major slave trade routes.

The Atlantic crossing, known as the Middle Passage, was brutal. Africans were chained below decks in cramped, filthy spaces. Overcrowding, disease, and despair claimed many lives. Some Africans mutinied, and others tried to starve themselves or jump overboard.

Connect to the Literature

What seems to be Equiano's attitude toward the captives who preferred death to slavery?

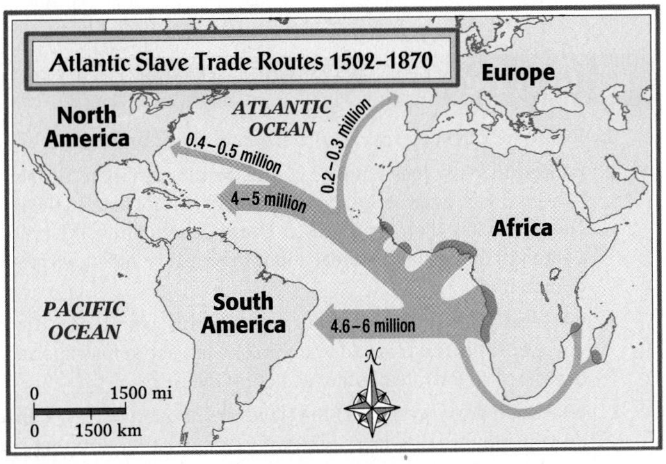

Reading Check

What do some slaves do to escape the misery of the Middle Passage?

2. **quadrant** (kwä′ drənt) *n.* an instrument used by navigators to determine the position of a ship.
3. **Bridgetown** *n.* the capital of Barbados.

⑩ Literature in context

The Slave Trade Between 1500 and 1800, about 15 million Africans were captured and shipped as slaves to the Western Hemisphere. Historians estimate that nearly two million slaves died during the middle passage before reaching their destinations. You may wish to point out that Equiano and others were months in transit prior to boarding the ship itself—and that they then spent several weeks on board before setting sail. Often pairs of adult captives were chained together at the ankles and wrists, and the shackles were removed only when one of the pair became very sick or died.

Connect to Literature Encourage students to examine Equiano's word choice before answering.
Possible response: Equiano calls the escaped slaves *wretches*. He also says many more slaves may have done the same thing, but he does not say that he wished to follow the escaped slaves to death. Equiano's attitude appears to be one of separateness. He does not see himself as being part of the group he describes. This attitude may be a means of protecting himself.

⑪ Reading Check

Answer: Some slaves choose to jump into the ocean and drown themselves rather than continue to endure the torture of the middle passage.

Differentiated Instruction Solutions for All Learners

Support for Less Proficient Readers
Help students make connections between the inset map and the information that appears in the Literature in Context box. Students should be able to recognize where the "middle passage" got its name and why it is so important to African Americans living in the United States.

Enrichment for Advanced Readers
Draw students' attention to the map, and point out that only a fraction of the total number of enslaved Africans came to what is now the United States. Encourage students to research the histories of these various populations of Africans and where their descendants live now.

⓬ Scholar's Insight

- Review the meaning of irony. Tell students that irony is a technique that involves amusing or surprising contradictions.
- Read the Scholar's Insight note to students. **Ask** them what is ironic about the bracketed passage. **Possible response:** Most Europeans felt that Africans were cannibals. It is ironic that the Africans think the men on the ship are going to eat them.

⓭ Critical Thinking
Drawing Conclusions

Ask students to explain what the presence of a variety of languages indicates about the slave trade.
Answer: Students should say that the slave trade was widespread throughout Africa.

ASSESS
Answers

1. Students may be impressed by Equiano's curiosity and eagerness to learn. They may also react to the high level of education that his writing shows he was able to obtain.
2. (a) Equiano believes that the traders' greed has led them to load the ships with more slaves than can comfortably fit. Thus their greed causes unsanitary conditions and illness. (b) The white crewmen view their captives as little more than cargo. (c) The captors do not seem to believe their cargo is human. They seem to believe that their captives' lives are only as valuable as the profit they bring.
3. (a) Equiano was granted certain privileges because of his age. For example, he was often kept on deck rather than in the cramped quarters below. (b) He probably felt lucky to be spared some of the degradation suffered by the other slaves.
4. (a) They preferred death to the misery aboard the ship. (b) The crew flogs newly rescued slaves to discourage others from attempting suicide.
5. **Possible response:** His strong constitution and instinct for survival are evident in his forceful prose.

⓬ parcels,[4] and examined us attentively. They also made us jump, and pointed to the land, signifying we were to go there. We thought by this, we should be eaten by these ugly men, as they appeared to us; and, when soon after we were all put down under the deck again, there was much dread and trembling among us, and nothing but bitter cries to be heard all the night from these apprehensions, insomuch, that at last the white people got some old slaves from the land to pacify us. They told us we were not to be eaten, but to work, and were soon to go on land, where we should see many of our country people. This report eased us much. And sure enough, soon after we were landed, there came to us Africans of all languages.

⓭ We were conducted immediately to the merchant's yard, where we were all pent up together, like so many sheep in a fold, without regard to sex or age. . . . We were not many days in the merchant's custody, before we were sold after their usual manner, which is this: On a signal given (as the beat of a drum), the buyers rush at once into the yard where the slaves are confined, and make choice of that parcel they like best. . . .

4. **parcels** (pär′ səlz) *n.* groups.

William L. Andrews
Scholar's Insight
This reversal of the well-established European stereotype of the African as cannibal is one of Equiano's most effective ironies.

Vocabulary Builder
pacify (pas′ ə fī′) *v.* calm; soothe

Critical Reading

1. **Respond:** Based on his narrative, what is your impression of Equiano?
2. **(a) Recall:** Why does Equiano blame the illness aboard the ship on the "improvident avarice" of the traders? **(b) Infer:** How do the white crewmen view their captives? **(c) Draw Conclusions:** What does the treatment of the slaves reveal about the captors' attitudes toward human life?
3. **(a) Recall:** How does Equiano's age affect his experiences during the voyage? **(b) Infer:** How do you think he felt about his experience compared to the fate of other slaves on the ship?
4. **(a) Recall:** Why do some of the slaves jump overboard? **(b) Infer:** Why do you suppose the slaves who were rescued after jumping overboard got flogged?
5. **Analyze:** How does Equiano prove his great zest for life despite his assertion that he wants to die? Provide examples from the story.
6. **Generalize:** Why is it important for people who are victims of such human injustices to record their experiences?

For: More about Olaudah Equiano
Visit: www.PHSchool.com
Web Code: ere-9210

Answers continued

6. **Possible response:** Through victims' recorded experiences, other people can understand history and learn how to prevent similar atrocities from recurring in the future.

Go Online Author Link For additional information about Olaudah Equiano, have students type in the Web Code, then select E from the alphabet, and then select Olaudah Equiano.

Apply the Skills

from *The Interesting Narrative of the Life of Olaudah Equiano*

Literary Analysis

Slave Narratives

1. According to Equiano's **slave narrative,** what was the general feeling of the slaves toward their situation?
2. Cite two examples of the slave traders' cruelty to the slaves.
3. Cite two examples that show the traders' concern for the slaves' well-being.
4. What might have motivated the traders' behavior toward their human cargo? Explain.

Connecting Literary Elements

5. **(a)** Using a chart like the one shown here, identify three examples of **emotional appeal** in Equiano's narrative. **(b)** What is the effect of these appeals on the reader?

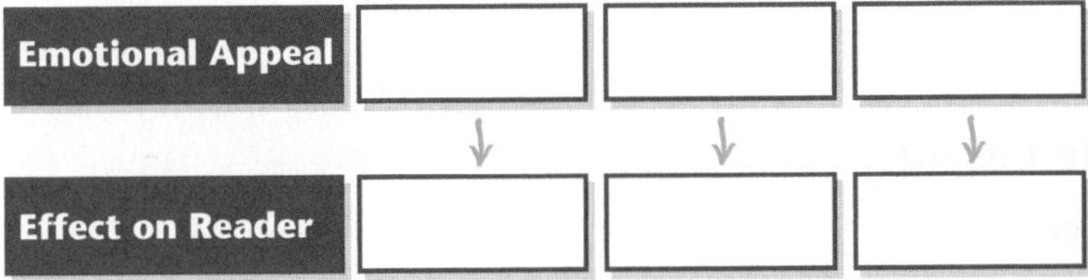

6. What aspect of the conditions aboard ship does Equiano stress in his account?
7. Explain how emotional appeals might strengthen Equiano's position against the slave trade.

Reading Strategy

Summarizing

8. Identify at least three main ideas the author conveys about the voyage.
9. **Summarize** the events that occur after the ship reached Bridgetown.

Extend Understanding

10. **Social Studies Connection:** How does Equiano's voyage compare with those of explorers and colonists?

QuickReview

A **slave narrative** is an autobiographical account of life as a slave.

Emotional appeals include vivid words and examples chosen for the feelings they inspire in readers.

To **summarize,** state main ideas and key details in your own words.

For: Self-test
Visit: www.PHSchool.com
Web Code: era-6207

Answers

1. The slaves felt complete despair. Many expressed a desire to die rather than endure conditions aboard the slave ship.
2. **Possible response:** The traders give the slaves very little living space on board ship. They routinely beat slaves to punish them.
3. The traders indulge Equiano's curiosity by allowing him to use the quadrant. They allow younger slaves to be kept out of chains and above deck.
4. The traders' main motivation is to make as much money as possible.
5. (a) **Possible response:** *so intolerably loathsome, absolutely pestilential,* and *wretched situation.* (b) These emotional appeals encourage the reader to empathize with the slaves. Another sample answer can be found on **Literary Analysis Graphic Organizer B,** p. 33 in ***Graphic Organizer Transparencies.***
6. Equiano stresses the unsanitary conditions.
7. Even eighteenth-century readers who accepted slavery as an economic idea might have been touched by Equiano's highly charged language. People's emotional reactions sometimes lead to changes in their opinions.
8. Summaries should include the following main points: Olaudah Equiano traveled across the Atlantic Ocean in a slave ship. The conditions on board were detestable; most slaves were confined to an overheated, cramped space. The crew treated the slaves as less than human, often flogging them for trespasses.
9. When the ship arrived on shore the frightened slaves were brought to auction and sold.
10. **Possible response:** Colonists and explorers did not know what they would find; however, they made the choice to take such a risk. Equiano's voyage is made against his will under horrible conditions.

Go Online Assessment Students may use the **Self-test** to prepare for **Selection Test A** or **Selection Test B.**

EXTEND/ASSESS

❶ Vocabulary Lesson

Word Analysis

1. Evidence can establish guilt because others can see proof of what took place.
2. People using video phones might become more concerned with their appearance before making a call.

Spelling Strategy

1. immortal
2. imbalanced
3. impossible
4. imprecise

Vocabulary Builder

1. synonyms
2. antonyms
3. antonyms
4. antonyms
5. synonyms
6. antonyms

❷ Grammar and Style Lesson

Suggested answers:

1. The crew permitted some of us to stay on the deck for fresh air.
2. The conditions soon reduced me so low.
3. The crew thought it necessary to keep me almost always on deck.
4. Crew members discovered them.
5. They saw flying fish.

Looking at Style

Answer: "We were conducted immediately . . ."; "We were all pent up together . . ."; "We were sold . . ." The passive voice emphasizes the helplessness and powerlessness of the slaves.

WG Writing and Grammar, Ruby Level

Students will find further instruction and practice on active and passive voice in Chapter 21, Section 4.

Build Language Skills

❶ Vocabulary Lesson

Word Analysis: Latin Root *-vid-*

The Latin root *-vid-*, from *videre*, means "to see." The word *provident* means "to have foresight." Considering the meaning of the root *-vid-*, answer these questions:

1. Why is *evidence* useful in establishing guilt?
2. How would *video* technology change telephone habits?

Spelling Strategy

Change the spelling of *in-*, a common prefix meaning "not," to *im-* when you add it to words beginning with *b*, *m*, or *p* (as in *improvident*). Using this strategy, spell the words described below:

1. not mortal
2. not balanced
3. not possible
4. not precice

Vocabulary Builder: Synonym or Antonym

Review the list of vocabulary words on page 159. Then, analyze the relationship between the words in each of the following pairs. Indicate whether the words are synonyms (words with similar meanings) or antonyms (words with opposite meanings).

1. loathesome, hateful
2. pestilential, sanitary
3. copious, sparse
4. improvident, cautious
5. avarice, greed
6. pacify, torment

❷ Grammar and Style Lesson

Active and Passive Voice

A verb is in the **active voice** when the subject of the sentence performs the action. A verb is in the **passive voice** when the subject receives the action.

Active Voice: They *tossed* the remaining fish into the sea.
(The subject, *they*, performs the action of the verb *tossed*.)

Passive Voice: This situation *was aggravated* by the galling of the chains.
(The subject, *situation*, receives the action of the verb *was aggravated*.)

Practice Rewrite the following sentences using the active voice. You may need to add words to indicate who performed the action.

1. Some of us had been permitted to stay on the deck for fresh air.
2. I was soon reduced so low here.
3. It was thought necessary to keep me almost always on deck.
4. They were discovered.
5. Flying fish were seen.

Looking at Style Find three examples of the passive voice in the final paragraph of the selection. What effect does the style have on your understanding of the slaves' experiences?

WG *Prentice Hall Writing and Grammar Connection: Chapter 21, Section 4*

Assessment Practice

Summarizing Written Texts: Implied Main Idea

When the main idea is not directly stated, students must infer the main focus of the passage. Some tests require students to identify the implied main idea of a reading passage. Have students reread p. 45. Then have them choose the implied main idea of the paragraph from the following responses:

A Most slaves were kept in the hold below the deck.

B Death seemed better than life to slaves on the African slave ships.

C Slave ships from Africa were filthy, overcrowded and cruelly managed, which caused many slaves to sicken and die.

D Equiano wrote a journal about life on an African slave ship.

Choice *A* is a supporting detail and choices *B* and *D* present background information. Choice *C* contains the implied main idea.

(For more practice, see *Standardized Test Preparation Workbook*, p. 3.)

Writing Lesson

Museum Placard

To educate today's audiences, museums present exhibits that document the slave trade of the 1800s. Write the introductory information for a large placard that visitors will read at an exhibit's beginning. Explain the sequence of events of the slave trade, from capture to slave auction.

Prewriting Use library sources to gather facts. Organize your findings in sequence, perhaps by drawing a map to trace the routes or marking dates and other key details on a timeline.

Drafting Create a timeline like the one shown to organize the events that occurred, listing them in chronological order. Begin with what happens first, and then continue in time order.

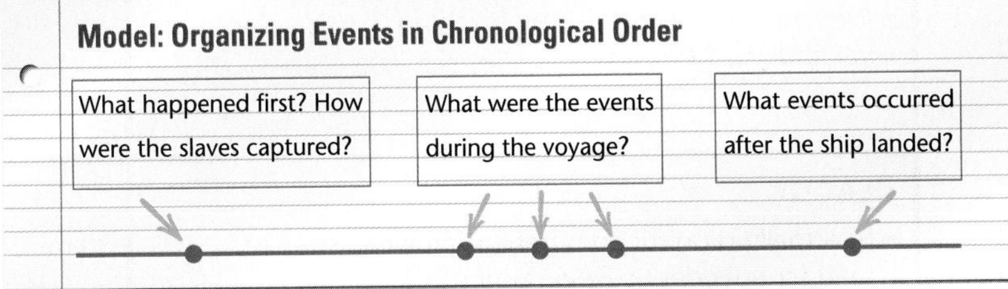
Model: Organizing Events in Chronological Order
What happened first? How were the slaves captured?
What were the events during the voyage?
What events occurred after the ship landed?

Revising Check that your placard highlights the important stages of the slave trade. Eliminate any confusing shifts in time sequence, and add transitions to sharpen that sequence.

WG *Prentice Hall Writing and Grammar Connection: Chapter 10, Section 3*

Extend Your Learning

Listening and Speaking With a small group, research the topic of the Middle Passage. Then, hold a **round-table discussion** in which you share what you have learned. Use the following tips:

- As a group, choose one student to coordinate the research and another to moderate.
- Listen respectfully without interrupting.
- Avoid monopolizing the discussion.
- Consider how you will communicate effectively to classmates whose cultural backgrounds may be different from your own.

Summarize your discussion for the rest of the class. **[Group Activity]**

Research and Technology Modern organizations such as Amnesty International work to increase awareness of injustices around the world. Use the Internet or the library to research the causes it publicizes. Develop charts or diagrams and give a **research presentation.**

Go Online
Research

For: An additional research activity
Visit: www.PHSchool.com
Web Code: erd-7206

Assessment Resources

The following resources can be used to assess students' knowledge and skills.

Unit 2 Resources
- **Selection Test A,** pp. 37–39
- **Selection Test B,** pp. 40–42

General Resources
- **Rubrics for Research Report,** pp. 49–50
- **Rubrics for Speaking: Delivering a Research Presentation,** p. 91

Go Online Assessment — Students may use the **Self-test** to prepare for **Selection Test A** or **Selection Test B.**

3 Writing Lesson

- To guide students in writing this museum placard, give them the **Support for Writing Lesson,** page 34, in ***General Resources.***
- Students' placards should use clear prose to present factual information in chronological order. Each placard should contain the most important actions and events of the slave trade, as well as key descriptive details.
- Remind students to use appropriate transition words to show the time order of events.
- Use the rubrics for Research Report, pages 49–50 in ***General Resources,*** to evaluate students' museum placards.

4 Research and Technology

- Students can find a wealth of information on Amnesty International's official Web site: www.amnesty.org. *We strongly recommend that you preview this and related sites before you send students to them.*
- Amnesty International was begun in Britain in 1961 with the goal of helping to free individuals "imprisoned solely because of their political or religious beliefs, gender, or racial or ethnic origin," though they had "neither used nor advocated violence." In 1977, the organization won the Nobel Peace Prize for its work.
- Students might organize their presentations according to particular causes, individuals, time periods, or geographic regions.
- The **Support for Extend Your Learning** page (***Unit 2 Resources,*** p. 35) provides guided note-taking opportunities to help students complete the Extend Your Learning Activities.
- Use the rubric for Speaking: Delivering A Research Presentation, page 91 in ***General Resources,*** to evaluate students' presentations.

Go Online Research — Have students type in the Web Code for another research activity.

Meeting Your Standards

Students will

1. **analyze and respond to literary elements.**
   - Literary Analysis: Persuasion
2. **read, comprehend, analyze, and critique speeches.**
   - Reading Strategy: Recognizing Charged Words
   - Reading Check questions
   - Apply the Skills questions
   - Assessment Practice (ATE)
3. **develop vocabulary.**
   - Vocabulary Lesson: Latin Root: *-fid-*
4. **understand and apply written and oral language conventions.**
   - Spelling Strategy
   - Grammar and Style Lesson: Parallelism
5. **develop writing proficiency.**
   - Writing Lesson: A Proposal to the Principal
6. **develop appropriate research strategies.**
   - Extend Your Learning: Précis
7. **understand and apply listening and speaking strategies.**
   - Extend Your Learning: News Reports

Block Scheduling: Use one 90-minute class period to preteach the skills and have students read the selection. Use a second 90-minute class period to assess students' mastery of skills, extend their learning, and monitor their progress.

Homework Suggestions

Following are possibilities for homework assignments.

- Support pages from *Unit 2 Resources:*
  Literary Analysis
  Reading Strategy
  Vocabulary Builder
  Grammar and Style
- An Extend Your Learning project and the Writing Lesson for this selection group may be completed over several days.

Step-by-Step Teaching Guide	Pacing Guide
PRETEACH	
• Administer Vocabulary and Reading Warm-ups as necessary.	5 min.
• Engage students' interest with the motivation activity.	5 min.
• Read and discuss author and background features. **FT**	10 min.
• Introduce the Literary Analysis Skill: Persuasion. **FT**	5 min.
• Introduce the Reading Strategy: Recognizing Charged Words. **FT**	10 min.
• Prepare students to read by teaching the selection vocabulary. **FT**	
TEACH	
• Informally monitor comprehension while students read independently or in groups. **FT**	30 min.
• Monitor students' comprehension with the Reading Check notes.	as students read
• Reinforce vocabulary with Vocabulary Builder notes.	as students read
• Develop students' understanding of persuasion with the Literary Analysis annotations. **FT**	5 min.
• Develop students' ability to recognize charged words with the Reading Strategy annotations. **FT**	5 min.
ASSESS/EXTEND	
• Assess students' comprehension and mastery of the Literary Analysis and Reading Strategy by having them answer the Apply the Skills questions. **FT**	15 min.
• Have students complete the Vocabulary Lesson and the Grammar and Style Lesson. **FT**	15 min.
• Apply students' ability to use forceful words by using the Writing Lesson. **FT**	45 min. or homework
• Apply students' understanding by using one or more of the Extend Your Learning activities.	20–90 min. or homework
• Administer Selection Test A or Selection Test B. **FT**	15 min.

Resources

PRINT

Unit 2 Resources

- Vocabulary Warm-up Word Lists [**L1, L2, EL**] . . . . .p. 43
- Vocabulary Warm-up Practice [**L1, L2, EL**] . . . . .p. 44
- Reading Warm-up A [**L1, L2, EL**] . . . . .p. 45
- Reading Warm-up B [**L1, L2, L3**] . . . . .p. 46

TRANSPARENCY

Graphic Organizer Transparencies

- Literary Analysis Graphic Organizer A [**L3**] . . . . .p. 36
- Literary Analysis Graphic Organizer B [**L1, L2, EL**] . . . . .p. 37
- Reading Strategy Graphic Organizer A [**L3**] . . . . .p. 34
- Reading Strategy Graphic Organizer B [**L1, L2, EL**] . . . . .p. 35

PRINT

Reader's Notebook [**L2**]
Reader's Notebook: Adapted Version [**L1**]
Reader's Notebook: English Learner's Version [**EL**]

Unit 2 Resources

- Literary Analysis [**L3**] . . . . .p. 47
- Reading Strategy [**L3**] . . . . .p. 48
- Vocabulary Builder [**L3**] . . . . .p. 49

TECHNOLOGY

Listening to Literature Audio CDs [**L2, EL**]
Reader's Notebook: Adapted Version Audio CD [**L1, L2**]

PRINT

Unit 6 Resources

- Grammar and Style [**L3**] . . . . .p. 50
- Support for Writing Lesson [**L3**] . . . . .p. 51
- Support for Extend Your Learning [**L3**] . . . . .p. 52
- Enrichment [**L4**] . . . . .p. 53
- Selection Test A [**L1, L2, EL**] . . . . .pp. 54–56
- Selection Test B [**L3, L4**] . . . . .pp. 57–59

General Resources

- Rubrics for Problem–Solution Essay [**L3**] . . . . .pp. 59–60
- Rubric for Evaluating a Media Presentation [**L3**] . . . . .p. 86

TECHNOLOGY

Go Online: Research [**L3**]
Go Online: Self-test [**L3**]
***ExamView®*, Test Bank** [**L3**]

Choosing Resources for Differentiated Instruction

[**L1**] Special Needs Students
[**L2**] Below-Level Students
[**L3**] All Students
[**L4**] Advanced Students
[**EL**] English Learners

FT Fast Track Instruction: To move the lesson more quickly, use the strategies and activities identified with **FT**.

Scaffolding for Less Proficient and Advanced Students

The leveled Critical Thinking questions after selections progress in the levels of thinking required to answer them. To address the needs of your different students, you may use the (a) level questions for your less proficient students and the (b) level questions with your on-level and advanced students. The occasional (c) level questions are appropriate for your advanced students.

PRENTICE HALL **TeacherEXPRESS™** Plan · Teach · Assess — Use this complete suite of powerful teaching tools to make lesson planning and testing quicker and easier.

Use the interactive textbook (online and on CD-ROM) to make selections and activities come alive with audio and video support and interactive questions.

PREPREACH

❶ Motivation

Jefferson and Paine wrote inspirational words that roused colonial Americans to action. Set the following scene for students. They are soldiers dressed in ragged clothes. It's winter; snow and ice surround them. A few have light jackets; some are barefoot. All are hungry, huddled in tents without floors. Badly defeated in the last battle, they think of home.

What spoken words could keep these desperate soldiers fighting for independence? Have students answer in their journals, writing in the first person as a soldier in the Revolutionary war. Discuss their responses. Then explain that they are about to read two writing selections that inspired those soldiers.

Background

More About the Authors

Though he spent nearly all his life in public service, Thomas Jefferson actually preferred life on his farm. He loved to read and owned a library of 6,400 books.

Thomas Paine's words aroused much passion in the hearts of his listeners. Not all of it was positive, however. Many hated Paine. Some found his personality offensive. Others disagreed with his views on religion. Perhaps it was Paine's dislike for compromise that earned him the most enemies.

❶ The Declaration of Independence • *from* The Crisis, Number 1

Thomas Jefferson (1743–1826)

When you look at all of Thomas Jefferson's achievements, it seems there was virtually nothing that he couldn't do. Not only did he help our nation win its independence and serve as its third president, but he also founded the University of Virginia, helped establish the public school system, designed his own home, invented a type of elevator for sending food from floor to floor, and created the decimal system for American money. He was a skilled violinist, an art enthusiast, and a brilliant writer.

Revolutionary Leader Born into a wealthy Virginia family, Jefferson attended the College of William and Mary and went on to earn a law degree. While serving in the Virginia House of Burgesses, he became an outspoken defender of American rights. When conflict between the colonists and the British erupted into revolution, Jefferson emerged as a leader in the effort to win independence.

Valued Statesman When the war ended, Jefferson served as the American minister to France for several years. He then served as the nation's first secretary of state and second vice president before becoming president in 1801. While in office, Jefferson nearly doubled the size of the nation by authorizing the purchase of the Louisiana Territory from France.

On the morning of July 4, 1826, the fiftieth anniversary of the Declaration of Independence, Jefferson died at the age of 83. John Adams, Jefferson's fellow contributor to the Declaration of Independence, died only several hours after his longtime friend. Adams's last words were "Thomas Jefferson still survives."

Thomas Paine (1737–1809)

Thomas Paine met Benjamin Franklin in London, and the introduction changed his life—and American history. Paine emigrated to the colonies from England in 1774. With a letter of introduction from Franklin, Paine began a career as a journalist. In January 1776, he published *Common Sense,* in which he argued that Americans must fight for independence. The pamphlet created a national mood for revolution.

Inspiring Essayist Paine enlisted in the American army toward the end of 1776. At that time, the army had just suffered a crushing defeat by the British in New Jersey and had retreated into Pennsylvania. The soldiers were suffering from freezing weather, a shortage of provisions, and low morale. Paine was writing the first of a series of essays entitled *The American Crisis.* Washington ordered Paine's essay read to his troops before they crossed the Delaware River to defeat the Hessians at the Battle of Trenton.

In 1787, several years after the end of the American Revolution, Paine traveled to Europe and became involved with the French Revolution. Though he wrote in support of the revolutionary cause in *The Rights of Man* (1791–1792), he was imprisoned for pleading against the execution of the overthrown French king. While in prison, he began writing *The Age of Reason* (1794), an attack on organized religion. The book turned American public opinion against him, and when he died in 1809, he was a broken man. Years later, however, Paine was once again recognized as a hero of the Revolution.

Preview

Connecting to the Literature

Today, we witness armed struggles for freedom through reports in the news media. The best way to experience what our own revolution was like, however, is to read documents, like these by Jefferson and Paine.

Literary Analysis

Persuasion

Persuasion is writing or speech meant to get readers or listeners to think or act in a certain way. A persuasive writer appeals to emotions or reason, offers opinions, and urges action. The writer must also back up his or her points with evidence. For example, to support his argument for independence, Jefferson presents a list of offenses committed by the British king.

> He has dissolved representative houses repeatedly, for opposing with manly firmness his invasions of the rights of the people.

In these works, notice how each writer appeals to both reason and emotion to persuade readers of the rightness of his position.

Comparing Literary Works

Jefferson's and Paine's writings argue in support of independence. They were, however, written for different **audiences.** Jefferson wrote to the British king, while Paine wrote for a broad colonial readership. As you read, look for the ways in which different audiences shape each document's message.

Reading Strategy

Recognizing Charged Words

Charged words are likely to produce a strong emotional response. For example, a word like *tyranny,* which means "oppressive power," may evoke feelings of outrage. To avoid being swayed by charged words, look for support to back up the words. Use a chart like the one shown to record charged words and their connotations, or the ideas they suggest.

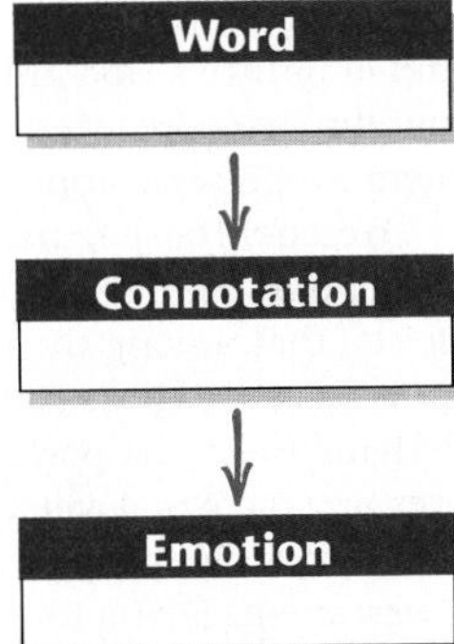

Vocabulary Builder

unalienable (un āl′ yən ə bəl) *adj.* not to be taken away (p. 170)

usurpations (yo͞o′ sər pā′ shənz) *n.* unlawful seizures of rights or privileges (p. 170)

perfidy (pur′ fə dē) *n.* betrayal of trust (p. 172)

redress (ri dres′) *n.* compensation for a wrong done (p. 172)

magnanimity (mag′ nə nim′ ə tē) *n.* ability to rise above pettiness or meanness (p. 172)

consanguinity (kän′ saŋ gwin′ ə tē) *n.* kinship (p. 173)

acquiesce (ak′ wē es′) *v.* agree without protest (p. 173)

impious (im′ pē əs) *adj.* lacking reverence for God (p. 175)

infidel (in′ fə del′) *n.* person who holds no religious belief (p. 175)

Differentiated Instruction Solutions for All Learners

Support for Special Needs Students
Have students read the adapted version of from *The Crisis, Number 1* in the ***Reader's Notebook: Adapted Version.*** This version provides basic-level instruction in an interactive format with questions and write-on lines. Completing these pages will prepare students to read the selection in the Student Edition.

Support for Less Proficient Readers
Have students read from *The Crisis Number 1* in the ***Reader's Notebook.*** This version provides basic-level instruction in an interactive format with questions and write-on lines. After students finish the selection in the ***Reader's Notebook***, have them complete the questions and activities in the Student Edition.

Support for English Learners
Have students read from *The Crisis Number 1* in the ***Reader's Notebook: English Learner's Version.*** This version provides basic-level instruction in an interactive format with questions and write-on lines. Completing these pages will prepare students to read the selection in the Student Edition.

2 Literary Analysis

Persuasion

- Tell students that in reading these selections by Jefferson and Paine, they will focus on persuasion: writing or speech meant to get readers or listeners to think or act a certain way.
- After reading aloud the instruction, have a volunteer read the quotation from Jefferson. Then read this Paine excerpt to students: ". . . if a thief breaks into my house, burns and destroys my property, and kills or threatens to kill me . . . am I to suffer it?" Discuss how both excerpts appeal to reason and emotion.
- Use the instruction for Comparing Literary Works to highlight other similarities and differences between the two selections.

3 Reading Strategy

Recognizing Charged Words

- Remind students that charged words inspire an emotional response. Usually these words carry strong connotations, or associated meanings.
- Point out to students that charged words can greatly advance a writer's persuasive goals by appealing to listeners' emotions. Demonstrate this by completing the chart from the student page using the word *tyranny.*
- Instruct students to complete their own charts as they read, inserting charged words from the selection and then identifying the connotations and emotions each inspires.
- Give students a copy of **Reading Strategy Graphic Organizer A,** p. 34 in ***Graphic Organizer Transparencies,*** to use as they read the selections.

Vocabulary Builder

- Pronounce each vocabulary word for students, and read the definition as a class. Have students identify any words with which they are already familiar.

TEACH

Learning Modalities
Visual/Spatial Learners For each point that Jefferson makes about King George and his treatment of the colonies, direct students to create one or more index cards. On each card, students can record each point and the evidence Jefferson uses to support it. Using various colors of either index cards or highlighter pens, students can organize the information for easy reference.

❶ About the Selection

Perhaps the most influential document in American history, *The Declaration of Independence* details the philosophy of the colonial revolutionaries and outlines their experiences with what they call a tyrannical king.

In this famous battlecry of freedom, Jefferson identifies what he calls "self-evident" truths, pointing out the equality of men and the tenuous contract of government. Then, in a list of the objectionable acts of King George III, arranged from least offensive to most, Jefferson outlines the reasons that the colonials are dissatisfied with their government. Jefferson reaches the reasoned conclusion that every rational means of reaching détente with Britain has failed, and, therefore, the United States of America must become independent of Britain.

❷ Literary Analysis
Persuasion

- Draw students' attention to the bracketed passage. Have students **paraphrase** the long sentence. **Possible response:** Because it isn't wise to change governments without serious reasons, people are likely to just go along with things even if they aren't entirely fair.
- Then **ask** students the Literary Analysis question: Why does Jefferson introduce the ideas that one does not change a government for "light" causes? **Answer:** Jefferson is arguing that the colonists' reasons for declaring independence are very serious.

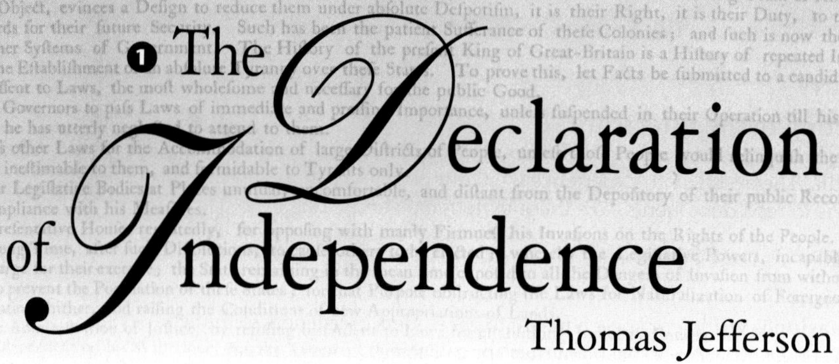

❶ The Declaration of Independence

Thomas Jefferson

Background In 1776, Jefferson was chosen (with Franklin, Adams, and others) to write a declaration of the colonies' independence. The draft presented to the Second Continental Congress was largely Jefferson's work. To his disappointment, however, Congress made changes before approving the document. They dropped Jefferson's condemnation of the British for tolerating a corrupt Parliament, and they struck out a strong statement against slavery.

When in the course of human events, it becomes necessary for one people to dissolve the political bands which have connected them with another, and to assume among the powers of the earth, the separate and equal station to which the laws of nature and of nature's God entitle them, a decent respect to the opinions of mankind requires that they should declare the causes which impel them to the separation.

We hold these truths to be self-evident: that all men are created equal; that they are endowed by their Creator with certain unalienable rights; that among these are life, liberty and the pursuit of happiness; that to secure these rights, governments are instituted among men, deriving their just powers from the consent of the governed; that whenever any form of government becomes destructive of these ends, it is the right of the people to alter or to abolish it, and to institute new government, laying its foundation on such principles and organizing its powers in such form, as to them shall seem most likely to effect their safety and happiness. ❷ Prudence, indeed, will dictate that governments long established should not be changed for light and transient causes; and accordingly all experience hath shown, that mankind are more disposed to suffer while evils are sufferable than to right themselves by abolishing the forms to which they are accustomed. But when a long train of abuses and usurpations, pursuing invariably the same object, evinces a design to reduce them under absolute despotism,[1] it is their

Vocabulary Builder
unalienable (un āl′ yən ə bəl) *adj.* not to be taken away

Literary Analysis
Persuasion Why does Jefferson introduce the idea that one does not change a government for "light" causes?

Vocabulary Builder
usurpations (yo͞o′ sər pā′ shənz) *n.* unlawful seizures of rights or privileges

1. **despotism** (des′ pət iz′ əm) *n.* tyranny.

Differentiated Instruction Solutions for All Learners

Accessibility at a Glance

	The Declaration of Independence	The Crisis, Number 1
Context	Philosophy of colonial revolutionaries	Call to arms
Language	18th-century vocabulary and sentence structure	18th-century vocabulary and sentence structure
Concept Level	Abstract (philosophical ideas)	Abstract (extended metaphor)
Literary Merit	Primary source	Classic example of persuasive writing
Lexile	1390	1200
Overall Rating	More challenging	Average

right, it is their duty, to throw off such government, and to provide new guards for their future security. Such has been the patient sufferance of these colonies; and such is now the necessity which constrains them to alter their former systems of government. The history of the present king of Great Britain is a history of repeated injuries and usurpations, all having in direct object the establishment of an absolute tyranny over these states. To prove this, let facts be submitted to a candid world.

Literary Analysis
Persuasion What does the statement about submitting facts to a "candid world" suggest about the intended audience?

He has refused his assent to laws the most wholesome and necessary for the public good.

He has forbidden his governors to pass laws of immediate and pressing importance, unless suspended in their operation till his assent should be obtained; and when so suspended, he has utterly neglected to attend to them.

The Declaration of Independence, John Trumbull, Yale University Art Gallery

He has refused to pass other laws for the accommodation of large districts of people, unless those people would relinquish the right of representation in the legislature, a right inestimable to them and formidable to tyrants only.

5 ▲ **Critical Viewing**
What is the mood of this painting? In what ways does the mood suit the occasion? **[Relate]**

He has called together legislative bodies at places unusual, uncomfortable, and distant from the depository of their public records, for the sole purpose of fatiguing them into compliance with his measures.

He has dissolved representative houses repeatedly, for opposing with manly firmness his invasions on the rights of the people.

He has refused for a long time after such dissolutions to cause others to be elected, whereby the legislative powers, incapable of annihilation, have returned to the people at large for their exercise, the state remaining in the mean time exposed to all the dangers of invasion from without, and convulsions within.

He has endeavored to prevent the population of these states; for that purpose obstructing the laws for naturalization of foreigners, refusing to pass others to encourage their migration hither, and raising the conditions of new appropriations of lands.

He has obstructed the administration of justice, by refusing his assent to laws for establishing judiciary powers.

He has made judges dependent on his will alone, for the tenure of their offices, and the amount and payment of their salaries.

He has erected a multitude of new offices, and sent hither swarms of officers to harass our people and eat out their substance.

He has kept among us in times of peace standing armies without the consent of our legislatures.

6 **Reading Check**
Why did Jefferson write this long list of facts?

3 Literary Analysis
Persuasion

- Write the bracketed text on the chalkboard. Review with students the meaning of the word *candid* and emphasize that Jefferson uses the word in the sense of "unbiased."
- **Ask** students the Literary Analysis question: What does the statement about submitting facts to a "candid world" suggest about the intended audience?
  Possible response: It suggests that Jefferson believed he was speaking to the world and that he believed the world would judge his words fairly and honestly.

4 Humanities

The Declaration of Independence, by John Trumbull

This painting is only thirty inches wide yet it contains forty-eight figures! Trumbull's placement of his subjects' heads and the sweep of banners in the background add action and excitement to the composition. Use these questions for discussion:

1. How does this painting add to your knowledge of the events surrounding Jefferson's work?
   Possible response: It shows that Jefferson spoke for many.
2. How does the composition of the painting heighten the impact of Jefferson's writing?
   Possible response: The dignity with which the figures are posed shows how important Jefferson's writing was to them.

5 Critical Viewing

Answer: The mood of this painting is dignified, stately, and triumphant, which suits the historic occasion.

6 Reading Check

Answer: He wanted to build a strong case against King George III in order to show that the colonists had no choice but to seek independence.

Differentiated Instruction
Solutions for All Learners

Strategy for Special Needs Students
As volunteers take turns reading aloud Jefferson's list of grievances, work with others to paraphrase and decode difficult language. Use the outline organizer in ***Graphic Organizer Transparencies,*** p. 309, to help students record the meaning of each grievance. As they reread, have students identify Jefferson's persuasive evidence.

Strategy for Less Proficient Readers
To help students understand Jefferson's list of grievances against King George III, model the use of an outline organizer from ***Graphic Organizer Transparencies,*** p. 309. Direct students to insert a subtopic name for each grievance, then list the supporting evidence Jefferson provides.

Strategy for Gifted/Talented Students
Have students read Jefferson's list of grievances, directing their attention to its paragraph structure. As they complete the outline organizer from ***Graphic Organizer Transparencies,*** p. 309, discuss how Jefferson's use of parallel structure adds impact to his writing.

7 The American Experience

Jefferson and Locke

Jefferson echoed Locke's views about natural rights with his phrase "unalienable rights." Like Locke, Jefferson advanced the idea that government has no right to give or take away such rights. Instead, the social contract allows communities to grant certain individuals the power to govern. If a ruler fails to act in the community's best interest, he has broken the social contract and should be removed from power.

Connect to Literature Help students outline the structure of Jefferson's argument on the board. **Possible response:** Jefferson echoes Locke's idea that people have the right to overthrow a government that breaks a social contract when he itemizes the wrongs done to the colonists by the King of England.

8 Literary Analysis

Persuasion

- Identify for students the bracketed text on this page and the earlier portion of the list on the previous page. Have students explain how each listed item is similar.
  Answer: They are all descriptions of how George III has mistreated the colonists.
- **Invite** students to recap Jefferson's main point in the selection's opening paragraph.
  Answer: When one people decides it must separate itself from the rule of another, it should explain why.
  Ask students the Literary Analysis question: What support does this catalog of offenses provide for Jefferson's argument?
  Answer: By showing the king as an unfit ruler who has imposed a series of unjust and oppressive measures on the colonists, Jefferson answers any argument readers may advance in favor of remaining loyal to Britain.

He has affected to render the military independent of, and superior to, the civil power. 7

He has combined with others to subject us to a jurisdiction foreign to our constitution and unacknowledged by our laws, giving his assent to their acts of pretended legislation: for quartering large bodies of armed troops among us; for protecting them by a mock trial from punishment for any murders which they should commit on the inhabitants of these states; for cutting off our trade with all parts of the world; for imposing taxes on us without our consent; for depriving us, in many cases, of the benefits of trial by jury; for transporting us beyond seas to be tried for pretended offenses; for abolishing the free system of English laws in a neighboring province,[2] establishing therein an arbitrary government, and enlarging its boundaries, so as to render it at once an example and fit instrument for introducing the same absolute rule into these colonies; for taking away our charters, abolishing our most valuable laws, and altering fundamentally the forms of our governments; for suspending our own legislatures, and declaring themselves invested with power to legislate for us in all cases whatsoever.

8 He has abdicated government here, by declaring us out of his protection and waging war against us.

He has plundered our seas, ravaged our coasts, burned our towns, and destroyed the lives of our people.

He is at this time transporting large armies of foreign mercenaries to complete the works of death, desolation, and tyranny, already begun with circumstances of cruelty and perfidy scarcely paralleled in the most barbarous ages, and totally unworthy the head of a civilized nation.

He has constrained our fellow citizens taken captive on the high seas to bear arms against their country, to become the executioners of their friends and brethren, or to fall themselves by their hands.

He has excited domestic insurrections amongst us, and has endeavored to bring on the inhabitants of our frontiers, the merciless Indian savages, whose known rule of warfare is an undistinguished destruction of all ages, sexes, and conditions.

In every stage of these oppressions we have petitioned for redress in the most humble terms. Our repeated petitions have been answered only by repeated injury.

A prince whose character is thus marked by every act which may define a tyrant is unfit to be the ruler of a free people.

Nor have we been wanting in attentions to our British brethren. We have warned them from time to time of attempts by their legislature to extend an unwarrantable jurisdiction over us. We have reminded them of the circumstances of our emigration and settlement here. We have appealed to their native justice and magnanimity and we have

2. **neighboring province** Quebec.

Jefferson, Locke, and the Social Contract

In writing the Declaration of Independence, Jefferson drew on a theory of government devised by earlier European political thinkers, especially the Englishman John Locke (1632–1704). Locke argued that all people are born with certain *natural rights* that are not the property of governments. Locke's concept of the *social contract* also contributed to Jefferson's notion that governments derive their power from "the consent of the governed." According to Locke, when a ruler breaks the social contract by acting abusively, the people have the right to revolt against his rule. In 1776, that is what the American colonists did.

Connect to the Literature

Where in the Declaration does Jefferson echo Locke's idea that the people have the right to overthrow a government that breaks the social contract?

Literary Analysis
Persuasion What support does this catalog of offenses provide for Jefferson's argument?

Vocabulary Builder

perfidy (pʉr′ fə dē) *n.* betrayal of trust

redress (ri dres′) *n.* compensation for a wrong done

magnanimity (mag′ nə nim′ ə tē) *n.* ability to rise above pettiness or meanness

Enrichment

A Spreading Flame of Freedom

When representatives from the thirteen colonies signed the Declaration of Independence, they were forging a path that other nations would soon follow. France, who helped the colonists defeat Great Britain, soon found itself amidst revolution against tyranny from within. The French Revolution began in 1789 and soon led to overthrow of the monarchy and to the establishment of democracy. In Latin America, a campaign for independence from Spain, led by Simón Bolívar, took shape early in the nineteenth century. His dream was to create a nation of united excolonies, a kind of United States of Central and South America.

For this reason, Bolívar is sometimes called "the George Washington of South America."

Ironically, although the French Revolution inspired many new independence movements, it was France's usurpation of the Spanish throne that prompted Bolívar to raise an army to liberate what are now the countries of Venezuela, Colombia, Ecuador, Peru, and Bolivia from Spanish rule.

conjured[3] them by the ties of our common kindred to disavow these usurpations which would inevitably interrupt our connections and correspondence. They too have been deaf to the voice of justice and of consanguinity. We must therefore acquiesce in the necessity which denounces our separation and hold them, as we hold the rest of mankind, enemies in war, in peace friends.

We, therefore, the representatives of the United States of America in general congress assembled, appealing to the Supreme Judge of the world for the rectitude of our intentions, do in the name and by authority of the good people of these colonies, solemnly publish and declare that these united colonies are and of right ought to be free and independent states; that they are absolved from all allegiance to the British Crown, and that all political connection between them and the state of Great Britain is and ought to be totally dissolved; and that as free and independent states, they have full power to levy war, conclude peace, contract alliances, establish commerce, and to do all other acts and things which independent states may of right do.

And for the support of this declaration, with a firm reliance on the protection of divine providence, we mutually pledge to each other our lives, our fortunes and our sacred honor.

Vocabulary Builder

consanguinity (kän′ saŋ gwin′ ə tē) *n.* kinship

acquiesce (ak′ wē es′) *v.* agree without protest

3. **conjured** *v.* solemnly appealed to.

Critical Reading

1. **Respond:** How would you have responded to the Declaration if you were **(a)** the king of England, **(b)** someone from a nation lacking in human rights, or **(c)** a Native American?
2. **(a) Recall:** What points about human rights does Jefferson make at the beginning of the Declaration? **(b) Analyze:** Why does he begin with these observations before addressing the colonists' situation?
3. **(a) Recall:** What does Jefferson claim has happened at "every stage of these oppressions"? **(b) Interpret:** What is Jefferson's purpose in presenting this information?
4. **(a) Evaluate:** What is the most convincing evidence that Jefferson cites to support his points? Explain. **(b) Evaluate:** How would you rate the overall effectiveness of his argument? Why?
5. **Synthesize:** The period in which this document was written is often referred to as the Age of Reason because of the emphasis on logic and discipline at the time. What elements of Jefferson's Declaration reflect a faith in reason?

For: More about Thomas Jefferson
Visit: www.PHSchool.com
Web Code: ere-9202

ASSESS

Answers

1. **Possible responses:** (a) I would have been insulted and angered as the Declaration paints me in a very negative light; (b) I would be first astonished and then envious that Americans believed themselves entitled to these rights; (c) I would have been angered by the hypocrisy toward my people suggested in the Declaration. It neither grants my people inalienable rights nor acknowledges that the colonists stole America's land from my people.
2. **Possible response:** (a) He says that some human rights are unalienable. (b) He wants to appeal to feelings about justice in the minds of listeners.
3. (a) At every stage the colonists have petitioned the king for redress. (b) He wants to show the colonists as reasonable and thereby justify their final decision to seek independence.
4. **Possible response:** (a) Jefferson's most convincing evidence is the last item about the king's dissolution of colonial representative houses when these oppose him. (b) Jefferson's argument is overwhelmingly effective. He first appeals to ideas about justice and humanity. Then he paints the king as an abusive ruler and the colonists as highly reasonable subjects. This contrast supports his argument that George III left the colonists no alternative but to seek independence.
5. Jefferson's detailed explanation of Great Britain's wrongs against the colonies set up a rational justification for the revolution. He clearly expects the reader to follow his reasonings.

Go Online Author Link For additional information about Thomas Jefferson, have students type in the Web Code, then select J from the alphabet, and then select Thomas Jefferson.

Differentiated Instruction Solutions for All Learners

Strategy for Special Needs Students
Have students work through the selection paragraph by paragraph to find the key ideas in each. Help students identify unfamiliar words or usage *before* they address the content of each paragraph.

Strategy for Less Proficient Readers
Encourage students to break down Jefferson's long sentences. One way to do this is by separating clauses. Using a random complex sentence, demonstrate how to identify and separate clauses. Ask students to paraphrase each clause. Then help them compose their own sentences using the paraphrasing.

❾ About the Selection

Paine's rhetoric, designed to build morale among the soldiers, promises that the severity of their situation makes triumph more glorious. He also vows that God would never desert those who fight for just causes. He criticizes Tories for being short sighted, because he believes revolution to be inevitable. He praises those who stand fast in their opposition to England and calls on all the states to put forth their best efforts to resist English rule. He labels those who step aside as evil, cold-hearted, cowardly, and unprincipled and concludes with an extended metaphor comparing the British to theives who must be punished.

❿ Humanities

Recruiting for the Continental Army by William T. Ranney

Ranney has captured what must have been the energy of the moment through artistic dramatization and excitement. The image resonates with patriotism. Since a recruit was paid less than seven dollars a month, from which the cost of his clothing was deducted, an appeal to patriotism was a chief recruiting strategy.

Use these questions for discussion:

1. How could Thomas Paine have used this painting to advance his position?
   Possible response: He could use it to show weary soldiers that many support them, even at cost to themselves, and that patriotic fervor remains strong.
2. Why is this painting an appropriate choice to illustrate Paine's essay?
   Possible response: The artist assumes the same fervor as Paine does in depicting the noble act of signing to fight for independence.

⓫ Critical Viewing

Answer: By placing a single recruit in the center and strongly lighting him and by placing the recruiter in an elevated position with his arms raised toward the heavens, the artist conveys the solemnity and intense feelings surrounding the revolutionary cause.

❾ from

The Crisis Number 1

Thomas Paine

❿

These are the times that try men's souls. ⓫ The summer soldier and the sunshine patriot will in this crisis, shrink from the service of his country; but he that stands it now, deserves the love and thanks of man and woman. Tyranny, like hell, is not easily conquered; yet we have this consolation with us, that the harder the conflict, the more glorious the triumph. What we obtain too cheap, we esteem too lightly; 'tis dearness only that gives everything its value. Heaven knows how to put a proper price upon its goods; and it would be strange indeed, if so celestial an article as FREEDOM should

▲ **Critical Viewing** What details in this image capture the patriotic fervor of Paine's essay? **[Connect]**

Enrichment

Revolutionary Blockbuster

Colonists began noticing Thomas Paine's extraordinary talents as a communicator nearly a year before the dark winter of his *Crisis* essay. Paine's pamphlet *Common Sense,* which in early 1776 had helped set the revolutionary mood, made a dramatic impact on colonists. The pamphlet spoke out fervently and frankly for independence, brooking no compromises or halfway measures—advocating only complete independence. Further, Paine criticized the entire concept of monarchy and called for the abolition of inherited class status. He said, "the birthday of a new world is at hand" and so it was.

not be highly rated. Britain, with an army to enforce her tyranny, has declared that she has a right (*not only* to TAX) but "to BIND *us in* ALL CASES WHATSOEVER," and if being *bound in that manner,* is not slavery, then is there not such a thing as slavery upon earth. Even the expression is <u>impious</u>, for so unlimited a power can belong only to God . . .

I have as little superstition in me as any man living, but my secret opinion has ever been, and still is, that God Almighty will not give up a people to military destruction, or leave them unsupportedly to perish, who have so earnestly and so repeatedly sought to avoid the calamities of war, by every decent method which wisdom could invent. Neither have I so much of the <u>infidel</u> in me, as to suppose that he has relinquished the government of the world, and given us up to the care of devils; and as I do not, I cannot see on what grounds the king of Britain can look up to heaven for help against us: a common murderer, a highwayman, or a housebreaker, has as good a pretense as he . . .

I once felt all that kind of anger, which a man ought to feel, against the mean[1] principles that are held by the Tories:[2] a noted one, who kept a tavern at Amboy, was standing at his door, with as pretty a child in his hand, about eight or nine years old, as I ever saw, and after speaking his mind as freely as he thought was prudent, finished with this unfatherly expression, "*Well! give me peace in my day.*" Not a man lives on the continent but fully believes that a separation must some time or other finally take place, and a generous parent should have said, "*If there must be trouble let it be in my day, that my child may have peace*"; and this single reflection, well applied, is sufficient to awaken every man to duty. Not a place upon earth might be so happy as America. Her situation is remote from all the wrangling world, and she has nothing to do but to trade with them. A man can distinguish himself between temper and principle, and I am as confident, as I am that God governs the world, that America will never be happy till she gets clear of foreign dominion. Wars, without ceasing, will break out till that period arrives, and the continent must in the end be conqueror; for though the flame of liberty may sometimes cease to shine, the coal can never expire . . .

I turn with the warm ardor of a friend to those who have nobly stood, and are yet determined to stand the matter out: I call not upon a few, but upon all; not on *this* state or *that* state, but on *every* state; up and help us; lay your shoulders to the wheel; better have too much force than too little, when so great an object is at stake. Let it be told to the future world, that in the depth of winter, when nothing but hope and virtue could survive, that the city and the country, alarmed at one common danger, came forth to meet and to repulse it. Say not that thousands are gone, turn out your tens of thousands; throw not the burden of the day upon Providence, but "*show your faith by your*

1. **mean** *adj.* here, small-minded.
2. **Tories** colonists who remained loyal to Great Britain.

Vocabulary Builder

impious (im′ pē əs) *adj.* lacking reverence for God

infidel (in′ fə dəl′) *n.* a person who holds no religious belief

Reading Strategy
Recognizing Charged Words In what ways might the word "foreign" help Paine inspire the colonists to fight against Great Britain?

14

Whom does Paine call to arms?

12 Vocabulary Builder
The Latin Word Root *-fid-*

- Draw students' attention to Paine's use of the word *infidel,* and tell students that the root *-fid-* comes from the Latin word *fides,* which means "faith."
- Remind students that the prefix *in-* adds the meaning of "not" or "without" to a word.
- Guide students to see that Paine uses the word to mean specifically "one who is unfaithful to his religion."
- Let students know that the root *-fid-* appears in many words containing the idea of faith or trust, such as *fidelity* (faithfulness) and *confidence* (faith in the self).

13 Reading Strategy
Recognizing Charged Words

- Invite a volunteer to stand and speak the words of the bracketed passage. Encourage the volunteer to put special emphasis on the word *foreign.*
- **Ask** students what associations they have with the word *foreign,* reminding students to be honest but sensitive in their responses.
  Possible response: Students may acknowledge associating the word *foreign* with things that are strange or alien to them but also with things that are exciting and interesting.
- **Ask** students the Reading Strategy question: In what ways might the word "foreign" help Paine inspire the colonists to fight against Great Britain?
  Possible response: With it, Paine casts the British as outsiders, when in fact most colonists were of British stock. By distancing the colonists' from their adversary, Paine appeals to the colonists' sense of themselves as an emerging nation. Casting Great Britain as a foreign power rather than as the colonists' legal government helps colonists avoid any sense of disloyalty.

14 Reading Check

Answer: He calls on every colonist in every state to help with this important cause.

Differentiated Instruction Solutions for All Learners

Support for Less Proficient Readers
Point out to students the many places in Paine's essay where he uses either all capital letters or italicized letters. Explain that Paine used these techniques to emphasize certain ideas. Thus, when students encounter a phrase such as "*not only* to TAX" they can use the special treatment of the letters to help them construct meaning.

Vocabulary for English Learners
Tell students that Paine uses figurative speech—words that have meaning beyond their literal definition—throughout his essay. Model how to decode this figurative language, using the example of the "summer soldier" and the "sunshine patriot." Then invite volunteers to take turns restating figurative language.

Enrichment for Advanced Learners
In a May 1777 address to the Continental Congress, George Washington said, "I am wearied to death. I think the game is pretty near up." Have students write a speech as if they were Washington, conveying their thoughts *after* hearing Paine's essay. Challenge them to quote from Paine's essay and to express a renewed dedication to the revolution.

ASSESS

Answers

1. **Possible response:** A Tory would probably be angered by Paine's remarks and would consider him a traitor to the crown.
2. (a) He says the king is as bad as a common murderer, a highwayman, or burglar. (b) It is exaggerated for effect. (c) Some students might find Paine a trustworthy reporter because he conveys the emotional immediacy of events. Others might argue that Paine is too committed to one side to give a balanced account.
3. (a) He says that the harder a goal is to achieve, the more worthy it is and that Britian's colonial policy amounts to slavery. (b) He refers to people who are available only when times are easy and who desert the cause in bleak, harsh, difficult circumstances.
4. **Possible responses:** (a) He appeals to the emotions of resentment and anger. (b) He appeals more to emotions. For example, he uses many charged words, such as *crisis, tyranny, hell, heaven, freedom,* and *slavery.*
5. (a) The main idea of the essay is that the colonists are fighting for a just cause; thus they should endure the difficult times and not lose sight of their purpose. (b) **Possible response:** He cites oppressive British policy; he suggests that separation from Britain is inevitable, and should be resolved now. (c) **Possible response:** Paine's vivid descriptions of the American predicament and his comparisons between British behavior and the actions of common criminals make his argument very persuasive.
6. **Possible response:** The image of America as a champion of freedom over tyranny still holds true today.

Go Online Author Link For additional information about Thomas Paine, have students type in the Web Code, then select P from the alphabet, and then select Thomas Paine.

works," that God may bless you. It matters not where you live, or what rank of life you hold, the evil or the blessing will reach you all. The far and the near, the home counties and the back, the rich and the poor, will suffer or rejoice alike. The heart that feels not now, is dead: the blood of his children will curse his cowardice, who shrinks back at a time when a little might have saved the whole, and made *them* happy. (I love the man that can smile at trouble; that can gather strength from distress, and grow brave by reflection.) 'Tis the business of little minds to shrink; but he whose heart is firm, and whose conscience approves his conduct, will pursue his principles unto death. My own line of reasoning is to myself as straight and clear as a ray of light. Not all the treasures of the world, so far as I believe, could have induced me to support an offensive war, for I think it murder; but if a thief breaks into my house, burns and destroys my property, and kills or threatens to kill me, or those that are in it, and to "*bind me in all cases whatsoever,*" to his absolute will, am I to suffer it? What signifies it to me, whether he who does it is a king or a common man: my countryman, or not my countryman; whether it be done by an individual villain or an army of them? If we reason to the root of things we shall find no difference; neither can any just cause be assigned why we should punish in the one case and pardon in the other.

Critical Reading

1. **Respond:** If you were a colonist who had remained loyal to the British how would you react to Paine's argument?
2. **(a) Recall:** In the second paragraph, what terms does Paine use to describe the British king? **(b) Analyze:** Is this description realistic or exaggerated? Explain. **(c) Draw Conclusions:** Is Paine trustworthy as a reporter of historical events? Explain.
3. **(a) Recall:** In the first paragraph, with what ideas does the author justify the struggle of revolution? **(b) Interpret:** What does Paine mean when he refers to "the summer soldier" and the "sunshine patriot"?
4. **(a) Classify:** Name two emotions to which Paine appeals in this essay. **(b) Make a Judgment:** Does Paine appeal more to emotion or to reason in this essay? Support your answer.
5. **(a) Interpret:** What is the main idea of this essay? **(b) Support:** What persuasive techniques does Paine use to develop his main idea? **(c) Evaluate:** In your opinion, how persuasive is Paine's essay?
6. **Connect:** Which of Paine's images of the American Revolution still hold true today? Why?

For: More about Thomas Paine
Visit: www.PHSchool.com
Web Code: ere-9203

Apply the Skills

The Declaration of Independence • from *The Crisis, Number 1*

Literary Analysis

Persuasion

1. **(a)** Why does Jefferson present such a long list of grievances? **(b)** Does this list make his argument more or less convincing? Why?
2. What strategy does Jefferson use to organize his list of grievances—for example, time order, order of severity, or order of importance—and why do you think he chose this organization?
3. An aphorism is a brief, pointed statement expressing a wise or clever observation. Use a chart like the one shown to identify three aphorisms Paine uses and to analyze how each one contributes to his overall message.

Aphorism	Meaning	Purpose
What we obtain too cheap, we esteem too lightly.	We value only those things that cost us dearly.	to emphasize the point that the struggle for freedom is worth it

Comparing Literary Works

4. **(a)** Who is the intended **audience** for each of these works? **(b)** What kinds of supporting evidence would you expect to see in writing meant for each audience? **(c)** Does each writer offer the type of support that is most convincing for his audience? Explain.
5. In what ways does the language of each document reflect its intended audience?

Reading Strategy

Recognizing Charged Words

6. These authors carefully selected **charged words** to stir readers' emotions. What responses do each of these words evoke in you?

   a. liberty **b.** justice **c.** honor **d.** barbarous

7. In describing the colonists' British rulers, how does Paine's use of the word *thief* evoke a different response than would the word *supporters*?

Extend Understanding

8. **Social Studies Connection:** The Declaration of Independence has been a source of inspiration throughout the world, and Paine's essay contains many frequently quoted sayings. Why do you think these documents have had such a lasting impact?

QuickReview

Persuasion is writing or speech meant to get readers or listeners to think or act in a certain way.

The **audience** of a literary work is the person or group of people the author intends to reach.

Charged words contain strong connotations likely to produce an emotional response.

For: Self-test
Visit: www.PHSchool.com
Web Code: era-6202

Go Online Assessment — Students may use the **Self-test** to prepare for **Selection Test A** or **Selection Test B.**

Answers

1. **Possible responses:** (a) He wants to make it clear that the colonists are justified in their position. (b) It makes his argument more convincing by showing how much the colonists have already tolerated.
2. **Possible response:** He organizes them in order of severity, from least offensive to most offensive. He chose that organization to build the intensity of his argument.
3. Students' charts should contain aphorisms from the text.

   Another sample answer can be found in **Literary Analysis Graphic Organizer B,** p. 37 in ***Graphic Organizer Transparencies.***
4. (a) Jefferson speaks to the world, while Paine speaks more specifically to those colonists already fighting and those who he hopes will fight. (b) **Possible response:** I would expect to see carefully constructed rational arguments in writing for the British king and the world stage, but more emotional and highly charged writing for soldiers in the field. (c) Yes, they do. Although both documents are moving, Jefferson's is more closely argued whereas Paine's is more rousing, aimed at the heart rather than the head.
5. **Possible response:** Jefferson uses the language of diplomacy while Paine uses more familiar language as if he were addressing readers personally.
6. **Possible response:** (a) *Liberty* suggests an ideal life characterized by freedom. (b) *Justice* can be associated with fairness, freedom, and equality. (c) *Honor* evokes a sense of morality and dignity. (d) *Barbarous* suggests cruel and animalistic behavior.
7. **Possible response:** *Supporters* is a kinder word that suggests caretaking, while *thief* suggests a negative image of Britain.
8. **Possible response:** These documents have had a lasting impact because they express ideals of freedom, equality, and justice, which are enduringly appealing. Also, both men use convincing arguments and employ memorable language in strong appeals to human emotion.

EXTEND/ASSESS

Answers

❶ Vocabulary Lesson

Word Analysis

1. *confident:* certain; self-assured
2. *fidelity:* faithful devotion
3. *confidential:* maintaining a trust

Spelling Strategy

1. acquaint
2. acknowledge
3. acquittal
4. acquire
5. acquiesce

Vocabulary Builder

1. True
2. True
3. True
4. False
5. False
6. False
7. False
8. False
9. False

❷ Grammar and Style Lesson

1. Jefferson was patriotic, intelligent, imaginative, and courageous.
2. He wrote the Declaration of Independence, designed his home, and co/founded a university.
3. Henry was a great speaker, Jefferson was a gifted writer, and Washington was a talented military leader.
4. Paine was passionate, eloquent, inspiring, and persuasive.
5. The Declaration accused King George III of tyranny, unfair taxation, military occupation, and bullying the legislature.

Writing Application

Students' opinions should be supported by facts and contain at least two examples of parallelism.

Build Language Skills

❶ Vocabulary Lesson

Word Analysis: Latin Root *-fid-*

The Latin root *-fid-* means "faith" or "trust." An *infidel* is a person without faith, and *perfidy* is a betrayal of trust. Use your understanding of this root to define the following words.

1. confident **2.** fidelity **3.** confidential

Spelling Strategy

When you join the prefix *ac-* to a word or root beginning with *q, k,* or hard *c,* retain the *c,* as in *acclaim.* Add *ac-* to each of the words or roots below.

1. -quaint
2. -knowledge
3. -quittal
4. -quire
5. -quiesce

Vocabulary Builder: True or False

Indicate which of the statements below are true and which are false. Explain your answers.

1. If a child *acquiesces* about being put to bed, she accepts her bedtime.
2. Leaders should have *magnanimity.*
3. There is no need for *redress* if no wrong has been committed.
4. American citizens would not be right to protest *usurpations* of their property.
5. Enemies have *consanguinity* toward one another.
6. The quality of *perfidy* is honorable.
7. *Unalienable* rights must be agreed upon annually.
8. *Infidels* observe certain religious holidays.
9. A pastor's *impious* behavior would be celebrated by his parishioners.

❷ Grammar and Style Lesson

Parallelism

Parallelism is the repetition of words, phrases, clauses, or sentences that are similar in structure or meaning.

Example: He has *plundered our seas, ravaged our coasts, burned our towns,* and *destroyed the lives of our people.* (parallel verb phrases: *verb-our-object*)

Practice Rewrite each sentence to correct errors in parallel structure.

1. Jefferson was patriotic, intelligent, imaginative, and he had courage.
2. He wrote the Declaration, designed his home, and was one of the people who founded a university.
3. Henry was a great speaker, Jefferson was a gifted writer, and the talented military leader was Washington.
4. Paine was passionate, eloquent, inspiring, and he was persuasive.
5. The Declaration accused King George III of tyranny, of unfair taxation, of military occupation, and it said he bullied the legislature.

Writing Application Write your opinion on an issue about which you have strong feelings. Use two examples of parallelism to emphasize ideas.

WG *Prentice Hall Writing and Grammar Connection: Chapter 20, Section 6*

Assessment Practice

Recognize Cause and Effect **(For more practice, see *Standardized Test Preparation Workbook*, p. 9.)**

To help students understand cause-and-effect relationships, have them reread pp. 170–171. Then ask:

Which of the following actions of the British king was NOT a cause of the American colonists' Declaration of Independence?

A His refusal to pass laws created by the colonists

B His dissolution of colonial houses of representatives

C His interference with the American justice system

D His personal visit to the thirteen colonies

Choices *A, B,* and *C* contributed to the Americans' decision to declare independence from Britain. Choice *D* is the correct choice, because it was NOT a cause of the revolution.

Writing Lesson

Timed Writing: A Proposal to the Principal

Like Jefferson and Paine, you can change your world with the persuasive use of words. Choose a problem or troubling situation in your school. Then, draft a proposal to the principal explaining why the situation needs attention and how you think it should be corrected. Use parallelism to emphasize your ideas. (*40 minutes*)

Prewriting *(10 minutes)* List the reasons that the situation in your school should be changed. Write details—facts, examples, explanations—supporting each reason. Keep word connotations in mind as you choose evidence.

Drafting *(20 minutes)* Use language with positive connotations to present ideas you would like your audience to accept; use language with negative connotations to present ideas you would like your audience to reject. Remember, however, that because you are writing for the principal, you should demonstrate respect.

Model: Drafting with Forceful Language

Separate lounges for upper- and lowerclassmen reflect superior planning. Wise thinkers recognize that each group needs a place to pursue age-appropriate activities.

Terms such as *superior* and *wise* reinforce the soundness of this proposal.

Revising *(10 minutes)* Review your proposal and revise any statements that seem unreasonable. Check that you have offered evidence in addition to using forceful language to support your argument.

Prentice Hall Writing and Grammar Connection: Chapter 7, Section 4

Extend Your Learning

Listening and Speaking With a group, write and deliver two **news reports**. First, recount the signing of the Declaration. Then, present the version of the story that might have appeared on London television. For each, remember these tips:

- Include the facts of the events.
- Consider what the news means to each specific audience.

Present both reports to classmates. **[Group Activity]**

Research and Technology A **précis** is a concise summary of essential points or statements. Research Thomas Paine's life, using library and Internet sources to gather information about his philosophies and activities. Then, write a précis detailing Paine's contributions to the Revolutionary cause.

For: An additional research activity
Visit: www.PHSchool.com
Web Code: erd-7202

3 Writing Lesson

You may use this Writing Lesson as timed-writing practice, or you may allow students to develop the essay as a writing assignment over several days.

- To guide students in writing this proposal, give them the **Support for Writing Lesson,** p. 51, in ***General Resources.*** Remind them to organize their evidence for the greatest impact as Jefferson did with his list of grievances.
- Use the Writing Lesson to guide students in developing their proposals.
- Use the Problem-Solution Essay rubrics, pp. 59–60 in ***General Resources,*** to evaluate students' proposals.

4 Listening and Speaking

- Divide each group into two teams. Have one team focus on the colonial news report and the other focus on the British report. Then, have the teams discuss the facts and events they want to include in their reports.
- Suggest some typical television news elements that students might want to include in their reports— for example, video footage, still photographs, voice-over narration, and mood music.
- Encourage students to create a script or storyboard for their report, noting how each visual will work with the spoken text.
- Have students rehearse their reports before making their final presentation to the class.
- Use the rubric for Evaluating a Media Presentation, p. 86 in ***General Resources,*** to evaluate students presentations.
- The **Support for Extend your Learning** page (***Unit 2 Resources,*** p. 52) provides guided note-taking opportunities to help students to use the Extend Your Learning Activities.

Go Online Research — Have students type in the Web Code for another research activity.

Assessment Resources

The following resources can be used to assess students' knowledge and skills.

Unit 2 Resources
- **Selection Test A,** pp. 54–56
- **Selection Test B,** pp. 57–59

General Resources
- **Rubrics for Problem–Solution Essay,** pp. 59–60
- **Rubric for Evaluating a Media Presentation,** p. 86

Go Online Assessment — Students may use the **Self-test** to prepare for **Selection Test A** or **Selection Test B.**

Meeting Your Standards

Students will

1. **analyze and respond to literary elements.**
   - Literary Analysis: Personification
2. **read, comprehend, analyze, and critique two poems.**
   - Reading Strategy: Clarifying Meaning
   - Reading Check questions
   - Apply the Skills questions
   - Assessment Practice (ATE)
3. **develop vocabulary.**
   - Vocabulary Lesson: Latin prefix *re-*
4. **understand and apply written and oral language conventions.**
   - Spelling Strategy
   - Grammar and Style Lesson: Subject and Verb Agreement
5. **develop writing proficiency.**
   - Writing Lesson: Inscription for a Monument
6. **develop appropriate research strategies.**
   - Extend Your Learning: Graphic Display
7. **understand and apply listening and speaking strategies.**
   - Extend Your Learning: Dramatic Reading

Block Scheduling: Use one 90-minute class period to preteach the skills and have students read the selection. Use a second 90-minute class period to assess students' mastery of skills, extend their learning, and monitor their progress.

Homework Suggestions

Following are possibilities for homework assignments.

- Support pages from *Unit 2 Resources:*
  Literary Analysis
  Reading Strategy
  Vocabulary Builder
  Grammar and Style
- An Extend Your Learning project and the Writing Lesson for this selection group may be completed over several days.

Step-by-Step Teaching Guide	Pacing Guide
PRETEACH	
• Administer Vocabulary and Reading Warm-ups as necessary.	5 min.
• Engage students' interest with the motivation activity.	5 min.
• Read and discuss author and background features. **FT**	10 min.
• Introduce the Literary Analysis Skill: Personification. **FT**	5 min.
• Introduce the Reading Strategy: Clarifying Meaning. **FT**	10 min.
• Prepare students to read by teaching the selection vocabulary. **FT**	
TEACH	
• Informally monitor comprehension while students read independently or in groups. **FT**	30 min.
• Monitor students' comprehension with the Reading Check notes.	as students read
• Reinforce vocabulary with Vocabulary Builder notes.	as students read
• Develop students' understanding of personification with the Literary Analysis annotations. **FT**	5 min.
• Develop students' ability to clarify meaning with the Reading Strategy annotations. **FT**	5 min.
ASSESS/EXTEND	
• Assess students' comprehension and mastery of the Literary Analysis and Reading Strategy by having them answer the Apply the Skills questions. **FT**	15 min.
• Have students complete the Vocabulary Development Lesson and the Grammar and Style Lesson. **FT**	15 min.
• Apply students' ability to use a persuasive tone by using the Writing Lesson. **FT**	45 min. or homework
• Apply students' understanding using by one or more of the Extend Your Learning activities.	20–90 min. or homework
• Administer Selection Test A or Selection Test B. **FT**	15 min.

Resources

PRINT

Unit 2 Resources

- Vocabulary Warm-up Word Lists [**L1, L2, EL**] .... p. 60
- Vocabulary Warm-up Practice [**L1, L2, EL**] .... p. 61
- Reading Warm-up A [**L1, L2, EL**] .... p. 62
- Reading Warm-up B [**L1, L2, L3**] .... p. 63

TRANSPARENCY

Graphic Organizer Transparencies

- Literary Analysis Graphic Organizer A [**L3**] .... p. 40
- Literary Analysis Graphic Organizer B [**L1, L2, EL**] .... p. 41
- Reading Strategy Graphic Organizer A [**L3**] .... p. 38
- Reading Strategy Graphic Organizer B [**L1, L2, EL**] .... p. 39

PRINT

Reader's Notebook [**L2**]
Reader's Notebook: Adapted Version [**L1**]
Reader's Notebook: English Learner's Version [**EL**]

Unit 2 Resources

- Literary Analysis [**L3**] .... p. 62
- Reading Strategy [**L3**] .... p. 63
- Vocabulary Builder [**L3**] .... p. 64

TECHNOLOGY

Listening to Literature Audio CDs [**L2, EL**]

PRINT

Unit 2 Resources

- Grammar and Style [**L3**] .... p. 67
- Support for Writing Lesson [**L3**] .... p. 68
- Support for Extend Your Learning [**L3**] .... p. 69
- Enrichment [**L4**] .... p. 70
- Selection Test A [**L1, L2, EL**] .... pp. 71–73
- Selection Test B [**L3, L4**] .... pp. 74–76

General Resources

- Rubrics for Descriptive Essay [**L3**] .... pp. 63–64

TECHNOLOGY

Go Online: Research [**L3**]
Go Online: Self-test [**L3**]
***ExamView*®, Test Bank** [**L3**]

Choosing Resources for Differentiated Instruction

[**L1**] Special Needs Students
[**L2**] Below-Level Students
[**L3**] All Students
[**L4**] Advanced Students
[**EL**] English Learners

FT Fast Track Instruction: To move the lesson more quickly, use the strategies and activities identified with **FT**.

Scaffolding for Less Proficient and Advanced Students

The leveled Critical Thinking questions after selections progress in the levels of thinking required to answer them. To address the needs of your different students, you may use the (a) level questions for your less proficient students and the (b) level questions with your on-level and advanced students. The occasional (c) level questions are appropriate for your advanced students.

PRENTICE HALL **TeacherEXPRESS™** Plan · Teach · Assess — Use this complete suite of powerful teaching tools to make lesson planning and testing quicker and easier.

PRENTICE HALL **StudentEXPRESS™** Learn · Study · Succeed — Use the interactive textbook (online and on CD-ROM) to make selections and activities come alive with audio and video support and interactive questions.

PRETEACH

Motivation

Understanding Wheatley's poems depends on students' ability to recognize personification. Write a list of common items on the board, such as rubber band, wind, table, cloud, car, newspaper, snow, rock, sparrow, leaf, and book. In small groups, ask students to provide sentences that give each item a human characteristic, such as "The *wind* gripped the tree and shook it violently." Put each group's sentences on the chalkboard. Compare the effect of various instances of personification. For instance, a leaf that dances in the wind takes on a different characteristic than one that hangs on tenaciously, shouldering the brutal buffeting of the wind.

❶ Background

More About the Author

Wheatley's prominent Massachusetts supporters—led by Governor Thomas Hutchinson—had administered an oral examination to her to persuade themselves of her intellectual and creative capacity. Impressed by her answers, they drafted a two-paragraph letter to the public stating, in part:

We . . . assure the World, that the POEMS specified in the following Page, were (as we verily believe) written by PHILLIS, a young Negro Girl, who was but a few Years since, brought . . . from *Africa.*

Build Skills *Poems*

❶ An Hymn to the Evening • To His Excellency, General Washington

Phillis Wheatley (1753?–1784)

Although she was an enslaved African whose native language was not English, Phillis Wheatley achieved success as a poet at an early age and went on to become one of the finest American poets of her day. This was an amazing feat, considering that few women in the colonies and even fewer slaves could read or write.

Born in West Africa, Wheatley was brought to America on a slave ship when she was about eight years old. She was purchased by John Wheatley, a Boston merchant, in 1761, probably as a gift for his wife Susannah. The Wheatleys gave Phillis their name and converted her to Christianity. They also recognized the girl's high intelligence and taught her to read and write. She avidly read the Bible, Latin and Greek classics, and works by contemporary English poets. At age thirteen, she saw her first poem published.

Fame Abroad at an Early Age In 1770, when she published a poem about the death of George Whitehead, a celebrated English clergyman, Wheatley became famous. Two years later, Wheatley met several British aristocrats who admired her poetry and helped her to publish *Poems on Various Subjects: Religious and Moral* in London in 1773. This was probably the first published work by an African in the colonies.

In a foreword to the book, the publisher claimed that persons who had read the poems felt that "Numbers would be ready to suspect they were not really the Writings of Phillis." Therefore, he offered an "attestation" to their authorship, which was signed by eighteen prominent Massachusetts men, among them John Hancock. Phillis Wheatley was well received by London society, and Benjamin Franklin visited her there. However, *Poems on Various Subjects: Religious and Moral* was not published in the United States until 1786, two years after her death.

The Story Behind the Poem During the Revolutionary War, Wheatley wrote a poem addressed to the commander of the American forces, George Washington. In October 1775, Wheatley sent the poem to Washington. He responded:

I thank you most sincerely for your polite notice of me in the elegant lines you enclosed; and however undeserving I may be of such encomium [high praise] and panegyric [tribute], the style and manner exhibit a striking proof of your poetical talents; in honor of which, and as a tribute justly due you, I would have published the poem, had I not been apprehensive that, while I only meant to give the world this new instance of your genius, I might have incurred the imputation of vanity. . . .

Slide From Glory Though she was freed in 1773, the last several years of Wheatley's life were filled with hardship and sorrow. Three of her children died in infancy, her husband was jailed for debt, and she fell into obscurity as a poet. Though she assembled a second collection of her poetry, the manuscript was lost before it could be published. With her husband in jail and her fame having faded, Phillis Wheatley died alone and impoverished in 1784.

In the centuries since Wheatley's death, her star has again risen. She is now seen as an important forerunner—the first writer of African origin to gain a voice in the United States.

Preview

Connecting to the Literature

A movie, a haircut, a joke—you may informally praise several things or people every day. At times you may express praise in a more formal way—in a song, essay, or poem—as Phillis Wheatley does in these selections.

Literary Analysis

Personification

Personification is a figure of speech that attributes human powers or qualities to something that is not human, such as an inanimate object, an aspect of nature, or an abstract idea. For instance, note the way Phillis Wheatley describes the ocean in these lines:

Enwrapp'd in tempest and a night of storms;
Astonish'd ocean feels the wild uproar . . .

Here, the poet personifies the sea by giving it a human emotion and sensibility. In both poems, notice how Wheatley uses personification to portray her subjects in human terms.

Comparing Literary Works

Beginning with the earliest epic poems, the **poem of praise** has had a long history in literature. Some poems of praise celebrate the deeds of a hero, others celebrate the natural world, and others celebrate ordinary objects. Though both of Wheatley's poems are tributes, their subjects are very different. As you read, think about how the subject matter leads Wheatley to use distinct descriptive language and to create very different moods and meaning in each poem.

Reading Strategy

Clarifying Meaning

When reading poetry, you may need to **clarify the meaning** of passages that at first seem unclear. In these poems, Wheatley often inverts common sentence order by placing a verb before its subject. Clarify meaning by rephrasing unusual word orders and checking the definitions of unfamiliar words. Use a chart like the one shown to aid your understanding.

Original Sentence
See mother earth her offspring's fate bemoan.

Define Words
offspring=children
bemoan=grieve

Reordered and Clarified Sentence
See mother earth grieve over her children's fate.

Vocabulary Builder

placid (plas′ id) *adj.* tranquil; calm; quiet (p. 182)

scepter (sep′ tər) *n.* a rod or staff held by rulers as a symbol of sovereignty (p. 182)

celestial (sə les′ chəl) *adj.* of the heavens (p. 185)

refulgent (ri ful′ jənt) *adj.* radiant; shining (p. 185)

propitious (prō pish′ əs) *adj.* favorably inclined or disposed (p. 185)

refluent (ref′ lo͞o ənt) *adj.* flowing back (p. 185)

pensive (pen′ siv) *adj.* thinking deeply or seriously (p. 186)

Differentiated Instruction — Solutions for All Learners

Support for Special Needs Students
Have students complete the **Preview** and **Build Skills** pages for the selections in the ***Reader's Notebook: Adapted Version.*** These pages provide a selection summary, an abbreviated presentation of the reading and literary skills, and the graphic organizer on the **Build Skills** page in the student book.

Support for Less Proficient Readers
Have students complete the **Preview** and **Build Skills** pages for the selections in the ***Reader's Notebook.*** These pages provide a selection summary, an abbreviated presentation of the reading and literary skills, and the graphic organizer on the **Build Skills** page in the student book.

Support for English Learners
Have students complete the **Preview** and **Build Skills** pages for the selections in the ***Reader's Notebook: English Learner's Version.*** These pages provide a selection summary, an abbreviated presentation of the skills, additional contextual vocabulary, and the graphic organizer on the **Build Skills** page in the student book.

❷ Literary Analysis

Personification

- Tell students that as they read Phillis Wheatley's poems, they will focus on personification, the attribution of human powers or qualities to something that is not human.
- Have students read the instruction about personification.
- Ask students to recall the Motivation activity and then **ask** what human qualities Wheatley attributes to the sea in the excerpt on this page.
  Answer: She gives it the capacity to feel astonishment and to experience *wild uproar.*
- Use the instruction for Comparing Literary Works to prepare students to read two very different Wheatley poems.

❸ Reading Strategy

Clarifying Meaning

- Help students recognize that they can clarify unusual poetic wording by focusing on word meaning and word order.
- Suggest that students begin by identifying and then defining unfamiliar words in the poems.
- Then, have students look for words that appear out of their usual order. Have students experiment with a variety of word orders and see which best clarifies the meaning.
- Give students a copy of **Reading Strategy Graphic Organizer A,** p. 38 in ***Graphic Organizer Transparencies,*** to use. Model the clarification process using the diagram on the student page, and direct students to use their own graphic organizer as they read.

Vocabulary Builder

- Pronounce each vocabulary word for students, and read the definitions as a class. Have students identify any words with which they are already familiar.

Learning Modalities
Visual/Spatial Learners
To acquaint students with personification, have them find a picture of a statue of the goddess Columbia. You might remind them that a statue of Columbia sits atop the dome of the Capitol in Washington, D.C. When they read "To His Excellency, General Washington," ask students to compare a sculptor's interpretation with Wheatley's.

❶ About the Selection

In "An Hymn to the Evening," Wheatley directs her attention to the close of day by describing a sunset and the night's restorative powers. Beginning after sunrise, storms have shaken the earth. After the rain, however, the aroma of blossoms, the sound of water in streams and the songs of birds make music. By evening, the western sky is the most beautiful—a deep red. Grateful to God for the light, the narrator asks for a peaceful night of sleep and to awaken the next morning refreshed and ready for the day's tasks.

❷ Literary Analysis
Personification

- Read the bracketed text aloud for students, pausing at punctuation to give the lines their proper rhythm.
- Have students paraphrase the lines if they can.
  Possible response: The west wind brings the scent of flowers on the air.
- **Ask** students the following question: How is the wind personified in these lines?
  Answer: The wind breathes and exhales incense.

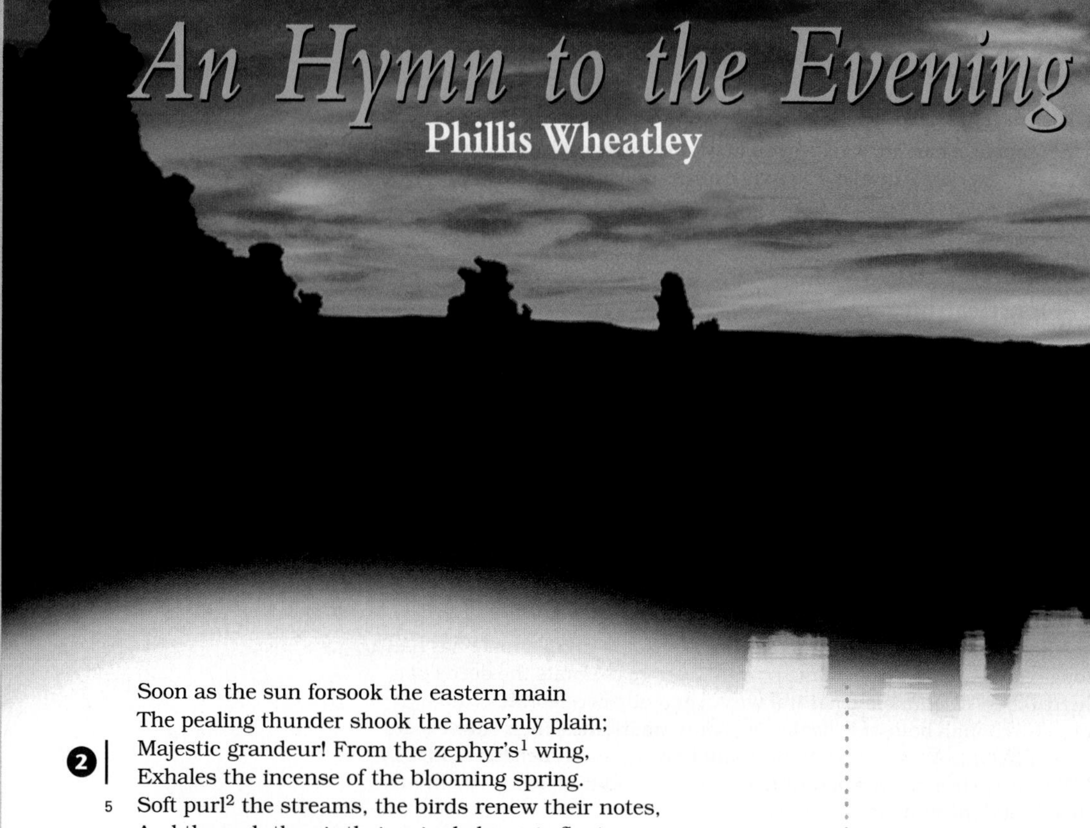

An Hymn to the Evening

Phillis Wheatley

Soon as the sun forsook the eastern main
The pealing thunder shook the heav'nly plain;
❷ Majestic grandeur! From the zephyr's[1] wing,
Exhales the incense of the blooming spring.
Soft purl[2] the streams, the birds renew their notes,
And through the air their mingled music floats.

Through all the heav'ns what beauteous dyes are spread!
But the west glories in the deepest red:
So may our breasts with ev'ry virtue glow,
The living temples of our God below!

Filled with the praise of him who gives the light;
And draws the sable curtains of the night,
Let placid slumbers soothe each weary mind,
At morn to wake more heav'nly, more refined;
So shall the labours of the day begin
More pure, more guarded from the snares of sin.

Night's leaden scepter seals my drowsy eyes,
Then cease, my song, till far *Aurora* rise.

Vocabulary Builder
placid (plas′ id) *adj.* tranquil; calm; quiet

scepter (sep′ tər) *n.* a rod or staff held by rulers as a symbol of sovereignty

1. **zephyr's** (zef′ ərz) *n.* belonging to the west wind.
2. **purl** (purl) *v.* to move in ripples or with a murmuring sound.

Differentiated Instruction Solutions for All Learners

Accessibility at a Glance

	An Hymn to the Evening	To His Excellency, General Washington
Context	Nature poem	Poem glorifying Revolutionary cause
Language	18th-century diction and syntax; rich vocabulary	18th-century diction and syntax; difficult vocabulary
Concept Level	Accessible (description of natural events)	Abstract (personification of America)
Literary Merit	historical importance; female African American colonial poet	historical importance; female African American colonial poet
Lexile	NP	NP
Overall Rating	Average	More challenging

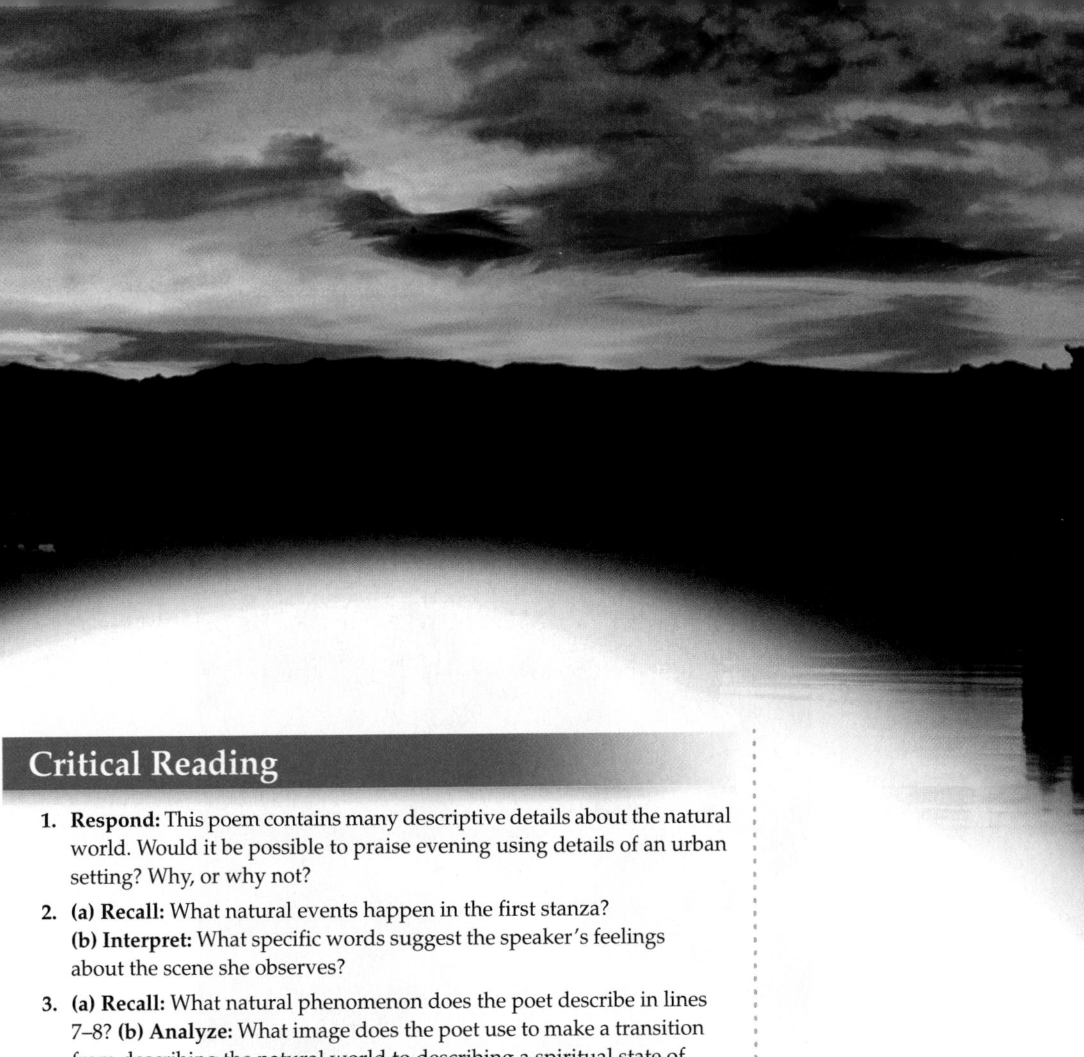

Critical Reading

1. **Respond:** This poem contains many descriptive details about the natural world. Would it be possible to praise evening using details of an urban setting? Why, or why not?
2. **(a) Recall:** What natural events happen in the first stanza? **(b) Interpret:** What specific words suggest the speaker's feelings about the scene she observes?
3. **(a) Recall:** What natural phenomenon does the poet describe in lines 7–8? **(b) Analyze:** What image does the poet use to make a transition from describing the natural world to describing a spiritual state of being? **(c) Draw Conclusions:** According to the poet, what are the "living temples of our God below"?
4. **(a) Recall:** What descriptive details does Wheatley use to describe the evening? **(b) Recall:** What details does she use to describe the morning? **(c) Compare and Contrast:** What mood or feeling does the poet connect with each time of day?
5. **(a) Recall:** When, according to Wheatley, are human beings more pure? **(b) Evaluate:** In your view, how accurate is Wheatley's contrast of a person's state of mind at night and in the morning?

Go Online
Author Link
For: More about Phillis Wheatley
Visit: www.PHSchool.com
Web Code: ere-9204

ASSESS

Answers

1. **Possible answer:** Yes, one can praise evening with urban details. For example, one can describe the changing light reflecting in buildings.
2. (a) On a spring afternoon, a brief thundershower occurs; the aroma of flowers is blown through the air by the wind; the sounds of streams and birds blend together. (b) The words "majestic grandeur" and "music" suggest Wheatley's positive feelings about the scene.
3. (a) She describes a sunset. (b) She uses the image of people glowing with virtue just as the sky glows with light. (c) People are "the living temples of our God below."
4. (a) Wheatley uses descriptive details such as "beauteous dyes" and "deepest red." (b) Wheatley describes people waking in a state of mind that is more "heav'nly, more refined" and "more pure, more guarded." (c) **Possible response:** She connects evening with an ability to soothe and refresh; morning with a feeling of purity.
5. (a) They are more pure in the morning. (b) **Possible response:** Students may cite their own experiences with the refreshing power of sleep.

Go Online **Author Link** For additional information about Phillis Wheatley, have students type in the Web Code, then select W from the alphabet, and then select Phillis Wheatley.

Differentiated Instruction Solutions for All Learners

Strategy for Special Needs Students

To help students clarify the meaning of difficult lines, use this strategy: Suggest that students write out any difficult lines and then use different colored markers to circle the subject, underline the verb, and double underscore the object of the verb. Afterward, suggest that they write the sentence again, reordering the words.

Strategy for Less Proficient Readers

Students might have an easier time understanding the meaning of this poem by making a chart in which they list the different parts of the day the poem mentions—the daylight hours, sunset, and night—as well as the corresponding line numbers of the poem. Students can then record details from the poem about these times of day.

Vocabalary for English Learners

Students will need help with Wheatley's use of apostrophes. For example, point out the words "heav'ns," "ev'ry," and "heav'nly." Explain that the apostrophes indicate missing letters. Then, help students complete each word and read the pertinent lines of the poem to reinforce comprehension.

❸ About the Selection

This poem glorifies the bravery and goodness of the revolutionary cause by personifying America as the goddess Columbia. The poet pictures Columbia as a daughter of Mother Earth, who sympathizes with her daughter's fight as she faces her enemies. The poem then praises George Washington as "first in peace and honors," famous for both his bravery and goodness, the perfect leader for a nation defended by heaven, a leader who has the moral support of other nations that hope America will win the war against Britain. The poem asks Washington to proceed, guided by the goddess; and Wheatley suggests that he will be rewarded with a crown, a mansion, and a golden throne.

❹ Humanities

Liberty and Washington

This folk art image glorifies Washington in many of the same ways as Wheatley's poem does. The light bathes the statue of George Washington and the woman standing above him as if to suggest their purity and inner light. Use these questions for discussion:

1. How do the words on the pedestal reflect Phillis Wheatley's attitude toward George Washington?
   Answer: They reinforce her admiration of Washington as a military leader, diplomat, and national hero.
2. What elements from the poem can you find in the painting?
   Possible responses: The painting displays a crown, a wreath of laurels, a flag, and the female goddess who suggests the figure of Columbia.

❺ Critical Viewing

Answer: Students may note that the goddess tramples the British crown underfoot while she places the laurel wreath, a symbol of victory, on Washington's head. This suggests Washington's leadership in the colonists' victory over England.

❸ To His Excellency, General Washington

PHILLIS WHEATLEY

❹

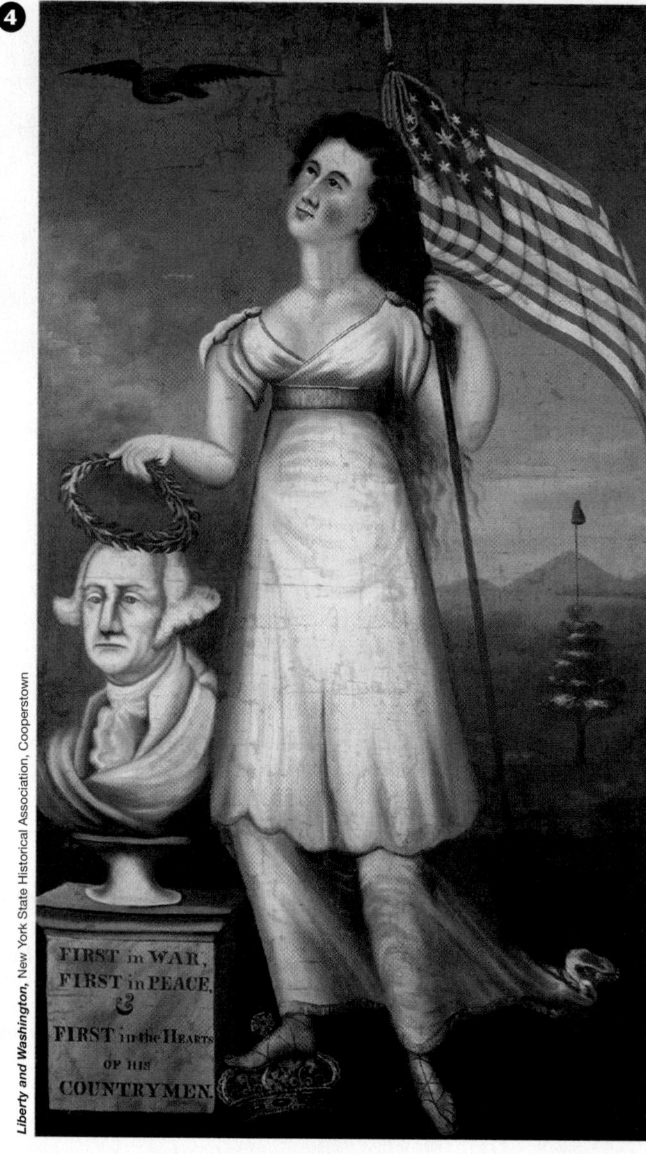

FIRST in WAR,
FIRST in PEACE,
&
FIRST in the HEARTS
OF HIS
COUNTRYMEN.

Liberty and Washington, New York State Historical Association, Cooperstown

❺ ◀ **Critical Viewing** Noting the symbols of the Revolutionary conflict, explain the action of the painting. **[Interpret]**

Differentiated Instruction Solutions for All Learners

Enrichment for Advanced Readers
Suggest that students read additional works by Phillis Wheatley. Provide student with the Life and Works of Phillis Wheatley or Memoir and Poems of Phillis Wheatley. You may wish to use **Authors In Depth,** *The American Experience,* which contains the following selections:

- "To the Right Honorable William, Earl of Dartmouth, His Majesty's Principal Secretary of State for North America"
- "To S.M., a Young African Painter, on Seeing His works.
- "On Imagination"
- "Letter" by John Wheatley

After students have read these or other works by Wheatley, review the instruction on Comparing Literary Works. Discuss whether the additional works students read are **poems of praise.** Invite students to provide specific details from the poems, such as descriptive language, to support their interpretation.

❻ **Background** Phillis Wheatley was the first poet to use the goddess Columbia to personify America. By giving the country's muse a name based on the explorer Columbus, Wheatley added to the new nation's mythology. The image caught on. In fact, a statue of Columbia sits atop the dome of the Capitol building in Washington, D.C.

Celestial choir! enthron'd in realms of light,
Columbia's scenes of glorious toils I write.
While freedom's cause her anxious breast alarms,
She flashes dreadful in refulgent arms.
See mother earth her offspring's fate bemoan,
And nations gaze at scenes before unknown!
See the bright beams of heaven's revolving light
Involved in sorrows and the veil of night!
The goddess comes, she moves divinely fair,
Olive and laurel binds her golden hair:
Wherever shines this native of the skies,
Unnumber'd charms and recent graces rise.
Muse![1] bow propitious while my pen relates
How pour her armies through a thousand gates,
❼ As when Eolus[2] heaven's fair face deforms,
Enwrapp'd in tempest and a night of storms;
Astonish'd ocean feels the wild uproar,
The refluent surges beat the sounding shore;
Or thick as leaves in Autumn's golden reign,
Such, and so many, moves the warrior's train.
In bright array they seek the work of war,
Where high unfurl'd the ensign[3] waves in air.
Shall I to Washington their praise recite?
Enough thou know'st them in the fields of fight.
Thee, first in peace and honors,—we demand
The grace and glory of thy martial band.
Fam'd for thy valor, for thy virtues more,
Hear every tongue thy guardian aid implore!
One century scarce perform'd its destined round,
When Gallic[4] powers Columbia's fury found;
And so may you, whoever dares disgrace
The land of freedom's heaven-defended race!

Vocabulary Builder

celestial (sə les′ chəl) *adj.* of the heavens

refulgent (ri ful′ jənt) *adj.* radiant; shining

Vocabulary Builder

propitious (prō pish′ əs) *adj.* favorably inclined or disposed

refluent (ref′ lo͞o ənt) *adj.* flowing back

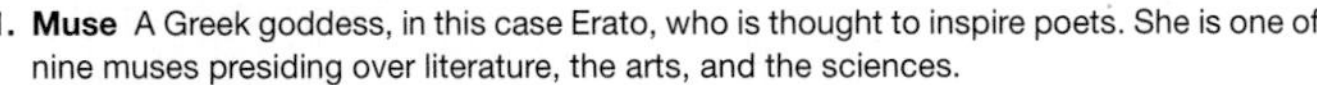

1. **Muse** A Greek goddess, in this case Erato, who is thought to inspire poets. She is one of nine muses presiding over literature, the arts, and the sciences.
2. **Eolus** (ē′ ə ləs) the Greek god of the winds.
3. **ensign** (en′ sin) flag.
4. **Gallic** (gal′ ik) French. The colonists, led by Washington, defeated the French in the French and Indian War (1754–1763).

❽ 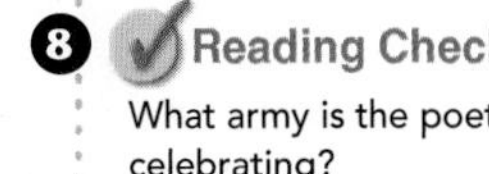
Reading Check

What army is the poet celebrating?

❻ Background
Culture

The publication of Phillis Wheatley's work merits special note for several reasons. First, she was female; few female authors anywhere had gained recognition by the eighteenth century. Second, she was African American; that group, too, had been denied literary recognition. Third, she was a slave; slaves generally could neither read nor write. Thus, Wheatley earned many "firsts." Nevertheless, for years she stood alone as an African American female author before other African American women joined the literary ranks.

❼ Literary Analysis
Personification

- Have students read the bracketed text aloud. Ask them to paraphrase the lines.
  Possible response: Strong winds and storms cause ocean turbulence and heavy surf.
- **Monitor Progress Ask** students how heaven, the ocean, and autumn are personified in the bracketed lines.
  Answer: Heaven has a "fair face"; the ocean is "astonished" by the wind's "wild uproar"; autumn has a "golden reign."

❽ Reading Check

Answer: She is celebrating the American Revolutionary army.

Differentiated Instruction
Solutions for All Learners

Support for Less Proficient Readers

Increase students' access and their enjoyment of Wheatley's poem by playing the Listening to **Literature/Audio CDs**. Encourage students to first listen to the poem with their eyes closed, trying to picture Wheatley's images. Then, have students listen again as they read along silently. Tell students that they can appreciate the mood and emotions these visual images evoke even when they don't entirely understand a poem's words or meaning.

Strategy for Gifted/Talented Students

In "To His Excellency, General Washington," Phillis Wheatley personifies elements of nature, such as the ocean, autumn, and the earth. Have students choose an object or idea of their own to personify. It might be something in nature or an abstract idea such as freedom. Encourage students to communicate their personification in performance or in art.

Fix'd are the eyes of nations on the scales,
For in their hopes Columbia's arm prevails.
Anon Britannia[5] droops the pensive head,
While round increase the rising hills of dead.
Ah! cruel blindness to Columbia's state!
Lament thy thirst of boundless power too late.
    Proceed, great Chief, with virtue on thy side,
Thy ev'ry action let the goddess guide.
A crown, a mansion, and a throne that shine,
With gold unfading, WASHINGTON! be thine.

Vocabulary Builder

pensive (pen′ siv) *adj.* thinking deeply or seriously

5. **Britannia** England.

Critical Reading

1. **Respond:** Do you think that Columbia and General Washington are worthy subjects of the poet's praise? Explain.
2. **(a) Recall:** In lines 9–12 of "To His Excellency, General Washington," how is Columbia described? **(b) Deduce:** What does this image of Columbia suggest about the speaker's view of America?
3. **(a) Recall:** In lines 13–20, to what natural phenomenon is the American army compared? **(b) Interpret:** What does this comparison suggest about the power of American military forces in battle?
4. **(a) Recall:** Note three instances where Wheatley indicates a relationship between God and the American cause. **(b) Analyze:** What is the nature of this relationship?
5. **(a) Infer:** What specific details in the last two lines reflect the influence of the British political system? **(b) Deduce:** What position in a new government does the speaker assume Washington will occupy? **(c) Synthesize:** Which details in this depiction of Washington suggest the debate about the kind of government to be established after the war?
6. **(a) Relate:** If you were going to write a poetic tribute, how would you personify the spirit of the United States today? **(b) Synthesize:** Whom would you choose for the subject of such a poetic tribute? Explain your choice.

For: More about Phillis Wheatley
Visit: www.PHSchool.com
Web Code: ere-9204

ASSESS

1. **Possible answer:** Columbia and Washington are worthy of praise because both stand for something invaluable—freedom.
2. (a) She is described as beautiful (fair), charming, and graceful with golden hair bound by olive and laurel. (b) America is beautiful and gracious.
3. (a) The army is compared to the constant beating of waves on the shore during a storm and to the continuous shower of leaves during autumn. (b) **Possible response:** They suggest that the American military forces are powerful and numerous.
4. (a) **Possible responses:** She uses the words "heaven-defended race," "a crown, a mansion, and a throne," and "heaven's revolving light." (b) **Possible response:** God supports the American cause.
5. (a) **Possible response:** They suggest that the new nation will create a government on the model of Britain's monarchy. (b) He will be its king. (c) It hints at a conflict between those seeking a monarchy and those desiring democracy.
6. (a) Students' answers will vary depending upon current events and their own points of view. (b) Students may select any person who seems worthy of such a tribute.

Go Online Author Link For additional information about Phillis Wheatley, have students type in the Web Code, then select W from the alphabet, and then select Phillis Wheatley.

Apply the Skills

An Hymn to the Evening • To His Excellency, General Washington

Literary Analysis

Personification

1. **(a)** In lines 9–12 of "To His Excellency, General Washington," how does the poet characterize Columbia? **(b)** What details does she use to describe Columbia's appearance?
2. Use a chart like the one shown to analyze other examples of **personification** that appear in "To His Excellency . . .".

Object/Idea	Human Qualities		Poet's Meaning
Eolus heaven's fair face deforms	The sky has a face.		Wind makes the sky turbulent.

3. Compare and contrast Wheatley's personification of America as the goddess Columbia with the common personification of the United States as Uncle Sam.

Comparing Literary Works

4. Compare the two poems in this section. Without seeing her name, could you tell they are by the same poet? Explain.
5. In what ways does the descriptive language and mood of each **poem of praise** reflect its distinct subject?
6. Both of these poems are written in couplets—two consecutive lines of poetry that rhyme. Do you think the couplet works equally well in both of these poems? Why, or why not?

Reading Strategy

Clarifying Meaning

7. **Clarify** lines 11–14 of "To His Excellency, General Washington" by explaining the meaning of *unnumber'd* and *graces* and reordering the sentence parts.
8. What effect does the inverted subject and verb order have on the reader of today?

Extend Understanding

9. **Social Studies Connection:** How might a historian's treatment of the British-American conflict differ from Wheatley's treatment of the same subject in "To His Excellency, General Washington"?

QuickReview

Personification is a figure of speech that attributes human powers or qualities to something that is not human.

Poems of praise are often written in tribute to heroes, the natural world, or even ordinary objects.

To **clarify the meaning** of poetry, define unfamiliar words and rephrase unusual word orders.

Go Online
Assessment

For: Self-test
Visit: www.PHSchool.com
Web Code: era-6203

Answers

1. (a) Columbia is characterized as a powerful, flashing, resplendent goddess. (b) The goddess moves divinely; her hair is gold and bound by olive and laurel leaves.
2. Students may cite Wheatley's personification of the United States as the goddess Columbia or any other use of personification in the poem.

   Another sample answer can be found on **Literary Analysis Graphic Organizer B,** p. 41 in ***Graphic Organizer Transparencies.***
3. **Possible response:** In personifying America as a goddess, Wheatley elevates the nation to a higher plane. She presents it as divinely featured and blessed. The image of America as Uncle Sam conjures a more everyday persona for the nation.
4. **Possible response:** Yes, the personification, references to classical literary figures, and inverted word orders mark both these poems as Wheatley's.
5. In "An Hymn to the Evening," Wheatley's descriptive language is highly sensual and largely natural. The mood is peaceful. In "To His Excellency, General Washington," Wheatley uses military descriptive language and the mood is celebratory.
6. Students may feel that the couplets work better in "To His Excellency, General Washing- ton" because they echo the marching rhythm of an army.
7. The word *unnumber'd* means "numerous" and *graces* means "beauties." *Wherever this native of the skies shines, unnumber'd charms and recent graces rise. Muse! bow propitious while my pen relates how her armies pour through a thousand gates.*
8. It makes the poetry more difficult for today's reader to understand. It also seems more flowery, more poetic, and less straightforward.
9. **Possible response:** A scholarly historian would probably rely almost entirely on facts and would attempt to avoid bias and the appearance of nationalism.

Go Online Assessment — Students may use the **Self-test** to prepare for **Selection Test A** or **Selection Test B.**

ASSESS

❶ Vocabulary Lesson

Word Analysis

1. c
2. b
3. a

Spelling Strategy

1. theater
2. center
3. meager

Vocabulary Builder

1. b
2. a
3. c
4. a
5. c
6. b
7. a

❷ Grammar and Style

1. thunder: shakes
2. powers: find
3. breasts: glow
4. slumbers: soothe
5. hills; increase

Writing Application

Possible response: Chicago, New York city, and San Francisco are the cities I have always wanted to visit. Last summer I was able to visit my cousin in Chicago. I was impressed by its size and the constant activity. It was not like home. My cousin loves living there.

WG Writing and Grammar, Ruby Level

Students will find further instruction and practice on subject and verb agreement in Chapter 23, Section 1.

Build Language Skills

❶ Vocabulary Lesson

Word Analysis: Latin Prefix *re-*

The prefix *re-*, which means "again" or "back," can help you define many words. The Latin word *fluere* means "to flow," and *refluent* can be defined as "flowing back." *Refulgent*, from the Latin word *refulgere*—"to flash back"—means "brilliant." Match each word in the left column with its definition in the right column.

1. revolve	a. repeat from memory
2. relate	b. link back to; connect
3. recite	c. turn or roll again and again

Spelling Strategy

The *-re* ending in British words like *sceptre* is usually spelled *-er* in American English: *scepter.* Rewrite each of these words with the correct American English spelling.

1. theatre 2. centre 3. meagre

Vocabulary Builder: Antonyms

Identify the word whose meaning is most nearly opposite that of the first word:

1. celestial: **(a)** heavenly, **(b)** earthbound, **(c)** windy
2. refulgent: **(a)** tarnished, **(b)** sparkling, **(c)** colorful
3. propitious: **(a)** evil, **(b)** lucky, **(c)** inopportune
4. refluent: **(a)** surging, **(b)** stagnant, **(c)** ebbing
5. pensive: **(a)** reflective, **(b)** mournful, **(c)** carefree
6. placid: **(a)** unfettered, **(b)** agitated, **(c)** generous
7. scepter: **(a)** trinket, **(b)** emblem, **(c)** wand

❷ Grammar and Style Lesson

Subject and Verb Agreement

Even in poetry, the rules of **subject-verb agreement** apply. Verbs become either singular or plural to agree with their subject in number. Singular subjects take singular verb forms; plural subjects take plural verb forms.

Singular: *She* flashes dreadful . . .
Plural: And *nations* gaze at scenes . . .

Practice Identify the subject in each sentence. Then, choose the correct form of the verb in parentheses.

1. The thunder (shake, shakes) the heavenly plain.
2. When Gallic powers Columbia's fury (find, finds).
3. So may our breasts with every virtue (glow, glows).
4. Slumbers (soothe, soothes) each weary mind.
5. While round (increase, increases) the rising hills of dead.

Writing Application Write a paragraph describing a visit you made to a site of historic importance. Circle at least three instances where you use correct subject-verb agreement.

WG Prentice Hall Writing and Grammar Connection: Chapter 23, Section 1

Assessment Practice

Predict Outcomes **(For more practice, see *Standardized Test Preparation Workbook*, p. 10.)**

Have students answer this sample test item.

Brought to America from West Africa on a slave ship when she was eight years old, Phillis Wheatley quickly learned to speak, read, and write English. She avidly read classic works, as well as those by contemporary English poets. When publishers did not believe she wrote the poems she claimed to have written, they gave her a test.

Wheatley most likely—

A failed the test.
B passed the test.
C refused to take the test.
D was too nervous to take the test.

Choices *A*, *C*, and *D* are possible outcomes, but they are not supported by textual evidence. Choice *B* is the most likely outcome based on the text.

Writing Lesson

Inscription for a Monument

Choose a figure from history whom you admire. Imagine you have been hired to write an inscription for a monument honoring this individual. Using Wheatley's poems as a model, convey the heroic qualities of this historical figure.

Prewriting Briefly research your chosen historical subject. Make a list of specific accomplishments and notable qualities—personal and professional—to persuade readers of your subject's historical importance.

Drafting Choose language that emphasizes the subject's greatness. Use forceful nouns (*trailblazer* instead of *worker*) and adjectives (*tireless* in place of *good*) that have positive connotations.

Model: Drafting with a Persuasive Tone

A man of supreme courage and skill, George Washington was an inspiring general, a true patriot, and a fearless leader. . . .

Charged words like *supreme* and *patriot* emphasize heroic qualities.

Revising Look for opportunities to be more economical, precise, and persuasive with word choices. Check to be sure you have included the figure's most important accomplishments.

WG *Prentice Hall Writing and Grammar Connection: Chapter 7, Section 4*

Extend Your Learning

Listening and Speaking When read aloud, poems gain richness because sound devices such as rhyme, meter, alliteration, and assonance become fully animated. Choose one of Wheatley's poems and prepare a **dramatic reading.** Use these tips to guide your rehearsal:

- Read the poem several times aloud to hear and identify the elements that make it musical.
- Mark a copy of the poem with notes about where to pause and where to change the tone of your voice.

As you present the poem to classmates, use body language and eye contact for dramatic effect.

4 **Research and Technology** Team up with two classmates to research George Washington's military career, political life, and youth. Using computer graphics software, create a **graphic display** that highlights important events from his life. With your classmates, integrate the displays into a fold-out presentation poster. **[Group Activity]**

For: An additional research activity
Visit: www.PHSchool.com
Web Code: erd-7203

3 Writing Lesson

- To guide students in writing this inscription, give them the **Support for Writing Lesson,** p. 68, in ***General Resources.***
- Refer students to the inscription in the painting on SE p. 184 for an example.
- Read through the Writing Lesson steps with students and clarify any confusion.
- Encourage students to work in pairs to brainstorm for powerful nouns and adjectives.
- Adapt the Descriptive Essay rubrics in **General Resources,** pp. 63–64, to evaluate students' inscription.

4 Research and Technology

- Help students divide up the research tasks, either by the listed aspects of Washington's life or, if students prefer, by source type.
- Encourage students to address no more than three or four events in each category. Suggest that they focus on events that lend them- selves to visual represen- tation, for example, important battles.
- Direct students to sketch out their presentation poster before developing the computerized material.
- Have each team present a guided tour of their poster for the class.
- The **Support for Extend Your Learning** page (***Unit 2 Resources,*** p. 69) porvide guided note-taking opportunities to help students complete the extended your

Go Online Research Have students type in the Web Code for another research activity.

Assessment Resources

The following resources can be used to assess students' knowledge and skills.

Unit 2 Resources
Selection Test A, pp. 71–73
Selection Test B, pp. 74–76

General Resources
Rubric for Descriptive Essay, pp. 63–64

Go Online Assessment Students may use the **Self-test** for prepare for **Selection Test A** or **Selection Test B.**

Meeting Your Standards

Students will

1. **understand and explain press releases.**
2. **read and interpret a press release.**

See Teacher Express™/Lesson View for a detailed lesson plan for Reading Informational Materials.

About Press Releases

- Have students read "About Press Releases."
- **Ask** students what information in a newspaper or on radio or television comes from a press release.
  Possible Response: Information about new shows, neighborhood festivals, or changes in public services may come from press releases.
- Explain that press releases are meant to be read by reporters and are organized to emphasize the most important facts.
- Explain to students that much of the news reported in newspapers or the electronic media originates in press releases. In addition, in the business world, students may encounter press releases announcing (among other things) special events and new products.

Reading Skill

Distinguishing Fact from Opinion

- Review the difference between fact and opinion.
- **Ask** why it is important to make this distinction when reading a press release.
  Answer: The purpose of a press release is often to present something in a favorable light. Therefore, press releases may mix verifiable, objective facts with unverifiable, subjective opinions. The reader cannot assume that a press release's claims are all fact.

Reading Informational Materials

Press Releases

About Press Releases

A **press release** is a document that an organization, company, or other group distributes to the news media. Sometimes known as a **news release,** a press release might announce

- an upcoming lecture, conference, or performance.
- a newly published book.
- the results of a scientific study.
- the recipients of awards or honors.
- a change in leadership at an organization or a company.

The purpose of a press release is to encourage the media to report on the event it announces. Therefore, press releases are often written not simply to inform reporters but also to influence the way writers cover the event. In fact, sometimes a newspaper simply reprints some of the press release in the form of a short news article. At other times, a reporter uses the information from the press release but recasts it into a news story that draws on other sources as well.

Reading Strategy

Distinguishing Between Fact and Opinion

Like all readers, journalists must carefully **distinguish between fact and opinion** when using press releases. A **fact** is a statement that can be verified, or proved true. An **opinion** is a judgment or viewpoint that cannot be proved, although it can be supported by facts and well-reasoned arguments. Like a responsible journalist, you should distinguish facts from opinions when reading a press release or any other public statement.

As you read the press release on pages 191–192, use the information in the following chart to help you distinguish between facts and opinions.

Identifying Facts and Opinions

Facts

- can be proved true
- can be verified through proof or experiment, or can be confirmed by an authoritative source

Example: "Professor Gates is coeditor . . . of the encyclopedia *Encarta Africana.*"

Opinions

- cannot be proved true or false
- are judgments or viewpoints
- may be supported by facts and well-reasoned arguments, or may be defended by persuasive emotional appeals

Example: Gates is a "relentless and outspoken champion for tolerance through understanding."

Differentiated Instruction Solutions for All Learners

Reading Support

Give students reading support with the appropriate version of the ***Reader's Notebooks:***

Reader's Notebook [L2, L3]

Reader's Notebook: Adapted Version [L1, L2]

Reader's Notebook: English Learner's Version [EL]

NEWS RELEASE

The Echo Foundation ***Voices Against Indifference Initiative***
The Henry Louise Gates, Jr., Project • November 11, 2003 • Charlottte, NC

THE ECHO FOUNDATION BRINGS HENRY LOUIS GATES, JR., TO CHARLOTTE;
Noted Scholar, Literary Critic To Hold Public Lecture, Student Dialogue Nov., 11th

September 26, 2003 (Charlotte, NC) - Henry Louis (Skip) Gates, Jr., chair of Harvard's African and Afro-American Studies department and director of the W.E.B. Du Bois Institute, will be in Charlotte, Tues., Nov. 11 for a public lecture, student dialogue and an adult leadership forum as part of The Echo Foundation's *Voices Against Indifference Initiative*. Nobel Laureate for literature Wole Soyinka will introduce Gates's lecture, "W.E.B. Du Bois and the *Encyclopedia Africana,*" at **7 P.M.** at Spirit Square's McGlohon Theatre, 345 N. College St. **Call 704. 372.1000 for reserved seats: individual ($20) and student groups ($5). Call 704.347.3844 for patron tickets ($65),** which include a pre-event reception with Gates and Soyinka at the Noel Gallery, 401 N. Tryon St.

Key facts answering the questions *who? what? when? where?* and *why?* appear at the beginning of the press release.

The ***Voices Against Indifference Initiative*** is an Echo Foundation program that brings speakers to Charlotte whose personal experience illuminates the power of the individual to have a positive impact on humanity, through moral courage, action, and words.

This statement explains the purpose of the program that sponsors Gates's speech.

Gates will share his story in several community venues, on Nov. 11. Some 400 students and teachers from Charlotte area private and public high schools are studying curriculum materials to prepare for the Gates dialogue at Providence Day School, from 11:15 - 12:30 P.M. Plans are also underway for an adult leadership forum with Gates about social capital issues, and he will be the featured guest on *Charlotte Talks* with Mike Collins at 9 A.M. on WFAE Radio (90.7 FM).

A relentless and outspoken champion for tolerance through understanding, Gates has earned numerous awards and accolades for broadening the discourse on African American literature and cultural tradition in his various roles as an educator, scholar, literary critic and writer. One recent accomplishment, the completion of *Encarta Africana,* is the result of his 25-year quest to realize the dream of W.E.B. Du Bois. The renowned early twentieth century black intellectual and civil rights leader envisioned a comprehensive encyclopedia about the entire black world that could be used as an instrument to fight racism by building greater awareness and understanding of the African culture. The 2.25 billion-word encyclopedia project, coedited by Gates and Princeton professor K. Anthony Appiah, and published in hardbound print and CD-ROM format, was dedicated in memory of Du Bois and in honor of Nelson Mandela on Martin Luther King's birthday, Jan. 19, 1999.

This paragraph presents a mix of facts and opinions about Gates's background and accomplishments. The first sentence might provide journalists with a good quotation for a news story.

###

NOTE TO THE EDITORS: The following page includes more detailed information about Gates and The Echo Foundation. Photos are available through The Echo Foundation.

The Echo Foundation
926 Elizabeth Avenue • Suite 403 • Charlotte, NC 28204
www.echofoundation.org

Reading Press Releases

- Have students read the press release announcing the talk by Henry Louis Gates, Jr. at the Echo Foundation. As they read paragraphs 1–4, **ask** students to identify several examples of facts and opinions.

Possible answers: Facts: Henry Louis Gates is the chair of Harvard's African and Afro-American Studies department. Gates will be lecturing in Charlotte on November 11 at 7 P.M. Students may mention the event time, location, ticket prices and reservation options.

They also may mention that Gates has won awards, and that he completed the *Encarta Africana* project.

Opinions may include the assertion in paragraph 2 that the foundation invites speakers whose personal experience illuminates the power of the individual to have a positive impact, and the description in paragraph 4 of Gates as a "champion for tolerance through understanding."

Differentiated Instruction Solutions for All Learners

Support for Special Needs Students

Draw students' attention to the portions of the release that represent opinions, and ask why these statements are opinions, rather than facts. Help students articulate the idea that words like "A relentless and outspoken champion for tolerance through understanding" are subjective. In addition, it is impossible to verify the truth of any of the words, since they are all open to interpretation. "Relentless" for one person might refer to an action that took place once or twice; for another person, it might refer to something that happened often. One person's "champion" is another person's "pest."

Vocabulary for English Learners

The Echo Foundation press release includes numerous words that may challenge English learners as they read. The use of *chair* to indicate a person who leads may be unfamiliar to students. Uses here of the words *forum, reception, illuminates,* and *impact* may also require explanations.

Help students identify which words in the press release tell who, what, where, when, and why. Ask students to identify words that are unfamiliar. Assist them in understanding the definitions of these words, and how the words affect the meaning of the selection.

Reading Press Releases
(cont.)

- Draw students' attention to the long list of Gates's achievements and honors. **Ask** how this factual information supports the favorable opinions presented of Gates in the press release.
Answer: The list of achievements and honors creates a favorable general impression of Gates but it does not directly prove that Gates is a "relentless and outspoken champion for tolerance through understanding." His commitment to sharing information about African American culture indirectly supports the idea that he has worked hard to spread understanding.

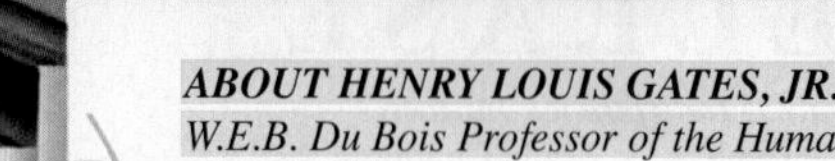

ABOUT HENRY LOUIS GATES, JR.
W.E.B. Du Bois Professor of the Humanities, Harvard University
Chair of Afro-American Studies
Director of the W.E.B. Du Bois Institute for Afro-American Research

This section summarizes Gates's academic credentials and introduces more detailed information about his publications and awards.

Professor Gates is coeditor with K. Anthony Appiah of the encyclopedia *Encarta Africana* published on CD-ROM by Microsoft (1999), and in book form by Basic Civitas Books under the title *Africana: The Encyclopedia of the African and African American Experience* (1999). He is the author of *Wonders of the African World* (1999), the book companion to the six-hour BBC/PBS television series of the same name.

Professor Gates is the author of several works of literary criticism, including *Figures in Black: Words, Signs and the 'Racial' Self* (Oxford University Press, 1987); *The Signifying Monkey: A Theory of Afro-American Literary Criticism* (Oxford, 1988), 1989 winner of the American Book Award; and *Loose Canons: Notes on the Culture Wars* (Oxford, 1992.) He has also authored *Colored People: A Memoir* (Knopf, 1994), which traces his childhood experiences in a small West Virginia town in the 1950s and 1960s; *The Future of the Race* (Knopf, 1996), coauthored with Cornel West; and *Thirteen Ways of Looking at a Black Man* (Random House, 1997). Professor Gates has edited several anthologies, including *The Norton Anthology of African American Literature* (W. W. Norton, 1996); and *The Oxford-Schomburg Library of Nineteenth Century Black Women Writers* (Oxford, 1991). In addition, Professor Gates is coeditor of *Transition* magazine. An influential cultural critic, Professor Gates's publications include a 1994 cover story for *Time* magazine on the new black Renaissance in art, as well as numerous articles for *The New Yorker.*

The press release includes information about the organization that is sponsoring the event and has distributed the press release.

Professor Gates earned his M.A. and Ph.D. in English Literature from Clare College at the University of Cambridge. He received a B.A. *summa cum laude* from Yale University in 1973 in English Language and Literature. Before joining the faculty of Harvard in 1991, he taught at Yale, Cornell, and Duke Universities. His honors and grants include a MacArthur Foundation "genius grant" (1981), the George Polk Award for Social Commentary (1993), Chicago Tribune Heartland Award (1994), the Golden Plate Achievement Award (1995), *Time* magazine's "25 Most Influential Americans" list (1997), a National Humanities Medal (1998), and election to the American Academy of Arts and Letters (1999).

ABOUT THE ECHO FOUNDATION
The Echo Foundation was founded in 1997 to carry on the message that Nobel Peace Prize winner Elie Wiesel brought to Charlotte that year—a call to action for human dignity, justice and moral courage. Its mission is "to sponsor and facilitate those voices which speak of human dignity, justice and moral courage in a way that will lead to positive action for humankind."

The Echo Foundation
926 Elizabeth Avenue • Suite 403 • Charlotte, NC 28204
www.echofoundation.org

192 ■ *A Nation Is Born (1750–1800)*

Tips for Test Taking

Explain that the press release's *who? what? when? where? how? why?* approach can be a very effective technique for crafting a thesis statement for a factual in-class essay or for the essay portion of a standardized test such as the SAT or ACT. Such an approach grounds the writer immediately and gives him or her a strong basis for developing this information with explanations and details.

The reading comprehension portions of standardized tests often students to decide whether or not certain information is provided in a piece of writing or whether a given statement represents a fact or an opinion. The practice gained from analyzing this press release can help students prepare for such prompts in the SAT or ACT.

Monitor Your Progress

Assessment Practice

Reading: Distinguishing Between Fact and Opinion

Directions: *Choose the letter of the best answer to each question about the press release.*

1. Which of the following is *not* a fact presented in paragraphs 1 or 2?
   A Henry Louis Gates will deliver a public lecture in Charlotte.
   B Henry Louis Gates is director of the W.E.B. Du Bois Institute.
   C Henry Louis Gates has had a positive impact on humanity.
   D Gates's visit is sponsored by the Echo Foundation.
2. Which of the following is an opinion presented in paragraphs 3 or 4?
   A Gates has earned numerous awards and accolades.
   B W.E.B. Du Bois envisioned an encyclopedia about the entire black world.
   C Gates worked for twenty-five years to create the encyclopedia.
   D An encyclopedia about the black world would be a useful tool.
3. Which of the following facts from the press release *best* supports the opinion that Gates is an influential cultural critic?
   A He won a MacArthur Foundation grant in 1981.
   B He has won numerous awards for his role as educator, scholar, literary critic, and writer.
   C He coedited an encyclopedia that contains 2.25 billion words.
   D He wrote a memoir about his childhood.
4. Which of the following is a *not* a fact about the Echo Foundation?
   A Its mission is to promote racial harmony and justice.
   B It was founded in 1997 to promote the message of Eli Wiesel.
   C It promotes human dignity, justice, and moral courage.
   D It sponsors the *Voices Against Indifference Initiative.*

Reading: Comprehension and Interpretation

Directions: *Write your answers on a separate sheet of paper.*

5. What is the topic of Henry Louis Gates's public lecture?
6. What can you infer from the press release about why he is speaking on this topic?
7. Why do you think the Echo Foundation invited Gates to speak? Base your answer on the facts and opinions presented in the press release.

Timed Writing: Explanation

Write a newspaper article that reports on the event announced in this press release. Include an informative headline, and answer the questions *who? what? when? where?* and *why?* You may include both facts and opinions, as long as you do not present opinions as facts. ***(30 minutes)***

Extend the Lesson

Writing

Have each student write a press release. As a class, brainstorm to create ideas for topics to explore and people to interview. Subject areas might include entertainment, music, any variety of local issues, politics, business, fashion, or automotive news. Encourage students to focus on events or stories that are accessible in terms of available information. Remind students that a press release often is meant to promote information from the perspective of the organization or person issuing the release. Have students consider their perspective when writing the piece. Will they be in the role of a reporter, company spokesperson, political aide, or sports agent? Allow students to share their finished press releases with the class.

ASSESS

Answers

Reading: Distinguishing Fact from Opinion

1. C
2. D
3. B
4. A

Reading: Comprehension and Interpretation

5. The topic of Gates's lecture is W.E.B. DuBois and the *Encyclopedia Africana.*
6. The reader can infer that Gates and the Echo Foundation believe that spreading knowledge of the culture and achievements of black people through works like the *Encyclopedia Africana* will promote tolerance among the races.
7. The Foundation invited Gates to participate in its initiative because he is a famous and widely honored scholar and member of the African American community. He is likely to attract a wide audience and deliver a knowledgeable, eloquent speech that will reflect credit on the Echo Foundation and its mission.

Timed Writing

- Students' explanations should clearly and accurately recapitulate the information presented in the press release, using the *who? what? when? where? how? why?* approach of the lead.
- Students might benefit from making brief working outlines to guide them as they write and help them decide which portions of the press release to use.
- Suggest that students plan their time to give 5 minutes to planning, 15 minutes to writing, and 10 minutes to reviewing and revising.

Meeting Your Standards

Students will

1. **understand the cultural and historical roles of proverbs.**
2. **recognize the fundamental characteristics that proverbs share.**

Connections
Literature Around the World

List on the board the following words: *friendship, love, thrift, greed, hard work,* and *responsibility.* Remind students that these universal concepts are reflected in not only Benjamin Franklin's Poor Richard's Almanack, but in literature throughout the World.

The Wisdom of Many

- Have students identify the major ideas in the text on this page.
- Ask students to think of a familiar proverb for each concept. Then, have students identify the African proverbs that address these concepts. Compare and contrast the language of each. It would be wise to collect several familiar proverbs in preparation for this activity in case students cannot think of enough.
- Remind students that although proverbs reflect distinguishing characteristics of their original cultures, they also share universal characteristics. Guide a class discussion to identify similarities among Franklin's proverbs and the African examples that appear in this feature.
- Have students **explain** why proverbs play an important role in cultures with active oral traditions of communication.
  Answer: Proverbs allow wisdom and guidance to be passed orally from one generation to the next.

Literature Around the World

Africa

The Wisdom of Many

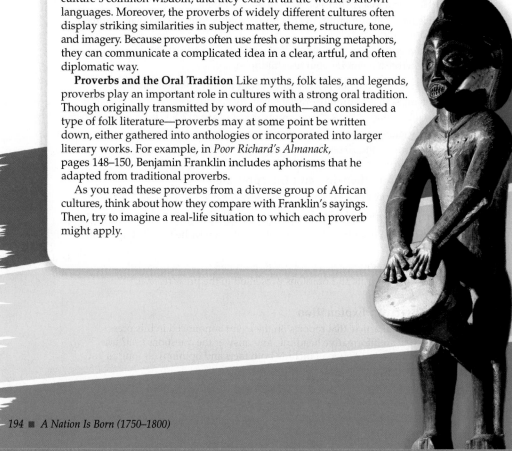

The eighteenth-century English statesman Lord John Russell defined a proverb as "one man's wit and all men's wisdom." Around 1600, the Spanish novelist Miguel de Cervantes, author of the classic novel *Don Quixote,* coined another pithy saying about proverbs when he defined them as "short sentences drawn from long experience." Both definitions, like proverbs themselves, are concise and memorable. They use repetition, balance, and contrast to make an insightful point.

A **proverb** is a traditional wise saying that offers cultural wisdom in the form of a practical truth about life. Proverbs are the distillation of a culture's common wisdom, and they exist in all the world's known languages. Moreover, the proverbs of widely different cultures often display striking similarities in subject matter, theme, structure, tone, and imagery. Because proverbs often use fresh or surprising metaphors, they can communicate a complicated idea in a clear, artful, and often diplomatic way.

Proverbs and the Oral Tradition Like myths, folk tales, and legends, proverbs play an important role in cultures with a strong oral tradition. Though originally transmitted by word of mouth—and considered a type of folk literature—proverbs may at some point be written down, either gathered into anthologies or incorporated into larger literary works. For example, in *Poor Richard's Almanack,* pages 148–150, Benjamin Franklin includes aphorisms that he adapted from traditional proverbs.

As you read these proverbs from a diverse group of African cultures, think about how they compare with Franklin's sayings. Then, try to imagine a real-life situation to which each proverb might apply.

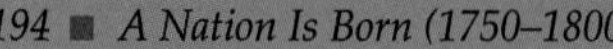

African Proverbs

Uganda: The Baganda

A small deed out of friendship is worth more than a great service that is forced.

One who loves you, warns you.

The one who has not made the journey calls it an easy one.

Where there are no dogs, the wild cats move about freely.

Words are easy, but friendship is difficult.

Thematic Connection
What does this proverb imply about the words that friends must sometimes use with one another?

Liberia: The Jabo

One who cannot pick up an ant and wants to pick up an elephant will someday see his folly.

The butterfly that flies among the thorns will tear its wings.

A man's ways are good in his own eyes.

Daring talk is not strength.

Children are the wisdom of the nation.

The one who listens is the one who understands.

South Africa: The Zulu

Do not speak of a rhinoceros if there is no tree nearby.

The one offended never forgets; it is the offender who forgets.

It never dawns in the same way.

Look as you fell a tree.

Eyes do not see all.

You cannot chase two gazelles.

What has happened before happens again.

No dew ever competed with the sun.

There is no foot which does not stumble.

Thematic Connection

Possible response: A genuine friend will prove his or her friendship through an act of kindness rather than an empty promise.

Thematic Connection

Possible response: Confronted with their failures, people will make excuses or blame others to save face.

Thematic Connection

Answer: Rain beats a leopard's skin, but it does not wash out the spots.

ASSESS

Answers

1. (a) African: A small deed out of friendship is worth more than a great service that is forced. Words are easy, but friendship is difficult. One who loves you, warns you. Franklin: Be slow in choosing a friend, slower in changing. An open foe may prove a curse, but a pretended friend is worse. A true friend is the best possession. (b) **Possible response:** Genuine friendship is a rare and cherished gift. (c) **Possible response:** Beware of friendship offered easily, for true friendship requires worthwhile effort.
2. (a) The one who has not made the journey calls it an easy one. If you cannot dance, you will say, "The drumming is poor." Words are easy, but friendship is difficult. (b) Well done is better than well said. A slip of the foot you may soon recover, but a slip of the tongue you may never get over. A good example is the best sermon.
3. Answers should be supported with reason.

Ghana: The Ashanti

Rain beats a leopard's skin, but it does not wash out the spots.

If you are in hiding, don't light a fire.

One falsehood spoils a thousand truths.

No one tests the depth of a river with both feet.

Nigeria: The Yoruba

The day on which one starts out is not the time to start one's preparations.

He who is being carried does not realize how far the town is.

Time destroys all things.

Little is better than nothing.

Tanzania and Kenya: The Masai

The hyena said, "It is not only that I have luck, but my leg is strong."

Baboons do not go far from the place of their birth.

We begin by being foolish and we become wise by experience.

The zebra cannot do away with his stripes.

Do not repair another man's fence until you have seen to your own.

It is better to be poor and live long than rich and die young.

Do not say the first thing that comes to your mind.

Thematic Connection
What does this proverb imply about human nature or human experience in general?

Thematic Connection
What other African proverb presented here teaches the same lesson as the fourth Masai proverb?

About the African Proverbs

The proverbs presented here reflect cultures throughout the African continent. The Masai and the Baganda live in the East African countries of Kenya, Tanzania, and Uganda; the Ashanti, the Yoruba, and the Jabo live in the West African countries of Ghana, Nigeria, and Liberia; and the Zulu live in South Africa. In many African cultures, proverbs are often embedded in the tales of oral storytellers, known as *griots* (grē′ ōz), who function as a living library for their communities. Proverbs have been used for centuries to teach children, offer advice, settle arguments, and even help resolve legal disputes.

Connecting Literature Around the World

1. **(a)** Identify three African proverbs and three aphorisms from *Poor Richard's Almanack* that deal with the theme of friendship. **(b)** What do these proverbs and aphorisms have to say about the value of true friendship? **(c)** What do they say about the pitfalls of friendship?
2. **(a)** Which African proverbs focus on the contrast between words and actions? **(b)** Which of Franklin's aphorisms address this theme?
3. Identify examples of sayings you know that have similar messages to some of these African proverbs. Explain what the sayings and the proverbs have in common.

Unit 2 Part 2

Focus on Literary Forms: Speeches

Selection Planning Guide

The selections in this section feature two of the finest orators in American history. In his famous "Speech in the Virginia Convention," Patrick Henry rouses his countrymen to battle for freedom. Benjamin Franklin then shows how the wisdom that comes with age can help resolve a clashing of the minds in "Speech in the Convention."

Humanities

George Washington Standing on the Platform

This painting depicts George Washington as President of the Constitutional Convention that met in the Pennsylvania State House in May, 1787. The words arching over the painting are taken from Washington's address to the Convention, in which he told the delegates to forge a worthy document that they could strongly support. Four months later, in September, 1787, the Constitution was signed by a majority of the men who had met to draft it.

Use these questions for discussion:

1. Compare the image of George Washington in this painting to that in Leutze's *Washington Crossing the Delaware*. What elements in this painting suggest that Washington will be a successful leader for the new nation?
   Possible response: His posture suggests confidence and vision. As in the Leutze painting, no head is higher than Washington's, and several of the delegates to the Convention have turned their heads to listen to him.
2. What is the effect of showing Washington's words as they are arranged here, arching over the speaker and his audience?
   Possible response: The painter suggests that these words in particular go to the heart of Washington's address and that they have become immortal.

Differentiated Instruction Solutions for All Learners

Accessibility at a Glance

More Challenging
- Speech in the Virginia Convention
- Speech in the Convention

Meeting Your Standards

Students will

1. **recognize and appreciate the types and elements of speeches.**
2. **apply strategies for reading speeches.**

❶ Types of Speeches

- Tell students that in Part 2 they will focus on speeches. Remind them that speeches are delivered orally, even though they will read printed versions of speeches. **Ask** students to explain how a speech is different from other nonfiction works, such as an essay.
  Possible answers: Speeches often have greater emotional impact than other nonfiction works. Speeches also draw as much attention to the language they use as to the ideas they express. Because they are spoken aloud, speeches usually give special emphasis to rhythm and other sound devices, unlike essays and other forms of nonfiction.
- Review types of speeches: the political speech, the address, the oration, and the sermon. Explain that some of these categories overlap; for example, a President's Inaugural Address has elements of a political speech and an oration, as well as an address. The "I Have a Dream" speech by Dr. Martin Luther King, Jr., has elements of all types of speeches.

❷ Rhetorical Devices

- Review the types of rhetorical devices described on these pages.
- Ask for volunteers to read aloud the examples of the rhetorical devices. Then **ask** students which ones seemed particularly effective, and discuss why they were powerful.

Focus on Literary Forms: Speeches

Defining Speeches

A **speech** is a nonfiction work that is delivered orally to an audience. Some speeches are composed in writing before they are spoken aloud. Others are composed more informally as they are presented, usually from notes.

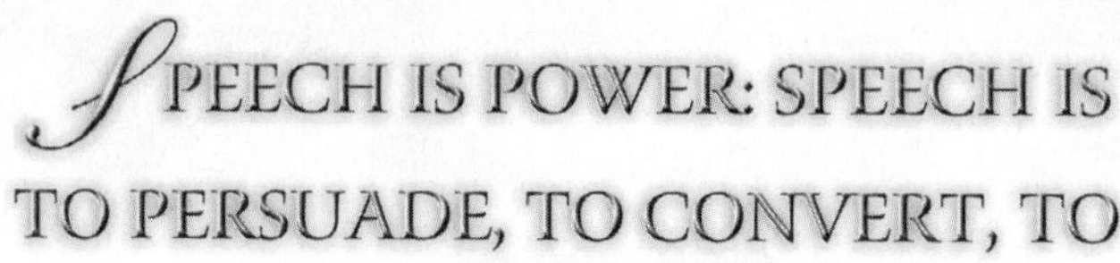

SPEECH IS POWER: SPEECH IS TO PERSUADE, TO CONVERT, TO COMPEL.

— *Ralph Waldo Emerson*

❶ Types of Speeches

Here are some common types of speeches:

- A **political speech** is a speech about an issue relating to government or politics. Usually, the speaker tries to persuade people to think or act in a certain way. During the Revolutionary War period, leaders such as Patrick Henry, Benjamin Franklin, and Thomas Paine gave inspiring and persuasive political speeches, such as Henry's "Speech in the Virginia Convention," page 202.
- An **address** is a formal speech that honors an occasion or the speaker. For example, Abraham Lincoln delivered his "Gettysburg Address," page 532 at the dedication of a military cemetery during the Civil War.
- A **sermon** is a speech that is usually based on a scriptural text and is intended to provide religious or moral instruction. Jonathan Edwards's "Sinners in the Hands of an Angry God," page 102, is an example of a sermon.

❸ Persuasive Techniques

Many speeches are examples of **persuasion**—speech or writing that tries to get the audience to think or act in a certain way. **Persuasive techniques** are the methods that a speaker or a writer uses to appeal to the audience. Most speeches use a mixture of persuasive appeals.

- A **logical appeal** builds a well-reasoned argument based on evidence, such as facts, statistics, or expert testimony.
- An **emotional appeal** attempts to arouse the audience's feelings, often by using rhetorical devices that evoke an emotional response or **loaded words** that convey strong positive or negative connotations.
- An **ethical appeal** is directed at the audience's sense of morality or values. This type of appeal is often linked to the audience's perception of the trustworthiness and moral character of the speaker or writer.

Extend the Lesson

Activity

- Ask students to watch, read, or listen to a contemporary speech—perhaps a political speech, an address at a school function, or a sermon.
- Have them develop their own set of standards as to what makes that speech—or any speech—effective. Tell them to focus particularly on rhetorical devices and persuasive appeals and to ask themselves the following questions:
  1. Am I more drawn to certain rhetorical devices than to others? Why?
  2. Which kinds of persuasive appeals do I find most effective?
- After each student lists his or her standards for an effective speech, have students work in groups to compile their ideas.
- Work with the class to come up with a comprehensive set of standards.

❷ **Rhetorical Devices**

Effective speeches typically include **rhetorical devices**—special patterns of words and ideas that create emphasis and stir the audience's emotions. The chart below shows some examples.

Rhetorical Device	Example
Repetition Restating an idea using the same words	"The war is inevitable—and let it come! I repeat it, sir, let it come!" —Patrick Henry, "Speech in the Virginia Convention," p. 202
Restatement Expressing the same idea in different words	"But, in a larger sense, we can not dedicate—we can not consecrate—we can not hallow—this ground." —Abraham Lincoln, "The Gettysburg Address," p. 532
Parallelism Repeating a grammatical structure	"With malice toward none; with charity for all; with firmness in the right . . ." —Abraham Lincoln, "Second Inaugural Address," p. 533
Antithesis Using strongly contrasting words, images, or ideas	"And so, my fellow Americans: ask not what your country can do for you—ask what you can do for your country." —John F. Kennedy, "Inaugural Address," p. 1228
Rhetorical questions Asking questions with obvious answers	"From such an assembly can a *perfect* production be expected?" —Benjamin Franklin, "Speech in the Convention," p. 207

❹ **Strategies for Reading Speeches**

Use these strategies as you read or listen to speeches.

Identify Persuasive Techniques Ask yourself whether the speaker depends primarily on logical appeals, emotional appeals, ethical appeals, or a combination of these techniques. If the speaker uses a logical appeal, evaluate whether it is based on sound arguments and evidence. If the speaker uses an emotional appeal, evaluate its effectiveness and consider whether it is manipulative as well as emotionally stirring. If the speaker uses an ethical appeal, identify the value that is stated or implied and decide whether it is truly connected to the topic of the speech.

Identify Rhetorical Devices Consider whether the speaker uses repetition, restatement, parallelism, antithesis, or rhetorical questions. If so, notice how these devices affect the sound and the meaning of the speech.

Refer to Patrick Henry's "Speech in the Virginia Convention" for examples of each. If necessary, tell students that Henry appeals to reason when he says that it seems unreasonable to hope that the British will treat the colonists more kindly, given their use of force over the past ten years. Henry makes an ethical appeal when he claims that "a just God" is on the colonists' side. He makes an emotional appeal in the memorable ending of his speech, when he cries out, "I know not what course others may take; but as for me, give me liberty or give me death!"

- Suggest that students use these pages as a reference when they read Part 2 and other speeches in this book.

❹ Strategies for Reading Speeches

- Tell students that speeches are intended to be read aloud. **Ask** how the speaker can increase the impact of a speech.
  Possible answers: The speaker can emphasize a speech's rhythm or rhetorical devices. A speaker can accent certain words or phrases to give them emphasis. A speaker also can pause to add emphasis or to change the pace at which he or she reads the speech. The speaker can add a particular emotional quality, such as sarcasm, anger, joy, or sorrow, tone, by the tone of his or her voice.
- **Ask** why readers need to think critically when they read speeches.
  Possible answer: Rhetorical devices and emotional appeals can mask the weakness of a speaker's argument. Students may mention that appeals that seem weak on paper may be more effective when spoken.
- Encourage students consider how the oral delivery of a speech can affect the audience's interpretation of the speech's written content.

Differentiated Instruction Solutions for All Learners

Strategies for Less Proficient Readers

The speeches in Part 2 may present challenges to students who are learning English. Have students listen to an oral reading of this speech on the **Listening to Literature CD** before they read it silently. Then, have them work with partners to break down long, complicated sentences into smaller segments, which are easier to paraphrase. Encourage partners to paraphrase these parts of the speech and to keep their written paraphrases in front of them as they follow along once again with the support of the **Listening to Literature CD**.

Strategies for Gifted/Talented Students

Have students with performing-arts skills read passages from the speeches in the text. Ask them to tell the class how it felt to deliver the speech—where they had to pay special attention to the rhythm, where the sentence was more difficult to speak aloud, where they decided to change their pace and volume, and why.

Meeting Your Standards

Students will

1. **analyze and respond to literary elements.**
   - Literary Analysis: Speeches
2. **read, comprehend, analyze, and critique speeches.**
   - Reading Strategy: Evaluating Persuasive Appeals
   - Reading Check questions
   - Apply the Skills questions
   - Assessment Practice (ATE)
3. **develop vocabulary.**
   - Vocabulary Lesson: Latin suffix: *-ity*
4. **understand and apply written and oral language conventions.**
   - Spelling Strategy
   - Grammar and Style Lesson: Double Negatives
5. **develop writing proficiency.**
   - Writing Lesson: Commentary on a Speech
6. **develop appropriate research strategies.**
   - Extend Your Learning: Display
7. **understand and apply listening and speaking strategies.**
   - Extend Your Learning: Debate

Block Scheduling: Use one 90-minute class period to preteach the skills and have students read the selection. Use a second 90-minute class period to assess students' mastery of skills, extend their learning, and monitor their progress.

Homework Suggestions

Following are possibilities for homework assignments.

- Support pages from *Unit 2 Resources:*
  Literary Analysis
  Reading Strategy
  Vocabulary Builder
  Grammar and Style
- An Extend Your Learning project and the Writing Lesson for this selection group may be completed over several days.

Step-by-Step Teaching Guide	Pacing Guide
PRETEACH	
• Administer Vocabulary and Reading Warm-ups as necessary.	5 min.
• Engage students' interest with the motivation activity.	5 min.
• Read and discuss author and background features. **FT**	10 min.
• Introduce the Literary Analysis Skill: Speeches. **FT**	5 min.
• Introduce the Reading Strategy: Evaluating Persuasive Appeals. **FT**	10 min
• Prepare students to read by teaching the selection vocabulary. **FT**	
TEACH	
• Informally monitor comprehension while students read independently or in groups. **FT**	30 min.
• Monitor students' comprehension with the Reading Check notes.	as students read
• Reinforce vocabulary with Vocabulary Builder notes.	as students read
• Develop students' understanding of speeches with the Literary Analysis annotations. **FT**	5 min.
• Develop students' ability to evaluate persuasive appeals with the Reading Strategy annotations. **FT**	5 min.
ASSESS/EXTEND	
• Assess students' comprehension and mastery of the Literary Analysis and Reading Strategy by having them answer the Apply the Skills questions. **FT**	15 min.
• Have students complete the Vocabulary Lesson and the Grammar and Style Lesson. **FT**	15 min.
• Apply students' ability to evaluate speeches by using the Writing Lesson. **FT**	45 min. or homework
• Apply students' understanding by using one or more of the Extend Your Learning activities.	20–90 min. or homework
• Administer Selection Test A or Selection Test B. **FT**	15 min.

Resources

PRINT

Unit 2 Resources

TRANSPARENCY

Graphic Organizer Transparencies

PRINT

Reader's Notebook [L2]
Reader's Notebook: Adapted Version [L1]
Reader's Notebook: English Learner's Version [EL]

Unit 2 Resources

TECHNOLOGY

Listening to Literature Audio CDs [L2, EL]
Reader's Notebook: Adapted Version Audio CD [L1, L2]

PRINT

Unit 2 Resources

General Resources

TECHNOLOGY

Go Online: Research **[L3]**
Go Online: Self-test **[L3]**
***ExamView*®, Test Bank [L3]**

Choosing Resources for Differentiated Instruction

[L1] Special Needs Students
[L2] Below-Level Students
[L3] All Students
[L4] Advanced Students
[EL] English Learners

FT Fast Track Instruction: To move the lesson more quickly, use the strategies and activities identified with **FT**.

Scaffolding for Less Proficient and Advanced Students

The leveled Critical Thinking questions after selections progress in the levels of thinking required to answer them. To address the needs of your different students, you may use the (a) level questions for your less proficient students and the (b) level questions with your on-level and advanced students. The occasional (c) level questions are appropriate for your advanced students.

PRENTICE HALL **TeacherEXPRESS**™ Plan · Teach · Assess Use this complete suite of powerful teaching tools to make lesson planning and testing quicker and easier.

PRENTICE HALL **StudentEXPRESS**™ Learn · Study · Succeed Use the interactive textbook (online and on CD-ROM) to make selections and activities come alive with audio and video support and interactive questions.

PRETEACH

Motivation

Patrick Henry concluded his speech with the famous words, "Give me liberty or give me death." Write these words on the board. Have students spend six or seven minutes freewriting in their journals in response to this question: What is worth dying for? Encourage students to share their thoughts, and then discuss the circumstances under which Henry spoke these words. Have students imagine that they were members of the Virginia Convention. Ask them what else Henry would have to say to convince them that they too should be willing to die for liberty.

❶ Background

More About the Authors

Patrick Henry was no stranger to conflict with the Crown. In 1765 he had been accused of treason when he delivered his fiery denunciation of the Stamp Act. On that occasion, Henry had referred to two leaders who had been killed for political reasons and declared that King George III might "profit by their example." This shocked the members of the audience so much that they screamed out, accusing Henry of treason. Henry is reported to have made the memorable reply, "If this be treason, make the most of it!"

It is difficult for many people to believe that Benjamin Franklin—scientist, journalist, educator, and statesman—started out as a penniless runaway in the English colonies. At age 12, Franklin had been apprenticed to his brother James, who operated a printing shop in Boston. James, however, often beat his brother when upset by his work. Franklin ran away, first traveling to New York and then on to Philadelphia. There, he found work as a printer's assistant. In a few years, he was able to open his own printing shop.

Build Skills *Speeches*

❶ Speech in the Virginia Convention • Speech in the Convention

Patrick Henry (1736–1799)

It was said that Patrick Henry could move his listeners to anger, fear, or laughter more easily than the most talented actor. Remembered most for his fiery battle cry—"Give me liberty or give me death"—Henry is considered to be the most powerful orator of the American Revolution. He helped to inspire colonists to unite in an effort to win their independence from Britain.

Voice of Protest In 1765, Henry was elected to the Virginia House of Burgesses. Shortly after his election, he delivered one of his most powerful speeches, declaring his opposition to the Stamp Act. The Stamp Act, which was passed by the British Parliament, required American colonists to pay a tax on every piece of printed paper they used. Legal documents, newspapers, and even playing cards were all subject to the tax. Over the protests of some of its most influential members, the Virginia House adopted Henry's resolutions.

A Call to Arms In 1775, Henry delivered his most famous speech at the Virginia Provincial Convention. While most of the speakers that day argued that the colony should seek a compromise with the British, Henry boldly urged armed resistance to England. His speech had a powerful impact on the audience, feeding the revolutionary spirit that led to the signing of the Declaration of Independence.

In the years that followed, Henry continued to be an important political leader, serving as governor of Virginia and member of the Virginia General Assembly.

Benjamin Franklin (1706–1790)

No other colonial American better embodied the promise of America than Benjamin Franklin. Through hard work, dedication, and ingenuity, Franklin was able to rise out of poverty to become a wealthy, famous, and influential person. Although he never received a formal education, Franklin made important contributions in the fields of literature, journalism, science, diplomacy, education, and philosophy.

A Persuasive Diplomat Franklin was a leader in the movement for independence. In 1776, Congress sent him to France to enlist aid for the American Revolution. Franklin's persuasive powers proved effective, as he was able to achieve his goal—a pivotal breakthrough that may have been the deciding factor in the war.

Helping Forge a Nation In 1783, Franklin signed the peace treaty that ended the war and established the new nation. He returned home to serve as a delegate to the Constitutional Convention in Philadelphia. There, as politicians clashed over plans for the new government, Franklin worked to resolve conflicts and ensure ratification of the Constitution.

In spite of his other contributions, Franklin is best remembered as a statesman and diplomat. He was the only American to sign all four documents that established the nation: the Declaration of Independence, the treaty of alliance with France, the peace treaty with England, and the Constitution. (For more on Franklin, see p. 140.)

Preview

Connecting to the Literature

Speeches, like Martin Luther King's "I have a dream," have helped to shape the American identity by expressing our goals as a people. As you read these speeches, think about the vital American principles they express.

Literary Analysis

Speeches

Speeches are written works that are delivered orally. An effective speaker uses a variety of techniques to emphasize key points:

- *Restatement:* repeating an idea in a variety of ways
- *Repetition:* restating an idea using the same words
- *Parallelism:* repeating grammatical structures
- *Rhetorical question:* asking a question whose answer is self-evident

Watch for examples of these techniques in these speeches.

Comparing Literary Works

Speeches from the same time period, even those addressing related topics, may sound very different. One reason for this is that a speaker's **diction**—the choice and arrangement of words—creates a personal stamp. Diction may be casual, formal, simple, or sophisticated, and is often altered to address the aims of the speech. Compare the diction of these speeches, evaluating how well each speaker's word choices support his purposes.

Reading Strategy

Evaluating Persuasive Appeals

To stir an audience, speakers may appeal to people's emotions, ethics, or sense of reason. When you read a persuasive speech, **evaluate** the **persuasive appeals** that the speaker makes. Assess the speaker's motivation in evoking emotions. Note the arguments and evidence offered, and evaluate how well the appeals suit the audience and occasion. Use a diagram like the one shown to record each speaker's persuasive appeals.

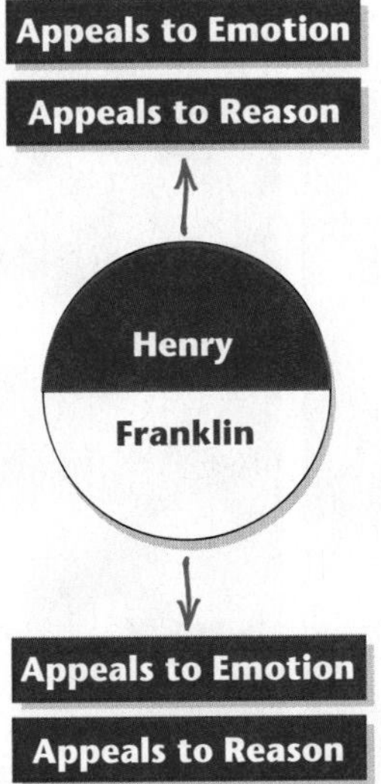

Vocabulary Builder

arduous (är′ jo͞o əs) *adj.* difficult (p. 204)

insidious (in sid′ ē əs) *adj.* deceitful; treacherous (p. 204)

subjugation (sub′ jə gā′ shən) *n.* the act of conquering (p. 204)

vigilant (vij′ ə lənt) *adj.* alert to danger (p. 205)

infallibility (in fal′ ə bil′ ə tē) *n.* inability to be wrong; reliability (p. 207)

despotism (des′ pət iz′ əm) *n.* absolute rule; tyranny (p. 207)

salutary (sal′ yo͞o ter′ ē) *adj.* beneficial; promoting a good purpose (p. 209)

unanimity (yo͞o′ nə nim′ ə tē) *n.* complete agreement (p. 209)

posterity (päs ter′ ə tē) *n.* all succeeding generations (p. 209)

manifest (man′ ə fest′) *adj.* evident; obvious; clear (p. 209)

Differentiated Instruction Solutions for All Learners

Support for Special Needs Students

Have students read the adapted version of "Speech in the Virginia Convention" in the ***Reader's Notebook: Adapted Version.*** This version provides basic-level instruction in an interactive format with questions and write-on lines. Completing these pages will prepare students to read the selection in the Student Edition.

Support for Less Proficient Readers

Have students read " Speech n the Virginia Convention" in the ***Reader's Notebook.*** This version provides basic-level instruction in an interactive format with questions and write-on lines. After students finish the selection in the ***Reader's Notebook,*** have them complete the questions and activities in the Student Edition.

Support for English Learners

Have students read "Speech in the Virginia Convention" in the ***Reader's Notebook: English Learner's Version.*** This version provides basic-level instruction in an interactive format with questions and write-on lines. Completing these pages will prepare students to read the selection in the Student Edition.

❷ Literary Analysis

Speeches

- Tell students they will read two speeches about critical issues in the birth of the United States. Remind students that speeches are written works meant to be delivered orally in front of an audience.
- Read the instruction about the different techniques used by speakers to emphasize key points. Encourage students to offer examples of each technique.
- Use the instruction from Comparing Literary Works to help students understand the importance of a speaker's choice of words.

❸ Reading Strategy

Evaluating Persuasive Appeals

- Explain to students that effective speakers use a variety of persuasive appeals in order to convince their audiences to believe in something or follow a particular course of action.
- Remind students that a speaker can persuade an audience by appealing to listeners' sense of reason or can sway them through emotional appeals.
- Then, discuss with students how a speaker might make this decision. Ask them to consider such things as the speaker's objective, the occasion, and the audience in evaluating the speaker's persuasive appeals.
- Give students a copy of **Reading Strategy Graphic Organizer A,** p. 42 in ***Graphic Organizer Transparencies,*** to record the different appeals each speaker makes as they read the selections.

Vocabulary Builder

- Pronounce each vocabulary word for students, and read the definitions as a class. Have students identify any words with which they are already familiar.

TEACH

Learning Modalities
Verbal/Linguistic Learners
Have students listen to the speech on **Listening to Literature CDs**. Then, have students rehearse and deliver one or two paragraphs of Henry's speech to the class. Have the class offer suggestions on ways to make each student's delivery more dramatic and persuasive.

❶ About the Selection

Patrick Henry's speech in the convention played a key role in turning colonial sentiment against negotiation with England and toward armed rebellion. He begins the speech with a respectful rebuttal to the previous speeches. He then defends his call for independence.

Henry argues that colonists have tried every argument but discussion is useless in averting the coming conflict. By establishing that the British are preparing for war, he asserts the war has already begun, undercutting any arguments for peaceful compliance.

❷ Humanities

Patrick Henry Before the Virginia House of Burgesses, by Peter F. Rothermel

In the mid-1800s Philadelphia had its own group of painters of historical subjects. The leader of these artists was Rothermel. In this painting, Rothermel presents his interpretation of Patrick Henry delivering his famous address.

Use this question for discussion:

How has the artist created a dramatic atmosphere in this painting?

Answer: Henry is on a raised platform; his lighted face is set against a dark background; his listeners are responding with animated expressions; the character in the foreground grips the chair and table; a glove lies forgotten on the floor.

❷

Patrick Henry Before the Virginia House of Burgesses, Peter F. Rothermel, Red Hill, The Patrick Henry National Memorial

❸ ▲ Critical Viewing Patrick Henry's dramatic speeches swayed sentiment away from loyalty to the British crown and toward armed resistance. What details in this painting convey the power of Henry's oratory? **[Analyze]**

Differentiated Instruction Solutions for All Learners

Accessibility at a Glance

	Speech in the Virginia Convention	Speech in the Convention
Context	Call to arms	Urges acceptance of Constitution
Language	Some difficult vocabulary	Difficult vocabulary and complicated sentences
Concept Level	Challenging (argues against negotiation in favor of armed rebellion)	Complex reasoning
Literary Merit	Cross-curricular: government;	Cross-curricular: government
Lexile	980	1500
Overall Rating	More challenging	More challenging

❶

Speech in the Virginia Convention

PATRICK HENRY

Background In this speech, delivered in 1775, Patrick Henry publicly denounces the British king and urges the colonists to fight for independence. Making such a declaration took tremendous bravery. England was the world's most powerful country at the time, and the odds against the colonists were overwhelming. If the colonies had failed to win independence, Henry could have been executed for treason.

Mr. President: No man thinks more highly than I do of the patriotism, as well as abilities, of the very worthy gentlemen who have just addressed the house. But different men often see the same subject in different lights; and, therefore, I hope it will not be thought disrespectful to those gentlemen, if, entertaining, as I do, opinions of a character very opposite to theirs, I shall speak forth my sentiments freely and
❹ without reserve. This is no time for ceremony. The question before the house is one of awful moment[1] to this country. For my own part, I consider it as nothing less than a question of freedom or slavery. And in proportion to the magnitude of the subject ought to be the freedom of the debate. It is only in this way that we can hope to arrive at truth, and fulfill the great responsibility which we hold to God and our country. Should I keep back my opinions at such a time, through fear of giving offense, I should consider myself as guilty of treason toward my country, and of an act of disloyalty toward the Majesty of Heaven, which I revere above all earthly kings.

Literary Analysis
Speeches and Diction Identify three phrases from this section that show Henry's use of sophisticated diction.

❺ 

Does Henry agree or disagree with those who spoke before him?

1. **moment** importance.

❸ Critical Viewing

Answer: Some students may say that the painting shows dramatic impact, with the speech causing incredulous characters to talk among themselves or to rise in reaction. Other students may classify those same depictions as examples of inattention.

❹ Literary Analysis
Speeches and Diction

- Remind students that diction is a writer's (or speaker's) choice of words. A speaker's word choice often depends on his or her subject, the occasion, and the audience.
- **Ask** students to identify both the speaker's purpose and his audience. Then, in view of these, ask students to discuss what diction they would expect the speaker to use.
  Answer: Henry is trying to persuade listeners to fight for independence. His audience is made up of Virginia statesmen. Henry's diction would most likely be formal and sophisticated.
- **Ask** the Literary Analysis question: Identify three phrases from this section that show Henry's use of sophisticated diction.
  Possible responses: "No man thinks more highly than I do . . . "; "I shall speak forth my sentiments . . . "; " . . . in proportion to the magnitude of the subject ought to be the freedom of the debate"

❺ Reading Check

Answer: Henry disagrees with those who spoke before him.

Differentiated Instruction
Solutions for All Learners

Strategy for Special Needs Students
Have students work in pairs to read through the speech, stopping at the end of each paragraph to review Henry's oratory techniques. Have students use the Two-column Chart in ***Graphic Organizer Transparencies***, p. 315. In the left column, have theme for write the technique in each paragraph. In the left-hand examples of each technique as they read.

Enrichment for Gifted/Talented Students
Challenge students to write a speech to be delivered in the United States Congress on an important contemporary issue. Suggest that students write a persuasive speech that appeals to both reason and emotion and deliver it to the class in much the same way Patrick Henry may have delivered his speech.

❻ Literary Analysis
Speeches

- Remind students that asking a rhetorical question is one technique a speaker can use in a speech. Rhetorical questions are questions to which the answer is evident. Because the answer is evident, these questions are often used to stir the emotions of listeners.
- Have a volunteer read aloud the bracketed passage. Encourage students to think about how these questions make them feel as they listen to them.
- Then, **ask** students the Literary Analysis question: What is the effect of the five rhetorical questions in this paragraph?
Answer: These questions counter any possible argument from those who still hesitate about going to war. They also help to stir up the indignation and frustration of the listeners.

Mr. President, it is natural to man to indulge in the illusions of hope. We are apt to shut our eyes against a painful truth, and listen to the song of that siren till she transforms us into beasts.[2] Is this the part of wise men, engaged in a great and arduous struggle for liberty? Are we disposed to be of the number of those who having eyes see not, and having ears hear not,[3] the things which so nearly concern their temporal salvation? For my part, whatever anguish of spirit it may cost, I am willing to know the whole truth; to know the worst and to provide for it.

I have but one lamp by which my feet are guided, and that is the lamp of experience. I know of no way of judging of the future but by the past. And judging by the past, I wish to know what there has been in the conduct of the British ministry for the last ten years to justify those hopes with which gentlemen have been pleased to solace themselves and the house? Is it that insidious smile with which our petition has been lately received? Trust it not, sir; it will prove a snare to your feet. Suffer not yourselves to be betrayed with a kiss.[4] Ask yourselves how this gracious reception of our petition comports with those warlike preparations which cover our waters and darken our land. Are fleets and armies necessary to a work of love and reconciliation? Have we shown ourselves so unwilling to be reconciled that force must be called in to win back our love? Let us not deceive ourselves, sir. These are the implements of war and subjugation—the last arguments to which kings resort.

I ask gentlemen, sir, what means this martial array, if its purpose be not to force us to submission? Can gentlemen assign any other possible motive for it? Has Great Britain any enemy in this quarter of the world, to call for all this accumulation of navies and armies? No, sir, she has none. They are meant for us: they can be meant for no other. They are sent over to bind and rivet upon us those chains which the British ministry have been so long forging.

❻ And what have we to oppose to them? Shall we try argument? Sir, we have been trying that for the last ten years. Have we anything new to offer upon the subject? Nothing. We have held the subject up in every light of which it is capable; but it has been all in vain. Shall we resort to entreaty and humble supplication? What terms shall we find which have not been already exhausted? Let us not, I beseech you, sir, deceive ourselves longer. Sir, we have done everything that could be done to avert the storm which is now coming on. We have petitioned; we have remonstrated; we have supplicated; we have prostrated ourselves before the throne, and have implored its interposition[5] to arrest the tyrannical hands of the ministry and Parliament. Our petitions

Vocabulary Builder
arduous (är′ jo͞o əs) *adj.* difficult

Vocabulary Builder
insidious (in sid′ ē əs) *adj.* deceitful; treacherous

Vocabulary Builder
subjugation (sub′ jə gā′ shən) *n.* the act of conquering

Literary Analysis
Speeches What is the effect of the five rhetorical questions in this paragraph?

2. **listen . . . beasts** In Homer's *Odyssey*, the enchantress Circe transforms men into swine after charming them with her singing.
3. **having eyes . . . hear not** In Ezekiel 12:2, those "who have eyes to see, but see not, who have ears to hear, but hear not" are addressed.
4. **betrayed with a kiss** In Luke 22:47–48, Jesus is betrayed with a kiss.
5. **interposition** intervention.

Enrichment

The Year 1775

The year 1775 was a momentous one in American history. It was on March 23 of 1775 that Patrick Henry rose to address the Virginia Convention. The issue before the legislative body was whether to arm the Virginia Militia in order to be ready to fight Great Britain. Less than a month after Henry's speech, on April 19, British troops marched to Lexington and Concord in search of hidden colonial arms and leaders. Before the year was over, the colonists appointed George Washington as Commander-in-Chief of the Continental Army. In Virginia, the local militia forced the Royal Governor to flee to the safety of a British warship off the coast. By the end of the year, it was clear to colonial leaders that there was no turning back. Patrick Henry's call for freedom or death had become reality.

have been slighted; our remonstrances have produced additional violence and insult; our supplications have been disregarded; and we have been spurned with contempt from the foot of the throne! In vain, after these things, may we indulge the fond[6] hope of peace and reconciliation. There is no longer any room for hope. If we wish to be free, if we mean to preserve inviolate those inestimable privileges for which we have been so long contending, if we mean not basely to abandon the noble struggle in which we have been so long engaged, and which we have pledged ourselves never to abandon until the glorious object of our contest shall be obtained—we must fight! I repeat it, sir, we must fight! An appeal to arms and to the God of Hosts is all that is left us!

AMERICA TRIUMPHANT and BRITANNIA in DISTRESS
EXPLANATION.
I America ſitting on that quarter of the globe with the Flag of the United States diſplayed over her head; holding in one hand the Olive branch, inviting the ſhips of all nations to partake of her commerce; and in the other hand ſupporting the Cap of Liberty.
II Fame proclaiming the joyful news to all the world.
III Britannia weeping at the loſs of the trade of America, attended with an evil genius.
IV The British flag ſtruck, on her ſtrong Fortreſses.
V French, Spaniſh, Dutch, &c. ſhipping in the harbours of America.
VI A view of New-York, wherein is exhibited the Traitor Arnold, taken with remorſe for ſelling his

7 ▲ **Critical Viewing** What details in this political cartoon convey the artist's opinion? **[Analyze]**

They tell us, sir, that we are weak—unable to cope with so formidable an adversary. But when shall we be stronger? Will it be the next week, or the next year? Will it be when we are totally disarmed, and when a British guard shall be stationed in every house? Shall we gather strength by irresolution and inaction? Shall we acquire the means of effectual resistance by lying supinely on our backs and hugging the delusive phantom of hope until our enemies shall have bound us hand and foot? Sir, we are not weak, if we make a proper use of those means which the God of nature hath placed in our power. Three millions of people, armed in the holy cause of liberty, and in such a country as that which we possess, are invincible by any force which our enemy can send against us. Besides, sir, we shall not fight our battles alone.
8 There is a just God who presides over the destinies of nations and who will raise up friends to fight our battles for us. The battle, sir, is not to the strong alone;[7] it is to the vigilant, the active, the brave. Besides, sir,

Vocabulary Builder
vigilant (vij′ ə lənt) *adj.* alert to danger

9 **Reading Check**
What measures, short of war, have the colonists tried?

6. **fond** foolish.
7. **The battle . . . alone** "The race is not to the swift, nor the battle to the strong." (Ecclesiastes 9:11)

7 Critical Viewing

Possible response: The depiction of Britain with an "evil genius," and America with an olive branch are two elements that reveal the artist's opinion.

8 Reading Strategy
Evaluating Persuasive Appeals

- Direct students' attention to Henry's use of the words *God* and *destinies*. Ask students to analyze what Henry is saying here.
  Possible response: Henry argues that God, who is on the side of the just, will favor their cause.

➤ **Monitor Progress:** Have students **evaluate** Henry's emotional appeal. How well do students think this appeal suits his audience and occasion?
Possible response: Students may say that listeners who foresaw the establishment of a new nation would have responded well to Henry's appeal.

9 Reading Check

Answer: The colonists have tried organizing protests and petitioning the king for justice.

Differentiated Instruction
Solutions for All Learners

Vocabulary for Less Proficient Readers
Direct students' attention to the paragraph on page 204 that begins "I ask gentlemen . . . ." Have the students work in pairs to use context clues to find out the meaning of *martial* and *forging*. Direct them to use *armies and navies* and *implements of war* to find the meaning of *martial,* and to use *chains* and *rivet* to find the meaning of *forging*.

Vocabulary for English Learners
Have students use each of the following vocabulary words in a sentence: *arduous, insidious, subjugation,* and *vigilant*. Then, have students work in pairs to write a paragraph about the American colonies in which they use each word.

Enrichment for Advanced Readers
Have students work in pairs to write a speech in rebuttal to Patrick Henry's. Have students do historical research to develop point-by-point rebuttals and encourage them to develop their own persuasive appeals, which should include appeals to emotion.

ASSESS

Answers

1. Students may say they would be swayed by the power of Henry's rhetoric and logic. They should refer to Henry's powerful appeals to patriotism and freedom.
2. (a) Henry says he thinks highly of their patriotism and abilities.
(b) Henry wants to give the impression that he has considered their arguments.
3. (a) Henry says they have "petitioned," "remonstrated," "supplicated," "prostrated," and "implored" the throne.
(b) The crown has shown it will not compromise and is intent on using force to gain submission.
4. (a) He wants the colonists to prepare for war. (b) He says that delay will allow the British to grow stronger.
5. (a) Students may say that Henry was committed to independence. In making that statement, in the context of the times, he was bringing a death sentence on himself if the colonists lost the war.
(b) Students may say it shows Henry was a man of courage who cared deeply about his country.
(c) Students' responses should show they understand the historical context of the speech.
6. Students should recognize that many people with close emotional ties to England likely supported the Tories.

Go Online Author Link For additional information about Patrick Henry, have students type in the Web Code, then select H from the alphabet, and then select Patrick Henry.

⑩ About the Selection

Benjamin Franklin uses his years of experience to urge his colleagues to accept the Constitution. Franklin admits that he does not entirely approve of the newly framed Constitution. He says that any legal document created by committee will have some inherent weaknesses although the government will more likely fail because of the people who administer it than because of the document that established it.

we have no election;[8] if we were base enough to desire it, it is now too late to retire from the contest. There is no retreat but in submission and slavery! Our chains are forged! Their clanging may be heard on the plains of Boston! The war is inevitable—and let it come! I repeat it, sir, let it come!

It is in vain, sir, to extenuate the matter. Gentlemen may cry, "Peace, peace"—but there is no peace. The war is actually begun! The next gale that sweeps from the north[9] will bring to our ears the clash of resounding arms! Our brethren are already in the field! Why stand we here idle? What is it that gentlemen wish? What would they have? Is life so dear, or peace so sweet, as to be purchased at the price of chains and slavery? Forbid it, Almighty God! I know not what course others may take; but as for me, give me liberty or give me death!

---

8. **election** choice.
9. **The next gale . . . north** In Massachusetts, some colonists had already shown open resistance to the British.

Critical Reading

1. **Respond:** If you had been in the audience, how would you have responded to Henry's speech? Why?
2. **(a) Recall:** What does Henry say about the previous speakers? **(b) Infer:** What does he hope to accomplish by commenting on the earlier speakers?
3. **(a) Recall:** What measures does Henry say the colonists have already tried in their dealings with England? **(b) Analyze:** What examples does Henry provide to support his position that compromise with the British is not a workable solution?
4. **(a) Infer:** What course of action does Henry want the colonists to take? **(b) Draw Conclusions:** What is Henry's answer to the objection that the colonists are not ready to fight against the British?
5. **(a) Speculate:** Do you think Henry was prepared to stand behind his words when he exclaimed, "Give me liberty or give me death"? Why, or why not? **(b) Deduce:** What does his willingness to make such an assertion reveal about his character? **(c) Extend:** If you had been in his place, would you have made such an assertion? Why, or why not?
6. **Speculate:** What types of people living in the colonies at the time of Henry's speech might have reacted negatively to his words? Why?

For: More about Patrick Henry
Visit: www.PHSchool.com
Web Code: ere-9206

Enrichment

The Constitution

Following the American Revolution, the newly independent states created their own constitution that gave most of the power to each state's elected legislative officials.

Congress was able to pass limited laws, but it had no power to tax the states or to regulate issues regarding trade and boundaries between states. These problems and other weaknesses inherent in the confederation resulted in the states sending delegates to a Constitutional Convention. This convention gave national government more power.

During the debate over ratification, two major sides emerged: the Federalists and anti-Federalists. Anti-Federalists were worried that the Constitution would give too much power to the federal government. The Federalists promised to add a Bill of Rights, which helped win ratification.

10

Speech in the Convention

Benjamin Franklin

Mr. President,

I confess, that I do not entirely approve of this Constitution at present; but, Sir, I am not sure I shall never approve it; for, having lived long, I have experienced many instances of being obliged, by better information or fuller consideration, to change my opinions even on important subjects, which I once thought right, but found to be otherwise. It is therefore that, the older I grow, the more apt I am to doubt my own judgment of others. Most men, indeed, as well as most sects in religion, think themselves in possession of all truth, and that wherever others differ from them, it is so far error. . . . Though many private Persons think almost as highly of their own infallibility as of that of their Sect, few express it so naturally as a certain French Lady, who, in a little dispute with her sister, said, "But I meet with nobody but myself that is *always* in the right." "*Je ne trouve que moi qui aie toujours raison.*"

Vocabulary Builder
infallibility (in fal′ ə bil′ ə tē) *n.* inability to be wrong; reliability

In these sentiments, Sir, I agree to this Constitution, with all its faults,—if they are such; because I think a general Government necessary for us, and there is no form of government but what may be a blessing to the people, if well administered; and I believe, farther, that this is likely to be well administered for a course of years, and can only end in despotism, as other forms have done before it, when the people shall become so corrupted as to need despotic government, being incapable of any other. I doubt, too, whether any other Convention we can obtain, may be able to make a better constitution; for, when you assemble a number of men, to have the advantage of their joint wisdom, you inevitably assemble with those men all their prejudices, their passions, their errors of opinion, their local interests, and their selfish views. From such an assembly can a *perfect* production be expected? It therefore astonishes me, Sir, to find this system approaching so near to perfection as it does; and I think it will astonish our enemies, who are waiting with confidence to hear, that our councils are confounded like those of the builders of Babel, and that our States are on the point of separation, only to meet hereafter for the purpose of cutting one another's throats. Thus I consent, Sir, to this Constitution, because I expect no better, and because I am not

Vocabulary Builder
despotism (des′ pət iz′ əm) *n.* absolute rule; tyranny

13  **Reading Check**
Why is Franklin so astonished by the high quality of the Constitution?

Differentiated Instruction Solutions for All Learners

Enrichment for Advanced Readers
Suggest that students read additional works by Benjamin Franklin. They can choose to read parts of Franklin's *Letters to the Press,* 1758–1775, V. W. Crane, editor. You may also wish to direct students to Authors In Depth, The American Experience, which contains the following selections:

- from *The Autobiography*
- "Information to Those Who Would Remove to America"
- "Speech in the Convention on the Subject of Salaries"

After students have read these or other works by Franklin, have them form discussion groups in which they compare and contrast the selections they have read. Suggest criteria for comparison, such as author's purpose or persuasive writing. To extend the activity, have volunteers read the speeches to the class, and then ask the class to analyze Franklin's effectiveness.

11 Reading Strategy
Evaluating Persuasive Appeals

- Have students read the bracketed passage to themselves. Then, have them paraphrase the passage's meaning.
- **Ask** students to identify Franklin's main points in this passage.
  Answer: Franklin says that he does not entirely approve of the Constitution. He also says that the older he gets, the more he doubts his judgements of others.
- **Ask** students to describe the appeal Franklin uses in this passage.
  Answer: Franklin appeals to his listeners' fears of making a grave error in voting to ratify the Constitution. By admitting to his own fallibility and the impossibility of perfect judgment, he neutralizes such fears, leaving his listeners free to compromise.

12 Vocabulary Builder
The Latin suffix *-ity*

- Draw students' attention to Franklin's use of the word *infallibility,* and read its definition.
- Have students **suggest** other words containing the suffix *-ity,* and write their suggestions on the chalkboard.
  Possible answers: *creativity, ingenuity, possibility*
- Break the suggested words down into their base word plus suffix. For example, creativity becomes creative + *-ity.* Based on these words, have students infer the meaning of the suffix *-ity.*
  Answer: When added to an adjective, the suffix -ity creates a noun indicating a state of being.

13 Reading Check

Answer: Franklin is astonished because he believes that when you assemble a group of people, their prejudices, passions, personal views, and selfish interests will color any achievements. A perfect product cannot come out of such an assembly. However, he believes that the Constitution is as close to perfect as one can get.

⓮ Humanities

***Benjamin Franklin (1706–90)–Overseeing the Printing of Poor Richard's Almanack,* oil on canvas, by Norman Rockwell (1894–1978)**

Norman Rockwell was born in New York City in 1894. He studied at the Art Students League and received his first free-lance assignment at age 17. Rockwell is most known for his illustrations for *The Saturday Evening Post*. He illustrated 317 covers for the magazine. Rockwell's paintings were of everyday people and small-town life. He treated his subjects with a little humor and paid meticulous attention to detail.

One of his most famous series was called *The Four Freedoms*. Posters of these paintings were distributed all over during World War II. The paintings were based on President Roosevelt's principles. Rockwell also illustrated the official *Boy Scout Calendar* for 50 years. Use this question for discussion:

- What particulars in this painting show Rockwell's attention to detail? **Possible response:** The pattern on Franklin's vest and the lace on his shirt are finely detailed. The wrinkles on his face are even visible.

⓯ Critical Viewing

Possible answer: Students may suggest that the depiction is what they imagined because of his action. He is reviewing a document with a critical eye like he probably reviewed the constitution. He also has a kind of gentleness to him that comes out in his speech.

⓮

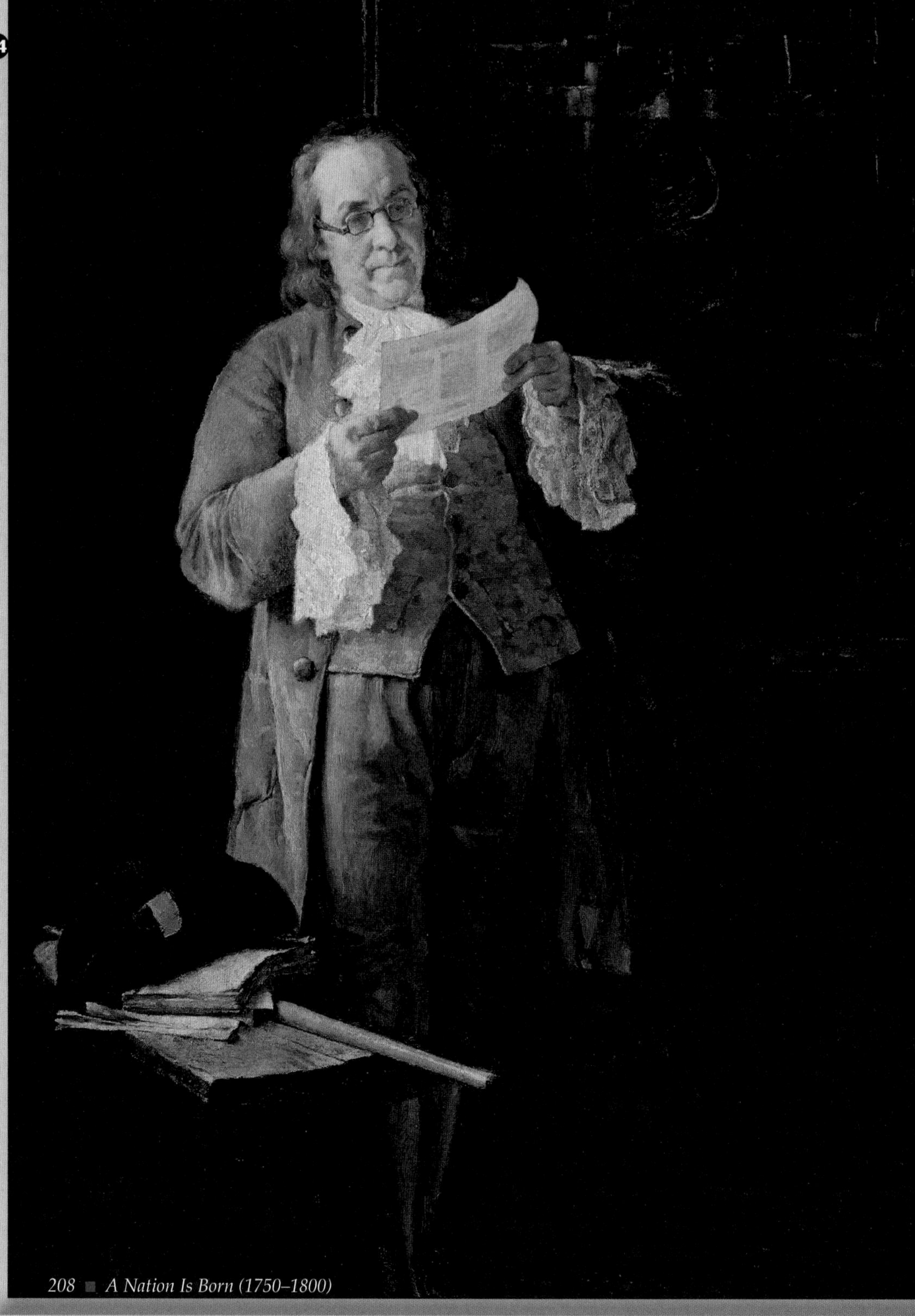

sure that it is not the best. The opinions I have had of its *errors* I sacrifice to the public good. I have never whispered a syllable of them abroad. Within these walls they were born, and here they shall die. If every one of us, in returning to our Constituents, were to report the objections he has had to it, and endeavour to gain Partisans in support of them, we might prevent its being generally received, and thereby lose all the salutary effects and great advantages resulting naturally in our favour among foreign nations, as well as among ourselves, from our real or apparent unanimity. Much of the strength and efficiency of any government, in procuring and securing happiness to the people, depends on *opinion*, on the general opinion of the goodness of that government, as well as of the wisdom and integrity of its governors. I hope, therefore, for our own sakes, as a part of the people, and for the sake of our posterity, that we shall act heartily and unanimously in recommending this Constitution, wherever our Influence may extend, and turn our future thoughts and endeavors to the means of having it *well administered.*

On the whole, Sir, I cannot help expressing a wish, that every member of the Convention who may still have objections to it, would with me on this occasion doubt a little of his own infallibility, and, to make *manifest* our *unanimity*, put his name to this Instrument.

15 **◀ Critical Viewing**
Does the artist's depiction of Franklin match your impression of him from his speech? Explain. **[Connect]**

Vocabulary Builder

salutary (sal′ yo͞o ter′ ē) *adj.* beneficial; promoting a good purpose

unanimity (yo͞o′ nə nim′ ə tē) *n.* complete agreement

posterity (päs ter′ ə tē) *n.* all succeeding generations

manifest (man′ ə fest′) *adj.* evident; obvious; clear

Critical Reading

1. **Respond:** Based on Franklin's argument, would you have ratified the Constitution? Why or why not?
2. **(a) Recall:** What confession does Franklin make in the first paragraph? **(b) Interpret:** What effect does Franklin achieve with this "confession"?
3. **(a) Recall:** Why does Franklin feel that unanimity among the delegates is essential to the success of the United States? **(b) Analyze:** What is Franklin's purpose in suppressing his "opinions" for the "public good"?
4. **(a) Recall:** Why, according to Franklin, would any document created by a committee be faulty? **(b) Draw Conclusions:** What is Franklin implying about human nature?
5. **(a) Recall:** What three reasons does Franklin give for finally agreeing to accept the Constitution? **(b) Evaluate:** How effectively does he convey the thought process that brought him from doubt about the Constitution to a decision to accept it? Explain.
6. **Take a Position:** Franklin says that government depends in part on the wisdom and integrity of its leaders. Do you agree? Explain.

For: More about Benjamin Franklin
Visit: www.PHSchool.com
Web Code: ere-9207

ASSESS

Answers

1. **Possible response:** In the spirit of pragmatism, students will likely agree that it was the best document available at the time and has certainly stood the test of time.
2. (a) He confesses that he does not entirely approve of the Constitution.
   (b) Students should see he disarms opponents by showing he is not rigid or inflexible.
3. (a) Unanimity will show citizens and the world that conflicting political interests do not prevent the nation's officials from working together.
   (b) Franklin does not want factions to arise as a result of lingering objections to this or that aspect of the Constitution's provisions.
4. (a) A committee brings not just its strengths but its weaknesses together.
   (b) Franklin implies that people have shortcomings as well as strengths in their character and abilities.
5. (a) The reasons he gives include that a general government is necessary; that no other convention could make a better constitution; and that enemies of the nation hope for a disagreement among the separate states.
   (b) Franklin effectively establishes positive reasons for approving the Constitution and eliminates any reasons for withholding approval. He does so by pointing out the impossibility of creating a perfect document by a committee and by stressing the importance of showing unanimity to Americans and the world.
6. Student responses will probably reflect the presence or absence of doubts that many people have about the political system.

Go Online Author Link For additional information about Benjamin Franklin, have students type in the Web Code, then select F from the alphabet, and then select Benjamin Franklin.

Apply the Skills

Speech in the Virginia Convention • Speech in the Convention

Literary Analysis

Speeches

1. Use a chart like the one shown to analyze each speaker's use of persuasive techniques.

	Example	Effect
Restatement		
Repetition		
Parallelism		

2. In what way does each speaker use "concession," or the acknowledgment of opposition arguments, to advance his position?
3. Based on this **speech,** do you think Henry's reputation as a great orator was deserved? Explain.

Comparing Literary Works

4. **(a)** To analyze the **diction** used by each speaker, find an example of ornate language from each speech. **(b)** Rewrite the passage in plain language. **(c)** Explain how the diction helps convey the message.
5. **(a)** Compare and contrast the endings of these speeches and weigh their impact on an audience. **(b)** Which do you think is more effective? Explain.
6. **(a)** What words does each speaker use to refer to the country's future? **(b)** How does each man see his responsibility—and that of his audience—to that future?
7. **(a)** How is Franklin's experience as a diplomat reflected in his speech? **(b)** How is Henry's experience as a lawyer reflected in his?

Reading Strategy

Evaluating Persuasive Appeals

8. Considering the purpose of Henry's speech, why are **persuasive appeals** to both emotions and reason appropriate?
9. What arguments does Franklin use to back up his emotional appeals?

Extend Understanding

10. **Social Studies Connection:** At times of crisis, what role can political speeches like those of Henry and Franklin play in public life? Explain.

QuickReview

Speeches are works of writing delivered orally. They often include techniques such as restatement, repetition, parallelism, and rhetorical questions.

Diction is a writer's or speaker's choice and arrangement of words.

Persuasive techniques include appeals to both the emotions and the reason of an audience.

For: Self-test
Visit: www.PHSchool.com
Web Code: era-6205

Answers

1. **Sample response:** (Henry) Restatement Mr. President, it is natural to indulge in the illusions of hope. We are apt to shut our eyes against a painful truth. **Effect:** It reinforces the point.
2. **Possible response:** Henry's "concession" to former speakers' patriotism and good intentions establishes his voice as one of considerate reasonableness pushed to extremes. Franklin's concession that those who oppose ratification have some valid arguments reinforces his position that some compromise is needed.
3. **Possible response:** Henry's reputation is deserved. The speech has dynamic imagery, powerful emotional appeals, and eloquent diction.
4. **Possible response:** (a) Students should choose effective and characteristic language from each speech. (b) Students' paraphrases should retain the meaning of the originals. (c) Students should recognize how the speakers use rhetorical devices to emphasize their points.
5. (a) Henry builds to an emotional climax with the final line. Franklin closes with a reasoned conclusion. (b) **Possible response:** Students will recognize that both accomplish their purposes.
6. (a) Franklin refers to *posterity,* and to the government's future administration. Henry speaks less directly about the future, but does refer to the great responsibility he and the others hold to achieve their aim of freedom. (b) Both men recognize that the future of the country hinges on decisions they and their peers will make.
7. (a) **Possible response:** Franklin's speech is logical, restrained, and respectful. (b) Henry's emotional appeal might sway a jury.
8. **Possible response:** Henry's well-educated audience needed a blend of reason and emotion to prompt them to act.

Answers continued

9. **Possible response:** Franklin appeals to the delegates' pride and vanity when he describes the Constitution as "so near to perfection."
10. **Possible response:** They can unite people in a common cause.

Go Online Assessment Students may use the **Self-test** to prepare for **Selection Test A** or **Selection Test B.**

Build Language Skills

Vocabulary Lesson

Word Analysis: Latin Suffix *-ity*

The Latin suffix *-ity* turns adjectives into nouns. Added to the adjective *infallible,* meaning "incapable of error," it creates the noun *infallibility,* meaning "the state of being infallible."

Define each of the following words:

1. complexity
2. flexibility
3. anonymity
4. adaptability

Spelling Strategy

When you add the suffix *-ity* to a word that ends in *-able* or *-ible,* drop the final *e* and insert *i* between the *b* and *l* (infallible + -ity = infallibility).

Add the suffix *-ity* to each word below.

1. legible
2. acceptable
3. reliable

Vocabulary Builder: Definitions

Match the vocabulary word with its definition.

1. insidious
2. subjugation
3. vigilant
4. infallibility
5. despotism
6. salutary
7. unanimity
8. manifest
9. arduous
10. posterity

a. evident; clear
b. deceitful; treacherous
c. complete agreement
d. tyranny
e. the act of conquering
f. alert to danger
g. reliability
h. beneficial
i. succeeding generations
j. very difficult

Grammar and Style Lesson

Double Negatives

Although it is no longer considered acceptable style, orators in the Revolutionary period sometimes used **double negatives**—two negatives where only one is needed—to stress their opinions. Look at these incorrect and correct examples. In both, the negatives are italicized:

Incorrect: I *don't hardly* know where to begin.

Correct: I *don't* know where to begin.

In the first example, there are two negatives. Remember to use only one negative to make a negative sentence.

Practice Revise each sentence that contains a double negative. If a sentence is correct, write "correct."

1. Don't sign nothing until you hear from me.
2. You don't have enough information.
3. I don't think you'll want hardly anything from me.
4. I didn't have any idea that he wouldn't show up.
5. It wouldn't make no difference to me if they cancelled the meeting.

Writing Application Write a paragraph in which you explain how the spirit of revolutionary Americans like Henry and Franklin does or does not still exist today. Use double negatives at least three times. Then, exchange your speech with a classmate and correct each other's mistakes.

WG *Prentice Hall Writing and Grammar Connection: Chapter 25, Section 1*

EXTEND/ASSESS

Answers

1 Vocabulary Lesson

Word Analysis

1. the quality of being complicated
2. the quality of being flexible; either changing shape or being receptive to change
3. the quality of being anonymous or unknown
4. the quality of being adaptable or changing to meet a situation

Spelling Strategy

1. legibility
2. acceptability
3. reliability

Vocabulary Builder

1. b
2. e
3. f
4. g
5. d
6. i
7. c
8. a
9. k
10. j

2 Grammar and Style Lesson

1. Don't sign anything until you hear from me.
2. correct
3. I don't think you'll want anything from me.
4. correct
5. It wouldn't make any difference to me if they cancelled the meeting.

Writing Application

See that students relate the revolutionary spirit to contemporary events. Also, make sure they include at least three double negatives in their paragraph.

WG **Writing and Grammar, Ruby Level**

Students will find further instruction and practice on double negatives in Chapter 25, Section 1.

Assessment Practice

Predict Outcomes **(For more practice, see the *Standardized Test Preparation Workbook*, p. 11.)**

Practice predicting with this sample test item:

> Have we [colonists] shown ourselves so unwilling to be reconciled that [English] force must be called in to win back our love? These are implements of war and subjugation—the last arguments to which kings resort.

Based on this passage, what will happen if the British assemble their armies and navies?

A The British will remain peaceful.
B The colonists will monitor the British military to avoid armed conflict.
C The British will decrease their show of strength after they threaten the colonists.
D The British will use force against the colonists, and the two sides will go to war.

Based on the text, *D* is the most likely choice.

❸ Writing Lesson

- To guide students in evaluating a speech, give them the **Support for Writing Lesson,** page 85, in ***General Resources.***
- Model a speech for students by reading John F. Kennedy's Inaugural Address on p. 1230.
- Show students how Kennedy uses many of the same techniques as Henry and Franklin do—restatement, repetition, and parallelism.
- Analyze the persuasive appeals Kennedy uses to make his points.
- Show students direct quotations can be used to illustrate points in support of their arguments.
- Have students use the Critique rubrics, pp. 75–76 in ***General Resources,*** to complete their commentaries.

❹ Research and Technology

- Have students brainstorm for a list of possible research topics. If they have difficulties, suggest that they focus on famous presidents (Washington, Lincoln, Theodore and Franklin Roosevelt, Woodrow Wilson) and other statesmen (Winston Churchill, Daniel Webster, Henry Clay, John C. Calhoun).
- Divide the class into groups and assign each group a research topic to pursue.
- Encourage students to research the context and historical situation in which each speech was made.
- Have students share their findings with the rest of the class.
- The **Support for Extend Your Learning** page (***Unit 2 Resources,*** p. 86) provides guided note-taking opportunities to help students complete the Extend Your Learning activities.

Go Online Research Have students type in the Web Code for another research activity.

SAT® PREP ACT

❸ Timed Writing: Writing Lesson

Commentary on a Speech

Choose a speech by a skilled modern orator and write a commentary that evaluates the way in which the speaker leads an audience to agree with his or her ideas. ***(40 minutes)***

Prewriting *(10 minutes)* Outline the speaker's key points and note the persuasive techniques used. Then, evaluate how effectively the speaker has supported those points and used persuasive techniques.

Drafting *(20 minutes)* Focus each paragraph on a single point—for example, one paragraph might focus on the speaker's appeals to emotions, another on the speaker's appeals to reason.

Revising *(10 minutes)* Review your commentary to make sure you have adequately supported your ideas. Identify places in your draft where you might strengthen your analysis with direct quotations from the speech.

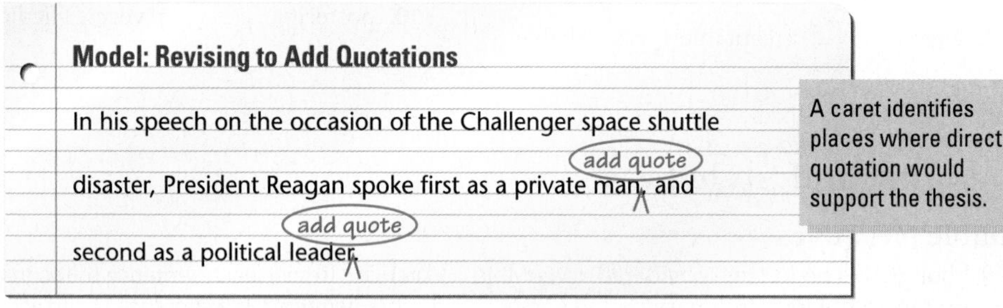

Model: Revising to Add Quotations
In his speech on the occasion of the Challenger space shuttle
add quote
disaster, President Reagan spoke first as a private man, and
add quote
second as a political leader.
A caret identifies places where direct quotation would support the thesis.

Prentice Hall Writing and Grammar Connection: Chapter 28, Section 1

❹ Extend Your Learning

Listening and Speaking With a group, prepare a **debate** about the value of independence or the ratification of the Constitution. Keep the following tips in mind:

- Choose evidence that supports your persuasive purpose.
- Include logical, ethical, and emotional appeals.

Present the debate to classmates. Maintain a positive atmosphere and control counter-productive emotional responses. **[Group Activity]**

Research and Technology Using electronic and online encyclopedias as sources, collect speeches from different periods of history. Incorporate photographs and audiotaped recordings of the speeches. Create a **display** highlighting key passages from the speeches.

For: An additional research activity
Visit: www.PHSchool.com
Web Code: erd-7204

Assessment Resources

The following resources can be used to assess students' knowledge and skills.

Unit 2 Resources
- **Selection Test A,** pp. 88–90
- **Selection Test B,** pp. 91–93

General Resources
- **Rubrics for Critique,** pp. 75–76

Go Online Assessment Students may use the **Self-test** to prepare for **Selection Test A** or **Selection Test B.**

Unit 2
Part
3

Defining an American

Selection Planning Guide

The selections in this section illustrate the American character that began to emerge in the eighteenth century. Abigail Adams's "Letter to Her Daughter from the New White House" illustrates both literally and figuratively that the United States was a country under construction. "Letters from an American Farmer" defines a new kind of person, an American.

Humanities

Eighteenth-century New England needlework

This needlework was made in the 1700s by a woman in New England. Help students see that the bright colors and loving detail of the work suggest the charm the creator saw in the land around her. The land is green, fertile, and abundant in both plant and animal life. The couple are happily reaping grain and picnicking. The natural scene—complete with serpent—recalls paradise in its beauty and innocence, suggesting America might be viewed as a New Eden.

Use these questions for discussion:

1. According to this needlework, what things were important to eighteenth-century Americans?
Possible responses: This needlework suggests that Americans valued the beauty of their land, its ability to provide for them, the animals that they encountered, both wild and domestic, their homes, and their family life.
2. Give this needlework a title appropriate to the idea of a new nation.
Possible responses: "A New Eden"; "A Day in an American Life"; "Adam and Eve in the New World."

Differentiated Instruction Solutions for All Learners

Accessibility at a Glance

Average	More Challenging
Letter to Her Daughter From the New White House	*from* Letters From an American Farmer

Meeting Your Standards

Students will

1. **analyze and respond to literary elements.**
   - Literary Analysis: Private and Public Letters (Epistles)
2. **read, comprehend, analyze, and critique nonfiction.**
   - Reading Strategy: Distinguishing Between Fact and Opinion
   - Reading Check questions
   - Apply the Skills questions
   - Assessment Practice (ATE)
3. **develop vocabulary.**
   - Vocabulary Lesson: Etymologies
4. **understand and apply written and oral language conventions.**
   - Spelling Strategy
   - Grammar and Style Lesson: Semicolons
5. **develop writing proficiency.**
   - Writing Lesson: Personal Letter
6. **develop appropriate research strategies.**
   - Extend Your Learning: Advertisements
7. **understand and apply listening and speaking strategies.**
   - Extend Your Learning: Interview

Block Scheduling: Use one 90-minute class period to preteach the skills and have students read the selection. Use a second 90-minute class period to assess students' mastery of skills, extend their learning, and monitor their progress.

Homework Suggestions

Following are possibilities for homework assignments.

- Support pages from *Unit 2 Resources:*
  Literary Analysis
  Reading Strategy
  Vocabulary Builder
  Grammar and Style
- An Extend Your Learning project and the Writing Lesson for this selection group may be completed over several days.

Step-by-Step Teaching Guide	Pacing Guide
PRETEACH	
• Administer Vocabulary and Reading Warm-ups as necessary.	5 min.
• Engage students' interest with the motivation activity.	5 min.
• Read and discuss author and background features. **FT**	10 min.
• Introduce the Literary Analysis Skill: Private and Public Letters (Epistles). **FT**	5 min.
• Introduce the Reading Strategy: Distinguishing Between Fact and Opinion. **FT**	10 min.
• Prepare students to read by teaching the selection vocabulary. **FT**	
TEACH	
• Informally monitor comprehension while students read independently or in groups. **FT**	30 min.
• Monitor students' comprehension with the Reading Check notes.	as students read
• Reinforce vocabulary with Vocabulary Builder notes.	as students read
• Develop students' understanding of private and public letters (epistles) with the Literary Analysis annotations. **FT**	5 min.
• Develop students' ability to distinguish between fact and opinion with the Reading Strategy annotations. **FT**	5 min.
ASSESS/EXTEND	
• Assess students' comprehension and mastery of the Literary Analysis and Reading Strategy by having them answer the Apply the Skills questions. **FT**	15 min.
• Have students complete the Vocabulary Development Lesson and the Grammar and Style Lesson. **FT**	15 min.
• Apply students' ability to use necessary context and background by using the Writing Lesson. **FT**	45 min. or homework
• Apply students' understanding by using one or more of the Extend Your Learning activities.	20–90 min. or homework
• Administer Selection Test A or Selection Test B. **FT**	15 min.

Resources

PRINT

Unit 2 Resources

Vocabulary Warm-up Word Lists **[L1, L2, EL]** . . . . .p. 94

Vocabulary Warm-up Practice **[L1, L2, EL]** . . . . .p. 95

Reading Warm-up A **[L1, L2, EL]** . . . . .p. 96

Reading Warm-up B **[L1, L2, L3]** . . . . .p. 97

TRANSPARENCY

Graphic Organizer Transparencies

Literary Analysis Graphic Organizer A **[L3]** . . . . .p. 48

Literary Analysis Graphic Organizer B **[L1, L2, EL]** . . . . .p. 49

Reading Strategy Graphic Organizer A **[L3]** . . . . .p. 46

Reading Strategy Graphic Organizer B **[L1, L2, EL]** . . . . .p. 47

PRINT

Reader's Notebook [L2]
Reader's Notebook: Adapted Version [L1]
Reader's Notebook: English Learner's Version [EL]

Unit 2 Resources

Literary Analysis **[L3]** . . . . .p. 98

Reading Strategy **[L3]** . . . . .p. 99

Vocabulary Builder **[L3]** . . . . .p. 100

TECHNOLOGY

Listening to Literature Audio CDs [L2, EL]
Reader's Notebook: Adapted Version Audio CD [L1, L2]

PRINT

Unit 2 Resources

Grammar and Style **[L3]** . . . . .p. 101

Support for Writing Lesson **[L3]** . . . . .p. 102

Support for Extend Your Learning **[L3]** . . . . .p. 103

Enrichment **[L4]** . . . . .p. 104

Selection Test A **[L1, L2, EL]** . . . . .pp. 105–107

Selection Test B **[L3, L4]** . . . . .pp. 108–110

General Resources

Rubrics for Business Letter **[L3]** . . . . .pp. 61–62

TECHNOLOGY

Go Online: Research **[L3]**
Go Online: Self-test **[L3]**
ExamView®, **Test Bank [L3]**

Choosing Resources for Differentiated Instruction

[L1] Special Needs Students
[L2] Below-Level Students
[L3] All Students
[L4] Advanced Students
[EL] English Learners

FT Fast Track Instruction: To move the lesson more quickly, use the strategies and activities identified with **FT**.

Scaffolding for Less Proficient and Advanced Students

The leveled Critical Thinking questions after selections progress in the levels of thinking required to answer them. To address the needs of your different students, you may use the (a) level questions for your less proficient students and the (b) level questions with your on-level and advanced students. The occasional (c) level questions are appropriate for your advanced students.

Use this complete suite of powerful teaching tools to make lesson planning and testing quicker and easier.

PRENTICE HALL
StudentEXPRESS™
Learn · Study · Succeed

Use the interactive textbook (online and on CD-ROM) to make selections and activities come alive with audio and video support and interactive questions.

PRETEACH

Motivation

Inform students that the selections provide windows through which they can catch a glimpse of early America. Ask students to imagine themselves receiving letters from early America. Have students make a list in response to the following questions:

For Adams: What is the new White House like?

For Crèvecoeur: What do you want to learn about American life?

Have students share their lists with the class. Discuss how such lists can be the basis of an informative letter.

1 Background

More About the Authors

Abigail Adams was born Abigail Smith, in Weymouth, Mass., on Nov. 11, 1744, the second of four children of Rev. William and Elizabeth Quincy Smith. Delicate in health, she never went to school. She married John Adams, a young Braintree lawyer, in 1764 when she was twenty, and bore him five children: two daughters, one of whom died as an infant, and three sons.

When Michel-Guillaume Jean de Crèvecoeur published *Letters From an American Farmer* he captured the imagination of downtrodden Europeans hungry for a better life. Life in America, however, was far from idyllic.

Because the country needed hard workers, not those seeking an easy life, it is no wonder that some American leaders worried about the effects of Crèvecoeur's glowing descriptions. George Washington himself called *Letters* "rather too flattering."

Build Skills | *Primary Sources*

1 Letter to Her Daughter From the New White House • *from* Letters From an American Farmer

Abigail Smith Adams (1744–1818)

Wife, mother, writer, first lady, revolutionary, women's rights pioneer—Abigail Smith Adams was all these and more. As the intelligent, outspoken wife of John Adams, the second president of the United States, and the mother of John Quincy Adams, the sixth president, Abigail Adams was one of the most influential women of her time.

Unequal Education Abigail Smith was born in Weymouth, Massachusetts. Although her father was a well-to-do minister and her mother came from an upper-class family, Abigail had no formal schooling. She often excused this shortcoming by saying that she was ill as a child. However, as a mother, she made sure that her daughter received as thorough an education as her four sons did—a privilege allotted to few American girls. Throughout her life, Adams vigorously supported women's rights to an education equal to the one men received.

A Political Wife At the age of twenty, Abigail married John Adams, whose political duties during and after the Revolution kept him from home for the better part of ten years. Abigail, therefore, became an avid correspondent, penning hundreds of letters to her husband and relatives and discussing everything from her opposition to slavery to her belief in women's rights. During the war, she even kept her husband posted on the movements of British troops.

Abigail Adams died in 1818. Twenty-two years after her death, her letters were collected and published. Today, she is a celebrated writer who is widely recognized as a pioneer of the American women's movement.

Michel-Guillaume Jean de Crèvecoeur (1735–1813)

The first writer to compare America to a melting pot, French aristocrat Michel-Guillaume Jean de Crèvecoeur (mē shel′ gē yōm zhän də krev kur) chronicled his experiences as a European immigrant adjusting to life in America. His idealistic descriptions confirmed a common vision of America as a land of great promise.

A Famous Farmer Born into a wealthy French family, Crèvecoeur emigrated to Canada and served for several years as a member of the French army in Quebec. After spending ten years traveling the colonies as a land surveyor and Indian trader, he married and settled on a farm in New York, where he began writing about his experiences in America. In 1780, Crèvecoeur sailed to London, where his *Letters From an American Farmer* was published two years later. This book, which was translated into several languages, made Crèvecoeur famous.

Returning To America In 1783, after visiting France, Crèvecoeur returned to America as a French Consul. Upon his return, he discovered that his farm had been burned, his wife killed, and his children sent to live with foster parents. When the French Revolution began in 1789, Crèvecoeur was obliged to return to Paris. He later fled to his family home in Normandy, where he continued to write about the adoptive country that he would never see again.

As France and the rest of Europe descended into the turmoil of the Napoleonic Wars, interest in the New World waned. Crèvecoeur spent the last years of his life largely forgotten amid the political turbulence.

Preview

Connecting to the Literature

Today, fewer and fewer people reach for pen and paper when they want to get in touch with someone. These selections, however, come from an era when letters were the only means of communicating over distances.

Literary Analysis

Private and Public Letters (Epistles)

Personal or **private letters** tend to be spontaneous, conversational, and intended only for the reader(s) to whom they are addressed. For example, Abigail Adams's language is conversational in this letter to her daughter:

> You must keep all this to yourself, and when asked how I like it, say that I write you the situation is beautiful, which is true.

By contrast, Crèvecoeur's *Letters* are **public letters** intended for a wide audience. Such literary works—essays written in letter form—are called **epistles.** By writing his essays in this form, Crèvecoeur maintains a personal approach while arguing public ideas.

Comparing Literary Works

The letters by Adams and the epistle by Crèvecoeur are both **primary source documents**—nonfiction works that are firsthand accounts of the era in which they were written. Some primary source documents, like the Declaration of Independence, speak solely to issues of public concern. Others reveal information about the private life of the writer. Compare and contrast the ways in which these letters detail the challenges of life in a new country.

3 Reading Strategy

Distinguishing Between Fact and Opinion

- A **fact** is something that can be proved.
- An **opinion** is a personal belief that can be supported but not proved. Opinions are usually indicated by words like "I think" or "it seems," suggesting individual judgment.

By **distinguishing between fact and opinion,** you can interpret the meaning of a literary work with greater accuracy. Use a chart like the one shown to record your observations about facts and opinions in these letters.

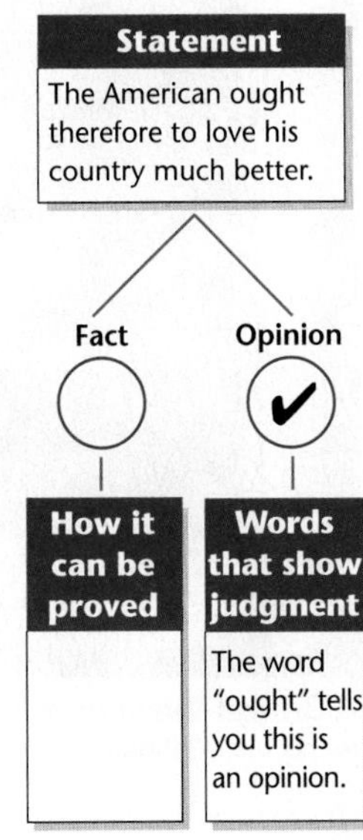

Vocabulary Builder

extricate (eks′ tri kāt′) *v.* set free (p. 217)

agues (ā′ gyo͞oz) *n.* fits of shivering (p. 218)

asylum (ə sī′ ləm) *n.* place of refuge (p. 220)

penury (pen′ yə rē) *n.* lack of money, property, or necessities (p. 220)

despotic (des pät′ ik) *adj.* harsh; cruel; unjust (p. 222)

subsistence (səb sis′ təns) *n.* means of support (p. 222)

2 Literary Analysis

Private and Public Letters (Epistles)

- Explain to students that in addition to private letters, with which students will be familiar, there are also public letters, known as epistles, which are written as an essay in the form of a letter to a general audience.
- Read the description of private letters and epistles together as a class. Draw students' attention to the examples provided.
- Use the instruction for Comparing Literary Works to familiarize students with primary source documents.

3 Reading Strategy

Distinguishing Between Fact and Opinion

- Review the definitions for fact and opinion with students.
- Explain the examples offered in the text, ensuring that students understand that factual statements are not necessarily true but they must be subject to proof.
- As they read the selections, have students use **Reading Strategy Graphic Organizer A,** p. 46 in ***Graphic Organizer Transparencies,*** to record facts and opinions and to help them distinguish between the two.

Vocabulary Builder

- Pronounce each vocabulary word for students, and read the definitions as a class. Have students identify any words with which they are unfamiliar.

Differentiated Instruction Solutions for All Learners

Support for Special Needs Students

Have students read the adapted versions of the selections in the ***Reader's Notebook: Adapted Version.*** This version provides basic-level instruction in an interactive format with questions and write-on lines. Completing these pages will prepare students to read the selection in the Student Edition.

Support for Less Proficient Readers

Have students read the selections in the ***Reader's Notebook.*** This version provides basic-level instruction in an interactive format with questions and write-on lines. After students finish the selection in the ***Reader's Notebook,*** have them complete the questions and activities in the Student Edition.

Support for English Learners

Have students read the selections in the ***Reader's Notebook: English Learner's Version.*** This version provides basic-level instruction in an interactive format with questions and write-on lines. Completing these pages will prepare students to read the selection in the Student Edition.

Learning Modalities
Verbal/Linguistic Learners
Abigail Adams' letters provide vivid firsthand accounts of history. Have students use Internet or library resources to find letters that capture the spirit of a period of history. Have students choose a letter and write a paragraph about what the letter reveals about the time in which it was written. Have students read their paragraphs aloud to the class. Students may also make the letters available to the class.

1 About the Selection

This letter provides an opportunity to examine the thoughts and feelings of the First Lady to occupy the White House. The beginning of the letter describes the difficulty Mrs. Adams's traveling party has in finding the way from Baltimore to Washington, a town made up at this time of nothing more than a few public buildings with crude residences scattered widely around it. The unfinished White House is huge but ill-equipped for living: there are thirty servants but no bells to ring for them, little firewood, and no fence or yard. Mrs. Adams, however, asks her daughter to keep these complaints between the two of them and to tell others only that the new White House and its city are beautiful. The first lady also shares with her daughter her active social life, including an invitation from Mrs. George Washington to visit Mount Vernon.

2 Critical Viewing

Possible response: With a sense of history, Abigail Adams may have expressed pride to be the first occupant of the White House. At the same time, she might have had some reservations about moving into an unfinished house without any conveniences in a town that was still under construction.

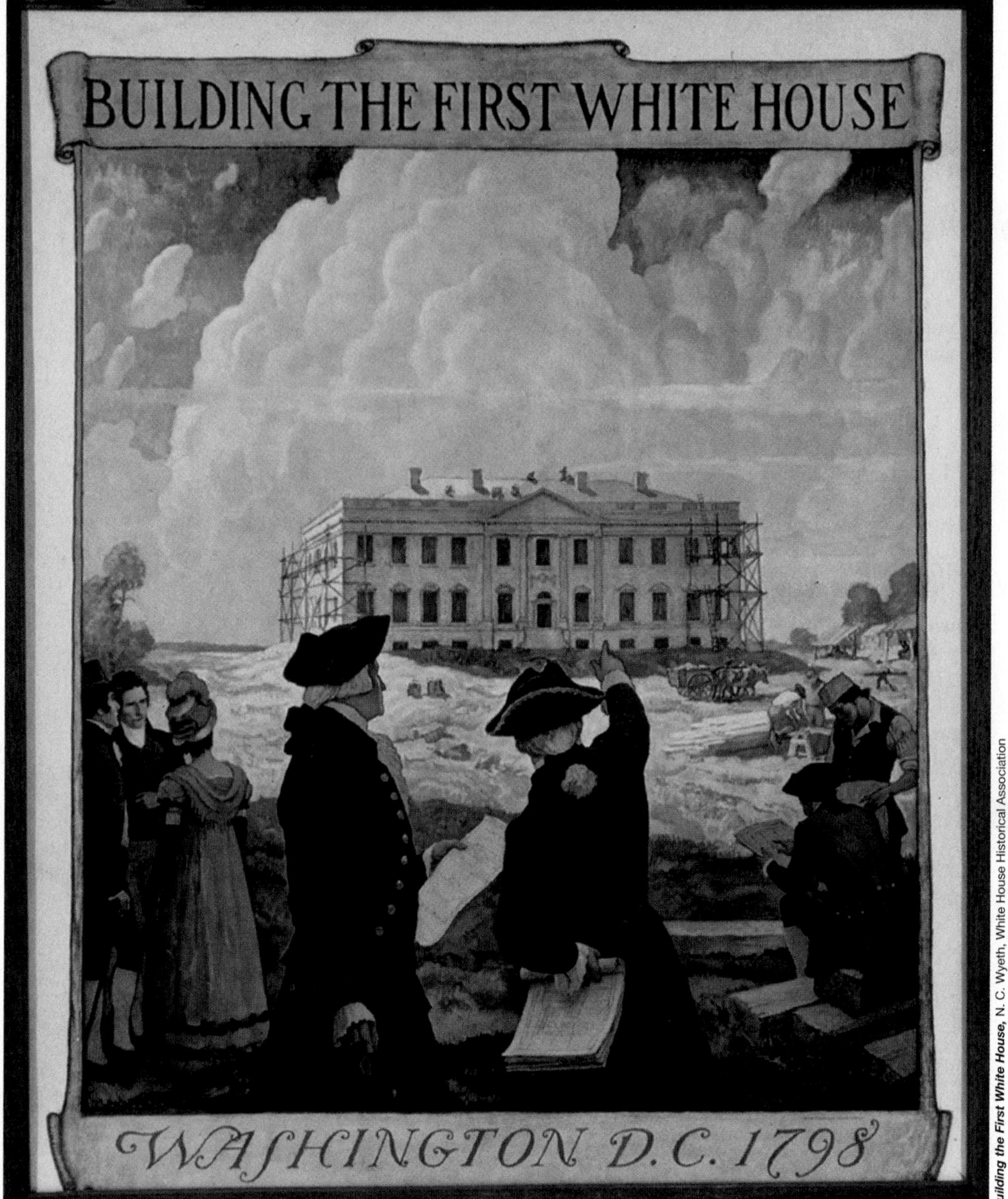

Building the First White House, N. C. Wyeth, White House Historical Association

2 ▲ Critical Viewing With what emotions might Abigail Adams have reacted to this scene? **[Speculate]** 3

Differentiated Instruction Solutions for All Learners

Accessibility at a Glance

	Letter to Her Daughter	Letters From an American Farmer
Context	Thoughts and feelings of first first lady	Immigrant experience
Language	Long sentences with embedded clauses	Difficult vocabulary
Concept Level	Accessible (description of daily events in life)	Accessible (America as land of opportunity)
Literary Merit	Primary source	Primary source
Lexile	1160	1050
Overall Rating	Average	More challenging

1 *Letter to Her Daughter From the New White House*

ABIGAIL ADAMS

Background When John Adams was elected president of the United States, he and Abigail became the first couple to live in the White House. At the time, the city of Washington consisted of a few public buildings and a scattered collection of crude residences. This letter to Adams's daughter describes the unfinished White House and captures the essence of life in the new nation.

Washington, 21 November, 1800

My Dear Child:

I arrived here on Sunday last, and without meeting with any accident worth noticing, except losing ourselves when we left Baltimore and going eight or nine miles on the Frederick road, by which means we were obliged to go the other eight through woods, where we wandered two hours without finding a guide or the path. Fortunately, a straggling black came up with us, and we engaged him as a guide to extricate us out of our difficulty; but woods are all you see from Baltimore until you reach the *city*, which is only so in name. Here and there is a small cot, without a glass window, interspersed amongst the forests, through which you travel miles without seeing any human being. In the city there are buildings enough, if they were

4 **Vocabulary Builder**
extricate (eks´ tri kāt´) *v.* set free

5 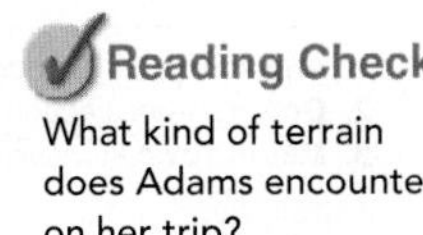
Reading Check
What kind of terrain does Adams encounter on her trip?

3 Humanities

Building the First White House, 1930, N.C. Wyeth

Newell Convers Wyeth was a famous and prolific American illustrator. One of his first commercial illustration commissions was to commemorate the Washington bicentennial year for the Pennsylvania Railroad. On May 1, 1930, the railroad advertised that "historical posters in full color, dealing with patriotic subjects have been designed by a well-known painter." In 1971 this painting appeared on the Christmas cards sent by then-President and Mrs. Nixon. Use the following questions for discussion:

1. What details in the painting clarify the time period?
   Answer: The lack of any other buildings in the vicinity, the clothes that the figures are wearing, and the wagon clarify the time period.
2. What effect does the placement of the figures have on the viewer?
   Answer: The figures help draw attention to the White House, especially the two figures standing in the center.

4 Vocabulary Builder

Word Analysis Etymologies

- Draw students' attention to the word *extricate,* and to its definition.
- Remind students that the Latin prefix *ex-* means *away from,* or *out of.*
- Let students know that the Latin root *tricae* means "a vexation or difficulty."
- Show students how from these definitions the meaning of the word can be inferred, "to remove or set free from a trouble or difficulty."

5 Reading Check

Answer: Adams travels through woods.

Differentiated Instruction
Solutions for All Learners

Strategy for Less Proficient Readers
Students may have difficulty with some of Adams's longer sentences. Encourage students to break down these long sentences to clarify their meaning. You may wish to model this process for students with the first sentence of the selection. Ask students to list events that Adams reports in each sentence segment:

- arrived last Sunday
- got lost leaving Baltimore
- went the wrong way on the Frederick road
- wandered for two hours in the woods

Enrichment for Gifted/Talented Students
Remind students that newspapers were few and far between, and all communications had to travel by horse and wagon. Explain to students that letters were the lifeline through which early Americans sent and received personal, professional, and political information. Have students analyze what the letters of Adams and Crévecoeur tell the reader about what it meant to be an American during our nation's early years.

6 Literary Analysis
Private and Public Letters (Epistles)

- Point out to students that the unfavorable comparison of Georgetown to Milton is a personal expression of opinion that would be entirely impolite to make in a public letter, especially as the author was the First Lady.
- **Ask** students the First Literary Analysis question: Why would this comment about "ladies" be found only in a private letter, never in an epistle?
  Answer: Adams's reports of her social visits are personal and would not appear in an epistle.

7 Literary Analysis
Letters and Primary Source Documents

- Explain to students that in 1800, Washington, D.C., was mostly rural. Adams was coming from Boston, one of the oldest and most developed of American cities.
- Encourage students to infer from the text what conveniences Adams had been accustomed to in her previous homes.
- Then, **ask** students the second Literary Analysis question: How does this statement about coming into a "new country" suggest a moment in time that is both historically and personally significant?
  Answer: Historically, the United States was a very young country and had a brand-new capital. Personally, the move to Washington was an adventure for Adams, and represented a very different kind of life than she had had in refined, cultivated Boston.

compact and finished, to accommodate Congress and those attached to it; but as they are, and scattered as they are, I see no great comfort for them. The river, which runs up to Alexandria,[1] is in full view of my window, and I see the vessels as they pass and repass. The house is upon a grand and superb scale, requiring about thirty servants to attend and keep the apartments in proper order, and perform the ordinary business of the house and stables; an establishment very well proportioned to the President's salary. The lighting of the apartments, from the kitchen to parlors and chambers, is a tax indeed; and the fires we are obliged to keep to secure us from daily agues is another very cheering comfort. To assist us in this great castle, and render less attendance necessary, bells are wholly wanting, not one single one being hung through the whole house, and promises are all you can obtain. This is so great an inconvenience, that I know not what to do, or how to do. The ladies from Georgetown[2] and in the city have many of them visited me. Yesterday I returned fifteen visits—but such a place as Georgetown appears—why, our Milton[3] is beautiful.

But no comparisons—if they will put me up some bells and let me have wood enough to keep fires, I design to be pleased. I could content myself almost anywhere three months; but, surrounded with forests, can you believe that wood is not to be had because people cannot be found to cut and cart it? Briesler entered into a contract with a man to supply him with wood. A small part, a few cords only, has he been able to get. Most of that was expended to dry the walls of the house before we came in, and yesterday the man told him it was impossible for him to procure it to be cut and carted. He has had recourse to coals; but we cannot get grates made and set. We have, indeed, come into a *new country.*

You must keep all this to yourself, and, when asked how I like it, say that I write you the situation is beautiful, which is true. The house is made habitable, but there is not a single apartment finished, and all withinside, except the plastering, has been done since Briesler came. We have not the least fence, yard, or other convenience without and the great unfinished audience room I make a drying-room of, to hang up the clothes in. The principal stairs are not up, and will not be this winter. Six chambers are made comfortable; two are occupied by the President and Mr. Shaw; two lower rooms, one for a common parlor, and one for a levee room. Upstairs there is the oval room, which is designed for the drawing room, and has the crimson furniture in it. It is a very handsome room now; but, when completed, it will be beautiful. If the twelve years, in which this place has been considered as the future seat of government had been improved, as they would have been if in New England, very many of the present inconveniences would have

1. **Alexandria** city in northeastern Virginia.
2. **Georgetown** section of Washington, D.C.
3. **Milton** town in Massachusetts.

Vocabulary Builder
agues (ā´ gyo͞oz) *n.* fits of shivering

Literary Analysis
Private and Public Letters (Epistles) Why would this comment about "ladies" be found only in a private letter, never in an epistle?

Literary Analysis
Private and Public Letters and Primary Source Documents In what ways does this statement about coming into a "new country" suggest a moment in time that is both historically and personally significant?

Enrichment
Adams and Women's Rights

In an era when most people believed that women needed little education, the Reverend William Smith saw to it that his daughter Abigail had the free use of his library. Under her father's guidance, she absorbed history, literature, philosophy, religion—and politics. John Adams was impressed with young Abigail's independent mind, and she became his wife and his chief advisor. In 1776 Abigail wrote to her husband of her vision of a new independence for women. "And by the way, in the new code of laws, which I suppose it will be necessary for you to make, I desire you would remember the ladies . . . Do not put such unlimited power into the hands of the husbands. Remember, all men would be tyrants if they could." Her complaint reflected her acute awareness that the era's law dictated that a married woman's rights were subsumed in her husband's; she could not vote, and any property she had when she married became her husband's absolutely.

been removed. It is a beautiful spot, capable of every improvement, and, the more I view it, the more I am delighted with it.

Since I sat down to write, I have been called down to a servant from Mount Vernon,[4] with a billet[5] from Major Custis, and a haunch of venison, and a kind, congratulatory letter from Mrs. Lewis, upon my arrival in the city, with Mrs. Washington's love, inviting me to Mount Vernon, where, health permitting, I will go before I leave this place.

Affectionately, your mother,

Abigail Adams

4. **Mount Vernon** home of George Washington, located in northern Virginia.
5. **billet** (bil′ it) *n.* brief letter.

Critical Reading

1. **Respond:** What, if anything, surprised you about Adams's description of the White House and the surrounding area?
2. **(a) Recall:** What details does Adams use to describe the area surrounding the White House? **(b) Generalize:** What does Adams's letter suggest about the difficulties facing those who were setting up a centralized national government?
3. **(a) Recall:** What does Adams instruct her daughter to tell those who ask about the White House? **(b) Speculate:** Why might Adams be greatly concerned about the opinions of others?
4. **(a) Classify:** Name two character traits that Adams exhibits as she faces the difficulties of life in her new home. **(b) Evaluate:** Adams is often referred to as a remarkable figure in our nation's history. Which character traits exhibited in this letter contribute to that assessment?
5. **(a) Apply:** Today, how are the White House and the city of Washington, D.C., different from the way they were when Adams lived there? **(b) Synthesize:** What do these differences tell you about changes in the United States since the eighteenth-century?
6. **Analyze:** In what ways does the construction of a home for its Presidents help the young nation to establish **(a)** its identity on the world stage, **(b)** symbolism, **(c)** tradition?
7. **Evaluate:** Is the continuity of the Presidential residence—the fact that every U.S. President lives in the White House—valuable? Explain.

For: More about Abigail Adams
Visit: www.PHSchool.com
Web Code: ere-9208

Differentiated Instruction Solutions for All Learners

Enrichment for Special Needs Students

Have students use the visual details in Adams's letter as the basis of a sketch or drawing of either the White House or her journey through the forest. Ask students to copy the details from the letter that they have illustrated on the bottom of their picture.

Strategy for English Learners

Have students choose a paragraph of the letter and identify the facts and opinions that Adams writes. For each fact and opinion, ask students to explain why they have identified each as such. Suggest that students use the Two-column Chart in ***Graphic Organizer Transparencies,*** labeling the left-hand column *Facts* and the right-hand column *Opinions.*

Enrichment for Gifted/Talented Students

John Adams's term as president was filled with controversy, as was the election of 1800 that was finally decided by the House of Representatives. Have students choose among the following issues on which to research and write a brief report: the XYZ Affair, the Alien and Sedition Acts, or the development of political parties.

Answers

1. Students may have been surprised by the degree to which the White House was unfinished. For example, students may be amused by the account of Abigail Adams drying laundry in the White House reception hall.
2. (a) The surrounding area is mostly wooded with just a few cottages interspersed throughout the forests, which are largely uninhabited. (b) Students should infer that those setting up the national government would not be able to show the world a national capital with the pomp and grandeur of other world cities.
3. (a) She tells her to say that the White House is located in a beautiful area. (b) Students should infer that as First Lady, Adams was in a political position in which the opinions of others carried great weight.
4. (a) She is plucky and flexible in adjusting to the situation. (b) She displays her intelligence, tact, and awareness of the difficulties of constructing the new nation's capital.
5. (a) Washington today is a modern, elegant city and the White House a beautifully preserved mansion. (b) The United States is now an established, developed nation.
6. (a) It shows the world that the country believes in a leader elected by the people who thus lives in the people's house. (b) It establishes a concrete image of the White House as the seat of American democracy and power. (c) It fixes a specific location for the presidential residence, thus establishing a sense of history and ongoing tradition.
7. Students should infer that it is appropriate that the President, who is elected by and should serve the people, lives during his term of office in the people's house.

Go Online Author Link For additional information about Abigail Adams, have students type in the Web Code, then select A from the alphabet, and then select Abigail Adams.

❽ About the Selection

In this essay, Crèvecoeur celebrates America as the land of opportunity. He describes the experience of immigrants to America, suffering from discrimination and poverty in Europe but finding opportunity and fair treatment in the United States.

❾ Humanities

Independence (Squire Jack Porter) 1858, by Frank Blackwell Mayer

Frank Blackwell Mayer (1827–1899) was born in Baltimore and studied in Paris. Because of his realistic portrayal of subjects from everyday life, Mayer was known as a genre painter.

This painting is a portrait of a prosperous farmer in western Maryland. The title suggests that Mayer wished to illustrate the American ideal discussed in Crèvecoeur's epistle. In the picture, a prospering landowner enjoys his hard-earned leisure. Use the following questions for discussion:

1. Although this painting was not created to illustrate *Letters from an American Farmer,* how does it relate to the text?
   Possible response: The painting shows a person who has obtained economic independence, as Crèvecoeur says that immigrants may do.
2. How would you define the mood of the painting?
   Possible response: The mood is one of quiet satisfaction.

❿ Critical Viewing

Answer: Students may note that the artist depicts a well-dressed gentleman-farmer at ease. In that respect, the painting correlates with Crèvecoeur's idyllic description of the American colonists.

❽ *from*

Letters From an American Farmer

Michel-Guillaume Jean de Crèvecoeur

❾

Independence (Squire Jack Porter), 1858, Frank Blackwell Mayer, National Museum of American Art, Smithsonian Institution

❿ ▲ **Critical Viewing** What connections do you see between this painting and Crèvecoeur's *Letters From an American Farmer*? **[Connect]**

In this great American asylum, the poor of Europe have by some means met together, and in consequence of various causes; to what purpose should they ask one another what countrymen they are? Alas, two thirds of them had no country. Can a wretch who wanders about, who works and starves, whose life is a continual scene of sore affliction or pinching penury, can that man call England or any other kingdom his country? A country that had no bread for him, whose fields

Vocabulary Builder

asylum (ə sī´ ləm) *n.* place of refuge

penury (pen´ yə rē) *n.* lack of money, property, or necessities

Enrichment

Immigrants

Crèvecoeur's letter shows that even in colonial times, immigrants came to America from a variety of countries. During the 1600s and 1700s, settlers came to the colonies from many parts of Europe, and enslaved Africans were taken to the Americas against their will.

In the 1840s, a potato famine in Ireland drove one-and-a-half million people to America's shores, and Chinese immigrants arrived in the 1860s to work on the transcontinental railroad.

In the 1870s, immigrants from Germany and Scandinavia came to the Great Plains as farmers or to the East as skilled workers. Another wave of immigrants came between 1880 and 1914.

By 1929, laws had reduced the annual quota of immigrants to 154,000. Immigration restrictions eased after World War II, however, as new prosperity increased the demand for labor. The United States continues to be a nation of immigrants.

procured him no harvest, who met with nothing but the frowns of the rich, the severity of the laws, with jails and punishments; who owned not a single foot of the extensive surface of this planet? No! Urged by a variety of motives, here they came. Everything has tended to regenerate
11 them; new laws, a new mode of living, a new social system; here they are become men: in Europe they were as so many useless plants, wanting vegetative mold[1] and refreshing showers; they withered, and were mowed down by want, hunger, and war; but now by the power of transplantation, like all other plants they have taken root and flourished!

Formerly they were not numbered in any civil lists[2] of their country, except in those of the poor; here they rank as citizens. By what invisible power has this surprising metamorphosis been performed? By that of the laws and that of their industry. The laws, the indulgent laws, protect them as they arrive, stamping on them the symbol of adoption; they receive ample rewards for their labors; these accumulated rewards procure them lands; those lands confer on them the title of freemen, and to that title every benefit is affixed which men can possibly require. This is the great operation daily performed by our laws. From whence proceed these laws? From our government. Whence the government? It is derived from the original genius and strong desire of the people ratified and confirmed by the crown. . . .

What attachment can a poor European emigrant have for a country where he had nothing? The knowledge of the language, the love of a few kindred as poor as himself, were the only cords that tied him: his country is now that which gives him land, bread, protection, and consequence: *Ubi panis ibi patria*[3] is the motto of all emigrants. What then is the American, this new man? He is either a European, or the descendant of a European, hence that strange mixture of blood, which you will find in no
12 other country. I could point out to you a family whose grandfather was an Englishman, whose wife was Dutch, whose son married a French woman, and whose present four sons have now four wives of different nations. *He* is an American, who, leaving behind him all his ancient prejudices and manners, receives new ones from the new mode of life he has embraced, the new government he obeys, and the new rank he holds. He becomes an American by being received in the broad lap of our great *Alma Mater.*[4] Here individuals of all nations are melted into a new race of men, whose labors and posterity will one day cause great changes in the world. Americans are the western pilgrims, who are carrying along with them that great mass of arts, sciences, vigor, and
13 industry which began long since in the east; they will finish the great circle. The Americans were once scattered all over Europe: here they

1. **vegetative mold** enriched soil.
2. **civil lists** lists of distinguished persons.
3. **Ubi . . . patria** (ū´ bē pä nis ib´ ē pä´ trē ə) "Where there is bread, there is one's fatherland" (Latin).
4. **Alma Mater** (al´ mə mät´ ər) "Fostering mother." Here, referring to America; usually used in reference to a school or college (Latin).

Literary Analysis
Private and Public Letters (Epistles) Does this passage describing Europeans coming to the "American asylum" address a public or a private concern?

Reading Strategy
Distinguishing Between Fact and Opinion
By referencing a family with roots in many nations, does the writer present a fact or an opinion? Explain.

14 
Reading Check
What kind of lives did Europeans have in their homelands?

11 Literary Analysis
Private and Public Letters (Epistles)

- **Ask** students to list the reasons that Crèvecoeur gives for Europeans coming to America.
- Then, **ask** students the Literary Analysis question: How does this passage describing Europeans coming to the "American asylum" address a public rather than a private concern?
  Answer: Crèvecoeur addresses social issues, such as poverty and famine, that provide motivation for coming to America. These are public, not private, concerns.

▶ **Monitor Progress: Ask** students how this passage might have been different if Crèvecoeur had been writing a private letter.

12 Reading Strategy
Distinguishing Between Fact and Opinion

- Remind students that a fact can be proven true.
- **Ask** students the Reading Strategy question: By referencing a family with roots in many nations, does the writer present a fact or an opinion? Explain.
  Answer: The description of the family is a factual statement because it can be proved that such a family exists.

13 Reading Strategy
Distinguishing Between Fact and Opinion

- Direct students' attention to the bracketed passage. **Ask** them if they think Crèvecoeur's statement about the population of America is a fact or an opinion.
- Then, **ask** students the following question: Which words indicate Crèvecoeur's expression of opinion in his discussion of the "finest systems of population?"
  Answer: finest, ever appeared, which will become distinct.

14 Reading Check

Answer: Europeans suffered without land or liberty.

Differentiated Instruction
Solutions for All Learners

Support for Less Proficient Readers
Have students use a comparison chart to help sort details of Crèvecoeur's contrast of life in Europe and America. Have students draw two columns down a page and write *Europe* on top of one column and *America* on top of the other. Then have them make entries on the chart as they read through the letter.

Background for English Learners
Volunteers might work in a group to discuss their own experiences about emigration or living in a different land and culture than the one in which their family originated. Do they agree or disagree with Crèvecoeur's main points?

Enrichment for Advanced Readers
Encourage students to write a cause-and-effect essay discussing the advantages and disadvantages of an open-door immigration policy. Have students gather background information by researching United States immigration history on the Internet or at the library.

are incorporated into one of the finest systems of population which has ever appeared, and which will hereafter become distinct by the power of the different climates they inhabit. The American ought therefore to love this country much better than that wherein either he or his forefathers were born. Here the rewards of his industry follow with equal steps the progress of his labor; his labor is founded on the basis of nature, *self-interest*; can it want a stronger allurement? Wives and children, who before in vain demanded of him a morsel of bread, now, fat and frolicsome, gladly help their father to clear those fields whence exuberant crops are to arise to feed and to clothe them all; without any part being claimed, either by a despotic prince, a rich abbot,[5] or a mighty lord. Here religion demands but little of him; a small voluntary salary to the minister, and gratitude to God; can he refuse these? The American is a new man, who acts upon new principles; he must therefore entertain new ideas, and form new opinions. From involuntary idleness, servile dependence, penury, and useless labor, he has passed to toils of a very different nature, rewarded by ample subsistence—This is an American.

Vocabulary Builder
despotic (des pät′ ik) *adj.* harsh; cruel; unjust

Vocabulary Builder
subsistence (səb sis′ təns) *n.* means of support

5. **abbot** *n.* the head of a monastery.

Critical Reading

1. **Respond:** If you were an eighteenth-century European, would this essay motivate you to relocate to the United States? Why or why not?
2. **(a) Recall:** To what natural objects does Crèvecoeur compare impoverished Europeans? **(b) Assess:** What is suggested through this imagery about Europeans' capacity to thrive in a new environment?
3. **(a) Recall:** What are the sources of the "invisible power" that is responsible for transforming humble Europeans into esteemed American "citizens"? **(b) Define:** How do you think Crèvecoeur would define a "citizen"?
4. **(a) Compare and Contrast:** How does the American population differ from that of Europe? **(b) Explain:** In what ways does Crèvecoeur believe the world will be invigorated by Americans?
5. **(a) Define:** How would you summarize Crèvecoeur's definition of an American? **(b) Evaluate:** Does Crèvecoeur's definition still hold true today? Explain. **(c) Take a Position:** Do you think that there can be a single definition of an American? Why or why not?
6. **Apply:** Do you think that eighteenth-century immigrants to America had the same goals as immigrants of today? Explain.

For: More about Michel-Guillaume Jean de Crèvecoeur
Visit: www.PHSchool.com
Web Code: ere-9209

ASSESS

Answers

1. Students should find that the letter is persuasive in establishing the opportunities that exist in America. They may cast doubt, however, on how accurately Crèvecoeur portrays the situation in Europe.
2. (a) Crèvecoeur compares the Europeans to withering plants lacking fertilizer and water that are mowed down by poverty and war. (b) Students should infer that the problem is not Europeans' abilities but the impoverished environment from which they fled.
3. (a) "New laws, a new mode of living, [and] a new social system" have regenerated the European immigrant. (b) Students should infer that Crèvecoeur would define a citizen as someone who not only lives in a place but contributes through his or her labor and earns his or her own living.
4. (a) The average European is impoverished and without rights, power, or dignity; Americans are free, productive citizens who through intermarriage have created a new race of people. (b) He believes Americans will continue the advance of civilization that began in the East and continued on to Europe.
5. (a) **Possible response:** An American is someone who has initiated a new social system through labor, industry, and self-interest. (b) Students should understand that in a very different world, there are many other things that make one an American, including living and participating in a social and political American milieu. (c) Students may point out that because the Americas stretch from Canada to Cape Horn, a single definition of an American is difficult to agree upon.
6. Students should understand that while the world has changed, some things remain the same, including many immigrants' desire for freedom and opportunity.

Go Online
Author Link
For additional information about Michel-Guillaume Jean de Crèvecoeur, have students type in the Web Code, then select C from the alphabet, and then select Michel-Guillaume Jean de Crèvecoeur.

Apply the Skills

Letter to Her Daughter From the New White House* • from *Letters From an American Farmer

Literary Analysis

Private and Public Letters (Epistles)

1. Use a chart like the one shown to explore ways in which you might rewrite Adams's **private letter** for a public audience.

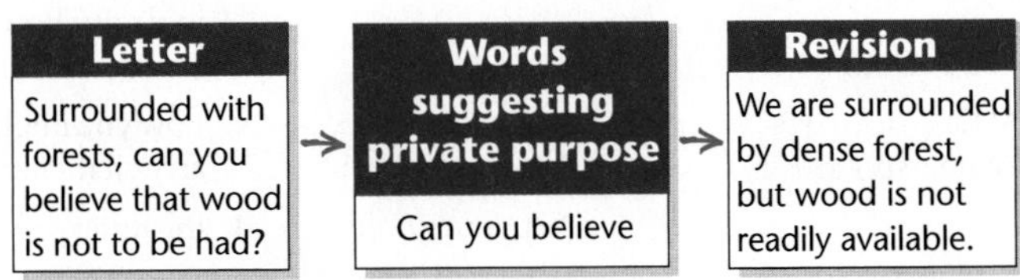

Letter
Surrounded with forests, can you believe that wood is not to be had?
Words suggesting private purpose
Can you believe
Revision
We are surrounded by dense forest, but wood is not readily available.

2. What kinds of information would Crèvecoeur have included in a private letter to a friend that are inappropriate for an **epistle**?
3. How does the epistle form allow Crèvecoeur to be more persuasive than a regular essay would permit?

Comparing Literary Works

4. **(a)** What character traits does Crèvecoeur hold up as being both typically American and admirable? **(b)** Are these character traits evident in Adams's descriptions? Explain.
5. **(a)** Which writer presents a more idealized view of America? Explain. **(b)** Which presents a more realistic view? Explain.

Reading Strategy

Distinguishing Between Fact and Opinion

6. Identify the **facts** and **opinions** in this statement.

   "The house is made habitable, but there is not a single apartment finished, and all withinside, except the plastering, has been done since Briesler came."
7. Identify at least one fact Crèvecoeur uses to support the following opinion: "here they are become men: in Europe they were as so many useless plants."

Extend Understanding

8. **Social Studies Connection:** Crèvecoeur implies that self-interest is valuable because it motivates people to work harder. Does modern society regard self-interest as a desirable quality? Explain your answer.

QuickReview

Private letters are intended only for the reader to whom they are addressed.

Public letters, or **epistles,** are essays written in the form of letters that are created for a wide audience.

Primary source documents are firsthand nonfiction accounts of events taking place at the time they were written.

A **fact** is something that can be proved. An **opinion** is a belief, feeling, or judgment that cannot be proved.

For: Self-test
Visit: www.PHSchool.com
Web Code: era-6206

Go Online Assessment Students may use the **Self-test** to prepare for **Selection test A** or **Selection Test B.**

Answers

1. Be sure students' charts contain specific sentences from Adams's letter and, for each sentence, a phrase suggesting private purpose as well as a suitable revision of that phrase.

   Another sample answer can be found on **Literary Analysis Graphic Organizer B,** p. 49 in ***Graphic Organizer Transparencies.***
2. **Possible response:** Crèvecoeur might have included personal comments, opinions, and complaints.
3. By using the form of the letter, Crèvecoeur can be persuasive in an intimate and personal manner. When reading a letter, readers have the sense that the author is speaking directly to them, which makes his words more persuasive.
4. (a) Crèvecoeur believes that Americans are hard workers who enjoy the fruits of their labors. Americans have initiated a new social system through labor, industry, and self-interest.
   (b) These traits are not evident in Adams's descriptions. Her letter describes all the things that are unfinished and missing in and around the White House. She even observes that the site had been chosen for the White House twelve years earlier yet little progress has been made.
5. Crèvecoeur offers a more idealized view of life in America. He feels that any industrious person can make a better life here. (b) Adams presents a more sober view by detailing all the problems she faces moving into the nation's new capital.
6. **Facts:** "not a single apartment finished"; "all withinside except the plastering has been done." **Opinion:** "The house is made habitable, . . ."
7. **Possible response:** In Europe, men were incapacitated by poverty, hunger, and war.
8. Students' responses will vary. Some will say that modern society regards self-interest as a desirable quality because it is seen as one important way of getting ahead. Others will say that society does not see self-interest as an admirable quality because it encourages people to be selfish and uncaring.

EXTEND/ASSESS

Answers

❶ Vocabulary Lesson

Word Analysis

1. *inter* (among) and *spargere* (scattered)
2. to scatter or distribute among other things

Spelling Strategy

1. observance
2. confidence
3. intelligence

Vocabulary Builder

1. e
2. b
3. d
4. f
5. a
6. c

❷ Grammar and Style Lesson

1. The travelers sought help finding Baltimore; the woods blocked their view of the city.
2. Six rooms were completed; two were not.
3. Adams thought she could be happy; however, the shortages caused her distress.
4. Crèvecoeur presents America as a land of opportunity; in fact, he shows how European immigrants have prospered.
5. Crèvecoeur wrote convincingly about the land; nevertheless, some felt he created an unrealistic picture of the quality of life.

Writing Application

Each sentence should present an opinion about, or insight into, America; there should be a semicolon in each of the four sentences.

WG Writing and Grammar, Ruby Level

Students will find further instruction and practice on semicolons in Chapter 27, Section 3.

Build Language Skills

❶ Vocabulary Lesson

Word Analysis: Etymologies

You can learn how words evolved by using a dictionary that shows etymologies, or word histories. Use this etymology for the word *interspersed* to answer the questions that follow.

< *interspersus,* pp. of *interspergere* < *inter-*, among + *spargere,* to scatter

1. *Interspersed* can be traced back to what two words or word parts?
2. What is the meaning of *interspersed*?

Spelling Strategy

The suffixes *-ance* and *-ence* are used to form nouns from adjectives. *Evident* becomes *evidence,* and *significant* becomes *significance.* Write the noun form of each adjective:

1. observant 2. confident 3. intelligent

Vocabulary Builder: Word Matching

Match each numbered word with the best lettered description.

1. extricate	a. how you support yourself
2. agues	b. what people who live in drafty houses suffer from
3. asylum	c. how you might describe an evil dictator
4. penury	d. the quiet privacy of your room
5. subsistence	e. to work your way out of an argument
6. despotic	f. poverty

❷ Grammar and Style Lesson

Semicolons

The **semicolon** can replace a comma and a coordinating conjunction to signal closely connected ideas. The semicolon can also be used to join independent clauses separated by a conjunctive adverb or a transitional expression.

> **Semicolon with conjunctive adverb:** Crèvecoeur was the first to express the concept of America as a melting pot; **however,** the term was not used until the twentieth century.

Practice Rewrite the following sentences, adding semicolons where needed.

1. The travelers sought help finding Baltimore the woods blocked their view of the city.
2. Six rooms were completed two were not.
3. Adams thought she could be happy however, the shortages caused her distress.
4. Crèvecoeur presents America as a land of opportunity in fact he shows how European immigrants have prospered.
5. Crèvecoeur wrote convincingly about the land nevertheless some felt he created an unrealistic picture of the quality of life.

Writing Application Write four sentences reflecting on what America means to you. Use a semicolon in each sentence.

WG Prentice Hall Writing and Grammar Connection: Chapter 27, Section 3

Assessment Practice

Recognize Cause and Effect

Successful readers understand that causal relationships are sometimes signaled by transitions such as "since" or "because." Use the following example to help students identify signal words as they look for causal relationships.

. . . if they will . . . let me have wood enough to keep fires, I design to be pleased. I could content myself almost anywhere three months; but surrounded with forests, can you believe that wood is not to be had because people cannot be found to cut and cart it?

Why does Abigail Adams lack firewood?

A There were no forests nearby.
B There was no one to cut the wood.
C People did not use firewood in Washington.
D Abigail Adams preferred coal.

Choices *A, C,* and *D* contain inaccurate information. *B* states the correct cause as it is given in the text.

Writing Lesson

Personal Letter

In a personal letter to either Adams or Crèvecoeur, provide an update on how an area of interest to the recipient has changed since his or her lifetime. Like a foreign pen pal, your reader lives in a different country—the country of the past—and will need help understanding your world.

Prewriting Decide on an appropriate subject for your letter. Outline the developments you will cover. Then, decide what background information your reader will need to understand your points.

Drafting Make sure to address the person to whom you are writing. You will need to include necessary context and background—the information a reader needs in order to make sense of the information you provide.

Model: Providing Context and Background

Unlike your contemporaries, who rarely worked outside the home, women today have many choices, Ms. Adams. While some stay home to raise children, others have full-time jobs.

Comparison-and-contrast examples establish context.

Revising Review your letter and decide whether the recipient would be able to understand the references you make. If necessary, add more detail to explain and prove your point.

WG *Prentice Hall Writing and Grammar Connection: Chapter 9, Section 2*

Extend Your Learning

Research and Technology With a group of classmates, use graphic design software to design **advertisements** that might have attracted immigrants to America in the late eighteenth century. As you plan, think about these questions:

- Who would have been the target groups for such ads?
- What messages and images would have persuaded them to make the journey?
- Would different ads have attracted different groups?

Display your ads for the class. **[Group Activity]**

Listening and Speaking Interview a recent immigrant to find out why and how he or she came to this country. Prepare your questions in advance, and ask follow-up questions as the interview progresses. With your subject's permission, you might take photographs of him or her as well. Record your **interview,** and then share it with your class.

For: An additional research activity
Visit: www.PHSchool.com
Web Code: erd-7205

❸ Writing Lesson

- To guide students in writing this personal letter, give them the **Support for Writing Lesson,** page 102, in ***General Resources.***
- Tell students that when they have selected a recipient for their letters, they should focus on an area of interest. Discourage students from addressing too many topics or areas of interest in their letter.
- Help students choose and narrow a topic, ensuring that the topic is one with sufficient context and background to meet the needs of the assignment.
- Adapt the rubrics for Business Letter, pages 61–62 in ***General Resources,*** to evaluate students' personal letters.
- When students have finished their letters, have them read the letters to the class.

❹ Listening and Speaking

- Have students work together to prepare questions. Encourage them to prepare general, open-ended questions to encourage their interviewee to feel more comfortable.
- If students record the interview, see that they have the proper equipment and know how to operate it. Instruct them to do a sample test at the interview site to make sure recording is taking place.
- The **Support for Extend Your Learning** page (***Unit 2 Resources,*** p. 103) provides guided note-taking opportunities to help students complete the Extend Your Learning activities.

Go Online Research Have students type in the Web Code for another research activity.

Assessment Resources

The following resources can be used to assess students' knowledge and skills.

Unit 2 Resources
- **Selection Test A,** pp. 105–107
- **Selection Test B,** pp. 108–110

General Resources
- **Rubrics for Business Letter,** pp. 61–62

Go Online Assessment Students may use the **Self-test** to prepare for **Selection test A** or **Selection Test B.**

Meeting Your Standards

Students will

1. write an essay evaluating authors' success in making the case for personal and/or political freedom.
2. use writing strategies to generate ideas and to plan, organize, evaluate, and revise the composition.

Prewriting

- Have a class discussion about the way the authors represented in this unit develop the theme of freedom in their writings and the degree to which they present compelling arguments. The discussion should help students identify topics for their essays.
- Help students clarify their thinking about personal and political freedom. Ask them to decide on the standard they will use to judge the authors' success in arguing for freedom. The standard might be the extent to which the authors have made their ideas clear and logical. Students can record their notes in the Three-column Chart on p. 312 of *Graphic Organizer Transparencies.*
- Suggest that students take notes on three or four authors whom they will use as examples in their essays.
- When they articulate their thesis statements, tell students to focus on both what these writers say about freedom and how well their messages are articulated.

Tips for Test Taking

A writing prompt on the SAT or ACT test may call on students to demonstrate their ability to analyze a topic, state a point of view about that topic, and develop and support that point of view with evidence. When writing under a time constraint, students will need to decide quickly on a thesis and find evidence that supports it. It would be helpful if they knew several selections well enough to refer to their most important points in these circumstances.

Writing About Literature

Evaluate Literary Themes

The writers of the Revolutionary period believed that they could—and should—take control of their destinies, both as individuals and as Americans. Belief in personal and political freedom gave these writers an enormous sense of optimism and energy. They saw all problems, from those of poor personal habits to those of political tyranny, as obstacles to be overcome rather than as circumstances to accept. In many respects, this sense of revolutionary optimism continues to characterize American political discourse. Review the literature in this unit to complete the assignment outlined in the box at the right.

Assignment: A Matter of Persuasion

Write an analytical essay that evaluates the success with which the authors in this unit make their cases for personal and/or political freedom.

Criteria:

- Include a thesis statement that states your opinion.
- Support your opinion with examples from the selections.
- Approximate length: 700 words.

Prewriting

Judge the selections. To evaluate literary works, follow these steps:

- First, determine the criterion upon which to base the evaluation.
- Second, analyze the authors' messages and methods.
- Finally, make judgments about the works in light of the stated criterion.

In this essay, your criterion is the success of the author's arguments in favor of freedom. Therefore, when you analyze each selection, focus on references to personal and political liberty.

Formulate a thesis. Use a chart like the one shown to organize your analysis of the references to freedom made by a number of authors. Then, state your judgment about the success with which the authors have argued for the rights of individuals to direct their own lives. Write your assessment in one sentence. Use this sentence as a working thesis.

Read to Write

Reread the texts, looking for the precise methods that the writers use to make their points about personal liberty.

Thesis: Jefferson and his colleagues are cautious men moved to radical action by extreme circumstances.

Model: Charting to Develop a Thesis

Selection	Reference	Method/Message
The Declaration of Independence	"Prudence, indeed, will dictate that governments long established should not be changed for light and transient causes."	Jefferson highlights idea of prudence, implying that reasons for declaring independence are not trivial.

Select powerful examples. Some of the selections you have analyzed will support your thesis better than others will. Pick the examples that most powerfully support your thesis statement.

Teaching Resources

The following resources can be used to extend or enrich the instruction for Writing About Literature.

General Resources

Rubrics for Response to Literature, pp. 65–66

Graphic Organizer Transparencies

Three-column Chart, p. 312

Drafting

Write an introduction. In your introduction, state your subject matter and purpose, and identify the works you will be evaluating—in this case, literature from the formative years of the United States. Then, assert your opinion of the success or failure of this literature in its argument that individuals should determine their own futures.

Present examples in order. Follow your introduction with the example that best supports your opinion. For example, if you think the writers in this unit fail to make a strong case for individual liberty, quote the argument that most clearly supports your point. Then, explain the reasons for your opinion.

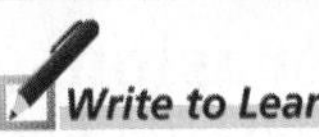

Write to Learn

You may find a selection to be more or less effective than you had originally thought. Allow for such changes in opinion; the writing process has given you a new perspective.

Revising and Editing

Review content: Make sure that you are evaluating your material. To be successful, an evaluative essay must assert a judgment about a subject, not just report on it. To make sure you are actually evaluating the literature, review each paragraph of your essay. Jot down the ideas you present in each paragraph. Then, use a highlighter to mark the sentences that contain evaluations. If you see too few highlighted sentences, go back and add well-supported judgments.

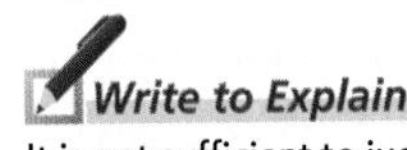

Write to Explain

It is not sufficient to judge a work in a casual way. Instead, justify your evaluations with examples from the selection.

Model: Revising to Add Evaluation

Paragraph
1. Jefferson wrote the Declaration as a message to the British king.
2. He portrays the colonists as cautious men who do not want to rebel, but feel they have no choice.
3. He says that the signers of the Declaration stake their lives and sacred honors on this document.
4. *This strategy is persuasive because it shows that freedom matters more than anything, including wealth or life itself.*

Review style: Use a variety of evaluative terms. An evaluative essay contains value-laden terms such as *effective, clear, convincing,* and *persuasive.* Review your draft, and underline your use of such terms. Replace vague adjectives, such as *good,* with more precise alternatives. If you have used certain words too often, replace them with synonyms.

Publishing and Presenting

Generate a literary magazine. With classmates, publish your essays in a literary magazine. Select a title for your magazine that indicates the scope and subject matter of the essays.

WG *Prentice Hall Writing and Grammar Connection: Chapter 14*

Drafting

Before students start writing, make sure that they have chosen their criterion for judging the authors' success in arguing for freedom, as well as the writings they will use to support their evaluation. Remind students that the assignment asks them not to judge the authors in the unit individually and not to decide who presents the best and worst arguments for freedom. Rather, they are to decide how well the authors in the unit, as a group, make the case for freedom and then choose the writings that best support their evaluation.

Revising and Editing

Have students exchange papers with a partner. Partners can help identify weak or unclear statements and digressions. They can also help students correct grammatical or mechanical problems. In particular, have students look for vague or neutral-sounding words to replace with more precise and value-laden terms. **Ask** students to list such alternatives to the word *good.* **Possible answers:** *compelling, clear, strong, convincing, reasonable, effective, persuasive, eloquent, moving, powerful.*

Publishing and Presenting

Organize students so that a range of varying evaluations is aired in class.

WG **Writing and Grammar, Ruby Level**

Students will find additional instruction on writing a response to literature essay in Chapter 14.

Writing and Grammar Interactive CD-ROM Students can use the following tools as they complete their evaluative essays:

- Transition Word Bin
- Comparatives Revising Tool
- Language Variety Revising Tool

Six Traits Focus

✓	Ideas	✓	Word Choice
✓	Organization		Sentence Fluency
	Voice	✓	Conventions

Assessing the Essay

To evaluate students' essays, use the Response to Literature rubric, pages 65–66 in ***General Resources.***

Differentiated Instruction
Solutions for All Learners

Support for Less Proficient Writers
Make sure students develop their ideas in their essays instead of rephrasing the same idea over and over. Make sure that they use at least three selections or authors in supporting their evaluations and that they use accurate quotations.

Support for English Learners
The eighteenth-century language of these selections poses special challenges for these writers. Have them to look up any unfamiliar words. Encourage them to bring in perspectives from their own cultures in judging the effectiveness of the American authors' arguments for freedom.

Support for Advanced Writers
Encourage students to make more original and less conventional choices in citing selections. For example, ask them to try to avoid using the Declaration of Independence and to look for statements defending freedom in other selections instead.

PREACH

Meeting Your Standards

Students will

1. write a persuasive essay.
2. use writing strategies to generate ideas and to plan, organize, evaluate, and revise the composition.
3. apply grammar skills.

 **From the Scholar's Desk**

William L. Andrews

Show students Segment 3 on William L. Andrews on *From the Author's Desk DVD.* Discuss Andrews's comments about how he revised his writing about Olaudah Equiano (see Equiano's writing, beginning on p. 160).

Writing Genres

Using the Form Point out to students that persuasive elements are included in many different kinds of writing. Mention these examples:

- Articles in magazines often include passages intended to persuade readers.
- College application essays frequently ask applicants to take a position on an issue.
- Autobiographies and biographies almost always offer a particular interpretation of events and people.

Writing Workshop

Persuasion: Persuasive Essay

During the Revolutionary period, American writers like Thomas Paine and Thomas Jefferson argued forcefully in favor of their political beliefs, trying to persuade readers to accept their viewpoint and take action against the British. Their writings are examples of **persuasive essays,** prose works that present a case for or against a position, using supporting evidence and compelling language. Follow the steps outlined in this workshop to write your own persuasive essay.

Assignment Write a persuasive essay that urges readers to accept your viewpoint on an issue and to take action on that issue.

What to Include Your persuasive essay should feature the following elements:

- a thesis statement that clearly states your position and the action you support
- an argument that takes into account the knowledge, experience, and concerns of your intended audience
- clearly organized evidence that supports your argument, such as facts, examples, statistics, and personal experience
- persuasive language that is compelling and convincing

To preview the criteria on which your persuasive essay may be assessed, see the rubric on page 235.

Using the Form

You may use elements of persuasion in these writing situations:

- letters to the editor
- newspaper editorials
- speeches
- college applications

To get a feel for persuasive writing, read the selection from *The Crisis: Number 1* by Thomas Paine, page 174.

Teaching Resources

The following resources can be used to enrich or extend the instruction for the Writing Workshop.

Unit 2 Resources
Writing Workshop, pp. 113–114

General Resources
Rubrics for Persuasive Essay, pp. 45–46

From the Author's Desk DVD
William L. Andrews, Segments 3 and 4

Prewriting

Choosing Your Topic

A good topic for a persuasive essay is an issue that you feel strongly about and that might even affect you personally. It should also be an issue that provokes disagreement. To choose a topic, use one of these strategies:

- **Make a "news" notebook.** Look at several newspapers and news magazines, skimming headlines and articles but also reading the editorials, letters to the editor, and op-ed pages. Watch television newscasts and listen to radio talk shows, particularly those that feature experts on both sides of an issue. Record interesting issues in a news notebook. Then, review your list, and choose an issue that you find compelling and that you can support with facts and arguments.
- **Conduct a round-table discussion.** Meet with a group of classmates to discuss school, community, national, or global issues. See which issues generate the most heated discussion—even if everyone in your group agrees with one another but disagrees with other people, such as school officials or politicians. Take notes on the discussion, and then choose a topic that provokes your own strong response.

Narrowing Your Topic

Once you have chosen a general topic, zero in on an aspect of that topic that you can cover effectively within the scope of your essay. To focus your topic, try a strategy called **looping**. Freewrite about your broad topic for five minutes. Read what you have written, and then circle the idea that you find most compelling. Then, freewrite for another five minutes about the idea you circled. Repeat the process until you arrive at a manageable topic for your persuasive essay.

Gathering Details

Compile your evidence. To gather evidence to support your position, research your topic. Use books, newspapers, magazines, Internet sources, personal interviews, and other resources to find out as much as you can about the issue. Look for facts and well-argued opinions.

- A **fact** is a statement that can be proved true.
- An **opinion** is a judgment or belief that cannot be proved, although it can be supported by facts and arguments.

Analyze both sides of the issue. In addition to gathering evidence that supports your position, find facts and arguments that attack or contradict your position so that you can prepare counterarguments. Use a T-chart like the one shown to help you organize the arguments for and against your viewpoint.

High school should start later in the morning.

Pro	Con
Teenagers are half-asleep at school because they are biologically wired to fall asleep late and wake up late.	Starting school later will create problems for students who do extracurriculars, play sports, or have jobs.

TEACH

Prewriting

- Have students choose topics by using the idea-generating strategies listed here.
- If they are reviewing a notebook of interesting news items, encourage volunteers to share ideas from their notebooks with classmates. Two students may choose to write about the same issue and perhaps even develop a "for" and "against" pair of persuasive essays.
- If a group of students is conducting a roundtable discussion, sit in briefly on their session to make sure the discussion is constructive. Encourage students to explore differing opinions about the issue they are discussing. If necessary, introduce opposing arguments into the mix.
- As students gather support for their opinions, make sure that they all understand the difference between a fact and an opinion. Model using a T-chart to stimulate opposing arguments by having volunteers offer positions about various issues. Have students evaluate the relative strengths of these arguments.

Six Traits Focus

✔	Ideas		Word Choice
✔	Organization		Sentence Fluency
	Voice		Conventions

WG Writing and Grammar, Ruby Level

Students will find additional instruction on prewriting for a persuasive essay in Chapter 7, Section 7. 2.

Writing and Grammar Interactive Textbook CD-ROM

Students can use the following tools as they complete their persuasive essays:

- T-Chart
- Descriptive Word Bin
- Language Variety Revising Tool

Tips for Using Rubrics

- Before students begin work on this assignment, have them preview the **Rubric for Self-Assessment** (p. 50) in ***Graphic Organizer Transparencies*** to know what is expected.
- Review the Assessment criteria in class. Before students use the **Rubric for Self-Assessment**, work with to rate the student model by applying one or more criteria to it.
- If you wish to assess students' persuasive essays with either a 4-point, a 5-point, or a 6-point scoring rubric, see ***General Resources***, pp. 45 and 46.

Writing Workshop

Drafting

Shaping Your Writing

State your position. Your opening paragraph should feature a strong **thesis statement** that identifies the issue and clearly states your position. You can begin with this statement or build up to it as the dramatic closing sentence of your paragraph. Aim for a thesis statement that captures your readers' interest by forcefully expressing the opinion you will defend in the rest of your essay. Try writing several practice statements to clarify your thinking and sharpen your focus.

Weak: Trials should not be televised.
Strong: Televised trials weaken the defendants' ability to gain a fair hearing because lawyers and judges play to the camera.

Organize to showcase your strongest arguments. The body of your persuasive essay provides the arguments that support your thesis statement. Acknowledge opposing opinions, but then refute them by showing why your arguments are stronger. In your concluding paragraph, restate your thesis and expand it by calling on readers to take action in support of your position. The organization shown here presents one effective way to structure the body and conclusion of your essay.

Organizing the Body and Conclusion of a Persuasive Essay

- Begin with your second strongest argument.
- Present your other arguments, in descending order of strength.
- Present and refute opposing viewpoints.
- Present your strongest argument last.
- End with a catchy paragraph that restates your thesis and presents a call to action.

Providing Elaboration

Use effective arguing techniques and appeals. You can use these types of arguments to build a strong case for your position:

- **Inductive reasoning:** specific facts used to lead to a general truth

  Example: Balanced nutrition helps maintain a healthy weight. Balanced nutrition provides necessary vitamins. Therefore, balanced nutrition is good.

- **Deductive reasoning:** a general truth applied to a particular case

  Example: Eating fruits and vegetables will help you stay healthy. Apples are fruits. If I eat apples, I will stay healthy.

You can use inductive or deductive reasoning to make the following kinds of appeals:

- **Logical appeal:** information based on reason
- **Ethical appeal:** information and language based on perceptions of what is right and wrong
- **Emotional appeal:** ideas and language meant to tap into feelings such as pride, fear, or revenge

Drafting

- Help students strengthen their thesis statements by encouraging them to elaborate on their opinions, as in the example given about televising trials. **Ask** students why the first thesis statement is weak.
  Answer: It is too general and lacks focus.
- Review the organization model with students. Encourage them to adapt the model. **Ask** why it is a good idea to begin with the "second-strongest argument."
  Answer: It provides a compelling beginning but saves the best point for later.
- Model inductive and deductive reasoning. Explain that inductive reasoning starts with specific observations and looks for a general truth: **Specific observations:** (a) Movies X, Y, and Z received many negative reviews. (b) They were not nominated for a Best Picture Oscar. **Inductive conclusion:** Reviewers and Oscar voters seem to agree about quality.

  On the other hand, deductive reasoning starts with a general principle and uses it to interpret a particular case. **General principle:** Critics and Oscar voters share similar standards. **Specific case:** Movie X received awful reviews.
  Deductive conclusion: Therefore, Movie X probably will not be nominated for Best Picture.
- Encourage students to practice coming up with logical, ethical, and emotional appeals. **Ask:** What are logical, ethical, and emotional appeals for the 13 American colonies to declare their independence from England?
  Answer: Logical appeal—the colonies are too far away from England to be properly governed. Ethical appeal—The colonists do not have fair representation under English law, and it is not right for England to tax them. Emotional appeal—It is time for the American colonists to stand up and fight against the tyranny of British rule.

Six Traits Focus

✔	Ideas	✔	Word Choice
✔	Organization		Sentence Fluency
	Voice		Conventions

WG Writing and Grammar, Ruby Level

Students will find additional instruction on drafting a persuasive essay in Chapter 7, Section 7.3.

From the Scholar's Desk

William L. Andrews on Revising for Accuracy

William L. Andrews

To mount a convincing attack on the transatlantic slave trade, Equiano highlighted his African origins and his firsthand experience of the Middle Passage. But some scholars of Equiano's life question whether he was born in or ever lived in Africa. Tracking every bit of surviving evidence about Equiano, these scholars have uncovered documents that make me wonder whether my own writings about Equiano the African should be revised. Since the controversy over Equiano's African origins hasn't been resolved, I can't present Equiano's version of his boyhood as an agreed-upon fact. At the same time, I can't say his autobiography is untrue. As the following passages show, in 2003 I had to revise a biographical note that I wrote about Equiano in 1997 to indicate that we may need to rethink Equiano's African identity.

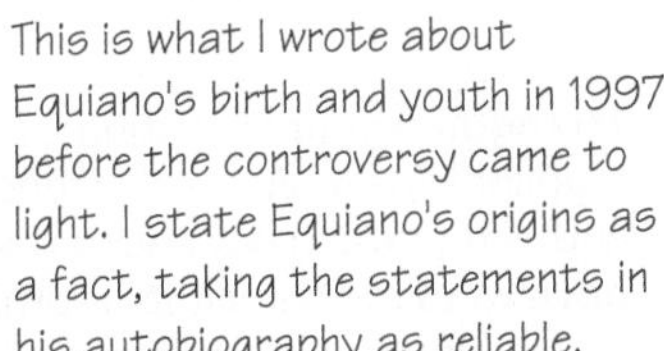

"To stay current and be accurate, you have to revise."

– William L. Andrews

Professional Model:

From *The Norton Anthology of African American Literature* (1997, 2003)

Born around 1745 in the village of Essaka in the interior of modern-day eastern Nigeria, Equiano grew up among the Ibo people before he was kidnapped at the age of eleven and sold as a slave to other Africans.

This is what I wrote about Equiano's birth and youth in 1997 before the controversy came to light. I state Equiano's origins as a fact, taking the statements in his autobiography as reliable.

Equiano claims to have been born around 1745 in the village of Essaka in the interior of modern-day eastern Nigeria, growing up among the Ibo people before being kidnapped at the age of eleven and sold as a slave to other Africans. Recent research, however, has raised questions about whether Equiano was born in Africa. The church record of his baptism on February 9, 1759, in Westminster, England, lists him as "Gustavus Vassa a Black born in Carolina 12 years old."

This is how I revised the same passage about Equiano's origins to reflect the uncertainty that's arisen about his African birth. "Equiano claims" doesn't mean his words are untrue. They're his claim, which we might still accept, but not without recognizing that the record of his baptism says something different.

From the Scholar's Desk

- Show students Segment 4 on William L. Andrews on **From the Author's Desk DVD.** Discuss his comments about why and how he revised his earlier writing about Olaudah Equiano because of new evidence that Equiano may not have been born in Africa.
- Draw students' attention to Andrews's presentation of his original and revised statements about Equiano's early years. **Ask:** What details are different in the two versions, and what are the other major differences?
  Answer: In the revised version, Andrews included both the information that Equiano had given and new information about baptismal records showing that he was born in England. In addition, the revision says that "Equiano claims to have been born around 1745 . . ." rather than "Born around 1745 . . ."
- **Ask** students to explain why persuasive writing could benefit from the kinds of adjustments Andrews made in his factual writing.
  Possible response: Persuasive writing needs to support its opinions with facts and logical arguments. If a fact supporting an opinion is called into question, the writer should acknowledge that the fact has been questioned, showing that he or she respects the truth and therefore is trustworthy. The writer must also weigh the possibility of not using the fact at all.

Differentiated Instruction Solutions for All Learners

Support for Special Needs Students

Encourage students to work in pairs and discuss a topic that is important to them. Be sure that they list each argument and counterargument. Review the difference between fact and opinion. *Fact*: George Washington was the first U.S. President. *Opinion:* George Washington was the greatest U.S. President. *Fact:* The Declaration of Independence was written in Philadelphia in 1776. *Opinion:* The Declaration of Independence is the most influential document in the world.

Enrichment for Advanced Writers

Have students examine one of the persuasive writings in this unit, such as the Declaration of Independence, Thomas Paine's "The Crisis," or Patrick Henry's "Speech in the Virginia Convention." Have students write a brief answer to one of these writers, replying to the original writer's argument, acknowledging his strong points, and finding counter-arguments.

Revising

- As students refine their arguments, remind them to address at least one argument opposing their opinion. Explain that if they don't anticipate arguments from the opposition, their argument may appear to be poorly conceived.
- Arrange for pairs of students to test one another's arguments by checking for faulty modes of persuasion. Test for circular reasoning by having students find specific ways in which each supporting argument does more than restate the main argument. To test for loaded language, point out that persuasive writing naturally uses language somewhat slanted to favor the writer's opinion. Loaded language, however, can be sarcastic in tone or uncritically praising. Explain that loaded language might be entertaining, but it also sounds unreasonable and may make readers reject the writer's opinion. Have students test the "loaded language" quotient of one another's papers, substituting balanced replacements for any questionable expressions.
- Emphasize the importance of transitions. Be sure that students understand that transitions connect ideas. Explain that transitions link supporting evidence in an argument much the way links in a chain hold a necklace together.

Six Traits Focus

✔	Ideas	✔	Word Choice
✔	Organization	✔	Sentence Fluency
✔	Voice	✔	Conventions

Writing and Grammar, Ruby Level

Students will find additional instruction on revising for a persuasive essay in Chapter 7, Section 7.4.

Writing Workshop

Revising

Revising Your Paragraphs

Eliminate faulty logic. When you write persuasively, you can get carried away with your passionate convictions instead of working to persuade your reader with carefully linked steps of logical thinking. To avoid errors in logic, look for the common mistakes listed in the chart below. Each is a technique that twists the facts or manipulates the reader's emotions.

Faulty Modes of Persuasion

Type	Definition	Example
loaded language	using words with strongly negative or positive connotations	"The firm's *horse-and-buggy* attitudes *tyrannize* mothers."
bandwagon appeal	urging readers to adopt a course of action because "everyone is doing it"	*"Every other high school* in the county has a soccer team; we need one too."
circular reasoning	supporting a point by merely stating it in other words	"The law *should be amended* because it needs *changing*."
post hoc, ergo propter hoc argument	assuming that because one event occurs after another, the first causes the second	"Since she became CEO, the value of our stock has fallen. It's time for her to resign."

Revising Your Word Choice

Strengthen your transitions. In persuasive writing, good transitions highlight the logic of an extended argument. Both between paragraphs and within them, you need transitions to make your reasoning more obvious to the reader, to improve sentence clarity, and to strengthen the connection between ideas.

Transitions that show contrast:	*however, although, despite*
Transitions that point to a reason:	*since, because, if*
Transitions that signal a conclusion:	*therefore, consequently, so, then, as a result*

Peer Review: Ask a group of three or four classmates to read your draft and identify places where you might improve your transitions. Make revisions as needed. Then, explain to the group how each of your revisions clarifies your logic or improves the connection between ideas.

Tips for Using Technology in Writing

Have students search the Internet for arguments supporting and opposing the opinions in their essays. They are likely to find a whole range of objective and subjective communications, some more trustworthy than others. If they find valid and effective arguments, encourage them to acknowledge these arguments, or use them to support their opinions, giving credit to the authors.

Developing Your Style

Using Parallelism

Create effective parallelism. Parallel structure is the repeated use of similar ideas in a similar grammatical form. In a persuasive essay, parallelism enhances the power of your language. Parallel expressions help you emphasize your arguments and create a compelling rhythm. In this example, similar ideas are expressed in phrases.

Not parallel: Philadelphia is famous for the First Continental Congress, housing the Liberty Bell, and publishing the country's first newspaper.

Parallel: Philadelphia is famous for hosting the First Continental Congress, housing the Liberty Bell, and publishing the country's first newspaper.

Review your draft to identify related or contrasting concepts. Consider expressing these concepts in parallel form by using the same grammatical structure. For example, you might use similar words, phrases, clauses, or sentences.

Find It in Your Reading Read or review the selection from *The Autobiography* by Benjamin Franklin on page 142.

1. Identify three sentences that use parallelism.
2. Write out the sentences, and underline the parallel elements.
3. Explain the way each sentence uses the same grammatical structure.

Apply It to Your Writing Review the draft of your persuasive essay to identify opportunities to link or contrast ideas using parallelism. Then, correct any unparallel constructions. For each paragraph in your essay, follow these steps:

1. Identify sentences or passages that express related or contrasting concepts.
2. If these concepts are in different sentences, use parallelism to combine them.
3. If the concepts are in the same sentence, make sure they have the same grammatical structure, as shown:

Without Parallelism: We rowed past the boathouse, under the bridge, and the boat crossed the finish line.

With Parallelism: We rowed past the boathouse, under the bridge, and across the finish line. (prepositional phrases)

Prentice Hall Writing and Grammar Connection: Chapter 20, Section 6

Developing Your Style

- Reinforce students' sense of parallelism by reviewing the examples in the text. **Ask:** Why is the first example sentence not parallel?
Answer: It ties together a trio of phrases, but the first phrase doesn't begin with a gerund, as do the other phrases (housing and publishing). The revision makes the statement parallel by beginning the first phrase with the gerund *hosting.*
- Examples of Parallelism in Franklin's Autobiography: "Lose no time; be always employed in something useful; cut off all unnecessary actions." These phrases are parallel because they all begin with imperative verbs.
- Have students read one another's persuasive essays to find examples of parallel structure as well as opportunities to use parallel structure.

Writing and Grammar, Ruby Level

Students will find additional instruction on revising for a persuasive essay in Chapter 7, Section 7.4.

Tips for Test Taking

Many standardized tests require students to revise errors in compositions. Some errors may be errors in parallelism. Parallel structures are often found in a series of ideas. Because errors in parallel structure often appear as words, phrases, or clauses in a series of ideas or actions, students should closely examine the word choices used to create the lists. For example, when students read a test item, they should check every series of ideas for parallelism. If they see a description using a series of one-word adjectives, they should be sure that the description does not include a prepositional phrase instead of a one-word adjective.

Student Model

- Explain that the student model is a sample and that persuasive essays may be longer.
- Have students notice the information that the author presents in his first paragraph. **Ask** them what important statement the author includes and why.
  Answer: The author makes a thesis statement in the first paragraph because he wants readers to know his position on an issue.
- Call students' attention to the author's word choice in the second paragraph. Explain that the author uses an emphatic statement in an attempt to create an emotional appeal that supports his opinion.
- Have students notice that in the third paragraph, the author continues to build his argument by creating a specific cause-and-effect scenario.
- Have students notice the language in the fourth paragraph. Explain that a successful argument needs more than a well-supported opinion. Having a good argument also requires using the right words to create a memorable appeal.
- Have students look at the last paragraph. **Ask** students what the author includes in this paragraph that he also includes in the first paragraph.
  Answer: The author restates his thesis from the first paragraph.
- Tell students that after supporting an opinion, it is best to restate that opinion at the end of the essay.

Writing Genres

Persuasive Essay Tell students that many jobs require persuasive skills. For example, people in business must write proposals supporting or opposing various measures. Attorneys must prepare arguments to support a particular viewpoint in court. Marketers use creative modes of persuasion when they craft advertisements.

Writing Workshop

Student Model: Shelby English
Black Mountain, North Carolina

Athletes and Their Effect on YOU!

How do the actions of professional athletes, the role models of today's society, affect the way people live? It is through their attitude and the way they present themselves in life. As children are growing up, they tend to look up to someone older than they are—usually someone famous, such as an athlete. For this reason, it is essential for those with the gift of being able to play a professional sport to make sure they set a good example.

> Shelby presents a thesis statement that states the opinion that she wants to persuade readers to accept.

Many people, children and adults alike, look at a professional athlete as the best thing ever to walk the planet. When you hear of a professional basketball player making the most points ever scored in a game, or watch a receiver win the Super Bowl by making a one-handed catch with five seconds left, you feel a sense of awe! Such events leave you wishing that you could have that same experience. When children see someone of that stature accomplishing such an extravagant goal, they think, "WOW! I want his jersey!" or "WOW! He is my favorite player!" They look up to that person and want to be exactly like him or her.

> Shelby gives a reason to support her opinion about why professional athletes must set a good example.

When athletes express themselves, they are showing people what's "cool"—what the new fad is, how to act, maybe even how to walk. When you see professional athletes investing their time and energy in the future of our needful society, you really admire them and think that they can do no wrong. Then, in this context, the news comes out that a "favorite player" has behaved badly, broken rules, or committed a crime. Admirers may transfer their thoughts to decide that not just the player but also the player's actions are cool and okay, and that they—the fans—should behave the same way. Young people definitely don't think about how such actions could ruin their future, leading them down the wrong path. They have tunnel vision that says, "Hey, man, if he can do it, then I can do it" or "It didn't hurt her, so it won't hurt me."

> The writer elaborates on her argument by providing specific examples of what happens when athletes *don't* set a good example.

When you see an interview on television that is about your role model, what do you think? When we look at people whom we admire and see them the way they really are inside, why we can't say, "No way, not for me"? Why do we keep thinking we want to be like these people? This is the way that today's outrageously dedicated fan, the person who loves the professional athlete as much as he or she loves his family, thinks. There is a sort of mind-block that just won't let you say, "Get away!" Instead, it tells you, "No, stay in there. Support this person, your role model, the athlete you are crazy about. Be exactly like him." The problem with this thinking is that one day you, too, will come out exactly where that erring athlete is—probably not as a superstar, but as a person who has messed up in life.

> Shelby appeals to her audience by using a catchy writing style.

The good role model, always leading by example, contributes immensely to the betterment of society. Such a person makes the distinction between what is good and bad, never blurring the lines. The good role model avoids the type of selfish behavior that leads to a negative outcome. Because of their impact, professional athletes must set a good example, always striving to be role models that people will be able to remember and say, "That person made a difference in my life." When an athlete becomes a player of great morals, he or she can show the next generation how to live life to its fullest.

> In her conclusion, Shelby restates her thesis and then strengthens her argument by explaining the positive consequences of the position she supports.

Differentiated Instruction Solutions for All Learners

Strategy for Less Proficient Learners
Encourage students to create outlines of their essays, beginning with the prewriting phase. Students can use these outlines to make sure that they have included all the components for their arguments. Each outline should state the student's opinion, list supporting arguments, and then address at least one opposing argument.

Enrichment for Gifted/Talented Students
Have students analyze the purpose and evaluate the support of the persuasive messages around them. For example, they might examine local billboards or current advertisements in magazines. Encourage them to identify a few ads that make appeals to logic. Then have them identify a few ads that make appeals to emotions. Be sure that students also identify to which emotions the ads appeal.

Editing and Proofreading

Review your persuasive essay to eliminate errors in grammar, spelling, or punctuation.

Focus on Commas: Make sure you have used commas to separate three or more parallel words, phrases, or clauses in a series.

Words: The train was crowded, noisy, and slow.
Phrases: We toured the town by bus, by car, and by train.
Clauses: The survey revealed that most residents approved of the mayor, that they supported her tax plan, and that they would vote for her again.

Publishing and Presenting

Consider one of the following ways to share your persuasive writing:

Publish in a newspaper. Modify your essay into an opinion piece that matches the length requirements of your local or school newspaper. Conclude your essay with a call to action and submit it for publication.
Deliver a speech. Use your persuasive essay as the basis for a speech. While delivering your speech, make frequent eye contact with your audience, and use hand gestures to emphasize your key points. If possible, record your delivery so that you can evaluate your own presentation.

Reflecting on Your Writing

Writer's Journal Jot down your thoughts on the experience of writing a persuasive essay. Begin by answering these questions:

- Did your opinion on your topic change as you wrote your essay? Explain.
- Has action been taken as a result of your essay? What has been done?

WG *Prentice Hall Writing and Grammar Connection: Chapter 27, Section 2*

Rubric for Self-Assessment

Evaluate your persuasive essay *using the following criteria and rating scale, or, with your classmates, determine your own reasonable evaluation criteria.*

Criteria	Rating Scale (not very – very)				
Focus: How clear is your thesis statement?	1	2	3	4	5
Organization: How effectively do you organize your arguments?	1	2	3	4	5
Support/Elaboration: How well do you use a variety of arguments to support your position?	1	2	3	4	5
Style: How well do you use parallel structure?	1	2	3	4	5
Conventions: How correct is your grammar, especially your use of commas?	1	2	3	4	5

Tips for Test-Taking

Students may encounter a test prompt that asks them to argue for or against an issue. Explain that they should read the question carefully so that they know exactly what they are being asked to do. Once they have taken a position, they should brainstorm for three or four points that support their position. Then they should write a thesis statement expressing their opinion and list each supporting point, presenting the strongest argument last. They should spend about one-fourth of their writing time for planning and organization. They should use about one-half of their time for writing the essay, and then use the remaining one-fourth for rereading, revising, and proofreading the essay.

Editing and Proofreading

- Have students carefully read their persuasive essays, making changes in grammar, spelling, word choice, and punctuation.
- Then, ask students to exchange papers and proofread one another's essays. Be sure that students look closely for errors in comma usage. When students have finished making proofreading changes, tell them to print a final copy of their essays.

Six Traits Focus

	Ideas		Word Choice
	Organization		Sentence Fluency
	Voice	✔	Conventions

ASSESS

Publishing and Presenting

- Ask students to consider how their audiences might react to their essays. **Ask:** Do you think you have persuaded members of this audience? Why or why not?
- Ask each student to exchange his or her essay with another student (a different student from the revising partner), and have that student evaluate the argument.
- Review the self-assessment criteria with students.
- Encourage students to plan and deliver an oral presentation of their persuasive essays.

Reflecting on Your Writing

- Ask students to explain what they learned about the issues they discussed in their persuasive essays. Did their positions on those issues change as they learned more and wrote more about them?
- **Ask** students these questions. Which part of persuasive writing seemed the easiest to do? Which seemed the most difficult? Which feature of their final essays are they proudest of? Why?

WG **Writing and Grammar, Ruby Level**

Students will find additional instruction on editing and proofreading, publishing, and presenting, and reflecting on a persuasive essay in Chapter 7, Section 7.5.

Meeting Your Standards

Students will

1. **learn the terms *recall, predict,* and *summarize.***
2. **apply knowledge of these terms in standardized-test situations.**

Knowing Your Terms: Recalling Information

Explain that the terms listed under Terms to Learn will be used in standardized-test situations when students are asked to recall information and extrapolate from it.

Terms to Learn

- Review *recall.* Tell students that recalling means accurately remembering information. When recalling information, suggest that students remember as closely as possible the words originally used.
- Review *predict.* Remind students that a predicting prompt asks them to take the logical next step from the information they were given. The prediction should be fully grounded in the given text.
- Review *summarize.* Emphasize that summarizing involves chronologically relating the most important points in the text in their own words. A summary does not cover the details of the text, only its essential points.

ASSESS

Answers

1. Franklin says that he cannot entirely approve of the Constitution, but he doubts that he can ever entirely approve of it since he changes his opinion.
2. It is likely that Franklin will ultimately vote for the Constitution with some reservations.
3. Franklin observes that individuals can never entirely agree with someone else's viewpoint, because each person feels that only he or she is right.

High-Frequency Academic Words

High-frequency academic words are words that appear often in textbooks and on standardized tests. Though you may already know the meaning of many of these words, they usually have a more specific meaning when they are used in textbooks and on tests.

Know Your Terms: Recalling and Using Text Details

Each of the words listed is a verb that tells you to show that you remember text details and can use them to answer questions. The words indicate the kind of details and information you should provide in your answer.

Terms to Learn

Recall Tell the details as you remember them.

Sample test item: ***Recall*** Jefferson's closing words in the *Declaration of Independence.*

Predict Tell what you think will happen based on details in the text.

Sample test item: Considering the evidence in Act I, what do you ***predict*** Macbeth and Lady Macbeth will do when King Duncan visits them?

Summarize Briefly state the most important information and ideas in the text.

Sample test item: ***Summarize*** Henry's argument about fighting for independence as presented in *Speech in the Virginia Convention.*

Practice

Directions: *Read the passage from Benjamin Franklin's speech to the Constitutional Convention. Then, on a separate piece of paper, answer questions 1–3.*

Mr. President,

I confess, that I do not entirely approve of this Constitution at present: but, Sir, I am not sure I shall never approve of it; for, having lived long, I have experienced many instances of being obliged, by better information or fuller consideration, to change my opinions even on important subjects, which I once thought right, but found to be otherwise. It is therefore that, the older I grow, the more apt I am to doubt my own judgment of others. Most men, indeed, as well as most sects in religion, think themselves in possession of all truth, and that wherever others differ from them, it is so far error.

1. *Recall* the opening words of Franklin's speech. What is his attitude toward the Constitution?
2. From this passage, *predict* what Franklin's final decision will be on the Constitution.
3. *Summarize* Franklin's observations about human nature and behavior.

Tips for Test Taking

- The reading-comprehension portions of standardized tests are meant to assess the students' ability to absorb what is on the page. Tell students that they will need to apply logic and common sense to this material but must always give highest priority to the original text. Remind them that reading-comprehension questions are not aimed at eliciting opinions or assessing originality; there is always only one right answer, and that answer is the one that accurately reflects the original text.
- Explain to students that when they are asked to choose the best prediction from items on a multiple-choice test, the most conservative choice is usually the best one.
- When students are asked to select the best summary of a given text, alert them to expect to see words different from but similar in meaning to those originally used.

Assessment Workshop

Critical Reading: Cause-and-Effect Relationships

The reading sections of some tests often require you to recognize cause-and-effect relationships and to predict probable outcomes based on the content of a passage. Use these strategies to answer test questions:

- As you read, recall and clarify the connections among events to help you identify the cause-and-effect relationships.
- Remember that a single cause can have many effects, and a single effect can have many causes.
- While other causes may be stated or implied, concentrate on the cause that has the most direct influence on the outcome.
- Look for words that indicate cause and effect, such as *causes, produces, affects, because of, as a result,* or *for this reason.* Try to use causes to predict effects.

Practice

Directions: *Read the passage, and then answer questions 1 and 2.*

The increasing growth of weeds in Cabot Lake threatens to turn it into a stagnant swamp. Ira North, a researcher for the Cabot Institute, cites an increase in phosphorus-based lawn fertilizers as the primary factor in the growth of lake weeds. "When it rains, fertilizer runs into the lake, causing aquatic plants to grow rapidly. Phosphorus-laden water from washing machines and dishwashers also contributes to the problem."

At this point, more than one third of Cabot Lake is overrun by weeds and is unsuitable for swimming. North says that as more people build homes in the area, the use of phosphorus-based lawn fertilizers will increase dramatically. The number of dishwashers and washing machines in use will also go up, putting additional strain on the ecosystem. North predicts that if nothing is done to control development and fertilizer use, the lake will be fully overrun with weeds within twenty-five years.

1. What is the main cause of weed overgrowth in Cabot Lake?

   A more homes
   C lawn fertilizers
   B rainwater runoff
   D dishwashers and washing machines

2. Why is one third of Cabot Lake unsuitable for swimming?

   A an increased number of lawns
   C increasing rainwater runoff
   B weeds in the lake
   D more people buying fertilizer

Test-Taking Strategies

- Identify connections between causes (an event or condition that produces a result) and effects (the result).
- Pause every once in a while to summarize one or more chains of cause and effect.

Meeting Your Standards

Students will

1. **identify and analyze cause-and-effect relationships in reading passages.**
2. **predict probable outcomes based on the content of a passage.**

Critical Reading

- Review the clue words signaling cause-and-effect relationships. **Ask** students to suggest additional words.
  Possible answers: The following words suggest causal relationships: *since, therefore, in order to, factor, influence, create, bring about,* and *consequence.*
- Remind students that in many cases, an effect in turn becomes a cause for a later effect. Similarly, a cause was probably the effect of some earlier action.
- When students are asked to predict probable outcomes based on the content of a passage, suggest that they try to find a pattern in the causes and events given in the passage. These cause-and-effect relationships will be clues to the answer, and students should expect that the pattern formed by these relationships will be repeated.
- Have students read the Practice passage and answer the questions.
- Point out that in question 1, the answer is C, because the phrase *primary factor* in the second sentence of the first paragraph points to lawn fertilizers as the chief cause of weed overgrowth in the lake.
- Point out that in question 2, the answer is *B,* as indicated by the first sentence in the second paragraph.

Tips for Test Taking

Tell students that reading-comprehension questions often can be simpler than they would expect and not to be discouraged when they see long passages of text in the SAT or ACT. Explain to students that in most cases, they should be able to point to specific words within a passage that make one answer clearly better than the others. Add that the practice of looking for clue words will be especially useful in long passages. This principle holds true for the questions in the Practice on this page. Both of the correct answers come from direct statements in the texts.

ASSESS

Answers

1. C
2. B

Meeting Your Standards

Students will

1. analyze persuasive techniques.
2. analyze the purpose of a persuasive speech based on the evidence presented by the speaker.
3. evaluate the support that a speaker provides for his or her claims.

Analyze Persuasive Purposes

- Review with students the bulleted list under "Analyze Persuasive Purposes." Make sure they understand each type of proposition on the list.
- **Ask** students to name instances when they've encountered or used one of the four types of propositions.
  Possible answer: Students might have encountered propositions of value in televised advertisements about political candidates. They might have used propositions in policy when talking with their parents about changes in household rules.

Evaluate Support

- Have students read the three questions for evaluating a speaker's support.
- Tell students that it might be helpful to take notes while listening to a persuasive speech. That way, they can thoroughly evaluate the speaker's evidence after the speech has ended.
- Encourage students to ask questions of the speaker when they encounter what is unclear or illogical.

Assess the Activity

To evaluate students' speeches, use the Peer Assessment: Speech rubric, p. 129 in ***General Resources.***

Analyze Persuasive Techniques

When speakers want to persuade you to accept their ideas, they can use a variety of **persuasive techniques.** The strategies noted below will help you recognize and evaluate four kinds of speech.

Analyze Persuasive Purposes

Persuasive speakers seek to convince audiences using one or more of these four types of ideas:

- **Proposition of fact:** The speaker wants listeners to accept a claim as either true or false.
- **Proposition of value:** The speaker wants listeners to accept a claim as either good or bad.
- **Proposition to illuminate a problem:** The speaker asks listeners to share a concern.
- **Proposition of policy:** The speaker wants listeners to agree to a change in policy regarding an issue.

As you listen to a persuasive speech, identify the speaker's main purpose.

Identify evidence. Each type of persuasive speech offers distinct kinds of evidence: For a proposition of fact, evidence should include hard data, examples, or testimony. For a proposition of value, evidence should include both facts and appeals to emotion, and will indicate the speaker's sense of values. For a proposition to illuminate a problem, the speaker must establish the existence of a threat or obstacle. Lastly, in a proposition of policy, the speaker must persuade listeners to take specific action. As you listen to a speech, identify the evidence presented, note whether it is suited to the speaker's purpose, and weigh its strength. Also evaluate the speech based on your assessment of the speaker's truthfulness and ethics.

Evaluating Persuasive Technique

Rating System
+ = Excellent ✓= average – = w

Goals and Organization
Purpose clearly presented ______
Thesis statement is clear ______
Logical organization of supporting material ______
Clear link to audience ______

Support
Proofs match speech type ______
Proofs support thesis ______
Language is compelling ______
Language is persuasive ______
Reasoning is sound ______

Answer the following questions:
Which type of persuasive speech did you find n compelling?
Which persuasive techniques did you find most effective?

Evaluate Support

Use these questions to evaluate the support a speaker provides:

- **Proof:** Does the speaker's proof pertain directly to the thesis?
- **Persuasive Language:** Does the speaker use strong language that urges agreement, and clear language that ensures understanding?
- **Reasoning:** Is the speaker's reasoning sound and logical?

Use a form like the one shown to assess the effectiveness of a speech.

Activity *Speak and Respond* In a group of four, present speeches of each type on a topic familiar to group members. Evaluate the effectiveness of each speech's organization and support.

Differentiated Instruction Solutions for All Learners

Strategy for Less Proficient Readers
Give students some practice with the terms on this page by having them analyze the persuasive selections in Unit 2 and identify which types of ideas and evidence are represented in each. Students can identify the purpose of each speech and discuss how successfully each writer supported his or her ideas.

Enrichment for Gifted/Talented Students
Have students analyze the purpose and evaluate the support of the persuasive messages around them. For example, they might examine local billboards or current advertisements on television or the radio. Which ads are well supported, and which simply have the appearance of being so?

Suggestions for Further Reading

Featured Titles:

Rights of Man

Thomas Paine *Penguin Books, 1984*

Philosophical Text Thomas Paine was one of the most eloquent and widely read political authors of all time. His pamphlet "Common Sense" helped inspire the Declaration of Independence, and the first installment of his *Crisis* papers encouraged George Washington's army when it was enduring a difficult winter at Valley Forge. After the American Revolution, Paine traveled to Europe and wrote *Rights of Man,* his defense of the French Revolution. In it, he argues against monarchy and for a republican form of government. He also sets forth ideas for curing society's ills, including a progressive income tax, popular education, and pensions. This book so infuriated the British government that it was banned. Today's readers, however, will marvel at Paine's prophetic insights.

The Federalist Papers

Alexander Hamilton, James Madison, and John Jay *Mentor, 1999*

Primary Source In 1787 and 1788, Alexander Hamilton, James Madison, and John Jay wrote eighty-five essays to persuade New Yorkers to adopt the new national Constitution. First published in newspapers, these articles were eventually collected in *The Federalist Papers.* Not only were they successful in their immediate purpose, but they have also survived more than 200 years as some of the wisest commentaries on government ever written.

The Anti-Federalist Papers and the Constitutional Convention Debates

Edited by Ralph Ketcham *Mentor, 1986*

Primary Source The perfect companion to *The Federalist Papers,* this volume provides a context for the debate surrounding the ratification of the Constitution. The introduction, for example, outlines both federalist principles and anti-federalist political thought. The many primary documents in the book itself are grouped into two sections: The Federal Convention of 1787, and Ratification of the Constitution.

Works Presented in Unit Two:

If sampling a portion of the following texts has built your interest, treat yourself to the full works.

The Interesting Narrative and Other Writings

Olaudah Equiano *Penguin Books, 1995*

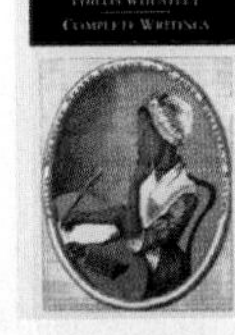

Complete Writings

Phillis Wheatley *Penguin Books, 2001*

The Autobiography and Other Writings

Benjamin Franklin *Penguin Books, 1986*

***Many of these titles are available in the* Prentice Hall/Penguin Literature Library.**
Consult your teacher before choosing one.

Planning Students' Further Reading

Discussions of literature can raise sensitive and often controversial issues. Before you recommend further reading to your students, consider the values and sensitivities of your community as well as the age, ability, and sophistication of your students. It is also good policy to preview literature before you recommend it to students. The notes below offer some guidance on specific titles.

Autobiography by Benjamin Franklin

Franklin alludes to sexuality and discusses the propriety of educating the female sex. There is extensive discussion of religion; some children may find the discussion challenging to their own beliefs, others may find passages too critical and be uncomfortable with Franklin's assertions. Students may perceive Franklin's tone as arrogant and preview discussion of the rational he gives for writing this autobiography should be helpful.

Lexile: 1370

Complete Writings by Phillis Wheatley

Lexile: N/A

Rights of Man by Thomas Paine

In referring to the rights of man, Paine is referring only to white men. Some of his opinions about the English monarchy and the Catholic Church may offend readers. There are also elements of anti-Semitism in the work.

Lexile: N/A

Federalist Papers by Alexander Hamilton

The framers of the Constitution did not include African Americans, Native Americans, or women in their concept of self-government. This historical and cultural limitation of the Constitution can serve as a fruitful point of departure for a discussion of the subsequent evolution of American democracy.

Lexile: 1450

Anti-Federalist Papers by Ralph Ketcham

Neither the framers of the Constitution nor their opponents among antifederalists included African Americans, Native Americans, or women in their concept of self-government. This historical and cultural limitation of the Constitution

Continued from right column

can serve as a fruitful point of departure for a discussion of the subsequent evolution of American democracy.

Lexile: N/A

Meeting Your Standards

Students will

1. read selections from the American literary tradition written between 1800 and 1870.
2. apply critical-reading strategies to these selections.
3. analyze literary elements.
4. use a variety of strategies to read unfamiliar words and build vocabulary.
5. learn elements of grammar, usage, and style.
6. use recursive writing processes to write in a variety of forms.
7. develop listening and speaking skills.
8. express and support responses to various types of texts.
9. prepare, organize, and present literary interpretations.

Unit Instructional Resources

In *Unit 2 Resources,* you will find materials to support students in developing and mastering the unit skills and to help you assess their progress.

Vocabulary and Reading

- **Vocabulary Warm-up Word Lists A and B** identify selection words for students who read at one or two grades below level.
- **Vocabulary Warm-up Practice (A and B)** provides practice on the Word List words.
- **Reading Warm-ups A and B** provide reading passages containing the Word List words, along with questions and activities for students working at one or two grades below level.

Selection Support

- Reading Strategy
- Literary Analysis
- Vocabulary Builder
- Grammar and Style
- Support for Writing
- Support for Extend Your Learning
- Enrichment

You may also access these resources on TeacherExpress.

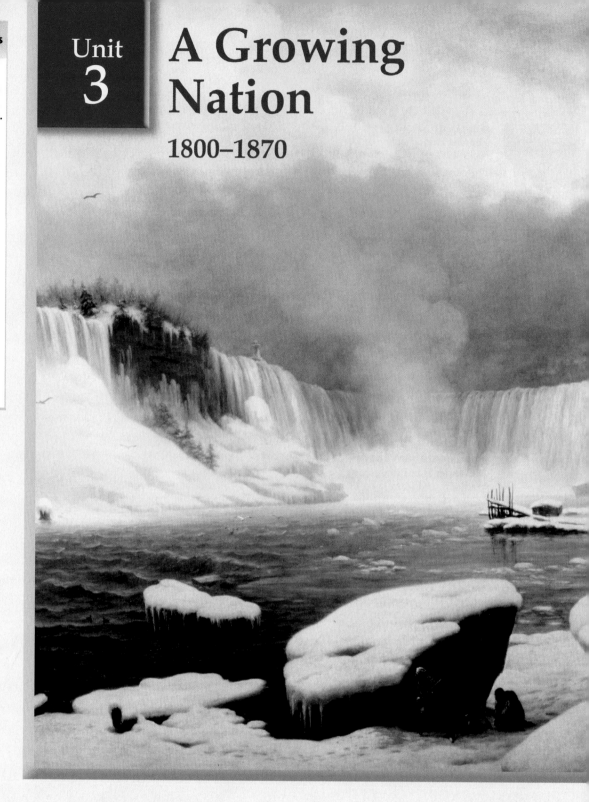

Unit 3 A Growing Nation

1800–1870

Nineteenth-Century Literature

"America is a land of wonders, in which everything is in constant motion and every change seems an improvement . . . . No natural boundary seems to be set to the efforts of man; and in his eyes what is not yet done is only what he has not yet attempted to do."

—Alexis de Tocqueville

◀ This painting, *Niagra Falls*, is by Hippolyte Victor Valentin Sebron, a French artist who painted in the United States from 1849 to 1855. This landscape captures the Romantic sensibility of the nineteenth century, with its emphasis on the awe-inspiring grandeur of nature.

Humanities

Winter at Niagara Falls, 1856, by Hippolyte Victor Valentin Sebron

Hippolyte Victor Valentin Sebron (1801–1897) was a French realist painter who moved to the United States in the nineteenth-century. Like many other European artists, Sebron came to paint the scenic landscapes of the country. During a six-year span, he traveled from New Orleans to Niagara Falls. Sebron produced a number of paintings of New York City, where he lived from 1854–1855.

- How does this painting convey the theme of a growing nation?
  Answer: It shows houses along the bank in the background, suggesting that Americans are spreading out and settling more and more land.

Introduce Unit 3

- Direct students' attention to the title and time period of this unit. Have a student read the quotations. **Ask** them: What does the quotation suggest about Americans at this point in their history?
  Possible response: The quotation suggests that Americans are exploring the natural wonders and developing the potential of the nation.
- Have students look at the art. Read the Humanities note to them, and **ask** the discussion question. Then **ask:** What kinds of literature or themes in literature do you think might come out of this period in American history?
  Possible response: Students probably will suggest themes concerning nature and exploration in the literature of this time period.

Unit Features

Connections

Use the information and questions on the Connections page to help students enrich their understanding of the selections presented in the unit.

Reading Informational Materials

These selections will help students learn to analyze and evaluate informational materials, such as workplace documents, technical directions, and consumer materials. They will expose students to the organization and features unique to nonnarrative texts.

In this unit, students will learn to read memorandums.

Introduce Gretel Ehrlich

- Gretel Ehrlich, a nature writer, introduces the unit and provides insights into the philosophy of Henry David Thoreau. As Americans became more aware of their expanding nation's natural wonders, some of America's most celebrated authors, like Thoreau, pondered deeply the connection between nature and the human spirit. Another commentary by Ehrlich appears on pages 402–403, where she introduces *Walden*.
- Have students read the introductory paragraph about Gretel Ehrlich. Tell students that Ehrlich spent seven years living on the Arctic island of Greenland, an experience she wrote about in *This Cold Heaven*. Her earlier book, *A Match to the Heart*, was inspired by her experience of being struck by lightning.
- Use the *From the Author's Desk DVD* to introduce Gretel Ehrlich. Show Segment 1 to provide insight into her career as a nature writer. After students have watched the segment, **ask:** How did Ehrlich's shyness as a child help her later as a writer?
  Answer: She learned to be a good listener and observer.

Telling the Stories that Come from the Earth

- Have students read Ehrlich's comments about the Inuit people and about Henry David Thoreau.
- Point out that Ehrlich is struck by the connections that both the Inuit and Thoreau find between nature and the human soul. **Ask:** What is the appeal of finding human meaning in natural fact?
  Answer: Finding human meaning in the natural world invests the natural world with spiritual value, rescuing it from being impersonal and faceless. It also makes human life in the world purposeful and significant.

Critical Viewing

Possible answer: Students may suggest peace, solitude, and oneness with nature.

Unit 3 features writing from a period in U.S. history when American writers were developing their own unique voices. In the following essay, Gretel Ehrlich introduces you to Henry David Thoreau, an important writer from this period who found great inspiration in nature. As you read her essay, the unit introduction that follows, and the literature in Unit 3, immerse yourself in this exciting time in American history.

From the Scholar's Desk
Gretel Ehrlich Talks About the Time Period

Gretel Ehrlich

Introducing Gretel Ehrlich (b. 1946) Born in California, Gretel Ehrlich has worked as a ranch hand, a sheepherder, and a documentary filmmaker. As a writer, she has been profoundly influenced by living in Wyoming, a place of intense extremes and breathtaking beauty. Ehrlich is best known for her nature writing, which has focused most recently on the island of Greenland.

▼ **Critical Viewing**
What "insights into human consciousness" might a nature writer achieve in the setting shown in this photograph? **[Speculate]**

Telling the Stories That Come From the Earth

We are all born on a particular spot on the planet with its unique seasons, weather, and topography. Mountains, rivers, rocks, storms, glaciers, skies, trees, and grasses, as well as all living things, help shape who we are, how we see, how we move through our days, and how we know who we are. Those of us who have been called "nature writers" are simply people who observe and write about the living planet, who witness the birth and death of its residents, who understand that we all share the earth equally, and who tell the stories that come from the earth.

From Natural Fact Comes Human Meaning The Inuit people of northern Greenland have a word, *sila,* that means "the power of nature, weather, and human and animal consciousness as one and the same": no separation between the "emotional weather" inside ourselves and the natural forces on the outside that affect us. Nature writers are always writing about two things at once: the ecosystem and continent that is our mind and body, and the greater one of the world surrounding us. They show us how human meaning can come from natural fact.

Teaching Resources

The following resources can be used to enrich or extend the instruction for the Unit 3 Introduction.

From the Author's Desk DVD
- **Gretel Ehrlich,** Segment 1

Unit 3 Resources
- **Unit Introduction: Names and Terms to Know,** p. 5
- **Unit Introduction: Focus Questions:** p. 6
- **Listening and Viewing,** p. 138

A One-Room Cabin on Walden Pond Henry David Thoreau was one of the great natural history writers of all time. Broken-hearted over a lost love, he went to live on Walden Pond in Concord, Massachusetts, for two years and two months. His friend and mentor, Ralph Waldo Emerson, a brilliant essayist, bought an eleven-acre field on the north shore of the pond, and in March of 1845, Thoreau, with Emerson's encouragement, built a ten-by-fifteen-foot one-room cabin. Then, he borrowed a horse and plow and planted two acres in white beans, corn, and potatoes.

An Inventory of the Natural World Thoreau was twenty-eight at the time, and he wanted to be free from the constraints of family and society. Reading widely, walking locally, writing obsessively—those were his priorities. He was not a great adventurer—others at the time were searching for the Northwest Passage in the Arctic, sailing the seas of the world, traveling by covered wagon across the country. Thoreau knew that his inventory of the natural world and his insights into human consciousness could be achieved right where he was: on Walden Pond. He wanted to live simply and quietly, to live deeply, to listen and observe, to become intimate with a place. In so doing, he allowed the outer landscape to shape the prose that came from within.

Where We Live Holds the Secrets of the Universe "I went to the woods because I wished to live deliberately," he wrote, "to front only the essential facts of life, and see if I could not learn what it had to teach, and not, when I came to die, discover that I had not lived." What we learn from Thoreau's life and writings is that anywhere we happen to live is good enough. We don't have to go to some exotic place to find ourselves or understand the world. It's all right here, for each of us. Each place holds all the secrets of the universe, the history of the world in a raindrop.

For: An online video
Visit: www.PHSchool.com
Web Code: ere-8301

For: More about Gretel Ehrlich
Visit: www.PHSchool.com
Web Code: ete-9312

Reading the Unit Introduction

Reading for Information and Insight Use the following terms and questions to guide your reading of the unit introduction on pages 246–253.

Names and Terms to Know
Alexis de Tocqueville
Louisiana Purchase
Sacajawea
War of 1812
Gold Rush
Seneca Falls Convention
Romanticism
Transcendentalism

Focus Questions As you read this introduction, use what you learn to answer these questions:

- In what ways did the growth in the size of the United States during this period affect the nation's view of itself?
- As a result of growing prosperity, what challenges confronted the United States in the mid-nineteenth century?
- In what ways does the literature of this period reflect the country's expansion?

Tell students that the terms and questions listed here are the key points in the introductory material. This information provides a context for the selections in the unit. Students should use the terms and questions as a guide to focus their reading of the unit introduction. When students have completed the unit introduction, they should be able to identify or explain each of these terms and answer the Focus Questions.

Concept Connector

After students have read the unit introduction, return to the Focus Questions to review the main points. For key points, see p. 253.

Go Online Author Link Typing in the Web Code when prompted will bring students to a video clip of Gretel Ehrlich.

Using the Timeline

The timeline can serve a number of instructional purposes, as follows:

Getting an Overview

Use the timeline to help students get a quick overview of themes and events of the period. This approach will benefit all students but may be especially helpful for visually oriented students, English-language learners, and those less proficient in reading. (For strategies in using the Timeline as an overview, see the bottom of this page.)

Thinking Critically

Have students answer critical-thinking questions about the timeline to help them establish the "so what" behind the "what happened." (For Critical Thinking and Critical Viewing questions, see the bottom and side columns of the facing page.)

Connecting to Selections

Have students refer back to the timeline when beginning to read individual selections. By consulting the timeline regularly, they will gain a better sense of the period's chronology. In addition, they will appreciate what was occurring in the world that gave rise to these works of literature.

Projects

Students can use the timeline as a launching pad for projects like these:

- **Annotated Map** Have students use this timeline and other sources to create annotated maps in their notebooks. Maps can show the growth of America from 1800 to 1870, with notes indicating when each state was added to the country.
- **Headline History** Have students scan the American Events section of the timeline for ten especially newsworthy items. Then ask them to write headlines dramatizing each of these items for readers living at the time.

American and World Events

1800 1810 1820

AMERICAN EVENTS

- 1803 Louisiana Purchase extends nation's territory to the Rocky Mountains.
- 1804 Lewis and Clark begin expedition exploring and mapping vast regions of the West. ▼

- 1807 Robert Fulton's steamboat makes first trip from New York City to Albany.
- 1812 U.S. declares war on Great Britain; early battles in War of 1812 are at sea.
- 1814 Bombardment of Fort McHenry inspires Francis Scott Key to write "The Star-Spangled Banner." ▼

- 1817 William Cullen Bryant publishes early draft of "Thanatopsis" in a Boston magazine.
- 1820 Missouri Compromise bans slavery in parts of new territories.

- 1825 Completion and success of Erie Canal spurs canal building throughout the nation. ▲
- 1827 Edgar Allan Poe publishes *Tamerlane*, his first collection of poems.

WORLD EVENTS

- 1804 France: Napoleon Bonaparte proclaims himself emperor. ▼

- 1813 England: Jane Austen publishes *Pride and Prejudice.*
- 1815 Belgium: French army under Napoleon routed at Waterloo.
- 1815 Austria: Congress of Vienna redraws map of Europe following Napoleon's downfall.
- 1816 France: René Läennec invents the stethoscope.
- 1818 England: Mary Wollstonecraft Shelley creates a legend with *Frankenstein.*
- 1829 England: George Stephenson perfects a steam locomotive for Liverpool-Manchester Railway. ▼

Getting an Overview of the Period

Introduction To give students an overview of the period, indicate the span of dates along the top of the timeline. Point out the division of the timeline into American and World Events, and have students practice scanning the timeline to look at both categories. Finally, tell them that the events in the timeline represent beginnings, turning points, and endings.

Key Events Have students select items in the American Events section that help tell the story of American expansion.

Possible answers: 1803, Louisiana Purchase; 1850, California admitted to the Union.

1830 1840 1850

- 1831 Cyrus McCormick invents mechanical reaper. ▼

- 1837 Samuel F. B. Morse patents electromagnetic telegraph.
- 1838 U.S. Army marches Cherokees of Georgia on long "Trail of Tears" to Oklahoma. ▶

- 1846 Mexican War begins.
- 1846 Abraham Lincoln first elected to Congress.
- 1848 Mexican War ends; United States expands borders.
- 1848 California Gold Rush begins.
- 1848 Women's Rights Convention held in Seneca Falls, New York.

- 1850 Nathaniel Hawthorne publishes *The Scarlet Letter.*
- 1850 California admitted to the Union.

- 1851 Herman Melville publishes *Moby-Dick.* ▲
- 1851 Nathaniel Hawthorne publishes *The House of the Seven Gables.*
- 1852 Harriet Beecher Stowe publishes *Uncle Tom's Cabin.*

- 1831 France: Victor Hugo publishes *Notre Dame de Paris.* ▼

- 1841 Antarctica: First explored by Englishman James Ross.
- 1842 Asia: Hong Kong becomes a British colony.
- 1845 Ireland: Famine results from failure of potato crop.
- 1847 Italy: Verdi's opera *Macbeth* first performed.
- 1847 England: Emily Brontë publishes *Wuthering Heights.*
- 1848 Belgium: Karl Marx and Friedrich Engels publish *The Communist Manifesto.*

- 1850 France: Life insurance introduced.
- 1850 England: Elizabeth Barrett Browning publishes *Sonnets from the Portuguese.*
- 1851 Australia: Gold discovered in New South Wales.
- 1853 Europe: Crimean War begins.
- 1854 Japan: Ports open to trade.
- 1855 England: Robert Browning publishes *Men and Women.*
- 1856 Crimean War ends.

Introduction ■ 245

size of the United States? (b) How would the United States have been different if this event had not taken place?
Answer: (a) 1803, Louisiana Purchase (b) The United States would not have been as powerful without the natural resources of the region.

2. (a) Which event between 1820 and 1830 affected the issue of slavery? (b) How was this event a harbinger of future conflict?
Answer: (a) 1820, Missouri Compromise banned slavery in new territories. (b) This foreshadowed future disputes over slavery.
3. (a) Indicate a date that relates to the invention of the telegraph. (b) Describe the effect the telegraph had on communication.
Answer: 1837, Morse patented his idea for telegraph. For the first time, people could send messages quickly over long distances.
4. (a) When were the words for "The Star-Spangled Banner" written? (b) Why was it an appropriate choice for the national anthem?
Answer: (a) The words were written in 1814. (b) Its description of the flag in the midst of battle made it the prefect choice for a national anthem.

Critical Viewing

1. What does the illustration of the Lewis and Clark expedition reveal about the American West?
Answer: It indicates the vastness and great natural beauty of the region.
2. What impression does his portrait give you of Napoleon?
Answer: He seems to have forgotten his revolutionary ideas and begun to think of himself as an absolute monarch.
3. What does the illustration of the forced march of the Cherokee suggest about government policy toward Native Americans?
Answer: The government forcibly removed whole peoples from their homelands in order to make way for white settlers.

claimed that America had produced few writers of distinction, Washington Irving was writing tales that would bring him international distinction. One of these tales appears on p. 258.

- The Louisiana Purchase was a key event of this period. Lewis's "Crossing the Great Divide," which describes the expedition's journey across this new territory, appears on p. 298.

Critical Viewing

Answer: The small chunk of present-day southern Arizona and New Mexico called the Gadsden Purchase was the last region on the map to be added to the United States.

In 1831, the Frenchman Alexis de Tocqueville, sent to report on America's prisons, ultimately wrote about something far more interesting: a bustling new nation full of individuals optimistically pursuing their destinies. His *Democracy in America* observed that Americans had "a lively faith in the perfectibility of man," believing "what appears to them today to be good may be superseded by something better tomorrow."

The bustling spirit that had enchanted Tocqueville in 1831 would make for a turbulent "tomorrow" in the decades to come: By 1870, industrialism, explosive population and economic growth, and the Civil War had all aged the nation's spirit. American literature also matured during this time. In 1831, Tocqueville wrote, "America has produced very few writers of distinction. . . . [The literature of England] still darts its rays into the forests of the New World." By 1870, America had produced many "writers of distinction": Irving, Cooper, Bryant, Poe, Emerson, Thoreau, Hawthorne, Melville, Dickinson, and Whitman—all of whom eventually shone their unmistakably American light into and far beyond "the forests of the New World."

Growth of the United States to 1853

CANADA
(Ceded by Britain, 1818)
OREGON COUNTRY
(Agreement with Britain, 1846)
LOUISIANA PURCHASE
(Purchased from France, 1803)
THE UNITED STATES, 1783
ORIGINAL 13 STATES
MEXICAN CESSION
(Treaty of Guadalupe-Hidalgo, 1848)
PACIFIC OCEAN
TEXAS ANNEXATION
(Annexed by Congress, 1845)
GADSDEN PURCHASE
(Purchased from Mexico, 1853)
FLORIDA
(Ceded by Spain, 18
MEXICO
GULF OF MEXICO
Present-day state boundaries
0 400 800 Miles
0 400 800 Kilometers

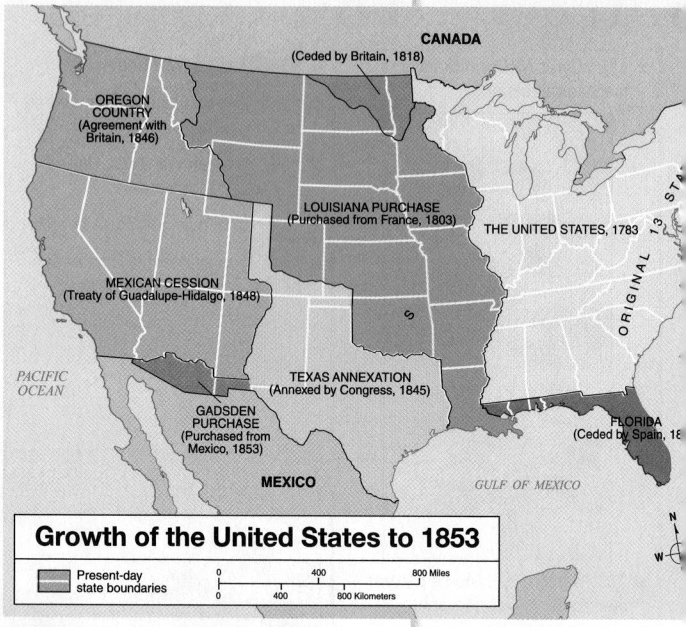

▲ **Critical Viewing** By 1848, the United States stretched from the Atlantic Ocean to the Pacific Ocean. What region of the map was the last to be added to the United States? **[Read a Map]**

Historical Background

In 1800, the United States consisted of sixteen states clustered near the east coast. In 1803, Thomas Jefferson doubled the nation's size by signing the Louisiana Purchase. The rapid growth of the nation inspired an upsurge in national pride and self-awareness. Improved transportation helped bind the old and the new states together. Canals, turnpikes, and railroads boomed during this period. Steamboats and sailing packets helped speed people and goods to their destinations.

The Growth of Democracy at Home: 1800–1840 As the nation expanded, Americans began to take more direct control of their government.

Enrichment

Old New York

In 1800, New York City had a population of 60,000, making it the second-largest city in the United States. A decade later, New York became the largest city, a rank it holds to this day. By 1840, New York was as heavily populated as Philadelphia and Boston combined.

The Dutch first settled the southern tip of Manhattan Island. By 1820, the city extended as far north as 14th Street. The buildings of the day were rarely more than four stories high.

Despite New York's prosperity, it was not looked on as a cultural capital. Alexis de Tocqueville saw it as "a center of all our greatest vices, without any of those interests which counteract their baleful influence."

The 1828 election of Andrew Jackson, "the People's President," ushered in the era of the common man, as property requirements for voting began to be eliminated. The democratic advances of the time, however, were confined to white males. Scant political attention was paid to women, and most African Americans remained enslaved. One of the most tragic policies of this period was "Indian removal," the forced westward migration of Native Americans from confiscated tribal lands—as in the 1838 "Trail of Tears," in which 4,000 of 15,000 Cherokee perished on the trek from Georgia to Oklahoma.

Young Nation on the World Stage Despite all this, the first decades of the 1800s were, on the whole, hopeful ones. The young republic seemed able to weather any storm.

The War of 1812 convinced Europeans that the United States was on the world stage to stay. In the Monroe Doctrine of 1823, President James Monroe warned Europe not to intervene in the new Latin American nations. In the 1830s, the U.S. became embroiled in a conflict over the secession of Texas from Mexico; in 1836, the Mexican Army made its famous assault on the Alamo, in which every Texan defender was killed. When Texas was admitted to the Union in 1845, the resulting war with

Close-up on History

Sacajawea, Guide for Lewis and Clark

Here is a sad contradiction: A Shoshone Indian woman named Sacajawea helped Lewis and Clark explore the territories bought in the Louisiana Purchase, but the westward movement inspired by this expedition eventually led to "Indian removal" and the confiscation of Indian lands.

In 1804, Sacajawea was staying with the Mandan Indians near present-day Bismarck, North Dakota. Meriwether Lewis and William Clark, who had been asked by President Thomas Jefferson to explore the new western lands, were overwintering with the Mandans. They worried about how they would cross the Rocky Mountains when they continued the expedition in the spring. Fortunately, Sacajawea offered to guide them. The Shoshones lived in the Rockies, and she knew the region well. She could also translate for them in their encounters with different Indian tribes.

Sacajawea contributed greatly to the success of the expedition, gathering wild vegetables and advising the men where to fish and hunt game. She also knew about the healing qualities of different herbs. When the party reached the mountains, Sacajawea recognized the lands of her people. Soon, she was reunited with her brother, and she persuaded her relatives to support the expedition with the food and horses it needed to continue.

After successfully crossing the Rockies, the explorers reached the west coast and returned to St. Louis in 1806. Thanks in large part to Sacajawea, their relations with Indians had been almost entirely peaceful. However, in the westward expansion to come, such peaceful relations were an early casualty.

Mill in California in January of 1848. In a few days, word of the gold strike spread to San Francisco. Carpenters threw down their tools, bakers left their loaves to burn, and schools emptied as teachers joined the rush to the gold fields.

The news quickly spread outward from San Francisco. More than 80,000 Americans, Europeans, and South Americans made the long journey to California in 1849. They became known as Forty-Niners.

The American Experience
Close-up on History

- Tell students that without Sacajawea, the Lewis and Clark expedition very likely would have failed to reach the Pacific Ocean, and certainly Lewis and Clark would not have gathered as much information about the people who were living in the west.
- **Ask** students how different attitudes about land may have led to the conflict in the decades that followed the early peaceful relations between explorers and the native people of the west. **Possible response:** Students may mention that native people did not see the land as property but as a common resource, whereas the settlers felt that the land where they lived was property.

Differentiated Instruction
Solutions for All Learners

Strategy for Less Proficient Readers
Ask each student to become an expert on a particular section of "A Growing Nation" by reading it several times and devising a comprehension test on it.

Support for English Learners
Draw a rough outline of the United States on the chalkboard. As students read about each new surge of expansion, shade in and date newly-acquired territory, so that students can see the course of growth.

Strategy for Advanced Readers
Challenge students to find links between this historical period and their own times. Students can look for parallels or cause-and-effect relationships. For example, why might people have hesitated to settle in the western frontier before the Louisiana Purchase?

period the story of westward expansion?
Answer: The Louisiana Purchase made westward expansion possible. Settlers continued spreading westward as the population grew. The war with Mexico resulted from westward expansion.

2. What link exists between westward expansion and conflicts over slavery?
Answer: Some people moving to new territories wanted slaves; others were against any expansion of slavery.

Critical Viewing

Possible answer: The poster depicts slavery as a brutal and terrifying experience.

Mexico (1846–1848) ended in a U.S. victory, which added more territory to the nation, including California. Soon after, the Gold Rush of 1849 drew hundreds of thousands to this new land of promise.

▲ **Critical Viewing** Harriet Beecher Stowe's novel *Uncle Tom's Cabin* (1851–1852) stirred anti-slavery sentiment in the North. What message regarding slavery is conveyed by this poster for an 1881 theatrical production of the novel? **[Analyze]**

The Way West and Economic Growth In a sense, the entire course of American history can be seen as a pageant rolling ever westward, as new territories opened up and transportation improved. The first white settlers sailed west from Europe, establishing their homes on the East Coast of the New World. All thirteen original states were on the eastern seaboard, hemmed in by mountain barriers blocking easy access to the interior. As late as 1845 the most western state in the Union was Texas. The last of the fifty states, Hawaii, lying far to the west of the North American continent, was at the time an independent kingdom.

During the early decades of the 1800s, transportation was steadily changing and improving. The Erie Canal, completed in New York in 1825, set off a wave of canal building. In the 1850s, the "iron horse"—the railroad—began to dominate long-distance American travel; by 1869, rail lines linked east and west coasts.

Advances in technology spurred social change. Factories sprang up all over the Northeast. The steel plow and reaper encouraged frontier settlement by making farming practical on the vast, sod-covered grasslands. The telegraph facilitated almost instant communication across great distances. Inventor Samuel F. B. Morse's message from Washington to Baltimore in 1844 could serve as the motto for this era: "What hath God wrought!"

Winds of Change It was evident to even the most cheerful observer that the United States at mid-century faced trouble as well as bright promise. The new prosperity unleashed fierce competition, leading to the creation of factories scarred by child labor and unsafe working conditions. In 1840, most women could not vote or file a lawsuit. The 1840s and 1850s saw an outburst of efforts promoting women's rights, notably the 1848 Seneca Falls Convention. Above all, the centuries-old institution of slavery bitterly divided the nation. The conflict between abolitionists, who opposed slavery, and the advocates of states' rights, who argued that the federal government could not bend states to its will, sharpened in the 1850s. The gathering storm finally burst into war in 1861, but it was a storm that had been building for 250 years, ever since the first slave was brought in chains to this continent.

Enrichment

Francis Lowell and American Industry

Britain's War of 1812 blockade of the United States provided a boost to American industry. Cut off from foreign suppliers, Americans had to produce more goods themselves.

As in Britain, advances occurred in the textile industry. A Boston merchant named Francis Cabot Lowell had toured the British textile mills, where he saw that workers at one factory spun thread while workers at another wove it into cloth. Lowell thought it would be more efficient to combine the spinning and weaving tasks under one roof.

Lowell and several partners built a textile mill in Waltham, Massachusetts. The nearby Charles River powered the machines that turned the raw cotton into finished cloth. Lowell died in 1817. In time, his company built an entire factory town on the Merrimack River and named it in his honor. By 1836, Lowell was a thriving town of more than 10,000 people.

Literature of the Period

American Literature Comes of Age Before 1800, American writers were not widely read—not even in America—but that situation soon began to change. The writers of this period would define the American voice—personal, idiosyncratic, bold—and its primary theme: the quest of the individual to define him- or herself.

Romanticism Despite their unmistakable differences, the writers of the early nineteenth century—Washington Irving, James Fenimore Cooper, William Cullen Bryant, and Edgar Allan Poe—can all be described as Romantics.

Romanticism was an artistic movement that dominated Europe and America during the nineteenth century. The name Romanticism can be a bit misleading because Romantics do not necessarily write about love. Romantic writers elevated the imagination over reason and intuition over fact. Washington Irving, the first American to be read widely overseas, made his mark with his *History of New York* (1809), which is not a dry historical record but a rollicking narrative that alters facts at will.

Point/Counterpoint

Edgar Allan Poe, Immature Genius or Mature Craftsman?

Was Edgar Allan Poe an immature genius who appeals to our childish love of mysteries and puzzles, or was he a mature craftsman who knew exactly what he wanted to achieve with every effect? Two critics—one of them, T.S. Eliot, a major poet himself—disagree about Poe's worth and craftsmanship.

An Immature Genius "That Poe had a powerful intellect is undeniable: but it seems to me the intellect of a highly gifted young person before puberty. The forms which his lively curiosity takes are those in which a pre-adolescent mentality delights: . . . puzzles and labyrinths, mechanical chess players . . . The variety and ardor of his curiosity delight and dazzle; yet in the end the eccentricity and lack of coherence of his interests tire. There is just that lacking which gives dignity to the mature man: a consistent view of life."

—T.S. Eliot, *To Criticize the Critic*

A Mature Craftsman "In the new picture of Poe, then, . . . we see somewhat less 'mad genius' and somewhat more 'commercial craftsman.' More wit, erudition, and philosophical consistency are evident in the new Poe, and far less compulsion. If we cannot entirely do away with the popular image of guttering candles and circling bats, in short, we should at least be able to point to craftsmanship, detachment, and humor . . . his brilliance is indisputable and his contribution to American and world literature, enormous."

—Stuart Levine, Introduction to *The Short Fiction of Edgar Allan Poe*

national literature, it also began establishing its own identity in the field of music. Among the Americans to contribute to this field was Frank Johnson (1792–1844).

One of the first of many prominent, successful African-American musicians, Johnson formed a woodwind band in the 1820s. In addition to playing throughout the United States, Johnson's band traveled to England and performed for the Queen.

Point/Counterpoint

Tell students that Edgar Allan Poe is a major figure in American literature and a father of modern mystery and horror stories. Explain that in addition to writing his own poems and stories Poe was a critic of literature who published many reviews during his lifetime. Then ask the following questions.

1. In what way are Eliot's and Levine's viewpoints different?
   Answer: Eliot considers Poe to be a bright but undeveloped writer; Levine believes that Poe has refined his writing.
2. Which of these two views shows a higher regard for Poe's writing craft?
   Answer: Levine believes that Poe made careful choices and that his writing has precisely the effects he wanted it to have, while Eliot believes that Poe resorted to gimmicks to engage readers.

a religious movement; it was a philosophical movement with religious overtones. Even though 100 years had passed since the death of Calvinist minister Jonathan Edwards, his teachings continued to influence people. William Ellery Channing, minister of Boston's Federal Street Church, had recently broken with Calvinist ideas like Edwards's. Channing had become the apostle of Unitarianism. His sermons and essays, promoting more tolerant religious attitudes and encouraging people to work in various social causes, helped to lay the groundwork for Transcendentalism.

Critical Viewing

Answer: The motto, "The birds and beasts will teach thee!" and a glowing, floating book inscribed "Nature" illustrate the Transcendental tenet that the natural world can teach people to see the presence of the "Over-Soul" in the creation.

The Romantics reveled in nature. William Cullen Bryant is best known for his lyric poems rejoicing in the healing powers of nature. Irving's "Rip Van Winkle" and "The Legend of Sleepy Hollow" sparked an interest in his beloved Hudson River Valley. James Fenimore Cooper's four *Leatherstocking Tales* feature the exploits of Natty Bumppo in the frontier forests of upstate New York. A man of absolute moral integrity, Natty Bumppo preferred nature over civilization, establishing the pattern for countless American heroes to come.

▲ **Critical Viewing** Above is a ticket to Charles Willson Peale's museum, which he ran to teach Americans how to learn by observing nature. How does this effort reflect Transcendentalist beliefs? **[Connect]**

Romantic writing often accented the fantastic aspects of human experience. The tortured genius Edgar Allan Poe remains popular to this day for his haunting poems and suspenseful stories whose characters, as one biographer has said, "are either grotesques or the inhabitants of another world than this."

New England Renaissance: 1840–1855 In 1837, Ralph Waldo Emerson, a former Boston minister, delivered his famous oration "The American Scholar," calling for American intellectual independence from Europe. Emerson believed that American writers should begin to interpret their own culture in new ways. As if in response to Emerson's call, an impressive burst of literary activity took place in and around Boston between 1840 and 1855. This "flowering of New England" would produce an array of great writers and enduring literature.

Transcendentalism Most, if not all, of these writers were influenced by the Transcendental movement then flourishing in New England. Emerson and Thoreau were the best-known Transcendentalists, but the ferment of Transcendental ideas affected many other writers.

Transcendentalism demands careful definition, yet it is very hard to define. It has many facets, many sources, and encompasses a range of beliefs whose specific principles depend on the individual writer or thinker. The term itself and some of the ideas came from the German philosopher Immanuel Kant. In his *Critique of Practical Reason* (1788), Kant defines the "transcendental" as the understanding a person gains intuitively because it lies beyond direct experience. American Transcendentalism drew on other thinkers as well: the ancient Greek philosopher Plato, the French mathematician Pascal, the Swedish mystic and scientist Swedenborg, and the anti-materialism of Buddhist thought. Philosophy, religion, and literature all merged in New England Transcendentalism, producing a native blend that was romantic, intuitive, mystical, and considerably easier to recognize than to explain.

For Transcendentalists the point was that the real truths, the most fundamental truths lie outside the experience of the senses, residing instead, as Emerson put it, in the "Over-Soul . . . a universal and benign omnipresence. . . ." If that seems a bit obscure, so did the essays in *The Dial,* the quarterly magazine of New England Transcendentalism. Published from 1840 to 1844, *The Dial* was first edited by Margaret Fuller, a dominant personality and zealous feminist who was an accepted member of the Transcendentalist group.

Walden The most influential expression of Transcendental philosophy came from Emerson and his younger friend and protégé, Henry David Thoreau, who withdrew from society to live by himself on the shores of Walden Pond. Thoreau undertook this way of life because he felt intensely the Transcendentalists' reverence for nature. He begins *Walden,* his account of this experience, by writing, "When I wrote the following pages . . . I lived alone, in the woods, a mile from any neighbor, in a house which I had built myself, on the shore of Walden Pond, in Concord, Massachusetts, and earned my living by the labor of my hands only." Published in 1854, *Walden* consists of eighteen essays about matters ranging from a battle between red and black ants to the individual's relation to society. Thoreau's observations of nature reveal his philosophy of individualism, simplicity, and passive resistance to injustice.

The American Experience — A Living Tradition

Walden Pond and Tinker Creek

About 120 years after Thoreau set himself the experiment of living "alone, in the woods . . . on the shore of Walden Pond," Annie Dillard undertook a similar experiment with nature and solitude: "I live by a creek, Tinker Creek, in a valley in Virginia's Blue Ridge." Just as Thoreau wrote *Walden* to describe his experiences, she, too, wrote a book about what she saw and thought, the best-selling *Pilgrim at Tinker Creek.* Near the beginning of the book, she describes the home base for her observations:

"An anchorite's hermitage [hermit's secluded retreat] is called an anchor-hold; some anchor-holds were simple sheds clamped to the side of a church like a barnacle to a rock. I think of this house clamped to the side of Tinker Creek as an anchor-hold. It holds me at anchor to the rock bottom of the creek itself and it keeps me steadied in the current, as a sea anchor does, facing the stream of light pouring down. It's a good place to live; there's a lot to think about. The creeks—Tinker and Carvin's—are an active mystery, fresh every minute."

read the excerpt from *Nature* by Ralph Waldo Emerson on p. 390.

- Students can read Thoreau's own description of his plan to live by Walden Pond in the excerpt from *Walden,* p. 406.

The American Experience
A Living Tradition

- Tell students that Annie Dillard's book *Pilgrim at Tinker Creek* is often compared to Thoreau's *Walden.*
- Point out that Dillard's *Pilgrim at Tinker Creek* continues a tradition of journal writing about personal experiences with the natural world that began with Thoreau and continues the legacy of the Transcendentalists of Thoreau's day. **Ask** students to speculate about how a modern person's interactions with nature might be different from Thoreau's in the 1840s.
  Possible response: Because people in the 1840s had less technology they were closer to nature in their daily lives than we are today.

Enrichment

American Music, New England Style

While American literature was blossoming in New England, Lowell Mason (1792–1872) of Boston and other New England musicians were reshaping American music. Determined to bring about universal musical literacy, Mason organized the Boston Academy of Music and added music to the curriculum of Boston public schools. Mason also prompted a change in the style of American church music by emphasizing the selection of easy and solemn songs that all members of a congregation could sing in harmony. He wrote thousands of musical pieces, including many hymns that have remained popular.

Background
Literature

The friendship between Hawthorne and Melville happened almost by accident. In his early thirties, Melville moved from New York City to Pittsfield, Massachusetts, where he wrote his monumental novel *Moby-Dick.* It was published in 1851, a year after Hawthorne's *The Scarlet Letter.* Hawthorne's novel was an immediate success, but Melville's would not receive its due until many years later. Melville approached Hawthorne, seeking solace and friendship. The two men became and remained friends.

Critical Viewing

Answer: The years between 1855 and 1860 saw the greatest growth in railroads, an increase of some 10,000 miles of track.

The Possibility of Evil Not everyone shared the Transcendentalists' optimistic views. Nathaniel Hawthorne and Herman Melville expressed the darker vision of those who, in Hawthorne's words, "burrowed into the depths of our common nature" and found the area not always shimmering, but often "dusky." Hawthorne's Puritan heritage was never far from his consciousness. His masterpiece, *The Scarlet Letter* (1850), set in Boston in the seventeenth century, deals with sin, concealed guilt, hypocrisy, and humility. In *The House of the Seven Gables,* he delves into seventeenth-century witchcraft, insanity, and a legendary curse.

Hawthorne became a kind of mentor to Melville. Depressed about the negative critical response to his novel *Moby-Dick* (1851), Melville approached the older, more successful writer. Both men saw human life in grim terms, but their personalities were quite different. Hawthorne, despite a tendency toward solitude, was stable and self-possessed, a shrewd man without illusions. Melville, by contrast, was a man at odds with the world, a tortured and cryptic personality. For a large part of his career, he raged against his fate, much as Captain Ahab in *Moby-Dick* unleashed his fury against the white whale that had maimed him.

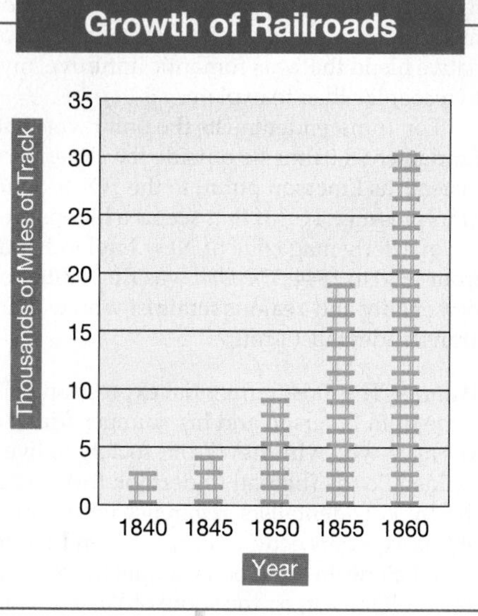

▲ Critical Viewing Railroads expanded rapidly after 1840. According to this graph, what five-year period saw the greatest growth in railroads? **[Read a Graph]**

At Home in Amherst While Thoreau was planting beans next to Walden Pond, Emily Dickinson was growing up in the nearby town of Amherst, Massachusetts. Her startling, intensely focused poetry catapulted her into the company of the greatest American poets—although not in her lifetime. A recluse for the second half of her life, Dickinson did not write for publication, or even for her family, but rather from a personal need to wrestle with questions about death, immortality, and the soul—questions unresolved by conventional religion.

Beyond New England Meanwhile, the quintessential American poet was tramping about the countryside, laboring at odd jobs to finance his poetry. In 1855, New Yorker Walt Whitman published his groundbreaking series of poems, *Leaves of Grass,* proudly broadcasting his "barbaric yawp" from Brooklyn to the universe. Most American readers ignored the irregular forms and frank language of this revolutionary poet, but Emerson knew an American original when he saw one and praised Whitman's work. Of all the poets of the period between 1800 and 1870, Whitman would have the most lasting effect on American literature—despite the fact that the first edition of *Leaves* sold fewer than twenty copies.

Fireside Poets Those were the literary giants of the period, as singled out by twentieth-century scholars. In 1850, however, the American reading public would probably have pointed instead to four other New England writers, known as the Fireside Poets: Henry Wadsworth Longfellow, a Harvard professor and tremendously popular poet; John Greenleaf Whittier, from a hardworking Quaker farm family; James Russell Lowell, born to wealth and position; and Oliver Wendell Holmes, a poet-physician and the unofficial laureate of the group.

After the Flowering As the war clouds gathered, the great burst of creativity in the Northeast began to subside. Antislavery writers, such as Emerson, Melville, Whittier, and Lowell, strongly supported the northern effort in the Civil War. Thoreau and Hawthorne died before the war ended. Whitman worked as a nurse in the war and incorporated war poems in his later editions of *Leaves of Grass*. Dickinson ignored the war in her poetry.

Oliver Wendell Holmes, energetic and cheerful, outlasted the rest of his renowned generation. He became "the last leaf upon the tree," to quote words he himself had written about Melville's grandfather, an old Revolutionary War veteran, in a poem published in 1831, when the poet and his country were still young.

▼ Critical Viewing
In this image, a freight train delivers ore to a foundry where it will be turned into steel. The railroad was a key to the growth of industry in the North. What other effects do you think the growth of the railroads had on northern life? **[Form a Hypothesis]**

Puritanism?
Answer: Transcendentalism replaced Puritan severity with optimism and tolerance.

2. Why is *Walden* an especially meaningful book today?
Possible answers: Thoreau's deep feeling for nature has influenced many and is embraced by today's environmental movement.
3. Where did most of America's great writers of this period live? Why?
Answer: Most were from New England or the Mid-Atlantic states. This was the first area of the country to be settled by Europeans and was therefore the most civilized and sophisticated area of the new country.

Critical Viewing

Possible answer: It would have greatly increased people's mobility, allowing suburbs to grow. It would also have contributed to the development of air pollution, from trains and from foundries.

Concept Connector

Have students return to the Focus Questions on p. 243. Ask them to use these questions to orally summarize the main points in the Unit Introduction. Students' summaries should include the following points:

How the Nation's Increased Size Changed its View of Itself

- The growth in size of the United States during the first half of the nineteenth century made Americans more aware of their country's position in relation to the established powers in Europe.
- The growth in the size of the nation also made Americans more confident of their own identity.

Challenges that Resulted from Mid-Nineteenth-Century Prosperity

- By the mid-nineteenth century, the United States faced the challenge of shifting from an agrarian to an industrial economy.
- The nation faced the challenge of dealing with different populations who sought opportunity in the United States.
- The westward expansion, a major factor in this growing prosperity, also intensified the struggle between North and South over slavery.
- The nation was also challenged to forge a national identity in an increasingly diverse country.

How Literary Movements Reflected the Country's Expansion

- The optimistic writing of many of the period's authors reflects the exhilaration of an expanding new nation.
- The darker musings of several authors portray the underside of this optimism—the uncertainty about the future, the sense that success does not come without a cost.

The Development of American English

The Truth About O.K.

BY RICHARD LEDERER

We Americans seem to have a passion for stringing initial letters together. We use *a.m.* and *p.m.* to separate light from darkness and B.C. and A.D. to identify vast stretches of time. We may listen to a deejay or veejay on *ABC, CBS, NBC,* or *MTV* or a crusading *DA* on *CNN, NPR,* or *PBS.*

Perhaps the most widely understood American word in the world is O.K. The explanations for its origin have been as imaginative as they have been various. Some have claimed that O.K. is a version of the Chocktaw affirmative *okeh.* Others have asserted that it is short for the Greek *olla kalla* ("all good") or *Orrin Kendall* crackers or *Aux Kayes* rum, or the name of chief *Old Keokuk.*

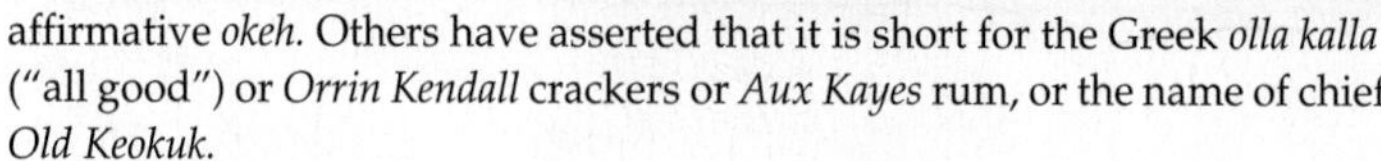

The truth is more politically correct than any of these theories.

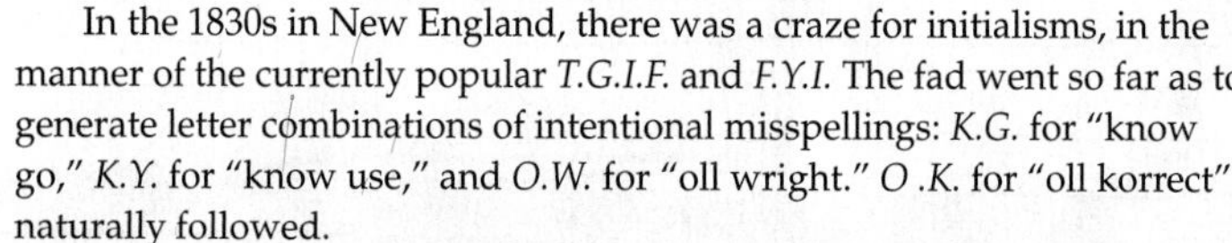

In the 1830s in New England, there was a craze for initialisms, in the manner of the currently popular *T.G.I.F.* and *F.Y.I.* The fad went so far as to generate letter combinations of intentional misspellings: *K.G.* for "know go," *K.Y.* for "know use," and *O.W.* for "oll wright." *O .K.* for "oll korrect" naturally followed.

Of all the loopy initialisms and misspellings of the time, *O.K.* alone survived. That's because of a presidential nickname that consolidated the letters in the national memory.

Martin Van Buren, elected our eighth president in 1836, was born in Kinderhook, New York, and, early in his political career, was dubbed "Old Kinderhook." Echoing the "Oll Korrect" initialism, *O.K.* became the rallying cry of the Old Kinderhook Club, a political organization supporting Van Buren during the 1840 campaign.

The coinage did Van Buren no good, and he was defeated in his bid for reelection. But the word honoring his name today remains what H. L. Mencken identified as "the most shining and successful Americanism ever invented."

Activity

1. In a dictionary, research what each of these initialisms stand for:
(a) A.D./B.C.
(b) aka
(c) GOP
(d) A.M./F.M.
(e) CD
(f) ERA
(g) a.m./p.m.
(h) IQ
(i) PS
(j) RIP
(k) RSVP
(l) UFO

2. Identify ten additional initialisms and the words each represents.

Critical Thinking

1. Why do you think Americans are so fond of abbreviations?
Answer: Americans are informal and like to save time.
2. What does the origin of the expression O.K. suggest about the relationship between new words and politics?
Answer: Since people remember an expression from a political campaign, it suggests that Americans are fascinated by politics and that they pay attention to campaigns.

Answers to Activity

1. (a) Anno Domini, Latin for "in the year of our Lord"/"before Christ" (b) also known as (c) Grand Old Party, meaning the Republican Party (d) in radio, amplitude modulation/frequency modulation (e) compact disk (f) Equal Rights Amendment (g) ante meridiem/post meridiem, Latin for "before/after noon" (h) intelligence quotient (i) postscript (j) requiescat in pace, Latin for "rest in peace" (k) répondez, s'il vous plaît, French for "please reply" (l) unidentified flying object.
2. **Possible answers:** ASAP, as soon as possible; PE, physical education; ID, identification; HQ, headquarters; COD, collect on delivery; PJs, pajamas; NBA, National Basketball Association; AWOL, absent without official leave; OJ, orange juice; DA, district attorney.

Unit 3 Part 1

Fireside and Campfire

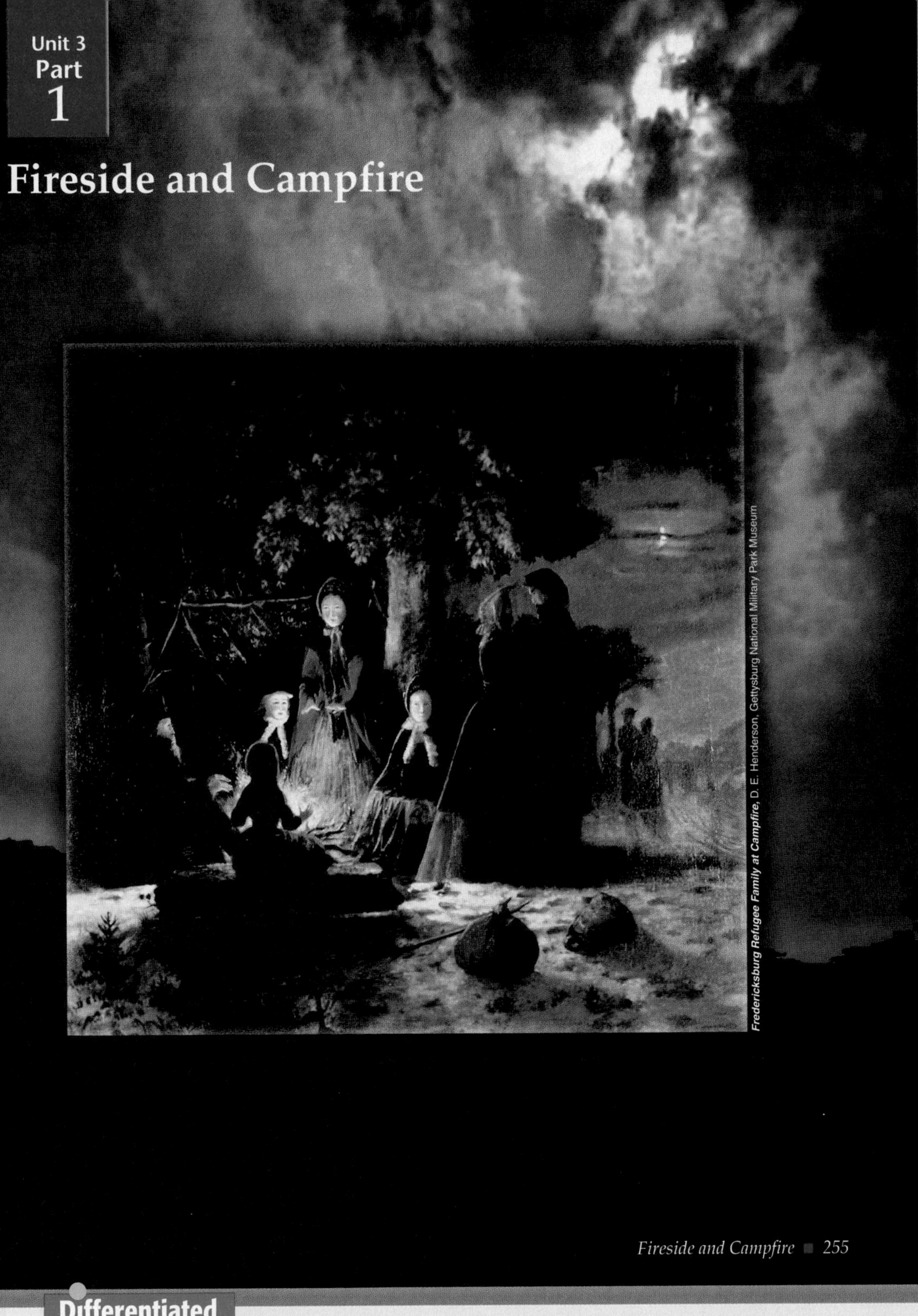

Fredericksburg Refugee Family at Campfire, D. E. Henderson, Gettysburg National Military Park Museum

Selection Planning Guide

The selections in this section reflect the literary and territorial expansion of the United States in the nineteenth century. Students will enjoy reading "The Devil and Tom Walker" by Washington Irving, one of the first of a new breed of purely American writers. The popular works of the Fireside Poets—Longfellow, Holmes, and Whittier—break new ground in American literature. "Crossing the Great Divide" and "The Most Sublime Spectacle on Earth" recount Lewis and Clark's exploration of the frontier.

Humanities

Untitled, by D. Henderson

This genre painting shows a refugee family around a campfire after the Civil War Battle of Fredericksburg, Virginia, which took place on December 13, 1862. The defeated Union forces, which outnumbered the Southern troops by two to one, continued to threaten Fredericksburg even after the battle. Although General Lee's Confederate troops held firm, the threat of more fighting persisted for months. The painting is a reminder of the terrible toll the war took on civilians in the South, where most of the battles were fought.

Use the following question for discussion:

- From what might the people in the painting be running?
  Answer: Their home may have been in the middle of a battle. Enemy soldiers might have commandeered their home for barracks or might have burned it down. They may have lost everything they had.

Differentiated Instruction Solutions for All Learners

Accessibility at a Glance

More Accessible	Average	More Challenging
The Tide Rises, The Tide Falls	The Devil and Tom Walker Old Ironsides *from* Snowbound Crossing the Great Divide The Most Sublime Spectacle on Earth	Thanatopsis

Meeting Your Standards

Students will

1. **analyze and respond to literary elements.**
   - Literary Analysis: Omniscient Point of View
2. **read, comprehend, analyze, and critique a short story.**
   - Reading Strategy: Inferring Cultural Attitudes
   - Reading Check questions
   - Apply the Skills questions
   - Assessment Practice (ATE)
3. **develop vocabulary.**
   - Vocabulary Lesson: Latin Prefix: *ex-*
4. **understand and apply written and oral language conventions.**
   - Spelling Strategy
   - Grammar and Style Lesson: Adjective Clauses
5. **develop writing proficiency.**
   - Writing Lesson: Modern Retelling of a Story
6. **develop appropriate research strategies.**
   - Extend Your Learning: Essay
7. **understand and apply listening and speaking strategies.**
   - Extend Your Learning: Enactment

Block Scheduling: Use one 90-minute class period to preteach the skills and have students read the selection. Use a second 90-minute class period to assess students' mastery of skills, extend their learning, and monitor their progress.

Homework Suggestions

Following are possibilities for homework assignments.

- Support pages from *Unit 3 Resources:*
  Literary Analysis
  Reading Strategy
  Vocabulary Builder
  Grammar and Style
- An Extend Your Learning project and the Writing Lesson for this selection group may be completed over several days.

Step-by-Step Teaching Guide	Pacing Guide
PRETEACH	
• Administer Vocabulary and Reading Warm-ups as necessary.	5 min.
• Engage students' interest with the motivation activity.	5 min.
• Read and discuss author and background features. **FT**	10 min.
• Introduce the Literary Analysis Skill: Omniscient Point of View. **FT**	5 min.
• Introduce the Reading Strategy: Inferring Cultural Attitudes. **FT**	10 min
• Prepare students to read by teaching the selection vocabulary. **FT**	
TEACH	
• Informally monitor comprehension while students read independently or in groups. **FT**	30 min.
• Monitor students' comprehension with the Reading Check notes.	as students read
• Reinforce vocabulary with Vocabulary Builder notes.	as students read
• Develop students'understanding of omniscient point of view with the Literary Analysis annotations. **FT**	5 min.
• Develop students' ability to infer cultural attitudes with the Reading Strategy annotations. **FT**	5 min.
ASSESS/EXTEND	
• Assess students' comprehension and mastery of the Literary Analysis and Reading Strategy by having them answer the Apply the Skills questions. **FT**	15 min.
• Have students complete the Vocabulary Lesson and the Grammar and Style Lesson. **FT**	15 min.
• Apply students' ability to include audience-appropriate details in their writing by using the Writing Lesson. **FT**	45 min. or homework
• Apply students' understanding by using one or more of the Extend Your Learning activities.	20–90 min. or homework
• Administer Selection Test A or Selection Test B. **FT**	15 min.

Resources

PRINT

Unit 3 Resources

Vocabulary Warm-up Word Lists [**L1, L2, EL**] ....p. 7
Vocabulary Warm-up Practice [**L1, L2, EL**] ....p. 8
Reading Warm-up A [**L1, L2, EL**] ....p. 9
Reading Warm-up B [**L1, L2, L3**] ....p. 10

TRANSPARENCY

Graphic Organizer Transparencies

Literary Analysis Graphic Organizer A [**L3**] ....p. 53
Literary Analysis Graphic Organizer B [**L1, L2, EL**] ....p. 54
Reading Strategy Graphic Organizer A [**L3**] ....p. 51
Reading Strategy Graphic Organizer B [**L1, L2, EL**] ....p. 52

PRINT

Reader's Notebook [L2]
Reader's Notebook: Adapted Version [L1]
Reader's Notebook: English Learner's Version [EL]

Unit 3 Resources

Literary Analysis [**L3**] ....p. 11
Reading Strategy [**L3**] ....p. 12
Vocabulary Builder [**L3**] ....p. 13

TECHNOLOGY

Listening to Literature Audio CDs [L2, EL]
Reader's Notebook: Adapted Version Audio CD [L1, L2]

PRINT

Unit 3 Resources

Grammar and Style [**L3**] ....p. 14
Support for Writing Lesson [**L3**] ....p. 15
Support for Extend Your Learning [**L3**] ....p. 16
Enrichment [**L4**] ....p. 17
Selection Test A [**L1, L2, EL**] ....pp. 18–20
Selection Test B [**L3, L4**] ....pp. 21–23

General Resources

Rubrics for Narration: Short Story [**L3**] ....pp. 57–58
Rubrics for Research Report [**L3**] ....pp. 49–50

TECHNOLOGY

Go Online: Research [**L3**]
Go Online: Self-test [**L3**]
***ExamView*®, Test Bank [L3]**

Choosing Resources for Differentiated Instruction

[**L1**] Special Needs Students
[**L2**] Below-Level Students
[**L3**] All Students
[**L4**] Advanced Students
[**EL**] English Learners

FT Fast Track Instruction: To move the lesson more quickly, use the strategies and activities identified with **FT**.

Scaffolding for Less Proficient and Advanced Students

The leveled Critical Thinking questions after selections progress in the levels of thinking required to answer them. To address the needs of your different students, you may use the (a) level questions for your less proficient students and the (b) level questions with your on-level and advanced students. The occasional (c) level questions are appropriate for your advanced students.

Use this complete suite of powerful teaching tools to make lesson planning and testing quicker and easier.

Use the interactive textbook (online and on CD-ROM) to make selections and activities come alive with audio and video support and interactive questions.

PRETEACH

Motivation

Dim the lights in the classroom and read aloud the paragraph on page 259 of "The Devil and Tom Walker," beginning "One day that . . ." The passage contains a detailed description of the gloomy swamp where Tom first encounters the Devil. Ask students to discuss the mood created by the description. What do they think will happen to Tom? Have students discuss their responses to the passage and make predictions about the story.

❶ Background

More About the Author

Although Irving's comic look at New York—usually referred to as *Knickerbocker's History of New York*—made him famous, it also offended many leading families by poking fun at their ancestors and heritage. Perhaps hoping to alleviate American criticism about his time spent abroad, Irving went to work for the U.S. government in Europe. He served as a U.S. diplomat first in Spain and later in London.

Build Skills *Short Story*

❶ The Devil and Tom Walker

Washington Irving (1783–1859)

Named after President George Washington, Washington Irving became the first American writer to achieve an international reputation.

Irving was born into a wealthy family, the youngest of eleven children. He began studying law at the age of sixteen. Although he had planned to be a lawyer, he found that he was more interested in travel and writing. Irving spent a great deal of time exploring New York's Hudson Valley, which became the setting for many of his stories. He also traveled throughout Europe and enjoyed European literature.

A Writing Career Blooms From 1807 to 1808, Irving wrote satirical essays using the pen name Jonathan Oldstyle. When he was twenty-four, he and his brother William anonymously began publishing the magazine *Salmagundi* (the name of a spicy appetizer), which carried humorous sketches and essays about New York society.

In 1809, using the pseudonym Diedrich Knickerbocker, he published his first major work, *A History of New York From the Beginning of the World to the End of the Dutch Dynasty.* The book, a humorous examination of New York during colonial times, was well received and made Irving famous.

Tour of Europe From 1815 to 1832, Irving lived in Europe. There, he traveled extensively and learned about European customs, traditions, and folklore. Inspired by the European folk heritage, Irving created two of his most famous stories, "The Legend of Sleepy Hollow" and "Rip Van Winkle." Both stories transform two traditional German tales into distinctly American narratives set in the Hudson Valley. Both Ichabod Crane, the nervous school teacher who hunts the headless horseman in Sleepy Hollow, and Rip Van Winkle, the colonist who sleeps for decades, have become classic figures of American literature. When Irving published these two stories in the *Sketchbook* (1820) under the pseudonym Geoffrey Crayon, writers and critics throughout Europe and the United States responded enthusiastically.

While living in Europe, Irving completed three other books, including *Tales of a Traveler*, which contains "The Devil and Tom Walker." In this story about ill-gotten wealth, Irving reshaped a German folk tale about a man who sells his soul to the Devil in exchange for earthly gain. Irving's adaptation of the story was timely in New England during the 1720s, when the Puritan belief in devoting one's life to God was being replaced by materialism and the desire for personal gain.

A Devoted American Because of the amount of time Irving spent abroad, some people questioned his patriotism. Irving offered this response:

> I am endeavoring to serve my country. Whatever I have written has been written with the feelings and published as the writing of an American. Is that renouncing my country? How else am I to serve my country—by coming home and begging an office of it: which I should not have the kind of talent or the business habits requisite to fill?—If I can do any good in this world it is with my pen.

Irving continued to publish after returning to the United States, and, like the original folk tales that inspired his work, his stories have remained popular for generations. His writing has become an important part of the American literary heritage.

Preview

Connecting to the Literature

Most of us know people who are consumed with making money. In this story, you will meet a character who is so filled with the desire for wealth that he will do virtually anything to attain it.

Literary Analysis

Omniscient Point of View

"The Devil and Tom Walker" uses an **omniscient point of view** in which an all-knowing narrator relates the events of the story. Stories told using this perspective have the following characteristics:

- A narrator who stands outside the action
- Details about the thoughts and feelings of all the characters
- The narrator's commentary about the events of the story

As you read the story, notice how Irving's use of an omniscient narrator allows you to see the conflicts in the story from several angles.

Connecting Literary Elements

Irving uses **characterization** to reveal the personality traits of his characters. In stories told using the third-person point of view, characterization is achieved in two primary ways.

- In **direct characterization,** the narrator tells the reader what the character is like.
- In **indirect characterization,** personality traits are revealed through the words, thoughts, and actions of the characters.

Notice how Irving makes use of both characterization methods.

Reading Strategy

Inferring Cultural Attitudes

This story reveals the **cultural attitudes** of New Englanders during the 1720s. Irving suggests these attitudes through descriptive details, the narrator's comments, and dialogue, and leaves it up to you to **make inferences,** or draw conclusions, based on these elements. For example, the colonists' belief in the Devil and the reference to Native Americans as "savages" reveal cultural attitudes. As you read, record details in a chart like the one shown, and draw conclusions about the cultural attitudes they represent.

Detail	Cultural Attitude

Vocabulary Builder

avarice (av′ ər is) *n.* greed (p. 262)

usurers (yo͞o′ zhər ərz) *n.* moneylenders who charge very high interest (p. 265)

extort (eks tôrt′) *v.* to obtain by threat or violence (p. 265)

ostentation (äs′ tən tā′ shən) *n.* boastful display (p. 266)

parsimony (pär′ sə mō′ nē) *n.* stinginess (p. 266)

❷ Literary Analysis
Omniscient Point of View

- Tell students that "The Devil and Tom Walker," is written from the third-person omniscient point of view. Explain to students that an omniscient narrator knows the characters' thoughts, feelings, and experiences.
- Point out that omniscient narration provides a writer with great flexibility and gives the reader access to all the characters and events in a story in a way that other types of narration cannot.
- Use the instruction for Connecting Literary Elements to point out that the third-person omniscient point of view greatly widens Irving's ability to use direct, as well as indirect, characterization.

❸ Reading Strategy
Inferring Cultural Attitudes

- Remind students that making inferences means drawing reasoned conclusions from the available evidence.
- To infer cultural attitudes, readers must focus on text clues about beliefs and values expressed in the story. Tell students that in this story, the characters' attitudes about money, for example, directly influence their behavior.
- Give students a copy of **Reading Strategy Graphic Organizer A,** p. 51 in ***Graphic Organizer Transparencies,*** to use as they read "The Devil and Tom Walker." Urge them to record story details that reveal cultural attitudes.

Vocabulary Builder

- Pronounce each vocabulary word for students, and read the definitions as a class. Have students identify any words with which they are unfamiliar.

Differentiated Instruction

Solutions for All Learners

Support for Special Needs Students
Have students read the adapted version of "The Devil and Tom Walker" in the ***Reader's Notebook: Adapted Version.*** This version provides basic-level instruction in an interactive format with questions and write-on lines. Completing these pages will prepare students to read the selection in the Student Edition.

Support for Less Proficient Readers
Have students read "The Devil and Tom Walker" in the ***Reader's Notebook.*** This version provides basic-level instruction in an interactive format with questions and write-on lines. After students finish the selection in the ***Reader's Notebook,*** have them complete the questions and activities in the Student Edition.

Support for English Learners
Have students read "The Devil and Tom Walker" in the ***Reader's Notebook: English Learner's Version.*** This version provides basic-level instruction in an interactive format with questions and write-on lines. Completing these pages will prepare students to read the selection in the Student Edition.

TEACH

Learning Modalities Logical/Mathematical Learners

Tell students that in this story characters make bargains—with themselves and with others. In each case, something is offered and something is expected in return. As students read the story, have them summarize each bargain on a two-column chart headed *Offered* and *Expected.* Have students discuss the terms of each bargain.

❶ About the Selection

Set in colonial Massachusetts, this story is Irving's retelling of the Faust legend. The miser Tom Walker, faced with an opportunity to acquire wealth, makes a pact with the Devil, whom he encounters in a swampy forest. Like other fictional characters who sell their souls, he obtains his heart's desire in exchange. The pact causes Walker to become even greedier, and he begins a campaign to fleece his neighbors of their property. Despite his tremendous wealth, Tom is just as stingy and miserly as ever. Although Tom later regrets his deal and attempts to reform his life, his efforts to save his soul are in vain; he cannot escape his terrible bargain, and must pay his inevitable debt to the Devil. The story illustrates the degree to which people may be overcome by greed and underlines the potentially devastating consequences of such an obsession.

The Devil and ❶ Tom Walker

Washington Irving

Background "The Devil and Tom Walker" is a variation of the Faust legend—a tale about a man who sells his soul to the Devil for earthly benefits. The legend was inspired by a real person, a wandering scholar and conjurer named Faust who lived in early sixteenth-century Germany. *Faustbach,* the first printed version of a Faust legend, was published in 1587. That story proposed that Faust had made a pact with the Devil for knowledge and power on Earth. Over the years, many variations of the Faust legend have appeared. Each retelling involves a person who trades his soul for experience, knowledge, or treasure. Adaptations do not share the same ending—in some, the protagonist is doomed; in others, he is redeemed.

A few miles from Boston in Massachusetts, there is a deep inlet, winding several miles into the interior of the country from Charles Bay, and terminating in a thickly wooded swamp or morass. On one side of this inlet is a beautiful dark grove; on the opposite side the land rises abruptly from the water's edge into a high ridge, on which grow a few scattered oaks of great age and immense size. Under one of these gigantic trees, according to old stories, there was a great amount of treasure buried by Kidd the pirate.[1] The inlet allowed a facility to bring the money in a boat secretly and at night to the very foot of the hill; the elevation of the place permitted a good look-out to be kept that no one was at hand;  while the remarkable trees formed good landmarks by which the place might easily be found again. The old stories add, moreover,

1. **Kidd the pirate** Captain William Kidd (1645–1701).

Differentiated Instruction Solutions for All Learners

Accessibility at a Glance

	The Devil and Tom Walker
Context	Early 19th-century story set in colonial times
Language	Some long sentences in description and narrative; accessible dialogue
Concept Level	Accessible: greed, usury, materialism, evil punished
Literary Merit	Classic; among earliest American short stories
Lexile	1130
Other	German folktale told in American context
Overall Rating	Average

that the Devil presided at the hiding of the money, and took it under his guardianship; but this it is well known he always does with buried treasure, particularly when it has been ill-gotten.

Be that as it may, Kidd never returned to recover his wealth; being shortly after seized at Boston, sent out to England, and there hanged for a pirate.

About the year 1727, just at the time that earthquakes were prevalent in New England, and shook many tall sinners down upon their knees, there lived near this place a meager, miserly fellow, of the name of Tom Walker. He had a wife as miserly as himself: they were so miserly that they even conspired to cheat each other. Whatever the woman could lay hands on, she hid away; a hen could not cackle but she was on the alert to secure the new-laid egg. Her husband was continually prying about to detect her secret hoards, and many and fierce were the conflicts that took place about what ought to have been common property. They lived in a forlorn-looking house that stood alone, and had an air of starvation. A few straggling savin trees, emblems of sterility, grew near it; no smoke ever curled from its chimney; no traveler stopped at its door. A miserable horse, whose ribs were as articulate as the bars of a gridiron, stalked about a field, where a thin carpet of moss, scarcely covering the ragged beds of puddingstone, tantalized and balked his hunger; and sometimes he would lean his head over the fence, look piteously at the passerby, and seem to petition deliverance from this land of famine.

The house and its inmates had altogether a bad name. Tom's wife was a tall termagant,[2] fierce of temper, loud of tongue, and strong of arm. Her voice was often heard in wordy warfare with her husband; and his face sometimes showed signs that their conflicts were not confined to words. No one ventured, however, to interfere between them. The lonely wayfarer shrunk within himself at the horrid clamor and clapperclawing;[3] eyed the den of discord askance; and hurried on his way, rejoicing, if a bachelor, in his celibacy.

One day that Tom Walker had been to a distant part of the neighborhood, he took what he considered a shortcut homeward, through the swamp. Like most shortcuts, it was an ill-chosen route. The swamp was thickly grown with great gloomy pines and hemlocks, some of them ninety feet high, which made it dark at noonday, and a retreat for all the owls of the neighborhood. It was full of pits and quagmires, partly covered with weeds and mosses, where the green surface often betrayed the traveler into a gulf of black, smothering mud; there were also dark and stagnant pools, the abodes of the tadpole, the bullfrog, and the watersnake; where the trunks of pines and hemlocks lay half-drowned, half-rotting, looking like alligators sleeping in the mire.

4 Tom had long been picking his way cautiously through this treacherous forest; stepping from tuft to tuft of rushes and roots, which

---

2. **termagant** (tʉr′ mə gənt) *n.* quarrelsome woman.
3. **clapperclawing** (klap′ ər klô′ iŋ) *n.* clawing or scratching.

Reading Strategy
Inferring Cultural Attitudes What does this reference to the Devil and money suggest about cultural attitudes toward wealth?

Literary Analysis
Omniscient Point of View What do you learn about Tom and his wife through this description?

Reading Check
Summarize what you have learned about the Walkers.

❷ Reading Strategy
Inferring Cultural Attitudes

- Have students paraphrase the bracketed passage.
  Possible response: Legend says the Devil loves money, especially if obtained illegally or immorally.
- **Ask** students whether they think that Irving's linking the figure of the Devil with money is a form of social commentary on wealth.
- Then, **ask** students the Reading Strategy question: What does this reference to the Devil and money suggest about cultural attitudes toward wealth?
  Answer: People in New England colonial society regarded a preoccupation with money as immoral and hence linked it with the Devil.

❸ Literary Analysis
Omniscient Point of View

- Have students read the bracketed passage. **Ask** them to note the details that they learn about Tom and his wife in this passage.
- **Ask** students the Literary Analysis question: What do you learn about Tom and his wife through this description?
  Possible response: They fight a lot. She picks on him verbally and physically. He suffers in these arguments.

Monitor Progress: Invite students to discuss how they know that this passage is told from the omniscient point of view.
Answer: The narrator uses pronouns such as *her, them, his,* and *himself.* The narrator knows not only intimate details about the Walkers' relationship, but how others responded to them.

❹ Reading Check

Answer: The Walkers are miserly, stingy people with a great love of money. They are unhappy, both individually and together. They fight a lot; no one likes them.

Differentiated Instruction
Solutions for All Learners

Strategy for Less Proficient Readers
Students may have difficulty with this long selection. Help sustain interest and concentration by encouraging students to summarize paragraphs. Remind them that in a summary, they should state the main idea in their own words and include only the most important information.

Vocabulary for English Learners
The dialogue includes words and expressions rarely used in modern conversation—for example, "Look yonder, and see how Deacon Peabody is faring." Using a two-column chart, have students jot down each unfamiliar term or expression and its meaning. Check students' understanding, clarifying as necessary.

Strategy for Advanced Readers
Encourage students to identify and analyze the symbolic language that Irving uses in his story. Have them share their observations and interpretations with the rest of the class.

5 Reading Strategy
Inferring Cultural Attitudes

- Point out the word *savages* and **ask** students to share their associations with this word. Ask them what they associate with the ritual of making sacrifices.
  Answer: Most students will associate the word *savages* with animalistic, inhuman people. Most will associate the custom of making sacrifices with cultures that are called primitive.
- **Ask** students the Reading Strategy question: What does the sentence beginning "Anyone but he" reveal about the colonists' attitudes toward Native Americans?
  Answer: The colonists saw the Native Americans as warlike savages who practiced unholy religious ceremonies characterized by magical chants and sacrifice.

6 Literary Analysis
Omniscient Point of View

- Read the bracketed passage aloud, instructing students to pay particular attention to the use of the words *he* and *his*. Tell them to listen to determine the antecedents to (or nouns replaced by) these pronouns.
  Answer: *He* and *him* refer first to Tom Walker and then to the man Tom meets.
- **Ask** students the Literary Analysis question: Whose thoughts and feelings—if anyone's —are revealed in this paragraph?
  Answer: The passage reveals Tom's thoughts and feelings. However, it also reveals details of the man's appearance.

afforded precarious footholds among deep sloughs; or pacing carefully, like a cat, along the prostrate trunks of trees; startled now and then by the sudden screaming of the bittern, or the quacking of a wild duck, rising on the wing from some solitary pool. At length he arrived at a piece of firm ground, which ran out like a peninsula into the deep bosom of the swamp. It had been one of the strongholds of the Indians during their wars with the first colonists. Here they had thrown up a kind of fort, which they had looked upon as almost impregnable, and had used as a place of refuge for their squaws and children. Nothing remained of the old Indian fort but a few embankments, gradually sinking to the level of the surrounding earth, and already overgrown in part by oaks and other forest trees, the foliage of which formed a contrast to the dark pines and hemlocks of the swamp.

5 It was late in the dusk of evening when Tom Walker reached the old fort, and he paused there awhile to rest himself. Anyone but he would have felt unwilling to linger in this lonely, melancholy place, for the common people had a bad opinion of it, from the stories handed down from the time of the Indian wars; when it was asserted that the savages held incantations here, and made sacrifices to the evil spirit.

Reading Strategy
Inferring Cultural Attitudes What does the sentence begining "Anyone but he" reveal about the colonists' attitudes toward Native Americans?

Tom Walker, however, was not a man to be troubled with any fears of the kind. He reposed himself for some time on the trunk of a fallen hemlock, listening to the boding cry of the tree toad, and delving with his walking staff into a mound of black mold at his feet. As he turned up the soil unconsciously, his staff struck against something hard. He raked it out of the vegetable mold, and lo! a cloven skull, with an Indian tomahawk buried deep in it, lay before him. The rust on the weapon showed the time that had elapsed since this deathblow had been given. It was a dreary memento of the fierce struggle that had taken place in this last foothold of the Indian warriors.

"Humph!" said Tom Walker, as he gave it a kick to shake the dirt from it.

6 "Let that skull alone!" said a gruff voice. Tom lifted up his eyes, and beheld a great black man seated directly opposite him, on the stump of a tree. He was exceedingly surprised, having neither heard nor seen anyone approach; and he was still more perplexed on observing, as well as the gathering gloom would permit, that the stranger was neither Negro nor Indian. It is true he was dressed in a rude half-Indian garb, and had a red belt or sash swathed round his body; but his face was neither black nor copper color, but swarthy and dingy, and begrimed with soot, as if he had been accustomed to toil among fires and forges. He had a shock of coarse black hair, that stood out from his head in all directions, and bore an ax on his shoulder.

Literary Analysis
Omniscient Point of View Whose thoughts and feelings—if anyone's—are revealed in this paragraph?

He scowled for a moment at Tom with a pair of great red eyes.

"What are you doing on my grounds?" said the black man, with a hoarse growling voice.

"Your grounds!" said Tom with a sneer, "no more your grounds than mine; they belong to Deacon Peabody."

Enrichment

The Massachusetts Bay Colony

The Puritans obtained a royal charter and established the Massachusetts Bay Colony in the Boston area in 1629. The successful colony grew and expanded into Massachusetts and Connecticut. The settlers soon began creating a new life without interference from England. However, they came into conflict with Native Americans already living in the region, whom they regarded as heathen obstacles to progress. Puritan and Native American ways of life contrasted dramatically.

In addition, the Puritans faced criticism for their treatment of Native Americans from the Quakers. This innovative religious sect believed in pacifism, justice, charity, and spiritual equality for all, including Native Americans. For these beliefs, they were persecuted in the colony, where four were executed. In Pennsylvania, however, Quakers prospered.

"Deacon Peabody be d—d," said the stranger, "as I flatter myself he will be, if he does not look more to his own sins and less to those of his neighbors. Look yonder, and see how Deacon Peabody is faring."

Tom looked in the direction that the stranger pointed, and beheld one of the great trees, fair and flourishing without, but rotten at the core, and saw that it had been nearly hewn through, so that the first high wind was likely to blow it down. On the bark of the tree was scored the name of Deacon Peabody, an eminent man, who had waxed wealthy by driving shrewd bargains with the Indians. He now looked round, and found most of the tall trees marked with the name of some great man of the colony, and all more or less scored by the ax. The one on which he had been seated, and which had evidently just been hewn down, bore the name of Crowninshield: and he recollected a mighty rich man of that name, who made a vulgar display of wealth, which it was whispered he had acquired by buccaneering.

"He's just ready for burning!" said the black man, with a growl of triumph. "You see I am likely to have a good stock of firewood for winter."

"But what right have you," said Tom, "to cut down Deacon Peabody's timber?"

"The right of a prior claim," said the other. "This woodland belonged to me long before one of your white-faced race put foot upon the soil."

"And pray, who are you, if I may be so bold?" said Tom.

"Oh, I go by various names. I am the wild huntsman in some countries; the black miner in others. In this neighborhood I am known by the name of the black woodsman. I am he to whom the red men consecrated this spot, and in honor of whom they now and then roasted a white man, by way of sweet-smelling sacrifice. Since the red men have been exterminated by you white savages, I amuse myself by presiding at the persecutions of Quakers and Anabaptists;[4] I am the great patron and prompter of slave dealers, and the grandmaster of the Salem witches."

"The upshot of all which is, that, if I mistake not," said Tom, sturdily, "you are he commonly called Old Scratch."

The Devil and Tom Walker, 1856, John Quidor, © The Cleveland Museum of Art

7

8 **▲ Critical Viewing**
This painting is called *The Devil and Tom Walker.* In what ways do the lighting and details reflect the mood of Irving's story? **[Analyze]**

9 

Reading Check
Who does Tom encounter in the woods?

4. **Quakers and Anabaptists** two religious groups that were persecuted for their beliefs.

7 Humanities

The Devil and Tom Walker, by John Quidor

This oil painting by American artist John Quidor (1801–1881) depicts Tom's initial meeting with the Devil in the swampy forest. The skull on the ground and the grinning, half-clothed creature holding an ax indicate that Tom's meeting is not a typical encounter. Use these questions for discussion:

1. What does the painting reveal about the story's setting?
   Answer: It highlights the dark, gloomy, wooded setting where Tom Walker first meets the Devil.
2. What does the painting reveal about the story's main character?
   Answer: It reveals the clothing worn during the time of the story and that Walker's physical appearance in the painting fits with his characterization as a greedy miser.

8 Critical Viewing

Answer: The gloomy lighting and sinister setting reflect the mood of the story, particularly the scenes set in the swamp. Students may note that although Tom is brightly lit, the Devil is in the shadows, symbolizing his association with evil.

9 Reading Check

Answer: Walker encounters the Devil in the woods.

Differentiated Instruction
Solutions for All Learners

Strategy for Special Needs Students

To clarify students' understanding of the selection, ask them to draw the scene described in the bracketed passage. Use their sketches to assess their comprehension of descriptive details. If you find that students have omitted details, have them revise their drawings.

Vocabulary for English Language Learners

Point out the word *impregnable,* line 8 on p. 260. Tell students to try to determine its meaning from context clues. Guide students to recognize that phrases such as "strongholds of the Indians during their wars," and "a kind of fort," all convey that *impregnable* means "not capable of being captured."

Strategy for Gifted/Talented Students

Ask students to identify the features that mark this character as the Devil. They can, for example, point to the coarse, animal-like hair; the soot from the fires of hell; and the red eyes. Have students suggest other physical features by which the Devil is represented in literature and in art.

⓾ Critical Thinking
Speculate

- Read aloud the bracketed passage. Discuss with students any speculations they can make about the fate of Mr. Crowninshield.
- **Ask:** Do you think Crowninshield, too, had dealings with Old Scratch?
  Answer: Most students will probably say that he did, based on Mr. Crowninshield's wealth and attitude toward it, as well as on the tree marked with Mr. Crowninshield's name and on the Devil's earlier reference to Mr. Crowninshield burning.

⓫ Literary Analysis
Omniscient Point of View

- Have students create a two-column chart headed Tom and *Mrs. Walker.* Read the bracketed passage aloud to them as they jot down details related to each character in the appropriate column.
- Point out that in this paragraph the narrator reveals both Tom's thoughts and his wife's attitudes.
- **Ask** students what they learn here about the relationship between Tom and his wife.
  Possible response: Both are selfish and untrusting, and neither has any interest in pleasing the other.

"The same, at your service!" replied the black man, with a half-civil nod.

Such was the opening of this interview, according to the old story; though it has almost too familiar an air to be credited. One would think that to meet with such a singular personage, in this wild, lonely place, would have shaken any man's nerves; but Tom was a hard-minded fellow, not easily daunted, and he had lived so long with a termagant wife, that he did not even fear the Devil.

It is said that after this commencement they had a long and earnest conversation together, as Tom returned homeward. The black man told him of great sums of money buried by Kidd the pirate, under the oak trees on the high ridge, not far from the morass. All these were under his command, and protected by his power, so that none could find them but such as propitiated his favor. These he offered to place within Tom Walker's reach, having conceived an especial kindness for him; but they were to be had only on certain conditions. What these conditions were may easily be surmised, though Tom never dis-closed them publicly. They must have been very hard, for he required time to think of them, and he was not a man to stick at trifles where money was in view. When they had reached the edge of the swamp, the stranger paused—"What proof have I that all you have been telling me is true?" said Tom. "There is my signature," said the black man, pressing his finger on Tom's forehead. So saying, he turned off among the thickets of the swamp, and seemed, as Tom said, to go down, down, down, into the earth, until nothing but his head and shoulders could be seen, and so on, until he totally disappeared.

When Tom reached home, he found the black print of a finger, burnt, as it were, into his forehead, which nothing could obliterate.

⓾ The first news his wife had to tell him was the sudden death of Absalom Crowninshield, the rich buccaneer. It was announced in the papers with the usual flourish, that "A great man had fallen in Israel."[5]

Tom recollected the tree which his black friend had just hewn down, and which was ready for burning, "Let the freebooter roast," said Tom, "who cares!" He now felt convinced that all he had heard and seen was no illusion.

⓫ He was not prone to let his wife into his confidence; but as this was an uneasy secret, he willingly shared it with her. All her avarice was awakened at the mention of hidden gold, and she urged her husband to comply with the black man's terms and secure what would make them wealthy for life. However Tom might have felt disposed to sell himself to the Devil, he was determined not to do so to oblige his

Walking stick, King Georges County, Virginia, 1846, Abby Aldrich Rockefeller Folk Art Center, Williamsburg, Virginia

Vocabulary Builder
avarice (av′ ə ris) *n.* greed

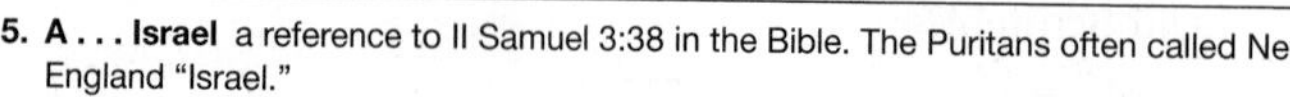

5. **A . . . Israel** a reference to II Samuel 3:38 in the Bible. The Puritans often called New England "Israel."

Enrichment

The Devil Across Cultures

In legend and literature, from the Bible to modern fiction, the Devil has appeared in many guises and under many names. Examples include Beelzebub, Mephistopheles, Satan, and Lucifer.

A pact with the Devil is a common theme in the folklore of many cultures. Although the Devil may go by different names, most cultures have their own tales about human encounters with an embodiment of evil. For some Native Americans, evil enters this world as a creature that can change shape and size at will. For example, Native American heroes from many various groups have been afraid of the water monster known as Unktehi in Nebraska and the Dakotas; others fear No Body, the Great Rolling Head of the prairies and mountains.

wife; so he flatly refused, out of the mere spirit of contradiction. Many and bitter were the quarrels they had on the subject, but the more she talked, the more resolute was Tom not to be damned to please her.

At length she determined to drive the bargain on her own account, and if she succeeded, to keep all the gain to herself. Being of the same fearless temper as her husband, she set off for the old Indian fort towards the close of a summer's day. She was many hours absent. When she came back, she was reserved and sullen in her replies. She spoke something of a black man, whom she had met about twilight, hewing at the root of a tall tree. He was sulky, however, and would not come to terms: she was to go again with a propitiatory offering, but what it was she forbore to say.

The next evening she set off again for the swamp, with her apron heavily laden. Tom waited and waited for her, but in vain; midnight came, but she did not make her appearance: morning, noon, night returned, but still she did not come. Tom now grew uneasy for her safety, especially as he found she had carried off in her apron the silver teapot and spoons, and every portable article of value. Another night elapsed, another morning came; but no wife. In a word, she was never heard of more.

What was her real fate nobody knows, in consequence of so many pretending to know. It is one of those facts which have become confounded by a variety of historians. Some asserted that she lost her way among the tangled mazes of the swamp, and sank into some pit or slough; others, more uncharitable, hinted that she had eloped with the household booty, and made off to some other province; while others surmised that the tempter had decoyed her into a dismal quagmire, on the top of which her hat was found lying. In confirmation of this, it was said a great black man, with an ax on his shoulder, was seen late that very evening coming out of the swamp, carrying a bundle tied in a checked apron, with an air of surly triumph.

The most current and probable story, however, observes that Tom Walker grew so anxious about the fate of his wife and his property, that he set out at length to seek them both at the Indian fort. During a long summer's afternoon he searched about the gloomy place, but no wife was to be seen. He called her name repeatedly, but she was nowhere to be heard. The bittern alone responded to his voice, as he flew screaming by; or the bullfrog croaked dolefully from a neighboring pool. At length, it is said, just in the brown hour of twilight, when the owls began to hoot, and the bats to flit about, his attention was attracted by the clamor of carrion crows hovering about a cypress tree. He looked up, and beheld a bundle tied in a checked apron, and hanging in the branches of the tree, with a great vulture perched hard by, as if keeping watch upon it. He leaped with joy; for he recognized his wife's apron, and supposed it to contain the household valuables.

Literary Analysis
Omniscient Point of View What does the narrator reveal about Mrs. Walker's thoughts and feelings here?

Teapot, Yale University Art Gallery, New Haven

13 ▲ **Critical Viewing** Tom Walker's wife packs up her valuables to take into the forest. Why might a teapot like this one be considered valuable? **[Support]**

14 ✓ **Reading Check** What action does Tom's wife take?

12 Literary Analysis
Omniscient Point of View

- Call on a volunteer to read aloud the bracketed passage. Have students **paraphrase** its meaning. **Answer:** Tom's wife planned to make her own deal with the Devil but to exclude Tom from its benefits. She went to the old Indian fort but would not discuss what occurred there.
- **Ask** students the Literary Analysis question: What does the narrator reveal about Mrs. Walker's thoughts and feelings here? **Answer:** The narrator reveals that Tom's wife will stop at nothing when money is at stake.

➤ **Monitor Progress: Ask** students to discuss how the story would be different if it were told only from Tom's point of view.

➤ **Reteach:** If students have trouble understanding the difference between a limited and omniscient third-person narrator, ask them to recall a conversation or event that they observed. Then ask them to describe that conversation or event. Explain that their version is limited because they see it only from their own point of view. They hear what is said or see what is happening, but they do not know what others are thinking or feeling beyond what is apparent. An omniscient narrator, on the other hand, knows all thoughts and feelings as well as sees and interprets all actions.

13 Critical Viewing

Possible response: The teapot appears to be made of a metal such as silver or pewter, which was costly for people like the Walkers.

14 Reading Check

Answer: Tom's wife collects the family valuables and brings them with her to bargain with the Devil.

Differentiated Instruction
Solutions for All Learners

Strategy for English Learners
Tell students that Irving's very long sentences may be difficult to understand. Point out, however, that Irving frequently uses semicolons to link clauses. Encourage students to break down long sentences into their several parts by separating them at the semicolons. They can read each clause for meaning before proceeding to the next clause.

Strategy for Gifted/Talented Students
Challenge students to deliver an unrehearsed speech about the dangers of greed, using details from Mrs. Walker's experience as supporting evidence. Invite students to present their speeches to the class, if possible without reference to notes. Afterward, have students share their experience of extemporaneous, or ad-libbed, speaking.

Enrichment for Advanced Readers
Share with students the following critic's remark: "One of Washington Irving's great gifts to prose is his ability to find humor even in the most grotesque circumstances." Have students write an essay about the selection in which they identify and discuss the effect of humorous elements.

15 Literary Analysis
Omniscient Point of View

- Remind students of the opening descriptions from p. 259 about the attitudes Tom and Mrs. Walker hold toward money and the relationship they have with each other. Then have students read the bracketed passage to themselves.
- Have students **identify** the losses to which the author alludes.
  Answer: Tom has lost his wife and the household's considerable valuable property.
- **Ask** students what the narrator reveals here about Tom's feelings.
  Answer: The narrator makes it clear that Tom is resigned to the loss of his goods only because it also means the loss of his wife, for which he feels no grief.

16 Critical Viewing

Possible response: Students can surmise that she is dead because her apron is attended by a vulture, a symbol of death.

"Let us get hold of the property," said he, consolingly to himself, "and we will endeavor to do without the woman."

As he scrambled up the tree, the vulture spread its wide wings, and sailed off screaming into the deep shadows of the forest. Tom seized the checked apron, but woeful sight! found nothing but a heart and liver tied up in it!

Such, according to the most authentic old story, was all that was to be found of Tom's wife. She had probably attempted to deal with the black man as she had been accustomed to deal with her husband; but though a female scold is generally considered a match for the Devil, yet in this instance she appears to have had the worst of it. She must have died game, however; for it is said Tom noticed many prints of cloven feet deeply stamped about the tree, and found handfuls of hair, that looked as if they had been plucked from the coarse black shock of the woodsman. Tom knew his wife's prowess by experience. He shrugged his shoulders, as he looked at the signs of a fierce clapperclawing. "Egad," said he to himself, "Old Scratch must have had a tough time of it!"

15 Tom consoled himself for the loss of his property, with the loss of his wife, for he was a man of fortitude. He even felt something like gratitude towards the black woodsman, who, he considered, had done him a kindness. He sought, therefore, to cultivate a further acquaintance with him, but for some time without success; the old blacklegs played shy, for whatever people may think, he is not always to be had for calling for: he knows how to play his cards when pretty sure of his game.

At length, it is said, when delay had whetted Tom's eagerness to the quick, and prepared him to agree to anything rather than not gain the promised treasure, he met the black man one evening in his usual woodsman's dress, with his ax on his shoulder, sauntering along the swamp, and humming a tune. He affected to receive Tom's advances with great indifference, made brief replies, and went on humming his tune.

By degrees, however, Tom brought him to business, and they began to haggle about the terms on which the former was to have the pirate's treasure. There was one condition which need not be mentioned, being generally understood in all cases where the Devil grants favors; but there were others about which, though of less importance, he was inflexibly obstinate. He insisted that the money found through his means should be employed in his service. He proposed, therefore, that Tom should employ it in the black traffic; that is to say, that he should

16 ▲ **Critical Viewing** The narrator describes "a great vulture perched hard by" and a checked apron hanging in the tree. What do you think happened to Tom Walker's wife? **[Infer]**

Enrichment

Loan Practices

Although usury such as that practiced by Tom Walker is illegal today, the legitimate financial services industry has a useful purpose and its loan practices are strictly monitored. Banks lend money to businesses and individuals for home mortgages, cars, tuition, renovations, and other large expenses. Rates for various loans are regulated by federal and state law.

In general, interest is charged at an annual percentage of the amount borrowed. For example, a loan of $100 at the 2% interest rate requires a repayment of $102 after a year. However, in Irving's story, the Devil seeks a rate of 2% a month, or 24% a year, which is an exorbitant rate. Tom Walker's rates, which add up to 48% a year, are even more extreme.

fit out a slave ship. This, however, Tom resolutely refused: he was bad enough in all conscience, but the Devil himself could not tempt him to turn slave-trader.

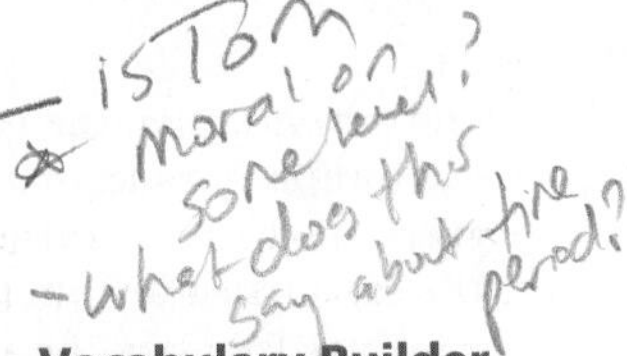

Finding Tom so squeamish on this point, he did not insist upon it, but proposed, instead, that he should turn usurer; the Devil being extremely anxious for the increase of usurers, looking upon them as his peculiar[6] people.

To this no objections were made, for it was just to Tom's taste.

"You shall open a broker's shop in Boston next month," said the black man.

"I'll do it tomorrow, if you wish," said Tom Walker.

"You shall lend money at two per cent a month."

"Egad, I'll charge four!" replied Tom Walker.

"You shall extort bonds, foreclose mortgages, drive the merchant to bankruptcy—"

"I'll drive him to the D——l," cried Tom Walker.

"You are the usurer for my money!" said the blacklegs with delight. "When will you want the rhino?"[7]

"This very night."

"Done!" said the Devil.

"Done!" said Tom Walker. So they shook hands and struck a bargain.

A few days' time saw Tom Walker seated behind his desk in a countinghouse in Boston.

His reputation for a ready-moneyed man, who would lend money out for a good consideration, soon spread abroad. Everybody remembers the time of Governor Belcher,[8] when money was particularly scarce. It was a time of paper credit. The country had been deluged with government bills; the famous Land Bank[9] had been established; there had been a rage for speculating; the people had run mad with schemes for new settlements, for building cities in the wilderness; land jobbers[10] went about with maps of grants, and townships, and El Dorados,[11] lying nobody knew where, but which everybody was ready to purchase. In a word, the great speculating fever which breaks out every now and then in the country, had raged to an alarming degree, and everybody was dreaming of making sudden fortunes from nothing. As usual the fever had subsided; the dream had gone off, and the imaginary fortunes with it; the patients were left in doleful plight, and the whole country resounded with the consequent cry of "hard times."

At this propitious time of public distress did Tom Walker set up as usurer in Boston. His door was soon thronged by customers. The needy

6. **peculiar** particular; special.
7. **rhino** (rī′ nō) slang term for money.
8. **Governor Belcher** Jonathan Belcher, the governor of Massachusetts Bay Colony from 1730 through 1741.
9. **Land Bank** a bank that financed transactions in real estate.
10. **land jobbers** people who bought and sold undeveloped land.
11. **El Dorados** (el′ də rä′ dōz) *n.* places that are rich in gold or opportunity. El Dorado was a legendary country in South America sought by early Spanish explorers for its gold and precious stones.

Vocabulary Builder
usurers (yo͞o′ zhər ərz) *n.* moneylenders who charge very high interest

18 **Vocabulary Builder**
extort (eks tôrt′) *v.* to obtain by threat or violence

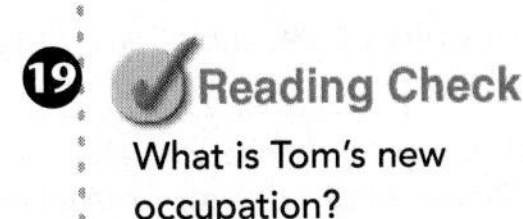

19 **Reading Check**
What is Tom's new occupation?

Differentiated Instruction
Solutions for All Learners

Support for Less Proficient Readers
Direct students to the text bracketed at 17. Guide students to understand that here Irving points out that the Devil embodies a range of bad qualities, that he is sly and manipulative. Ask students to note that the Devil and Tom Walker seem to agree well together. Emphasize to students that Irving wishes the reader to recognize that the two characters have much in common.

Strategy for Advanced Readers
Have students write a character comparison/contrast of Tom Walker and the Devil. To get students started, pose questions such as these: In what ways are the two similar? Why, for example, would the Devil bargain with Tom but not with Mrs. Walker?

17 Reading Strategy
Inferring Cultural Attitudes

- Have two students read aloud the conversation between the Devil and Tom Walker. **Ask** students to share any prior knowledge they have about colonial attitudes toward brokers and usurers.

Monitor Progress: Have students determine what the bracketed dialogue reveals about colonial attitudes toward brokers and usurers.

Reteach: If students have difficulty contributing to the discussion, post the graphic organizer from p. 257. Help students list details about Tom and the Devil that suggest colonial attitudes. Charts should look similar to the one shown below.

Detail or Description	Cultural Attitude
Davil suggests usury; greedy Tom is eager to be a usurer; the word *extort*	colonists frowned on usury, considering it the work of the Devil

18 Vocabulary Builder
Word Analysis: Latin Prefix *ex-*

- Draw students' attention to the word extort and its definition.
- Let students know that the Latin prefix *ex-* means "out." Show students how together with the Latin root *torquere,* which means "to twist," the prefix forms a word meaning literally "to twist (something) out."
- Have students volunteer other words containing the prefix *ex-*. **Possibilities include:** exhale, expand, exude, excel, and excess.
- Then, have students infer how the prefix contributes to the meanings of these words. The prefix *ex-* of the word "exhale" shows that the word means, "breathe out."
- Finally, if students cannot infer the significance of the prefix in the meanings of the listed words, have them look up the explanations in a dictionary.

19 Reading Check

Answer: Tom has become a loan shark who charges exceptionally high rates because he lends money to people who cannot borrow it anywhere else.

20 Reading Strategy
Inferring Cultural Attitudes

- Stress to students that people often have mixed feelings about money. Remind students, for example, that their discusssion of p. 259 included how colonists linked money with the Devil. Point out, however, that here Irving seems to suggest that parsimony is no more admirable than ostentation.
- **Ask** students the Reading Strategy question: From the paragraph beginning "As Tom waxed old," what can you infer about the attitudes of the day about money?
Answer: Tom's onrush of guilt about his ill-gotten gains—and his consequent bout of church-going—indicate that the people of the day took literally the biblical idea that the love of money is the root of all evil.

21 Literary Analysis
Omniscient Point of View and Characterization

- Have students read the bracketed passage carefully. Help them list topics about which Tom Walker cares deeply, whether positively or negatively.
Possible response: He hates his wife passionately, he desires money above all else, he becomes rigidly religious.
- **Ask** students the Literary Analysis question: What do you learn about Tom's character from the narrator's description of his religious zeal?
Possible response: You learn that he is as rigid, narrow-minded, and cold-hearted in his religiosity as he is in his money-making.

Monitor Progress: Encourage students to discuss whether this passage is an example of direct characterization, indirect characterization, or both.

and adventurous, the gambling speculator, the dreaming land jobber, the thriftless tradesman, the merchant with cracked credit, in short, everyone driven to raise money by desperate means and desperate sacrifices, hurried to Tom Walker.

Thus Tom was the universal friend of the needy, and acted like a "friend in need"; that is to say, he always exacted good pay and good security. In proportion to the distress of the applicant was the hardness of his terms. He accumulated bonds and mortgages; gradually squeezed his customers closer and closer, and sent them at length, dry as a sponge, from his door.

20 In this way he made money hand over hand, became a rich and mighty man, and exalted his cocked hat upon 'Change.[12] He built himself, as usual, a vast house, out of ostentation; but left the greater part of it unfinished and unfurnished, out of parsimony. He even set up a carriage in the fullness of his vainglory, though he nearly starved the horses which drew it; and as the ungreased wheels groaned and screeched on the axletrees, you would have thought you heard the souls of the poor debtors he was squeezing.

As Tom waxed old, however, he grew thoughtful. Having secured the good things of this world, he began to feel anxious about those of the next. He thought with regret on the bargain he had made with his black friend, and set his wits to work to cheat him out of the conditions. He became, therefore, all of a sudden, a violent churchgoer. He prayed loudly and strenuously, as if heaven were to be taken by force of lungs. Indeed, one might always tell when he had sinned most during the week, by the clamor of his Sunday devotion. The quiet Christians who had been modestly and steadfastly traveling Zionward,[13] were struck with self-reproach at seeing themselves so suddenly outstripped in their career by this new-made convert. 21 Tom was as rigid in religious as in money matters; he was a stern supervisor and censurer of his neighbors, and seemed to think every sin entered up to their account became a credit on his own side of the page. He even talked of the expediency of reviving the persecution of Quakers and Anabaptists. In a word, Tom's zeal became as notorious as his riches.

Still, in spite of all this strenuous attention to forms, Tom had a lurking dread that the Devil, after all, would have his due. That he might not be taken unawares, therefore, it is said he always carried a small Bible in his coat pocket. He had also a great folio Bible on his countinghouse desk, and would frequently be found reading it when people called on business; on such occasions he would lay his green spectacles in the book, to mark the place, while he turned round to drive some usurious bargain.

Some say that Tom grew a little crackbrained in his old days, and that fancying his end

12. **'Change** exchange where bankers and merchants did business.
13. **Zionward** (zī′ ən wərd) toward heaven.

Vocabulary Builder
ostentation (äs′ tən tā′ shən) *n.* boastful display
parsimony (pär′ sə mō′ nē) *n.* stinginess

Reading Strategy
Inferring Cultural Attitudes From the paragraph beginning "As Tom waxed old," what can you infer about the attitudes of the day about money?

Literary Analysis
Omniscient Point of View and Characterization What do you learn about Tom's character from the narrator's description of his religious zeal?

Enrichment

Changing Views

Washington Irving wrote this story in the early nineteenth century, but the story's setting is 100 years earlier. As a result, Irving's attitudes about certain key cultural issues contrast sharply with those of his characters. For example, by 1824, antislavery and abolitionist attitudes had grown strong in the Northeast. Thus, when Tom Walker refuses to turn slave-trader, his attitude reflects the abolitionist sentiments of Irving and his northern contemporaries more than the mores of eighteenth-century colonists.

Irving's distance from Tom Walker's time allowed him to comment critically on that culture. He knew that in the early eighteenth century, many colonists were beginning to replace Puritanism with a philosophy of commercialism and capitalism. Thus, when Tom Walker first meets the Devil and sees his wealthy neighbors' names scored into the trees, Irving can satirize the hypocrisy of those Puritans who used their prominence to amass wealth. He continues by describing Tom's own ostentatious behavior once he becomes wealthy.

approaching, he had his horse newly shod, saddled and bridled, and buried with his feet uppermost; because he supposed that at the last day the world would be turned upside down, in which case he should find his horse standing ready for mounting, and he was determined at the worst to give his old friend a run for it. This, however, is probably a mere old wives' fable. If he really did take such a precaution, it was totally superfluous; at least so says the authentic old legend, which closes his story in the following manner.

One hot summer afternoon in the dog days, just as a terrible black thunder-gust was coming up, Tom sat in his counting-house in his white linen cap and India silk morning gown. He was on the point of foreclosing a mortgage, by which he would complete the ruin of an unlucky land speculator for whom he had professed the greatest friendship. The poor land jobber begged him to grant a few months' indulgence. Tom had grown testy and irritated, and refused another day.

"My family will be ruined and brought upon the parish," said the land jobber.

"Charity begins at home," replied Tom; "I must take care of myself in these hard times."

"You have made so much money out of me," said the speculator.

Tom lost his patience and his piety—"The Devil take me," said he, "if I have made a farthing!"

Just then there were three loud knocks at the street door. He stepped out to see who was there. A black man was holding a black horse, which neighed and stamped with impatience.

"Tom, you're come for," said the black fellow, gruffly. Tom shrunk back, but too late. He had left his little Bible at the bottom of his coat pocket, and his big Bible on the desk buried under the mortgage he was about to foreclose: never was sinner taken more unawares. The black man whisked him like a child into the saddle, gave the horse the lash, and away he galloped, with Tom on his back, in the midst of the thunderstorm. The clerks stuck their pens behind their ears, and stared after him from the windows. Away went Tom Walker, dashing down the streets, his white cap bobbing up and down, his morning gown fluttering in the wind, and his steed striking fire out of the pavement at every bound. When the clerks turned to look for the black man he had disappeared.

Tom Walker never returned to foreclose the mortgage. A countryman who lived on the border of the swamp, reported that in the height of the thunder-gust he had heard a great clattering of hoofs and a howling along the road, and running to the window caught sight of a figure, such as I have described, on a horse that galloped like mad across the fields, over the hills and down into the black hemlock swamp towards the old

The American Experience

22 ***The European Influence on American Literature***

Washington Irving lived in Europe for many years, joining a trend of American writers and artists who left home to study or travel abroad. This trend was sparked by an American desire to maintain ties to European roots, to model English styles, and to find publishers and readers abroad. Through their travels, Irving, and other writers such as Nathaniel Hawthorne and the Fireside Poets, brought new themes and ideas to American literature. Under the pseudonym Geoffrey Crayon, Irving later wrote,

> ". . . Europe held for the charms of storied and poetical association. There were to be seen the masterpieces of art, the refinements of highly cultivated society, the quaint peculiarities of ancient and local custom. My native country was full of youthful promise; Europe was rich in the accumulated treasures of age."

Connect to the Literature

Explain how the theme of Irving's story shows the influence of the European literary and folk tradition. In what ways is his story distinctly American?

23 **Reading Check**

According to legend, how does the Devil catch up with Tom?

22 The American Experience

The European Influence on American Literature

European influence appeared in many of Irving's works. In addition to the German folktale behind this story, Irving explored Italian folk themes in other *Tales of a Traveller*. Later, while serving the United States in Spain, Irving focused on Spanish literary themes. There he produced works such as *The Conquest of Granada* (1829) and *The Alhambra* (1832). In his later years, however, Irving apparently decided that America's promise was worthy of study. His final work—historical and biographical rather than fictional—followed the life of American hero George Washington.

Connect to the Literature Encourage students to recall what they learned about Washington Irving in Build Skills, p. 256.

Possible response: Irving's "The Legend of Sleepy Hollow" and "Rip Van Winkle" are based on German tales but set in colonial New York. "The Devil and Tom Walker, too, is based on a German story but set in colonial New England during a time when materialism was beginning to replace religious belief.

23 Reading Check

Answer: Tom calls up the Devil by using him to prove his own truthfulness, even though he is in fact lying.

Differentiated Instruction

Solutions for All Learners

Strategy for Less Proficient Readers

Students will benefit from rereading all or parts of the story and filling in any missing elements of their story timelines. In reviewing the story, prompt students to focus on specific elements, such as cultural attitudes, Tom Walker's attitudes, or how the omniscient narrator contributes to the story.

Background for English Learners

Explain that a farthing was equal to about a fourth of a cent in American money. Then explain that Tom speaks figuratively. He refers to the Devil taking him as an example of something that would never happen in order to stress that he is speaking the truth. Help students recognize the irony of the statement.

Strategy for Advanced Readers

Ask students to identify the scary details in the description of Tom's capture and contrast them with those that are sardonic. Suggest that they list their contrasting details in a two-column chart with the headings *Scary* and *Sardonic*.

ASSESS

Answers

1. **Possible response:** No. He behaves quite characteristically throughout, showing his single-mindedness and self-absorbtion.
2. (a) He offers to make Tom Walker rich by giving him the pirate's treasure. (b) The Devil's conditions are hard and Tom wants to think about them before accepting.
3. (a) The Devil kills her. (b) **Possible response:** You learn that he cares more about money than about people.
4. (a) Tom agrees to sell his soul to the Devil in exchange for the pirate's treasure and also to use the treasure as a moneylender in the Devil's service. (b) **Possible response:** He begins to regret his bargain and hopes that religious zeal will protect him from the Devil.
5. (a) He prays loudly and strenuously. (b) He becomes a stern supervisor of the spiritual accounts of his neighbors and is willing to persecute other sects, just as he harasses his debtors.
6. **Possible response:** They were selfish, greedy, and callous. All their actions were self-serving, whether in seeking money or in seeking escape from a bargain.
7. (a) **Possible response:** Anyone willing to bargain with the Devil deserves his fate. (b) **Possible response:** One might think this to be a more acceptable bargain because knowledge seems more worthy. On reflection, however, any bargain in which someone sells his or her soul will likely prove dangerous in the end.

Go Online Author Link For additional information about Washington Irving, have students type in the Web Code, then select I from the alphabet, and then select Washington Irving.

Indian fort; and that shortly after a thunderbolt falling in that direction seemed to set the whole forest in a blaze.

The good people of Boston shook their heads and shrugged their shoulders, but had been so much accustomed to witches and goblins and tricks of the Devil, in all kind of shapes from the first settlement of the colony, that they were not so much horror struck as might have been expected. Trustees were appointed to take charge of Tom's effects. There was nothing, however, to administer upon.

On searching his coffers all his bonds and mortgages were found reduced to cinders. In place of gold and silver his iron chest was filled with chips and shavings; two skeletons lay in his stable instead of his half-starved horses, and the very next day his great house took fire and was burned to the ground.

Such was the end of Tom Walker and his ill-gotten wealth. Let all griping money brokers lay this story to heart. The truth of it is not to be doubted. The very hole under the oak trees, whence he dug Kidd's money, is to be seen to this day; and the neighboring swamp and old Indian fort are often haunted in stormy nights by a figure on horseback, in morning gown and white cap, which is doubtless the troubled spirit of the usurer. In fact, the story has resolved itself into a proverb, and is the origin of that popular saying, so prevalent throughout New England, of "The Devil and Tom Walker."

Critical Reading

1. **Respond:** Were you surprised by Tom's actions in this story? Why or why not?
2. **(a) Recall:** What does the Devil offer Tom Walker? **(b) Analyze:** What factors contribute to Tom's initial refusal?
3. **(a) Recall:** What happens to Tom's wife? **(b) Interpret:** What do you learn about Tom, based on his reaction to the loss of his wife?
4. **(a) Recall:** What agreement does Tom Walker ultimately make with the Devil? **(b) Draw Conclusions:** As the story progresses, why do you think Tom begins to go to church and carry a Bible around with him at all times?
5. **(a) Recall:** What does Tom do to cause the narrator to call him a "violent churchgoer"? **(b) Interpret:** In what way is Tom's approach to religion similar to his approach to financial dealings?
6. **Evaluate:** What kind of people do you think Tom Walker and his wife are? Explain.
7. **(a) Take a Position:** Do you feel that Tom Walker deserved his fate? Why or why not? **(b) Defend:** Would you have felt more sympathy for Tom if he had sold his soul for knowledge instead of money? Explain.

Go Online Author Link

For: More about Washington Irving
Visit: www.PHSchool.com
Web Code: ere-9301

Apply the Skills

The Devil and Tom Walker

Literary Analysis

Omniscient Point of View

1. Using a diagram like the one shown, give two examples in which the **omniscient point of view narrator** reveals the thoughts and feelings of the characters in the story.

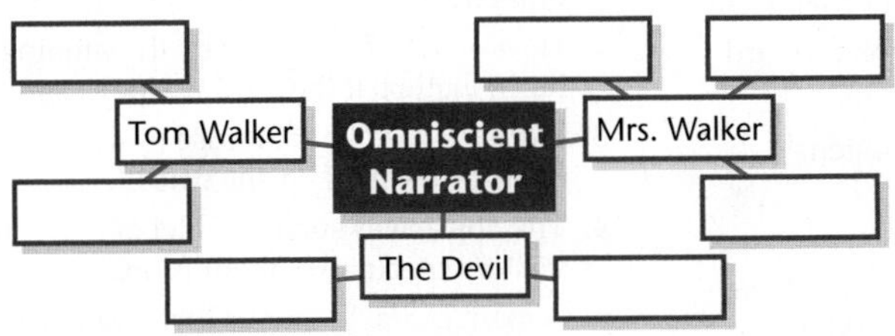

2. Find two places in the story where the narrator reveals Tom Walker's plans.
3. Find one place in the story where the narrator reveals the thoughts or unspoken plans of Tom Walker's wife.

Connecting Literary Elements

4. Identify three things you learn about Tom through **direct characterization.**
5. **(a)** Characterize Tom's wife based on the narrator's comments. **(b)** What do you learn about the relationship of Tom and his wife through **indirect characterization**? Explain.
6. What does the narrator's description of the Walker's house and the condition of their horse tell you about their personalities?

Reading Strategy

Inferring Cultural Details

7. What inferences can you draw about the **cultural attitudes** of New Englanders during the 1720s, especially in the area of religion? Explain.
8. **(a)** What can you infer about the attitudes of people toward moneylenders in Tom Walker's time? **(b)** Which details in the story lead you to draw this inference?

Extend Understanding

9. **Career Connection:** In what way might a banker today respond to Irving's suggestion that moneylenders are greedy?

QuickReview

In a story told from the **omniscient point of view,** the narrator is all-knowing, stands outside the action, and relates the thoughts and feelings of all the characters.

Characterization is the art of revealing character. With **direct characterization,** a writer simply states what a character is like. With **indirect characterization,** a writer reveals personality traits through the characters' thoughts, words, and actions, and through what other characters say about them.

By drawing conclusions about the details describing people in a story, you can **infer cultural attitudes.**

Go Online Assessment

For: Self-test
Visit: www.PHSchool.com
Web Code: era-6301

Students may use the **Self-test** to prepare for **Selection Test A** or **Selection Test B.**

Answers

1. **Possible response:** Tom Walker: is greedy for money; attends church and reads the Bible out of fear. Mrs. Walker: dislikes her husband; wants money more than anything else. The Devil: lies and manipulates people; exacts his due no matter what.

   Another sample answer can be found on **Literary Analysis Graphic Organizer B,** p. 54 in ***Graphic Organizer Transparencies.***
2. **Possible responses:** The narrator states that Tom seeks to cultivate a further acquaintance with the Devil. Later the narrators states that Tom plans to avoid the consequences of his bargain through his religious behavior.
3. **Possible response:** The narrator states that she decided to drive a bargain with the Devil and to keep all the gain for herself.
4. **Possible response:** You learn that he is crafty, selfish, and greedy.
5. (a) **Possible response:** She is greedy, with a violent temper, a nasty manner, and distorted values. (b) **Possible response:** That they fight is learned from the reactions of passers-by and neighbors who avoid the Walkers' home at all costs.
6. The description shows that the Walkers are too miserly and too mean to care for their house and field or to feed their horse.
7. **Possible response:** New Englanders prided themselves on their piety and religious faith. They regarded worldly success as possibly being of the Devil.
8. **Possible response:** (a) People of Tom Walker's time saw moneylenders as people who took advantage of people's weakness. (b) The author's ironic tone, the Devil's delight at Tom's willingness to be a money lender, and Tom's own guilty conscience show that money lending was not admired.
9. A banker would probably object to Irving's implications. Today's bankers are employees of financial institutions and do not personally profit from lending; banking and lending are carefully regulated industries.

ASSESS/EXTEND

Answers

1 Vocabulary Lesson

Word Analysis

1. b
2. d
3. a
4. e
5. c

Spelling Strategy

1. excerpt
2. ex-marine
3. excavate

Vocabulary Builder

1. usurers
2. extort
3. parsimony
4. ostentation
5. avarice

2 Grammar and Style Lesson

1. which ran out like a peninsula into the . . . deep bosom of the swamp; modifies *ground*
2. who would lend money out for a good consideration; modifies *man*
3. whom she had met about twilight; modifies *man*
4. that stood out from his head in all directions; modifies *hair*
5. which is doubtless the troubled spirit of the usurer; modifies *figure*

Writing Application

Paragraphs should contain at least three adjective clauses with *who, whom, whose, which,* or *that* in them.

Writing and Grammar, Ruby Level

Students will find further instruction and practice on pronoun case in Chapter 19, Section 3.

Build Language Skills

1 Vocabulary Lesson

Word Analysis: Latin Prefix *ex-*

The Latin prefix *ex-* means "out," as in *extort*, which means "to squeeze out." Match the words on the left with their definitions on the right.

1. exceed	**a.** elevate; glorify
2. exact	**b.** go beyond normal limits
3. exalt	**c.** look out; look forward
4. expedite	**d.** wring; pry out
5. expect	**e.** speed up; hasten

Spelling Strategy

When the prefix *ex-* means "out," do not use a hyphen after it: *extort, export, extract.* When it means "former," use a hyphen: *ex-president, ex-wife.* Add the prefix *ex-* to the following words, using a hyphen if it is needed.

1. cerpt **2.** marine **3.** cavate

Vocabulary Builder: Context

Select the word from the vocabulary list on page 257 that best completes each sentence.

1. Unfortunately, we had borrowed money from __?__, who charged an excessive rate of interest.
2. He would __?__ money by threatening to harm victims if they did not pay.
3. Her __?__ led her to refuse to send for a doctor—even when she was ill.
4. The house was such a model of __?__ that visitors speculated about its excessive cost.
5. A main characteristic of Mrs. Walker's personality was __?__.

2 Grammar and Style Lesson

Adjective Clauses

An **adjective clause** is a subordinate clause that modifies a noun or a pronoun. Adjective clauses are introduced with relative pronouns: *who* or *whom, whose, which,* or *that.*

> ADJECTIVE CLAUSE
> **Example:** A miserable horse, whose ribs stuck out, stalked about a field. (modifies horse)

Practice Identify the adjective clause and the word it modifies in each of the following sentences.

1. At length he arrived at a piece of firm ground, which ran out like a peninsula into the . . . deep bosom of the swamp.
2. His reputation for a ready-moneyed man, who would lend money out for a good consideration, soon spread abroad.
3. She spoke something of a black man, whom she had met about twilight . . .
4. He had a shock of coarse black hair, that stood out from his head in all directions . . .
5. The . . . swamp and the old Indian fort are often haunted . . . by a figure on horseback, which is doubtless the troubled spirit of the usurer.

Writing Application Write a paragraph about another character who makes a deal at a high price. Use three adjective clauses that contain the relative pronouns *who, whom, whose, which,* or *that.*

Prentice Hall Writing and Grammar Connection: Chapter 19, Section 3

Assessment Practice

Make Inferences and Generalizations (For more practice, see *Standardized Test Preparation Workbook*, p. 15.)

An inference is a reasonable guess based on facts. Use this sample test item.

> A miserable horse, whose ribs were as articulated as the bars of a gridiron, stalked about a field . . . and sometimes he would lean his head over the fence . . . and seem to petition deliverance from this land of famine.

According to the passage, why is the horse so miserable?

A He misses his former owner.
B He is kept in the barn all day.
C He lives in the country.
D He is starving.

The excerpt makes no mention of any information found in choices *A, B,* and *C.* The horse's ribs show, and the author describes a "land of famine." Students should infer that the horse is not well fed and choose *D*.

Writing Lesson

Modern Retelling of a Story

Write an updated version of Irving's story with new plot elements and character details. Use your story to convey the same theme as Irving, but in a way that addresses a modern audience.

Prewriting Outline the plot of the original story. Consider the best way to update each plot event you list. For example, instead of meeting in a forest, Tom Walker might encounter the Devil at the mall.

Drafting Write your story, making sure your characters' dialogue, dress, and actions reflect modern times. Include references to food, clothes, and current events.

Writing Model: Updating a Story

Tom was sitting at his computer, downloading promissory notes. Suddenly, he saw a pair of beady eyes glaring at him from the screen. Then, pixel by pixel, a strange-looking face took shape.

While maintaining the intent of the story, modern elements such as "pixel" and "computer" update the setting.

Revising Confirm that your draft balances the original story elements with the new details that update it. Check to see that the conflict and the message are the same, but make sure the language and setting reflect today's world.

WG *Prentice Hall Writing and Grammar Connection: Chapter 5, Section 2*

Extend Your Learning

Listening and Speaking Speculate about what happens when Mrs. Walker meets the Devil. Prepare an **enactment** of the scene as you think it would occur.

- Write dialogue to show what might take place between the two characters.
- Choose a classmate to perform the scene with you.

Practice the scene; then perform it for your class.
[Group Activity]

Research and Technology In addition to providing the basis for this story, the Faust legend has inspired plays, operas, and even a Broadway musical. Research these works, and write an **essay** reporting your findings. Include photographs, illustrations, and other art with your essay.

For: An additional research activity
Visit: www.PHSchool.com
Web Code: erd-7301

3 Writing Lesson

- To guide students in writing this story, give them the **Support for Writing Lesson,** p. 15 in ***Unit 3 Resources.***
- Remind students that a story must have a beginning, a middle, and an end. Review the central conflict and message in Irving's story.
- To aid prewriting, have students use the Plot Diagram in ***Graphic Organizer Transparencies,*** p. 278 to outline the original story plot.
- Urge students to use descriptive detail to set the scene in modern times and to use both direct and indirect characterization to develop their characters.
- Use the Narration: Short Story rubric in ***General Resources,*** pp. 57–58, to evaluate students' stories.

4 Research and Technology

- Help students choose a manageable number of works to research. Add poetry and novels to the list of genre choices.
- Encourage students to focus on topic headings before conducting their research. Logical topics might include author background, audience reception, basic story line, story outcome.
- Direct students to outline their essay before writing, using the Outline in ***Graphic Organizer Transparencies,*** p. 309.
- Use the Research Report rubrics, pages 49–50 of ***General Resources,*** to evaluate students' reports.
- The **Support for Extend Your Learning** page (***Unit 3 Resources,*** p. 16) provides guided note-taking opportunities to help students complete the Extend Your Learning activities.

Go Online Research — Have students type in the Web Code for another research activity.

Assessment Resources

The following resources can be used to assess students' knowledge and skills.

Unit 3 Resources
Selection Test A, pp. 18–20
Selection Test B, pp. 21–23

General Resources
Rubrics for Narration:
Short Story, pp. 57–58
Rubrics for Research Report, pp. 49–50

Students may use the **Self-test** to prepare for **Selection Test A** or **Selection Test B.**

Meeting Your Standards

Students will

1. **analyze and respond to literary elements.**
   - Literary Analysis: Meter
2. **read, comprehend, analyze, and critique poetry.**
   - Reading Strategy: Summarizing
   - Reading Check questions
   - Apply the Skills questions
   - Assessment Practice (ATE)
3. **develop vocabulary.**
   - Vocabulary Lesson: Latin Word Root: *-patr-*
4. **understand and apply written and oral language conventions.**
   - Spelling Strategy
   - Grammar and Style Lesson: Participles as Adjectives
5. **develop writing proficiency.**
   - Writing Lesson: Précis
6. **develop appropriate research strategies.**
   - Extend Your Learning: Oral Presentation
7. **understand and apply listening and speaking strategies.**
   - Extend Your Learning: Dramatic Reading

Block Scheduling: Use one 90-minute class period to preteach the skills and have students read the selection. Use a second 90-minute class period to assess students' mastery of skills, extend their learning, and monitor their progress.

Homework Suggestions

Following are possibilities for homework assignments.

- Support pages from ***Unit 3 Resources:***
  Literary Analysis
  Reading Strategy
  Vocabulary Builder
  Grammar and Style
- An Extend Your Learning project and the Writing Lesson for this selection group may be completed over several days.

Step-by-Step Teaching Guide	Pacing Guide
PRETEACH	
• Administer Vocabulary and Reading Warm-ups as necessary.	5 min.
• Engage students' interest with the motivation activity.	5 min.
• Read and discuss author and background features. **FT**	10 min.
• Introduce the Literary Analysis Skill: Meter. **FT**	5 min.
• Introduce the Reading Strategy: Summarizing. **FT**	10 min.
• Prepare students to read by teaching the selection vocabulary. **FT**	
TEACH	
• Informally monitor comprehension while students read independently or in groups. **FT**	30 min.
• Monitor students' comprehension with the Reading Check notes.	as students read
• Reinforce vocabulary with Vocabulary Builder notes.	as students read
• Develop students'understanding of meter with the Literary Analysis annotations. **FT**	5 min.
• Develop students' ability to summarize with the Reading Strategy annotations. **FT**	5 min.
ASSESS/EXTEND	
• Assess students' comprehension and mastery of the Literary Analysis and Reading Strategy by having them answer the Apply the Skills questions. **FT**	15 min.
• Have students complete the Vocabulary Lesson and the Grammar and Style Lesson. **FT**	15 min.
• Apply students' ability to use a clear beginning, middle, and end by using the Writing Lesson. **FT**	45 min. or homework
• Apply students' understanding by using one or more of the Extend Your Learning activities.	20–90 min. or homework
• Administer Selection Test A or Selection Test B. **FT**	15 min.

Resources

PRINT

Unit 3 Resources

- Vocabulary Warm-up Word Lists [**L1, L2, EL**] .... p. 24
- Vocabulary Warm-up Practice [**L1, L2, EL**] .... p. 25
- Reading Warm-up A [**L1, L2, EL**] .... p. 26
- Reading Warm-up B [**L1, L2, L3**] .... p. 27

TRANSPARENCY

Graphic Organizer Transparencies

- Reading Strategy Graphic Organizer A [**L3**] .... pp. 55–57
- Reading Strategy Graphic Organizer B [**L1, L2, EL**] .... pp. 56–58

PRINT

Reader's Notebook [L2]
Reader's Notebook: Adapted Version [L1]
Reader's Notebook: English Learner's Version [EL]

Unit 3 Resources

- Literary Analysis [**L3**] .... p. 28
- Reading Strategy [**L3**] .... p. 29
- Vocabulary Builder [**L3**] .... p. 30

TECHNOLOGY

Listening to Literature Audio CDs [L2, EL]
Reader's Notebook: Adapted Version Audio CD [L1, L2]

PRINT

Unit 3 Resources

- Grammar and Style [**L3**] .... p. 31
- Support for Writing Lesson [**L3**] .... p. 32
- Support for Extend Your Learning [**L3**] .... p. 33
- Enrichment [**L4**] .... p. 34
- Selection Test A [**L1, L2, EL**] .... pp. 35–37
- Selection Test B [**L3, L4**] .... pp. 38–40

General Resources

- Rubric for Summary [**L3**] .... pp. 71–72

TECHNOLOGY

Go Online: Research [**L3**]
Go Online: Self-test [**L3**]
***ExamView*®, Test Bank** [**L3**]

Choosing Resources for Differentiated Instruction

[**L1**] Special Needs Students
[**L2**] Below-Level Students
[**L3**] All Students
[**L4**] Advanced Students
[**EL**] English Learners

FT Fast Track Instruction: To move the lesson more quickly, use the strategies and activities identified with **FT**.

Scaffolding for Less Proficient and Advanced Students

The leveled Critical Thinking questions after selections progress in the levels of thinking required to answer them. To address the needs of your different students, you may use the (a) level questions for your less proficient students and the (b) level questions with your on-level and advanced students. The occasional (c) level questions are appropriate for your advanced students.

PRENTICE HALL **TeacherEXPRESS™** Plan · Teach · Assess Use this complete suite of powerful teaching tools to make lesson planning and testing quicker and easier.

PRENTICE HALL **StudentEXPRESS™** Learn · Study · Succeed Use the interactive textbook (online and on CD-ROM) to make selections and activities come alive with audio and video support and interactive questions.

PRETEACH

Motivation

Have some students bring to class a recording of or lyrics to a contemporary song that has special meaning to them. Ask volunteers to share their songs. Discuss how some musical artists give voice to the concerns and ideals of an entire generation of listeners. To which musical artists do students feel such a connection? Explain to students that the poets whose work they are about to read popularized poetry as a family entertainment long before families could turn to CDs, radio, television, movies, or other technological diversions. They expressed the values, emotions, and concerns of those who lived in earlier eras.

❶ Background

More About the Authors

Longfellow showed his literary promise early. He published his first poem when he was only 13 and entered Bowdoin College at age 15. In a letter written from college to his father, Longfellow declared his wish to spend his life writing.

Longfellow's childhood home in Portland, Maine, was located at the seashore. Perhaps this explains the poet's lifelong knowledge of and interest in the sea. "The Tide Rises, The Tide Falls" is only one of several poems Longfellow wrote about the sea.

William Cullen Bryant helped to establish an American literary tradition by producing poems that were a match for the work of the best European poets of his day. Perhaps his early lessons in Greek and Latin, taught by his country doctor father, gave him added linguistic dexterity. Certainly his father helped launch Bryant's career by submitting "Thanatopsis" and another poem to a Boston magazine. Shocked that an American could draft such compelling verse, the magazine nonetheless published Bryant's poem in its first version—minus some of the introductory lines and the final stanza.

Build Skills | *Poems*

❶ The Tide Rises, The Tide Falls • Thanatopsis • Old Ironsides • *from* Snowbound

Henry Wadsworth Longfellow (1807–1882)

Henry Wadsworth Longfellow enjoyed a long and successful career as a poet, publishing his first collection of poems, *Voices in the Night,* in 1839. By writing poetry that soothed and encouraged readers, Longfellow became the first American poet to reach a wide audience and create a national interest in poetry. His popular anthology *The Poets and Poetry of Europe,* published in 1845, accomplished his goal of bringing non-English poetry to the ordinary American reader.

Born and raised in Portland, Maine, Longfellow graduated from Bowdoin College and went on to teach modern languages at Harvard University for eighteen years, often writing and publishing his own textbooks for his classes. He also translated foreign literature into English, finding in foreign poetry inspirational models for his own work.

Longfellow experimented with adapting traditional European verse forms and themes to uniquely American subjects. Many of his narrative poems, such as *The Song of Hiawatha* (1855), *The Courtship of Miles Standish* (1858), and "Paul Revere's Ride" (1860), gave a romanticized view of America's early history and democratic ideals.

Longfellow Legacy Longfellow's poetry has been criticized for being overly optimistic and sentimental. Yet it was his optimism and sentimentality that made Longfellow the most popular poet of his day. In fact, Longfellow was so popular in his time that his seventy-fifth birthday was celebrated as if it were a national holiday.

William Cullen Bryant (1794–1878)

As a journalist and political activist, William Cullen Bryant fought to ensure that industrialization did not obscure America's democratic values. Bryant began writing poetry at the age of nine and drafted the first version of "Thanatopsis," his most famous poem, when he was only nineteen. To support himself, Bryant practiced law for ten years while continuing to write poetry in his spare time. In 1825, he moved to New York City and became a journalist; by 1829, he had become editor-in-chief and part owner of the New York newspaper the *Evening Post.*

Voice for Justice Bryant used his position as an influential journalist to defend human rights and personal freedoms. He was an outspoken advocate of women's rights and a passionate foe of slavery. Bryant was the first American poet to win worldwide critical acclaim, and his work helped establish the Romantic Movement in America.

Oliver Wendell Holmes (1809–1894)

Oliver Wendell Holmes made important contributions to both literature and medicine. A descendant of the poet Anne Bradstreet (page 96), he briefly studied law and then completed a medical degree at Harvard University in 1836, the same year his first collection of poetry was published.

Holmes enjoyed a long teaching career at Harvard, becoming a leading medical researcher and continuing his literary pursuits. Along with

James Russell Lowell, Holmes founded *The Atlantic Monthly.* His love of exaggeration and quotable statements made his essays popular with readers.

In 1830, Holmes wrote "Old Ironsides" to protest the planned destruction of the battleship *Constitution,* nicknamed "Old Ironsides" for its ability to withstand British attacks during the War of 1812. The poem saved the ship and earned Holmes national recognition as a poet.

John Greenleaf Whittier (1807–1892)

John Greenleaf Whittier was born in poverty. As a child, he worked on his family's debt-ridden farm near Haverhill, Massachusetts and received virtually no formal education. As a Quaker, Whittier believed in hard work, simplicity, pacifism, religious devotion, and social justice.

Whittier was more deeply involved in the social issues of his day than were his fellow poets. He was elected to the Massachusetts State Legislature in 1835. For twenty-five years, he worked diligently for the abolition of slavery. Because of his devotion to the abolitionist cause, he did not gain national prominence until after the Civil War. When the Civil War ended, Whittier focused on writing poetry, earning national fame with the 1866 publication of *Snowbound,* which depicts the simple warmth of rural New England life. In the poem, Whittier remembers with fondness the life he spent as a boy in his family's farmhouse. As the way of life captured in Whittier's poetry disappeared, the popularity of his poems grew.

Background

Until the third decade of the nineteenth century, America had little real literature to call its own. The Fireside Poets—Henry Wadsworth Longfellow, Oliver Wendell Holmes, John Greenleaf Whittier, and James Russell Lowell—represented a literary coming of age for the young country. This first generation of acclaimed American poets took their name from the popularity of their works, which were widely read both as fireside family entertainment and in the schoolroom, where generations of children memorized them.

The four poets—all New England born and bred—chose uniquely American settings and subjects. Their themes, meter, and imagery, however, borrowed heavily from the English tradition. Though their reliance on conservative literary styles prevented them from being truly innovative, the Fireside Poets were literary giants of their day. In their own time, and for decades afterward, they ranked as America's most read and best-loved poets.

The Four Seasons of Life, Currier & Ives

More About the Authors (cont.)

Although nationally recognized for his poetry, Oliver Wendell Holmes took greater pride in his medical achievements. In particular, his ideas about improving medical practices in childbirth—doctors began to wash their hands and wear sterile clothing to deliver babies—saved many lives. Holmes's medical students loved him as much as did the readers of his poetry. As a result, he always taught his classes at times when students would be most tired—Holmes's witty style kept them interested!

John Greenleaf Whittier expressed his passionate antislavery views through his poetry, as well as his political activities. In one poem, "Massachusetts to Virginia," he criticizes Virginia for forgetting the democratic ideals on which America had been founded. In another, "Ichabod," Whittier upbraids a U.S. senator for supporting legislation that would return runaway slaves to their owners. These political poems, contrasting with his more sentimental New England poems, added depth to Whittier's reputation.

❷ Literary Analysis
Meter

- Tell students that as they read the poems, they should focus on meter, that is, the systematic arrangement of stressed and unstressed syllables in poetry.
- Read aloud the instruction about meter. Then read aloud the *Snowbound* example and help students hear its meter.
- Model the process of identifying meter. Explain to students that reading aloud a poem can help them identify its meter.
- Discuss the instruction under Comparing Literary Works and invite students to give some examples of mood in other poetry they have read.

❸ Reading Strategy
Summarizing

- Remind students that summarizing can help them understand a poet's key points.
- Direct students to use charts like the one on the student page to summarize as they read the poems of the Fireside Poets.
- Give students a copy of **Reading Strategy Graphic Organizer A,** p. 55 in ***Graphic Organizer Transparencies*** to use as they read the selections.

Vocabulary Builder

- Pronounce each vocabulary word for students, and read the definitions as a class. Have students identify any words with which they are familiar.

Preview

Connecting to the Literature

Do the lyrics or attitudes of your favorite musicians reflect *your* feelings, and *your* views? Gifted musicians and writers often give voice to a generation. Similarly, in the early nineteenth century, the Fireside Poets gave voice to the sentiments of their age.

❷ Literary Analysis

Meter

In poetry, a systematic arrangement of stressed (′) and unstressed (˘) syllables is called **meter.** The basic unit of meter is the foot, which usually consists of one stressed and one or more unstressed syllables. The most frequently used foot in American verse is the *iamb*—one unstressed syllable followed by a stressed syllable. The type and number of feet in the lines of a poem determine its meter. For example, a pattern of four iambs per line, as in this excerpt from *Snowbound,* is known as iambic tetrameter.

Thĕ sún thăt bríef Dĕcémbĕr dáy
Rŏse chéerlĕss óvĕr hílls ŏf gráy

Read each poem aloud to discover its meter, listening for metrical patterns that repeat.

Comparing Literary Works

While these poems were written during the same period in history, they each present a different mood. **Mood,** or atmosphere, is the feeling created in a reader by a literary work. Setting, tone, subject, or word choice can influence mood. As you read, notice the similarities and differences in the mood of each poem and how each poem makes you feel.

❸ Reading Strategy

Summarizing

To check your understanding of what you have read, **summarize** the work or parts of the work by briefly stating the main ideas and supporting details in your own words. Use an organizer like the one shown to summarize each poem.

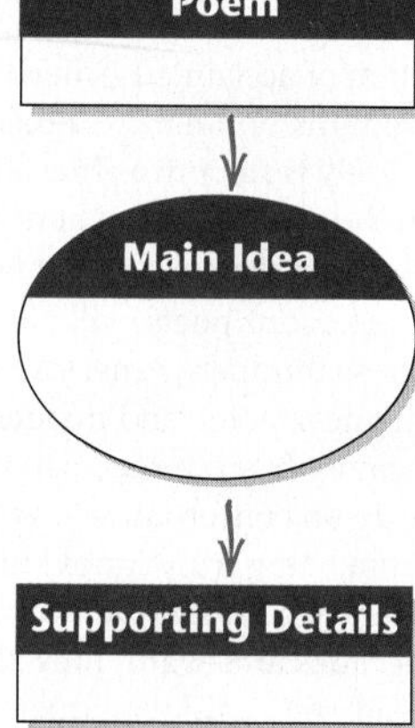

Vocabulary Builder

efface (ə fās′) *v.* erase, wipe out (p. 276)

sepulcher (sep′əl kər) *n.* tomb (p. 278)

pensive (pen′ siv) *adj.* expressing deep thoughtfulness (p. 278)

venerable (ven′ ər ə bəl) *adj.* worthy of respect (p. 278)

ominous (äm′ ə nəs) *adj.* threatening (p. 283)

querulous (kwer′ yo͞o ləs) *adj.* complaining (p. 284)

patriarch (pā′ trē ärk′) *n.* the father and ruler of a family or tribe (p. 286)

Differentiated Instruction
Solutions for All Learners

Support for Special Needs Students
Have students use the support pages for these selections in the ***Reader's Notebook: Adapted Version.*** Completing these pages will prepare students to read the selection in the Student Edition.

Support for Less Proficient Readers
Have students use the support pages for these selections in the ***Reader's Notebook.*** After students finish the selection in the ***Reader's Notebook,*** have them complete the questions and activities in the Student Edition.

Support for English Learners
Have students use the support pages in the ***Reader's Notebook: English Learner's Version.*** Completing these pages will prepare students to read the selection in the Student Edition.

The Tide Rises, The Tide Falls

Henry Wadsworth Longfellow

4

The tide rises, the tide falls.
The twilight darkens, the curlew[1] calls;
Along the sea sands damp and brown
The traveler hastens toward the town,
And the tide rises, the tide falls.

1. **curlew** (kʉr′ lo͞o′) *n.* large wading bird associated with the evening.

3 ▼ **Critical Viewing** What questions come to mind as you view this painting? Consider both the subject matter and the artist's technique. **[Generate Questions]**

TEACH

Learning Modalities
Verbal/Linguistic Learners

Play the **Listening to Literature Audio CDs** for students. Have students listen carefully to the cadence and rhythm of the poem. In particular talk with students about the refrain in "The Tide Rises, The Tide Falls." Ask how the refrain emphasizes Longfellow's main points.

1 About the Selection

The mysterious sea, with its endless cycle of tides, is the setting for "The Tide Rises, The Tide Falls," which suggests or implies the idea that, though a person may die, life continues. The recurring pauses, frequent repetition of words, and refrain combine with strong metrical rhythm to create a rising and falling rhythm, like the breaking of waves on the shore.

2 Humanities

Maximilien Luce

Born in Paris, Maximilien Luce (1858–1941) became a lithographer and draftsman. Encouraged by influential artists, he devoted himself to painting. At the invitation of Georges Seurat and Paul Signac, Luce became a founding member of the Neo-Impressionist movement. These artists were often referred to as the Pointillists due to their scientific study of light and revolutionary technique of painting using a multitude of tiny paint dots to create a composition. His prolific body of work celebrates landscapes and empathetic portrayals of the urban working class. Use the following question for discussion.

- How are the images and ideas from the poem reflected in the painting? **Possible responses:** Both the painting and the poem share a twilight setting. Both reflect a sea with similar characteristics. Both portray man as insignificant when compared to the vast permanence of the sea.

3 Critical Viewing

Possible responses: How long did it take the artist to compose the painting? Is this painting of a specific location? What effect does the technique have on the mood of the painting?

Differentiated Instruction Solutions for All Learners

Accessibility at a Glance

	The Tide Rises	Thanatopsis	Old Ironsides	Snowbound
Context	Early American romantic poetry	Discusses death and nature	Famous poem about battleship	Glorification of nature and family
Language	Accessible	Poetic syntax; vocabulary	Declamatory	Accessible; strict and regular rhyme
Concept Level	Accessible (metaphors)	Challenging (death; nature)	Accessible (plea to save ship)	Accessible (nature and family)
Literary Merit	Classic	Classic	Classic	Narrative poem
Lexile	NP	NP	NP	NP
Over all Rating	Accessible	More challenging	Average	Average

4 Literary Analysis
Meter and Mood

- Tell students that poets often change the meter from one line to the next. Generally, such a change indicates that the poet wishes to draw the reader's attention to something in the line, to note a difference between that line and the one that preceded it.
- Have three volunteers each read aloud a stanza of the poem. Ask the other students to listen carefully to the change in meter of the final line of each stanza. **Ask** the literary analysis question: In what way does the change of meter in lines 5, 10, and 15 affect the mood of the poem?
  Possible response: The change of meter emphasizes the line and slows down the pace of the other lines in the stanza. The poet is emphasizing the slower, constant, eternal rhythm of the tides as contrasted with the faster pace of human beings.

ASSESS
Answers

1. **Possible response:** It evoked images of waves breaking on the beach.
2. (a) The tide rises and falls; evening brings darkness; a night bird calls; a traveler approaches a town. (b) **Possible response:** The darkening of the sky and sound of the night suggest the ending of a life. (c) Darkness has settled, and the waves have erased the traveler's footprints.
3. (a) "And the tide rises, the tide falls" is repeated. (b) Mirroring the repeated motion of the tide reminds the reader of the never-ending cycle of life on earth.
4. (a) The little waves are like hand that erase footprints in the sand. (b) It further emphases the cyclical nature of human life and nature's eternal presence.
5. (a) **Possible responses:** The day returns, but the traveler does not. (b) Humans come and go, but the rhythms of nature endure. Humans are mortal; nature is eternal.

continued

Darkness settles on roofs and walls,
But the sea, the sea in the darkness calls:
The little waves, with their soft, white hands,
Efface the footprints in the sands,
    And the tide rises, the tide falls.

The morning breaks; the steeds in their stalls
Stamp and neigh, as the hostler[2] calls:
The day returns, but nevermore
Returns the traveler to the shore,
    And the tide rises, the tide falls.

2. **hostler** (häs′ lər) *n.* person who tends horses at an inn or stable.

Vocabulary Builder
efface (ə fās′) *v.* erase; wipe out

Literary Analysis
Meter and Mood In what way does the change of meter in lines 5, 10, and 15 affect the mood of the entire poem?

Critical Reading

1. **Respond:** What images did this poem evoke for you?
2. **(a) Recall:** Which events occur in the first stanza?
   (b) Interpret: Which details suggest that the traveler is nearing death?
   (c) Support: Which details suggest that he has died?
3. **(a) Recall:** Which line does the speaker repeat throughout the poem?
   (b) Evaluate: What effect does this repetition have on the message of the poem?
4. **(a) Analyze:** In the second stanza, how does the speaker portray the sea and the waves? **(b) Evaluate:** How does this portrayal affect the meaning of the poem?
5. **(a) Contrast:** In the third stanza, what is the difference between the traveler and the day? **(b) Draw Conclusions:** What does the poem suggest about humanity and nature?
6. **Evaluate:** What do you think Longfellow's outlook on life and death was when he wrote this poem? Explain.

For: More about Henry Wadsworth Longfellow
Visit: www.PHSchool.com
Web Code: ere-9302

Answers continued

6. (a) **Possible response:** Longfellow seems to view the life and death of a single human being as a small part of a vast, timeless cycle of nature. In this poem, Longfellow evokes the relative insignificance of a single human life against the background of the long, slow turning of time and tide.

Go Online — Author Link For additional information about Henry Wadsworth Longfellow, have students type in the Web Code, then select L from the alphabet, and then select Henry Wadsworth Longfellow.

❺

Thanatopsis

William Cullen Bryant

❻

Kindred Spirits, Asher B. Durand, New York Public Library

To him who in the love of Nature holds
Communion with her visible forms, she speaks
A various language; for his gayer hours
She has a voice of gladness, and a smile
And eloquence of beauty, and she glides
Into his darker musings, with a mild
And healing sympathy, that steals away
Their sharpness, ere[1] he is aware. When thoughts
Of the last bitter hour come like a blight
Over thy spirit, and sad images
Of the stern agony, and shroud, and pall,
And breathless darkness, and the narrow house,[2]
Make thee to shudder, and grow sick at heart—
Go forth, under the open sky, and list
To Nature's teachings, while from all around—
Earth and her waters, and the depths of air—

❼ **▲ Critical Viewing**
This painting pays tribute to the friendship between the poet Bryant and landscape painter Thomas Cole. What does the painting suggest about the two men's shared interests? **[Infer]**

❽ **Reading Check**
Who has "a voice of gladness" and a "healing sympathy"?

1. **ere** before.
2. **narrow house** coffin.

❺ About the Selection

"Thanatopsis" presents the poet's thoughts on death and its links to nature. Nature brings joy and comfort to those who love it. When people think of death, nature teaches them that everyone and everything must die and become part of the earth again. As all of nature is intertwined, so are the bodies and spirits of all who die. Death need not be feared or despised.

❻ Humanities

Kindred Spirits, by Asher B. Durand

This portrait-in-nature shows artist Thomas Cole and poet William Cullen Bryant. Durand, Cole, and Bryant were close friends who encouraged and supported one another's work. Use this question for discussion:

- What inspirations might Bryant have taken from this scene?
  Answer: Perhaps he developed ideas for poems on nature or friendship.

❼ Critical Viewing

Answer: Because Cole was a landscape painter, he, like Bryant, must have had deep feelings about nature. The two, standing on a rock overlooking a beautiful valley might be sharing their views on the relationship between nature and art.

❽ Reading Check

Answer: Nature has a voice of gladness and a healing sympathy.

Differentiated Instruction
Solutions for All Learners

Support for Special Needs Students
To help students appreciate this poem, focus on its rhythm before addressing its meaning. Have students listen to Bryant's poem on **Listening to Literature Audio CDs.** Discuss students' reactions to hearing the poem. Then guide them in reading the poem for meaning.

Vocabulary for Less Proficient Readers
Students may find the poetic language of these poems challenging. Point out some examples in lines 8 and 14 (*ere* and *list,* meaning "before" and "listen"). Explain that poetic language—language used in some older, traditional poetry but not in speech—includes words such as these, which poets include for the sake of rhyme or meter.

Enrichment for Gifted/Talented Students
Tell students that the painting belongs to the Hudson River School. Although this group of artists received little respect, their skill in portraying the wilderness helped make landscape an honorable subject in American art. Encourage students to complete the Research and Technology activity on p. 291.

9 Reading Strategy
Summarizing

- Invite a volunteer to read aloud the bracketed text.
- Have students identify the main idea and the details that support this idea.
- **Tell** students to do the Reading Strategy task: Summarize the meaning of lines 22–30. **Possible response:** We return to nature when we die.

10 Literary Analysis
Meter and Mood

- Before addressing the text, have students review the instruction about meter and mood on p. 274.
- **Ask** students to identify the mood of the poem up to line 30. Then, draw their attention to the word *Yet* in line 31. Tell students that this signal word indicates a shift in the poem's mood.
- In the bracketed text, focus students' attention on words such as *magnificent, kings, wise,* and *good.* Urge them to think about the mood these words suggest.
- Have students **respond** to the Literary Analysis direction: Describe the shift in mood in lines 31–35. **Possible response:** Here the mood becomes hopeful and positive as the poet describes an eternal resting place, in contrast to the previous lines in which the mood was somber and even grim in discussing earthly burial.

Comes a still voice—Yet a few days, and thee
The all-beholding sun shall see no more
In all his course; nor yet in the cold ground,
Where thy pale form was laid, with many tears,
Nor in the embrace of ocean, shall exist
Thy image. Earth, that nourished thee, shall claim
Thy growth, to be resolved to earth again,
And, lost each human trace, surrendering up
9 Thine individual being, shalt thou go
To mix forever with the elements,
To be a brother to the insensible rock
And to the sluggish clod, which the rude swain[3]
Turns with his share,[4] and treads upon. The oak
Shall send his roots abroad, and pierce thy mold.

Yet not to thine eternal resting place
10 Shalt thou retire alone, nor couldst thou wish
Couch[5] more magnificent. Thou shalt lie down
With patriarchs of the infant world—with kings,
The powerful of the earth—the wise, the good,
Fair forms, and hoary seers of ages past,
All in one mighty sepulcher. The hills
Rock-ribbed and ancient as the sun—the vales
Stretching in pensive quietness between;
The venerable woods—rivers that move
In majesty, and the complaining brooks
That make the meadows green; and, poured round all,
Old Ocean's gray and melancholy waste—
Are but the solemn decorations all
Of the great tomb of man. The golden sun,
The planets, all the infinite host of heaven,
Are shining on the sad abodes of death,
Through the still lapse of ages. All that tread
The globe are but a handful to the tribes
That slumber in its bosom. Take the wings
Of morning,[6] pierce the Barcan[7] wilderness,
Or lose thyself in the continuous woods
Where rolls the Oregon,[8] and hears no sound,
Save his own dashings—yet the dead are there:
And millions in those solitudes, since first
The flight of years began, have laid them down

Reading Strategy
Summarizing Summarize the meaning of lines 22–30.

Literary Analysis
Meter and Mood Describe the shift in mood in lines 31–35.

Vocabulary Builder

sepulcher (sep′əl kər) *n.* tomb

pensive (pen′ siv) *adj.* expressing deep thoughtfulness

venerable (ven′ər ə bəl) *adj.* worthy of respect

3. **swain** country youth.
4. **share** plowshare.
5. **couch** bed.
6. **Take . . . morning** allusion to Psalm 139:9.
7. **Barcan** (bär′ kən) referring to Barca, a desert region in North Africa.
8. **Oregon** river flowing between Oregon and Washington, now known as the Columbia River.

Enrichment

Cultural Views of Death

Many cultures have looked upon death with as much interest as William Cullen Bryant does in this poem. In many ancient civilizations, death was seen as a passage to another life. The Egyptians built huge pyramids as tombs for their pharaohs and stocked them with all the comforts needed for the afterlife, including pets and servants.

The position in which the dead are buried also has significance. In some African cultures, men are buried on their right side, facing east, so the rising sun will wake them in the afterlife to hunt and farm. Women are buried facing west, so the setting sun will remind them to prepare the evening meal.

In their last sleep—the dead reign there alone.
So shalt thou rest, and what if thou withdraw
In silence from the living, and no friend
Take note of thy departure? All that breathe
Will share thy destiny. The gay will laugh
When thou art gone, the solemn brood of care
Plod on, and each one as before will chase
His favorite phantom; yet all these shall leave
Their mirth and their employments, and shall come
And make their bed with thee. As the long train
Of ages glide away, the sons of men,
The youth in life's green spring, and he who goes
In the full strength of years, matron and maid,
The speechless babe, and the gray-headed man—
Shall one by one be gathered to thy side,
By those, who in their turn shall follow them.

So live, that when thy summons comes to join
The innumerable caravan, which moves
To that mysterious realm, where each shall take
His chamber in the silent halls of death,
11 Thou go not, like the quarry-slave at night,
Scourged to his dungeon, but, sustained and soothed
By an unfaltering trust, approach thy grave,
Like one who wraps the drapery of his couch
About him, and lies down to pleasant dreams.

Reading Strategy
Summarizing How would you restate the poet's message in the final stanza?

Critical Reading

1. **Respond:** Did this poem make you think of nature in a new way? Explain.
2. **(a) Recall:** Identify the various languages Nature speaks to those who love her. **(b) Interpret:** How does the speaker find comfort in Nature's "various language"?
3. **(a) Recall:** According to the "still voice" introduced in line 17 what will happen to the individual being? **(b) Interpret:** In what ways do the images in lines 27–30 reinforce this idea?
4. **(a) Recall:** In the end, who shares the individual being's destiny? **(b) Draw Conclusions:** How would you summarize the poet's attitudes toward life and death?
5. **(a) Connect:** The title combines the Greek words *thanatos* (death) and *opsis* (a vision). Explain the title's connection to the poem. **(b) Apply:** In what ways can Nature provide insight into the mysteries of life and death?

Go Online
Author Link
For: More about William Cullen Bryant
Visit: www.PHSchool.com
Web Code: ere-9303

Differentiated Instruction
Solutions for All Learners

Strategy for Less Proficient Readers
Point out Bryant's extensive use of figurative language. Review the definition of metaphor: a thing is spoken of as though it were something else. For example, the poet describes the earth metaphorically as "the great tomb of man." Help students locate and decipher other metaphors in "Thanatopsis."

Strategy for English Learners
Tell students that Bryant personifies Earth, nature, and ocean in this poem. Review with students that in using personification, poets attribute human qualities to inanimate objects. Help students understand that with personification, Bryant can portray Earth having feelings or taking actions that it cannot really have or take.

Strategy for Advanced Readers
Challenge students to develop a character analysis of Nature as Bryant portrays her. What feelings does he ascribe to her? Is she seen as beautiful and inviting or as threatening? Ask volunteers to read their analyses aloud for the class. Poll the class to see how many students agree with each writer's interpretation of the poem.

11 Reading Strategy
Summarizing

- Read aloud the bracketed text, striving to convey the poem's meter and to create its uplifting final mood.
- **Ask** students the Reading Strategy question: How would you restate the poet's message in the final stanza?
  Possible response: Be aware that death is a natural process that comes to all, and you can accept it peacefully when it comes.

ASSESS
Answers

1. Responses should reflect new insights gained in students' reading.
2. (a) Nature has a voice of gladness and a still voice. (b) Nature can rejoice with us when we are happy and comfort us when we are sad.
3. (a) He or she will die, be buried, and become part of nature's elements. (b) They describe a buried body's return to the earth.
4. (a) "All that breathe"—anyone who lives—share that destiny. (b) The poet seems to have accepted his place in the life cycle. He recognizes that it is his destiny to return to the earth at death so that his mortal body may in some way become part of nature's immortality.
5. (a) The poet is examining his beliefs about death and man's place in the world. He conveys his own philosophy or "vision" of death: that mortal man must die and become part of immortal nature. (b) **Possible response:** In life, nature comforts and heals us. Through nature, we come to understand our place in the life cycle and how, with our deaths, our bodies return to it.

Go Online **Author Link** For additional information about William Cullen Bryant, have students type in the Web Code, then select B from the alphabet, and then select William Cullen Bryant.

⓬ About the Selection

Written when the War of 1812 was still a living memory, the poem "Old Ironsides" pays homage to the valiant role the ship U.S.S. *Constitution* played in American history. The poet pleads to let it sink at sea rather than suffer ignominious demolition.

⓭ Critical Viewing

Answer: Students may cite lines 2–4 and lines 9–14.

⓬ OLD IRONSIDES

Oliver Wendell Holmes

⓭ ▲ **Critical Viewing** To celebrate the 200th anniversary of her October 1797 launch, the U.S.S. *Constitution* took a five-hour sail around Massachusetts Bay in July 1997. Before that date, the ship had not sailed under its own power in more than 116 years. Which lines from the poem still apply to "Old Ironsides" today?

Enrichment

The U.S.S. *Constitution*

America has always been proud of the great ships its workers have built. Certain ships stand out as praiseworthy examples of this complex craft. The U.S.S. *Constitution,* nicknamed "Old Ironsides," is foremost among them. This 44-gun warship, ordered by President George Washington and completed in 1797, first won fame battling Barbary pirates in Tripoli, a victory celebrated in the Marine Corps hymn. The *Constitution* is probably best remembered for its role in the War of 1812, when it outsailed British ships to win several decisive battles for the U.S. Navy.

Though Oliver Wendell Holmes helped win the war to save the *Constitution* from peril, a century later it was in peril again. The deteriorating ship was in need of major repairs. This time, America's schoolchildren came to the rescue, by contributing money that they had collected to restore the ship to its original conditions. The restored *Constitution* is still on display at Charlestown Navy Yard, Charlestown, Massachusetts.

Ay, tear her tattered ensign down!
Long has it waved on high,
And many an eye has danced to see
That banner in the sky;
Beneath it rung the battle shout,
And burst the cannons roar;—
The meteor of the ocean air
Shall sweep the clouds no more.

Her deck, once red with heroes' blood,
Where knelt the vanquished foe,
When winds were hurrying o'er the flood,
And waves were white below,
14 No more shall feel the victor's tread,
Or know the conquered knee;—
The harpies[1] of the shore shall pluck
The eagle of the sea!

15 Oh, better that her shattered hulk
Should sink beneath the wave;
Her thunders shook the mighty deep,
And there should be her grave;
Nail to the mast her holy flag.
Set every threadbare sail,
And give her to the god of storms,
The lightning and the gale!

1. **harpies** (här′ pēz) In Greek mythology, hideous, half-woman, half bird monsters.

Literary Analysis
Meter Why do you think Holmes occasionally alters the meter in "Old Ironsides"?

Reading Strategy
Summarizing Summarize the last stanza of the poem.

Critical Reading

1. **Respond:** If you had been alive in 1830, would this poem have inspired you to protest the ship's demolition? Explain.
2. **(a) Recall:** In the first stanza, what does the speaker suggest doing with the ship? **(b) Infer:** Is he being sincere?
3. **(a) Recall:** By what names does the speaker refer to the ship? **(b) Infer:** What do these names imply?
4. **(a) Draw Conclusions:** Which do you think is more important to the speaker—the ship itself or its historic role? Explain. **(b) Analyze:** In what ways does the poet appeal to the American sense of patriotism?
5. **Evaluate:** This poem was instrumental in saving *Old Ironsides.* Could a poem have such an effect today? Explain.

For: More about Oliver Wendell Holmes
Visit: www.PHSchool.com
Web Code: ere-9304

14 Literary Analysis
Meter

- Have volunteers identify which lines vary the meter.
  Possible response: Lines 7, 13, and 21 vary the meter.
- **Ask** students the Literary Analysis question: Why do you think Holmes occasionally alters the meter in "Old Ironsides"?
  Possible response: Holmes may have varied the meter to capture readers' attention and thus stress an important idea.

15 Reading Strategy
Summarizing

- Have students read the bracketed passage several times.
- Then, **offer** students the Reading Strategy prompt: Summarize the last stanza of the poem.
  Possible response: Let the ship go down in a storm to a dignified death.

ASSESS
Answers

1. Students should support their responses with well-reasoned explanations.
2. (a) He suggests tearing down the ship's ragged flag. (b) No, he is being ironic.
3. (a) He calls it "the meteor of the ocean air" and "the eagle of the sea." (b) **Possible response:** They imply that the *Constitution* was a swift ship.
4. (a) His references to the important battles in which the ship took part show that he thinks of the ship as an American symbol. (b) He reminds the reader of important battles in which the ship played a key role.
5. **Possible response:** Because fewer people now read poetry, a poem probably would not have so powerful an effect.

Go Online Author Link For additional information about Oliver Wendell Holmes, have students type in the Web Code, then select H from the alphabet, and then select Oliver Wendell Holmes.

Differentiated Instruction
Solutions for All Learners

Strategy for Less Proficient Readers
Have students summarize the first stanza of "Old Ironsides." If students have difficulty summarizing, encourage them to paraphrase the lines in the stanza before they begin their summaries. Help them do the same thing for each stanza of "Old Ironsides." Then, lead a class discussion on the poem's overall message.

Enrichment for English Learners
Help students visualize the action Holmes evokes. Help them make sketches of the ship's flag, the cannon fire, the battling sailors and vanquished foes. Then, have them use the photograph on page 280 as a guide to sketch the sinking ship as Holmes describes it.

Enrichment for Advanced Readers
Invite interested students to learn more about the 200th birthday sail of the *Constitution* on July 21, 1997. That was the first time since 1881 that the nation's oldest commissioned warship sailed under its own power. Students might prepare a presentation about the event for the class.

16 About the Selection

This narrative poem commemorates a way of life and a close-knit family. A December snowstorm isolates a family on a New England farm. Despite extra efforts they must make to care for their animals and keep warm, the family relishes its cozy home and the beauties of nature's artistry.

17 Humanities

Old Holley House, Cos Cob, by John Henry Twachtman

The artist uses soft colors in this painting. At first glance, the picture seems flat, but closer examination reveals depth and vibrancy, such as might be seen on the bright snowy day after Whittier's snowstorm. Use these questions for discussion:

1. How do the artist and the poet use color to describe snow?
   Answer: The artist uses shades of blue, white, gray, pink, and purple while Whittier mostly refers to the snow as either white or crystalline (clear).
2. What words from the poem also describe this picture?
   Possible response: *Hills of gray, white drift, glistening, dazzling crystal, snow-mist,* and *frost line*

18 Critical Viewing

Answer: Students may say that the mood inside the speaker's home is cozy, warm, merry, and content. The painting conveys an exterior that is cold, lonely, and unwelcoming.

17

Old Holley House, Cos Cob, John Henry Twachtman, Cincinnati Art Museum

18 ▲ **Critical Viewing** At the end of this poem, the speaker describes the inside of his home. Contrast that interior with the exterior of the house in this painting. **[Contrast]**

Differentiated Instruction Solutions for All Learners

Enrichment for Advanced Readers

In his poem "A Fable for Critics," James Russell Lowell wrote about his contemporary, John Greenleaf Whittier. Read these lines to students:

There was ne'er a man born who had more of the swing
Of the true lyric bard and all that kind of thing;
And his failures arise (though he seem not to know it)
From the very same cause that has made him a poet,—

Challenge students to find the complete poem and read it independently. Then, lead a brief discussion in which you invite students to ask questions if there are lines or passages they don't understand. Finally, have them answer the following question in their journals: Do you think Lowell's criticism of Whittier is reasonable or unreasonable? Why or why not?

from SNOWBOUND

John Greenleaf Whittier

A Winter Idyll

19

The sun that brief December day
Rose cheerless over hills of gray,
And, darkly circled, gave at noon
A sadder light than waning moon.
Slow tracing down the thickening sky
Its mute and <u>ominous</u> prophecy,

A portent seeming less than threat,
It sank from sight before it set.
A chill no coat, however stout,
Of homespun stuff could quite shut out,
A hard, dull bitterness of cold,
That checked, mid-vein, the circling race
Of lifeblood in the sharpened face,
The coming of the snowstorm told.
The wind blew east; we heard the roar
Of Ocean on his wintry shore,
And felt the strong pulse throbbing there
Beat with low rhythm our inland air.

Meanwhile we did our nightly chores—
Brought in the wood from out of doors,
Littered the stalls, and from the mows
Raked down the herd's-grass for the cows:
Heard the horse whinnying for his corn;
And, sharply clashing horn on horn,
Impatient down the stanchion[1] rows
The cattle shake their walnut bows;
While, peering from his early perch

Vocabulary Builder
ominous (äm′ ə nəs) *adj.* threatening

20

Reading Check
What signals the coming of the snowstorm?

1. **stanchion** (stan′ chən) restraining device fitted around the neck of a cow to confine it to its stall.

19 Literary Analysis
Meter and Mood

- Have students read bracketed text to themselves.
- Encourage students to reflect on their emotional responses to the text, focusing on such words and phrases as *brief December day, cheerless, grey hills, darkly circled, sadder light,* and *ominous.*
- **Ask** students to identify the mood of these six lines.
  Answer: The mood is ominous, threatening, and gloomy.

20 Reading Check
Answer: The sky's thickening, the gray light, a chill in the air, the hard and dull cold, the wind blowing east and a sound like the sea all signal the coming snowstorm.

Differentiated Instruction Solutions for All Learners

Strategy for Less Proficient Readers
To help students understand this lengthy poem, treat the selection in sections. You may divide the poem as follows:

1. Signs of the coming storm (lines 1–3)
2. Description of the storm and the family's response to it (lines 31–115)
3. Lighting a fire in the fireplace (lines 116–142)
4. Description of the outside world (lines 143–154)
5. Description of the world inside (lines 155–174)

As they read each section, have students note how the poet appeals to the senses. They might make a graphic organizer in which they list sense imagery.

21 Literary Analysis
Meter

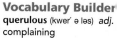

- Read aloud lines 35–36. Have students comment on both the meter and the action of these lines.
- Have students identify what is being described in these lines. **Answer:** The movement of the snow in the wind is being described.
- **Ask** students the Literary Analysis question: The pattern of meter changes at lines 35 and 36. In what ways does this change in meter correspond with the action described in these lines? **Answer:** The changing meter suggests the back and forth movement of snow in the wind.

Upon the scaffold's pole of birch,
The cock his crested helmet bent
And down his querulous challenge sent.

Unwarmed by any sunset light
The gray day darkened into night,
A night made hoary with the swarm
And whirl-dance of the blinding storm,
21 As zigzag, wavering to and fro,
Crossed and recrossed the winged snow:
And ere the early bedtime came
The white drift piled the window frame,
And through the glass the clothesline posts
Looked in like tall and sheeted ghosts.

So all night long the storm roared on:
The morning broke without a sun;
In tiny spherule[2] traced with lines
Of Nature's geometric signs,
in starry flake, and pellicle,[3]
All day the hoary meteor fell;

Vocabulary Builder
querulous (kwer′ ə ləs) *adj.* complaining

Literary Analysis
Meter The pattern of the meter changes at lines 35 and 36. In what ways does this change correspond with the action described in these lines?

2. **spherule** (sfer′ o͞ol) small sphere.
3. **pellicle** (pel′ i kəl) thin film of crystals.

Enrichment

Musical "Descriptions"

Many of the wintry descriptions John Greenleaf Whittier created with words, the Italian composer Antonio Vivaldi (1678–1741) created with music. His famous *Four Seasons* concerto is rich with dynamic, tonal, and rhythmic effects. This piece, based on a cycle of four sonnets that Vivaldi himself may have written, offers musical images of spring, summer, autumn, and winter.

Play "Winter" for the class. Challenge students to listen for musical illustrations of icy snow, chilling winds, and chattering teeth. Discuss the musical devices Vivaldi used to convey his imagery.

And, when the second morning shone,
We looked upon a world unknown,
On nothing we could call our own.
Around the glistening wonder bent
The blue walls of the firmament,
No cloud above, no earth below—
A universe of sky and snow!
The old familiar sights of ours
Took marvelous shapes; strange domes and towers
22 Rose up where sty or corncrib stood,
Or garden wall, or belt of wood;
A smooth white mound the brush pile showed,
A fenceless drift what once was road;
The bridle post an old man sat
With loose-flung coat and high cocked hat;
The wellcurb had a Chinese roof;
And even the long sweep,[4] high aloof,
In its slant splendor, seemed to tell
Of Pisa's leaning miracle.[5]

A prompt, decisive man, no breath
Our father wasted: "Boys, a path!"
Well pleased (for when did farmer boy
23 Count such a summons less than joy?)
Our buskins[6] on our feet we drew;
With mittened hands, and caps drawn low,
To guard our necks and ears from snow,

4. **sweep** pole with a bucket at one end, used for raising water from a well.
5. **Pisa's leaning miracle** famous leaning tower of Pisa in Italy.
6. **buskins** high-cut leather shoes or boots.

Literary Analysis
Meter and Mood What mood is conveyed in the morning light? Which words create this mood?

Reading Strategy
Summarizing Why are the boys so excited by their father's order to make a path through the snow?

24 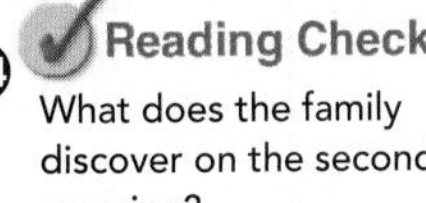
Reading Check
What does the family discover on the second morning?

22 Literary Analysis
Meter and Mood

- After students read the bracketed text silently, call on a volunteer to read aloud the lines. Urge the other students to close their eyes as they listen and to visualize the new morning.
- Encourage students to identify the feelings they associate with the following words and phrases: *glistening wonder, universe of sky and snow, marvelous shapes,* and *slant splendor.*
- Then, **ask** students the Literary Analysis questions: What mood is conveyed in the morning light? Which words create this mood?
  Answer: The mood is one of wonder and fascination at the transformation wrought by the snow. Words such as *glistening wonder, universe of sky and snow, marvelous, strange, splendor,* and *miracle* all contribute to this mood.

23 Reading Strategy
Summarizing

- Have students reread the bracketed text. Then ask them to summarize its contents.
  Answer: The father asks his sons to make a path through the snow. They eagerly get warmly dressed to tackle the task.
- **Ask** students the Reading Strategy question: Why are the boys so excited by their father's order to make a path through the snow?
  Answer: This is not a typical farm chore; it evokes a sense of excitement and mystery and stimulates their imaginations.

24 Reading Check

Answer: They discover that their farm has been transformed by the heavy snowfall.

Differentiated Instruction Solutions for All Learners

Strategy for Special Needs Students
Students may more easily visualize the playful, stunning imagery of the snow-covered farm by sketching the scene Whittier describes in lines 50–65. Before students begin their sketching, work through each line word by word to define and explore the meanings of Whittier's highly evocative language. Suggest that students write down the meanings of all unfamiliar words and refer to their lists as they sketch. Ask them to illustrate in their sketches at least five of these words of a others in the poem.

Support for Less Proficient Readers
To help students access Whittier's description of the snowbound setting, remind them to use the Reading Strategy: Summarizing. Explain that by summarizing the main ideas and key details of Whittier's description, they can build a clear visual image of the setting. Model this process on lines 50–65.

25 Vocabulary Builder
The Latin Word Root *-patr-*

- Call students' attention to the word *patriarch* and its definition. Let students know that the root comes from the Latin word for father, *pater.*
- **Ask** students to volunteer any other words they may know that incorporate this word root. **Possibilities include:** patronage, paternal, and patriot.
- Have students write short explanations of how the idea of fatherhood influenced the formation of words such as *patronage* and *patriot.*

26 Reading Strategy
Summarizing

- Direct students' attention to the bracketed text. As they read it, urge students to note words that describe or convey sound. **Possible answers:** The words *no welcome sound, sharpest ear, could not hear, music, almost human tone* connote sound.
- **Ask** the Reading Strategy question: How do the sounds of the world change as a result of the snowstorm? **Answer:** The wind shrieks, boughs moan, sleet beats against the window. Also, the snow's blanket quiets certain sounds such as those of church bells or the brook.

We cut the solid whiteness through.
And, where the drift was deepest, made
A tunnel walled and overlaid
With dazzling crystal: we had read
Of rare Aladdin's[7] wondrous cave,
And to our own his name we gave,
With many a wish the luck were ours
To test his lamp's supernal powers.
We reached the barn with merry din,
And roused the prisoned brutes within,
The old horse thrust his long head out,
And grave with wonder gazed about;
The cock his lusty greeting said,
And forth his speckled harem led;
The oxen lashed their tails, and hooked,
And mild reproach of hunger looked;
25 The hornèd patriarch of the sheep,
Like Egypt's Amun[8] roused from sleep,
Shook his sage head with gesture mute,
And emphasized with stamp of foot.

All day the gusty north wind bore
The loosening drift its breath before:
Low circling round its southern zone,
The sun through dazzling snow-mist shone.
No church bell lent its Christian tone
To the savage air, no social smoke
Curled over woods of snow-hung oak
A solitude made more intense
By dreary-voicèd elements,
The shrieking of the mindless wind,
The moaning tree boughs swaying blind,
26 And on the glass the unmeaning beat
Of ghostly fingertips of sleet.
Beyond the circle of our hearth
No welcome sound of toil or mirth
Unbound the spell, and testified
Of human life and thought outside.
We minded that the sharpest ear
The buried brooklet could not hear,
The music of whose liquid lip
Had been to us companionship,
And, in our lonely life, had grown
To have an almost human tone.

Vocabulary Builder
patriarch (pā′ trē ärk′) *n.* the father and ruler of a family or tribe

Reading Strategy
Summarizing How do the sounds of the world change as a result of the snowstorm?

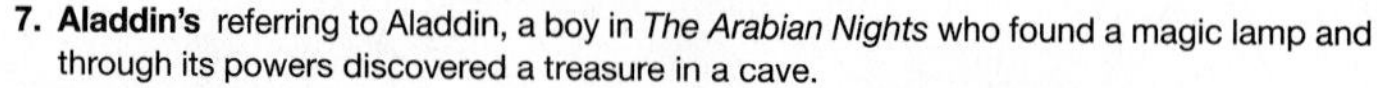

7. **Aladdin's** referring to Aladdin, a boy in *The Arabian Nights* who found a magic lamp and through its powers discovered a treasure in a cave.
8. **Amun** Egyptian god with a ram's head.

As night drew on, and, from the crest
Of wooded knolls that ridged the west,
The sun, a snow-blown traveler, sank
From sight beneath the smothering bank,
We piled, with care, our nightly stack
Of wood against the chimney back—
The oaken log, green, huge, and thick,
And on its top the stout backstick;
The knotty forestick laid apart,
26 And filled between with curious art
The ragged brush; then, hovering near,
We watched the first red blaze appear,
Heard the sharp crackle, caught the gleam
27 On whitewashed wall and sagging beam,
Until the old, rude-furnished room
Burst, flowerlike, into rosy bloom;
While radiant with a mimic flame
28 Outside the sparkling drift became,
And through the bare-boughed lilac tree
Our own warm hearth seemed blazing free.
The crane and pendent trammels[9] showed,
The Turks' heads[10] on the andirons glowed;
While childish fancy, prompt to tell
The meaning of the miracle,
Whispered the old rhyme: *"Under the tree,*
When fire outdoors burns merrily,
There the witches are making tea."

The moon above the eastern wood
Shone at its full; the hill range stood
Transfigured in the silver flood,
Its blown snows flashing cold and keen,
Dead white, save where some sharp ravine
Took shadow, or the somber green
Of hemlocks turned to pitchy black
Against the whiteness at their back.
For such a world and such a night
Most fitting that unwarming light,
Which only seemed where'er it fell
To make the coldness visible.

Shut in from all the world without,
We sat the clean-winged hearth[11] about,

9. **trammels** (tram′ əlz) *n.* adjustable pothooks hanging from the movable arm, or crane, attached to the hearth.
10. **Turks' heads** turbanlike knots at the top of the andirons.
11. **clean-winged hearth** a turkey wing was used for the hearth broom.

Literary Analysis
Meter and Mood What mood is conveyed by nightfall, the crackling fire, and the warm hearth?

Reading Strategy
Summarizing Summarize the action in lines 116–142

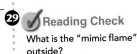

29 **Reading Check**
What is the "mimic flame" outside?

27 Literary Analysis
Meter and Mood

- Play the **Listening to Literature Audio CDs,** so that students can hear the bracketed lines read aloud. Encourage students to visualize the speaker's surroundings as they listen.
- Invite volunteers to highlight especially evocative words from the bracketed text.
  Possible responses: *snow-blown traveler; nightly stack; first red blaze; sharp crackle; burst, flowerlike, into rosy bloom; radiant with a mimic flame; warm hearth*
- **Ask** students the Literary Analysis question: What mood is conveyed by nightfall, the crackling fire, and the warm hearth?
  Answer: A mood of warmth and coziness is conveyed.

28 Reading Strategy
Summarizing

- Make sure students understand that a summary, whether for an entire work or part of a work, should include only the main idea and any important details that support this idea.
- Remind students of the audio reading they listened to when responding to the Literary Analysis question above. Then **ask** students to respond to the Reading Strategy prompt: Summarize the action in lines 116–142.
  Possible response: Night falls as the family gathers wood for the night, builds a fire, and warms the house's interior against the storm.

29 Reading Check

Answer: The speaker is describing the reflection of the hearth flames in the windowpanes.

Differentiated Instruction
Solutions for All Learners

Strategy for English Learners

Help students gain oral proficiency by having them read aloud lines 116–142 and then lines 143–154. After they read, lead a comparison discussion about the colors the speaker mentions in the two stanzas. Make sure that students know the colors named, using classroom objects or photographs to indicate examples. Then point out that the speaker uses color imagery to contrast the mood of the two stanzas, using white, silver, and black to describe the outdoors and rose, red, and gold to describe the indoors. Help students assign moods to these color groups as a way of understanding the text. For example, the outside colors are cold colors that suggest a stark, cold, detached mood. The inside colors are warm, glowing colors that suggest an embracing, welcoming mood.

30 Literary Analysis
Meter and Mood

- After students read the bracketed text, **ask** them what feelings the lines evoke in the reader.
Possible responses: security, warmth
- **Ask** students what the lasting mood of the final lines of this poem is?
Answer: happy, contented

ASSESS
Answers

1. Students may reply that it might be fun for a short time; others may not like the idea of being confined to their homes.
2. (a) There is hardly any sun, and the sky is thickening. (b) They hint at the possibility of danger.
3. (a) They contain and feed the animals; they gather wood. (b) They suggest that the family lives in harmony with nature.
4. (a) **Possible response:** "Shut in from all the world without" and "the red logs before us beat/ The frost line back with tropic heat" convey these feelings. (b) **Possible response:** "No cloud above, no earth below" and "Around the glistening wonder bent/The blue walls of firmament" show the narrator's sense of wonder. (c) They enjoy the time to step outside daily routine and be together.
5. (a) People today may more often feel that a snowbound day is an inconvenience. (b) **Possible response:** When such storms occur, people might avail themselves of snow blowers, SUVs, and other equipment to cope with the severe conditions. Likewise, people might communicate with neighbors and government agencies through the use of the telephone or Internet. (c) **Possible response:** Some students may observe that people are much less affected by weather than in Whittier's day. Others may point out that most people today cannot cook or heat their homes without electricity, and that a blizzard may therefore leave many at nature's mercy.

Content to let the north wind roar
In baffled rage at pane and door,
While the red logs before us beat
The frost line back with tropic heat;
And ever, when a louder blast
Shook beam and rafter as it passed,
The merrier up its roaring draft
The great throat of the chimney laughed;
30 The house dog on his paws outspread
Laid to the fire his drowsy head.
The cat's dark silhouette on the wall
A couchant tiger's seemed to fall:
And, for the winter fireside meet,
Between the andirons' straddling feet.
The mug of cider simmered slow.
The apples sputtered in a row.
And, close at hand, the basket stood
With nuts from brown October's wood.

Critical Reading

1. **Respond:** Would you find it pleasant to be isolated, like the narrator and his family, by a powerful snowstorm? Why or why not?
2. **(a) Recall:** What weather conditions forewarn the narrator of the approaching snowstorm? **(b) Connect:** In what way do these "previews" build suspense in the poem?
3. **(a) Recall:** In what ways does the family prepare for and cope with the storm? **(b) Draw Conclusions:** What do these responses to the storm suggest about the family's relationship with nature?
4. **(a) Recall:** Which details in the poem convey a sense of warmth, security, and family closeness? **(b) Analyze:** Which descriptive details in lines 47–80 convey the narrator's sense of wonder upon viewing the snow-covered landscape? **(c) Infer:** What are the family's feelings about being snowbound?
5. **(a) Assess:** In what ways has life changed since *Snowbound* was written in 1865? **(b) Extend:** Today, influenced as we are by modern technologies, how would people cope with the consequences such a storm could pose? **(c) Take a Position:** Are people still at the mercy of nature, as they were in Whittier's day? Explain your answer.

For: More about John Greenleaf Whittier
Visit: www.PHSchool.com
Web Code: ere-9305

Go Online Author Link For additional information about John Greenleaf Whittier, have students type in the Web Code, then select W from the alphabet, and then select John Greenleaf Whittier.

Apply the Skills

The Tide Rises, The Tide Falls • *Thanatopsis* • *Old Ironsides* • from *Snowbound*

Literary Analysis

Meter

1. Copy these lines from "Thanatopsis" and mark the stressed and unstressed syllables of the **meter:** So shalt thou rest, and what if thou withdraw / In silence from the living, and no friend.
2. Copy these lines from *Snowbound.* Mark the stressed and unstressed syllables: Beyond the circle of our hearth / No welcome sound of toil or mirth.
3. **(a)** In the second stanza of "Old Ironsides," which lines are in iambic tetrameter (four iambs)? **(b)** Which are iambic trimeter (three iambs)?

Comparing Literary Works

4. **(a)** Contrast the **moods** of Longfellow's poem "The Tide Rises, The Tide Falls" and the excerpt from *Snowbound.* **(b)** How does the setting in each poem contribute to these moods?
5. **(a)** What shift in mood occurs in line 31 of "Thanatopsis"? **(b)** How does this mood shift offer comfort?
6. Which of the other poems in this grouping best matches the mood of "The Tide Rises, The Tide Falls"? Why?

Reading Strategy

Summarizing

7. Using a chart like the one shown, write a **summary** of the first two stanzas of the excerpt from *Snowbound.*

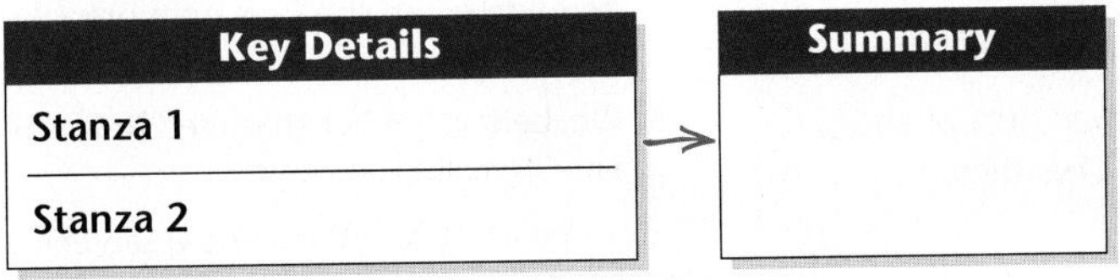

8. Summarize the main idea of "Thanatopsis." Consider your summary as a prereading guide for someone who is unfamiliar with the poem.

Extend Understanding

9. **Cultural Connection:** What value do historical monuments and symbols have to American society?

QuickReview

Meter in poetry is a systematic arrangement of stressed and unstressed syllables.

Mood, or atmosphere, is the feeling created in a reader by a literary work.

To **summarize,** briefly state the main ideas and supporting details in your own words.

For: Self-test
Visit: www.PHSchool.com
Web Code: era-6302

Answers

1. Sŏ shált thŏu rést, ănd whát ĭf thŏu wĭthdráw
   Ĭn sílĕnce fróm thĕ lívĭng, ănd nŏ fríend
2. Bĕyónd thĕ círclĕ óf oŭr héarth
   Nŏ wélcŏme sóund ŏf tóil ŏr mírth.
3. (a) Lines 9, 11, 13, and 15 are in iambic tetrameter. (b) Lines 10, 12, 14, and 16 are in iambic trimeter.
4. (a) "The Tide Rises, The Tide Falls" has a somber mood of resignation whereas *Snowbound* conveys a cozy, festive mood. (b) "The Tide Rises, The Tide Falls" is set on the seashore, isolated and constant *Snowbound* is set during an exciting snowstorm.
5. (a) **Possible response:** The mood shifts from grim to exalted. (b) The new mood offers comfort to those grieving or facing death.
6. "The Tide Rises, The Tide Falls" best matches the mood of "Thanatopsis" because it, too, deals with the inevitability of death.
7. **Possible response:** Students should cite key details from stanzas 1 and 2 in writing their summaries.
   Another sample answer can be found on **Reading Strategy Graphic Organizer B,** p. 58 in ***Graphic Organizer Transparencies.***
8. **Possible response:** In "Thanatopsis," the speaker details his thoughts about death and man's place in the world. He begins by exploring the role of nature, stating that nature's cycle naturally includes man's death, and his resulting return to nature. Finally, the speaker urges people to live fully so that they can accept death peacefully.
9. Historical monuments remind us of our rich history.

Go Online Assessment Students may use the **Self-test** to prepare for **Selection Test A** or **Selection Test B.**

EXTEND/ASSESS

Answers

1 Vocabulary Lesson

Word Analysis

1. patriots
2. paternal
3. patronage

Vocabulary Builder

1. synonyms
2. antonyms
3. antonyms
4. antonyms
5. synonyms
6. antonyms
7. synonyms

Spelling Strategy

1. dividable
2. sensible
3. usable

2 Grammar and Style Lesson

1. *circled* modifies *sun; waning* modifies *moon*
2. *resting* modifies *place*
3. *healing* modifies *sympathy*
4. *all-beholding* modifies *sun*
5. *shattered* modifies *hulk*

Writing Application

The *dazzling* snow reflected the sunlight from every *crusted* branch and *drifted* slope. As I squinted into the *chilling* wind, I could barely make out the *ice-coated* snow bank that used to be my front steps.

Writing and Grammar, Ruby Level

Students will find further instruction and practice on participles as adjectives in Chapter 19, Section 2.

Build Language Skills

1 Vocabulary Lesson

Word Analysis: Latin Root *-patr-*

The Latin root *-patr-*, comes from the word *pater,* meaning "father." This root is found in many English words, including *patriarch.* Complete each sentence by writing one of the *-patr-* words listed below in the blank.

patronage paternal patriot

1. People who love their fatherland are called __?__ .
2. My father's mother is my __?__ grandmother.
3. The mayor has the authority to give out certain __?__ jobs to his supporters.

Vocabulary Builder: Antonyms or Synonyms?

Decide whether the words in each pair are *antonyms* (opposites) or *synonyms* (similar).

1. sepulcher, tomb
2. pensive, frivolous
3. venerable, contemptible
4. efface, destroy
5. ominous, forbidding
6. querulous, content
7. patriarch, father

Spelling Strategy

The suffix *-able* / *-ible* is used to form adjectives, such as *biodegradable* and *visible.* Use the roots below to write adjectives that end with *-able* / *-ible.*

1. divide 2. sense 3. use

2 Grammar and Style Lesson

Participles as Adjectives

A **participle** is a verb form that can act as an adjective and answers the question *What kind?* or *Which one?* about the noun or pronoun it modifies. **Present participles** end in *-ing,* as in *dazzling.* **Past participles,** like *walled* and *overlaid,* may end in *-ed, -d, -t,* or *-en.* Notice the participles in this example.

Example: "A tunnel *walled* and *overlaid* / With *dazzling* crystal . . ."

Practice Identify the participles in each item, along with the noun each participle modifies.

1. The sun . . . / Rose cheerless . . . , / And, darkly circled, gave at noon / A sadder light than waning moon.
2. Yet not to thine eternal resting place / Shalt thou retire alone, . . .
3. Into his darker musings, with a mild / And healing sympathy, . . .
4. . . .Yet a few days, and thee / The all-beholding sun shall see no more / In all his course; . . .
5. Oh, better that her shattered hulk / Should sink beneath the wave; . . .

Writing Application Write three sentences describing a snow-covered landscape. Use participial forms of the following verbs as adjectives: *dazzle, coat, crust, drift, chill.* Draw arrows from the participles to the words they modify.

Prentice Hall Writing and Grammar Connection: Chapter 19, Section 2

Assessment Practice

Make Inferences and Generalizations

(For more practice, see *Standardized Test Preparation Workbook*, p. 17.)

Many tests require students to make valid generalizations based on specific evidence in a text. Explain that a valid generalization is supported by information found in the passage. Use this sample test item:

Which of the following most accurately describes Old Ironsides's record of service?

A inactive
B unremarkable
C distinguished
D brief

A, B, and *D* are not supported by the poem. The ship survived difficult battles and won many victories at sea. Therefore, *C* is correct.

Writing Lesson

Précis

Write a précis (prā sē′)—a concise abridgment or brief summary of a longer work—of the selection from *Snowbound.* Include all the main ideas and key details a reader would need in order to understand the events in the poem. Your summary should have a clear beginning, middle, and end.

Prewriting For each stanza, or group of lines, of the poem, list the main ideas and key details you will include in your précis. Try to convey a series of details with a single phrase or sentence.

Model: Identifying Beginning, Middle, and End

Beginning	Middle	End
Darkening	Chores, blizzard	
December sky,	starts, roars	
cold, windy . . .	through night . . .	

A clear beginning, middle, and end are especially important to a précis, which should reflect the structure or progression of the original work.

Drafting Set the mood for the poem's impending storm by summarizing the poem's opening stanza. Refer to your prewriting notes to avoid confusing the sequence of events as you draft the middle and end.

Revising Evaluate whether your précis accurately reflects the phases of the storm. Add details to convey the wonder of the snowy landscape and the coziness of the farmhouse hearth.

WG *Prentice Hall Writing and Grammar Connection: Chapter 31, Section 1*

Extend Your Learning

Listening and Speaking With a partner, convey Holmes's patriotic fervor in a **dramatic reading** of "Old Ironsides." Use these tips as you rehearse:

- Read with appropriate rhythm, meter, flow, and pronunciation.
- Use a tone, pitch, and pace suited to the work.
- Alternate stanzas with your partner, keeping the same mood and pace.

Ask classmates to critique your reading. **[Group Activity]**

Research and Technology The painting on page 277 depicts William Cullen Bryant and Thomas Cole. Research Cole and the Hudson River School of artists to determine the basis for Cole's claim to kinship with Bryant. Present your findings in an **oral presentation.**

Go Online Research **For:** An additional research activity **Visit:** www.PHSchool.com **Web Code:** erd-7302

3 Writing Lesson

- To guide students in writing this précis, give them the **Support for Writing Lesson,** p. 32 in ***Unit 3 Resources.***
- Review the Reading Strategy: Summarizing instruction on p. 274 with students.
- After discussing the steps in the Writing Lesson, emphasize the importance of careful detail selection. Stress that students should select enough details to convey the feel of the poem but not so many that their writing becomes cluttered.
- Use the Summary rubrics in ***General Resources,*** pp. 71–72, to evaluate student work.

4 Listening and Speaking

- Organize students in groups to summarize and discuss Holmes's poem and the emotions it conveys. Urge students to build on the discussion as they prepare their readings.
- Pair students to rehearse. Partners can take turns prompting each other with the words or suggesting possible places for emphasis.
- The **Support for Extend Your Learning** page (***Unit 3 Resources,*** p. 33) provides guided note-taking opportunities to help students complete the Extend Your Learning activities.

Go Online Research Have students type in the Web Code for another research activity.

Assessment Resources

The following resources can be used to assess students' knowledge and skills.

Unit 3 Resources
- **Selection Test A,** pp. 35–37
- **Selection Test B,** pp. 38–40

General Resources
- **Rubrics for Summary,** pp. 71–72

Go Online Assessment Students may use the **Self-test** to prepare for **Selection Test A** or **Selection Test B.**

Meeting Your Standards

Students will

1. **understand and explain memorandums.**
2. **read and interpret a memorandum from Thomas Jefferson to Meriwether Lewis.**

*See **Teacher Express™/Lesson View** for a detailed lesson plan for Reading Informational Materials.*

About Memorandums

- Write the word memorandum on the board. Underline the first five letters, and point out the link to the words *memory and remember.* A memorandum is a note that will help the recipient remember something important.
- **Ask** students to list situations in which memorandums might be useful.
  Possible answers: Any time you have to remember something, it is helpful to have a written record of it. Memorandums of agreements made in meetings are important so that misunderstandings can be avoided.

Reading Skill

Analyzing Text Structures: Patterns of Organization

- Explain to students that memos are usually organized according to one of three methods: chronological order, order of importance, and enumeration.
- Review the basic structure of each method of organization.
- **Ask** students to suggest situations that require each method of organization.
  Possible answers: Chronological—instructions for a process, a timetable; order of importance—prioritized list, justification for a certain action, persuasive memo; enumeration—inventories of items, lists of names; descriptions of multiple tasks of equal importance.

Reading Informational Materials

Memorandums

About Memorandums

You may already have a job, or you may be planning for your career. Either way, you are likely to read memorandums, or memos, in your workplace.

In today's workplace, the average memorandum is brief and rather informal in tone. It usually contains a heading beginning with these recognizable lines:

TO: (naming the recipient/s of the memo)

FROM: (naming the sender)

DATE:

TOPIC:

The body of the note contains only a few facts—for example, an announcement of a time change for a staff meeting or a reminder about a deadline.

The memorandums that you read today may differ from those written in the past. Historical memorandums may be more formal, longer, and more detailed. You will find these qualities in the following memorandum, written by President Thomas Jefferson when he assigned Meriwether Lewis to undertake the exploration of the Missouri River.

Reading Strategy

Analyzing Text Structures: Patterns of Organization

Informative writing of any length can follow several different patterns of organization. Three patterns are described below.

Common Patterns of Organization

Pattern of Organization	Structure	Type of Writing in Which It Is Found
Chronological Order	Details appear in the sequence in which they occur.	do-it-yourself instructions
Order of Importance	Information is arranged so that ideas flow from most to least important, or build from least to most important.	persuasive writing
Enumeration	Supporting details are provided in list form.	brochures or sales documents

Differentiated Instruction Solutions for All Learners

Reading Support

Give students reading support with the appropriate version of the *Reader's Notebooks:*

Reader's Notebook **[L2, L3]**

Reader's Notebook: Adapted Version **[L1, L2]**

Reader's Notebook: English Learner's Version **[EL]**

Commission of Meriwether Lewis

Thomas Jefferson

Historic Memorandum

June 20, 1803

To Meriwether Lewis, esquire, captain of the first regiment of infantry of the United States of America: Your situation as secretary of the president of the United States, has made you acquainted with the objects of my confidential message of January 18, 1803, to the legislature; you have seen the act they passed, which, though expressed in general terms, was meant to sanction those objects, and you are appointed to carry them into execution.

. . .

Although this historical memorandum does not have the same format as a modern memorandum, it still begins with the date and the name of the recipient.

The object of your mission is to explore the Missouri river, and such principal streams of it, as, by its course and communication with the waters of the Pacific ocean, whether the Columbia, Oregan [*sic*], Colorado, or any other river, may offer the most direct and practicable water-communication across the continent, for the purposes of commerce.

Beginning at the mouth of the Missouri, you will take observations of latitude and longitude, at all remarkable points on the river, and especially at the mouths of rivers, at rapids, at islands, and other places and objects distinguished by such natural marks and characters, of a durable kind, as that they may with certainty be recognized hereafter. The courses of the river between these points of observation may be supplied by the compass, the log-line, and by time, corrected by the observations themselves. The variations of the needle, too, in different places, should be noticed.

The interesting points of the portage between the heads of the Missouri, and of the water offering the best communication with the Pacific Ocean, should also be fixed by observation; and the course of that water to the ocean, in the same manner as that of the Missouri.

Your observations are to be taken with great pains and accuracy; to be entered distinctly and intelligibly for others as well as yourself; to comprehend all the elements necessary, with the aid of the usual tables, to fix the latitude and longitude of the places at which they were taken; and are to be rendered to the war-office, for the purpose of having the calculations made concurrently by proper persons within the United States. Several copies of these, as well as of your other notes, should be made at leisure times, and put into the care of the most trustworthy of your attendants to guard, by multiplying them against the accidental losses to which they will be exposed. A further guard would be, that one of these copies be on the cuticular membranes of the paper-birch, as less liable to injury from damp than common paper.

Jefferson takes the time in this memorandum to explain not only what is required but also why it is required.

The commerce which may be carried on with the people inhabiting the line you will pursue, renders a knowledge of those people important. You will therefore endeavor to make yourself acquainted, as far as a diligent pursuit of your journey shall admit, with the names of the nations and their numbers;

The extent and limits of their possessions;

Their relations with other tribes or nations;

Their language, traditions, monuments;

Their ordinary occupations in agriculture, fishing, hunting, war, arts, and the implements for these;

Their food, clothing, and domestic accommodations;

The diseases prevalent among them, and the remedies they use;

Moral and physical circumstances which distinguish them from the tribes we know;

READING INFORMATIONAL MATERIALS

Reading Memorandums

- Point out that Jefferson lays out in specific detail what he expects Lewis to do.
- As they read, **ask** students to list what they think are the most important requests Jefferson makes of Lewis. **Possible answer:** Students might list information about the landscape of their route; river access through the territory; the natural resources; and in particular, the customs, languages, and land possessions of the native tribes whom the explorers encounter.

Differentiated Instruction Solutions for All Learners

Strategy for Special-Needs Students

As they read, have each student make a list of the various tasks that Jefferson requests Lewis to perform. Have students work in small groups, dividing the memorandum so that each group concentrates on the tasks listed in one portion of the memo. Groups can then exchange lists, compare tasks, and make any needed corrections.

Enrichment for Advanced Writers

Have students write a memorandum that reminds employees of their company why they must perform particular tasks, such as offering free services or merchandise or planning a public event. Tell students to choose a pattern or organization and to be sure that it matches the purpose for the memo. Encourage students to share their memos with the class.

Reading Memorandums

(cont.)

- Draw students' attention to Jefferson's concern about the interaction between the explorers and the Indians. **Ask** why Jefferson would go to such lengths to suggest how Lewis's group should treat any people whom they meet. **Possible answer:** Jefferson says that he would like to promote trade between the inhabitants of the territory and the United States. He is also very concerned about the safety of the explorers, so he wants them to avoid inciting violence. He may also have a genuine interest in learning about different cultures and promoting information exchange between the Indians' culture and his own.

Peculiarities in their laws, customs, and dispositions;

And articles of commerce they may need or furnish, and to what extent.

And, considering the interest which every nation has in extending and strengthening the authority of reason and justice among the people around them, it will be useful to acquire what knowledge you can of the state of morality, religion, and information among them; as it may better enable those who may endeavor to civilize and instruct them, to adapt their measures to the existing notions and practices of those on whom they are to operate.

Like today's memorandums, this historical memorandum focuses on precise facts.

Other objects worthy of notice will be—The soil and face of the country, its growth and vegetable productions, especially those not of the United States;

The animals of the country generally, and especially those not known in the United States;

The remains and accounts of any which may be deemed rare or extinct;

The mineral productions of every kind, but more particularly metals, limestone, pit-coal, and saltpeter; salines and mineral waters, noting the temperature of the last, and such circumstances as may indicate their character;

Volcanic appearances;

Climate, as characterized by the thermo-meter, by the proportion of rainy, cloudy, and clear days; by lightning, hail, snow, ice; by the access and recess of frost; by the winds prevailing at different seasons; the dates at which particular plants put forth, or lose their flower or leaf; times of appearance of particular birds, reptiles or insects.. . .

In all your [dealings] with the natives, treat them in the most friendly and conciliatory manner which their own conduct will admit; allay all jealousies as to the object of your journey; satisfy them of its innocence; make them acquainted with the position, extent, character, peaceable and commercial dispositions of the United States; of our wish to be neighborly, friendly, and useful to them, and of our dispositions to a commercial [relationship] with them; confer with them on the points most convenient as mutual emporiums, and the articles of most desirable interchange for them and us. If a few of their influential chiefs, within practicable distance, wish to visit us, arrange such a visit with them, and furnish them with authority to call on our officers on their entering the United States, to have them conveyed to this place at the public expense. If any of them should wish to have some of their young people brought up with us, and taught such arts as may be useful to them, we will receive, instruct, and take care of them. Such a mission, whether of influential chiefs, or of young people, would give some security to your own party. Carry with you some matter of the kine-pox; inform those of them with whom you may be of its efficacy as a preservative from the small-pox, and instruct and encourage them in the use of it. This may be especially done wherever you winter.

As it is impossible for us to for esee in what manner you will be received by those people, whether with hospitality or hostility, so is it impossible to prescribe the exact degree of perseverance with which you are to pursue your journey. We value too much the lives of citizens to offer them to probable destruction. Your numbers will be sufficient to secure you against the unauthorized opposition of individuals, or of small parties; but if a superior force, authorized, or not authorized, by a nation, should be arrayed against your further passage, and inflexibly determined to arrest it, you must decline its further pursuit and return. In the loss of yourselves we should lose also the information you will have acquired. By returning safely with that, you may enable us to renew the essay with better calculated means. To your own discretion, therefore, must be left the degree of danger you may risk, and the point at which you should decline, only saying, we wish you to err on the side of your safety, and to bring back your party safe, even if it be with less information. . . .

Tips for Using Technology

Many word processing programs give students the ability to create auto text, which allows them to use preset text formats, such as the format for a memo. Students can save these formats and insert them into a document whenever they need that particular format. This is helpful for people who regularly write memos, letters, and other informational materials.

Assessment Practice

Reading: Analyzing Text Structures: Patterns of Organization

Directions: *Choose the letter of the best answer to each question about the memorandum.*

1. According to this memo, what is Lewis's most important objective?
   - A to observe and befriend the Indians
   - B to observe the landscape
   - C to collect data for accurate maps
   - D to find the waterway to the Pacific
2. What is the **overall** pattern of organization in this memorandum?
   - A order of importance
   - B enumeration
   - C chronological order
   - D least to most important order
3. Which is an example of enumeration from the memorandum?
   - A the directions to Lewis to make multiple copies of his notes
   - B the lists of what Lewis is to note about the Indians and landscape
   - C the order to take great care with his safety and that of his party
   - D the description of precautions to take against smallpox
4. What key point does Jefferson save for the last paragraph of the memo?
   - A You represent the country; be brave and generous.
   - B Fight all those who face and oppose you.
   - C Bring back all the information you can gather.
   - D Your safety is more important than your complete success.

Reading: Comprehension and Interpretation

Directions: *Write your answers on a separate sheet of paper.*

5. Why does Jefferson want Lewis to explore the Missouri River?
6. **(a)** What information does Jefferson consider so important that he wants Lewis to make multiple copies of it? **(b)** Why might this information be valuable to Jefferson?
7. **(a)** How is Lewis instructed to treat the Native Americans he meets? **(b)** How do you interpret Jefferson's motivation or motivations for making this instruction?

Timed Writing: Summary

Choose a topic from Jefferson's memorandum, such as *interaction with Indians* or *plants and animals.* Write a brief summary of this topic that Lewis could use as instructional material to share with his exploration party. Be sure to cover the most important related points from the memorandum. Use a pattern of organization that best suits the presentation of this information. **(*25 minutes*)**

ASSESS

Answers

Reading: Analyzing Text Structures: Patterns of Organization

1. D
2. A
3. B
4. D

Reading: Comprehension and Interpretation

5. He wants Lewis to find a waterway to the Pacific Ocean and to take accurate notes of everything he encounters along the way.
6. (a) He wants all Lewis's notes copied, especially the latitude and longitude of the places he sees. (b) Perhaps Jefferson wants to know the location of strategic features such as rivers or mountains in order to defend the new lands. Perhaps he wants to know where to find useful resources to aid in future commerce.
7. (a) He is to be "friendly and conciliatory." (b) Friendly overtures will be more likely to encourage friendship from the tribes and discourage aggression. Jefferson seems very concerned about the safety of the explorers. He may also feel that the native tribes have their own claim to the territory and so wants to establish a policy of peaceful co-existence.

Timed Writing

- Review the instructions in the text with the students, and answer any questions they might have.
- Suggest that students plan their time to allow 5 minutes for planning, 10 minutes for writing, and 10 minutes for reviewing and revising.

Extend the Lesson

Demonstration

To give students further practice with directions, have students demonstrate following instructions for a device they have available. Along with their demonstration they should provide a comprehensive set of instructions for operating or assembling the device. Remind students to make eye contact with the audience while giving their demonstration.

Meeting Your Standards

Students will

1. **analyze and respond to literary elements.**
   - Literary Analysis: Description
2. **read, comprehend, analyze, and critique nonfiction.**
   - Reading Strategy: Noting Spatial Relationships
   - Reading Check questions
   - Apply the Skills questions
   - Assessment Practice (ATE)
3. **develop vocabulary.**
   - Vocabulary Lesson: Latin Prefix: *multi-*
4. **understand and apply written and oral language conventions.**
   - Spelling Strategy
   - Grammar and Style Lesson: Participial Phrases
5. **develop writing proficiency.**
   - Writing Lesson: Description of a Natural Wonder
6. **develop appropriate research strategies.**
   - Extend Your Learning: Expedition Map
7. **understand and apply listening and speaking strategies.**
   - Extend Your Learning: Tourism Presentation

Block Scheduling: Use one 90-minute class period to preteach the skills and have students read the selection. Use a second 90-minute class period to assess students' mastery of skills, extend their learning, and monitor their progress.

Homework Suggestions

Following are possibilities for homework assignments.

- Support pages from *Unit 3 Resources:*
  Literary Analysis
  Reading Strategy
  Vocabulary Builder
  Grammar and Style
- An Extend Your Learning project and the Writing Lesson for this selection group may be completed over several days.

Step-by-Step Teaching Guide	Pacing Guide
PRETEACH	
• Administer Vocabulary and Reading Warm-ups as necessary.	5 min.
• Engage students' interest with the motivation activity.	5 min.
• Read and discuss author and background features. **FT**	10 min.
• Introduce the Literary Analysis Skill: Description. **FT**	5 min.
• Introduce the Reading Strategy: Noting Spatial Relationships. **FT**	10 min.
• Prepare students to read by teaching the selection vocabulary. **FT**	
TEACH	
• Informally monitor comprehension while students read independently or in groups. **FT**	30 min.
• Monitor students' comprehension with the Reading Check notes.	as students read
• Reinforce vocabulary with Vocabulary Builder notes.	as students read
• Develop students' understanding of description with the Literary Analysis annotations. **FT**	5 min.
• Develop students' ability to note spatial relationships with the Reading Strategy annotations. **FT**	5 min.
ASSESS/EXTEND	
• Assess students' comprehension and mastery of the Literary Analysis and Reading Strategy by having them answer the Apply the Skills questions. **FT**	15 min.
• Have students complete the Vocabulary Lesson and the Grammar and Style Lesson. **FT**	15 min.
• Apply students' ability to use transitions by using the Writing Lesson. **FT**	45 min. or homework
• Apply students' understanding by using one or more of the Extend Your Learning activities.	20–90 min. or homework
• Administer Selection Test A or Selection Test B. **FT**	15 min.

Resources

PRINT

Unit 3 Resources

Vocabulary Warm-up Word Lists **[L1, L2, EL]** .... p. 41
Vocabulary Warm-up Practice **[L1, L2, EL]** .... p. 42
Reading Warm-up A **[L1, L2, EL]** .... p. 43
Reading Warm-up B **[L1, L2, L3]** .... p. 44

TRANSPARENCY

Graphic Organizer Transparencies

Literary Analysis Graphic Organizer A **[L3]** .... p. 59
Literary Analysis Graphic Organizer B **[L1, L2, EL]** .... p. 60
Reading Strategy Graphic Organizer A **[L3]** .... p. 61
Reading Strategy Graphic Organizer B **[L1, L2, EL]** .... p. 62

PRINT

Reader's Notebook [L2]
Reader's Notebook: Adapted Version [L1]
Reader's Notebook: English Learner's Version [EL]

Unit 3 Resources

Literary Analysis **[L3]** .... p. 45
Reading Strategy **[L3]** .... p. 46
Vocabulary Builder **[L3]** .... p. 47

TECHNOLOGY

Listening to Literature Audio CDs [L2, EL]

PRINT

Unit 3 Resources

Grammar and Style **[L3]** .... p. 48
Support for Writing Lesson **[L3]** .... p. 49
Support for Extend Your Learning **[L3]** .... p. 50
Enrichment **[L4]** .... p. 51
Selection Test A **[L1, L2, EL]** .... pp. 52–54
Selection Test B **[L3, L4]** .... pp. 55–57

General Resources

Rubrics for Descriptive Essay **[L3]** .... pp. 63–64

TECHNOLOGY

Go Online: Research **[L3]**
Go Online: Self-test **[L3]**
***ExamView*®, Test Bank [L3]**

Choosing Resources for Differentiated Instruction

[L1] Special Needs Students
[L2] Below-Level Students
[L3] All Students
[L4] Advanced Students
[EL] English Learners

FT Fast Track Instruction: To move the lesson more quickly, use the strategies and activities identified with **FT**.

Scaffolding for Less Proficient and Advanced Students

The leveled Critical Thinking questions after selections progress in the levels of thinking required to answer them. To address the needs of your different students, you may use the (a) level questions for your less proficient students and the (b) level questions with your on-level and advanced students. The occasional (c) level questions are appropriate for your advanced students.

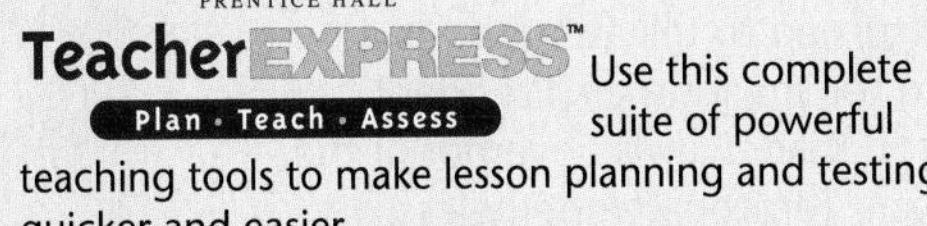

Use this complete suite of powerful teaching tools to make lesson planning and testing quicker and easier.

Use the interactive textbook (online and on CD-ROM) to make selections and activities come alive with audio and video support and interactive questions.

PRETEACH

Motivation

Show students a portion of the PBS *Nova* episode entitled "Rafting Through the Grand Canyon" (which includes several excerpts from John Wesley Powell's journal) or any other documentary program about the canyon. Then ask students to write a brief postcard from the Grand Canyon describing to a friend what they have just seen. Have volunteers share their postcard messages. Ask students to discuss how it would feel to be the first person to see such a sight. Explain that the journals that they are about to read are the literary equivalent of postcards from the American frontier.

1 Background

More About the Authors

Despite Captain Lewis's sense of failure about the expedition, historians credit Lewis and Clark with great leadership skills. They led the expedition across thousands of miles, through the lands of many different Native American peoples, and returned to tell about it. As a reward for the journey, President Jefferson made Lewis governor of the Louisiana Territory. Nonetheless, Lewis did not feel satisfied. Recent research suggests that Lewis's fatal gunshot wound in 1809 was probably self-inflicted.

As a result of his journeys to study the geology of the west, John Wesley Powell developed a profound interest in the Native Americans living on those lands. In fact, he was the first to truly study and classify Native American languages. His expertise contributed to a new government department, the U.S. Bureau of Ethnology, of which he was the first director.

Build Skills Primary Sources

1 Crossing the Great Divide • The Most Sublime Spectacle on Earth

Meriwether Lewis (1774–1809)

Meriwether Lewis, along with William Clark and a team of hearty former soldiers, completed a two-year, 8,000-mile expedition across the uncharted territory that the United States acquired in the Louisiana Purchase. Between 1804 and 1806, Lewis and Clark traveled from St. Louis up the Missouri River to its source, then across Rocky Mountain passes to the Pacific coast. When they returned to St. Louis, they brought back valuable information about the Pacific Northwest and the other lands through which they had passed.

An American Expedition Captain Lewis's efforts were sponsored by President Thomas Jefferson, for whom Lewis had served as personal secretary. Jefferson gave Lewis and his team a rigorous assignment: map a passage to the Pacific Ocean, collect scientific information about the regions he traveled, trace the boundaries of the Louisiana territory, and claim the Oregon territory for the United States.

Along his journey, Lewis documented plants, animals, and minerals. To complement Lewis's naturalist interests, Clark provided strong map skills and created detailed sketches of the regions they crossed. The men also encountered a variety of Indian nations on the frontier with whom they traded gifts and information.

Mixed Results When Meriwether Lewis returned to Washington, D.C., after the expedition had concluded, he was received as a national hero. However, because he had not found what Jefferson sought—an all-water route to the Pacific Ocean—he himself thought the journey was a failure.

John Wesley Powell (1834–1902)

As a Union soldier fightin[g] in the Civil War, John Wesley Powell lost an arm at the Battle of Shiloh. Despite this injury, he was the first to navigate and chart the Colorado River and the Grand Canyo[n].

Exploring the Grand Canyon Powell was a geologist who conducted a daring and dangerou[s] three-month journey on the Colorado River in 1869. Financed by the Smithsonian Institution and Congress, Powell led a party of ten men in four boats. In a reflective moment before he entered the canyon, Powell described the experience ahead of him as "an unknown distance yet to run; an unknown river yet to explore." Entering the Grand Canyon by boat, the explorers faced raging rapids, towering waterfalls, and dangerously sharp rock formations. Once in the canyon, Powell's expedition party split up. Thos[e] who had become too terrified of the river went overland at "Separation Rapids" and eventually perished. Powell and the others who remained o[n] the river survived and completed the expedition.

An Early Conservationist Later, in other expeditions, Powell surveyed the Rocky Mountains and the canyons of the Green River. In the 1870s, he directed a federal geographic survey of western lands in the public domain, urging the government to develop plans for using the land. Powell had a profound understanding of the American West, and he warned the government of the hazards of economic exploitation of the region. He spent the rest of his life trying to communicate his message of responsible development of that magnificent bu[t] arid, unpredictable, and fragile land.

Preview

Connecting to the Literature

If you have ever had an outdoor adventure while backpacking or mountain climbing, you know how exciting it is to experience the power of nature. Imagine what it would have been like to chart new territory like the adventurers who blazed a trail across the western frontier.

Literary Analysis

Description

Description in writing captures the physical sensations of sight, sound, smell, taste, and touch. Consider this example from Powell's journal:

> But form and color do not exhaust all the divine qualities of the Grand Canyon. It is the land of music. The river thunders in perpetual roar . . .

Look for similar examples of descriptive language that bring scenes to life in these selections. Use a chart like the one shown to record descriptive details.

Descriptions	
Sight	
Sound	
Smell	
Taste	
Touch	

Comparing Literary Works

Both of the men who wrote these selections were working under government commissions to explore uncharted lands. In writing these journals, both explorers sought to describe the amazing sights and experiences of their expeditions to readers in cities and towns far away. While their motives for writing were similar, their styles differ greatly. As you read, note the effects of each writer's **style**—word choice, level of formality, and imagery—on your perception of his experiences.

Reading Strategy

Noting Spatial Relationships

Noting spatial relationships as you read can help to clarify the size, distance, and location of the features being described. Using this information will help you form an accurate mental picture of the subject. Note the spatial relationships in these selections to gain a better understanding of the features they describe.

Vocabulary Builder

conspicuous (kən spik′ yo͞o əs) *adj.* obvious; easy to see or perceive (p. 300)

sublime (sə blīm′) *adj.* inspiring awe or admiration through grandeur or beauty (p. 301)

labyrinth (lab′ ə rinth′) *n.* intricate network of winding passages; maze (p. 301)

excavated (eks′ kə vāt′ id) *v.* dug out; made a hole (p. 301)

demarcation (dē′ mär kā′ shən) *n.* separation (p. 302)

multifarious (mul′ tə far′ ē əs) *adj.* having many parts; diverse (p. 304)

multitudinous (mul′ tə to͞od′ ′n əs) *adj.* numerous (p. 304)

2 Literary Analysis
Description

- Tell students that as they read these journal entries, they will focus on description, writing that captures the physical sensations of an experience or setting.
- Have a volunteer read aloud the excerpted text from Powell's journal. Help students identify sensory words in the excerpt.
- Use the instruction for Comparing Literary Works to prepare students to appreciate the writers' styles in two very different journal excerpts.
- Give students a copy of **Literary Analysis Graphic Organizer A,** p. 59 in ***Graphic Organizer Transparencies,*** to use as they read the journals. Model its use by placing details from the Powell excerpt in the correct place.

3 Reading Strategy
Noting Spatial Relationships

- Remind students that noting spatial relationships can help them track events and visualize settings.
- Draw students' attention to the three types of spatial relationships mentioned: size, distance, and location. Remind them to pay attention to all three as they read.
- Tell students to jot down spatial relationship clues under the headings *Size, Distance,* and *Location.*

Vocabulary Builder

- Pronounce each vocabulary word for students, and read the definitions as a class. Have students identify any words with which they are familiar.

Differentiated Instruction
Solutions for All Learners

Support for Special Needs Students
Have students complete the **Preview** and **Build Skills** pages for these selections in the ***Reader's Notebook: Adapted Version.*** These pages provide a selection summary, an abbreviated presentation of the reading and literary skills, and the graphic organizer on the **Build Skills** page in the student book.

Support for Less Proficient Readers
Have students complete the **Preview** and **Build Skills** pages for these selections in the ***Reader's Notebook.*** These pages provide a selection summary, an abbreviated presentation of the reading and literary skills, and the graphic organizer on the **Build Skills** page in the student book.

Support for English Learners
Have students complete the **Preview** and **Build Skills** pages for these selections in the ***Reader's Notebook: English Learner's Version.*** These pages provide a selection summary, an abbreviated presentation of the skills, additional contextual vocabulary, and the graphic organizer on the **Build Skills** page in the student book.

TEACH

Learning Modalities
Musical/Rhythmic Learners

Students can enhance their appreciation of Powell's journal entry by listening to music composed to celebrate the Grand Canyon. For example, they can listen to *Grand Canyon Suite* by Ferdi Grofé or *Canyon Trilogy* by the Navajo-Ute flutist Carlos Nakai.

❶ About the Selection

Lewis kept an intermittent but very detailed, descriptive, and informative journal of his expedition. Here he describes one of the expedition's many interactions with Native Americans. It is characteristic of Lewis's efforts to persuade Native Americans of the powers of his government and of the advantages of cooperating with him in his mission to reach the Pacific.

❷ Humanities

Lewis and Clark With Sacagawea at the Great Falls of the Missouri, by Olaf Seltzer

This painting depicts a scene that took place some time during the spring of 1805. Sacagawea, a Shoshone teenager, served as a guide to Lewis and Clark. The fourth figure, York, was Clark's slave and lifelong companion. Use this question for discussion:

- If you were Lewis, how might you describe the landscape in your journal?
  Possible response: Students may mention the barren, treeless, rugged landscape; the brown, rocky bluffs; and the white mesas far in the distance that suggest a desertlike terrain.

❷ Critical Viewing

Answer: Students should note that the figures in the painting appear to be at ease with one another. The text, which describes the explorers' friendship with and dependence on the Native Americans, is reflected in the painting.

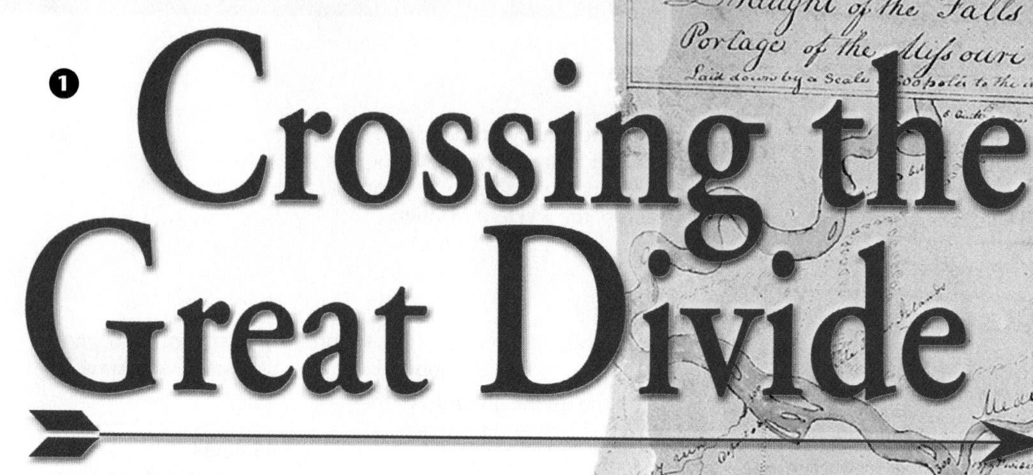

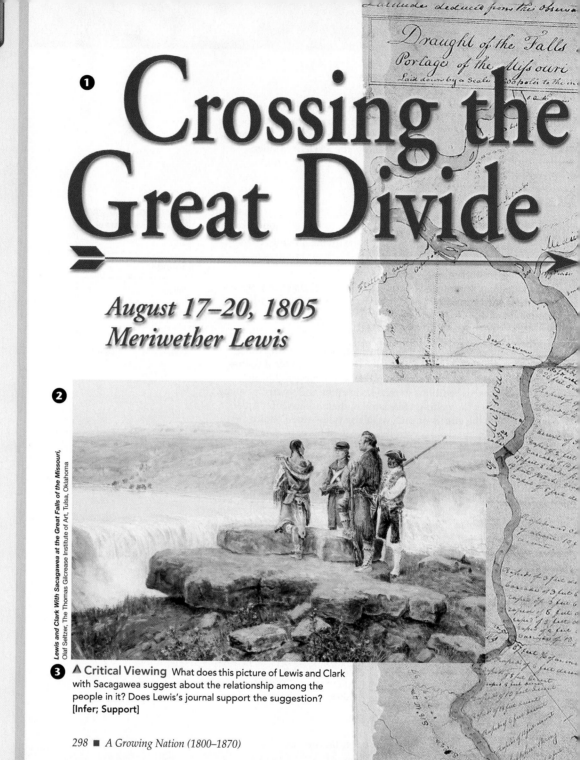

❶ Crossing the Great Divide

August 17–20, 1805
Meriwether Lewis

❷

Lewis and Clark With Sacagawea at the Great Falls of the Missouri, Olaf Seltzer, The Thomas Gilcrease Institute of Art, Tulsa, Oklahoma

❸ ▲ **Critical Viewing** What does this picture of Lewis and Clark with Sacagawea suggest about the relationship among the people in it? Does Lewis's journal support the suggestion? **[Infer; Support]**

Differentiated Instruction Solutions for All Learners

Accessibility at a Glance

	Crossing the Great Divide	The Most Sublime Spectacle
Context	Journal of Lewis and Clark	Canyon
Language	Simple sentence structure	Detailed descriptions; long sentences
Concept Level	Accessible (Lewis's negotiations)	Historic description of the Grand Canyon
Literary Merit	Primary source: journal	Primary source: journal
Lexile	1450	1280
Overall Rating	Average	Average

Background In 1803, the United States doubled the amount of territory it controlled with a single purchase of land from the French. Looking for money to finance its wars against other European nations, France sold land to the United States for a total price of $15 million—less than three cents an acre. Known as the Louisiana Purchase, the acquisition began an era of westward expansion that lasted for nearly a century. These accounts detail what the explorers found in the newly purchased territory.

Saturday, August 17th, 1805

This morning I arose very early and dispatched Drewyer and the Indian down the river. Sent Shields to hunt. I made McNeal cook the remainder of our meat which afforded a slight breakfast for ourselves and the Chief. Drewyer had been gone about 2 hours when an Indian who had straggled some little distance down the river returned and reported that the white men were coming, that he had seen them just below. They all appeared transported with joy, and the chief repeated his fraternal hug. I felt quite as much gratified at this information as the Indians appeared to be. Shortly after Capt. Clark arrived with the Interpreter Charbono, and the Indian woman, who proved to be a sister of the Chief Cameahwait. The meeting of those was really affecting, particularly between Sah-ca-ga-we-ah and an Indian woman, who had been taken prisoner at the same time with her, and who had afterwards escaped from the Minnetares and rejoined her nation. At noon the canoes arrived, and we had the satisfaction once more to find ourselves all together, with a flattering prospect of being able to

◀ **Critical Viewing** What do visuals like maps and illustrations add to the narrative of exploration accounts? **[Interpret]**

❹ ▲ **Critical Viewing**
What does the placement and size of this sketch in Clark's journal reveal about his purpose in creating it? **[Infer]**

❺ 
Reading Check
What information does the Indian bring to Lewis and his group?

❹ Critical Viewing

Answer: The size of the sketch suggests that Clark wished to make the image large enough to show details. The placement of the image inside the journal's text reveals that he needed to use each piece of paper fully, since he could not obtain more.

❺ Reading Check

Answer: He has seen a small part of their group, including both Capt. Clark and his interpreters, on the way back to the main camp.

Differentiated Instruction Solutions for All Learners

Vocabulary for Special Needs Students
Point out that Lewis's writing—even in a journal—is more formal than most modern writing. Draw students' attention to words such as *gratified,* which simply means "pleased." Help students work through the text on p. 299 word by word to find synonyms for challenging terms. Encourage the use of a dictionary and thesaurus.

Vocabulary for Less Proficient Readers
Help students identify familiar words used in unfamiliar ways. Examples include *affecting* ("emotionally moving") and *flattering* ("favorable"). Have volunteers read aloud the sentences from p. 299 that contain each word. Guide students to use context clues to determine the meanings of each usage.

Vocabulary for Advanced Readers
Have students identify vocabulary on this page that reflects Lewis's era either through archaic word usage or especial formality. Then challenge students to list as many synonyms or paraphrases for these words or phrases as they can. Have students share these keys to comprehension with the class.

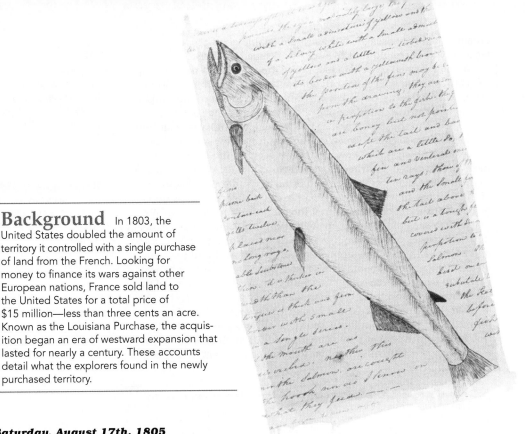

❻ Reading Strategy
Noting Spatial Relationships

- Read the bracketed passage with students.
- **Ask** students the Reading Strategy question: Which words help readers gain a clearer picture of the campsite?
  Answer: Words such as *just below, Lard. side, here, on shore,* and *in the ground* help readers get a clear picture.

➤ **Monitor Progress:** Have students sketch the scene described in the bracketed text, identifying the words and details they used to help them determine the spatial relationships between the objects mentioned in the passage.

ASSESS

Answers

1. **Possible response:** Some students might observe that Lewis disguised his real motives.
2. (a) He is pleased and relieved.
   (b) He now has hopes of obtaining enough horses to continue the voyage by land if necessary.
3. (a) He tells them his goal is to improve trade routes for the Indians' benefit.
   (b) **Possible response:** Lewis is not being completely candid. Lewis hints at how he misled the Indians when he says that he "gave them as a reason . . . to examine and find out a more direct way to bring merchandise to them."
4. (a) He told them to expect trade, defense, and comfort.
   (b) **Possible response:** He wants them to understand their dependence on the U.S. for certain goods, and to appreciate the government's strength. Thus, he hopes to obtain their help.
5. (a) He expected friendliness, horses, guidance through unfamiliar territory, supplies.
   (b) **Possible response:** He is very persuasive in his bid to convince the Native Americans to cooperate.

Go Online Author Link For additional information about Meriwether Lewis, have students type in the Web Code, then select L from the alphabet, and then select Meriwether Lewis.

obtain as many horses shortly as would enable us to prosecute our voyage by land should that by water be deemed unadvisable.

❻ We now formed our camp just below the junction of the forks on the Lard. side[1] in a level smooth bottom covered with a fine turf of greensward. Here we unloaded our canoes and arranged our baggage on shore; formed a canopy of one of our large sails and planted some willow brush in the ground to form a shade for the Indians to sit under while we spoke to them, which we thought it best to do this evening. Accordingly about 4 P.M. we called them together and through the medium of Labuish, Charbono and Sah-ca-ga-we-ah, we communicated to them fully the objects which had brought us into this distant part of the country, in which we took care to make them a conspicuous object of our own good wishes and the care of our government. We made them sensible of their dependence on the will of our government for every species of merchandise as well for their defense and comfort; and apprised them of the strength of our government and its friendly dispositions towards them. We also gave them as a reason why we wished to penetrate the country as far as the ocean to the west of them was to examine and find out a more direct way to bring merchandise to them. That as no trade could be carried on with them before our return to our homes that it was mutually advantageous to them as well as to ourselves that they should render us such aids as they had it in their power to furnish in order to hasten our voyage and of course our return home.

1. **Lard. side** abbreviation for larboard, the port side of a ship. From their perspective, they camped on the left side of the river.

Reading Strategy
Noting Spatial Relationships Which words help readers gain a clearer picture of the campsite?

Vocabulary Builder
conspicuous (kən spik′ yo͞o əs) *adj.* obvious; easy to see or perceive

Critical Reading

1. **Respond:** What did you think of the way Lewis negotiated with the Indians? Explain.
2. **(a) Recall:** How did Lewis feel about being reunited with his party? **(b) Analyze:** What were his reasons for feeling as he did?
3. **(a) Recall:** What did Lewis tell the Indians was the reason for the expedition? **(b) Infer:** Was he being candid in his explanation? Explain.
4. **(a) Recall:** What did Lewis tell the Indians to expect from the United States government? **(b) Speculate:** Why do you think he told the Indians the things he did?
5. **(a) Generalize:** What did Lewis expect from the Indians? **(b) Evaluate:** How would you rate Lewis as a negotiator?

Go Online Author Link
For: More about Meriwether Lewis
Visit: www.PHSchool.com
Web Code: ere-9306

Enrichment

A Formidable Landscape

In 1804, President Thomas Jefferson and his advisers knew almost nothing about the lands Lewis was to explore. For one thing, they thought that there was an all-water route to the Pacific. For another, they thought Lewis and Clark might encounter mastodons. Geographically, all they really knew was the latitude and longitude of the mouth of the Columbia River, St. Louis, and the Mandan peoples' villages along the Missouri River. With so much yet to discover, Jefferson made choices. For example, he chose not to seek gold or silver. Instead, he instructed Lewis to focus on the possibility of establishing trade with the Native Americans.

7

The Most Sublime Spectacle on Earth

John Wesley Powell

The Grand Canyon of the Colorado is a canyon composed of many canyons. It is a composite of thousands, of tens of thousands, of gorges. In like manner, each wall of the canyon is a composite structure, a wall composed of many walls, but never a repetition. Every one of these almost innumerable gorges is a world of beauty in itself. In the Grand Canyon there are thousands of gorges like that below Niagara Falls, and there are a thousand Yosemites. Yet all these canyons unite to form one grand canyon, the most sublime spectacle on the earth. Pluck up Mt. Washington by the roots to the level of the sea and drop it headfirst into the Grand Canyon, and the dam will not force its waters over the walls. Pluck up the Blue Ridge and hurl it into the Grand Canyon, and it will not fill it.

The carving of the Grand Canyon is the work of rains and rivers. The vast labyrinth of canyon by which the plateau region drained by the Colorado is dissected is also the work of waters. Every river has excavated its own gorge and every creek has excavated its gorge. When a shower comes in this land, the rills carve canyons—but a little at each storm; and though storms are far apart and the heavens above are cloudless for most of the days of the year, still, years are plenty in the ages, and an intermittent rill called to life by a shower can do much work in centuries of centuries.

Vocabulary Builder

sublime (sə blīm′) *adj.* inspiring admiration

labyrinth (lab′ ə rinth) *n.* network of passages; maze

excavated (eks′ kə vāt′ id) *v.* dug out; made a hole

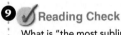

9 **Reading Check**

What is "the most sublime spectacle" on earth?

7 About the Selection

In this excerpt, Powell provides a rich description of the grandeur of the Grand Canyon. He writes of its size, the many different layers and formations of rock, its colors, and its shapes. In his attempt to describe its majesty to people who have never seen anything like it, Powell admits to the inadequacy of words.

8 Literary Analysis

Description

- After students read the text on this page, have them reread it, looking for ways in which Powell uses description to help readers appreciate the size and grandeur of the Grand Canyon.
- **Ask** students to identify the descriptive strategies that Powell uses to help readers appreciate the size and grandeur of the Grand Canyon.
  Answer: Powell uses relative sizes, for example, by saying "thousands, tens of thousands, of gorges"; he uses recognizable landmarks such as Niagara Falls to provide benchmarks for readers; he uses vivid sensory details to paint a picture of the place for readers.

Monitor Progress: Have students complete the **Literary Analysis Graphic Organizer**, p. 59 in ***Graphic Organizer Transparencies,*** with details from these paragraphs to explore the sensory imagery that Powell uses to describe the Grand Canyon.

9 Reading Check

Answer: The Grand Canyon is the "most sublime spectacle" on Earth.

Differentiated Instruction Solutions for All Learners

Background for Less Proficient Readers

Increase students' comprehension by providing the following context: Powell is attempting a written description of a vast and constantly changing landscape that his original readers have never seen. To convey his awestruck impression, he invites the reader to imagine various details of geologic phenomena, sights, and sounds. He imparts information by giving readers statistics, comparisons, and detailed descriptions of colors, sounds, and movements. Help students access this multilayered descriptive text by suggesting that they take time to imagine the visual images and the sounds the author provides. Direct students to specific descriptions on this page, such as the comparison of the Canyon to familiar landmarks or the image of water carving out gorges a little at a time. Help students practice visualizing.

10 Literature in Context
The Hudson River School

Also known as Romantic Realists, the artists of the Hudson River school loved the untainted and untamed American wilderness. They combined detailed panoramic landscapes with the moral messages found in the literature of the time. The style of the Hudson River artists led to the creation of the National Academy of Design. An 1836 exhibit held by the academy was praised by writers such as William Cullen Bryant and James Fenimore Cooper.

Connect to Literature Have students look carefully at the painting and describe it. **Ask** them what aspects of Powell's description are visible in it.
Possible response: The striking colors, the connection of the mountains to the clouds, and the sense of enormity and depth appear in the painting. The painting and the journal seem to convey a similar sense of awe.

11 Reading Strategy
Noting Spatial Relationships

- Invite a volunteer to read aloud the bracketed passage. Urge students to jot down spatial word clues as they hear them.
- **Ask** students to identify the words or phrases that help them visualize the rock formations and other geologic features of the grand vista Powell describes.
  Possible responses: *below, the foundation, crowned, covered, from below, seem to graduate, a portion, vast, wall to wall, spanning, blended, vast.*

10 The erosion represented in the canyons, although vast, is but a small part of the great erosion of the region, for between the cliffs blocks have been carried away far superior in magnitude to those necessary to fill the canyons. Probably there is no portion of the whole region from which there have not been more than a thousand feet degraded, and there are districts from which more than 30,000 feet of rock have been carried away. Altogether, there is a district of country more than 200,000 square miles in extent from which on the average more than 6,000 feet have been eroded. Consider a rock 200,000 square miles in extent and a mile in thickness, against which the clouds have hurled their storms and beat it into sands and the rills have carried the sands into the creeks and the creeks have carried them into the rivers and the Colorado has carried them into the sea. We think of the mountains as forming clouds about their brows, but the clouds have formed the mountains. Great continental blocks are upheaved from beneath the sea by internal geologic forces that fashion the earth. Then the wandering clouds, the tempest-bearing clouds, the rainbow-decked clouds, with mighty power and with wonderful skill, carve out valleys and canyons and fashion hills and cliffs and mountains. The clouds are the artists sublime.

11 In winter some of the characteristics of the Grand Canyon are emphasized. The black gneiss[1] below, the variegated quartzite, and the green or alcove sandstone form the foundation for the mighty red wall. The banded sandstone entablature is crowned by the tower limestone. In winter this is covered with snow. Seen from below, these changing elements seem to graduate into the heavens, and no plane of demarcation between wall and blue firmament[2] can be seen. The heavens constitute a portion of the facade and mount into a vast dome from wall to wall, spanning the Grand canyon with empyrean blue. So the earth and the heavens are blended in one vast structure.

When the clouds play in the canyon, as they often do in the rainy season, another set of effects is produced. Clouds creep out of canyons and wind into other canyons. The heavens seem to be alive, not moving as move the heavens over a plain, in one direction with the wind, but following the multiplied courses of these gorges. In this manner the little clouds seem to be individualized, to have wills and souls of their own, and to be going on diverse errands—a vast assemblage of self-willed clouds, faring here and there, intent upon purposes hidden in their own breasts. In the imagination the clouds belong to the sky, and when they are in the canyon the skies come down into

1. **gneiss** (nīs) *n.* coarse-grained metamorphic rock resembling granite, consisting of alternating layers of minerals such as feldspar, quartz, and mica and having a banded appearance.
2. **firmament** (fʉrm′ ə mənt) *n.* sky.

10 Literature in Context

Humanities Connection

The Hudson River School

Writers and explorers were not the only ones who responded to the beauty of the American landscape—artists were inspired by it as well. In 1825, British-born American painter Thomas Cole founded the Hudson River School, a group of artists who painted strikingly beautiful images of the Hudson River Valley and America's wilderness and western frontier. These paintings—such as the one shown on page 303—featured the effects of sunsets and dramatic weather on mountains, ravines, and rivers. Cole and his fellow artists searched for exciting and uniquely American images and helped to create an artistic identity for the young nation.

Connect to the Literature

The Hudson River School painter Thomas Moran accompanied Powell on his second expedition to the Grand Canyon in 1873. Do you think Moran's painting on page 303 conveys the same tone as Powell's description? Explain.

Vocabulary Builder

demarcation (dē′ mär kā′ shən) *n.* separation

Enrichment

The Grand Canyon

Located in northwest Arizona, the Grand Canyon is nearly one mile deep, up to 18 miles wide, and 277 miles long.

Around 6 million years ago, the Colorado River began carving its way through the rock to form the Grand Canyon. The warping of Earth's crust steepened the river's path, increasing the water's velocity and volume. The rushing river, which carried large amounts of abrasive mud, sand, and gravel, wore away the soft rock, cutting sharp, deep channels. The almost rainless climate preserved the steep pitch of the canyon walls, which otherwise would have been softened or even entirely eroded by rain wash, leaving only gentle hills behind.

The layers of rock in the canyon's walls contain a historical record of geological events. The oldest rocks at the bottom of the canyon may be as many as four billion years old.

Grand Canyon With Rainbow, 1912 (detail), Thomas Moran, Fine Arts Museum of San Francisco

▲ **Critical Viewing** Compare Powell's description with the painter's interpretation of the same natural wonder. **[Compare]**

⓬ Humanities

Grand Canyon With Rainbow, by Thomas Moran

English immigrant Thomas Moran traveled to Yellowstone Park in 1871 and—like Powell—was captivated by its natural beauty. In this powerful landscape painting, Moran captures the vivid colors and beauty of the Grand Canyon. Use this question for discussion:

- Would Powell have approved of this painting as an illustration for his journal passage? Explain. **Possible response:** He probably would have approved of the painting because it captures the striking colors and forms that he describes in such detail.

⓭ Critical Viewing

Answer: Students may respond that the painting vividly captures the beautiful colors, forms, and unusual cloud formations Powell describes. The painting does not, however, convey how the scene changes under different conditions, nor does it convey the "music" of the canyon's waters—both of which are important parts of Powell's written description of the Grand Canyon.

14 Vocabulary Builder

The Latin prefix *multi-*

- Call students' attention to the word *multifarious* and to its definition. Let students know that the prefix *multi-* derives from the Latin word *multus* meaning "much" or "many."
- **Ask** students to volunteer words with which they are familiar that begin with this prefix.
  Possibilities include: multiple, multilingual, multimedia, multimillionaire, and multicultural.
- List student words on the chalkboard as they are mentioned. When the list is complete, erase the prefix *multi-* from the words. Guide students to recognize how the addition of the prefix adds the idea of "many" to nouns.

15 Literary Analysis

Description

- Read aloud for students the bracketed paragraph.
- Tell students to listen for words and phrases that appeal to the visual and auditory senses.
- **Ask** students the Literary Analysis Question: Which descriptive details in this paragraph appeal to the reader's senses?
  Possible response: Students may mention the colors of rocks, the blue sky and clouds, and the sounds of water rushing, rippling, and plunging. Students may also mention that a musical metaphor describes the relationship between the profile of the canyon and the sky.

16 Reading Check

Answer: Powell hears many sounds of nature in the Grand Canyon.

the gorges and cling to the cliffs and lift them up to immeasurable heights, for the sky must still be far away. Thus they lend infinity to the walls.

The wonders of the Grand Canyon cannot be adequately represented in symbols of speech, nor by speech itself. The resources of the graphic art are taxed beyond their powers in attempting to portray its features. Language and illustration combined must fail. The elements that unite to make the Grand Canyon the most sublime spectacle in nature are
14 multifarious and exceedingly diverse. The Cyclopean forms which result from the sculpture of tempests through ages too long for man to compute, are wrought into endless details, to describe which would be a task equal in magnitude to that of describing the stars of the heavens or the multitudinous beauties of the forest with its traceries of foliage presented by oak and pine and poplar, by beech and linden and hawthorn, by tulip and lily and rose, by fern and moss and lichen. Besides the elements of form, there are elements of color, for here the colors of the heavens are rivaled by the colors of the rocks. The rainbow is not more replete with hues. But form and color do not exhaust all the divine qualities of the Grand Canyon. It is the land of music. The river thunders in perpetual roar, swelling in floors of music when the storm gods play upon the rocks and fading away in soft and low murmurs when the infinite blue of heaven is unveiled. With the melody of the great tide rising and falling, swelling and vanishing forever, other melo-
15 dies are heard in the gorges of the lateral[3] canyons, while the waters plunge in the rapids among the rocks or leap in great cataracts. Thus the Grand Canyon is a land of song. Mountains of music swell in the rivers, hills of music billow in the creeks, and meadows of music murmur in the rills that ripple over the rocks. Altogether it is a symphony of multitudinous melodies. All this is the music of waters. The adamant foundations of the earth have been wrought into a sublime harp, upon which the clouds of the heavens play with mighty tempests or with gentle showers.

The glories and the beauties of form, color, and sound unite in the Grand Canyon—forms unrivaled even by the mountains, colors that vie with sunsets, and sounds that span the diapason[4] from tempest to tinkling raindrop, from cataract to bubbling fountain. But more: it is a vast district of country. Were it a valley plain it would make a state. It can be seen only in parts from hour to hour and from day to day and from week to week and from month to month. A year scarcely suffices to see it all. It has infinite variety, and no part is ever duplicated. Its colors, though many and complex at any instant, change with the ascending and declining sun; lights and shadows appear and vanish with the passing clouds, and the changing seasons mark their passage in changing colors. You cannot see the Grand Canyon in one view, as 16

Vocabulary Builder

multifarious (mul′ tə far′ ē əs) *adj.* having many parts; diverse

multitudinous (mul′ tə to͞od′ ’n əs) *adj.* numerous

Literary Analysis

Description Which descriptive details in this paragraph appeal to the reader's senses?

Reading Check

Why does Powell describe the Grand Canyon as the "land of song"?

3. **lateral** (lat′ ər əl) *adj.* of, from, or at the sides.
4. **diapason** (dī′ ə pā′ zən) *n.* entire range of a musical instrument.

Differentiated Instruction

Solutions for All Learners

Background for Less Proficient Readers

Help students build background for reading Powell's journal. Read the Enrichment information on TE p. 302 to students, answering any questions they have. Then model for students how to use the Cause-and-Effect Flowchart from ***Graphic Organizer Transparencies,*** p. 305 to track the canyon's formation.

Background for English Learners

Distribute the Cause-and-Effect Flowchart in ***Graphic Organizer Transparencies,*** p. 305. Instruct students to enter "Formation of the Grand Canyon" under "Major Event." Then, have students carefully reread pages 302–303, identifying causes of the formation of the canyon and entering them in the appropriate boxes.

Background for Advanced Readers

Have students look into current ecological issues related to the Grand Canyon, specifically, the effects of the Glen Canyon Dam. Provide students with the Cause-and-Effect Flowchart from ***Graphic Organizer Transparencies,*** p. 305, as a framework in which to organize their findings.

if it were a changeless spectacle from which a curtain might be lifted, but to see it you have to toil from month to month through its labyrinths. It is a region more difficult to traverse than the Alps or the Himalayas, but if strength and courage are sufficient for the task, by a year's toil a concept of sublimity can be obtained never again to be equaled on the hither side of Paradise.

Critical Reading

1. **(a) Respond:** Why do you think Powell says much about the Grand Canyon but almost nothing about his journey? **(b) Speculate:** What do you think that choice says about him?
2. **(a) Recall:** List three aspects of the Grand Canyon that Powell describes at length. **(b) Analyze:** To what senses does Powell appeal in those descriptions?
3. **(a) Recall:** Powell describes two special visual effects that are produced seasonally. What are they? **(b) Evaluate:** What is effective about the descriptions?
4. **(a) Interpret:** What point does Powell make when he writes that, in portraying the Grand Canyon, "Language and illustration combined must fail"?
   (b) Draw Conclusions: What do you think it meant to Powell to explore the Grand Canyon?
5. **(a) Compare and Contrast:** What might a painting of the Grand Canyon show that a written description cannot?
   (b) Compare and Contrast: What can a description of the Grand Canyon or any setting reveal that a painting cannot?
6. **(a) Assess:** If you were reading this description without any prior knowledge of the Grand Canyon, what information and insight would Powell's words effectively convey? **(b) Criticize:** What further questions about the Grand Canyon do you think you might have?

For: More about John Wesley Powell
Visit: www.PHSchool.com
Web Code: ere-9307

ASSESS

Answers

1. **Possible responses:** (a) Powell was driven by the need to make the reader understand the scope and magnificence of the Grand Canyon. (b) He was inspired by the sight of the Grand Canyon.
2. (a) He describes the form, color, and sounds of the canyon.
   (b) He appeals to sight and to hearing.
3. (a) One effect is the blending of canyon walls into sky in the winter; the other is the effect of clouds playing in the canyons during the rainy season.
   (b) Powell effectively conveys the varied sights, sounds, and ever-changing quality of these features of the Grand Canyon.
4. (a) The details that make up the beauty of the Grand Canyon are too many and too varied for language or illustration to adequetly describe. (b) Powell's journey seems to have been an awe-inspiring experience.
5. (a) **Possible response:** A painting can capture the colors, the forms, and the play of light and shadow in a way that words cannot. (b) A description can convey changes that take place over time, as well as the sounds that are part of the Grand Canyon experience.
6. **Possible responses:** (a) They would effectively convey the size and grandeur of the Grand Canyon, as well as its varied physical features. (b) What kind of animals live there? What peoples, if any, make their home along the river's edge?

Go Online Author Link For additional information about John Wesley Powell, have students type in the Web Code, then select P from the alphabet, and then select John Wesley Powell.

Answers

1. (a) Students should choose passages rich in descriptive imagery. (b) Examples should include vivid sensory details and clear spatial orientation.
2. Students should identify a passage that describes Lewis's camp.
3. **Possible response:** Lowell occasionally uses phrases or incomplete sentences, in true journal format, while Powell writes more formally in longer and more complex sentences.
4. Lewis seems more focused on portraying a view of himself while Powell wants only to describe his surroundings.
5. His style is factual; it conveys information rather than emotions.
6. Students may find Powell's account more effective because of its detailed description.
7. The erosion of the region is greater. Powell states that one is greater than the other.
8. **Possible responses:** Description: Powell's description of the behavior of clouds in the Grand Canyon during rain. Spatial Relationships: Out of canyons, into other canyons, over a plain, in one direction, multiplied courses, vast, here and there, the skies come down, lift them up, far away, infinity. In My Own Words: During the rainy season, the canyon is filled with clouds that spread into all its crevices. Because clouds are usually seen in the sky, this image of the canyon makes it look as if the sky had come down into the canyon and as if its walls stretched upward forever.

   Another sample answer can be found on **Reading Strategy Graphic Organizer B**, p. 62 in *Graphic Organizer Transparencies*.
9. **Possible response:** Antarctica is largely unexplored, as are many parts of the ocean. Both these places merit exploration.

Apply the Skills

Crossing the Great Divide • The Most Sublime Spectacle on Earth

Literary Analysis

Description

1. **(a)** Choose three passages of **description** in "The Most Sublime Spectacle on Earth." **(b)** What makes each one effective?
2. Lewis is not as descriptive as Powell, but he does include some descriptive elements in his writing. Identify a passage in Lewis's journal that helps readers see his camp.

Comparing Literary Works

3. Based on these accounts, what differences do you see in the writers' **styles**?
4. Judging by the amount of description each writer includes, what would you guess is the purpose of each piece? Support your answer with references from the selections.
5. Considering Lewis's word choice, tone, and level of formality, how would you categorize his style of writing?
6. Which of the two accounts do you find more effective, and why? Support your answer with evidence from the selections.

Reading Strategy

Noting Spatial Relationships

7. **Noting relationships** of space and size as Powell describes them, determine which is greater—the erosion of the canyons or the erosion of the region? Explain.
8. Using a chart like the one shown, note details that indicate size and spatial relationships of the Grand Canyon. Then, describe these relationships in your own words.

Description	Spatial Relationships	In My Own Words

Extend Understanding

9. **Social Studies Connection:** Where are some unexplored areas in the world today? Upon which of these do you think we should focus the most attention? Why?

QuickReview

Description is language that uses details that appeal to the senses.

A writer's **style** includes such elements as word choice, tone, level of formality, figurative language, imagery, and sentence structure.

To **note spatial relationships**, pay attention to the description of sizes, distances, and locations of features.

For: Self-test
Visit: www.PHSchool.com
Web Code: era-6303

Go Online Assessment Students may use the **Self-test** to prepare for **Selection Test A** or **Selection Test B**.

Build Language Skills

Vocabulary Lesson

Word Analysis: Latin Prefix *multi-*

The word *multitudinous* contains the common Latin prefix *multi-*, which means "many" or "much." The word "multitudinous" means "numerous." Write definitions for each of the following words.

1. multiply
2. multicultural
3. multimedia

Spelling Strategy

In general, use *-tion* to spell the sound of *shun*, as in *portion*. Use *-sion* to spell the sound of *zhun*, as in *erosion*. Complete each word with: *-tion* or *-sion*.

1. *vi__*
2. *explo__*
3. *examina__*
4. *situa__*
5. *dimen__*
6. *explana__*

Vocabulary Builder: Word Meanings

Review the vocabulary list on p. 297. Then, answer the following questions. Explain each answer, referring to the meaning of italicized word in the question.

1. Are *conspicuous* omissions easy to find?
2. Is a graduation-day rainstorm a *sublime* experience?
3. How would you prepare before entering an unexplored *labyrinth*?
4. What tools are used to *excavate* a sandbox?
5. Is a fence a sign of *demarcation*?
6. Is your wardrobe *multifarious*?
7. Are the inhabitants of an anthill *multitudinous*?

Grammar and Style Lesson

Participial Phrases

A **participial phrase** consists of a participle (a verb form used as an adjective to modify a noun or pronoun) and its complements and modifiers. Participial phrases can add details to descriptions.

Past Participle: The Grand Canyon is a canyon composed of many canyons. (modifies *canyon*)

Practice Identify each participial phrase, and explain the word it modifies.

1. Sights described by Powell can be seen today.
2. Lewis's expedition would fail without the woman known as Sacagawea.
3. Begun in 1804, the expedition to explore uncharted territories of the United States took two years.
4. Deeply moved by what he saw, Powell produced a poetic description.
5. Powell's description of the Grand Canyon, published years after his visit, set off a wave of tourism.

Writing Application Write a paragraph describing something that you recently witnessed. In your writing, include sensory images and at least three participial phrases.

WG Prentice Hall Writing and Grammar Connection: Chapter 19, Section 2

Assessment Practice

Make Inferences and Generalizations

Many tests ask students to make inferences about implied information. After students read "Crossing the Great Divide," ask: Why does Lewis emphasize the U.S. government's "friendly disposition" toward the Indians in his meeting with them?

- **A** He wants them to help his expedition.
- **B** He wants to join their community.
- **C** He wants them to join the United States.
- **D** He wants to take their land.

(For more practice, see *Standardized Test Preparation Workbook*, p. 18.)

B, C, and *D* are not supported by the passage. Lewis explains that if the Indians help the explorers reach the Pacific Ocean and then return home, the government will provide them with many benefits. Thus, choice *A* is correct.

EXTEND/ASSESS

Answers

1 Vocabulary Lesson

Word Analysis

1. increase something many times
2. having or characterized by many different cultures
3. a combination of many different types of media, such as television, radio, print, and photography

Spelling Strategy

1. vision
2. explosion
3. examination
4. situation
5. dimension
6. explanation

Vocabulary Builder

1. Yes, because they are obvious.
2. It is not, because a storm might delay celebrations.
3. One should have a compass, utensils to make a map, and enough food to last for some time.
4. A bucket and a shovel are usually used to dig out a sandbox.
5. Yes it is, because it clearly defines and separates adjoining spaces.
6. Yes; I like to wear many different types of clothes.
7. Yes, anthills are occupied by swarms of ants.

2 Grammar and Style Lesson

1. "described by Powell"/*sights*
2. "known as Sacagawea"/*woman*
3. "Begun in 1804"/*expedition*
4. "deeply moved by what he saw"/ *Powell*
5. "published years after his visit"/ *description*

Writing Application

Paragraphs should be free of major mechanical errors and should contain at least three participial phrases.

❸ Writing Lesson

- To guide students in writing this description, give them the **Support for Writing Lesson,** p. 49 in ***Unit 3 Resources.***
- Reread a portion of Powell's description to remind students of its descriptive elements.
- Offer students the scene in **Fine Art Transparencies,** Volume 1, Art Transparency 2, as an alternative visual stimulus or provide books depicting the world's great natural wonders.
- Read through the Writing Lesson steps with students and clarify any confusion.
- Use the Descriptive Essay rubrics in ***General Resources,*** pp. 63–64, to evaluate students' descriptions.

❹ Research and Technology

- Help students identify likely research avenues, for example, historical sites or even those from government geological or historical departments. Historical atlases are also rich information sources.
- Provide students with sample maps of the complexity level you expect to see from them. These maps should be relatively simple with political boundaries and very major geographical landmarks labeled.
- Direct students to sketch their maps before they attempt to create a computerized version.
- Have each student present his or her map and brochure to the class in a guided tour.
- The **Support for Extend Your Learning** page (***Unit 3 Resources,*** p. 50) provides guided note-taking opportunities to help students complete the Extend Your Learning activities.

Go Online Research — Have students type in the Web Code for another research activity.

❸ Writing Lesson

Description of a Natural Wonder

Have you ever seen a natural wonder—something so amazing that it leaves you searching for words to describe it? Choose a natural wonder that you have observed directly, learned about through research, or seen on film. Like Powell, write a description of it, using sensory images so that your readers can share your experience.

Prewriting Picture the natural wonder you are going to describe. Create a rough sketch of your subject, and jot down some details. Also jot down the feelings your subject evoked in you.

Drafting Decide which feature you will describe first, and continue logically and spatially from that point. Use transitions such as *behind, next to, in front of,* or *at the bottom* to show the relationship of details in your description.

Model: Using Transitions to Show Place

The solitary rock, as tall as a skyscraper, stood guard *at the foot* of the canyon, *just to the east* of the rushing river. We looked past the lone sentinel, *up the canyon,* to the plateau *in the distance.*

The transitions *at the foot, just to the east, past, up,* and *in the distance* aid and enhance the description by clarifying spatial relationships.

Revising Review your work, adding or changing your sensory details to make the description more clear. Look for places where you can add transitions to clarify the spatial relationships.

WG *Prentice Hall Writing and Grammar Connection: Chapter 6, Section 2*

❹ Extend Your Learning

Listening and Speaking In a small group, create a **tourism presentation** about a Grand Canyon sightseeing tour by raft. Address the following aspects of the tour:

- Present a vivid description of the sights.
- Provide an explanation of what rafting through the Grand Canyon will be like.
- Offer a list of the clothing and equipment to take along.

Use slides and photos of the canyon to enrich your presentation. **[Group Activity]**

Research and Technology Prepare a map showing Lewis and Clark's expedition route from its start in St. Louis, Missouri, to its conclusion at the Oregon coast. Use the Internet to gather details about the journey. If possible, use a desktop publishing program to produce an **expedition map** and an informative brochure to accompany it.

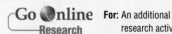

For: An additional research activity
Visit: www.PHSchool.com
Web Code: erd-7303

Assessment Resources

The following resources can be used to assess students' knowledge and skills.

Unit 3 Resources
- **Selection Test A,** pp. 52–54
- **Selection Test B,** pp. 55–57

General Resources
- **Rubrics for Descriptive Essay,** pp. 63–64

Go Online Assessment — Students may use the **Self-test** to prepare for **Selection Test A** or **Selection Test B.**

Unit 3
Part
2

Shadows of the Imagination

Shadows of the Imagination ■ 309

Differentiated Instruction Solutions for All Learners

Accessibility at a Glance

Average
The Raven

More Challenging
The Fall of the House of Usher
The Minister's Black Veil
from Moby Dick

Selection Planning Guide

The selections in this section deal with the ominous side of human emotions. Here we find characters who are tortured individuals ruled by the menacing shadows of their imaginations. "The Fall of the House of Usher" introduces Roderick Usher, a physically deteriorating person who knows he is losing his mind and tries anything, including burying his twin sister alive, to escape death. In "The Raven," Poe presents a man whose grief for his deceased beloved knows no bounds. His wounded psyche proves far too fragile to survive the shattering blows of the single negative word uttered repeatedly by an uninvited guest. The last selection provides a close-up of obsession at its most dangerous. In an excerpt from the novel *Moby-Dick,* Captain Ahab is driven to revenge at any cost, including the lives of most of his crew and himself.

Humanities

Mysterious Night,
Elliott Daingerfield

Ask students what they see in this painting, and generate a list of possibilities on the board for students to compile situations from. Then use these questions to spark discussion.

1. Imagine that a person lurks underneath the white shape on the right. Make up a story idea explaining what he or she is doing out on this foggy night.
   Possible response: He is waiting to meet someone who has the other half of a treasure map.
2. Describe the mood of this painting. What details and elements contribute most to this mood?
   Possible response: The mood of the painting is mysterious, haunting, ominous. Details that contribute to the mood include the fog or mist; the large, shadowy tree; the pool of light in the middle of the painting.

Meeting Your Standards

Students will

1. **analyze and respond to literary elements.**
   - Literary Analysis: Single Effect
2. **read, comprehend, analyze, and critique a short story and a poem.**
   - Reading Strategy: Breaking Down Long Sentences
   - Reading Check questions
   - Apply the Skills questions
   - Assessment Practice (ATE)
3. **develop vocabulary.**
   - Vocabulary Lesson: Latin Word Root: *-voc-*
4. **understand and apply written and oral language conventions.**
   - Spelling Strategy
   - Grammar and Style Lesson: Coordinate Adjectives
5. **develop writing proficiency.**
   - Writing Lesson: Literary Criticism
6. **develop appropriate research strategies.**
   - Extend Your Learning: Discussion
7. **understand and apply listening and speaking strategies.**
   - Extend Your Learning: Dramatic Reading

Block Scheduling: Use one 90-minute class period to preteach the skills and have students read the selection. Use a second 90-minute class period to assess students' mastery of skills, extend their learning, and monitor their progress.

Homework Suggestions

Following are possibilities for homework assignments.

- Support pages from ***Unit 3 Resources:***
  Literary Analysis
  Reading Strategy
  Vocabulary Builder
  Grammar and Style
- An Extend Your Learning project and the Writing Lesson for this selection group may be completed over several days.

Step-by-Step Teaching Guide	Pacing Guide
PRETEACH	
• Administer Vocabulary and Reading Warm-ups as necessary.	5 min.
• Engage students' interest with the motivation activity.	5 min.
• Read and discuss author and background features. **FT**	10 min.
• Introduce the Literary Analysis Skill: Single Effect. **FT**	5 min.
• Introduce the Reading Strategy: Breaking Down Long Sentences. **FT**	10 min.
• Prepare students to read by teaching the selection vocabulary. **FT**	
TEACH	
• Informally monitor comprehension while students read independently or in groups. **FT**	30 min.
• Monitor students' comprehension with the Reading Check notes.	as students read
• Reinforce vocabulary with Vocabulary Builder notes.	as students read
• Develop students' understanding of single effect with the Literary Analysis annotations. **FT**	5 min.
• Develop students' ability to break down long sentences with the Reading Strategy annotations. **FT**	5 min.
ASSESS/EXTEND	
• Assess students' comprehension and mastery of the Literary Analysis and Reading Strategy by having them answer the Apply the Skills questions. **FT**	15 min.
• Have students complete the Vocabulary Lesson and the Grammar and Style Lesson. **FT**	15 min.
• Apply students' ability to write appropriately for a medium by using the Writing Lesson. **FT**	45 min. or homework
• Apply students' understanding by using one or more of the Extend Your Learning activities.	20–90 min. or homework
• Administer Selection Test A or Selection Test B. **FT**	15 min.

Resources

PRINT

Unit 3 Resources

Vocabulary Warm-up Word Lists **[L1, L2, EL]** .... p. 58
Vocabulary Warm-up Practice **[L1, L2, EL]** .... p. 59
Reading Warm-up A **[L1, L2, EL]** .... p. 60
Reading Warm-up B **[L1, L2, L3]** .... p. 61

TRANSPARENCY

Graphic Organizer Transparencies

Literary Analysis Graphic Organizer A **[L3]** .... p. 65
Literary Analysis Graphic Organizer B **[L1, L2, EL]** .... p. 66
Reading Strategy Graphic Organizer A **[L3]** .... p. 63
Reading Strategy Graphic Organizer B **[L1, L2, EL]** .... p. 64

PRINT

Reader's Notebook [L2]
Reader's Notebook: Adapted Version [L1]
Reader's Notebook: English Learner's Version [EL]

Unit 3 Resources

Literary Analysis **[L3]** .... p. 62
Reading Strategy **[L3]** .... p. 63
Vocabulary Builder **[L3]** .... p. 64

TRANSPARENCY

Graphic Organizer Transparencies

Outline .... p. 309

TECHNOLOGY

Listening to Literature Audio CDs [L2, EL]
Reader's Notebook: Adapted Version Audio CD [L1, L2]

PRINT

Unit 3 Resources

Grammar and Style **[L3]** .... p. 65
Support for Writing Lesson **[L3]** .... p. 66
Support for Extend Your Learning **[L3]** .... p. 67
Enrichment **[L4]** .... p. 68
Selection Test A **[L1, L2, EL]** .... pp. 69–71
Selection Test B **[L3, L4]** .... pp. 72–74

TRANSPARENCY

Graphic Organizer Transparencies

Outline .... p. 309

General Resources

Rubrics for Response to Literature **[L3]** .... pp. 65–66
Rubric for Dramatic Performance **[L3]** .... p. 131

TECHNOLOGY

Go Online: Research **[L3]**
Go Online: Self-test **[L3]**
***ExamView*®, Test Bank [L3]**

Choosing Resources for Differentiated Instruction

[L1] Special Needs Students
[L2] Below-Level Students
[L3] All Students
[L4] Advanced Students
[EL] English Learners

FT Fast Track Instruction: To move the lesson more quickly, use the strategies and activities identified with **FT**.

Scaffolding for Less Proficient and Advanced Students

The leveled Critical Thinking questions after selections progress in the levels of thinking required to answer them. To address the needs of your different students, you may use the (a) level questions for your less proficient students and the (b) level question with your on-level and advanced students. The occasional (c) level questions are appropriate for your advanced students.

PRENTICE HALL **TeacherEXPRESS**™ Plan · Teach · Assess — Use this complete suite of powerful teaching tools to make lesson planning and testing quicker and easier.

PRENTICE HALL **StudentEXPRESS**™ Learn · Study · Succeed — Use the interactive textbook (online and on CD-ROM) to make selections and activities come alive with audio and video support and interactive questions.

PREVIEW

Motivation

The odd deterioration of Roderick Usher and the madness of the narrator of "The Fall of the House of Usher" are shrouded in as much mystery and horror as any psychological thriller students may have encountered on the page or screen. Engage students' interest in Poe by writing the following passages on the chalkboard:

"Having deposited our mournful burden . . . within this region of horror, we partially turned aside the yet unscrewed lid of the coffin, and looked upon the face of the tenant."

"Deep into that darkness peering, long I stood there wondering, fearing,

Doubting, dreaming dreams no mortal ever dared to dream before . . . ."

Have students use the passages to make predictions about the story and poem.

1 Background

More About the Author

Edgar Allan Poe's writing contains a fascinating duality. On one hand, Poe was an idealist whose sensitivity led him to write touching lyrics, most notably "Annabel Lee." Yet he was intrigued by dark escapes from reality as well. He was irresistibly drawn to eerie thoughts, impulses, and fears in writing his daring tales of wickedness, anguish, crime, and death.

1 The Fall of the House of Usher • The Raven

Edgar Allan Poe (1809–1849)

When Edgar Allan Poe died, Rufus Griswold wrote a slanderous obituary of the eccentric writer. He claimed that Poe had been expelled from college, that he had neither good friends nor good qualities, and that he committed flagrant acts of plagiarism. Suspicious of this unconventional obituary, some have speculated that Poe orchestrated the death notice himself to keep his name in the public eye. Yet, Poe's real life was almost as dark and dismal as the possibly false obituary described it.

A Troubled Childhood Poe was born in Boston in 1809, the son of impoverished traveling actors. Shortly after Poe's birth, his father deserted the family; a year later, his mother died. Young Edgar was taken in—though never formally adopted—by the family of John Allan, a wealthy Virginia merchant. Poe lived with the Allans in England from 1815 to 1820, when they returned to the United States. It was from John Allan that Poe received his middle name. The Allans also provided for Poe's education; however, when his stepfather refused to pay Poe's large gambling debts at the University of Virginia, the young man was forced to leave the school.

Building a Literary Career In 1827, after joining the army under an assumed name, Poe published his first volume of poetry, *Tamerlane and Other Poems*. Two years later, he published a second volume, *Al Aaraaf*. In 1830, John Allan helped Poe win an appointment to the United States Military Academy at West Point. Within a year, however, Poe was expelled for academic violations, and his dismissal resulted in an irreparable break with his stepfather.

An Unhappy Ending During the second half of his short life, Poe pursued a literary career in New York, Richmond, Philadelphia, and Baltimore, barely supporting himself by writing and working as an editor for several magazines. After his third volume of poetry, *Poems* (1831), failed to bring him either money or acclaim, he turned from poetry to fiction and literary criticism. Five of his short stories were published in newspapers in 1832, and in 1838 he published his only novel, *The Narrative of Arthur Gordon Pym*. Although his short stories gained him some recognition and his poem "The Raven" (1845) was greeted with enthusiasm, Poe could never escape from poverty. He suffered from bouts of depression and madness. Then, in 1849, two years after the death of his beloved wife, Virginia, Poe died in Baltimore, alone and unhappy.

A Legacy Since his death, Poe's work has been a magnet for attention. Poe is widely accepted as the inventor of the detective story, and his psychological thrillers have been imitated by scores of modern writers. His work has been translated into nearly every language, and dozens of film adaptations have been made of his stories. Although critics have not always agreed about Poe, the Mystery Writers of America have honored their best and brightest by conferring upon them the "Edgar" award for great achievement in mystery writing.

Poe's work has provoked intense critical debate. Some scholars have harshly criticized his writing, while others have celebrated his use of vivid imagery and sound effects, as well as his tireless exploration of altered mental states and the dark side of human nature. Despite Poe's uncertain status among critics, his work has remained extremely popular among generations of American readers.

Preview

Connecting to the Literature

It is natural to feel anxiety, but in extreme circumstances, "nerves" can become a destructive part of a person's personality. Such is the case for the characters in the selections that follow.

Literary Analysis

Single Effect

Poe argued that a short story should be constructed to achieve "a certain unique or **single effect.**" He believed that every character, incident, and detail should contribute to this effect. As you read, examine the ways in which Poe heeds his own advice.

Comparing Literary Works

Although one is a story and the other a poem, both "The Fall of the House of Usher" and "The Raven" exemplify the literary genre known as the **Gothic**. The Gothic style is characterized by the following elements:

- The story is set in bleak or remote places.
- The plot involves macabre or violent incidents.
- Characters are in psychological and/or physical torment.
- A supernatural or otherworldly element is often present.

As you read, examine how both the story and the poem emphasize different elements of the Gothic style.

Reading Strategy

Breaking Down Long Sentences

Long, intricate sentences can challenge your understanding. It may help to **break down long sentences** into logical parts. First, look for a sentence's core: its subject and verb. Then, look for clues in punctuation, conjunctions, and modifying words. Use a chart like the one shown to break down Poe's lengthy sentences into more manageable parts.

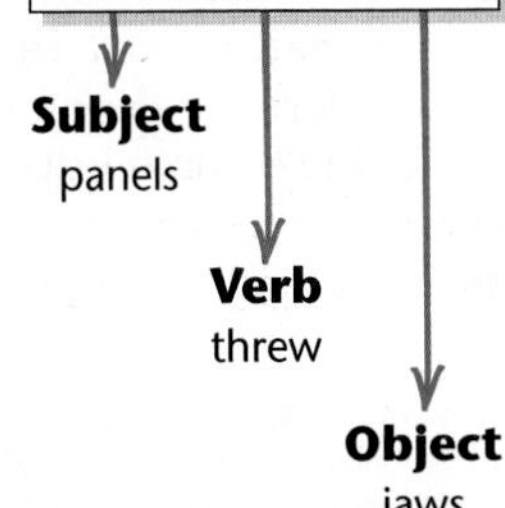
Sentence
As if . . . there had been found the potency of a spell, the huge antique panels to which the speaker pointed threw slowly back, upon the instant, their ponderous and ebony jaws.
Subject
panels
Verb
threw
Object
jaws

Vocabulary Builder

importunate (im pôr′ cho͞o nit) *adj.* insistent (p. 314)

munificent (myo͞o nif′ ə sənt) *adj.* generous (p. 314)

equivocal (ē kwiv′ ə kəl) *adj.* having more than one possible interpretation (p. 315)

appellation (ap′ ə lā′ shən) *n.* name or title (p. 315)

specious (spē′ shəs) *adj.* seeming to be good or sound without actually being so (p. 315)

anomalous (ə näm′ ə ləs) *adj.* abnormal (p. 318)

sentience (sen′ shəns) *n.* capacity of feeling (p. 322)

obeisance (ō bā′ səns) *n.* gesture of respect (p. 331)

craven (krā′ vən) *adj.* very cowardly (p. 331)

Differentiated Instruction Solutions for All Learners

Support for Special Needs Students
Have students read the adapted version of "The Raven" in the ***Reader's Notebook: Adapted Version.*** This version provides basic-level instruction in an interactive format with questions and write-on lines. Completing these pages will prepare students to read the selection in the Student Edition.

Support for Less Proficient Readers
Have students read "The Raven" in the ***Reader's Notebook.*** This version provides basic-level instruction in an interactive format with questions and write-on lines. After students finish the selection in the ***Reader's Notebook,*** have them complete the questions and activities in the Student Edition.

Support for English Learners
Have students read "The Raven" in the ***Reader's Notebook: English Learner's Version.*** This version provides basic-level instruction in an interactive format with questions and write-on lines. Completing these pages will prepare students to read the selection in the Student Edition.

❷ Literary Analysis

Single Effect

- Explain to students that as they read the two selections, they will focus on the single effect that Poe believed should be achieved by a short story.
- Let students know that Edgar Allan Poe was the first writer to define the short story as a distinct literary genre and to argue that it deserved the same status as a poem or a novel.
- Read the instruction on single effect together as a class. Point out that Poe believed not only that every character and incident should contribute to this effect but also each detail in every sentence. If not, Poe wrote, "then [the writer] has failed."
- Invite students as they read to identify and characterize the particular effect Poe set out to achieve in each of these works.

❸ Reading Strategy

Breaking Down Long Sentences

- Read aloud with students the instruction on breaking down long sentences. Point out that Poe's style is notable for its use of long, complicated sentences.
- Point out that rereading a challenging sentence several times can help readers appreciate its structure, as well as its main idea.
- Also encourage students to read aloud difficult sentences to allow them to *hear* the sentence's essential meaning.
- Remind students that identifying a sentence's subject and predicate can help them distinguish the sentence's main idea from various details. Give students a copy of **Reading Strategy Graphic Organizer A**, p. 63, in ***Graphic Organizer Transparencies,*** to use as they read the selections.

Vocabulary Builder

- Pronounce each vocabulary word for students, and read the definitions as a class. Have students identify any words with which they are already familiar.

TEACH

Learning Modalities
Visual/Spatial Learners

Invite students to compare and contrast the descriptions of the Usher house at the beginning and end of the tale in order to identify a crucial example of the story's total effect. Encourage students to take special note of descriptive details such as the unusual lighting effects, the vast house standing alone in shadow, the fissure in the wall, and the sullen silence with which the waters of the tarn close over the ruins of the House of Usher.

❶ About the Selection

In Poe's classic journey into the inner reaches of a decaying mind, the narrator honors a request from a boyhood friend to visit him during an oppressive illness. The narrator arrives at a remote, gloomy mansion next to a dark lake and finds Roderick Usher in poor physical and mental health. Usher is not unaware that his mind is disintegrating. After the apparent death of his twin sister, Usher and the narrator bear a coffin containing her body to a vault in the lower reaches of the mansion. After several days of unexplained sounds emanating from the vault, Usher admits that she may have been buried alive. On a subsequent stormy night, she escapes the vault, appears in the doorway before them, and (with Roderick) suddenly dies. The narrator flees the house as it collapses into the dark lake.

❷ Literary Analysis
Single Effect

- Write a list on the chalkboard of students' ideas about what words and phrases in this sentence create a distinct atmosphere. Students' responses might include *dull dark, soundless, clouds hung oppressively low, alone, dreary, shades, evening,* and *melancholy.*
- **Ask** students the Literary Analysis question: What single effect does Poe create in the very first sentence?
  Answer: The first sentence establishes the gloominess of the story's setting.

❶

The Fall of the House of Usher

Edgar Allan Poe

Background In 1839, Poe lived in Philadelphia and became coeditor of *Burton's Gentleman's Magazine*, a journal that published essays, fiction, reviews, and poems, as well as articles on sailing, hunting, and cricket. Poe's articles ran the gamut of topics. He explained the parallel bars, mused about the mysteries of Stonehenge, and reviewed more than eighty books on a variety of topics. It was in this magazine, in 1839, that Poe first published "The Fall of the House of Usher."

Son Coeur est un luth suspendu:
Sitôt qu'on le touche il résonne.[1]

❷ During the whole of a dull, dark, and soundless day in the autumn of the year, when the clouds hung oppressively low in the heavens, I had been passing alone, on horseback, through a singularly dreary tract of country, and at length found myself, as the shades of evening drew on, within view of the melancholy House of Usher. I know not how it was—but, with the first glimpse of the building, a sense of insufferable gloom pervaded my spirit. I say insufferable; for the feeling was unrelieved by any of that half-pleasurable, because poetic, sentiment, with which the mind usually receives even the sternest natural images of the desolate or terrible. I looked upon the scene before me—upon the mere house, and the simple landscape features of the domain—upon the bleak walls—upon the vacant eyelike windows—upon a few rank sedges[2]—and upon a few white trunks of decayed trees—with an utter depression of soul, which I can

Literary Analysis
Single Effect What single effect does Poe create in the very first sentence?

1. ***Son . . . résonne*** "His heart is a lute strung tight: As soon as one touches it, resounds." From "Le Refus" by Pierre Jean de Béranger (1780–1857).
2. **sedges** (sej´ iz) *n.* grasslike plants.

Differentiated Instruction Solutions for All Learners

Accessibility at a Glance

	The Fall of the House of Usher	The Raven
Context	Early tale of gloom and psychological suspense	Famous nineteenth-century narrative poem
Language	Challenging (long, intricate sentences; much description)	Accessible (narrative poem, contains much alliteration and imagery)
Concept Level	Challenging (descent into madness caused by guilt and grief)	Challenging (speaker's monologue about loss, grief, and madness)
Literary Merit	Classic tale of mental disintegration and madness	Classic narrative poem describing sorrow and madness
Lexile	1410	N/P
Overall Rating	More challenging	Average

3

"I at length...," Edgar Allan Poe's Tales of Mystery and Imagination, Arthur Rackham, The New York Public Library

4 ▲ **Critical Viewing** What mood does the artist's choice of shapes and colors create in this painting? Which details of the story's opening paragraph does the painter convey? **[Analyze]**

3 Humanities

"I at length . . ." Edgar Allan Poe's Tales of Mystery and Imagination, 1935, by Arthur Rackham

London-born Arthur Rackham (1867–1939) was one of the best known illustrators of his day, and his work is still familiar to millions of readers. Some of his most famous works are the illustrations for *Grimm's Fairy Tales* (1900) and for limited editions of German legends and Christmas stories. Rackham's imaginative, fanciful style was well suited to whimsical, grotesque, and gruesome subjects. For example, his use of form and color in this illustration for "The Fall of the House of Usher" dramatically captures the tortured mood of the story.

1. How does Rackham's rendition of this scene compare with the image Poe creates?
   Possible answer: The scene is gloomy, remote, and eerie, much as Poe describes it.
2. Often Rackham's trees have twisted or otherwise misshapen trunks. How do the trees contribute to the overall effect of this scene?
   Answer: Students may say that the trees suggest death and distortion.

4 Critical Viewing

Answer: The artist's choice of shapes and colors creates a gloomy and forbidding mood. Details from the story's opening paragraph that appear in the picture include the dark sky, the narrator on horseback, the House of Usher's bleak walls and vacant windows, and the decayed trees.

Differentiated Instruction Solutions for All Learners

Vocabulary for English Learners

Help students orient themselves at the start of Poe's story by pointing out and discussing key words in the story's opening sentences. After discussing the definitions of words such as *oppressively, melancholy, gloom, insufferable,* and *decayed,* invite students to create picture cards for each term. Explain that understanding the meaning of these few words puts readers on track to understand the single effect sought by the author.

Enrichment for Gifted/Talented Students

Have students speculate on why Poe opens the story with the French couplet from "Le Rufus." Why might he have chosen this particular quotation? As they read, have students try to determine which character the author intends to evoke with the quotation. Is it the narrator or Roderick Usher who is extraordinarily sensitive to impressions? Students might also do research to learn more about Pierre Jean de Béranger and his literary works.

5 Reading Strategy
Breaking Down Long Sentences

- Have two student volunteers read aloud the sentence beginning "It was possible, I reflected . . . ."
- **Ask** students the first Reading Strategy question: What are the subjects and verbs in the sentence beginning "It was possible, I reflected"?
  Answer: The sentence's subjects and predicates are as follows: *It/was; I/reflected; arrangement/would be.*

Monitor Progress: Ask students to paraphrase the meaning of this sentence.
Possible response: I thought that maybe if the house and its surroundings were looked at from another point of view they might look less grim: but when I looked at them reflected in the tarn they looked even worse.

6 Reading Strategy
Breaking Down Long Sentences

- Read aloud the sentence beginning "It was the manner" two or three times with students.
- Encourage students to momentarily ignore the nonessential parts of this sentence (for example, "and much more," as well as the phrase marked off by dashes), to help them focus on the core of the sentence.
- Then, **ask** students the second Reading Strategy question: What is the core of the sentence beginning "It was the manner"?
  Answer: The core of the sentence is "It was the manner in which all of this was said which allowed me no room for hesitation."

compare to no earthly sensation more properly than to the afterdream of the reveler upon opium—the bitter lapse into everyday life—the hideous dropping off of the veil. There was an iciness, a sinking, a sickening of the heart—an unredeemed dreariness of thought which no goading of the imagination could torture into aught[3] of the sublime. What was it—I paused to think—what was it that so unnerved me in the contemplation of the House of Usher? It was a mystery all insoluble; nor could I grapple with the shadowy fancies that crowded upon me as I pondered. I was forced to fall back upon the unsatisfactory conclusion, that while, beyond doubt, there are combinations of very simple natural objects which have the power of thus affecting us, still the analysis of this power lies among considerations beyond our depth. 5 It was possible, I reflected, that a mere different arrangement of the particulars of the scene, of the details of the picture, would be sufficient to modify, or perhaps to annihilate its capacity for sorrowful impression; and, acting upon this idea, I reined my horse to the precipitous brink of a black and lurid tarn[4] that lay in unruffled luster by the dwelling, and gazed down—but with a shudder even more thrilling than before—upon the remodeled and inverted images of the gray sedge, and the ghastly tree stems, and the vacant and eyelike windows.

Nevertheless, in this mansion of gloom I now proposed to myself a sojourn of some weeks. Its proprietor, Roderick Usher, had been one of my boon companions in boyhood; but many years had elapsed since our last meeting. A letter, however, had lately reached me in a distant part of the country—a letter from him—which, in its wildly importunate nature, had admitted of no other than a personal reply. The MS[5] gave evidence of nervous agitation. The writer spoke of acute bodily illness—of a mental disorder which oppressed him—and of an earnest desire to see me, as his best and indeed his only personal friend, with a view of attempting, by the cheerfulness of my society, some alleviation of his malady. 6 It was the manner in which all this, and much more, was said—it was the apparent *heart* that went with his request—which allowed me no room for hesitation; and I accordingly obeyed forthwith what I still considered a very singular summons.

Although, as boys, we had been even intimate associates, yet I really knew little of my friend. His reserve had been always excessive and habitual. I was aware, however, that his very ancient family had been noted, time out of mind, for a peculiar sensibility of temperament, displaying itself, through long ages, in many works of exalted art, and manifested, of late, in repeated deeds of munificent yet unobtrusive charity, as well as in a passionate devotion to the intricacies, perhaps even more than to the orthodox and easily recognizable

3. **aught** (ôt) anything.
4. **tarn** (tärn) *n.* small lake.
5. **MS.** *abbr.* manuscript.

Reading Strategy
Breaking Down Long Sentences What is the subject and what are the verbs in the sentence beginning "It was possible, I reflected"?

Vocabulary Builder
importunate (im pôr′ chə nit) *adj.* insistent

Reading Strategy
Breaking Down Long Sentences What is the core of the sentence beginning "It was the manner"?

Vocabulary Builder
munificent (myo͞o nif′ ə sənt) *adj.* generous

beauties, of musical science. I had learned, too, the very remarkable fact, that the stem of the Usher race, all time-honored as it was, had put forth, at no period, any enduring branch: in other words, that the entire family lay in the direct line of descent, and had always, with very trifling and very temporary variations, so lain. It was this deficiency, I considered, while running over in thought the perfect keeping of the character of the premises with the accredited character of the people, and while speculating upon the possible influence which the one, in the long lapse of centuries, might have exercised upon the other—it was this deficiency, perhaps of collateral issue,[6] and the consequent undeviating transmission, from sire to son, of the patrimony[7] with the name,
7 which had, at length, so identified the two as to merge the original title of the estate in the quaint and equivocal appellation of the "House of Usher"—an appellation which seemed to include, in the minds of the peasantry who used it, both the family and the family mansion.

I have said that the sole effect of my somewhat childish experiment—that of looking down within the tarn—had been to deepen the first singular impression. There can be no doubt that the consciousness of the rapid increase of my superstition—for why should I not so term it?—served mainly to accelerate the increase itself. Such, I have long known, is the paradoxical law of all sentiments having terror as a basis. And it might have been for this reason only, that, when I again uplifted my eyes to the house itself, from its image in the pool, there grew in my mind a strange fancy—a fancy so ridiculous, indeed, that I but mention it to show the vivid force of the sensations which oppressed me. I had so worked upon my imagination as really to believe that about the whole mansion and domain there hung an atmosphere peculiar to themselves and their immediate vicinity—an atmosphere which had no affinity with the air of heaven, but which had reeked up from the decayed trees, and the gray wall, and the silent tarn—a pestilent and mystic vapor, dull, sluggish, faintly discernible and leaden-hued.

Shaking off from my spirit what *must* have been a dream, I scanned more narrowly the real aspect of the building. Its principal feature seemed to be that of an excessive antiquity. The discoloration of ages had been great. Minute fungi overspread the whole exterior, hanging in a fine tangled web-work from the eaves. Yet all this was apart from any extraordinary dilapidation. No portion of the masonry
8 had fallen; and there appeared to be a wild inconsistency between its still perfect adaptation of parts, and the crumbling condition of the individual stones. In this there was much that reminded me of the specious totality of old woodwork which has rotted for long years in some neglected vault, with no disturbance from the breath of the

Vocabulary Builder
equivocal (i kwiv′ ə kəl) *adj.* having more than one possible interpretation

appellation (ap′ ə lā′ shən) *n.* name or title

Vocabulary Builder
specious (spē′ shəs) *adj.* seeming to be good or sound without actually being so

9 
Reading Check
What is the physical condition of the House of Usher?

6. **collateral** (kə lat′ ər əl) **issue** descended from the same ancestors but in a different line.
7. **patrimony** (pat′ rə mō′ nē) *n.* property inherited from one's father.

7 Vocabulary Builder
The Latin Word Root *-voc-*

- Call students' attention to the word *equivocal* and its definition. Tell students that the Latin word root *-voc-* comes from the Latin word for "voice," *vox.*
- **Ask** students to volunteer words or phrases that contain this root, and list them on the blackboard. **Possibilities include:** vocal, vocation, vocabulary.
- Have students discuss how the meaning of the root *-voc-* contributes to the definitions of words such as *vocation* and *equivocate.*

8 Literary Analysis
Single Effect

- Have a student volunteer read aloud this paragraph. Ask the class to think about what single effect Poe aims to achieve as the volunteer reads this passage.
- Read the paragraph aloud a second time. Help students recognize that Poe describes the house as an old, decaying wreck whose "barely perceptible fissure" suggests a fatal flaw.
- Discuss how the author repeatedly emphasizes the isolation of the house. Encourage students to think about what these clues may suggest about the inhabitants.

9 Reading Check

Answer: The house is notable for its extreme age, its rotting and discolored shell, and the evidence of decay in many of the individual stones of which its walls are made up.

Differentiated Instruction
Solutions for All Learners

Support for Special Needs Students
Have students in small groups listen as you read the story's opening paragraphs. Point out that despite all of the gloom described in the opening passages, the narrator plans to stick to his decision to stay for some weeks. Have students discuss why he makes this choice. Encourage them to see that he may feel loyalty to his old friend, that he may not want to let the gloom frighten him away, or that his curiosity may compel him to stay on.

Enrichment for Advanced Readers
Challenge students to trace and analyze a common theme in Poe's work: a narrator preyed upon by malevolent outside forces, as well as by his own disordered or obsessive thoughts or those of another character. Have students look for examples of such outside forces in this story and in the poem that follows.

10 The American Experience
Poe and the Gothic Tradition

Despite the fact that British writers established the Gothic novel and produced most of its famous examples—including Mary Shelley's *Frankenstein* and Bram Stoker's *Dracula*—the form took hold in the United States as well. Several notable writers set about the task of discovering Gothic effects in the newly explored American landscape.

Edgar Allan Poe and Nathaniel Hawthorne are the two best-known American authors who fashioned tales using dark, mysterious, and sometimes ghastly subjects and settings. Yet before either of these men was born, Charles Brockden Brown crafted full-length Gothic narratives such as *Wieland, or The Transformation* (1798) and *Edgar Huntly* (1799). Sometimes called "the father of the American novel," Brown wove into his tales eerie topics and grisly special effects (prefiguring later American works ranging from Poe's to John Carpenter's) such as mass murder, religious mania, spontaneous combustion, ventriloquism, and psychological terror.

Connect to the Literature
Encourage students to talk about Suspenseful movies they have seen. Ask them what made the film especially spellbinding.
Possible response: Students may mention classic suspense film directors like Alfred Hitchcock or more contemporary directors such as M. Night Shyamalan, Wes Craven, Jim Gillespie, and Michael Cooney.

11 Reading Strategy
Breaking Down Long Sentences

- Write the bracketed sentence on the chalkboard. Have a volunteer read aloud this sentence.
- Show students that they can omit the nonessential phrases and clauses in order to clarify its meaning. On the chalkboard, cross out "Upon my entrance," "on which he had been lying at full length," "which had much in it," "I at first thought," and "of the constrained effort of the *ennuyé* man of the world."
- Lead students to see that the sentence's essential meaning is as follows: *Usher got up to greet me with too much warmth.*

external air. Beyond this indication of extensive decay, however, the fabric gave little token of instability. Perhaps the eye of a scrutinizing observer might have discovered a barely perceptible fissure, which, extending from the roof of the building in front, made its way down the wall in a zigzag direction, until it became lost in the sullen waters of the tarn. 10

Noticing these things, I rode over a short causeway to the house. A servant in waiting took my horse, and I entered the Gothic[8] archway of the hall. A valet, of stealthy step, then conducted me, in silence, through many dark and intricate passages in my progress to the studio of his master. Much that I encountered on the way contributed, I know not how, to heighten the vague sentiments of which I have already spoken. While the objects around me—while the carvings of the ceilings, the somber tapestries of the walls, the ebon blackness of the floors, and the phantasmagoric[9] armorial trophies which rattled as I strode, were but matters to which, or to such as which, I had been accustomed from my infancy—while I hesitated not to acknowledge how familiar was all this—I still wondered to find how unfamiliar were the fancies which ordinary images were stirring up. On one of the staircases, I met the physician of the family. His countenance, I thought, wore a mingled expression of low cunning and perplexity. He accosted me with trepidation and passed on. The valet now threw open a door and ushered me into the presence of his master.

The room in which I found myself was very large and lofty. The windows were long, narrow, and pointed, and at so vast a distance from the black oaken floor as to be altogether inaccessible from within. Feeble gleams of encrimsoned light made their way through the trellised panes, and served to render sufficiently distinct the more prominent objects around; the eye, however, struggled in vain to reach the remoter angles of the chamber, or the recesses of the vaulted and fretted[10] ceiling. Dark draperies hung upon the walls. The general furniture was profuse, comfortless, antique, and tattered. Many books and musical instruments lay scattered about, but failed to give any vitality to the scene. I felt that I breathed an atmosphere of sorrow. An air of stern, deep, and irredeemable gloom hung over and pervaded all.

11 Upon my entrance, Usher arose from a sofa on which he had been lying at full length, and greeted me with a vivacious warmth which had much in it, I at first thought, of an overdone cordiality—of the constrained effort of the *ennuyé*[11] man of the world. A glance, however, at his countenance convinced me of his perfect

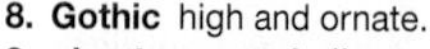

8. **Gothic** high and ornate.
9. **phantasmagoric** (fan taz′ mə gôr′ ik) *adj.* fantastic or dreamlike.
10. **fretted** (fret′ id) *v.* ornamented with a pattern of small, straight, intersecting bars.
11. ***ennuyé*** (än′ wē ā′) *adj.* bored (French).

10 ***Poe and the Gothic Tradition***

Gothic fiction first appeared in England in the late 1700s in works like *Castle of Otranto* (1764) by Horace Walpole and *The Mysteries of Udolpho* (1794) by Ann Radcliffe. It has never gone away.

The word *Gothic* was borrowed from architecture, where it is used to describe buildings that were created during the late Middle Ages. To later generations, their cold chambers and secret passages held mysteries—dark tales of vengeance and passion. Gothic novels are often set in such buildings, populated by the insane, the lovelorn, the terrified—and, often, the dead.

Edgar Allan Poe translated the imagery and atmosphere of British Gothic into an American landscape. His work paved the way for an American Gothic tradition that has been a mainstay of popular culture. Contemporary writers like Stephen King and Anne Rice are in a direct line of descent from Poe, and so are many of Hollywood's most successful filmmakers.

Connect to the Literature

What contemporary filmmaker would you choose to direct a movie based on "The Fall of the House of Usher"? Why?

Enrichment

Gothic Architecture

Introduce students to the characteristics of Gothic architecture—as found in European cathedrals built between the twelfth and sixteenth centuries—such as interior pillars, side aisles, radiating chapels, soaring ceilings, flying buttresses, and luminous windows. If possible, display pictures of famous Gothic structures, such as the cathedrals of Notre Dame (Paris), Chartres, Reims, and Amiens in France; the cathedrals of Salisbury, Gloucester, and Canterbury, as well as Westminster Abbey (London) in England; the cathedrals of Avila, Barcelona, Toledo, and Palma da Majorca in Spain; the cathedrals of Santa Croce (Florence) and Milan in Italy; and Town Hall in Brussels, Belgium. Discuss how these structures affect people who approach or enter them, and make an effort to link these responses to students' responses to Poe's work.

sincerity. We sat down; and for some moments, while he spoke not, I gazed upon him with a feeling half of pity, half of awe. Surely, man had never before so terribly altered, in so brief a period, as had Roderick Usher! It was with difficulty that I could bring myself to admit the identity of the wan being before me with the companion of my early boyhood. Yet the character of his face had been at all times remarkable. A cadaverousness of complexion; an eye large, liquid, and luminous beyond comparison; lips somewhat thin and very pallid, but of a surpassingly beautiful curve; a nose of a delicate Hebrew model, but with a breadth of nostril unusual in similar formations; a finely molded chin, speaking, in its want of prominence, of a want of moral energy; hair of a more than weblike softness and tenuity—these features, with an inordinate expansion above the regions of the temple, made up altogether a countenance not easily to be forgotten. And now in the mere exaggeration of the prevailing character of these features, and of the expression they were wont to convey, lay so much of change that I doubted to whom I spoke. The now ghastly pallor of the skin, and the now miraculous luster of the eye, above all things startled and even awed me. The silken hair, too, had been suffered to grow all unheeded, and as, in its wild gossamer texture, it floated rather than fell about the face, I could not, even with effort, connect its Arabesque[12] expression with any idea of simple humanity.

In the manner of my friend I was at once struck with an incoherence—an inconsistency; and I soon found this to arise from a series of feeble and futile struggles to overcome an habitual trepidancy—an excessive nervous agitation. For something of this nature I had indeed been prepared, no less by his letter than by reminiscences of certain boyish traits, and by conclusions deduced from his peculiar physical conformation and temperament. His action was alternately vivacious and sullen. His voice varied rapidly from a tremulous indecision (when the animal spirits seemed utterly in abeyance) to that species of energetic concision—that abrupt, weighty, unhurried, and hollow-sounding enunciation—that leaden, self-balanced, and perfectly modulated guttural utterance, which may be observed in the lost drunkard, or the irreclaimable eater of opium, during the periods of his most intense excitement.

It was thus that he spoke of the object of my visit, of his earnest desire to see me, and of the solace he expected me to afford him. He entered, at some length, into what he conceived to be the nature of his malady. It was, he said, a constitutional and a family evil and one for which he despaired to find a remedy—a mere nervous affection,[13] he immediately added, which would undoubtedly soon pass off. It displayed itself in a host of unnatural sensations. Some of these, as he detailed them, interested and bewildered me; although, perhaps, the terms and the general manner of their narration had their weight. He

12. **Arabesque** (ar′ ə besk′) *adj.* of complex and elaborate design.
13. **affection** affliction.

Reading Strategy
Breaking Down Long Sentences In your own words, restate the meaning of the sentence beginning "His voice varied."

14 **Reading Check**
In what ways has Roderick Usher changed since the speaker last saw him?

12 Literary Analysis
Single Effect

- Slowly read aloud this detailed description of Roderick Usher's appearance.
- Help students with the complexity of Poe's descriptive prose by encouraging them to keep close track of the focus on Usher's features and on the effect created by these details.
- **Invite** students to find parallels between the descriptions of Roderick Usher and those of the house. Explain to students that this likeness is another manifestation of Poe's use of single effect.
  Possible responses: Usher's web-like hair is like the tangled web of fungi on the house; the ghastly pallor of his skin is like the house's bleak walls.

13 Reading Strategy
Breaking Down Long Sentences

- Have a student volunteer read the sentence beginning "His voice varied."
- Draw students' attention to the fact that the sentence is designed to distinguish two styles of speaking.
- Have students copy the sentence onto a piece of paper. Ask them to break down the sentence by writing each of the sentence's parts on a separate line. Students can then recognize the meaning of these shorter parts in order to understand the main idea of the sentence.
- Then, **ask** students to respond to the Reading Strategy instruction: In your own words, restate the meaning of the sentence beginning "His voice varied."
  Possible response: His voice alternated quickly between an uncertain, halting quality and an unnaturally deliberate, hollow, heavy quality.

14 Reading Check

Answer: Usher has grown "wan," and each of his facial features has been exaggerated by time. Especially notable are Usher's "ghastly pallor," the " miraculous luster of the eye," and disheveled "silken hair."

Differentiated Instruction Solutions for All Learners

Strategy for Less Proficient Readers
Help students infer the kind of background or upbringing the narrator has had based on his comments and observations. Students may notice the narrator's awareness of and familiarity with elements of wealth and finery to which "[he] has been accustomed from [his] infancy." They can conclude that he has been raised in a well-to-do family.

Strategy for Gifted/Talented Students
Challenge students to write dialogue for the scene on this page between the speaker and Roderick Usher. Suggest that students reread the text several times to develop dialogue that reveals the characters' backgrounds, personalities, and present emotions as described in the narrative. Allow interested students to perform their dialogue for the class.

15 Literary Analysis
Single Effect and Gothic Style

- Ask one or more student volunteers to summarize Roderick Usher's mental state. Students' responses should focus on his nervousness, distraction, hypersensitivity, and apparent weakness of spirit.
- Then, have one or more other students characterize the condition and appearance of the Usher house in a single sentence. Students' responses might focus on the grimness of the building and its situation, the layer of moss covering the entire house, and so forth.

Monitor Progress: Ask students the Literary Analysis question: In what ways do Usher's mental state and the house itself typify a work of Gothic literature?
Answer: Both are characterized by gloom and decay, as is Gothic literature itself.

suffered much from a morbid acuteness of the senses; the most insipid food was alone endurable; he could wear only garments of certain texture; the odors of all flowers were oppressive; his eyes were tortured by even a faint light; and there were but peculiar sounds, and these from stringed instruments, which did not inspire him with horror.

To an anomalous species of terror I found him a bounden slave. "I shall perish," said he, "I *must* perish in this deplorable folly. Thus, thus, and not otherwise, shall I be lost. I dread the events of the future, not in themselves, but in their results. I shudder at the thought of any, even the most trivial, incident, which may operate upon this intolerable agitation of soul. I have, indeed, no abhorrence of danger, except in its absolute effect—in terror. In this unnerved, in this pitiable, condition I feel that the period will sooner or later arrive when I must abandon life and reason together, in some struggle with the grim phantasm, FEAR."

15 I learned, moreover, at intervals, and through broken and equivocal hints, another singular feature of his mental condition. He was enchained by certain superstitious impressions in regard to the dwelling which he tenanted, and whence, for many years, he had never ventured forth—in regard to an influence whose supposititious[14] force was conveyed in terms too shadowy here to be restated—an influence which some peculiarities in the mere form and substance of his family mansion had, by dint of long sufferance, he said, obtained over his spirit—an effect which the physique of the gray walls and turrets, and of the dim tarn into which they all looked down, had at length, brought about upon the morale of his existence.

He admitted, however, although with hesitation, that much of the peculiar gloom which thus afflicted him could be traced to a more natural and far more palpable origin—to the severe and long-continued illness—indeed to the evidently approaching dissolution—of a tenderly beloved sister, his sole companion for long years, his last and only relative on earth. "Her decease," he said, with a bitterness which I can never forget, "would leave him (him, the hopeless and the frail) the last of the ancient race of the Ushers." While he spoke, the lady Madeline (for so was she called) passed through a remote portion of the apartment, and, without having noticed my presence, disappeared. I regarded her with an utter astonishment not unmingled with dread; and yet I found it impossible to account for such feelings. A sensation of stupor oppressed me as my eyes followed her retreating steps. When a door, at length, closed upon her, my glance sought instinctively and eagerly the countenance of the brother; but he had buried his face in his hands, and I could only perceive that a far more than ordinary wanness had overspread the emaciated fingers through which trickled many passionate tears.

The disease of the lady Madeline had long baffled the skill of her physicians. A settled apathy, a gradual wasting away of the person,

Vocabulary Builder
anomalous (ə näm′ ə ləs) *adj.* abnormal

Literary Analysis
Single Effect and Gothic Style In what ways do Usher's mental state and the house itself typify a work of Gothic literature?

14. **supposititious** (sə päz′ ə tish′ əs) *adj.* supposed.

Enrichment

Carl Maria von Weber
Poe mentions the music of German Romantic composer Carl Maria von Weber (1786–1826). Play excerpts of his work, such as the overtures from his operas *Der Freischütz* (The Freeshooter) and *Oberon*. Tell students that von Weber had a great influence on later Romantic composers, much like Poe had on writers who followed him. Or you might play the works of other Romantic composers such as Frédéric Chopin, Franz Liszt, Robert Schumann, and Hector Berlioz. Have students respond to the moods evoked by musical works such as these. Ask students whether they think Romantic music is designed to evoke a strong emotional response. Help them recognize that the melodious—and at times poignant—aspects of much Romantic music seem intended to elicit a strong emotional response in listeners.

16 and frequent although transient affections of a partially cataleptical[15] character were the unusual diagnosis. Hitherto she had steadily borne up against the pressure of her malady, and had not betaken herself finally to bed; but on the closing in of the evening of my arrival at the house, she succumbed (as her brother told me at night with inexpressible agitation) to the prostrating power of the destroyer; and I learned that the glimpse I had obtained of her person would thus probably be the last I should obtain—that the lady, at least while living, would be seen by me no more.

For several days ensuing, her name was unmentioned by either Usher or myself; and during this period I was busied in earnest endeavors to alleviate the melancholy of my friend. We painted and read together, or I listened, as if in a dream, to the wild improvisations of his speaking guitar. And thus, as a closer and still closer intimacy admitted me more unreservedly into the recesses of his spirit, the more bitterly did I perceive the futility of all attempt at cheering a mind from which darkness, as if an inherent positive quality, poured forth upon all objects of the moral and physical universe in one unceasing radiation of gloom.

I shall ever bear about me a memory of the many solemn hours I thus spent alone with the master of the House of Usher. Yet I should fail in any attempt to convey an idea of the exact character of the studies, or of the occupations, in which he involved me, or led me the way. An excited and highly distempered ideality[16] threw a sulfureous[17] luster over all. His long improvised dirges will ring forever in my ears. Among other things, I hold painfully in mind a certain singular perversion and amplification of the wild air of the last waltz of von Weber.[18] From the paintings over which his elaborate fancy brooded, and which grew, touch by touch, into vaguenesses at which I shuddered the more thrillingly, because I shuddered knowing not why—from these paintings (vivid as their images now are before me) I would in vain endeavor to educe more than a small portion which should lie within the compass of merely written words. By the utter simplicity, by the nakedness of his designs, he arrested and overawed attention. If ever mortal painted an idea, that mortal was Roderick Usher. For me at least, in the circumstances then surrounding me, there arose out of the pure abstractions which the hypochondriac contrived to throw upon his canvas, an intensity of intolerable awe, no shadow of which felt I ever yet in the contemplation of the certainly glowing yet too concrete reveries of Fuseli.[19]

15. **cataleptical** (kat′ əl ep′ tik əl) *adj.* in a state in which consciousness and feeling are suddenly and temporarily lost and the muscles become rigid.
16. **ideality** (ī dē al′ i tē) *n.* something that is ideal and has no reality.
17. **sulfureous** (sul fyo͞or′ ē əs) *adj.* greenish-yellow.
18. **von Weber** (fôn vā′ bər) Karl Maria von Weber (1786–1826), a German Romantic composer whose music was highly emotional and dramatic.
19. **Fuseli** (fo͞o ze′ lē) Johann Hinrich Fuseli (1741–1825), also known as Henry Fuseli, Swiss-born painter who lived in England and was noted for his depictions of dreamlike and sometimes nightmarish images.

Literary Analysis
Single Effect In what way does Madeline's surrender on this night contribute to a single effect?

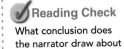

17 **Reading Check**
What conclusion does the narrator draw about Usher's mental state?

16 Literary Analysis
Single Effect

- Have students reread the two paragraphs beginning "The disease of the Lady Madeline." Make sure students understand that Madeline's disease is mysterious, even to her physicians.
- With students, write on the chalkboard a list of the disease's symptoms and characteristics.
- **Ask** students the Literary Analysis question: In what way does Madeline's surrender on this night contribute to a single effect?
  Answer: Students may say that her mysterious (and apparently final) appearance in the house adds to the narrator's sense of anxiety and foreboding.

17 Reading Check

Answer: The narrator concludes that Usher is agitated, terrified, melancholic, and hypochondriacal. He correlates Usher's mental state both with the condition and atmosphere of the house and with the condition of his sister.

Differentiated Instruction
Solutions for All Learners

Strategy for Less Proficient Readers
Read aloud with students the paragraphs beginning "For several days" and "I shall ever bear." Help students focus on the activities that the narrator and Roderick Usher perform together—reading, playing music, and painting. Then lead students in a discussion of the narrator's conclusion that Usher is so deeply rooted in gloom that not even gestures of friendship can cheer him up. Students may say that a person so fraught with emotional turmoil is unlikely to change—even with the attentions of a devoted friend.

Enrichment for Gifted/Talented Students
Have students read carefully the two last paragraphs on p. 319. Invite them to create a work of art, for example a lyric or musical composition fitting the term *dirge* ("a song of grief") or a painting fitting Poe's description of Usher's work. Encourage students to share their finished works with classmates. Interested students might research the paintings of Johann Hinrich Fuseli and compare them with their own work.

18 Background

Literature

Tell students that Poe's poem that appears here, "The Haunted Palace," was published separately five months before it appeared in this short story (in fact, it is possible that the poem inspired the tale). In one of his letters, Poe says that the palace in the poem's title symbolizes the human mind: ". . . by the Haunted Palace I mean to imply a mind haunted by phantoms—a disordered brain." Invite students to use this detail to interpret the poem and then to relate its meaning to the theme of the story.

One of the phantasmagoric conceptions of my friend, partaking not so rigidly of the spirit of abstraction, may be shadowed forth, although feebly, in words. A small picture presented the interior of an immensely long and rectangular vault or tunnel, with low walls, smooth, white and without interruption or device. Certain accessory points of the design served well to convey the idea that this excavation lay at an exceeding depth below the surface of the earth. No outlet was observed in any portion of its vast extent, and no torch or other artificial source of light was discernible; yet a flood of intense rays rolled throughout, and bathed the whole in a ghastly and inappropriate splendor.

I have just spoken of that morbid condition of the auditory nerve which rendered all music intolerable to the sufferer, with the exception of certain effects of stringed instruments. It was, perhaps, the narrow limits to which he thus confined himself upon the guitar which gave birth, in great measure, to the fantastic character of his performances. But the fervid facility of his impromptus could not be so accounted for. They must have been, and were, in the notes, as well as in the words of his wild fantasias (for he not unfrequently accompanied himself with rhymed verbal improvisations), the result of that intense mental collectedness and concentration to which I have previously alluded as observable only in particular moments of the highest artificial excitement. The words of one of these rhapsodies I have easily remembered. I was, perhaps, the more forcibly impressed with it as he gave it because, in the under or mystic current of its meaning, I fancied that I perceived, and for the first time, a full consciousness on the part of Usher of the tottering of his lofty reason
18 upon her throne. The verses, which were entitled "The Haunted Palace," ran very nearly, if not accurately, thus:

20 ▲ **Critical Viewing** In what ways do the colors and shapes in this image suggest Roderick Usher's tormented mental condition? **[Interpret]**

I

In the greenest of our valleys,
By good angels tenanted,
Once a fair and stately palace—
19 *Radiant palace—reared its head.*
In the monarch Thought's dominion—
It stood there!
Never seraph[20] *spread a pinion*
Over fabric half so fair.

20. seraph (ser′ əf) angel.

II

Banners yellow, glorious, golden,
On its roof did float and flow
(This—all this—was in the olden
Time long ago)
And every gentle air that dallied,
In that sweet day,
Along the ramparts plumed and pallid,
A winged odor went away.

III

Wanderers in that happy valley
Through two luminous windows saw
Spirits moving musically
To a lute's well-tunéd law;
Round about a throne, where sitting
(Porphyrogene!)[21]
In state his glory well befitting,
The ruler of the realm was seen.

IV

And all with pearl and ruby glowing
Was the fair palace door,
Through which came flowing, flowing, flowing
And sparkling evermore,
A troop of Echoes whose sweet duty
Was but to sing,
In voices of surpassing beauty,
The wit and wisdom of their king.

V

But evil things, in robes of sorrow,
Assailed the monarch's high estate;
(Ah, let us mourn, for never morrow
Shall dawn upon him, desolate!)
And, round about his home, the glory
That blushed and bloomed
Is but a dim-remembered story
Of the old time entombed.

VI

And travelers now within that valley,
Through the red-litten[22] *windows see*

Literary Analysis
Single Effect Which details of this poem contribute to the story's style effect?

21 **Reading Check**
What is "The Haunted Palace"?

21. **Porphyrogene** (pôr fər ō jēn′) born to royalty or "the purple."
22. **litten** lighted.

19 Literary Analysis
Single Effect

- Remind students that the narrator identifies these stanzas as the lyrics to a song sung by Roderick Usher.
- Guide students to notice in what ways the poem reflects the same atmosphere and emotions as those in the story. In this way the verse augments Poe's intended single effect.
- **Ask** students the Literary Analysis question: Which details of this poem contribute to the story's style effect?
  Answer: Examples include the reference to a lute (stanza III), which echoes the opening French couplet, and the words "But evil things, in robes of sorrow,/Assailed the monarch's high estate" (stanza V), which mirror the eerie mood at the Usher mansion.

20 Critical Viewing

Answer: The artist's use of dark colors and twisted shapes reflects Roderick Usher's melancholia and distorted thinking.

21 Reading Check

Answer: "The Haunted Palace" is a song sung by Roderick Usher. The lyrics of the song describe the mysterious, desolate palace of a doomed king.

Differentiated Instruction Solutions for All Learners

Enrichment for Special Needs Students

These students might gain greater appreciation of "The Haunted Palace" if they accompany the words with music, as was done by Roderick Usher. Groups of students might do a choral reading of the words accompanied by a recording of appropriate—melancholy or softly moody—background music. Students can evaluate whether the music enhances the mood of the words.

Strategy for English Learners

Help students read the poem stanza by stanza, identifying subjects and verbs and analyzing unusual sentence structures. Encourage students to color-code rhyming words at the ends of lines and to take note of Poe's use of sound devices (such as the many examples of repetition and alliteration). Finally, invite students to work in pairs to read the poem aloud. Partners might proceed by reading alternate stanzas.

22 Reading Strategy
Breaking Down Long Sentences

- Read aloud with students the sentence beginning "But, in his disordered fancy."
- Help students identify the sentence's subject (*idea*) and its compound predicate (*had assumed, [had] trespassed*).
- Then, have students identify and paraphrase key words and phrases, such as *disordered fancy*, *more daring character*, *trespassed*, and *kingdom* of *inorganization*.

Monitor Progress: Ask students to restate the meaning of the entire sentence.
Possible answer: Usher's confused mind has led him to believe that not only *living* things but also inanimate objects possess the ability to think and feel.

23 Literary Analysis
Single Effect

- **Ask** students to summarize the single effect Poe sets out to achieve in this story.
- Then, **ask** students to recall how (earlier in the story) Poe linked Roderick Usher and the house in which he lives. If necessary, review passages in which the man and the structure are described as having similar characteristics.
- Finally, **ask** students the Literary Analysis question: What details of this philosophical discussion contribute to the story's single effect?
Answer: Students should note that Usher's delusions about the stones, the fungus on them, the decayed trees, and the house's reflection in the tarn link the house even more closely with the decay of its inhabitants.

24 Background
Literature

An octavo edition is a book whose page size is six by nine inches. A quarto Gothic book has a page size of about nine by twelve inches; the words appear in Gothic type.

Vast forms that move fantastically
To a discordant melody;
While, like a rapid ghastly river,
Through the pale door,
A hideous throng rush out forever,
And laugh—but smile no more.

I well remember that suggestions arising from this ballad led us into a train of thought wherein there became manifest an opinion of Usher's which I mention not so much on account of its novelty (for other men have thought thus), as on account of the pertinacity with which he maintained it. This opinion, in its general form, was that of the sentience of all vegetable things. But, in his disordered fancy the 22 idea had assumed a more daring character, and trespassed, under certain conditions, upon the kingdom of inorganization.[23] I lack words to express the full extent, or the earnest abandon of his persuasion. The belief, however, was connected (as I have previously hinted) with the gray stones of the home of his forefathers. The conditions of the sentience had been here, he imagined, fulfilled in the method of collocation of these stones—in the order of their arrangement, as well as in that of the many fungi which overspread them, and of the 23 decayed trees which stood around—above all, in the long undisturbed endurance of this arrangement, and in its reduplication in the still waters of the tarn. Its evidence—the evidence of the sentience—was to be seen, he said (and I here started as he spoke), in the gradual yet certain condensation of an atmosphere of their own about the waters and the walls. The result was discoverable, he added, in that silent yet importunate and terrible influence which for centuries had molded the destinies of his family, and which made him what I now saw him—what he was. Such opinions need no comment, and I will make none.

Our books—the books which, for years, had formed no small portion of the mental existence of the invalid—were, as might be supposed, in strict keeping with this character of phantasm. We pored together over such works as the *Ververt et Chartreuse*[24] of Gresset; the *Belphegor* of Machiavelli; the *Heaven and Hell* of Swedenborg; the *Subterranean Voyage of Nicholas Klimm* by Holberg; the *Chiromancy* of Robert Flud, of Jean D'Indaginé and of De la Chambre; the *Journey into the Blue Distance* of Tieck; and the *City of the Sun* of Campanella. One favorite volume was a small octavo edition of the *Directorium Inquisitorium*, by the Dominican Eymeric de Gironne; and there were passages in Pomponius Mela, about the old 24 African Satyrs and Œgipans, over which Usher would sit dreaming for hours. His chief delight, however, was found in the perusal of an exceedingly rare and curious book in quarto Gothic—the manual

Vocabulary Builder
sentience (sen′ shəns) *n.* capacity of feeling

Literary Analysis
Single Effect Which details of this philosophical discussion contribute to the story's single effect?

23. **inorganization** (in′ ôr gə ni zā′ shən) *n.* inanimate objects.
24. ***Ververt et Chartreuse,* etc.** All the books listed deal with magic or mysticism.

Enrichment
Film Adaptations of Poe's Work
The vivid images in Edgar Allan Poe's stories and poems and his exploration of macabre, gruesome, and chilling themes have made his literary works appealing to filmmakers, and some works have been adapted more than once. Films based on Poe's works include *The Raven* (1935, 1963), *The Tell-Tale Heart* (1962), *The Fall of the House of Usher* (1982), *Murders in the Rue Morgue* (1932, 1971, 1986), *The Masque of the Red Death* (1964, 1989), and *The Pit and the Pendulum* (1961).

Invite interested students to read the original poem or tale and then to watch a film adaptation of it. Then, have students write a critical essay that analyzes the strengths and weaknesses of the film version.

of a forgotten church—the *Vigilae Mortuorum secundum Chorum Ecclesiae Maguntinae.*

I could not help thinking of the wild ritual of this work, and of its probable influence upon the hypochondriac, when, one evening, having informed me abruptly that the lady Madeline was no more, he stated his intention of preserving her corpse for a fortnight (previously to its final interment), in one of the numerous vaults within the main walls of the building. The worldly reason, however, assigned for this singular proceeding, was one which I did not feel at liberty to dispute. The brother had been led to his resolution (so he told me) by consideration of the unusual character of the malady of the deceased, of certain obtrusive and eager inquiries on the part of her medical men, and of the remote and exposed situation of the burial ground of the family. I will not deny that when I called to mind the sinister countenance of the person whom I met upon the staircase, on the day of my arrival at the house, I had no desire to oppose what I regarded as at best but a harmless, and by no means an unnatural precaution.

At the request of Usher, I personally aided him in the arrangements for the temporary entombment. The body having been encoffined, we two alone bore it to its rest. The vault in which we placed it (and which had been so long unopened that our torches, half smothered in its oppressive atmosphere, gave us little opportunity for investigation) was
25 small, damp, and entirely without means of admission for light; lying, at great depth, immediately beneath that portion of the building in which was my own sleeping apartment. It had been used, apparently, in remote feudal times, for the worst purposes of a donjon-keep, and, in later days, as a place of deposit for powder, or some other highly combustible substance, as a portion of its floor, and the whole interior of a long archway through which we reached it, were carefully sheathed with copper. The door, of massive iron, had been, also, similarly protected. Its immense weight caused an unusually sharp, grating sound, as it moved upon its hinges.

Having deposited our mournful burden upon trestles within this region of horror, we partially turned aside the yet unscrewed lid of the coffin, and looked upon the face of the tenant. A striking similitude between the brother and sister now first arrested my attention; and Usher, divining, perhaps, my thoughts, murmured out some few words from which I learned that the deceased and himself had been twins, and that sympathies of a scarcely intelligible nature had always existed between them. Our glances, however, rested not long upon the dead—for we could not regard her unawed. The disease which had thus entombed the lady in the maturity of youth, had left, as usual in all maladies of a strictly cataleptical character, the mockery of a faint blush upon the bosom and the face, and that suspiciously lingering smile upon the lip which is so terrible in death. We replaced and screwed down the lid, and, having secured the door of iron, made our way, with toil, into the scarcely less gloomy apartments of the upper portion of the house.

Reading Strategy
Breaking Down Long Sentences Clarify the main idea of the sentence beginning "The vault in which we placed it."

26 **Reading Check**
What does the narrator notice about Madeline's appearance in her coffin?

25 Reading Strategy
Breaking Down Long Sentences

- Begin by reading aloud each of this paragraph's first two sentences, encouraging students to visualize Poe's descriptions of physical actions and other details. Make sure students understand the difference between a *coffin* and a *vault* ("a burial chamber or other underground storage compartment").
- Invite one or more students to read aloud the sentence beginning "The vault in which we placed it."
- **Direct** students to respond to the Reading Strategy instruction: Clarify the main idea of the sentence beginning "The vault in which we placed it."
  Answer: The vault where Madeline's body will be temporarily entombed is dark, small, damp, and long unused. Students may also note the location of the vault directly below the room where the narrator sleeps.

26 Reading Check
Answer: The narrator notices her close resemblance to her brother, as well as the way the corpse retains a slight smile on her mouth and small patches of color on her skin.

Differentiated Instruction Solutions for All Learners

Enrichment for Gifted/Talented Students
Have students do research for an essay on the Gothic novel. Point out that they will need to use a variety of literary resources. Have students brainstorm for ideas about what they want to find out, how they might find resources, and the ways in which they will conduct their research. Ideas should include using the library, the Internet, and other print and non-print resources.

Have students generate a list of questions related to the history of the Gothic novel, for example:

- How and where did the Gothic novel originate?
- Who were the first authors of Gothic novels, and how did this genre grow in Europe and in the United States?
- What Gothic novels are still popular?

Suggest that students organize information in an outline that includes dates for important literary works. Encourage them to use the Outline graphic organizer in ***Graphic Organizer Transparencies***, p. 309.

27 Critical Thinking
Speculate

- **Ask** students to recall and discuss Roderick Usher's behavior and appearance earlier in the story. Students will probably note his nervousness and apparent ill health.
- Read aloud the paragraph beginning "And now, some days of bitter grief." **Invite** students to speculate on what may have caused this deterioration.
  Answer: Students may say that grief has overwhelmed him, that his twin's death has made him fear for his own life, and that he is harboring a terrible secret that torments him.

28 Critical Thinking
Analyze Cause and Effect

- Draw students' attention to the fact that the narrator says that he is not only terrified but also "infected" by Usher's condition.
- **Ask** students this question: How might one "catch" another's mood?
  Answer: Students might say that being with someone for a number of days could influence one's emotional state.

29 Literary Analysis
Single Effect and Gothic Style

- Have a student volunteer read aloud the paragraph beginning "It was, especially." Encourage other students to listen carefully for descriptions of the narrator's physical and mental condition.
- Then **ask** students the Literary Analysis question: Which elements of Gothic literature do the narrator's physical and mental state reflect?
  Answer: The narrator is feeling a growing psychological and physical torment. Moreover, his physical and mental symptoms have begun to feed one another in a destructive cyclical manner. This repetitive process is echoed by the narrator's pacing back and forth across the floor.

And now, some days of bitter grief having elapsed, an observable change came over the features of the mental disorder of my friend. His ordinary manner had vanished. His ordinary occupations were neglected or forgotten. He roamed from chamber to chamber with hurried, unequal, and object-less step. The pallor of his countenance had assumed, if possible, a more ghastly hue—but the luminousness of his eye had utterly gone out. The once occasional huskiness of his tone was heard no more; and a tremulous quaver, as if of extreme terror, habitually characterized his utterance. There were times, indeed, when I thought his unceasingly agitated mind was laboring with some oppressive secret, to divulge which he struggled for the necessary courage. At times, again, I was obliged to resolve all into the mere inexplicable vagaries[25] of madness, for I beheld him gazing upon vacancy for long hours, in an attitude of the profoundest attention, as if listening to some imaginary sound. It was no wonder that his condition terrified—that it infected me. I felt creeping upon me, by slow yet uncertain degrees, the wild influences of his own fantastic yet impressive superstitions.

It was, especially, upon retiring to bed late in the night of the seventh or eighth day after the placing of the lady Madeline within the donjon, that I experienced the full power of such feelings. Sleep came not near my couch—while the hours waned and waned away. I struggled to reason off the nervousness which had dominion over me. I endeavored to believe that much, if not all of what I felt, was due to the bewildering influence of the gloomy furniture of the room—of the dark and tattered draperies, which, tortured into motion by the breath of a rising tempest, swayed fitfully to and fro upon the walls, and rustled uneasily about the decorations of the bed. But my efforts were fruitless. An irrepressible tremor gradually pervaded my frame; and, at length, there sat upon my very heart an incubus[26] of utterly causeless alarm. Shaking this off with a gasp and a struggle, I uplifted myself upon the pillows, and, peering earnestly within the intense darkness of the chamber, hearkened—I know not why, except that an instinctive spirit prompted me—to certain low and indefinite sounds which came, through the pauses of the storm, at long intervals, I knew not whence. Overpowered by an intense sentiment of horror, unaccountable yet unendurable, I threw on my clothes with haste (for I felt that I should sleep no more during the night), and endeavored to arouse myself from the pitiable condition into which I had fallen by pacing rapidly to and fro through the apartment.

I had taken but few turns in this manner, when a light step on an adjoining staircase arrested my attention. I presently recognized it as that of Usher. In an instant afterward he rapped, with a gentle touch, at my door, and entered, bearing a lamp. His countenance was, as usual, cadaverously wan—but, moreover, there was a species of mad hilarity in his eyes—an evidently restrained hysteria in his whole demeanor. His

Literary Analysis
Single Effect and Gothic Style Which elements of Gothic literature do the narrator's physical and mental states reflect?

---

25. vagaries (vā′ ger ēz) *n.* odd, unexpected actions or notions.
26. incubus (iŋ′ kyə bəs) *n.* something nightmarishly burdensome.

air appalled me—but anything was preferable to the solitude which I had so long endured, and I even welcomed his presence as a relief.

"And you have not seen it?" he said abruptly, after having stared about him for some moments in silence—"you have not then seen it?—but, stay! you shall." Thus speaking, and having carefully shaded his lamp, he hurried to one of the casements, and threw it freely open to the storm.

30 The impetuous fury of the entering gust nearly lifted us from our feet. It was, indeed, a tempestuous yet sternly beautiful night, and one wildly singular in its terror and its beauty. A whirlwind had apparently collected its force in our vicinity; for there were frequent and violent alterations in the direction of the wind; and the exceeding density of the clouds (which hung so low as to press upon the turrets of the house) did not prevent our perceiving the lifelike velocity with which they flew careering from all points against each other, without passing away into the distance. I say that even their exceeding density did not prevent our perceiving this—yet we had no glimpse of the moon or stars, nor was there any flashing forth of the lightning. But the under surfaces of the huge masses of agitated vapor, as well as all terrestrial objects immediately around us, were glowing in the unnatural light of a faintly luminous and distinctly visible gaseous exhalation which hung about and enshrouded the mansion.

"You must not—you shall not behold this!" said I, shuddering, to Usher, as I led him, with a gentle violence, from the window to a seat. "These appearances, which bewilder you, are merely electrical phenomena not uncommon—or it may be that they have their ghastly origin in the rank miasma[27] of the tarn. Let us close this casement:—the air is chilling and dangerous to your frame. Here is one of your favorite romances. I will read, and you shall listen:—and so we will pass away this terrible night together."

The antique volume which I had taken up was the *Mad Trist* of Sir Launcelot Canning;[28] but I had called it a favorite of Usher's more in sad jest than in earnest; for, in truth, there is little in its uncouth and unimaginative prolixity which could have had interest for the lofty and spiritual ideality of my friend. It was, however, the only book immediately at hand; and I indulged a vague hope that the excitement which now agitated the hypochondriac, might find relief (for the history of mental disorder is full of similar anomalies) even in the extremeness of the folly which I should read. Could I have judged, indeed, by the wild overstrained air of vivacity with which he hearkened, or apparently hearkened, to the words of the tale, I might well have congratulated myself upon the success of my design.

I had arrived at that well-known portion of the story where Ethelred, the hero of the Trist, having sought in vain for peaceable admission into the dwelling of the hermit, proceeds to make good an

27. **miasma** (mī az′ mə) *n.* unwholesome atmosphere.
28. ***Mad Trist* of Sir Launcelot Canning** fictional book and author.

Literary Analysis
Single Effect In what way does the description of the storm contribute to the growing sense of terror?

31  **Reading Check**
Which odd or unnatural sight does the narrator see when the curtains are opened?

30 Literary Analysis
Single Effect

- Invite a student volunteer to summarize Edgar Allan Poe's theory about a single effect in literary works. If necessary, remind students that Poe's theory asserts that every character, incident and description in a story must contribute to the single effect being achieved in the story.
- **Ask** students the Literary Analysis question: In what way does the description of the storm contribute to the growing sense of terror? **Answer:** Students may say that Poe describes the storm with many of the same words he used to describe the mansion and Roderick Usher, such as *agitated, luminous, ghastly, rank, chilling,* and *dangerous.*

31 Reading Check

Answer: The narrator sees strangely dense clouds, whirlwinds, and other effects of a terrible storm taking place on this "sternly beautiful night."

Differentiated Instruction Solutions for All Learners

Enrichment for Advanced Readers

Tell students that whirlpools and whirlwinds are recurring symbols in Poe stories. Because they draw things toward their center, they stand for destructive collapse. Poe believed that the universe was destined to collapse in on itself. He wrote about his theories of cosmology in his book *Eureka*. His ideas about the origin and end of the universe are remarkable because they anticipated the Big Bang theory by many years. Have students read and report on another piece of Poe's short fiction that uses whirlpool or whirlwind imagery, such as "A Descent Into the Maelstrom." Encourage students to give short oral presentations in which they summarize the story and explain how this particular imagery relates to the story's plot, themes, or characters.

32 Literary Analysis

Single Effect

- Have three or four student volunteers read these four paragraphs as classmates listen to and record Poe's descriptive details.
- **Ask** students the Literary Analysis question: Which words and details from this description of the unusual sounds add to the single effect?
Answer: Words and details include: *echo; cracking and ripping sound; coincidence; rattling; increasing storm; disturbed; shriek so horrid and harsh; piercing; dreadful noise; wild amazement; low and apparently distant . . . grating sound; and dragon's unnatural shriek.*

entrance by force. Here, it will be remembered, the words of the narrative run thus:

"And Ethelred, who was by nature of a doughty heart, and who was now mighty withal, on account of the powerfulness of the wine which he had drunken, waited no longer to hold parley with the hermit, who, in sooth, was of an obstinate and maliceful turn, but feeling the rain upon his shoulders, and fearing the rising of the tempest, uplifted his mace outright, and, with blows, made quickly room in the plankings of the door for his gauntleted hand; and now pulling therewith sturdily, he so cracked, and ripped, and tore all asunder, that the noise of the dry and hollow-sounding wood alarumed and reverberated throughout the forest."

At the termination of this sentence I started and, for a moment, paused; for it appeared to me (although I at once concluded that my excited fancy had deceived me)—it appeared to me that, from some very remote portion of the mansion, there came, indistinctly to my ears, which might have been, in its exact similarity of character, the echo (but a stifled and dull one certainly) of the very cracking and ripping sound which Sir Launcelot had so particularly described. It was, beyond doubt, the coincidence alone which had arrested my attention; for, amid the rattling of the sashes of the casements, and the ordinary commingled noises of the still increasing storm, the sound, itself, had nothing, surely, which should have interested or disturbed me. I continued the story:

"But the good champion Ethelred, now entering within the door, was sore enraged and amazed to perceive no signal of the maliceful hermit; but, in the stead thereof, a dragon of a scaly and prodigious demeanor, and of a fiery tongue, which sate in guard before a palace of gold, with a floor of silver; and upon the wall there hung a shield
32 of shining brass with this legend enwritten—

Who entereth herein, a conqueror
hath bin;
Who slayeth the dragon, the shield
he shall win.

And Ethelred uplifted his mace, and struck upon the head of the dragon, which fell before him, and gave up his pasty breath, with a shriek so horrid and harsh, and withal so piercing, that Ethelred had fain to close his ears with his hands against the dreadful noise of it, the like whereof was never before heard."

Here again I paused abruptly, and now with a feeling of wild amazement—for there could be no doubt whatever that, in this instance, I did actually hear (although from what direction it proceeded I found it impossible to say) a low and apparently distant, but harsh, protracted, and most unusual screaming or grating sound—the exact counterpart of what my fancy had already conjured up for the dragon's unnatural shriek as described by the romancer.

Literary Analysis
Single Effect Which words and details from this description of the unusual sounds add to the single effect?

Enrichment

Dragons

In the story within this tale, Poe describes a dragon slain by Ethelred. Though dragons are imaginary creatures that appear in myths and legends of many cultures, not all dragons are alike. In the Chinese and Japanese cultures, dragons symbolize wisdom, power, and the mysteries of the universe. They possess courage, impart knowledge, and are assumed to be fabulously rich. Their strength is thought to explain forces of nature such as lightning and wind.

Unlike the benevolent Eastern dragon, the typical Western dragon is unmercifully evil. This dragon has a hideous, scaly body with angular wings. Its breath is so foul that the stench—or the blast of red-hot fire—from its mouth can kill. Western legends place dragons in habitats such as caves or underground in tunnels, cellars, or wells. Some live above ground in trees, fields, or mountains. Like Eastern dragons, some Western dragons live in or near lakes, rivers, swamps, or oceans.

Separation, 1896, Edvard Munch, Munch Museet, Oslo, Norway

Oppressed, as I certainly was, upon the extraordinary coincidence, by a thousand conflicting sensations, in which wonder and extreme terror were predominant, I still retained sufficient presence of mind to avoid exciting, by an observation, the sensitive nervousness of my companion. I was by no means certain that he had noticed the sounds in question; although, assuredly, a strange alteration had, during the last few minutes, taken place in his demeanor. From a position fronting my own, he had gradually brought round his chair; so as to sit with his face to the door of the chamber; and thus I could but partially perceive his features, although I saw that his lips trembled as if he were murmuring inaudibly. His head had dropped upon his breast—yet I knew that he was not asleep, from the wide and rigid opening of the eye as I caught a glance of it in profile. The motion of his body, too, was at

34 **▲ Critical Viewing**
Describe the ways in which this painting conveys the same unnatural sense of terror Poe creates in the story. **[Analyze]**

35 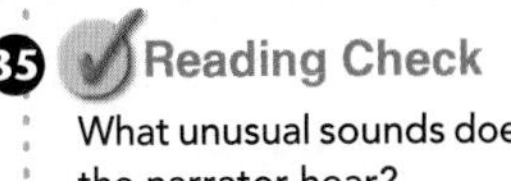

Reading Check
What unusual sounds does the narrator hear?

33 Humanities

Separation, 1896, by Edvard Munch

Edvard Munch (1863–1944) was a painter and graphic artist who studied in Paris, as well as in his native Norway. Munch's complex psychological style is considered one of the earliest manifestations of Expressionism, a movement in art marked by the use of symbols and images that are distorted to convey emotion and inner experience. Like Poe, Munch drew his identity as an artist from an obsession with depression, fear, and death; his exploration of these dark themes infuses his art with a harrowing power.

Like so many of Munch's works, *Separation* focuses on the emotional effects of a situation. The dark colors and drawn expression of the person in the foreground create a mood ofdespair. Use these questions for discussion:

1. How does the artist create contrast in the painting?
   Answer: Students may note that one person is dressed in dark clothes and is stationary. The other figure's dress is light; she is in motion; and her face and fingers are only suggested. Students may also point out the painting's contrasting settings.
2. In what ways is the image related to Poe's tale?
   Answer: Roderick Usher is a man in despair; his sister Madeline is isolated by illness. The story describes their "separation."

34 Critical Viewing

Answer: The painting shows two people. One seems to have a troubled expression; the other appears to be a faceless ghost. Both the painting and Poe's story evoke a sense of supernatural dread and anguish.

35 Reading Check

Answer: The narrator hears a "cracking and ripping sound," "a shriek so horrid and harsh," and "a low and apparently distant, but harsh, protracted, and most unusual screaming or grating sound."

Differentiated Instruction

Solutions for All Learners

Enrichment for Advanced Readers

The French poet Charles Baudelaire saw Poe as both an outlaw and a hero. In an essay published in the *Paris Review* in 1852, Baudelaire observed:

"Poe usually suppresses the minor details or gives them a minimal value. Because of this harsh severity, the generating idea is more evident and the subject stands out vividly against the bare background. In Poe's books the style is condensed, tightly linked. The ill will or laziness of the reader cannot slip through the mesh of this logically woven net. All ideas, like obedient arrows, fly to the same target."

Read aloud Baudelaire's critique and work with students to paraphrase it. Then have students discuss or write about the following question:

Does Poe "suppress the minor details"? Explain. Which details might he have suppressed in "The Fall of the House of Usher.

36 Reading Strategy
Breaking Down Long Sentences

- Read aloud for students the paragraph beginning "And now, the champion." Remind students that these words likewise are being read aloud to Roderick Usher by the narrator from a book called *Mad Trist*.
- **Direct** students to respond to the Reading Strategy question: Summarize the action of the paragraph-long sentence beginning "And now, the champion." **Possible response:** Ethelred thinks of the magical shield, removes the dragon's corpse, and walks toward the shield hanging on the castle wall, during which time the shield crashes to the floor at his feet.

37 Critical Thinking
Draw Conclusions

- Read aloud this passage, in which Roderick Usher claims—excitedly and repeatedly—that he did not dare to speak of his fearful realization.
- **Ask** students why Usher may have been unable to speak out, given that he took careful precautions to ensure that he did not bury his sister alive. **Answer:** Students may say that Roderick feels guilty about what he has done but fears exposing the gruesome act to his one friend or that he intentionally kept silent because he wanted his sister to be dead.

38 Literary Analysis
Single Effect and Gothic Style

- Read aloud the paragraph beginning "As if in the superhuman energy."
- **Ask** students the Literary Analysis question: What elements of Gothic literature are evident in this passage about Madeline Usher? **Answer:** This passage features elements such as macabre or violent plot details (*blood upon her white robes, some bitter struggle, violent and now final death agonies*), characters in physical or psychological torment (Madeline and Roderick), and the presence of a supernatural or otherworldly element (*superhuman energy*).

variance with this idea—for he rocked from side to side with a gentle yet constant and uniform sway. Having rapidly taken notice of all this, I resumed the narrative of Sir Launcelot, which thus proceeded:

36 "And now, the champion, having escaped from the terrible fury of the dragon, bethinking himself of the brazen shield, and of the breaking up of the enchantment which was upon it, removed the carcass from out of the way before him, and approached valorously over the silver pavement of the castle to where the shield was upon the wall; which in sooth tarried not for his full coming, but fell down at his feet upon the silver floor, with a mighty great and terrible ringing sound."

No sooner had these syllables passed my lips, than—as if a shield of brass had indeed, at the moment, fallen heavily upon a floor of silver—I became aware of a distinct, hollow, metallic, and clangorous, yet apparently muffled, reverberation. Completely unnerved, I leaped to my feet; but the measured rocking movement of Usher was undisturbed. I rushed to the chair in which he sat. His eyes were bent fixedly before him, and throughout his whole countenance there reigned a stony rigidity. But, as I placed my hand upon his shoulder, there came a strong shudder over his whole person; a sickly smile quivered about his lips; and I saw that he spoke in a low, hurried, and gibbering murmur, as if unconscious of my presence. Bending closely over him I at length drank in the hideous import of his words.

37 "Not hear it?—yes, I hear it, and have heard it. Long—long—long—many minutes, many hours, many days, have I heard it—yet I dared not—oh, pity me, miserable wretch that I am!—I *dared* not—I dared not speak! *We have put her living in the tomb!* Said I not that my senses were acute? I *now* tell you that I heard her first feeble movement in the hollow coffin. I heard them—many, many days ago—yet I dared not—*I dared not speak!* and now—tonight—Ethelred—ha! ha!—the breaking of the hermit's door, and the death cry of the dragon, and the clangor of the shield—say, rather, the rending of her coffin, and the grating of the iron hinges of her prison, and her struggles within the coppered archway of the vault! Oh! wither shall I fly? Will she not be here anon? Is she not hurrying to upbraid me for my haste? Have I not heard her footstep on the stair? Do I not distinguish that heavy and horrible beating of her heart? Madman!"—here he sprang furiously to his feet, and shrieked out his syllables, as if in the effort he were giving up his soul—"*Madman! I tell you that she now stands without the door!*"

38 As if in the superhuman energy of his utterance there had been found the potency of a spell, the huge antique panels to which the speaker pointed threw slowly back, upon the instant, their ponderous and ebony jaws. It was the work of the rushing gust—but then without those doors there *did* stand the lofty and enshrouded figure of the lady Madeline of Usher. There was blood upon her white robes, and the evidence of some bitter struggle upon every portion of her emaciated frame. For a moment she remained trembling and reeling to and fro upon the threshold—then, with a low moaning cry, fell heavily inward

Reading Strategy
Breaking Down Long Sentences Summarize the action of the paragraph-long sentence beginning "And now, the champion."

Literary Analysis
Single Effect and Gothic Style Which elements of Gothic literature are evident in this passage about Madeline Usher?

Enrichment

Literary Critics

A literary critic reads, analyzes, evaluates, and comments on literature for both general and specialized audiences. He or she does so online, in magazines or newspapers, on radio or television, or in professional journals. Have students read some literary criticism about Edgar Allan Poe's "The Fall of the House of Usher" or "The Raven" to get a better grasp of a critic's objectives and style of writing. Tell students that literary critics usually support their opinions—whether positive or negative—about a literary work with citations from the text.

Invite students to brainstorm for a list of traits that a good literary critic should possess. Students who have an interest in this field might be encouraged to submit their own literary reviews to a school newspaper.

upon the person of her brother, and in her violent and now final death agonies, bore him to the floor a corpse, and a victim to the terrors he had anticipated.

From that chamber, and from that mansion, I fled aghast. The storm was still abroad in all its wrath as I found myself crossing the old causeway. Suddenly there shot along the path a wild light, and I turned to see whence a gleam so unusual could have issued; for the vast house and its shadows were alone behind me. The radiance was that of the full, setting, and bloodred moon, which now shone vividly through that once barely discernible fissure, of which I have before spoken as extending from the roof of the building, in a zigzag direction, to the base. While I gazed, this fissure rapidly widened—there came a fierce breath of the whirlwind—the entire orb of the satellite burst at once upon my sight—my brain reeled as I saw the mighty walls rushing asunder—there was a long tumultuous shouting sound like the voice of a thousand waters—and the deep and dank tarn at my feet closed sullenly and silently over the fragments of the *"House of Usher."*

Critical Reading

1. **Respond:** In this story, the narrator barely escapes being drawn into Roderick's fantasy world. Were you drawn into the fantasy world of the story? Explain.
2. **(a) Recall:** Why has the narrator gone to visit Usher? **(b) Assess:** Does the narrator succeed in his purpose? **(c) Analyze:** What is the significance of the detail that the narrator finds himself becoming affected by Usher's condition?
3. **(a) Analyze:** In the description of the exterior of the house, which words suggest the presence of decay in the structure itself? **(b) Connect:** In what ways does this description foreshadow, or hint at, the ending of the story?
4. **(a) Interpret:** Which descriptive details of the interior of the house suggest that the narrator has entered a realm that is quite different from the ordinary world? **(b) Infer:** Which details in Usher's appearance suggest that he has been cut off from the outside world for many years? **(c) Connect:** In what ways is the appearance of the interior of the house related to Usher's appearance and to the condition of his mind?
5. **(a) Speculate:** Poe chose to characterize Roderick and Madeline as twins, not simply as brother and sister. Why do you think he made this choice? **(b) Support:** What evidence is there to support the claim of some critics who have argued that Madeline and Roderick are actually physical and mental components of the same being?

For: More about Edgar Allan Poe
Visit: www.PHSchool.com
Web Code: ere-9308

ASSESS

Answers

1. Students may say that they *were* drawn into the fantasy world. The unbroken span of terror in this story may have made students imagine the frightening scene all too clearly.
2. (a) The narrator arrives to lessen the effects of the "malady" of Usher, his boyhood friend. (b) He is powerless to stop Usher's descent into madness and death. (c) It indicates that a person can become infected by another person's psychological maladies.
3. (a) Students might point to words such as *excessive antiquity, discoloration of ages, minute fungi overspread the whole exterior, crumbling condition of individual stones, barely perceptible fissure . . . extending from the roof . . . down the wall in a zigzag fashion.* (b) Especially the final detail hints that the house may be vulnerable to collapse.
4. (a) Students might cite details such as *dark and intricate passages; phantasmagoric armorial trophies; feeble beams of encrimsoned light;* and *an air of stern, deep, and irredeemable gloom.* (b) **Possible responses** include *overdone cordiality, cadaverousness of complexion, ghastly pallor of the skin, silken hair . . . suffered to grow all unheeded.* (c) Like Usher's physical appearance, the house is in a state of decay; like his mind, the house is gloomy and full of sorrow.
5. (a) **Possible response:** Making the Ushers twins increases the horror of Roderick's inability (or unwillingness) to save his sister; moreover it suggests a self-destructive or suicidal impulse in Roderick.
(b) **Possible response:** Roderick seems always to know what Madeline is experiencing; he does not attempt to rescue her because he knows they are both doomed; he mentions the extremely intuitive feelings that have always been between them.

Go Online Author Link For additional information about Edgar Allan Poe, have students type in the Web Code, then select P from the alphabet, and then select Edgar Allan Poe.

39 About the Selection

On one level, "The Raven" tells of a man who grieves for his lost love, Lenore. A mysterious talking raven appears at the speaker's door, prompting him to question the bird about Lenore. The raven responds to each question—including the question of whether the speaker will ever see Lenore again—with the single word *Nevermore,* leaving the speaker broken and devoid of hope. On another level, the poem explores how grief and loneliness can turn to madness. Poe depicts a mind going to pieces—and watching itself in the process.

40 Critical Thinking

Infer

- Help students infer from the clues in these five lines what kind of person the speaker is.
- As they discuss this issue and return to the text for evidence, encourage students to consider every part of both lines—not just the adjectives that describe the speaker directly. **Response:** Students may say that the speaker is prone to melancholy and self-absorption or that he seems lonely.

41 Literary Analysis

Single Effect

- Tell students that poets use sound devices—such as alliteration, assonance, consonance, repetition, internal rhyme, and onomatopoeia—to give a musical quality to their writing. Sound devices please the ear and reinforce meaning by emphasizing key sounds, ideas, words, or images.
- **Ask** students the Literary Analysis question: In what way does Poe's use of sound devices contribute to the creation of a single effect? **Answer:** Poe's use of all of these devices creates a hypnotic effect that draws readers into the speaker's world. As a result, Poe persuades readers temporarily to abandon their notions of reality to accept the speaker's demented vision.

39

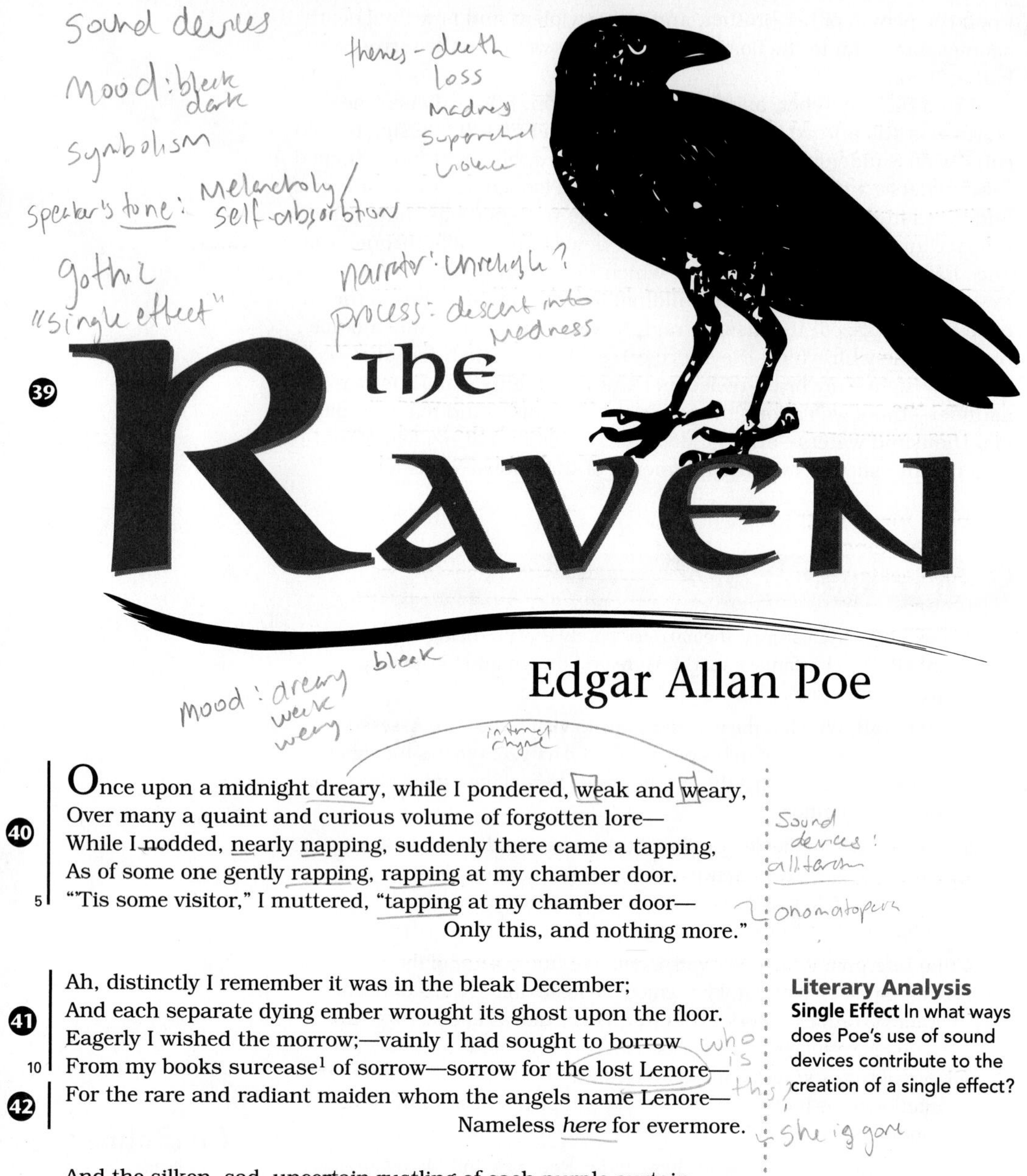

The Raven

Edgar Allan Poe

40

Once upon a midnight dreary, while I pondered, weak and weary,
Over many a quaint and curious volume of forgotten lore—
While I nodded, nearly napping, suddenly there came a tapping,
As of some one gently rapping, rapping at my chamber door.
"'Tis some visitor," I muttered, "tapping at my chamber door—
Only this, and nothing more."

41

Ah, distinctly I remember it was in the bleak December;
And each separate dying ember wrought its ghost upon the floor.
Eagerly I wished the morrow;—vainly I had sought to borrow
From my books surcease[1] of sorrow—sorrow for the lost Lenore—

42

For the rare and radiant maiden whom the angels name Lenore—
Nameless *here* for evermore.

And the silken, sad, uncertain rustling of each purple curtain
Thrilled me—filled me with fantastic terrors never felt before;
So that now, to still the beating of my heart, I stood repeating
"'Tis some visitor entreating entrance at my chamber door—

Literary Analysis
Single Effect In what ways does Poe's use of sound devices contribute to the creation of a single effect?

1. **surcease** (sur sēs′) end.

Enrichment

The Raven

Point out that when Edgar Allan Poe wrote this poem, he drew from a long tradition that viewed the raven as a bird of ill omen. Yet, in some cultures, the raven enjoys a more positive image. In the Bible, ravens feed the prophet Elijah in the desert; Christian art depicts ravens as symbols of God's providence. When Vikings were lost at sea, they would set free a raven and the bird would fly toward land, leading the Vikings to safety. The Vikings prized ravens highly and featured them on their flags.

Discuss with students the symbolic meanings, both positive and negative, of ravens and other birds in various cultures. You might speak of such birds as the albatross, bluebird, crow, nightingale, owl, and parrot. Individual students might be assigned to research the symbolism of one type of bird and to report their findings to the class.

Some late visitor entreating entrance at my chamber door;—
This it is and nothing more."

Presently my soul grew stronger; hesitating then no longer,
"Sir," said I, "or Madam, truly your forgiveness I implore;
But the fact is I was napping, and so gently you came rapping,
And so faintly you came tapping, tapping at my chamber door,
That I scarce was sure I heard you"—here I opened wide the door;—
Darkness there and nothing more.

Deep into that darkness peering, long I stood there wondering, fearing,
Doubting, dreaming dreams no mortal ever dared to dream before;
But the silence was unbroken, and the stillness gave no token,
And the only word there spoken was the whispered word, "Lenore?"
This I whispered, and an echo murmured back the word, "Lenore!"
Merely this and nothing more.

Back then into the chamber turning, all my soul within me burning,
Soon again I heard a tapping somewhat louder than before.
"Surely," said I, "surely that is something at my window lattice;
Let me see, then, what thereat is, and this mystery explore—
Let my heart be still a moment and this mystery explore;—
'Tis the wind and nothing more!"

Open here I flung the shutter, when, with many a flirt and flutter,
In there stepped a stately Raven of the saintly days of yore;
Not the least obeisance made he; not a minute stopped or stayed he;
But, with mien of lord or lady, perched above my chamber door—
Perched upon a bust of Pallas[2] just above my chamber door—
Perched, and sat, and nothing more.

Then this ebony bird beguiling[3] my sad fancy into smiling,
By the grave and stern decorum of the countenance[4] it wore,
"Though thy crest be shorn and shaven, thou," I said, "art sure no craven,
Ghastly grim and ancient Raven wandering from the Nightly shore—
Tell me what thy lordly name is on the Night's Plutonian[5] shore!"
Quoth the Raven, "Nevermore."

Reading Strategy
Breaking Down Long Sentences Summarize the action of the stanza-long sentence beginning "Presently my soul grew stronger."

Vocabulary Builder
obeisance (ō bā′ səns) *n.* gesture of respect

Vocabulary Builder
craven (krā′ vən) *adj.* very cowardly

2. **Pallas** (pal′ əs) Pallas Athena, the ancient Greek goddess of wisdom.
3. **beguiling** (bi gīl′ iŋ) *part.* charming.
4. **countenance** (koun′ tə nəns) *n.* facial expression.
5. **Plutonian** (plo͞o tō′ nē ən) *adj.* like the underworld or infernal regions; refers to Pluto, Greek and Roman god of the underworld.

44 **Reading Check**
What is the speaker's first reaction to the Raven?

42 Background
Literature

In his poems and fictional prose works, Poe often depicts the death of a beautiful young woman. He considered this to be the greatest tragic theme, perhaps as a result of his wife's fragile health or his mother's early death.

43 Reading Strategy
Breaking Down Long Sentences

- Have students listen to the fourth stanza read aloud by a classmate, by you, or by a professional reader (on the **Listening to Literature Audio CD**).
- **Direct** students to respond to the Reading Strategy task: Summarize the action of the stanza-long sentence beginning "Presently my soul grew stronger."
  Answer: The speaker feels bolder, stops hesitating, and speaks to his undiscovered visitor. Then he opens the door and sees nothing but darkness.

44 Reading Check

Answer: The speaker smiles at its apparent "grave and stern decorum."

Differentiated Instruction
Solutions for All Learners

Strategy for Special Needs Students

Encourage students to choose a stanza—or even a single line—and to identify in it examples of repeated sounds or letter sequences. In line 37, for instance, students might note the three words beginning with the letters *fl,* the two words containing the sequence of letters *u-t-t-e-r,* and the two words starting with *w.* Have students listen to the line (or stanza) spoken aloud more than once, and have them practice saying it themselves.

Strategy for Advanced Readers

Have students identify examples of Poe's use of assonance, consonance, and alliteration. Students might point to the repetition of vowel sounds in the words *flung, shutter,* and *flutter* as an example of assonance; the repetition of consonant sounds in the words *shutter, flirt,* and *flutter* is an example of consonance; the repetitions of initial consonant sounds in the words *when* and *with* and *flirt* and *flutter* are examples of alliteration. These devices give the poem a driving rhythm and a musical flair.

45 Humanities

***The Raven*, 1845, by Edmund Dulac**

This picture of a raven features bold lines that give the bird a frenzied or disheveled quality while at the same time symbolically evoking a troubled or discordant mind.

Use these questions for discussion:

1. What images from the poem does the artist evoke?
   Answer: Students may say that the raven sits on a bust; its open mouth suggests speech; its ruffled appearance fits the line about the "ungainly fowl"; the brightness behind it recalls "lamp-light o'er him streaming."
2. Why is the raven off-center?
   Answer: Students may say that the unbalanced scene suggests the speaker's unbalanced mind.

46 Critical Viewing

Answer: The lines going at many angles convey the feeling of chaos or frenzy. The shading lets the raven stand out from the vortex-like background at the same time that it is clearly part of it. The mood of the illustration—that of brooding or lurking evil—clearly matches that of the poem.

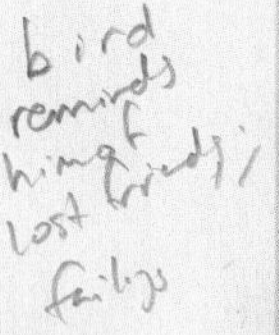

45 ***The Raven,*** Edmund Dulac

Much I marveled this ungainly fowl to hear discourse so plainly,
Though its answer little meaning—little relevancy bore;
For we cannot help agreeing that no living human being
Ever yet was blessed with seeing bird above his chamber door—
Bird or beast upon the sculptured bust above his chamber door,
With such name as "Nevermore."

But the Raven, sitting lonely on the placid bust, spoke only
That one word, as if his soul in that one word he did outpour.
Nothing farther than he uttered—not a feather then he fluttered—
Till I scarcely more than muttered, "Other friends have flown before—
On the morrow *he* will leave me, as my Hopes have flown before."
Then the bird said, "Nevermore."

46 ▲ Critical Viewing
Explain the effect produced by the lines and shading of this drawing. Does the mood of the illustration match that of the poem? Explain. **[Assess]**

Differentiated Instruction Solutions for All Learners

Enrichment for Advanced Readers

Suggest that students read additional works by Edgar Allan Poe such as "The Black Cat," "The Pit and the Pendulum, "The Bells, " or "The Cask of Amontillado." You may also wish to use ***Authors In Depth,*** *The American Experience,* which contains the following selections:

- Preface from *Lyrical Ballads*
- from "Chapter of Suggestions"
- "Alone"
- "Eldorado"
- "To Helen"

After students read these or other works by Poe, have them form discussion groups in which they compare and contrast the selections they have read. Suggest criteria for comparison, such as setting, theme, characters, and mood. To extend the activity, have volunteers present to the class brief oral reports on their favorite Poe selections.

Startled at the stillness broken by reply so aptly spoken,
"Doubtless," said I, "what it utters is its only stock and store
Caught from some unhappy master whom unmerciful Disaster
Followed fast and followed faster till his songs one burden bore—
Till the dirges of his Hope that melancholy burden bore
Of 'Never—nevermore.'"

But the Raven still beguiling my sad fancy into smiling,
Straight I wheeled a cushioned seat in front of bird, and bust and door;
Then, upon the velvet sinking, I betook myself to linking
Fancy unto fancy, thinking what this ominous[6] bird of yore—
What this grim, ungainly, ghastly, gaunt, and ominous bird of yore
47 Meant in croaking "Nevermore."

This I sat engaged in guessing, but no syllable expressing
To the fowl whose fiery eyes now burned into my bosom's core;
This and more I sat divining, with my head at ease reclining
On the cushion's velvet lining that the lamp-light gloated o'er,
But whose velvet-violet lining with the lamp-light gloating o'er,
She shall press, ah, nevermore!

Then, methought, the air grew denser, perfumed from an unseen censer
Swung by seraphim whose foot-falls tinkled on the tufted floor.
"Wretch," I cried, "thy God hath lent thee—by these angels he hath sent thee
Respite—respite and nepenthe[7] from thy memories of Lenore;
Quaff, oh quaff this kind nepenthe and forget this lost Lenore!"
Quoth the Raven, "Nevermore."

"Prophet!" said I, "thing of evil!—prophet still, if bird or devil!—
Whether Tempter sent, or whether tempest tossed thee here ashore,
48 Desolate yet all undaunted, on this desert land enchanted—
On this home by Horror haunted—tell me truly, I implore—
Is there—*is* there balm in Gilead?[8]—tell me—tell me, I implore!"
Quoth the Raven, "Nevermore."

"Prophet!" said I, "thing of evil!—prophet still, if bird or devil!
By that Heaven that bends above us—by that God we both adore—
Tell this soul with sorrow laden if, within the distant Aidenn,[9]

Literary Analysis
Single Effect and Gothic Style Which aspects of the Gothic style are evident in the speaker's relationship to the Raven?

6. **ominous** (äm′ ə nəs) *adj.* threatening; sinister.
7. **nepenthe** (ni pen′ thē) *n.* drug that the ancient Greeks believed could relieve sorrow.
8. **balm in Gilead** (gil′ ē əd) in the Bible, a healing ointment made in Gilead, a region of ancient Palestine.
9. **Aidenn** (ā′ den) Arabic for Eden or heaven.

49 **Reading Check**
What does the speaker want the Raven to tell him?

47 Reading Strategy
Breaking Down Long Sentences

- To aid in students' understanding, suggest that students break down long sentences into phrases that tell about the key ideas: who, what, and why. Using this visual device will help students focus on the ideas for restatement:

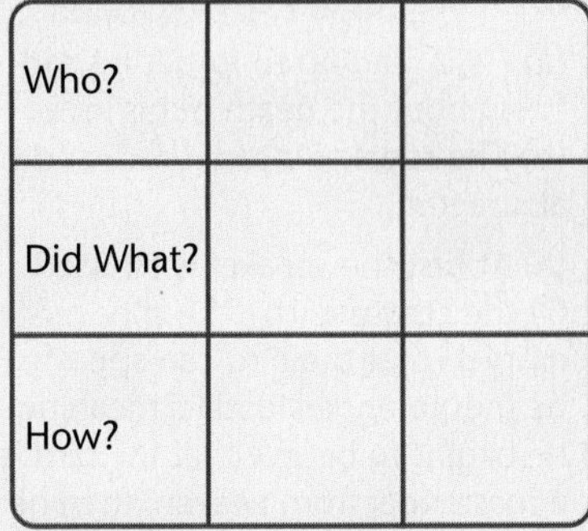

Who?		
Did What?		
How?		

- Explain that by separating out the nonessential information or details, students can more easily restate a passage in their own words.
- Have students use the organizer to break down lines 67–78 into phrases or segments of information. Then have students summarize the text in their own words.

48 Literary Analysis
Single Effect and Gothic Style

- Have students pair up and review stanzas 7–15 of the poem, noting how the speaker and the Raven interact and how the Raven affects the speaker's thoughts and emotions.
- **Ask** students the Literary Analysis question: Which aspects of the Gothic style are evident in the speaker's relationship to the Raven?
Answer: Students may note the macabre effect of the Raven's repetition of the word *nevermore,* the psychological torment the speaker feels because of the Raven's implacability, and the otherworldly overtones in the creature's presence in the speaker's chamber.

49 Reading Check

Answer: The speaker wants the Raven to say whether there is "balm in Gilead"—in other words, whether there is a prospect of relief from his grief.

It shall clasp a sainted maiden whom the angels name Lenore—
Clasp a rare and radiant maiden whom the angels name Lenore."
Quoth the Raven, "Nevermore."

"Be that word our sign of parting, bird or fiend!" I shrieked, upstarting—
"Get thee back into the tempest and the Night's Plutonian shore!
Leave no black plume as a token of that lie thy soul hath spoken!
Leave my loneliness unbroken!—quit the bust above my door!
Take thy beak from out my heart, and take thy form from off my door!"
Quoth the Raven, "Nevermore."

And the Raven, never flitting, still is sitting, *still* is sitting
On the pallid bust of Pallas just above my chamber door;
And his eyes have all the seeming of a demon's that is dreaming;
And the lamp-light o'er him streaming throws his shadow on the floor;
And my soul from out that shadow that lies floating on the floor
Shall be lifted—nevermore!

Critical Reading

1. **Respond:** This poem has been popular for more than one hundred years. Explain why you think the poem does or does not merit this continued attention.
2. **(a) Recall:** Why is the speaker reading at the beginning of the poem? **(b) Assess:** What is his emotional state as the poem begins?
3. **(a) Recall:** With what emotion does the speaker first greet the Raven? **(b) Interpret:** During the course of the poem, how does the speaker's attitude toward the Raven change? **(c) Analyze Cause and Effect:** In what way is the word *nevermore* related to these emotional changes?
4. **(a) Recall:** What does the speaker eventually order the Raven to do? **(b) Analyze:** At the end of the poem, what does the speaker mean when he says the Raven "still is sitting" above the door?
5. **(a) Interpret:** What is the relationship between the raven's shadow and the speaker's soul at the end of the poem? **(b) Analyze:** What does the Raven finally come to represent?
6. **Apply:** Do you think grief can truly cause a person to permanently lose the ability to reason? Explain.

Go Online
Author Link

For: More about Edgar Allan Poe
Visit: www.PHSchool.com
Web Code: ere-9308

ASSESS

Answers

1. Students might suggest that many generations of readers have responded to the poem's sound effects and rhythm, as well as to its fantastic elements, especially the enigmatic and maddening utterances of the raven.
2. (a) He is reading to forget his sadness about the death of his lover. (b) The speaker is sad, tired, and abstracted.
3. (a) At first the speaker is amused by the creature. (b) The speaker marvels that the bird can speak; he tries to understand its meaning; he begins to believe that the bird is a messenger from heaven; then he thinks it is evil; finally he becomes angry and orders the bird to leave. (c) The speaker grows increasingly agitated by the Raven's use of this word—because of the unvarying quality of its response, as well as because the speaker's queries to the bird grow more and more important as the poem progresses.
4. (a) He orders the Raven to leave. (b) Students might say that the Raven has, in fact, never left the chamber—or that the creature so disturbed the speaker's mind that now he believes the Raven is still there, although actually it has departed.
5. (a) The effect of the Raven's visit, symbolized by its shadow, has been to permanently darken the speaker's soul. (b) It comes to represent the speaker's permanent state of madness and despair.
6. Most students will say that normally grief abates with time.

Go Online **Author Link** For additional information about Edgar Allan Poe, have students type in the Web Code, then select P from the alphabet, and then select Edgar Allan Poe.

Apply the Skills

The Fall of the House of Usher • The Raven

Literary Analysis

Single Effect

1. Describe the ways in which the following elements contribute to the **single effect** of a growing sense of terror in "The Fall of the House of Usher": **(a)** the description of the house, **(b)** Madeline's entombment, **(c)** the storm.
2. In "The Raven," how do both the tapping and the Raven's fiery eyes contribute to the speaker's deteriorating emotional state?

Comparing Literary Works

3. Use a chart like the one shown to compare the **Gothic** elements in both the story and the poem. Is one of these works more typical of the Gothic style than the other? Explain.

Gothic Element	House of Usher	Raven
Setting		
Violence		
Characterization		
The Supernatural		

4. Are the narrators of these works reliable or unreliable? Explain.
5. **(a)** When Madeline appears at the end of the story, is she there in actuality or is she a hallucination? Explain. **(b)** At the end of "The Raven," do you think the bird is actually still in the room? Why or why not?

Reading Strategy

Breaking Down Long Sentences

6. **Break down this sentence** from the story and restate it in your own words.

   At times, again, I was obliged to resolve all into the mere inexplicable vagaries of madness, for I beheld him gazing upon vacancy for long hours, in an attitude of the profoundest attention, as if listening to some imaginary sound.

Extend Understanding

7. **Psychology Connection:** Both this story and this poem suggest that the imagination is capable of producing false perceptions of reality. Do you agree with this suggestion? Why or why not?

QuickReview

In writing constructed to achieve a **single effect**, every character, incident, and detail contributes to an overall impression.

The **Gothic style** is characterized by remote settings, violent or macabre acts, tormented characters, and, often, the presence of supernatural elements.

To **break down a long sentence,** identify logical parts and analyze the relationship of these parts.

For: Self-test
Visit: www.PHSchool.com
Web Code: era-6304

Answers

1. (a) The description of the house gives the story an ominous start and establishes a mood of gloom and bleakness. (b) Madeline's entombment provides a sense of the ultimate horror for Roderick (as well as for many readers)—the fear of being buried alive. (c) The storm reinforces the growing terror inside the house and eventually accompanies the story's climax.
2. The increasing volume of the tapping emphasizes an increasingly acute sensitivity to sensory stimuli. The detail of the Raven's "fiery eyes" shows that the speaker is now attributing unlikely expressions (in the form of otherworldly effects) to the bird's eyes.
3. Students should fill their charts with specific details and textual references. They may assert that the poem's occasional (albeit dark) humor makes it less typical of the Gothic style than the story.

   Another sample answer can be found on **Literary Analysis Graphic Organizer B**, p. 66 in ***Graphic Organizer Transparencies.***
4. Given that the speaker of the poem descends into madness, clearly he is unreliable. The narrator of the story *seems* largely reliable, though he admits being influenced by Roderick Usher's melancholy and mental illness.
5. (a) There is no way of knowing for certain. Students should support either conclusion with clear reasoning and textual citations. (b) Students should support either interpretation with reasons and with details taken from the text.
6. **Possible response:** "Sometimes I thought that everything was just the quirks of insanity, because I saw him looking at nothing for hours in rapt attention, as if listening to an imaginary sound."
7. Students should support their answers with clear explanations, reasons, and examples.

Go Online Assessment: Students may use the **Self-test** to prepare for **Selection Test A** or **Selection Test B.**

ASSESS/EXTEND

Answers

❶ Vocabulary Lesson

Word Analysis

1. uttered or produced by the *voice*
2. to *voice* vague terms to deceive or mislead
3. using a loud or vehement *voice* in making one's feelings known
4. a call, or *voice;* a feeling of being summoned to enter a certain career

Spelling Strategy

1. gracious
2. mention
3. suspicion
4. malicious

Vocabulary Builder

1. antonyms
2. synonyms
3. synonyms
4. synonyms
5. antonyms
6. synonyms
7. synonyms
8. antonyms
9. synonyms

❷ Grammar and Style Lesson

1. *Correct*
2. He gazed longingly at the clear, placid lake.
3. She marveled at the low, smooth, white walls of the tunnel.
4. The guests noticed her wild, theatrical manner.
5. The dry, hollow-sounding wood splintered and crashed.

Writing Application

Possible response: Sickly, despondent Roderick Usher died last night. As might be expected, it was a dark, stormy night.

WG Writing and Grammar, Ruby Level

Students will find further instruction and practice on coordinate adjectives in Chapter 27, Section 2.

Build Language Skills

❶ Vocabulary Lesson

Word Analysis: Latin Root *-voc-*

The word *equivocal* contains the Latin root *-voc-*, which derives from the Latin word *vox*, meaning "voice." *Equivocal* can be defined as "equal voices" or "having two or more interpretations."

Explain how the root *-voc-* influences the meaning of each of the following words.

1. vocal
2. equivocate
3. vociferous
4. vocation

Spelling Strategy

The sound of *sh* is sometimes spelled *ci*, as in *specious*, or *ti*, as in *sentience*. Complete each word with the correct spelling of the *sh* sound.

1. gra__ous
2. men__on
3. suspi__on
4. mali__ous

Vocabulary Builder: Synonyms or Antonyms?

Identify each of the following pairs of words as either synonyms (words with similar meanings) or antonyms (words with opposite meanings).

1. anomalous, normal
2. appellation, title
3. craven, weak
4. equivocal, ambiguous
5. importunate, yielding
6. munificent, charitable
7. obeisance, reverence
8. specious, sound
9. sentience, emotion

❷ Grammar and Style Lesson

Coordinate Adjectives

Coordinate adjectives are adjectives of equal rank that separately modify the noun they precede. They should always be separated by commas. To determine whether adjectives are coordinate, switch their order or add *and* between them. If the sentence still makes sense, the adjectives are coordinate.

Example: During the whole of a *dull, dark,* and *soundless* day . . .

Example: . . . about the whole mansion and domain there hung an atmosphere . . . a pestilent and mystic vapor, *dull, sluggish, faintly discernible,* and *leaden-hued.*

Practice In each item, identify which adjectives are coordinate. Then, insert commas where necessary. If a sentence needs no commas, write *Correct.*

1. I was his only personal friend.
2. He gazed longingly at the clear placid lake.
3. She marveled at the low smooth white walls of the tunnel.
4. The guests noticed her wild theatrical manner.
5. The dry hollow-sounding wood splintered and crashed.

Writing Application Write an obituary of Roderick Usher. Include at least two sentences that contain coordinate adjectives.

WG *Prentice Hall Writing and Grammar Connection: Chapter 27, Section 2*

Assessment Practice

Make Inferences and Generalizations

(For more practice, see *Standardized Test Practice Workbook*, p. 17.)

Many tests require students to make inferences—to fill in information not stated by the author—about written texts. Students can practice making inferences by completing the following exercise:

> While he spoke, the lady Madeline . . . passed through a remote portion of the apartment, and without having noticed my presence, disappeared. I regarded her with an utter astonishment not unmingled with dread . . . .

In this passage, Madeline most resembles

A a movie star
B a ghost
C a dancer
D a servant

A and *D* are incorrect. Madeline silently enters, then "disappears," causing a feeling of dread in the speaker. *B* is correct.

/riting Lesson

med Writing: Literary Criticism

Since its publication in 1839, "The Fall of the House of Usher" has prompted many tical views. Some say it is the narrator who is insane, not Usher. Others say that each aracter represents a separate aspect of human psychology—the conscious mind, the conscious mind, and the soul. Write an essay in which you defend or refute one of ese critical views. ***(40 minutes)***

Prewriting *(10 minutes)* Reread the story, noting passages and details that support your critical interpretation.

Drafting *(20 minutes)* In your introduction, note the critical viewpoint you will address, and state whether or not you agree with it. Elaborate upon your reasoning in each body paragraph, using details from the text.

Model: Refuting an Argument

The idea that the narrator of Poe's famous story is himself insane is compelling. After all, that would explain the story's strangeness: It is all in the narrator's mind. Unfortunately, that view is unconvincing.

The writer shows an understanding of the opinion being critiqued. The essay to follow will support the analysis.

Revising *(10 minutes)* Review your draft, making sure you have supported your ideas with details from the text. Note places where you might address readers who hold opposing viewpoints.

Prentice Hall Writing and Grammar Connection: Chapter 14, Section 2

xtend Your Learning

stening and Speaking Present a **dramatic ading** of "The Raven" that captures the poem's nsion and brings to life its unique rhymes and ythms. Use the following technique to prepare:

Record yourself on audio- or videotape, and review your presentation for possible lack of clarity or dramatic effect.

Use body language to help convey the poem's meaning.

s you perform, speak clearly, and allow your ice to reflect the poem's rising emotion.

Research and Technology In a group, watch a film by director Alfred Hitchcock. Then, lead a **discussion** in which you analyze the techniques Hitchcock uses to produce suspense and fear, and compare Hitchcock's techniques with Poe's. With classmates, discuss whether print or film is a better medium for horror. **[Group Activity]**

For: An additional research activity
Visit: www.PHSchool.com
Web Code: erd-7304

Assessment Resources

The following resources can be used to assess students' knowledge and skills.

Unit 3 Resources
- **Selection Test A,** pp. 69–71
- **Selection Test B,** pp. 72–74

General Resources
- **Rubrics for Response to Literature,** pp. 65–66
- **Rubric for Dramatic Performance,** p. 131

Go Online Assessment: Students may use the **Self-test** to prepare for **Selection Test A** or **Selection Test B.**

3 Writing Lesson

You may use this Writing Lesson as timed-writing practice, or you may allow students to develop the response as a writing assignment over several days.

- To guide students in writing this critical essay, give them the **Support for Writing Lesson,** p. 66 in ***Unit 3 Resources.***
- Students' critical essays should present one of the noted critical views of "The Fall of the House of Usher" and then defend or refute this view clearly, logically, and thoroughly. If students choose to refute a view, their essay should indicate a more convincing interpretation.
- Encourage students to use an outline to organize the main ideas of their critical essay. Provide them with the Outline Graphic Organizer on p. 309 of ***Graphic Organizer Transparencies.*** Details culled from the text can be indicated briefly on these outlines.
- Use the rubrics for Response to Literature in ***General Resources,*** pp. 65–66 to evaluate students' essays.

4 Listening and Speaking

- You might have students photocopy the text so that they have wide margins in which to write notes and instructions to themselves.
- Encourage students to identify the exposition, the rising action, the climax, and the resolution. Explain that knowing how Poe structured his poem will help them make decisions about how to interpret the poem orally.
- The **Support for Extend Your Learning** page (***Unit 3 Resources,*** p. 67) provides guided note-taking opportunities to help students complete the Extend Your Learning activities.
- Use the rubric for Dramatic Performance, p. 131 in ***General Resources,*** to evaluate student work.

Go Online Research: Have students type in the Web Code for another research activity.

The Minister's Black Veil

Meeting Your Standards

Students will

1. **analyze and respond to literary elements.**
    - Literary Analysis: Parable
2. **read, comprehend, analyze, and critique a short story.**
    - Reading Strategy: Drawing Inferences About Meaning
    - Reading Check questions
    - Apply the Skills questions
    - Assessment Practice (ATE)
3. **develop vocabulary.**
    - Vocabulary Lesson: Latin Word Root: *equi-*
4. **understand and apply written and oral language conventions.**
    - Spelling Strategy
    - Grammar and Style Lesson: Varying Sentence Openers
5. **develop writing proficiency.**
    - Writing Lesson: Response to a Short Story
6. **develop appropriate research strategies.**
    - Extend Your Learning: Oral Presentation
7. **understand and apply listening and speaking strategies.**
    - Extend Your Learning: Monologue

Block Scheduling: Use one 90-minute class period to preteach the skills and have students read the selection. Use a second 90-minute class period to assess students' mastery of skills, extend their learning, and monitor their progress.

Homework Suggestions

Following are possibilities for homework assignments.

- Support pages from *Unit 3 Resources:*
  Literary Analysis
  Reading Strategy
  Vocabulary Builder
  Grammar and Style
- An Extend Your Learning project and the Writing Lesson for this selection group may be completed over several days.

Step-by-Step Teaching Guide	Pacing Guide
PRETEACH	
• Administer Vocabulary and Reading Warm-ups as necessary.	5 min.
• Engage students' interest with the motivation activity.	5 min.
• Read and discuss author and background features. **FT**	10 min.
• Introduce the Literary Analysis Skill: Parable. **FT**	5 min.
• Introduce the Reading Strategy: Drawing Inferences About Meaning. **FT**	10 min.
• Prepare students to read by teaching the selection vocabulary. **FT**	
TEACH	
• Informally monitor comprehension while students read independently or in groups. **FT**	30 min.
• Monitor students' comprehension with the Reading Check notes.	as students read
• Reinforce vocabulary with Vocabulary Builder notes.	as students read
• Develop students' understanding of parables with the Literary Analysis annotations. **FT**	5 min.
• Develop students' ability to draw inferences about meaning with the Reading Strategy annotations. **FT**	5 min.
ASSESS/EXTEND	
• Assess students' comprehension and mastery of the Literary Analysis and Reading Strategy by having them answer the Apply the Skills questions. **FT**	15 min.
• Have students complete the Vocabulary Lesson and the Grammar and Style Lesson. **FT**	15 min.
• Apply students' ability to use exact quotations by using the Writing Lesson. **FT**	45 min. or homework
• Apply students' understanding by using one or more of the Extend Your Learning activities.	20–90 min. or homework
• Administer Selection Test A or Selection Test B. **FT**	15 min.

Resources

PRINT

Unit 3 Resources

Vocabulary Warm-up Word Lists [**L1, L2, EL**] . . . . p. 75
Vocabulary Warm-up Practice [**L1, L2, EL**] . . . . p. 76
Reading Warm-up A [**L1, L2, EL**] . . . . p. 77
Reading Warm-up B [**L1, L2, L3**] . . . . p. 78

TRANSPARENCY

Graphic Organizer Transparencies

Literary Analysis Graphic Organizer A [**L3**] . . . . p. 69
Literary Analysis Graphic Organizer B [**L1, L2, EL**] . . . . p. 70
Reading Strategy Graphic Organizer A [**L3**] . . . . p. 67
Reading Strategy Graphic Organizer B [**L1, L2, EL**] . . . . p. 68

PRINT

Reader's Notebook [L2]
Reader's Notebook: Adapted Version [L1]
Reader's Notebook: English Learner's Version [EL]

Unit 3 Resources

Literary Analysis [**L3**] . . . . p. 79
Reading Strategy [**L3**] . . . . p. 80
Vocabulary Builder [**L3**] . . . . p. 81

TECHNOLOGY

Listening to Literature Audio CDs [L2, EL]

PRINT

Unit 3 Resources

Grammar and Style [**L3**] . . . . p. 82
Support for Writing Lesson [**L3**] . . . . p. 83
Support for Extend Your Learning [**L3**] . . . . p. 84
Enrichment [**L4**] . . . . p. 85
Selection Test A [**L1, L2, EL**] . . . . pp. 86–88
Selection Test B [**L3, L4**] . . . . pp. 89–91

General Resources

Rubrics for Response to Literature [**L3**] . . . . pp. 65–66
Rubric for Peer Assessment: Dramatic Performance [**L3**] . . . . p. 131

TECHNOLOGY

Go Online: Research [**L3**]
Go Online: Self-test [**L3**]
***ExamView®*, Test Bank [L3]**

Choosing Resources for Differentiated Instruction

[**L1**] Special Needs Students
[**L2**] Below-Level Students
[**L3**] All Students
[**L4**] Advanced Students
[**EL**] English Learners

FT Fast Track Instruction: To move the lesson more quickly, use the strategies and activities identified with **FT**.

Scaffolding for Less Proficient and Advanced Students

The leveled Critical Thinking questions after selections progress in the levels of thinking required to answer them. To address the needs of your different students, you may use the (a) level questions for your less proficient students and the (b) level questions with your on-level and advanced students. The occasional (c) level questions are appropriate for your advanced students.

PRENTICE HALL **TeacherEXPRESS™** Plan · Teach · Assess Use this complete suite of powerful teaching tools to make lesson planning and testing quicker and easier.

PRENTICE HALL **StudentEXPRESS™** Learn · Study · Succeed Use the interactive textbook (online and on CD-ROM) to make selections and activities come alive with audio and video support and interactive questions.

PREETEACH

Motivation

Write the following quotation on the chalkboard:

"But what has good Parson Hooper got upon his face?" cried the sexton in astonishment.

When Parson Hooper appears one day wearing a black veil, it causes quite a stir among his congregation. Invite students to imagine that someone they know appears unexpectedly wearing a mask. Ask them to predict how they would react. What might they wish to ask or say to this person?

❶ Background

More About the Author

Nathaniel Hawthorne was a master of symbolism and allegory. He wrote throughout his life, nearly always with the same result—critical acclaim coupled with monetary failure. The literary critic Edward H. Davidson has written: "That a century after he lived he should be included in a collection of major writers of America would have baffled Hawthorne . . . Hawthorne himself had been so consistently ignored, that to be a subject for literary study . . . and to be termed a 'classic' among American writers, would have seemed nothing short of grotesque . . . Indeed, his literary reputation has maintained its high place more steadily than that of any other major American writer."

❶ The Minister's Black Veil

Nathaniel Hawthorne (1804–1864)

Along with Herman Melville, Nathaniel Hawthorne is sometimes referred to as an Anti-Transcendentalist. Although he lived at a time when many intellectuals glorified the power of the human spirit, as it was described by Transcendentalists like Ralph Waldo Emerson, Hawthorne found it impossible to adopt such an optimistic worldview. Despite his admiration for Emerson, Hawthorne believed that evil was a dominant force in the world, and his fiction expresses a gloomy vision of human affairs.

Inherited Guilt Born in Salem, Massachusetts, Hawthorne was descended from a prominent Puritan family. One of Hawthorne's ancestors was a Puritan judge who played a key role in the Salem witchcraft trials. Another ancestor was a judge known for his persecution of Quakers. Both Hawthorne's character and his focus as a writer were shaped by a sense of inherited guilt. He was haunted by the intolerance and cruelty of these ancestors, even though he himself was not a Puritan and was born 112 years after the Salem witchcraft trials.

The Long Seclusion After graduation from Maine's Bowdoin College in 1825, Hawthorne secluded himself at his mother's house in Salem and wrote a novel, *Fanshawe*. Soon after the book's anonymous publication in 1828, the young author was seized by shame and abruptly burned most available copies of it. During the nine years that followed, Hawthorne single-mindedly honed his writing skills, working in a room he called "the dismal chamber" on the third floor of his mother's house. These labors resulted in a collection of stories entitled *Twice-Told Tales*, which was published in 1837. Although the book sold poorly, it established Hawthorne as a respected writer and gave him sufficient resources and encouragement to continue his writing.

Moving in Transcendentalist Society After moving out of his mother's house, Hawthorne lived briefly at Brook Farm, the utopian community designed by the Transcendentalists. Then, in 1842, he married Sophia Peabody and moved to the Old Manse at Concord, Massachusetts, where Emerson had once lived. During his years in Concord, Hawthorne spent time with both Emerson and Henry David Thoreau, but their vastly different spiritual philosophies remained an obstacle to deeper friendship. While in Concord, Hawthorne published a second collection of stories, *Mosses From an Old Manse* (1846), and celebrated the birth of his first daughter, Una.

Man of Letters When he was appointed surveyor at the Salem customhouse, Hawthorne moved with his family back to his birthplace. In 1850, after a change in administration forced him out of office, he published his masterpiece, *The Scarlet Letter*, a powerful novel about sin and guilt among early Puritans. The book was extremely successful, earning its author international fame. He soon wrote two more novels, *The House of the Seven Gables* (1851) and *The Blithedale Romance* (1852).

When his college friend Franklin Pierce became president, Hawthorne was named the American consul at Liverpool, England. He spent several years in England and traveled through Italy before returning to Massachusetts. He used his Italian experiences in the novel *The Marble Faun* (1860). Hawthorne died in his sleep four years later, while on a carriage tour in New Hampshire. He left four unfinished novels among his belongings.

Preview

Connecting to the Literature

A secret, when kept too long, can take on mysterious significance. If unrevealed, it can cause people to fill in the missing story and draw their own untrue conclusions. In "The Minister's Black Veil," a Puritan parson keeps a secret from an entire village for his whole life.

Literary Analysis

Parable

A **parable** is a simple, usually brief, story that teaches a moral lesson. Unlike a fable, which features animal characters, a parable is populated by human beings. A parable is a type of **allegory**—a story with both a literal and a symbolic meaning. In subtitling this story "A Parable," Hawthorne indicates that the moral message it conveys is important. As you read, think about the lesson Hawthorne wants his story to communicate.

Connecting Literary Elements

The veil that Mr. Hooper vows never to remove is a **symbol**—something that has meaning in itself while also standing for something greater. To understand the message expressed in Hawthorne's parable, you must analyze the veil's symbolic meaning, which is revealed through the responses of the parishioners and in the minister's own deathbed explanation:

"I look around me, and, lo! on every visage a Black Veil!"

To discover the veil's symbolic meaning, notice Hawthorne's descriptions of the veil and its effects on the characters in the story.

Reading Strategy

Drawing Inferences About Meaning

When the message of a work of fiction is conveyed indirectly, as it is in this symbolic story, the reader must **draw inferences,** or conclusions, by looking closely at details, especially description and dialogue. Use a chart like the one shown to draw inferences about the story's characters and events.

Description/ Dialogue

"He has changed himself into something awful, only by hiding his face."

↓

Inference

Villagers are frightened by the veil.

Vocabulary Builder

venerable (ven′ ər ə bəl) *adj.* commanding respect (p. 342)

iniquity (i nik′ wi tē) *n.* sin (p. 343)

indecorous (in dek′ ə rəs) *adj.* improper (p. 343)

ostentatious (äs′ tən tā′ shəs) *adj.* intended to attract notice; showy (p. 343)

sagacious (sə gā′ shəs) *adj.* shrewd; perceptive (p. 343)

vagary (və ger′ ē) *n.* unpredictable occurrence (p. 344)

tremulous (trem′ yo͞o ləs) *adj.* characterized by trembling (p. 345)

waggery (wag′ ər ē) *n.* mischievous humor (p. 345)

impertinent (im pʉrt′ ′n ənt) *adj.* not showing proper respect (p. 346)

obstinacy (äb′ stə nə sē) *n.* stubbornness (p. 347)

Differentiated Instruction — Solutions for All Learners

Support for Special Needs Students
Have students complete the **Preview** and **Build Skills** pages for the selection in the ***Reader's Notebook: Adapted Version.*** These pages provide a selection summary, an abbreviated presentation of the reading and literary skills, and the graphic organizer on the **Build Skills** page in the student book.

Support for Less Proficient Readers
Have students complete the **Preview** and **Build Skills** pages for the selection in the ***Reader's Notebook.*** These pages provide a selection summary, an abbreviated presentation of the reading and literary skills, and the graphic organizer on the **Build Skills** page in the student book.

Support for English Learners
Have students complete the **Preview** and **Build Skills** pages for the selection in the ***Reader's Notebook: English Learner's Version.*** These pages provide a selection summary, an abbreviated presentation of the skills, additional contextual vocabulary, and the graphic organizer on the **Build Skills** page in the student book.

❷ Literary Analysis

Parable

- Tell students that they will focus on the parable as they read Hawthorne's short story.
- Read the instruction about parables together as a class. Lead students in a discussion of other stories they have read that carry a moral lesson. What topics are writers likely to touch on as they convey moral messages to readers?
- Help students understand that because its purpose is moral instruction, a parable often contains some characters and events that are more symbolic than realistic.
- As they read, invite students to relate to the views and feelings of Parson Hooper (as well as of other Milford residents), using their own prior knowledge about clashes between private belief and public reputation.

❸ Reading Strategy

Drawing Inferences About Meaning

- Remind students that drawing inferences is a way of interpreting a character's behavior, statements, or an author's message. You might wish to point out that Hawthorne delights in presenting people and situations that are cloaked in ambiguity. Thus it is imperative that readers draw inferences about his meaning.
- Explain the importance of focusing special attention on characters' words and on descriptions of characters' actions as students attempt to draw inferences about the story. Often a reader can find meaning in the disparity between characters' words and their actions.
- Give students a copy of **Reading Strategy Graphic Organizer A,** p.67 in ***Graphic Organizer Transparencies,*** to use as they read the story.

Vocabulary Builder

- Pronounce each vocabulary word for students, and read the definitions as a class. Have students identify any words with which they are already familiar.

Learning Modalities
Visual/Spatial Learners

Invite students to create a picture that evokes the eerie atmosphere of this story. Have the students draw or paint a scene such as a chance meeting between the minister and a parishioner on a village street. Remind students to decide what emotion the person will feel when confronted by the veiled minister: Will he or she betray feelings of fear, surprise, curiosity, or terror?

1 About the Selection

In this parable, Mr. Hooper, a highly respected minister in a small Puritan community, suddenly appears wearing a black veil, a mask he vows never to remove. The veil has a powerful, gloomy effect on his parishioners; they are stunned and unable to ask him directly why he is wearing it. Even Hooper's fiancée turns from him because of the veil. The veil's symbolic meaning—a reminder of the secret sins each soul carries to the grave—is revealed through the speech and actions of Hooper and his parishioners, as well as in his deathbed explanation.

1 The Minister's Black Veil

A PARABLE

Nathaniel Hawthorne

Background Set in the 1600s, in a typical village of Puritan New England, this story reflects Hawthorne's deep awareness of his Puritan ancestry. The Puritans lived stern lives, emphasizing hard work and religious devotion. They believed that only certain people were predestined by God to go to heaven. This belief led Puritans to search their souls continually for signs that God had chosen them. At the same time, those who behaved unusually were often thought to be controlled by evil forces. This attitude contributed to the Salem witchcraft trials of 1692, during which at least twenty accused witches were executed. In this story, Hawthorne explores how such attitudes probably led to other, more commonplace acts of cruelty.

The sexton[1] stood in the porch of Milford meetinghouse, pulling busily at the bell rope. The old people of the village came stooping along the street. Children, with bright faces, tripped merrily beside their parents, or mimicked a graver gait, in the conscious dignity of their Sunday clothes. Spruce bachelors looked sidelong at the pretty maidens, and fancied that the Sabbath sunshine made them prettier than on weekdays. When the throng had mostly streamed into the porch, the sexton began to toll the bell, keeping his eye on the

1. **sexton** (seks′ tən) *n.* person in charge of the maintenance of a church.

Differentiated Instruction Solutions for All Learners

Accessibility at a Glance

	The Minister's Black Veil
Context	Nineteenth-century tale about sin and damnation
Language	Challenging dialogue; dense, formal narration; nineteenth-century diction
Concept Level	Challenging (abstract, religious, philosophical considerations about sin and damnation)
Literary Merit	Classic
Lexile	1250
Other	Provocative tale about religion
Overall Rating	More challenging

Reverend Mr. Hooper's door. The first glimpse of the clergyman's figure was the signal for the bell to cease its summons.

"But what has good Parson Hooper got upon his face?" cried the sexton in astonishment.

All within hearing immediately turned about, and beheld the semblance of Mr. Hooper, pacing slowly his meditative way towards the meetinghouse. With one accord they started, expressing more wonder than if some strange minister were coming to dust the cushions of Mr. Hooper's pulpit.

"Are you sure it is our parson?" inquired Goodman[2] Gray of the sexton.

"Of a certainty it is good Mr. Hooper," replied the sexton. "He was to have exchanged pulpits with Parson Shute, of Westbury; but Parson Shute sent to excuse himself yesterday, being to preach a funeral sermon."

2. **Goodman** title of respect similar to "Mister."

❷ 

As the story begins, what weekly event is about to take place?

❸ ▼ Critical Viewing

Identify the elements or details of this painting that correspond to those in Hawthorne's story. **[Connect]**

Winter Sunday in Norway, Maine, Unidentified artist, New York State Historical Association, Cooperstown

❹

❷ Reading Check

Answer: Reverend Hooper's regular Sunday church service is about to begin at Milford meetinghouse.

❸ Critical Viewing

Answer: Students can point to the painting's cold, gray, and gloomy setting, as well as to the stiff, proper appearance of the people.

❹ Humanities

Winter Sunday in Norway, Maine, artist unidentified

This painting is by an anonymous folk artist. Folk artists provide a link between the past and the present by reflecting social history. Folk art paintings offer intimate views of events through the eyes of ordinary people. Thus, images in folk art tend to be simple, homey, deeply felt, and untutored. Folk art incorporates common scenes and materials, native designs, and artisanship. Use these questions for discussion:

1. How would you describe the mood of this scene?
   Answer: Students may say that it is a dreary, somber winter day in a small town where the church plays a prominent role. Students may notice that the insides of the church and houses are as colorless as the bleak landscape.
2. What seems to be missing from this scene?
   Answer: Students may notice that no smoke comes from the chimneys and that there appears to be a lack of warmth inside and out.

Differentiated Instruction Solutions for All Learners

Support for Special Needs Students

Students will benefit from hearing dialogue read aloud; in many cases it will help them to hear a passage read aloud more than once. Point out how Hawthorne uses dialogue skillfully for dramatic effect. For example, the veil is first mentioned and the minister's identity first questioned in the story's initial line of dialogue.

Strategy for English Learners

Encourage students to create a two-column graphic organizer to track characters and dialogue. Have them record the name of each character as it is mentioned in the text, together with notes about their actions and dialogue. Students should also note new vocabulary and definitions that appear in the story.

Strategy for Advanced Readers

To help students make inferences about the story, encourage them to speculate about the thoughts of Milford residents as they read. Have students use a two-column graphic organizer. Have students note characters' spoken words in one column and jot down speculations about their inner thoughts in the other.

5 Literary Analysis
Parable

- Slowly read aloud the first paragraph on this page. Encourage students to listen for descriptive details about Mr. Hooper, the veil, and the reactions of townspeople.
- **Ask** students the first Literary Analysis question: What does this first detailed description of the veil indicate about its effect on the community?
  Answer: The description makes the veil seem strange and significant.

6 Literary Analysis
Parable and Symbol

- Remind students that when an object takes on significance outside itself and stands for something greater, it is being used as a symbol.
- **Ask** one or more student volunteers to read aloud carefully the passage beginning "That mysterious emblem." Urge students to take note of how Hawthorne has chosen to describe the effect of the veil.
- **Ask** students the second Literary Analysis question: The passage beginning "That mysterious emblem" is the first suggestion that the veil is a symbol. What might the veil symbolize?
  Answer: Hawthorne's descriptions delineate how the veil creates an "unnatural" separation between Hooper and the subject of his current attention (speaking the psalm, reading the page of the Bible, looking up to God). Thus the veil may symbolize something that has come between the minister and ordinary life.

The cause of so much amazement may appear sufficiently slight. Mr. Hooper, a gentlemanly person, of about thirty, though still a bachelor, was dressed with due clerical neatness, as if a careful wife had starched his band, and brushed the weekly dust from his Sunday's garb. There was but one thing remarkable in his appearance. Swathed about his forehead, and hanging down over his face, so low as to be shaken by his breath, Mr. Hooper had on a black veil. On a
5 nearer view it seemed to consist of two folds of crape,[3] which entirely concealed his features, except the mouth and chin, but probably did not intercept his sight, further than to give a darkened aspect to all living and inanimate things. With this gloomy shade before him, good Mr. Hooper walked onward, at a slow and quiet pace, stooping somewhat, and looking on the ground, as is customary with abstracted men, yet nodding kindly to those of his parishioners who still waited on the meetinghouse steps. But so wonderstruck were they that his greeting hardly met with a return.

"I can't really feel as if good Mr. Hooper's face was behind that piece of crape," said the sexton.

"I don't like it," muttered an old woman, as she hobbled into the meetinghouse. "He has changed himself into something awful, only by hiding his face."

"Our parson has gone mad!" cried Goodman Gray, following him across the threshold.

A rumor of some unaccountable phenomenon had preceded Mr. Hooper into the meetinghouse, and set all the congregation astir. Few could refrain from twisting their heads towards the door; many stood upright, and turned directly about; while several little boys clambered upon the seats, and came down again with a terrible racket. There was a general bustle, a rustling of the women's gowns and shuffling of the men's feet, greatly at variance with that hushed repose which should attend the entrance of the minister. But Mr. Hooper appeared not to notice the perturbation of his people. He entered with an almost noiseless step, bent his head mildly to the pews on each side, and bowed as he passed his oldest parishioner, a white-haired great-grandsire, who occupied an armchair in the center of the aisle. It was strange to observe how slowly this venerable man became conscious of something singular in the appearance of his pastor. He seemed not fully to partake of the prevailing wonder, till Mr. Hooper had ascended the stairs, and showed himself in the pulpit, face to face with his congregation, except for the black veil. That mysterious emblem was never once withdrawn. It shook with his measured breath, as he gave out the psalm; it threw
6 its obscurity between him and the holy page, as he read the Scriptures; and while he prayed, the veil lay heavily on his uplifted countenance. Did he seek to hide it from the dread Being whom he was addressing?

Such was the effect of this simple piece of crape, that more than one woman of delicate nerves was forced to leave the meetinghouse.

3. **crape** (krāp) *n.* piece of black cloth worn as a sign of mourning.

Literary Analysis
Parable What does this first detailed description of the veil indicate about its effect on the community?

Vocabulary Builder
venerable (ven′ ər ə bəl) *adj.* commanding respect

Literary Analysis
Parable and Symbol The passage beginning "That mysterious emblem" is the first suggestion that the veil is a symbol. What might the veil symbolize?

Enrichment

Veils

A veil can be defined as "a piece of light fabric, as of net or gauze, worn especially by women over the face or head or draped from a hat to conceal, protect, or enhance the face." Traditionally veils have been worn for a variety of reasons in different cultures. Often they are worn at weddings, funerals, and other religious ceremonies. People may wear veils to express modesty or mourning.

Have students do research to find out more about why, when, how, and by whom veils are worn in different cultures. When students complete their research, they may share their findings with their classmates during a class discussion.

Yet perhaps the palefaced congregation was almost as fearful a sight to the minister, as his black veil to them.

Mr. Hooper had the reputation of a good preacher, but not an energetic one: he strove to win his people heavenward by mild, persuasive influences, rather than to drive them thither by the thunders of the Word. The sermon which he now delivered was marked by the same characteristics of style and manner as the general series of his pulpit oratory. But there was something, either in the sentiment of the discourse itself, or in the imagination of the auditors, which made it greatly the most powerful effort that they had ever heard from their
7 pastor's lips. It was tinged, rather more darkly than usual, with the gentle gloom of Mr. Hooper's temperament. The subject had reference to secret sin, and those sad mysteries which we hide from our nearest and dearest, and would fain conceal from our own consciousness, even forgetting that the Omniscient[4] can detect them. A subtle power was breathed into his words. Each member of the congregation, the most innocent girl, and the man of hardened breast, felt as if the preacher had crept upon them, behind his awful veil, and discovered their
8 hoarded iniquity of deed or thought. Many spread their clasped hands on their bosoms. There was nothing terrible in what Mr. Hooper said, at least, no violence; and yet, with every tremor of his melancholy voice, the hearers quaked. An unsought pathos came hand in hand with awe. So sensible were the audience of some unwonted attribute in their minister, that they longed for a breath of wind to blow aside the veil, almost believing that a stranger's visage would be discovered, though the form, gesture, and voice were those of Mr. Hooper.

At the close of the services, the people hurried out with indecorous confusion, eager to communicate their pent-up amazement, and conscious of lighter spirits the moment they lost sight of the black veil. Some gathered in little circles, huddled closely together, with their mouths all whispering in the center; some went homeward alone, wrapt in silent meditation; some talked loudly, and profaned the Sabbath day with ostentatious laughter. A few shook their sagacious heads, intimating that they could penetrate the mystery; while one or two affirmed that there was no mystery at all, but only that Mr. Hooper's eyes were so weakened by the midnight lamp, as to require a shade. After a brief interval, forth came good Mr. Hooper also, in the rear of his flock. Turning his veiled face from one group to another, he paid due reverence to the hoary heads, saluted the middle-aged with kind dignity as their friend and spiritual guide, greeted the young with mingled authority and love, and laid his hands on the little children's heads to bless them. Such was always his custom on the Sabbath day. Strange and bewildered looks repaid him for his courtesy. None, as on former occasions, aspired to the honor of walking by their pastor's side. Old Squire Saunders, doubtless by an

4. **Omniscient** (äm ni′ shənt) all-knowing God.

Reading Strategy
Drawing Inferences About Meaning Has Mr. Hooper truly changed? What inferences can you draw based on this description of his sermon?

Vocabulary Builder
iniquity (i nik′ wi tē) *n.* sin

Vocabulary Builder
indecorous (in dek′ ə rəs) *adj.* improper

ostentatious (äs′ tən tā′ shəs) *adj.* intended to attract notice; showy

sagacious (sə gā′ shəs) *adj.* shrewd; perceptive

9 
Reading Check
What change has occurred in Mr. Hooper's appearance?

7 Reading Strategy
Drawing Inferences About Meaning

- **Ask** a students to summarize how readers can determine meanings in a work of fiction when the author's message is conveyed indirectly.
  Answer: The reader must draw inferences after examining textual details, particularly the writer's use of description and dialogue.
- Invite students to listen closely to an oral reading of the first paragraph on this page.
- Then, **ask** them the Reading Strategy question: Has Mr. Hooper truly changed? What inferences can you draw based on this description of his sermon?
  Possible answer: Some students may feel that Mr. Hooper has changed, and point to the choice of sermon and the reaction of parishioners. Others may feel that the sight of the veil is causing the villagers' response.

8 Vocabulary Builder
Latin Root *-equi-*

- Point out the word *iniquity* in the bracketed sentence. Explain that this word means "sin."
- Tell students that the Latin word root *-equi-* means "equal." Have students use a dictionary to find out how the meaning of this root word comes to bear on the word *iniquity*.
  Answer: *Iniquity* means "uneven" or "unjust" and has come to be defined as "wickedness" or "sin."
- Have students identify other words that contain this Latin word root.
  Possibilities include: *equable, equity, equivocate, equinox,* and *equilateral.*

9 Reading Check

Answer: Mr. Hooper has draped a black veil across his face from his forehead.

Differentiated Instruction
Solutions for All Learners

Strategy for Less Proficient Readers
Help students draw inferences about meaning by drawing their attention to the three lines of dialogue on p. 342. Point out the strong reactions, both verbal and physical, that the townspeople have toward the veil. Ask students to think about what these reactions reveal about Hooper's parishioners. Help students appreciate that these reactions reveal the parishioners' superstitious thoughts, as well as their inability to accept change or tolerate differences.

Strategy for Advanced Readers
Hawthorne's focus on the superstitious character of the Puritans provides much of the mystery and tension in his stories. Guide students to recognize the elements of tension Hawthorne uses to build suspense throughout "The Minister's Black Veil." Then, remind students that mystery is created both by description and by information that is deliberately omitted. Urge students to identify both of these strategies in Hawthorne's story.

⑩ The American Experience

Jonathan Edwards In *Jonathan Edwards, Pastor,* author Patricia Tracy discusses how Edwards achieved the "terrifying effects" of his sermon: "Although it conveys the reek of brimstone, the sermon does not say that God will hurl man into everlasting fires—on the contrary, doom will come from God's indifference . . . He holds man above the pit as by a spider's thread, and should He become weary of protecting worthless man, that abominable insect will *drop of his own weight.* Man's preservation lay in God's whim of mercy, and the terror of this message derived from the insecurity of being temporarily protected by an all-powerful being who had an infinite anger. (Was the control of such strong feelings something that Edwards's audience found difficult to understand or to trust?)" Tracy suggests that because the Puritans held such a dim view of human beings' ability to control their feelings, they were all the more anxious about God's ability to control His anger.

Connect to the Literature

Have a volunteer read the note aloud. Then, ask students how the black veil is a sign of sin or evil, even though the Reverend Hooper is a mild and benevolent man.

Possible response: People might fear something that appears to be a mark of sin because it could signify damnation despite an individual's apparent goodness or religious observance.

accidental lapse of memory, neglected to invite Mr. Hooper to his table, where the good clergyman had been wont to bless the food, almost every Sunday since his settlement. He returned, therefore, to the parsonage, and, at the moment of closing the door, was observed to look back upon the people, all of whom had their eyes fixed upon the minister. A sad smile gleamed faintly from beneath the black veil, and flickered about his mouth, glimmering as he disappeared.

"How strange," said a lady, "that a simple black veil, such as any woman might wear on her bonnet, should become such a terrible thing on Mr. Hooper's face!"

"Something must surely be amiss with Mr. Hooper's intellects," observed her husband, the physician of the village. "But the strangest part of the affair is the effect of this vagary, even on a sober-minded man like myself. The black veil, though it covers only our pastor's face, throws its influence over his whole person, and makes him ghostlike from head to foot. Do you not feel it so?"

"Truly do I," replied the lady; "and I would not be alone with him for the world. I wonder he is not afraid to be alone with himself!"

"Men sometimes are so," said her husband.

The afternoon service was attended with similar circumstances. At its conclusion, the bell tolled for the funeral of a young lady. The relatives and friends were assembled in the house, and the more distant acquaintances stood about the door, speaking of the good qualities of the deceased, when their talk was interrupted by the appearance of Mr. Hooper, still covered with his black veil. It was now an appropriate emblem. The clergyman stepped into the room where the corpse was laid, and bent over the coffin, to take a last farewell of his deceased parishioner. As he stooped, the veil hung straight down from his forehead, so that, if her eyelids had not been closed forever, the dead maiden might have seen his face. Could Mr. Hooper be fearful of her glance, that he so hastily caught back the black veil? A person who watched the interview between the dead and living, scrupled not to affirm, that, at the instant when the clergyman's features were disclosed, the corpse had slightly shuddered, rustling the shroud and muslin cap, though the countenance retained the composure of death. A superstitious old woman was the only witness of this prodigy. From the coffin Mr. Hooper passed into the chamber of the mourners, and thence to the head of the staircase; to make the funeral prayer. It was a tender and heart-dissolving prayer, full of sorrow, yet so imbued with celestial hopes, that the music of a heavenly harp, swept by the fingers of the dead, seemed faintly to be heard among the saddest accents of the minister. The people trembled, though they but darkly understood him when he prayed that they, and himself, and all of mortal race, might be ready, as he trusted this young maiden

⑩ ***Jonathan Edwards, Puritans, and Sermons of Fear***

The congregation's fear of Mr. Hooper's veil recalls Jonathan Edwards, one of the greatest preachers of the colonial period. Edwards used his sermons to inspire fear of eternal damnation in the minds of his listeners. He insisted that the evidence they saw as proof of God's grace in their lives was false. According to Edwards, personal comfort, success, health, and a sense of being a good person were no proof that one was saved. Rather, these satisfactions in the earthly realm were mere distractions, providing comfort, but no substance, to the ignorant.

Though Hawthorne describes Mr. Hooper as a mild and benevolent preacher—certainly no spouter of fire-and-brimstone like Edwards—his veil inspires a similar fear and trembling among the villagers. You can read an excerpt of Jonathan Edwards's "Sinners in the Hands of an Angry God" on page 102.

Connect to the Literature

People in Hooper's congregation are taught to fear eternal damnation—and to look for signs of evil in themselves and others. Why would they be inclined to fear anything that appears to be a mark of sin?

Vocabulary Builder

vagary (və ger′ ē) *n.* unpredictable occurrence

Enrichment

The Clergy

Like most members of the clergy—such as ministers, rabbis, and priests—Mr. Hooper is a central figure in his community. In addition to offering religious instruction and counseling to their congregations, the clergy preside over weddings, funerals, and other rites of passage. Many are involved in education and social service. Today, as in Hooper's time, a minister is a public figure whose words and actions are observed by all.

Have students interview members of the clergy in your area to find out how they view the breadth of their responsibilities. Students might ask them to describe various interactions with their congregations and with other members of their communities. Students can compare notes to identify characteristics that are shared by effective clergy and to gain a better understanding of their leadership roles.

had been, for the dreadful hour that should snatch the veil from their faces. The bearers went heavily forth, and the mourners followed, saddening all the street, with the dead before them, and Mr. Hooper in his black veil behind.

"Why do you look back?" said one in the procession to his partner.

"I had a fancy," replied she, "that the minister and the maiden's spirit were walking hand in hand."

"And so had I, at the same moment," said the other.

That night, the handsomest couple in Milford village were to be joined in wedlock. Though reckoned a melancholy man, Mr. Hooper had a placid cheerfulness for such occasions, which often excited a sympathetic smile where livelier merriment would have been thrown away. There was no quality of his disposition which made him more beloved than this. The company at the wedding awaited his arrival with impatience, trusting that the strange awe, which had gathered over him throughout the day, would now be dispelled. But such was not the result. When Mr. Hooper came, the first thing that their eyes rested on was the same horrible black veil, which had added deeper gloom to the funeral, and could portend nothing but evil to the wedding. Such was its immediate effect on the guests that a cloud seemed to have rolled duskily from beneath the black crape, and dimmed the light of the candles. The bridal pair stood up before the minister. But the bride's cold fingers quivered in the tremulous hand of the bridegroom, and her deathlike paleness caused a whisper that the maiden who had been buried a few hours before was come from her grave to be married. If ever another wedding were so dismal, it was that famous one where they tolled the wedding knell.[5] After performing the ceremony, Mr. Hooper raised a glass of wine to his lips, wishing happiness to the new-married couple in a strain of mild pleasantry that ought to have brightened the features of the guests, like a cheerful gleam from the hearth. At that instant, catching a glimpse of his figure in the looking glass, the black veil involved his own spirit in the horror with which it overwhelmed all others. His frame shuddered, his lips grew white, he spilt the untasted wine upon the carpet, and rushed forth into the darkness. For the Earth, too, had on her Black Veil.

The next day, the whole village of Milford talked of little else than Parson Hooper's black veil. That, and the mystery concealed behind it, supplied a topic for discussion between acquaintances meeting in the street, and good women gossiping at their open windows. It was the first item of news that the tavernkeeper told to his guests. The children babbled of it on their way to school. One imitative little imp covered his face with an old black handkerchief, thereby so affrighting his playmates that the panic seized himself, and he well nigh lost his wits by his own waggery.

5. **If . . . knell** reference to Hawthorne's short story "The Wedding Knell." A knell is the slow ringing of a bell, as at a funeral.

Reading Strategy
Drawing Inferences About Meaning What inferences can you draw from this dialogue about the veil's intensifying impact on the villagers?

Vocabulary Builder
tremulous (trem´ yoo ləs) *adj.* characterized by trembling

Vocabulary Builder
waggery (wag´ ər ē) *n.* mischievous humor

13 

Why is the black veil an appropriate emblem for a funeral?

11 Reading Strategy
Drawing Inferences About Meaning

- Have two students read this dialogue in quiet, discreet voices.
- Encourage students to pay attention to the reference to the spirit of the dead maiden. Have them consider why the villager might have made this statement.
- Then **ask** students the Reading Strategy question: What inferences can you draw from this dialogue about the veil's increasing impact on the villagers?
  Answer: A reader might infer that the veil has started to work on villagers' imaginations. Though the minister has said nothing yet regarding the meaning of the veil, parishioners are creating increasingly detailed scenarios that might explain the veil and Hooper's behavior.

12 Critical Thinking
Compare and Contrast

- Ask students to brainstorm a list of words, phrases, ideas, and feelings they associate with the word *wedding*.
- **Ask** students: Why might the fearful effect of the black veil be more intense at the wedding than at the funeral?
  Possible response: People expect such dismal attire (as well as sadness) at a funeral. A wedding, however, is ordinarily a time of joy. Therefore, the minister's black veil at the wedding inverts everyone's sense of normalcy and makes the veil's effect even more upsetting than it would be at a funeral.

13 Reading Check

Answer: In the context of a funeral, a black veil is appropriate as a symbol of mourning.

Differentiated Instruction
Solutions for All Learners

Support for Less Proficient Readers
Have students reread the dialogue near the top of p. 345, in order to discuss whether the lines suggest a link between the maiden's death and Mr. Hooper's wearing the veil. Help them understand that the mourners are only gossiping and that the remarks are pure speculation. You may wish to explain that Hawthorne may be invoking the Salem witch trials, in which innocent people were condemned by the specious and hysterical testimony of neighbors.

Enrichment for Advanced Readers
Hawthorne's short story "The Wedding Knell" is one of the pieces Hawthorne chose to include in his first published volume, *Twice-Told Tales.* Have students choose another of Hawthorne's short stories to read and analyze. Tales that are especially interesting in comparison and contrast to "The Minister's Black Veil" include "The Maypole of Merry Mount," "The Birthmark," "Rappaccini's Daughter," and "Ethan Brand."

14 Literary Analysis
Parable

- Encourage students to look carefully for details that reveal the character of Mr. Hooper's fiancée.
- Then, **ask** students to identify any possible connections between these details and the symbolism represented by the veil.
- **Ask** students the Literary Analysis question: What might these details about Mr. Hooper's fiancée add to the parable's moral?
  Answer: The description of how directly and simply Hooper's fiancée approaches the topic of the veil and the revelation that the minister refuses to explain his reasons even to her reinforce the symbolic power of the veil.

It was remarkable that of all the busybodies and impertinent people in the parish, not one ventured to put the plain question to Mr. Hooper, wherefore he did this thing. Hitherto, whenever there appeared the slightest call for such interference, he had never lacked advisers, nor shown himself averse to be guided by their judgment. If he erred at all, it was by so painful a degree of self-distrust that even the mildest censure would lead him to consider an indifferent action as a crime. Yet, though so well acquainted with this amiable weakness, no individual among his parishioners chose to make the black veil a subject of friendly remonstrance. There was a feeling of dread, neither plainly confessed nor carefully concealed, which caused each to shift the responsibility upon another, till at length it was found expedient to send a deputation of the church, in order to deal with Mr. Hooper about the mystery, before it should grow into a scandal. Never did an embassy so ill discharge its duties. The minister received them with friendly courtesy, but became silent, after they were seated, leaving to his visitors the whole burden of introducing their important business. The topic, it might be supposed, was obvious enough. There was the black veil swathed round Mr. Hooper's forehead, and concealing every feature above his placid mouth, on which, at times, they could perceive the glimmering of a melancholy smile. But that piece of crape, to their imagination, seemed to hang down before his heart, the symbol of a fearful secret between him and them. Were the veil but cast aside, they might speak freely of it, but not till then. Thus they sat a considerable time, speechless, confused, and shrinking uneasily from Mr. Hooper's eye, which they felt to be fixed upon them with an invisible glance. Finally, the deputies returned abashed to their constituents, pronouncing the matter too weighty to be handled, except by a council of the churches, if, indeed, it might not require a general synod.[6]

Vocabulary Builder
impertinent (im purt' 'n ənt) *adj.* not showing proper respect

14 But there was one person in the village unappalled by the awe with which the black veil had impressed all beside herself. When the deputies returned without an explanation, or even venturing to demand one, she, with the calm energy of her character, determined to chase away the strange cloud that appeared to be settling round Mr. Hooper, every moment more darkly than before. As his plighted wife,[7] it should be her privilege to know what the black veil concealed. At the minister's first visit, therefore, she entered upon the subject with a direct simplicity, which made the task easier both for him and her. After he had seated himself, she fixed her eyes steadfastly upon the veil, but could discern nothing of the dreadful gloom that had so overawed the multitude: it was but a double fold of crape, hanging down from his forehead to his mouth, and slightly stirring with his breath.

Literary Analysis
Parable What might these details about Mr. Hooper's fiancée add to the parable's moral?

"No," said she aloud, and smiling, "there is nothing terrible in this piece of crape, except that it hides a face which I am always glad to

6. **synod** (sin' əd) *n.* high governing body in certain Christian churches.
7. **plighted wife** fiancée.

look upon. Come, good sir, let the sun shine from behind the cloud. First lay aside your black veil; then tell me why you put it on."

Mr. Hooper's smile glimmered faintly.

"There is an hour to come," said he, "when all of us shall cast aside our veils. Take it not amiss, beloved friend, if I wear this piece of crape till then."

"Your words are a mystery, too," returned the young lady. "Take away the veil from them, at least."

"Elizabeth, I will," said he, "so far as my vow may suffer me. Know, then, this veil is a type and a symbol, and I am bound to wear it ever, both in light and darkness, in solitude and before the gaze of multitudes, and as with strangers, so with my familiar friends. No mortal eye will see it withdrawn. This dismal shade must separate me from the world: even you, Elizabeth, can never come behind it!"

"What grievous affliction hath befallen you," she earnestly inquired, "that you should thus darken your eyes forever?"

"If it be a sign of mourning," replied Mr. Hooper, "I, perhaps, like most other mortals, have sorrows dark enough to be typified by a black veil."

"But what if the world will not believe that it is the type of an innocent sorrow?" urged Elizabeth. "Beloved and respected as you are, there may be whispers that you hide your face under the consciousness of secret sin. For the sake of your holy office, do away this scandal!"

The color rose into her cheeks as she intimated the nature of the rumors that were already abroad in the village. But Mr. Hooper's mildness did not forsake him. He even smiled again—that same sad smile, which always appeared like a faint glimmering of light, proceeding from the obscurity beneath the veil.

"If I hide my face for sorrow, there is cause enough," he merely replied; "and if I cover it for secret sin, what mortal might not do the same?"

And with this gentle, but unconquerable obstinacy did he resist all her entreaties. At length Elizabeth sat silent. For a few moments she appeared lost in thought, considering, probably, what new methods might be tried to withdraw her lover from so dark a fantasy, which, if it had no other meaning, was perhaps a symptom of mental disease. Though of a firmer character than his own, the tears rolled down her cheeks. But in an instant, as it were, a new feeling took the place of sorrow: her eyes were fixed insensibly on the black veil, when, like a sudden twilight in the air, its terrors fell around her. She arose, and stood trembling before him.

"And do you feel it then, at last?" said he mournfully.

She made no reply, but covered her eyes with her hand, and turned to leave the room. He rushed forward and caught her arm.

"Have patience with me, Elizabeth!" cried he, passionately. "Do not desert me, though this veil must be between us here on earth. Be mine, and hereafter there shall be no veil over my face, no darkness

Reading Strategy
Drawing Inferences About Meaning In his reply to Elizabeth, what does Mr. Hooper suggest about the veil's meaning?

Vocabulary Builder
obstinacy (äb′ stə nə sē) *n.* stubbornness

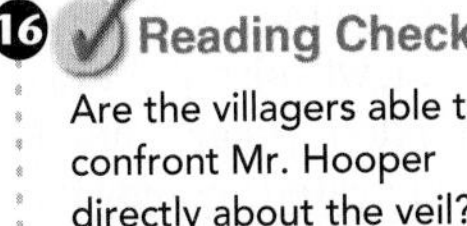

16 **Reading Check**
Are the villagers able to confront Mr. Hooper directly about the veil? Why or why not?

15 Reading Strategy
Drawing Inferences About Meaning

- **Ask** two students to read aloud the dialogue between Mr. Hooper and his fiancée.
- Then **ask** students the Reading Strategy question: In his reply to Elizabeth, what does Mr. Hooper suggest about the veil's meaning?
  Possible response: He suggests that the veil possesses a deep, serious, and universal meaning. Moreover, he implies that its meaning relates to the contrast between his relationship with God and his relationship with human society.

➤ **Monitor Progress: Ask** students to explain what Mr. Hooper's responses say about Hawthorne's view of humanity.
Answer: Hawthorne seems to believe that people everywhere know sorrow, but more importantly, that they live burdened with secret sins.

16 Reading Check

Answer: The villagers see the veil as "the symbol of a fearful secret between him and them" and so are unable to confront him directly about it.

Differentiated Instruction Solutions for All Learners

Support for Special Needs Students

These students may need help focusing the central ideas underlying this pivotal scene between Elizabeth and Mr. Hooper. Read aloud the scene, stopping to clarify and discuss how Elizabeth tries to elicit an explanation from Hooper first by using a simple, direct approach based on her position as his beloved and fiancée and secondly by suggesting that a scandal may result if some people are led to believe that he is hiding a secret sin.

Then spend time discussing with students Mr. Hooper's question "what mortal might not do the same?" Help students see that Hooper expresses the belief (no doubt Hawthorne's own) that people everywhere carry the consciousness of their own sins with them.

17 Humanities

Cemetery, 1970, by Peter McIntyre

Peter McIntyre (1910–) was born in New Zealand. He studied art in London, where he became involved in illustrating books and magazines, as well as in stage design. He was an "Official War Artist" during World War II. He served in that capacity in Greece, Crete, North Africa, and Italy. Cemetery was completed during a trip to the United States and published in the book *Peter McIntyre's West.* Use this question for discussion:

- How do you think the artist's perspective and his feelings about this place suggest that he has attempted to achieve more than a photographic likeness?
  Answer: Students may point to the vivid contrast between the menacing, overgrown, disorderly graveyard and the serene village in the background, and they may say that the artist creates the impression that there may be something ominous in the town's past—or perhaps its future.

18 Critical Viewing

Answer: Students may say that the artist has created a gloomy atmosphere in which death and dying hover menacingly over a sleepy village. In Hawthorne's story, an atmosphere of gloom, mistrust, and foreboding blankets the village.

19 Literary Analysis

Parable

- Read aloud the passage beginning "But even amid his grief."
- **Ask** students the Literary Analysis question: What message is conveyed by the passage beginning "But even amid his grief"?
  Answer: Hawthorne's pessimistic view of human nature is revealed. Marital bliss is denied the minister and his fiancée because of his refusal to provide a direct answer about the veil. Thus, a "material emblem" destroys happiness. Hawthorne may be suggesting that true happiness is impossible in this imperfect material world.

17

Cemetery, Peter McIntyre, Courtesy of the artist

18 ▲ **Critical Viewing** In what ways does the atmosphere in this painting reflect the mood of the story? **[Connect]**

between our souls! It is but a mortal veil—it is not for eternity! O! you know not how lonely I am, and how frightened, to be alone behind my black veil. Do not leave me in this miserable obscurity forever!"

"Lift the veil but once, and look me in the face," said she.

"Never! It cannot be!" replied Mr. Hooper.

"Then farewell!" said Elizabeth.

She withdrew her arm from his grasp, and slowly departed, pausing at the door, to give one long shuddering gaze, that seemed almost to penetrate the mystery of the black veil. But, even amid his grief,
19 Mr. Hooper smiled to think that only a material emblem had separated him from happiness, though the horrors, which it shadowed forth,

Literary Analysis
Parable What message is conveyed by the passage beginning "But, even amid his grief"?

Enrichment

Hawthorne

"The Minister's Black Veil" reflects Hawthorne's intense awareness of the distrustfulness and intolerance of his Puritan ancestors. You may wish to share with students this excerpt from Hawthorne's celebrated introduction to *The Scarlet Letter:*

It is nearly two centuries and a quarter since the original Briton, the earliest emigrant of my name, made his appearance in the wild and forest-bordered settlement . . . The figure of that first ancestor, invested by family tradition with a dim and dusky grandeur, was present to my boyish imagination, as far back as I can remember. It still haunts me, and induces a sort of home-feeling with the past . . . He was a soldier, legislator, judge; he was a ruler in the Church; he had all the Puritanical traits, both good and evil. He was likewise a bitter persecutor . . . His son, too, inherited the persecuting spirit, and made himself so conspicuous in the martyrdom of the witches, that their blood may fairly be said to have left a stain upon him . . .

must be drawn darkly between the fondest of lovers. From that time no
20 attempts were made to remove Mr. Hooper's black veil, or, by a direct appeal, to discover the secret which it was supposed to hide. By persons who claimed a superiority to popular prejudice, it was reckoned merely an eccentric whim, such as often mingles with the sober actions of men otherwise rational, and tinges them all with its own semblance of insanity. But with the multitude, good Mr. Hooper was irreparably a bugbear.[8] He could not walk the street with any peace of mind, so conscious was he that the gentle and timid would turn aside to avoid him, and that others would make it a point of hardihood to throw themselves in his way. The impertinence of the latter class compelled him to give up his customary walk at sunset to the burial ground; for when he leaned pensively over the gate, there would always be faces behind the gravestones, peeping at his black veil. A fable went the rounds that the stare of the dead people drove him thence. It grieved him, to the very depth of his kind heart, to observe how the children fled from his approach, breaking up their merriest sports, while his melancholy figure was yet afar off. Their instinctive dread caused him to feel more strongly than aught else, that a preternatural[9] horror was interwoven with the threads of the black crape. In truth, his own antipathy to the veil was known to be so great that he never willingly passed before a mirror, nor stooped to drink at a still fountain, lest, in its peaceful bosom, he should be affrighted by himself. This was what gave plausibility to the whispers, that Mr. Hooper's conscience tortured him for some great crime too horrible to be entirely concealed, or otherwise than so obscurely intimated. Thus, from beneath the black veil, there rolled a cloud into the sunshine, an ambiguity of sin or sorrow, which
21 enveloped the poor minister, so that love or sympathy could never reach him. It was said that ghost and fiend consorted with him there. With self-shudderings and outward terrors, he walked continually in its shadow, groping darkly within his own soul or gazing through a medium that saddened the whole world. Even the lawless wind, it was believed, respected his dreadful secret, and never blew aside the veil. But still good Mr. Hooper sadly smiled at the pale visages of the worldly throng as he passed by.

Among all its bad influences, the black veil had the one desirable effect, of making its wearer a very efficient clergyman. By the aid of his mysterious emblem—for there was no other apparent cause—he became a man of awful power over souls that were in agony for sin. His converts always regarded him with a dread peculiar to themselves, affirming, though but figuratively, that, before he brought them to celestial light, they had been with him behind the black veil. Its gloom, indeed, enabled him to sympathize with all dark affections. Dying sinners cried aloud for Mr. Hooper, and would not yield their

8. **bugbear** *n.* something causing needless fear.
9. **preternatural** (prēt′ ər năch′ ər əl) *adj.* supernatural.

Reading Strategy
Drawing Inferences About Meaning What can you infer about the people in the community based on their fear of Mr. Hooper's veil?

Literary Analysis
Parable Why is it significant that nature, as represented by the wind, respects the veil?

22 

How does Mr. Hooper feel about the veil?

20 Reading Strategy
Drawing Inferences About Meaning

- Have a student volunteer read the first three sentences of the paragraph beginning "She withdrew her arm from his grasp." Then help students summarize the reactions of various townspeople and acquaintances of Hooper, as described by Hawthorne so far.
- **Ask** students the Reading Strategy question: What can you infer about the people in the community based on their fear of Mr. Hooper's veil?
  Possible response: One might infer that Milford residents are guilt ridden, superstitious, or reluctant to admit the possibility of shame or sin in themselves or in those around them.

21 Literary Analysis
Parable

- Read aloud with students the passage beginning "In truth, his own antipathy." Ask students to listen in order to identify Hawthorne's use of nature imagery. If necessary, draw students' attention to the words *cloud into the sunshine, shadow,* and *lawless wind.*
- **Ask** students the Literary Analysis question: Why is it significant that nature, as represented by the wind, respects the veil?
  Possible response: If even such a powerful and "lawless" force as Nature respects the veil, one might feel confident inferring that Hooper is hiding a secret or sin of great significance.

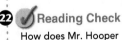

22 Reading Check

Answer: He feels such horror and loathing toward the veil that he avoids any situation in which he might be confronted with a reflection of himself.

Differentiated Instruction
Solutions for All Learners

Support for Special Needs Students
Students may need help to understand why the black veil makes Mr. Hooper "a very efficient clergyman." After reading aloud the paragraph beginning "Among all its bad influences," use discussion to guide students to understand the effect the veiled minister has upon people who suffer from overwhelming guilt. For these people, the minister's veil symbolizes their own sense of sin, suffering, and shame.

Enrichment for Advanced Readers
Point out that Parson Hooper is a religious leader commanding the utmost respect. Yet his action throws the village into confusion and anxiety. Invite students to stage a debate on whether a leader has the right to take such an action. Should a leader publicly acknowledge his or her own wrongdoing while continuing to serve in an official capacity? Students may wish to conduct research to support their viewpoints. History provides ample evidence for and against the rights and responsibilities of leaders.

23 Literary Analysis
Parable

- Spend time reading aloud and discussing the final paragraph on this page. Help students recognize that Hawthorne is setting the stage for the story's climactic scene.
- **Ask** students the Literary Analysis question: What message is Hawthorne conveying in his description of the veil as a partition, setting Mr. Hooper off from "cheerful brotherhood"? **Possible response:** Hawthorne highlights an awful irony; although Mr. Hooper wears a veil symbolizing the guilt and sin that all people share, the veil separates him from humanity.

breath till he appeared; though ever, as he stooped to whisper consolation, they shuddered at the veiled face so near their own. Such were the terrors of the black veil, even when Death had bared his visage! Strangers came long distances to attend service at his church, with the mere idle purpose of gazing at his figure, because it was forbidden them to behold his face. But many were made to quake ere they departed! Once, during Governor Belcher's[10] administration, Mr. Hooper was appointed to preach the election sermon. Covered with his black veil, he stood before the chief magistrate, the council, and the representatives, and wrought so deep an impression that the legislative measures of that year were characterized by all the gloom and piety of our earliest ancestral sway.

In this manner Mr. Hooper spent a long life, irreproachable in outward act, yet shrouded in dismal suspicions; kind and loving, though unloved, and dimly feared; a man apart from men, shunned in their health and joy, but ever summoned to their aid in mortal anguish. As years wore on, shedding their snows above his sable veil, he acquired a name throughout the New England churches, and they called him Father Hooper. Nearly all his parishioners, who were of mature age when he was settled, had been borne away by many a funeral: he had one congregation in the church, and a more crowded one in the churchyard; and having wrought so late into the evening, and done his work so well, it was now good Father Hooper's turn to rest.

Several persons were visible by the shaded candlelight, in the death chamber of the old clergyman. Natural connections[11] he had none. But there was the decorously grave, though unmoved physician, seeking only to mitigate the last pangs of the patient whom he could not save. There were the deacons, and other eminently pious members of his church. There, also, was the Reverend Mr. Clark, of Westbury, a young and zealous divine, who had ridden in haste to pray by the bedside of the expiring minister. There was the nurse, no hired handmaiden of death, but one whose calm affection had endured thus long in secrecy, in solitude, amid the chill of age, and would not perish, even at the dying hour. Who, but Elizabeth! And there lay the hoary head of good Father Hooper upon the death pillow, with the black veil still swathed about his brow, and reaching down over his face, so that each more difficult gasp of his faint breath caused it to stir. All through life that piece of crape had hung between him and the world: it had separated him from cheerful brotherhood and woman's love, and kept him in that saddest of all prisons, his own heart; and still it lay upon his face, as if to deepen the gloom of his darksome chamber, and shade him from the sunshine of eternity.

Literary Analysis
Parable What message is Hawthorne conveying in his description of the veil as a partition, setting Mr. Hooper off from "cheerful brotherhood"?

10. **Governor Belcher** Jonathan Belcher (1682–1757), the royal governor of the Massachusetts Bay Colony, from 1730 to 1741.
11. **Natural connections** relatives.

For some time previous, his mind had been confused, wavering doubtfully between the past and the present, and hovering forward, as it were, at intervals, into the indistinctness of the world to come. There had been feverish turns, which tossed him from side to side, and wore away what little strength he had. But in his most convulsive struggles, and in the wildest vagaries of his intellect, when no other thought retained its sober influence, he still showed an awful solicitude lest the black veil should slip aside. Even if his bewildered soul could have forgotten, there was a faithful woman at his pillow, who, with averted eyes, would have covered that aged face, which she had last beheld in the comeliness of manhood. At length the death-stricken old man lay quietly in the torpor of mental and bodily exhaustion, with an imperceptible pulse, and breath that grew fainter and fainter, except when a long, deep, and irregular inspiration seemed to prelude the flight of his spirit.

The minister of Westbury approached the bedside.

"Venerable Father Hooper," said he, "the moment of your release is at hand. Are you ready for the lifting of the veil that shuts in time from eternity?"

Father Hooper at first replied merely by a feeble motion of his head; then, apprehensive, perhaps, that his meaning might be doubtful, he exerted himself to speak.

"Yea," said he, in faint accents, "my soul hath a patient weariness until that veil be lifted."

"And is it fitting," resumed the Reverend Mr. Clark, "that a man so given to prayer, of such a blameless example, holy in deed and thought, so far as mortal judgment may pronounce; is it fitting that a father in the church should leave a shadow on his memory, that may seem to blacken a life so pure? I pray you, my venerable brother, let not this thing be! Suffer us to be gladdened by your triumphant aspect as you go to your reward. Before the veil of eternity be lifted, let me cast aside this black veil from your face!"

And thus speaking, the Reverend Mr. Clark bent forward to reveal the mystery of so many years. But, exerting a sudden energy, that made all the beholders stand aghast, Father Hooper snatched both his hands from beneath the bedclothes, and pressed them strongly on the black veil, resolute to struggle, if the minister of Westbury would contend with a dying man.

"Never!" cried the veiled clergyman. "On earth, never!"

"Dark old man!" exclaimed the affrighted minister, "with what horrible crime upon your soul are you now passing to the judgment?"

Father Hooper's breath heaved; it rattled in his throat; but, with a mighty effort, grasping forward with his hands, he caught hold of life, and held it back till he should speak. He even raised himself in bed; and there he sat, shivering with the arms of death around him, while the black veil hung down, awful, at that last moment, in the gathered terrors of a lifetime. And yet the faint, sad smile, so often

physical veil
spiritual veil

Literary Analysis
Parable and Symbol What does the minister of Westbury's question suggest about the veil's symbolic meaning?

25 **Reading Check**
On his deathbed, does Mr. Hooper wish the veil to be removed?

24 Literary Analysis
Parable and Symbol

- Read aloud the bracketed passage to students. **Ask** them what they think the minister of Westbury means when he says that the moment of Mr. Hooper's "release" is near.
  Answer: Mr. Hooper is about to die.
- Spend time discussing the question the minister asks Mr. Hooper, "Are you ready for the lifting of the veil that shuts in time from eternity?" Help students realize that in this solemn moment he alludes to the lifting of the veil between life and death—"time and eternity"—more than he does to the physical veil worn by Mr. Hooper.
- **Ask** students the Literary Analysis question: What does the minister of Westbury's question suggest about the veil's symbolic meaning?
  Possible responses: Students may say that it suggests that the veil symbolizes the division or veil between life and death.

25 Reading Check

Answer: Hooper musters all his strength to resist having the veil removed from his face before death.

Differentiated Instruction Solutions for All Learners

Strategy for English Learners
Read aloud the key sentence beginning "Nearly all his parishioners" on p. 350. Help students work through and paraphrase the sentence. Help students recognize the use of metaphor in Hawthorne's description of Hooper's "congregations," alive and dead. Tell students that Hawthorne's reference to Hooper's having "wrought so late into the evening" is a way of comparing his life to a single working day. Hooper is very old and about to die.

Strategy for Advanced Readers
Remind students that Hawthorne's writing reflects his preoccupation with the superstitions, cruelty, and character flaws of his Puritan ancestors. Invite students to identify and analyze examples of this preoccupation in "The Minister's Black Veil." Also, point out that Hawthorne incorporated his keen awareness of human flaws into his work. Encourage students to keep these ideas in mind as they read.

ASSESS

Answers

1. (a) Some students may say that they would have reacted to the veil with fear or shock. Others may say that they would not have been alarmed by the veil. (b) Students may say that as a Puritan clergyman, they would have tried to persuade Hooper (much as Reverend Clark did) to remove the veil and bring to an end the mystery, gossip, suspicions, and sense of dread that had infected the village.
2. (a) His congregation held him in high esteem. (b) The veil separates him from them; they grow fearful of him and of his apparent secret. Also the performance of his ordinary duties as a minister begins to have a greater and keener impact on the members of his congregation.
3. (a) The sermon's subject is secret sin. (b) His sermon arouses feelings of guilt, fear, and remorse. (c) The minister's wearing of an unexplained black veil is shocking and provocative, and it causes his listeners to react in unexpected, dramatic ways.
4. (a) It makes him a very efficient clergyman. (b) Students may say that the veil impels Hooper's listeners to question why he wears the veil, to relate the words of his sermon to his wearing the veil, and to relate both the sermon and the veil to their private knowledge about their own secret sins.
5. (a) The veil has a powerful effect on people because it reminds them of their secret sins. (b) Students may respond that they do agree with the suggestion, because all people have some thoughts and concerns that they feel they have to keep to themselves.
6. Students may say that guilt could have benefits for a person if it led him or her to admit fault or to change destructive behavior.

Go Online Author Link For additional information about Nathaniel Hawthorne, have students type in the Web Code, then select H from the alphabet, and then select Nathaniel Hawthorne.

there, now seemed to glimmer from its obscurity, and linger on Father Hooper's lips.

"Why do you tremble at me alone?" cried he, turning his veiled face round the circle of pale spectators. "Tremble also at each other! Have men avoided me, and women shown no pity, and children screamed and fled, only for my black veil? What, but the mystery which it obscurely typifies, has made this piece of crape so awful? When the friend shows his inmost heart to his friend; the lover to his best beloved; when man does not vainly shrink from the eye of his Creator, loathsomely treasuring up the secret of his sin; then deem me a monster, for the symbol beneath which I have lived, and die! I look around me, and, lo! on every visage a Black Veil!"

While his auditors shrank from one another, in mutual affright, Father Hooper fell back upon his pillow, a veiled corpse, with a faint smile lingering on the lips. Still veiled, they laid him in his coffin, and a veiled corpse they bore him to the grave. The grass of many years has sprung up and withered on that grave, the burial stone is moss-grown, and good Mr. Hooper's face is dust; but awful is still the thought that it moldered beneath the Black Veil!

Critical Reading

1. **Respond:** How would you have reacted to the veil if you had been **(a)** a member of Mr. Hooper's congregation or **(b)** another Puritan clergyman?
2. **(a) Recall:** How did his congregation regard Mr. Hooper before he began wearing the veil? **(b) Analyze:** In what ways does the veil affect Mr. Hooper's relationship with his congregation?
3. **(a) Recall:** What is the subject of Mr. Hooper's sermon on the day he first wears the veil? **(b) Compare and Contrast:** What emotions does Mr. Hooper evoke in his congregation that he never did before? **(c) Draw Conclusions:** To what do you attribute Mr. Hooper's new found ability to affect his listeners?
4. **(a) Recall:** According to the narrator, what is the veil's "one desirable effect"? **(b) Infer:** Why does the veil make Mr. Hooper a more effective minister?
5. **(a) Interpret:** Why does the veil have such a powerful effect on people? **(b) Synthesize:** Hawthorne suggests that all people carry secrets they choose not to reveal to anyone. Do you agree or disagree with this suggestion? Explain.
6. **Take a Position:** At some point in our lives, most human beings will feel guilty about something. Do you think that guilt is ever beneficial? Explain.

For: More about Nathaniel Hawthorne
Visit: www.PHSchool.com
Web Code: ere-9309

Apply the Skills

The Minister's Black Veil

Literary Analysis

Parable

1. In what ways does this **parable** convey the message that people possess the potential for both good and evil?
2. Why do you think Hawthorne does not reveal the reason Parson Hooper begins wearing the veil?
3. The Anti-Transcendentalists believed that the truths of existence are both elusive and disturbing. What disturbing truth does Hawthorne convey through Parson Hooper and his black veil?

Connecting Literary Elements

4. **(a)** With what emotions does Elizabeth regard the veil at first and later on? **(b)** What do her reactions suggest about the veil as a **symbol**?
5. **(a)** Use a chart like the one shown to analyze the emotional associations contained in three descriptions of the veil. **(b)** Is the veil symbolic of a single idea, or does it offer a range of possible interpretations?

Descriptive Detail	Emotional Associations	Symbolic Meaning

6. On his deathbed, Mr. Hooper says, "I look around me, and lo! on every visage a Black Veil!" What does this statement suggest about the veil's symbolic meaning?

Reading Strategy

Drawing Inferences About Meaning

7. Based on the villagers' reactions to Parson Hooper, **draw inferences** about human nature as Hawthorne sees it.
8. What can you infer about the author's attitude toward the Puritans from this story? Support your answer.

Extend Understanding

9. **Cultural Connection: (a)** Do you think a community's expectations that its leaders be without any guilt are realistic? **(b)** Are they fair? Explain.

QuickReview

A **parable** is a short, simple story with a moral message.

A **symbol** is something that has meaning in and of itself and also stands for something else.

To **draw inferences about meaning,** use details from the text as clues to an author's larger purpose.

For: Self-test
Visit: www.PHSchool.com
Web Code: era-6305

Answers

1. **Possible responses:** The behavior and actions of Parson Hooper alone show that human beings have the potential for both evil (his implied albeit unspecified "secret sin") and good (his lifetime of honesty and good works). The actions and behavior of Elizabeth and of the other townspeople also show the potential for good and evil, respectively.
2. By not revealing Hooper's motive, Hawthorne creates ambiguity and forces the reader to infer the reason by examining the evidence in the story.
3. All people have committed some acts that they regret as sinful, and all put some barriers between themselves and others.
4. (a) She regards the veil with determination, embarrassment, sorrow, and finally fear. (b) Her reactions suggest that the veil is a symbol characterized by ambiguity and great power.
5. (a) Students' charts should contain accurate details drawn from the story, and insightful inferences about emotional associations and symbolic meanings.
   Another sample answer can be found on **Literary Analysis Graphic Organizer B,** p. 70 in ***Graphic Organizer Transparencies.***
   (b) The veil takes on different meanings and associations at various times during the story.
6. It suggests that the veil symbolizes the secret sin that lies in the heart of every human being.
7. Hawthorne seems to see human nature as marked by negative characteristics such as suspicion, pettiness, ignorance, and cowardice.
8. One can infer that Hawthorne took a negative view of the Puritans, because many characters are hypocritical and lack compassion.
9. (a and b) Students should support their responses with clear reasoning and examples.

Go Online Assessment Students may use the **Self-test** to prepare for **Selection Test A** or **Selection Test B.**

EXTEND/ASSESS

Answers

❶ Vocabulary Lesson

Word Analysis

1. *equidistant*—equally distant
2. *equivalent*—equal in value, quantity, force, meaning, etc.
3. *equate*—to make equal
4. *equilibrium*—a state of balance or equality between opposing forces

Spelling Strategy

1. impertinent
2. iniquity
3. indecorous
4. impassive

Vocabulary Builder

1. c
2. f
3. g
4. j
5. a
6. d
7. e
8. i
9. b
10. h

❷ Grammar and Style Lessson

Answers should include the following: **(1)** two paragraphs from the selection; **(2)** a list of the types of openers of the sentences; **(3)** two rewritten paragraphs, both with sentences containing the same type of opener; **(4)** an explanation of the ineffectiveness of the rewritten paragraphs.

Writing Application

Students' paragraphs should engage readers and use a variety of sentence openers.

WG Writing and Grammar, Ruby Level

Students will find further instruction and practice on varying sentence openers Chapter 20, Section 3.

Build Language Skills

❶ Vocabulary Lesson

Word Analysis: Latin Root *-equi-*

The Latin root *-equi-* means "equal." The spelling of the root changes slightly in the word ***iniquity,*** meaning "sin or gross injustice." Using your knowledge of this root, define the following words:

1. equidistant
2. equivalent
3. equate
4. equilibrium

Spelling Strategy

The prefix *in-*, meaning "not," as in *indecorous,* changes to *im-* before many words beginning with *p*, such as *impersonal*, or with *m*, such as *immature.* Complete the words below by adding the correct prefix.

1. __pertinent (impolite)
2. __iquity (evil)
3. __decorous (vulgar)
4. __passive (emotionless)

Vocabulary Builder: Synonyms

Review the vocabulary list on page 339. Then, select the letter of the best synonym for each numbered word.

1. venerable	**a.** wise
2. iniquity	**b.** rude
3. indecorous	**c.** honorable
4. ostentatious	**d.** whim
5. sagacious	**e.** timid
6. vagary	**f.** evil
7. tremulous	**g.** uncouth
8. waggery	**h.** stubbornness
9. impertinent	**i.** humor
10. obstinacy	**j.** showy

❷ Grammar and Style Lesson

Varying Sentence Openers

By **varying sentence openers,** you can avoid a repetitive rhythm and enliven your writing. In addition to beginning a sentence with a subject followed by a verb, use one of these types of sentence openers:

Prepositional Phrase: *At the close of the services,* the people hurried out . . .

Participial Phrase: *Turning his veiled face from one group to another,* he paid due reverence . . .

Subordinate Clause: *As he stooped,* the veil hung straight down from his forehead . . .

Looking at Style Review the story, and select a paragraph that contains at least three different types of sentence openers. Identify the type of opener used in each sentence. Then, rewrite the paragraph so that all of the sentences have the same type of opener. Finally, explain why the rewritten paragraph is less effective than the original one.

Writing Application Write the opening paragraph of a short story. Engage readers by using a variety of sentence openers. Then, underline and identify each type.

WG *Prentice Hall Writing and Grammar Connection: Chapter 20, Section 3*

Assessment Practice

Make Inferences and Generalizations

(For more practice, see *Standardized Test Preparation Workbook*, p. 20.)

Many tests require students to make generalizations—that is, general statements based on specific information from the written passage. A generalization is a general idea that is supported by textual evidence. Use the following sample question about Hawthorne's story to show students how to make generalizations about a written text:

What effect does the appearance of Minister Hooper's black veil have on his congregation?

A They are afraid and confused.
B They are indifferent.
C They are quietly supportive.
D They are angry and violent.

Choices *B, C,* and *D* contain information not found in the text. *A* is correct. The veil is mysterious and makes Mr. Hooper appear more threatening and powerful.

Writing Lesson

Timed Writing: Response to a Short Story

Some aspects of this dark and powerful story probably made a distinct impression on you. Perhaps you were fascinated by the spectacle of the veil or upset by Parson Hooper's (or the villagers') behavior. Write a short paper in which you present your response to an element of the story. Support your response with specific details from the story. (***40 minutes***)

Prewriting (*10 minutes*) Review the story, and note your thoughts and feelings about the characters, setting, plot, and symbols. Choose one element to address. Then, find details that you can use to help explain your reactions.

Drafting (*20 minutes*) In an introductory paragraph, identify the element on which you are focusing and explain your reaction to it. Then, explain the role of this element in the story, citing specific details for support.

Revising (*10 minutes*) Revise your response to make certain that you have included enough passages and details from the story to explain your reaction.

Model: Using Exact Quotations

Hawthorne never tells us why Parson Hooper decides to wear the veil. We know only that the veil conceals his entire face except for his chin and mouth.

, which Hawthorne describes as a "gloomy shade"

The most effective way to cite details from a literary work is to use word-for-word quotations.

WG Prentice Hall Writing and Grammar Connection: Chapter 14, Section 2

Extend Your Learning

Listening and Speaking As Elizabeth, present a **monologue** in which you appeal to your fiancé to remove his black veil.

- Use a familiar tone of address.
- Maintain an appropriately Puritan air of restraint.
- Refer to Elizabeth's history with Mr. Hooper and her hopes for their future.

Give a dramatic presentation to the class.

Research and Technology Read "The Wedding Knell"—another story in Hawthorne's *Twice-Told Tales*. Compare and contrast it with "The Minister's Black Veil." Then, prepare and deliver an **oral presentation** in which you discuss the two stories.

For: An additional research activity
Visit: www.PHSchool.com
Web Code: erd-7305

❸ Writing Lesson

You may use this Writing Lesson as timed-writing practice, or you may allow students to develop the response as a writing assignment over several days.

- To guide students in writing this response to a short story, give them the **Support for Writing Lesson**, p. 83 in ***Unit 3 Resources.***
- Students' responses should focus on Hawthorne's use of a literary element. Their papers should include not only explanations and descriptions of their responses, but also a variety of supporting textual details.
- Use the Response to Literature rubrics in ***General Resources,*** pp. 65–66, to evaluate student work.

❹ Listening and Speaking

- Urge students to reread carefully each of the two scenes in which Elizabeth plays a role. They should take special note of her dialogue, in order to clarify its content and familiarize themselves with the style of her words.
- Pairs of students might benefit from improvising dialogue between Elizabeth and Hooper. If students record some of these improvisations, they may discover material that can be used later in their monologues.
- Give students a copy of the Peer Assessment: Dramatic Performance rubric on p. 131 of ***General Resources.***
- Have students use The **Support for Extend Your Learning** page (***Unit 3 Resources,*** p. 84) provides guided note-taking opportunities to help students complete the Extend Your Learning activities.

Go Online Research — Have students type in the Web Code for another research activity.

Assessment Resources

The following resources can be used to assess students' knowledge and skills.

Unit 3 Resources
- **Selection Test A,** pp. 86–88
- **Selection Test B,** pp. 89–91

General Resources
- **Rubrics for Response to Literature,** pp. 65–66
- **Rubric for Peer Assessment: Dramatic Performance** p. 131

Go Online Assessment — Students may use the **Self-test** to prepare for **Selection Test A** or **Selection Test B.**

Meeting Your Standards

Students will

1. **analyze and respond to literary elements.**
   - Literary Analysis: Symbol
2. **read, comprehend, analyze, and critique an excerpt from a novel.**
   - Reading Strategy: Recognizing Symbols
   - Reading Check questions
   - Apply the Skills questions
   - Assessment Practice (ATE)
3. **develop vocabulary.**
   - Vocabulary Lesson: Latin Prefix: *mal-*
4. **understand and apply written and oral language conventions.**
   - Spelling Strategy
   - Grammar and Style Lesson: Agreement With Collective Nouns
5. **develop writing proficiency.**
   - Writing Lesson: A Character Study
6. **develop appropriate research strategies.**
   - Extend Your Learning: Report
7. **understand and apply listening and speaking strategies.**
   - Extend Your Learning: Monologue

Block Scheduling: Use one 90-minute class period to preteach the skills and have students read the selection. Use a second 90-minute class period to assess students' mastery of skills, extend their learning, and monitor their progress.

Homework Suggestions

Following are possibilities for homework assignments.

- Support pages from *Unit 3 Resources:*
  Literary Analysis
  Reading Strategy
  Vocabulary Builder
  Grammar and Style
- An Extend Your Learning project and the Writing Lesson for this selection may be completed over several days.

Step-by-Step Teaching Guide	Pacing Guide
PRETEACH	
• Administer Vocabulary and Reading Warm-ups as necessary.	5 min.
• Engage students' interest with the motivation activity.	5 min.
• Read and discuss author and background features. **FT**	10 min.
• Introduce the Literary Analysis Skill: Symbol **FT**	5 min.
• Introduce the Reading Strategy: Recognizing Symbols **FT**	10 min
• Prepare students to read by teaching the selection vocabulary. **FT**	
TEACH	
• Informally monitor comprehension while students read independently or in groups. **FT**	30 min.
• Monitor students' comprehension with the Reading Check notes.	as students read
• Reinforce vocabulary with Vocabulary Builder notes.	as students read
• Develop students' understanding of symbol with the Literary Analysis annotations. **FT**	5 min.
• Develop students' ability to recognize symbols with the Reading Strategy annotations. **FT**	5 min.
ASSESS/EXTEND	
• Assess students' comprehension and mastery of the Literary Analysis and Reading Strategy by having them answer the Apply the Skills questions. **FT**	15 min.
• Have students complete the Vocabulary Lesson and the Grammar and Style Lesson. **FT**	15 min.
• Apply students' ability to write a summary by using the Writing Lesson. **FT**	45 min. or homework
• Apply students' understanding by using one or more of the Extend Your Learning activities.	20–90 min. or homework
• Administer Selection Test A or Selection Test B. **FT**	15 min.

Resources

PRINT

Unit 3 Resources

- Vocabulary Warm-up Word Lists [**L1, L2, EL**] .... p. 101
- Vocabulary Warm-up Practice [**L1, L2, EL**] .... p. 102
- Reading Warm-up A [**L1, L2, EL**] .... p. 103
- Reading Warm-up B [**L1, L2, L3**] .... p. 104

TRANSPARENCY

Graphic Organizer Transparencies

- Literary Analysis Graphic Organizer A [**L3**] .... p. 73
- Literary Analysis Graphic Organizer B [**L1, L2, EL**] .... p. 74
- Reading Strategy Graphic Organizer A [**L3**] .... p. 71
- Reading Strategy Graphic Organizer B [**L1, L2, EL**] .... p. 72

PRINT

Reader's Notebook [**L2**]

Reader's Notebook: Adapted Version [**L1**]

Reader's Notebook: English Learner's Version [**EL**]

Unit 3 Resources

- Literary Analysis [**L3**] .... p. 105
- Reading Strategy [**L3**] .... p. 106
- Vocabulary Builder [**L3**] .... p. 107

TRANSPARENCY

Graphic Organizer Transparencies

- Series of Events Chain .... p. 311

TECHNOLOGY

Listening to Literature Audio CDs [**L2, EL**]

PRINT

Unit 3 Resources

- Grammar and Style [**L3**] .... p. 108
- Support for Writing Lesson [**L3**] .... p. 109
- Support for Extend Your Learning [**L3**] .... p. 110
- Enrichment [**L4**] .... p. 111
- Selection Test A [**L1, L2, EL**] .... p. 112
- Selection Test B [**L3, L4**] .... p. 115

General Resources

- Rubrics for Response to Literature [**L3**] .... pp. 65–66
- Rubrics for Peer Assessment Dramatic Performance [**L3**] .... p. 131

TECHNOLOGY

Go Online: Research [**L3**]

Go Online: Self-test [**L3**]

***ExamView®*, Test Bank** [**L3**]

Choosing Resources for Differentiated Instruction

[**L1**] Special Needs Students

[**L2**] Below-Level Students

[**L3**] All Students

[**L4**] Advanced Students

[**EL**] English Learners

FT Fast Track Instruction: To move the lesson more quickly, use the strategies and activities identified with **FT**.

Scaffolding for Less Proficient and Advanced Students

The leveled Critical Thinking questions after selections progress in the levels of thinking required to answer them. To address the needs of your different students, you may use the (a) level questions for your less proficient students and the (b) level questions with your on-level and advanced students. The occasional (c) level questions are appropriate for your advanced students.

PRENTICE HALL **TeacherEXPRESS™** Plan · Teach · Assess

Use this complete suite of powerful teaching tools to make lesson planning and testing quicker and easier.

Use the interactive textbook (online and on CD-ROM) to make selections and activities come alive with audio and video support and interactive questions.

PRETEACH

Motivation

Ahab says, "Death to Moby-Dick! God hunt us all, if we do not hunt Moby-Dick to his death!" After reading this quotation, tell students that Ahab is a man obsessed. Invite students to think of people (or fictional characters) they know who have worked intensely to reach a goal. You might mention people like Midori, Tiger Woods, and Gary Kasparov, as well as world-class ice skaters, musicians, gymnasts, and others whose intense, single-minded efforts began at an early age. Ask students whether they see a distinction between concentrated effort and obsession. Does one need to be obsessed to reach lofty goals?

❶ Background

More About the Author

After an unsuccessful job search and a brief stint as a teacher, Melville sailed on the whaler *Acushnet* to the South Seas in 1841, anchoring in the Marquesas Islands. On this voyage, he joined an uprising that landed him in a Tahitian jail. After escaping, Melville roamed throughout French Polynesia, during which time he became deeply embittered at the mistreatment of native Polynesian peoples by colonists and missionaries.

In addition to his novels and short stories, Melville wrote verse. His first volume of poetry, *Battle-Pieces and Aspects of the War* (1866), concerned the Civil War. His last prose work, *Billy Budd, Foretopman,* was not published until 1924.

Build Skills *Novel*

❶ *from* Moby-Dick

Herman Melville (1819–1891)

Herman Melville is one of America's greatest novelists. Unfortunately, his work was never fully appreciated during his lifetime, and he lived a life that was often filled with frustration and despair.

Melville was born in New York City, the son of a wealthy merchant. His family's comfortable financial situation changed drastically in 1830, however, when his father's import business failed. Two years later, Melville's father died, leaving the family in debt. Forced to leave school, Melville spent the rest of his childhood working as a clerk, a farmhand, and a teacher to help support his family.

Whaling in the South Pacific Melville became a sailor at the age of nineteen and spent several years working on whaling ships and exploring the South Pacific. He returned to the United States in 1844, after a brief period of service in the navy.

Soon thereafter, Melville began his career as a writer, using his adventures in the South Seas as material for his fiction. He quickly produced two popular and financially successful novels, *Typee* (1846) and *Omoo* (1847), both set in the Pacific islands. His third novel, *Mardi* (1849), was considerably more abstract and symbolic. When readers rejected the book and his fame began to fade, Melville grew increasingly melancholy. He continued writing, however, turning out two more novels, *Redburn* (1849) and *White-Jacket* (1850), over the next two years.

Writing in the Berkshires Using the profits from his popular novels, Melville bought a farm, known as Arrowhead, near Pittsfield, Massachusetts. There, he befriended the author Nathaniel Hawthorne, who lived in a neighboring village. Greatly encouraged by Hawthorne's interest and influenced by his reading of Shakespeare, Melville redoubled his own creative energies. He began producing deeper and more sophisticated works. In 1851, he published his masterpiece, *Moby-Dick,* under the title *The Whale.*

Moby-Dick is a complex novel with several layers of meaning. On the surface, it is the story of the fateful voyage of a whaling ship. On another level, it is the story of a bitter man's quest for vengeance and truth. On still another level, it is a philosophical examination of humanity's relationship to the natural world and the conflict between creativity and cruelty.

A Moment of Pride When he finished the book, Melville sensed the magnitude of his achievement. Unfortunately, his pleasure in his work was short-lived. Unable to appreciate the novel's depth, nineteenth-century readers responded unfavorably to *Moby-Dick.* It did not attract a wide audience.

Audiences also rejected his next two novels, *Pierre* (1852) and *The Confidence Man* (1857). Melville fell into debt and was forced to accept a job as an inspector at the New York customs house. Some of the short stories Melville published between 1852 and 1855—including "Bartleby the Scrivener," "The Encantadas," and "Benito Cereno"—reflect the author's circumstances at the time, including his contempt for hypocrisy and materialism.

Rediscovered Disillusioned and bitter, Melville turned away from writing fiction during the latter part of his life. He privately published several volumes of poetry. He also produced a handful of short stories and the moving novella *Billy Budd.* Melville died in 1891, unappreciated and unnoticed. In the 1920s, however, his novels and tales were rediscovered and hailed by scholars, and he finally received the recognition he deserved. Today, *Moby-Dick* is widely regarded as one of the finest novels in all of American literature.

Preview

Connecting to the Literature

Some situations demand fierce concentration. However, as this excerpt from one of literature's most famous works of fiction illustrates, when one focuses *too* intensely on a goal, attention can become obsession.

Literary Analysis

Symbol

A **symbol** is a person, place, or thing that has its own meaning and also represents something larger. Writers often use symbols that appear in the literature of many different cultures. Such symbols are called **archetypes.** For example, Melville's whale is like the whale that swallows Jonah in the Bible. However, Moby-Dick is an extremely complex symbol. To understand its meaning, examine every aspect of the whale's behavior and appearance.

- Moby-Dick is massive, threatening, and awe-inspiring yet beautiful.
- Moby-Dick seems unpredictable but is controlled by natural laws.
- Moby-Dick seems immortal and indifferent to human suffering.

Analyzed in this way, Moby-Dick seems to symbolize all that is mysterious and uncontrollable in life.

Connecting Literary Elements

A **theme** is a central message revealed by a literary work, and is often expressed through the use of symbols, as well as characters' actions, descriptions, and imagery. In *Moby-Dick,* Melville explores the enormous theme of the mysteries of existence. As you read, look for points at which Melville addresses such ideas as good, evil, sacrifice, and revenge.

Reading Strategy

Recognizing Symbols

To **recognize symbols,** look for characters, places, or objects that are mentioned repeatedly or linked to larger concepts. For example, Ahab's description of Moby-Dick gives the whale symbolic meaning:

> I see in him outrageous strength, with an inscrutable malice sinewing it. That inscrutable malice is chiefly what I hate . . .

From this description, you might guess that Moby-Dick symbolizes nature's destructive power. Use a chart like the one shown to recognize and interpret symbols.

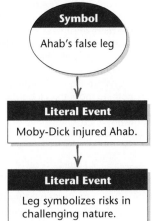

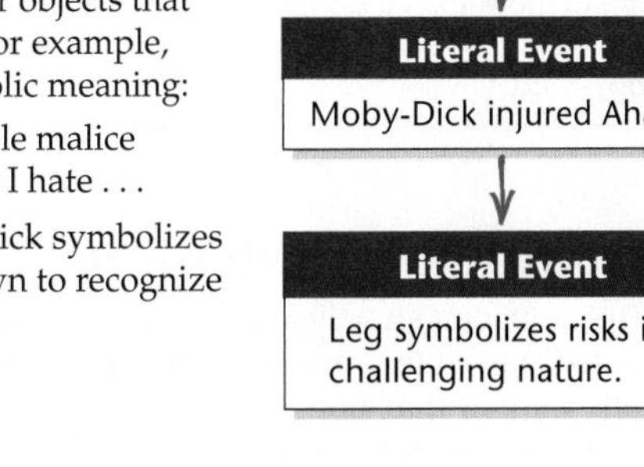

Symbol
Ahab's false leg
Literal Event
Moby-Dick injured Ahab.
Literal Event
Leg symbolizes risks in challenging nature.

Vocabulary Builder

inscrutable (in skro͞ot′ ə bəl) *adj.* not able to be easily understood (p. 362)

maledictions (mal′ ə dik′ shənz) *n.* curses (p. 364)

prescient (presh′ ənt) *adj.* having foreknowledge (p. 368)

pertinaciously (pʉr′ tə nā′ shəs lē) *adv.* unyieldingly (p. 370)

❷ Literary Analysis
Symbol

- Tell students that they will focus on symbol as they read the excerpts from *Moby-Dick* in this selection. You may want students to review what they learned about symbols when they read Hawthorne's "The Minister's Black Veil."
- Urge students to analyze each symbol to identify its literal meaning, as well as its deeper or larger meaning.
- Before they begin reading, you might wish to encourage students to use prior knowledge to list and reflect on some common symbols in our culture today. Examples include flags; colors; fashions; vehicles; cellular phones; fences, walls, and bridges; and so on.

❸ Reading Strategy
Recognizing Symbols

- As they read Melville's narrative, have students take note of characters, places, objects, images, and actions that are mentioned repeatedly, explained in detail, or linked to larger concepts.
- Explain that symbols can range from relatively simple to very complex. Point out that Melville portrays the great white whale in such a way that it takes on many shades of symbolic meaning. To help students recognize and interpret the symbols as they read the excerpt from *Moby-Dick,* give them a copy of **Reading Strategy Graphic Organizer A,** p. 71 in ***Graphic Organizer Transparencies.***

Vocabulary Builder

- Pronounce each vocabulary word for students, and read the definitions as a class. Have students identify any words with which they are already familiar.

Differentiated Instruction
Solutions for All Learners

Support for Special Needs Students
Have students complete the **Preview** and **Build Skills** pages for the selection in the ***Reader's Notebook: Adapted Version.*** These pages provide a selection summary, an abbreviated presentation of the reading and literary skills, and the graphic organizer on the **Build Skills** page in the student book.

Support for Less Proficient Readers
Have students complete the **Preview** and **Build Skills** pages for the selection in the ***Reader's Notebook.*** These pages provide a selection summary, an abbreviated presentation of the reading and literary skills, and the graphic organizer on the **Build Skills** page in the student book.

Support for English Learners
Have students complete the **Preview** and **Build Skills** pages for the selection in the ***Reader's Notebook: English Learner's Version.*** These pages provide a selection summary, an abbreviated presentation of the skills, additional contextual vocabulary, and the graphic organizer on the **Build Skills** page in the student book.

Learning Modalities
Intrapersonal Learners To promote active reading, invite students to keep a reader's response journal. Guide them to focus their observations about Ahab's desire for revenge and on Starbuck's responses to Ahab. Encourage them to record their own opinions of Ahab's quest and the reactions of the other sailors.

❶ About the Selection

Widely regarded as one of the finest American novels ever written, *Moby-Dick* expresses the view that, despite people's desire to do so, they will never be able to control nature or understand it completely. In "The Quarter-Deck," one of the novel's key early chapters, Ahab becomes the novel's dominant character, and Melville reveals Ahab's vengeful, obsessive personality and his conflict with Moby-Dick. At this turning point, readers and sailors alike learn the true purpose of the *Pequod's* voyage. "The Chase—Third Day" is the book's last chapter. There the novel reaches its climax in the final catastrophic contest with Moby-Dick.

❷ Background
History

In Melville's day, the captain of a ship had unlimited authority—and all aboard ship knew this to be the case. Failing to follow orders brought harsh and perhaps arbitrary punishment, and most crew members were careful not to challenge the captain directly.

❶

FROM

MOBY-DICK

Herman Melville

Background *Moby-Dick* is the story of a man's obsession with the dangerous and mysterious white whale that years before had taken off one of his legs. The man, Captain Ahab, guides the *Pequod*, a whaling ship, and its crew in relentless pursuit of this whale, Moby-Dick. Among the more important members of the crew are Starbuck, the first mate; Stubb, the second mate; Flask, the third mate; Queequeg, Tashtego, and Daggoo, the harpooners; and Ishmael, the young sailor who narrates the book.

When the crew signed aboard the *Pequod*, the voyage was to be nothing more than a business venture. However, in the following excerpt, Ahab makes clear to the crew that his purpose is to seek revenge against Moby-Dick.

from The Quarter-Deck

❷ One morning shortly after breakfast, Ahab, as was his wont, ascended the cabin gangway to the deck. There most sea captains usually walk at that hour, as country gentlemen, after the same meal, take a few turns in the garden.

Soon his steady, ivory stride was heard, as to and fro he paced his old rounds, upon planks so familiar to his tread, that they were all over dented, like geological stones, with the peculiar mark of his walk. Did you fixedly gaze, too, upon that ribbed and dented brow;

Differentiated Instruction Solutions for All Learners

Accessibility at a Glance

	from Moby-Dick
Context	Nineteenth-century whaling voyage
Language	Challenging (similes and metaphors; whaling/seamen's language and vocabulary; long compound and complex sentences
Concept Level	Challenging (Moby-Dick as a symbol of nature's beauty, power, and immortality)
Literary Merit	Classic, influential American novel
Lexile	970
Other	Powerful struggle between humankind and nature
Overall Rating	More challenging

there also, you would see still stranger footprints—the footprints of his one unsleeping, ever-pacing thought.

But on the occasion in question, those dents looked deeper, even as his nervous step that morning left a deeper mark. And, so full of his thought was Ahab, that at every uniform turn that he made, now at the mainmast and now at the binnacle,[1] you could almost see that thought turn in him as he turned, and pace in him as he paced; so completely possessing him, indeed, that it all but seemed the inward mold of every outer movement.

"D'ye mark him, Flask?" whispered Stubb; "the chick that's in him pecks the shell. 'Twill soon be out."

The hours wore on—Ahab now shut up within his cabin; anon, pacing the deck, with the same intense bigotry of purpose[2] in his aspect.

It drew near the close of day. Suddenly he came to a halt by the bulwarks, and inserting his bone leg into the auger hole there, and with one hand grasping a shroud, he ordered Starbuck to send everybody aft.

"Sir!" said the mate, astonished at an order seldom or never given on shipboard except in some extraordinary case.

"Send everybody aft," repeated Ahab. "Mastheads, there! come down!"

When the entire ship's company were assembled, and with curious and not wholly unapprehensive faces, were eyeing him, for he looked not unlike the weather horizon when a storm is coming up, Ahab, after rapidly glancing over the bulwarks, and then darting his eyes among the crew, started from his standpoint; and as though not a soul were nigh him resumed his heavy turns upon the deck. With bent head and half-slouched hat he continued to pace, unmindful of the wondering whispering among the men; till Stubb cautiously whispered to Flask, that Ahab must have summoned them there for the purpose of witnessing a pedestrian feat. But this did not last long. Vehemently pausing, he cried:

"What do ye do when ye see a whale, men?"

"Sing out for him!" was the impulsive rejoinder from a score of clubbed voices.

"Good!" cried Ahab, with a wild approval in his tones; observing the hearty animation into which his unexpected question had so magnetically thrown them.

"And what do ye next, men?"

"Lower away, and after him!"

"And what tune is it ye pull to, men?"

"A dead whale or a stove[3] boat!"

More and more strangely and fiercely glad and approving, grew the countenance of the old man at every shout; while the mariners began to

1. **binnacle** (bin′ ə kəl) *n.* case enclosing a ship's compass.
2. **bigotry of purpose** complete single-mindedness.
3. **stove** *v.* broken; smashed.

Literary Analysis
Symbol What might the "dents" on Ahab's furrowed brow symbolize?

Reading Check
Why are the *Pequod's* planks dented?

3 Literary Analysis
Symbol

- Have a student volunteer read aloud the paragraph beginning "Soon his steady, ivory stride was heard." Make sure students understand the cause of the "dents" mentioned by Melville's narrator; these are the dents in the wooden planks of the ship's deck caused by Ahab's peg leg.
- Point out that the repetition of the image of dents indicates the presence of a symbol. Draw students' attention to the language Melville uses—*the footprints of his one unsleeping, ever-pacing thought*—to describe the wrinkles in Ahab's brow.
- In addition, point out the connection Melville draws between Ahab's dented brow and the deeper marks left by Ahab's "nervous" steps.
- **Ask** students the Literary Analysis question: What might the "dents" on Ahab's furrowed brow symbolize?
Answer: The dents might symbolize psychological injuries Ahab has suffered in his battle with the great whale.

4 Reading Check

Answer: Ahab has dented them walking back and forth with his "bone leg."

Differentiated Instruction
Solutions for All Learners

Support for Less Proficient Readers
Discuss with students why the men are curious and apprehensive. The reasons include that it is unusual for the men to be gathered on this particular deck (the "aft" deck at the stern, or rear, of the ship). Also, the men are wary of Ahab's peculiar behavior as he continues to pace about as if not noticing them.

Point out how Melville establishes early on an atmosphere of psychological tension, together with the idea that Ahab is a man with powerful feelings.

Support for English Learners
Draw students' attention to Melville's use of metaphor and simile to describe Ahab's growing tension (a chick pecking the shell, a stormy horizon). Also draw their attention to possibly confusing descriptive phrasing in the text ("not wholly unapprehensive"). Explain that these writing techniques were common in the nineteenth century. Encourage students to read slowly and carefully and to paraphrase the story whenever possible.

5 Humanities

Captain Ahab on the Deck of the Pequod, 1930, by Rockwell Kent

Rockwell Kent made many pen-and-ink drawings, including those that appear in this selection, for the 1930 Lakeside Press edition of *Moby-Dick,* published by Random House, Chicago. Kent was a painter, printmaker, author, illustrator, explorer, and political activist. Use the following question for discussion:

- What evidence of symbolism can you find in this image?
  Possible answer: Ahab's looming shadow might symbolize the destructive effects of his obsession with Moby-Dick.

6 Critical Viewing

Answer: Students may say that the illustration captures Ahab's implacable, obssesive nature very well.

7 Reading Strategy
Recognizing Symbols

- Point out that the narrator mentions several times a gold coin brandished by Ahab.
- **Ask** students the Reading Strategy question: What does Ahab's treatment of the gold coin suggest about its presence as a symbol?
  Answer: Ahab's nailing of the coin to the mast of the *Pequod* ensures its central and continual presence throughout the voyage. The gold, worth a fortune to the sailors, thus symbolizes the value that the quest has for Ahab, and the extreme nature of his desire for vengeance.

gaze curiously at each other, as if marveling how it was that they themselves became so excited at such seemingly purposeless questions.

But, they were all eagerness again, as Ahab, now half-revolving in his pivot hole, with one hand reaching high up a shroud,[4] and tightly, almost convulsively grasping it, addressed them thus:

5

Captain Ahab on the Deck of the Pequod, Rockwell Kent

"All ye mastheaders have before now heard me give orders about a white whale. Look ye! d'ye see this Spanish ounce of gold?"—holding up a broad bright coin to the sun—"it is a sixteen-dollar piece, men. D'ye see it? Mr. Starbuck, hand me yon topmaul."

While the mate was getting the hammer, Ahab, without speaking, was slowly rubbing the gold piece against the skirts of his jacket, as if to heighten its luster, and without using any words was meanwhile lowly humming to himself, producing a sound so strangely muffled and inarticulate that it seemed
7 the mechanical humming of the wheels of his vitality in him.

Receiving the topmaul from Starbuck, he advanced towards the mainmast with the hammer uplifted in one hand, exhibiting the gold with the other, and with a high raised voice exclaiming: "Whosoever of ye raises me a white-headed whale with a wrinkled brow and a crooked jaw; whosoever of ye raises me that white-headed whale, with three holes punctured in his starboard fluke[5]—look ye, whosoever of ye raises me that same white whale, he shall have this gold ounce, my boys!"

"Huzza! huzza!" cried the seamen, as with swinging tarpaulins they hailed the act of nailing the gold to the mast.

"It's a white whale, I say," resumed Ahab, as he threw down the topmaul: "a white whale. Skin your eyes for him, men; look sharp for white water; if ye see but a bubble, sing out."

All this while Tashtego, Daggoo, and Queequeg had looked on with even more intense interest and surprise than the rest, and at the mention of the wrinkled brow and crooked jaw they had started as if each was separately touched by some specific recollection.

"Captain Ahab," said Tashtego, "that white whale must be the same that some call Moby-Dick."

"Moby-Dick?" shouted Ahab. "Do ye know the white whale then, Tash?"

8 "Does he fantail[6] a little curious, sir, before he goes down?" said the Gay-Header deliberately.

6 ▲ **Critical Viewing**
In what ways does this portrait of Ahab compare or contrast with your mental image of him? **[Compare and Contrast]**

Reading Strategy
Recognizing Symbols
What does Ahab's treatment of the gold coin suggest about its presence as a symbol?

4. **shroud** *n.* set of ropes from a ship's side to the masthead.
5. **starboard fluke** (flo͝ok) *n.* right half of a whale's tail.
6. **fantail** *v.* to spread the tail like a fan.

Enrichment

Nantucket

The *Pequod* sails from the island of Nantucket, which is situated in the Atlantic Ocean off the southern coast of Massachusetts, about twenty miles south of Cape Cod and just east and south of Martha's Vineyard. In the late 1700s and early 1800s, Nantucket was one of the world's major whaling centers. At one point during this period, well over one hundred whaling ships used the island as their main port. In the mid-1800s, the whaling industry began to decline and the island developed its other resources.

Invite students to do research on the Internet and elsewhere to find whaling museums or restored seaports that feature whaling ships, tools, and other objects associated with the whaling industry. You might have students send for brochures on various items and exhibits. Such institutions include the Kendall Whaling Museum in Sharon, Massachusetts; the New Bedford Whaling Museum in New Bedford, Massachusetts; and the Cold Spring Harbor Whaling Museum in Cold Spring Harbor, New York.

"And has he a curious spout, too," said Daggoo, "very bushy, even for a parmacetty,[7] and mighty quick, Captain Ahab?"

"And he have one, two, tree—oh! good many iron in him hide, too, Captain," cried Queequeg disjointedly, "all twiske-tee betwisk, like him—him—" faltering hard for a word, and screwing his hand round and round as though uncorking a bottle—"like him—him—"

"Corkscrew!" cried Ahab, "aye, Queequeg, the harpoons lie all twisted and wrenched in him; aye, Daggoo, his spout is a big one, like a whole shock of wheat, and white as a pile of our Nantucket wool after the great annual sheepshearing; aye, Tashtego, and he fantails like a split jib in a squall. Death and devils! men, it is Moby-Dick ye have seen—Moby-Dick—Moby-Dick!"

"Captain Ahab," said Starbuck, who, with Stubb and Flask, had thus far been eyeing his superior with increasing surprise, but at last seemed struck with a thought which somewhat explained all the wonder. "Captain Ahab, I have heard of Moby-Dick—but it was not Moby-Dick that took off thy leg?"

"Who told thee that?" cried Ahab; then pausing, "Aye, Starbuck; aye, my hearties all round; it was Moby-Dick that dismasted me; Moby-Dick that brought me to this dead stump I stand on now. Aye, aye," he shouted with a terrific, loud, animal sob, like that of a heart-stricken moose; "Aye, aye! it was that accursed white whale that razeed me; made a poor pegging lubber[8] for me forever and a day!" Then tossing both arms, with measureless imprecations he shouted out: "Aye, aye! and I'll chase him round Good Hope, and round the Horn, and round the Norway Maelstrom, and round perdition's flames before I give him up. And this is what ye have shipped for, men! to chase that white whale on both sides of land, and over all sides of earth, till he spouts black blood and rolls fin out. What say ye, men, will ye splice hands on it, now? I think ye do look brave."

"Aye, aye!" shouted the harpooneers and seamen, running closer to the excited old man: "A sharp eye for the white whale; a sharp lance for Moby-Dick!"

"God bless ye," he seemed to half sob and half shout. "God bless ye, men. Steward! go draw the great measure of grog. But what's this long face about, Mr. Starbuck; wilt thou not chase the white whale? art not game for Moby-Dick?"

"I am game for his crooked jaw, and for the jaws of Death too, Captain Ahab, if it fairly comes in the way of the business we follow; but I came here to hunt whales, not my commander's vengeance. How many barrels will thy vengeance yield thee even if thou gettest it, Captain Ahab? it will not fetch thee much in our Nantucket market."

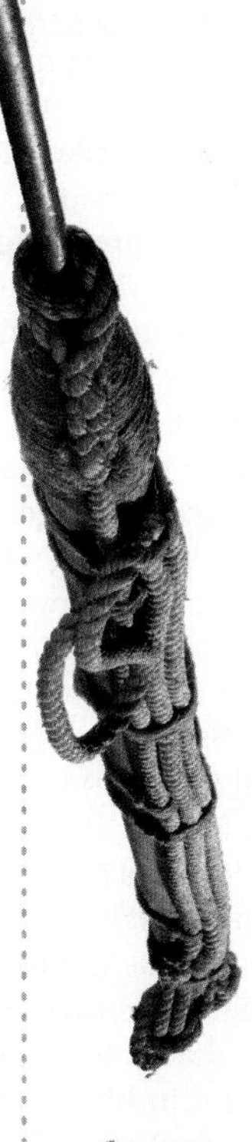

Literary Analysis
Symbol What image of Moby-Dick is created in this discussion?

10 **Reading Check**
What does Ahab say is his real purpose for making the voyage?

7. **parmacetty** (pär′ mə set′ ē) *n.* dialect for spermaceti, a waxy substance taken from a sperm whale's head and used to make candles.
8. **lubber** (lub′ ər) *n.* slow, clumsy person.

8 Literary Analysis
Symbol

- Invite listeners to focus on the details about Moby-Dick that are offered by each speaker. Suggest that students use a graphic organizer like one shown on p. 357 to record these details.
- **Ask** students the Literary Analysis question: What image of Moby-Dick is created in this discussion? **Possible answer:** The image of Moby-Dick as an almost supernatural being is created.

9 Background
History

Discuss with students why Ahab's command would surprise the crew. Point out that sailors on a whaler signed on for a share of the net profits. Although some probably hoped for adventure, most sailors simply hoped to capture as many whales as possible so they could sell the valuable whale oil, whalebone, and other whale byproducts. It would be understandable if Ahab's crew were to show reluctance to chase a single whale.

10 Reading Check

Answer: The real purpose is to chase and kill the great white whale, Moby-Dick.

Differentiated Instruction Solutions for All Learners

Strategy for Less Proficient Readers
To help students comprehend the text, have them list and discuss the physical traits that Ahab and the crew members say distinguish Moby-Dick from other whales. These include his white color; his unique way of fanning his tail before submerging; his unusual, large, and "bushy" spout; his quickness; and his hide, which contains several iron harpoons.

Strategy for English Learners
Help improve students' comprehension with the Series of Events Chain Graphic Organizer in ***Graphic Organizer Transparencies,*** p. 311. Use this to help students connect the events in the story.

11 Literary Analysis
Symbol and Theme

- Have students read this passage and identify references to money and commerce (*Nantucket market, money's, accountants, computed, countinghouse, guineas, premium*).
- Then, **ask** students how they know Ahab is using business metaphors to emphasize the strength of his desire to catch and kill Moby-Dick. If necessary, point out his explicit reference to "my vengeance" and his physical indication of his heart.
- **Ask** students the first Literary Analysis question: What do Ahab's comments say about the value of money compared with great desire?
  Answer: Ahab views desire—even if it is considered "vengeance"— as far more valuable than money.

12 Literary Analysis
Symbol

- Read aloud the passage more than once, so that students can focus on the key ideas of Ahab's speech.
- Help students understand Ahab's references to masks. These tell the reader that the captain believes that the whale's behavior shows it to be acting in response to a mind and will, rather than by animal instincts.
- **Ask** students the second Literary Analysis question: What insights into the whale's symbolic meaning can you gain from a close reading of this passage?
  Answer: Close reading indicates that Ahab (and the reader) must view the whale on both real and symbolic levels. Ahab declares here that he does not care whether the whale acts on its own out of malice or at the direction of another greater will ("Talk not to me of blasphemy, man; I'd strike the sun if it insulted me"). Indeed, the unknowability of the whale's—and by implication God's—motives are the very thing Ahab hates. Because it is hate that drives Ahab, his quest is cast symbolically in this passage as *hubris,* or the placing of the self above the will of God as revealed in nature, including the white whale.

11 "Nantucket market! Hoot! But come closer, Starbuck; thou requirest a little lower layer. If money's to be the measurer, man, and the accountants have computed their great countinghouse the globe, by girdling it with guineas, one to every three parts of an inch; then, let me tell thee, that my vengeance will fetch a great premium *here!*"

"He smites his chest," whispered Stubb, "what's that for? methinks it rings most vast, but hollow."

"Vengeance on a dumb brute!" cried Starbuck, "that simply smote thee from blindest instinct! Madness! To be enraged with a dumb thing, Captain Ahab, seems blasphemous."

12 "Hark ye yet again—the little lower layer. All visible objects, man, are but as pasteboard masks. But in each event—in the living act, the undoubted deed—there, some unknown but still reasoning thing puts forth the moldings of its features from behind the unreasoning mask. If man will strike, strike through the mask! How can the prisoner reach outside except by thrusting through the wall? To me, the white whale is that wall, shoved near to me. Sometimes I think there's naught beyond. But 'tis enough. He tasks me; he heaps me; I see in him outrageous strength, with an inscrutable malice sinewing it. That inscrutable thing is chiefly what I hate; and be the white whale agent, or be the white whale principal, I will wreak that hate upon him. Talk not to me of blasphemy, man; I'd strike the sun if it insulted me. For could the sun do that, then could I do the other; since there is ever a sort of fair play herein, jealousy presiding over all creations. But not my master, man, is even that fair play. Who's over me? Truth hath no confines. Take off thine eye! more intolerable than fiends' glarings is a doltish stare! So, so; thou reddenest and palest; my heat has melted thee to anger-glow. But look ye, Starbuck, what is said in heat, that thing unsays itself. There are men from whom warm words are small indignity. I meant not to incense thee. Let it go. Look! see yonder Turkish cheeks of spotted tawn—living, breathing pictures painted by the sun. The pagan leopards—the unrecking and unworshiping things, that live, and seek, and give no reasons for the torrid life they feel! The crew, man, the crew! Are they not one and all with Ahab, in this matter of the whale? See Stubb! he laughs! See yonder Chilean! he snorts to think of it. Stand up amid the general hurricane, thy one tossed sapling cannot, Starbuck! And what is it? Reckon it. 'Tis but to help strike a fin; no wondrous feat for Starbuck. What is it more? From this one poor hunt, then, the best lance out of all Nantucket, surely he will not hang back, when every foremasthand has clutched a whetstone. Ah! constrainings seize thee; I see! the billow lifts thee! Speak, but speak!—Aye, aye! thy silence, then, that voices thee. *(Aside)* Something shot from my dilated nostrils, he has inhaled it in his lungs. Starbuck now is mine; cannot oppose me now, without rebellion."

"God keep me!—keep us all!" murmured Starbuck, lowly.

But in his joy at the enchanted, tacit acquiescence of the mate, Ahab did not hear his foreboding invocation; nor yet the low laugh

Literary Analysis
Symbol and Theme What do Ahab's comments say about the value of money compared with great desire?

Vocabulary Builder
inscrutable (in skro͞ot′ ə bəl) *adj.* not able to be easily understood

Literary Analysis
Symbol What insights into the whale's symbolic meaning can you gain from a close reading of this passage?

Enrichment

Hunting Rituals

Ahab gathers his crew on the quarter-deck to begin the hunt for Moby-Dick. The gathering has ceremonial aspects that echo the tradition of centuries of pre-hunt rituals. Tell students that ever since the earliest Americans drummed and sang to address the animal spirits before a hunt, many peoples have believed in the power of ritual to aid their success. For example, before buffalo hunts, the Blackfeet and other Plains Indians held celebrations in which they prayed, danced, sang, smoked, and made offerings to ensure that the animals would come near enough to be taken.

Have students find out more about pre-hunt rituals in North America or elsewhere. Have them look for similarities and differences among them. Invite students to make class presentations of their findings.

from the hold; nor yet the presaging vibrations of the winds in the cordage; nor yet the hollow flap of the sails against the masts, as for a moment their hearts sank in. For again Starbuck's downcast eyes lighted up with the stubbornness of life; the subterranean laugh died away; the winds blew on; the sails filled out; the ship heaved and rolled as before. Ah, ye admonitions and warnings! why stay ye not when ye come? But rather are ye predictions than warnings, ye shadows! Yet not so much predictions from without, as verifications of the fore-going things within. For with little external to constrain us, the innermost necessities in our being, these still drive us on.

"The measure! the measure!" cried Ahab.

Receiving the brimming pewter, and turning to the harpooneers, he ordered them to produce their weapons. Then ranging them before him near the capstan,[9] with their harpoons in their hands, while his three mates stood at his side with their lances, and the rest of the ship's company formed a circle round the group; he stood for an instant searchingly eyeing every man of his crew. But those wild eyes met his, as the bloodshot eyes of the prairie wolves meet the eye of their leader, ere he rushes on at their head in the trail of the bison; but, alas! only to fall into the hidden snare of the Indian.

"Drink and pass!" he cried, handing the heavy charged flagon to the nearest seamen. "The crew alone now drink. Round with it, round! Short drafts—long swallows, men; 'tis hot as Satan's hoof. So, so; it goes round excellently. It spiralizes in ye; forks out at the serpent-snapping eye. Well done; almost drained. That way it went, this way it comes. Hand it me—here's a hollow! Men, ye seem the years; so brimming life is gulped and gone. Steward, refill!

"Attend now, my braves. I have mustered ye all round this capstan; and ye mates, flank me with your lances; and ye harpooneers, stand there with your irons; and ye, stout mariners, ring me in, that I may in some sort revive a noble custom of my fishermen fathers before me. O men, you will yet see that—Ha! boy, come back? bad pennies come

9. **capstan** (kap′ sten) *n.* large cylinder, turned by hand, around which cables are wound.

13 Reading Check

With whom does Ahab share a drink? For what purpose?

13 Reading Check

Answer: Ahab shares a pre-hunt drink with his crew in order to get them to pledge their success in the hunt for Moby-Dick.

Differentiated Instruction Solutions for All Learners

Strategy for Less Proficient Readers

Moby-Dick is a huge novel, and when it is read in its entirety, the characters grow in detail and fullness before the reader's eyes. In excerpts like these, students may need help delineating the characters. For especially challenging passages, have students read each paragraph twice—once silently and once aloud. Help students identify any fragments of dialogue or description that seem important or suggestive about a particular character.

Strategy for Advanced Readers

Point out that Ahab could be described as suffering what the Greeks called *hubris,* or excessive pride. Invite these students to define the term, to identify other tragic heroes who share this character trait, and to lead the class in a discussion of how hubris might be said to apply to Ahab.

14 Literature in Context

Melville When the *Acushnet* rounded Cape Horn and crossed the Pacific Ocean to the Marquesas Islands in 1842, Melville deserted the ship and headed inland. There he encountered the Typees, an island tribe rumored to be cannibals. To Melville's surprise, the people were peaceful and generous. He was to use this experience later as the basis for his 1846 novel *Typee.*

Connect to the Literature Review with students Ahab's perception of Moby-Dick's behavior. Encourage them to cite examples of animals who have behaved in an extraordinary way, whether good or bad.
Answer: Students should support their answers with appropriate reasoning and examples.

15 Literary Analysis
Symbol

- Encourage students to visualize or model what the harpooners are doing, as well as what Ahab has in mind.
- If necessary, help students understand that the harpooners are removing the iron part of their harpoons and up-ending the sockets to use as cups, which Ahab will fill with drink.
  Ask students the Literary Analysis question: What is Ahab's symbolic purpose in having his harpooners drink from their weapons?
  Answer: Ahab may wish them to participate in a pre-hunt ritual that symbolizes a common mission and allegiance. The act of drinking from their weapons symbolically binds them together as extensions of Ahab's vision and vengeance. Students may mention that the drinking from the "chalices" is reminiscent of religious rituals.

16 Vocabulary Builder
Latin Prefix *mal-*

- Point out the word *maledictions* in the bracketed sentence. Tell students that *mal-* means "bad."
- Have students look up this word in a dictionary.
- As a class, have students suggest other words that contain *mal-*.
  Possibilities include: malicious, malign, malodorous, maladroit.

not sooner. Hand it me. Why, now, this pewter had run brimming again, wer't not thou St. Vitus' imp[10]—away, thou ague![11]

"Advance, ye mates! cross your lances full before me. Well done! Let me touch the axis." So saying, with extended arm, he grasped the three level, radiating lances at their crossed center; while so doing, suddenly and nervously twitched them; meanwhile glancing intently from Starbuck to Stubb; from Stubb to Flask. It seemed as though, by some nameless, interior volition, he would fain have shocked into them the same fiery emotion accumulated within the Leyden jar[12] of his own magnetic life. The three mates quailed before his strong, sustained, and mystic aspect. Stubb and Flask looked sideways from him; the honest eye of Starbuck fell downright.

"In vain!" cried Ahab; "but, maybe, 'tis well. For did ye three but once take the full-forced shock, then mine own electric thing, *that* had perhaps expired from out me. Perchance, too, it would have dropped ye dead. Perchance ye need it not. Down lances! And now, ye mates, I do appoint ye three cupbearers to my three pagan kinsmen there—yon three most honorable gentlemen and noblemen, my valiant harpooneers. Disdain the task? What, when the great Pope washes the feet of beggars, using his tiara for ewer? Oh, my sweet cardinals! your own condescension, that shall bend ye to it. I do not order ye; ye will it. Cut your seizings and draw the poles, ye harpooneers!"

Silently obeying the order, the three harpooneers now stood with the detached iron part of their harpoons, some three feet long, held, barbs up, before him.

"Stab me not with that keen steel! Cant them; cant them over! know ye not the goblet end? Turn up the socket! So, so; now, ye cupbearers, advance. The irons! take them; hold them while I fill!"
15 Forthwith, slowly going from one officer to the other, he brimmed the harpoon sockets with the fiery waters from the pewter.

"Now, three to three, ye stand. Commend the murderous chalices! Bestow them, ye who are now made parties to this indissoluble league. Ha! Starbuck! but the deed is done! Yon ratifying sun now waits to sit upon it. Drink, ye harpooneers! drink and swear, ye men that man the deathful whaleboat's bow—Death to Moby-Dick! God hunt us all, if we do not hunt Moby-Dick to his death!" The long, barbed steel goblets were lifted; and to cries and maledictions against the white whale, the
16 spirits were simultaneously quaffed down with a hiss. Starbuck paled, and turned, and shivered. Once more, and finally, the replenished pewter went the rounds among the frantic crew; when, waving his free hand to them, they all dispersed; and Ahab retired within his cabin.

---

10. **St. Vitus' imp** offspring of St. Vitus, the patron saint of people stricken with the nervous disorder chorea, which is characterized by irregular, jerking movements.
11. **ague** (ā′ gyo͞o) *n.* a chill or fit of shivering.
12. **Leyden** (līd′ ən) **jar** *n.* glass jar coated inside and out with tinfoil and having a metal rod connected to the inner lining; used to condense static electricity.

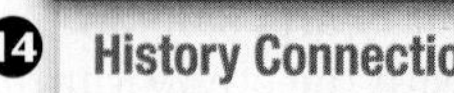

14 **History Connection**

The Legend of the White Whale

Herman Melville's whaling experiences in the South Pacific provided him with rich material for his writing. While working aboard the whaling ship *Acushnet*, he often heard stories about an elusive, monstrous white whale. Melville expanded this legend—adding his knowledge of the day-to-day workings of a whaler—into his best-known work, *Moby-Dick.*

Melville also based his novel on an actual whaling disaster: the 1820 sinking of a Nantucket whaling ship, the *Essex*, by a sperm whale. Melville had read a first-person account of the disaster written by the ship's first mate—one of eight survivors. The whale's attack on the ship was believed to be both intentional and unprovoked.

Connect to the Literature

Do you think it is possible for an animal such as a whale to act with destructive and even malicious intent? Explain.

Literary Analysis
Symbol What is Ahab's symbolic purpose in having his harpooners drink from their weapons?

Vocabulary Builder
maledictions (mal′ ə dik′ shənz) *n.* curses

Enrichment

Moby-Dick

Moby-Dick is a long and complex novel that can be divided into five parts. In the first part, the reader meets Ishmael, the story's narrator, and learns of his relationship with the harpooner Queequeg. The chapter "The Quarter-Deck" appears in the next part of the book, the section that develops the character of Ahab and the conflict between Ahab and Moby-Dick. Parts three and four are concerned with the business of the *Pequod* and the general subject of whales and whaling. "The Chase—Third Day" is the last chapter of the fifth and final part, in which Melville focuses on the search for—and confrontation with—the great whale. In a one-page epilogue, Ishmael tells how he survived to tell his tale: He was rescued by another ship, the *Rachel,* "that in her retracing search after her missing children, only found another orphan."

Melville's reference is to the Bible's book of Jeremiah in which Rachel is said to be weeping for her children, "because they were not."

17

After Moby-Dick has been sighted in the Pacific Ocean, the Pequod's boats pursue the whale for two days. One of the boats has been sunk, and Ahab's ivory leg has been broken off. However, as the next day dawns, the chase continues.

Moby-Dick, Rockwell Kent

The Chase—Third Day

The morning of the third day dawned fair and fresh, and once more the solitary night man at the foremasthead was relieved by crowds of the daylight lookouts, who dotted every mast and almost every spar.

"D'ye see him?" cried Ahab; but the whale was not yet in sight.

"In his infallible wake, though; but follow that wake, that's all. Helm there; steady, as thou goest, and hast been going. What a lovely day again! were it a new-made world, and made for a summerhouse to the angels, and this morning the first of its throwing open to them, a fairer day could not dawn upon that world. Here's food for thought, had Ahab time to think; but Ahab never thinks; he only feels, feels, feels; that's tingling enough for mortal man! to think's audacity. God only has that right and privilege. Thinking is, or ought to be, a coolness and a calmness; and our poor hearts throb, and our poor brains beat too much for that. And yet, I've sometimes thought my brain was very calm—frozen calm, this old skull cracks so, like a glass in which the contents turned to ice, and shiver it. And still this hair is growing now; this moment growing, and heat must breed it; but no, it's like that sort of common grass that will grow anywhere, between the earthy clefts of Greenland ice or in Vesuvius lava. How the wild winds blow it; they whip it about me as the torn shreds of split sails lash the tossed ship they cling to. A vile wind that has no doubt blown ere this through prison corridors and cells, and wards of hospitals, and ventilated them, and now comes blowing hither as innocent as fleeces.[13] Out upon it!—it's tainted. Were I the wind, I'd blow no more on such a wicked, miserable world. I'd crawl somewhere to a cave, and slink there. And yet, 'tis a noble and heroic thing, the wind! who ever conquered it? In every fight it has the last and bitterest blow. Run tilting at it, and you but run through it. Ha! a coward wind that strikes stark-naked men, but will not stand to receive a single blow. Even Ahab is a braver thing—a

13. **fleeces** (flēs′ əz) *n.* sheep.

18 ▲ **Critical Viewing**
Draw an inference about the size of the whale pictured. On what details do you base your inference? **[Infer]**

Reading Strategy
Recognizing Symbols
What does the wind symbolize to Ahab?

20 **Reading Check**
For how long has the *Pequod* pursued Moby-Dick?

17 Humanities

Moby-Dick, 1930, by Rockwell Kent

Throughout his life, Kent tested his devotion to nature. He spent extended time in some of the planet's coldest and most remote, severe environments. Kent captured these experiences in his drawings, paintings, illustrations, and prints in some of the most authentic evocations of nature's power in twentieth-century art. Use the following question for discussion:

- What evidence of symbolism can you find in this image?
  Possible answer: The small whales are fleeing Moby-Dick as the giant surfaces. The act of surfacing might represent the destiny of the whale in this novel.

18 Critical Viewing

Answer: Students may infer that the whale pictured here is huge. Their inference might be based on the proximity of three small whales. If these are swimming in the vicinity of the large one, then the latter is indeed enormous.

19 Reading Strategy
Recognizing Symbols

- Have a student volunteer read this passage as you—or students—write on the chalkboard words and phrases that Melville uses to characterize the wind.
- Lead students to see that these images include *wild winds, vile wind, tainted, noble and heroic thing, coward wind, bodiless, most special . . . most cunning, glorious and gracious,* and so on.

➤ **Monitor Progress: Ask** students the Reading Strategy question: What does the wind symbolize to Ahab?
Answer: The wind symbolizes the maddening, sometimes ineffable, noble, and glorious power of nature. He absolves it of malice, however, unlike Moby-Dick.

20 Reading Check

Answer: The *Pequod* is in its third day of pursuing Moby-Dick.

Differentiated Instruction **Solutions for All Learners**

Support for Special Needs Students
These students may benefit from seeing some or all of a dramatized version of Melville's sprawling story. Of course, *Moby-Dick* has all the elements of a blockbuster movie—compelling characters, exotic locations, and one of the largest movie "villains" imaginable—and filmmakers have tried a number of times to bring to the screen Melville's tale of the great white whale.

One of the best attempts was made by director John Huston, who cast Gregory Peck as Ahab in the 1956 film *Moby Dick.* Screen a video of this production for students. Have students view one or more scenes in order to help them appreciate the characterizations of Ahab, Starbuck, and Ishmael; the evocations of the whale as a symbol of nature's power and of the untamable; and the various conflicts that drive the story forward.

21 Literature in Context
The Whale as Archetype

In the biblical tale, the great fish is portrayed as the embodiment of evil. Jonah is sent by God to the city of Ninevah to prophesy about the city's wickedness. To escape God's order, Jonah heads in the opposite direction. However, his ship is engulfed by an extraordinary storm. Knowing that his disobedience has caused the storm, Jonah asks to be thrown overboard. He is swallowed by a "great fish," stays inside it for three days and nights, and is finally vomited onto land. The ninth chapter of Melville's *Moby-Dick* addresses the story of Jonah directly.

Connect to the Literature Ask students how they react to the image of a whale. How might it different from their reactions to a huge, mysterious, fearsome creature about whom they know very little?
Possible answer: Because of scientific advances, modern readers know more about whales and their behavior. Many modern readers probably have seen whales at aquariums and do not fear them. However, a whale's size and power might still inspire awe.

22 Literary Analysis
Symbol

- Have a student volunteer read this passage in which Ahab addresses the masthead and then begins to compare himself to it.
- **Ask** students the Literary Analysis question on p. 367: What symbolic meaning do you find in the comparison between Ahab and the mast?
- As students consider the question, you might list words and phrases from their responses in a Venn diagram on the chalkboard. This diagram can help students see the similarities and differences between Ahab and the masthead.
Answer: Students may say that to Ahab the mast represents his resolve in his quest for Moby-Dick. The mast stands alone, tall, strong, and long lasting, as he does in his single-mindedness.

nobler thing than *that*. Would now the wind but had a body but all the things that most exasperate and outrage mortal man, all these things are bodiless, but only bodiless as objects, not as agents. There's a most special, a most cunning, oh, a most malicious difference! And yet, I say again, and swear it now, that there's something all glorious and gracious in the wind. These warm trade winds, at least, that in the clear heavens blow straight on, in strong and steadfast, vigorous mildness; and veer not from their mark, however the baser currents of the sea may turn and tack, and mightiest Mississippis of the land swift and swerve about, uncertain where to go at last. And by the eternal poles! these same trades that so directly blow my good ship on; these trades, or something like them—something so unchangeable, and full as strong, blow my keeled soul along! To it! Aloft there! What d'ye see?"

"Nothing, sir."

"Nothing! and noon at hand! The doubloon[14] goes a-begging! See the sun! Aye, aye, it must be so. I've oversailed him. How, got the start? Aye, he's chasing me now; not I, him—that's bad; I might have known it, too. Fool! the lines—the harpoons he's towing.

Aye, aye, I have run him by last night. About! about! Come down, all of ye, but the regular lookouts! Man the braces!"

Steering as she had done, the wind had been somewhat on the Pequod's quarter, so that now being pointed in the reverse direction, the braced ship sailed hard upon the breeze as she rechurned the cream in her own white wake.

"Against the wind he now steers for the open jaw," murmured Starbuck to himself, as he coiled the new-hauled main brace upon the rail. "God keep us, but already my bones feel damp within me, and from the inside wet my flesh. I misdoubt me that I disobey my God in obeying him!"

"Stand by to sway me up!" cried Ahab, advancing to the hempen basket.[15] "We should meet him soon."

"Aye, aye, sir," and straightway Starbuck did Ahab's bidding, and once more Ahab swung on high.

A whole hour now passed; gold-beaten out to ages. Time itself now held long breaths with keen suspense. But at last, some three points off the weather bow, Ahab descried the spout again, and instantly from the three mastheads three shrieks went up as if the tongues of fire had voiced it.

"Forehead to forehead I meet thee, this third time, Moby-Dick! On deck there!—brace sharper up; crowd her into the

14. **doubloon** (du blōōn′) *n.* old Spanish gold coin. (Ahab offered it as a reward to the first man to spot the whale.)
15. **hempen basket** rope basket. (The basket was constructed earlier by Ahab, so that he could be raised, by means of a pulley device, to the top of the mainmast.)

Literature in Context

21 Humanities Connection

The Whale as Archetype

An archetype is an image, a symbol, a character, or a plot that recurs so consistently across cultures and time that it is considered universal. The term comes from Swiss psychologist Carl Jung (1875–1961), who believed that certain human experiences have become a shared genetic memory. According to Jung, this "collective unconscious" explains why archetypes evoke strong feelings in people of all cultures.

The whale had made many appearances in myth, folklore, literature, and art well before Melville used it as a central symbol in *Moby-Dick*. Perhaps the most famous is the biblical tale in which Jonah is swallowed by a whale and then cast ashore. Because the whale is the largest of all animals, its image evokes fear and awe, as well as a sense of the power of nature. In *Moby-Dick*, Melville used these archetypal associations to create fiction of enduring power.

Connect to the Literature

Do you think modern readers react with fear and awe to the image of a whale? Explain.

Enrichment

Whales

In existence for over ten million years, whales are among the world's most ancient and intelligent animals. They also are the largest: The blue whale is heavier and longer than any known dinosaur. Invite students to find out more about these amazing mammals. They can find interesting information as they work to answer questions like these:

1. How do whales keep warm? How deep do they dive?
2. How are the swimming methods of whales and of fish different? How far can whales swim?
3. What is the world's whale population today? Are whales in danger of extinction?
4. How do whales, porpoises, and dolphins differ?
5. How do whales communicate with one another?

Invite students to share their findings.

wind's eye. He's too far off to lower yet, Mr. Starbuck. The sails shake! Stand over that helmsman with a topmaul! So, so; he travels fast, and I must down. But let me have one more good round look aloft here at the sea; there's time for that. An old, old sight, and yet somehow so young; aye, and not changed a wink since I first saw it, a boy, from the sand hills of Nantucket! The same!—the same!—the same to Noah as to me. There's a soft shower to leeward. Such lovely leewardings! They must lead somewhere—to something else than common land, more palmy than the palms. Leeward! the white whale goes that way; look to windward, then; the better if the bitterer quarter. But good-bye, good-bye, old masthead! What's this?—green? aye, tiny mosses in these warped cracks. No such green weather stains on Ahab's head! There's the
22 difference now between man's old age and matter's. But aye, old mast, we both grow old together; sound in our hulls, though, are we not, my ship? Aye, minus a leg, that's all. By heaven this dead wood has the better of my live flesh every way. I can't compare with it; and I've known some ships made of dead trees outlast the lives of men made of the most vital stuff of vital fathers. What's that he said? he should still go before me, my pilot; and yet to be seen again? But where? Will I have eyes at the bottom of the sea, supposing I descend those endless stairs? and all night I've been sailing from him, wherever he did sink to. Aye,
23 aye, like many more thou told'st direful truth as touching thyself, O Parsee; but, Ahab, there thy shot fell short. Good-bye, masthead—keep a good eye upon the whale, the while I'm gone. We'll talk tomorrow, nay, tonight, when the white whale lies down there, tied by head and tail."

He gave the word; and still gazing round him, was steadily lowered through the cloven blue air to the deck.

In due time the boats were lowered; but as standing in his shallop's stern, Ahab just hovered upon the point of the descent, he waved to the mate—who held one of the tackle ropes on deck—and bade him pause.

"Starbuck!"

"Sir?"

"For the third time my soul's ship starts upon this voyage, Starbuck."

"Aye, sir, thou wilt have it so."

"Some ships sail from their ports, and ever afterwards are missing, Starbuck!"

"Truth, sir: saddest truth."

"Some men die at ebb tide; some at low water; some at the full of the flood—and I feel now like a billow that's all one crested comb, Starbuck. I am old—shake hands with me, man."

Their hands met; their eyes fastened; Starbuck's tears the glue.

"Oh, my captain, my captain!—noble heart—go not—go not!—see, it's a brave man that weeps; how great the agony of the persuasion then!"

"Lower away!"—cried Ahab, tossing the mate's arm from him. "Stand by the crew!"

In an instant the boat was pulling round close under the stern.

Literary Analysis
Symbol What symbolic meaning do you find in the comparison between Ahab and the mast?

25 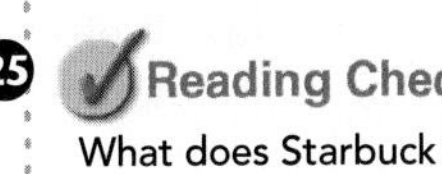
Reading Check
What does Starbuck beg Ahab to do?

23 Background
Literature

The Parsee is a Persian sailor who disappeared in the previous chapter of the novel. Earlier in the book, a prediction was made that he would die before Ahab but that Ahab would see him once more before his own death.

24 Critical Thinking
Analyze

- Have three students—playing Ahab, Starbuck, and the narrator—read aloud this passage.
- **Ask** students to explain what is happening in this exchange between Ahab and Starbuck.
Answer: Students may respond that Ahab is expressing fear and apprehension prior to this (his next attempt to kill Moby-Dick) and that Starbuck is making one last futile effort to persuade Ahab to forgo the quest.

25 Reading Check

Answer: Starbuck begs Ahab not to pursue Moby-Dick in a small harpooning boat.

26 Reading Strategy
Recognizing Symbols

- As you read aloud this passage, **ask** students to think about the possible symbolic meaning of the sharks that surround Ahab and follow him in his small boat.
- Help students understand that the sharks separate Ahab further from his crew. Moreover, they suggest in a symbolic way that Ahab's pursuit of the white whale is foolish and doomed. The sharks add an extra element of danger; they are harbingers of death.

27 Humanities

Moby-Dick, 1930, by Rockwell Kent

This is another of Rockwell's pen-and-ink drawings for the Lakeside Press edition of *Moby-Dick.* Use the following question for discussion.

- What evidence of symbolism can you find in this image?
  Possible answer: Although the whale is largely out of sight, it is responsible for the chaos and destruction portrayed in the image. The whale's partial concealment beneath the sea may symbolize the "masked," "inscrutable" malice that Ahab sees in Moby-Dick's actions.

28 Critical Viewing

Answer: Students may respond that the artist used many details from *Moby-Dick* to create this illustration, among them the descriptions of the boats, harpoons, and lines, as well as the descriptions of the size, speed, and power of Moby-Dick as he dives and surfaces.

29 Reading Strategy
Recognizing Symbols

- Tell students that three is a traditional symbol echoing the trinity in Christian belief. The third number often represents finality.
- **Ask** students to explain the significance of Starbuck's reference to the number three here.
  Answer: Usually the voice of practicality, Starbuck now recognizes the grim meaning of the three-day chase. Ahab and the crew are now in the third day, and Starbuck seems to sense a mystical significance in the length of time the chase has taken.

"The sharks! the sharks!" cried a voice from the low cabin window there; "O master, my master, come back!"

But Ahab heard nothing; for his own voice was high-lifted then; and the boat leaped on.

26 Yet the voice spake true; for scarce had he pushed from the ship, when numbers of sharks, seemingly rising from out the dark waters beneath the hull, maliciously snapped at the blades of the oars, every time they dipped in the water; and in this way accompanied the boat with their bites. It is a thing not uncommonly happening to the whaleboats in those swarming seas; the sharks at times apparently following them in the same prescient way that vultures hover over the banners of marching regiments in the east. But these were the first sharks that had been observed by the *Pequod* since the White Whale had been first descried; and whether it was that Ahab's crew were all such tiger-yellow barbarians, and therefore their flesh more musky to the senses of the sharks—a matter sometimes well known to affect them—however it was, they seemed to follow that one boat without molesting the others.

29 "Heart of wrought steel!" murmured Starbuck gazing over the side, and following with his eyes the receding boat—"canst thou yet ring boldly to that sight?—lowering thy keel among ravening sharks, and followed by them, open-mouthed to the chase; and this the critical third day?—For when three days flow together in one continuous intense pursuit; be sure the first is the morning, the second the noon, and the third the evening and the end of that thing—be that end what it may. Oh! my God! what is this that shoots through me, and leaves me so deadly calm, yet expectant—fixed at the top of a shudder! Future things swim before me, as in empty outlines and skeletons; all the past is somehow grown dim. Mary, girl; thou fadest in pale glories behind me; boy! I seem to see but thy eyes grown wondrous blue.[16] Strangest problems of life seem clearing; but clouds sweep between—Is my journey's end coming? My legs feel faint; like his who has footed it all day. Feel thy heart—beats it yet? Stir thyself, Starbuck!—stave it off—move, move! speak aloud!—Masthead there! See ye my boy's hand on the hill?—Crazed—aloft there!—keep thy

Vocabulary Builder
prescient (presh′ənt) *adj.* having foreknowledge

27 

Moby-Dick, Rockwell Kent

28 **▲ Critical Viewing**
What details from *Moby-Dick* did the artist probably use to create this illustration? **[Hypothesize]**

16. Mary . . . blue reference to Starbuck's wife and son.

Enrichment

Whale Songs

Some people—scientists and musicians alike—are fascinated by the mysterious, mournful, musical sounds whales make as they communicate with one another. Their groans, yips, and wails can carry many miles through and across the water. Humpback whales, in particular, are skillful performers: Each male sings its own unique song (which can last for up to thirty-five minutes) over and over again.

Obtain recordings of whale songs to play for students. For example, on the Judy Collins album *Whales and Nightingales,* the traditional sea song "Farewell to Tarwathie" incorporates melodies of the humpback whale. Invite students to freewrite in response to the sounds they hear.

keenest eye upon the boats—mark well the whale!—Ho! again!—drive off that hawk! see! he pecks—he tears the vane"—pointing to the red flag flying at the maintruck—"Ha, he soars away with it!—Where's the old man now? see'st thou that sight, oh Ahab!—shudder, shudder!"

The boats had not gone very far, when by a signal from the mastheads—a downward pointed arm, Ahab knew that the whale had sounded; but intending to be near him at the next rising, he held on his way a little sideways from the vessel; the becharmed crew maintaining the profoundest silence, as the head-beat waves hammered and hammered against the opposing bow.

"Drive, drive in your nails, oh ye waves! to their uttermost heads drive them in! ye but strike a thing without a lid; and no coffin and no hearse can be mine:—and hemp only can kill me! Ha! ha!"

Suddenly the waters around them slowly swelled in broad circles; then quickly upheaved, as if sideways sliding from a submerged berg of ice, swiftly rising to the surface. A low rumbling sound was heard; a subterraneous hum; and then all held their breaths; as bedraggled with trailing ropes, and harpoons, and lances, a vast form shot length-
30 wise, but obliquely from the sea. Shrouded in a thin drooping veil of mist, it hovered for a moment in the rainbowed air; and then fell swamping back into the deep. Crushed thirty feet upwards, the waters flashed for an instant like heaps of fountains, then brokenly sank in a shower of flakes, leaving the circling surface creamed like new milk round the marble trunk of the whale.

"Give way!" cried Ahab to the oarsmen, and the boats darted forward to the attack; but maddened by yesterday's fresh irons that corroded in him, Moby-Dick seemed combinedly possessed by all the angels that fell from heaven. The wide tiers of welded tendons overspreading his broad white forehead, beneath the transparent skin, looked knitted together; as head on, he came churning his tail among the boats; and once more flailed them apart; spilling out the irons and lances from the two mates' boats, and dashing in one side of the upper part of their bows, but leaving Ahab's almost without a scar.

While Daggoo and Queequeg were stopping the strained planks; and as the whale swimming out from them, turned, and showed one entire flank as he shot by them again; at that moment a quick cry went up. Lashed round and round to the fish's back; pinioned in the turns upon turns in which, during the past night, the whale had reeled the involutions of the lines around him, the half-torn body of the Parsee was seen; his sable
31 raiment frayed to shreds; his distended eyes turned full upon old Ahab.

The harpoon dropped from his hand.

"Befooled, befooled!"—drawing in a long lean breath—"Aye, Parsee! I see thee again—Aye, and thou goest before; and this, this then is the hearse that thou didst promise. But I hold thee to the last letter of thy word. Where is the second hearse? Away, mates, to the ship! those boats are useless now; repair them if ye can in time, and return to me; if not, Ahab is enough to die—Down, men! the first thing that but offers

Literary Analysis
Symbol What symbolic meaning is suggested by the description of the whale's behavior as he breaks the water's surface?

Reading Strategy
Recognizing Symbols What does Ahab realize when he sees Parsee's body lashed to Moby-Dick?

32 **Reading Check**
What happens to Parsee?

30 Literary Analysis
Symbol

- If necessary, draw students' attention to the import of what is about to happen: Moby-Dick is about to surface. Point out that—given the symbolic associations Melville has established already for the white whale—the descriptive details of the whale's appearance are bound to carry symbolic meaning.
- **Ask** students the Literary Analysis question: What symbolic meaning is suggested by the description of the whale's behavior as he breaks the water's surface?
  Answer: The description of the whale's behavior, rising slowly at first so that the water shows mysterious portents of his presence, then bursting from the sea into the air and seeming to hang suspended there, symbolizes Moby-Dick's near-supernatural status as Ahab's nemesis.

31 Reading Strategy
Recognizing Symbols

- If necessary, remind students of the identity of the Parsee and of his prophecy regarding his own and Ahab's death (see p. 367).
- **Ask** students the Reading Strategy question: What does Ahab realize when he sees the Parsee's body lashed to Moby-Dick?
  Answer: He realizes that his own death is at hand.

32 Reading Check

Answer: He has died and remains lashed to the body of Moby-Dick.

Differentiated Instruction
Solutions for All Learners

Strategy for Less Proficient Readers
The paragraph beginning "Suddenly the waters" marks the start of the dramatic final clash with Moby-Dick. Encourage students to pause here to picture the sudden appearance of the whale and its powerful movements. Invite them to imagine the spray, the sounds, and the changing textures of the surface of the water as the giant emerges from, and then dives back into, the depths. You might encourage students to draw their own illustrations of this dramatic passage.

Strategy for English Learners
Encourage students to use the illustrations accompanying the selection to help them picture and understand the action. Have them note key details that they find in the illustrations that add meaning to what they encounter in the text. Then have students share and discuss these details with other students.

33 Literary Analysis
Symbol and Theme

- Remind sudents that every symbol functions on two levels—a literal meaning and a larger meaning—and that a theme is one of a literary work's central messages.
- **Ask** students the Literary Analysis question: What does Melville mean when he describes Ahab as being tormented by "far other hammers?"
  Possible response: He means that Ahab briefly feels a stab of regret and remorse when he passes the *Pequod* and sees his men working hard to repair damage Moby-Dick has done.

34 Critical Thinking
Speculate

- Read this passage aloud and **ask** students to identify the surprising idea that the narrator seems to be suggesting. If necessary, point out that Ishmael is suggesting that Moby-Dick may be giving up the fight.
- Invite students to say what they think will happen next.
  Answer: Students might respond that because of what has happened up to this point, the fight with Moby-Dick is far from over. In fact, catastrophe may yet result.

to jump from this boat I stand in, that thing I harpoon. Ye are not other men, but my arms and my legs; and so obey me—Where's the whale? gone down again?"

But he looked too nigh the boat; for as if bent upon escaping with the corpse he bore, and as if the particular place of the last encounter had been but a stage in his leeward voyage, Moby-Dick was now again steadily swimming forward; and had almost passed the ship—which thus far had been sailing in the contrary direction to him, though for the present her headway had been stopped. He seemed swimming with his utmost velocity, and now only intent upon pursuing his own straight path in the sea.

"Oh! Ahab," cried Starbuck, "not too late is it, even now, the third day, to desist. See! Moby-Dick seeks thee not. It is thou, thou, that madly seekest him!"

Setting sail to the rising wind, the lonely boat was swiftly impelled to leeward, by both oars and canvas. And at last when Ahab was sliding by the vessel, so near as plainly to distinguish Starbuck's face as he leaned over the rail, he hailed him to turn the vessel about, and follow him, not too swiftly, at a judicious interval. Glancing upwards he saw Tashtego, Queequeg, and Daggoo, eagerly mounting to the three mast-heads; while the oarsmen were rocking in the two staved boats which had just been hoisted to the side, and were busily at work in repairing them, one after the other, through the portholes, as he sped, he also caught flying glimpses of Stubb and Flask, busying themselves on deck among bundles of new irons and lances. As he saw all this; as he heard
33 the hammers in the broken boats; far other hammers seemed driving a nail into his heart. But he rallied. And now marking that the vane or flag was gone from the main masthead, he shouted to Tashtego, who had just gained that perch, to descend again for another flag, and a hammer and nails, and so nail it to the mast.

34 Whether fagged by the three days' running chase, and the resistance to his swimming in the knotted hamper he bore; or whether it was some latent deceitfulness and malice in him: whichever was true, the White Whale's way now began to abate, as it seemed, from the boat so rapidly nearing him once more; though indeed the whale's last start had not been so long a one as before. And still as Ahab glided over the waves the unpitying sharks accompanied him; and so pertinaciously stuck to the boat; and so continually bit at the plying oars, that the blades became jagged and crunched, and left small splinters in the sea, at almost every dip.

"Heed them not! those teeth but give new rowlocks to your oars. Pull on! 'tis the better rest, the sharks' jaw than the yielding water."

"But at every bite, sir, the thin blades grow smaller and smaller!"

"They will last long enough! pull on!—But who can tell"—he muttered—"whether these sharks swim to feast on the whale or on Ahab?—But pull on! Aye, all alive, now—we near him. The helm! take the helm! let me pass"—and so saying, two of the oarsmen helped him forward to the bows of the still flying boat.

Literary Analysis
Symbol and Theme What does Melville mean when he describes Ahab as being tormented by "far other hammers?"

Vocabulary Builder
pertinaciously (pur' tə nā' shəs lē) *adv.* unyieldingly

Enrichment

Cetology

Cetology is the branch of zoology that deals with the study of cetaceans, a mammalian order that includes whales and dolphins. Oceanography is the study of the ocean environments, including analysis of the water, ocean depths, sea beds, animals, and plants. Invite interested students to research what kinds of work scientists at the cutting edge of these branches of science are doing currently. To research today's cetology or oceanography issues, students can use the Internet, books, scientific journals, or magazines such as *Nature or Natural History.* Students might even interview scientists who are doing research in either field. Suggest that students get started on their research by talking with their science teachers about the best research paths to follow.

At length as the craft was cast to one side, and ran ranging along with the White Whale's flank, he seemed strangely oblivious of its advance—as the whale sometimes will—and Ahab was fairly within the smoky mountain mist, which, thrown off from the whale's spout, curled round his great Monadnock[17] hump; he was even thus close to him; when, with body arched back, and both arms lengthwise high-lifted to the poise, he darted his fierce iron, and his far fiercer curse into the hated whale. As both steel and curse sank to the socket, as if sucked into a morass, Moby-Dick sidewise writhed; spasmodically rolled his nigh flank against the bow, and, without staving a hole in it, so suddenly canted the boat over, that had it not been for the elevated part of the gunwale to which he then clung, Ahab would once more have been tossed into the sea. As it was, three of the oarsmen—who foreknew not the precise instant of the dart, and were therefore unprepared for its effects—these were flung out; but so fell, that, in an instant two of them clutched the gunwale again, and rising to its level on a combing wave, hurled themselves bodily inboard again; the third man helplessly dropping astern, but still afloat and swimming.

Almost simultaneously, with a mighty volition of ungraduated, instantaneous swiftness, the White Whale darted through the weltering sea. But when Ahab cried out to the steersman to take new turns with the line, and hold it so; and commanded the crew to turn round on
35 their seats, and tow the boat up to the mark; the moment the treacherous line felt that double strain and tug, it snapped in the empty air!

"What breaks in me? Some sinew cracks!—'tis whole again; oars! oars! Burst in upon him!"

Hearing the tremendous rush of the sea-crashing boat, the whale wheeled round to present his blank forehead at bay; but in that evolution, catching sight of the nearing black hull of the ship; seemingly seeing in it the source of all his persecutions; bethinking it—it may be—a larger and nobler foe; of a sudden, he bore down upon its advancing prow, smiting his jaws amid fiery showers of foam.

Ahab staggered; his hand smote his forehead. "I grow blind; hands! stretch out before me that I may yet grope my way. Is't night?"

"The whale! The ship!" cried the cringing oarsmen.

"Oars! oars! Slope downwards to thy depths. O sea that ere it be forever too late, Ahab may slide this last, last time upon his mark! I see: the ship! the ship! Dash on, my men! will ye not save my ship?"

But as the oarsmen violently forced their boat through the sledge-hammering seas, the before whale-smitten bow-ends of two planks burst through, and in an instant almost, the temporarily disabled boat lay nearly level with the waves; its half-wading, splashing crew, trying hard to stop the gap and bale out the pouring water.

Meantime, for that one beholding instant, Tashtego's masthead
36 hammer remained suspended in his hand; and the red flag, half wrapping him as with a plaid, then streamed itself straight out from

17. **Monadnock** (mə nad′ näk) mountain in New Hampshire.

Literary Analysis
Symbol What symbolic connection between his own body and the boat does Ahab seem to feel?

Reading Strategy
Recognizing Symbols What is symbolized by the red flag streaming out from Tashtego?

37 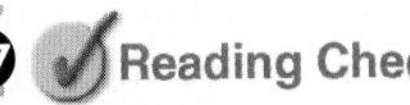
Reading Check
What happens to the boat carrying Ahab when it nears Moby-Dick?

35 Literary Analysis
Symbol

- Have students note the rapid chain of events in the bracketed passage: Moby-Dick, having nearly turned the boat over, swims swiftly away. Ahab orders the line connecting the boat to the whale to be pulled taut, to pull the boat closer to the whale. The rope snaps in two, and Ahab cries out.
- Then, **ask** students the Literary Analysis question: What symbolic connection between his own body and the boat does Ahab seem to feel?
  Answer: Ahab seems to feel as though the boat is an extension of his body.

36 Reading Strategy
Recognizing Symbols

- Draw students' attention back to the passage on p. 370 in which Ahab instructs Tashtego to nail another flag to the main masthead, since a hawk has torn down the other and flown away with it.
- **Ask** students the Reading Strategy question: What is symbolized by the red flag streaming out from Tashtego?
  Answer: Students might say that the flag symbolizes the passionate desire of Tashtego, the crew, and Ahab's to vanquish the white whale; others might say that the flag symbolizes Ahab's life, which is about to be lost to the vast ocean.

37 Reading Check

Answer: The boat is nearly capsized by the whale's rolling motion.

Differentiated Instruction
Solutions for All Learners

Enrichment for Gifted/Talented Students
Students might enjoy acting out part of the exciting action of this chapter. Have students prepare a script, using correct conventions and style to indicate dialogue and stage directions. Use page 91 in ***Writing and Grammar,*** Ruby Level, to help students draft their scripts. Guide students to rehearse lines and actions before performing their scenes for the class. If possible, have students include props to make their performances more realistic.

Support for Advanced Readers
Guide students to appreciate that the action is becoming increasingly kaleidoscopic. Have them notice that readers now catch only brief bits of the action, much as a sailor at the scene would do in the midst of the chaos of battle. Also help students note that Ahab's statements become increasingly disjointed. Aside from the frantic chase of the white whale, what do students think is causing Ahab's strange, sometimes incomprehensible statements?

38 Literary Analysis
Symbol

- Point out that Ahab himself articulates the symbolic nature of the great whale in a conversation with Starbuck (see p. 362): "I see in him outrageous strength, with an inscrutable malice sinewing it."
- After reteaching symbol, read aloud with students the bracketed passage and **ask** students the first Literary Analysis question: What details in this paragraph suggest that the whale has become a symbol of retribution?
  Answer: Students may point to details such as the whale's "swift vengeance" and the "eternal malice [of] his whole aspect."
- Remind students that it is the narrator, Ishmael, who is telling the story. **Ask** students what is suggested by Ishmael's description of the whale as malicious and vengeful.
  Possible response: Students may point out that Ishmael's account suggests that he has joined Ahab in his view of the whale as a deliberate agent of destruction.

39 Literary Analysis
Symbol and Theme

- Read aloud this stirring speech, or play the recording of it on the **Listening to Literature Audio CDs.**
- **Ask** students the second Literary Analysis question: What thematic elements come together in Ahab's climactic speech?
  Possible response: In Ahab's speech, Melville touches on thematic elements such as personal loyalty, death, humanity's search for meaning in life, the mysteries of nature, and good and evil.

him, as his own forward-flowing heart; while Starbuck and Stubb, standing upon the bowsprit beneath, caught sight of the down-coming monster just as soon as he.

"The whale, the whale! Up helm, up helm! Oh, all ye sweet powers of air, now hug me close! Let not Starbuck die, if die he must, in a woman's fainting fit. Up helm I say—ye fools, the jaw! the jaw! Is this the end of all my bursting prayers? all my lifelong fidelities? Oh, Ahab, Ahab, lo, thy work. Steady! helmsman, steady. Nay, nay! Up helm again! He turns to meet us! Oh, his unappeasable brow drives on towards one, whose duty tells him he cannot depart. My God, stand by me now!"

"Stand not by me, but stand under me, whoever you are that will now help Stubb; for Stubb, too, sticks here. I grin at thee, thou grinning whale! Who ever helped Stubb, or kept Stubb awake, but Stubb's own unwinking eye? And now poor Stubb goes to bed upon a mattress that is all too soft; would it were stuffed with brushwood! I grin at thee, thou grinning whale! Look ye, sun, moon, and stars! I call ye assassins of as good a fellow as ever spouted up his ghost. For all that, I would yet ring glasses with thee, would ye but hand the cup! Oh, oh! oh, oh! thou grinning whale, but there'll be plenty of gulping soon! Why fly ye not, O Ahab! For me, off shoes and jacket to it; let Stubb die in his drawers! A most moldy and oversalted death, though—cherries! cherries! cherries! Oh, Flask, for one red cherry ere we die!"

"Cherries? I only wish that we were where they grow. Oh, Stubb, I hope my poor mother's drawn my part-pay ere this; if not, few coppers will now come to her, for the voyage is up."

38 From the ship's bows, nearly all the seamen now hung inactive; hammers, bits of plank, lances, and harpoons, mechanically retained in their hands, just as they had darted from their various employments; all their enchanted eyes intent upon the whale, which from side to side strangely vibrating his predestinating head, sent a broad band of overspreading semicircular foam before him as he rushed. Retribution, swift vengeance, eternal malice were in his whole aspect, and spite of all that mortal man could do, the solid white buttress of his forehead smote the ship's starboard bow, till men and timbers reeled. Some fell flat upon their faces. Like dislodged trucks, the heads of the harpooneers aloft shook on their bull-like necks. Through the breach, they heard the waters pour, as mountain torrents down a flume.

Literary Analysis
Symbol What details in this paragraph suggest that the whale has become a symbol of retribution?

"The ship! The hearse!—the second hearse!" cried Ahab from the boat; "its wood could only be American!"

Diving beneath the settling ship, the whale ran quivering along its keel; but turning under water, swiftly shot to the surface again, far off the other bow, but within a few yards of Ahab's boat, where, for a time, he lay quiescent.

39 "I turn my body from the sun. What ho, Tashtego! let me hear thy hammer. Oh! ye three unsurrendered spires of mine; thou uncracked keel; and only god-bullied hull; thou firm deck, and haughty helm, and Polepointed prow—death-glorious ship! must ye then perish, and

Literary Analysis
Symbol and Theme What thematic elements come together in Ahab's climactic speech?

Enrichment

Impacts on Whale Hunting

A decade after *Moby-Dick* was published, a Norwegian whaling captain developed two inventions that revolutionized the whaling industry. One was a new harpoon tipped with an exploding bomb to kill whales more quickly; the other was a faster, steam-powered whaling boat. As a result, more whales were killed in the first forty years of the twentieth century than in the four preceding centuries.

For humanitarian reasons, many nations, including the United States, Canada, and most of Europe, have stopped hunting whales. Japan and the former Soviet Union still do hunt, although international pressure to outlaw whaling increases each year. Have students find out what whale products are used today and the current size of the world's whale population. Ask them to give and support their opinion on whether or not whaling should be prohibited internationally.

without me? Am I cut off from the last fond pride of meanest shipwrecked captains? Oh, lonely death on lonely life! Oh, now I feel my topmost greatness lies in my topmost grief. Ho, ho! from all your furthest bounds, pour ye now in, ye bold billows of my whole foregone life, and top this one piled comber of my death! Towards thee I roll, thou all-destroying but unconquering whale; to the last I grapple with thee; from hell's heart I stab at thee; for hate's sake I spit my last breath at thee. Sink all coffins and all hearses to one common pool! and since neither can be mine, let me then tow to pieces, while still chasing thee, though tied to thee, thou damned whale! *Thus*, I give up the spear!"

The harpoon was darted; the stricken whale flew forward; with igniting velocity the line ran through the groove;—ran foul. Ahab stooped to clear it; he did clear it; but the flying turn caught him round the neck, and voicelessly as Turkish mutes bowstring their victim, he was shot out of the boat, ere the crew knew he was gone. Next instant, the heavy eye splice in the rope's final end flew out of the stark-empty tub, knocked down an oarsman, and smiting the sea, disappeared in its depths.

For an instant, the tranced boat's crew stood still; then turned. "The ship? Great God, where is the ship?" Soon they through dim, bewildering mediums saw her sidelong fading phantom, as in the gaseous fata morgana,[18] only the uppermost masts out of water: while fixed by infatuation, or fidelity, or fate, to their once lofty perches, the pagan harpooneers still maintained their sinking lookouts on the sea. And now, concentric circles seized the lone boat itself, and all its crew, and each floating oar, and every lance pole, and spinning, animate and inanimate, all round and round in one vortex, carried the smallest chip of the *Pequod* out of sight.

But as the last whelmings intermixingly poured themselves over the sunken head of the Indian at the mainmast, leaving a few inches of the erect spar yet visible, together with long streaming yards of the flag, which calmly undulated, with ironical coincidings, over the destroying billows they almost touched—at that instant, a red arm and a hammer hovered backwardly uplifted in the open air, in the act of nailing the flag faster and yet faster to the subsiding spar. A sky hawk that tauntingly had followed the main-truck downwards from its natural home among

41 Reading Check
What happens to the *Pequod*?

40 ▼ Critical Viewing
In this image from a film version of *Moby-Dick*, how do the filmmakers use a sense of scale to suggest the whale's overwhelming power? **[Analyze]**

18. **fata morgana** (fät′ ə môr gän′ ə) *n.* mirage seen at sea.

40 Critical Viewing

Answer: The filmmakers show Moby-Dick's huge jaw closing upon Ahab's tiny boat, which will clearly be barely a mouthful for the great whale.

41 Reading Check

Answer: The *Pequod* sinks in a vortex of swirling water.

Differentiated Instruction Solutions for All Learners

Strategy for Less Proficient Readers
Using repeated oral readings, help students understand how Ahab dies. Guide them to see that he is caught around the neck by the harpoon line and jerked from the boat. He dies throwing a harpoon into a fleeing Moby-Dick and declaring his eternal hatred of the animal. Have students use the same technique to recognize the fate of the *Pequod.*

Vocabulary for Gifted/Talented Students
Invite students to review the text in order to create a glossary of nautical and other technical terms for readers of *Moby-Dick.* Students' entries might include such terms as *capstan, harpoon,* and *keel.*

ASSESS

Answers

1. Students should support their responses with clear reasons and examples from the text.
2. (a) Ahab offers a Spanish coin made from one ounce of gold. (b) He may sense that they do not feel as strong a motivation as he does to hunt down this particular whale.
3. (a) He lost one of his legs. (b) It reveals that he is a stubborn, angry, and bitter man. (c) Starbuck is practical and realistic and is disturbed by Ahab's obsession; in contrast, Ahab is obsessive and volatile.
4. (a) Starbuck sees the obsession as vengeance against a dumb animal. (b) Starbuck obeys because he is loyal and has served Ahab a long time; he also cares about Ahab, and may unwillingly admire his courage.
5. (a) Ahab is caught by the fouled, or tangled, harpoon line, is yanked out of the boat and disappears; with the harpoon in him, Moby-Dick disappears; the *Pequod* sinks. (b) **Possible response:** Nature endures in the face of human mortality and is indifferent to human suffering.
6. (a) He surfaces and then disappears. (b) In his obsession, Ahab feels pursued and tormented by Moby-Dick; in reality, Moby-Dick is trying to escape his pursuers.
7. (a) Ahab means that he—like many human beings—is powerless to resist following his emotions. Ahab implies that thought is a "higher" process that is best left to God. (b) Students should support their opinions with evidence from the selection.
8. Many students may agree with this assessment, given that the last years of Ahab's life are dedicated to his journey to find and kill Moby-Dick.

Go Online — Author Link For additional information about Herman Melville, have students type in the Web Code, then select M from the alphabet, and then select Hermen Melville.

the stars, pecking at the flag, and incommoding Tashtego there: this bird now chanced to intercept its broad fluttering wing between the hammer and the wood: and simultaneously feeling that ethereal thrill, the submerged savage beneath, in his deathgasp, kept his hammer frozen there: and so the bird of heaven, with archangelic shrieks, and his imperial beak thrust upwards, and his whole captive form folded in the flag of Ahab, went down with his ship, which, like Satan, would not sink to hell till she had dragged a living part of heaven along with her, and helmeted herself with it.

Now small fowls flew screaming over the yet yawning gulf; a sullen white surf beat against its steep sides; then all collapsed, and the great shroud of the sea rolled on as it rolled five thousand years ago.

Critical Reading

1. **Respond:** Do you admire, despise, or pity Captain Ahab? Explain.
2. **(a) Recall:** What does Ahab offer to the crew member who spots Moby-Dick? **(b) Infer:** Why does Ahab feel it necessary to offer this incentive to his crew?
3. **(a) Recall:** What happened to Ahab in his previous encounter with Moby-Dick? **(b) Interpret:** What does Ahab's obsession with Moby-Dick reveal about his character? **(c) Compare and Contrast:** In what ways is Starbuck different from Ahab?
4. **(a) Recall:** How does Starbuck interpret Ahab's obsession with Moby-Dick? **(b) Analyze:** Why does Starbuck obey Ahab even though he disagrees with him?
5. **(a) Recall:** What happens to Ahab, Moby-Dick, and the *Pequod* at the end? **(b) Analyze:** What does the final paragraph indicate about the relationship between humanity and nature?
6. **(a) Recall:** What is Moby-Dick's reaction when the *Pequod* first approaches his flank? **(b) Compare and Contrast:** How does Moby-Dick's reaction to the ship illuminate the differences between the whale in reality and in Ahab's imagination?
7. **(a) Interpret:** What does Ahab mean when he says, "Ahab never thinks; he only feels, feels, feels; that's tingling enough for mortal man! to think's audacity." **(b) Evaluate:** Do you think Ahab's beliefs about human nature are true? Explain.
8. **Take a Position:** This novel has been called a "voyage of the soul." Would you agree or disagree with that assessment? Explain.

For: More about Herman Melville
Visit: www.PHSchool.com
Web Code: ere-9310

Apply the Skills

from *Moby-Dick*

Literary Analysis

Symbol

1. What omens appear **(a)** as Ahab's whaleboat pulls away from the *Pequod* and **(b)** when Moby-Dick surfaces? **(c)** What is Ahab's reaction to these omens?
2. The color white is often used as a **symbol** for innocence, as well as for absence and death. What contradictory symbolic meanings does the whale's whiteness convey?
3. If the crew of the *Pequod* symbolizes humanity and Moby-Dick symbolizes nature, what do you think the ship's voyage symbolizes?

Connecting Literary Elements

4. **(a)** Use a chart like the one shown to compare and contrast the characters of Starbuck and Ahab. **(b)** What **theme** is Melville expressing through these contrasting characters?

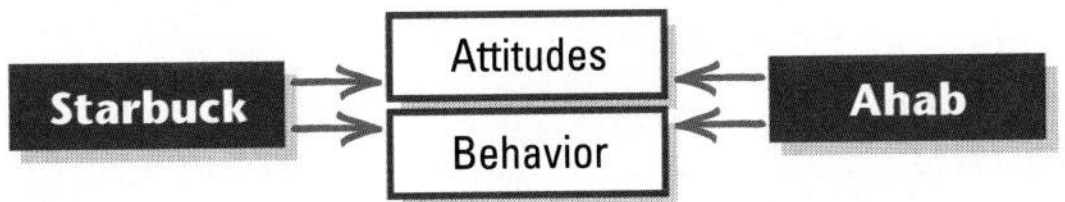

5. Considering the journey's symbolic meaning and its terrible outcome, speculate about the novel's overall theme, or central idea.

Reading Strategy

Recognizing Symbols

6. Identify events, dialogue, or descriptions that lead you to **recognize** Moby-Dick as a **symbol** of **(a)** nature's beauty, **(b)** nature's power, and **(c)** nature's immortality. Explain your reasoning.
7. How does this statement by Ishmael suggest a way to look at the symbolic nature of the events he describes:

   "Ah, ye admonitions and warnings! why stay ye not when ye come? But rather are ye predictions than warnings, ye shadows! Yet not so much predictions from without, as verifications of the foregoing things within."

Extend Understanding

8. **Psychology Connection: (a)** With what goals are people obsessed today? **(b)** In what cases, if any, are obsessions helpful?

QuickReview

A **symbol** is a person, place, or thing that has meaning in itself and also represents something larger.

A **theme** is a central message or insight revealed by a literary work.

To **recognize symbols,** look for characters, places, or objects that are stressed, mentioned repeatedly, or linked to larger ideas.

For: Self-test
Visit: www.PHSchool.com
Web Code: era-6306

Answers

1. (a) Sharks appear and surround his boat; Starbuck sees visions of his family. (b) Ahab sees the corpse of the Parsee. (c) Though he acknowledges each omen, he says that the last part of the omen has not been seen, and he continues to pursue the whale.
2. **Sample answer:** Despite Ahab's obsession with avenging what he sees as the whale's evil action, Moby-Dick is innocent: He is merely a creature following its instincts. On the other hand, the whale's whiteness represents death not only for Ahab, but also for the entire crew of the *Pequod* —with the exception of Ishmael.
3. The ship's voyage may symbolize humanity's efforts to explain and control nature.
4. (a) Whereas Starbuck is practical, realistic, and thoughtful, Ahab is stubborn, angry, and bitter.
   (b) **Sample answer:** With these contrasting characters, Melville touches on themes such as good vs. evil, loyalty, and sacrifice.

   Another sample answer can be found on **Literary Analysis Graphic Organizer B,** p. 74 in ***Graphic Organizer Transparencies.***
5. **Possible response:** The *Pequod's* journey suggests that the most impassioned and determined human will is dwarfed and easily subdued by the vast, mysterious powers of nature.
6. (a) One example might be "There's a soft shower to leeward. Such lovely leewardings! They must lead somewhere—to something else than common land, more palmy than the palms. Leeward! the white whale goes that way; look to windward, then . . ." (b) One example might be " . . . it was Moby-Dick that dismasted me; Moby-Dick that brought me to this dead stump I stand on now . . . ."
   (c) Students may mention Moby-Dick's disappearance—but not death—at the end of the fight with Ahab.
7. **Sample answer:** Ishmael's comments suggest that humanity is itself responsible for much of what it sees as tragic or evil in the world.
8. (a) Many people are obsessed with attaining financial prosperity; many others focus on getting political power or fame.

Answers continued

(b) Students may mention that obsession could be helpful insofar as it keeps a person focused on a goal; the danger is that obsession can throw a person's sense of judgment out of balance.

Go Online Assessment Students may use the **Self-test** to prepare for **Selection Test A** or **Selection Test B.**

EXTEND/ASSESS

Answers

❶ Vocabulary Lesson

Word Analysis

1. d 4. b
2. c 5. a
3. e

Vocabulary Builder

1. b 3. a
2. d 4. c

Spelling Strategy

1. *ss* 3. *sh*
2. *sk*

❷ Grammar and Style Lesson

Practice

1. crew *line* up
2. team *draws*
3. crew *is*
4. flock *glides*
5. crowd *gathers*

Writing Application

Possible responses: The audience is utterly silent./The house manager would prefer that the audience enter through several doors simultaneously. A herd of mustangs could be seen in the distance./The herd ranges from one-day-old foals to twenty-five-year-old stallions.The foreman said, "The jury finds the defendant not guilty."/The jury spend much of their time sequestered in their rooms at the hotel.

WG Writing and Grammar, Ruby Level

Students will find further instruction and practice on participial phrases in Chapter 23, Section 1.

Build Language Skills

❶ Vocabulary Lesson

Word Analysis: Latin Prefix *mal-*

The Latin prefix *mal-* means "bad" or "badly." The word *malady* means illness and the word *maladjusted* means "badly adjusted." Select the letter of the definition that best matches each word below.

1. malcontent	**a.** active ill will
2. malevolent	**b.** likely to cause death
3. malign	**c.** wishing harm to others
4. malignant	**d.** dissatisfied
5. malice	**e.** to slander

Vocabulary Builder: Synonyms

Select the best synonym from the column on the right for each vocabulary word.

1. maledictions	**a.** tenaciously
2. prescient	**b.** curses; bad words
3. pertinaciously	**c.** mysterious
4. inscrutable	**d.** prophetic

Spelling Strategy

The letters *sc* usually make the sound of *sk,* as in *describe.* Sometimes, however, *sc* makes the sound of *sh,* as in *prescient,* or *s,* as in *science.* Indicate the sound *sc* makes in each of these words.

1. muscles **2.** mascot **3.** omniscient

❷ Grammar and Style Lesson

Agreement With Collective Nouns

Collective nouns—such as *team* or *flock*—name a group of people or things. A collective noun may be either singular or plural, depending on whether the group it names is seen as a unit (singular) or as a collection of individuals (plural). The verb must always agree in number with the intended meaning of the collective noun.

> **Plural:** When the entire ship's company *were* assembled . . .
>
> **Singular:** The company *consists* of 150 sailors.

Practice Identify the collective noun in each sentence. Then, write the verb form that agrees with it.

1. The crew __?__ up. (lines, line)
2. A team of horses __?__ the hearse. (draws, draw)
3. The crew of the whaling ship __?__ composed of fine, experienced sailors from all over the world. (is, are)
4. A flock of gulls __?__ over the ship. (glides, glide)
5. A curious and horrified crowd __?__ quickly near the site of the grisly accident. (gathers, gather)

Writing Application Use each of these collective nouns—*audience, herd, jury*—in two different sentences. In the first, construct a situation that calls for a singular verb; in the second, construct a sentence that requires a plural verb.

WG *Prentice Hall Writing and Grammar Connection: Chapter 23, Section 1*

Assessment Practice

Make Inferences and Generalizations

(For more practice, see *Standardized Test Preparation Workbook*, p. 19.)

Many tests require students to make generalizations about a written passage. Use this sample test item:

> . . . to and fro he paced his old rounds, upon planks so familiar to his tread, that they were all over dented, like geological stones, with the peculiar mark of his walk. Did you fixedly gaze, too, upon that ribbed and dented brow; there also, you would see still stranger footprints—the footprints of his one unsleeping, ever-pacing thought.

Which of the following best describes Ahab?

A rational and energetic
B calm and powerful
C reverent and self-effacing
D tormented and obsessed

A, B, and *C* are not supported by the text. Ahab's pacing shows his obsession. *D* is correct.

Writing Lesson

Timed Writing: Character Study

For some readers, Ahab's obsession with Moby-Dick borders on madness. For others, his persistence borders on greatness. Write an essay in which you make your own judgement of Ahab's character. To ensure that your readers understand your ideas, include a brief summary of the story. (***40 minutes***)

Prewriting (*10 minutes*) Gather and interpret details about Ahab. Organize your interpretations into a statement of opinion. This will serve as your working thesis.

Drafting (*20 minutes*) Include information from the beginning, middle, and end of the story to create a brief summary. Then, state your thesis in your introduction. Use one body paragraph to develop each of your supporting ideas about Ahab's character.

Model: Writing a Summary

Beginning: The *Pequod* sets out.

Middle: Ahab tells the crew that he will kill Moby-Dick.

End: In a struggle with Moby-Dick, the ship is destroyed.

Summary: In Ahab's search for Moby-Dick, the *Pequod* is destroyed, and most of her crew killed.

To write an effective summary, select key elements from the beginning, middle, and end of a text.

Revising (*10 minutes*) Review your essay, making sure that your summary provides the necessary context, and that your opinion is supported by the text.

WG *Prentice Hall Writing and Grammar Connection: Chapter 14, Section 2*

Extend Your Learning

Listening and Speaking Present a **monologue** that Ishmael might have spoken to the whalers who rescued him. As you prepare, pay attention to the following elements:

- Use nautical terms like Melville's.
- Replicate Ishmael's tone.
- Describe the order of events clearly.
- Add descriptive details about the characters.

Write a monologue that is clear, dramatic, and forceful. Then, share it with the class.

Research and Technology Write a **report** concerning the species of whales that face possible extinction today and what efforts, if any, are being made to save them. Use a series of clear questions to direct your research. Locate answers using field studies, interviews, and news reports from written and electronic sources.

For: An additional research activity
Visit: www.PHSchool.com
Web Code: erd-7306

Assessment Resources

The following resources can be used to assess students' knowledge and skills.

Unit 3 Resources
- **Selection Test A,** pp. 112–114
- **Selection Test B,** pp. 115–117

General Resources
- **Rubrics for Response to Literature,** pp. 65–66
- **Rubric for Peer Assessment: Dramatic Performance** p. 131

Go Online Assessment: Students may use the **Self-test** to prepare for **Selection Test A** or **Selection Test B.**

3 Writing Lesson

You may use this Writing Lesson as timed-writing practice, or you may allow students to develop the character study as a writing assignment over several days.

- To guide students in writing this character study, give them the **Support for Writing Lesson,** p. 109 in ***Unit 3 Resources.***
- Students' character studies should include a brief summary of the story, as well as establish and explain their ideas and insights about Ahab's character.
- Remind students to take into account Ahab's position as the captain of the *Pequod* as they develop their theses. Point out, also, that students should support their theses by citing Ahab's actions, behavior, and speech.
- Use the Response to Literature rubrics in ***General Resources,*** pp. 65–66, to evaluate student work.

4 Listening and Speaking

- You might recommend that students begin by sketching out the order of events first as a reference point. Then, they might consider whether Ishmael would place more emphasis on certain events and less emphasis on others as he speaks to his rescuers.
- Encourage students to reread a variety of narrative passages from the selection to re-familiarize themselves with Ishmael's tone.
- Have students attempt to capture the rhythm and style of Ishmael's account. Urge them to rehearse their monologues as a way of making decisions about how to revise them.
- Have students use the Peer Assessment rubric for Dramatic Performance, p. 131, in ***General Resources.***
- The **Support for Extend Your Learning** page (***Unit 3 Resources,*** p. 110) provides guided note-taking opportunities to help students complete the Extend Your Learning activities.

Go Online Research: Have students type in the Web Code for another research activity.

Meeting Your Standards

Students will

1. understand the connections between the Gothic Tradition in England and in the United States.
2. students will read an example of English Gothic literature.

Connections
Literature Around the World

Students might review "The Fall of the House of Usher" and "The Raven." Like those selections, Mary Shelley's *Frankenstein* contains an atmosphere of gloom and foreboding common to the gothic novel. Explain to students that as they read this passage by Shelley, they will concentrate on the Gothic tradition in literature, a genre featuring supernatural events.

The Gothic Tradition

- Tell students that Gothic literature is often set in castles, dark passages, and other places with mysterious atmospheres. The name *Gothic* describes the style of architecture used in many European castles, and the literary tradition was given this name for its use of such castles as settings.
- Have students recall that Poe's works contain these same characteristics. Elements of mystery and terror are foundations for Gothic traditions, and authors of Gothic novels and stories employ these elements.
- In this introduction to her novel *Frankenstein,* Mary Shelley offers readers firsthand insight into the process. She reports her emotionally charged reactions to her own idea, as well as the events leading up to her inspiration.

British Literature

England

The Gothic Tradition

The Gothic style emerged in both British and American literature during the Romantic Movement. It developed first in England during the late eighteenth century, pioneered by Horace Walpole, whose *Castle of Otranto* (1764) is considered the first Gothic novel. In words that foreshadowed Mary Shelley's introduction to *Frankenstein* sixty years later, Walpole explained his creative process: "I gave rein to my imagination; visions and passions choked me." Filled with ghosts, giants, terror, and anguish, Walpole's novel enjoyed spectacular success and was wildly imitated.

The Gothic style first appeared in American literature in the works of Charles Brockden Brown (1771–1810). His novels strongly foreshadowed Edgar Allan Poe's fascination with obsession, madness, and horror (page 310), as well as Nathaniel Hawthorne's exploration of evil, guilt, and moral despair (page 338).

Mystery and Terror Works in the Gothic style feature macabre plots, remote settings filled with crumbling castles and secret passageways, and an atmosphere of mystery and terror. In Gothic literature, the "spell" of reason is broken as characters plunge into the supernatural. This rejection of reason is a key feature of Romanticism. The Romantics put their faith, not in rational thought, but in the power of the imagination, which they likened to the creative force of nature and which they viewed as the source of truth and morality.

Mary Shelley and *Frankenstein* Mary Shelley, the wife of the English Romantic poet Percy Bysshe Shelley, wrote within the Gothic tradition and also within the broader context of Romanticism. As you read Shelley's introduction to her novel *Frankenstein,* consider how her account reflects some of the key themes and features of both the Gothic tradition and the Romantic Movement, as well as how it enriches your reading of Poe in this unit.

▶ Critical Viewing
Based on the second paragraph of her essay, do you think Shelley might have liked this painting? Why or why not? **[Speculate]**

Introduction to Frankenstein

Mary Wollstonecraft Shelley

The Publishers of the Standard Novels, in selecting *Frankenstein* for one of their series, expressed a wish that I should furnish them with some account of the origin of the story. I am the more willing to comply, because I shall thus give a general answer to the question, so very frequently asked me: "How I, then a young girl, came to think of, and to dilate upon, so very hideous an idea?" It is true that I am very averse to bringing myself forward in print; but as my account will

A View of Chamonix and Mt. Blanc, Ludwig Ferdinand Schnorr von Carolsfeld, Austrian Gallery, Vienna

CONNECTIONS

Humanities

A View of Chamonix and Mt. Blanc, by Julius Schnorr von Carolsfeld

Julius Schnorr von Carolsfeld (1794–1872) was a German Nazarene painter. The Nazarenes were a group of Viennese artists who sought a return to the art of the early Renaissance. They occupied an abandoned monastery in Rome and worked as artist-monks.

Von Carolsfeld painted *A View of Chamonix and Mt. Blanc* in 1824. Beautifully detailed, it is a moonlit view of a famous glacier-covered mountain and a small village in the French Alps. As is common in German Romanticism, the scene takes on a mysterious feeling, in part because of the extreme realism.

Use this question for discussion:

- What relationship does this Romantic painting suggest between people and nature? **Answer:** The human figure and the houses in the valley seem almost insignificant beside the mountains and the trees, suggesting that human beings are a tiny part of a much larger universe.

Critical Viewing

Answer: Shelley may have found this painting appealing because it shows off the Alps to great effect, and she has fond memories of her time there.

Differentiated Instruction Solutions for All Learners

Support for Special Needs Students
Review with students the various elements of the Gothic tradition. Then, direct students to the descriptions of ghost stories in the "Introduction to *Frankenstein*." Help students read each description, and focus on aspects of these stories that seem especially Gothic. As you read with students, have volunteers list examples of Gothic elements on the board.

Enrichment for Gifted/Talented Students
Remind students that Shelley described in detail the scene she imagined, which inspired her to write *Frankenstein*. Encourage students to illustrate one aspect of Shelley's imagined scene that is especially Gothic in its mood. Review with students their understandings of the Gothic tradition for additional guidance. Have students display their Gothic art.

Thematic Connection

Possible response: Rainy, dreary conditions provide the dark and gloomy atmosphere that is often part of the Gothic tale.

Literary Analysis
The Gothic Tradition

- Review with students elements of the Gothic tradition, including a dark, mysterious, foreboding atmosphere and a setting that might include ruined castles.
- Then **ask** students what elements of the Gothic tradition are incorporated in the image of a shape "lost beneath the shadow of the castle walls."
  Answer: The setting includes a castle, typical of the Gothic tradition. In addition, the concealment of a figure in the shadows adds the mysterious, threatening atmosphere characteristic of the genre.

only appear as an appendage to a former production, and as it will be confined to such topics as have connection with my authorship alone, I can scarcely accuse myself of a personal intrusion. . . .

In the summer of 1816, we[1] visited Switzerland, and became the neighbors of Lord Byron. At first we spent our pleasant hours on the lake or wandering on its shores; and Lord Byron, who was writing the third canto of *Childe Harold,* was the only one among us who put his thoughts upon paper. These, as he brought them successively to us, clothed in all the light and harmony of poetry, seemed to stamp as divine the glories of heaven and earth, whose influences we partook with him.

But it proved a wet, ungenial summer, and incessant rain often confined us for days to the house. Some volumes of ghost stories, translated from the German into French,[2] fell into our hands. There was "The History of the Inconstant Lover," who, when he thought to clasp the bride to whom he had pledged his vows, found himself in the arms of the pale ghost of her whom he had deserted. There was the tale of the sinful founder of his race,[3] whose miserable doom it was to bestow the kiss of death on all the younger sons of his fated house, just when they reached the age of promise. His gigantic, shadowy form, clothed like the ghost in Hamlet, in complete armor but with the beaver[4] up, was seen at midnight, by the moon's fitful beams, to advance slowly along the gloomy avenue. The shape was lost beneath the shadow of the castle walls; but soon a gate swung back, a step was heard, the door of the chamber opened, and he advanced to the couch of the blooming youths, cradled in healthy sleep. Eternal sorrow sat upon his face as he bent down and kissed the foreheads of the boys, who from that hour withered like flowers snapped upon the stalk. I have not seen these stories since then, but their incidents are as fresh in my mind as if I had read them yesterday.

"We will each write a ghost story," said Lord Byron; and his proposition was acceded to. There were four of us.[5] The noble author began a tale, a fragment of which he printed at the end of his poem of Mazeppa. Shelley, more apt to embody ideas and sentiments in the radiance of brilliant imagery, and in the music of the most melodious verse that adorns our language, than to invent the machinery of a story, commenced one founded on the experiences of his early life. Poor Polidori had some terrible idea about a skull-headed lady, who was so punished for peeping through a keyhole—what to see I forget—something very shocking and wrong of course; but when she was reduced to a worse condition than the renowned Tom of Coventry,[6]

Vocabulary Builder
appendage (ə pen′ dij) *n.* something added on

Vocabulary Builder
ungenial (un jēn′ yəl) *adj.* disagreeable; characterized by bad weather

Thematic Connection
In what way does the weather provide an appropriate setting for reading ghost stories?

Vocabulary Builder
acceded (ak sēd′ id) *v.* yielded (to); agreed

1. **we** Mary Shelley, her husband Percy Bysshe Shelley, and their two children.
2. **volumes . . . French** *Fantasmagoriana,* or *Collected Stories of Apparitions of Specters, Ghosts, Phantoms, Etc.,* published anonymously in 1812.
3. **the tale . . . race** "Family Portraits."
4. **beaver** hinged piece of armor that covers the face.
5. **four of us** Byron, the two Shelleys, and John William Polidori, Byron's physician.
6. **Tom of Coventry** "Peeping Tom" who, according to legend, was struck blind for looking at Lady Godiva as she rode naked through Coventry.

Enrichment

Contemporary Research on Life

Mary Shelley describes Dr. Frankenstein as "the pale student of unhallowed arts" whose experiments "mock" the creator. The uneasy reaction of modern critics to developments such as cloning and genetic engineering shares a good deal with Shelley's reaction to her own vision. When humans reshape the character of life, their actions challenge some people's sense that life is a gift from a creator. Without this sense, some people believe that humanity becomes dangerously arrogant. Defenders of such research emphasize the value of inquiry and of improving the quality of life.

he did not know what to do with her, and was obliged to despatch her to the tomb of the Capulets,[7] the only place for which she was fitted. The illustrious poets also, annoyed by the platitude of prose, speedily relinquished their uncongenial task.

I busied myself to *think of a story*—a story to rival those which had excited us to this task. One which would speak to the mysterious fears of our nature and awaken thrilling horror—one to make the reader dread to look round, to curdle the blood, and quicken the beatings of the heart. If I did not accomplish these things, my ghost story would be unworthy of its name. I thought and pondered—vainly. I felt that blank incapability of invention which is the greatest misery of authorship, when dull Nothing replies to our anxious invocations. *Have you thought of a story?* I was asked each morning, and each morning I was forced to reply with a mortifying negative. . . .

Many and long were the conversations between Lord Byron and Shelley, to which I was a devout but nearly silent listener. During one of these, various philosophical doctrines were discussed, and among others the nature of the principle of life and whether there was any probability of its ever being discovered and communicated. They talked of the experiments of Dr. Darwin.[8] (I speak not of what the Doctor really did or said that he did, but, as more to my purpose, of what was then spoken of as having been done by him), who preserved a piece of vermicelli in a glass case till by some extraordinary means it began to move with voluntary motion. Not thus, after all, would life be given. Perhaps a corpse would be reanimated: galvanism[9] had given token of such things. Perhaps the component parts of a creature might be manufactured, brought together, and endued with vital warmth.

Night waned upon this talk, and even the witching hour had gone by, before we retired to rest. When I placed my head on my pillow, I did not sleep, nor could I be said to think. My imagination, unbidden, possessed and guided me, gifting the successive images that arose in my mind with a vividness far beyond the usual bounds of reverie. I saw—with shut eyes but acute mental vision—I saw the pale student of unhallowed arts kneeling beside the thing he had put together. I saw the hideous phantasm of a man stretched out, and then, on the working of some powerful engine, show signs of life and stir with an uneasy, half vital motion. Frightful must it be, for supremely frightful would be the effect of any human endeavor to mock the stupendous mechanism of the Creator of the world. His success would terrify the artist; he would rush away from his odious handiwork, horror-stricken. He would hope that, left to itself, the slight spark of life which he had communicated would fade; that this thing, which had received such imperfect animation, would subside into dead matter; and he might sleep in the

7. **tomb of the Capulets** the place where Romeo and Juliet died.
8. **Dr. Darwin** The physician, botanist, and poet Erasmus Darwin (1731–1802), grandfather of the Charles Darwin who pioneered the theory of evolution.
9. **galvanism** use of electric current to induce twitching in dead muscles.

Vocabulary Builder
platitude (plat′ ə to͞od′) *n.* statement lacking originality

Thematic Connection
How do Mary Shelley's goals for her story fit into the Gothic tradition in literature?

Thematic Connection
To what power or force does Shelley attribute her inspiration?

Vocabulary Builder
phantasm (fan′ taz′ əm) *n.* supernatural form or shape; ghost; figment of the mind

Reading Check
Why does the author have trouble falling a sleep?

Thematic Connection

Possible response: She hopes to produce a story that is mysterious and frightening, one that will "make the reader dread to look round, to curdle the blood, and quicken the beatings of the heart."

Thematic Connection

Possible response: Shelley overhears a discussion about the possibility of creating artificial life. Shelley's imagination then fuels her visions. Her experience is so unusually vivid that she frightens herself.

Background
Science

The Romantics held more faith in the power of the imagination than in the power of rational thought. This faith in imagination colored their approach to science, too. For example, Erasmus Darwin spent part of his life in Lichfield, England, where he built a botanical garden for which "the general design . . . is to enlist imagination under the banner of science." In 1791, he published a long poem titled *The Botanic Garden.* In the poem, the goddess of Botany descends to Earth and explores various natural phenomena.

Reading Check

Answer: Shelley imagines that she sees a person use a great machine to spark life from a corpse.

Differentiated Instruction
Solutions for All Learners

Strategy for English Learners

Direct students' attention to Shelley's use of the word *phantasm,* which means "supernatural form or shape; ghost; or figment of the imagination." Explain to students that *phantasm* is related to the word *fantasy.* Both words have their origin in the Greek and Latin word *phantasma,* meaning "image" or "spectre," and both words allude to an illusion or something that is not real. Speakers of romance languages should be familiar with the Latin origin. Have students find other words that are related to *phantasm* or *fantasy*. Students may mention *phantom, phantasmagoria, fantastic, fantasia,* or *fanciful.*

Enrichment for Advanced Students

Have interested students read a segment of the novel *Frankenstein.* Then, ask them to prepare book reviews in which they compare *Frankenstein* to Shelley's description of it in her introduction. Ask students to describe Frankenstein's monster and then compare the story with other horror stories they have read.

ASSESS

Answers

1. Shelley's idea includes the Gothic elements of mystery, terror, and the supernatural. The story centers on the strange plot of a person creating life from a corpse. This "creator" then becomes horrified when the creature comes to life.
2. Both authors approach the power of the imagination as a force that can affect how people view reality. Shelley approaches the imagination as a creative force that reveals truth. In fact, Shelley describes herself as "possessed" by her own imagination when she sees her vision, and her imagination produces a story without her conscious, rational involvement. In contrast, Poe approaches the power of the imagination as a destructive force that alters reality. Poe's works suggest that the imagination leads the speaker in the poem and the narrator in the story to produce false perceptions, leading them to madness.
3. **Possible response:** Horror stories are the type of stories that keep people excited. The elements of horror, mystery, and macabre plots can create thrilling stories in which readers or viewers are drawn in, anticipating what will happen next.

belief that the silence of the grave would quench forever the transient existence of the hideous corpse which he had looked upon as the cradle of life. He sleeps; but he is awakened; he opens his eyes; behold the horrid thing stands at his bedside, opening his curtains, and looking on him with yellow, watery, but speculative eyes.

I opened mine in terror. The idea so possessed my mind, that a thrill of fear ran through me, and I wished to exchange the ghastly image of my fancy for the realities around. I see them still: the very room, the dark parquet,[10] the closed shutters, with the moonlight struggling through, and the sense I had that the glassy lake and white high Alps were beyond. I could not so easily get rid of my hideous phantom: still it haunted me. I must try to think of something else. I recurred to my ghost story—my tiresome unlucky ghost story! O! if I could only contrive one which would frighten my reader as I myself had been frightened that night!

Swift as light and as cheering was the idea that broke in upon me. "I have found it! What terrified me will terrify others, and I need only describe the specter which had haunted my midnight pillow." On the morrow I announced that I had *thought of a story.* I began that day with the words, *It was on a dreary night of November,* making only a transcript of the grim terrors of my waking dream.

At first I thought but of a few pages—of a short tale—but Shelley urged me to develop the idea at greater length. I certainly did not owe the suggestion of one incident, nor scarcely of one train of feeling, to my husband, and yet but for his incitement, it would never have taken the form in which it was presented to the world. From this declaration I must except the preface. As far as I can recollect, it was entirely written by him.

And now, once again, I bid my hideous progeny go forth and prosper. I have an affection for it, for it was the offspring of happy days, when death and grief were but words, which found no true echo in my heart. Its several pages speak of many a walk, many a drive, and many a conversation, when I was not alone; and my companion was one who, in this world, I shall never see more. But this is for myself: my readers have nothing to do with these associations.

Vocabulary Builder
incitement (in sīt′ mənt) *n.* act of urging; encouragement

Mary Wollstonecraft Shelley (1797–1851)

Mary Wollstonecraft Shelley was the daughter of William Godwin, a political philosopher, and Mary Wollstonecraft Godwin, one of Britain's first feminist writers. When she was sixteen, she met a young poet, Percy Bysshe Shelley, who admired her father's social theories. The couple eloped and settled in Italy. Mary Shelley's *Frankenstein* was first published to great success in 1818. Four years later, after her husband's death in a drowning accident, Mary Shelley returned to England and continued to write. Although the novel *The Last Man* (1826) is often considered her best work, *Frankenstein* is her most famous. It has thrilled countless readers and been interpreted by generations of filmmakers.

10. **parquet** (pär kā′) flooring made of wooden pieces arranged in a pattern.

Connecting British Literature

1. Explain why Shelley's idea for *Frankenstein* fits into the Gothic tradition.
2. Compare and contrast the ways in which Shelley, in her introduction to *Frankenstein,* and Poe, in "The Fall of the House of Usher" and "The Raven," view the power of the imagination.
3. In your opinion, why do so many people enjoy horror stories and movies? Explain your answer.

Unit 3
Part
3

The Human Spirit and the Natural World

Early Morning at Cold Spring, 1850, Asher B. Durand, Montclair Art Museum, Montclair, New Jersey

Selection Planning Guide

The section introduces students to two of the most influential writers of the nineteenth century. Ralph Waldo Emerson and Henry David Thoreau helped define the American character by inspiring people to turn to nature in order to better understand both themselves and the universal truths. Students may be surprised to find that they share many of the views on nature and individuality Emerson expresses in *Nature* and "Self-Reliance." "Concord Hymn" and "The Snowstorm" reveal the poetic—and perhaps more accessible—side of Emerson's literary talent. Thoreau's views in *Walden* on how to live a productive life may intrigue students. Encourage them to assess the validity of his evaluation of government in *Civil Disobedience*.

Humanities

Early Morning at Cold Spring,
Asher B. Durand

One of the founders of the Hudson River school of painting, Asher B. Durand (1796–1886) began his career as an engraver, reproducing paintings by others and engraving banknotes; in fact, U.S. currency incorporates a number of the designs he developed. In his middle age, Durand turned to landscape painting and became one of the leaders of a group of northeastern artists who painted scenes from the Hudson River, Adirondack Mountains, and New England. Cold Spring is a city north of New York City along the Hudson River, a favorite haunt for Durand and his colleagues.

Use these questions for discussion:

1. Why might the artist have painted a solitary man, rather than a group of people, in such a setting?
   Possible response: He probably wanted to portray an individual quietly contemplating the beauty of the landscape.
2. What does the human figure add to this tranquil landscape painting?
   Possible responses: The figure adds a human dimension—it represents the human mind responding to or interacting with the beauty of nature.

Differentiated Instruction
Solutions for All Learners

Accessibility at a Glance

Average	More Challenging
from Nature *from* Self-Reliance Concord Hymn The Snowstorm *from* Civil Disobedience	*from* Walden

Students will

1. understand the beginnings of Transcendentalism in America.
2. discuss the role of the individual in society.

Background
History

One of Margaret Fuller's closest friends was Elizabeth Palmer Peabody (1804–1894), the eldest of three remarkable sisters. A writer of an extraordinary collection of letters and a tireless correspondent with many of the foremost thinkers of her day, Elizabeth remained energetic until her death, teaching, running a literary bookshop, and eventually founding the first kindergartens in the United States. Mary Peabody Mann (1806–1887) worked with Elizabeth in the kindergarten movement. She also taught and wrote a book about the Paiute tribe based on interviews with Sarah Winnemucca, a Paiute leader and educator. Mary married a man who became famous: Horace Mann, the educator. Sophia Peabody (1809–1871) married Nathaniel Hawthorne after a long courtship. She wanted to become an artist, and later encouraged similar ambitions in her daughter Rose Hawthorne.

Critical Viewing

Possible response: Life was very simple and without modern conveniences.

Transcendentalism: The Seekers

For the Transcendentalists, the loose-knit group of writers, artists, and reformers who flourished in the 1830s and 1840s, the individual was at the center of the universe, more powerful than any institution, whether political or religious. So it is fitting that the most influential literary and philosophical movement in American history began with the struggles of one man.

A Crisis of Confidence In the early 1830s, a young Boston pastor found himself wrestling with his faith. His beloved wife had died, and he began questioning his beliefs. At the time, many institutions downplayed the importance of the individual. The Industrial Revolution had shown that machines could actually replace people, that individuals did not matter.

▼ Critical Viewing Judging from this image of a replica of Thoreau's cabin, what do you think life was like on Walden Pond? **[Speculate]**

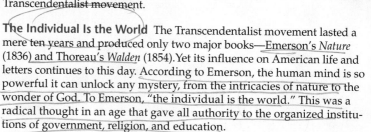

> *"According to Emerson, the Human Mind is so Powerful it can Unlock any Mystery, from the Intricacies of Nature to the Wonder of God."*

The pastor was troubled by this notion. He believed, on the contrary, that the human mind was the most important force in the universe. The pastor was so passionate about his search for a new way of thinking that he resigned his position and traveled to Europe to visit with some of the great philosophers of the day.

That pastor was Ralph Waldo Emerson, and his crisis of confidence became a revolution in American thought. When Emerson returned to the United States in 1833, he helped forge the Transcendentalist movement.

The Individual Is the World The Transcendentalist movement lasted a mere ten years and produced only two major books—Emerson's *Nature* (1836) and Thoreau's *Walden* (1854). Yet its influence on American life and letters continues to this day. According to Emerson, the human mind is so

powerful it can unlock any mystery, from the intricacies of nature to the wonder of God. To Emerson, "the individual is the world." This was a radical thought in an age that gave all authority to the organized institutions of government, religion, and education.

Emerson first proposed his ideas in 1833 in a speech at Harvard University. Then, he took his ideas further, proposing that every soul and all of nature was part of an "Over-Soul," a universal spirit to which all beings return after death. In other words, every being is part of God's mind.

Meetings of Great Minds Many people denounced Emerson as a heretic, but his supporters flocked to his home in Concord, Massachusetts.

Enrichment

Louisa May Alcott

The fame of Transcendentalist Amos Bronson Alcott was far eclipsed by his daughter Louisa May. Louisa's novel *Little Women,* and its sequels outsold the writing of Emerson, Hawthorne, Melville, and Thoreau combined, and have never gone out of print.

Popular though her children's stories were, Alcott preferred writing Gothic fiction. Because she was a woman, scandal would have resulted if she had published her thrilling tales of mesmerism, murder, adultery, and the supernatural under her own name. Her stories all appeared anonymously or under the pen name A.M. Barnard. Late in the 20th century, scholars identified her as the author of *A Modern Mephistopheles* and a number of Gothic tales by studying her journals and correspondence. Today these stories and novels are published as Alcott would have wished, under her own name.

Emerson looks kind, thoughtful, and good-humored, because of his smile. They may say that Fuller's cast-down eyes make her look thoughtful and introspective.

During the height of Transcendentalist activities, Concord attracted so many great minds that it was dubbed the "Athens of America."

Among Emerson's admirers was Amos Bronson Alcott, whose beliefs about education revolutionized American schools. Alcott insisted that students should not be taught through routine memorization, but should instead be challenged to think, debate, and discuss. Feminist author and editor Margaret Fuller was another eminent Transcendentalist. Along with Emerson, Fuller was the driving force behind the Transcendentalist journal *The Dial.*

Emerson's most famous protégé was Henry David Thoreau. As a twenty-year-old student, Thoreau heard Emerson speak at Harvard and was thrilled by his ideas. Not content merely to discuss Transcendentalist philosophy, Thoreau wanted to put it into action. In 1845, he built a rough cottage in the woods at Walden Pond and went there to live alone, in harmony with nature, untied to material things. Thoreau lived at Walden Pond for two years and wrote about his experiences in his collection of essays, *Walden.*

A Lasting Legacy Like other Transcendentalists, Thoreau was a fierce abolitionist. To protest slavery and the Mexican War, he refused to pay taxes and was imprisoned. Although Thoreau spent only one night in jail, the experience gave him insights into the relationship of individuals to government. The theory of nonviolent civil disobedience that he developed has had a profound effect on society throughout the world. During India's struggle for independence in the 1940s, Mahatma Gandhi adopted Thoreau's ideas. In America, nonviolent protest served as the guiding principle for Martin Luther King, Jr., during the civil rights movement.

The influence of the Transcendentalists is so woven into the fabric of American culture that we take it for granted. Yet whenever we celebrate the individual, look to the natural world as a mirror of human lives, or state a belief in the power of intuition to grasp fundamental truths, we owe a debt to the great, brief meeting of minds in Concord.

▲ **Critical Viewing**
What personality traits are conveyed in these images of Ralph Waldo Emerson and Margaret Fuller? Explain your responses. **[Interpret]**

Activity

The Power of One

The Transcendentalists believed that no institution should be as powerful as the individual. With a group, discuss the role of the individual in our society. Use these questions to guide your discussion:

- How much power do political, religious, and corporate institutions wield in our society? Support your position with examples.
- Can one person make a difference in our society? If so, how?
- Should individuals have more power than they do? Why or why not?

Choose a point person to share your group's conclusions with the class.

Critical Thinking

1. Why do you think the Transcendentalist movement appealed to people like Emerson and Alcott?
   Answer: They were concerned about the age of industrialization that threatened to reduce the individual to a mechanized state. Transcendentalism offered man the opportunity to make the most of mind and spirit.
2. What does the prominence of Margaret Fuller in the Transcendentalist movement suggest about it?
   Answer: Transcendentalists were willing to treat women as intellectual equals.

Activity

- Encourage students to track their thoughts by using charts. In one column of a chart, have them write how much power political, religious, and corporate institutions have in society. Tell them to list examples in a second column. In a third column, have them list the power that each should have in society.
- Students can create a similar chart to track the power of individuals in society.

From the Scholar's Desk

CHARLES JOHNSON
on Ralph Waldo Emerson

Charles Johnson

Charles Johnson has published a range of work, including cartoon collections, philosophical and literary studies, screenplays, and novels like *Middle Passage,* winner of the National Book Award in 1990.

Emerson Gave Me Permission to Question Everything

At age sixteen, when I was an Illinois boy trying to figure out where my place might be in the tempestuous, rapidly changing decade of the 1960s, and long before I became a black American novelist and philosopher, my teachers at Evanston Township High School placed the essays of Ralph Waldo Emerson in front of me. I'm thankful they did.

In grand fashion, "Self-Reliance" gave me permission to be a free thinker and to rigorously question *every*thing around me—from the status quo to social cliques in my school, from neighborhood gangs to eighty-year-old social "conventions" that enshrined racial segregation in the South and in the North. Emerson gave me the courage to resist the pressure to conform to things that were unreasonable, to always trust myself, to dream "impossible dreams," and to value my own individual voice and vision, even if doing so resulted in disapproval and being unpopular with the hip "in crowd."

Challenging Us to Go Beyond the Ordinary Just as he served me well in my teens, Emerson's belief in "the infinitude of the private man," and his identification with all forms of life, proved to be reliable guides during my adult years. First, that's because he defined so beautifully the values that eight generations of Americans regard as the basis for our national character and core beliefs, particularly his devotion to what he called "the republic of Man." He condemned the institution of slavery, championed the right of women to vote, and spoke out against the "wicked Indian policy."

In his journal, Emerson dreamed of an America that would one day be an "asylum of all nations, the energy of Irish, Germans, Swedes, Poles & Cossacks, & all the European tribes—of the Africans, & of the Polynesians [who] will construct a new race, a new religion, a new State, a new literature, which will be as vigorous as the new Europe which came out of the smelting pot of the Dark Ages. . . ." He truly believed, and made *me* see, how "It is our duty to be discontented, with the measure we have of knowledge & virtue, to forget the things behind & press toward those before."

Secondly, Emerson has long inspired me—as he does anyone with an adventurous spirit—because he challenges us to be flexible and resourceful, like the "sturdy lad from New Hampshire or Vermont,

From the Scholar's Desk
Charles Johnson

- Tell students that Charles Johnson, a prize-winning novelist and teacher, was born in 1948 and so came of age during the Civil Rights movement of the 1960s. Johnson's novel *Middle Passage,* which won the prestigious National Book Award in 1990, treats the subject of slavery from the unconventional viewpoint of a freed slave who leaves his life in New Orleans and travels to Africa on a slave ship. In 1998 Johnson received a MacArthur Foundation "genius" grant—so-called because the grants are given to individuals with decidedly original minds—something of which Ralph Waldo Emerson would have approved.

Emerson Gave Me Permission to Question Everything

- Have students read Johnson's comments about the influence of Emerson on his life. **Ask:** What might be the advantages and disadvantages in believing as Johnson and Emerson do that "It is our duty to be discontented"?
  Answer: The advantages of being discontented are that you are always challenging yourself, never resting on your achievements, and so always striving for improvement of self and the human condition. The disadvantages might be that such an attitude is stressful and difficult to maintain, that others may perceive you as selfish, immature, or chronically negative.

Critical Viewing

Possible response: Emerson must have been a captivating speaker because the audience is listening attentively. His stance, expression, and hand gesture show his ease in front of the crowd.

◀ Critical Viewing This print shows Emerson delivering a lecture. What details reveal what he might have been like as a speaker? **[Analyze]**

who in turn tries all the professions, who *teams* it, *farms* it, *peddles,* keeps a school, preaches, edits a newspaper, goes to Congress, buys a township, and so forth, in successive years, and always, like a cat, falls on his feet" (from "Self-Reliance").

All those *are* our possibilities. There is nothing, Emerson says, that we cannot achieve if we believe in ourselves. As a Transcendentalist, he was a restless and superbly civilized man who went beyond (or transcended) the ordinary, the outdated, and the unoriginal, for, in his own words, he chose to "unsettle all things. No facts are to me sacred, none are profane; I simply experiment, an endless seeker, with no Past at my back" (from "Circles").

Author Link

For: More about Charles Johnson
Visit: www.PHSchool.com
Web Code: ete-9316

Thinking About the Commentary

1. (a) Recall: When Johnson was a teenager, what three important lessons did he learn from Emerson? **(b) Connect:** What important life-lessons have you learned from a favorite author?

2. (a) Recall: What two qualities does Emerson's "sturdy lad from New Hampshire or Vermont" display? **(b) Speculate:** Are these qualities still part of our "core beliefs" as Americans? Why or why not?

As You Read the Selections by Emerson . . .

3. Think about whether Emerson's work is still as relevant to today's high school students as it was to the young Charles Johnson.

Challenging Us to Go Beyond the Ordinary

- Have students read Johnson's comments on Emerson's theory on transcending "the ordinary."
Ask: What does Emerson mean when he tells us to go beyond the ordinary?
Answer: Emerson is encouraging us to believe in ourselves and achieve all that is within our grasp. We should not settle for mediocrity, but always strive to achieve perfection. As a nation, we must purge ourselves of practices or beliefs that cause us to fall short of perfection.

ASSESS

Answers

1. (a) As a teenager, Johnson learned to be a free-thinker and question everything around him, including high-school social cliques and societal norms such as segregation. He also learned to resist the pressure to conform; he learned to trust himself and "dream 'impossible dreams.'" (b) Students should cite a specific author whose writing has taught them something about living—for example, they might indicate how *The Diary of Anne Frank* shows the power and persistence of hope.
2. (a) Emerson's "sturdy lad from New Hampshire displays flexibility and resourcefulness. (b) Most students will probably feel that these qualities are still central to the American character, because Americans continue to show the ability to adapt to new circumstances and find solutions to new problems as they arise.
3. As they read Emerson, encourage students to look for the qualities that Johnson singles out in the author's writing and think of instances in their own lives when they resisted conforming and instead thought independently.

Meeting Your Standards

Students will

1. **analyze and respond to literary elements.**
   - Literary Analysis: Transcendentalism
2. **read, comprehend, analyze, and critique nonfiction and poetry**
   - Reading Strategy: Challenging the Text
   - Reading Check questions
   - Apply the Skills questions
   - Assessment Practice (ATE)
3. **develop vocabulary.**
   - Vocabulary Lesson: Latin Root: *-radi-*
4. **understand and apply written and oral language conventions.**
   - Spelling Strategy
   - Grammar and Style Lesson: Varying Sentence Length
5. **develop writing proficiency.**
   - Writing Lesson: Critical Evaluation of a Philosophical Essay
6. **develop appropriate research strategies.**
   - Extend Your Learning: Profile
7. **understand and apply listening and speaking strategies.**
   - Extend Your Learning: Public Service Announcement

Block Scheduling: Use one 90-minute class period to preteach the skills and have students read the selection. Use a second 90-minute class period to assess students' mastery of skills, extend their learning, and monitor their progress.

Homework Suggestions

Following are possibilities for homework assignments.

- Support pages from *Unit 3 Resources:*
  Literary Analysis
  Reading Strategy
  Vocabulary Builder
  Grammar and Style
- An Extend Your Learning project and the Writing Lesson for this selection group may be completed over several days.

Step-by-Step Teaching Guide	Pacing Guide
PRETEACH	
• Administer Vocabulary and Reading Warm-ups as necessary.	5 min.
• Engage students' interest with the motivation activity.	5 min.
• Read and discuss author and background features. **FT**	10 min.
• Introduce the Literary Analysis Skill: Transcendentalism. **FT**	5 min.
• Introduce the Reading Strategy: Challenging the Text. **FT**	10 min.
• Prepare students to read by teaching the selection vocabulary. **FT**	
TEACH	
• Informally monitor comprehension while students read independently or in groups. **FT**	30 min.
• Monitor students' comprehension with the Reading Check notes.	as students read
• Reinforce vocabulary with Vocabulary Builder notes.	as students read
• Develop students' understanding of Transcendentalism with the Literary Analysis annotations. **FT**	5 min.
• Develop students' ability to challenge the text with the Reading Strategy annotations. **FT**	5 min.
ASSESS/EXTEND	
• Assess students' comprehension and mastery of the Literary Analysis and Reading Strategy by having them answer the Apply the Skills questions. **FT**	15 min.
• Have students complete the Vocabulary Lesson and the Grammar and Style Lesson. **FT**	15 min.
• Apply students' ability to support their writing with relevant examples by using the Writing Lesson. **FT**	45 min. or homework
• Apply students' understanding by using one or more of the Extend Your Learning activities.	20–90 min. or homework
• Administer Selection Test A or Selection Test B. **FT**	15 min.

Resources

PRINT

Unit 3 Resources

TRANSPARENCY

Graphic Organizer Transparencies

PRINT

Reader's Notebook [L2]
Reader's Notebook: Adapted Version [L1]
Reader's Notebook: English Learner's Version [EL]

Unit 3 Resources

TECHNOLOGY

Listening to Literature Audio CDs [L2, EL]
Reader's Notebook: Adapted Version Audio CD [L1, L2]

PRINT

Unit 3 Resources

General Resources

TECHNOLOGY

Go Online: Research [**L3**]
Go Online: Self-test [**L3**]
***ExamView®*, Test Bank [L3]**

Choosing Resources for Differentiated Instruction

[**L1**] Special Needs Students
[**L2**] Below-Level Students
[**L3**] All Students
[**L4**] Advanced Students
[**EL**] English Learners

FT Fast Track Instruction: To move the lesson more quickly, use the strategies and activities identified with **FT**.

Scaffolding for Less Proficient and Advanced Students

The leveled Critical Thinking questions after selections progress in the levels of thinking required to answer them. To address the needs of your different students, you may use the (a) level questions for your less proficient students and the (b) level questions with your on-level and advanced students. The occasional (c) level questions are appropriate for your advanced students.

PRENTICE HALL **TeacherEXPRESS™** Plan · Teach · Assess Use this complete suite of powerful teaching tools to make lesson planning and testing quicker and easier.

PRENTICE HALL **StudentEXPRESS™** Learn · Study · Succeed Use the interactive textbook (online and on CD-ROM) to make selections and activities come alive with audio and video support and interactive questions.

Motivation

In his writings, Emerson touches on an issue that is especially relevant to high-school students: conformity, that is, behaving according to societal rules and customs. Write the word *conformity* on the chalkboard. Create a two-column chart with the headings Advantages and Disadvantages. Then have the class brainstorm for a list of as many advantages and disadvantages of conformity as they can think of. Take a vote to see whether students think that the advantages of conformity outweigh the disadvantages, or vice versa. Let students know that the writer whose works they're about to read is one of history's greatest champions of nonconformity.

1 Background

More About the Author

Emerson published the ninety-five page book *Nature* anonymously in Boston. It predates *The Dial*—the journal of the Transcendentalist Club—by four years. Almost everything Emerson wrote after *Nature* amplified or extended the ideas that appeared in it.

1 *from* Nature • *from* Self-Reliance • Concord Hymn • The Snowstorm

Ralph Waldo Emerson (1803–1882)

Individuality, independence, and an appreciation for the wonders of nature—these are just a few of the principles that Ralph Waldo Emerson helped to ingrain in our nation's identity. Although his ideas were sometimes considered controversial, he had a tremendous influence on the young people of his time, and his beliefs have continued to inspire people to this day.

Throughout his life, Emerson's mind was constantly in motion, generating new ideas and defining and redefining his view of the world. His natural eloquence in expressing these ideas—in essays, lectures, and poetry—makes him one of the most quoted writers in American literature.

A New England Childhood The son of a Unitarian minister, Emerson was born in Boston. When Emerson was seven, his father died. The boy turned to a brilliant and eccentric aunt, Mary Moody Emerson, who encouraged his independent thinking. At fourteen, Emerson entered Harvard, where he began the journal he was to keep all his life. After postgraduate studies at Harvard Divinity School, he became pastor of the Second Church of Boston.

Finding His Niche Emerson's career as a minister was short-lived. Grief-stricken at the death of his young wife, and dissatisfied with what he saw as the spiritual restrictions in Unitarianism, Emerson resigned after three years. He then went to Europe, where he met the English writers Thomas Carlyle, Samuel Taylor Coleridge, and William Wordsworth. On his return to the United States, Emerson settled in Concord, Massachusetts. He married again and began his lifelong career of writing.

Emerson's second wife, Lydia Jackson of Plymouth, provided a supportive and secure family life. Emerson was now receiving money from his first wife's legacy and, for the first time in his life, was not living in poverty. The Emerson household welcomed a slowly widening circle of friends and admirers that included many of the country's most important thinkers.

In time, Emerson became widely sought as a lecturer throughout the nation. In fact, many of his essays began as lectures. Emerson kept working on the ideas until he had honed them into essay form. His talks attracted people of many ages and social classes, but it was the young people of his time who were most receptive to the thoughts of this often controversial philosopher.

An Independent Thinker Emerson was a soft-spoken man, given to neither physical nor emotional excess. Beneath his calm, sober demeanor existed a restless, highly individualistic mind that resisted conformity. "Good men," he once wrote, "must not obey the laws too well."

Emerson first achieved national fame in 1841, when he published *Essays,* a collection based on material from his journals and lectures. He went on to publish several more volumes of nonfiction, including *Essays, Second Volume* (1844), *Representative Men* (1849), and *The Conduct of Life* (1860).

Though Emerson was known mostly for his essays and lectures, he considered himself primarily a poet. "I am born a poet," he once wrote, "of a low class without doubt, yet a poet. That is my nature and my vocation." He published two successful volumes of poetry, *Poems* (1847) and *May-Day and Other Pieces* (1867). Like his essays, Emerson's poems express his beliefs in individuality and in humanity's spiritual connection to nature.

Preview

Connecting to the Literature

"Be true to yourself." "Follow your dream." Most of us have faced the choices these sentiments address: whether to conform to the expectations of others, or follow our own inner voice. Emerson's writings address such choices. He comes down squarely in favor of nonconformity.

Literary Analysis

Transcendentalism

Transcendentalism was an intellectual movement founded by Emerson. These are the cornerstones of Transcendentalist beliefs:

- Human senses are limited; they convey knowledge of the physical world, but deeper truths can be grasped only through intuition.
- The observation of nature illuminates the nature of human beings.
- God, nature, and humanity are united in a shared universal soul, or Over-Soul.

These beliefs pervade all of Emerson's work.

Comparing Literary Works

The essays that appear here are concerned with the nature of the individual, but they explore two different arenas. In one, Emerson looks at the individual's relationship to nature, and in the other, he explores the individual's relationship to society. As you read, compare how Emerson depicts the individual in nature versus the way he describes the individual among his or her fellow human beings.

Reading Strategy

Challenging the Text

When you read a work that presents an argument, do not simply accept the ideas—challenge them. To **challenge a text**, question the author's assertions and reasoning. Compare the evidence the author offers with your personal experience or other reading. Then, decide whether you agree. Use a chart like the one shown here to record your thinking.

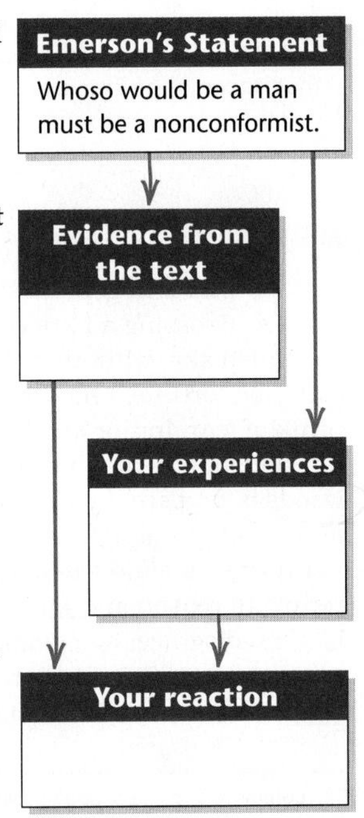

Vocabulary Builder

blithe (blīth) *adj.* carefree (p. 390)

connate (kän′ āt′) *adj.* existing naturally; innate (p. 391)

chaos (kā′ äs′) *n.* disorder of matter and space, supposed to have existed before the ordered universe (p. 393)

aversion (ə vʉr′ zhən) *n.* object arousing an intense dislike (p. 394)

suffrage (suf′ rij) *n.* vote or voting (p. 394)

divines (də vīnz′) *n.* clergy (p. 394)

radiant (rā′ dē ənt) *adj.* shining brightly (p. 397)

tumultuous (to͞o mul′ cho͞o əs) *adj.* rough; stormy (p. 397)

bastions (bas′ chənz) *n.* fortifications (p. 398)

❷ Literary Analysis

Transcendentalism

- Tell students that as they read Emerson's essays and poems, they will focus on Transcendentalism, an intellectual movement that guided the writer's work. Read aloud the instruction about Transcendentalism. Then tell students that Transcendentalism affected most of the writers of Emerson's day. Have volunteers read aloud the basic precepts of the movement.
- Discuss the instruction under Comparing Literary Works and stress the comparison between individual-nature and individual-society.

❸ Reading Strategy

Challenging the Text

- Remind students that challenging the text will make them more engaged and involved readers.
- Provide this example from "Self-Reliance": "Whoso would be a man must be a nonconformist." Model ways to challenge the statement, such as by examining Emerson's supporting evidence.
- Direct students to use **Reading Strategy Graphic Organizer A,** p. 75 in ***Graphic Organizer Transparencies,*** to challenge Emerson's text as they read the selections.

Vocabulary Builder

- Pronounce each vocabulary word for students, and read the definitions as a class. Have students identify any words with which they are already familiar.

Differentiated Instruction

Solutions for All Learners

Support for Special Needs Students

Have students use the support pages for these selections in the ***Reader's Notebook: Adapted Version.*** Completing these pages will prepare students to read the selection in the Student Edition.

Support for Less Proficient Readers

Have students use the support pages for these selections in the ***Reader's Notebook.*** After students finish the selection in the ***Reader's Notebook,*** have them complete the questions and activities in the Student Edition.

Support for English Learners

Have students use the support pages for these selections in the ***Reader's Notebook: English Learner's Version.*** Completing these pages will prepare students to read the selection in the Student Edition.

TEACH

Learning Modalities
Kinesthetic Learners Tell students that they can respond more fully to Emerson's views about nature by reading the poems in a natural setting. Encourage students to find such a setting, whether in a park, backyard, or even on a city stoop. Challenge them to study their surroundings for elements of nature, such as clouds, sky, trees, squirrels, or weather.

❶ About the Selection

In this excerpt from his book *Nature,* Emerson expresses his belief that the meaning of existence can be found by exploring the natural world. He describes how, through his exploration of nature, he has discovered that he is spiritually connected with the universe, with God, and with every living thing.

❷ Literary Analysis
Transcendentalism

- Read the bracketed passage aloud. **Ask** students to identify the jarring image in the passage and to explain what Emerson means by it. **Possible response:** "I become a transparent eyeball" is a jarring image. Emerson means that he sees everything; the metaphor suggests the poet is like a single, huge eye.
- **Ask** students the Literary Analysis question: According to this passage, what is the relationship between Emerson and nature? **Possible response:** Emerson feels spiritually a part of nature and every living thing, as well as God.

from Nature ❶

Ralph Waldo Emerson

Background During the 1830s and 1840s, Emerson and a small group of like-minded friends gathered regularly in his study to discuss philosophy, religion, and literature. Among them were Emerson's protégé, Henry David Thoreau, as well as educator Bronson Alcott, feminist writer Margaret Fuller, and ex-clergyman and author George Ripley. The intimate group, known as the Transcendental Club, developed a philosophical system that stressed intuition, individuality, and self-reliance. In 1836, Emerson published *Nature*, the lengthy essay (excerpted here) that became the Transcendental Club's unofficial statement of belief.

Nature is a setting that fits equally well a comic or a mourning piece. In good health, the air is a cordial of incredible virtue. Crossing a bare common,[1] in snow puddles, at twilight, under a clouded sky, without having in my thoughts any occurrence of special good fortune, I have enjoyed a perfect exhilaration. I am glad to the brink of fear. In the woods, too, a man casts off his years, as the snake his slough, and at what period soever of life is always a child. In the woods is perpetual youth. Within these plantations of God, a decorum and sanctity reign, a perennial festival is dressed, and the guest sees not how he should tire of them in a thousand years. In the woods, we return to reason and faith. There I feel that nothing can befall me in life—no disgrace, no calamity (leaving me my eyes), which nature cannot repair. Standing on the bare ground—my head bathed by the blithe air and uplifted into infinite space—all mean egotism vanishes.

Literary Analysis
Transcendentalism
According to this passage, what is the relationship between Emerson and nature?

Vocabulary Builder
blithe (blīth) *adj.* carefree

1. **common** *n.* piece of open public land.

Differentiated Instruction Solutions for All Learners

Accessibility at a Glance

	from Nature	Self-Reliance	Concord Hymn	The Snowstorm
Context	Transcendentalism	Nineteenth-century individualism	American Revolution	Extended metaphor
Language	Accessible (metaphors)	Formal diction	Poetic diction and syntax	Figurative language
Concept Level	Challenging (oneness with nature)	Accessible (nonconformity)	Accessible (bravery)	Accessible (nature's powers)
Literary Merit	Classic	Classic	Classic	Classic
Lexile	960	980	NP	NP
Overall Rating	Average	Average	Average	Average

I become a transparent eyeball; I am nothing; I see all; the currents of the Universal Being circulate through me; I am part or parcel of God. The name of the nearest friend sounds then foreign and accidental: to be brothers, to be acquaintances, master or servant, is then a trifle and a disturbance. I am the lover of uncontained and immortal beauty. In the wilderness, I find something more dear and connate than in the streets or villages. In the tranquil landscape, and especially in the distant line of the horizon, man beholds somewhat as beautiful as his own nature.

The greatest delight which the fields and woods minister is the suggestion of an occult relation between man and the vegetable. I am not alone and unacknowledged. They nod to me, and I to them. The

Vocabulary Builder
connate (kän′ āt′) *adj.* existing naturally; innate

3 **Reading Check**
Which emotions does Emerson experience when in the woods?

Sunset, Frederick E. Church, Munson-Williams-Proctor Institute Museum of Art, Utica, New York

▲ **Critical Viewing** Emerson says that nature often allows us to become transparent eyeballs, seeing all, but remaining detached from the business of the world. In what ways does this image reinforce his statement? **[Support]**

Differentiated Instruction Solutions for All Learners

Enrichment for Less Proficient Readers

Given our fast-paced, technological society, students may have trouble understanding the basis of Transcendentalism. Explain that this philosophy centers on gaining spiritual knowledge through recognizing one's connection to the universe, God, and the surrounding world. One way to achieve this is to reduce the unnecessary clutter in one's life, striving for simplicity and a return to the basics. Create activities that encourage students to experience life in a more direct sense. For example, you could have them walk to a destination rather than ride in a car. They could also write their assignments out in longhand rather than type them. Encourage students to cook dinner or begin a craft. All these exercises will help them regain a transcendental connection to daily life. As they pursue such activities, students might consider whether they believe that all living things are connected, and if so, how.

3 Reading Check

Answer: Emerson experiences delight.

4 Critical Viewing

Answer: Students may refer to the painting's serenity, its apparent meshing of land and heavens, the reflection of the landscape in the water, and the complete absence of any traces of humankind.

5 Humanities

Sunset, by Frederic E. Church

Frederic Church, a student of Hudson River School leader Thomas Cole, became a key member of that group. This painting reveals his deep love of nature and his belief that painting should depict the natural world in a grand way. The painting glows with the vibrancy of nature at the most colorful moment of the day—sunset. Use this question for discussion:

- Is this painting an appropriate illustration for Emerson's essay? Why or why not?
  Answer: Some students may say that the painting is appropriate because it portrays the enduring grandeur of nature. Others may say that a painting portraying a person appreciating nature would be more appropriate.

6 Reading Strategy
Challenging the Text

- According to Emerson, from where does the power to produce "this delight" come?
  Answer: The power comes from human beings, not nature, or from a combination of both.
- Then, **ask** students the Reading Strategy question: Do you agree or disagree with this statement about a harmony between human beings and nature? Explain.
  Possible response: Students may say that the power to produce delight resides in nature, but the ability to experience it resides in us.

ASSESS
Answers

1. Students' responses will vary.
2. (a) It vanishes in the woods. (b) Students should identify it as petty narcissism. (c) It's replaced with divinity and delight.
3. (a) He becomes this after he sheds "mean egotism" amidst nature. (b) He feels connected to nature and to God. (c) Emerson, like everyone and everything, is connected to the Universal Being.
4. (a) It comes from a harmony of man and nature. (b) **Possible response:** He means that it is forever linked and intertwined, but not necessarily that it is serene.
5. (a) No, sometimes nature is less welcoming. It depends, on nature's mood and on the emotions we bring in. (b) He means that nature reflects our emotions or mood.
6. (a) **Possible response:** Nature teaches us how we are connected to everyone and everything around us. (b) Responses should be supported by their evaluation of Emerson's ideas.
7. Students may mention the environmental movement and the popularity of outdoor activities.

Go Online — Author Link For additional information about Ralph Waldo Emerson, have students type in the Web Code, then select E from the alphabet, and then select Ralph Waldo Emerson.

waving of the boughs in the storm is new to me and old. It takes me by surprise, and yet is not unknown. Its effect is like that of a higher thought or a better emotion coming over me, when I deemed I was thinking justly or doing right.

6 Yet it is certain that the power to produce this delight does not reside in nature, but in man, or in a harmony of both. It is necessary to use these pleasures with great temperance. For nature is not always tricked[2] in holiday attire, but the same scene which yesterday breathed perfume and glittered as for the frolic of the nymphs is overspread with melancholy today. Nature always wears the colors of the spirit. To a man laboring under calamity, the heat of his own fire hath sadness in it. Then there is a kind of contempt of the landscape felt by him who has just lost by death a dear friend. The sky is less grand as it shuts down over less worth in the population.

– mimetic quality

2. **tricked** *v.* dressed.

Reading Strategy
Challenging the Text Do you agree or disagree with this statement about a harmony between human beings and nature? Explain.

Critical Reading

1. **Respond:** Which of your experiences have made you "glad to the brink of fear"? Explain.
2. **(a) Recall:** Under what circumstances, according to Emerson, does "mean egotism" vanish? **(b) Define:** How would you define Emerson's idea of "mean egotism"? **(c) Analyze Cause and Effect:** In nature, with what emotional state does Emerson suggest that "mean egotism" is replaced?
3. **(a) Recall:** When does Emerson become a "transparent eyeball"? **(b) Analyze:** What are the characteristics of this experience? **(c) Connect:** In what ways does this description reflect the Transcendentalist belief in an Over-Soul?
4. **(a) Recall:** Where does the power to produce nature's delight come from? **(b) Define:** In stating that there is a harmony between human beings and nature, do you think Emerson means the relationship is always serene, or not? Explain.
5. **(a) Infer:** According to Emerson, is our experience with nature the same every time we go to the woods? Explain. **(b) Interpret:** What does Emerson mean when he says that "Nature always wears the colors of the spirit"?
6. **(a) Evaluate:** What is Emerson's main point in this essay? **(b) Assess:** Do you find Emerson's message convincing? Explain why you do or do not accept his ideas about nature.
7. **Take a Position:** Do you find any evidence of Emerson's reverence for nature in American culture today? Explain.

Go Online — Author Link
For: More about Ralph Waldo Emerson
Visit: www.PHSchool.com
Web Code: ere-9311

Enrichment

Emerson's Abolitionist Views

After the passage of the Fugitive Slave Act, which required people to return runaway slaves to the owners, Emerson became an active and vocal abolitionist. He remarked that anyone building a house should include space in it for fugitive slaves. Prompt students to discuss how Emerson's position on slavery relates to his statement in this essay that "Nothing is at last sacred but the integrity of your own mind."

Encourage interested students to find out more about the details of the Fugitive Slave Act and the Compromise of 1850 of which it was part. Have them research how abolitionists responded to the law. Invite students to share any incidents and anecdotes they encounter.

from

7 # Self-Reliance

RALPH WALDO EMERSON

There is a time in every man's education when he arrives at the conviction that envy is ignorance; that imitation is suicide; that he must take himself for better, for worse, as his portion; that though the wide universe is full of good, no kernel of nourishing corn can come to him but through his toil bestowed on that plot of ground which is given to him to till. The power which resides in him is new in nature, and none but he knows what that is which he can do, nor does he know until he has tried. Not for nothing one face, one character, one fact makes much impression on him, and another none. This sculpture in the memory is not without preestablished harmony. The eye was placed where one ray should fall, that it might testify of that particular ray. We but half express ourselves, and are ashamed of that divine idea which each of us represents. It may be safely trusted as proportionate and of good issues, so it be faithfully imparted, but God will not have his work made manifest by cowards. A man is relieved and gay when he has put his heart into his work and done his best; but what he has said or done otherwise, shall give him no peace. It is a deliverance which does not deliver. In the attempt his genius deserts him; no muse befriends; no invention, no hope.

Trust thyself: every heart vibrates to that iron string. Accept the place the divine providence has found for you; the society of your contemporaries, the connection of events. Great men have always done so and confided themselves childlike to the genius of their age, betraying their perception that the absolutely trustworthy was stirring at their heart, working through their hands, predominating in all their being. And we are now men, and must accept in the highest mind the same transcendent destiny; and not minors and invalids in a protected corner, but guides, redeemers, and benefactors. Obeying the Almighty effort and advancing on chaos and the Dark. . . .

9 Society everywhere is in conspiracy against the manhood of every one of its members. Society is a joint-stock company in which the members agree for the better securing of his bread to each shareholder,

Literary Analysis
Transcendentalism
What does the passage beginning "Trust thyself" tell you about Emerson's belief in the importance of the individual?

Vocabulary Builder
chaos (kā´ äs´) *n.* disorder of matter and space, supposed to have existed before the ordered universe

Reading Check
What does Emerson believe about being true to oneself?

7 About the Selections

In his essay, "Self-Reliance," which echoes a theme common to many of his works, Emerson exhorts readers to avoid blindly conforming to the ideas and behavior dictated by society or peers. Instead, he urges people to think and act independently.

In the poems "Concord Hymn" and "The Snowstorm," Emerson continues his celebration of country and nature. In "Concord Hymn," Emerson praises the bravery of the minutemen who fought at Lexington and Concord. The poem conveys the message that people who make great sacrifices for noble causes such as freedom will never be forgotten. In "The Snowstorm," Emerson develops an extended metaphor in which he compares nature's force during a snowstorm to an architect crafting a building. The poem conveys the message that nature is capable of creating works of amazing beauty that parallel or surpass those produced by human beings.

8 Literary Analysis
Transcendentalism

- Read aloud the bracketed text to students, and then reread the opening two words: "Trust thyself." Urge students to find evidence in the paragraph for this opening exhortation.
- To help students, go around the classroom and have volunteers express the meaning of each sentence in their own words.
- **Ask** students the Literary Analysis question: What does the passage beginning "Trust thyself" tell you about Emerson's belief in the importance of the individual? **Possible response:** He believes the individual's importance is from God and that people must therefore honor it and trust in it.

9 Reading Check

Answer: Emerson believes it produces the best work and the most spiritual peace. He believes that unless one is true to oneself, one will never find inspiration.

Differentiated Instruction
Solutions for All Learners

Strategy for Special Needs Students
Have students read the essay in small groups, pausing at the end of each paragraph to identify the sentence that best sums up its meaning. Students should then try to restate the meaning of each topic sentence in their own words. Circulate to check on the progress of the groups and clarify any misinterpretations.

Strategy for Less Proficient Readers
Encourage students to look closely at the first sentence of each paragraph. These sentences essentially serve as an outline of the key points in the essay. By grasping the ideas in these sentences, students will be well on their way to identifying Emerson's main ideas. Have students draft a list of the main points.

Enrichment for Gifted/Talented Students
Ask students to review what they have learned about Emerson's life and writings. Then, challenge them to give a brief talk to the class in which they relate information about Emerson's personal experiences to the ideas he discusses in *Nature* and *Self-Reliance*.

ASSESS

Answers

1. Students may cite our society's tendency to admire "self-made" people.
2. (a) He describes it as a joint-stock company. (b) Its purpose is to conspire against individual self-reliance. (c) People should not care how others perceive them.
3. (a) They were all misunderstood. (b) He points out that some of the greatest people who ever lived were misunderstood.
4. (a) It is important because it distinguishes between a rational consistency of thought and purpose and an unreasoning, compulsory conformity.
   (b) **Possible response:** Emerson clearly said that a *foolish* consistency was to be avoided. He would be unlikely to advocate inconsistency in scholarship, for example, or in friendships or family life.
5. (a) For Emerson, the divine is God's idea of what each of us might be if we had the courage to live up to our full creative potential. (b) **Possible response:** He would say that the reason for living is to seek out God's purpose for us and to pursue it without fear of society's pressures and opinions. Students' explanations should be supported with references from the text.
6. Students' responses should reflect a careful reading of the essay.

Go Online Author Link For additional information about Ralph Waldo Emerson, have students type in the Web Code, then select E from the alphabet, and then select Ralph Waldo Emerson.

to surrender the liberty and culture of the eater. The virtue in most request is conformity. Self-reliance is its aversion. It loves not realities and creators, but names and customs.

Whoso would be a man must be a nonconformist. He who would gather immortal palms must not be hindered by the name of goodness, but must explore if it be goodness. Nothing is at last sacred but the integrity of your own mind. Absolve you to yourself, and you shall have the suffrage of the world. . . .

A foolish consistency is the hobgoblin of little minds, adored by little statesmen and philosophers and divines. With consistency a great soul has simply nothing to do. He may as well concern himself with his shadow on the wall. Speak what you think now in hard words and tomorrow speak what tomorrow thinks in hard words again, though it contradict everything you said today. "Ah, so you shall be sure to be misunderstood?"—is it so bad, then, to be misunderstood? Pythagoras was misunderstood, and Socrates, and Jesus, and Luther, and Copernicus, and Galileo, and Newton,[1] and every pure and wise spirit that ever took flesh. To be great is to be misunderstood. . . .

1. **Pythagoras . . . Newton** individuals who made major contributions to scientific, philosophical, or religious thinking.

Vocabulary Builder

aversion (ə vur′ zhən) *n.* object arousing an intense dislike

suffrage (suf′ rij) *n.* vote or voting

divines (də vīnz′) *n.* clergy

Critical Reading

1. **Respond:** Which aspects, if any, of today's American culture reflect Emerson's belief in self-reliance?
2. **(a) Recall:** What terms does Emerson use to describe society? **(b) Interpret:** According to Emerson, what is society's main purpose? **(c) Draw Conclusions:** In what ways does Emerson believe people should be affected by the way others perceive them?
3. **(a) Recall:** According to Emerson, what do Pythagoras, Socrates, Jesus, Luther, Copernicus, Galileo, and Newton have in common? **(b) Support:** What evidence does Emerson use to support his claim that "to be great is to be misunderstood"?
4. **(a) Make a Judgment:** How important is Emerson's use of the adjective "foolish" in his discussion of consistency? **(b) Speculate:** Do you think there would be any circumstances in which Emerson would advocate the benefits of consistency? Explain.
5. **(a) Interpret:** According to Emerson, what role does the "divine" have in determining each person's circumstances? **(b) Generalize:** What would Emerson say is each person's reason for living? Explain.
6. **Apply:** Which of Emerson's statements, if any, would you choose as a guideline for personal conduct? Explain.

For: More about Ralph Waldo Emerson
Visit: www.PHSchool.com
Web Code: ere-9311

Enrichment

Early Revolutionary Battles

In April 1775, a British military force marched to confiscate colonial arms they knew were stockpiled in Concord, Massachusetts. Along the way, they were confronted at dawn on April 19 by a small group of militia on the Lexington green. The British dispersed the Americans, killing ten, and then moved on to Concord, five miles away. There, they were met by a larger contingent of militia, who attacked them at the North Bridge. At this spot, the first British blood of the Revolution was spilled. The British retreated to Boston. On the way, they were repeatedly attacked by thousands of American militia. Many years later, sculptor Daniel Chester French created his commemorative statue with the support of a Concord resident who wished to memorialize the spot where Americans fell.

Concord Hymn

Sung at the Completion of the Battle Monument, July 4, 1837

Ralph Waldo Emerson

By the rude[1] bridge that arched the flood,
Their flag to April's breeze unfurled,
Here once the embattled farmers stood,
And fired the shot heard round the world.

The foe long since in silence slept;
Alike the conqueror silent sleeps;
And Time the ruined bridge has swept
Down the dark stream which seaward creeps.

On this green bank, by this soft stream,
We set today a votive[2] stone;
That memory may their deed redeem,
When, like our sires, our sons are gone.

Spirit, that made those heroes dare
To die, and leave their children free,
Bid Time and Nature gently spare
The shaft we raise to them and thee.

1. **rude** (ro͞od) *adj.* crude or rough in form or workmanship.
2. **votive** (vōt′ iv) *adj.* dedicated in fulfillment of a vow or pledge.

⑪ ▲ Critical Viewing
In 1875, the first verse of "Concord Hymn" was carved into the base of this statue commemorating the Minutemen who fought the British in Lexington and Concord on April 19, 1775. What aspects of the sculpture communicate the emotions of the poem? **[Connect]**

Critical Reading

1. **Respond:** What do you think of war monuments? Explain.
2. **(a) Recall:** What event took place by the "rude bridge"? **(b) Interpret:** What does the poet mean by the image of "the shot heard round the world"?
3. **(a) Recall:** What has happened to the bridge since the battle that took place there? **(b) Analyze:** How does the poem's organization reflect a sense of the passage of time?
4. **(a) Recall:** In the last stanza, whom does the poet address directly? **(b) Infer:** In what way does this direct address reflect Transcendentalist beliefs in an Over-Soul?
5. **Apply:** Which aspects of "Concord Hymn" would be appropriate for the dedication of other war monuments?

Go Online
Author Link
For: More about Ralph Waldo Emerson
Visit: www.PHSchool.com
Web Code: ere-9311

⑩ Humanities

Minute Man, 1871–1875, by Daniel Chester French

Daniel Chester French completed this commemorative statue for the centennial of the American Revolution. The project was funded by a Concord resident who wished to mark the spot where Americans fell. *Minute Man* was cast using bronze from a decommissioned Civil War cannon. Emerson, a member of the committee that requested the work, praised the statue at its unveiling. Guide students to notice the position of the soldier's feet and the plow on which his hand rests. Then, ask these questions:

1. What is the significance of the minuteman's firm grip on the plow?
   Answer: It symbolizes that he is a peaceful farmer who took up a rifle because his land and freedom were threatened.
2. Why do you think the minuteman's foot is in a raised position?
   Answer: It shows that the soldier is ready to fight.

⑪ Critical Viewing

Answer: Students should note that, like the poem, the statue captures the courage and devotion of the minutemen.

ASSESS

Answers

1. **Possible response:** It is important to honor those who die defending their countries.
2. (a) Americans fell to British guns. (b) It heralded the founding of a new nation.
3. (a) It has fallen apart. (b) It acknowledges that the events are long past but that people today still revere them.
4. (a) He addresses a "Spirit." (b) It assumes that this spirit created the brave and nonconforming indivdvuals who fought at Concord and Lexington.
5. **Possible response:** The idea that we should honor those who have died for freedom could fit on any war memorial.

Differentiated Instruction Solutions for All Learners

Strategy for Special Needs Students
Work with students stanza by stanza to paraphrase the lines in the poem. Pause after each stanza to invite questions and suggestions about paraphrasing. Continue until all four stanzas have been paraphrased. Then, help students read the complete selection.

Strategy for Less Proficient Readers
Have students read aloud the final stanza of the poem. Help them paraphrase the wish that Emerson expresses in this stanza. Point out that he asks the same Creator or Spirit who inspired the bravery of the minutemen to command time and nature to spare the monument from the ravages of time and the elements.

Strategy for English Learners
Direct students' attention to words such as *rude*. Remind students that words can have multiple meanings. In this case, Emerson has used an uncommon meaning for *rude*. Point out the definition in footnote #1: crude or rough in form or workmanship. Then help students paraphrase the first line. (By a simple bridge over a creek.)

12 Literary Analysis
Transcendentalism

- Read aloud the bracketed passage. Point out that Emerson describes nature's impact on the human experience.
- **Ask** students this Literary Analysis question: How does Emerson's description of the storm and the snowbound people reflect his Transcendentalist beliefs? **Possible answer:** It suggests that nature—which here keeps everyone inside—illuminates human experience by providing a moment of peace within the storm.

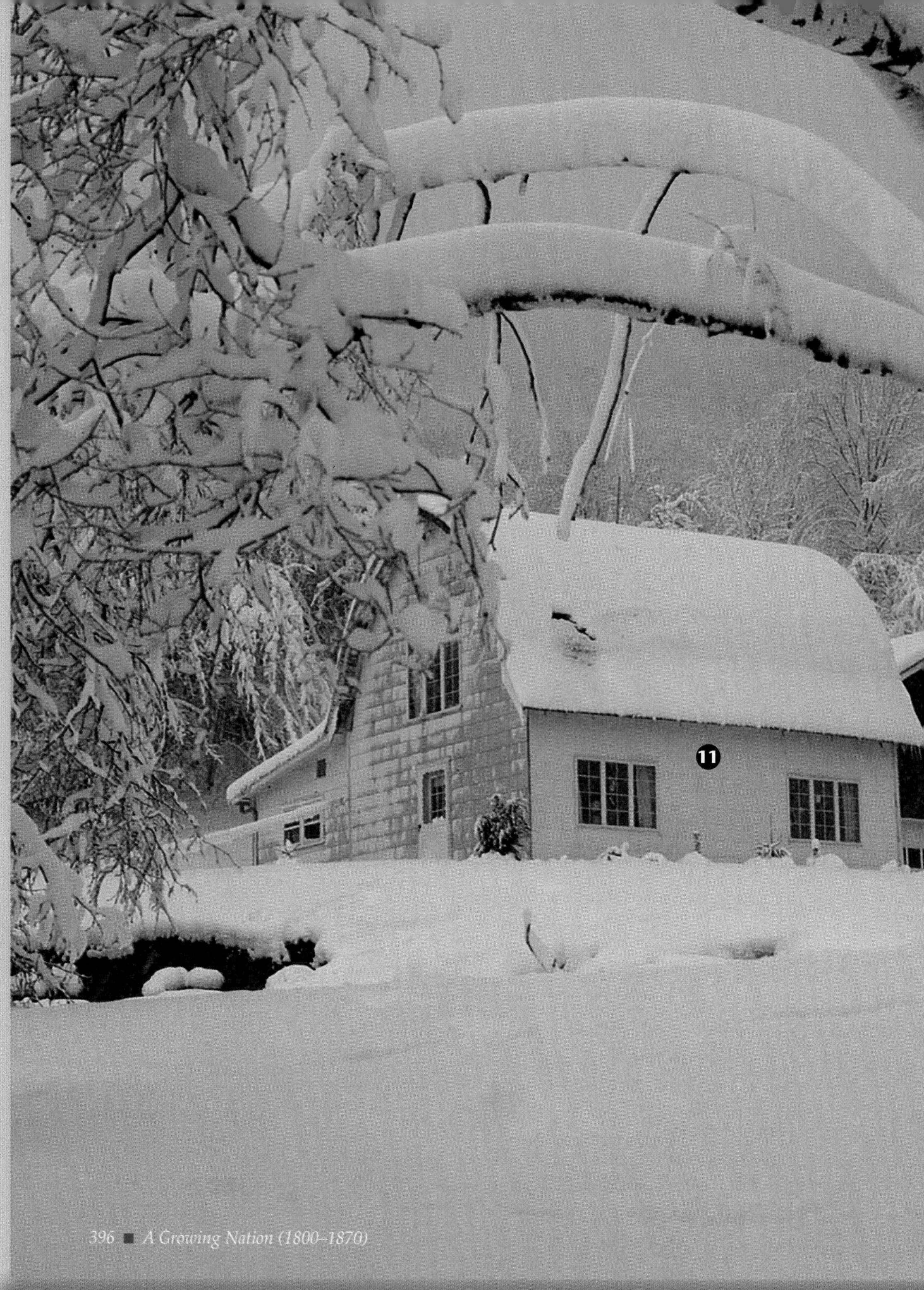

Enrichment

New England Weather

Based on Emerson's description of this snowstorm, it probably qualified as a blizzard. Today, the National Weather Service defines a blizzard as any storm containing strong winds and large amounts of snow. Winds must be blowing steadily at more than thirty-five miles per hour while visibility must be reduced to one-quarter mile over a period of at least three hours.

While some may argue that New England's weather has changed in the years since Emerson wrote "The Snowstorm," the region still has plenty of snowy days and even a few blizzards. For example, the city of Boston has received an average of forty-two inches of snow each year since records have been kept. Other places in New England get significantly more snow, such as Caribou, Maine, which received more than one hundred inches of snow in 1998. About ten of those inches fell in one day during a late January storm.

The Snowstorm

Ralph Waldo Emerson

12 Announced by all the trumpets of the sky,
Arrives the snow, and, driving o'er the fields,
Seems nowhere to alight: the whited air
Hides hills and woods, the river, and the heaven,
And veils the farmhouse at the garden's end.
The sled and traveler stopped, the courier's feet
Delayed, all friends shut out, the house mates sit 14
13 Around the radiant fireplace, enclosed
In a tumultuous privacy of storm.

Vocabulary Builder
radiant (rā′ dē ənt) *adj.* shining brightly

tumultuous (to͞o mul′ cho͞o əs) *adj.* rough; stormy

Reading Check
What action of the wind and snow does the speaker describe?

13 Vocabulary Builder
Latin Root *-radi-*

- Call students' attention to the word *radiant* and its definition.
  Tell students that the Latin word root *-radi-* means "spoke" or "ray."
- Challenge students to suggest other words containing this root.
  Possible answers: radial, radiate, radiator, radio, radiology
- **Ask** students how the word *radiant* contributes to the meaning of the stanza.
  Possible response: It evokes a cozy mood by suggesting that the fireplace's heat and security radiate through the room to shield occupants from the storm.

14 Reading Check
Answer: He describes the arrival of the snow and wind, the wind's blowing of the snow, the snow's covering of buildings and landscape.

Differentiated Instruction Solutions for All Learners

Support for Less Proficient Readers
As students read the poem, help them understand Emerson's extended metaphor. Direct students' attention to the final stanza. Guide students to understand that the snowstorm, by coating everything with snow, has created the illusion that it has formed from snow in a single night buildings that would take people years to build.

Strategy for English Learners
Review the definition of metaphor with students and explain that sometimes writers extend a metaphor throughout a work. In "The Snowstorm," Emerson compares nature to a human architect. Help students find examples of the metaphor, such as Emerson's description of the "north wind's masonry."

Enrichment for Advanced Readers
Draw students' attention to the extended metaphor Emerson uses to describe the effect of the snowstorm. Then, remind students of reading the excerpt from *Snowbound* (p. 282). Challenge students to compare and contrast the figurative language each poet uses to describe snow and snowstorms.

ASSESS

Answers

1. **Possible response:** I am similarly fascinated by the visual effects snow can create, although at times these cause me inconvenience.
2. (a) The sled and traveler must stop; the courier is delayed; the house mates remain inside together.
   (b) **Possible response:** He means that the storm's disturbance creates privacy by keeping visitors away and keeping residents from leaving.
3. (a) The following words relate to the design and construction of buildings: *masonry, quarry, furnished with tile, artificer, bastions, projected roof, work, number or proportion, coop or kennel, wall to wall.*
   (b) They suggest that he views the snowstorm as a gifted creator or artisan.
4. (a) It leaves human artists and architects to imitate, slowly and with difficulty, what the storm created overnight.
   (b) It reflects the idea that humans can find a parallel to their own creative force in nature and vice versa.
5. **Possible response:** Snowstorms can cause tremendous damage to buildings and to nature, as well as to business through transportation delays, stranded employees, and lack of commerce.

Go Online Author Link For additional information about Ralph Waldo Emerson, have students type in the Web Code, then select E from the alphabet, and then select Ralph Waldo Emerson.

Come see the north wind's masonry.
Out of an unseen quarry evermore
Furnished with tile, the fierce artificer
Curves his white bastions with projected roof
Round every windward stake, or tree, or door.
Speeding, the myriad-handed, his wild work
So fanciful, so savage, nought cares he
For number or proportion. Mockingly,
On coop or kennel he hangs Parian[1] wreaths;
A swan-like form invests the hidden thorn;
Fills up the farmer's lane from wall to wall.

Maugre[2] the farmer's sighs; and at the gate
A tapering turret overtops the work.
And when his hours are numbered, and the world
Is all his own, retiring, as he were not,
Leaves, when the sun appears, astonished Art
To mimic in slow structures, stone by stone,
Built in an age, the mad wind's nightwork,
The frolic architecture of the snow.

1. **Parian** (per′ ē ən) *adj.* referring to a fine, white marble of the Greek city Paros.
2. **Maugre** (mô′ gər) *prep.* in spite of.

Vocabulary Builder
bastions (bas′ chənz) *n.* fortifications

Critical Reading

1. **Respond:** How does your attitude toward snow compare with Emerson's?
2. **(a) Recall:** In the first stanza, what effect does the storm have on the "sled and traveler," the "courier," and the "house mates"?
   (b) Analyze: Explain what Emerson means when he refers to the "tumultuous privacy of the storm" in line 9.
3. **(a) Recall:** In the second stanza, which words relate to the design and construction of buildings? **(b) Analyze:** What do these words suggest about the comparison the poet is making between the storm and an architect or artist?
4. **(a) Recall:** According to lines 25–28, what has the storm left behind "when the sun appears"? **(b) Synthesize:** Which aspects of Emerson's Transcendentalist beliefs does this image reflect?
5. **Speculate:** Emerson expresses a favorable attitude toward the snowstorm. Why might some people living in northern climates not share Emerson's attitude?

For: More about Ralph Waldo Emerson
Visit: www.PHSchool.com
Web Code: ere-9311

Apply the Skills

from *Nature* • from *Self-Reliance* • *Concord Hymn* • *The Snowstorm*

Literary Analysis

Transcendentalism

1. What does "Nature" reveal about the **Transcendentalist** attitude toward nature? Support your answers with examples from the text.
2. Emerson writes: "Speak what you think now in hard words and tomorrow speak what tomorrow thinks in hard words, though it contradict everything you said today." In what ways does this statement reflect the Transcendentalist belief in intuition?
3. Does the image of a "transparent eyeball" effectively convey the Transcendentalist idea of a universal Over-Soul? Explain.

Comparing Literary Works

4. **(a)** Use a chart like the one shown to compare and contrast Emerson's descriptions of the bonds between people in society and those between people and nature. **(b)** Which bonds would Emerson say are more important? Explain.

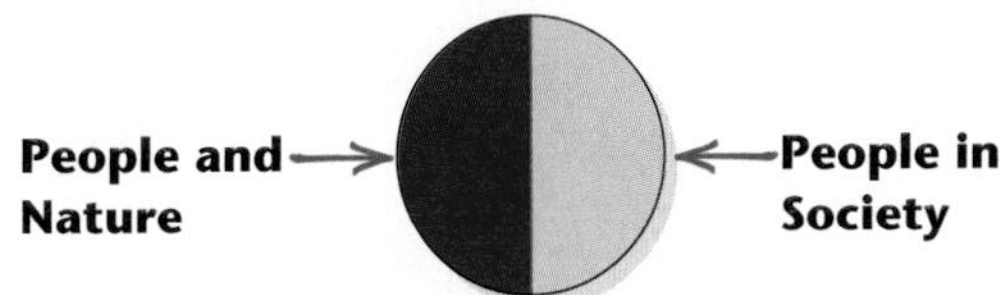

5. In "Nature," Emerson says the woods are the "plantations of God," and in "Self-Reliance," he portrays individuals as "that divine idea which each of us represents." Do these passages express similar ideas about the relationship of God to people and the world? Explain.

Reading Strategy

Challenging the Text

6. Consider this assertion from "Self-Reliance": "A foolish consistency is the hobgoblin of little minds." **Challenge the text** by answering these questions: **(a)** What evidence does Emerson provide to support his position? **(b)** Offer two arguments against this statement. **(c)** Do you agree with this statement? Support your answer.

Extend Understanding

7. **Cultural Connection:** Some cultures view children as innocents, and others view them as inherently bad. How do you think the Transcendentalists viewed childhood? Support your answer.

QuickReview

The **Transcendentalist** philosophy asserts that knowledge of fundamental reality is beyond the reach of a person's limited senses and is derived through intuition rather than sensory experience.

To **challenge the text,** question the author's assertions and decide whether or not you agree with them.

Go Online Assessment

For: Self-test
Visit: www.PHSchool.com
Web Code: era-6307

Students may use the **Self-test** to prepare for **Selection Test A** or **Selection Test B.**

Answers

1. The Transcendentalists loved nature and were interested in humanity's relationship to it. Emerson says that nature has the power to fill him with joy and childlike wonder. He also believes that nature reflects personal moods.
2. The Transcendentalists believed that since real truths cannot be found in physical reality, we must trust intuition.
3. The image suggests that the speaker sees all, but can also blend with everything around him, merging into the universal Over-Soul.
4. (a) Emerson suggests that our relationship to nature transcends personal relationships, since social ties are largely expedients for material survival, whereas our relationship to nature binds us to the spiritual foundation of life.
(b) Emerson seems to have regarded the relationship between people and nature as more essential than the relationships between people in society.

   Another sample answer can be found on **Literary Analysis Graphic Organizer B,** p. 78 in ***Graphic Organizer Transparencies.***
5. Both phrases suggest that Emerson believed in a God who had some role in creating both humans and nature.
6. (a) Emerson claims that only small-minded people are consistent; people with great minds speak their opinions, even if they change with time. Inconsistency will cause you to be misunderstood as the greatest and wisest people have been.
(b) **Possible response:** People who are inconsistent don't take the time to think before they speak. Misunderstood people are not necessarily great; they may have poorly organized ideas.
(c) Students should explain the reasoning behind their responses.
7. **Possible response:** They probably viewed childhood as a time free of the constraints of social convention and abundant in the leisure to explore nature.

EXTEND/ASSESS

Answers

❶ Vocabulary Lesson

Word Analysis

1. A radiator projects heat into a room.
2. To radiate is to send out rays of light, heat, or other energy.
3. A radio receives waves from a transmitter and converts them into sound that radiates from its speakers.
4. The radius of a circle is the measurement from the center to the periphery.
5. Radiation is the process by which energy in the form of rays of light, heat, etc. is emitted.
6. Matter is radioactive when it gives off radiation.

Spelling Strategy

1. breathe
2. clothe
3. lithe
4. writhe
5. seethe
6. lathe

Vocabulary Builder

1. antonyms
2. synonyms
3. synonyms
4. synonyms
5. antonyms
6. antonyms
7. synonyms
8. antonyms
9. synonyms

❷ Grammar and Style Lesson

Looking at Style

Students should identify passages in which sentence length varies by at least ten words and describe their effect on the reader.

Writing Application

Paragraphs should focus on a short journey and should contain at least three sentences that vary in length by more than ten words from the other sentences. Students should correctly highlight short and long sentences.

WG Writing and Grammar, Ruby Level

Students will find further instruction and practice on coordinate adjectives in Chapter 20, Section 3.

Build Language Skills

❶ Vocabulary Lesson

Word Analysis: Latin Root *-radi-*

The Latin root *-radi-* means "spoke" or "ray." This root contributes to the meaning of *radiant*—"shining brightly" or "giving off rays of light."

Knowing the meaning of the root *-radi-*, write a definition for each of these words.

1. radiator
2. radiate
3. radio
4. radius
5. radiation
6. radioactive

Spelling Strategy

A final silent *e* often helps create the sound of a long vowel followed by a voiced *th*—for example, as in *blithe*. Follow this principle to complete the spelling of each word.

1. brea__
2. clo__
3. li__
4. wri__
5. see__
6. la__

Vocabulary Builder: Antonyms or Synonyms?

Review the vocabulary list on page 389. Then, study each item below to identify which of the following word pairs are antonyms and which are synonyms.

1. chaos, order
2. aversion, repugnance
3. suffrage, vote
4. divines, ministers
5. blithe, anxious
6. connate, acquired
7. radiant, luminous
8. tumultuous, serene
9. bastions, bulwarks

❷ Grammar and Style Lesson

Varying Sentence Length

In "Nature" and "Self-Reliance," Emerson often follows a very long sentence with one or more short ones. **Varying sentence length** enables Emerson to sustain the reader's interest and to establish rhythm. In addition, he often uses a short sentence to clarify or emphasize ideas he has expressed in the longer sentence preceding it. Notice this pattern in the example from "Nature":

> Crossing a bare common, in snow puddles, at twilight, under a clouded sky, without having in my thoughts any occurrence of special good fortune, I have enjoyed a perfect exhilaration. I am glad to the brink of fear.

Looking at Style Find three passages from Emerson's essays in which he varies the length of his sentences. Explain the effect of the sentence variations in each passage.

Writing Application Write one paragraph describing your walk home from school or some other short journey. Vary your sentence length to create rhythm and maintain reader interest.

After you draft, highlight your short sentences in one color and your long sentences in another color to see the pattern you have established. In what ways does varying your sentence length improve your writing?

WG Prentice Hall Writing and Grammar Connection: Chapter 20, Section 3

Assessment Practice

Make Inferences and Generalizations **(For more practice, see *Standardized Test Preparation Workbook*, p.22.)**

The reading sections of tests often require students to make inferences that are drawn from implied information in written texts. For example, students might be asked to recognize implied messages found in poetry.

According to the third stanza of "Concord Hymn," what is the purpose of the monument?

A to remember the sacrifices made by Revolutionary War soldiers

B to add support to the crumbling Lexington bridge

C to commemorate the British soldiers who died in the American Revolution

D to direct visitors to the towns of Lexington and Concord

The last three answers contain incorrect information. *A* is supported by the lines, "That memory may their deed redeem/When, like our sires, our sons are gone."

Writing Lesson

Timed Writing: Critical Evaluation of a Philosophical Essay

Ever since they were first published, Emerson's essays have incited argument, and inspired imitation. Now, it is your turn to add your voice. Write a critical evaluation of "Self-Reliance." Include a summary of Emerson's points, a statement of opinion, and an assessment of the ways in which the argument is made. ***(40 minutes)***

Prewriting ***(10 minutes)*** Reread "Self-Reliance," noting key ideas from the beginning, middle, and end. Observe how Emerson leads the reader from one thought to the next. Then, write one sentence that summarizes Emerson's argument. Phrase his ideas in your own words.

Drafting ***(20 minutes)*** In your introduction, state the goals of your essay. Then, write out your summary of Emerson's essay. Follow the summary with a statement of your opinion of his ideas and how he presents them. Support your ideas with citations from the text.

Model: Using Relevant Citations

Emerson pays tribute to the value of being true to oneself. While most of us would agree with him in theory, how many of us withstand the pressures to conform? Emerson notes, "The virtue in most request is conformity."

Citations specific to the argument keep the writing focused.

Revising ***(10 minutes)*** Highlight any citations that do not effectively support your point. Replace weak citations with more relevant support.

WG Prentice Hall Writing and Grammar Connection: Chapter 14, Section 3

Extend Your Learning

Listening and Speaking Create a **public service announcement** urging people to resist conformity. Strengthen your position with two types of reasoning:

- inductive reasoning (use evidence to arrive at a general conclusion)
- deductive reasoning (start with a premise and then support it with evidence)

Begin your announcement with a catchy phrase that will stick in listeners' minds. Then, record your announcement and share it with the class.

Research and Technology According to Emerson, the misunderstood individual joins the ranks of Pythagoras, Socrates, Jesus, Joan of Arc, and others. With a group, research and write a **profile** of one of these "great souls" to learn how or why the person was misunderstood. Share your profile with other groups. **[Group Activity]**

For: An additional research activity
Visit: www.PHSchool.com
Web Code: erd-7307

3 Writing Lesson

You may use this Writing Lesson as timed-writing practice, or you may allow students to develop the critical evaluation as a writing assignment over several days.

- To guide students in writing this critical evaluation, give them the **Support for Writing Lesson,** p. 128 in ***Unit 3 Resources***.
- Review the essay with students, confirming their understanding of its main ideas. Then remind them to use the Reading Strategy, Challenging the Text, to build arguments for their analysis.
- After discussing the steps in the Writing Lesson, emphasize the importance of building clear arguments that are solidly supported by evidence from the text.
- Use the Response to Literature rubrics in ***General Resources***, pp. 65–66, to evaluate student essays.

4 Research and Technology

- Organize students into groups to research an individual from the provided list. You might also mention Martin Luther, Copernicus, Galileo, and Isaac Newton as possible topics.
- Encourage students to explore online and electronic resources, downloading original writings by or about their featured individual.
- Have the group organize a brief report and present it to the class.
- Have students use the Research Report rubrics in ***General Resources,*** pp. 49–50.
- The **Support for Extend Your Learning** page (***Unit 3 Resources,*** p. 129) provides guided note-taking opportunities to help students complete the Extend Your Learning activities.

Go Online Research — Have students type in the Web Code for another research activity.

Assessment Resources

The following resources can be used to assess students' knowledge and skills.

Unit 3 Resources
Selection Test A, pp. 131–133
Selection Test B, pp. 134–136

General Resources
Rubrics for Response to Literature, pp. 65–66
Rubrics for Research Report, pp. 49–50

Go Online Assessment — Students may use the **Self-test** to prepare for **Selection Test A** or **Selection Test B.**

Meeting Your Standards

Students will

1. **analyze and respond to literary elements.**
   - Literary Analysis: Style
2. **read, comprehend, analyze, and critique a journal and an essay.**
   - Reading Strategy: Evaluating the Writer's Statement of Philosophy
   - Reading Check questions
   - Apply the Skills questions
   - Assessment Practice (ATE)
3. **develop vocabulary.**
   - Vocabulary Lesson: Latin Root: *-flu-*
4. **understand and apply written and oral language conventions.**
   - Spelling Strategy
   - Grammar and Style Lesson: Infinitives and Infinitive Phrases
5. **develop writing proficiency.**
   - Writing Lesson: Editorial
6. **develop appropriate research strategies.**
   - Extend Your Learning: Oral Presentation
7. **understand and apply listening and speaking strategies.**
   - Extend Your Learning: Debate

Block Scheduling: Use one 90-minute class period to preteach the skills and have students read the selection. Use a second 90-minute class period to assess students' mastery of skills, extend their learning, and monitor their progress.

Homework Suggestions

Following are possibilities for homework assignments.

- Support pages from *Unit 3 Resources:*
  Literary Analysis
  Reading Strategy
  Vocabulary Builder
  Grammar and Style
- An Extend Your Learning project and the Writing Lesson for this selection group may be completed over several days.

Step-by-Step Teaching Guide	Pacing Guide
PRETEACH	
• Administer Vocabulary and Reading Warm-ups as necessary.	5 min.
• Engage students' interest with the motivation activity.	5 min.
• Read and discuss author, background, and From the Scholar's Desk features. **FT**	10 min.
• Introduce the Literary Analysis Skill: Style. **FT**	5 min.
• Introduce the Reading Strategy: Evaluating the Writer's Statement of Philosophy. **FT**	10 min.
• Prepare students to read by teaching the selection vocabulary. **FT**	
TEACH	
• Informally monitor comprehension while students read independently or in groups. **FT**	30 min.
• Monitor students' comprehension with the Reading Check notes.	as students read
• Reinforce vocabulary with Vocabulary Builder notes.	as students read
• Develop students' understanding of style with the Literary Analysis annotations. **FT**	5 min.
• Develop students' ability to evaluate the writer's statement of philosophy with the Reading Strategy annotations. **FT**	5 min.
ASSESS/EXTEND	
• Assess students' comprehension and mastery of the Literary Analysis and Reading Strategy by having them answer the Apply the Skills questions. **FT**	15 min.
• Have students complete the Vocabulary Lesson and the Grammar and Style Lesson. **FT**	15 min.
• Apply students' ability to identify cause and effect by using the Writing Lesson. **FT**	45 min. or homework
• Apply students' understanding by using one or more of the Extend Your Learning activities.	20–90 min. or homework
• Administer Selection Test A or Selection Test B. **FT**	15 min.

Resources

PRINT

Unit 3 Resources

From the Scholar's Desk . . . . p. 137
Listening and Viewing . . . . p. 138
Vocabulary Warm-up Word Lists **[L1, L2, EL]** . . . . p. 139
Vocabulary Warm-up Practice **[L1, L2, EL]** . . . . p. 140
Reading Warm-up A **[L1, L2, EL]** . . . . p. 141
Reading Warm-up B **[L1, L2, L3]** . . . . p. 142

TRANSPARENCY

Graphic Organizer Transparencies

Literary Analysis Graphic Organizer A **[L3]** . . . . p. 81
Literary Analysis Graphic Organizer B **[L1, L2, EL]** . . . . p. 82
Reading Strategy Graphic Organizer A **[L3]** . . . . p. 79
Reading Strategy Graphic Organizer B **[L1, L2, EL]** . . . . p. 80

TECHNOLOGY

From the Scholar's Desk DVD . . . . Gretel Ehrlich, Segment 2

PRINT

Reader's Notebook [L2]
Reader's Notebook: Adapted Version [L1]
Reader's Notebook: English Learner's Version [EL]

Unit 3 Resources

Literary Analysis **[L3]** . . . . p. 143
Reading Strategy **[L3]** . . . . p. 144
Vocabulary Builder **[L3]** . . . . p. 145

TECHNOLOGY

Listening to Literature Audio CDs [L2, EL]
Reader's Notebook: Adapted Version Audio CD [L1, L2]

PRINT

Unit 3 Resources

Grammar and Style **[L3]** . . . . p. 146
Support for Writing Lesson **[L3]** . . . . p. 147
Support for Extend Your Learning **[L3]** . . . . p. 148
Enrichment **[L4]** . . . . p. 149
Selection Test A **[L1, L2, EL]** . . . . pp. 150–152
Selection Test B **[L3, L4]** . . . . pp. 153–55

TRANSPARENCY

Graphic Organizer Transparencies

Cause-and-Effect Flowchart . . . . p. 305

General Resources

Rubrics for Persuasion: Persuasive Essay **[L3]** . . . . pp. 45–46
Rubrics for Speaking Presenting Pros and Cons **[L3]** . . . . p. 92

TECHNOLOGY

Go Online: Research **[L3]**
Go Online: Self-test **[L3]**
***ExamView®*, Test Bank [L3]**

Choosing Resources for Differentiated Instruction

[L1] Special Needs Students
[L2] Below-Level Students
[L3] All Students
[L4] Advanced Students
[EL] English Learners

FT Fast Track Instruction: To move the lesson more quickly, use the strategies and activities identified with **FT**.

Scaffolding for Less Proficient and Advanced Students

The leveled Critical Thinking questions after selections progress in the levels of thinking required to answer them. To address the needs of your different students, you may use the (a) level questions for your less proficient students and the (b) level questions with your on-level and advanced students. The occasional (c) level questions are appropriate for your advanced students.

PRENTICE HALL **TeacherEXPRESS™** Plan · Teach · Assess — Use this complete suite of powerful teaching tools to make lesson planning and testing quicker and easier.

PRENTICE HALL **StudentEXPRESS™** Learn · Study · Succeed — Use the interactive textbook (online and on CD-ROM) to make selections and activities come alive with audio and video support and interactive questions.

 From the Scholar's Desk

Introduce Gretel Ehrlich

- You might wish to have students reread Ehrlich's introduction to this unit on pages 242–243.
- Gretel Ehrlich, an eloquent nature writer, comments on Henry David Thoreau's great and influential work, *Walden* (page 406). Other commentaries by Ehrlich appear elsewhere in this book, on pages 242, 243, and 459.
- Have students read the introductory paragraph about Gretel Ehrlich. She lived a number of years in Greenland, a place of great and desolate beauty. Living in such an environment was influential to her work; many of her books carry naturalistic themes.
- Use the *From the Author's Desk DVD* to introduce Gretel Ehrlich. Show Segment 2 to provide insight into her writing. After students have watched the segment, **ask:** What does the writing of Gretel Ehrlich reveal about her attitude toward nature? **Answer:** Her writing shows that understanding nature can help people understand themselves. Ehrlich organized her book *This Cold Heaven* according to seasons of the year.

Living from the Inside Out

- After students have read about the effect of Thoreau's writing on Ehrlich, **Ask:** What does Ehrlich mean when she talks about living "from the inside out?"
  Answer: She means that people should focus their energies on taking in the world, thinking about it, and responding to it rather than being distracted by external forces, such as the quest for status or material goods.

Critical Viewing

Possible response: The snow and ice-covered trees and the stillness of the lake capture Thoreau's "auroral character."

From the Scholar's Desk

GRETEL EHRLICH INTRODUCES
from Walden *by Henry David Thoreau*

Discovering Thoreau

When I was in high school, my parents took me to look at colleges on the east coast, and on that trip, we visited Walden Pond. I'd bought a collection of Thoreau's essays at a bookstore in Boston, and standing at the edge of the pond, I read *Walden*. My parents had lived nearby before I was born, but I grew up on the central California coast. Thoreau's landscape was not familiar to me, and yet the ideas he expressed in his book-length essay *Walden* spoke to me as no others had.

Living From the Inside Out An essay is essentially a way of asking a question. It is an attempt to understand the nature of things: the human condition and the natural world. Thoreau's questions to me, the reader, asked me to think about where I lived and how I lived in that place. That "owning" land or a house is not as important as becoming friends with that place. That rich and poor are unimportant, but that how you meet your life and how you live from moment to moment, day to day, is most important of all.

Living comes from the inside out, not from an outsider's view of who you are. Life is change. The weather changes, our relationships

Gretel Ehrlich

Gretel Ehrlich is the author of more than a dozen works of nonfiction, fiction, and poetry, including the essay collection *The Solace of Open Spaces* and *The Future of Ice: A Journey Into Cold.*

▼ **Critical Viewing**
What details in this early hand-painted photograph of Walden Pond capture what Thoreau calls "the auroral character" of the setting? **[Connect]**

Teaching Resources

The following resources can be used to enrich or extend the instruction for From the Scholar's Desk.

Unit 3 Resources
- **From the Scholar's Desk** p. 137
- **Listening and Viewing,** p. 138

From the Author's Desk DVD
- **Gretel Ehrlich, Segment 2**

with one another change, our bodies change. To be static is to be dead. To live in harmony with nature means to roll with those changes daily, yearly, moment by moment.

Contemplating One Ripple in the Pond These days we go about our lives with so much speed and so much extraneous information that it's difficult to contemplate just one thing, one sight, one evening or morning, one ripple in the pond. Thoreau would have us simplify, slow down, become quiet, and burrow into the heart of things with our minds. Not to "dumb down," but the opposite: to stop, listen, and see; to turn off the monologue in our minds; to erase our idea about how things are; to live in others' shoes.

Building a Fire in the Mind Thoreau would have us think like a river, a pond, a tree, another animal or human; to adopt their point of view instead of our own; to build a fire in the mind with real wood and a match that cannot be extinguished. Then, the fresh, dawnlike nature of things— what Thoreau calls "the auroral character"— will keep radiating, piercing the difficulties in our lives with new songs. A hut in the woods, a still pond, a fresh breeze: these morning winds carry poems, music, love, and loss into our days. Not a dreaminess, but the direct experience of life as it is.

Marching to a Different Drummer Thoreau encourages us to advance confidently in the direction of our dreams. He encourages each of us to be our own person—distinct, unique, thoughtful, precise, and passionate about what we love in the world. It is good to march to "a different drummer," if that's where our feet take us. To live fully, deeply, profoundly, unafraid to be ourselves—this is advice that travels forward for centuries, through all our lives.

Thinking About the Commentary

1. **(a) Recall:** What do Thoreau's questions ask Ehrlich—and all readers—to think about? **(b) Interpret:** In what way might Thoreau's questions help readers live "from the inside out"?
2. **(a) Recall:** What would Thoreau have people do in a complex world? **(b) Speculate:** How might following Thoreau's advice change the way you live in the twenty-first century?

As You Read *from* Walden . . .

3. Consider what relevance Thoreau's ideas have in today's world and in your own life.
4. Think about the ways in which Ehrlich's commentary enriches your reading of Thoreau.

ASSESS

Answers

1. (a) Thoreau's questions ask readers to think about where they live and how they live. (b) Thoreau's questions focus not on the material world or the world of achievement and striving, but on the connection between people and nature. The questions make people think about and respond to the world around them.
2. (a) Thoreau would have people "simplify" their lives. (b) Possible answer: Thoreau might inspire twenty-first century people to view less mediocre television, spend less time in trivial activities, think less about material gain. His writings might also encourage people to create a mental haven from the constant motion of our world, as he did in withdrawing to Walden Pond, in order to find what is really essential.
3. **Possible answer:** Thoreau still seems relevant, because the world today is even more distracting than his was, and his advice to step back and think about what is essential is as needed as ever.
4. **Possible answer:** Ehrlich's commentary shows how Thoreau's words resonated with someone living in a different time and place from him. As a contemporary woman, she creates a bridge to Thoreau.

PRETEACH

Motivation

Share with students the following quotation from Thoreau: "I went to the woods because I wished to live deliberately, to front only the essential facts of life." Have students imagine that they are about to spend some time alone in the wilderness. Ask them to tell what essentials they would bring with them other than the necessities associated with food and shelter. Prompt them to predict what the experience would be like, physically, emotionally, and spiritually. Invite students who have spent any time in wilderness areas to tell about it. Explain that the works they are about to read are drawn from the ideas and philosophies Thoreau developed while voluntarily living a life of rustic isolation.

❶ Background

More About the Author

In "Civil Disobedience," Thoreau questions the government's right to tell him what to do. In life, he also questioned its right to tax him, especially when those taxes supported policies with which he disagreed. In 1846, Thoreau—who opposed slavery—put his beliefs into practice by refusing to pay taxes that might in some way support slavery policies. For this passive resistance, Thoreau spent one night in jail.

Build Skills | Nonfiction

❶ *from* Walden • *from* Civil Disobedience

Henry David Thoreau (1817–1862)

From the time he was a child, Henry David Thoreau was known by his Concord, Massachusetts, neighbors as an eccentric. He rarely followed rules. He was independent and strong-willed but casual about his studies. It was his mother's drive and encouragement that convinced him to pursue an education. Thoreau attended Concord Academy, a college preparatory school. Five years later, he enrolled at Harvard, where he pursued his studies in his own unique style. Although Harvard University's code called for students to wear black coats, Thoreau wore a green one.

Questioning Authority Thoreau always questioned the rules that were presented to him. When his objection to corporal punishment forced him to quit his first teaching job, Thoreau and his older brother John opened their own school in Concord. The school was quite successful, but they had to close it when John became ill.

In 1841, Thoreau moved into the house of another famous Concord resident, Ralph Waldo Emerson. He lived there for two years, performing odd jobs to pay for his room and board. While there, Thoreau became fascinated by Emerson's Transcendentalist beliefs. Soon, Thoreau became Emerson's close friend and devoted disciple. Deciding not to go back to teaching and refusing to pursue another career, Thoreau dedicated himself to testing the Transcendentalist philosophy through personal experience. By simplifying his needs, Thoreau was able to devote the rest of his life to exploring and writing about the spiritual relationship between humanity and nature and supporting his political and social beliefs.

On Walden Pond From 1845 to 1847, Thoreau lived alone in a cabin he built himself at Walden Pond outside of Concord. Thoreau's experiences during this period provided him with the material for his masterwork, *Walden* (1854). Condensing his experiences at Walden Pond into a single year, Thoreau used the four seasons as a structural framework for the book. A unique blend of natural observation, social criticism, and philosophical insight, *Walden* is now generally regarded as the supreme work of Transcendentalist literature.

Thoreau wrote throughout his life, but only *A Week on the Concord and Merrimack Rivers* and some poems were published—at Thoreau's own expense—during his lifetime. *The Maine Woods, Cape Cod*, and *A Yankee in Canada* were published posthumously. Carefully and deliberately crafted, Thoreau's work reflects the economy for which he strove throughout his life and about which he wrote in *Walden*.

A Noble Soul When Henry David Thoreau died of tuberculosis at the age of forty-four, his work had received little recognition. Yet he had achieved an inner success that few others have experienced. Speaking at Thoreau's funeral, Ralph Waldo Emerson commented, "The country knows not yet, or in the least part, how great a son it has lost. . . . But he, at least, is content. His soul was made for the noblest society; he had in a short life exhausted the capabilities of this world; wherever there is knowledge, wherever there is virtue, wherever there is beauty, he will find a home."

Thoreau's reputation has steadily grown since his death. His work has inspired writers, environmentalists, and social and political leaders. It has made generations of readers aware of the possibilities of the human spirit and the limitations of society.

Preview

Connecting to the Literature

In today's world, we use countless modern conveniences—cellular phones, computers, the Internet—often without stopping to think whether or not we truly need them. Thoreau took time to stop to think about what was truly essential in life.

Literary Analysis

Style

Style refers to the manner in which a writer puts his or her thoughts into words. Thoreau constructs paragraphs so that the sentences build to a climax. Thoreau also repeats his main ideas to reinforce his message. As you read his works, watch for these signposts of Thoreau's style.

Comparing Literary Works

While both of these selections reveal Thoreau's style, each is written for a different purpose. One selection is descriptive and poetic, presenting ideas at a leisurely pace. The other, in contrast, is logical, advancing a focused argument. In both cases, Thoreau uses **metaphors**—figures of speech that compare two unlike things without using *like* or *as*.

- Time is but the stream I go a-fishing in . . .
- [Government] is a sort of a wooden gun to the people themselves . . .

As you read, compare the metaphors Thoreau uses and notice how they reveal the author's distinct reasons for writing.

Reading Strategy

Evaluating the Writer's Statement of Philosophy

As a reader, you are not bound to accept everything you see in print. In fact, when reading essays written about ideas, you should **evaluate the writer's philosophy.** To do this, pay special attention to the support the writer provides to back up his or her outlook. As you read Thoreau's works, compare his ideas and supporting details with your own experiences. Use a chart like the one shown here to organize your comparison.

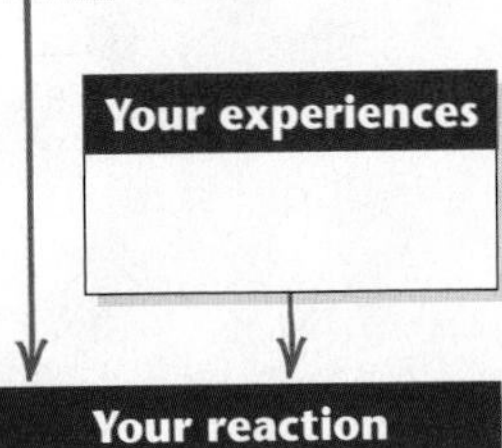

Vocabulary Builder

dilapidated (də lap′ə dāt′ id) *adj.* in disrepair (p. 408)

sublime (sə blīm′) *adj.* noble; majestic (p. 410)

superfluous (sə pʉr′flo͞o əs) *adj.* excessive; not necessary (p. 410)

evitable (ev′i tə bəl) *adj.* avoidable (p. 410)

magnanimity (mag′nə nim′ə tē) *n.* generosity (p. 413)

expedient (ek spē′ dē ənt) *n.* resource (p. 416)

posterity (päs ter′ə tē) *n.* all succeeding generations (p. 416)

alacrity (ə lak′rə tē) *n.* speed (p. 417)

❷ Literary Analysis

Style

- Tell students that as they read, they will focus on style, the manner in which a writer puts his or her ideas into words. Style can include sentence or paragraph structure, word choice, figurative language, rhythm, and imagery.
- After students read the Literary Analysis instruction, point out that Thoreau's style is intrinsic to his purpose, which is to encourage us to examine how we live and think.
- Review the stylistic device of metaphor with students as you introduce the instruction for **Comparing Literary Works.**

❸ Reading Strategy

Evaluating the Writer's Statement of Philosophy

- Give students a copy of **Reading Strategy Graphic Organizer A,** p. 79 in ***Graphic Organizer Transparencies*** to use as they read the selections.
- Remind students that evaluating the writer's statement of philosophy can help them read critically and respond more effectively to essays.
- Draw students' attention to the graphic organizer in the minor column of their page. Clarify the information suited to each cell and direct students to complete their own organizer as they read.
- Explain that a philosophy is a system of beliefs and values that guide a person's life and actions. Emphasize that after evaluating a writer's philosophy—exploring the supporting evidence and considering their own experiences—students may still decide that they agree with it.

Vocabulary Builder

- Pronounce each vocabulary word for students, and read the definitions as a class. Have students identify any words with which they are already familiar.

Differentiated Instruction Solutions for All Learners

Support for Special Needs Students
Have students read the adapted version of the excerpt from *Walden* in the ***Reader's Notebook: Adapted Version.*** This version provides basic-level instruction in an interactive format with questions and write-on lines. Completing these pages will prepare students to read the selection in the Student Edition.

Support for Less Proficient Readers
Have students read the excerpt from *Walden* in the ***Reader's Notebook.*** This version provides basic-level instruction in an interactive format with questions and write-on lines. Completing these pages will prepare students to read the selection in the Student Edition.

Support for English Learners
Have students read the excerpt from *Walden* in the ***Reader's Notebook: English Learner's Version.*** This version provides basic-level instruction in an interactive format with questions and write-on lines. Completing these pages will prepare students to read the selection in the Student Edition.

TEACH

Learning Modalities
Kinesthetic Learners Tell students that Thoreau conducts a great deal of real estate business in *Walden*. He considers different properties, weighs their features, negotiates their purchase, but he does it all in his imagination. As they read, challenge students to think about how reviewing a process mentally differs from completing that process or task physically.

❶ About the Selection

Walden was published in 1854, seven years after Thoreau's two-year residence at Walden Pond. During the intervening years, Thoreau reflected upon and revised the journals he had kept at Walden. A celebration of life and nature, *Walden* presents Thoreau's views on society and his philosophy of life. In the sections that follow, Thoreau expresses the belief that society has become too complex and fast-paced and that people should do everything possible to simplify their lives. He also stresses the need to resist conformity and to follow our own inner voices, and he suggests that by doing so people can experience a spiritual awakening.

Differentiated Instruction
Solutions for All Learners

Accessibility at a Glance

	from Walden	*from* Civil Disobedience
Context	Nineteenth-century transcendentalism	Nineteenth-century individualism
Language	First-person narrative; formal language	Some long sentences
Concept Level	Challenging (transcendental philosophy	Average political/social movements
Literary Merit	Classic	Influential document
Lexile	1190	1050
Overall Rating	More challenging	Average

❶ *from*

Walden

Henry David Thoreau

from Where I Lived, and What I Lived For

At a certain season of our life we are accustomed to consider every spot as the possible site of a house. I have thus surveyed the country on every side within a dozen miles of where I live. In imagination I have bought all the farms in succession, for all were to be bought, and I knew their price. I walked over each farmer's premises, tasted his wild apples, discoursed on husbandry[1] with him, took his farm at his price, at any price, mortgaging it to him in my mind; even put a higher price on it—took everything but a deed of it—took his word for his deed, for I dearly love to talk—cultivated it, and him too to some extent, I trust, and withdrew when I had enjoyed it long enough, leaving him to carry it on. This experience entitled me to be regarded as a sort of real-estate broker by my friends. Wherever I sat, there I might live, and the landscape radiated from me accordingly. What is a house but a sedes, a seat?—better if a country seat. I discovered many a site for a house not likely to be soon improved, which some might have thought too far from the village, but to my eyes the village was too far from it. Well, there might I live, I said; and there I did live, for an hour, a summer and a winter life; saw how I could let the years run off, buffet the winter through, and see the spring come in. The future inhabitants of this region, wherever they may place their houses, may be sure that they have been anticipated. An afternoon

seasonal change; natural timescales – blurring effect

1. husbandry (huz´ bən drē) *n.* farming.

◀ **Critical Viewing** Based on this picture of Walden Pond, what do you think it would be like to live in such a place? **[Speculate]**

Gretel Ehrlich
Scholar's Insight
Thoreau is saying that every rock is our home, every vista is ours to drink in. And as a result, the landscape comes into us, and pours out again as an image, a poem, a bit of music.

❹ **Reading Check**
Did Thoreau truly intend to purchase a farm?

❷ Scholar's Insight

- Draw students' attention to the Scholar's Insight note. **Ask** students if they have ever had an experience in nature that resulted in a poem or song.
- Discuss with students the idea of oneness with nature. **Ask** if they agree with this philosophy. **Possible response:** Students should give reasons to support their answers.

❸ Critical Viewing

Answer: Students may respond that it must have been beautiful yet isolated. Others may say that it would be boring to live so far from society and modern conveniences.

❹ Reading Check

Answer: No, he was merely enjoying mental speculation about the land around him.

Differentiated Instruction Solutions for All Learners

Strategy for Less Proficient Readers
Point out the sentence beginning "I walked over each farmer's premises. . . ." Note with students that it continues for seven lines of text. Help students work phrase by phrase, clause by clause, to build meaning from the sentence: I explored each farm, spoke with the farmer, negotiated for each farm but never actually completed the sale.

Strategy for Special Needs Students
Thoreau uses dashes and semicolons to string many sentence parts into a single long sentence. Explain that readers can treat dashes as if they were commas while semicolons reflect more significant pauses in the writer's ideas. Have students reread long sentences as you help them recognize breaks and build meaning.

Strategy for Advanced Readers
Challenge students to edit Thoreau's long sentences into more accessible text. Remind them, however, that an editor must avoid imprinting his or her own style on an author's work. Students should avoid the temptation to merely replace long sentences with shorter ones. Instead, they might reword or repunctuate for clarity.

5 Reading Strategy
Evaluating the Writer's Statement of Philosophy

- Read the bracketed passage with students and invite them to paraphrase it.
  Answer: The fewer encumbrances there are on one's life, the richer and freer that life will be.
- **Ask** students the Reading Strategy question: Do you think this philosophical statement about a man's wealth applies in today's world? Can Thoreau support it?
  Possible answer: Given today's emphasis on material possessions, students may have a different attitude from Thoreau's. If students express disagreement, encourage them to cite evidence to support their position. Thoreau supports his position by demonstrating in his own life that he feels richer and freer as he gives up material attachments.

6 Literary Analysis
Style

- Have a volunteer read aloud the bracketed passage. Invite listeners to raise their hands each time Thoreau repeats his main point about the Hollowell farm.
- Have students discuss possible reasons for Thoreau's use of repetition in this passage.
- Then, **ask** students the Literary Analysis question: What point does Thoreau make through his use of repetition in his description of the Hollowell farm?
  Possible answer: Repetition helps Thoreau make the point that he likes this farm because it is very isolated and private.

sufficed to lay out the land into orchard woodlot and pasture, and to decide what fine oaks or pines should be left to stand before the door, and whence each blasted tree could be seen to the best advantage; and then I let it lie, fallow[2] perchance, for a man is rich in proportion to the number of things which he can afford to let alone.

My imagination carried me so far that I even had the refusal of several farms—the refusal was all I wanted—but I never got my fingers burned by actual possession. The nearest that I came to actual possession was when I bought the Hollowell Place, and had begun to sort my seeds, and collected materials with which to make a wheelbarrow to carry it on or off with; but before the owner gave me a deed of it, his wife—every man has such a wife—changed her mind and wished to keep it, and he offered me ten dollars to release him. Now, to speak the truth, I had but ten cents in the world, and it surpassed my arithmetic to tell, if I was that man who had ten cents, or who had a farm, or ten dollars, or all together. However, I let him keep the ten dollars and the farm too, for I had carried it far enough; or rather, to be generous, I sold him the farm for just what I gave for it, and, as he was not a rich man, made him a present of ten dollars, and still had my ten cents, and seeds, and materials for a wheelbarrow left. I found thus that I had been a rich man without any damage to my poverty. But I retained the landscape, and I have since annually carried off what it yielded without a wheelbarrow. With respect to landscapes:

> "I am monarch of all I *survey*,
> My right there is none to dispute."[3]

I have frequently seen a poet withdraw, having enjoyed the most valuable part of a farm, while the crusty farmer supposed that he had got a few wild apples only. Why, the owner does not know it for many years when a poet has put his farm in rhyme, the most admirable kind of invisible fence, has fairly impounded it, milked it, skimmed it, and got all the cream, and left the farmer only the skimmed milk.

The real attractions of the Hollowell farm, to me, were: its complete retirement, being about two miles from the village, half a mile from the nearest neighbor, and separated from the highway by a broad field; its bounding on the river, which the owner said protected it by its fogs from frosts in the spring, though that was nothing to me; the gray color and ruinous state of the house and barn, and the dilapidated fences, which put such an interval between me and the last occupant; the hollow and lichen-covered apple trees, gnawed by rabbits, showing what kind of neighbors I should have; but above all, the recollection I had of it from my earliest voyages up the river, when the house was concealed behind a dense grove of red maples, through which I heard the house-dog bark. I was in haste to buy it, before the proprietor finished getting out some rocks, cutting down

Reading Strategy
Evaluating the Writer's Statement of Philosophy Do you think this philosophical statement about a man's wealth applies in today's world? Does Thoreau support it?

Literary Analysis
Style What point does Thoreau make through his use of repetition in his description of the Hollowell farm?

Vocabulary Builder
dilapidated (də lap′ ə dāt′ id) *adj.* in disrepair

2. **fallow** (fal′ ō) *adj.* left uncultivated or unplanted.
3. **"I . . . dispute"** from William Cowper's *Verses Supposed to Be Written by Alexander Selkirk.*

Enrichment

Touring Walden Pond

Today, tourists come from all over the world to visit Walden Pond. Some are drawn by the natural beauty of the place; others by its literary and historical significance. The pond and the surrounding forestland are now a public park preserve, the Walden Pond State Reservation. There are guided walks along the many pathways surrounding the pond, and visitors are welcome to swim, boat, picnic, and hike. During the summer months, large numbers of people from the area go to Walden Pond to sunbathe on the public beaches.

A re-creation of Thoreau's cabin stands a few dozen feet from the site of his original home. In a tradition begun decades ago, visitors still leave rocks and notes to Thoreau piled on the site. Above the house site, the stumps of some of the 400 white pines Thoreau planted can still be seen; they were wiped out by the great hurricane of 1938.

the hollow apple trees, and grubbing up some young birches which had sprung up in the pasture, or, in short, had made any more of his improvements. To enjoy these advantages I was ready to carry it on; like Atlas,[4] to take the world on my shoulders—I never heard what compensation he received for that—and do all those things which had no other motive or excuse but that I might pay for it and be unmolested in my possession of it; for I knew all the while that it would yield the most abundant crop of the kind I wanted if I could only afford to let it alone. But it turned out as I have said.

All that I could say, then, with respect to farming on a large scale (I have always cultivated a garden) was that I had had my seeds ready. Many think that seeds improve with age. I have no doubt that time discriminates between the good and the bad; and when at last I shall plant, I shall be less likely to be disappointed. But I would say to my fellows, once for all, As long as possible live free and uncommitted. It makes but little difference whether you are committed to a farm or the county jail.

Old Cato,[5] whose "De Re Rustica" is my "Cultivator," says, and the only translation I have seen makes sheer nonsense of the passage, "When you think of getting a farm, turn it thus in your mind, not to buy greedily; nor spare your pains to look at it, and do not think it enough to go round it once. The oftener you go there the more it will please you, if it is good." I think I shall not buy greedily, but go round and round it as long as I live, and be buried in it first, that it may please me the more at last. . . .

I do not propose to write an ode to dejection, but to brag as lustily as chanticleer[6] in the morning, standing on his roost, if only to wake my neighbors up.

When first I took up my abode in the woods, that is, began to spend my nights as well as days there, which, by accident, was on Independence Day, or the fourth of July, 1845, my house was not finished for winter, but was merely a defense against the rain, without plastering or chimney, the walls being of rough weatherstained boards, with wide chinks, which made it cool at night. The upright white hewn studs and freshly planed door and window casings gave it a clean and airy look, especially in the morning, when its timbers were saturated with dew, so that I fancied that by noon some sweet gum would exude from them. To my imagination it retained throughout the day more or less of this auroral[7] character, reminding me of a certain house on a mountain which I had visited the year before. This was an airy and unplastered cabin, fit to entertain a traveling god, and where a goddess might trail her garments. The winds which passed over my dwelling were such as sweep over the ridges of mountains, bearing the broken strains, or celestial parts only, 8

4. **Atlas** (at′ ləs) from Greek mythology, a Titan who supported the heavens on his shoulders.
5. **Old Cato** Roman statesman (234–149 B.C.). "De Re Rustica" is Latin for "Of Things Rustic."
6. **chanticleer** (chan′ tə klir′) *n.* rooster.
7. **auroral** (ô rôr′ əl) *adj.* resembling the dawn.

Reading Strategy
Evaluating the Writer's Statement of Philosophy
What difference do you see between a person's commitment to a farm and to a jail?

Reading Check
What was the state of Thoreau's house in the woods when he first took up residence?

7 Reading Strategy
Evaluating the Writer's Statement of Philosophy

- Direct students to read the bracketed text several times. Then, have them paraphrase the passage.
- Have students use a copy of **Reading Strategy Graphic Organizer A** to explore their reactions to Thoreau's statement. Charts should look similar to the following:

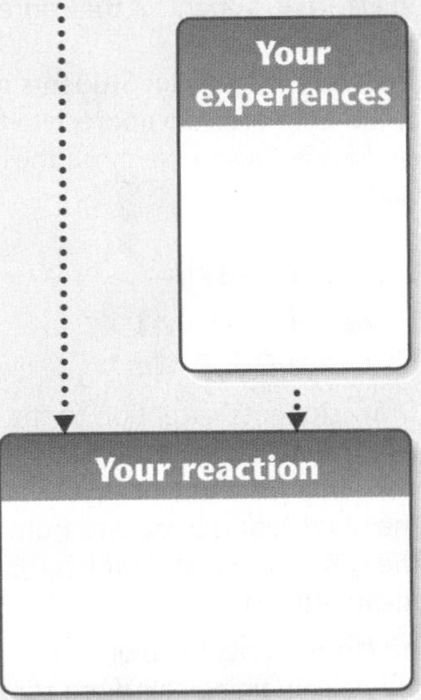

- **Ask** students to answer the Reading Strategy question: What difference do you see between a person's commitment to a farm and to a jail?
  Possible Answer: While both curtail your freedom through commitment, you are free to leave the farm or to sell it while you are not free to leave jail.

8 Reading Check
Answer: It was unfinished, without the insulation or inside walls that provide winter protection.

Differentiated Instruction Solutions for All Learners

Support for Less Proficient Readers
Help students respond to Thoreau's ideas. For example, point out the lengthy paragraph about the Hallowell Farm. Lead students toward an understanding of the central point of this paragraph: Thoreau considers an ideal property one that is isolated and in a natural "unimproved condition."

Support for English Learners
Help these students understand and develop responses to Thoreau's comments about the Hallowell Farm. Use the Literary Analysis: Style question and the TE instruction on p. 408 to help students identify Thoreau's main point. Point out each incidence of repetition for those students who need this additional help.

Strategy for Advanced Readers
Post these quotations on the chalkboard: "a man is rich in proportion to the number of things he can afford to let alone"; "time discriminates between the good and the bad [seeds]." Challenge students to deduce the implications of these comments and to decide whether they agree or disagree with Thoreau.

❾ Scholar's Insight

- Point out Ehrlich's comment on writers. **Ask** students if they agree with her idea that all writers must be students.
  Possible response: Students may agree with Ehrlich because writers must be open to all aspects of an experience. Better writing comes from one who lets go of preconceptions.
- After reading the excerpt *from Walden,* ask students if they feel Thoreau acted as a student of the world. Have them select passages that support their assertions.

❿ Scholar's Insight

- Have a student read Ehrlich's note aloud to the class. Discuss Thoreau's opinion that people should face the good and the bad in life. **Ask** students if they agree with this notion.
  Possible response: Students may feel that in order to appreciate the good one must experience the bad.

⓫ Vocabulary Development

The Latin Root *-flu-*

- Draw students' attention to the word *superfluous* and to its definition. Let students know that the word root *-flu-* derives from the Latin word *fluere,* which means "to flow."
- **Invite** students to volunteer words containing this word root, and list them on the chalkboard.
  Possibilities include: *fluid, influence, fluctuate,* and *fluency.*
- Next, have students look up the meanings of these words in a dictionary, and write a short paragraph for each word, describing how the word root contributes to the word's definition.

of terrestrial music. The morning wind forever blows, the poem of creation is uninterrupted; but few are the ears that hear it. Olympus[7] is but the outside of the earth everywhere. . . .

❾ I went to the woods because I wished to live deliberately, to front only the essential facts of life, and see if I could not learn what it had to teach, and not, when I came to die, discover that I had not lived. I did not wish to live what was not life, living is so dear; nor did I wish to practice resignation, unless it was quite necessary. I wanted to live deep and suck out all the marrow of life, to live so sturdily and Spartanlike[8] as to put to rout all that was not life, to cut a broad swath and shave close, to drive life into a corner, and reduce it to its lowest terms, and, if it proved to be mean, why then to get the whole and genuine meanness of it, and publish its meanness to the world; or if ❿ it were sublime, to know it by experience, and be able to give a true account of it in my next excursion. For most men, it appears to me, are in a strange uncertainty about it, whether it is of the devil or of God, and have *somewhat hastily* concluded that it is the chief end of man here to "glorify God and enjoy him forever."[9]

Still we live meanly, like ants; though the fable tells us that we were long ago changed into men; like pygmies we fight with cranes:[10] it ⓫ is error upon error, and clout upon clout, and our best virtue has for its occasion a superfluous and evitable wretchedness. Our life is frittered away by detail. An honest man has hardly need to count more than his ten fingers, or in extreme cases he may add his ten toes, and lump the rest. Simplicity, simplicity, simplicity! I say, let your affairs be as two or three, and not a hundred or a thousand; instead of a million count half a dozen, and keep your accounts on your thumbnail. In the midst of this chopping sea of civilized life, such are the clouds and storms and quicksands and thousand-and-one items to be allowed for, that a man has to live, if he would not founder and go to the bottom and not make his port at all, by dead reckoning,[11] and he must be a great calculator indeed who succeeds. Simplify, simplify. Instead of three meals a day, if it be necessary eat but one; instead of a hundred dishes, five; and reduce other things in proportion. Our life is like a German Confederacy,[12] made up of petty states, with its boundary forever fluctuating, so that even a German cannot tell you how it is bounded at any moment. The nation itself, with all its so-called internal improvements, which, by the way, are all external and superficial, is just such an unwieldy and overgrown establishment, cluttered with furniture and tripped up by its own traps, ruined by luxury and heedless expense, by

8. **Spartanlike** like the people of Sparta, an ancient Greek state whose citizens were known to be hardy, stoical, simple, and highly disciplined.
9. **"glorify . . . forever"** the answer to the question "What is the chief end of man?" in the Westminster catechism.
10. **like . . . cranes** In the *Iliad,* the Trojans are compared to cranes fighting against pygmies.
11. **dead reckoning** navigating without the assistance of stars.
12. **German Confederacy** At the time, Germany was a loose union of thirty-nine independent states, with no common government.

***Gretel Ehrlich* Scholar's Insight**
Thoreau comes to Walden Pond with a "beginner's mind." He allows the earth to instruct him in its ways, leaving preconceptions behind. That is how writers must approach all things, as a student of the world.

***Gretel Ehrlich* Scholar's Insight**
Thoreau encourages us to face all that life brings to us, both its painful and beautiful sides. There cannot be one without the other.

Vocabulary Builder

sublime (sə blīm′) *adj.* noble; majestic

superfluous (so͞o pur′ flo͞o əs) *adj.* excessive; not necessary

evitable (ev′ i tə bəl) *adj.* avoidable

Enrichment

Geology

As the glacier that covered New England 12,000 years ago slowly melted, one huge block of ice remained behind on the site that is now Walden Pond. Streams of melted water—filled with once-embedded sand and gravel—ran off the main glacier. This gravelly sediment built up around the base of the detached ice-block; when the block melted, a steep-sided, water-filled basin, about 100 feet deep, remained.

Unlike other ponds, the water level of Walden Pond changes little. Walden's water also remains pure and clear. Science can explain Walden's mysteries. Because its permeable sandbanks quickly absorb water, draining rainwater does not rush down its banks, washing dirt and debris into the pond. The absence of any tributary streams or shoreline development protects Walden's water quality. The stable water level can also be explained: Walden Pond intersects a water table, so its levels are relatively unaffected by short-term wet and dry spells.

want of calculation and a worthy aim, as the million households in the land; and the only cure for it as for them is in a rigid economy, a stern and more than Spartan simplicity of life and elevation of purpose. It lives too fast. Men think that it is essential that the *Nation* have commerce, and export ice, and talk through a telegraph, and ride thirty miles an hour, without a doubt, whether *they* do or not; but whether we should live like baboons or like men, is a little uncertain. If we do not get out sleepers,[13] and forge rails, and devote days and nights to the work, but go to tinkering upon our *lives* to improve *them*, who will build railroads? And if railroads are not built, how shall we get to heaven in season? But if we stay at home and mind our business, who will want railroads? We do not ride on the railroad; it rides upon us. . . .

Time is but the stream I go a-fishing in. I drink at it; but while I drink I see the sandy bottom and detect how shallow it is. Its thin current slides away, but eternity remains. I would drink deeper; fish in the sky, whose bottom is pebbly with stars. I cannot count one. I know not the first letter of the alphabet. I have always been regretting that I was not as wise as the day I was born. The intellect is a cleaver; it discerns and rifts its way into the secret of things. I do not wish to be any more busy with my hands than is necessary. My head is hands and feet. I feel all my best faculties concentrated in it. My instinct tells me that my head is an organ for burrowing, as some creatures use their snout and fore-paws, and with it I would mine and burrow my way through these hills. I think that the richest vein is somewhere hereabouts; so by the divining rod[14] and thin rising vapors I judge; and here I will begin to mine. . . .

from The Conclusion

I left the woods for as good a reason as I went there. Perhaps it seemed to me that I had several more lives to live, and could not spare any more time for that one. It is remarkable how easily and insensibly we fall into a particular route, and make a beaten track for ourselves. I had not lived there a week before my feet wore a path from my door to the pondside; and though it is five or six years since I trod it, it is still quite distinct. It is true, I fear that others may have fallen into it, and so

13. **sleepers** (slē′ pərz) *n.* ties supporting railroad tracks.
14. **divining rod** a forked branch or stick alleged to reveal underground water or minerals.

Literature in Context

Humanities Connection

♦ ***Olympus***

When he describes his home in the woods, Thoreau rhapsodizes about another mountain cabin he had seen, an airy place where a "goddess might trail her garments." Thoreau goes on to say, "Olympus is but the outside of the earth everywhere."

Mount Olympus is both a real mountain in northern Greece and an important setting in ancient Greek mythology. The home of the gods, Olympus was off-limits to mortals. The ancient Greeks pictured their gods in human form with human flaws, so Olympus was far from perfect. But as a place of relative beauty, harmony, and enlightenment, it was better than earth.

Connect to the Literature

What attitude toward nature does Thoreau express with his metaphor about Olympus? How is it related to his statement elsewhere in *Walden:* "Heaven is under our feet as well as over our heads"?

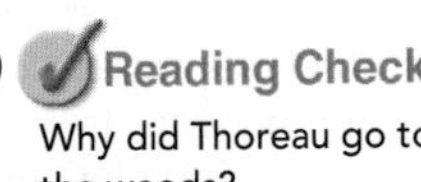

Reading Check

Why did Thoreau go to the woods?

12 Literature in Context

Olympus

In the ancient Greek stories to which Thoreau refers, each Greek god was closely associated with a specific aspect of nature—such as the sun or the moon—or with specific emotions—such as love or anger.

The educated people of Thoreau's day would have been familiar with Greek language and lore, so a reference to Greek mythology in a discussion about nature would have been seen—then as now—as totally appropriate.

Connect to the Literature Review with students Thoreau's views on nature. **Possible response:** Thoreau thinks that nature embodies ideals of harmony, enlightenment, and beauty. Thoreau describes "heaven" as nature, that it is all around us every day, visible and tangible, as well as something abstract.

13 Reading Check

Answer: He went to the woods to live simply and deliberately, to try to understand the essential facts of life.

Differentiated Instruction Solutions for All Learners

Strategy for Less Proficient Readers

Point out the first sentence of Thoreau's "Conclusion," and review the reasons Thoreau came to Walden Pond. If necessary, have students reread the paragraph on p. 410 in which Thoreau states his purpose for coming to Walden. Stress to students that it is helpful to reread for referenced information.

Strategy for English Language Learners

To help students identify Thoreau's purpose in living at Walden, suggest that students complete the sentence stem "I went to the woods because . . ." with phrases from the text. For example, "I went to the woods because I wished to live deep."

Enrichment for Gifted/Talented Students

The beliefs that Thoreau expresses in these passages are echoed in the theme of the film *Dead Poets Society.* You may wish to show portions of this film or have students view it on their own. Be aware, however, that the film addresses some sensitive issues. Preview the film to determine its suitability for your students.

14 Literary Analysis
Style and Metaphor

- **Direct** students to read the bracketed passage. Ask students to define *metaphor*.
  Answer: A metaphor is a figure of speech in which one thing is described as being something else.
- **Ask** them the Literary Analysis question: What metaphor does Thoreau use in the sentence beginning, "If a man does not keep pace with his companions"?
  Answer: He speaks of life as though it were a march in time with music—as though people were soldiers.

Monitor Progress: Have students explain Thoreau's metaphor. What two things is he comparing? Then, have students rephrase this metaphor as a simile.
Answer: He is comparing life to a sea journey, with the ship's deck as full participation of life while a cabin passage would be a sheltered, hidden interaction with life.

15 Critical Viewing

The aerial photograph reveals little modern development on Walden Pond. The photo suggests that inhabitants of the area have chosen to preserve the natural splendor of the landscape, perhaps in deference to Thoreau's ideas about honoring nature.

helped to keep it open. The surface of the earth is soft and impressible by the feet of men; and so with the paths which the mind travels. How worn and dusty, then, must be the highways of the world, how deep the ruts of tradition and conformity! I did not wish to take a cabin passage, but rather to go before the mast and on the deck of the world, for there I could best see the moonlight amid the mountains. I do not wish to go below now.

I learned this, at least, by my experiment; that if one advances confidently in the direction of his dreams, and endeavors to live the life which he has imagined, he will meet with a success unexpected in common hours. He will put some things behind, will pass an invisible boundary; new, universal, and more liberal laws will begin to establish themselves around and within him; or the old laws be expanded, and interpreted in his favor in a more liberal sense, and he will live with the license of a higher order of beings. In proportion as he simplifies his life, the laws of the universe will appear less complex, and solitude will not be solitude, nor poverty poverty, nor weakness weakness. If you have built castles in the air, your work need not be lost; that is where they should be. Now put the foundations under them. . . .

Why should we be in such desperate haste to succeed, and in such
14 desperate enterprises? If a man does not keep pace with his companions, perhaps it is because he hears a different drummer. Let him step to the music which he hears, however measured or far away. It is not important that he should mature as soon as an apple tree or an oak. Shall he turn his spring into summer? If the condition of things which we were made for is not yet, what were any reality which we can substitute? We will not be shipwrecked on a vain reality. Shall we with pains

15 ▲ Critical Viewing
What elements in this aerial photograph of Walden Pond reveal conventional notions of progress? What details suggest that the community has applied some of Thoreau's ideas? **[Analyze]**

Literary Analysis
Style and Metaphor
What metaphor does Thoreau use in the sentence beginning "If a man does not keep pace with his companions . . ."?

erect a heaven of blue glass over ourselves, though when it is done we shall be sure to gaze still at the true ethereal heaven far above, as if the former were not? . . .

However mean your life is, meet it and live it; do not shun it and call it hard names. It is not so bad as you are. It looks poorest when you are richest. The faultfinder will find faults even in paradise. Love your life, poor as it is. You may perhaps have some pleasant, thrilling, glorious hours, even in a poorhouse. The setting sun is reflected from the windows of the almshouse[15] as brightly as from the rich man's abode; the snow melts before its door as early in the spring. I do not see but a quiet mind may live as contentedly there, and have as cheering thoughts, as in a palace. The town's poor seem to me often to live the most independent lives of any. Maybe they are simply great enough to receive without misgiving. Most think that they are above being supported by the town; but it oftener happens that they are not above supporting themselves by dishonest means, which should be more disreputable. Cultivate poverty like a garden herb, like sage. Do not trouble yourself much to get new things, whether clothes or friends. Turn the old; return to them. Things do not change; we change. Sell your clothes and keep your thoughts. God will see that you do not want society. If I were confined to a corner of a garret[16] all my days, like a spider, the world would be just as large to me while I had my thoughts about me. The philosopher said: "From an army of three divisions one can take away its general, and put it in disorder; from the man the most abject and vulgar one cannot take away his thought." Do not seek so anxiously to be developed, to subject yourself to many influences to be played on; it is all dissipation. Humility like darkness reveals the heavenly lights. The shadows of poverty and meanness gather around us, "and lo! creation widens to our view."[17] We are often reminded that if there were bestowed on us the wealth of Croesus,[18] our aims must still be the same, and our means essentially the same. Moreover, if you are restricted in your range by poverty, if you cannot buy books and newspapers, for instance, you are but confined to the most significant and vital experiences; you are compelled to deal with the material which yields the most sugar and the most starch. It is life near the bone where it is sweetest. You are defended from being a trifler. No man loses ever on a lower level by magnanimity on a higher. Superfluous wealth can buy superfluities only. Money is not required to buy one necessary of the soul. . . .

The life in us is like the water in the river. It may rise this year higher than man has ever known it, and flood the parched uplands; even this may be the eventful year, which will drown out all our

15. **almshouse** *n.* home for people too poor to support themselves.
16. **garret** (gar′ it) *n.* attic.
17. **"and . . . view"** from the sonnet "To Night" by British poet Joseph Blanco White (1775–1841).
18. **Croesus** (krē′ səs) King of Lydia (d. 546 B.C.), believed to be the wealthiest person of his time.

Gretel Ehrlich
Scholar's Insight
To cultivate poverty is a radical thought and one that has been alive throughout history. Poverty in this sense means simplicity, like the "poverty" of an animal that wears only its own fur coat. The mind and the imagination are our true wealth.

Reading Strategy
Evaluating the Writer's Statement of Philosophy
Thoreau has strong opinions about how people should live, as shown in his advice to "cultivate poverty." Has he convinced you? Explain.

Vocabulary Builder
magnanimity (mag′ nə nim′ ə tē) *n.* generosity

18  **Reading Check**
What does Thoreau feel about superfluous wealth?

16 Scholar's Insight

- Have a student read the bracketed passage aloud to the class. Then, read Ehrlich's Insight note. Tell students that Thoreau is using this example to further explain his philosophy. **Ask** students if they feel readers of the time would be moved by Thoreau's explanation.
Possible response: Students may suggest that the radical idea, no matter how it is expressed, would not affect people.

17 Reading Strategy
Evaluating the Writer's Statement of Philosophy

- Ask a volunteer to read aloud the bracketed passage. Invite listening students to share their initial reactions to Thoreau's position.
- Encourage students to analyze Thoreau's support for his ideas and then compare it with their own experience in order to evaluate the writer's philosophy.
- **Ask** students the Reading Strategy question: Thoreau has strong opinions about how people should live, as shown in his advice to "cultivate poverty." Has he convinced you?
Possible response: Students may or may not be convinced that poverty is preferable to wealth.

18 Reading Check

Answer: It is unimportant because it only buys unnecessary things. Money cannot buy the truly necessary items of the spirit.

Differentiated Instruction Solutions for All Learners

Support for Less Proficient Readers
Read students the text beginning "In proportion as he simplifies. . . ." Then focus on building an understanding of the metaphor "castles in the air." Guide students to understand that Thoreau is urging people to simplify their lives, to dream, and then to follow their dreams by building foundations for them.

Vocabulary for English Language Learners
Point out the sentence: "If a man does not keep pace with his companions, perhaps it is because he hears a different drummer." Tell students that the metaphor of hearing a different drummer has become common, signifying that someone approaches life differently than do most people.

Strategy for Advanced Readers
Tell students that although not wealthy, Thoreau did have a Harvard education and a family business. Discuss with students how economic conditions today might lead Thoreau to change his advice about poverty. Ask students: How would living in a city affect one's ability to cope with poverty?

19 Literary Analysis
Style and Metaphor

- Read aloud the passage on pp. 414–415 in which Thoreau describes the egg deposited long ago in the wood later used for a table. Pause to emphasize the word *egg* when it appears.
- **Ask** students the question: To what does Thoreau compare the long-buried egg?
  Answer: He compares it to our human vitality, to our life energy, which can seem dead and buried but is still capable of emerging afresh.

20 Critical Viewing

The cabin is extremely humble—plain, small, and unadorned. Such a cabin would provide only the most basic shelter and require little attention, leaving its inhabitant to focus on matters of the mind and spirit.

muskrats. It was not always dry land where we dwell. I see far inland the banks which the stream anciently washed, before science began to record its freshets. Everyone has heard the story which has gone
19 the rounds of New England, of a strong and beautiful bug which came out of the dry leaf of an old table of apple-tree wood, which had stood in a farmer's kitchen for sixty years, first in Connecticut, and afterward in Massachusetts—from an egg deposited in the living tree many years

▼ Critical Viewing In what ways does this replica of Thoreau's cabin reflect his desire to "front only the essential facts of life"? **[Interpret]**

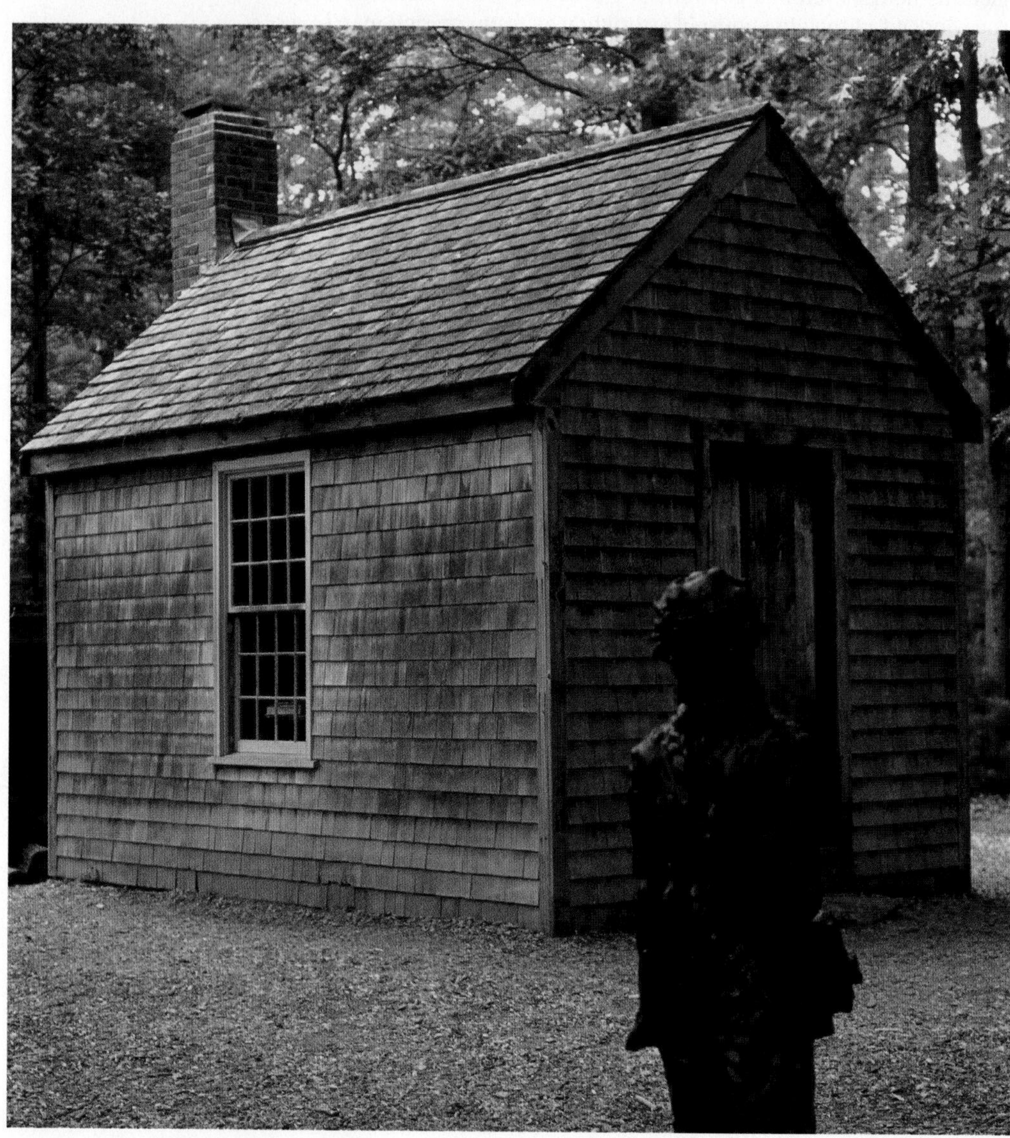

Enrichment

Gandhi

Thoreau's beliefs have influenced people throughout the world in the decades since his death. For example, his concept of civil disobedience, which is vividly described in the selection that follows, greatly influenced Indian leader Mohandas Gandhi in his campaign against British rule in his homeland. Drawing on Thoreau's ideas, Gandhi formulated his philosophy of *Satyagraha* ("The Devotion to Truth" in Sanskrit, an ancient Indian language) in 1906. Guided by this philosophy, Gandhi called for massive boycotts of British goods and British-run institutions in India that treated Indians unfairly. Thousands of Gandhi's supporters and Gandhi himself repeatedly went to prison without resistance. When India won its independence in 1947, it was largely due to Gandhi's nonviolent protests.

earlier still, as appeared by counting the annual layers beyond it; which was heard gnawing out for several weeks, hatched perchance by the heat of an urn. Who does not feel his faith in a resurrection and immortality strengthened by hearing of this? Who knows what beautiful and winged life, whose egg has been buried for ages under many concentric layers of woodenness in the dead dry life of society, deposited at first in the alburnum[19] of the green and living tree, which has been gradually converted into the semblance of its well-seasoned tomb—heard perchance gnawing out now for years by the astonished family of man, as they sat round the festive board— may unexpectedly come forth from amidst society's most trivial and handselled furniture, to enjoy its perfect summer life at last!

I do not say that John or Jonathan[20] will realize all this; but such is the character of that morrow which mere lapse of time can never make to dawn. The light which puts out our eyes is darkness to us. Only that day dawns to which we are awake. There is more day to dawn. The sun is but a morning star.

19. **alburnum** (al bur′ nəm) *n.* soft wood between the bark and the heartwood, where water is conducted.
20. **John or Jonathan** average person.

Critical Reading

1. **Respond:** From your point of view, what would be the advantages and disadvantages of spending two solitary years in a natural setting?
2. **(a) Recall:** What advice does Thoreau offer to his "fellows" about ownership of land or property? **(b) Interpret:** What does Thoreau mean by his comment, "It makes but little difference whether you are committed to a farm or the county jail"?
3. **(a) Recall:** What advice does Thoreau offer to those who live in poverty? **(b) Analyze:** What does this advice suggest about Thoreau's definition of true wealth?
4. **(a) Recall:** According to Thoreau, by what is our life "frittered away"? **(b) Interpret:** What does Thoreau mean by his advice to "Simplify, simplify."?
5. **(a) Deduce:** What did Thoreau hope to achieve by living at Walden Pond? **(b) Make a Judgment:** Do you believe Thoreau felt his time at Walden was well spent? Explain.
6. **(a) Apply:** How would you define those things that are necessary to the soul? **(b) Take a Position:** Do you agree with Thoreau that "Money is not required to buy one necessary of the soul"? Explain.

For: More about Henry David Thoreau
Visit: www.PHSchool.com
Web Code: ere-9313

ASSESS

Answers

1. **Possible response:** Advantages include having a chance to get an intimate view of nature and develop one's inner resources. Disadvantages include being separated from family, friends, and modern conveniences.
2. (a) He tells them to avoid the commitments of ownership. (b) **Possible answer:** He means that all commitments create restrictions and demands.
3. (a) They should love life and find the best in it. (b) **Possible response:** He believes that true wealth is spiritual rather than financial.
4. (a) It is "frittered away" by detail. (b) **Possible response:** He means that people should reduce both their material possessions and the external demands of their lives.
5. (a) He hoped to identify and experience the very essence of life. (b) **Possible response:** Yes, he seems to feel that he's learned a great deal from his experience, for example, to "advance in the direction of his dreams" and "live the life which he has imagined."
6. **Possible response:** (a) Such things as truth, justice, beauty, and love are necessary to the soul. (b) Most students will agree that while the body must have its basic needs met, the soul needs nothing money can buy.

Go Online Author Link For additional information about Henry David Thoreau, have students type in the Web Code, then select T from the alphabet, and then select Henry David Thoreau.

Differentiated Instruction Solutions for All Learners

Enrichment for Special Needs Students

Take students for a walk to a natural setting. While outside, read aloud the final selection paragraph and work with students to build comprehension. Then, ask students to describe their reactions to nature. How do they feel when they are in natural settings? Does it give them hope, as it does Thoreau?

Strategy for Less Proficient Readers

For students who find Thoreau's comparison of the hidden egg to life's energy difficult to comprehend, return to the paragraph's opening sentence. Highlight its subject "the life in us." Explain that this remains the subject of comparison throughout the paragraph.

Strategy for Gifted/Talented Students

Point out Thoreau's use of figurative language in "The Conclusion." For example, list or ask these students to list some of the metaphors that Thoreau uses for life. Discuss which of these—life is a road or path, a ship, a parade, a bone, a river, a day, and the seasons of the year—students find most effective.

21 About the Selection

This selection is excerpted from a long essay, about twenty pages in length, in which Thoreau advocates civil disobedience—the deliberate and public refusal to obey laws that violate one's personal principles. In the portions included here, Thoreau expresses his belief that government has been no more than an impediment to the productivity and achievements of the American people. Philosophically, he stands opposed to government. Practically, he urges readers to try to make a better government, one that commands respect.

22 Reading Strategy
Evaluating the Writer's Statement of Philosophy

- Have students read the bracketed passage. Explain that recognizing their initial personal response to a writer's philosophy can help readers respond to evidence.
- **Encourage** students to paraphrase Thoreau's statement of philosophy about government.
  Possible response: He believes that there should be as little government as possible, because it generally creates more problems than it solves.
- **Ask** students the Reading Strategy question: Before you read Thoreau's supporting arguments, do you think you will agree with his philosophy about government? Explain.
  Possible response: I disagree with Thoreau because in our modern, rapidly growing, fast-paced society, many tasks can be best accomplished by government.

21 from CIVIL DISOBEDIENCE

Henry David Thoreau

Background The Mexican War was a conflict between Mexico and the United States that took place from 1846 to 1848. The war was caused by a dispute over the boundary between Texas and Mexico, as well as by Mexico's refusal to discuss selling California and New Mexico to the United States. Believing that President Polk had intentionally provoked the conflict before gaining congressional approval, Thoreau and many other Americans strongly objected to the war. In protest, Thoreau refused to pay his taxes and was forced to spend a night in jail. After that experience, Thoreau wrote "Civil Disobedience," urging people to resist governmental policies with which they disagree.

22 I heartily accept the motto, "That government is best which governs least";[1] and I should like to see it acted up to more rapidly and systematically. Carried out, it finally amounts to this, which also I believe: "That government is best which governs not at all"; and when men are prepared for it, that will be the kind of government which they will have. Government is at best but an expedient; but most governments are usually, and all governments are sometimes, inexpedient. The objections which have been brought against a standing army, and they are many and weighty, and deserve to prevail, may also at last be brought against a standing government. The standing army is only an arm of the standing government. The government itself, which is only the mode which the people have chosen to execute their will, is equally liable to be abused and perverted before the people can act through it. Witness the present Mexican war, the work of comparatively a few individuals using the standing government as their tool; for in the outset, the people would not have consented to this measure.

This American government—what is it but a tradition, though a recent one, endeavoring to transmit itself unimpaired to posterity, but each instant losing some of its integrity? It has not the vitality and force of a single living man; for a single man can bend it to his will. It is a sort of wooden gun to the people themselves; and, if ever they should use it in earnest as a real one against each other, it will surely split.

Reading Strategy
Evaluating the Writer's Statement of Philosophy
Before you read Thoreau's supporting arguments, do you think you will agree with his philosophy about government? Explain.

Vocabulary Builder
expedient (ek spē′ dē ənt) *n.* resource

Vocabulary Builder
posterity (päs ter′ ə tē) *n.* all succeeding generations

1. **"That . . . least"** the motto of the *United States Magazine and Democratic Review,* a literary-political journal.

Enrichment

Government

Discuss whether government is, as Thoreau contends, an impediment to our freedoms and progress or whether citizens can improve their local, state, and federal governments by exercising their right to participate. Explain that citizens have many opportunities to make their voices heard, particularly on the local level. Discuss the following ways groups and individuals can influence public policy. Ask students to add their own suggestions to this list:

- Write a letter to a civic leader
- Organize or sign a petition
- Submit a letter to the editor of a local paper
- Speak out at a town meeting
- Exercise the right to vote

Have students think about their own responses to governmental issues. Ask them whether they have ever signed a petition or written a letter voicing their feelings on a particular issue. Have students discuss their views on what roles and responsibilities individuals have as citizens in a democracy.

But it is not the less necessary for this; for the people must have some complicated machinery or other, and hear its din, to satisfy that idea of government which they have. Governments show thus how successfully men can be imposed on, even impose on themselves, for their own advantage. It is excellent, we must all allow; yet this government never of itself furthered any enterprise, but by the alacrity with which it got out of its way. *It* does not keep the country free. *It* does not settle the West. *It* does not educate. The character inherent in the American people has done all that has been accomplished; and it would have done somewhat more, if the government had not sometimes got in its way. For government is an expedient by which men would fain succeed in letting one another alone; and, as has been said, when it is most expedient, the governed are most let alone by it. Trade and commerce, if they were not made of India rubber,[2] would never manage to bounce over the obstacles which legislators are continually putting in their way; and, if one were to judge these men wholly by the effects of their actions, and not partly by their intentions, they would deserve to be classed and punished with those mischievous persons who put obstructions on the railroads.

But, to speak practically and as a citizen, unlike those who call themselves no government men, I ask for, not at once no government, but *at once* a better government. Let every man make known what kind of government would command his respect, and that will be one step toward obtaining it. . . .

Vocabulary Builder
alacrity (ə lak′ rə tē) *n.* speed

2. **India rubber** a form of crude rubber.

Critical Reading

1. **Respond:** What kind of government commands your respect? Why?
2. **(a) Recall:** What motto does Thoreau accept? **(b) Analyze:** How would he like to see that motto implemented?
3. **(a) Recall:** How does Thoreau define the best possible kind of government? **(b) Draw Conclusions:** According to Thoreau, when will Americans get the best possible kind of government?
4. **(a) Summarize:** What is Thoreau asking his readers to do? **(b) Evaluate:** Does Thoreau present a convincing argument for acting on one's principles?
5. **(a) Criticize:** What arguments might you use to counter Thoreau's objections to the idea of a standing government? **(b) Support:** What examples might you provide to support an argument that government benefits individuals?

For: More about Henry David Thoreau
Visit: www.PHSchool.com
Web Code: ere-9313

ASSESS

Answers

1. Students should explain the reasoning behind their opinions.
2. (a) He accepts the motto "That government is best, which governs least." (b) He would like to see it implemented quickly and systematically.
3. (a) A government that governs least is the best possible kind of government. (b) Thoreau says that when people are ready, they will dispense with government altogether.
4. (a) He's asking them to step forward and state what they want from government. (b) Students should support their responses with an evaluation of Thoreau's arguments
5. (a) **Possible response:** Without a standing government, the nation cannot prepare itself for war, cannot make plans for future needs and cannot organize national elections. (b) **Possible response:** Governments provide schools, military and civil defense and transportation systems.

Go Online Author Link For additional information about Henry David Thoreau, have students type in the Web Code, then select T from the alphabet, and then select Henry David Thoreau.

Answers

1. **Possible responses:** (a) He begins with a simile about ants and proceeds to a statement about detail. He urges simplicity and gives examples about simplifying individual lives. He makes another comparison and decries the complexities of progress. (b) The paragraph that begins "however mean your life" on p. 413 builds to a climax that expresses the meaning of the paragraph.
2. (a) Suggested responses include the first paragraph from "The Conclusion" of *Walden.* (b) Yes, it invites reader support with details before reaching "larger truth."
3. Students' should explain Thoreau's metaphors.

   Another sample answer can be found on **Literary Analysis Graphic Organizer B,** p. 78 in ***Graphic Organizer Transparencies.***
4. The "wooden gun" metaphor is logical. The "chopping sea of civilized life" is artistic.
5. (a) He makes more use of metaphor in *Walden.* (b) Metaphor is more suited to *Walden,* in which spiritual and physical journeys intertwine. *Civil Disobedience* is a persuasive essay about Thoreau's public views.
6. (a) He claims that details distract us from real living. As evidence he describes simplifying his life and experiencing greater freedom. (b) **Possible responses:** The details of living add richness to our lives. (c) Students should defend their responses.
7. (a) He contends that government is too easily perverted by a few individuals. (b) Students should explain the reasoning behind their reponses.
8. Students may feel that today, life is too complex.

Apply the Skills

from *Walden* • from *Civil Disobedience*

Literary Analysis

Style

1. **(a)** Explain how the paragraph on simplicity in *Walden* demonstrates Thoreau's tendency to make sentences build to a climax. **(b)** Find another example in *Walden* of Thoreau's climactic **style.**
2. Thoreau often starts a paragraph with specific examples. He then applies them to a larger truth. **(a)** Find one such paragraph. **(b)** Do you think this approach is effective? Explain.

Comparing Literary Works

3. Use a chart like the one shown here to examine the meanings of Thoreau's **metaphors.**

Metaphor	Things compared	Meaning
I wanted to live deep and suck out all the marrow of life		

4. In *Civil Disobedience,* Thoreau describes government as "a wooden gun." In *Walden,* he describes "this chopping sea of civilized life." Does each of these metaphors function primarily as a logical or an artistic tool? Explain.
5. **(a)** In which essay does Thoreau make more elaborate use of metaphor? **(b)** How does this choice reflect the purpose of the essay?

Reading Strategy

Evaluating the Writer's Statement of Philosophy

6. Thoreau writes that people should simplify their lives. **(a)** What support for this belief does he provide? **(b)** How could you argue against this idea? **(c)** Is his argument convincing? Explain.
7. **(a)** What evidence does Thoreau use to support his contention that "That government is best which governs not at all"? **(b)** Do you agree with Thoreau? Explain.

Extend Understanding

8. **World Events Connection:** Would it be possible for Thoreau to conduct his "experiment" of living at Walden Pond in today's society? Why or why not?

QuickReview

Style is the manner in which a writer puts his or her thoughts into words.

Metaphors compare two unlike things, without the use of *like* or *as.*

To **evaluate the writer's statement of philosophy,** weigh the writer's supporting evidence and your own experience. Decide whether you agree or disagree.

For: Self-test
Visit: www.PHSchool.com
Web Code: era-6309

Go Online Assessment Students may use the **Self-test** to prepare for **Selection Test A** or **Selection Test B.**

Build Language Skills

Vocabulary Lesson

Word Analysis: Latin Root *-flu-*

The Latin root *-flu-*, found in words like *fluid*, means "flow." The word *superfluous* means "overflowing" or "exceeding what is sufficient." Match each of the words with its definition. Check your answers in a dictionary.

a. affluence **b.** confluence **c.** fluent

1. a flowing together, as in two streams
2. wealth; an abundant flow; prosperity
3. effortlessly smooth; flowing

Spelling Strategy

If a word ends in *-ent*, such as the word *expedient*, its parallel forms end in *-ence (expedience)* or *-ency (expediency)*. For each of these words, correctly spell the parallel forms.

1. resident **2.** dependent **3.** excellent

Vocabulary Builder: Synonyms

Select the word or phrase below whose meaning is closest to that of the first word.

1. dilapidated: **(a)** depressed, **(b)** in disrepair, **(c)** new
2. sublime: **(a)** tight, **(b)** filthy, **(c)** majestic
3. superfluous: **(a)** superb, **(b)** unnecessary, **(c)** wanted
4. evitable: **(a)** avoidable, **(b)** evident, **(c)** fair
5. magnanimity: **(a)** spontaneity, **(b)** horror, **(c)** kindness
6. expedient: **(a)** resource, **(b)** expense, **(c)** implosive
7. posterity: **(a)** future generations, **(b)** ancestors, **(c)** current generations
8. alacrity: **(a)** awareness, **(b)** readiness, **(c)** suspicion

Grammar and Style Lesson

Infinitives and Infinitive Phrases

Thoreau makes frequent use of infinitives and infinitive phrases. **Infinitive phrases** combine an **infinitive** (the basic form of the verb preceded by the word *to*) and its complements and modifiers. Infinitive phrases function as nouns, adjectives, or adverbs. In the examples below, the infinitive phrases are in italics.

Noun: I dearly love *to talk.* (object of the verb *love*)

Adjective: I had several more lives *to live.* (modifies the noun *lives*)

Adverb: This was an airy . . . cabin, fit *to entertain a traveling god.* (modifies the participle *fit*)

Practice Find at least six infinitives or infinitive phrases in the paragraph of *Walden* (page 410) that begins "I went to the woods . . . " Identify the grammatical function of the infinitive in each phrase.

Writing Application Write two paragraphs describing how you plan to achieve a difficult goal. Use infinitive phrases such as *to shine* in persuasive statements: "Give my plan an opportunity to *shine.*"

After you draft, highlight the infinitives and infinitive phrases in your paragraphs. For each, identify the function it serves in the sentence.

WG *Prentice Hall Writing and Grammar Connection: Chapter 19, Section 2*

Assessment Practice

Make Inferences and Generalizations

(For more practice, see *Standardized Test Preparation Workbook*, p. 23.)

To help students practice making generalizations, have them complete this sample test item.

> I heartily accept the motto, "That government is best which governs least"; and I should like to see it acted up to more rapidly and systematically.

Based on this statement, Thoreau probably believes that—

A governments should be more involved in the lives of the people.
B people could do more if governments did less.
C the American people need help from the government to improve their country.
A government should be abolished.

B is the most accurate generalization because it is based on details from the passage.

EXTEND/ASSESS

Answers

❶ Vocabulary Lesson

Word Analysis

1. b 3. c
2. a

Spelling Strategy

1. residence, residency
2. dependence, dependency
3. excellence, excellency

Vocabulary Builder

1. b 5. c
2. c 6. a
3. b 7. a
4. a 8. b

❷ Grammar and Style Lesson

Possible responses: to live deliberately (noun); to front only the essential facts of life(noun); [to] see if I could not learn (noun); to teach (noun); to die (adverb); [to] discover that I had not lived (noun); to practice resignation (noun); to live deep (noun); [to] suck out all the marrow of life (noun); to live so sturdily and Spartanlike (noun); to put (adverb); to cut a broad swatch (noun); [to] shave close (noun); to drive life into a corner (noun); [to] reduce it to its lowest terms (noun); to be mean (adjective)

Writing Application

Paragraphs should be free of major mechanical errors and should contain at least three infinitive phrases. Phrases should be accurately highlighted and labeled with correct grammatical function.

WG **Writing and Grammar, Ruby Level**

Students will find further instruction and practice on infinitives and infinitive phrases in Chapter 19, Section 2.

❸ Writing Lesson

You may use this Writing Lesson as timed-writing practice, or you may allow students to develop the editorial as a writing assignment over several days.

- To guide students in writing this editorial, give them the **Support for Writing Lesson**, p. 147 in ***Unit 3 Resources.***
- Discuss with students two possible organizations for their paper: begin with the cause and then discuss its effect OR begin with effects and then prove the cause.
- Provide students with the Cause-and-Effect Flowchart, p. 305, in ***Graphic Organizer Transparencies*** as an additional tool for organizing their prewriting notes. Provide students also with the rubrics for Persuasion: Persuasive Essay in ***General Resources,*** pp. 45–46.
- Read through the Writing Lesson steps with students and clarify any confusion.
- Encourage students to work in pairs to try out their editorials on an audience.

❹ Listening and Speaking

- Give students a copy of the Speaking: Presenting Pros and Cons rubric on page 92 in ***General Resources.***
- Consider assigning students to groups that require them to argue against their personal views. This can encourage more thorough investigation of persuasive arguments and force more rigorous logic.
- Encourage students to identify evidence that can support their arguments.
- Direct groups to sequence their arguments, with the strongest first or last, and to assign these elements to strong speakers.
- Conduct the debates as a class with yourself or a student as moderator. Remind students of courteous debate behavior.
- The **Support for Extend Your Learning** page (***Unit 3 Resources,*** p. 148) provides guided note-taking opportunities to help students complete the Extend Your Learning activities.

Go Online Research Have students type in the Web Code for another research activity.

SAT® PREP ACT

❸ Writing Lesson

Timed Writing: Editorial

In the century-and-a-half-since Thoreau wrote *Walden,* life for most Americans has become increasingly complex rather than simpler. Write an editorial for a major newspaper either advocating or rejecting Thoreau's ideas of simplicity for today's world. Refer to the texts of *Walden* and *Civil Disobedience* to support your ideas. ***(40 minutes)***

Prewriting ***(10 minutes)*** Decide whether you think Thoreau was right or wrong, and brainstorm for a list of examples that support your point of view.

Drafting ***(20 minutes)*** Introduce Thoreau and outline his ideas. Use quotations from his work to illustrate your points. Make a strong statement either advocating or refuting his ideas, using your list of examples. Anticipate and answer the arguments of those who may disagree with you.

Model: Anticipating Opponents' Arguments

Today, Thoreau's ideas fall on deaf ears because everyone is glued to a cell phone. Instead of hearing his wisdom, people say, "But I can't live without my fax machine. It makes my life easier." Yet, people have less time with family, and less time for the simple pleasures of life than ever before.

Anticipating and answering opponents' arguments creates a more persuasive piece of writing.

Revising ***(10 minutes)*** Reread your editorial, adding examples, anecdotes, or quotations as necessary to sharpen your argument.

WG *Prentice Hall Writing and Grammar Connection: Chapter 7, Section 2*

❹ Extend Your Learning

Listening and Speaking With a group, stage a **debate** to argue the pros and cons of civil disobedience as a form of protest. Keep the following strategies in mind as you work:

- Develop several key arguments supporting your position.
- Use analogies, or comparisons, to familiar situations to clarify your points.

As you listen to your opponents' arguments, take notes on their main idea and supporting details so that you will be prepared to make your rebuttal. **[Group Activity]**

Research and Technology Conduct research to find out what Walden Pond is like today and what efforts have been made to preserve it. Share your findings with the class in an **oral presentation.** Follow with a discussion of the way Walden Pond has changed since Thoreau's day.

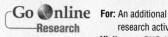

For: An additional research activity
Visit: www.PHSchool.com
Web Code: erd-7308

Assessment Resources

The following resources can be used to assess student's knowledge and skills.

Unit 3 Resources
- **Selection Test A,** pp. 150–152
- **Selection Test B,** pp. 153–155

General Resources
- **Rubrics for Persuasion: Persuasive Essay,** pp. 45–46
- **Rubric for Speaking: Presenting Pros and Cons,**p. 92

Go Online Assessment Students may use the **Self-test** to prepare for **Selection Test A** or **Selection Test B.**

Unit 3 Part 4

Focus on Literary Forms: Poetry

Walden Pond Revisited, 1942, N. C. Wyeth, Brandywine River Museum

Selection Planning Guide

The selections in this section reveal the range of two of the nation's most famous poets. Emily Dickinson's poetry explores the vast inner landscape. "The Brain—is wider than the Sky—" asserts that the human soul can encompass all things in the natural world and an individual identity. In "Because I could not stop for Death—" and "I heard a Fly buzz when I died—," the poet describes the somber journey from life to death. Rich in imagery and symbolism and innovative in its form, Dickinson's poetry has been celebrated and emulated long after the poet's death. Similarly, Walt Whitman broke the poetic conventions of his time. Whitman's strong belief in the connection between humanity and nature as well as his unique catalog style are evident in the excerpt from "Song of Myself" and "I Hear America Singing."

Humanities

Walden Pond Revisited, N.C. Wyeth

Newell Convers Wyeth (1882–1945) was the premiere book illustrator of his day. Born in Needham, Massachusetts, Wyeth knew early on that he wanted to be an artist, and so he studied with the great American illustrator Howard Pyle, often visiting Pyle at his home in Chadds Ford, Pennsylvania. Wyeth eventually settled his family in this beautiful area.

This painting, a mixture of egg-based tempera and other media, is somewhat surrealistic in its style. Wyeth renders various natural elements in careful detail, but the unnaturally crowded composition and dramatic lighting of the painting suggest a kind of dreamscape. Painted nearly a century after Thoreau's historic sojourn at Walden Pond, this work reveres the writer as a kind of philosopher saint, setting him in an idealized landscape.

- Based on this painting, what would you say Wyeth felt about Thoreau, and what elements in the painting led you to this idea?
  Possible response: Wyeth seems to admire Thoreau, and this admiration is conveyed by the halo-like light that surrounds the writer.

1. recognize and appreciate the types and elements of poetry.
2. apply strategies for reading poetry.

❶ Types of Poetry

- Tell students that in Part 4 they will focus on poetry. **Ask** students to explain how poetry is different from prose—aside from its appearance on the page. **Possible answers:** Poetry uses figurative language and expresses an idea more succinctly than prose does. Poetry uses rhyme and rhythm to create musical effects.
- Review the types of poetry with students: narrative poetry, dramatic poetry, and lyric poetry.
- Tell them that the poetry of Emily Dickinson and Walt Whitman is lyric poetry.

❷ Elements of Poetry

- Review the elements of poetry presented on these pages. Suggest that students use these pages as a reference when they read Part 4 and other poetry throughout these units.
- Point out that Walt Whitman's poetry is an example of free verse, poetry that uses irregular meter and line lengths.
- Point out that Emily Dickinson's poetry often uses slant rhyme, in which words rhyme approximately rather than exactly, such as *One/Stone* and *is/Paradise.*

Defining Poetry

Poetry, prose, and drama are the three major genres, or forms, of literature. Poets usually use highly charged language different from that of everyday speech, arranging their words in lines that form verses and stanzas.

❶ Types of Poetry

Most poems fall into one of three categories:

- **Narrative poetry** tells a story. Narrative poetry includes ballads, epics, and verse romances.
- **Dramatic poetry** uses the techniques of drama to present the speech of one or more characters.
- **Lyric poetry** expresses the thoughts and feelings of a single speaker. Lyric poetry includes sonnets, odes, elegies, and haiku.

IF I FEEL PHYSICALLY AS IF THE TOP OF MY HEAD WERE TAKEN OFF, I KNOW THAT IS POETRY. —*Emily Dickinson*

❷ Elements of Poetry

Here are some of the most common poetic elements.

Meter

Meter is the regular pattern of stressed (/) and unstressed (˘) syllables in each poetic line. You can describe a poem's meter this way:

Name its main type of **foot,** or unit of rhythm. These are the most common English feet:

- iamb (˘/) as in *around*
- trochee (/˘) as in *broken*
- spondee (//) as in *airship*
- dactyl (/˘˘) as in *argument*
- anapest (˘˘/) as in *understand*

Count the number of feet in each line.

- monometer (one foot)
- dimeter (two feet)
- trimeter (three feet)
- tetrameter (four feet)
- pentameter (five feet)

Groups of poetic lines are called **stanzas**. You can describe some stanzas by counting the number of lines they contain:

- couplets (two lines)
- tercets (three)
- quatrains (four)
- sestets (six)

Extend the Lesson

Activity

- Read aloud Emily Dickinson's poem "There is a Solitude of Space" on p. 433, emphasizing the meter. Then **ask** students the following questions:
  1. What category of poetry does this poem represent?
     Answer: This poem represents lyric poetry.
  2. What makes this poem an example of lyric poetry?
     Answer: It is a short poem expressing the thoughts and feelings of one speaker, who can be identified with the writer, Dickinson.

Sound Devices

Sound devices are elements that enhance a poem's meaning by adding a musical quality to the language.

- **rhyme:** repetition of sounds at the ends of words, as in *top* and *drop*.
- **alliteration:** repetition of initial consonant sounds, as in *weak* and *weary*.
- **consonance:** repetition of final consonant sounds, as in *pull* and *fall*.
- **assonance:** repetition of similar vowel sounds, as in *low* and *tow*.
- **onomatopeoia:** use of a word that sounds like what it means, as in *fizz* and *hiss*.

Imagery and Figurative Language

Imagery is language that uses **images:** words or phrases that appeal to one or more of the senses of sight, hearing, touch, taste, or smell. **Figurative language** is language that is used imaginatively instead of literally and includes one or more **figures of speech:**

- A **simile** is a figure of speech that compares two apparently unlike things by using *like* or *as*, as in *I wandered lonely as a cloud*.
- A **metaphor** is a figure of speech that compares two apparently unlike things without using *like* or *as*, as in *Life is a broken-winged bird*.
- **Personification** is a figure of speech that gives human traits to something nonhuman, as in *Let the rain sing you a lullaby*.
- An **oxymoron** is a figure of speech that combines two contradictory words, as in *wise fool*. An oxymoron often expresses a **paradox:** an idea that seems contradictory but is actually true.

3

Strategies for Reading Poetry

Use these strategies as you read poetry.

Respond Read with your body as well as your mind. Experience the rhythms, as you do with music. Tap out the beat as you read silently or aloud. Notice how the poem looks on the page—does it sprawl or fall neatly into stanzas?

Compare and Contrast Putting poems side by side will help you to understand them. Compare and contrast poets like Whitman and Dickinson—one outward-looking and the other introspective.

- Tell students that poetry is intended to be read differently from prose.
- Encourage students to respond by actively involving their senses as they read a poem. Suggest that they read it aloud in order to hear the sounds. Help them find examples of imagery, engaging as many senses as possible.
- In addition to comparing and contrasting poems and poets, tell students to look for the comparisons that poets make within a single poem. For example, poets use similes and metaphors to compare two differing items.
- Also encourage students to compare and contrast poems with other literary forms when both are addressing the same topic or theme. For example, compare and contrast Walt Whitman's joyful individualism in his poem "Song of Myself" with Emerson's or Thoreau's essays on the same theme.

Emily Dickinson's Poetry

Meeting Your Standards

Students will

1. **analyze and respond to literary elements.**
   - Literary Analysis: Slant Rhyme
2. **read, comprehend, analyze, and critique poems.**
   - Reading Strategy: Analyzing Images
   - Reading Check questions
   - Apply the Skills questions
   - Assessment Practice (ATE)
3. **develop vocabulary.**
   - Vocabulary Lesson: Latin Word Root: *-finis-*
4. **understand and apply written and oral language conventions.**
   - Spelling Strategy
   - Grammar and Style Lesson: Gerunds
5. **develop writing proficiency.**
   - Writing Lesson: Letter to an Author
6. **develop appropriate research strategies.**
   - Extend Your Learning: Report
7. **understand and apply listening and speaking strategies.**
   - Extend Your Learning: Poetry Reading

Block Scheduling: Use one 90-minute class period to preteach the skills and have students read the selection. Use a second 90-minute class period to assess students' mastery of skills, extend their learning, and monitor their progress.

Homework Suggestions

Following are possibilities for homework assignments.

- Support pages from *Unit 3 Resources:*
  Literary Analysis
  Reading Strategy
  Vocabulary Builder
  Grammar and Style
- An Extend Your Learning project and the Writing Lesson for this selection group may be completed over several days.

Step-by-Step Teaching Guide	Pacing Guide
PRETEACH	
• Administer Vocabulary and Reading Warm-ups as necessary.	5 min.
• Engage students' interest with the motivation activity.	5 min.
• Read and discuss author and background features. **FT**	10 min.
• Introduce the Literary Analysis Skill: Slant Rhyme. **FT**	5 min.
• Introduce the Reading Strategy: Analyzing Images. **FT**	10 min.
• Prepare students to read by teaching the selection vocabulary. **FT**	
TEACH	
• Informally monitor comprehension while students read independently or in groups. **FT**	30 min.
• Monitor students' comprehension with the Reading Check notes.	as students read
• Reinforce vocabulary with Vocabulary Builder notes.	as students read
• Develop students' understanding of slant rhyme with the Literary Analysis annotations. **FT**	5 min.
• Develop students' ability to analyze images with the Reading Strategy annotations. **FT**	5 min.
ASSESS/EXTEND	
• Assess students' comprehension and mastery of the Literary Analysis and Reading Strategy by having them answer the Apply the Skills questions. **FT**	15 min.
• Have students complete the Vocabulary Lesson and the Grammar and Style Lesson. **FT**	15 min.
• Apply students' ability to use clear and logical organization by using the Writing Lesson. **FT**	45 min. or homework
• Apply students' understanding by using one or more of the Extend Your Learning activities.	20–90 min. or homework
• Administer Selection Test A or Selection Test B. **FT**	15 min.

Resources

PRINT

Unit 3 Resources

Vocabulary Warm-up Word Lists [**L1, L2, EL**] .... p. 156
Vocabulary Warm-up Practice [**L1, L2, EL**] .... p. 157
Reading Warm-up A [**L1, L2, EL**] .... p. 158
Reading Warm-up B [**L1, L2, L3**] .... p. 159

TRANSPARENCY

Graphic Organizer Transparencies

Literary Analysis Graphic Organizer A [**L3**] .... p. 85
Literary Analysis Graphic Organizer B [**L1, L2, EL**] .... p. 86
Reading Strategy Graphic Organizer A [**L3**] .... p. 83
Reading Strategy Graphic Organizer B [**L1, L2, EL**] .... p. 84

PRINT

Reader's Notebook [**L2**]
Reader's Notebook: Adapted Version [**L1**]
Reader's Notebook: English Learner's Version [**EL**]

Unit 3 Resources

Literary Analysis [**L3**] .... p. 160
Reading Strategy [**L3**] .... p. 161
Vocabulary Builder [**L3**] .... p. 162

TECHNOLOGY

Listening to Literature Audio CDs [**L2, EL**]
Reader's Notebook: Adapted Version Audio CD [**L1, L2**]

PRINT

Unit 3 Resources

Grammar and Style [**L3**] .... p. 163
Support for Writing Lesson [**L3**] .... p. 164
Support for Extend Your Learning [**L3**] .... p. 165
Enrichment [**L4**] .... p. 166
Selection Test A [**L1, L2, EL**] .... pp. 167–169
Selection Test B [**L3, L4**] .... pp. 170–172

General Resources

Rubrics for Business Letter [**L3**] .... pp. 61–62
Rubrics for Research: Research Report [**L3**] .... pp. 49–50

TECHNOLOGY

Go Online: Research [**L3**]
Go Online: Self-test [**L3**]
***ExamView*®, Test Bank** [**L3**]

Choosing Resources for Differentiated Instruction

[**L1**] Special Needs Students
[**L2**] Below-Level Students
[**L3**] All Students
[**L4**] Advanced Students
[**EL**] English Learners

FT Fast Track Instruction: To move the lesson more quickly, use the strategies and activities identified with **FT**.

Scaffolding for Less Proficient and Advanced Students

The leveled Critical Thinking questions after selections progress in the levels of thinking required to answer them. To address the needs of your different students, you may use the (a) level questions for your less proficient students and the (b) level questions with your on-level and advanced students. The occasional (c) level questions are appropriate for your advanced students.

Use this complete suite of powerful teaching tools to make lesson planning and testing quicker and easier.

Use the interactive textbook (online and on CD-ROM) to make selections and activities come alive with audio and video support and interactive questions.

Motivation

Many of Emily Dickinson's poems address the idea of solitude. Ask students to consider their personal response to the word *alone*. Each student should list the five words that first come to mind. Then elicit these words from each student. As you write responses on the chalkboard, ask the class to classify each response as positive or negative. When you have collected at least one response from every student, ask students to determine whether the word *alone* has a more positive or more negative connotation. Ask students to consider both aspects of solitude—independence and isolation—as they approach Emily Dickinson's poetry.

❶ Background

More About the Author

Although Emily Dickinson's reclusive lifestyle was most likely of emotional origin, it also may have been encouraged by the mores of the day. In the mid-nineteenth century, as an unmarried woman, Dickinson had little choice but to live with her family. Her decision to isolate herself may also have been the result of the inability of those around her to understand her. One eminent scholar and critic has said, "The poet Emily Dickinson complained that everybody said: 'What?' to her, until finally she practically gave up trying to talk altogether and confined herself to writing notes." Such an explanation is supported by Dickinson's poem on p. 431, "The soul selects her own society."

❶ Emily Dickinson's Poetry

Emily Dickinson (1830–1886)

Of the 1,775 poems Emily Dickinson wrote during her lifetime, only seven were published before her death—and these few appeared anonymously. Dickinson was a private person who was extremely reluctant to reveal herself or her work to the world. As a result, few people outside her family and a small circle of friends knew of her poetic genius until after her death. Today, however, she is widely regarded as one of the greatest American poets.

A Life Apart Dickinson was born in Amherst, Massachusetts, the daughter of a prominent lawyer. As a child, she was energetic and enjoyed the tasks of daily life—cooking, sewing, playing with friends, winter sports, even studying at a boarding school. Her childhood was normal in many respects. However, as an adult she became increasingly isolated. Though she traveled as a young woman to Boston, Washington, D.C., and Philadelphia to visit friends, she rarely left her hometown as she grew older. In fact, after her father's death in 1874, she seldom left the house, and during the last ten years of her life, she remained entirely within her house and garden. Dickinson's circle of friends grew smaller and smaller, and she communicated with the few that remained mainly through notes and fragments of poems. She dressed only in white and would not allow her neighbors or any strangers to see her. When her health failed, she allowed her doctor to examine her only by observing her from a distance. Dickinson was fond of children, however, and sometimes lowered a basket of candy or fruit to them from her upstairs window.

Her Talent Is Recognized Though she chose to live most of her life in virtual isolation, Emily Dickinson was a deeply energetic, intense person. She possessed a clear sense of purpose—to write poetry—and devoted most of her time to doing so. Yet because she shared her work with few people, she sometimes doubted her abilities. In 1862, she sent four poems to Thomas Wentworth Higginson, an influential literary critic, and asked him to tell her whether her verse was "alive." Like the editors who first published her work after her death, Higginson sought to change her unconventional style—her eccentric use of punctuation and irregular meter and rhyme. He did not understand that she had crafted her poetry with great precision and that her unique style, marked by unconventional capitalization and the use of dashes, was an important element of her poetry. Still, he did recognize her talent and encouraged her to keep writing.

Dickinson's Legacy In 1886, after fighting illness for two years, Emily Dickinson died in the same house in which she had been born. After her death, her sister Lavinia discovered packets of poems in the drawers of Emily's dresser. Dickinson had given instructions that her poems were to be destroyed after her death. Nevertheless, the poems were organized and edited by various family members and were published in small installments. However, it was not until 1955, when *The Poems of Emily Dickinson* was published, that her work as a whole was revealed to the world and her genius fully recognized.

The Belle of Amherst In the years since the publication of her work, Dickinson has become the subject of numerous plays, novels, and poems that have romanticized her life and celebrated her genius with varying amounts of sentimentality and accuracy. But for the poets who came after her, Dickinson has no peer. She is a voice of intense delicacy and urgency, rising out of stillness.

Preview

Connecting to the Literature

Although you may not often share your private thoughts about life's "big topics," you probably have many ideas about them. In her poems, Emily Dickinson shines light on her shadowy "private" thoughts as well as on ideas about such vast subjects as death, solitude, consciousness, and the soul.

Literary Analysis

Slant Rhyme

Poets use rhyme to create pleasant musical sounds and to unify groups of lines or stanzas. **Exact rhyme** occurs when two words have identical sounds in their final accented syllables. In **slant rhyme** (also called **half rhyme** or **approximate rhyme**), the final sounds are similar but not identical.

Exact rhyme: *glove/above*

Slant rhyme: *glove/prove*

Dickinson uses both exact and slant rhyme in her poetry. Her independence from strict rhyme is one of the reasons her poems are so surprising. As you read her poems, pay attention to her uses of both kinds of rhyme and consider the effects they create.

Comparing Literary Works

In all of her work, Dickinson explored different aspects of human consciousness. In some poems, Dickinson saw human consciousness as an infinite universe. In others, she saw it as a small, isolated presence. In all of her poems, the conscious mind of the individual is "Where the meanings are." As you read these poems, compare the differing ways in which Dickinson defines human awareness.

Reading Strategy

Analyzing Images

Poets often link abstract concepts such as love, life, and death to concrete images, or word pictures. In reading poetry, it is helpful to **analyze images** to clarify the abstract meaning the author is conveying. As you read Dickinson's poems, use a chart like the one shown here to help you understand her images.

Image	Abstract Idea
Carriage, slow journey	Death
School-children, grain, sunset	Life

Vocabulary Builder

cornice (kôr′ nis) *n.* projecting decorative molding along the top of a building (p. 427)

surmised (sər mīzd′) *v.* guessed (p. 427)

oppresses (ə pres′ əz) *v.* weighs heavily on the mind (p. 430)

finite (fī′ nīt) *adj.* having measurable or definable limits (p. 433)

infinity (in fin′ i tē) *n.* endless or unlimited space, time, or distance (p. 433)

2 Literary Analysis

Slant Rhyme

- Tell students that as they read Emily Dickinson's poems, they will focus on slant rhyme, in which final ending sounds are related but not identical.
- Have volunteers read aloud the Literary Analysis instruction and excerpts. Help students hear the difference between exact and slant rhymes.
- Discuss the instruction under Comparing Literary Works and use it to help students connect Dickinson's poetic structure to her exploration of human consciousness.

3 Reading Strategy

Analyzing Images

- Remind students that analyzing images can help them understand poetry's deeper, often symbolic, meanings.
- Explain to students that they can analyze images by questioning the emotions each image evokes. For example, a shiver in response to the image of the chill of nightfall might suggest the idea of a life ending.
- Direct students to use **Reading Strategy Graphic Organizer A** in ***Graphic Organizer Transparencies***, p. 83, to analyze images as they read Dickinson's poetry.

Vocabulary Builder

- Pronounce each vocabulary word for students, and read the definitions as a class. Have students identify any words with which they are already familiar.

Differentiated Instruction

Solutions for All Learners

Support for Special Needs Students
Have students use the support pages for these selections in the ***Reader's Notebook: Adapted Version.*** Completing these pages will prepare students to read the selections in the Student Edition.

Support for Less Proficient Readers
Have students use the support pages for these selections in the ***Reader's Notebook.*** Completing these pages will prepare students to read the selections in the Student Edition.

Support for English Learners
Have students use the support pages for these selections in the ***Reader's Notebook: English Learner's Version.*** Completing these pages will prepare students to read the selections in the Student Edition.

TEACH

Learning Modalities
Interpersonal Learners Remind students that Dickinson spoke directly to fewer and fewer people as her life progressed. Have students compose imaginary dialogues in which Dickinson discusses her work and her ideas and students express in their turn what they might wish to tell the poet about the effect her poems have had on them.

❶ About the Selection

In this poem, Dickinson captures the inevitability of death and suggests a belief in an eternal afterlife through the personification of Death as a coach driver who carries people toward their final resting place.

❷ Critical Viewing

Possible response: As in the poem, the horse and carriage wait outside the house. In the painting, the house seems isolated, almost unearthly, surrounded by clouds. The viewer is struck by the apparent simplicity of the scene and of the painter's style, but both belie the consummate skill of the artist.

❶ Because I could not stop for Death

Emily Dickinson

Waiting Outside No. 12, Anonymous, Crane Kalman Gallery

Background The extent of Emily Dickinson's gift was not generally recognized until 1955, when a new edition of her poems was published under the guidance of Thomas H. Johnson. Previous editors had changed Dickinson's poems to reflect conventional ideas about poetry, but Johnson's edition restored the poet's original versions. For the first time, Dickinson's poetry was printed as she had meant it to be read, and the world experienced the power of her complex mind captured in concrete imagery and simple but forceful language. Dickinson's work is often compared with that of the modern poets, and she is now acknowledged as a visionary who was far ahead of her time.

Because I could not stop for Death—
He kindly stopped for me—
The Carriage held but just Ourselves—
And Immortality.

❷ ▲ **Critical Viewing** In what ways do the details of this painting mirror Dickinson's poem? **[Analyze]**

Differentiated Instruction Solutions for All Learners

Accessibility at a Glance

	Death, Slant, Life, Soul	Fly, Brain, Solitude
Context	Innovative nineteenth-century works	Innovative nineteenth-century works
Language	Accessible (forceful, direct; concrete imagery)	Accessible (some ususual diction and syntax; concrete images)
Concept Level	Challenging (abstract concepts translated into concrete imagery)	Accessible (concrete, familiar concepts)
Literary Merit	One of most important American voices; original style; strong influence on generations	One of most important American voices; original style; strong influence on generations
Lexile	NP	NP
Overall Rating	More challenging	Average

We slowly drove—He knew no haste
And I had put away
My labor and my leisure too,
For his Civility—

We passed the School, where Children strove
At Recess—in the Ring—
We passed the Fields of Gazing Grain—
We passed the Setting Sun—

❸ Or rather—He passed Us—
The Dews drew quivering and chill—
For only Gossamer,[1] my Gown—
My Tippet[2]—only Tulle[3]—

We paused before a House that seemed
A Swelling of the Ground—
The Roof was scarcely visible—
The Cornice—in the Ground—

Since then—'tis Centuries—and yet
Feels shorter than the Day
I first surmised the Horses Heads
Were toward Eternity—

Reading Strategy
Analyzing Images What idea do the images of Gossamer and Tulle suggest?

Vocabulary Builder
cornice (kôr′ nis) *n.* projecting decorative molding along the top of a building

surmised (sər mīzd′) *v.* guessed

1. **Gossamer** *n.* very thin, soft, filmy cloth.
2. **Tippet** *n.* scarflike garment worn over the shoulders and hanging down in front.
3. **Tulle** (to͞ol) *n.* thin, fine netting used for scarves.

Critical Reading

1. **Respond:** Which images in this poem were the most vivid for you? Why?
2. **(a) Recall:** In the first two lines, what adverb defines Death's actions? **(b) Analyze:** In what sense is this depiction ironic?
3. **(a) Recall:** What three scenes does the carriage pass in stanza three? **(b) Interpret:** What is the significance of these images?
4. **(a) Recall:** How much time passes for the speaker in this poem? **(b) Speculate:** Why do you think the speaker notes that the time "feels shorter than the Day"? **(c) Compare and Contrast:** What does the speaker seem to feel about the experience of death in contrast with life?
5. **(a) Draw Conclusions:** What is the message of this poem? **(b) Take a Position:** Do you agree with the message? Explain.

For: More about Emily Dickinson
Visit: www.PHSchool.com
Web Code: ere-9314

❸ Reading Strategy
Analyzing Images

- Read the poem aloud for students. Then reread just the bracketed lines. Help students use the footnotes to define the words *gossamer, tippet,* and *tulle.*
- **Ask** students the Reading Strategy question: What idea do the images of gossamer and tulle suggest?
  Possible answer: They suggest fragile fabrics such as those that were used in making shrouds.

ASSESS
Answers

1. Students should identify specific images and provide support for their responses.
2. (a) The adverb "kindly" describes Death's actions. (b) **Possible response:** Death is usually personified in negative terms.
3. (a) It passes "the School," "the Fields," and "the Setting Sun." (b) These details could represent the stages of life.
4. (a) It has been centuries since the speaker died. (b) The speaker depicts the timeless nature of eternity. (c) The speaker suggests that both life and death are journeys but that death's journey is free of the busy pace of life.
5. **Possible responses:**
   (a) The poem presents death as the coming of a friend who brings the dead to a new home.
   (b) Students should support their responses.

Go Online Author Link For additional information about Emily Dickinson, have students type in the Web Code, then select D from the alphabet,

Differentiated Instruction Solutions for All Learners

Strategy for Special Needs Students
Point out Dickinson's unusual use of capitalization. Explain that the capitalized words serve either rhythmic purposes or provide emphasis on particular images and ideas. Encourage students to first read the poem as if the capitalization were not there. Then help them reread to understand the purpose of each incidence.

Support for Less Proficient Readers
Students may find Dickinson's frequent use of dashes to be confusing. Explain that dashes may be treated as commas, to suggest a brief pause. Play the recording of the poem on **Listening to Literature Audio CDs.** Direct students to follow along in their texts, listening for the pauses at each dash.

Strategy for Gifted/Talented Students
Have students prepare this poem as one of their choices for the Listening and Speaking activity on p. 437. Remind them to pay careful attention to both the dashes and capitalization that Dickinson uses to convey meaning and cadence.

❹ About the Selection

In this poem, Dickinson describes the final moments between life and death. A fly, an almost trivial symbol of life, is what the speaker is most aware of before death.

❺ Humanities

Room With a Balcony, by Adolph von Menzel

Like von Menzel's other work, this painting is distinguished by its expressiveness, accurate details, and use of light and shade for subtle effects. It captures the contrasting ordinariness and extraordinariness of death. Use these questions for discussion:

1. How is the overall impression of the painting similar to that of the poem?
   Answer: Both the image and the poem convey stillness. There appears to be no life in the painted room. The chairs and lamps are placed symmetrically around the mirror. The curtains do not move; this detail reinforces the "Stillness."
2. What might the image of an open window mean in a room in which someone has died?
   Possible answer: It suggests that something or someone may have just entered or left the room.

❻ Critical Viewing

Answer: The mirrored image of a couch and painting, which are no longer in the room but are still suggested by shadows, reflect the poem's idea of death taking away life but leaving behind some mark of the departed.

I heard a Fly buzz—when I died

Emily Dickinson

❹

❺

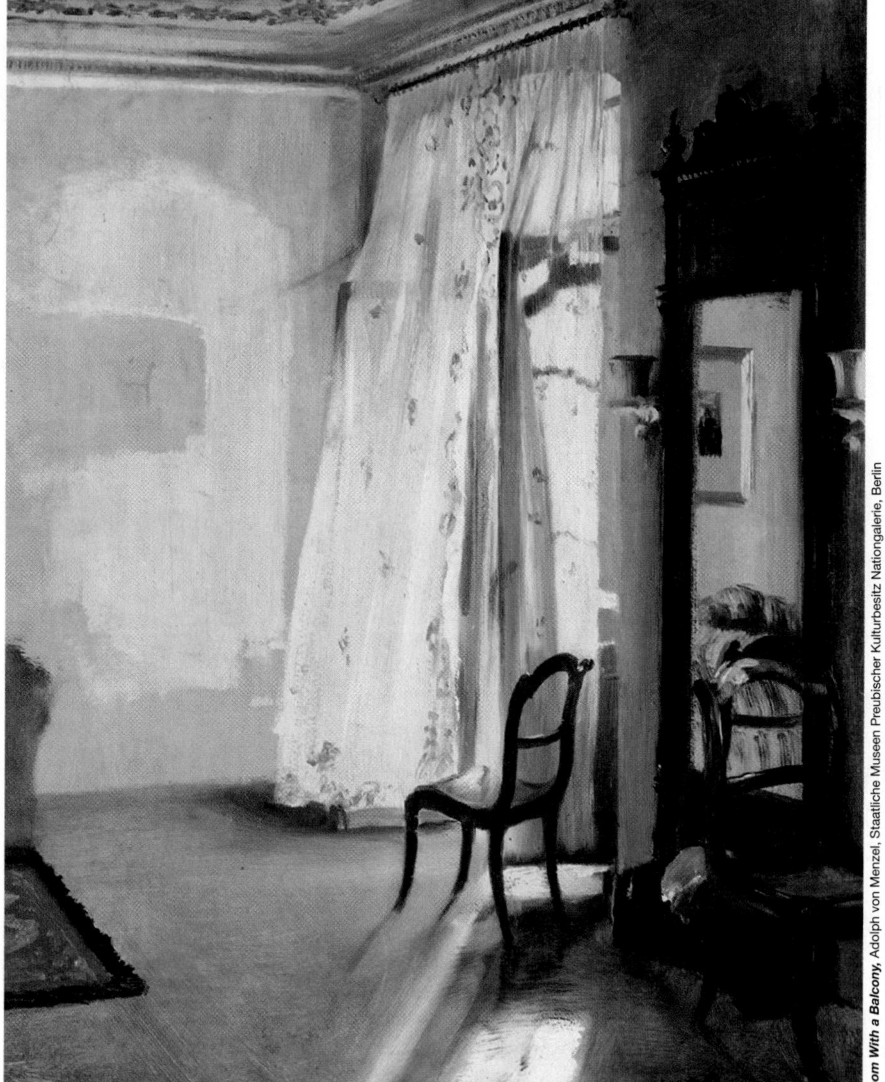

Room With a Balcony, Adolph von Menzel, Staatliche Museen Preubischer Kulturbesitz Nationgalerie, Berlin

❻ ▲ **Critical Viewing** What details in this painting serve as an appropriate illustration for Dickinson's poem? **[Support]**

I heard a Fly buzz—when I died—
The Stillness in the Room
Was like the Stillness in the Air—
Between the Heaves of Storm—

The Eyes around—had wrung them dry—
And Breaths were gathering firm
For that last Onset—when the King
Be witnessed—in the Room—

I willed my Keepsakes—Signed away
What portion of me be
Assignable—and then it was
There interposed a Fly—

With Blue—uncertain stumbling Buzz—
Between the light—and me—
And then the Windows failed—and then
I could not see to see—

7 Literary Analysis
Slant Rhyme What two words form a slant rhyme in the first stanza?

Critical Reading

1. **Respond:** What was your first reaction to this poem? Explain.
2. **(a) Recall:** What do the speaker and those in attendance expect to experience when "the last Onset" occurs? **(b) Recall:** What happens instead? **(c) Analyze:** In what ways is this turn of events ironic?
3. **(a) Recall:** What actions has the speaker taken in preparation for death? **(b) Interpret:** Which "portion" of the speaker is "assignable," or able to be willed to others, and which is not?
4. **(a) Recall:** In the final stanza, what adjectives does the speaker use to describe the buzzing of the fly? **(b) Draw Conclusions:** What statement about dying is Dickinson making in this poem?
5. **Speculate:** If you were describing a deathbed scene from the perspective of the dying person, would you mention the buzzing of a fly? Why or why not?

For: More about Emily Dickinson
Visit: www.PHSchool.com
Web Code: ere-9314

7 Literary Analysis
Slant Rhyme

- Have students read the bracketed passage.
- **Ask** them the Literary Analysis Question. What two words form a slant rhyme in the stanza?
  Answer: *Be* and *fly* form a slant rhyme.

ASSESS
Answers

1. Students should support their responses with evidence from the text.
2. (a) They expect to witness the speaker's death. (b) A fly begins to buzz. (c) It suggests that death is highly ordinary, even pedestrian.
3. (a) The speaker wills away keepsakes and other worldly goods. (b) **Possible response:** The material aspects are "assignable," but the spirit is not.
4. (a) The speaker describes the fly with *Blue, uncertain, stumbling,* and *Buzz.* (b) **Possible response:** She shows that death is an everyday event; she points out that the experience does not match people's expectations.
5. Students should support their responses.

Go Online Author Link For additional information about Emily Dickinson, have students type in the Web Code, then select D from the alphabet, and then select Emily Dickinson.

Differentiated Instruction
Solutions for All Learners

Background for Less Proficient Readers
Explain that Emily Dickinson did not title her poems. Because an editorial decision was later made to use the first lines as titles, they do not reflect traditional capitalization for titles. Make sure that students follow the exact punctuation and capitalization shown in their book when writing about the poems.

Vocabulary for English Learners
Point out the word *heaves* in line 4 to students. In the poem's context, the word means "to rise and fall rhythmically." Explain that Dickinson refers to the calm between waves of rain or thunder in a storm.

Strategy for Advanced Readers
Provide students with the factual background in the column for Less Proficient Readers. Ask them to develop their own title for this poem. Suggest that they discuss the circumstances in which a person might become aware of the sound of a fly. Urge them to think about what a fly might represent as they search for an appropriate title.

❽ About the Selections

The first poem describes an unbearable hurt that fills the soul, and comes with winter, when the world is cold and still. The poet decribes the hurt as a divine visitation, sent to teach the meaning of our own mortality. The second poem conveys the sense of pain that comes from parting with a loved one. The final poem is a meditation on the nature of the human soul. The poet depicts the soul as a feminine entity, separate from and indifferent to worldly claims on her attention. Dickinson portrays the soul as choosing, for unknowable reasons, a single person to share her society, and rejecting all others.

❾ Literary Analysis

Slant Rhyme

- After students read the entire poem "There's a certain Slant of light," direct them to reread the final bracketed stanza.
- Then, have students locate two words that form a slant rhyme in the stanza.
  Answer: The words *listens* and *Distance* form a slant rhyme.

❽ There's a certain Slant of light

Emily Dickinson

There's a certain Slant of light,
Winter Afternoons—
That oppresses, like the Heft
Of Cathedral Tunes—

Heavenly Hurt, it gives us—
We can find no scar,
But internal difference,
Where the Meanings, are—

None may teach it—Any—
'Tis the Seal Despair—
An imperial affliction
Sent us of the Air—

❾
When it comes, the Landscape listens—
Shadows—hold their breath—
When it goes, 'tis like the Distance
On the look of Death—

Vocabulary Builder
oppresses (ə pres′ əz) *v.* weighs heavily on the mind

❽ My life closed twice before its close

Emily Dickinson

My life closed twice before its close—
It yet remains to see
If Immortality unveil
A third event to me.

So huge, so hopeless to conceive
As these that twice befell.
Parting is all we know of heaven.
And all we need of hell.

Enrichment

Seasonal Affective Disorder

In "There's a certain Slant of light," Emily Dickinson describes an emotional response that resembles a medical condition unknown to her or to the doctors of her time. In the nineteenth century, a person who felt lethargic and depressed during winter months might be referred to as having "cabin fever." However, in the 1980s, doctors diagnosed this depression as a mood disorder that is triggered by a lack of sunlight. The major symptoms of this condition, called Seasonal Affective Disorder (SAD), are low energy and fatigue, difficulty concentrating, increased sensitivity to social rejection and avoidance of social situations, and change in appetite and weight gain. SAD usually occurs in late fall and lasts through early winter. One treatment for SAD is bright light therapy. Other treatments for depression, such as counselling and exercise, also can be effective for persons with SAD.

The Soul selects her own Society

Emily Dickinson

The Soul selects her own Society—
Then—shuts the Door—
To her divine Majority—
Present no more—

10
Unmoved—she notes the Chariots—pausing—
At her low Gate—
Unmoved—an Emperor be kneeling
Upon her Mat—

I've known her—from an ample nation—
Choose One—
Then—close the Valves of her attention—
Like Stone—

Literary Analysis
Slant Rhyme What words create slant rhymes in the second stanza?

Critical Reading

1. **Respond:** How does "My life closed twice before its close—" connect details of personal history to ideas about eternity?
2. **(a) Recall:** According to the speaker of "There's a certain Slant of light," in what ways does the winter light affect people? **(b) Analyze:** What does this light seem to represent to the speaker?
3. **(a) Interpret:** What is the third event to which the speaker of "My life closed before its close—" refers? **(b) Connect:** What is the relationship between the three events?
4. **(a) Recall:** In "The Soul selects her own Society—," what leaves the soul "unmoved"? **(b) Analyze:** How would you describe the soul's attitude toward the world's attractions?
5. **(a) Recall:** What happens after the soul makes her choice? **(b) Assess:** What adjectives would you use to characterize the speaker based on this choice?
6. **Relate:** Our culture places a premium on popularity for its own sake. What do Dickinson's poems suggest about other ways to view human relationships?

Go Online Author Link

For: More about Emily Dickinson
Visit: www.PHSchool.com
Web Code: ere-9314

10 Critical Thinking

Interpret

- Read the poem aloud for students at least twice.
- **Discuss** the central meaning of the poem and have students restate it in their own words.
Possible response: The soul's role in our choice of friends is mysterious.
- **Ask** students to describe the kind of person the speaker is.
Possible response: Students may say that the speaker, like the soul, is proud, defiant, solitary, and highly selective.

11 Literary Analysis

Slant Rhyme

- Ask a student to read the second stanza aloud to the class. Then, **ask** the Literary Analysis question: What words create slant rhymes in the second stanza?
Answer: The words are *gate* and *mat*.

ASSESS

Answers

1. The speaker connects life experiences of loss to her expectations of heaven and hell.
2. (a) It oppresses them. (b) It seems to represent her own mortality.
3. (a) The third event is her death. (b) They are each kinds of endings.
4. (a) Chariots and emperors leave the soul unmoved. (b) The soul is indifferent to the world's attractions.
5. (a) The soul shuts the door. (b) **Possible response:** Sudents may suggest the adjectives *private, picky, detached,* or *divine.*
6. **Possible response:** The poems suggest that human relationships are complex, and that a single close friend may be more valuable than a whole group of less meaningful acquaintances.

Go Online Author Link — For additional information about Emily Dickinson, have students type in the Web Code, then select D from the alphabet, and then select Emily Dickinson.

Differentiated Instruction

Solutions for All Learners

Strategy for Special Needs Students

Highlight Dickinson's use of a gerund, *parting,* in line 7 of "My life closed twice before its close." To help these students understand Dickinson's use of present participle verbs, both as gerunds and as verbs, present the Grammar and Style Lesson on Gerunds, p. 436.

Strategy for Less Proficient Readers

Point out the gerund *parting* in line 7 of "My life closed twice before its close." Identify *parting* as the subject of the sentence. Then help students understand the lines: Death is all we know of heaven because we remain on Earth, yet it is all we need of hell because no hell could be as painful as losing someone deeply beloved.

Strategy for English Learners

With your students, review gerunds. Point out that the gerund *parting* in line 7 of "My life closed twice before its close" is the subject of the sentence. Emphasize that other *-ing* words in Dickinson's poems, such as *pausing* and *kneeling* in "The soul selects her own society" are not gerunds but present participles.

12 About the Selections

The first poem contrasts the brain, as a metaphor for the soul, with the sky and the sea to arrive at the notion that the human soul is infinite, like God, and by implication it is of God. The second poem says that the strongest solitude is the solitude of inner loneliness.

13 Humanities

Twilight in the Wilderness, by Frederic E. Church

This painting, like other early works by Church, is a panoramic composition with emphatic visual effects. Some critics call this Church's finest sunset painting. Use this question for discussion:

- How does the painting suit both "There is a solitude of space" and "The Brain—is wider than the Sky—"?
  Possible answer: Church's expansive view echoes the widness of the sky Dickinson describes in the first poem and reflects the solitude central to the second poem.

14 Reading Strategy
Analyzing Images

- Have a volunteer read aloud the bracketed stanza.
- **Ask** students to identify Dickinson's comparison and suggest its effects on readers.
  Possible answer: Dickinson compares the human brain to the sky and sea. She suggests that the brain's capacity is unrelated to its size.

15 Critical Viewing

Answer: Students may cite general feelings of serenity, beauty, awe, or solemnity.

12 The Brain—is wider than the Sky

Emily Dickinson

13

Twilight in the Wilderness, Frederick E. Church

14

The Brain—is wider than the Sky—
For—put them side by side—
The one the other will contain
With ease—and You—beside—

The Brain is deeper than the sea—
For—hold them—Blue to Blue—
The one the other will absorb—
As Sponges—Buckets—do—

The Brain is just the weight of God—
For—Heft them—Pound for Pound—
And they will differ—if they do—
As Syllable from Sound—

15 ▲ **Critical Viewing** What feelings do the sweep of sky, mountains, and water in this painting evoke in you? **[Respond]**

Enrichment

The Human Brain

In "The Brain—is wider than the Sky—," Dickinson compares the human brain's scope or size to the sky and the sea. In fact, the adult human brain weighs an average of about three pounds. The brain grows rapidly in a person's first six years, adding many nerve cells as well as a system of supporting and connecting cells. While representing just 2 percent of an adult's average total body weight, the brain requires 20 percent of the oxygen consumed by the body and can suffer serious damage in just three to five minutes without sufficient supply.

Many of the perceptions to which Dickinson refers arise from the cerebral cortex. The cortex receives and responds to sensory messages. It also controls motor functions and allows humans to think, speak, and remember. Recent brain research suggests some interesting physical differences between the brains of men and women. These differences may explain why, in general, men find spatial tasks easier and women excel at verbal tasks.

There is a solitude of space

Emily Dickinson

There is a solitude of space
A solitude of sea
A solitude of death, but these
Society shall be
Compared with that profounder site
That polar privacy
A soul admitted to itself—
Finite Infinity.

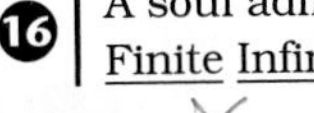

Vocabulary Builder

finite (fī′ nīt′) *adj.* having measurable or definable limits

infinity (in fin′ i tē) *n.* endless or unlimited space, time, or distance

Critical Reading

1. **Respond:** Do you think it is a good idea for people to seek solitude? Why or why not?
2. **(a) Recall:** What comparisons does the speaker make in "The Brain is Wider Than the Sky"? **(b) Interpret:** What role does a surprising use of scale and size play in these comparisons?
3. **(a) Recall:** According to the poet, how is the brain wider than the sky? **(b) Recall:** How is the brain deeper than the sea? **(c) Interpret:** What do these images suggest about the power of the human mind and heart?
4. **(a) Compare and Contrast:** In what ways does the poet's comparison of the brain to God differ from the comparisons made in the earlier stanzas? **(b) Interpret:** What is the poet suggesting about the relationship between human consciousness and divinity?
5. **(a) Recall:** In "There is a solitude of space," what three things does the speaker compare to "polar privacy"? **(b) Contrast:** How does the solitude of "a soul admitted to itself" differ from the other solitudes described?
6. **Modify:** Dickinson did not give her poems titles, though her editors sometimes used a poem's first line. What titles would you give these two poems? Why?

For: More about Emily Dickinson
Visit: www.PHSchool.com
Web Code: ere-9314

16 Vocabulary Builder

The Latin Root *-finis-*

- Call students' attention to Dickinson's use of the related words *finite* and *infinity,* and their definitions.
- Let students know that the Latin root of each word is *finis,* which means "end."
- **Invite** students to volunteer other words containing this root. **Possiblities include:** *infinitude, final, finish, confine, refine*
- Make sure students recognize how prefixes act to change the meanings of words formed with the root *finis.* Have students look up etymologies for these words in the dictionary and record them in their journals.

ASSESS

Answers

1. Students should support their opinions.
2. (a) The speaker compares the brain to the sky, to the sea, and to God. (b) The speaker compares the brain to things that seem at first to be much larger.
3. (a) The brain can contain the sky with ease. (b) It can absorb the sea's blue. (c) The human mind and heart can hold images and experiences of limitless scope and size.
4. (a) The first two comparisons suggest that the brain is wider or deeper, while the third suggests a difference in substance rather than in size. (b) **Possible response:** Human consciousness has some similarity of scope to divinity, though it may be vastly different in substance.
5. (a) Privacy is compared to the solitude of space, sea, and death. (b) While the solitude of a "soul admitted to itself" cannot be shared, the other kinds of solitude can.
6. Students should be able to explain their title choices.

Go Online Author Link For additional information about Emily Dickinson, have students type in the Web Code, then select D from the alphabet, and then select Emily Dickinson.

Differentiated Instruction

Solutions for All Learners

Strategy for Less Proficient Readers

Use a concept map or web to show students how abstract concepts can be linked to concrete images in poetry and literature. Explain that by analyzing the images, a reader learns what the author is conveying.

Have students analyze the images in "There is a solitude of space" by Dickinson. Using a diagram like the one shown, help students link abstract words to concrete images and then tell what is being compared.

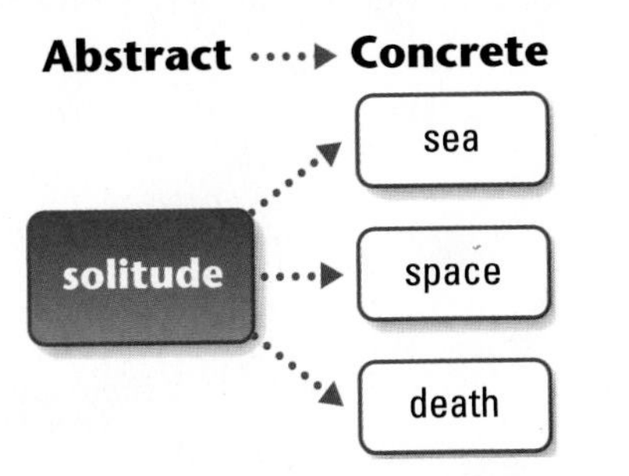

17 About the Selection

This poem suggests that comparison and contrast are useful ways to learn; we can only learn things by comparing them with very different things.

18 Critical Thinking

Analyze

- Direct students to read the bracketed text.
- **Challenge** students to explain the meaning of the last line.
  Possible answer: Fallen snow is cold, still, and lifeless, while birds are vibrant, lovely, and contrast starkly with the snow.

ASSESS

Answers

1. Students' answers will vary.
2. (a) In each line, the speaker states that each line's first word is learned from the words that follow. (b) **Possible responses:** One knows a thing by its absence, by its opposite, or by need. Things have meaning only in context. (c) Students should be able to support their positions.
3. (a) Students may mention study skills they have learned only when these skills were necessary or people they recognized they cared about only when the people were absent (b) Students' additions should be consistent with the form and message of the poem.

Go Online Author Link For additional information about Emily Dickinson, have students type in the Web Code, then select D from the alphabet, and then select Emily Dickinson.

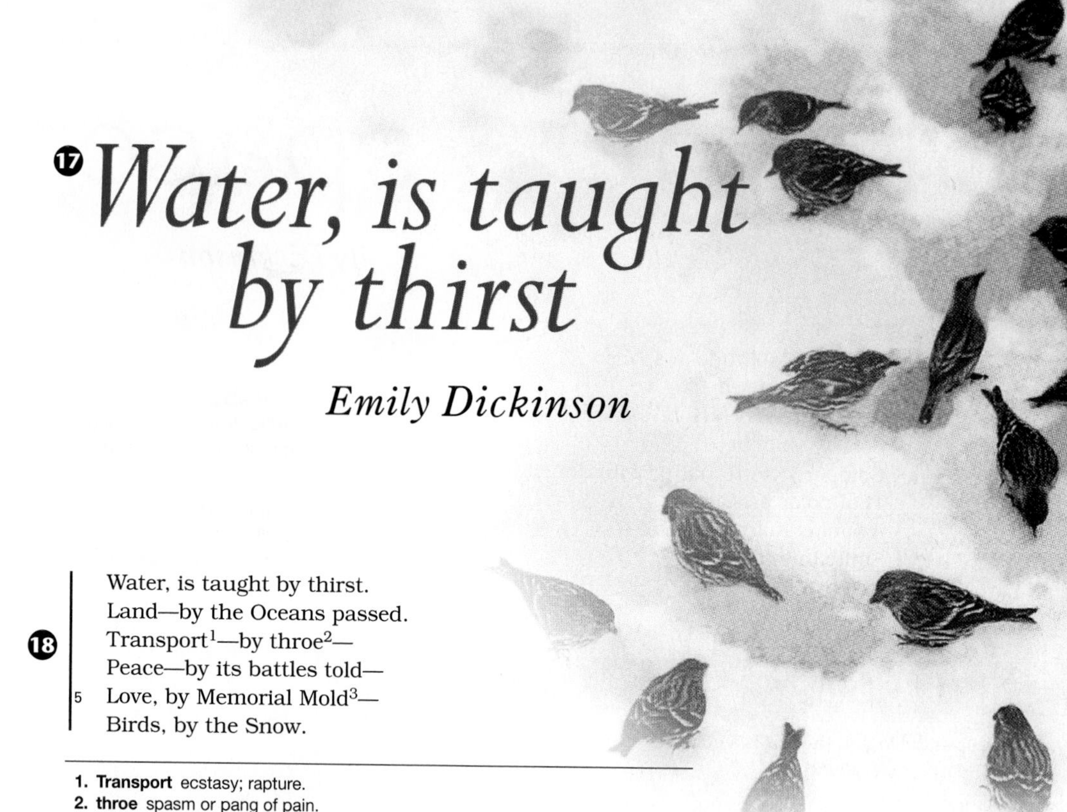

17 *Water, is taught by thirst*

Emily Dickinson

18

Water, is taught by thirst.
Land—by the Oceans passed.
Transport[1]—by throe[2]—
Peace—by its battles told—
Love, by Memorial Mold[3]—
Birds, by the Snow.

1. **Transport** ecstasy; rapture.
2. **throe** spasm or pang of pain.
3. **Memorial Mold** memorial grounds or cemetery.

Critical Reading

1. **Respond:** How many lines did you read before you understood the title of this poem?
2. **(a) Recall:** What is the relationship between each line's first word and the following words? **(b) Interpret:** What is the theme or message of this poem? **(c) Take a Position:** Do you agree or disagree with this message? Explain.
3. **(a) Relate:** What situations or experiences in your daily life demonstrate the theme of this poem? **(b) Extend:** Based on these situations, add two lines to this poem that are in keeping with the theme.

For: More about Emily Dickinson
Visit: www.PHSchool.com
Web Code: ere-9314

Apply the Skills

Emily Dickinson's Poetry

Literary Analysis

Slant Rhyme

1. In "Because I could not stop for Death," what three words create **slant rhymes** for *Immortality, Civility,* and *Eternity*?
2. **(a)** Using a chart like the one here and the abc system it models for notating rhyme scheme, examine the pattern of rhyme in "There's a certain Slant of light." **(b)** What is the effect of Dickinson's patterned use of both slant and full rhyme?

	Stanza One	Two	Three	Four
Line 1	*light* (a)			
Line 2	*noons* (b)			
Line 3	*Heft* (a-slant)			
Line 4	*Tunes* (b-full)			

Comparing Literary Works

3. Does *soul* have the same meaning in both "The Soul selects her own Society" and "There is a solitude of space"? Explain.
4. **(a)** Which poems present human consciousness as something boundless? **(b)** Which present consciousness as something limited? **(c)** How would you define Dickinson's view of the individual self?

Reading Strategy

Analyzing Images

5. What **image** does Dickinson use to describe a gravesite in "Because I could not stop for Death"?
6. **(a)** Identify two images in "Water, is taught by thirst." **(b)** Identify two images in "The Brain—is wider than the Sky." **(c)** How do these images help the speaker communicate a specific abstract idea?

Extend Understanding

7. **Humanities Connection:** In real life, people select a wide variety of different "societies." **(a)** What are some of the "societies" people enjoy in your community? **(b)** What do you think this tendency indicates about human beings?

QuickReview

Slant rhyme occurs when two words sound alike but do not rhyme exactly.

To **analyze images,** determine whether—and how—they relate to larger ideas.

For: Self-test
Visit: www.PHSchool.com
Web Code: era-6310

Answers

1. *Me, away,* and *day* are slant rhymes for these words.
2. (a)

Stanza One	Stanza Two
light (a)	us (a)
noons (b)	scar (b)
Heft (a-slant)	difference (a-slant)
Tunes (b-full)	are (b-full)

Stanza Three	Stanza Four
any (a)	listens (a)
Despair (b)	breath (b)
affliction (c)	Distance (a-slant)
Air (b-full)	Death (b-full)

(b) The poem has a repetitive, musical quality.

Another sample answer can be found on **Literary Analysis Graphic Organizer B**, p. 86 in ***Graphic Organizer Transparencies.***

3. Yes, both discuss the nature of the soul as the innermost core of our being.
4. (a) "There is a solitude of space," "The Soul selects her own Society" and "The Brain—is wider than the Sky—" present human consciousness as boundless. (b) "There's a certain Slant of light," and "I heard a Fly buzz—when I died—" present human consciousness as limited by mortality. (c) **Possible response:** The self presented through these poems is engaged with the world but always aware of eternity and human mortality.
5. She uses the image of a house below ground.
6. (a) Each line of the poem presents an image. (b) Each stanza of the poem presents an image. (c) These images use concrete objects to illustrate abstract ideas.
7. Students may mention athletic groups, clubs, peer groups, or work colleagues. The choice of a variety of "societies" indicates that humans are diverse.

Go Online Assessment — Students may use the **Self-test** to prepare for **Selection Test A** or **Selection Test B.**

EXTEND/ASSESS

Answers

1 Vocabulary Lesson

Word Analysis

1. *Finish* means "end."
2. *Confine* means "to limit or enclose."
3. *Final* means "of or coming at the end, last."
4. *Refinement* means "elegance of speech, manners, etc."

Spelling Strategy

1. confessor
2. processor
3. depressor
4. professor

Vocabulary Builder

1. a
2. b
3. b
4. c
5. c

2 Grammar and Style Lesson

1. *Swelling* is a predicate nominative.
2. *Writing* is a subject.
3. *Parting* is a subject.
4. *Cooking* is a predicate nominative.
5. *Traveling* is a direct object.

Writing Application

Students should identify the gerunds in their paragraphs.

Possible response: I am often found working on my *sewing*. *Choosing* a pattern and actually *creating* something to wear can be rewarding. I like *seeing* the smile on a friend's face when I give her a gift I've made.

WG Writing and Grammar, Ruby Level

Students will find further instruction and practice on gerunds in Chapter 19, Section 2.

Build Language Skills

1 Vocabulary Lesson

Word Analysis: Latin Root *-finis-*

In "There is a solitude of space," Dickinson uses the words *finite* and *infinity*, both of which contain the Latin root *-finis-*, meaning "end" or "limit." A *finite* entity is limited in time or space; *infinity* is limitless. Explain the meaning of each of the following words, and then note how the root *-finis-* relates to the meaning of each one.

1. finish
2. confine
3. final
4. refinement

Spelling Strategy

When writing the noun forms of verbs ending in *-ess*, you will usually add the suffix *-or*, as in *oppress* + *-or* = *oppressor*. Write the noun form for each of the verbs listed below. Check your spelling in a dictionary.

1. confess
2. process
3. depress
4. profess

Vocabulary Builder: Synonyms

Review the vocabulary list on page 425. Then, identify the word or phrase whose meaning is most nearly the same as that of the first word in each item below.

1. cornice: **(a)** decorative ledge, **(b)** functional door, **(c)** elaborate spire
2. surmised: **(a)** explained, **(b)** inferred, **(c)** reduced
3. oppresses: **(a)** inhabits, **(b)** troubles, **(c)** judges
4. finite: **(a)** heavenly, **(b)** endless, **(c)** limited
5. infinity: **(a)** mystery, **(b)** multitude, **(c)** endlessness

2 Grammar and Style Lesson

Gerunds

A **gerund** is a verb form that ends in *-ing* and is used as a noun. Like nouns, gerunds function in sentences as subjects, direct objects, predicate nominatives, and objects of prepositions. The gerunds are italicized in the following examples.

Subject: *Writing* requires discipline.

Direct Object: Dickinson left her *writing* in her dresser.

Object of Preposition: She learned about *writing* by *practicing*.

Practice Identify each gerund below and tell how it is used in the sentence.

1. We paused before a House that seemed / A Swelling of the Ground—.
2. Writing was Dickinson's great passion.
3. Parting is all we know of heaven.
4. Her favorite activity was cooking.
5. Dickinson avoided traveling great distances.

Writing Application Write a paragraph of at least three sentences in which you describe a hobby—skiing or painting, for example. Include at least three gerunds.

WG *Prentice Hall Writing and Grammar Connection: Chapter 19, Section 2*

Assessment Practice

Make Inferences and Generalizations

(For more practice, see *Standardized Test Practice Workbook*, p. 24.)

The reading sections of many tests require students to make inferences. Explain to students that making inferences will help them understand poetry because poets often leave much of their message unstated. Use the following example to help students make inferences about "There's a certain Slant of light," on p. 430:

Which of the following best describes the effect of the light?

A overwhelming
B uplifting
C encouraging
D energizing

The last three answers cannot be supported by details from the text. The light is oppressive and feels heavy, so *A* is the best choice.

Writing Lesson

Letter to an Author

Dickinson's poetry may have stirred your emotions, challenged you to think about an idea or aspect of existence, or helped you to better understand yourself. Imagine that Dickinson is still alive. Write a letter to the poet in which you express your reactions to her verse. Be sure to use a clear organization in presenting your ideas.

Prewriting Focus on one poem. Explore your thoughts and feelings about the poem and its effect on you. Edit your reactions down to three or four important points; then, consider how your notes support each idea.

Model: Creating Clear and Logical Organization

Salutation: Dear Emily Dickinson,

Intro: Explain that I admire her poetry.

First paragraph: Her poems explore complex ideas.

Second paragraph: Her imagery gives me new ways to think.

Conclusion: Thank her, and tell her to keep writing.

An effective letter is organized clearly and logically.

Drafting Open your letter with an explanation of why you are writing. Then, develop and support each important idea in a separate paragraph.

Revising Check your tone and word choice. Confirm that you have conveyed your thoughts in a clear and logical way, with appropriate transitions from one paragraph to the next.

Prentice Hall Writing and Grammar Connection: Chapter 14, Section 3

Extend Your Learning

Listening and Speaking Choose three Dickinson poems to present in a **poetry reading.** Consider the meaning of each idea, image, and punctuation mark. Keep these tips in mind:

- Experiment with volume and tone until you achieve the desired effect.
- Speak clearly, letting the poem's meaning show in your emphasis and pacing.

Give a reading that you feel is as close as possible to the author's intention.

Research and Technology Dickinson was close to her brother Austin. Using a variety of sources, research him and their relationship. Then, select two of Dickinson's poems that seem to speak to her relationship with her brother. Combine your research and the poems in a **report.**

For: An additional research activity
Visit: www.PHSchool.com
Web Code: erd-7309

3 Writing Lesson

- To guide students in writing this letter to a poet, give them the **Support for Writing Lesson,** p. 164 in ***Unit 3 Resources.***
- Organize students into groups. Have them exchange reactions to the poems as a way to choose a poem on which to focus.
- Suggest that students use the Outline organizer in ***Graphic Organizer Transparencies,*** p. 309, to structure their ideas.
- Use the Business Letter rubrics, in ***General Resources,*** pp. 61–62, to evaluate work.

4 Research and Technology

- Suggest that students use the Internet as a research source.
- Encourage students to focus very specifically on historical evidence of the relationship between Emily and Austin, rather than on providing simple biographical information.
- Direct students to poem indices in your library or online that can help them identify pertinent Dickinson poems.
- If time allows, invite students to present oral versions of their reports to the class.
- Use the rubrics for Research: Research Reports in ***General Resources,*** pp. 49–50.
- The **Support for Extend Your Learning** page (***Unit 3 Resources,*** p. 165) provides guided note-taking opportunities to help students complete the Extend Your Learning activities.

Go Online Research Activity: Have students type in the Web Code for another research activity.

Assessment Resources

The following resources can be used to assess students' knowledge and skills.

Unit 3 Resources
- **Selection Test A,** pp. 167–169
- **Selection Test B,** pp. 170–172

General Resources:
- **Rubrics for Business Letter,** pp. 61–62
- **Rubrics for Research: Research Report,** pp. 49–50

Go Online Assessment: Students may use the **Self-test** to prepare for **Selection Test A** or **Selection Test B.**

Meeting Your Standards

Students will

1. **analyze and respond to literary elements.**
   - Literary Analysis: Free Verse
2. **read, comprehend, analyze, and critique poems.**
   - Reading Strategy: Inferring the Poet's Attitude
   - Reading Check questions
   - Apply the Skills questions
   - Assessment Practice (ATE)
3. **develop vocabulary.**
   - Vocabulary Lesson: Latin Root: *-fus-*
4. **understand and apply written and oral language conventions.**
   - Spelling Strategy
   - Grammar and Style Lesson: Pronoun and Antecedent Agreement
5. **develop writing proficiency.**
   - Writing Lesson: Imitation of an Author's Style
6. **develop appropriate research strategies.**
   - Extend Your Learning: Report
7. **understand and apply listening and speaking strategies.**
   - Extend Your Learning: Collage

Block Scheduling: Use one 90-minute class period to preteach the skills and have students read the selection. Use a second 90-minute class period to assess students' mastery of skills, extend their learning, and monitor their progress.

Homework Suggestions

Following are possibilities for homework assignments.

- Support pages from *Unit 3 Resources:*
  Literary Analysis
  Reading Strategy
  Vocabulary Builder
  Grammar and Style
- An Extend Your Learning project and the Writing Lesson for this selection group may be completed over several days.

Step-by-Step Teaching Guide	Pacing Guide
PRETEACH	
• Administer Vocabulary and Reading Warm-ups as necessary.	5 min.
• Engage students' interest with the motivation activity.	5 min.
• Read and discuss author and background features. **FT**	10 min.
• Introduce the Literary Analysis Skill: Free Verse. **FT**	5 min.
• Introduce the Reading Strategy: Inferring the Poet's Attitude. **FT**	10 min.
• Prepare students to read by teaching the selection vocabulary. **FT**	
TEACH	
• Informally monitor comprehension while students read independently or in groups. **FT**	30 min.
• Monitor students' comprehension with the Reading Check notes.	as students read
• Reinforce vocabulary with Vocabulary Builder notes.	as students read
• Develop students' understanding of free verse with the Literary Analysis annotations. **FT**	5 min.
• Develop students' ability to infer the poet's attitude with the Reading Strategy annotations. **FT**	5 min.
ASSESS/EXTEND	
• Assess students' comprehension and mastery of the Literary Analysis and Reading Strategy by having them answer the Apply the Skills questions. **FT**	15 min.
• Have students complete the Vocabulary Lesson and the Grammar and Style Lesson. **FT**	15 min.
• Apply students' ability to use a consistent style by using the Writing Lesson. **FT**	45 min. or homework
• Apply students' understanding by using one or more of the Extend Your Learning activities.	20–90 min. or homework
• Administer Selection Test A or Selection Test B. **FT**	15 min.

Resources

PRINT

Unit 3 Resources

- Vocabulary Warm-up Word Lists [**L1, L2, EL**] .p. 173
- Vocabulary Warm-up Practice [**L1, L2, EL**] .p. 174
- Reading Warm-up A [**L1, L2, EL**] .p. 175
- Reading Warm-up B [**L1, L2, L3**] .p. 176

TRANSPARENCY

Graphic Organizer Transparencies

- Literary Analysis Graphic Organizer A [**L3**] .p. 89
- Literary Analysis Graphic Organizer B [**L1, L2, EL**] .p. 90
- Reading Strategy Graphic Organizer A [**L3**] .p. 87
- Reading Strategy Graphic Organizer B [**L1, L2, EL**] .p. 88

PRINT

Reader's Notebook [L2]
Reader's Notebook: Adapted Version [L1]
Reader's Notebook: English Learner's Version [EL]

Unit 3 Resources

- Literary Analysis [**L3**] .p. 177
- Reading Strategy [**L3**] .p. 178
- Vocabulary Builder [**L3**] .p. 179

TECHNOLOGY

Listening to Literature Audio CDs [L2, EL]

PRINT

Unit 3 Resources

- Grammar and Style [**L3**] .p. 180
- Support for Writing Lesson [**L3**] .p. 181
- Support for Extend Your Learning [**L3**] .p. 182
- Enrichment [**L4**] .p. 183
- Selection Test A [**L1, L2, EL**] .pp. 184–186
- Selection Test B [**L3, L4**] .pp. 187–189

General Resources

- Rubrics for Poem [**L3**] .pp. 73–74
- Rubric for Delivering a Research Presentation [**L3**] .p. 92

TECHNOLOGY

Go Online: Research [**L3**]
Go Online: Self-test [**L3**]
***ExamView*®, Test Bank** [**L3**]

Choosing Resources for Differentiated Instruction

[**L1**] Special Needs Students
[**L2**] Below-Level Students
[**L3**] All Students
[**L4**] Advanced Students
[**EL**] English Learners

FT Fast Track Instruction: To move the lesson more quickly, use the strategies and activities identified with **FT**.

Scaffolding for Less Proficient and Advanced Students

The leveled Critical Thinking questions after selections progress in the levels of thinking required to answer them. To address the needs of your different students, you may use the (a) level questions for your less proficient students and the (b) level questions with your on-level and advanced students. The occasional (c) level questions are appropriate for your advanced students.

PRENTICE HALL **TeacherEXPRESS**™ Plan · Teach · Assess Use this complete suite of powerful teaching tools to make lesson planning and testing quicker and easier.

PRENTICE HALL **StudentEXPRESS**™ Learn · Study · Succeed Use the interactive textbook (online and on CD-ROM) to make selections and activities come alive with audio and video support and interactive questions.

PREETEACH

Motivation

Walt Whitman's poetry celebrates his vision of the United States. Brainstorm with students for images or metaphors for a poem about America by completing this line:

America is ________.

Students may suggest ideas such as "America is energy," "America is a struggle for freedom," "America is another chance," and so forth. List the variety of responses on the board. Then examine them for both positive and negative images and examples of the dignity, intensity, diversity, and democracy that Whitman evokes in his poetry.

❶ Background

More About the Author

In some of his poems, Whitman uses a form reflected in the poetry of the Hebrew Bible (sometimes known as the Old Testament). This form is also reminiscent of the *Bhagavad-Gita* (India's sacred books), which historians speculate Whitman read in translation. Given the lyrical and emotional nature of Whitman's poems, the undulating rhythm of this form fits well.

Build Skills Nonfiction • Poems

❶ Walt Whitman's Poetry

Walt Whitman (1819–1892)

In the preface to his first volume of poetry, the 1855 edition of *Leaves of Grass,* Walt Whitman wrote: "The proof of a poet is that his country absorbs him as affectionately as he absorbed it." Whitman's hopes for such proof of his own merit as a poet were deferred: He was harshly denounced for his first volume of poetry, but in the following decades, his poems gained popularity, and he became famous as "the Good Gray Poet" and "the Bard of Democracy." In his later years, Whitman was admired by writers and intellectuals on both sides of the Atlantic. Today, he is widely recognized as one of the greatest and most influential poets the United States has ever produced.

The Poet at Work Whitman was born on Long Island and raised in Brooklyn, New York. His education was not formal, but he read widely, including the works of Sir Walter Scott, Shakespeare, Homer, and Dante. Trained to be a printer, Whitman spent his early years alternating between printing jobs and newspaper writing. When he was twenty-seven, he became the editor of the Brooklyn *Eagle,* a respected newspaper, but the paper fired him in 1848 because of his opposition to slavery. After accepting a position on a paper in New Orleans, Whitman traveled across the country for the first time, observing the diversity of America's landscapes and people.

Whitman soon returned to New York City, however, and in 1850 quit journalism to devote his energy to writing poetry. Impressed by Ralph Waldo Emerson's prophetic description of a new kind of American poet, Whitman had been jotting down ideas and fragments of verse in a notebook for years. His work broke every poetic tradition of rhyme and meter as it celebrated America and the common man. When the first edition of *Leaves of Grass* was published in 1855, critics attacked Whitman's subject matter and abandonment of traditional poetic devices and forms. Noted poet John Greenleaf Whittier hated Whitman's poems so much that he hurled his copy of *Leaves of Grass* into the fireplace. Emerson, on the other hand, responded with great enthusiasm, remarking that the collection was "the most extraordinary piece of wit and wisdom that America has yet contributed."

The Bard of Democracy Though Whitman did publish other works in the course of his career, his life's work proved to be *Leaves of Grass,* which he continually revised, reshaped, and expanded until his death in 1892. The poems in later editions became less confusing, repetitious, and raucous, and more symbolic, expressive, and universal. He viewed the volume as a single long poem that expressed his evolving vision of the world. Using his poetry to convey his passionate belief in democracy, equality, and the spiritual unity of all forms of life, he celebrated the potential of the human spirit. Though Whitman's philosophy grew out of the ideas of the Transcendentalists, his poetry was mainly shaped by his ability to absorb and comprehend everything he observed. From its first appearance as twelve unsigned and untitled poems, *Leaves of Grass* grew to include 383 poems in its final, "death-bed" edition (1892). The collection captures the diversity of the American people and conveys the energy and intensity of all forms of life. In the century since Whitman's death, *Leaves of Grass* has become one of the most highly regarded collections of poetry ever written. There is little doubt that, according to his own definition, Whitman has proven himself as a poet.

Preview

Connecting to the Literature

You probably learn something new about yourself, your world, or life in general every day. As you will discover, Walt Whitman devoted his life and work to making new discoveries and reaching new understandings.

Literary Analysis

Free Verse

In contrast to verse written with a fixed meter and line length, **free verse** is poetry that has an irregular meter and line length. Free verse is designed to re-create the cadences of natural speech. Thus, Whitman uses whatever rhythms and line lengths are appropriate to his message:

Do I contradict myself?
Very well then I contradict myself...

Though free verse is as old as the Psalms in the Bible, Whitman was the first American poet to use it. It proved to be the perfect form for this individualist, allowing him to express himself without formal restraints.

Comparing Literary Works

Along with his use of free verse, Whitman's **diction**—word choice and arrangement—also plays a key role in his voice. Whitman's diction is characterized by the use of two main techniques:

- The use of catalogs, or long lists
- The use of **parallelism**—the repetition of phrases or sentences with similar structures or meanings.

In his poems, Whitman addresses a wide range of subjects, modifying his diction to complement each one. In some poems, his diction emphasizes important ideas. In others, it builds crescendos of emotion. As you read, compare the ways in which the poet's diction varies from poem to poem in order to serve the purpose and meaning of each work.

Reading Strategy

Inferring the Poet's Attitude

You can infer a poet's attitude toward a subject by examining his or her choice of words and details. Consider this passage from Whitman's "Song of Myself":

I jump from the crossbeams and seize the clover and timothy,
And roll head over heels . . .

Use a chart like the one shown to note key words and images in Whitman's poems and to clarify the attitudes each reveals.

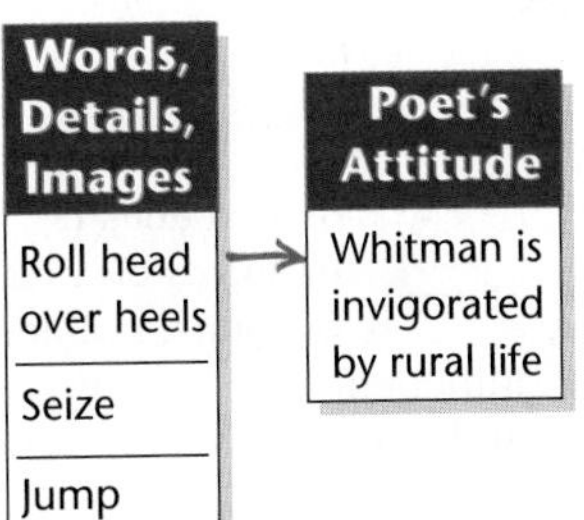

Vocabulary Builder

abeyance (ə bā′ əns) *n.* temporary suspension (p. 442)

effuse (e fyo͞oz′) *v.* pour out (p. 445)

❷ Literary Analysis

Free Verse

- Tell students that as they read Walt Whitman's poems, they will focus on free verse which uses irregular meter and line length.
- Share with students the More About the Author information from ATE p. 438. Explain that as with these other works, Whitman's poetry reflects the rise and fall of speech.
- Have volunteers read aloud the Literary Analysis instruction and excerpts. Help students hear the rhythm in the excerpt.
- Discuss the instruction under Comparing Literary Works and use it to help students understand how diction and free verse work together to create Whitman's unique poetic voice.

❸ Reading Strategy

Inferring the Poet's Attitude

- Remind students that inferring the poet's attitude can help them recognize a writer's unstated messages.
- Explain to students that they can infer a poet's attitude in much the same way as they make other inferences—by combining text clues and life experience for reasonable conclusions.
- Direct students to the excerpt on the student page. Point out, for example, that from words and phrases such as *jump, seize,* and *roll head over heels* readers can infer that Whitman is invigorated by rural life.
- Give students a copy of **Reading Strategy Graphic Organizer A,** p. 87 in ***Graphic Organizer Transparencies,*** to use as they read the selections.

Vocabulary Builder

- Pronounce each vocabulary word for students, and read the definitions as a class. Have students identify any words with which they are already familiar.

Differentiated Instruction

Solutions for All Learners

Support for Special Needs Students

Have students complete the **Preview** and **Build Skills** pages for the these selections in the ***Reader's Notebook: Adapted Version.*** These pages provide a selection summary, an abbreviated presentation of the reading and literary skills, and the graphic organizer on the **Build Skills** page in the student book.

Support for Less Proficient Readers

Have students complete the **Preview** and **Build Skills** pages for these selections in the ***Reader's Notebook.*** These pages provide a selection summary, an abbreviated presentation of the reading and literary skills, and the graphic organizer on the **Build Skills** page in the student book.

Support for English Learners

Have students complete the **Preview** and **Build Skills** pages for these selections in the ***Reader's Notebook: English Learner's Version.*** These pages provide a selection summary, an abbreviated presentation of the skills, additional contextual vocabulary, and the graphic organizer on the **Build Skills** page in the student book.

TEACH

Learning Modalities
Musical/Rhythmic Learners
Have students read the poems aloud to listen for poetic devices such as alliteration, assonance, consonance, and repetition.

Ask students what music they might choose to accompany a reading of the poem.

❶ About the Selection

In this preface to his historic 1855 Edition of *Leaves of Grass,* Whitman says that America has never been static. It is an ever-growing nation of people, ideas, and beliefs that evolve as the nation itself changes. Americans perceive that old ways are passing and strong new ways approaching. Whitman comments that the United States is a great poem, a nation characterized by activity, diversity, and the gifts of its rich natural bounties.

❷ Literary Analysis
Free Verse and Diction

- **Invite** volunteers to read each of the phrases in turn, then read all the phrases aloud yourself. Help students identify repeated words in the phrases.
  Answer: The words *that it* or *that its* are repeated.
- **Ask** students the Literary Analysis question: How does Whitman's use of parallel phrases beginning with "perceives" help establish an uplifting tone?
  Possible answer: The parallel structure and repetition create a crescendo in which each phrase adds to those previous. This rhythmic crescendo creates an uplifting tone.

❶

from Preface to the 1855 Edition of Leaves of Grass

Walt Whitman

Background In his lifetime, Whitman's poetry, which broke traditional rules of rhythm and rhyme, provoked both glowing reviews and fiercely negative reactions. After receiving his complimentary copy of *Leaves of Grass*, Ralph Waldo Emerson had abundant praise for this poet. In a letter to Whitman, Emerson wrote:

> . . . I give you joy of your free and brave thought, I have great joy in it. I find incomparable things said incomparably well, as they must be. I find the courage of treatment, which so delights me, and which large perception only can inspire. I greet you at the beginning of a great career. . . .

More than a century after his death, Whitman's poetry is still regarded as some of the bravest, most generous, and most stirring in American literature.

America does not repel the past or what it has produced under its forms or amid other politics or the idea of castes or the old religions. . . . accepts the lesson with calmness . . . is not so impatient as has been supposed that the slough still sticks to opinions and manners and literature while the life which served its requirements has passed into the new life of the new forms . . . perceives that the corpse is slowly borne from the eating and sleeping rooms of the house . . . perceives that it waits a little while in the door . . . that it
❷ was fittest for its days . . . that its action has descended to the stalwart and well-shaped heir who approaches . . . and that he shall be fittest for his days.

Literary Analysis
Free Verse and Diction How does Whitman's use of parallel phrases beginning with "perceives" help establish an uplifting tone?

Differentiated Instruction Solutions for All Learners

Accessibility at a Glance

	from Leaves of Grass,	*from* Song of Myself, I Hear America Singing,	Bivouac	Learned Astronomer, Spider
Language	Metaphor; difficult vocabulary; long sentences	Easily read free verse; minimal poetic syntax	Long sentences in free verse	Easily read free verse
Concept Level	Challenging (description of American soul)	Average (individual and American spirit)	Accessible (sentry thinks of home)	Accessible (nature versus scientific thought)
Literary Merit	Classic	Classic	Intimate Civil War poem	Classic
Lexile	NP	NP	NP	NP
Overall Rating	Challenging	Average	Average	Accessible

The Americans of all nations at any time upon the earth have probably the fullest poetical nature. The United States themselves are essentially the greatest poem. In the history of the earth hitherto the largest and most stirring appear tame and orderly to their ampler largeness and stir. Here at last is something in the doings of man that corresponds with the broadcast doings of the day and night. Here is not merely a nation but a teeming nation of nations. Here is action untied from strings necessarily blind to particulars and details magnificently moving in vast masses. Here is the hospitality which forever indicates
3 heroes. . . . Here are the roughs and beards and space and ruggedness and nonchalance that the soul loves. Here the performance disdaining the trivial unapproached in the tremendous audacity of its crowds and groupings and the push of its perspective spreads with crampless and flowing breadth and showers its prolific and splendid extravagance. One sees it must indeed own the riches of the summer and winter, and need never be bankrupt while corn grows from the ground or the orchards drop apples or the bays contain fish or men beget children upon women. . . .

Reading Strategy
Inferring the Poet's Attitude What can you infer about Whitman's attitude toward America from his use of the images of "roughs and beards and space and ruggedness"? Explain.

Critical Reading

1. **Respond:** Do you think that Whitman's characterization of the United States is still accurate? Why or why not?
2. **(a) Recall:** What subject does Whitman address in the first paragraph? **(b) Interpret:** What does Whitman mean when he says "the corpse is slowly borne from the eating and sleeping rooms of the house"?
3. **(a) Recall:** According to Whitman, what makes America different from all other nations? **(b) Interpret:** What is the meaning of Whitman's notion that the United States "is not merely a nation but a teeming nation of nations"?
4. **(a) Recall:** What riches do the seasons offer? **(b) Interpret:** What does the poet's mention of these riches suggest about his vision of America's promise?
5. **(a) Recall:** According to Whitman, what is the greatest of all poems? **(b) Analyze:** Based on this statement, how is Whitman redefining the idea of a poem?
6. **Extend:** What parallels can you draw between Whitman's ideas about the United States and those expressed by Michel-Guillaume Jean de Crèvecoeur in *Letters From an American Farmer* on p. 220?
7. **Compare and Contrast:** How does Whitman's idea of the United States compare with your idea? Explain.

For: More about Walt Whitman
Visit: www.PHSchool.com
Web Code: ere-9315

3 Reading Strategy
Inferring the Poet's Attitude

- Direct students to read the bracketed text alone and then in the context of the surrounding paragraph. Guide them to understand the literal meanings of Whitman's images.
  Answer: *Roughs* and *beards* are Americans, living in rough conditions, probably off the land and on the move, and perhaps wearing beards as did Whitman.
- **Ask** students the Reading Strategy question: What can you infer about Whitman's attitude toward America from his use of the images of "roughs and beards and space and ruggedness."
  Possible answer: He views America as rough but vital.

ASSESS
Answers

1. Students should support their responses with evidence.
2. (a) Possible response: The speaker addresses the subject of the past. (b) Possible response: He means that old habits die hard and that history is not quickly forgotten.
3. (a) It has the fullest poetical nature. (b) In this line, Whitman refers to the cultural diversity of the American people.
4. (a) The seasons offer food and the promise of new life. (b) He thinks America has the promise to grow and nurture its population.
5. (a) According to the speaker, "the United States themselves are essentially the greatest poem." (b) Usually a poem is a highly organized group of words on a page. Whitman's metaphor seems to replace lines with land and words with human beings.
6. Both writers view the United States as a country that welcomes people of different backgrounds, and both consider the land to be a rich source of food and opportunity.
7. Students should support their responses with examples.

Differentiated Instruction Solutions for All Learners

Support for Less Proficient Readers
Help students access Whitman's ideas by providing support in understanding his style. For example, demonstrate how to interpret the ideas separated by ellipses by inserting a missing subject or verb to clarify meaning: "[America] accepts the lesson with calmness . . ." or "[perceives] that it was fittest for its days."

Support for English Learners
Point out to students that Whitman sometimes implies, rather than states, ideas. Words may be missing or simply suggested by the surrounding context. For example, when Whitman repeats *Here* in the second paragraph, he means here in the United States.

Enrichment for Gifted/Talented Students
Give students the opportunity to read *Death of President Lincoln* in **Authors In Depth,** *The American Experience,* p. 85. Ask students to find additional examples of Whitman's inclination to leave out words or imply ideas. What effect does the use of such ellipses in the text have on the reader?

4 About the Selection

In these sections from "Song of Myself," the poet gives his evolving vision of life through the perspective of a vast set of encounters and observations. Its tone is optimistic, exuberant, and energetic; its subject, the poet himself. Yet the poem reaches beyond individual experience to all humankind. Whitman conveys his belief in the limitless potential of the human spirit to embrace the world and to grow from everything it experiences.

5 Critical Viewing

Answer: Students may respond that Whitman looks like a rugged free spirit who shuns the formal dress of his time for simple clothing that suits his wandering.

6 Literary Analysis

Free Verse

- Call on a volunteer to read aloud Section 6. Point out the question and answer pattern in the text.
- **Ask** students the Literary Analysis question: In Section 6, how does Whitman's rhythm reflect the natural cadences of speech?
  Answer: The question and answer pattern makes Section 6 sound like a conversation, in this case, between the poet and himself.

4 *from* Song of Myself

Walt Whitman

1

I celebrate myself, and sing myself,
And what I assume you shall assume,
For every atom belonging to me as good belongs to you.

I loaf and invite my soul,
I lean and loaf at my ease observing a spear of summer grass.

My tongue, every atom of my blood, formed from this soil, this air,
Born here of parents born here from parents the same, and their
  parents the same,
I, now thirty-seven years old in perfect health begin,
Hoping to cease not till death.

Creeds and schools in abeyance,
Retiring back a while sufficed at what they are, but never forgotten,
I harbor for good or bad, I permit to speak at every hazard,
Nature without check with original energy.

6

6

A child said *What is the grass?* fetching it to me with full hands,
How could I answer the child? I do not know what it is any
  more than he.

I guess it must be the flag of my disposition, out of hopeful
  green stuff woven.

Or I guess it is the handkerchief of the Lord,
A scented gift and remembrancer[1] designedly dropped,

5 ▲ **Critical Viewing** This illustration depicts Walt Whitman as a young man. What can you conclude about his attitudes and personality from this picture? How are they reflected in this poem? **[Infer; Support]**

Vocabulary Builder

abeyance (ə bā′ əns) *n.* temporary suspension

Literary Analysis

Free Verse In Section 6, how does the rhythm reflect the natural cadences of speech?

1. **remembrancer** reminder.

Enrichment

Farming in Today's America

The largely agrarian society in which Walt Whitman lived for most of his life has almost disappeared from today's America. Although some Americans still live in rural areas, few still operate farms; those who do, work in vastly different ways from the way they did in the nineteenth century.

Farming—the sowing, tending, and harvesting of crops—is now largely mechanized. In 1992, one hundred years after Whitman's death, only 7 percent of rural residents lived on farms.

Have students research population trends in America over the past century. Students should consider such issues as changes in the percentage of people who live in urban, suburban, and rural areas; changes in the number of active family farms; variations in population density; and so forth. Students can share their findings orally, accompanied by graphs, tables, or charts.

Bearing the owner's name someway in the corners, that we may see
and remark, and say *Whose?*

. . .

What do you think has become of the young and old men?
And what do you think has become of the women and children?

They are alive and well somewhere,
The smallest sprout shows there is really no death,
And if ever there was it led forward life, and does not wait at the end to arrest it,
And ceas'd the moment life appear'd.
All goes onward and outward, nothing collapses,
And to die is different from what anyone supposed, and luckier.

Reading Strategy
Inferring the Poet's Attitude What attitude toward the cycle of life is suggested by Whitman's use of the words "onward," "outward," and "luckier"? Explain.

9

The big doors of the country barn stand open and ready,
The dried grass of the harvest-time loads the slow-drawn wagon.
The clear light plays on the brown gray and green intertinged,
The armfuls are pack'd to the sagging mow.

I am there, I help, I came stretch'd atop of the load,
I felt its soft jolts, one leg reclined on the other,
I jump from the crossbeams and seize the clover and timothy,
And roll head over heels and tangle my hair full of wisps.

14

The wild gander leads his flock through the cool night,
Ya-honk he says, and sounds it down to me like an invitation,
The pert may suppose it meaningless, but I listening close,
Find its purpose and place up there toward the wintry sky.

The sharp-hoof'd moose of the north, the cat on the house-sill, the chickadee, the prairie dog,
The litter of the grunting sow as they tug at her teats,
The brood of the turkey hen and she with her half-spread wings,
I see in them and myself the same old law.

The press of my foot to the earth springs a hundred affections,
They scorn the best I can do to relate them.

I am enamor'd of growing outdoors,
Of men that live among cattle or taste of the ocean or woods,
Of the builders and steerers of ships and the wielders of axes and mauls, and the drivers of horses,
I can eat and sleep with them week in and week out.

8 Reading Check
What aspects of life does the poet celebrate in this poem?

7 Reading Strategy
Inferring the Poet's Attitude

- Have all students pause in their reading to study the bracketed passage.
- Elicit from students their ideas about the connotations of "onward," "outward," and "luckier."
- Then, **ask** students the Reading Strategy question: What attitude toward the cycle of life is suggested by Whitman's use of the words "onward," "outward," and "luckier"?
  Answer: These words have positive, hopeful connotations. His attitude toward the life cycle is that it is natural and that it moves us ever forward.

8 Reading Check

Answer: He celebrates the natural aspects of life, those found in outdoor activities, in life's natural cycles, in animals, and in agriculture.

Differentiated Instruction
Solutions for All Learners

Vocabulary for Special Needs Students
Point out to students how Whitman uses contractions such as *sharphoof'd* and *enamor'd.* Explain to students that the apostrophes represent missing letters, in these two cases the letter *e*. Encourage students to try inserting the letter *e* in Whitman's other contractions, reading out the resulting word to check for sense.

Strategy for Less Proficient Readers
Tell students to note Whitman's use of italics to suggest the sounds of his poem and its speech. Point out the child's question in Section 6, line 1, and the gander's call of *Yahonk* in Section 14, line 1. Explain that the italics invite readers to hear these lines as if they were spoken aloud by the indicated character.

Enrichment for Gifted/Talented Students
Literary scholar James E. Miller, Jr., characterizes "Song of Myself" as a drama in which the poet is the main character. The complete work has fifty-two numbered sections that can be viewed as acts in the play. Challenge students to perform part or all of this excerpt from "Song of Myself."

❾ Literary Analysis
Free Verse and Diction

- Call on a volunteer to read aloud the bracketed passage. Have students identify the parallel structures in Section 17.
  Answer: Lines 1–4 contain the phrase "they are not." Lines 5–6 begin with "This is the."
- **Direct** students to answer the first Literary Analysis question: In what way does Whitman's use of parallel structure in Section 17 emphasize the ideas he is expressing?
  Answer: It creates repetition that drives home Whitman's ideas.

❿ Literary Analysis
Free Verse

- **Direct** students to read the bracketed lines silently. Ask students what characterizes free verse.
  Answer: Free verse lacks regular meter or line length.
- **Ask** students to paraphrase lines 2–3 of Section 52.
  Answer: I won't be tamed or made to follow rules in expressing my ideas.
- **Invite** students' responses to the second Literary Analysis question: In what ways does Whitman's use of free verse in lines 2–3 of section 52 emphasize the ideas he is expressing?
  Answer: Both reflect the same unwillingness to be tethered.

What is commonest, cheapest, nearest, easiest, is Me,
Me going in for my chances, spending for vast returns,
Adorning myself to bestow myself on the first that will take me,
Not asking the sky to come down to my good will,
Scattering it freely forever.

17

❾
These are really the thoughts of all men in all ages and lands, they are not original with me,
If they are not yours as much as mine they are nothing, or next to nothing,
If they are not the riddle and the untying of the riddle they are nothing,
If they are not just as close as they are distant they are nothing.
This is the grass that grows wherever the land is and the water is,
This is the common air that bathes the globe.

51

The past and present wilt—I have fill'd them, emptied them,
And proceed to fill my next fold of the future.

Listener up there! what have you to confide to me?
Look in my face while I snuff the sidle of evening,[2]
(Talk honestly, no one else hears you, and I stay only a minute longer.)

Do I contradict myself?
Very well then I contradict myself,
(I am large, I contain multitudes.)
I concentrate toward them that are nigh,[3] I wait on the door-slab.

Who has done his day's work? who will soonest be through with his supper?
Who wishes to walk with me?

Will you speak before I am gone? will you prove already too late?

52

The spotted hawk swoops by and accuses me, he complains of my gab and my loitering.

❿
I too am not a bit tamed, I too am untranslatable,
I sound my barbaric yawp over the roofs of the world.

Literary Analysis
Free Verse and Diction In what ways does Whitman's use of parallel structures in Section 17 emphasize the ideas he is expressing?

Literary Analysis
Free Verse In what ways does Whitman's use of free verse in lines 2–3 of section 52 emphasize the ideas he is expressing?

2. **snuff . . . evening** put out the hesitant last light of day, which is moving sideways across the sky.
3. **nigh** near.

Enrichment

Taoism

Walt Whitman found much inspiration in Asian philosophy and thought. Whitman believed in the sacredness of the self and in placing the individual above society, ideas that echo the beliefs of the Chinese philosophy of Taoism. Tao, or the Way, is the central force that makes each thing in the universe unique but also brings everything together in a whole that is reality. Taoist poetry, like Whitman's, shows a love of the beauty of nature and the importance of living one's life in harmony with it. Whitman also espoused the belief in a spiritual unity that connects all things. Such universal philosophy gives Whitman's poetry broad appeal.

Invite interested students to learn more about the principles of Taoism. They can use their research to create a report examining the similarities between Taoist philosophy and poetry and Whitman's ideas.

The last scud[4] of day holds back for me,
It flings my likeness after the rest and true as any on the
shadow'd wilds,
It coaxes me to the vapor and the dusk.

11 I depart as air, I shake my white locks at the runaway sun,
I effuse my flesh in eddies, and drift it in lacy jags.

12 I bequeath myself to the dirt to grow from the grass I love,
If you want me again look for me under your boot soles.

You will hardly know who I am or what I mean,
But I shall be good health to you nevertheless,
And filter and fiber your blood.

Failing to fetch me at first keep encouraged,
Missing me one place search another,
I stop somewhere waiting for you.

---

4. **scud** low, dark, wind-driven clouds.

Vocabulary Builder
effuse (e fyo͞oz′) *v.* to pour out

Critical Reading

1. **Respond:** Which of the ideas expressed in "Song of Myself" do you find most—and least—appealing?
2. **(a) Recall:** From what does Whitman say his tongue and blood are formed? **(b) Analyze:** How does he view his relationship with nature? **(c) Analyze:** How does he view his relationship with other people?
3. **(a) Recall:** In Section 17, what natural images does Whitman use to communicate the idea that his thoughts belong to everyone? **(b) Generalize:** Which elements of these images convey a belief in the spiritual unity of all natural forms?
4. **(a) Recall:** In the second stanza of Section 51, where does the speaker use apostrophe—a direct address to an absent person? **(b) Infer:** Whom do you think the speaker is addressing in this stanza? Explain.
5. **(a) Recall:** In Section 52, where does the speaker say readers can find him? **(b) Infer:** What does he suggest will happen to his spirit and message after he is gone?
6. **Evaluate:** In Section 52, Whitman proudly characterizes his poetry as "barbaric yawp." What terms would you use to describe and evaluate his work?

For: More about Walt Whitman
Visit: www.PHSchool.com
Web Code: ere-9315

11 Vocabulary Builder
Latin Root *-fus-*

- Call students' attention to the word *effuse.* Let students know that the word root *-fus-* comes from a Latin word, *effusus,* which means "poured out."
- **Ask** students to volunteer words containing this word root. **Possiblilities include:** *infuse, diffuse,* or *profusion*

12 Critical Thinking
Synthesize

- Point out in the bracketed lines that the speaker bequeaths himself "to the dirt."
- Then, **ask**: How does this statement take the grass and the speaker full cycle?
  Possible response: The speaker began by speculating about the meaning of the grass; by bequeathing himself to it—in the eternal circle of life, he will become one with the earth.

ASSESS
Answers

1. Students' responses will reflect their attitudes toward life.
2. (a) He says they are formed from American soil and air. (b) He views himself as part of nature. (c) He views all people as being part of the same life cycle.
3. (a) He refers to the grass that grows everywhere and the air that everyone breathes. (b) **Possible response:** Whitman links these images to the "thoughts of all men in all ages and lands."
4. (a) He speaks directly to the "Listener up there!" (b) The "listener" may be God or Nature.
5. (a) He says they can find him under their boot soles in the earth. (b) He suggests that he will be "somewhere waiting."
6. Students should respond with evaluations of Whitman's ideas.

Go Online Author Link For additional information about Walt Whitman, have students type in the Web Code, then select W from the alphabet, and then select Walt Whitman.

Differentiated Instruction
Solutions for All Learners

Strategy for Special Needs Students
Students may be confused about who is who as they read Whitman's many pronouns. To help these students form a clear picture of the narrative, have them perform a choral reading of the poem. Each time a new pronoun appears, such as *I* or *you,* introduce a new reader. Help students understand to whom Whitman refers in each line.

Strategy for Less Proficient Readers
Clarify Whitman's use of pronouns by helping students identify antecedents. Point out the words *These, they,* and *this is* in Section 17. Remind students of Whitman's personal connections to nature—his belief in its power. Explain that Whitman's pronouns refer to spiritual bonds that link humanity and nature.

Support for English Learners
In Section 51, Whitman uses the pronoun "I" to refer to both himself and the developing nation. Point out to students that Whitman believes both to be full of growing pains and contradictions. He also believes that for both, these contradictions lead to a treasured richness.

⓭ About the Selections

In the first poem, the speaker reveals that he prefers imagining and experiencing the mystery of the stars to knowing the precise scientific facts an expert scientist can teach. "By the Bivouac's Fitful Flame" contrasts a sentry's physical surroundings in an army camp with the procession of "tender and wondrous thoughts" of life, love, home, family, and friends that carry him back to the life left behind.

⓮ Humanities

The Lawrence Tree, by Georgia O'Keeffe

Georgia O'Keeffe discovered early that she could say things with color and shape that she could not say in any other way. The painting evokes O'Keeffe's memories of lying on a bench and looking up into this tree to the stars beyond. Like Whitman, O'Keeffe reveals her very personal experiences through her art. Use this question for discussion.

- What is O'Keeffe saying about nature in this work? Do you think Whitman would agree?
  Possible response: Nature is lofty. Its grandness and majesty dwarf people on Earth. Whitman would agree that nature is grand, but I think he feels more a part of nature and less dwarfed by it than does O'Keeffe.

⓯ Critical Viewing

Answer: Both the artist and the poet view the stars with awe as they gaze upward at the canopy of the night sky. From such an angle, the viewer seems small and insignificant, while the stars appear very distant and mysterious.

⓮

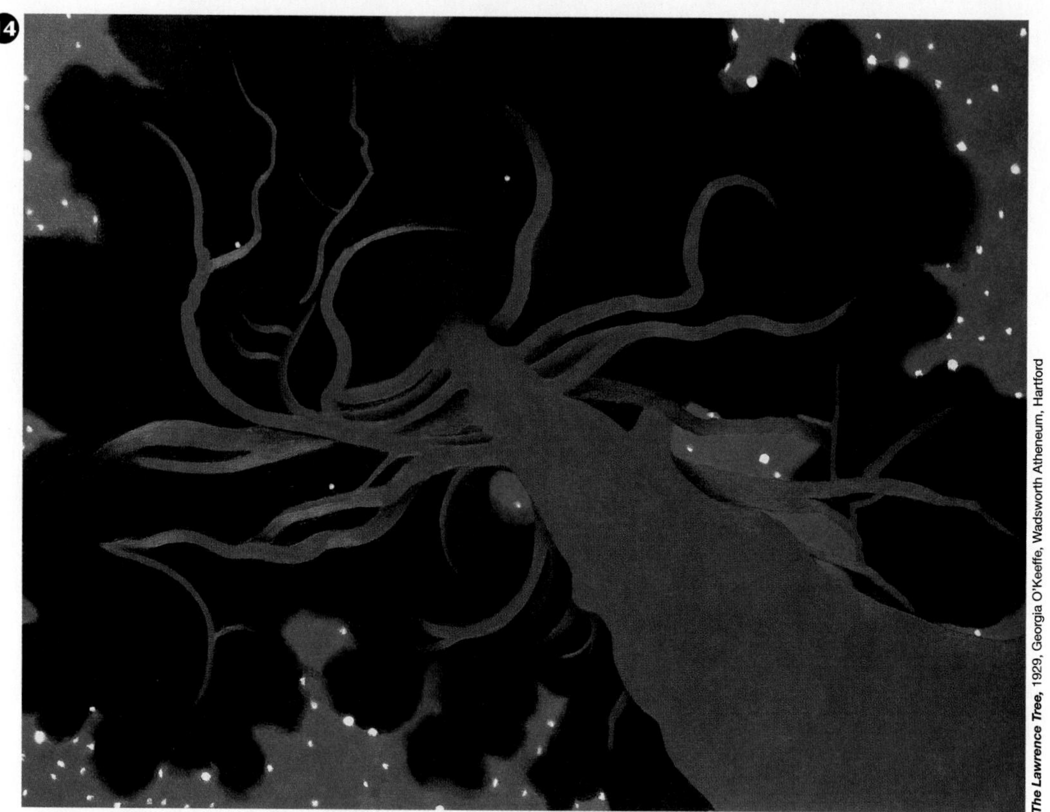

The Lawrence Tree, 1929, Georgia O'Keeffe, Wadsworth Atheneum, Hartford

⓭ *When I Heard the Learn'd Astronomer*

Walt Whitman

When I heard the learn'd astronomer,
When the proofs, the figures, were ranged in columns before me,
When I was shown the charts and diagrams, to add, divide and measure them,
When I sitting heard the astronomer where he lectured with much applause in the lecture room,
How soon unaccountable I became tired and sick,
Till rising and gliding out I wander'd off by myself,
In the mystical moist night air, and from time to time,
Look'd up in perfect silence at the stars.

⓯ ▲ **Critical Viewing** In what ways does the artist's viewpoint in this painting compare with Whitman's in "When I Heard the Learn'd Astronomer"? **[Connect]**

⓭ *By the Bivouac's Fitful Flame*

Walt Whitman

By the bivouac's[1] fitful flame,
A procession winding around me, solemn and sweet and slow—but first I note,
The tents of the sleeping army, the fields' and woods' dim outline,
The darkness lit by spots of kindled fire, the silence,
Like a phantom far or near an occasional figure moving,
The shrubs and trees, (as I lift my eyes they seem to be stealthily watching me,)
While wind in procession thoughts, O tender and wondrous thoughts,
Of life and death, of home and the past and loved, and of those that are far away;
A solemn and slow procession there as I sit on the ground,
By the bivouac's fitful flame.

1. **bivouac** (biv´ wak´) *n.* night guard to prevent surprise attacks.

Critical Reading

1. **Respond:** To which of these poems do you relate most strongly? Why?
2. **(a) Recall:** In "When I Heard the Learn'd Astronomer," what does the speaker do in reaction to the lecture? **(b) Connect:** What do his actions reveal about his character?
3. **(a) Compare and Contrast:** In what ways does the "perfect silence" in the last line contrast with the lecture? **(b) Draw Conclusions:** What is the speaker saying about the value of science versus a personal experience with nature?
4. **(a) Recall:** In lines 3–4 of "By the Bivouac's Fitful Flame," what sights does the speaker look upon? **(b) Infer:** What is the procession to which he refers in line 2?
5. **(a) Recall:** Where does the speaker's mind go as he gazes upon the scene before him? **(b) Analyze:** Is the procession he refers to in line 9 the same one referred to earlier? Explain.
6. **Make a Judgment:** Whitman is known as a poet who celebrated life. Are these poems celebratory? If so, of what?

For: More about Walt Whitman
Visit: www.PHSchool.com
Web Code: ere-9315

Answers

1. Students should explain their responses.
2. (a) He leaves the lecture hall to look at the stars himself. (b) It suggests that he wants to experience things personally.
3. (a) One is silent, while the other is filled with numbers and words. (b) He is saying that personal experience with nature is more important than science.
4. (a) He looks upon an army camp, the camp's fire, and the darkness around him. (b) The reader doesn't yet know.
5. (a) It goes to his friends and family at home. (b) Yes, it is revealed that the procession is one of the speaker's thoughts.
6. **Possible response:** Yes. "When I Heard the Learn'd Astronomer" celebrates nature's wonder, while "By the Bivouac's Fitful Flame" celebrates the human capacity for memory and for love.

Go Online Author Link For additional information about Walt Whitman, have students type in the Web Code, then select W from the alphabet, and then select Walt Whitman.

Differentiated Instruction Solutions for All Learners

for Advanced Readers

Suggest that students read additional works by Walt Whitman. Provide students with the following titles: *Leaves of Grass, Drum Taps* and *Good-Bye, My Fancy.* You may also wish to use ***Authors In Depth**, The American Experience,* which contains the following selections:

- "As I Ebb'd with the Ocean of Life" (poem, p. 79)
- "Broadway" (poem, p. 82)
- "Beat! Beat! Drums!" (poem, p. 83)
- "As Toilsome I Wander'd Virginia's Woods" (poem, p. 84)
- *Death of President Lincoln* (nonfiction, p. 85)

Before students read, have them choose particular issues or literary elements on which to focus. They might, for example, wish to study Whitman's use of free verse and diction, as well as his attitudes in the additional works they read. Lead a round-table discussion in which students can share their analysis of Whitman's other works.

16 About the Selection

This poem celebrates Whitman's joyous view of the indomitable American spirit. People distinguish themselves by their work, perform tasks that build the future, and demonstrate an exuberance of skill and purpose that makes each of them a vibrant contributor to the spirit of a proud nation.

ASSESS

Answers

1. Whitman's message might celebrate the same American spirit, but would probably mention new kinds of work.
2. (a) Whitman mentions mechanics, a carpenter, a mason, a boatman, a shoemaker, a wood-cutter, a ploughboy, a mother, and a wife. (b) His list suggests that he views America as a vigorous and vast place to be tamed by great physical energy.
3. (a) He uses the word "singing." (b) Singing suggests a vibrant, hearty, and proud mood.
4. (a) At night, the workers share leisure time singing. (b) Whitman wants to emphasize his celebratory vision of America and its workers by leaving readers with an image of singing.
5. **Possible response:** Yes, he presents laborers as always happy and singing.

Go Online Author Link For additional information about Walt Whitman, have students type in the Web Code, then select W from the alphabet, and then select Walt Whitman.

16 I Hear America Singing

Walt Whitman

I hear America singing, the varied carols I hear,
Those of mechanics, each one singing his as it should be blithe and strong,
The carpenter singing his as he measures his plank or beam,
The mason singing his as he makes ready for work, or leaves off work,
The boatman singing what belongs to him in his boat, the deckhand singing on the steamboat deck,
The shoemaker singing as he sits on his bench, the hatter[1] singing as he stands,
The wood-cutter's song, the ploughboy's on his way in the morning, or at noon intermission or at sundown,
The delicious singing of the mother, or of the young wife at work, or of the girl sewing or washing,
Each singing what belongs to him or her and to none else,
The day what belongs to the day—at night the party of young fellows, robust, friendly,
Singing with open mouths their strong melodious songs.

1. **hatter** person who makes, sells, or cleans hats.

Critical Reading

1. **Respond:** If Whitman were to write this poem today, do you think his message would be the same? Explain.
2. **(a) Recall:** What occupations does Whitman attribute to Americans? **(b) Draw Conclusions:** What does his catalog of occupations suggest about his vision of America?
3. **(a) Recall:** What word does Whitman use to describe all the workers' actions? **(b) Analyze:** In what ways does this word affect the poem's mood?
4. **(a) Recall:** What does Whitman describe the laborers doing at night? **(b) Analyze:** Why do you think the poem ends as it does?
5. **Evaluate:** Do you think Whitman romanticizes the life of a laborer? Explain your answer.

Go Online Author Link

For: More about Walt Whitman
Visit: www.PHSchool.com
Web Code: ere-9315

Enrichment

A Man of the People

Clearly, Whitman loved and admired his nation. He believed in its peoples and relished the opportunity to mingle with them. Whitman attended countless events just for the pleasure of being with other Americans. According to one story, he even rode on stagecoaches and ferries just so that he could talk with ordinary people.

Whitman tried to imbue his poetry with the vibrant energy and diversity of American democracy. In an 1856 letter to Ralph Waldo Emerson, Whitman outlined this poetic goal. He wrote, "Every day I go among the people of Manhattan Island, Brooklyn, and other cities, and among the young men, to discover the spirit of them, and to refresh myself . . . In poems, the young men of The States shall be represented, for they out-rival the best of the rest of the earth."

The Reaper, Louis C. Tiffany, National Academy of Design, New York City

17 ◄ Critical Viewing What might Whitman say about the work of this farmer? **[Speculate]**

17 Critical Viewing

Answer: Whitman would probably praise the merits of physical labor done in the great outdoors.

18 Humanities

The Reaper, by Louis C. Tiffany

Tiffany, though known best for his work in decorative glass, was also an accomplished painter. This oil-on-canvas painting celebrates the harvest. The farmhand stands surrounded by grain in the midst of the field, sharpening his blade in preparation for harvesting.

Use this question for discussion:

- What parallels can you draw between the artist's and the poet's attitudes toward their subjects? **Answer:** Both men seem to have admired and respected those who earn their livings through manual labor.

Differentiated Instruction Solutions for All Learners

Vocabulary for English Learners

Students may be unfamiliar with the words Whitman uses to label various workers. List some of these on the chalkboard: *mechanics, mason, deckhand, wood-cutter, ploughboy.* Use visual images, such as the painting on p. 449 and Fine Art Transparency 12, to convey information about the kind of work each laborer undertakes.

Strategy for Gifted/Talented Students

After students have read "I Hear America Singing," challenge them to list as many "singing" references in the poem as they can. Emphasize that Whitman referred to everyday people, pursuing everyday activities. Then display Art Transparency 12, pointing out the "everyday" look of the scene, the "slice of life" character of the sculpture. Remind students that according to Whitman, everyone has "strong melodious songs" that belong "to him or her and to none else." Ask students to speculate what song the farmer could be singing.

⓳ About the Selection

Watching a spider spin its thread, the speaker in "A Noiseless Patient Spider" compares the insect to his soul. Like the spider, he stands in oceans of space, throwing out threads, seeking connections to the universe.

ASSESS

Answers

1. Some students may admire the spider's efforts, as Whitman does. Others may regard spiders as pests.
2. (a) A huge vast open space surrounds the spider. (b) They are the world around the soul, the world of people to whom the soul must forge a connection.
3. (a) It spins filament to explore its surroundings. (b) Both the speaker's soul and the spider are poised in isolation, and both seek to explore and connect themselves to the world.
4. (a) He uses *stood, mark'd, explore, launch'd forth, unreeling, speeding.* (b) He uses *stand, musing, venturing, throwing, seeking, connect, form'd hold, fling.* (c) The spider's exploration is purely physical, while the soul's journey is spiritual.
5. (a) The poet addresses his own soul. (b) The speaker wants the soul to succeed in forming a bridge.
6. The spider's physical efforts mirror the human soul's spiritual efforts to connect to the surrounding world.
7. Students should be able to support their responses with details from the poem and their own experiences.

Go Online Author Link For additional information about Walt Whitman, have students type in the Web Code, then select W from the alphabet, and then select Walt Whitman.

⓳ A Noiseless Patient Spider

Walt Whitman

A noiseless patient spider,
I mark'd where on a little promontory it stood isolated,
Mark'd how to explore the vacant vast surrounding,
It launch'd forth filament, filament, filament, out of itself,
Ever unreeling them, ever tirelessly speeding them.

And you O my soul where you stand,
Surrounded, detached, in measureless oceans of space,
Ceaselessly musing, venturing, throwing, seeking the spheres
    to connect them,
Till the bridge you will need be form'd, till the ductile anchor hold,
Till the gossamer thread you fling catch somewhere, O my soul.

Critical Reading

1. **Respond:** Would your reaction to watching a spider spin a web be similar to Whitman's? Why or why not?
2. **(a) Recall:** In line three, what surrounds the spider? **(b) Interpret:** In line 6, what are the "measureless oceans of space" with which the speaker's soul is surrounded?
3. **(a) Recall:** Why does the spider "tirelessly" spin out filament? **(b) Connect:** How is the speaker's soul similar to the spider?
4. **(a) Recall:** What verbs does Whitman use to describe the spider's actions? **(b) Recall:** What verbs does he use to describe the activities of his soul? **(c) Compare and Contrast:** How are the two explorations the same, and how are they different?
5. **(a) Recall:** Who—or what—does the poet address directly? **(b) Interpret:** What is the speaker's attitude toward the recipient of this direct address?
6. **Synthesize:** Like the Transcendentalists, Whitman believed that the human spirit was mirrored in the world of nature. What aspects of "A Noiseless Patient Spider" reflect this belief?
7. **Evaluate:** Do you think the parallel Whitman draws between his soul and the spider is convincing? Explain.

Go Online Author Link
For: More about Walt Whitman
Visit: www.PHSchool.com
Web Code: ere-9315

Apply the Skills

Walt Whitman's Poetry

Literary Analysis

Free Verse

1. In what ways does the use of **free verse** allow the poet to express his ideas more freely in "Song of Myself"?
2. How would the impact of "When I Heard the Learn'd Astronomer" be different if it had regular meter and line length?

Comparing Literary Works

3. Use a chart like the one shown to analyze Whitman's use of catalogs, or lists, in both "By the Bivouac's Fitful Flame" and "When I Heard the Learn'd Astronomer."

Poem	Cataloging	What the Details Share	Effect

4. In what ways does the **diction** in "When I Heard the Learn'd Astronomer," especially the use of parallel structures in the first four lines, reinforce Whitman's description of the astronomer?
5. What effect does the catalog of workers in "I Hear America Singing" have on the poem's message?
6. In your opinion, which poem represents the best match between subject and diction? Explain.

Reading Strategy

Inferring the Poet's Attitude

7. **(a)** In Section 14, lines 11–14, of "Song of Myself," what can you **infer** about Whitman's **attitude** toward people who work outdoors? **(b)** What language helps you draw this inference?
8. Note at least five descriptive words or phrases in "When I Heard the Learn'd Astronomer" that help you infer Whitman's attitude toward the science of astronomy and his feelings about the stars.

Extend Understanding

9. **Literature Connection:** It has been said that Whitman's entire body of work was a spiritual autobiography. Do you think this assessment is accurate? Explain.

QuickReview

Free verse is poetry that has an irregular meter and line length.

Diction involves the writer's choice and arrangement of words, and includes the use of such devices as catalogs and parallelism.

You can **infer the poet's attitude** by noting his or her choice of subjects, details, and words.

For: Self-test
Visit: www.PHSchool.com
Web Code: era-6311

Answers

1. The use of free verse emphasizes Whitman's free, unconventional, and unconfined approach to the wonders of nature.
2. It would seem to support the scientist's approach to nature rather than the poet's unconventional point of view.
3. Possible response for "When I heard . . .": Cataloging: the proofs, the figures; the charts and diagrams; What the Details Have in Common: They all relate to organizing information; Effect: They support Whitman's attitude that science takes the mystery out of nature.

   Another sample answer can be found on **Literary Analysis Graphic Organizer B,** p. 90 in ***Graphic Organizer Transparencies.***
4. Repeated use of the opening words *When I* set up the readers' expectation of the speaker's response to the astronomer's facts and figures.
5. It gives it a singsong, musical quality that reinforces Whitman's message about the poetry in everyday Americans.
6. Students' responses should be supported with examples from their chosen poem.
7. (a) Whitman values physical labor; he seems to exult in the work and the workers he observes. (b) The catalog of workers singing at their jobs helps one draw the inference.
8. **Possible responses:** to *add, divide, and measure them; sitting; tired and sick; rising and gliding; the mystical moist night air;* and *in perfect silence.*
9. Students should be able to support their responses with examples from the poems.

Go Online Assessment Students may use the **Self-test** to prepare for **Selection Test A** or **Selection Test B.**

EXTEND/ASSESS

Answers

❶ Vocabulary Lesson

Word Analysis

1. a
2. d
3. c
4. b

Vocabulary Builder

1. No, because her ruling temporarily overturns the law.
2. Light that effuses spreads through the room.

Spelling Strategy

1. puny
2. feud
3. youth
4. value

❷ Grammar and Style Lesson

1. she, *mare*
2. their, the *woman and* child
3. its, *life*
4. his, *shoemaker*
5. they, *the laborers*

Writing Application

Students' sentences should be free of mechanical errors and should each contain a pronoun that correctly matches its antecedent.

Writing and Grammar, Ruby Level

Students will find further instruction and practice on pronoun and antecedent agreement in Chapter 23, Section 2.

Build Language Skills

❶ Vocabulary Lesson

Word Analysis: Latin Root *-fus-*

In "Song of Myself" Whitman writes, "I effuse my flesh in eddies, and drift it in lacy jags." The word *effuse* means "pour" or "spread." It is based on the Latin root *-fus-*, meaning "pour," combined with the prefix *e-*, which means "out" or "away."

Each of the words in the left column is based on the root *-fus-*. Match each word with its definition in the right column.

1. profusion	**a.** rich or lavish supply
2. infuse	**b.** dispersed
3. effusive	**c.** gushing
4. diffuse	**d.** fill

Vocabulary Builder: Denotations

Answer the following questions. Then, explain your answers.

1. If a judge hands down a ruling in *abeyance* of a particular law, is she enforcing that law?
2. Does light that *effuses* from a lamp spread softly or shine in a sharply focused beam?

Spelling Strategy

The sound of *y* followed by long *u* is often created by the letter *u* alone, as in *effuse.* Other spellings include *ew, ue, eu,* and *ou.* Complete each word below with the correct spelling.

1. p__ny (small)
2. f__d (major argument)
3. y__th (a child)
4. val__ (worth)

❷ Grammar and Style Lesson

Pronoun and Antecedent Agreement

A **pronoun** must **agree** in number with its **antecedent**—the word to which it refers—in the following ways:

- in number—singular or plural
- in gender—masculine or feminine

Singular:	The *shoemaker* (ANTECEDENT) singing as *he* (PRONOUN) sits on *his bench.* (masculine, singular)
Plural:	. . .The *past* and *present* (ANTECEDENT) wilt— I have fill'd *them* (PRONOUN) . . .

Two singular antecedents joined by *and* take a plural pronoun. Two singular antecedents joined by *or* take a singular pronoun.

Practice Choose the correct pronoun for each sentence below. Then, identify its antecedent.

1. The mare awoke, and then (she, it) stepped toward the door of the stall.
2. The woman and child opened (his, their) books and began to sing.
3. Life has (its, their) challenges and gratifications.
4. The shoemaker went on (their, his) lunch break.
5. All of the laborers received pay increases after (he, they) made requests.

Writing Application Write five sentences describing the work of various friends or family members. For each, use pronouns that correctly match their antecedents.

Prentice Hall Writing and Grammar Connection: Chapter 23, Section 2

Assessment Practice

Make Inferences and Generalizations (For more practice, see *Standardized Test Preparation Workbook*, p. 25.)

Many tests require students to make inferences about a written passage. Explain that sometimes inferences need to be drawn concerning an author's point of view, opinions, or attitudes. Have students read "I Hear America Singing" on p. 442, then ask them the following question:

What is the poet's attitude toward the American workers about whom he writes?

A uncertain
B celebratory
C dismissive
D somber

The poet emphatically proclaims his admiration for the laborers. Thus *A, C,* and *D* cannot be correct. The best choice is *B.*

Writing Lesson

Imitation of an Author's Style

Write a poem in which you imitate Walt Whitman's unique style. Choose several elements of his style—diction, tone, degree of formality, rhythm, use of catalogs, or structure—and use them throughout your poem.

Prewriting Decide on a "Whitmanesque" topic, and review the characteristics of free verse. List or diagram sensory details and images related to your topic.

Model: Using a Cluster Diagram to Gather Details

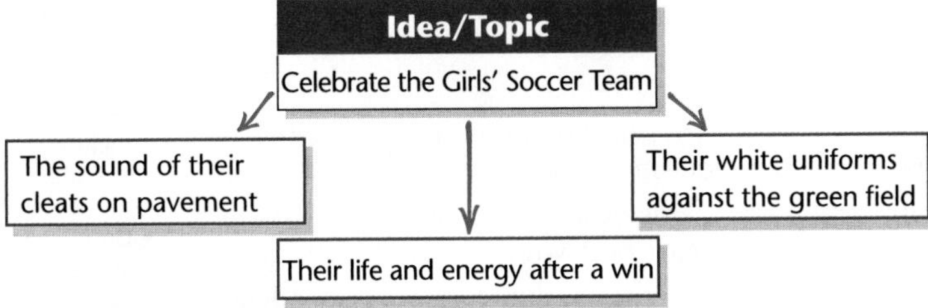

Drafting Maintain a consistent style and tone, and let your meaning determine the lengths of lines and stanzas.

Revising Read your poem aloud. Listen for natural rhythms of speech rather than formal rhythms or grammatical structures. Make any changes necessary to maintain the natural-sounding rhythms.

WG Prentice Hall Writing and Grammar Connection: Chapter 3, Section 3

Extend Your Learning

Listening and Speaking Whitman's poems capture America at the dawn of the Industrial Age. With a group, look through magazines for images that capture America's essence today. Make a **collage.** Then, present your findings to the class. Let the following tips guide your presentation:

- Explain why you included each image.
- Discuss how the themes of the collage compare to Whitman's vision of the country.

Include passages from Whitman's poetry that speak to the images you present. **[Group Activity]**

Research and Technology Compare the rhyme and meter of Emily Dickinson's poetry with the unrhymed free verse of Whitman's poetry. Use the Internet to locate and listen to oral readings of the two poets. Then, research the ways in which each poet has influenced American poetry. Deliver a **report** of your findings to the class.

For: An additional research activity
Visit: www.PHSchool.com
Web Code: erd-7310

❸ Writing Lesson

- To guide students in writing this poem, give them the **Support for Writing Lesson,** p. 181 in ***Unit 3 Resources.***
- Have volunteers read aloud their favorite of the Whitman poems. Discuss with students the aspects of Whitman's style that they enjoy.
- Suggest exuberance, reflection, or wonder as possible tones to adopt in writing a Whitmanlike poem.
- Review the Writing Lesson to guide students in developing their poems. Offer students **Fine Art Transparencies, Volume1,** Transparency 19, *Builders in the City,* as an inspiration for their poems.
- Adapt the rubrics for Poem (Rhyming), pp. 73–74 in ***General Resources,*** to evaluate students' poems.

❹ Listening and Speaking

- Encourage groups to focus on a few areas of American life before they begin their image search.
- Provide students with a variety of magazines or suggest that they look at home or at rummage sales for old magazines.
- Remind students to refer frequently to their collages as they speak.
- Provide students with the rubric for Delivering a Research Presentation in ***General Resources,*** p. 91.
- The **Support for Extend Your Learning** page (***Unit 3 Resources,*** p. 182) provides guided note-taking opportunities to help students complete the Extend Your Learning activities.

Go Online Research Activity Have students type in the Web Code for another research activity.

Assessment Resources

The following resources can be used to assess students' knowledge and skills.

Unit 3 Resources
- **Selection Test A,** pp. 184–186
- **Selection Test B,** pp. 187–189

General Resources
- **Rubrics for Poem (Rhyming),** pp 73–74
- **Rubric for Delivering a Research Presentation,** p. 92

Go Online Assessment Students may use the **Self-test** to prepare for **Selection Test A** or **Selection Test B.**

Meeting Your Standards

Students will

1. **write an essay comparing and contrasting American literature of the 1800s with a more traditional school of literature of the same era.**
2. **use writing strategies to generate ideas and to plan, organize, evaluate, and revise the composition.**

Prewriting

- To give students guidance in developing this assignment, give them the **Writing About Literature** support pages in ***Unit 3 Resources.***
- Discuss with students how selections that they have read in this unit show characteristics that are particularly "American." Then discuss the ways that authors represented in this unit conform to and depart from traditional European styles of the same period. Review as many authors and works as possible.
- Suggest that students take notes on three or four authors whom they will use as examples in their essays. Tell them to organize their notes in the Five-column Chart on p. 308 of ***Graphic Organizer Transparencies.***
- When students are thinking about trends to compare and contrast, tell them to consider using selections from different genres, such as fiction, nonfiction, poetry, or essay.

Tips for Test Taking

A writing prompt on a standardized test may ask students to write a compare-and-contrast essay. Remind students that it is important to quickly develop a thesis and sketch out an outline. Also, a "subject-by-subject" approach is generally easier to execute. If the similarities in the essay are more striking than the differences, conclude with the similarities. If the differences are more striking, conclude with them.

Writing About Literature

Compare and Contrast Literary Trends

In its formative years, American literature comprised a fairly random assortment of individual efforts. There were no literary movements, and there was no strong sense of a distinctly American literature. By the early to mid 1800s, this had changed, and American writers began to produce a distinctive body of work. The stories, poems, and essays published during these decades explored a range of themes and set their ideas within a uniquely American landscape.

Using the assignment outlined in the yellow box, write an essay to address this period in American literary history.

Assignment: Old vs. New in American Literature

Write an analytical essay that compares and contrasts one of the more distinctly American literary trends of this period with one of the more traditional schools of literature. Your essay will focus on two different trends and may require support from more than two authors.

Criteria:

- Include a thesis statement that identifies the trends and authors you will compare.
- Compare and contrast your subjects point by point, with references and quotations from the works.
- Approximate length: 700 words.

Prewriting

Identify trends. Review each selection in this unit to see how it fits into a larger trend. These questions may help frame your review:

- Are the setting and theme explicitly American, or could the selection just as easily have been written by an English author?
- Does the work reflect American values such as independence and optimism, or does it reflect a traditional, European outlook on life?
- Is the author's voice personal and strongly individualistic? If so, in what ways is this expressed?
- What other literary works in the unit does the selection resemble? In what ways?

Use your review of each selection and your knowledge of history and literature to classify the pieces in this unit according to the trends they exemplify.

Select trends to compare or contrast. After classifying the selections that appear in this unit, determine which ones you want to explore in your essay. Decide whether you are more interested in comparing points of similarity between two emerging trends or in contrasting extreme differences between the old and the new.

Read to Write

Reread the texts carefully, looking for ways in which they reveal—or do not reveal—distinctly American sensibilities.

Focus on similarities and differences. Once you have identified the selections you intend to analyze, use a chart like the one shown to closely analyze specific features.

Unique to Emerson	Similarities	Unique to Poe
Emerson's belief in the power of the individual expresses a core American value.	Both writers believed that some aspects of the truth were beyond the realm of physical reality.	Allusions to European art, music, and architecture in "The Fall of the House of Usher" show Poe's kinship with European traditions.

Teaching Resources

The following resources can be used to extend or enrich the instruction for Writing About Literature.

Unit 3 Resources
- **Writing About Literature**, pp. 190–191

General Resources
- **Rubrics for Comparison-and-Contrast Essay**, pp. 69–70

Graphic Organizer Transparencies
- **Five column Chart**, p. 308
- **Outline**, p. 309

Drafting

Outline. Use the information from your chart to create a working outline. In the major headings of the outline, indicate the most important points of similarity or difference between the two trends under discussion. Beneath each heading, list the supporting details from the literature.

Model: Devising a Working Outline

I. Similarities between Poe and Emerson
  A. belief in aspects of truth that are beyond physical reality
  B. (other similarities)
II. Differences between Poe and Emerson
  A. Emerson exhibits new American value of self-determination.
  B. Poe's stories reflect the European belief in fate.

Write to Learn
If you have trouble finding details to support a conclusion, reconsider your ideas. Maybe you have jumped to a conclusion based on insufficient evidence. If so, rethink your argument.

Refer to historical context. Writers are individuals, but they also reflect the times and places in which they live. As you draft, analyze the extent to which each writer's work expresses ideas that were either shared by their contemporaries or that were innovative—even radical—at the time.

Revising and Editing

Review content: Check the accuracy of details. All the opinions in your essay must be supported with accurate details from the selections. Verify the accuracy of details by going back and checking the source.

Review style: Vary sentence length and structure. Review your draft to evaluate your sentences. If you find too many long sentences in a row, break some of them down into shorter sentences. If you find a string of short, choppy sentences, combine some of them.

Repetitive sentence length and structure: American writing flourished during the 1800s. Poe wrote disturbing horror stories. Emerson produced striking essays.

Improved sentence variety: During the 1800s, American writing flourished. Poe wrote disturbing horror stories, while Emerson produced original and striking essays.

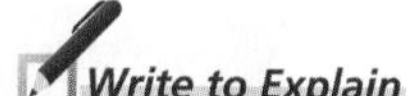
Write to Explain
The reader cannot follow your thought process; he or she can only follow the arguments you note on the page. Make sure that you explain your reasons for drawing conclusions, and do not omit any steps in your thought process.

Publishing and Presenting

Create a comparison and contrast poster. To share your analysis with others, take the major points from your essay and distill them into brief statements. Place the statements on a poster, with comparisons in one section and contrasting points in another section. Use graphic elements to draw visual attention to your main points.

Prentice Hall Writing and Grammar Connection: Chapter 9

Differentiated Instruction Solutions for All Learners

Support for Special-Needs Students

Make the task of comparing and contrasting as straightforward as possible. Show students two selections that are very different, such as a Fireside poem focusing on landscape and a story by Poe. Students should be able to see that the Fireside poem portrays an American subject, such as a New England winter, while Poe's story could take place anywhere.

Enrichment for Advanced Writers

Encourage students to make a list of questions they might ask about American versus European literary styles in the nineteenth century. They might start with specific writers, such as Whitman or Poe. What makes Whitman's poetry different from that of an English writer? Does Poe sound more American when he writes his stories and more "European" when he writes poetry (or vice versa)? Do some writers use American themes but place them in conventional literary patterns?

Drafting

Make sure that before studen[...] writing, they create an outline. U[...] the Outline transparency on p. 309 in ***Graphic Organizer Transparencies.*** Explain that students can organize comparison-and-contrast essays by identifying the most important *traits* that create similarities or differences among selections. Another way they can discuss all the traits for each *selection* before discussing the next selection. The model discusses Emerson and Poe using a trait-by-trait approach. The outline moves from the traits both authors share to the traits that differentiates them.

Revising and Editing

Have students exchange papers with partners. Partners can help identify whether opinions are supported by details. They can also help each other spot grammatical or mechanical errors. In particular, have students look for repetitive sentence structures, especially the frequent use of short, choppy sentences with repetitive sentence openers.

Publishing and Presenting

Organize the class into groups to reflect a good mix of authors and trends and to promote the airing of a range of views.

Writing and Grammar, Ruby Level

Students will find added instruction on comparison-and-contrast essays in Chapter 9, Sections 1–7.

Writing and Grammar Interactive CD-ROM

Students can use the following tools as they complete their comparison-contrast essays:

- Customizable Outliner
- Sentence Openers Variety
- Language Variety Revising Tool

Six Traits Focus

✓	Ideas		Word Choice
✓	Organization	✓	Sentence Fluency
	Voice	✓	Conventions

Assessing the Essay

To evaluate students' essays, use the rubrics for Comparison-and-Contrast, pp. 69–70, in ***General Resources.***

TEACH

ng Your Standards

1. write a reflective essay.
2. use writing strategies to generate ideas and to plan, organize, evaluate, and revise the composition.
3. apply grammar skills.

From the Scholar's Desk

Gretel Ehrlich

Show students Segment 3 on Gretel Ehrlich on *From the Author's Desk DVD.* Discuss Ehrlich's comments about how she extracted meaning from details as she wrote her essay, "The Solace of Open Spaces."

Writing Genres

Using the Form Point out to students that reflective narration is often included in different forms of writing. Mention these examples:

- Autobiographical narratives consist largely of the author's reflections about his or her personal experiences.
- Essays about personal history written for college or other applications often include several paragraphs of reflection about an event.
- Nature essays such as those by Gretel Ehrlich often focus on a particular natural environment and the writer's reflections about it.

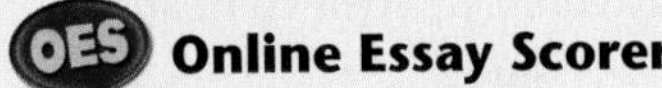

Online Essay Scorer

A writing prompt for this mode of writing can be found on the *PH Online Essay Scorer* at PHSuccessNet.com.

Writing Workshop

Narration: Reflective Essay

The thoughtful essays of Ralph Waldo Emerson and Henry David Thoreau, included in this unit, provide fascinating insights into the writers' personalities. These **reflective essays** do more than report events: they interpret them and consider their larger meaning. Follow the steps outlined in this workshop to write your own reflective essay.

Assignment Write a reflective essay in which you explore a personal experience or an event, and reflect on its broader significance or deeper meaning.

What to Include Your reflective essay should feature the following elements:

- the writer as the main character
- the personal feelings, thoughts, or views of the writer
- connections between specific incidents and broader themes
- insights gained during reflection
- a balance between specific incidents and abstract ideas

To preview the criteria on which your reflective essay may be assessed, see the rubric on page 463.

Using the Form

You may use elements of a reflective essay in these writing situations:

- memoirs
- travelogues
- personal narratives
- autobiographical incidents

To get a feel for the reflective essay, read the selection from *Walden* by Henry David Thoreau, page 406.

Teaching Resources

The following resources can be used to enrich or extend the instruction for the Writing Workshop.

Unit 3 Resources
- **Writing Workshop**, pp. 192–193

General Resources
- **Rubrics for Reflective Essay**, p. 47–48

Graphic Organizer Transparencies
- **Rubric for Self-Assessment**, p. 91
- **Timeline**, p. 314
- **Outline**, p. 309

From the Author's Desk DVD
- **Gretel Ehrlich**, Segments 3 and 4

Prewriting

Choosing Your Topic

To choose an event for your reflective essay, use one of the following strategies:

- **Listing and Itemizing** Start a list of meaningful events by chronicling your daily life. List the activities that fill your week, itemizing notable incidents that happened during these activities. Choose one event that has a wider meaning to explore in your reflective essay.
- **Freewriting About Personal Milestones** Freewrite about your personal history. Consider the important moments you have experienced in your life, such as first friends, lost loved ones, or tough choices. Ask yourself how these moments have changed your life. Consult family members or friends to help you retrace your thinking during these momentous changes. Then, choose one of these milestones as the topic for your reflective essay.

Narrowing Your Topic

From your list or your freewriting, select a moment from your life that you want to explore. Find an insight in your experience—an instant that caused you to learn something new about yourself or to see the world in a different light. Review your notes, and then write a sentence that identifies the event and the lesson it taught you. As you write, limit your focus to these two ideas: the event and the insight.

Example: When I saw how far I could travel by car, I admired the pioneers who had plodded west on horseback.

Gathering Details

Draw comparisons. Once you have selected an experience to explore, use a diagram like the one shown to consider themes in the world at large that might compare to your own experience.

Exploring Back Roads

In My Life	In the World
• Be like my brothers • Learn to navigate my world	• Connect to history • Create sense of family continuity between generations

Do some research. To connect your personal event with an incident in the outside world, you may need to do some research. Consult friends, family, the library, or the Internet and incorporate any relevant information into your draft.

TEACH

Prewriting

- Have students choose topics by using the idea-generating strategies listed here.
- Use pp. 192 and 193 from ***Unit 3 Resources*** for lesson support.
- If students are using a list to generate writing ideas, guide them by mentioning areas of life that may yield memorable events for example: family life, school, sports, competitions, jobs, or travel.
- If students are freewriting about personal milestones in order to generate ideas, suggest that they use the Timeline, p. 314, in ***Graphic Organizer Transparencies,*** to help them remember important childhood events.
- In narrowing the topic, students should focus on those events or observations that produced a lasting impact on them, creating a noticeable change in their thinking or perspective about someone or something.

Six Traits Focus

✔	Ideas		Word Choice
✔	Organization		Sentence Fluency
	Voice		Conventions

WG Writing and Grammar, Ruby Level

Students will find additional instruction on prewriting for a reflective essay in Chapter 4, Section 2.

Writing and Grammar Interactive CD-ROM

Students can use the following tools as they complete their reflective essays:

- Timeline
- Outline
- Language Variety Revising Tool

Tips for Using Rubrics

- Before students begin work on this assignment, have them preview the **Rubric for Self-Assessment** (p. 463) to know what is expected.
- Review the Assessment criteria in class. Before students use the **Rubric for Self-Assessment,** work with them to rate the student model by applying one or more criteria to it.
- If you wish to assess students' reflective essays with either a 4-, 5-, or 6-point scoring rubric, see ***General Resources***, pp. 47 and 48.

Drafting

- Go over the organization model in the textbook with the students. Encourage them to adapt the model if the structure is a good fit for their essays. They may wish to use the Outline transparency, p. 309, in ***Graphic Organizer Transparencies.***
- Suggest other organizational approaches, such as beginning with the insight and then relating the experience that produced it. Mention presenting several different experiences that, taken together, had an impact on their lives.
- Help students extend and elaborate ideas by giving them more practice in using this process. For instance, ask them to provide personal observations that elaborate on the idea that members of their class view their school quite differently from the way ninth-graders see it.
- Encourage students to use concrete sensory details and dialogue to enliven the narrative portions of their essays.
- Tell students to use language that is natural to them so that their personalities come through to the reader and their writing sounds sincere.

Six Traits Focus

✔	Ideas	✔	Word Choice
✔	Organization		Sentence Fluency
✔	Voice		Conventions

WG Writing and Grammar, Ruby Level

Students will find additional instruction on drafting a reflective essay in Chapter 4, Section 3.

Writing Workshop

Drafting

Shaping Your Writing

Organize your reflection. Develop a draft that follows a logical organization and that places the incident you are describing in a broader thematic context. The organizational format shown here is an effective way to build a reflective essay.

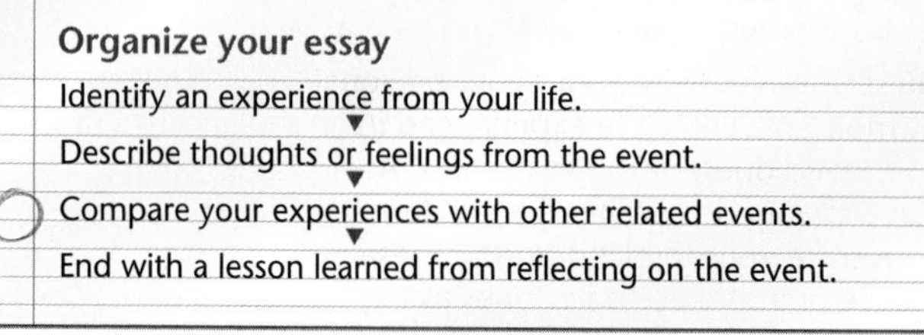

Organize your essay

Identify an experience from your life.

Describe thoughts or feelings from the event.

Compare your experiences with other related events.

End with a lesson learned from reflecting on the event.

To read the complete student model, see page 462.

Begin with a compelling lead. Reflective writing gives you the opportunity to interest someone in your life. A simple but catchy opening sentence can provide just the right amount of information to grab a reader's attention.

Examples: Whenever I hear the song "Memory," I burst into laughter.
My sister refuses to wear the color purple.

Providing Elaboration

Make your writing personal. As you draft your essay, include details such as the thoughts and feelings you remember experiencing during the event. Interpret small moments through your own personal prism. Note sensory images that will make details more vivid. Refer back to the notes you took during prewriting, and add these thoughts, feelings, and images to your draft.

Use the SEE technique to add details. Expand ideas by using *Statement—Extension—Elaboration* to dig deeper into your personal feelings, thoughts, and views. Begin by stating a main idea. Then, extend it by restating or developing it. Finally, elaborate on it further to amplify or expand the original idea.

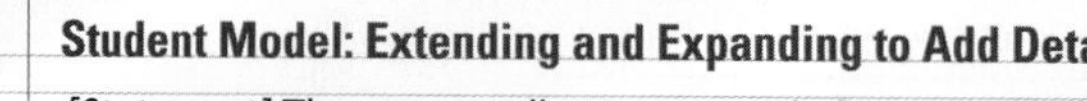

Student Model: Extending and Expanding to Add Details

[Statement] They are small country roads *[Extension]*—the ones that change color *[Expansion]* and ride when you cross a simple parish line. *[Expansion]* They have four-ton limits. . .

Extending and expanding the definition with personal observations provides a more vivid picture of the country road.

Gretel Ehrlich

From the Scholar's Desk
Gretel Ehrlich on Using Layers of Meaning

These are the closing paragraphs of the title essay of my book the *Solace of Open Spaces.* Here, I stepped back from the details in the essay—those of anecdote and description—to contemplate the larger meaning of "space" and the way it shapes our minds and our experience of the world—the "internal weather" of our lives.

"Writing is an act of seeing through to the other side of our lives, then coming back and putting an expression of that otherness on the page."

—— Gretel Ehrlich

Professional Model:

From *The Solace of Open Spaces*

At night, by moonlight, the land is whittled to slivers—a ridge, a river, a strip of grassland stretching to the mountains, then the huge sky. One morning a full moon was setting in the west just as the sun was rising. I felt precariously balanced between the two as I loped (my horse) across a meadow. For a moment, I could believe that the stars, which were still visible, work like cooper's bands, holding together everything above Wyoming.

Space has a spiritual equivalent and can heal what is divided and burdensome in us. My grandchildren will probably use space shuttles for a honeymoon trip or to recover from heart attacks, but closer to home we might also learn how to carry space inside ourselves in the effortless way we carry our skins. Space represents sanity, not a life purified or dull, or "spaced out," but one that might accommodate intelligently any idea or situation.

In this paragraph, I turn the concept of "space" in four directions: as a spiritual guide, as a healer of physical maladies, as an actual component of our body's makeup, and as a state of mind.

From the clayey soil of northern Wyoming is mined bentonite, which is used as a filler in candy, gum, and lipstick. We Americans are great on fillers, as if what we have, what we are, is not enough. We have the cultural tendency toward denial, but, being affluent, we strangle ourselves with what we can buy. . . . We fill up space as if it were a pie shell, with things whose opacity further obstructs our ability to see what is already there.

Here I take an actual geological substance—bentonite, which is a kind of clay—and use it metaphorically: to indicate the way we pack our heads, hearts, and homes with things we don't need.

Here I am reminding the reader that "space" does not represent an "absence" but something positive.

From the Author's Desk

- Show students Segment 4 on Gretel Ehrlich on **From the Author's Desk DVD.** Discuss her comments about how she elaborated on the concept of space as both a physical and mental entity.
- Draw students' attention to Ehrlich's striking use of the information about bentonite to elaborate on her ideas about space. She provides an interesting detail about a little-known substance to create a clever analogy illustrating how people compulsively fill up their lives with trivia. Just as Ehrlich uses this detail to comment on our waste of physical and mental space, authors make ideas easier to grasp and more memorable by elaborating on them with extended details and creative figures of speech.
- Review Ehrlich's comments about treating space as if it were a pie shell, to be filled with things whose opacity further obstructs our ability to see what is actually there. **Ask** students to give other examples of things that interfere with clear perception and thought.
  Possible answer: Students might mention the frenzy to buy the latest fashions and consumer items, or the hours spent watching television, chatting online, or playing video games.

Differentiated Instruction
Solutions for All Learners

Strategy for Less Proficient Writers

Have students choose partners to whom they will tell the stories they are using as the basis for their reflective essays. Telling their stories as part of the prewriting activity will help students organize and focus their ideas, eliminate less relevant details, shape the plots of their narratives, and express their insights and reflections more coherently.Have each student make a timeline to use as a guide when writing and list two or three important ideas or insights about the story they will write. Tell students to put those ideas or insights on their timelines first.

Tell partners to help each other make certain that their timelines show events in the proper order. Partners can ask each other questions to make sure of accurate chronology and to draw out meaningful information.

Revising

- Arrange the schedule to allow students at least 24 hours before they reread them with an eye toward revision. Time away from a piece of writing helps the writer to see his or her work with fresh eyes and new energy.
- Remind students that the more concrete and specific their writing is, the more lifelike and appealing it will seem to their readers. Urge students to find places to add additional details and specific observations.
- Suggest that students practice varying sentence beginnings; remind them of alternative ways of starting a sentence. Ask them to find examples of the following sentence openers in the Student Model: a subordinate clause, a prepositional phrase, a participial phrase, an adverb,or a transition. **Possible response:** Students may find the following: subordinate clause: "Whether we went and looked at natural gas wells"; prepositional phrase: "In a blue and gray Ford truck"; participial phrase: "Looking back"; adverb: "Now and again"; transition: "So"

Six Traits Focus

✔	Ideas	✔	Word Choice
✔	Organization		Sentence Fluency
	Voice		Conventions

Writing and Grammar, Ruby Level

Students will find additional guidance for revising a reflective essay in Chapter 4, Section 4.

Writing Workshop

Revising

Revising Your Overall Structure

Take a balanced approach. Review your draft to find the connections between your own personal experiences and broader themes, insights, or events in the world at large. Use this strategy to create a balance in your draft between the narration of your experiences and your reflections about their meaning:

1. Place a blue star next to sentences that develop your own experiences.
2. Place a red check next to sentences that refer to related outside experiences or to reflections about the meaning of your own experiences.
3. Check that your draft effectively balances descriptions of your own experiences with reflections on larger themes that relate to those experiences. If you have too few checks, add more statements that broaden your focus.
4. As you revise your draft, be prepared to cut commentary that strays too far from the main idea of your essay.

To read the complete student model, see page 462.

Model: Revising for Balance

☆Now I am driving.☆Those old Bienville roads have acquired new meaning.✓I know that if I hang a right at the T, I can get to the cemetery that holds my relations from 150 years back, the same people that first helped settle North Louisiana.☆None of my brothers ever knew about the cemetery, but I do.☆I even know three ways to get to Minden that my brother Judd did not teach me.✓*On the roads that my family has traveled for over a century, I am just starting to find my way of traveling. . . .*

The writer added information that enlarges upon the specific experiences he describes.

Revising Your Sentences

Vary sentences. Even though your reflective essay is about an event that happened to you, avoid beginning every sentence with *I*. Highlight the first word in every sentence in your draft, and vary sentence beginnings to make your writing more interesting.

Example: I remember the door. I remember it was locked. I remember being curious.
The door was locked, and I remember being curious.

Peer Review: Convene a group of three or four classmates, and have them read your work. Ask them to identify places in your draft where you might improve sentence variety. Revise based on your classmates' feedback. Be prepared to justify your revision choices by explaining how your changes improve your writing style.

Tips for Using Technology in Writing

At the revision stage, students using word processors can use the Thesaurus tool to expand their word choice options. In particular, if they discover repetition of words or phrases within the space of a sentence or two, they can find a replacement. In addition, students can use the Word Count command to determine whether their essays meet required length. If they are more than one hundred words over or under the limit, they can review their essays, looking for ways to shorten or expand certain sections. Students can also use the organizing tools and revision checkers on **Writing and Grammar *i*Text.**

Developing Your Style

Keeping Voice and Tone Consistent

Write in your own voice. A writer's voice produces a unique effect, much like the individual style of a person's speaking voice. When you call a friend on the telephone, he or she can probably recognize your voice without even seeing your face. To create a literary personality of word choices, pace, and patterns of vowels and consonants, make your writing voice as distinctive as your speaking voice, and use the same voice consistently throughout your reflective essay.

Use an appropriate tone. Your tone is the attitude you convey toward your subject and your reader. Treat them both with respect. Establish a tone for your reflective essay—for example, serious, lighthearted, humorous, formal, or informal—and use that tone consistently throughout.

Serious: Snow fell quietly, covering the ugly remnants of the fire.

Lighthearted: That snowy hillside reminded me, with a thrill, of all the fun we used to have sledding and snowboarding.

Review your essay, and circle any words that do not correctly convey the tone you have chosen. Replace them with choices that project the tone you intend.

Find It in Your Reading Read or review the selection from *Walden* by Henry David Thoreau, page 406.

1. Identify three sentences that demonstrate Thoreau's voice. For each sentence, notice the word choice and any identifiable patterns.
2. Identify the tone in *Walden.* List words and details that convey the writer's attitude toward the subject or the audience.

Apply It to Your Writing Review your draft of a reflective essay. For each paragraph in your draft, follow these steps:

1. Locate sentences or phrases that reveal your voice. Look for writing that sounds like you or reflects your thinking.
2. Review your work for elements of tone. Read parts aloud to hear your particular way of saying things. Isolate the words that suggest that tone. Be sure that your essay has a tone appropriate to both personal reflection and the larger themes you discuss.
3. If your essay lacks a detectable personal voice, revise it to create writing that sounds more like you.
4. If your tone seems inappropriate, match it to your purpose. Informal and friendly tones usually work best with personal observations, whereas formal or distant tones keep your far-reaching comments from sounding flip or insincere.

WG *Prentice Hall Writing and Grammar Connection: Chapter 3, Section 4*

Developing Your Style

- Reinforce students' sense of tone by reminding them that tone refers to the attitude a writer takes toward his or her subject and audience.
- Organize students into pairs, and have partners read their essays to each other. Have students define the tone that comes across to the reader.
- Have partners read their essays aloud again, with each partner listening for passages that do not fit the overall tone. Encourage partners to suggest revisions for each other.
- Discuss with students how sentence structure and variety contribute to the pace, tone, and mood of a piece of writing. Have students read each other's essays aloud to listen for monotonous or awkward sentence structure.

Six Traits Focus

✔	Ideas	✔	Word Choice
✔	Organization	✔	Sentence Fluency
✔	Voice		Conventions

WG Writing and Grammar, Ruby Level

Students will find additional instruction on keeping voice and tone consistant in Chapter 4, Section 4.

Tips for Test Taking

Remind students to budget their time when they take a timed essay test. Do not spend too much time on any one phase of the writing process. Choose a topic quickly. Elaborate on a first instinct. Students should allow half of the allotted time for writing and the rest for rereading, revising, and proofreading their essays.

Student Model

- Explain that the student model is a sample and that many reflective essays may be longer.
- Note that the author does not focus on any one particular event in this reflective essay. **Ask** students to summarize the experiences the author relates in his essay.
Possible response: The essay describes the backroads that Graham Walker rode with his brothers; as he grew older and came to know the roads better, he began to connect more with his brothers. **Ask** students to explain the insight that Graham expresses by describing the backroads.
Possible response: Graham's insight has to do with a stronger sense of his own identity and his roots a journey to who he is, where he has come from, and, eventually, where he is headed.

Writing Genres

Reflective Essay Tell students that professional writers often include reflective passages in personal essays, memoirs, and travelwriting. Often reflective essays are published in magazines or on the opinion pages of newspapers. Journals and diaries also are often enlivened and enriched by short, reflective essays.

Student Model: Graham Walker, Ruston, Louisiana

Back Roads to Tomorrow

They are small country roads—the ones that change color and ride when you cross a simple parish line. They have four-ton limits assigned to small bridges that hop over waters like Bear Creek and Black Lake Bayou. Their ragged shoulders are missing chunks of pavement and rise three inches above the packed red clay that supports the asphalt. Bright ribbons of tape hang from the lower limbs of pine trees to escort log trucks to jobs. Now and again a color will halt at a worn path entering a clean-bottomed plot of trees, but the others remain loyal to the country road.

This descriptive language creates a strong sense of place and establishes a personal tone.

These are the roads I grew up on.

Graham is the main character in his essay.

It was usually just my oldest brother, Judd, and me. In a blue and gray Ford truck, we would branch out from our home in Taylor, Louisiana, with the windows down. Whether we went and looked at natural gas wells or whether we shot big turtles sunning themselves on logs in a bayou, it never took too much to keep us rolling along on those old Bienville back roads.

Graham uses sensory details to convey a vivid picture of his experience.

But it was not pure riding experience that I enjoyed so much. It was the infinite knowledge of the roads that I believed I gained from those trips. I was in Back Roads 101: Knowing the Road. I made sure that I asked my brother whether we would take a right here or keep straight at the intersections. I felt that I had to know three different ways to get to Minden, ten miles away, or which way the T below our house would take me in case I wanted to slip off for a spin in my pre-double digit years.

Looking back, I realize it was not my concern for my future driving years that led me to study those roads so intently and to map them in my memory. It was one of the lengths I went to so I could be like my three older brothers. All three of them knew the lay of the pavement throughout the Bienville Parish. They could tell me how to get wherever I wished by a back road route—even to Shreveport, I am sure. And more than I wanted to get to Shreveport, I wanted to be like them.

Graham begins to draw connections between the specific experience and a deeper meaning.

So I soon knew most of the roads they knew. I could tell anyone three different ways to get to Minden, or which way the T would take me. But I was mapping more than Bienville Parish.

Now I am driving. Those old Bienville roads have acquired new meaning. I know that if I hang a right at the T, I can get to the cemetery that holds my relations from 150 years back, the same people that first helped settle North Louisiana. None of my brothers ever knew about the cemetery, but I do. I even know three ways to get to Minden that my brother Judd did not teach me. On the roads that my family has traveled for over a century, I am just starting to find my way of traveling. That journey, I now understand, is what all my rides with my brothers were really about.

Graham extends his personal experience into the abstract realm of family, identity, and history.

Differentiated Instruction Solutions for All Learners

Strategy for English Learners

Encourage students to use vocabulary words with which they are comfortable, rather than try to include new and unfamiliar words. However, use this assignment as an opportunity for English learners to add a few words to their vocabularies. Help them by having them tell you their stories. Identify points in the narrative that could be refined by finding a synonym. Ask students to consult a thesaurus or a dictionary to find useful synonyms. Assist them in distinguishing the nuances in meaning and usage.

Strategy for Gifted/Talented Students

Students with a strong visual sense may find it helpful to look at family photographs to stimulate their memories of certain experiences. Students with musical abilities might recall music they associate with an important milestone. In presenting their papers to the class, students with visual or musical talents should be encouraged to include images and recordings to add emotional power to their written words. Students who can write music might be interested in creating musical accompaniments for other students' writings.

Editing and Proofreading

Review your essay to eliminate errors in grammar, spelling, or punctuation.

Focus on Fragments: To create an intimate, reflective tone, you may be tempted to use sentence fragments for effect. Review your work to correct fragments. One way is to join a fragment to another sentence.

Publishing and Presenting

Consider one of the following ways to share your writing:

Deliver an oral presentation. Read your reflective essay aloud to your classmates. After you have finished, ask them to identify other themes that relate to the personal experience you have explored.

Publish a literary magazine. Gather a variety of reflective essays to create a classroom magazine. Have small committees share the tasks of designing the magazine's format, creating a cover and illustrations, proofreading, and distributing copies to other classes.

Reflecting on Your Writing

Writer's Journal Jot down your thoughts on the experience of writing a reflective essay. Begin by answering these questions:

- What insight into your own life has writing this essay given you?
- What did you learn about writing in your own voice?

WG *Prentice Hall Writing and Grammar Connection: Chapter 20, Section 2*

Rubric for Self-Assessment

Evaluate your reflective essay *using the following criteria and rating scale, or, with your classmates, determine your own reasonable evaluation criteria.*

Criteria	Rating Scale (*not very* – *very*)
Focus: How well do you establish yourself as the main character?	1 2 3 4 5
Organization: How well have you organized your feelings, thoughts, and views?	1 2 3 4 5
Support/Elaboration: How effectively do you use specific incidents to connect to broader themes?	1 2 3 4 5
Style: How well do you describe the insights you gained?	1 2 3 4 5
Conventions: How correct is your use of grammar, especially your use of complete sentences?	1 2 3 4 5

Editing and Proofreading

- Have students read their reflective essays carefully, marking them for line to line edits, including changes in word choice and corrections in grammar, spelling, and punctuation.
- Ask students to exchange papers so a more objective reader can proofread them. Then, have students provide a final copy.
- Have students read essays aloud to one another to listen for coherence.

Six Traits Focus

	Ideas	✓	Word Choice
✓	Organization		Sentence Fluency
	Voice	✓	Conventions

ASSESS

Publishing and Presenting

- Remind students that the purpose of a reflective essay is to elicit an emotional response from readers so that readers understand why the experience is important means so much to the writer.
- Ask students to exchange papers with a classmate who has not seen the essay, read each other's essays, and have readers describe the emotional effect of the essays they have read.
- Encourage students to plan and deliver an oral presentation of their reflective essays to their classmates. Invite students to add music and visual aids to their presentations.

Reflecting on Your Writing

- Ask students to compare this experience of writing a reflective essay with past experiences of writing about personal events. What did they do differently this time?

WG **Writing and Grammar, Ruby Level**

Students will find additional instruction on editing and proofreading, publishing and presenting, and reflecting on a reflective essay in Chapter 4, Section 5.

Tips for Test Taking

A writing prompt on a standardized test may ask the student to write a reflective essay, communicating an insight gained from a past experience. Help students develop a method for writing a strong reflective essay in a relatively short time period by reviewing the process they followed in writing this essay. Remind them of the important steps in this process and suggest that they remember particularly effective methods they used to choose a subject for and organize their reflective essays. Suggest that when possible they write about something they have already written about so that they have topic and an idea of what to say and how to say it.

Meeting Your Standards

Students will

1. **learn the terms *differentiate, analyze,* and *infer.***
2. **apply knowledge of these terms in standardized-test situations.**

Know Your Terms: Analyzing Information

Explain that the terms listed under Terms to Learn will be used in standardized-test situations when students are asked to analyze information and draw logical conclusions from it.

Terms to Learn

- Review *differentiate.* Tell students that to differentiate is to distinguish between or among comparable items or qualities.
- Review *analyze.* Explain that the verb *analyze* means to break down something whole into its' essential parts. Students analyze when they dissect an animal or diagram a sentence.
- Review *infer* and *inference.* Explain to students that to infer is to derive as a conclusion based on facts or premises that alone only imply. The inference is the conclusion.

ASSESS

Answers

1. The character is a man who lacks imagination. He understands facts, but not their implication. These traits prevent him from appreciating the gravity of his dilemma.
2. The author suggests that the severe cold is life-threatening.
3. The writer sees the larger implications—that freezing cold threatens life. Meanwhile, the character cannot project or contemplate consequences.

Go Online Vocabulary **For:** An Interactive Crossword Puzzle
Visit: PHSchool.com
Web Code: tk

SAT® PREP ACT

Vocabulary Workshop

High-Frequency Academic Words

High-frequency academic words are words that appear often in textbooks and on standardized tests. Though you may already know the meaning of many of these words, they usually have a more specific meaning when they are used in textbooks and on tests.

Know Your Terms: Demonstrating Understanding

Each of the words listed is a verb that tells you to use examples to show your understanding. The words indicate the kinds of details and information you should provide in your answer.

Terms to Learn

Apply Tell how you use information in a specific situation.

Sample test item: ***Apply*** the information in the chart to explain the change in population density.

Demonstrate Use examples to show that you understand how the information works in a specific situation.

Sample test item: In a paragraph, ***demonstrate*** how Martin Luther King, Jr., relied on Henry David Thoreau's theory of civil disobedience.

Illustrate Give examples that show what information means.

Sample test item: ***Illustrate*** Emily Dickinson's use of slant rhyme, using three examples.

Practice

Directions: *Read the passage from Ralph Waldo Emerson's essay "Self-Reliance." Then, answer questions 1–3.*

A foolish consistency is the hobgoblin of little minds, adored by little statesmen and philosophers and divines. With consistency a great soul has simply nothing to do. He may as well concern himself with his shadow on the wall. Speak what you think now in hard words and tomorrow speak what tomorrow thinks in hard words again, though it contradict everything you said today. "Ah, so you are sure to be misunderstood?"—is it so bad, then, to be misunderstood? Pythagoras was misunderstood, and Socrates, and Jesus, and Luther, and Copernicus, and Galileo, and Newton, and every pure and wise spirit that ever took flesh. To be great is to be misunderstood. . . .

1. Use details from the passage to *demonstrate* Emerson's view of consistency.
2. Emerson says, "To be great is to be misunderstood. . . ." Use a figure from American history to *illustrate* his point.
3. *Apply* Emerson's comments to a situation in current events.

Tips for Test Taking

- Remind students that when they are taking a test that asks them to analyze, differentiate, or infer, certain transitional and clarifying words will be associated with answers and will help them make their points more precisely, creating clearer and more effective essays.
- When the prompt is *analyze,* students should plan to use such cause-effect words as *because, reason, as a result, therefore, consequently,* and *since.* If they are asked to analyze a process, they should use words such as *before, after, first, next, last, when,* and *then.*
- When the prompt is *differentiate,* they should use such transitions as *different from* (never *different than*), *distinguish, contrast, rather than, on the one hand, on the other hand.*
- When the prompt is *infer,* appropriate transitions include *imply, inference, hint, suggest, deduce, conclude,* and so on.

Critical Reading:
Inferences and Generalizations

The reading sections of some tests often require you to read a passage of fiction and draw inferences and generalizations about the plot, setting, characters, and mood. Use the following strategies:

- As you read fiction, remember that to infer is to read between the lines, recognizing the implied message. Differentiate between what is stated and what is implied in a literary work.
- Look in the passage for clues about the characters, setting, plot, and mood. Apply these clues to draw inferences and make generalizations.
- Significant word choices, patterns of events, and other clues can help you understand the writer's implied message. When you make an inference, demonstrate its validity to yourself by examining the evidence that such clues provide.

Practice

Directions: *Read the passages, and then answer questions 1–3.*

Passage A. A weak rain drizzled outside the cabin, and Dan sat at the kitchen table, trying to gather courage. The idea of quitting his new job filled him with fear. He thought returning home to Oregon would help. But as the thunder boomed outside, he tried in vain to overcome his worries. He was simply too afraid of failure to quit—even if he disliked his new boss and felt indifferent toward his co-workers.

Passage B. Ellen's plan to garden on the dusty plot of Oklahoma clay didn't surprise anyone. When the rain rotted her tomato sprouts, she simply planted more. When the deer nibbled her corn, she built a strong fence around the garden bed. When the summer skies withheld rain, she lugged bucketfuls of water from a nearby spring. And when the town amateur gardening contest gave out blue ribbons, Ellen won them all.

1. In Passage A, Dan's main conflict is with

A the wilds of Oregon. **C** his new boss.
B himself. **D** his co-workers.

2. In Passage B, which of the following most accurately describes Ellen?

A talented **C** determined
B lucky **D** strong

3. Which of the following inferences does Passage B support?

A Ellen lives with a large family. **C** Oklahoma clay presents difficulties.
B Gardening is financially rewarding. **D** Tomatoes are easy to harvest.

Test-Taking Strategies

- Before answering questions, review the passage and highlight the main points.
- Look for descriptive details to help you make inferences about character, setting, plot, and mood.

Meeting Your Standards

Students will

1. **draw inferences from a reading passage to find the writer's implied message.**
2. **make generalizations from a reading passage to extend an idea beyond the text.**

Critical Reading

- Explain that when students are asked to make an inference, they should read the passage for hints and implications. They should pay particular attention to words and phrases that hint at positive or negative attitudes on the part of the writer.
- When students are asked to generalize, they should look for an idea that runs through the passage or for statements that have something in common.
- Have students read the Practice passages and answer the questions.
- Point out that in question 1, each possible answer refers in some way to one of the difficulties mentioned in the passage, but the only answer that can be applied to the entire passage is B, "himself."
- Point out that in question 2, all four qualities may describe Ellen accurately, but the main point of the passage is to show her determination. The correct answer, then, is C.
- Point out that in question 3, there is no mention of Ellen's family or financial reward, ruling out items *A* and *B,* while the passage's content actually contradicts *D.* The correct answer must, therefore, be *C.*

Tips for Test Taking

Very often, as in item 3 above, process of elimination will help students narrow down answers in a multiple-choice test. Explain to students that usually one answer among the choices is blatantly wrong. In the case of reading-comprehension questions, the blatantly wrong answer might directly contradict something in the passage and so should be ruled out immediately. In addition, if the question asks about the passage as a whole, answer options that refer to only a part of the passage, as in item 1, must likewise be wrong.

ASSESS

Answers

1. B
2. C
3. C

Meeting Your Standards

Students will:

1. analyze media.

Analyze Purpose

- Explain to students that the main purpose of all forms of media is to extend their audience. Makers of television shows want more people to watch; publishers of newspapers want more people to buy and read them; advertisers want to sell their products. All media are produced by companies whose main motivation is to stay in business and to make greater profits. Informing, entertaining, and persuading are secondary purposes.

Analyze Techniques

- Discuss the examples of techniques listed in the textbook. Have students give examples of effective uses of each technique.
- Have students discuss criteria that newscasters use when they choose someone to interview.
- Discuss what *format* means and how a format affects the message of a show.

Assess the Activity

To evaluate students' performance use the Analyzing Media Messages rubric, p. 84 in ***General Resourses.***

Analyzing Media

Every day, most of us are bombarded with media messages, from advertisements to radio talk shows to television news broadcasts. All of these different forms of media are created for specific purposes. The following strategies will help you to analyze the purposes and identify the techniques media makers use to advance their aims.

Analyze Purpose

Most forms of media seek to persuade, inform, or entertain. To identify media purposes, use the following guidelines:

- **Define media types.** Persuasive media seeks to convince you to think or act in a particular way. Informative media explains or describes a topic. Entertainment media creates enjoyment for the audience.
- **Identify uses of language.** Word choice can provide signals about the purpose of a media presentation. For example, persuasive media may contain evaluative terms, informative media may include technical language, and entertainment media may contain emotional language.
- **Consider strategies.** Look for the reasoning behind the media maker's choices. For example, even in news broadcasts, set design and lighting create a specific environment.

Analyze Techniques

As you observe media, evaluate the use of these techniques.

- **Interviews.** Real people help viewers identify with the message of a presentation. Informative media such as newscasts might use interviews with people who have played a role in the story and who can share their personal reactions.
- **Format.** Performers may choose media to heighten dramatic or comedic effect. For example, radio disc jockeys might focus on amusing word plays, while comedians in a theater might use sight gags.
- **Music and sound effects.** The music used in a presentation should help to reinforce the tone. For example, advertisements directed at children may use high-spirited music, while those conveying public safety messages might use somber music.

Evaluation Form for Media Analysi

Name of Media ________
Media Type and Purpose ________
Intended Audience ________

Signal Characteristics

Word/content choice ________
Tone ________

Reasoning:
Why do you think the media maker made specifi choices about structure, content, and style? ____

Techniques:

Interviews ________
Format ________
Music/sound effects ________

Were the techniques used in this presentatior effective? Did they advance the purpose you identified above?

Activity *View and Analyze* Watch television for a week as an active viewer. For each show you see, note the intended audience, the show's purpose, and the techniques used, and their intended effects. Use an evaluation form like the one shown to aid your analysis. Notice whether the verbal and nonverbal messages reinforce or contradict one another.

Differentiated Instruction Solutions for All Learners

Strategy for English Learners
Watching television is a good way to learn a new language. Most news shows include printed text of headlines and other messages. Students can use these printed titles and headlines to improve their vocabularies.

Suggestions for Further Reading

Featured Titles:

The Journals of Lewis and Clark
Edited by John Bakeless
Mentor, 1964

Nonfiction In 1803, Thomas Jefferson doubled the size of the United States by purchasing a tract of land west of the Mississippi River. Jefferson then sent Captains Meriwether Lewis and William Clark on an expedition to explore this vast, new territory. Readers will feel as if they are accompanying this historic expedition every step of the way as they read the journal entries of its two leaders. On this trek from the Missouri River to the Pacific coast, encounters with friendly and unfriendly Native Americans, awe-inspiring scenery, and grizzly bears are part of the daily routine.

The Scarlet Letter
Nathaniel Hawthorne *Pearson Prentice Hall, 2000*

Novel They were very few in number, but their courage, hard work, and intense perseverance enabled the Puritans who landed at Plymouth in 1620 to establish a colony. Though *The Scarlet Letter* was published in 1850, Nathaniel Hawthorne chose this setting—a world in which people lived simple lives and followed a strict moral code—for his masterpiece. The novel tells the story of Hester Prynne, who is branded as an outcast and struggles to create her own redemption.

Works Presented in Unit Three:

If sampling a portion of the following texts has built your interest, treat yourself to the full works.

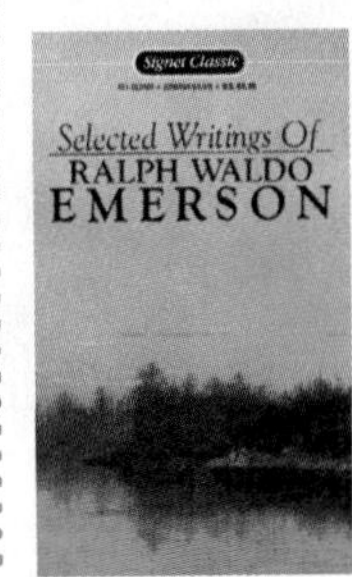

Selected Writings of Ralph Waldo Emerson
Edited by William H. Gilman
Signet Classic, 1965

Walden and Civil Disobedience
Henry David Thoreau *Signet Classic, 1999*

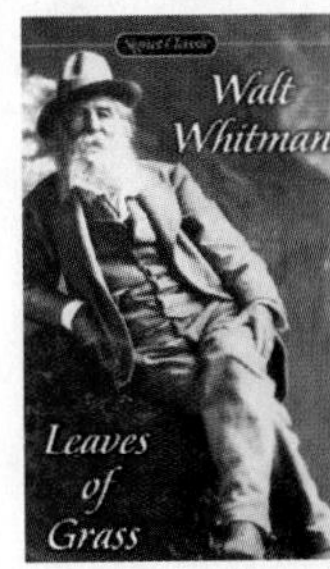

Leaves of Grass
Walt Whitman *Signet Classic, 2000*

***Many of these titles are available in the* Prentice Hall/Penguin Literature Library.**
Consult your teacher before choosing one.

Planning Students' Further Reading

Discussions of literature can raise sensitive and often controversial issues. Before you recommend further reading to your students, consider the values and sensitivities of your community as well as the age, ability, and sophistication of your students. It is also good policy to preview literature before you recommend it to students. The notes below offer some guidance on specific titles.

***The Journals of Lewis and Clark* Edited by John Bakeless**

The authors of the journals occasionally Express negative comments about the "savage" lifestyle and customs of the Native Americans. They also focus on fertility rites, eating habits, or other practices that other students may find objectionable. Make sure students understand that the journals were written at a time when most white people knew very little about Native Americans and were often fearful of them.

Lexile: 1000

***The Scarlet Letter* by Nathaniel Hawthorne**

Remind students that the scarlet letter A stands for adultery, or consensual sexual relations between a married person and someone other than his or her spouse. Some students may feel that Hester's punishment is too severe. Point out that adultery, prohibited by one of the Ten Commandments, was considered a capital crime by the Puritans of seventeenth–century Massachusetts. If students ask whether the term "Black Devil" was designed to mask racial prejudice On Hawthorne's part, assure them that this is not the case. Inform them that classical writers often used the expressions "black," "dark," and "darkness" to refer to evil and "white," "pure," and "purify" to refer to goodness or virtue. Adapted: Remind students that the scarlet letter A stands for adultery. Point out that adultery, prohibited by one of the Ten Commandments, was considered a capital crime by the Puritans of seventeenth–century Massachusetts. If students ask whether the term "Black Devil" was designed to mask racial prejudice On Hawthorne's part, assure them that this is not the case. Inform them that classical writers

continued

continued from right column

often used the expressions "black," "dark," and "darkness" to refer to evil and "white," "pure," and "purify" to refer to goodness or virtue.

Lexile: RL 3–8

***Selected Writings of Ralph Waldo Emerson* Edited by William H. Gilman**

Emerson espouses religious beliefs that are contrary to most mainstream religious doctrines. Some students may be sensitive to this.

Lexile: N/A

***Walden and Civil Disobedience* By Henry David Thoreau**

Lexile: 1420 and 1200

***Leaves of Grass* by Walt Whitman**

Whitman's poems contain details about human Sexuality, drinking, crime, slavery, the violence of war, suicide, prostitution, venereal disease, and various bodily functions. He occasionally uses dated ethnic, racial, and religious language and stereotypes that may be problematic.

Lexile: RL 9

Meeting Your Standards

Students will

1. read selections from American literature written during the period (1850–1914).
2. apply a variety of reading strategies, particularly interactive reading strategies, appropriate for reading these selections.
3. analyze literary elements.
4. use a variety of strategies to read unfamiliar words and to build vocabulary.
5. learn elements of grammar, usage, and style.
6. use recursive writing processes to write in a variety of forms.
7. develop listening and speaking skills.
8. express and support responses to various types of texts.
9. prepare, organize, and present literary interpretations.

Unit Instructional Resources

In *Unit 4 Resources,* you will find materials to support students in developing and mastering the unit skills and to help you assess their progress.

Vocabulary and Reading

- **Vocabulary Warm-up Word Lists A and B** identify selection words for students who read at one or two grades below level.
- **Vocabulary Warm-up Practice (A and B)** provides practice on the Word List words.
- **Reading Warm-ups A and B** provide reading passages containing the Word List words, along with questions and activities for students working at one or two grades below level.

Selection Support

- Reading Strategy
- Literary Analysis
- Vocabulary Builder
- Grammar and Style
- Support for Writing
- Support for Extend Your Learning
- Enrichment

PRENTICE HALL TeacherEXPRESS™ Plan · Teach · Assess You may also access these resources on TeacherExpress.

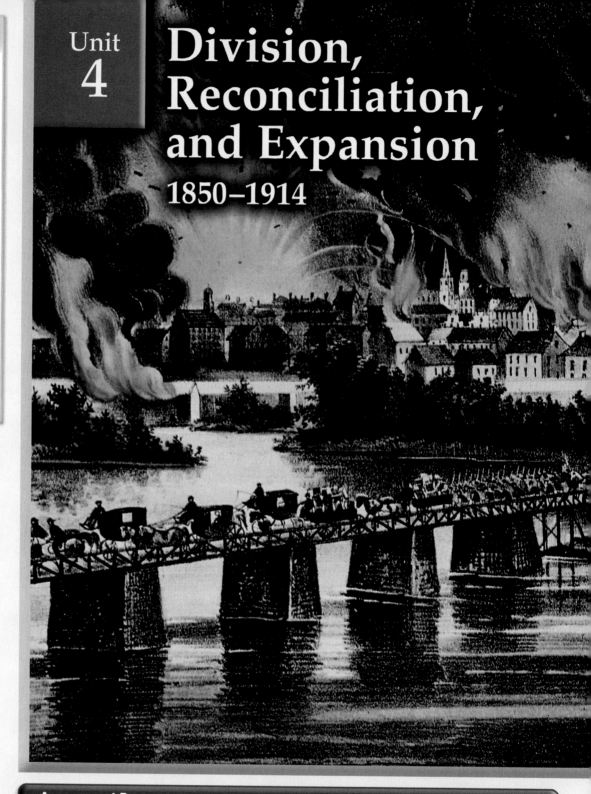

Unit 4 Division, Reconciliation, and Expansion 1850–1914

Assessment Resources

Listed below are the resources available to assess and measure students' progress in meeting the unit objectives and your state standards.

Skills Assessment

Unit 4 Resources
Selection Tests A and B

TeacherExpress™
ExamView® Test Bank Software

Adequate Yearly Progress Assessment

Unit 4 Resources
Diagnostic Tests
Benchmark Tests

Standardized Assessment

Standardized Test Preparation Workbook

The Age of Reason

"If we do not make common cause to save the good old ship of the Union on this voyage, nobody will have a chance to pilot her on another voyage."

—Abraham Lincoln, President of the United States of America. July 15, 1861

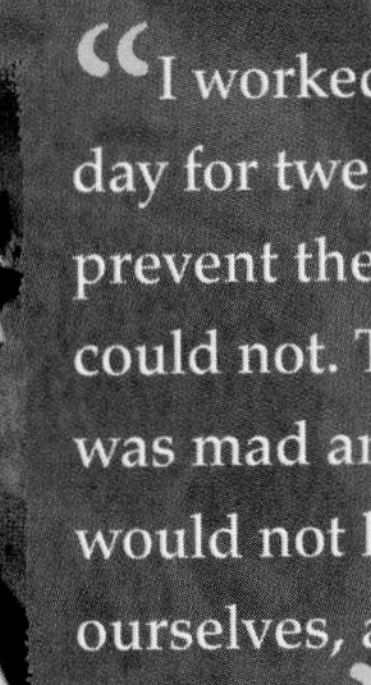

"I worked night and day for twelve years to prevent the war, but I could not. The North was mad and blind, would not let us govern ourselves, and so the war came."

—Jefferson Davis, President of the Confederate States of America, July 17, 1864

◀ This famous print, *The Fall of Richmond* by Nathaniel Currier and James Marritt Ives, depicts the Union army's capture of the Confederate capital, Richmond, Virginia, during the Civil War.

Introduce Unit 4

- Direct students' attention to the title and time period of this unit. Have a student read the quotations.
  Ask them: What do the quotations suggest about Americans at this point in their history?
  Possible response: The quotation suggests that Americans are on the verge of war.
- Have students look at the art. Read the Humanities note to them, and **ask** the discussion question.
- Then **ask:** What kinds of literature or themes in literature do you think might come out of this period in American history?
  Possible response: Students probably will suggest themes concerning war and the division between the North and the South.

Humanities

The Fall of Richmond, by Nathaniel Currier and James Merritt Ives

Nathaniel Currier (1813–188) and James Merritt Ives (1824–1895) were nineteenth-century lithographers who created many popular prints. Currier hired Ives as a bookkeeper for his print publishing company in New York City. Five years later, Ives was made a partner. Together they printed depictions of recent events, political satires, and scenes such as sleigh rides and boxing matches. Their prints became valuable historical records of America.

- Based on what you see in the painting, speculate about the impression of war this painter intended to create.
  Possible response: The painter focuses on the confusion, panic, and destruction of war rather than on the heroism or fighting.

Unit Features

Nell Irvin Painter
Each unit features commentary by a contemporary writer or scholar under the heading "From the Author's Desk." Author Nell Irvin Painter introduces Unit 4 in Setting the Scene, in which she discusses how and why historians divide history into periods. Later in the unit she introduces Sojourner Truth's *Account of an Experience with Discrimination.* She also contributes her insights on p. 685 in the Writing Workshop.

Connections
Every unit contains a feature that connects the American literature of the period to World Literature. In this unit, students will connect twentieth-century Italian writer Luigi Pirandello's "War" with thoughts of Civil War era American writers.

Use the information and questions on the Connections pages to help students enrich their understanding of the selections presented within the unit.

Reading Informational Materials
These selections will help students learn to analyze and evaluate informational texts, such as workplace documents, technical directions, and consumer materials. They will expose students to the organization and features unique to nonnarrative texts.

In this unit, the focus is on public documents.

Introduce Nell Irvin Painter

- Nell Irvin Painter, a well-known historian, introduces the unit by providing insight into historians' thought processes when they organize history into periods. Later in this unit, on pages 546–547, Painter introduces Sojourner Truth's "Account of an Experience with Discrimination." She also comments on using research to achieve a specific purpose in the Writing Workshop.
- Have students read the introductory paragraph about Nell Irvin Painter. Tell students that Painter is a noted historian with wide-ranging interests that include late nineteenth-century American social patterns, ideas of race and ethnicity, and the life and times of Sojourner Truth.
- Use the ***From the Author's Desk DVD*** to introduce Nell Irvin Painter. Show Segment 1 to provide insight into her career as a historian and teacher. After the students have watched the segment, **ask:** What events and circumstances in Nell Irvin Painter's youth might have contributed to her scholarly interests as an adult?
  Possible responses: Her family had a history of scholarship; her grandfather had been a professor. She grew up in an environment that fostered learning: the neighborhood around The University of California at Berkeley.

Timing Is Everything

- Have students read Painter's comments about how historians structure the study of the past, in which she explains how she came up with the time span of 1877 to 1919 for her book *Standing at Armageddon.* This period signaled the shift when the focus of politics shifted from land to labor.
- **Ask:** What are the benefits of organizing the past into "meaningful" units?
  Answer: Organizing the past into meaningful units allows historians to define and highlight trends or patterns in human development.

Setting the Scene

Unit 4 features writing from one of the most dramatic periods in American history. The following essay by historian Nell Irvin Painter discusses major trends that help define this era. As you read her essay, the unit introduction that follows, and the literature in Unit 4, think about how this period witnessed both the division of America and its dramatic growth.

From the Scholar's Desk
Nell Irvin Painter Talks About the Time Period

Nell Irvin Painter

Introducing Nell Irvin Painter (b. 1942) Nell Irvin Painter served as the director of Princeton University's Program in African American Studies from 1997 to 2000. She is the author of *Southern History Across the Color Line* and *Sojourner Truth: A Life, A Symbol.*

Timing Is Everything

One of my most-read books, *Standing at Armageddon: The United States, 1877–1919,* showed me how politics changes as the times change. (The word *Armageddon* in the title refers to the end of the world, and the phrase *Standing at Armageddon* comes from a statement Theodore Roosevelt made in 1912.)

Historians, of course, know that timing is everything. We call one of our specialties "periodization," meaning the breaking up of the past into meaningful chunks of time. Historians decided that certain dates—in this textbook, for example, 1750, 1800, 1850, 1870, 1914, and 1946—carried special meaning, that what came before was different from what came afterward. The periodization in this unit (1850–1914) generally corresponds to the periodization of my book (1877–1919), although this unit includes the Civil War and Reconstruction and my book does not.

I made my own discoveries as I was just starting to work on *Standing at Armageddon.* I had to decide where to start and end a book on the period that covered roughly 1885 to 1915. The years 1885 and 1915 had no particular resonance: Nothing earthshaking occurred in either of those years to change the course of United States history. So I set about finding meaningful years by reading newspapers and news magazines, where I could follow the news of the day as it unfolded, day by day and week by week.

A Shift from Land to Labor Issues At the beginning of the 1870s, the news still bristled with violence related to the politics of the Civil War, as Democrats attacked Republicans and killed off the people associated with Reconstruction. Reconstruction—the reorganization of Southern states from 1867 to 1877—was dying a bloody death in the South, as Democrats

Teaching Resources

The following resources can be used to enrich or extend the instruction for the Unit 4 introduction.

From the Author's Desk DVD
- **Nell Irvin Painter,** Segment 1

Unit 4 Resources
- **Unit Introduction: Names and Terms to Know,** p. 5
- **Unit Introduction: Focus Questions,** p. 6
- **Listening and Viewing,** p. 93

took back by force the power they had held before the war. In 1877, however, new conflicts eclipsed the focus on Southern political terrorism. The news also revealed a great deal of labor conflict outside the South. A nationwide strike of railroad workers occurred in 1877 that began a whole new era in which politics revolved around working people and strikes. Before the Civil War, politics had been about land and access to land. After Reconstruction, postwar politics focused on industries and workers; 1877—the year national attention shifted from land to labor—became the starting point for *Standing at Armageddon.*

▶ **Critical Viewing** Explain how this photograph of a railroad strike reflects Painter's discussion of American workers. **[Connect]**

What about the end? Where should my period and my book end? Still reading the newspapers and news magazines, I found an echo of 1877's strikes and riots in 1919, the year contemporaries called the "Great Upheaval." There was the end of my period, a time in which working people and their issues once again dominated American politics.

Go Online
Author Link

For: An online video
Visit: www.PHSchool.com
Web Code: ere-8101

For: More about Nell Irvin Painter
Visit: www.PHSchool.com
Web Code: ete-9424

Organized Labor Becomes a Force Before 1877, American politics revolved around questions of land. But after 1877, politics revolved around industry and the people who worked in it. Organized labor became a force in U. S. politics between 1877 and 1919 and, building on this foundation, labor unions would surge to the fore in the 1930s. My periodization of 1877–1919 reflects my belief that working people and their concerns lie at the heart of the politics of the era. I begin and end *Standing at Armageddon* at moments in which workers attract the attention of Americans as a whole.

Reading the Unit Introduction

Reading for Information and Insight Use the following terms and questions to guide your reading of the unit introduction on pages 474–481.

Names and Terms to Know
Fugitive Slave Act (1850)
Civil War
Abraham Lincoln
Transcontinental Railroad
Second Industrial Revolution
Frederick Douglass
Gettysburg Address
Mark Twain
Realism
Naturalism

Focus Questions As you read this introduction, use what you learn to answer these questions:

- What differences between the North and the South led to the Civil War?
- In the fifty years after the Civil War, what factors caused the most dramatic changes in American life?
- How did the Civil War, westward expansion, and the Second Industrial Revolution help shape the literary movements known as Realism and Naturalism?

Reading the Unit Introduction

Tell students that the terms and questions listed here are the key points in this introductory materials. This information provides a context for the selections in the unit. Students should use the terms and questions as a guide to focus their reading of the unit introduction. When students have completed the unit introduction, they should be able to identify or explain each of these terms and answer or discuss the Focus Questions.

Concept Connector

After students have read the unit introduction, return to the Focus Questions to review the main points. For key points, see p. 481.

Go Online **Author Link** Typing in the Web Code when prompted will bring students to a video clip of Nell Irvin Painter.

Getting an Overview

Use the Timeline to help students get a quick overview of themes and events of the period. This approach will benefit all students but may be especially helpful for Visual/Spatial Learners, English Learners, and Less Proficient Readers. (For strategies in using the Timeline as an overview, see the bottom of this page.)

Thinking Critically

Questions are provided on the facing page. Use these questions to have students review the events, discuss their significance, and examine the *so what* behind the *what happened*.

Connecting to Selections

Have students refer back to the Timeline when they begin to read individual selections. By consulting the Timeline regularly, they will gain a better sense of the period's chronology. In addition, they will appreciate what was occurring in the world that gave rise to these works of literature.

Projects

Students can use the Timeline as a launching pad for projects like these:

- **Cause-and-Effect Connections** Have students scan the Timeline and speculate about cause-and-effect connections among events. They may want to diagram these links using the Cause-and-Effect Flowchart, p. 305 in **Graphic Organizer Transparencies**.
- **Additional Illustrations** Have students search for additional illustrations for items in the Timeline. They can find such illustrations in biographies of the figures mentioned in the Timeline, encyclopedias, books on American history, and books on the history of technology. Students should be prepared to justify each new illustration they suggest.

1850 1860 1870

AMERICAN EVENTS

- 1855 Walt Whitman publishes first edition of *Leaves of Grass.*
- 1855 *My Bondage and My Freedom*, Frederick Douglass's second autobiography, makes its appearance. ▼

- 1858 Lincoln-Douglas debates help make Abraham Lincoln a national figure.
- 1859 John Brown, an abolitionist, leads a raid on federal arsenal at Harpers Ferry, Virginia; he is hanged for treason.
- 1860 Republican Abraham Lincoln is elected United States president.
- 1860 South Carolina secedes from the Union.
- 1861 Civil War begins in April with firing on Fort Sumter.
- 1863 Lincoln issues the Emancipation Proclamation.
- 1865 General Robert E. Lee surrenders to General Ulysses S. Grant at Appomattox. ▼

MARK TWAIN
KNOWN TO EVERYONE–LIKED BY ALL

- 1876 Mark Twain publishes *The Adventures of Tom Sawyer.* ▲
- 1876 Baseball's National League founded.
- 1877 The Compromise of 1877 ends military occupation of the South.
- 1877 Thomas Edison patents the phonograph.

WORLD EVENTS

- 1857 France: Gustave Flaubert completes *Madame Bovary*, a classic novel of realism.
- 1859 England: Charles Dickens adds to his fame with *A Tale of Two Cities.*
- 1859 England: Charles Darwin introduces theory of evolution in *The Origin of Species.*
- 1862 France: Louis Pasteur proposes modern germ theory of disease.
- 1865 England: Lewis Carroll completes *Alice's Adventures in Wonderland.*
- 1865 Germany: Karl Benz builds first automobile powered by the internal-combustion engine.
- 1869 Russia: Leo Tolstoy publishes *War and Peace.*
- 1874 France: Claude Monet gathers Impressionist painters for first exhibition.
- 1877 England: First tennis championship held at Wimbledon.

Getting an Overview of the Period

Introduction To give students an overview of the period, indicate the span of dates in the title of the Timeline. Next, point out that the Timeline is divided into American Events (on top) and World Events (on bottom). Have students scan the Timeline, looking both at the American Events and the World Events. Finally, point out that the events in the Timeline often represent beginnings, turning points, and endings.

Key Events Have students identify key events related to division, reconciliation, and expansion.

Possible responses: division—South Carolina secedes from the Union (1860), Civil War begins (1861); reconciliation—Compromise of 1877 ends military occupation of the South (1877); expansion—last major battle between U.S. troops and Native Americans (1890), Henry Ford build his first Model T (1908).

1880 1890 1900

- 1883 Railroads adopt standard time zones.
- 1883 The Brooklyn Bridge is opened.
- 1884 Mark Twain publishes *The Adventures of Huckleberry Finn*.

- 1886 Statue of Liberty dedicated in New York Harbor. ▲
- 1888 Great mid-March blizzard in eastern United States piles 30-foot drifts in New York's Herald Square.

- 1890 Last major battle between U.S. troops and Native Americans fought at Wounded Knee, South Dakota.
- 1895 Stephen Crane publishes *The Red Badge of Courage*.
- 1895 First professional football game played in Latrobe, Pennsylvania.
- 1896 *The Country of the Pointed Firs*, Sarah Orne Jewett's masterpiece, appears.

- 1903 Jack London publishes *The Call of the Wild*.

- 1903 Wright Brothers stay aloft for 852 feet in their airplane at Kitty Hawk, North Carolina. ▲
- 1908 Henry Ford builds his first Model T. ▼

- 1885 French scientist Louis Pasteur administers the first successful rabies vaccination. ▶
- 1886 Russia: Leo Tolstoy completes *The Death of Ivan Ilyich*.

- 1891 England: Thomas Hardy publishes *Tess of the D'Urbervilles*.
- 1894 Sino-Japanese War breaks out; Japanese army easily defeats Chinese.
- 1895 Germany: Wilhelm Roentgen discovers X-rays.
- 1898 France: Pierre and Marie Curie discover radium and polonium.

- 1901 Italy: First transatlantic radio telegraphic message is achieved by Marconi.
- 1903 Spain: Pablo Picasso paints *The Old Guitarist*.
- 1904 Russo-Japanese War begins.
- 1905 Germany: Albert Einstein proposes his relativity theory.

Critical Viewing

1. What does the portrait of Frederick Douglass suggest about the writer's character? Explain. **[Analyze]**
Possible response: Douglass appears confident and proud in the portrait.
2. What details in the picture of the Statue of Liberty (1886) suggest that its dedication was a festive occasion? **[Analyze]**
Answer: The sky seems to be filled with fireworks in honor of the occasion, and there are many ships in the harbor.
3. Which has more in common with its modern replacement, the first plane (1903) or the first mass-produced car (1908)? **[Compare and Contrast]**
Possible response: The car, which has many recognizable features.

during the decade 1850–1860 that relate to the conflict over slavery. (b) Explain how these events might have set the stage for the Civil War. **[Speculate]**
Answer: (a) In 1855, Frederick Douglass's second autobiography appears; in 1859, John Brown led his raid on Harper's Ferry.
(b) **Possible response:** Douglass's revelations about slavery may have encouraged abolitionists. John Brown's raid may have strengthened the resolve of the South to defend slavery.

2. (a) What key Civil War event occurred in 1863? (b) What does this event suggest about the course of the war? **[Infer]**
Answer: (a) Lincoln issued the Emancipation Proclamation.
(b) **Possible response:** It suggests that freeing the slaves had become a priority for the Union.
3. (a) Looking at both American and World Events, name two key sporting events that occurred during the decade 1870–1880.
(b) What is the importance of these events for us today? **[Relate]**
Answer: (a) In 1876, baseball's National League was founded, and in 1877, the first tennis championship was held at Wimbledon. (b) Baseball and the National League are still going strong, and tennis championships are still held at Wimbledon.
4. (a) What important battle was fought by in America in 1890? (b) In what way did this battle indicate that the frontier period was ending? **[Interpret]**
Answer: (a) The last major battle between U.S. troops and Native Americans. (b) Native Americans were no longer in a position to oppose settlers, as they had during the period of the expanding frontier.
5. (a) Name two developments in transportation that occurred during the early 1900s. (b) What impact did these developments have? **[Connect]**
Answer: (a) In 1903, first flight, brothers', and in 1908, first Model T. (b) **Possible response:** Because of these developments, America is a land of people on the move.

realistic view of the Civil War.

- The spirituals "Swing Low, Sweet Chariot," and "Go Down, Moses," will help students better understand the situation and aspirations of enslaved African Americans.
- In the excerpt from *My Bondage and My Freedom,* students will learn about slavery from the first-person account of Frederick Douglass.

Critical Viewing

Possible response: A sixteen-year-old might become very homesick and might be shocked by the realities of wartime life.

The years between 1850 and 1914 witnessed a transformation of the United States. During those years, America changed from a decentralized, mostly agricultural nation to the modern industrial nation that we know today. This transformation began in the period leading up to the Civil War. In that war, Americans took up arms against one another to determine which should prevail: North or South? the federal Union or states' rights? freedom or slavery? The North won, the Union held, and slavery was abolished, but at a devastating cost to the nation.

Historical Background

Prelude to War By the mid-nineteenth century, it was evident that the North and the South had developed along very different lines. In the North, commerce, was king; in the South, cotton ruled. The Industrial Revolution and cheap transportation had helped turn northern towns and cities into centers of bustling activity. Education, banking, science, and reform movements—all were topics of interest and concern. Immigration, too, was changing the face of the North. A rising tide of Irish and German immigrants, among others, came seeking new lives in the United States. Most of these newcomers landed at seaports between Boston and Baltimore and settled in the northern states.

The South, in contrast, was a slower-paced region of plantations and small farms. There were cities, to be sure, but the area was defined by its cotton plantations, large and small. Sugar, rice, and tobacco were also important crops. The march of technological progress, with its hotly debated social issues and problems, had little impact on the prewar South. One issue, however, made an indelible impression: slavery. The South believed its lifeblood depended on the institution of slavery.

Disagreements between North and South over slavery were nothing new, but the controversy was rekindled in 1850 by the passage of the Fugitive Slave Act. It required all citizens—of free states as well as slave states—to help catch runaway slaves. Southerners saw the law as just; Northerners considered it an outrage.

The expansion of slavery into the West was hotly contested. In 1854, when the Kansas-Nebraska Act opened up a vast area of previously free western land to slavery, the argument became a fight. "We will engage in competition for the virgin soil of Kansas," a senator from New York insisted. The "competition" turned Kansas into a bloody battleground.

Just as it dominated politics and preoccupied the nation, the controversy over slavery influenced the literature of the day, and in one classic case, literature fueled the controversy. Harriet Beecher Stowe's novel *Uncle Tom's Cabin,* published in 1852, vividly depicted

▼ Critical Viewing This picture shows a young Confederate soldier. Most of the soldiers in both armies were between the ages of 18 and 21. Some were even younger. What problems do you think a 16-year-old Union or Confederate soldier might have faced? **[Relate]**

Enrichment

The North and the South

The northern and southern United States had developed along different economic lines. In the North, commerce was king. The Industrial Revolution and cheap transportation had caused explosive urban growth. Immigration, too, was changing the face of the North. A rising tide of Irish and German immigrants, among others, were seeking new lives in northern cities.

The South was a slower-paced region of plantations and small farms. There were cities, but the area was most truly defined by its cotton plantations. Sugar, rice, and tobacco were also important crops. Technological progress, with its social issues and problems, had little impact on the prewar South.

Have students consider what these differences suggest about the outcome of a war between these regions. Guide students to recognize that the North, with its greater population and more developed industry, would have an advantage in a war.

the cruelty of slavery. The book became a powerful antislavery weapon, selling more than 300,000 copies within a year. Its impact was such that, within three years, no fewer than thirty southern novels came out attempting to counter its influence.

The deep national division intensified in 1859 when a group of antislavery extremists raided a federal arsenal at Harpers Ferry, West Virginia. Led by John Brown, the group had intended to provoke an armed slave revolt. The attempt failed and Brown was executed for treason, but his death only fed the controversy, which now threatened to escalate out of control.

The Union Is Dissolved The conflict between North and South came to a head when Abraham Lincoln was elected in 1860. Lincoln represented the newly formed Republican party, which had dedicated itself to halting the spread of slavery. South Carolina had threatened to secede if Lincoln was elected, and in December it did so. Five states followed South Carolina out of the Union. In February 1861, the secessionist states established the Confederate States of America.

Fighting began on April 12, 1861, when Confederate artillery fired on Union troops holding Fort Sumter, in Charleston Harbor. Many on both sides anticipated a short war ending in victory. No one could know what lay ahead: the carnage of Antietam, where more than 26,000 men fell in a single day; the deprivation of the siege of Vicksburg, where people survived by eating dogs and rats; the wholesale destruction of Georgia, when Union general William T. Sherman's troops marched to the sea. In fact, the devastating war would last four long years.

By the time Confederate general Robert E. Lee surrendered to Union general Ulysses S. Grant in the spring of 1865, nearly 620,000 soldiers on both sides had lost their lives. About 500,000 had been wounded. The South lay in ruins, its cities razed, its farms and plantations destroyed.

Lincoln guided the nation through the worst crisis in its history. He did not, however, have the chance to reconstruct the Union. Just days after Lee's surrender, Lincoln was assassinated. He died on April 15, 1865. The nation, war-torn and weary, would have to face the daunting tasks of reconciliation and reconstruction without him.

An Expanding America If conflict characterized the Civil War years, change—on an astonishing scale—characterized the period that followed. During the fifty-year period following the war, physical expansion and industrialization transformed the American landscape, economy, society, and identity.

The Homestead Act of 1862 promised 160 acres to anyone who would live on the land for a certain period and make minimal improvements to it.

▲ Critical Viewing
Robert E. Lee (left) and Ulysses S. Grant (right) were the leaders of the Confederate and Union armies, respectively. What can you infer about their different personalities and backgrounds by comparing and contrasting these photographs? Explain. **[Compare and Contrast]**

war in which black troops fought in large numbers. By the end of the war, there were some 180,000 black soldiers in more than a hundred Union regiments. On the Confederate side, both slaves and free blacks accompanied the army as cooks, teamsters, and laborers.

Background
Science

The South desperately needed a way to break the Union blockade of its ports. One method it tried was the ironclad ship. Confederates covered the *Merrimack,* an abandoned Union ship, with iron plates 4 inches thick and sent it into battle. On March 8, 1862, the *Merrimack* sank one Union ship, drove another aground, and forced a third to surrender. Cannonballs bounced harmlessly off the *Merrimack's* metal skin.

The Union countered with its own ironclads. One of these, the *Monitor,* struck back at the *Merrimack* in the waters off Hampton Roads, Virginia. In the end, neither ship seriously damaged the other, and both withdrew. Yet ironclad ships had changed naval warfare forever. Both sides rushed to build more of them. The South, however, never mounted a serious attack against the Union navy, and the Union blockade held.

Critical Viewing

Possible response: Lee's upright posture suggests that he is more formal than Grant, who leans informally against a tree. Also, Lee looks more aristocratic than Grant.

Differentiated Instruction
Solutions for All Learners

Strategy for Less Proficient Readers
Have students preview the heads and subheads on pp. 474–481. Then, have them make connections between the "Historical Background" subheads and those under "Literature of the Period." For example, "The Union Is Dissolved" (p. 475) suggests the war that gave rise to "Wartime Voices" (p. 478).

Strategy for English Learners
Have students study the illustrations on pp. 474–481 to gain a better understanding of the themes of this period. Then, have them read the subheads under "Literature of the Period." Encourage them to draw connections between the illustrations and the literary themes.

Strategy for Advanced Readers
Instruct these students to read pp. 474–481 independently, noting key ways in which national identity changed during those years. Then, have students discuss ways they might expect to find those changes expressed in the literature of the period.

difficult periods of American history, and is widely regarded as one of the United States' greatest presidents. Then, **ask** the following questions.

1. In what way are these two view points different?
   Answer: Sandburg seems more enthusiastic about the genius and skill of Lincoln, while Oates seems more focused on Lincoln's problems.
2. In what way are these views similar?
   Answer: Both historians agree that Lincoln was a great and heroic man.
3. Can you imagine scholars having this argument about the legacy of a contemporary leader? Explain.
   Possible response: Most students will find it difficult to imagine any scholar arguing that a contemporary leader is as flawless and towering a figure as Sandburg's Lincoln. We know too much about the personal lives of our leaders today to see them in those terms.

Background
History

People had to be strong to survive the hardships of life on the Great Plains. With few stores, women had to make clothing, quilts, soap, candles, and other goods by hand. They also had to cook and preserve all the food needed through the long winter.

Women had many other duties. They educated the children. With no doctors nearby, they treated the sick and injured. Women also helped with the planting and harvesting. When needed, they helped build sod houses.

Critical Viewing

Possible response: As the picture suggests, the West offered African Americans the hope of owning their own house and land.

Point/Counterpoint

Abraham Lincoln—Legendary Hero or "Flawed and Complex Man"

Was Abraham Lincoln a legendary hero, someone to be compared with such historic figures as Lao-tse or Caesar, or was he a flawed human being? Two biographers disagree on the answer to this question.

Legendary Hero

"Perhaps no human clay pot has held more laughter and tears.

"The facts and myths of his life are to be an American possession, shared widely over the world, for thousands of years, as the tradition of Knute or Alfred, Lao-tse or Diogenes, Pericles or Caesar, are kept. This because he was not only a genius in the science of neighborly human relationships and an artist in the personal handling of life from day to day, but a strange friend and a friendly stranger to all forms of life that he met."

—Carl Sandburg, *A Lincoln Preface*

Flawed and Complex Man

"The historical Lincoln, as I have tried to approximate him, was a flawed and complex man who had the gift of vision that let him see things few others ever see. When I say that he was flawed, I am not profaning his memory, as many of my correspondents have accused me of doing. On the contrary, the historical Lincoln comes out more heroic than the immortal Man of the People, because we see him overcoming his deficiencies and self-doubts, often against tremendous odds."

—Stephen B. Oates, *Abraham Lincoln: The Man Behind the Myths*

This shifted the westward movement into high gear. Half a million farmers, including tens of thousands of emancipated African Americans, staked claims on the Great Plains. Miners went west by the thousands, lured by the prospect of striking it rich in gold. Still others moved west to become cattle ranchers. Westward expansion was boosted by completion of the first transcontinental railroad in 1869. As the national railroad system grew, the covered wagon—symbol of the American pioneer—was replaced by the train as the principal means of transportation.

The Disappearing Frontier By 1890, the frontier as Americans had known it for centuries had ceased to exist. The steady influx of settlers, the burgeoning railroads, the growth of mining and cattle ranching—all had combined to transform the West. Gone were the great herds of buffalo. Gone was the expanse of open range. In its place was an enormous patchwork of plowed fields and grazing lands, separated by miles of barbed wire fencing.

Gone, too, were the Indian nations, many of which had depended on the buffalo for survival. By 1890, virtually all the Native Americans in the

Enrichment

Songs of the Civil War

Play for students renditions of the spirituals "Swing Low, Sweet Chariot" and "Go Down, Moses," from the **Listening to Literature CD.**

Explain to students that spirituals were created among groups of enslaved African Americans, and that singers customarily embellish on the word and melody of spirituals. Consequently, each rendition of "Swing Low, Sweet Chariot" and "Go Down, Moses" is unique.

Ask students how all three songs throw new light on the Civil War.
Possible response: Students may respond that the spirituals reveal the deep feeling with which African Americans yearned for freedom, and that Foster's song discloses the personal sadness caused by wartime separations.

West had been forced from their land. Decades of fierce and bloody resistance had ultimately proved futile. "I am tired of fighting," Chief Joseph of the Nez Percé reportedly said after being hunted down by the United States Army in 1877. Like others before them, Chief Joseph and his people were sent to live in Indian Territory, in what is now Oklahoma. However, even Indian Territory, which Congress had set aside in 1834, was not safe from white encroachment. In 1889, unassigned land in Indian Territory was opened up to settlers.

The frontier may have disappeared, but its legacy lived on in a rich western folk tradition. Larger-than-life folk heros like Pecos Bill were celebrated in tall tales and legends. The frontier survived, too, in the songs of sod busters, railroad workers, cowpokes, and miners.

▲ Critical Viewing
Some African Americans traveled to the West. In this picture, the Shores family poses in front of their Nebraska sod house. What opportunities might the West have offered African Americans that the East did not? **[Analyze a Situation]**

A Changing American Society With the introduction of electricity in the 1880s, the second Industrial Revolution began in earnest. Electricity replaced steam power in many manufacturing industries. The now-familiar trappings of modern life began to make their appearance: electric lights, telephones, automobiles, motion pictures, and phonographs. The mass production of consumer goods sparked the rise of an important new medium: advertising. Skyscrapers, department stores, and mass transportation became part of city life—as did noise, traffic jams, air pollution, crime, and slums.

The country's industrial and urban growth was also fueled by immigration. In 1880, the population of the United States was just over 50 million. By the turn of the century, it was just under 76 million. A significant portion of this increase was due to the more than 9 million immigrants who came to the country during this twenty-year period. Most of the newcomers settled in cities. In the same period, millions of Americans left farms and small towns and moved to the cities to seek work. This influx swelled urban populations and provided an inexhaustible supply of cheap labor for industry.

The industrial boom of the late nineteenth century created new extremes of wealth and poverty. The wages of industrial workers were so low that a single worker, or even two, often could not support a family. Child labor became the norm among the poor working class. Immigrant families often lived in small, dark, unventilated apartments with no toilets. In these conditions, disease was rampant.

Meanwhile, a relative handful of men—the owners of big industrial corporations—made fortunes and lived like royalty. Their ostentatious displays of wealth led Mark Twain to dub this period "The Gilded Age," implying a thin veneer of glitter over something of poor quality.

Critical Thinking

1. Why was literature such an important part of the conflict? **[Support]**
   Possible response: Books such as Douglass's autobiography and Stowe's *Uncle Tom's Cabin* fueled antislavery sentiment and widened national division.
2. If America had been a smaller country, without a frontier, how might its history have been different? **[Speculate]**
   Possible response: It might have been urbanized more quickly, but it might not have attracted as many immigrants.
3. What were drawbacks to America's industrialization and expansion? **[Analyze]**
   Possible response: Drawbacks included mistreatment of Native Americans and poverty among African Americans and immigrants.

Background
History

As farmers spread across the Plains, fewer areas remained to be settled. The last major land rush took place in 1889, in Oklahoma. Late in April, as many as 100,000 land seekers waited at the Oklahoma border. The government had announced that farmers could claim free homesteads in Oklahoma starting at noon on April 22. As the "boomers" charged in, they found to their surprise that others were already there. "Sooners" had sneaked in and staked out much of the best land.

The 1890 census reported that the United States no longer had a frontier. For 100 years, the frontier had absorbed immigrants, adventurers, and city folks. Now the frontier was closed.

Literature of the Period

- Students will find alternative views of the expansion of the United States and the closing of the frontier in Miriam Davis Colt's "Heading West," and Chief Joseph's "I Will Fight No More Forever."
- Both "The Story of an Hour," by Kate Chopin, and "A Wagner Matinée," by Willa Cather, have themes related to the changes sweeping American society in this period.

Historical Background
Comprehension Check

1. What major transformation did America undergo in the years between 1850 and 1914?
   Answer: It changed from a mostly agricultural nation to the urban, industrial nation that we know.
2. In what way did the Civil War surprise both sides?
   Answer: It was longer and more costly than either side anticipated.
3. What three factors combined to transform the West in the years after the Civil War?
   Answer: The influx of settlers, the burgeoning railroads, and the growth of mining and cattle ranching transformed the West.
4. Why did Mark Twain call the late 1800s "The Gilded Age"?
   Answer: A few powerful men displayed their wealth, but underneath this veneer, people were in need.

Answer: (a) Among the most prosperous years were 1872, 1881, 1886, 1890, 1891, and 1900. (b) Severe depression struck in 1865, 1876–1878, 1884, 1893, and 1896.

Background
History

Perhaps surprisingly, Lincoln's two most able commanders—Ulysses S. Grant and William T. Sherman—produced memoirs that are still regarded as models of their kind. In fact, the quality of the writing done by high-ranking officers on both sides is remarkable.

A great many patriotic songs were written and sung during the war. Among the most popular ones in the North were "The Battle Cry of Freedom" and "Tenting Tonight on the Old Campground." The most famous Union song of all is probably Julia Ward Howe's stirring "The Battle Hymn of the Republic." Among southerners, "The Bonnie Blue Flag" and "The Yellow Rose of Texas" were favorites, as was the well-known "Dixie."

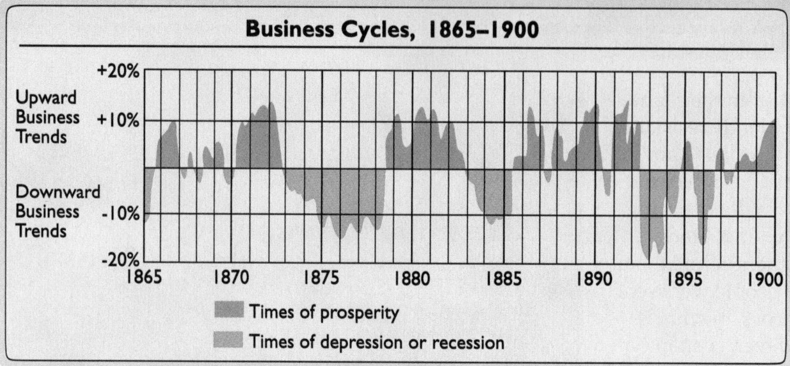

▲ Critical Viewing The ups and downs of the economy, known as business cycles, were felt more sharply as the nation industrialized and more people worked for wages. (a) Which years were the most prosperous? (b) In which years did severe depression strike? **[Read a Graph]**

Indeed, just below the surface of the nation's prosperity, discontentment grew. Women, African Americans, and workers agitated for changes in their social, economic, and political status: Women still did not have the vote; most African Americans, despite emancipation, were hardly better off in 1914 than they had been in 1850; labor reform was desperately needed. Bitter struggles erupted between emerging workers' unions and management.

Literature of the Period

Oh, Freedom! Of the blacks who lived in slavery in the 1850s, a significant number worked on cotton plantations. On these plantations and elsewhere, the slaves developed a unique style of music, the black spiritual. Spirituals fused traditional African music with such sources as the Bible, Protestant hymns, and popular music of the day. To enslaved African Americans, spirituals were—in addition to moving expressions of faith—work songs, war songs, laments, lullabies, and funeral dirges.

Not all of the black voices of the period surfaced in spirituals. One of the great black abolitionist leaders was Frederick Douglass. Born into slavery in Maryland, Douglass escaped as a young man and settled in the North, where he became a persuasive orator against slavery. In 1845, he published the first version of *Narrative of the Life of Frederick Douglass,* his eloquent autobiography that was also an indictment of slavery.

Wartime Voices Thousands of diaries, letters, journals, and speeches were produced during the war, providing a richly detailed and moving record of what Americans—from the lowliest private to General Lee himself—experienced. The lengthy diary of Mary Chesnut, the wife of a high-ranking Confederate officer, is a notable example of the extraordinary literary output of the Civil War years.

One of the greatest masters of the language at mid-century was President Lincoln. His speeches and letters are models of clarity and eloquence. His Gettysburg Address, a mere ten sentences in length, has become a classic expression of the meaning of American democracy.

Enrichment

Whitman in the Civil War

Walt Whitman was a northern poet who wrote movingly about the war. Whitman's younger brother George had enlisted in the Union army. When George was wounded at the Battle of Fredericksburg, Whitman went to Virginia to care for him. He remained in Washington, D.C., for the rest of the war, working as a volunteer in military hospitals. Out of this experience came such masterpieces as "Cavalry Crossing a Ford," "By the Bivouac's Fitful Flame," and "Beat! Beat! Drums!"

Upon the assassination of Lincoln, Whitman wrote "O Captain! My Captain" and the elegy "When Lilacs Last in the Dooryard Bloom'd."

Ask students how Whitman, a noncombatant, could have written so vividly about Civil War scenes.

Possible response: The poet's contact with wounded soldiers may have given him a strong sense of what the war was like.

Frontier Voices As America expanded westward, so, too, did America's literature. During this period, a number of writers represented the Midwest and the Far West for the first time. Some, like Bret Harte and Willa Cather, were born in the East or the South but later moved west. As a young man, Harte moved from New York to California. Cather moved from Virginia to Nebraska as a child. Mark Twain, one of the greatest writers in all of American literature, grew up in Hannibal, Missouri, but traveled widely, settling in a Nevada mining town during the Civil War. Twain drew on the colorful language and outsized sensibility of the West for his first short story, "The Notorious Jumping Frog of Calaveras County."

Not all the frontier voices were those of European settlers. Mexican Americans living in the Southwest had their own legends and tales. They also had songs, such as "The Legend of Gregorio Cortez," that can take their place beside such famous western ballads as "The Streets of Laredo." Also, few speeches in American history have been as eloquent as that given by Chief Joseph of the Nez Percé when accepting the terms of surrender from federal troops in 1877.

Realism and Naturalism The harsh reality of frontier life, coupled with artists' reactions to the Civil War—in fiction like Ambrose Bierce's "Incident at

A Living Tradition

N. Scott Momaday and the Indian Oral Tradition

In an essay entitled "On Indian-White Relations: A Point of View," N. Scott Momaday, the Pulitzer Prize-winning author of Kiowa ancestry, responds to the beauty of the Indian oral tradition and of Indian oratory. The speech he cites was spoken by Satanta, a nineteenth-century Kiowa chief, but Momaday's observations might apply equally well to the famous speech by Chief Joseph on p. 614.

> The American Indian has a highly developed oral tradition. . . . One who has only an oral tradition thinks of language in this way: my words exist at the level of my voice. If I do not speak with care, my words are wasted. If I do not listen with care, my words are lost. If I do not remember carefully, the very purpose of words is frustrated. . . . [Momaday goes on to compare the elaborateness of a written executive order from the President, dated 1968, with the directness of the following speech by Satanta, who expresses his unwillingness to settle on a reservation.]
>
> > I have heard that you intend to settle us on a reservation near the mountains. I don't want to settle. I love to roam over the prairies. There I feel free and happy, but when we settle down we grow pale and die. I have laid aside my lance, bow, and shield, and yet I feel safe in your presence. I have told the truth. I have no little lies hid about me, but I don't know how it is with the commissioners. Are they as clear as I am?
>
> [Satanta's speech] is in the plain style, a style that preserves, in its way, the power and beauty of language.

this period, immigrants from Mexico developed a rich tradition of folklore. The tales and legends—or *cuentos*—of the Mexican-American Southwest include both stories with complex religious and social morals and fantasies filled with magic and the supernatural. This folk culture had its roots in the Old World, but the tales had developed their own flavor in the physical and social landscape of Mexico and the Southwest. Surviving texts, such as "The Legend of Gregorio Cortez," can be read today, but on the frontier they were spoken aloud and performed. Suggest that students try to imagine the frontier and the people who lived there as they read these selections.

The American Experience
A Living Tradition

- Tell students that in oral cultures the development of precise memory skills was important because without them there was no way to preserve or share information or stories.
- **Ask** students how the development of writing may have affected the use of memory among people in literate cultures. **Possible response:** Students may mention that people depend less on memory skills in literate cultures, and therefore people in literate cultures may not develop memory as extensively. Students might mention that people in literate cultures use memory to access information by remembering how to find it stored in written form.

record of the Civil War from the perspective of those who experienced it?
Answer: diaries, letters, journals, and speeches provide such a record.

2. What are two qualities that make Lincoln's speeches and letters so memorable?
Answer: They are models of clarity and eloquence.
3. Which region of the country most influenced Mark Twain's colorful language and use of humorous exaggeration?
Answer: The West influenced Twain in this manner.
4. (a) In literature, what is Realism? (b) What event turned American writers toward Realism?
Answer: (a) Writers in the Realist movement strove to describe the lives of ordinary people in an honest, objective way. (b) The Civil War turned writers toward Realism.
5. (a) Which literary movement was an offshoot of Realism? (b) What did writers in this new movement attempt to do?
Answer: (a) Naturalism was an offshoot of Realism. (b) Writers showed how forces such as nature, heredity, and fate shaped individuals.

Critical Viewing

Answer: (a) The Chisolm Trail ended in Abilene; the Goodnight-Loving Trail ended in Cheyenne. (b) Cattle trails tend to end at prominent railroad stations, so that cattle could be easily transported. Mining centers are often, but not always, close to railroad lines. This would make it easier to transport ore.

Owl Creek Bridge" and Stephen Crane's *The Red Badge of Courage*, for example—gave rise to a new movement in American literature called Realism. Realism in literature began after the Civil War. Although the outcome of the war had given the nation a hard-won sense of unity, the enormous cost in human life had shattered the nation's idealism. Young writers turned away from the Romanticism that was popular before the war. Instead, writers began to focus on portraying "real life" as ordinary people lived it and attempted to show characters and events in an honest, objective, almost factual way. Willa Cather, for example, was a Realist noted for her unflinching portrayal of the loneliness and cultural isolation of life on the prairie. In "A Wagner Matinée," she contrasts this isolation with the cultural richness of an eastern city.

Edith Wharton wrote fiction in the Realist vein, not about Western frontier life but about the Eastern high society into which she had been born. In *The House of Mirth* (1905), for example, she wrote about conflicts between the newly rich and the old aristocracy and about how social customs can prevent individuals from fulfilling themselves.

An important literary offshoot of Realism was Naturalism. Naturalist writers also depicted real people in real situations, but they believed that forces larger than the individual—nature, fate, heredity—shaped individual destiny. Jack London, for example, set much of his fiction in Alaska, where the environment was cruel and unforgiving. The theme of human endurance in the face of overwhelming natural forces pervades his fiction, including the short story "To Build a Fire."

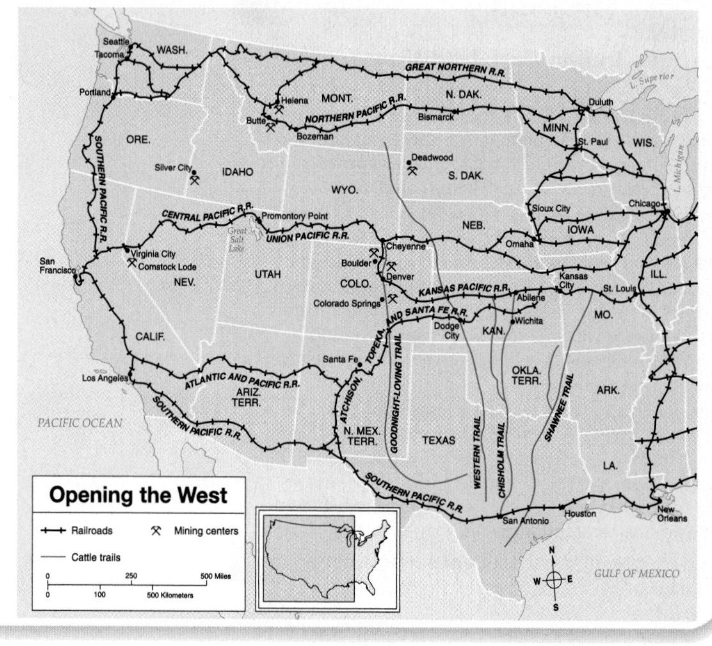

◀ Critical Viewing Transportation by rail, mining, and cattle grazing helped open the Great Plains for settlement, as shown on this map. (a) Which cattle trail ended in Abilene? In Cheyenne? (b) What relationship do you see between railroads and cattle trails? Between railroads and mining centers? **[Read a Map]**

Enrichment

Naturalism Around the World

Naturalism flourished in Europe during the late nineteenth and early twentieth centuries. In fact, scholars point to France as the birthplace of the movement. The writer Emile Zola was its leading practitioner. His approach to literature, was similar to a scientist's approach to an experiment. Characters should be subjected to tests, Zola suggested, and the author should record their reactions objectively.

Overall, naturalism drew on advances in the world of science. Scientific principles were imported into literature, and writers created characters whose lives were shaped and actions dictated by powerful forces—heredity and nature, but also social and economic pressure—entirely beyond their control. Major American Naturalist authors included Jack London, Stephen Crane, Frank Norris, and Theodore Drieser.

Art in the Historical Context

The Ashcan School and Realism in Painting

At the beginning of the twentieth century, a group of artists working in Philadelphia and New York developed a Realist vision in their work. These painters realized that America was becoming increasingly urban, and they wanted to depict this new urban reality. Some critics insultingly called them the Ashcan School (*ashcan* means "garbage can"). This name has endured, but it is no longer considered an insult.

One prominent member of this movement was John Sloan (1871–1951). Sloan said that he saw a city as a "vast stage set where all sorts of lively business was in progress." His painting *Six O'Clock* (c. 1912) shows the "lively business" of a New York City rush hour.

Make an Inference What qualities of urban life does Slaon capture?

Six O' Clock, John Sloan, Phillips Collection, Washington, D.C.

If the reality these writers depicted seemed always to be a harsh one, it was because hardship influenced their artistic vision. It was a vision rooted in war, in the frontier, and, increasingly, in America's growing cities.

Literature of Discontent The social ills that grew out of industrialization came under the sharp eye and pen of many talented writers of the day. Kate Chopin's writing, for example, explored women's desire for equality and independence. The Naturalists saw industrialization as a force against which individuals were powerless.

In 1897, one of the finest of all volumes of American poems appeared, Edwin Arlington Robinson's *The Children of the Night.* This volume contains unsparing and unforgettable psychological portraits of a variety of small-town characters. Eighteen years later, *Spoon River Anthology* by Edgar Lee Masters presented a disturbingly candid portrait of small-town life in the form of epitaphs spoken by the dead themselves.

By 1914, America had grown up, and in a sense, American literature had, too. The Civil War, the closing of the frontier, and industrialization had brought about a loss of innocence, a shift from idealism to pragmatism in the American character. In their rejection of Romanticism and their embrace of Realism, American writers reflected this change.

- Tell students that John Sloan began his artistic career at a Philadelphia newspaper as a commercial artist, and that studied with the artist Robert Henri. When Henri left Philadelphia for New York City, Sloan moved with him. There, the artists were central to the Ashcan School.
- The first two decades of the twentieth century proved to be Sloan's most important period. He became best known for his paintings of New York City and its daily routines. His paintings were realistic, and showed his sympathy for ordinary, working-class people, but on occasion his paintings would reflect a quiet sadness.
- **Ask** students to describe the mood of this painting.
  Possible response: The mood is claustrophobic or melancholy, suggesting that Sloan is ambivalent about technology and its impact on people's lives. Students may support this by noting the painting's darkness.

Critical Thinking

1. How does the saying "Less is more" relate to Lincoln's Gettysburg Address? **[Connect]**
   Possible response: The speech supports the saying. It shows how a brief address, if eloquently written, can be more memorable than a long speech.

Concept Connector

Have students discuss the Focus Questions on p. 471. Students' discussions should include the following points:

Regional Differences that Led to the Civil War

- By the early nineteenth century, slavery was no longer legal in the Northern states.
- Slavery was the bedrock of the economy of the Southern states.
- The Northern states had moved toward an industrial economy while the Southern states remained primarily agrarian.

Factors that Caused Dramatic Changes in American Life after the Civil War

- The loss of Lincoln shocked the people.
- Reconstruction after the war left lasting racial and regional divisions.
- Westward expansion followed by the closing of the frontier caused dramatic changes in the availability of resources and opportunities.
- Industry and the rise in immigration fueled the growth of cities.
- Indstrialization changed the ways people worked and how and where they lived.

How Civil War and Post-war Changes Shaped Literary Movements

These factors encouraged a literary focus on the working-class. Americans had to deal with the challenges posed by nature and with the societal challenges arising from clashes between different ethnic and economic groups.

The Development of American English

Mark Twain and the American Language

BY RICHARD LEDERER

AMERICAN LITERATURE COMES OF AGE

On February 18, 1885, thirty thousand copies of Mark Twain's *The Adventures of Huckleberry Finn* were released in the United States. The novel turned out to be Twain's masterpiece, and it changed the direction of American letters. Twain captured the everyday speech of characters, instead of the more formal, standard English that writers before him used. In *The Adventures of Huckleberry Finn,* Twain used seven distinct dialects to reflect the speech patterns of various characters, and he also became the first important author to show the freshness and vitality of the new American idiom in narrative as well as in dialogue. Just as Geoffrey Chaucer's *The Canterbury Tales* is the first significant work written in English, *Huckleberry Finn* is the first novel of world rank to be written entirely in American.

READIN', WRITIN', AND TWAIN

Twain held strong opinions about a passel of subjects, and he possessed the gift of being able to state these views in memorable ways: "It's better to keep your mouth shut and appear stupid than to open it and remove all doubt"; "Be careful about reading health books. You may die of a misprint."

Twain also had a lot to say about style, literature, and the American language that he, more than any other writer, helped to shape.

- *On American English, compared with British English:* The property has gone into the hands of a joint stock company, and we own the bulk of the shares.
- *On dialects:* I have traveled more than anyone else, and I have noticed that even the angels speak English with an accent.
- *On choosing words:* The difference between the almost right word and the right word is really a large matter—'tis the difference between the lightning-bug and the lightning.
- *On style* (in a letter to a twelve-year-old boy): I notice that you use plain, simple language, short words, and brief sentences. That is the way to write English—it is the modern way and the best way. Stick to it; and don't let fluff and flowers and verbosity creep in.
- *On being concise:* A successful book is not made of what is in it, but what is left out of it.
- *On using short words:* I never write metropolis for seven cents when I can get the same for city. I never write policeman because I can get the same for cop.
- *On reading:* The man who does not read good books has no advantage over the man who can't read them.

Activity

1. With a group, discuss Twain's statement on dialects. Include some of the characteristics of the dialect you speak, and contrast it to standard American English.
2. Use one of Mark Twain's statements about writing or language as the thesis for an essay or discussion on the subject.
3. In 1885, Twain wrote in his notebook, "My works are like water. The works of the great masters are like wine. But everyone drinks water." Choose a passage from one of Twain's stories or essays, and show how that passage exemplifies the author's philosophy of style.

Critical Thinking

1. Why was it important that Twain "captured the everyday speech of characters"? **[Speculate]**
   Possible response: If a writer hopes to capture a country's life, then his books ought to talk the way people do.
2. What did Twain mean by his observation about American English compared with British English? **[Interpret]**
   Possible response: Twain meant that Americans would now influence the future development of the English language even more than the British would.
3. Why do you think Twain favored short words over long ones? **[Speculate]**
   Possible response: He seems to have felt that long words were pretentious, flowery, and perhaps more European than American.

Critical Viewing

- Instruct students to look at the picture of Twain on this page. **Ask:** Does he look the way he sounds in the quotations? **[Connect]**
  Possible response: Obviously, there is no "correct" answer, but students may say that Twain looks like a down-to-earth, no-nonsense person, and these are qualities reflected in the quotations.

Answers to the Activity

1. Before students begin the discussion, be sure that they understand the quotation. Its gist is that dialects are ubiquitous. Define the word *dialect* for students, or help them to define it for themselves: the form or variety of a spoken language peculiar to a region, social group, or occupational group.
2. Be sure that students understand the quotations they choose. Essays should be focused on elaborating upon and supporting Twain's position.
3. Students should show how the passage exemplifies the down-to-earth directness of Twain's style—the way that his writing is, "like water," meant for everybody.

Enrichment

More of Twain's Wit and Wisdom

Share these additional quotations from Mark Twain with students. Students interested in pursuing Activity 3 might choose one of these passages:

> Soap and education are not as sudden as a massacre, but they are more deadly in the long run.
>
> —*The Facts Concerning the Recent Resignation*
>
> Work consists of whatever a body is obliged to do . . . Play consists of whatever a body is not obliged to do.
>
> —*The Adventures of Tom Sawyer*
>
> Hain't we got all the fools in town on our side? And ain't that a big enough majority in every town?
>
> —*The Adventure of Huckleberry Finn*
>
> War talk by men who have been in a war is always interesting; whereas moon talk by a poet who has not been in the moon is likely to be dull.
>
> —*Life on the Mississippi*

Unit 4
Part
1

A Nation Divided

Fight for the Standard, Wadsworth Atheneum, Hartford, Connecticut

Selection Planning Guide

The selections in this section show the many faces of a nation divided. Stephen Crane's "An Episode of War" portrays the battlefront. The spirituals and Frederick Douglass excerpt provide a candid look at the divisive issue of slavery. "An Occurrence at Owl Creek Bridge" will have students debating whether all is really fair in love and war. Two of the war's greatest figures—Abraham Lincoln and Robert E. Lee—reveal in their own words the issues at the heart of the Civil War.

Humanities

Fight for the Standard, by Daniel Wadsworth

In old-fashioned warfare, capturing the opponents' flag was meant to throw the other side into despair and confusion. Help students to see that this traditional painting seems posed for dramatic effect, with two cavalrymen emerging from a smoky background to fight. Point out that the Confederate soldier holding the flag is about to be mortally wounded by the Union soldier on the white horse.

Have students link the painting to the theme "A Nation Divided" by answering the following questions:

1. Do you think the painter favored one side over the other in this painting? What leads you to that impression?
   Possible response: Some students will say that the balance of the composition projects a balanced view of the fight. Others may point to details that favor the Northerner—he rides a white horse, his face and not the Southerner's is visible, and he is about to win.
2. Does this artist create a realistic or romanticized view of war? Explain.
   Possible response: Details like the excitement of hand-to-hand combat, the beautiful horses, and the almost knightly sabers support a romanticized view of warfare. The Southerner's imminent death reflects a realistic view.

Differentiated Instruction Solutions for All Learners

Accessibility at a Glance

More Accessible	Average	More Challenging
Willie Has Gone to the War	An Episode of War	*from* My Bondage and My Freedom
Swing Low, Sweet Chariot	Go Down, Moses	Second Inaugural Address
	An Occurrence at Owl Creek Bridge	Letter to his Son
	The Gettysburg Address	

Meeting Your Standards

Students will

1. **analyze and respond to literary elements.**
   - Literary Analysis: Realism and Naturalism
2. **read, comprehend, analyze, and critique a short story and lyrics.**
   - Reading Strategy: Recognizing Historical Details
   - Reading Check questions
   - Apply the Skills questions
   - Assessment Practice (ATE)
3. **develop vocabulary.**
   - Vocabulary Lesson: Latin Root: *-greg-*
4. **understand and apply written and oral language conventions.**
   - Spelling Strategy
   - Grammar and Style Lesson: Usage: *Like* and *As*
5. **develop writing proficiency.**
   - Writing Lesson: Field Report on Hospital Conditions
6. **develop appropriate research strategies.**
   - Extend Your Learning: Definition Essay
7. **understand and apply listening and speaking strategies.**
   - Extend Your Learning: Musical Presentation

Block Scheduling: Use one 90-minute class period to preteach the skills and have students read the selection. Use a second 90-minute class period to assess students' mastery of skills, extend their learning, and monitor their progress.

Homework Suggestions

Following are possibilities for homework assignments.

- Support pages from ***Unit 4 Resources:***
  Literary Analysis
  Reading Strategy
  Vocabulary Builder
  Grammar and Style
- An Extend Your Learning project and the Writing Lesson for this selection group may be completed over several days.

Step-by-Step Teaching Guide	Pacing Guide
PRETEACH	
• Administer Vocabulary and Reading Warm-ups as necessary.	5 min.
• Engage students' interest with the motivation activity.	5 min.
• Read and discuss author and background features. **FT**	10 min.
• Introduce the Literary Analysis Skill: Realism and Naturalism. **FT**	5 min.
• Introduce the Reading Strategy: Recognizing Historical Details. **FT**	10 min.
• Prepare students to read by teaching the selection vocabulary. **FT**	
TEACH	
• Informally monitor comprehension while students read independently or in groups. **FT**	30 min.
• Monitor students' comprehension with the Reading Check notes.	as students read
• Reinforce vocabulary with Vocabulary Builder notes.	as students read
• Develop students' understanding of Realism and Naturalism with the Literary Analysis annotations. **FT**	5 min.
• Develop students' ability to recognize historical details with the Reading Strategy annotations. **FT**	5 min.
ASSESS/EXTEND	
• Assess students' comprehension and mastery of the Literary Analysis and Reading Strategy by having them answer the Apply the Skills questions. **FT**	15 min.
• Have students complete the Vocabulary Lesson and the Grammar and Style Lesson. **FT**	15 min.
• Apply students' ability to use precise details by using the Writing Lesson. **FT**	45 min. or homework
• Apply students' understanding by using one or more of the Extend Your Learning activities.	20–90 min. or homework
• Administer Selection Test A or Selection Test B. **FT**	15 min.

Resources

PRINT

Unit 4 Resources

- Vocabulary Warm-up Word Lists [**L1, L2, EL**] .... p. 7
- Vocabulary Warm-up Practice [**L1, L2, EL**] .... p. 8
- Reading Warm-up A [**L1, L2, EL**] .... p. 9
- Reading Warm-up B [**L1, L2, L3**] .... p. 10

TRANSPARENCY

Graphic Organizer Transparencies

- Literary Analysis Graphic Organizer A [**L3**] .... p. 94
- Literary Analysis Graphic Organizer B [**L1, L2, EL**] .... p. 95
- Reading Strategy Graphic Organizer A [**L3**] .... p. 92
- Reading Strategy Graphic Organizer B [**L1, L2, EL**] .... p. 93

PRINT

Reader's Notebook [L2]
Reader's Notebook: Adapted Version [L1]
Reader's Notebook: English Learner's Version [EL]

Unit 4 Resources

- Literary Analysis [**L3**] .... p. 11
- Reading Strategy [**L3**] .... p. 12
- Vocabulary Builder [**L3**] .... p. 13

TECHNOLOGY

Listening to Literature Audio CDs [L2, EL]
Reader's Notebook: Adapted Version Audio CD [L1, L2]

PRINT

Unit 4 Resources

- Grammar and Style [**L3**] .... p. 14
- Support for Writing Lesson [**L3**] .... p. 15
- Support for Extend Your Learning [**L3**] .... p. 16
- Enrichment [**L4**] .... p. 17
- Selection Test A [**L1, L2, EL**] .... pp. 18–20
- Selection Test B [**L3, L4**] .... pp. 21–23

General Resources

- Rubrics for Descriptive Essay [**L3**] .... pp. 63–64
- Rubric for Listening: Evaluating a Media Presentation [**L3**] .... p. 86

TECHNOLOGY

Go Online: Research [**L3**]
Go Online: Self-test [**L3**]
***ExamView®*, Test Bank [L3]**

Choosing Resources for Differentiated Instruction

[**L1**] Special Needs Students
[**L2**] Below-Level Students
[**L3**] All Students
[**L4**] Advanced Students
[**EL**] English Learners

FT Fast Track Instruction: To move the lesson more quickly, use the strategies and activities identified with **FT**.

Scaffolding for Less Proficient and Advanced Students

The leveled Critical Thinking questions after selections progress in the levels of thinking required to answer them. To address the needs of your different students, you may use the (a) level questions for your less proficient students and the (b) level questions with your on-level and advanced students. The occasional (c) level questions are appropriate for your advanced students.

PRENTICE HALL **TeacherEXPRESS™** Plan · Teach · Assess — Use this complete suite of powerful teaching tools to make lesson planning and testing quicker and easier.

Use the interactive textbook (online and on CD-ROM) to make selections and activities come alive with audio and video support and interactive questions.

PREFACH

Motivation

Play the scene from the 1993 film *Gettysburg* in which General Longstreet visits General Hood as the latter recovers from an amputation in a Confederate field hospital. Use this scene—which occurs at the beginning of Part 2—to help students gain an awareness of the conditions in a Civil War field hospital. Invite them to share their reactions to what they see and hear. Then, tell them that they are about to read a story in which an injured soldier makes a frightening journey to such a medical facility.

1 Background

More About the Authors

Crane received firsthand experience fighting forces beyond his control when a boat on which he was traveling sank off the Florida coast. He and three other passengers spent nearly thirty hours afloat in a dinghy before landing safely at Daytona.

At one point, Stephen Foster's financial difficulties grew so extreme that he nearly starved to death while living on the streets of New York City. Although he worked with a collaborator on this Civil War ballad, he often wrote both lyrics and music for his songs.

Build Skills *Short Story • Song*

1 An Episode of War • Willie Has Gone to the War

Stephen Crane (1871–1900)

Stephen Crane had not even been born when the last battle of the American Civil War was fought, yet he is best remembered for his compelling depiction of the conflict. During his brief life, Crane worked to establish himself as both a leader of the Naturalist movement and one of the greatest writers of his time.

Early in his career, Crane worked as a newspaper writer in New York City. His experiences there inspired his first novel, *Maggie: A Girl of the Streets* (1893). Its grimly realistic portrayal of life in the city's slums was so frank and shocking that Crane was unable to find a publisher, so he printed the book at his own expense.

The Red Badge of Courage Crane's second novel, published in 1895, was *The Red Badge of Courage: An Episode of the American Civil War.* A psychological exploration of a young soldier's mental and emotional reactions under enemy fire, the wildly successful novel earned international acclaim for the twenty-four-year-old writer. Although Crane had never experienced military combat, he interviewed Civil War veterans and studied photographs, battle plans, and biographical accounts before writing the realistic battle scenes.

Crane later viewed war firsthand when he served as a newspaper correspondent during the Greco-Turkish War in 1897 and the Spanish-American War in 1898. His war experiences provided material for a collection of poetry, *War Is Kind* (1899), but they took their toll on his health. He died of tuberculosis at the age of twenty-eight.

An Untimely Death Knowing he was going to die, Crane worked intensely in the last years of his life. His novels, short stories, poems, and other writings fill twelve volumes. He is considered a literary prodigy who wrote as quickly and passionately as he lived. Like other Naturalists, Crane depicts characters who are manipulated by forces that are beyond their understanding or control. His most common themes include the harsh reality of war, the degradation of humanity, social rebellion, betrayal, and guilt. Crane also wrote of the physical emotional, and intellectual responses of people under extreme pressure.

Stephen Foster (1826–1864)

Stephen Foster was born in Pennsylvania on July 4, 1826—the fiftieth anniversary of American independence and the day that both Thomas Jefferson and John Adams died. As a young man, Foster worked as a bookkeeper but experienced little success. In fact, throughout his life he was plagued by financial failure. Music publishers took advantage of Foster, who never achieved monetary success to match his musical talent.

The popular minstrel songs and sentimental ballads that he wrote earned Foster an honored place in American music. Foster composed about 200 songs in his rather short lifetime, including such classics as "The Old Folks at Home" (popularly known as "Way Down Upon the Swanee River"), "Camptown Races," "Oh! Susanna," "My Old Kentucky Home," and "Jeanie With the Light Brown Hair."

Although Foster often wrote his own lyrics, he also collaborated with lyricist **George Cooper (1838–1927)** on many songs, including the Civil War ballad "Willie Has Gone to the War."

Preview

Connecting to the Literature

Being in control of a situation and making responsible decisions helps you take command of your life. This luxury was not granted to the Civil War soldiers who had very little control over their own destinies in battle.

Literary Analysis

Realism and Naturalism

In reaction to Romanticism—a movement that emphasized emotion, imagination, and nature—two literary movements emerged during the mid- to late-nineteenth century: **Realism** and **Naturalism.**

- Realism sought to portray life as faithfully and accurately as possible, focusing on ordinary people suffering the harsh realities of everyday life.
- Naturalism also sought to portray ordinary people's lives, but suggested that environment, heredity, and chance, or forces they could neither understand nor control, determined people's fate.

As you read, look for elements related to these two literary movements.

Comparing Literary Works

Both of these selections are set against a backdrop of the Civil War, but each presents a different perspective on the bloodiest conflict ever fought on American soil. As you read, determine which writer presents the more accurate description of events and which one presents a more idealized version of life during that bitter moment in history.

Reading Strategy

Recognizing Historical Details

The social and political climate surrounding these Civil War snapshots form part of their setting and context. When you **recognize historical details,** you determine how the attitudes of both writers and characters reflect the ideas of their day. As you read, use a chart like the one shown to record events that suggest historical context.

Event	Historical Context
Battles	
Medical Practices	
Political Situations	
Social Attitudes	

Vocabulary Builder

precipitate (prē sip′ ə tāt′) *v.* cause to happen before expected or desired (p. 488)

aggregation (ag′ rə gā′ shən) *n.* group of distinct objects or individuals (p. 488)

inscrutable (in skro͞ot′ ə bəl) *adj.* impossible to see (p. 489)

disdainfully (dis dān′ fəl ē) *adv.* showing scorn or contempt (p. 490)

glade (glād) *n.* open space in a wood or forest (p. 492)

❷ Literary Analysis
Realism and Naturalism

- Tell students that they will be exploring the literary movements of Realism and Naturalism as they read the two works in this grouping. Both Realists and Naturalists sought to portray real life as accurately as possible. Naturalists also believed that human lives are determined by chance, fate, or other forces beyond our control.
- As they read, encourage students to consider how accurately each selection portrays "real life."
- Invite students to think about a wide range of stories, novels, films, and television programs with which they are familiar. Might any of these works be deemed examples of Realism or Naturalism? Do any of them present real life accurately? Do any of them convey the idea that people's fates are determined by chance or by forces they cannot control?

❸ Reading Strategy
Recognizing Historical Details

- Give students a copy of **Reading Strategy Graphic Organizer A** from the ***Graphic Organizer Transparencies,*** p. 92, to use as they read "An Episode of War."
- Point out to students that recognizing historical details will enrich their appreciation of a literary work, and will help them to better understand descriptions, characters, events, and themes.
- Remind students that the most obvious historical details are references to events, ideas,persons, or things. Less conspicuous (but equally important) are descriptions of social attitudes, political situations, and cultural practices.
- Invite students to look for details that indicate historical context in these works by Crane and Foster.

Vocabulary Builder

- Pronounce each vocabulary word for students, and read the definitions as a class. Have students identify any words with which they are already familiar.

Differentiated Instruction Solutions for All Learners

Support for Special Needs Students
Have students use the support pages for these selections in the ***Reader's Notebooks.*** Completing these pages will prepare students to read the selections in the Student Edition.

Support for Less Proficient Readers
Have students use the support pages for these selections in the ***Reader's Notebooks.*** After students finish the selection in the Reader's Notebooks, have them complete the questions and activities in the Student Edition.

Support for English Learners
Have students use the support pages for these selections in the ***Reader's Notebooks: English Learner's Version.*** Completing these pages will prepare students to read the selections in the Student Edition.

Learning Modalities
Visual/Spatial Learners

Encourage students to use the photographs and fine art to help them picture the setting, characters, and events in the story. Make sure that they understand that the two photographs depict real soldiers who fought in the Civil War. Have students discuss how the photographs add to the details that Crane provides in his story. You may also wish to conduct a more general discussion about the differences between written and visual records of historical events.

❶ About the Selection

This stark account of how a Civil War lieutenant loses his arm to amputation is detached and impersonal, yet hauntingly moving. The lieutenant is rationing coffee when a stray bullet hits his arm and changes his life forever. So begins his dreamlike journey toward the field hospital. Although the nameless lieutenant appears numb, the reader can imagine his dread as he anticipates the medical attention he will receive. Despite his protests and the doctor's false assurances, the lieutenant loses his arm in just another "episode of war." Through his depiction of this gripping series of events, Crane conveys an important message about the tragedy of war and the helplessness of those caught up in the fighting.

❷ Critical Viewing

Answer: Students may say that the soldiers' facial expressions and the way the men recline in crowded and unsanitary conditions indicate that they are not receiving quality treatment.

❶ An Episode of War

Stephen Crane

Background Both of these selections were inspired by the American Civil War, the bloodiest conflict in American history. The war claimed the lives of 600,000 soldiers—more American casualties than the combined total of all other wars in which the United States has fought. Hundreds of thousands more were left maimed by battle wounds and crude medical care.

When the war began, neither side was prepared to care for the wounded. The conditions were terrible, and twice as many Civil War soldiers died of infections as of combat wounds. As you read "An Episode of War," keep in mind that amputation was routine treatment for injured limbs. A wounded soldier knew that he faced the high probability of losing his arm or leg to a surgeon's saw.

Differentiated Instruction Solutions for All Learners

Accessibility at a Glance

	"An Episode of War"	"Willie Has Gone to War"
Context	U.S. Civil War	U.S. Civil War
Language	Footnotes For Vocabulary	Poetic Diction
Concept Level	Accessible (realisitic description)	Accessible (romance view of war)
Literary Merit	Noted Author	Noted Composer
Lexile	1100	NP
Overall Rating	Average	More accessible

The lieutenant's rubber blanket lay on the ground, and upon it he had poured the company's supply of coffee. Corporals and other representatives of the grimy and hot-throated men who lined the breast-work[1] had come for each squad's portion.

The lieutenant was frowning and serious at this task of division. His lips pursed as he drew with his sword various crevices in the heap, until brown squares of coffee, astoundingly equal in size, appeared on the blanket. He was on the verge of a great triumph in mathematics, and the corporals were thronging forward, each to reap a little square, when suddenly the lieutenant cried out and looked quickly at a man near him as if he suspected it was a case of personal assault. The others cried out also when they saw blood upon the lieutenant's sleeve.

He had winced like a man stung, swayed dangerously, and then straightened. The sound of his hoarse breathing was plainly audible. He looked sadly, mystically, over the breast-work at the green face of a wood, where now were many little puffs of white smoke. During this moment the men about him gazed statuelike and silent, astonished and awed by this catastrophe which happened when catastrophes were not expected—when they had leisure to observe it.

As the lieutenant stared at the wood, they too swung their heads, so that for another instant all hands, still silent, contemplated the distant forest as if their minds were fixed upon the mystery of a bullet's journey.

The officer had, of course, been compelled to take his sword into his left hand. He did not hold it by the hilt. He gripped it at the middle of the blade, awkwardly. Turning his eyes from the hostile wood, he looked at the sword as he held it there, and seemed puzzled as to what to do with it, where to put it. In short, this weapon had of a sudden become a strange thing to him. He looked at it in a kind of stupefaction, as if he had been endowed with a trident, a sceptre,[2] or a spade.

Finally he tried to sheathe it. To sheathe a sword held by the left hand, at the middle of the blade, in a scabbard hung at the left hip, is a feat worthy of a sawdust ring.[3] This wounded officer engaged in a desperate struggle with the sword and the wobbling scabbard, and during the time of it breathed like a wrestler.

But at this instant the men, the spectators, awoke from their stone-like poses and crowded forward sympathetically. The orderly-sergeant

1. **breast-work** low wall put up quickly as a defense in battle.
2. **a trident, a sceptre** (trīd′ ənt; sep′ tər) three-pronged spear; decorated ornamental rod or staff symbolizing royal authority.
3. **sawdust ring** ring in which circus acts are performed.

Reading Strategy
Recognizing Historical Details What details in this passage set the story at the time of the Civil War?

2 ◀ **Critical Viewing** This is an actual photograph of a temporary Civil War hospital. Do you think that soldiers received quality treatment in this setting? On what details do you base your answer? **[Assess]**

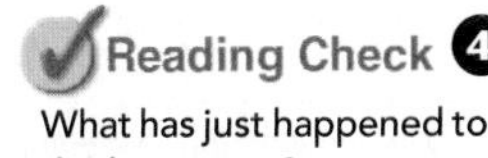
Reading Check **4**
What has just happened to the lieutenant?

3 Reading Strategy
Recognizing Historical Details

- Have a student volunteer read the paragraph aloud slowly and clearly. Tell students to listen for details in the passage that establish the story's time and place.
- Then, **ask** students the Reading Strategy question: What details in this passage set the story at the time of the Civil War?
  Answer: Students should mention the lieutenant's possessing a sword.
- If necessary, help students understand that the terms *trident* and *sceptre* do not relate to the Civil War setting. (The former was a weapon used in ancient Rome; the latter is an object used as a symbol of British royalty.) Crane includes these two images—as well as that of a humble digging tool, the spade—to emphasize the lieutenant's disorientation.

4 Reading Check

Answer: The lieutenant has been shot in the arm.

Differentiated Instruction
Solutions for All Learners

Background for Special Needs Students
Inform students that a Civil War officer in uniform customarily carried a sword, and that when not in use, the sword rested in a scabbard slung at the officer's hip. Help students picture the lieutenant's maneuvers as he grasps and then attempts to sheathe his sword by having them act out his movements. After they perform these gestures, invite them to explain in their own words why the officer's wounded arm made him feel so awkward.

Enrichment for Gifted/Talented Students
Stephen Crane opens this tale with a brief portrait of life in a military camp. The story begins during a lull just before shooting breaks out. Have students describe the activities in which the soldiers are engaged prior to the onset of gunfire. Then, encourage them to draw or create a tableau—based on Crane's description—that captures the ordinariness of camp life.

5 Background
The Red Badge of Courage

Inform students that Civil War officers, for the most part, were Victorian gentlemen who held romantic notions about war. To some, a wound was a sign of bravery and glory (hence, Crane's title *The Red Badge of Courage*). Tell students that as the bloody war raged on, this notion gradually began to lose its appeal.

6 Reading Strategy
Recognizing Historical Details

- Encourage students to review the story so far to try to find detailed references to the lieutenant's wound. If necessary, help students recognize that—other than a single allusion to "blood upon the lieutenant's sleeve" and references to his holding the arm gingerly—Crane provides no details about the wound.

Monitor Progress: Ask students the Reading Strategy question: Using your knowledge of the historical context, what do you think is the potential outcome of the lieutenant's injury?
Answer: Students may mention amputation—or even death as a result of an infection.

7 Vocabulary Builder
Latin Root *-greg-*

- Draw students' attention to Crane's use of the word *aggregation,* and read its definition. Then, tell students that the root *-greg-* derives from the Latin word meaning "herd," or "flock." The prefix *ag-* is equivalent to *ad-* and means "near," or "to," and the suffix *-ion* means a "state" or "condition."
- Invite students to brainstorm for a list of other words that share the root *-greg-*. Have them explain the ways in which all these words relate to the meaning of the root.

took the sword and tenderly placed it in the scabbard. At the time, he leaned nervously backward, and did not allow even his finger to brush the body of the lieutenant. A wound gives strange dignity to him who bears it. Well men shy from his new and terrible majesty. It is as if the wounded man's hand is upon the curtain which hangs before the revelations of all existence—the meaning of ants, potentates,[4] wars, cities, sunshine, snow, a feather dropped from a bird's wing; and the
5 power of it sheds radiance upon a bloody form, and makes the other men understand sometimes that they are little. His comrades look at him with large eyes thoughtfully. Moreover, they fear vaguely that the weight of a finger upon him might send him headlong, precipitate the tragedy, hurl him at once into the dim, grey unknown. And so the orderly-sergeant, while sheathing the sword, leaned nervously backward.

There were others who proffered assistance. One timidly presented his shoulder and asked the lieutenant if he cared to lean upon it, but the latter waved him away mournfully. He wore the look of one who knows he is the victim of a terrible disease and understands his helplessness. He again stared over the breast-work at the forest, and then, turning, went slowly rearward. He held his right wrist tenderly in his left hand as if the wounded arm was made of very brittle glass.

6 And the men in silence stared at the wood, then at the departing lieutenant; then at the wood, then at the lieutenant.

As the wounded officer passed from the line of battle, he was enabled to see many things which as a participant in the fight were unknown to him. He saw a general on a black horse gazing over the lines of blue infantry at the green woods which veiled his problems. An aide galloped furiously, dragged his horse suddenly to a halt, saluted, and presented a paper. It was, for a wonder, precisely like a historical painting.

To the rear of the general and his staff a group, composed of a bugler, two or three orderlies, and the bearer of the corps standard,[5] all upon maniacal horses, were working like slaves to hold their ground, preserve their respectful interval, while the shells boomed in the air about them, and caused their chargers to make furious quivering leaps.

A battery, a tumultuous and shining mass, was swirling toward the right. The wild thud of hoofs, the cries of the riders shouting blame and praise, menace and encouragement, and, last, the roar of the wheels, the slant of the glistening guns, brought the lieutenant to an intent pause. The battery swept in curves that stirred the heart; it made halts
7 as dramatic as the crash of a wave on the rocks, and when it fled onward this aggregation of wheels, levers, motors had a beautiful unity, as if it were a missile. The sound of it was a war-chorus that reached into the depths of man's emotion.

Vocabulary Builder
precipitate (prē sip′ ə tāt′) *v.* cause to happen before expected or desired

Reading Strategy
Recognizing Historical Details Using your knowledge of the historical context, what do you think is the potential outcome of the lieutenant's injury?

Vocabulary Builder
aggregation (ag′ grə gā′ shən) *n.* group of distinct objects or individuals

4. **potentates** (pōt′ ən tāts) *n.* rulers; powerful people.
5. **corps standard** (kôr) flag or banner representing a military unit.

Enrichment

Photojournalism

The work of photographers such as Mathew Brady (see pp. 486 and 489) and Alexander Gardner brought the horrors of the Civil War into parlors across the United States of America. Like their earlier counterparts, today's photojournalists capture news events or explore timely issues through images rather than words. Although some work as staff photographers for newspapers and magazines, most work as freelancers. These photojournalists may be hired for an assignment, or they may sell images to individual publications or to photo services that then distribute them to subscribers.

Invite students to discuss the idea of working as a photojournalist. Ask them to talk about the kinds of events they would most like to cover. Would they prefer to work as a staff or freelance photographer? Why? Suggest that they contact modern-day photojournalists to learn more about the nature and history of this career.

8

The lieutenant, still holding his arm as if it were of glass, stood watching this battery until all detail of it was lost, save the figures of the riders, which rose and fell and waved lashes over the black mass.

Later, he turned his eyes toward the battle, where the shooting sometimes crackled like bush-fires, sometimes sputtered with exasperating irregularity, and sometimes reverberated like the thunder. He saw the smoke rolling upward and saw crowds of men who ran and cheered, or stood and blazed away at the inscrutable distance.

He came upon some stragglers, and they told him how to find the field hospital. They described its exact location. In fact, these men, no longer having part in the battle, knew more of it than others. They told the performance of every corps, every division, the opinion of every general. The lieutenant, carrying his wounded arm rearward, looked upon them with wonder. 11

At the roadside a brigade was making coffee and buzzing with talk like a girls' boarding school. Several officers came out to him and

9 **Critical Viewing** What connections do you see between this photograph and Crane's description of the wounded lieutenant being helped by his men? **[Connect]**

Vocabulary Builder
inscrutable (in skrōōt´ ə bəl) *adj.* impossible to see

Reading Check
Why does the lieutenant look upon the stragglers with wonder?

Differentiated Instruction Solutions for All Learners

Support for Less Proficient Readers
Students may need help determining the essential meaning of some of Crane's poetic passages. For instance, guide them through his description of the effect of the wound, on p. 488—particularly the sentence beginning *It is as if the wounded man's hand.* Point out the phrase *as if* and explain that the author uses an imaginative word picture (a hand upon a curtain hanging in front of the answers to life's questions) to convey an important idea. Guide students through the list of nouns—*ants, wars,* and so on—and invite them to suggest what the "meaning" of each might be.

Make sure students understand Crane's essential point that a wound carries with it a strange power: Other people believe that the wounded person stands closer to the essence of life itself. Moreover, Crane is suggesting that in the final analysis, human beings may not "mean" more than an insect or an inanimate object such as a feather.

8 Humanities
Photographs by Mathew Brady

The Civil War was the first war to be captured in photographs. Due to the limitations of the photographic process at that time, photographers rarely captured action or battle scenes. They took pictures of events behind the scenes or photographed the carnage that remained after battle. Have students contrast the photographs that accompany this story with photographs they have seen of later wars.

9 Critical Viewing

Answer: Like the men in the story, this soldier expresses aloofness in his body language, as though proximity to the wounded man will cause his own doom. Nevertheless, he still attempts to help his fallen comrade by giving him water from a canteen, much as the soldiers in the story offer timid assistance to their lieutenant.

10 Critical Thinking
Analyze Causes and Effects

- Have a student volunteer read the first three paragraphs on this page. Guide students to recognize that the lieutenant makes a variety of observations as he is walking.
- Then, **ask** students to explain why the stragglers might know more about the battle than the lieutenant does. Is their information reliable?
Answer: Students may say that the stragglers, removed as they are from the thick of battle, have seen more of the larger conflict than the lieutenant has. Others may suggest that these men may not have accurate information and know little of what the generals are thinking.

11 Reading Check

Possible answer: He looks upon them with wonder because of the breadth of their information and because he sees everything anew in light of his wound.

⓬ Literary Analysis
Realism and Naturalism

- Invite one or two student volunteers to explain the definitions of Realism and Naturalism. Ensure that students recognize the similarities as well as the fundamental difference between these two literary movements.
- You might wish to have students use a Venn diagram to clarify the similarities and differences between the two movements.

➤ Monitor Progress: Ask students the Literary Analysis question: What details of this description reflect the ideas of the Naturalists?

Answer: Details include the "deep mud" (environment) or the chance collision of two ambulances that could hasten the death of wounded soldiers.

⓭ Critical Viewing

Answer: This set of surgical instruments highlights the brutality and crudeness of Civil War medical practices. In particular, both the small hatchet and the saw suggest the frequency with which amputations were performed.

inquired concerning things of which he knew nothing. One, seeing his arm, began to scold. "Why, man, that's no way to do. You want to fix that thing." He appropriated the lieutenant and the lieutenant's wound. He cut the sleeve and laid bare the arm, every nerve of which softly fluttered under his touch. He bound his handkerchief over the wound, scolding away in the meantime. His tone allowed one to think that he was in the habit of being wounded every day. The lieutenant hung his head, feeling, in this presence, that he did not know how to be correctly wounded.

12 The low white tents of the hospital were grouped around an old schoolhouse. There was here a singular commotion. In the foreground two ambulances interlocked wheels in the deep mud. The drivers were tossing the blame of it back and forth, gesticulating and berating, while from the ambulances, both crammed with wounded, there came an occasional groan. An interminable crowd of bandaged men were coming and going. Great numbers sat under the trees nursing heads or arms or legs. There was a dispute of some kind raging on the steps of the schoolhouse. Sitting with his back against a tree a man with a face as grey as a new army blanket was serenely smoking a corncob pipe. The lieutenant wished to rush forward and inform him that he was dying.

Literary Analysis
Realism and Naturalism What details of this description reflect the ideas of the Naturalists?

A busy surgeon was passing near the lieutenant. "Good-morning," he said, with a friendly smile. Then he caught sight of the lieutenant's arm, and his face at once changed. "Well, let's have a look at it." He seemed possessed suddenly of a great contempt for the lieutenant. This wound evidently placed the latter on a very low social plane. The doctor cried out impatiently, "What mutton-head had tied it up that way anyhow?" The lieutenant answered, "Oh, a man."

When the wound was disclosed the doctor fingered it disdainfully. "Humph," he said. "You come along with me and I'll 'tend to you." His voice contained the same scorn as if he were saying: "You will have to go to jail."

Vocabulary Builder
disdainfully (dis dān′ fəl ē) *adv.* showing scorn or contempt

The lieutenant had been very meek, but now his face flushed, and he looked into the doctor's eyes. "I guess I won't have it amputated," he said. 13

▼ Critical Viewing What do these Civil War surgical instruments suggest about the nature of the medical treatment the lieutenant faces? **[Interpret]**

"Nonsense, man! Nonsense! Nonsense!" cried the doctor. "Come along, now. I won't amputate it. Come along. Don't be a baby."

"Let go of me," said the lieutenant, holding back wrathfully, his glance fixed upon the door of the old schoolhouse, as sinister to him as the portals of death.

And this is the story of how the lieutenant lost his arm. When he reached home, his sisters, his mother, his wife, sobbed for a long time at the sight of the flat sleeve. "Oh, well," he said, standing shamefaced amid these tears, "I don't suppose it matters so much as all that."

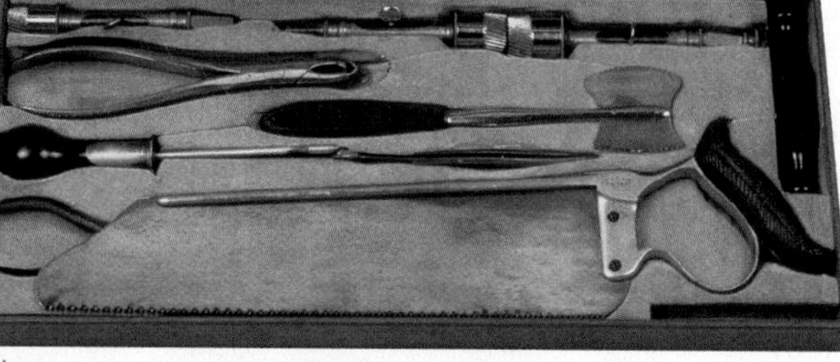

© Museum of the Confederacy, Richmond, Virginia

Enrichment

Stephen Foster

Stephen Foster is widely regarded as the first great American songwriter. In the wealth of songs that Foster composed, one can hear the beginnings of popular music, jazz melodies based on folk tunes, even the first hints of American musical theater. Foster was influenced strongly by the Anglo-Irish folk tradition as well as by the music and speech of African Americans. He drew on these influences to create distinctly American music.

In turn, Foster influenced nearly every other great American songwriter who followed, from Irving Berlin, the composer of such favorites as "White Christmas" and "Easter Parade," to Broadway composer Jerome Kern to 1960s folk-rock icon Bob Dylan.

Obtain a copy of *American Dreamer: Songs of Stephen Foster.* Invite students to listen to these songs and to note the rich melodies and the variety of emotions they evoke.

Willie Has Gone to the War

Words by George Cooper

Music by Stephen Foster

Young Soldier: Separate Study of a Soldier Giving Water to a Wounded Companion, 1861, Winslow Homer, Cooper-Hewitt, National Museum of Design, Smithsonian Institution

The blue bird is singing his lay,[1]
To all the sweet flow'rs of the dale,
The wild bee is roaming at play,
And soft is the sigh of the gale;
I stray by the brookside alone,
Where oft we have wander'd before,
And weep for my lov'd one, my own,
My Willie has gone to the war!

Willie has gone to the war, Willie,
Willie my lov'd one, my own;
Willie has gone to the war, Willie,
Willie my lov'd one is gone!

'Twas here, where the lily bells grow,
I last saw his noble young face,
And now while he's gone to the foe,
Oh! dearly I love the old place;
The whispering waters repeat
The name that I love o'er and o'er,
And daisies that nod at my feet,
Say Willie has gone to the war!

1. **lay** *n.* song or melody.

16 **Critical Viewing** This teenaged Union soldier may have enlisted in the army hoping to find glory on the battlefield. In what way does "Willie Has Gone to the War" show another side to the experience of war? **[Contrast]**

17 **Reading Check**
Where does the speaker wait for Willie?

14 About the Selection

Using a stanza and chorus format, lyricist George Cooper and composer Stephen Foster created this Civil War ballad that romanticizes the idea of waiting for a loved one to return from war.

15 Humanities

Young Soldier, by Winslow Homer

Considered one of the greatest painters of the nineteenth century, Homer (1836–1910) is best known for his watercolors. His first claim to fame, however, came as an illustrator. After an apprenticeship to a lithographer, he worked as a freelance illustrator for such publications as *Harper's Weekly.* During the Civil War, he abandoned this lucrative career to serve as an artist for the Army of the Potomac. His work, mostly drawings and oil sketches done at or near the front lines and in the encampments, was superior to the lifeless depictions of other wartime illustrators. Homer's renderings featured unsentimental images of the fear and despair that permeated the life of the Civil War soldier.

Use these questions for discussion:

1. What emotions does the artist capture in this image?
   Possible answer: Homer captures the shyness and exhaustion of the young Union soldier.
2. The lightest area on this canvas is the soldier's face. Why might the artist have wished to lead the viewer's eye to the soldier's face?
   Answer: The soldier's face not only shows his tender age but also suggests his feelings.

16 Critical Viewing

Answer: Students may say that the eager young volunteers soon came to understand all too well that "glory on the battlefield" was not to be. By contrast, the song suggests a romantic, but still painful experience, of waiting for a soldier's return.

17 Reading Check

Answer: The speaker waits for Willie "by the brookside" where they "have wander'd before."

Differentiated Instruction — Solutions for All Learners

Support for Special Needs Students

Students may need help clarifying and articulating the essential difference between the story's and the song's portrayal of the Civil War. If necessary, guide them to see that Crane reflects the harsh realities experienced by the soldiers who fought the war, whereas Foster reflects a romanticized vision of war cherished by those at home. Ask students to speculate why those at home might prefer the version of war Foster expresses.

Enrichment for Advanced Readers

Encourage students to write song lyrics or a poem that Willie might send back to the person who misses him. Suggest that they review Crane's story for details of battle, soldiers' behaviors, important incidents, and the setting of both encampment and battlefield that Willie could mention in his lyrics or poem. Have students think about the variety of ways in which a young soldier might convey his experiences to someone back home who worries for his life and safety. Invite interested students to share their work with the class.

ASSESS

Answers

1. Students may be disturbed by the soldiers' and the doctor's attitude toward the wounded lieutenant or by the amputation itself.
2. (a) A bullet hits his arm as he apportions coffee to various squads of soldiers. (b) Because the lieutenant is wounded while working at a humble task, his wound seems especially unjust.
3. (a) The lieutenant waves him off "mournfully." (b) **Possible answer:** He is already dreading the amputation of his arm.
4. (a) **Possible answer:** He sees the battle as though it were a painting, and he looks at others "with wonder"; the doctor treats the lieutenant with contempt once he realizes that he is injured; the lieutenant tries to downplay the importance of his injury; his empty sleeve is a lifelong reminder of how he is different from other people. (b) These examples suggest that the lieutenant is seen not only as separate from other people, but also as less human than they are.
5. The song is idealized and sentimental; it doesn't portray the hardships that face those left at home.
6. **Possible answer:** The nameless lieutenant symbolizes an unfortunate Everyman, helpless to prevent his injury, to sheathe his own sword, or to avoid amputation. He is wounded by chance and swept toward a fate he is powerless to escape.
7. Students should support their responses with specific reasons and with references to the text.

Go Online Author Link For additional information about Stephen Crane and Stephen Foster, have students type in the Web Code, then select C and F from the alphabet, and then select Stephen Crane and Stephen Foster.

Willie has gone to the war, Willie,
Willie my lov'd one, my own;
Willie has gone to the war, Willie,
Willie my lov'd one is gone!

The leaves of the forest will fade,
The roses will wither and die,
But spring to our home in the glade,
On fairy like pinions[2] will fly;
And still I will hopefully wait
The day when these battles are o'er,
And pine like a bird for its mate,
Till Willie comes home from the war!

Willie has gone to the war, Willie,
Willie my lov'd one, my own;
Willie has gone to the war, Willie,
Willie my lov'd one is gone!

2. **pinions** (pin′ yənz) *n.* antiquated term meaning "wings."

Vocabulary Builder
glade (glād) *n.* open space in a wood or forest

Critical Reading

1. **Respond:** Which aspects of "An Episode of War" did you find particularly tragic or unsettling? Explain.
2. **(a) Recall:** What happens to cause the lieutenant's injury? **(b) Analyze:** How does the manner in which the lieutenant is wounded make him a sympathetic character?
3. **(a) Recall:** Describe the lieutenant's reaction when a soldier offers him a helpful shoulder. **(b) Infer:** What accounts for his mournful detachment?
4. **(a) Recall:** Note three examples of the lieutenant's distance from the uninjured people around him. **(b) Interpret:** What do these examples suggest about the way that he is seen by others, and the way in which he sees himself?
5. **Analyze:** In what ways does "Willie Has Gone to the War" romanticize the monotony and anguish of waiting for a soldier to return from war?
6. **Apply:** According to the Naturalists, humans are weak and ineffectual beings at the mercy of mysterious forces. In what way might this statement apply to "An Episode of War"?
7. **Take a Position:** In your view, is the story—in which no battle is described—more or less frightening than contemporary war movies? Explain.

For: More about Stephen Crane and Stephen Foster
Visit: www.PHSchool.com
Web Code: ere-9401

Apply the Skills

An Episode of War • Willie Has Gone to the War

Literary Analysis

Realism and Naturalism

1. Explain how the lieutenant's rationing coffee at the time of his injury contributes to the quality of **Realism** in "An Episode of War."
2. In what way can the same situation be used to support the assertion that this story is distinctly **Naturalistic**?
3. Give two examples that show how the lieutenant exhibits the quiet, courageous endurance typical of characters in Naturalistic works.
4. Use a chart like the one shown to note two examples each of Realistic and Naturalistic characterization from the story.

Realism	Naturalism

5. Citing examples from the lyrics to support your argument, refute the statement that "Willie Has Gone to the War" reflects Realism.

Comparing Literary Works

6. **(a)** What details in the selections suggest that they were written about the same period of time? **(b)** What details make it seem as if the writers describe different historical events?
7. In your opinion, which selection would be more useful to historians? Explain.

Reading Strategy

Recognizing Historical Details

8. Using your knowledge of Civil War medical practices, why do you think the doctor promises the lieutenant that he will not amputate?
9. What does the lieutenant's struggle to resheath his sword tell you about battle practices of the Civil War?
10. How does the orderly-sergeant's sympathetic attitude to the lieutenant reflect the romantic notions Civil War officers had of their role in the war?

Extend Understanding

11. **Science Connection:** In what ways might a doctor describe the task of caring for the Civil War wounded?

QuickReview

Realism depicts ordinary people coping with everyday realities.

Naturalism focuses on people's helplessness in the face of chance.

To **recognize historical details,** look for elements that indicate the time period, and determine how the attitudes of both writers and characters reflect the ideas of their day.

For: Self-test
Visit: www.PHSchool.com
Web Code: era-6401

Answers

1. Soldiers did not spend all their time in battle; they were often busy with ordinary tasks.
2. It is a random bullet—the type of chance event characteristic of Naturalistic literature—that causes the lieutenant's injury.
3. He submits to the doctor, even when he suspects his worst fear is about to be made real. Later, he downplays the trauma so that his family won't be unduly upset.
4. **Possible responses:**

Realism	Naturalism
Injured soldier smoking a corncob pipe	The men's fearful reaction to the wound

5. The ballad is a sentimental depiction of a woman whose longing for her loved one is reflected in idealized nature. There is no mention of true hardship.
6. **Possible answers:** (a) The story clearly documents The Civil War in the mid-1800s. The romantic language of the song, with words like "lay" and "pinions," suggests a work from that time period. (b) Details from the song include *blue bird, wild bee is roaming at play* and from the story include *winced like a man stung, victim of a terrible disease.*
7. The Crane story would be more useful because it presents a realistic portrait of a few hours in the life of a Union soldier.
8. It was probably the only way for the doctor to get the lieutenant to agree to be treated.
9. **Possible answer:** His struggle indicates that there was a certain formality to one's behavior in battle. It seems that a certain level of decorum was expected of officers.
10. The orderly-sergeant behaves as if the lieutenant's wound is a sign of bravery.
11. A phsician might focus on the risk of infection, the volume of injuries, and the difficulty work in makeshift facilities.

Go Online Assessment Students may use the **Self-test** to prepare for **Selection Test A** or **Selection Test B.**

ASSESS

Answers

❶ Vocabulary Lesson

Word Analysis

congregated; gregarious; aggregate

Vocabulary Builder

1. disdainfully
2. inscrutable
3. glade
4. precipitate
5. aggregation

Spelling Strategy

1. precipitate
2. staid
3. aggregate

❷ Grammar and Style Lesson

1. The lieutenant divided the coffee evenly, just as he promised he would.
2. *Correct*
3. The men stood like stones, frightened as though they had never seen a man wounded in battle.
4. The lieutenant stumbled toward the field hospital like a man in a trance.
5. *Correct*

Writing Application

Students' descriptions should describe a chance event and should use *like, as, as if,* or *as though* correctly at least three times.

WG Writing and Grammar, Ruby Level

Students will find further instruction and practice on usage of *like* and *as* in Chapter 25, Section 2.

Build Language Skills

❶ Vocabulary Lesson

Word Analysis: Latin Root *-greg-*

The word *aggregation* contains the root *-greg-*, meaning "herd" or "flock." An *aggregation* is a group of people or things considered as a whole, while a *congregation* is a group and a *gregarious* person enjoys being part of a crowd.

Copy the paragraph below, filling in each blank with the appropriate -greg- word from the following list.

aggregate gregarious congregated

The wounded soldiers __?__ on the steps, waiting to see the doctor. They were silent, except for one __?__ private who described his injury to everyone. In the __?__, a nearby orderly reflected, wounded men are a quiet bunch, though there is always an exception.

Vocabulary Builder: Analogies

Copy the following analogies, completing each one with the appropriate vocabulary word.

1. *Quickly* is to *rapidly* as __?__ is to *scornfully.*
2. *Hidden* is to *revealed* as __?__ is to *obvious.*
3. *Brook* is to *stream* as __?__ is to *meadow.*
4. *Laugh* is to *cry* as __?__ is to *delay.*
5. *Sum* is to *parts* as __?__ is to *individual.*

Spelling Strategy

The long *a* sound can be spelled *a*-consonant-*e*, as in *glade*, or it can be spelled *ai*, as in *disdain*. In your notebook, complete the spelling of these words.

1. precipit__ 2. st__d 3. aggreg__

❷ Grammar and Style Lesson

Usage: *Like* and *As*

Like and *as, as if,* and *as though* are often used interchangeably, but they actually serve different purposes. ***Like*** is a preposition; it should be followed by a noun, pronoun, or noun phrase—not a verb. ***As, as if,*** and ***as though*** are subordinating conjunctions that introduce clauses. In a comparison, use *as* (not *like*) if what follows contains a verb.

Like: He had winced *like a man stung. . . .* (preposition)

As if: [The lieutenant] looked quickly at a man near him *as if he suspected it was a case of personal assault.* (introduces a clause)

As though: The men regarded him *as though their hearts would break.* (introduces a clause)

Practice Rewrite the following sentences, correcting any errors in the use of *like, as, as if,* or *as though.* Write "correct" for sentences without errors.

1. The lieutenant divided the coffee evenly, just like he promised he would.
2. He staggered as though weak with fatigue.
3. The men stood as stones, frightened like they had never seen a man wounded.
4. The lieutenant stumbled toward the field hospital as if a man in a trance.
5. Like any wounded man, he dwelled on the possibility of amputation.

Writing Application Use *like, as, as if,* or *as though* at least three times in a description of a chance event you experienced.

WG *Prentice Hall Writing and Grammar Connection: Chapter 25, Section 2*

Assessment Practice

Context **(For more practice, see *Standardized Test Preparation Workbook*, p. 26.)**

The reading sections of some tests require students to use context to determine the meaning of figurative language. Remind students that the words surrounding the targeted expression can provide clues to its meaning. Use the following sample test item to demonstrate.

But at this instant the men, the spectators, awoke from their stone-like poses and crowded forward sympathetically.

In this passage, "awoke from their stone-like poses" most nearly means

A got off their stone beds.
B moved suddenly after being still.
C got up to look at statues.
D posed for a sculpture.

The men, referred to as impassive "spectators," were like "stone" until they "awoke" and roused themselves from their stupor. Context clues support *B*.

Writing Lesson

Field Report on Hospital Conditions

Imagine that a Civil War colonel wants to know why so many of his soldiers are dying from minor wounds. As the lieutenant, report to the colonel on the treatment you received and the problems you observed at the army hospital.

Prewriting Review the Background on page 486 and the photographs in the selection to develop a list of issues for your report. Jot down the precise details from the story you will use to support each issue. If necessary, consult a Civil War reference book for more facts.

Drafting State your report's purpose in an introduction. Then, present each issue and supporting details in a separate paragraph. Use precise details. Summarize your main points in the conclusion.

Model: Using Precise Details

We must have better conditions immediately or more men will die. The wounded are often neglected and forced to lie on filthy beds, or even the floor, for hours and even days at a time without being fed, bathed, or treated.

Rather than simply stating that wounded soldiers are neglected, precise details like the ones highlighted provide a complete picture.

Revising Reread your report, checking for logical order and sufficiently precise supporting details. Take steps to improve your organization and strengthen or clarify your writing.

 *Prentice Hall Writing and Grammar Connection: Chapter 6, Section 3*

Extend Your Learning

Listening and Speaking Among the most famous Civil War songs are "Battle Hymn of the Republic" and "Dixie." In a **musical presentation,** provide historic context and a discussion of a Civil War song of your choice.

- Evaluate several songs before choosing one.
- Consider the musical qualities of the song, such as the tempo and the mood.
- Provide background on the song's origins.

Play a recording of the song as part of your presentation. **[Group Activity]**

Research and Technology In the library or on the Internet, research the definition of Naturalism and its presence in literature. Then, write a **definition essay,** defining Naturalism and giving examples of it from "An Episode of War." Be sure to include events in the story that reflect the belief that humankind is helpless in the face of events it cannot control.

For: An additional research activity
Visit: www.PHSchool.com
Web Code: erd-7401

Assessment Resources

Unit 4 Resources
Selection Test A, pp. 18–20
Selection Test B, pp. 21–23

General Resources
Rubrics for Descriptive Essay, pp. 63–64
Rubric for Listening: Evaluating a Media Presentation, p. 86

Go Online Assessment: Students may use the **Self-test** to prepare for **Selection Test A** or **Selection Test B.**

3 Writing Lesson

- To guide students in writing this field report, give them the **Support for Writing Lesson** from ***Unit 4 Resources,*** p. 15.
- Students' field reports should convey a sense of the overall situation facing army hospitals on Civil War battlefields, as well as appropriate details that support each point.
- Remind students to put themselves in the position of the lieutenant, a proper Civil War officer. They must see the relevant medical issues through his eyes and express views about the situation as he might have done.
- Use the Writing Lesson as well as the Descriptive Essay rubrics in ***General Resources,*** pp. 63–64 to guide students in developing their essays.

4 Listening and Speaking

- Point out that the Civil War produced a wealth of songs. Many have been recorded. Two albums that attempt to re-create the music of the Civil War period are the *Original Soundtrack Recording: The Civil War,* produced by Ken Burns and John Colby, and *The Blue and the Gray in Black and White,* by Sparky and Rhonda Rucker.
- Conduct student presentations. Have students introduce their songs and then play or sing them for the class. If they have found more than one version of a song, invite them to play both and discuss which seems most authentic.
- Adapt the Listening: Evaluating a Media Presentation rubric in ***General Resources,*** p. 86 to evaluate students' presentations.
- The **Support for Extend Your Learning** page (***Unit 4 Resources,*** p. 16) provides guided note-taking opportunities to help students complete the Extend Your Learning activities.

Go Online Research: Have students type in the Web Code for another research activity.

Meeting Your Standards

Students will

1. **analyze and respond to literary elements.**
   - Literary Analysis: Refrain
2. **read, comprehend, analyze, and critique song lyrics.**
   - Reading Strategy: Listening
   - Reading Check questions
   - Apply the Skills questions
   - Assessment Practice (ATE)
3. **develop vocabulary.**
   - Vocabulary Lesson: Latin Root: *-press-*
4. **understand and apply written and oral language conventions.**
   - Spelling Strategy
   - Grammar and Style Lesson: Direct Address
5. **develop writing proficiency.**
   - Writing Lesson: Reflective Essay
6. **develop appropriate research strategies.**
   - Extend Your Learning: Anthology
7. **understand and apply listening and speaking strategies.**
   - Extend Your Learning: Choral Reading

Block Scheduling: Use one 90-minute class period to preteach the skills and have students read the selection. Use a second 90-minute class period to assess students' mastery of skills, extend their learning, and monitor their progress.

Homework Suggestions

Following are possibilities for homework assignments.

- Support pages from ***Unit 4 Resources:***
  Literary Analysis
  Reading Strategy
  Vocabulary Builder
  Grammar and Style
- An Extend Your Learning project and the Writing Lesson for this selection group may be completed over several days.

Step-by-Step Teaching Guide	Pacing Guide
PRETEACH	
• Administer Vocabulary and Reading Warm-ups as necessary.	5 min.
• Engage students' interest with the motivation activity.	5 min.
• Read and discuss author and background features. **FT**	10 min.
• Introduce the Literary Analysis Skill: Refrain. **FT**	5 min.
• Introduce the Reading Strategy: Listening. **FT**	10 min.
• Prepare students to read by teaching the selection vocabulary. **FT**	
TEACH	
• Informally monitor comprehension while students read independently or in groups. **FT**	30 min.
• Monitor students' comprehension with the Reading Check notes.	as students read
• Reinforce vocabulary with Vocabulary Builder notes.	as students read
• Develop students' understanding of refrain with the Literary Analysis annotations. **FT**	5 min.
• Develop students' ability to listen with the Reading Strategy annotations. **FT**	5 min.
ASSESS/EXTEND	
• Assess students' comprehension and mastery of the Literary Analysis and Reading Strategy by having them answer the Apply the Skills questions. **FT**	15 min.
• Have students complete the Vocabulary Lesson and the Grammar and Style Lesson. **FT**	15 min.
• Apply students' ability to freewrite to tap personal experiences by using the Writing Lesson. **FT**	45 min. or homework
• Apply students' understanding by using one or more of the Extend Your Learning activities.	20–90 min. or homework
• Administer Selection Test A or Selection Test B. **FT**	15 min.

Resources

PRINT

Unit 4 Resources

- Vocabulary Warm-up Word Lists [**L1, L2, EL**] .... p. 24
- Vocabulary Warm-up Practice [**L1, L2, EL**] .... p. 25
- Reading Warm-up A [**L1, L2, EL**] .... p. 26
- Reading Warm-up B [**L1, L2, L3**] .... p. 27

TRANSPARENCY

Graphic Organizer Transparencies

- Reading Strategy Graphic Organizer A [**L3**] .... pp. 96, 98
- Reading Strategy Graphic Organizer B [**L1, L2, EL**] .... pp. 97, 99

PRINT

Reader's Notebook [L2]
Reader's Notebook: Adapted Version [L1]
Reader's Notebook: English Learner's Version [EL]

Unit 4 Resources

- Literary Analysis [**L3**] .... p. 28
- Reading Strategy [**L3**] .... p. 29
- Vocabulary Builder [**L3**] .... p. 30

TECHNOLOGY

Listening to Literature Audio CDs [L2, EL]

PRINT

Unit 4 Resources

- Grammar and Style [**L3**] .... p. 31
- Support for Writing Lesson [**L3**] .... p. 32
- Support for Extend Your Learning [**L3**] .... p. 33
- Enrichment [**L4**] .... p. 34
- Selection Test A [**L1, L2, EL**] .... pp. 35–37
- Selection Test B [**L3, L4**] .... pp. 38–40

General Resources

Rubrics for Reflective Essay [**L3**] .... pp. 47–48

TECHNOLOGY

Go Online: Research [**L3**]
Go Online: Self-test [**L3**]
***ExamView®*, Test Bank [L3]**

Choosing Resources for Differentiated Instruction

[**L1**] Special Needs Students
[**L2**] Below-Level Students
[**L3**] All Students
[**L4**] Advanced Students
[**EL**] English Learners

FT Fast Track Instruction: To move the lesson more quickly, use the strategies and activities identified with **FT**.

Scaffolding for Less Proficient and Advanced Students

The leveled Critical Thinking questions after selections progress in the levels of thinking required to answer them. To address the needs of your different students, you may use the (a) level questions for your less proficient students and the (b) level questions with your on-level and advanced students. The occasional (c) level questions are appropriate for your advanced students.

Use this complete suite of powerful teaching tools to make lesson planning and testing quicker and easier.

PRENTICE HALL
StudentEXPRESS™
Learn · Study · Succeed

Use the interactive textbook (online and on CD-ROM) to make selections and activities come alive with audio and video support and interactive questions.

Motivation

The best way to engage students' interest in the spirituals is by having them listen to the songs. Play "Go Down, Moses" and "Swing Low, Sweet Chariot" on the **Listening to Literature Audio CDs.** As students listen, have them focus more on the sound of the spirituals than on the meanings of the lyrics. Follow with a discussion in which you help students explore why spirituals have remained popular for so long. With whom are they most likely to be popular? Why? Why have spirituals been so strong an influence on other types of music? After you've completed the discussion, have students read the texts of the spirituals.

❶ Background

More About the Literature

Cultural historian Bernice Johnson Reagon writes, "Spirituals were songs created as leverage, as salve, as voice, as a bridge over troubles one could not endure without the flight of song and singing. . . . [They] record the struggle of a people to survive, but like no other histories, have the power to touch the soul and stir the emotions of the people who sing and hear them."

❶ Swing Low, Sweet Chariot • Go Down, Moses

Spirituals

Spirituals are folk songs that originated among enslaved and oppressed African Americans. They are one of the earliest and most widely known forms of American folk song to have survived to the twenty-first century. Spirituals took on the forms of anthems, ballads, shouts, and jubilees to reflect different moods and circumstances. Containing both social and religious content, spirituals helped to shape the conscious identity of an enslaved people; they also helped slaves persevere under the physical and psychological pressures of their daily life. These songs conveyed the singers' pain, their yearning for freedom, and their rage against slavery. In doing so, they brought to life the emotional impact of slavery, which divided our nation for decades and played a key role in causing the Civil War. Frederick Douglass, a slave who became one of the most important writers of his time, said of the spirituals, "Every tone was a testimony against slavery and a prayer to God for deliverance from chains." At the same time, the songs helped to replace lost African religious traditions and allowed men and women to maintain a connection to their musical heritage.

Song of the Fields Plantation owners, fearing discontent among their slaves, encouraged field hands to sing while they picked cotton or sugar, reasoning that people who were busy singing could not plot escape or rebellion. They generally accepted spirituals because the songs had religious content. The slaves, however, found ways to benefit from singing. Their songs provided an outlet for the grief and frustration they often kept bottled up inside. Spirituals also fostered a sense of personal self-worth by portraying slaves as innocents of a mighty God, deserving of a heavenly reward for their earthly labors. By grafting their memories of traditional African music and rhythms onto religious hymns of early nineteenth-century Christian revivalists, enslaved Africans managed to hold on to part of their heritage. In addition, the language in some songs provided a means to communicate forbidden thoughts and feelings.

A Double Message Many spirituals had a double meaning. Most included references to people, places, or events in the Bible. They frequently referred to Moses, who in the Old Testament led the Jews out of slavery in Egypt. Slaves identified with the ancient Israelites, who had once been the slaves of the Egyptians. Singing about the Israelites was a safe way to voice their own yearning for liberty. For example, in spirituals such as "Swing Low, Sweet Chariot" and "Go Down, Moses," slaves expressed their hope that they would someday escape to their own "promised land," just as the Israelites escaped to ancient Israel. References to figures and events in the Bible thus became a kind of code for the slaves' own experience. One work song did more than just express discontent; it gave directions for escape: In "Follow the Drinking Gourd," fugitive slaves were advised to follow the Big Dipper north to freedom.

Path to Popularity Spirituals were almost unknown outside the South until after the Civil War. In 1867, a collection of African American music called *Slave Songs of the United States* was published. In 1871, a black choral group, the Jubilee Singers from Fisk University, traveled throughout the United States and to England and Germany singing spirituals to raise money for their school. The Jubilee Singers were extremely gifted, and became highly successful, even singing for Queen Victoria in England. Students from other schools followed their example and helped popularize the spiritual. Today, spirituals are performed by gospel singers, and their influence is apparent in contemporary music forms such as blues and jazz.

Preview

Connecting to the Literature

Songs have an amazing power to sway our emotions. They can soothe us when we are feeling sad or bring back special memories. As these two spirituals demonstrate, songs can even help people endure great hardships. As you read, think about a song that had a strong emotional impact on you.

2 Literary Analysis

Refrain

If you are searching for the meaning of a song or poem, you will often find it in the **refrain**—a word, phrase, line, or group of lines repeated at regular intervals throughout the work. Refrains serve these key functions:

- They emphasize the most important ideas.
- They help establish the rhythm of the song.

Most spirituals contain at least one refrain. For example, the line "Coming for to carry me home" is repeated throughout "Swing Low, Sweet Chariot." As you read these songs, think about the message each refrain conveys.

Comparing Literary Works

Most spirituals were not meant to be sung alone. Instead, the refrain facilitated a call-and-response format in which a leader sang the verses and the rest of the group acted like a chorus and sang the refrain. Each song produced a different mood or feeling within the group: some songs focused more on the pain or rage caused by the conditions of slavery, while other songs looked hopefully toward the future. Compare the mood of these two songs and imagine how you might feel as you sang or heard them.

3 Reading Strategy

Listening

Since songs are created for the ear and not the eye, **listening** is an especially important skill for appreciating lyrics.

- Read each spiritual aloud, listening to its rhythm.
- Pay attention to rhymes and other repeated sounds. For example, the opening line in "Go Down, Moses" contains three stressed syllables in a row.

Often, the rhythms and sounds of a song suggest a specific mood. As you read these spirituals, think about the different moods and effects that the sounds of the songs create. Record some of these effects in a chart like the one shown.

Song Text
Go down, Moses, Way down in Egypt land Tell old Pharoah To let my people go

↓

Mood Conveyed

Vocabulary Builder

oppressed (ə prest′) *v.* kept down by cruel or unjust power (p. 500)

smite (smīt) *v.* to kill by a powerful blow (p. 500)

Differentiated Instruction Solutions for All Learners

Support for Special Needs Students
Have students complete the **Preview** and **Build Skills** pages for these selections in the ***Reader's Notebook: Adapted Version.*** These pages provide a selection summary, an abbreviated presentation of the reading and literary skills, and the graphic organizer on the **Build Skills** page in the student book.

Support for Less Proficient Readers
Have students complete the **Preview** and **Build Skills** pages for these selections in the ***Reader's Notebook.*** These pages provide a selection summary, an abbreviated presentation of the reading and literary skills, and the graphic organizer on the **Build Skills** page in the student book.

Support for English Learners
Have students complete the **Preview** and **Build Skills** pages for these selections in the ***Reader's Notebook: English Learner's Version.*** These pages provide a selection summary, an abbreviated presentation of the skills, additional contextual vocabulary, and the graphic organizer on the **Build Skills** page in the student book.

2 Literary Analysis

Refrain

- Explain that students will focus on refrains as they study the two songs in this grouping.
- Invite students to draw on their prior knowledge of music to explain what they know about refrains. Many students may be familiar with the refrain's primary defining characteristic: the repetition of words, phrases, or lines at regular intervals.
- Encourage students to think of examples of songs they know that contain memorable refrains. Have students review the lyrics of the songs to see how the refrain emphasizes or complements each song's most important ideas.

3 Reading Strategy

Listening

- Give students a copy of **Reading Strategy Graphic Organizer A** from the ***Graphic Organizer Transparencies,*** p. 96, to use as they read these selections.
- Point out to students that all language contains rhythm. Good songwriters link a song's melody with the inherent rhythms of the lyrics.
- Thus, students should understand that rhythm in songs is not limited to the melody or instrumental passages. Students can hear rhythm in the language of the lyrics, as well.
- Explain that listening is a skill that is often taken for granted. Encourage students to reflect on how their own experiences prove the profound difference between close and distracted listening.

Vocabulary Builder

- Pronounce each vocabulary word for students, and read the definitions as a class. Have students identify any words with which they are already familiar.

TEACH

Learning Modalities
Musical/Rhythmic Learners
Invite students to look for ways in which today's rhythm and blues, gospel, jazz, or hip-hop music reflects the influence of spirituals. Challenge them to identify specific musical elements that are common to all these styles.

❶ About the Selection

This spiritual, constructed around the refrain "Coming for to carry me home," expresses both a desire for eternal salvation in heaven and a longing for freedom from slavery. The "sweet chariot" and the "band of angels" are symbols for the Underground Railroad. This song is based on an Old Testament story in which the prophet Elijah is taken to heaven in a fiery chariot.

❷ Critical Viewing

Answer: One can infer that fugitive slaves had difficult lives and few material possessions.

❸ Background

Spirituals

In his autobiography, former slave Frederick Douglass discusses why enslaved Africans sang spirituals as they worked: "Slaves are generally expected to sing as well as to work. A silent slave is not liked by masters or overseers. . . . The remark is not unfrequently made, that slaves are the most contented and happy laborers in the world. They dance and sing, and make all manner of joyful noise—so they do; but it is a great mistake to suppose them happy because they sing. The songs of the slave represent the sorrows rather than the joys, of his heart; and he is relieved by them, only as an aching heart is relieved by its tears."

❶ Swing Low, Sweet Chariot

Spiritual

❷ ▲ Critical Viewing
Looking at the people in this photograph, what can you infer about their lives? **[Infer]**

Background Africans first came to this country as slaves in 1619. Although the slave trade was banned in 1808, slavery remained legal. In response to slave rebellions of the 1820s and 1830s, many southern states enacted tough new laws that deprived slaves of nearly all their rights. In the years before the Civil War, many enslaved Africans fled captivity. They were hidden and transported by the Underground Railroad, a secret network of ❸ activists dedicated to helping fugitives reach freedom in the North and in Canada.

One of those activists was Harriet Tubman, who was born a slave around 1820. Tubman was called the Moses of her people. In the Bible, Moses led the Israelites out of captivity in Egypt. Following Moses' example, Tubman escaped along the Underground Railroad and then risked her life to return for her family. Driven by the desire to help others still oppressed, she returned to the South again and again to rescue other enslaved Africans, eventually leading more than 300 people to freedom.

Differentiated Instruction Solutions for All Learners

Accessibility at a Glance

	"Swing Low, Sweet Chariot"	"Go Down, Moses"
Context	Song of slavery	Song of slavery
Language	Poetic diction/allegory	Poetic diction/allegory
Concept Level	Accessible (allegory)	Accessible (allegory)
Literary Merit	Spiritual	Spiritual
Lexile	NP	NP
Overall Rating	More accessible	Average

Swing low, sweet chariot,
Coming for to carry me home,
Swing low, sweet chariot,
Coming for to carry me home.

I looked over Jordan[1] and what did I see
Coming for to carry me home,
A band of angels coming after me,
Coming for to carry me home.

4

If you get there before I do,
Coming for to carry me home,
Tell all my friends I'm coming too,
Coming for to carry me home.

Swing low, sweet chariot,
Coming for to carry me home,
Swing low, sweet chariot,
Coming for to carry me home.

Literary Analysis
Refrain In what ways does the song's refrain emphasize the speaker's yearning?

1. **Jordan** river of the Near East that flows from the Lebanon Mountains through the Sea of Galilee to the Dead Sea. Many spirituals use the phrase "crossing over Jordan" as a metaphor for crossing the Ohio River to freedom or going to heaven.

Critical Reading

1. **Respond:** What mood did this spiritual evoke in you? Explain.
2. **(a) Recall:** Where does the speaker want to go? **(b) Infer:** What do you think this place represents?
3. **(a) Recall:** In what vehicle will the speaker travel "home"? **(b) Interpret:** What do you think this vehicle represents?
4. **(a) Recall:** Who is coming over Jordan to carry the speaker home? **(b) Interpret:** If the song is an expression of the slaves' desire for escape, what do these figures represent?
5. **Interpret:** Knowing that spirituals were often "code" songs for escape, do you think there are any hidden messages in this song? Explain.
6. **Apply:** In what ways do you think such a song could offer comfort to the slaves?

4 Literary Analysis
Refrain

- Have students participate in a choral reading of "Swing Low, Sweet Chariot."

Monitor Progress: Ask students the Literary Analysis question: How does the song's refrain emphasize the speaker's yearning?
Answer: The repetition emphasizes the steady hope or belief that release will come—either through literal freedom or through death and an afterlife in heaven.

ASSESS
Answers

1. Students should be specific about the mood the song evoked in them.
2. (a) The speaker wants to go "home." (b) *Home* represents either heaven or a place where African Americans are no longer enslaved.
3. (a) The speaker will be carried in a chariot. (b) This vehicle may represent death or the Underground Railroad.
4. (a) "A band of angels" is coming across the Jordan River to carry the speaker home. (b) The angels might be abolitionists or those helping fugitives on the Underground Railroad.
5. This song seems to contain secret messages about the Underground Railroad's helping slaves escape to freedom.
6. The song offers the hope of freedom and reunion with friends.

Differentiated Instruction
Solutions for All Learners

Vocabulary for Special Needs Students
You may wish to clarify for students a few examples of vocabulary and usage in the spirituals. For instance, students may be confused by the antiquated phrase *coming for;* explain that the phrase means simply "coming." You might point out that—in this context—a *band* is "a group of people joined together for a common purpose" and that the archaic verb *saith* means "says."

Enrichment for Gifted/Talented Students
Moses does not just "tell old Pharaoh" to let his people go; he threatens that the Lord will "smite" Pharaoh's first-born child. Can nonviolent methods be used to end oppression, or is violence an inevitable result? What are the moral choices inherent in a struggle against oppression? Challenge students to debate these issues, using their knowledge of oppression in any historical period.

5 About the Selection

These lyrics refer to the biblical account of Moses leading the Hebrews out of bondage. In this song, the Pharaoh is a metaphor for any slaveholder; the Israelites are the slaves; Moses is a redeemer or savior; and Egypt represents the American South.

6 Literary Analysis

Refrain

- Have students listen to the spiritual as it is read aloud.

Monitor Progress: **Ask** students to identify the refrain and to explain how they can recognize it.
Answer: The refrain is found in the first four lines, and again in lines 8–12 and 16–20. This is the refrain because it is the part that repeats.

7 Vocabulary Builder

Latin Root *-press-*

- Draw students' attention to the use of the word *oppressed,* and read its definition. Then, tell students that the root *-press-* derives from the Latin word *premere* meaning "to press."
- In small groups, have students **brainstorm** for a list of other words that share the root *-press-*. As each group reports its list, write the words on the chalkboard.
Possible responses: *pressure, suppress, repress, impress*

ASSESS

Answers

1. Students should support their answers with details.
2. (a) The people of Israel are oppressed. (b) The two groups share the experience of slavery.
3. (a) He will destroy their "first-born." (b) enslaved African Americans
4. (a) Moses issues his demand to Pharaoh. (b) Pharaoh represents slave owners.
5. The song uses both informal language, such as *Way down in Egypt land,* and formal language, such as *smite.* Students may find this an effective way to differentiate between the voice of the speaker and that of Moses.

5 GO DOWN, MOSES

SPIRITUAL

Go down, Moses,
Way down in Egypt land
Tell old Pharaoh
To let my people go.

When Israel was in Egypt land
Let my people go
Oppressed so hard they could not stand
Let my people go.

Go down, Moses,
Way down in Egypt land
Tell old Pharaoh
"Let my people go."

"Thus saith the Lord," bold Moses said,
"Let my people go;
If not I'll smite your first-born dead
Let my people go."

Go down, Moses,
Way down in Egypt land,
Tell old Pharaoh,
"Let my people go!"

Vocabulary Builder
oppressed (ə prest′) *v.* kept down by cruel or unjust power

Vocabulary Builder
smite (smīt) *v.* to kill by a powerful blow

Critical Reading

1. **Respond:** What emotions does this song most strongly convey to you? Explain.
2. **(a) Recall:** Who is oppressed in this song? **(b) Connect:** What connection might these oppressed people have with the slaves?
3. **(a) Recall:** With what punishment does the Lord threaten the Egyptians if they refuse to free the Israelites? **(b) Interpret:** Whom do the Israelites represent?
4. **(a) Recall:** Whom does Moses tell to "let my people go"? **(b) Interpret:** If this song is related to the slaves, whom might this figure represent?
5. **Evaluate:** Explain the effectiveness of the mix of formal and informal language in "Go Down, Moses."

Apply the Skills

Swing Low, Sweet Chariot • *Go Down, Moses*

Literary Analysis

Refrain

1. What **refrains,** both lines and entire stanzas, are used in "Swing Low, Sweet Chariot"?
2. List the refrains, both lines and entire stanzas, used in "Go Down, Moses."
3. What idea or message is emphasized through the single-line refrain in "Go Down, Moses"?

Comparing Literary Works

4. In each **spiritual,** which lines might have been sung by a soloist and which by the chorus? Explain.
5. **(a)** What symbolic words do you note in each of the spirituals? **(b)** What do you think the symbols represent?
6. How might these spirituals soothe the feelings of longing, sadness, and injustice they express?
7. Compare the moods of these two spirituals.

Reading Strategy

Listening

8. Explain how each of the songs uses rhythm, rhyme, and repetition to reinforce meaning.
9. Using the sound elements you identified in both songs, compare the musical qualities of "Go Down, Moses" with those of "Swing Low, Sweet Chariot." Record your ideas in a chart like the one shown.

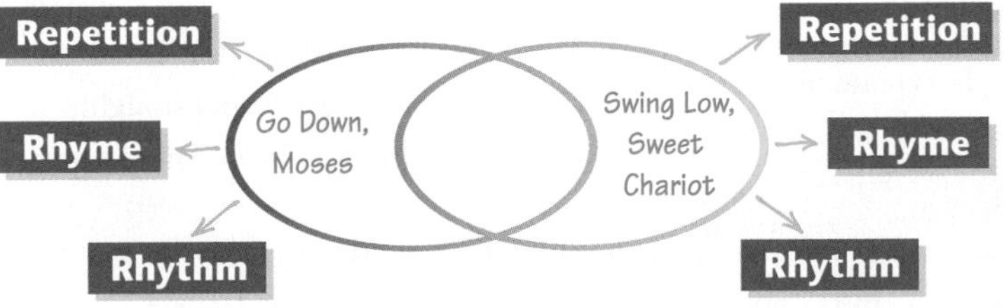

Extend Understanding

10. **Social Studies Connection:** Harriet Tubman once said, "We got to be free or die. And freedom's not bought with dust." What other American heroes would agree with her words? Explain your choices.

QuickReview

The **refrain** is a word, phrase, line, or group of lines repeated at regular intervals in a poem or song.

Spirituals are folk songs developed by enslaved Africans that often feature Biblical references and a call-and-response format.

Listening to a song's rhyme, rhythm, and repetition helps you appreciate its message and mood.

For: Self-test
Visit: www.PHSchool.com
Web Code: era-6402

Go Online Assessment Students may use the **Self-test** to prepare for **Selection Test A** or **Selection Test B.**

Answers

1. The entire first stanza is a refrain that appears twice in "Swing Low, Sweet Chariot." The line "Coming for to carry me home" is also used as a refrain.
2. The entire first stanza is a refrain that appears three times in the song. The line "let my people go" is also a refrain.
3. The refrain "let my people go" expresses the slaves' desire for freedom. This is the main idea of the song.
4. The soloist would probably sing the verses, which tell the story. The refrains would be sung by a chorus to reinforce the theme of the song.
5. (a) Students may mention words such as *chariot, home, Jordan, band of angels,* and all of the proper nouns in "Go Down, Moses." (b) The chariot represents the Underground Railroad; home represents freedom; Jordan represents the Ohio River; the band of angels represents conductors on the Underground Railroad; the Pharaoh and Egyptians represent slave owners; Egypt represents the United States of America; the Israelites represent enslaved African Americans.
6. The songs offer the hope of freedom.
7. "Go Down, Moses" is dignified and determined in mood, while "Swing Low" is calmer and more melancholy.
8. **Possible response:** In both songs, the refrain, which is repeated many times, clearly states the theme. Rhyme is used to frame the refrains and to reinforce the meaning of the other lines. The rhythms support the messages by drawing readers into the songs.
9. Both spirituals repeat single lines and entire stanzas; both use end rhymes extensively; both feature strong, regular rhythms. The rhythm of "Swing Low" is smoother and gentler.
10. Students might mention Martin Luther King Jr., or Abraham Lincoln, because both held strong beliefs in freedom and equality.

EXTEND/ASSESS

Answers

❶ Vocabulary Lesson

Word Analysis

1. impress
2. compress
3. depress
4. repress

Vocabulary Builder

1. b
2. c

Spelling Strategy

1. c, *installed*
2. b, *bossed*
3. a, *possessed*

❷ Grammar and Style Lesson

1. Selena, sing slowly and with great feeling.
2. The choir performed well, Ms. Dodd.
3. Choir members, please stand straight.
4. Everyone agrees, Joe, that you have a great voice.
5. Still, Mr. Jones, I'd rather play the guitar.

Writing Application

Students' sentences should discuss a particular musical genre, and each one should contain a correctly punctuated example of direct address.

WG Writing and Grammar, Ruby Level

Students will find further instruction and practice on Direct Address in Chapter 27, Section 2.

Build Language Skills

❶ Vocabulary Lesson

Word Analysis: Latin Root *-press-*

The root *-press-* means "push." People who are *oppressed* are pushed or kept down. Copy each sentence, completing each blank with an appropriate word formed with the root *-press-* and one of the prefixes defined below.

com- (together) *re-* (back)
de- (down) *im-* (into)

1. __?__ the metal seal on the hot wax to make your mark.
2. Watch as I __?__ the paper into a tight ball.
3. When you __?__ the button, a buzzer sounds.
4. The enthusiastic fans weren't able to __?__ their squeals.

Vocabulary Builder: Antonyms

Select the word that is the closest antonym, or opposite, of the first word.

1. oppressed: **(a)** crushed, **(b)** assisted, **(c)** punished
2. smite: **(a)** hit, **(b)** question, **(c)** caress

Spelling Strategy

When adding *-ed* to a word ending in a double consonant, keep both consonants, as in *oppress + ed = oppressed.* Match the correct word for each definition given below, adding *-ed* to each word to form a new word.

1. fixed in position — **a.** possess
2. ordered — **b.** boss
3. owned — **c.** install

❷ Grammar and Style Lesson

Direct Address

In both these spirituals, the speaker uses **direct address** by speaking directly to someone or something by name.

When you use direct address, put a comma after the name if it comes first in the sentence, before the name if it comes last in the sentence, and on both sides of the name if it comes in the middle of the sentence.

Examples: Swing low, *sweet chariot,*
Coming for to carry me home.
Go down, *Moses,*
Way down in Egypt land.
Lord, hear our prayer.

Practice Copy these sentences in your notebook. Underline the words of direct address and add punctuation where necessary.

1. Selena sing slowly and with great feeling.
2. The choir performed well Ms. Dodd.
3. Choir members please stand straight.
4. Everyone agrees Joe that you have a great voice.
5. Still Mr. Jones I'd rather play the guitar.

Writing Application Write three sentences or questions related to your interest in music. Include direct address, with correct punctuation, in each sentence.

WG *Prentice Hall Writing and Grammar Connection: Chapter 27, Section 2*

Assessment Practice

Context Clues **(For more practice, see *Standardized Test Preparation Workbook*, p. 27.)**

Many tests require students to use context clues to determine the meaning of unfamiliar words. Use the following sample test item to give students practice in this skill.

. . . bold Moses said,
"Let my people go;
If not I'll smite your first-born dead
Let my people go."

In this passage, smite most nearly means—

A build **C** cure
B strike **D** affect

From the context of this passage, students should be able to determine that *smite* means a violent, destructive action. Even if they are not certain of the meaning of *strike,* students should recognize that none of the other choices fits this definition. Guide students to recognize that *B* is the correct answer.

Writing Lesson

Reflective Essay

Imagine that you are a free person living in the South before the Civil War. You hear these spirituals, and for the first time, truly pay attention to the lyrics. In a reflective essay, analyze what the songs have taught you about the realities of slavery.

Prewriting Freewrite about the songs by writing quickly and continuously for five minutes. Review your notes to choose a few ideas to explore.

Model: Freewriting to Tap Personal Experiences

I think "Go Down, Moses" expresses several emotions—pride, anger, sorrow, yearning. . . . That refrain, "Let my people go," really sums it up. Someone else is keeping me and my people from freedom. Let my people go. I can hardly imagine having to live my life like that . . .

To capture ideas, freewriting relaxes the rules of grammar. Errors can be edited later.

Drafting In your introduction, summarize the songs. Then, in the body of your essay, discuss the insights the songs have revealed to you.

Revising A reflective essay should indicate the significance of an experience. Review your draft. If necessary, add more information to show what the songs mean to you, or how they might change your life.

WG *Prentice Hall Writing and Grammar Connection: Chapter 4, Section 2*

Extend Your Learning

Listening and Speaking With a small group, conduct a **choral reading** of a spiritual. Use a call-and-response format, with one student calling out the verses and the rest answering with the refrains. Each "soloist" should improvise to create at least one new verse. Use these tips to prepare:

- Determine who will say which lines.
- Memorize your lines.
- Emphasize the call-and-response format.

After you have practiced, perform the spiritual for your class. **[Group Activity]**

Research and Technology Using the Internet or other library resources, find several other spirituals to present in an **anthology.** For each song you include, write a brief introduction that provides background information or necessary context for readers.

For: An additional research activity
Visit: www.PHSchool.com
Web Code: erd-7402

3 Writing Lesson

- To guide students in writing this Reflective Essay, give them the **Support for Writing Lesson** from ***Unit 4 Resources,*** p. 32.
- Students' reflective essays should express the personal significance of their listening to the spirituals. They should also include details about the experience of slavery that helped students come to a new understanding of the topic.
- Suggest that students do their freewriting as they listen to the recordings of the spirituals on the **Listening to Literature Audio CDs.**
- Use the Reflective Essay rubrics in ***General Resources,*** pp. 47–48 to evaluate students' reflective essays.

4 Research and Technology

- Students might find examples of spirituals in a variety of forms, including audio recordings, sheet music, poetry anthologies, and nonfiction and reference books.
- Remind students to review each of the spirituals they select for words, idioms and other unusual syntax, and historical allusions. Any such elements will need to be illuminated in students' introductory passages.
- The **Support for Extend Your Learning** page (***Unit 4 Resources,*** p. 33) provides guided note-taking opportunities to help students complete the Extend Your Learning activities.

Go Online Research Have students type in the Web Code for another research activity.

Assessment Resources

Unit 4 Resources
Selection Test A, pp. 35–37
Selection Test B, pp. 38–40

General Resources
Rubrics for Reflective Essay, pp. 47–48

Go Online Assessment Students may use the **Self-test** to prepare for **Selection Test A** or **Selection Test B.**

Meeting Your Standards

Students will

1. **analyze and respond to literary elements.**
   - Literary Analysis: Autobiography
2. **read, comprehend, analyze, and critique nonfiction.**
   - Reading Strategy: Establishing a Purpose
   - Reading Check questions
   - Apply the Skills questions
   - Assessment Practice (ATE)
3. **develop vocabulary.**
   - Vocabulary Lesson: Latin Root: *-bene-*
4. **understand and apply written and oral language conventions.**
   - Spelling Strategy
   - Grammar and Style Lesson: Correlative Conjunctions
5. **develop writing proficiency.**
   - Writing Lesson: College Admission Essay
6. **develop appropriate research strategies.**
   - Extend Your Learning: Multimedia Presentation
7. **understand and apply listening and speaking strategies.**
   - Extend Your Learning: Oral Presentation

Block Scheduling: Use one 90-minute class period to preteach the skills and have students read the selection. Use a second 90-minute class period to assess students' mastery of skills, extend their learning, and monitor their progress.

Homework Suggestions

Following are possibilities for homework assignments.

- Support pages from *Unit 4 Resources:*
  Literary Analysis
  Reading Strategy
  Vocabulary Builder
  Grammar and Style
- An Extend Your Learning project and the Writing Lesson for this selection may be completed over several days.

Step-by-Step Teaching Guide	Pacing Guide
PRETEACH	
• Administer Vocabulary and Reading Warm-ups as necessary.	5 min.
• Engage students' interest with the motivation activity.	5 min.
• Read and discuss author and background features. **FT**	10 min.
• Introduce the Literary Analysis Skill: Autobiography. **FT**	5 min.
• Introduce the Reading Strategy: Establishing a Purpose. **FT**	10 min.
• Prepare students to read by teaching the selection vocabulary. **FT**	
TEACH	
• Informally monitor comprehension while students read independently or in groups. **FT**	30 min.
• Monitor students' comprehension with the Reading Check notes.	as students read
• Reinforce vocabulary with Vocabulary Builder notes.	as students read
• Develop students' understanding of an autobiography with the Literary Analysis annotations. **FT**	5 min.
• Develop students' ability to establish a purpose with the Reading Strategy annotations. **FT**	5 min.
ASSESS/EXTEND	
• Assess students' comprehension and mastery of the Literary Analysis and Reading Strategy by having them answer the Apply the Skills questions. **FT**	15 min.
• Have students complete the Vocabulary Lesson and the Grammar and Style Lesson. **FT**	15 min.
• Apply students' ability to plan clear and logical organization by using the Writing Lesson. **FT**	45 min. or homework
• Apply students' understanding by using one or more of the Extend Your Learning activities.	20–90 min. or homework
• Administer Selection Test A or Selection Test B. **FT**	15 min.

Resources

PRINT

Unit 4 Resources

TRANSPARENCY

Graphic Organizer Transparencies

PRINT

Reader's Notebook [L2]
Reader's Notebook: Adapted Version [L1]
Reader's Notebook: English Learner's Version [EL]

Unit 4 Resources

TECHNOLOGY

Listening to Literature Audio CDs [L2, EL]
Reader's Notebook: Adapted Version Audio CD [L1, L2]

PRINT

Unit 4 Resources

General Resources

TECHNOLOGY

Go Online: Research [**L3**]
Go Online: Self-test [**L3**]
***ExamView*®, Test Bank** [**L3**]

Choosing Resources for Differentiated Instruction

[**L1**] Special Needs Students
[**L2**] Below-Level Students
[**L3**] All Students
[**L4**] Advanced Students
[**EL**] English Learners

FT Fast Track Instruction: To move the lesson more quickly, use the strategies and activities identified with **FT**.

Scaffolding for Less Proficient and Advanced Students

The leveled Critical Thinking questions after selections progress in the levels of thinking required to answer them. To address the needs of your different students, you may use the (a) level questions for your less proficient students and the (b) level questions with your on-level and advanced students. The occasional (c) level questions are appropriate for your advanced students.

PRENTICE HALL **TeacherEXPRESS**™ Plan · Teach · Assess Use this complete suite of powerful teaching tools to make lesson planning and testing quicker and easier.

PRENTICE HALL **StudentEXPRESS**™ Learn · Study · Succeed Use the interactive textbook (online and on CD-ROM) to make selections and activities come alive with audio and video support and interactive questions.

PRETEACH

Motivation

Engage students' interest by sharing an idea of Douglass's that is seemingly paradoxical: both slaves and slaveholders were victims of slavery. Have students react to this idea and consider questions such as, how can slaveholders be perceived as victims of a system from which they benefit? Invite students to speculate about what evidence Douglass might offer to support his point. Then, have them read the selection to find out. When they've finished reading, conduct a follow-up discussion in which students explain whether their views have been changed in any way by Douglass's argument.

1 Background

More About the Author

Frederick Bailey was born on the Eastern Shore of Maryland, on land facing west toward Chesapeake Bay. His first owner was Aaron Anthony, who worked for the wealthy planter Edward Lloyd. Before his years with Sophie and Hugh Auld in Baltimore, Frederick lived on Lloyd's plantation. At fifteen, Douglass was sent to St. Michaels on the Eastern Shore to work for Thomas Auld. There, he was hired out as a laborer to a number of farmers, and there, he attempted to escape his bondage for the first time. At twenty, Frederick Bailey took the name Frederick Douglass.

Build Skills *Autobiography*

1 *from* My Bondage and My Freedom

Frederick Douglass (1818–1895)

Frederick Douglass rose out of slavery to become one of the most gifted writers and orators of his time. Using these talents, he dedicated his life to fighting for the abolition of slavery and for civil rights. Douglass's life served as an inspiration and example for both blacks and whites throughout the country.

Early Years Douglass was born on a Maryland plantation. Historians believe that his name at birth was Frederick Augustus Bailey. At the age of eight, he was sent as a slave to the Baltimore home of the Auld family. While there, Douglass learned to read and write, at first with the strong encouragement of Mrs. Auld and later despite her objections. Learning soon became an unquenchable thirst for Douglass. He often traded biscuits for reading lessons from his playmates.

His reading fueled a quest for freedom. At age twenty, he escaped to Massachusetts, a free state, and took the surname Douglass to avoid arrest as a fugitive.

A Public Life Although he had never spoken in public before, Douglass delivered a tremendously powerful and moving debut speech at the 1841 convention of an abolitionist organization. Despite the constant fear of being arrested as a fugitive slave, he spent the next four years lecturing against slavery and arguing for the need for civil rights for all people.

Rumors spread that a man of such eloquence could not possibly have been a slave. In response, Douglass published his first autobiography, *Narrative of the Life of Frederick Douglass, an American Slave, Written By Himself* (1845). Fearing that the book would lead to his re-enslavement, Douglass then fled to England, where he spent years trying to gain British support for the abolitionist movement in the United States.

Freedom at Last After English friends raised money to buy his freedom, Douglass returned to the United States, established a newspaper for African Americans, and resumed lecturing. In 1855, he published *My Bondage and My Freedom,* an updated version of his autobiography.

During the Civil War, Douglass helped recruit African American soldiers for the Union army. After slavery was abolished, he fought vigorously for civil rights for African Americans. He became a consultant to President Lincoln and held several government positions, including United States minister to Haiti.

A Vision for the Future As an abolitionist, orator, and journalist, Douglass favored political methods for emancipating the slaves and bringing them into the mainstream of American life—a goal he was determined they should reach. In 1883, speaking as a vigorous fighter for civil rights, Douglass commented that the American people "must learn, or neglect to do so at their own peril. . . . The American people must stand each for all and all for each, without respect to color or race. . . . I expect to see the colored people of this country enjoying the same freedom, voting at the same ballot-box, using the same cartridge-box, going to the same schools, attending the same churches, . . . proud of the same country, fighting the same foe, and enjoying the same peace and all its advantages. . . ."

Douglass did not limit himself to fighting for the civil rights of African Americans. He also helped women in their battle to win the vote. Because he did not segregate his causes, Douglass is a model for all who struggle against injustice.

Preview

Connecting to the Literature

Imagine another person denying your right to read just as you were discovering the power of learning. If you were enslaved like Frederick Douglass, you would have no choice but to submit (or at least appear to submit) to your owner's wishes.

Literary Analysis

Autobiography

An **autobiography** is a person's written account of his or her own life, focusing on the events the author considers most significant. Because the writer's life is presented as he or she views it, the portrayal of people and events is colored by the author's feelings and beliefs. Usually, writers of autobiographies believe that their lives are interesting or important and can in some way help others. Frederick Douglass wrote his autobiography because he believed that his life proved that blacks were no less perceptive, intelligent, or capable than whites, as he states directly in these lines:

> I could talk and sing; I could laugh and weep; I could reason and remember . . .

As you read about the experiences that shaped Douglass's life, notice how they might serve as examples for others.

Connecting Literary Elements

When reading autobiographies, you can usually detect a clear **tone**—the writer's attitude toward the subject, characters, or audience. Tone is created through a choice of words and details. It may be formal or informal, friendly or distant. As you read, listen for Douglass's tone just as you would if he were speaking to you aloud.

Reading Strategy

Establishing a Purpose

Establishing a purpose for reading gives you an idea or concept on which to focus. For example, as you read from Douglass's autobiography, establish the purpose of learning about his special qualities and expanding your understanding of what it was like to be a slave. Record details that reflect this purpose in a chart like the one shown.

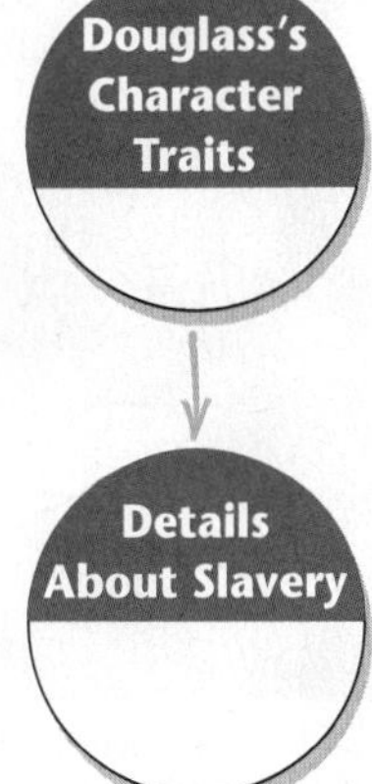

Vocabulary Builder

congenial (kən jēn′ yəl) *adj.* agreeable (p. 507)

benevolent (bə nev′ ə lənt) *adj.* kindly; charitable (p. 507)

stringency (strin′ jən sē) *n.* strictness; severity (p. 507)

depravity (dē prav′ ə tē) *n.* corruption; wickedness (p. 507)

consternation (kän′ stər nā′ shən) *n.* great fear or shock that makes one feel helpless or bewildered (p. 509)

redolent (red′ əl ənt) *adj.* suggestive (p. 511)

Differentiated Instruction
Solutions for All Learners

Support for Special Needs Students
Have students read the adapted version of the excerpt from *My Bondage and My Freedom* in the ***Reader's Notebook: Adapted Version.*** This version provides basic-level instruction in an interactive format with questions and write-on lines. Completing these pages will prepare students to read the selection in the Student Edition.

Support for Less Proficient Readers
Have students read from *My Bondage and My Freedom* in the ***Reader's Notebook.*** This version provides basic-level instruction in an interactive format with questions and write-on lines. After students finish the selection in the ***Reader's Notebook,*** have them complete the questions and activities in the Student Edition.

Support for English Learners
Have students read from *My Bondage and My Freedom* in the ***Reader's Notebook: English Learner's Version.*** This version provides basic-level instruction in an interactive format with questions and write-on lines. Completing these pages will prepare students to read the selection in the Student Edition.

2 Literary Analysis
Autobiography

- Tell students that they will focus on autobiography—a person's written account of his or her own life—as they read this excerpt from Frederick Douglass's *My Bondage and My Freedom.*
- Read the instruction about autobiography aloud. Point out the sentences concerning the subjective nature of autobiographical writing. Encourage students to discuss the range of choices a writer must make in the process of planning and drafting an autobiography. Speculate about the process a writer might use to select specific life experiences on which to focus.
- As they read Douglass's narrative, encourage students to take note of the episodes, ideas, people, and emotions on which Douglass has placed his emphasis.

3 Reading Strategy
Establishing a Purpose

- Give students a copy of **Reading Strategy Graphic Organizer A,** p. 100 in ***Graphic Organizer Transparencies,*** to use as they read the selection.
- Ask student volunteers to suggest examples of texts—such as a technical manual for using software, a lyric poem, or the autobiography of a former slave—that require readers to set a variety of purposes. As discussion ensues, list and categorize these purposes on the chalkboard.
- Remind students that setting purposes for reading is a way for them to exert control over their literary experiences. If they realize early in a text that their chosen purpose is inappropriate, they are free to set another purpose for reading.

Vocabulary Builder

- Pronounce each vocabulary word for students, and read the definitions as a class. Have students identify any words with which they are already familiar.

Learning Modalities
Interpersonal Learners
Douglass wrote that his mistress was a "most kind and tenderhearted woman. . . ." Have students discuss whether it is possible for a slave owner to be a "good" person or, more broadly, whether it is possible for a good person to do bad things.

❶ Humanities

The Chimney Corner, by Eastman Johnson

Eastman Johnson (1824–1906) was the son of a wealthy Maine politician. He studied art in Germany, Holland, and France, and he returned to the United States well-trained in genre painting. Johnson painted portraits of some of the most notable Americans of his time, including John Quincy Adams and Henry Wadsworth Longfellow. During the Civil War, he used his talents to record topical scenes and events.

Use these questions for discussion:

1. Do you think this man is a slave? Explain.
   Possible answer: Students may say that because the painting dates from 1863, the man may be a slave who, by the look of his clothing, works in a house. Perhaps he has found a moment of privacy to indulge a love of reading. If he is not a slave, he may be a house servant who was not discouraged from reading.
2. How would you describe the mood of the painting?
   Possible answer: Students may say that the dark, uncomfortable corner provides a sense of privacy and calm. The man is quietly engrossed in his book, despite the meanness of his surroundings.

❷ Critical Viewing

Answer: Students might say that the light shining on this man reading in a dark chamber symbolizes the beacon of knowledge, an awakening of understanding, or a glimmer of hope.

❶

The Chimney Corner, 1863, Eastman Johnson, Munson-Williams-Proctor Institute Museum of Art, Utica, New York

❷ ▲ **Critical Viewing** What might the light shining on the reader symbolize? **[Interpret]**

Differentiated Instruction Solutions for All Learners

Accessibility at a Glance

	My Bondage and My Freedom
Context	Chronicle of Slavery
Language	Complicated sentence structure
Concept Level	Challenging (social philosophy)
Literary Merit	Personal saga, historical
Lexile	1130
Overall Rating	More challenging

3

from My Bondage and My Freedom

Frederick Douglass

Background Frederick Douglass was perhaps the most prominent African American leader of the nineteenth century, and his influence is still felt. As a crusader for human rights, Douglass served as a role model for African American leaders such as Booker T. Washington and W.E.B. DuBois. In our own era, the civil rights movement has drawn inspiration from Douglass, who opposed segregation decades before other voices were raised. As a young man, Douglass protested segregated seating on trains by sitting in cars reserved for whites until the authorities forcibly removed him. Later, he fought job discrimination against African Americans, protested segregation in school, and fought for civil rights for all Americans.

I lived in the family of Master Hugh, at Baltimore, seven years, during which time—as the almanac makers say of the weather—my condition was variable. The most interesting feature of my history here, was my learning to read and write, under somewhat marked disadvantages. In attaining this knowledge, I was compelled to resort to indirections by no means congenial to my nature, and which were really humiliating to me. My mistress—who had begun to teach me—was suddenly checked in her benevolent design, by the strong advice of her husband. In faithful compliance with this advice, the good lady had not only ceased to instruct me, herself, but had set her face as a flint against my learning to read by any means. It is due, however, to my mistress to say, that she did not adopt this course in all its stringency at the first. She either thought it unnecessary, or she lacked the depravity indispensable to shutting me up in mental darkness. It was, at least, necessary for her to have some training, and some hardening, in the exercise of the slaveholder's prerogative, to make her equal to forgetting my human nature and character, and to treating me as a thing destitute of a moral or an intellectual nature. Mrs. Auld—my

Vocabulary Builder

congenial (kən jēn′ yəl) *adj.* agreeable

4 **benevolent** (bə nev′ ə lənt) *adj.* kindly; charitable

stringency (strin′ jən sē) *n.* strictness; severity

depravity (di prav′ ə tē) *n.* corruption; wickedness

5 **Reading Check**

Why did Douglass's mistress stop teaching him to read and write?

3 About the Selection

In this excerpt from his second autobiography, Douglass tries to show that slavery corrupted, dehumanized, and victimized everyone—including slaveholders. The passage describes how his master's kind wife, Mrs. Auld, feels compelled to abandon her efforts to educate young Frederick. Convinced by her husband that slavery and education are incompatible, she attempts to block any learning opportunities for the young boy, even though such hard-heartedness goes against her nature. Douglass continues to learn from his white playmates, trading biscuits for lessons. Influenced by the ideas he discovers through his reading, Douglass becomes consumed by a constant yearning for freedom and thoughts about the evils of slavery. He grows to hate the institution of slavery, which has made enemies of him and his mistress, who might otherwise have been friends.

4 Vocabulary Builder

Latin Root *-bene-*

- Draw students' attention to Douglass's use of the word *benevolent,* and read its definition. Then, tell students that the root *-bene-* derives from the Latin word meaning "well," or "good."
- Invite students to suggest other words that Douglass might have used to convey his meaning, and list these words on the chalkboard. Possibilities include *kind, good-hearted,* and *generous.*
- Guide students to see that the word *benevolent* encompasses the ideas of both kindness and generosity. Douglass uses it to emphasize his mistress's natural greatness of heart.

5 Reading Check

Answer: The mistress's husband insisted that she stop.

Differentiated Instruction Solutions for All Learners

Vocabulary for English Learners

Help students use context clues and a dictionary to decode the meanings of unfamiliar words such as *marked, checked,* and *waxed,* used here by Douglass in less familiar ways. Then, have them brainstorm for other words that Douglass might have used to convey similar meanings. For example, for the word *marked,* students might provide the synonyms *noticeable, striking,* or *distinct.* For the word *checked,* students might suggest words such as *prevented, stopped,* or *prohibited.*

Strategy for Advanced Readers

Encourage students to look closely at Douglass's opening paragraph, examining it for the ways in which he begins to convey his essential message about the unnaturalness of slavery. Ask students to answer this question: What does Douglass say his mistress must undergo in order to become an effective slaveholder? Then, invite students to speculate about what might be involved in such "training." Why is it essential that a slaveholder "forget" the "human nature and character" of a slave?

6 Background
History
Help students put this remarkable statement into historical perspective. In 1825, many whites in the United States of America, in their ignorance, did not believe that people with dark skin were truly human. Through her experience with Frederick, Mrs. Auld learned the truth.

7 Critical Viewing
Possible response: The painting suggests that plantation owners lived lives of luxury that contrasted sharply with the experiences of the slaves.

8 Humanities
A Home on the Mississippi, 1871, by Currier and Ives

Nathaniel Currier (1813–1888) and James Ives (1824–1895) started the firm of Currier and Ives in 1857 to produce commercially countless lithographic chronicles of nineteenth-century American life. Hand-colored scenes like this one were immensely popular with the American public. People obtained them by mail order, from traveling salespeople, and from the partners' shop in New York City. A favorite Currier and Ives theme was the home. *A Home on the Mississippi* was reproduced more than 3.5 billion times on the label of a popular beverage. The scene is filled with typical Southern atmosphere accentuated by the gracious verandah on the house and the Spanish moss hanging from the trees.

Use these questions for discussion:

1. What impression of southern living does this print convey? **Possible answer:** Students may say that it suggests a calm, genteel, leisurely lifestyle.
2. Do you think this view of the South matches Frederick Douglass's? Why or why not? **Answer:** Students may say that it does in that it shows the southern gentry riding in elegant carriages while the slaves walk along the side of the road or stand outside the fences.

mistress—was, as I have said, a most kind and tender-hearted woman; and, in the humanity of her heart, and the simplicity of her mind, she set out, when I first went to live with her, to treat me as she supposed one human being ought to treat another.

It is easy to see, that, in entering upon the duties of a slaveholder, some little experience is needed. Nature has done almost nothing to prepare men and women to be either slaves or slaveholders. Nothing but rigid training, long persisted in, can perfect the character of the one or the other. One cannot easily forget to love freedom; and it is as hard to cease to respect that natural love in our fellow creatures. On entering upon the career of a slaveholding mistress, Mrs. Auld was singularly deficient; nature, which fits nobody for such an office, had done less for her than any lady I had known. It was no easy matter to induce her to think and to feel that the curly-headed boy, who stood by her side, and even leaned on her lap; who was loved by little Tommy, and who loved little Tommy in turn; sustained to her only the relation of a chattel. I was *more* than that, and she felt me to be more than that. I could talk and sing; I could laugh and weep; I could reason and remember; I could love and hate. I was human, and she, dear lady, knew and felt me to be so. How could she, then, treat me as a brute, without a mighty struggle with all the noble powers of her own soul. That struggle came, and the will and power of the husband was victorious. Her noble soul was

7 ▼ **Critical Viewing** How does this idealized picture of plantation life contrast with Douglass's experiences as an enslaved African American? **[Contrast]**

8

Enrichment
Slavery
Slavery neither began nor ended with southern plantation owners. A common practice since ancient times, slavery originated with conquest; it was the fate that awaited the conquered. Slave markets existed by the time of the first Babylonian Empire, more than three thousand years ago. Sadly, slavery continues to exist in parts of the world even today.

Students have read about one slave's reaction to his circumstances. Invite them to find out how other slaves have responded to their bondage. They might, for instance, obtain a copy of a Haggadah (the narrative of the Exodus from Egypt that is read every year at the Jewish festival of Passover) to read about what the slave Nachshon did to obtain his freedom. Or they can research one of the several slave revolts in America; in particular, they can find out about the only sustained slave revolt in American history, the 1831 rebellion led by Nat Turner.

overthrown; but, he that overthrew it did not, himself, escape the consequences. He, not less than the other parties, was injured in his domestic peace by the fall.

When I went into their family, it was the abode of happiness and contentment. The mistress of the house was a model of affection and tenderness. Her fervent piety and watchful uprightness made it impossible to see her without thinking and feeling—"that woman is a Christian." There was no sorrow nor suffering for which she had not a tear, and there was no innocent joy for which she did not [have] a smile. She had bread for the hungry, clothes for the naked, and comfort for every mourner that came within her reach. Slavery soon proved its ability to divest her of these excellent qualities, and her home of its early happiness. Conscience cannot stand much violence. Once thoroughly broken down, *who* is he that can repair the damage? It may be broken toward the slave, on Sunday, and toward the master on Monday. It cannot endure such shocks. It must stand entire, or it does not stand at all. If my condition waxed bad, that of the family waxed not better. The first step, in the wrong direction, was the violence done to nature and to conscience, in arresting the benevolence that would have enlightened my young mind. In ceasing to instruct me, she must begin to justify herself *to* herself; and, once consenting to take sides in such a debate, she was riveted to her position. One needs very little knowledge of moral philosophy, to see *where* my mistress now landed. She finally became even more violent in her opposition to my learning to read, than was her husband himself. She was not satisfied with simply doing as *well* as her husband had commanded her, but seemed resolved to better his instruction. Nothing appeared to make my poor mistress—after her turning toward the downward path—more angry, than seeing me, seated in some nook or corner, quietly reading a book or a newspaper. I have had her rush at me, with the utmost fury, and snatch from my hand such newspaper or book, with something of the wrath and consternation which a traitor might be supposed to feel on being discovered in a plot by some dangerous spy.

Mrs. Auld was an apt woman, and the advice of her husband, and her own experience, soon demonstrated, to her entire satisfaction, that education and slavery are incompatible with each other. When this conviction was thoroughly established, I was most narrowly watched in all my movements. If I remained in a separate room from the family for any considerable length of time, I was sure to be suspected of having a book, and was at once called upon to give an account of myself. All this, however, was entirely *too late.* The first, and never to be retraced, step had been taken. In teaching me the alphabet, in the days of her simplicity and kindness, my mistress had given me the "inch," and now, no ordinary precaution could prevent me from taking the "ell."[1]

compassion civility intelligence

Literary Analysis
Autobiography Douglass blames the institution of slavery, rather than Mrs. Auld for the changes in the household. What does this tell you about him?

Vocabulary Builder
consternation (kän′ stər nā′ shən) *n.* great fear or shock that makes one feel helpless or bewildered

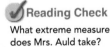

10 **Reading Check**
What extreme measure does Mrs. Auld take?

1. **ell** *n.* former English measure of length, equal to forty-five inches.

9 Literary Analysis
Autobiography

- Have a student volunteer read this passage aloud, and invite students to listen for the distinctive tone of civility, intelligence, compassion, and determination in the narrative voice of Frederick Douglass.
- **Ask** students the Literary Analysis question: Douglass blames the institution of slavery, rather than Mrs. Auld, for the changes in the household. What does this tell you about him?
  Answer: Students may respond that Douglass has a positive view of human nature despite his experiences as a slave.

10 Reading Check

Answer: Mrs. Auld becomes "even more violent [than Mr. Auld] in her opposition" to Douglass's reading.

Differentiated Instruction Solutions for All Learners

Strategy for Special Needs Students
Frederick Douglass makes frequent use of long sentences that may pose a challenge for students. Help them break down the long sentences by identifying the core of each one—its subject and verb—and stating the main action described. Then, have students look at how the other groups of words in the sentence relate to the subject and the verb.

Enrichment for Gifted/Talented Students
Guide students to appreciate Douglass's views on the intrinsic right of an individual to acquire knowledge and on the negative effects of denying a person that right. Invite students to discuss why the Aulds' decision regarding Douglass's education places them in a "condition" Douglass views as worse than his own. Encourage students to create a drawing or other visual image that captures the power of knowledge and the opposing relationships of the Aulds and Douglass.

11 The American Experience

Slave Narratives The first known slave narrative—*A Narrative of the Uncommon Sufferings and Surprising Deliverance of Briton Hammon, a Negro Man*—appeared in 1760 in Boston. Other notable examples of this sub-genre of autobiography include *A Narrative of the Lord's Wonderful Dealings with J. Murrant, a Black, Taken Down from His Own Relation* (1784), *Incidents in the Life of a Slave Girl, Written by Herself* (1861) by Harriet Jacobs, and *Scenes in the Life of Harriet Tubman* (1869).

Connect to the Literature

Encourage students to consider why children whose own parents were slaveholders did not support keeping people in bondage.

Possible answer: By showing children's opposition to slavery, Douglass may have wanted readers to observe that support for slavery was learned, not natural.

12 Critical Thinking

Interpret/Support

- Invite students to explain the meaning of the expression "Give [him] an inch and [he'll] take a mile" and to support their definitions with examples.
- Then, point out that this saying summarizes Mr. Auld's fears regarding the potential results of Douglass's education. Auld once said that if Frederick learned to read "there would be no keeping him. . . . If you learn him how to read, he'll want to know how to write; and this accomplished, he'll be running away with himself."

13 Background

History

Remind students that Maryland was *not* one of the states that seceded from the United States of America to join the Confederacy. Point out that although slavery was present in Maryland, it was not as prevalent as it was in states of the Deep South.

Seized with a determination to learn to read, at any cost, I hit upon many expedients to accomplish the desired end. The plea which I mainly adopted, and the one by which I was most successful, was that of using my young white playmates, with whom I met in the street, as teachers. I used to carry, almost constantly, a copy of Webster's spelling book in my pocket; and, when sent on errands, or when play time was allowed me, I would step, with my young friends, aside, and take a lesson in spelling. I generally paid my *tuition fee* to the boys, with bread, which I also carried in my pocket. For a single biscuit, any of my hungry little comrades would give me a lesson more valuable to me than bread. Not everyone, however, demanded this consideration, for there were those who took pleasure in teaching me, whenever I had a chance to be taught by them. I am strongly tempted to give the names of two or three of those little boys, as a slight testimonial of the gratitude and affection I bear them, but prudence forbids; not that it would injure me, but it might, possibly, embarrass them; for it is almost an unpardonable offense to do anything, directly or indirectly, to promote a slave's freedom, in a slave state. It is enough to say, of my warm-hearted little play fellows, that they lived on Philpot Street, very near Durgin & Bailey's shipyard. 11

Although slavery was a delicate subject, and very cautiously talked about among grownup people in Maryland, I frequently talked about it—and that very freely—with the white boys. I would, sometimes, say to them, while seated on a curbstone or a cellar door, "I wish I could be free, as you will be when you get to be men." "You will be free, you know, as soon as you are twenty-one, and can go where you like, but I am a slave for life. Have I not as good a right to be free as you have?" Words like these, I observed, always troubled them; and I had no small satisfaction in wringing from the boys, occasionally, that fresh
13 and bitter condemnation of slavery, that springs from nature, unseared and unperverted.[2] Of all consciences let me have those to deal with which have not been bewildered by the cares of life. I do not remember ever to have met with a *boy*, while I was in slavery, who defended the slave system; but I have often had boys to console me, with the hope that something would yet occur, by which I might be made free. Over and over again, they have told me, that "they believed *I* had as good a right to be free as *they* had"; and that "they did not believe God ever made anyone to be a slave." The reader will easily see, that such little conversations with my play fellows, had no tendency to weaken my love of liberty, nor to render me contented with my condition as a slave.

Slave Narratives

From 1760 to the end of the Civil War, when slavery was officially abolished, the testimonies of hundreds of fugitive and former slaves appeared in the form of slave narratives. Like the precedent-setting *Interesting Narrative of the Life of Olaudah Equiano* (page 160), these slave narratives exposed the inhumanities of the slave system. Former slaves recorded the oppressive conditions they suffered under their owners, not only to document their experiences but also to ensure that the reunified nation would not soon forget. The Federal Writers Project of the 1920s and 1930s gathered the narratives and documented them, creating an archive attesting to the terrible experience of American slavery.

Connect to the Literature

Douglass intended his narrative to be read by both black and white audiences. What do you think was his purpose in describing the white boys' attitude toward slavery?

2. **unperverted** (un′ pər vurt′ id) *adj.* uncorrupted; pure.

When I was about thirteen years old, and had succeeded in learning to read, every increase of knowledge, especially respecting the free states, added something to the almost intolerable burden of the thought—"I am a slave for life." To my bondage I saw no end. It was a terrible reality, and I shall never be able to tell how sadly that thought chafed my young spirit. Fortunately, or unfortunately, about this time in my life, I had made enough money to buy what was then a very popular schoolbook, the *Columbian Orator.* I bought this addition to my library, of Mr. Knight, on Thames street, Fell's Point, Baltimore, and paid him fifty cents for it. I was first led to buy this book, by hearing some little boys say they were going to learn some little pieces out of it for the exhibition. This volume was, indeed, a rich treasure, and every opportunity afforded me, for a time, was spent in diligently perusing it . . . The dialogue and the speeches were all redolent of the principles of liberty, and poured floods of light on the nature and character of slavery. As I read, behold! the very discontent so graphically predicted by Master Hugh, had already come upon me. I was no longer the light-hearted, gleesome boy, full of mirth and play, as when I landed first at Baltimore. Knowledge had come . . . This knowledge opened my eyes to the horrible pit, and revealed the teeth of the frightful dragon that was ready to pounce upon me, but it opened no way for my escape. I have often wished myself a beast, or a bird—anything, rather than a slave. I was wretched and gloomy, beyond my ability to describe. I was too thoughtful to be happy. It was this everlasting thinking which distressed and tormented me; and yet there was no getting rid of the subject of my thoughts. All nature was redolent of it. Once awakened by the silver trump[3] of knowledge, my spirit was roused to eternal wakefulness. Liberty! the inestimable birthright of every man, had, for me, converted every object into an asserter of this great right. It was heard in every sound, and beheld in every object. It was ever present, to torment me with a sense of my wretched condition. The more beautiful and charming were the smiles of nature, the more horrible and desolate was my condition. I saw nothing without seeing it, and I heard nothing without hearing it. I do not exaggerate, when I say, that it looked from every star, smiled in every calm, breathed in every wind, and moved in every storm.

I have no doubt that my state of mind had something to do with the change in the treatment adopted, by my once kind mistress toward me. I can easily believe, that my leaden, downcast, and discontented look, was very offensive to her. Poor lady! She did not know my trouble, and I dared not tell her. Could I have freely made her acquainted with the real state of my mind, and given her the reasons therefor, it might have been well for both of us. Her abuse of me fell upon me like the blows of the false prophet upon his ass; she did not know that an *angel* stood in 15

3. **trump** trumpet.

Vocabulary Builder
redolent (red´ əl ənt) *adj.* suggestive

Literary Analysis
Autobiography and Tone
What does Douglass's tone here reveal about the importance of reading this book?

Reading Check
What significant changes take place in Douglass after reading *Columbian Orator?*

14 Literary Analysis
Autobiography and Tone

- Ask a strong reader to read aloud this powerful, impassioned passage from Douglass's autobiography. Invite students to describe Douglass's tone using details in the passage to support their ideas.

Monitor Progress Then, **ask** students the Literary Analysis question: What does Douglass's tone here reveal about the importance of reading this book?
Answer: For Douglass, reading the book was crucial: it validated his private thoughts and feelings and fueled his determination to break the bonds of slavery.

15 Reading Check

Answer: He grows "wretched and gloomy" and "too thoughtful to be happy."

Differentiated Instruction Solutions for All Learners

Vocabulary for Special Needs Students
Clarify the meaning of the term *nature* for students by pointing out that Douglass is not using it in the strict sense as a reference to the natural world. Instead, he uses *nature* to mean all of creation—the natural world as well as the human. On page 512, when he states that "Nature had made us friends," he is referring to "human nature"—the qualities all human beings share.

Strategy for Less Proficient Readers
In the long paragraph that begins at the top of this page, Douglass presents one of the key ideas of this selection: reading the *Columbian Orator* caused him to develop an overpowering desire for freedom. This point is made toward the middle of the paragraph, and it is restated and reinforced in the sentences that follow. Assist students in identifying the main idea and noting the ways in which Douglass develops and supports it.

ASSESS

Answers

1. Students should offer clear, solid reasons to back up their points of view.
2. (a) He is first taught by Mrs. Auld and later, by young white playmates. (b) At first, she approves of it and actively supports it. (c) In order to compensate for her initial, natural reaction of support, Mrs. Auld adopts an attitude even more extreme than her husband's. In this way she may hope to fool herself into thinking that she is comfortable with suppressing the intellectual curiosity of a boy.
3. (a) They believe slavery is wrong and that black and white children are inherently equal. (b) Students may point out that a human being's "natural" or "pure" impulse is to treat other people as equals. Children may be closer to this state of purity.
4. (a) He reads a book about liberty and realizes he can no longer tolerate his bondage. (b) Knowledge opens his eyes to the pain and evil of slavery, but gives him few tools—at least initially—with which to escape it.
5. (a) He is consumed by his desire for freedom. (b) The ability to read gives Douglass access to voices and ideas that challenge and condemn the institution of slavery. Without education, he would have remained ignorant of these ideas and received no validation for his innate desire to be free.
6. Some students may observe that, in one sense, Douglass was free because he realized his self-worth and saw slavery as an invalid system. This awareness led him to seek actual freedom. Many other students will respond that Douglass was not free while still in bondage.

Go Online Author Link For additional information about Frederick Douglass, have students type in the Web Code, then select D from the alphabet, and then select Frederick Douglass.

the way;[4] and—such is the relation of master and slave—I could not tell her. Nature had made us *friends*; slavery made us *enemies*. My interests were in a direction opposite to hers, and we both had our private thoughts and plans. She aimed to keep me ignorant; and I resolved to know, although knowledge only increased my discontent. My feelings were not the result of any marked cruelty in the treatment I received; they sprung from the consideration of my being a slave at all. It was *slavery*—not its mere *incidents*—that I hated. I had been cheated. I saw through the attempt to keep me in ignorance . . . The feeding and clothing me well, could not atone for taking my liberty from me. The smiles of my mistress could not remove the deep sorrow that dwelt in my young bosom. Indeed, these, in time, came only to deepen my sorrow. She had changed; and the reader will see that I had changed, too. We were both victims to the same overshadowing evil—*she*, as mistress, *I*, as slave. I will not censure her harshly; she cannot censure me, for she knows I speak but the truth, and have acted in my opposition to slavery, just as she herself would have acted, in a reverse of circumstances.

4. **blows . . . the way** allusion to a biblical tale (Numbers 22:21–35) about an ass that cannot move, though she is beaten by her master, because her path is blocked by an angel.

Critical Reading

1. **Respond:** Do you think it is possible to be a benevolent slaveholder? Why or why not?
2. **(a) Recall:** How does Douglass learn to read? **(b) Recall:** What does Mrs. Auld initially think about Douglass's reading? **(c) Draw Conclusions:** Why do you think she was later "violent in her opposition" to Douglass's reading?
3. **(a) Recall:** What is the attitude toward slavery of the white boys who help Douglass learn to read? **(b) Analyze:** Why do you think they have that attitude toward the slaves?
4. **(a) Recall:** What circumstance transforms Douglass from "light-hearted" to "wretched and gloomy"? **(b) Connect:** What does knowledge do for him?
5. **(a) Recall:** What consumed Douglass once he obtained knowledge? **(b) Support:** How does his experience prove his mistress's belief that education and slavery are incompatible?
6. **Apply:** Mahatma Gandhi wrote, "The moment the slave resolves that he will no longer be a slave, his fetters fall." Explain whether or not you feel Douglass was free even while in bondage.

For: More about Frederick Douglass
Visit: www.PHSchool.com
Web Code: ere-9403

Apply the Skills

from *My Bondage and My Freedom*

Literary Analysis

Autobiography

1. Douglass is relatively well cared for as a slave. In what way does he use his **autobiography** to make his case against slavery?
2. Find a passage in which Douglass conveys his opposition to slavery through his description of events.
3. In what ways would this account be different if it had been written by Mrs. Auld?

Connecting Literary Elements

4. **(a)** Describe Douglass's attitude toward Mrs. Auld. **(b)** Why do you think he feels as he does?
5. **(a)** What is the **tone** of the end of the selection? **(b)** Which specific words and phrases reveal Douglass's attitude toward slavery?
6. How does the tone—including word choice—of this selection support Douglass's desire to serve as a model?

Reading Strategy

Establishing a Purpose

7. Which of Douglass's special qualities are conveyed through this section of his autobiography? Explain.
8. Using a chart like the one shown, identify what you learned about the effects of slavery from Douglass's account.

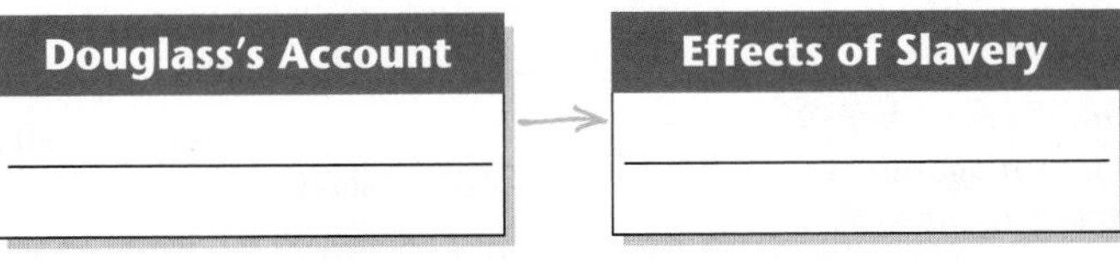

9. In what ways did reading this selection add to your understanding of the effects of slavery? Expain.

Extend Understanding

10. **Social Studies Connection:** Many writers have paid tribute to Douglass's ideas. **(a)** Why do you think his messsage strikes such a chord with Americans? **(b)** In what ways does it reflect the core values on which America was founded?

QuickReview

An **autobiography** is a person's written account of his or her life.

The **tone** of a work reflects the author's attitude toward the subject, characters, or audience.

Establish a purpose for reading by choosing an idea or concept on which to focus.

For: Self-test
Visit: www.PHSchool.com
Web Code: era-6403

Go Online Assessment Students may use the **Self-test** to prepare for **Selection Test A** or **Selection Test B.**

Answers

1. He uses his relationship with his mistress as an example of the many ways in which slavery forces people to betray their natural tendencies—hers toward kindness and his toward liberty.
2. The paragraph that begins "When I went into their family" is one example of this approach.
3. **Possible response:** She may have denied any change in her personality and would have seen her actions as proper.
4. (a) He does not blame her for becoming an oppressor. Instead, he sees her as another victim of the institution of slavery. (b) **Possible answer:** He feels this way because he has witnessed her earlier, natural response.
5. (a) To describe Douglass's tone, students might use words such as *determined, steadfast,* and *intense.* (b) Words and phrases include *like the blows of the false prophet upon his ass; it was* slavery—*not its mere* incidents—*that I hated.*
6. Douglass's eloquent telling of his life's story reflects his intelligence and his ability to understand human nature. It illustrates that African Americans of Douglass's time were capable of achieving great things despite great obstacles.
7. **Possible answer:** It reveals his intelligence, persistence, and ingenuity.
8. **Possible answer:** Douglass's Account: *I was compelled to resort to indirections by no means congenial to my nature;* Effects: Sometimes slavery caused African Americans to act in ways that they considered to be morally offensive.
9. Students should support their answers with details from the text.
10. (a) Students may mention Douglass's evenhandedness and clarity, as well as his compassion and sympathy. (b) Douglass's central ideas concern the fundamental humanity of African Americans and the basic impulse of human beings to regard each other as equals.

EXTEND/ASSESS

Answers

❶ Vocabulary Lesson

Word Analysis

1. "a positive effect"
2. "someone who does good things for someone or something"
3. "a blessing"

Spelling Strategy

1. stringency
2. leniency
3. insistence
4. reverence

Vocabulary Builder

congenial; consternation; redolent; benevolent; depravity; stringency

❷ Grammar and Style Lesson

1. Neither . . . nor
2. Not only . . . but also
3. Whether . . . or
4. Just as . . . so
5. Either . . . or

Writing Application

Check to see that students have used correlative conjunctions in proper pairs.

WG **Writing and Grammar,** Ruby Level

Students will find further instruction and practice on correlative conjunctions in Chapter 17, Section 4.

Build Language Skills

❶ Vocabulary Lesson

Word Analysis: Latin Root *-bene-*

The Latin root *-bene-* means "well" or "good." The word *benevolent* literally means "with good wishes" or "kindly."

Define each of the following words, incorporating the meaning of the root *-bene-* into your definition.

1. benefit **2.** benefactor **3.** benediction

Spelling Strategy

When creating the noun form of an adjective that ends in *-ent,* replace the *t* with *-ce* or *-cy: benevolent* becomes *benevolence.* Add the *-ce* or *-cy* ending to each adjective below.

1. stringent
2. lenient
3. insistent
4. reverent

Vocabulary Builder: Sentence Completion

Copy the following passage and fill in the blanks with the appropriate vocabulary words from the list on page 505.

I could see my otherwise __?__ neighbor scowling with a look of __?__, so I knew something was wrong. Her well-manicured garden was usually __?__ with the fragrance of roses, which she was __?__ enough to share with me. The previously robust bushes were cut to the ground! I was stunned by the __?__ of the deed—and by the __?__ of her message as she sadly tacked up a KEEP OUT sign.

❷ Grammar and Style Lesson

Correlative Conjunctions

Correlative conjunctions—pairs of connecting words—link similar kinds of words and word groups and connect ideas. In this example, the italicized words show the relationship between the two actions in the sentence.

Example: . . . the good lady had *not only* ceased to instruct me, herself, *but* had set her face as a flint against my learning to read by any means.

Correlative conjunctions are usually used in these combinations:

- *either . . . or*
- *not only . . . but (also)*
- *whether . . . or*
- *neither . . . nor*
- *just as . . . so*

Practice For each item, create a logical sentence by adding a pair of correlative conjunctions from the italicized list.

1. __?__ slave __?__ mistress was truly free.
2. __?__ Maryland __?__ Mississippi and Tennessee were slave states.
3. __?__ a slave __?__ a slaveholder, all people are harmed by slavery.
4. __?__ Douglass worked to abolish slavery, __?__ did Sojourner Truth.
5. __?__ Mrs. Auld __?__ Mr. Auld would win the moral struggle.

Writing Application Write an original paragraph about slavery, using each of the five pairs of correlative conjunctions listed.

WG *Prentice Hall Writing and Grammar Connection: Chapter 17, Section 4*

Assessment Practice

Context (For more practice, see *Standardized Test Preparation Workbook*, p. 28.)

Many tests require students to use context to determine the appropriate meaning of a multiple-meaning word. Use the following sample test item to give students practice in this skill.

I was compelled to resort to indirections by no means congenial to my nature, and which were really humiliating to me.

In this passage, congenial most nearly means—

A friendly **C** kindred
B sympathetic **D** suited

The word *humiliating* provides a context clue that the indirections are not suited to the speaker's nature or temperament. Although the other choices are also definitions of *congenial, D* is the appropriate meaning in the context of this passage.

Writing Lesson

College Admission Essay

A college application often requires you to write about an experience that helped shape you as a person. Just as Douglass described how knowledge freed him, you, too, can identify a key event or shaping force in your life, and write an essay explaining it.

Prewriting Outline the details of the event, and describe its effect on you. List the details in chronological order to establish organization.

Model: Planning a Clear and Logical Organization

A. Worked in local campaign office
   1. Met the candidate; was inspired
   2. Distributed flyers; polled voters
   3. Phoned residents to encourage voting
B. Learned team work and the power of democracy

Chronological order makes it easy for readers to follow an essay.

Drafting Introduce the experience and explain why you are writing about it. Then, write the body paragraphs to follow your outline. Conclude with a paragraph that insightfully sums up the impact of the experience on your life.

Revising Add time transition words like *first, next,* and *finally* to show chronological order and cause-effect words like *since* and *therefore* to reinforce the way this event helped shape you.

WG *Prentice Hall Writing and Grammar Connection: Chapter 4, Section 3*

Extend Your Learning

Listening and Speaking Select a passage from Douglass's autobiography, and imagine that you are reading it at an abolitionist convention. Introduce your reading with a few comments that emphasize Douglass's purpose. Consider the following:

- Use your voice and body language to convey Douglass's tone.
- Use persuasive language to inspire your audience to take action.

Deliver the **oral presentation** to your class.

Research and Technology Using words, pictures, and sounds, work with a group to create a **multimedia presentation** that expresses the importance of literacy. Draw your materials from printed sources such as magazines, newspapers, and photographs. Consider recordings of speeches that will add vitality to your presentation. **[Group Activity]**

For: An additional research activity
Visit: www.PHSchool.com
Web Code: erd-7403

3 Writing Lesson

- To guide students in writing this college admission essay, give them the **Support for Writing Lesson** page from ***Unit 4 Resources***, p. 49.
- Students' college admission essays should describe an event that had great significance for them and should explain in detail the impact of the event on their lives.
- Remind students that their audience knows nothing about the context in which this key event occurred. Therefore, early in their essays, students must describe what their lives and viewpoints were like *before* the event. Readers will then understand both the nature of the event and its significance in their lives.
- Use the Writing Lesson, as well as reflective the essay rubrics in ***General Resources***, pp. 47–48, to guide students in their essays.

4 Research and Technology

- Encourage students to review the passages in this selection that deal with the power of reading. Have students list words and phrases that Douglass uses to convey his ideas.
- Then, have students gather in small groups to generate lists of their own thoughts and feelings about literacy.
- Finally, invite groups to brainstorm for ways to express both Douglass's and their own ideas, using visual images or sound.
- Use the Multimedia Presentation rubric in ***General Resources***, pp. 51–52, to evaluate students' multimedia presentations.
- The **Support for Extend Your Learning** page (***Unit 4 Resources***, p. 50) provides guided note-taking opportunities to help students complete the Extend Your Learning activities.

Go Online Research — Have students type in the Web Code for another research activity.

Assessment Resources

Unit 4 Resources
- **Selection Test A,** pp. 52–54
- **Selection Test B,** pp. 55–57

General Resources
- **Rubrics for Reflective Essay,** pp. 47–48
- **Rubrics for Multimedia Presentation,** pp. 51–52

Go Online Assessment — Students may use the **Self-test** to prepare for **Selection Test A** or **Selection Test B.**

Meeting Your Standards

Students will

1. **analyze and respond to literary elements.**
   - Literary Analysis: Point of View
2. **read, comprehend, analyze, and critique a short story.**
   - Reading Strategy: Identifying Chronological Order
   - Reading Check questions
   - Apply the Skills questions
   - Assessment Practice (ATE)
3. **develop vocabulary.**
   - Vocabulary Lesson: Latin Root: *-summa-*
4. **understand and apply written and oral language conventions.**
   - Spelling Strategy
   - Grammar and Style Lesson: Semicolons in Compound Sentences
5. **develop writing proficiency.**
   - Writing Lesson: Critical Essay
6. **develop appropriate research strategies.**
   - Extend Your Learning: Visual Model
7. **understand and apply listening and speaking strategies.**
   - Extend Your Learning: Summary

Block Scheduling: Use one 90-minute class period to preteach the skills and have students read the selection. Use a second 90-minute class period to assess students' mastery of skills, extend their learning, and monitor their progress.

Homework Suggestions

Following are possibilities for homework assignments.

- Support pages from *Unit 4 Resources:*
  Literary Analysis
  Reading Strategy
  Vocabulary Builder
  Grammar and Style
- An Extend Your Learning project and the Writing Lesson for this selection may be completed over several days.

Step-by-Step Teaching Guide	Pacing Guide
PRETEACH	
• Administer Vocabulary and Reading Warm-ups as necessary.	5 min.
• Engage students' interest with the motivation activity.	5 min.
• Read and discuss author and background features. **FT**	10 min.
• Introduce the Literary Analysis Skill: Point of View. **FT**	5 min.
• Introduce the Reading Strategy: Identifying Chronological Order. **FT**	10 min.
• Prepare students to read by teaching the selection vocabulary. **FT**	
TEACH	
• Informally monitor comprehension while students read independently or in groups. **FT**	30 min.
• Monitor students' comprehension with the Reading Check notes.	as students read
• Reinforce vocabulary with Vocabulary Builder notes.	as students read
• Develop students' understanding of point of view with the Literary Analysis annotations. **FT**	5 min.
• Develop students' ability to identify chronological order with the Reading Strategy annotations. **FT**	5 min.
ASSESS/EXTEND	
• Assess students' comprehension and mastery of the Literary Analysis and Reading Strategy by having them answer the Apply the Skills questions. **FT**	15 min.
• Have students complete the Vocabulary Lesson and the Grammar and Style Lesson. **FT**	15 min.
• Apply students' ability to incorporate quotations from the story by using the Writing Lesson. **FT**	45 min. or homework
• Apply students' understanding by using one or more of the Extend Your Learning activities.	20–90 min. or homework
• Administer Selection Test A or Selection Test B. **FT**	15 min.

Resources

PRINT

Unit 4 Resources

Vocabulary Warm-up Word Lists [**L1, L2, EL**] .... p. 58
Vocabulary Warm-up Practice [**L1, L2, EL**] .... p. 59
Reading Warm-up A [**L1, L2, EL**] .... p. 60
Reading Warm-up B [**L1, L2, L3**] .... p. 61

TRANSPARENCY

Graphic Organizer Transparencies

Literary Analysis Graphic Organizer A [**L3**] .... p. 106
Literary Analysis Graphic Organizer B [**L1, L2, EL**] .... p. 107
Reading Strategy Graphic Organizer A [**L3**] .... p. 104
Reading Strategy Graphic Organizer B [**L1, L2, EL**] .... p. 105

PRINT

Reader's Notebook [L2]
Reader's Notebook: Adapted Version [L1]
Reader's Notebook: English Learner's Version [EL]

Unit 4 Resources

Literary Analysis [**L3**] .... p. 62
Reading Strategy [**L3**] .... p. 63
Vocabulary Builder [**L3**] .... p. 64

TECHNOLOGY

Listening to Literature Audio CDs [L2, EL]

PRINT

Unit 4 Resources

Grammar and Style [**L3**] .... p. 65
Support for Writing Lesson [**L3**] .... p. 66
Support for Extend Your Learning [**L3**] .... p. 67
Enrichment [**L4**] .... p. 68
Selection Test A [**L1, L2, EL**] .... pp. 69–71
Selection Test B [**L3, L4**] .... pp. 72–74

General Resources

Rubrics for Response to Literature [**L3**] .... pp. 65–66

TECHNOLOGY

Go Online: Research [**L3**]
Go Online: Self-test [**L3**]
***ExamView®*, Test Bank [L3]**

Choosing Resources for Differentiated Instruction

[**L1**] Special Needs Students
[**L2**] Below-Level Students
[**L3**] All Students
[**L4**] Advanced Students
[**EL**] English Learners

FT Fast Track Instruction: To move the lesson more quickly, use the strategies and activities identified with **FT**.

Scaffolding for Less Proficient and Advanced Students

The leveled Critical Thinking questions after selections progress in the levels of thinking required to answer them. To address the needs of your different students, you may use the (a) level questions for your less proficient students and the (b) level questions with your on-level and advanced students. The occasional (c) level questions are appropriate for your advanced students.

PRENTICE HALL TeacherEXPRESS™ Plan · Teach · Assess Use this complete suite of powerful teaching tools to make lesson planning and testing quicker and easier.

Use the interactive textbook (online and on CD-ROM) to make selections and activities come alive with audio and video support and interactive questions.

PRETEACH

Motivation

Play the opening scene of the video *An Occurrence at Owl Creek Bridge.* Pause the video after the noose is placed around the civilian's neck. Have students discuss possible reasons the man is in this situation. Then, tell students to read the story to discover the man's fate.

❶ Background

More About the Author

Ernest Hopkins, an editor and author who has specialized in the work of Ambrose Bierce, claims that Bierce's general philosophy was a "realistic, pessimistic, hard-boiled attitude toward life. This first-handed approach made him rather difficult to work with, no doubt, but it did make his writings refreshingly original and does so today—to read Bierce is to enter a different world."

Build Skills *Short Story*

❶ An Occurrence at Owl Creek Bridge

Ambrose Bierce

(1842–1914?)

Ambrose Bierce's writing and philosophy were shaped by his career as a Union officer in the Civil War. The extreme poverty in which he was raised helped to foster Bierce's unsentimental, pessimistic view of the world; the brutality he saw during the war only cemented his cynicism. Bierce explored themes of cruelty and death in his writing, earning himself the nickname "Bitter Bierce."

A Civil War Soldier Bierce was born in Ohio and raised on a farm in Indiana. Having educated himself by reading his father's books, he left the farm while in his teens to attend a military academy in Kentucky. When the Civil War broke out, he enlisted in the Union army. Bierce fought in several important battles, rose from private to lieutenant, and won many awards for bravery. Toward the end of the war he was seriously wounded, but he returned to battle a few months later.

Poisoned Pen After the war, Bierce settled in San Francisco as a journalist. His "Prattler" column, which appeared in *The Argonaut* (1877–1879), the *Wasp* (1881–1886), and the San Francisco *Sunday Examiner* (1887–1896), mixed political and social satire, literary reviews, and gossip. The broodingly handsome writer was dubbed "the wickedest man in San Francisco" for his cynical and often malicious commentary. Though his journalistic barbs angered many key political and business figures, Bierce's dark reputation only added to his personal popularity. He was a magnetic figure who charmed those around him despite the malice of his words.

Establishing His Legacy Although Bierce published many of his finest short stories in his column, he decided in the early 1890s to publish his collected short stories in two volumes entitled *Tales of Soldiers and Civilians* (1891) and *Can Such Things Be?* (1893). The concise, carefully plotted stories in these collections, set for the most part during the Civil War, capture the cruelty and futility of war and the indifference of death. Bierce's pessimism is also reflected in *The Devil's Dictionary* (1906), a book of humorous and cynical definitions, and in a book of quotations published after his death. Challenging, spiteful, or merely macabre, these comments more than justify Bierce's reputation as a hard-nosed, hard-boiled critic of nearly everything.

The Perfect Cynic Writer George Sterling wrote of Bierce, his longtime friend, that he "never troubled to conceal his justifiable contempt of humanity. . . . Bierce was a 'perfectionist,' a quality that in his case led to an intolerance involving merciless cruelty. He demanded in all others, men or women, the same ethical virtues that he found essential to his own manner of life. . . . To deviate from his point of view, indeed, to disagree with him even in slight particulars, was the unpardonable sin."

While he was successful professionally, Bierce found little happiness in a world where so few people met his expectations. His marriage ended in divorce, and both of his sons died at an early age. In 1913, at age 71, the lonely writer traveled to Mexico, a country in the midst of a bloody civil war. To this day, his fate is unknown, although a reasonable speculation is that he was killed during the siege of Ojinaga in 1914. "An Occurrence at Owl Creek Bridge" may foreshadow that death during wartime.

Preview

Connecting to the Literature

"All's fair in love and war." This phrase has been used to excuse everything from trivial lies to wide-scale atrocities. Do you think there are times when the rules of the game involve no rules at all?

2 Literary Analysis

Point of View

In this story, Bierce uses his main character's warped perception of time to distort the reader's sense of reality. The way that you perceive time in a story may depend on the **point of view** from which it is told.

- In stories told from an *omniscient point of view,* the narrator is an objective observer of everything that happens.
- In stories told from a *limited third-person point of view,* the narrator relates the inner thoughts and feelings of a single character.

As the point of view in this story shifts from omniscient to limited third-person, the emotional tone and sense of time change as well.

Connecting Literary Elements

In order to convey the strange and stressful events of this story, Bierce uses a literary technique known as **stream of consciousness.** Using this style, Bierce reports thoughts and ideas the way the human mind experiences them—in short bursts, without full sentences, and often without clear or logical connections. As you read, try to fill in the missing pieces by considering which events spark the thoughts or feelings the narrator describes.

3 Reading Strategy

Identifying Chronological Order

In Bierce's story, the action jumps backward and forward in time. To see the true **chronological order,** reorder events to represent the sequence in which they occurred. To understand the order of events in this story, create a timeline like the one shown.

Event

Vocabulary Builder

etiquette (et′ i kit) *n.* appropriate behavior and ceremonies (p. 519)

deference (def′ ər əns) *n.* respect; courtesy; regard (p. 519)

imperious (im pir′ ē əs) *adj.* urgent; imperative (p. 520)

dictum (dik′ təm) *n.* formal statement of fact or opinion (p. 521)

summarily (sə mer′ ə lē) *adv.* promptly and without formality (p. 521)

effaced (ə fāsd′) *adj.* erased; wiped out (p. 522)

oscillation (äs′ ə lā′ shən) *n.* act of swinging back and forth (p. 522)

apprised (ə prīzd′) *v.* informed; notified (p. 522)

malign (mə līn′) *adj.* malicious; very harmful (p. 525)

ineffable (in ef′ ə bəl) *adj.* too overwhelming to be spoken (p. 526)

2 Literary Analysis

Point of View

- Tell students that as they read this story, they will focus on the author's artful use of point of view to convey the main character's unique experience.
- Read the instruction about point of view together as a class. Draw students' attention to the distinctions between the omniscient and the limited third-person points of view. Ensure that students understand that an author might choose to shift between two points of view in a single story to create a particular effect.
- As they read the story, invite students to look for words that indicate distortions in the main character's perceptions of time and space.

3 Reading Strategy

Identifying Chronological Order

- Give students a copy of **Reading Strategy Graphic Organizer A** in ***Graphic Organizer Transparencies,*** p.104, to use as they read "An Occurrence at Owl Creek Bridge."
- Inform students that an author may choose to present the events of a narrative in an order that is significantly different from the sequence in which they occurred in real time.
- Encourage students to understand that authors alter chronological order to create dramatic effects of one kind or another.

Vocabulary Builder

- Pronounce each vocabulary word for students, and read the definitions as a class. Have students identify any words with which they are already familiar.

Differentiated Instruction Solutions for All Learners

Support for Special Needs Students
Have students read the adapted version of "An Occurrence at Owl Creek Bridge" in the ***Reader's Notebook: Adapted Version.*** This version provides basic-level instruction in an interactive format with questions and write-on lines. Completing these pages will prepare students to read the selection in the Student Edition.

Support for Less Proficient Readers
Have students read "An Occurrence at Owl Creek Bridge" in the ***Reader's Notebook.*** This version provides basic-level instruction in an interactive format with questions and write-on lines. After students finish the selection in the ***Reader's Notebook,*** have them complete the questions and activities in the Student Edition.

Support for English Learners
Have students read "An Occurrence at Owl Creek Bridge" in the ***Reader's Notebook: English Learner's Version.*** This version provides basic-level instruction in an interactive format with questions and write-on lines. Completing these pages will prepare students to read the selection in the Student Edition.

TEACH

Learning Modalities
Bodily/Kinesthetic Learners
Students may be better able to imagine the events that occur on the bridge if they clearly identify the positions, stances, and actions of the soldiers standing near the condemned man. Instruct a small group of students to use textual clues to "block" the scene, much as a director blocks a play.

❶ About the Selection

Ambrose Bierce creates a compelling depiction of the Civil War hanging of a Southern planter who has attempted (and failed at) an act of sabotage. Bierce explores the rapid movement of people's thoughts in the moments before death and the way in which the perception of time can become distorted in traumatic situations. As the character, Peyton Farquhar, falls toward his death by hanging, he imagines that the rope breaks and sets him free. In his fantasy, Farquhar plunges into the stream below, swims to safety, and returns home. Unaware that the events are taking place in the condemned man's imagination, the reader is surprised by the story's abrupt ending, when Farquhar's thoughts suddenly stop. Bierce describes Farquhar's dead body swinging "gently from side to side beneath the timbers of the Owl Creek bridge."

❶ An Occurrence at OWL CREEK BRIDGE

Ambrose Bierce

Background The senseless violence, death, and destruction Ambrose Bierce witnessed during the American Civil War (1861–1865) convinced him that war was terrible and futile. He set much of his best fiction, including this story, against the backdrop of this divisive war in which the agricultural South, whose economy was based on slavery, battled the more industrialized North. Fought mostly in the South, the war caused hundreds of thousands of casualties on both sides.

I

A man stood upon a railroad bridge in northern Alabama, looking down into the swift water twenty feet below. The man's hands were behind his back, the wrists bound with a cord. A rope closely encircled his neck. It was attached to a stout cross timber above his head and the slack fell to the level of his knees. Some loose boards laid upon the sleepers supporting the metals of the railway supplied a footing for him and his executioners—two private soldiers of the Federal army, directed by a sergeant who in civil life may have been a deputy sheriff. At a short remove upon the same temporary platform was an officer in the uniform of his rank, armed. He was a captain. A sentinel at each end of the bridge stood with his rifle in the position known as "support," that is to say, vertical in front of the left shoulder, the hammer resting on the forearm thrown straight across the chest—a formal and unnatural position, enforcing an erect carriage of the body. It did not appear to be the duty of these two men to know what was occurring at the center of the bridge; they merely blockaded the two ends of the foot planking that traversed it.

Beyond one of the sentinels nobody was in sight; the railroad ran straight away into a forest for a hundred yards, then, curving, was lost to view. Doubtless there was an out-post farther along. The other bank of the stream was open ground—a gentle acclivity[1] topped with a stockade of vertical

1. **acclivity** (ə kliv′ ə tē) *n.* upward slope.

Differentiated Instruction Solutions for All Learners

Accessibility at a Glance

	"An Occurrence at Owl Creek Bridge"
Context	Historical information, setting
Language	Stream of consciousness
Concept Level	Abstract (death)
Literary Merit	Classic
Lexile	1010
Overall Rating	Average

tree trunks, loopholed for rifles, with a single embrasure through which protruded the muzzle of a brass cannon commanding the bridge. Midway of the slope between bridge and fort were the spectators—a single company of infantry in line, at "parade rest," the butts of the rifles on the ground, the barrels inclining slightly backward against the right shoulder, the hands crossed upon the stock. A lieutenant stood at the right of the line, the point of his sword upon the ground, his left hand resting upon his right. Excepting the group of four at the center of the bridge, not a man moved. The company faced the bridge, staring stonily, motionless. The sentinels, facing the banks of the stream, might have been statues to adorn the bridge. The captain stood with folded arms, silent, observing the work of his subordinates, but making no sign. Death is a dignitary who when he comes announced is to be received with formal manifestations of respect, even by those most familiar with him. In the code of military etiquette silence and fixity are forms of deference.

The man who was engaged in being hanged was apparently about thirty-five years of age. He was a civilian, if one might judge from his habit, which was that of a planter. His features were good—a straight nose, firm mouth, broad forehead, from which his long, dark hair was combed straight back, falling behind his ears to the collar of his well-fitting frock coat. He wore a mustache and pointed beard, but no whiskers; his eyes were large and dark gray, and had a kindly expression which one would hardly have expected in one whose neck was in the hemp. Evidently this was no vulgar assassin. The liberal military code makes provision for hanging many kinds of persons, and gentlemen are not excluded.

The preparations being complete, the two private soldiers stepped aside and each drew away the plank upon which he had been standing. The sergeant turned to the captain, saluted and placed himself immediately behind that officer, who in turn moved apart one pace. These movements left the condemned man and the sergeant standing on the two ends of the same plank, which spanned three of the crossties of the

Vocabulary Builder

etiquette (et′ i kit) *n.* appropriate behavior and ceremonies

deference (def′ ər əns) *n.* respect; courtesy; regard

3 **▼ Critical Viewing**
Which of the men in this photo seem to show an attitude of military etiquette? Explain. **[Interpret]**

4 **Reading Check**
What event is about to take place on the bridge?

2 Background
History
During the Civil War, executions were always carried out according to strict military code. In that war, as in most others, civilian attempts at sabotage were treated harshly; the culprits were immediately hanged or shot. Saboteurs knew the extreme penalty for their deeds.

3 Critical Viewing
Answer: The posture and bearing of the figure at far right suggests a formal military etiquette. The other men, engaged in preparing their weapons, reveal less formal postures and attitudes.

4 Reading Check
Answer: A civilian is about to be hanged by members of the Federal army.

Differentiated Instruction
Solutions for All Learners

Strategy for Less Proficient Readers
Suggest that as they read independently, students use self-sticking notes to mark any passages that present them with confusing ideas or vocabulary but do not stop reading. Sustained reading like this may clarify many ambiguous points. If students remain confused about certain passages, they can use the self-sticking notes to return to these pages and to ask questions during a class discussion.

Enrichment for Advanced Readers
Invite students to analyze the second paragraph in which Bierce carefully describes the preparations for the man's hanging. Have them consider both Bierce's style and the content of the passage by addressing these questions: In what ways does Bierce's precise language echo the actions he describes? What does Bierce mean by the idea of "Death" being a "dignitary"? Is such a sentiment particular to the military—especially in wartime—or does it find application in ordinary life?

❺ Literary Analysis
Point of View

- Ask a student volunteer to explain the difference between the omniscient and the limited third-person points of view. Then, ask students which point of view Bierce has employed in the story so far (objective).
- **Ask** students the Literary Analysis question: What phrase indicates that the point of view has shifted from omniscient to limited third-person? Explain.
  Answer: Students may point to the phrase *fix his last thoughts upon his wife and children* as a clear indication that the point of view has shifted. This shift allows Bierce to introduce the man's thoughts and emotions.

❻ Critical Thinking
Make Connections

- Guide students to notice the man's over-acute senses: A watch's ticking sounds to him like *the stroke of a blacksmith's hammer upon the anvil.* Invite students to explain what this description indicates about Farquhar.
  Answer: Students may say that Farquhar's perceptions are compromised by the trauma he is experiencing.
- **Ask** students to compare the man's heightened senses with those of other characters depicted in this textbook.
  Answer: Students may recall Roderick's ability to hear his sister in Poe's "Fall of the House of Usher."

❼ Reading Strategy
Identifying Chronological Order

- Read these two sentences for the class. Then, help students clarify the action described.
- Point out that the first sentence contains information about the first "action" (the condemned man's thinking) and the second action (the captain's nod). The third action occurs when the sergeant steps off the plank.
- If necessary, help students visualize the effect of this third action: with the sergeant's weight removed, the plank will tilt and send the man tumbling to his death by hanging.

bridge. The end upon which the civilian stood almost, but not quite, reached a fourth. This plank had been held in place by the weight of the captain; it was now held by that of the sergeant. At a signal from the former the latter would step aside, the plank would tilt and the condemned man go down between two ties. The arrangement commended itself to his judgment as simple and effective. His face had not been covered nor his eyes bandaged. He looked a moment at his "unsteadfast footing," then let his gaze wander to the swirling water of the stream racing madly beneath his feet. A piece of dancing driftwood caught his attention and his eyes followed it down the current. How slowly it appeared to move! What a sluggish stream!

❺ He closed his eyes in order to fix his last thoughts upon his wife and children. The water, touched to gold by the early sun, the brooding mists under the banks at some distance down the stream, the fort, the soldiers, the piece of drift—all had distracted him. And now he became conscious of a new disturbance. Striking through the thought of his dear ones was a sound which he could neither ignore nor understand, a sharp, distinct, metallic percussion like the stroke of a blacksmith's hammer upon the anvil; it had the same ringing quality. He wondered what it was, and whether immeasurably distant or near by—it seemed both. Its recurrence was regular, but as slow as the tolling of a death knell. He awaited each ❻ stroke with impatience and—he knew not why—apprehension. The intervals of silence grew progressively longer; the delays became maddening. With their greater infrequency the sounds increased in strength and sharpness. They hurt his ear like the thrust of a knife; he feared he would shriek. What he heard was the ticking of his watch.

He unclosed his eyes and saw again the water below him. "If I could free my hands," he thought, "I might throw off the noose and spring into the stream. By diving I could evade the bullets and, swimming vigorously, reach the bank, take to the woods and get away home. My home, thank God, is as yet outside their lines; my wife and little ones are still beyond the invader's farthest advance."

❼ As these thoughts, which have here to be set down in words, were flashed into the doomed man's brain rather than evolved from it the captain nodded to the sergeant. The sergeant stepped aside.

II

Peyton Farquhar was a well-to-do planter, of an old and highly respected Alabama family. Being a slave owner and like other slave owners a politician he was naturally an original secessionist and ardently devoted to the Southern cause. Circumstances of an imperious nature, which it is unnecessary to relate here, had prevented him from taking service with the gallant army that had fought the disastrous campaigns ending with the fall of Corinth,[2] and he chafed

Literary Analysis
Point of View What phrase indicates that the point of view has shifted from omniscient to limited third-person? Explain.

Vocabulary Builder
imperious (im pir′ ē əs) *adj.* urgent; imperative

2. **Corinth** Mississippi town that was the site of an 1862 Civil War battle.

Enrichment

Civil War Geography

The Civil War was fought in thousands of places all over the United States of America. Have students find out about ways in which the war affected the area in which you live. Guide their exploration with the following questions:

- Were any battles fought in your community, region, or state?
- What roads or railroads were built at the time?
- What historical structures were destroyed?
- Which factories were built to respond to the demands of the war, or were quickly retooled to make ammunition or uniforms?
- Which buildings became temporary hospitals?
- After which leaders and generals were streets or schools named?

Have students share their findings with the class.

under the inglorious restraint, longing for the release of his energies, the larger life of the soldier, the opportunity for distinction. That opportunity, he felt, would come, as it comes to all in war time. Meanwhile he did what he could. No service was too humble for him to perform in aid of the South, no adventure too perilous for him to undertake if consistent with the character of a civilian who was at heart a soldier, and who in good faith and without too much qualification assented to at least a part of the frankly villainous dictum that all is fair in love and war.

One evening while Farquhar and his wife were sitting on a rustic bench near the entrance to his grounds, a gray-clad soldier rode up to the gate and asked for a drink of water. Mrs. Farquhar was only too happy to serve him with her own white hands. While she was fetching the water her husband approached the dusty horseman and inquired eagerly for news from the front.

"The Yanks are repairing the railroads," said the man, "and are getting ready for another advance. They have reached the Owl Creek bridge, put it in order and built a stockade on the north bank. The commandant has issued an order, which is posted everywhere, declaring that any civilian caught interfering with the railroad, its bridges, tunnels or trains will be summarily hanged. I saw the order."

"How far is it to the Owl Creek bridge?" Farquhar asked.

"About thirty miles."

"Is there no force on this side the creek?"

"Only a picket post[3] half a mile out, on the railroad, and a single sentinel at this end of the bridge."

"Suppose a man—a civilian and student of hanging—should elude the picket post and perhaps get the better of the sentinel," said Farquhar, smiling, "what could he accomplish?"

The soldier reflected. "I was there a month ago," he replied. "I observed that the flood of last winter had lodged a great quantity of driftwood against the wooden pier at this end of the bridge. It is now dry and would burn like tow."[4]

The lady had now brought the water, which the soldier drank. He thanked her ceremoniously, bowed to her husband and rode away. An hour later, after nightfall, he repassed the plantation, going northward in the direction from which he had come. He was a Federal scout.

III

As Peyton Farquhar fell straight downward through the bridge he lost consciousness and was as one already dead. From this state he

3. **picket post** troops sent ahead with news of a surprise attack.
4. **tow** (tō) *n.* coarse, broken fibers of hemp or flax before spinning.

Literature in Context

8 History Connection

The Battle of Shiloh

Owl Creek is the stream that runs through Tennessee at the sight of one of the bloodiest battles of the Civil War—the Battle of Shiloh—where more than 20,000 soldiers died. Railroad bridges like Owl Creek Bridge were important because they gave the armies access over bodies of water.

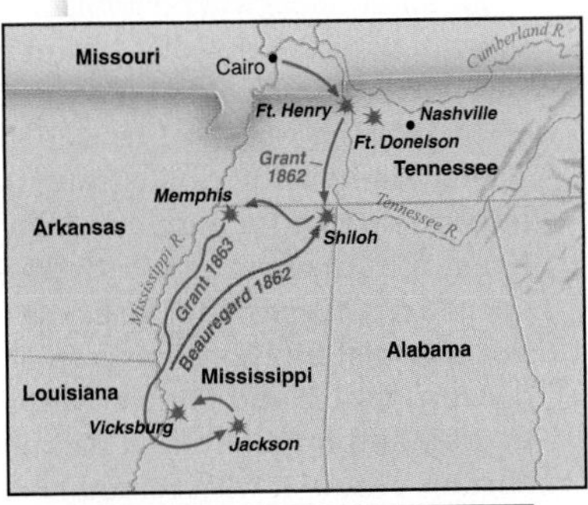

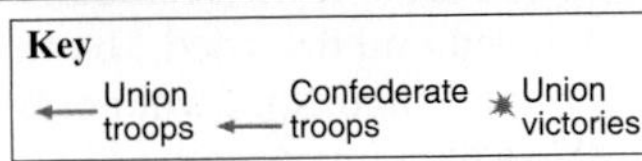

Connect to the Literature

Why does Farquhar ask so many questions about the bridge?

Vocabulary Builder

dictum (dik′ təm) *n.* formal statement of fact or opinion

summarily (sə mer′ ə lē) *adv.* promptly and without formality

11  **Reading Check**

In the war that divides his nation, which side does Farquhar support?

8 Literature in Context

The Battle of Shiloh In early April 1862, Union troops were headed toward Corinth—an Alabama town that was strategically important because two key railroads crossed at that point. On their journey, the Union soldiers collided with Confederate troops at Shiloh. Soon after the Battle of Shiloh, a Federal army occupied and then defended Corinth. They held the town until it was no longer strategically important.

Connect to the Literature
Encourage students to find information in the story about Farquhar's situation that supports their answers. **Possible response:** Farquhar wants to help the Confederate cause and is trying to determine whether he can sabotage the bridge.

9 Vocabulary Builder

Latin Word Root *-summa-*

- Draw attention to the word *summarily*, and read its definition. Then, tell students that *-summa-* comes from the Latin word *summa*, meaning "sum," or "whole."
- Remind students that the suffix *-ily* indicates that the word is an adverb, modifying the manner in which an action takes place.
- Guide students to see that Bierce's use of the word indicates the swiftness—or wholeness—with which punishment will be meted out to civilian saboteurs.

10 Reading Strategy

Identifying Chronological Order

- Discuss with students how the first paragraph of the story's second section differs from the preceding paragraphs.
- If necessary, explain that here, for the first time, Bierce provides background information on Peyton Farquhar.
- **Ask** students this question: Does the encounter with the "gray-clad soldier" take place before or after the opening scene on the bridge?
Answer: This scene occurs before the story's opening events. Here, the reader learns what generated Farquhar's interest in the bridge and can infer the reason for his execution.

11 Reading Check

Answer: Farquhar supports the Confederacy.

Differentiated Instruction Solutions for All Learners

Support for Less Proficient Readers
Students may need to reread (or to act out) the paragraph that begins on p. 519 with the words *The preparations being complete* in order to understand the procedure for hanging the man. Make sure students understand that when the sergeant steps off the plank, the condemned man will fall to his death.

Support for Special Needs Students
Help students understand that the Federal scout plants an idea in Farquhar's mind. The reader is expected to infer that Farquhar then set about to burn the bridge and that the scout reported this possibility to Union officers. Guide students to understand that Farquhar's capture is the result of the scout's trickery.

Support for Gifted/Talented Students
Students should note that Bierce describes the waters of Owl Creek as *swirling* and *racing* and then as *sluggish.* This contradiction hints that things may not be what they seem and that the man's perceptions of his environment and the events taking place may not be altogether reliable.

⓬ Reading Strategy
Identifying Chronological Order

- **Ask** a student volunteer to summarize the information Bierce conveys in section II of the story.
- Then, have students **respond** to the Reading Strategy question: Describe the shift in time that occurs between sections II and III.
Answer: Students may respond that the scene shifts back abruptly to the "present," in which Farquhar stands with a noose around his neck in the middle of Owl Creek Bridge and is about to be hanged.

was awakened—ages later, it seemed to him—by the pain of a sharp pressure upon his throat, followed by a sense of suffocation. Keen, poignant agonies seemed to shoot from his neck downward through every fiber of his body and limbs. These pains appeared to flash along well-defined lines of ramification[5] and to beat with an inconceivably rapid periodicity. They seemed like streams of pulsating fire heating him to an intolerable temperature. As to his head, he was conscious of nothing but a feeling of fullness—of congestion. These sensations were unaccompanied by thought. The intellectual part of his nature was already effaced: he had power only to feel, and feeling was torment. He was conscious of motion. Encompassed in a luminous cloud, of which he was now merely the fiery heart, without material substance, he swung through unthinkable arcs of oscillation, like a vast pendulum. Then all at once, with terrible suddenness, the light about him shot upward with the noise of a loud plash; a frightful roaring was in his ears, and all was cold and dark. The power of thought was restored; he knew that the rope had broken and he had fallen into the stream. There was no additional strangulation; the noose about his neck was already suffocating him and kept the water from his lungs. To die of hanging at the bottom of a river!—the idea seemed to him ludicrous. He opened his eyes in the darkness and saw above him a gleam of light, but how distant, how inaccessible! He was still sinking, for the light became fainter and fainter until it was a mere glimmer. Then it began to grow and brighten, and he knew that he was rising toward the surface—knew it with reluctance, for he was now very comfortable. "To be hanged and drowned," he thought, "that is not so bad; but I do not wish to be shot. No; I will not be shot; that is not fair."

He was not conscious of an effort, but a sharp pain in his wrist apprised him that he was trying to free his hands. He gave the struggle his attention, as an idler might observe the feat of a juggler, without interest in the outcome. What splendid effort!—what magnificent, what superhuman strength! Ah, that was a fine endeavor! Bravo! The cord fell away; his arms parted and floated upward, the hands dimly seen on each side in the growing light. He watched them with a new interest as first one and then the other pounced upon the noose at his neck. They tore it away and thrust it fiercely aside, its undulations resembling those of a watersnake. "Put it back, put it back!" He thought he shouted these words to his hands, for the undoing of the noose had been succeeded by the direst pang that he had yet experienced. His neck ached horribly; his brain was on fire; his heart, which had been fluttering faintly, gave a great leap, trying to force itself out at his mouth. His whole body was racked and wrenched with an insupportable anguish! But his disobedient hands gave no heed to the command. They beat the water vigorously with quick, downward

5. **flash along well-defined lines of ramification** spread out quickly along branches from a central point.

Reading Strategy
Identifying Chronological Order Describe the shift in time that occurs between sections II and III.

Vocabulary Builder
effaced (ə fāsd′) *adj.* erased; wiped out

oscillation (äs′ ə lā′ shən) *n.* act of swinging back and forth

Vocabulary Builder
apprised (ə prīzd′) *v.* informed; notified

strokes, forcing him to the surface. He felt his head emerge; his eyes were blinded by the sunlight; his chest expanded convulsively, and with a supreme and crowning agony his lungs engulfed a great draft of air, which instantly he expelled in a shriek!

He was now in full possession of his physical senses. They were, indeed, preternaturally[6] keen and alert. Something in the awful disturbance of his organic system had so exalted and refined them that they made record of things never before perceived. He felt the ripples upon his face and heard their separate sounds as they struck. He looked at the forest on the bank of the stream, saw the individual trees, the leaves and the veining of each leaf—saw the very insects upon them: the locusts, the brilliant-bodied flies, the gray spiders stretching their webs from twig to twig. He noted the prismatic colors in all the dewdrops upon a million blades of grass. The humming of the gnats that danced above the eddies of the stream, the beating of the dragonflies' wings, the strokes of the water spiders' legs, like oars which had lifted their boat—all these made audible music. A fish slid along beneath his eyes and he heard the rush of its body parting the water.

He had come to the surface facing down the stream; in a moment the visible world seemed to wheel slowly round, himself the pivotal point, and he saw the bridge, the fort, the soldiers upon the bridge, the captain, the sergeant, the two privates, his executioners. They were in silhouette against the blue sky. They shouted and gesticulated, pointing at him. The captain had drawn his pistol, but did not fire; the others were unarmed. Their movements were grotesque and horrible, their forms gigantic.

Suddenly he heard a sharp report and something struck the water smartly within a few inches of his head, spattering his face with spray. He heard a second report, and saw one of the sentinels with his rifle at his shoulder, a light cloud of blue smoke rising from the muzzle. The man in the water saw the eye of the man on the bridge gazing into his own through the sights of the rifle. He observed that it was a gray eye and remembered having read that gray eyes were keenest, and that all famous marksmen had them. Nevertheless, this one had missed.

A counterswirl had caught Farquhar and turned him half round; he was again looking into the forest on the bank opposite the fort. The sound of a clear, high voice in a monotonous singsong now rang out behind him and came across the water with a distinctness that pierced and subdued all other sounds, even the beating of the ripples in his ears. Although no soldier, he had frequented camps enough to know the dread significance of that deliberate, drawling, aspirated

6. **preternaturally** (prēt′ ər nach′ ər əl ē) *adv.* abnormally; extraordinarily

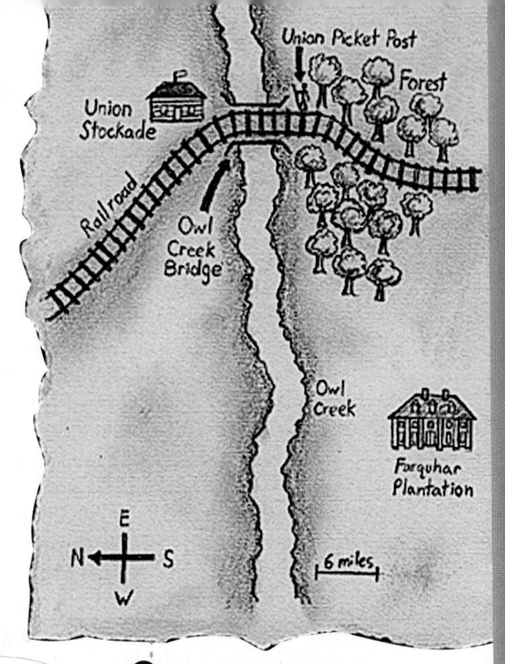

13 **Critical Viewing**
Based on this map, why is the bridge so important to the Union army? **[Interpret]**

14 **Reading Check**
What unusual event happens upon Farquhar's hanging?

13 Critical Viewing

Answer: Students should note that this bridge supports railroad tracks. Since trains were critical to the movement of troops and supplies, both Federal and Confederate forces would have wanted control of this bridge. However, the Union would be especially concerned about maintaining access, because one of their stockades lay within a few miles of the river.

14 Reading Check

Answer: Apparently, the rope breaks, and he falls into the water below.

Differentiated Instruction Solutions for All Learners

Vocabulary for English Learners

The term *report* is one of several examples in this story of a familiar word used in an unfamiliar way. *Habit,* smartly, *sleepers,* and *bank* are others. Guide students to use context clues or to consult a dictionary to ascertain the meanings of these words as Bierce uses them.

Enrichment for Advanced Readers

Students may enjoy reading Edgar Allan Poe's short story "The Tell-Tale Heart" to appreciate another striking example of a character who is "preternaturally keen and alert." As his mental condition deteriorates, the narrator of Poe's famous story hears "all things in heaven and hell." Likewise, students may draw comparisons to Usher's ability to hear his sister in Poe's "Fall of the House of Usher." Invite students to compare and contrast the reasons for these heightened senses in all three characters.

15 Reading Strategy
Identifying Chronological Order

- Ask one or more students to review the story so far to find passages that describe the locations and weaponry of the Union soldiers. For example, students might identify this passage from the story's first paragraph: *A sentinel stood at each end of the bridge . . . with his rifle in the position known as "support." . . .*
- **Ask** students the Reading Strategy question: What event might these words announce?
  Answer: These words probably announce the commencement of gunfire aimed at Farquhar by the company of Federal soldiers.

16 Background
History

In 1862, soldiers fired muzzle-loading rifles, so a capable marksman could get off just two shots per minute. Thus, after the men on the bridge fire once, Farquhar has about thirty seconds of safety before the next round of shots.

17 Literary Analysis
Point of View and Stream of Consciousness

- Read aloud this paragraph, in which Bierce describes Farquhar's perceptions of and reactions to various physical phenomena. Have students evaluate the reliability of the narrator as you read.

➤ **Monitor Progress: Ask** students the Literary Analysis question: What clues does Bierce give you to suggest that the speaker may not be totally reliable as a witness?
Answer: Students may note details such as the narrator's use of exclamation points and his presentation of patently absurd information *(heard the deflected shot humming through the air ahead, and in an instant it was cracking and smashing . . . in the forest beyond).*

chant; the lieutenant on shore was taking a part in the morning's work. How coldly and pitilessly—with what an even, calm intonation, presaging,[7] and enforcing tranquillity in the men—with what accurately measured intervals fell those cruel words:

15 "Attention, company! . . . Shoulder arms! . . . Ready! . . . Aim! . . . Fire!"

Farquhar dived—dived as deeply as he could. The water roared in his ears like the voice of Niagara, yet he heard the dulled thunder of the volley and, rising again toward the surface, met shining bits of metal, singularly flattened, oscillating slowly downward. Some of them touched him on the face and hands, then fell away, continuing their descent. One lodged between his collar and neck; it was uncomfortably warm and he snatched it out.

16 As he rose to the surface, gasping for breath, he saw that he had been a long time under water; he was perceptibly farther down stream—nearer to safety. The soldiers had almost finished reloading; the metal ramrods flashed all at once in the sunshine as they were drawn from the barrels, turned in the air, and thrust into their sockets. The two sentinels fired again, independently and ineffectually.

The hunted man saw all this over his shoulder; he was now swimming vigorously with the current. His brain was as energetic as his arms and legs; he thought with the rapidity of lightning.

"The officer," he reasoned, "will not make that martinet's[8] error a second time. It is as easy to dodge a volley as a single shot. He has probably already given the command to fire at will. God help me, I cannot dodge them all!"

17 An appalling plash within two yards of him was followed by a loud, rushing sound, *diminuendo,*[9] which seemed to travel back through the air to the fort and died in an explosion which stirred the very river to its deeps! A rising sheet of water curved over him, fell down upon him, blinded him, strangled him! The cannon had taken a hand in the game. As he shook his head free from the commotion of the smitten water he heard the deflected shot humming through the air ahead, and in an instant it was cracking and smashing the branches in the forest beyond.

"They will not do that again," he thought; "the next time they will use a charge of grape.[10] I must keep my eye upon the gun; the smoke will apprise me—the report arrives too late; it lags behind the missile. That is a good gun."

Suddenly he felt himself whirled round and round—spinning like a top. The water, the banks, the forests, the now distant bridge, fort and men—all were commingled and blurred. Objects were represented

Reading Strategy
Identifying Chronological Order What event might these words announce?

Literary Analysis
Point of View and Stream of Consciousness What clues does Bierce give you to suggest that the speaker may not be totally reliable as a witness?

7. **presaging** (prē sāj′ iŋ) predicting; warning.
8. **martinet** (märt′ 'n et′) strict military disciplinarian.
9. ***diminuendo*** (də min′ yo͞o en′ dō) musical term used to describe a gradual reduction in volume.
10. **charge of grape** cluster of small iron balls—"grape shot"—that disperse once fired from a cannon.

Enrichment

Civil Engineers

During the Civil War, armies regularly blew up bridges and destroyed tracks to set back the pursuing armies. Civil engineers rapidly put these structures together again. Today, people with advanced mathematics skills can find work in several different engineering fields.

Share these distinctions with students:

- ***Civil engineers*** plan and implement municipal projects such as highways and airport runways.
- ***Mechanical engineers*** plan the design of engines and machinery such as elevators and water-sprinkler and irrigation systems.
- ***Electrical engineers*** design power systems and lighting for bridges and stadiums.
- ***Aeronautical engineers*** design aircraft, helicopters, and spacecraft.

Have interested students find out more about the work of engineers today.

by their colors only; circular horizontal streaks of color—that was all he saw. He had been caught in a vortex and was being whirled on with a velocity of advance and gyration that made him giddy and sick. In a few moments he was flung upon the gravel at the foot of the left bank of the stream—the southern bank—and behind a projecting point which concealed him from his enemies. The sudden arrest of his motion, the abrasion of one of his hands on the gravel, restored him, and he wept with delight. He dug his fingers into the sand, threw it over himself in handfuls and audibly blessed it. It looked like diamonds, rubies, emeralds; he could think of nothing beautiful which it did not resemble. The trees upon the bank were giant garden plants; he noted a definite order in their arrangement, inhaled the fragrance of their blooms. A strange, roseate[11] light shone through the spaces among their trunks and the wind made in their branches the music of aeolian harps.[12] He had no wish to perfect his escape—was content to remain in that enchanting spot until retaken.

A whiz and rattle of grapeshot among the branches high above his head roused him from his dream. The baffled cannoneer had fired him a random farewell. He sprang to his feet, rushed up the sloping bank, and plunged into the forest.

All that day he traveled, laying his course by the rounding sun. The forest seemed interminable; nowhere did he discover a break in it, not even a woodman's road. He had not known that he lived in so wild a region. There was something uncanny in the revelation.

By night fall he was fatigued, footsore, famishing. The thought of his wife and children urged him on. At last he found a road which led him in what he knew to be the right direction. It was as wide and straight as a city street, yet it seemed untraveled. No fields bordered it, no dwelling anywhere. Not so much as the barking of a dog suggested human habitation. The black bodies of the trees formed a straight wall on both sides, terminating on the horizon in a point, like a diagram in a lesson in perspective. Overhead, as he looked up through this rift in the wood, shone great golden stars looking unfamiliar and grouped in strange constellations. He was sure they were arranged in some order which had a secret and malign significance. The wood on either side was full of singular noises, among which—once, twice, and again, he distinctly heard whispers in an unknown tongue.

His neck was in pain and lifting his hand to it he found it horribly swollen. He knew that it had a circle of black where the rope had bruised it. His eyes felt congested: he could no longer close them. His tongue was swollen with thirst; he relieved its fever by thrusting it forward from between his teeth into the cold air. How softly the turf

Vocabulary Builder
malign (mə līn′) *adj.* malicious; very harmful

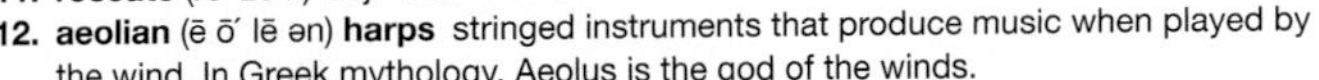

11. **roseate** (rō′ zē it) *adj.* rose-colored.
12. **aeolian** (ē ō′ lē ən) **harps** stringed instruments that produce music when played by the wind. In Greek mythology, Aeolus is the god of the winds.

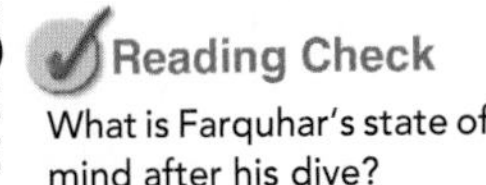

19 **Reading Check**
What is Farquhar's state of mind after his dive?

18 Critical Thinking

Interpret

- Draw students' attention to language that indicates the foreignness of Farquhar's surroundings. Invite students to speculate about why everything seems so unfamiliar to Farquhar, even though he is not far from home.
- Have students identify a handful of examples of sensory details that convey the idea that the man's flight is marked by strangeness and wonder. Encourage students to use a chart like the one shown to record these sensory details.

Sense	Detail
Touch	
Sight	great golden stars
Taste	
Smell	
Sound	

Possible answer: The details students select should be well-observed and clearly related to each of the five senses.

- **Ask** students to explain what these details may indicate (or have them refer back to this passage after they have finished reading).
Answer: Students may say that Farquhar's journey is more dreamlike than real. This sense of unreality is suggested by the fact that the surroundings seem unfamiliar, the journey seems endless, and the path seems untraveled.

19 Reading Check

Answer: He seems exhausted and perhaps delirious.

Differentiated Instruction Solutions for All Learners

Strategy for Special Needs Students
Once students know how the story ends, they can go back and read it a second time. During this second reading, encourage them to look for clues that indicate which elements are real and which exist only in Farquhar's imagination. Make sure students understand that nearly all of Farquhar's actions, observations, and thoughts described in Section III occur solely in his mind.

Strategy for Advanced Readers
After completing a first reading, suggest that students go back through the story and look for clues that show what was actually happening to Farquhar as he was imagining his escape. For example, in the passage in which he gasps for breath after rising to the surface of the water, Farquhar in reality may have been gasping because of the tightened noose. Later in the story, his swollen neck, congested eyes, and swollen tongue are all symptoms of death by hanging.

had carpeted the untraveled avenue—he could no longer feel the roadway beneath his feet!

Doubtless, despite his suffering, he had fallen asleep while walking, for now he sees another scene—perhaps he has merely recovered from a delirium. He stands at the gate of his own home. All is as he left it, and all bright and beautiful in the morning sunshine. He must have traveled the entire night. As he pushes open the gate and passes up the wide white walk, he sees a flutter of female garments: his wife, looking fresh and cool and sweet, steps down from the veranda to meet him. At the bottom of the steps she stands waiting, with a smile of ineffable joy, an attitude of matchless grace and dignity. Ah, how beautiful she is! He springs forward with extended arms. As he is about to clasp her he feels a stunning blow upon the back of the neck; a blinding white light blazes all about him with a sound like the shock of a cannon—then all is darkness and silence!

Peyton Farquhar was dead; his body, with a broken neck, swung gently from side to side beneath the timbers of the Owl Creek bridge.

Vocabulary Builder
ineffable (in ef´ ə bəl) *adj.* too overwhelming to be spoken

Critical Reading

1. **Respond:** With what emotions did you respond to the story's ending? Explain your answer.
2. **(a) Recall:** In Part I, what do you learn about the condemned man? **(b) Analyze:** Bierce makes deliberate decisions about what information to reveal and when to reveal it. How do his choices create suspense?
3. **(a) Recall:** Identify one example of Farquhar's distorted perceptions. **(b) Interpret:** What causes this distortion?
4. **(a) Recall:** What does Farquhar visualize moments before he is hanged? **(b) Connect:** In what way is his journey connected with this earlier vision?
5. **(a) Recall:** What sensation does Farquhar experience "with terrible suddenness" after he has been hanged? **(b) Distinguish:** What details suggest that Farquhar's escape occurs in his mind?
6. **Evaluate:** Do you think the portrayal of Farquhar's final thoughts is realistic? Why or why not?
7. **(a) Extend:** What does this story suggest about the psychology of a person facing a life or death situation? **(b) Speculate:** Are such insights applicable in daily life, or merely in extreme circumstances, like those of war? Explain.

For: More about Ambrose Bierce
Visit: www.PHSchool.com
Web Code: ere-9404

ASSESS

Answers

1. Most students will probably say that they were shocked by the story's ending.
2. (a) The reader learns only that a man who is about to be hanged is a 35-year-old civilian with a wife and children, as well as various details of his appearance. (b) They make the reader want to read on to learn more about the man and what is happening to him.
3. (a) **Possible answer:** He mistakes the ticking of his watch for "a sharp, distinct, metallic percussion like the stroke of a blacksmith's hammer upon the anvil." (b) **Possible answer:** His perceptions are distorted by his fear.
4. (a) He visualizes freeing his hands, releasing the noose, and fleeing. (b) His journey is an extended, detailed version of this brief visualization.
5. (a) He sees light shoot "upward" and hears "the noise of a loud plash" and "a frightful roaring" in his ears before everything goes "cold and dark." (b) **Possible answers:** The narrator says that he "was one already dead" and that he experienced a "sense of suffocation."
6. Many students will respond that this portrayal seems realistic because it suggests that someone who knows he is about to die could lapse into a dreamlike state.
7. (a) The story suggests that someone facing imminent death may escape the trauma and express the longing to live by lapsing into a dreamlike state. (b) These insights are especially apt for extreme circumstances, but also suggest the power of the imagination to create an alternate reality—one that is preferable to ordinary life.

Go Online Author Link For additional information about Ambrose Bierce, have students type in the Web Code, then select B from the alphabet, and then select Ambrose Bierce.

Apply the Skills

An Occurrence at Owl Creek Bridge

Literary Analysis

Point of View

1. Analyze the story to find examples of the two different **points of view** Bierce uses. Complete the chart below to identify the effects of these choices.

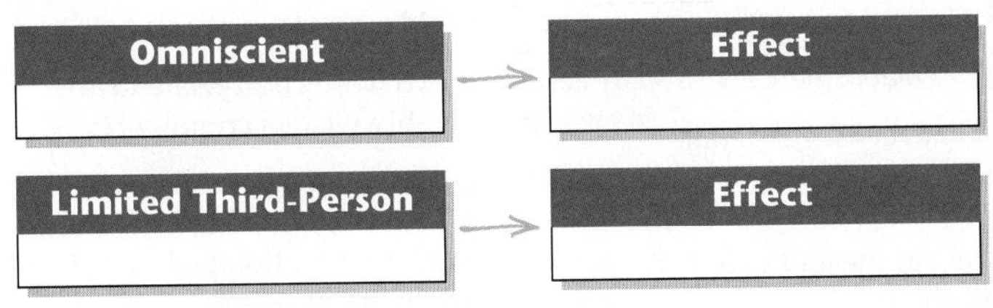

2. What is the effect of the shift in point of view in the last paragraph of the story?

Connecting Literary Elements

3. **(a)** What details in the second paragraph of section III are revealed through the use of **stream of consciousness**? **(b)** What "sharp pain" sparks Farquhar's thoughts? **(c)** In what ways does this passage mimic the natural, jumbled flow of thoughts?
4. Why is stream-of-consciousness technique particularly appropriate for this story?

Reading Strategy

Identifying Chronological Order

5. Which takes place first: Farquhar's encounter with the Federal scout or his preoccupation with the ticking of his watch?
6. How much real time do you estimate elapses from the opening to the closing scene of the story? Explain.
7. How did the story's ending change your initial perception of the sequence and duration of the events it describes?

Extend Understanding

8. **Social Studies Connection:** Farquhar was a civilian in the war—not a soldier. Do you think his death was justified? Why or why not?

QuickReview

Point of view is the vantage point from which a story is told.

In the **omniscient point of view,** the narrator is an objective observer.

In the **limited third-person point of view,** the narrator reveals the thoughts of a single character.

The **stream-of-consciousness** technique of narration captures the chaotic nature of the human thought process by jumping from one idea to another without transition.

To **identify chronological order,** reorder events into the proper time sequence.

For: Self-test
Visit: www.PHSchool.com
Web Code: era-6404

Answers

1. **Possible responses:** Omniscient—*A man stood upon a railroad bridge . . . twenty feet below;* Effect: conveys a sense of straightforward reporting, as well as a dry emotional tone; Limited—*A piece of dancing driftwood . . . What a sluggish stream!;* Effect: conveys a sense of wonder, as well as an emotionally engaging personal tone.

   Another sample answer can be found on **Literary Analysis Graphic Organizer B,** p. 107 in ***Graphic Organizer Transparencies.***
2. The abrupt shift surprises the reader and emphasizes the finality of Farquhar's death.
3. (a) Examples include *gave the struggle his attention, as an idler might observe the feat of a juggler* and *Bravo! The cord fell away.* (b) The sharp pain is caused by the rope tightening around his neck. (c) The passage moves from straightforward description of a physical sensation to the thoughts, and admonishments it triggers. There is a feeling of informality and exuberant disorder in the connections between sentences.
4. Stream of consciousness is appropriate for this story because Bierce's protagonist suffers a warped sense of time and reality. That distorted sense of reality is effectively conveyed through the stream-of-consciousness technique.
5. The encounter comes first.
6. A few minutes elapse.
7. The ending makes it clear that the events have taken place in a matter of seconds, rather than hours.
8. Students should support their answers with clear reasons.

Go Online Assessment Students may use the **Self-test** to prepare for **Selection Test A** or **Selection Test B.**

EXTEND/ASSESS

Answers

❶ Vocabulary Lesson

Word Analysis

1. false
2. false
3. false

Spelling Strategy

1. malign
2. align
3. resign

Vocabulary Builder

1. etiquette, deference, summarily, dictum
2. malign, ineffable
3. apprised, imperious, effaced
4. oscillation

❷ Grammar and Style Lesson

Peyton Farquhar desperately surveyed the landscape; plans of escape rushed through his mind.

Peyton Farquhar dropped from the bridge to the stream below; the shock of the cold water jolted him.

The silent interminable moment ended; a thunderous roar shattered the calm.

Writing Application

Students' paragraphs should use vivid descriptive language, including numerous compound sentences joined by semicolons.

WG Writing and Grammar, Ruby Level

Students will find further instruction and practice on semicolons in compound sentences in Chapter 27, Section 3.

Build Language Skills

❶ Vocabulary Lesson

Word Analysis: Latin Root *-summa-*

Summary suggests a brief, general idea. Likewise, *summarily* describes an action taken hastily or promptly. These words derive from the Latin word *summa*, meaning "sum, whole." Use your understanding of this root to decide whether each of the following statements is true or false.

1. *Consummate* professionals do poor work.
2. When you *summarize,* you elaborate.
3. A court *summation* covers every legal detail.

Spelling Strategy

When *gn* follows the vowel *i* at the end of a word, as in *sign,* you do not need a final *e* to make the vowel long. Complete the words below.

1. to speak evil of: mal__
2. to bring into line: al__
3. to give up one's position: res__

Vocabulary Builder: Context

Review the vocabulary words on page 517. Then, use them to answer these questions. Use each word from the list only once, and explain your answers.

1. Which four words best relate to a book entitled *Lady Windmere's Authoritative Guide to Manners for Servants?*
2. Which two words best relate to an unspeakably vicious comment?
3. Which three words best relate to a court clerk who hastily interrupts a judge to inform her that audiotaped evidence had been accidentally erased?
4. Which word relates to a table fan that revolves to cool an entire room?

❷ Grammar and Style Lesson

Semicolons in Compound Sentences

Compound sentences are sometimes formed by linking independent clauses—clauses that can stand alone as sentences—with a **semicolon** rather than a comma and a conjunction. This style is used to connect two closely related ideas.

Example: They hurt his ear like the thrust of a knife; he feared he would shriek.

Practice Choose from among the independent clauses below to create compound sentences. Use semicolons to join clauses that will form powerful sentences.

1. Plans of escape rushed through his mind.
2. Peyton Farquhar dropped from the bridge to the stream below.
3. The silent, interminable moment ended.
4. The shock of the cold water jolted him.
5. A thunderous roar shattered the calm.
6. Peyton Farquhar surveyed the landscape.

Writing Application Write a paragraph describing a scary experience. Mimic Bierce's style by using compound sentences joined by semicolons.

Looking at Style Bierce makes effective use of compound sentences in the objective parts of the story, where the pattern of short, linked clauses creates a rhythm like that of gunfire.

WG *Prentice Hall Writing and Grammar Connection: Chapter 27, Section 3*

Assessment Practice

Context **(For more practice, see *Standardized Test Preparation Workbook*, p. 29.)**

Use the following sample item to teach students how to use context clues to determine the meanings of specialized terms.

> The two private soldiers stepped aside and each drew away the plank upon which he had been standing. The sergeant turned to the captain, saluted and placed himself immediately behind that officer.

Which answer lists the soldiers in order from lowest to highest in rank?

A captain, sergeant, private
B sergeant, private, captain
C private, sergeant, captain
D private, captain, sergeant

The privates perform duties, the sergeant salutes the captain, and the captain is an officer. The correct answer is C.

Writing Lesson

Timed Writing: Critical Essay

Bierce was one of the first writers to use stream of consciousness—a style that imitates the natural flow of thoughts, images, and feelings. In an essay, explain how this style makes the story more dramatic. Use details from the story to support your ideas. ***(40 minutes)***

Prewriting *(10 minutes)* Reread the story and generate a list of passages where the use of stream of consciousness helps you to understand the speaker's thoughts. Then, select two or three passages to discuss.

Drafting *(20 minutes)* Focus on one passage at a time. Explain why the use of stream of consciousness reveals the character's thoughts with heightened realism and drama.

Revising *(10 minutes)* As you review your draft, note points where quotations from the story will help support your opinions and analysis. Make strong connections between your opinions and the passage you are quoting.

Model: Incorporating Quotations From the Story

Through stream of consciousness, Bierce enables readers to empathize with Farquhar as he desperately imagines a struggle to save his life. The moment of full peace when he reunites with his wife is especially powerful.

In his own words, Farquhar thinks he "must have traveled the entire night."

Appropriate quotations from the story create strong connections between the writer's opinions and the text.

WG Prentice Hall Writing and Grammar Connection: Chapter 14, Section 3

Extend Your Learning

Listening and Speaking Locate scientific reports about the ways in which perceptions of time change when people are under duress. Write a **summary** of your findings and their connections to this story.

- Summarize the reports you have reviewed.
- Summarize the distortions of time that Farquhar experiences.
- Note the ways in which Bierce's use of time supports or contradicts the research.

Share your summary with the class.

Research and Technology Use the map on page 523 to estimate how long it would have taken Farquhar to reach the bridge, destroy it, and return home. Include key information, such as Farquhar's mode of travel (on horse or foot) and rate of speed. Then, use slide show software or manual art materials to create a **visual model** of Farquhar's journey.

For: An additional research activity
Visit: www.PHSchool.com
Web Code: erd-7404

❸ Writing Lesson

You may use this Writing Lesson as timed-writing practice, or you may allow students to develop the essay as a writing assignment over several days.

- To guide students in writing this critical essay, give them the **Support for Writing Lesson,** p. 66 in ***Unit 4 Resources.***
- Students' critical essays should analyze various passages from the story to explain the dramatic effect of Bierce's use of stream of consciousness.
- Encourage students to scour Bierce's story for passages that show how the use of stream of consciousness captures Peyton Farquhar's experience better than a conventional narrative approach would do.
- To guide students in developing their critical essays.
- Use the Response to Literature rubrics in ***General Resources,*** pp. 65–66, to evaluate student's critical essays.

❹ Research and Technology

- Urge students to study the map closely and to start by calculating the distance between Farquhar's plantation and the Owl Creek bridge according to one or more routes.
- Encourage pairs or small groups of students to put themselves in Farquhar's position and reflect on the best possible route and means of travel to accomplish the destruction of the bridge.
- The **Support for Extend Your Learning** page (***Unit 4 Resources,*** p. 67) provides guided note-taking opportunities to help students complete the Extend Your Learning activities.

Go Online Research — Have students type in the Web Code for another research activity.

Assessment Resources

Unit 4 Resources
Selection Test A, pp. 69–71
Selection Test B, pp. 72–74

General Resources
Rubrics for Response to Literature, pp. 65–66

Go Online Assessment — Students may use the **Self-test** to prepare for **Selection Test A** or **Selection Test B.**

Meeting Your Standards

Students will

1. **analyze and respond to literary elements.**
   - Literary Analysis: Diction
2. **read, comprehend, analyze, and critique speeches and a letter.**
   - Reading Strategy: Using Background Knowledge
   - Reading Check questions
   - Apply the Skills questions
   - Assessment Practice (ATE)
3. **develop vocabulary.**
   - Vocabulary Lesson: Greek Word Part: *-archy-*
4. **understand and apply written and oral language conventions.**
   - Spelling Strategy
   - Grammar and Style Lesson: Parallel Structure
5. **develop writing proficiency.**
   - Writing Lesson: Diary Entry
6. **develop appropriate research strategies.**
   - Extend Your Learning: Web site
7. **understand and apply listening and speaking strategies.**
   - Extend Your Learning: Mock Supreme Court Hearing

Block Scheduling: Use one 90-minute class period to preteach the skills and have students read the selection. Use a second 90-minute class period to assess students' mastery of skills, extend their learning, and monitor their progress.

Homework Suggestions

Following are possibilities for homework assignments.

- Support pages from *Unit 4 Resources:*
  Literary Analysis
  Reading Strategy
  Vocabulary Builder
  Grammar and Style
- An Extend Your Learning project and the Writing Lesson for this selection group may be completed over several days.

Step-by-Step Teaching Guide	Pacing Guide
PRETEACH	
• Administer Vocabulary and Reading Warm-ups as necessary.	5 min.
• Engage students' interest with the motivation activity.	5 min.
• Read and discuss author and background features. **FT**	10 min.
• Introduce the Literary Analysis Skill: Diction. **FT**	5 min.
• Introduce the Reading Strategy: Using Background Knowledge. **FT**	10 min.
• Prepare students to read by teaching the selection vocabulary. **FT**	
TEACH	
• Informally monitor comprehension while students read independently or in groups. **FT**	30 min.
• Monitor students' comprehension with the Reading Check notes.	as students read
• Reinforce vocabulary with Vocabulary Builder notes.	as students read
• Develop students' understanding of diction with the Literary Analysis annotations. **FT**	5 min.
• Develop students' ability to use background knowledge with the Reading Strategy annotations. **FT**	5 min.
ASSESS/EXTEND	
• Assess students' comprehension and mastery of the Literary Analysis and Reading Strategy by having them answer the Apply the Skills questions. **FT**	15 min.
• Have students complete the Vocabulary Lesson and the Grammar and Style Lesson. **FT**	15 min.
• Apply students' ability to use persuasive language by using the Writing Lesson. **FT**	45 min. or homework
• Apply students' understanding by using one or more of the Extend Your Learning activities.	20–90 min. or homework
• Administer Selection Test A or Selection Test B. **FT**	15 min.

Resources

PRINT

Unit 4 Resources

Vocabulary Warm-up Word Lists [**L1, L2, EL**] .... p. 75
Vocabulary Warm-up Practice [**L1, L2, EL**] .... p. 76
Reading Warm-up A [**L1, L2, EL**] .... p. 77
Reading Warm-up B [**L1, L2, L3**] .... p. 78

TRANSPARENCY

Graphic Organizer Transparencies

Literary Analysis Graphic Organizer A [**L3**] .... p. 110
Literary Analysis Graphic Organizer B [**L1, L2, EL**] .... p. 111
Reading Strategy Graphic Organizer A [**L3**] .... p. 108
Reading Strategy Graphic Organizer B [**L1, L2, EL**] .... p. 109

PRINT

Reader's Notebook [L2]
Reader's Notebook: Adapted Version [L1]
Reader's Notebook: English Learner's Version [EL]

Unit 4 Resources

Literary Analysis [**L3**] .... p. 79
Reading Strategy [**L3**] .... p. 80
Vocabulary Builder [**L3**] .... p. 81

TECHNOLOGY

Listening to Literature Audio CDs [L2, EL]

PRINT

Unit 4 Resources

Grammar and Style [**L3**] .... p. 82
Support for Writing Lesson [**L3**] .... p. 83
Support for Extend Your Learning [**L3**] .... p. 84
Enrichment [**L4**] .... p. 85
Selection Test A [**L1, L2, EL**] .... pp. 86–88
Selection Test B [**L3, L4**] .... pp. 89–91

General Resources

Rubrics for Response to Literature [**L3**] .... pp. 65–66
Rubric for Speaking: Presenting Pros and Cons .... p. 92

TECHNOLOGY

Go Online: Research [**L3**]
Go Online: Self-test [**L3**]
***ExamView®*, Test Bank [L3]**

Choosing Resources for Differentiated Instruction

[**L1**] Special Needs Students
[**L2**] Below-Level Students
[**L3**] All Students
[**L4**] Advanced Students
[**EL**] English Learners

FT Fast Track Instruction: To move the lesson more quickly, use the strategies and activities identified with **FT**.

Scaffolding for Less Proficient and Advanced Students

The leveled Critical Thinking questions after selections progress in the levels of thinking required to answer them. To address the needs of your different students, you may use the (a) level questions for your less proficient students and the (b) level questions with your on-level and advanced students. The occasional (c) level questions are appropriate for your advanced students.

PRENTICE HALL
TeacherEXPRESS™ Plan · Teach · Assess
Use this complete suite of powerful teaching tools to make lesson planning and testing quicker and easier.

PRENTICE HALL
StudentEXPRESS™ Learn · Study · Succeed
Use the interactive textbook (online and on CD-ROM) to make selections and activities come alive with audio and video support and interactive questions.

PRETEACH

Motivation

If you can obtain a taped version of Ward and Burns's documentary *The Civil War,* you might wish to use it to give students some sense of the carnage and destruction that the war created. Tell students that the selections presented here address the turmoil caused by a war between two opposed groups of states. Ask students to discuss the ways in which a civil war might be considered more devastating than a war with an "external" enemy.

❶ Background

More About the Authors

Stories abound regarding Lincoln's drafting of the Gettysburg Address: He wrote it the week before; he wrote it the night before; he wrote it on the train; he wrote it on a piece of scrap paper. Certainly, we know that he was still revising it even as he spoke, adding the phrase "under God" to describe the nation. An experienced orator, Lincoln probably anticipated the positive effect this suggestion of divine approval of the United States and its goals of freedom would have on the audience.

It has been computed that Lincoln's printed speeches and writings contain 1,078,365 words. This figure is even more impressive when one considers that his writing style is admired especially for its precision and conciseness.

Robert E. Lee may have been the most respected and admired Southerner of his time. Even Ulysses S. Grant remarked, "There was not a man in the Confederacy whose influence with the whole people was as great as his."

Build Skills | *Speeches • Letter*

❶ The Gettysburg Address • Second Inaugural Address • Letter to His Son

Abraham Lincoln (1809–1865)

Serving as president during one of the most tragic periods in American history, Abraham Lincoln fought to reunite a nation torn apart by war. His courage, strength, and dedication in the face of an overwhelming national crisis have made him one of the most admired and respected American presidents.

A man of humble origins, Lincoln developed an early interest in politics. He served in the Illinois state legislature and the United States Congress, where he earned a reputation as a champion of emancipation. In 1858, he ran for the United States Senate against Stephen Douglas. Lincoln lost the election, but his heated debates with Douglas brought him national recognition and helped him win the presidency in 1860.

Troubled Times Shortly after his election, the Civil War erupted. Throughout the war, Lincoln showed great strength and courage. He also demonstrated his gift for oratory. He was invited to make "a few appropriate remarks" in November 1863 for a dedication of the Gettysburg battle-field as a national cemetery. The world has long remembered what he said there.

Lincoln's great care as a writer shows in the Gettysburg Address, as it does in many of his other speeches. He worked diligently and thoughtfully to prepare messages that would have the effect he desired. Two important aspects of the Gettysburg speech are its brevity—just 272 words—and its reaffirmation of the democratic principles at the heart of American government. Lincoln was killed by an assassin's bullet in 1865 while attending the theater with his wife.

Robert E. Lee (1807–1870)

Robert E. Lee was born into a respected Virginia family and graduated with high honors from the United States Military Academy at West Point. During the Mexican War, Lee established a reputation as one of the finest military leaders in the United States Army.

Divided Loyalties Despite his military traditions, the job of commanding the Confederate army during the Civil War was not one that Robert E. Lee wanted. As the dispute over slavery grew, Lee was torn. A descendant of a number of distinguished patriots and statesmen, he believed in the Union and opposed both slavery and secession. Still, when President Lincoln offered him command of the Union forces, Lee refused to lead an army against his native state and resigned from the army, vowing to fight only in defense of Virginia.

A Difficult Task Unlike many Confederate leaders, Lee had no illusions about the South's power. Serving initially as commander of the army of northern Virginia and later of all the Confederate armies, he expected the widespread bloodshed and destruction caused by the war. He was an extraordinary military leader whose accomplishments and personal integrity in the face of overwhelming odds inspired great loyalty in both soldiers and civilians.

An avid letter writer, Lee wrote frequently to family members explaining his actions and expressing his feelings. On the eve of resigning his U.S. Army commission, Lee explored his divided loyalties in "Letter to His Son." After the war, Lee served as president of Washington College (now Washington and Lee) until his death.

Preview

Connecting to the Literature

Imagine being swept up in a conflict like the Civil War that pits friends and family members against each other. Divided loyalties, like those expressed by Robert E. Lee, were painfully common.

Literary Analysis

Diction

Diction, a writer's choice and arrangement of words, gives a piece of writing its unique quality. Whether formal or informal, concrete or abstract, the words a writer chooses help to convey feelings beyond the ideas presented. Look at these examples from the selections:

- **Lincoln:** To . . . extend this interest was the object for which the insurgents would rend the Union . . .
- **Lee:** I see that four states have declared themselves out of the Union . . .

As you read, contrast the ways in which each writer's diction reflects the different audiences, purposes, and occasions of his writing.

Comparing Literary Works

Lee's diction in writing to his son is more informal than the public speech drafted by President Lincoln. Despite this contrast, both documents provide a window into the private and public conflicts of the Civil War. Compare and contrast the information and insights these selections provide about the nation's great war.

Reading Strategy

Using Background Knowledge

If you read a historical document without understanding the situations that inspired it, you may miss most of its underlying value and meaning. **Use prior background knowledge** of the Civil War to analyze ideas, actions, and decisions in historical context. Complete a chart like the one shown to organize your ideas.

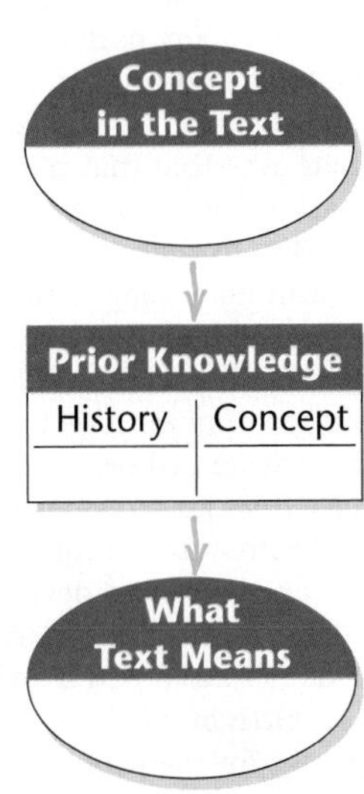

Vocabulary Builder

consecrate (kän′ si krāt′) *v.* cause to be revered or honored (p. 532)

hallow (hal′ ō) *v.* honor as sacred (p. 532)

deprecated (dep′ rə kāt′ id) *v.* expressed disapproval of; (p. 534)

insurgents (in sur′ jənts) *v.* rebels; those who revolt against authority (p. 534)

discern (di surn′) *v.* receive or recognize; make out clearly (p. 534)

scourge (skurj) *n.* cause of serious trouble or affliction (p. 534)

malice (mal′ is) *n.* ill will; spite (p. 534)

anarchy (an′ ər kē) *n.* absence of government (p. 535)

redress (ri dres′) *n.* atonement; rectification (p. 535)

Differentiated Instruction Solutions for All Learners

Support for Special Needs Students
Have students complete the **Preview** and **Build Skills** pages for these selections in the ***Reader's Notebook: Adapted Version.*** These pages provide a selection summary, an abbreviated presentation of the reading and literary skills, and the graphic organizer on the **Build Skills** page in the student book.

Support for Less Proficient Readers
Have students complete the **Preview** and **Build Skills** pages for these selections in the ***Reader's Notebook.*** These pages provide a selection summary, an abbreviated presentation of the reading and literary skills, and the graphic organizer on the **Build Skills** page in the student book.

Support for English Learners
Have students complete the **Preview** and **Build Skills** pages for these selections in the ***Reader's Notebook: English Learner's Version.*** These pages provide a selection summary, an abbreviated presentation of the skills, additional contextual vocabulary, and the graphic organizer on the **Build Skills** page in the student book.

2 Literary Analysis

Diction

- Tell students that as they read the two speeches and the personal letter in this grouping, they will focus on the diction of Lincoln and Lee.
- Read the instruction about diction aloud. Draw students' attention to the ways in which word choice and arrangement relate to a writer's audience and to his or her purpose in writing. Inform students that it is inaccurate to say that formal, abstract words create better diction than do informal, concrete ones (or vice versa). Instead, a writer's diction can be judged based on its appropriateness to the purpose and audience.
- As they read, suggest that students note and draw conclusions about each writer's word choices and style.

3 Reading Strategy

Using Background Knowledge

- Give students a copy of **Reading Strategy Graphic Organizer A** from the ***Graphic Organizer Transparencies,*** p. 108 to use as they read these selections.
- Help students recognize that they already possess knowledge about the Civil War. To do so, lead the class in a brainstorming session about the war. As discussion ensues, list and organize information on the chalkboard.
- Encourage students to offer not only factual information about the war but also any associations, impressions, thoughts, and feelings they have about the nation's geographical and ideological split during the middle of the nineteenth century.
- You might wish to have students examine photographs of various Civil War subjects to spur their ideas.

Vocabulary Builder

- Pronounce each vocabulary word for students, and read the definitions as a class. Have students identify any words with which they are already familiar.

Learning Modalities
Musical/Rhythmic Learners Like Lincoln's moving speeches, the lyrics of popular songs can carry the cry for peace to large audiences. Ask students to discuss why popular music can be a powerful tool for political ends.

❶ About the Selection

Lincoln's short but powerful Gettysburg Address places the Civil War into the historical context of the American fight for freedom. Lincoln asserts that the war is a test of the ideals for which colonials fought in 1776—in a sense, it is a continuation of the American Revolution. In an attempt to give direction to his divided country, Lincoln urges Americans to devote themselves to the task begun but not completed—to preserve freedom for *all* Americans.

❷ Literary Analysis

Diction

- Explain that "four score and seven years" is eighty-seven years. (A score equals twenty years.) Eighty-seven years before 1863 was the year 1776, the year the Declaration of Independence was signed.
- **Ask** students the Literary Analysis question: What impression do you get of the speaker from the level of diction in "four score and seven years ago"?
  Answer: Students should note that these formal words add to the eloquence of the speech.

❶

The Gettysburg Address

Abraham Lincoln November 19, 1863

Background The battle of Gettysburg, Pennsylvania, fought in July 1863, was an important Union victory and marked a turning point in the war. More than 51,000 soldiers were injured in the battle. On November 19, 1863, while the war still raged, a military cemetery on the battlefield was dedicated. Unsure of President Lincoln's availability, the dedication organizers slated him as a secondary speaker, asking him to make only "a few appropriate remarks." In drafting that brief address, Lincoln wanted to lead the 15,000 American citizens attending the dedication through an emotional, final rite of passage. He also needed to gain continuing support for a bloody conflict that was far from over.

❷ Four score and seven years ago our fathers brought forth on this continent a new nation, conceived in Liberty, and dedicated to the proposition that all men are created equal.

Now we are engaged in a great civil war, testing whether that nation, or any nation so conceived and so dedicated, can long endure. We are met on a great battle-field of that war. We have come to dedicate a portion of that field, as a final resting place for those who here gave their lives that that nation might live. It is altogether fitting and proper that we should do this.

But, in a larger sense, we can not dedicate—we can not consecrate—we can not hallow—this ground. The brave men, living and dead, who struggled here, have consecrated it, far above our poor power to add or detract. The world will little note, nor long remember what we say here, but it can never forget what they did here. It is for us the living, rather, to be dedicated here to the unfinished work which they who fought here have thus far so nobly advanced. It is rather for us to be here dedicated to the great task remaining before us—that from these honored dead we take increased devotion to that cause for which they gave the last full measure of devotion—that we here highly resolve that these dead shall not have died in vain—that this nation, under God, shall have a new birth of freedom—and that government of the people, by the people, for the people, shall not perish from the earth.

Literary Analysis
Diction What impression do you get of the speaker from the level of diction in "four score and seven years ago"?

Vocabulary Builder
consecrate (kän′ si krāt′) *v.* cause to be revered or honored

hallow (hal′ ō) *v.* honor as sacred

Differentiated Instruction Solutions for All Learners

Accessibility at a Glance

	Gettysburg Address	Second Inaugural	Letter to His Son
Context	U. S. Civil War	U. S. Civil War	U. S. Civil War
Language	Formal, use of parallelism	Complicated sentence structure	Formal
Concept Level	Accessible (war)	Challenging (war)	Challenging (war)
Literary Merit	Exemplary Speech	Exemplary speech	Cross generational
Lexile	1500	1130	1110
Overall Rating	Average	More challenging	More challenging

❸ Second Inaugural Address

Abraham Lincoln

March 4, 1865

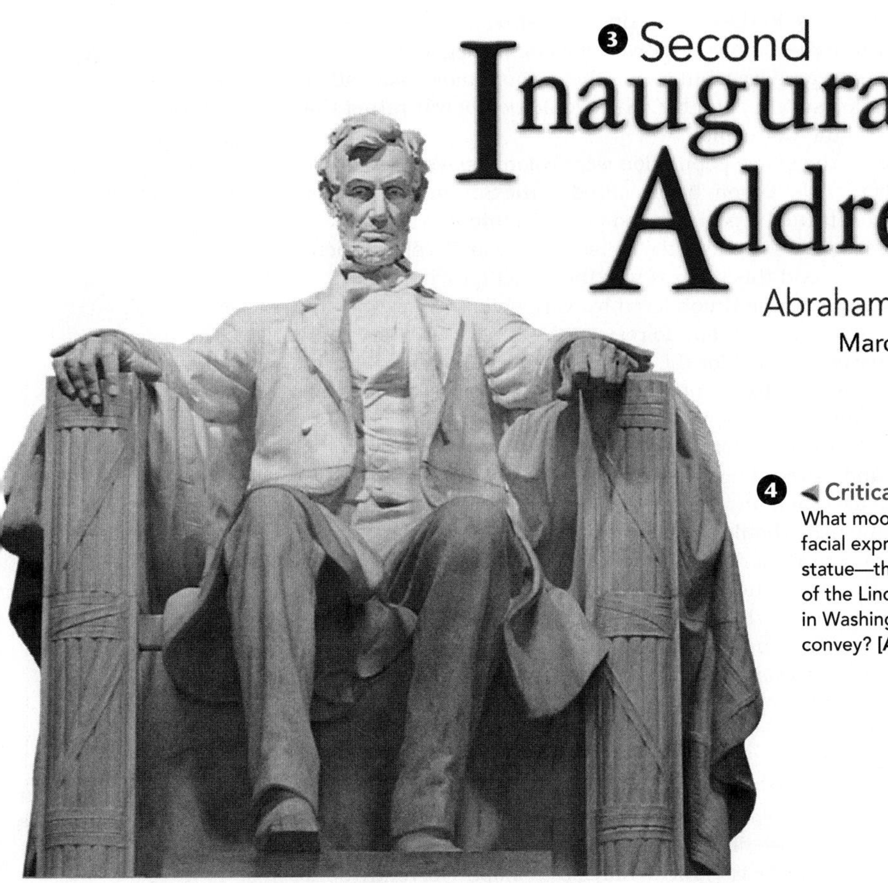

❹ ◀ Critical Viewing
What mood does the facial expression of this statue—the centerpiece of the Lincoln Memorial in Washington, D.C.—convey? **[Analyze]**

At this second appearing to take the oath of the presidential office, there is less occasion for an extended address than there was at the first. Then a statement, somewhat in detail, of a course to be pursued, seemed fitting and proper. Now, at the expiration of four years, during which public declarations have been constantly called forth on every point and phase of the great contest which still absorbs the attention, and engrosses the energies of the nation, little that is new could be presented. The progress of our arms, upon which all else chiefly depends, is as well known to the public as to myself; and it is, I trust, reasonably satisfactory and encouraging to all. With high hope for the future, no prediction in regard to it is ventured.

On the occasion corresponding to this four years ago, all thoughts were anxiously directed to an impending civil war. All dreaded it—all sought to avert it. While the inaugural address was being delivered from this place, devoted altogether to *saving* the Union without war,

❺ Reading Check
Why does Lincoln say there is less call for an extended address than there was at his first inauguration?

❸ About the Selection

In his Second Inaugural Address, delivered a month before his death, Lincoln recalls the issues that challenged the country four years earlier, acknowledges slavery as the real cause of the ongoing war, and laments the suffering caused by the war. He expresses hope for the end of the conflict and urges Americans to strive for a lasting peace.

❹ Critical Viewing

Answer: Students might describe Lincoln's facial expression with words such as *grave, serious, resolute, concerned,* and *solemn.*

❺ Reading Check

Answer: In the intervening four years, he has made numerous public declarations about the course he believes the nation must take.

Differentiated Instruction
Solutions for All Learners

Background for Special Needs Students
Invite students to reflect on what they may already know about how personal and political freedom is protected by law in the United States of America. Point out Lincoln's reference to the Declaration of Independence ("Four score . . ."), which demands freedom for all. Lincoln implies that Americans should seek to promote the views of that document rather than those of the Constitution, which does not recognize the rights of all people.

Background for English Learners
Encourage students to share with the class any background knowledge they may have about inaugurations. If students don't have much background, tell them that the President and Vice-President are sworn into office in an inauguration ceremony and that this ceremony is the occasion of the President's inaugural address. The Twentieth Amendment to the Constitution, ratified in 1933, set the terms of President and Vice President to begin on January 20.

❻ Background
History

Inform students that when Lincoln was elected, the country boasted a population of about thirty-one million, of which nine million lived in southern states. Of that nine million, four million were slaves. By the time of Lincoln's first inauguration, seven states had already seceded and others were on the verge of joining those in the newly formed Confederacy.

❼ Literary Analysis
Diction

- Have a strong reader deliver this section of Lincoln's speech clearly and slowly to the rest of the class.
- Point out that Lincoln not only alludes to God and to the Bible, but also uses a Biblical quote to support his point about the Civil War.

Monitor Progress: Ask students the Literary Analysis question: What can you infer about Lincoln from his diction in the passage beginning "It may seem Strange"?
Answer: Lincoln's diction shows that he is intelligent, well-educated, and knowledgeable about (as well as respectful toward) Biblical scripture.

insurgent agents were in the city seeking to *destroy* it without war—seeking to dissolve the Union, and divide effects, by negotiation. Both parties deprecated war; but one of them would *make* war rather than let the nation survive; and the other would *accept* war rather than let it perish. And the war came.

❻ One eighth of the whole population were colored slaves, not distributed generally over the Union, but localized in the Southern part of it. These slaves constituted a peculiar and powerful interest. All knew that this interest was, somehow, the cause of the war. To strengthen, perpetuate, and extend this interest was the object for which the insurgents would rend the Union, even by war; while the government claimed no right to do more than to restrict the territorial enlargement of it. Neither party expected for the war, the magnitude, or the duration, which it has already attained. Neither anticipated that the *cause* of the conflict might cease with, or even before, the conflict itself should cease. Each looked for an easier triumph, and a result less fundamental and astounding. Both read the same Bible, and pray to the same God; and each invokes His aid against the other. ❼ It may seem strange that any men should dare to ask a just God's assistance in wringing their bread from the sweat of other men's faces; but let us judge not that we be not judged. The prayers of both could not be answered; that of neither has been answered fully. The Almighty has his own purposes. "Woe unto the world because of offences! for it must needs be that offences come; but woe to that man by whom the offence cometh!"[1] If we shall suppose that American Slavery is one of those offences which, in the providence of God,[2] must needs come, but which, having continued through His appointed time, He now wills to remove, and that He gives to both North and South, this terrible war, as the woe due to those by whom the offence came, shall we discern therein any departure from those divine attributes which the believers in a Living God always ascribe to Him? Fondly do we hope—fervently do we pray—that this mighty scourge of war may speedily pass away. Yet, if God wills that it continue, until all the wealth piled by the bond-man's two hundred and fifty years of unrequited toil shall be sunk, and until every drop of blood drawn with the lash, shall be paid by another drawn with the sword, as was said three thousand years ago, so still it must be said "the judgments of the Lord, are true and righteous altogether."[3]

With malice toward none; with charity for all; with firmness in the right, as God gives us to see the right, let us strive on to finish the work we are in; to bind up the nation's wounds; to care for him who shall have borne the battle, and for his widow, and his orphan—to do all which may achieve and cherish a just and lasting peace, among ourselves, and with all nations.

Vocabulary Builder
deprecated (dep′ rə kāt′ id) *v.* expressed disapproval of

insurgents (in sʉr′ jənts) *n.* rebels; those who revolt against authority

Literary Analysis
Diction What can you infer about Lincoln from his diction in the passage beginning "It may seem strange"?

Vocabulary Builder
discern (di sʉrn′) *v.* receive or recognize; make out clearly

scourge (skʉrj) *n.* cause of serious trouble or affliction

malice (mal′ is) *n.* ill will; spite

1. **"Woe unto the world . . . offence cometh"** from Matthew 18:7 of the King James Version of the Bible.
2. **providence of God** benevolent care or wise guidance of God.
3. **"The judgments . . . altogether"** from Psalm 19:9.

Enrichment
Aaron Copland

At the outbreak of World War II, American composer Aaron Copland (1900–1990) was commissioned to write a musical portrait of a great American. In response, Copland chose Abraham Lincoln as his subject. "A Lincoln Portrait" blends original music with familiar American folk tunes to accompany a script based on Lincoln's own words. In his notes about the work, Copland explained the structure he attempted to create: "In the opening section I wanted to suggest something of the mysterious sense of fatality that surrounds Lincoln's personality. . . . The quick middle section briefly sketches in the background of the times he lived in. This merges into the concluding section where my sole purpose was to draw a simple but impressive frame about the words of Lincoln himself."

Invite students to listen to a recording of the piece and determine whether or not Copland succeeded in creating the effects he intended.

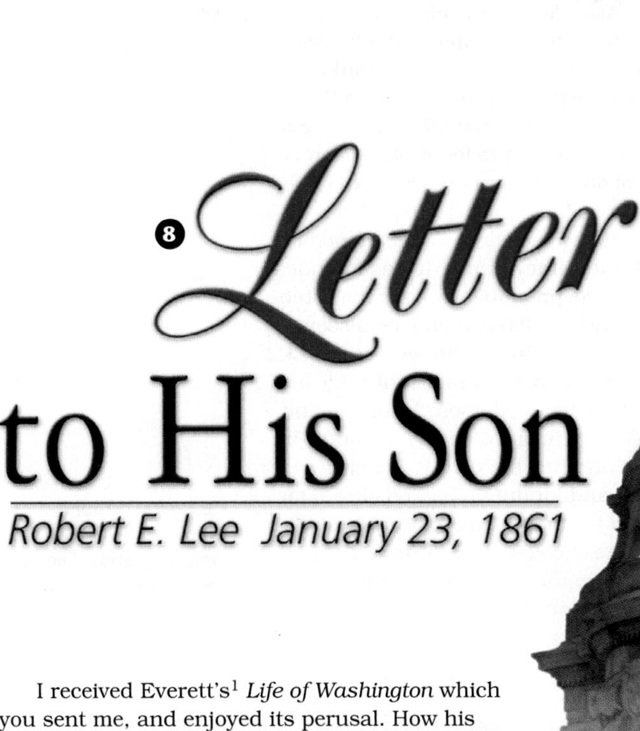

8 Letter to His Son

Robert E. Lee January 23, 1861

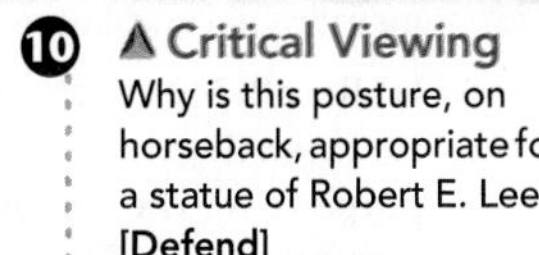

I received Everett's[1] *Life of Washington* which you sent me, and enjoyed its perusal. How his spirit would be grieved could he see the wreck of his mighty labors! I will not, however, permit myself to believe, until all ground of hope is gone, that the fruit of his noble deeds will be destroyed, and that his precious advice and virtuous example will so soon be forgotten by his countrymen. As far as I can judge by the papers, we are between a state of anarchy and civil war. May God avert both of these evils from us! I fear that mankind will not for years be sufficiently Christianized to bear the absence of restraint and force. I see that four states[2] have declared themselves out of the Union; four more will apparently follow their example. Then, if the border states are brought into the gulf of revolution, one half of the country will be arrayed against the other. I must try and be patient and await the end, for I can do nothing to hasten or retard it.

The South, in my opinion, has been aggrieved by the acts of the North, as you say. I feel the aggression and am willing to take every proper step for redress. It is the principle I contend for, not individual or private benefit. As an American citizen, I take great pride in my

10 ▲ **Critical Viewing**
Why is this posture, on horseback, appropriate for a statue of Robert E. Lee? **[Defend]**

Vocabulary Builder
anarchy (an′ ər kē) *n.* absence of government

redress (ri dres′) *n.* atonement; rectification

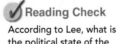

12 **Reading Check**
According to Lee, what is the political state of the country?

1. **Everett's** referring to Edward Everett (1794–1865), an American scholar and orator who made a long speech at Gettysburg before Lincoln delivered his famous address.
2. **four states** South Carolina, Mississippi, Florida, and Alabama.

8 About the Selection

In this letter Robert E. Lee addresses the difficult decision he faces as the country approaches a war that will pit the states against each other. The most respected officer in the United States Army, Lee explains that despite his strong belief in the Constitution and in preserving the Union, his strongest loyalty is to his home state of Virginia. He expresses his willingness to take up arms to defend his state. The letter illustrates Lee's dignity, loyalty, and bravery.

9 Vocabulary Builder

Greek Root *-archy-*

- Draw students' attention to Lee's use of the word *anarchy,* and read its definition. Then, tell students that the root *-archy-* derives from the Greek word meaning "rule" or "government."
- Write these words that share the root *-archy-* on the chalkboard: *patriarchy, oligarchy,* and *matriarchy.*
- Have students research each word's prefix and determine the meaning it adds to the root. Then, instruct them to write their own definitions of each word.
  Answer: *Pater* is Latin for "father"; a patriarchy is a government led by a strong male figure. *Oligos,* from the Greek, means "few"; an oligarchy is government ruled by a small faction. *Mater* is Latin for "mother"; a matriarchy is a government led by women.

10 Critical Viewing

Answer: Students may note that this posture accentuates the bravery, power, and heroism of the man.

11 Background

History

Just four days before Lee wrote this letter, Georgia seceded from the United States, joining South Carolina, Mississippi, Florida, and Alabama. Virginia seceded in April, 1861.

12 Reading Check

Answer: He states that it is "between a state of anarchy and civil war."

Differentiated Instruction Solutions for All Learners

Strategy for Less Proficient Readers
Read Lee's letter aloud, working paragraph by paragraph or even sentence by sentence, so that students can recognize Lee's formal tone, his sense of regret, and his deep respect for his state and its rights. You may wish to clarify that as a trained military leader, Lee would not actually "draw [his] sword," but rather would lead an army into battle from a position on horseback. Lee is, thus, speaking figuratively.

Strategy for Advanced Readers
Have students identify textual examples that reflect Lincoln's solid understanding of his audience's thoughts and emotions. Students may note that Lincoln recognizes the suffering people have endured and the losses they have experienced. In keeping with the times, he also invokes religious sentiments and appeals for divine inspiration. Encourage students to infer the issues, values, and goals Lincoln's audience held dear.

⓭ Reading Strategy
Using Background Knowledge

- Help students proceed through this dense paragraph in order to clarify the two warring impulses within Lee—his loyalty to both his nation and to his home state.
- **Ask** students the Reading Strategy question: Given what you know about Lee, why was he so committed to the Union and to Virginia? **Answer:** Lee was trained for the military in the North and served the Union Army as an officer in Mexico. Many of his ancestors were statesmen and American patriots. Yet, Lee was a proud native of Virginia, and this "simple" fact led him to defend the Confederacy rather than the Union.

ASSESS

Answers

1. Students should support their responses with clear reasons.
2. (a) The first was delivered after the Battle of Gettysburg; the second was delivered toward the end of the war, after he had been reelected. (b) His purpose was to rally the American public around the cause of winning the war. (c) His purpose was to lead people to recognize the need to heal the nation's wounds.
3. (a) He describes a vision of the nation as healthy, peaceful, and free. (b) This expression of hope and optimism effectively ends both speeches because it emphasizes the idea of regaining national unity.
4. (a) "Secession is nothing but revolution." (b) He argues that secession conflicts with the goals of the Constitution.
5. (a) He has given him a biography of Washington. (b) Lee asserts that Washington would be upset if he knew that the Union, that Washington worked so hard to create, might soon be destroyed.
6. **Possible answer:** Today's addresses are longer and usually far less eloquent.

country, her prosperity and institutions, and would defend any state if her rights were invaded. But I can anticipate no greater calamity for the country than a dissolution of the Union. It would be an accumulation of all the evils we complain of, and I am willing to sacrifice everything but honor for its preservation. I hope, therefore, that all constitutional means will be exhausted before there is a resort to force. Secession is nothing but revolution. The framers of our Constitution never exhausted so much labor, wisdom, and forbearance in its formation, and surrounded it with so many guards and securities, if it was intended to be broken by every member of the Confederacy at will. It was intended for "perpetual union," so expressed in the preamble, and for the establishment of a government, not a compact, which can only be dissolved by revolution or the consent of all the people in convention assembled. ⓭ It is idle to talk of secession. Anarchy would have been established, and not a government, by Washington, Hamilton, Jefferson, Madison, and the other patriots of the Revolution. . . . Still, a Union that can only be maintained by swords and bayonets, and in which strife and civil war are to take the place of brotherly love and kindness, has no charm for me. I shall mourn for my country and for the welfare and progress of mankind. If the Union is dissolved, and the government disrupted, I shall return to my native state and share the miseries of my people; and, save in defense, will draw my sword on none.

Reading Strategy
Using Background Knowledge Given what you know about Lee, why was he so committed to the Union and to Virginia?

Critical Reading

1. **Respond:** Which phrases in Lincoln's speeches do you find the most memorable? Explain your response.
2. **(a) Recall:** Briefly describe the occasion for each of Lincoln's speeches. **(b) Infer:** Beyond the stated reasons, what was Lincoln's underlying purpose in "The Gettysburg Address"? **(c) Infer:** What was his main purpose in the "Second Inaugural Address"?
3. **(a) Recall:** What vision of the nation does Lincoln describe at the close of both speeches? **(b) Connect:** In what way does an expression of this vision further his purpose?
4. **(a) Recall:** How does Lee define secession? **(b) Summarize:** In your own words, explain Lee's argument against secession.
5. **(a) Recall:** What gift has Lee's son given him? **(b) Connect:** Explain the line of reasoning that links Lee's acknowledgment of his son's gift to an argument against secession.
6. **Apply:** In what ways, if any, are Lincoln's speeches different from modern presidential addresses? Explain.

Go Online
Author Link
For: More about Abraham Lincoln and Robert E. Lee
Visit: www.PHSchool.com
Web Code: ere-9405

Go Online **Author Link** For additional information about Abraham Lincoln and Robert E. Lee, have students type in the Web Code, then select L from the alphabet, and then select Abraham Lincoln and Robert E. Lee.

Apply the Skills

The Gettysburg Address • Second Inaugural Address • Letter to His Son

Literary Analysis

Diction

1. Using a chart like the one shown here, analyze the **diction** of each writer.

	Examples of Diction	Audience	Purpose
Lincoln			
Lee			

2. In what ways does each writer's diction reflect and suit his audience and purpose?

Comparing Literary Works

3. **(a)** What words does Lincoln use to describe the war? **(b)** What words does Lee use to describe it?
4. **(a)** Based on the ideas and insights revealed in these selections, what personal qualities do you think Lee and Lincoln share? **(b)** In what ways do they differ?
5. Which voice do you find more engaging, Lincoln's or Lee's? Why?

Reading Strategy

Using Background Knowledge

6. **Using background knowledge,** explain why President Lincoln wrote such a short speech for his address at Gettysburg.
7. Why did Lincoln connect the honoring of the Gettysburg dead with the goal of continuing the war toward a Union victory?
8. In the "Second Inaugural Address," why did Lincoln suggest that both the war and an end to slavery were part of God's plan?
9. Why was Lee so opposed to secession?

Extend Understanding

10. **Social Studies Connection:** Lee describes the relationship between the states and the Union as "a government, not a compact." What are some of the ways in which people, organizations, and governments make compacts with one another?

QuickReview

Diction is a writer's choice and arrangement of words.

To **use background knowledge,** refer to information you already know about a subject to help you create meaning for current reading.

For: Self-test
Visit: www.PHSchool.com
Web Code: era-6405

Answers

1. **Possible answers:** Lincoln—Diction: we cannot consecrate—we cannot hallow this ground; we here highly resolve that these dead shall not have died in vain; Audience: several thousand Union supporters; Purpose: to help further the mourning process for the slain soldiers, and to gain support for the war. Lee—Diction: It is the principle I contend for, not individual or private benefit; Audience: his son; Purpose: to explain his support of the Confederacy.

   Another sample answer can be found on **Literary Analysis Graphic Organizer B,** p. 111 in ***Graphic Organizer Transparencies.***
2. Lincoln's address is intended for a general audience; Lee's writing is intended only for his son.
3. (a) Lincoln describes the war as *a great civil war, the great task remaining before us, the great contest,* and *this mighty scourge of war.* (b) Lee describes the war with the word *evils.*
4. (a) **Possible answer:** Both are dignified, thoughtful, and courageous.
   (b) **Possible answer:** Perhaps because of his military background, Lee seems to revile war more deeply and personally than does Lincoln; never does Lee describe a military effort in glorified terms. By contrast, Lincoln does so occasionally.
5. Students should support their answers with clear reasons and with details from the texts.
6. He was asked only to "make a few appropriate remarks."
7. As president, he wanted to see the nation survive. He did not want the enormous loss of life to have been in vain.
8. **Possible answer:** He did so because both sides shared the same religious beliefs.
9. Having served in the United States military and having descended from generations of loyal Americans, Lee felt strong ties to the Union.
10. Students might mention marriage, mergers, and treaties.

Go Online Assessment Students may use the **Self-test** to prepare for **Selection Test A** or **Selection Test B.**

EXTEND/ASSESS

Answers

❶ Vocabulary Lesson

Word Analysis

1. government with one ruler
2. a family or culture in which the father possesses ultimate authority
3. a government in which a select few hold all power

Spelling Strategy

1. confess
2. distress
3. stress
4. compress

Vocabulary Builder

1. b 2. a 3. a 4. c 5. b 6. a 7. c 8. c 9. a

❷ Grammar and Style Lesson

1. Fondly do we hope/fervently do we pray
2. we cannot dedicate/we cannot consecrate/we cannot hallow
3. until all the wealth/until every drop
4. all dreaded/all sought
5. of the people/by the people/for the people

Writing Application

Check student responses for faulty parallelism.

Looking at Style

Make sure students have chosen a clear example of parallelism, explained why it is parallel, and how it is effective.

WG Writing and Grammar, Ruby Level

Students will find further instruction and practice on active and passive voice in Chapter 8, Section 4.

Build Language Skills

❶ Vocabulary Lesson

Word Analysis: Greek Word Part *-archy-*

The word *anarchy* derives from the Greek word *archein*, meaning "to rule" or "to govern." With the prefix *an-*, meaning "without," *anarchy* means "without government." Use your knowledge of the root and the supplied information to write a definition for each word below.

1. monarchy (*mono* = single; one)
2. patriarchy (*patri* = father)
3. oligarchy (*olig* = few)

Spelling Strategy

Except when forming plurals, use *ss* to spell the *s* sound at the end of a word, as in *redress*. In your notebook, complete the spelling of the words below.

1. confe__
2. distre__
3. stre__
4. compre__

Vocabulary Builder: Synonyms

Review the vocabulary list on p. 531. Then, choose the word that is the best synonym, or word with similar meaning, for each first word.

1. consecrate: **(a)** destroy, **(b)** bless, **(c)** join
2. hallow: **(a)** honor, **(b)** greet, **(c)** enlarge
3. deprecated: **(a)** condemned, **(b)** proved, **(c)** enlarged
4. insurgents: **(a)** patriots, **(b)** loyalists, **(c)** rebels
5. discern: **(a)** hear, **(b)** understand, **(c)** ask
6. scourge: **(a)** punishment, **(b)** reward, **(c)** desire
7. malice: **(a)** grace, **(b)** scent, **(c)** spite
8. anarchy: **(a)** honor, **(b)** order, **(c)** chaos
9. redress: **(a)** atonement, **(b)** fear, **(c)** disturbance

❷ Grammar and Style Lesson

Parallel Structure

Parallel structure is the repeated expression of similar ideas in a similar grammatical form. Parallelism can involve the repeated use of similar words, phrases, clauses, or sentences. In the example, each phrase begins with the word *with*.

> *With* malice toward none; *with* charity for all; *with* firmness in the right . . .

Practice Identify the parallel structures in each of the following items.

1. Fondly do we hope—fervently do we pray—that this mighty scourge . . .
2. . . . we cannot dedicate—we cannot consecrate—we cannot hallow—this ground . . .
3. . . . until all the wealth piled by the bondman's . . . and until every drop of blood . . .
4. All dreaded it—all sought to avert it.
5. . . . that government of the people, by the people, for the people . . .

Writing Application Rewrite a sentence from "Letter to His Son," using parallel structure to emphasize Lee's ideas.

Looking at Style Review Lincoln's speeches to find a particularly strong example of parallel structure. Explain your choice, noting the effect of the example you have chosen.

WG Prentice Hall Writing and Grammar Connection: Chapter 8, Section 4

Assessment Practice

Context **(For more practice, see *Standardized Test Preparation Workbook*, p. 30.)**

Many tests require students to use context clues such as synonyms and antonyms to determine the meanings of unfamiliar words. Write the following passage from p. 524 on the chalkboard. Then, ask students the question that follows.

> Both parties deprecated war; but one of them would *make* war rather than let the nation survive; and the other would *accept* war rather than let it perish.

In this passage, the word perish means–

A flourish **C** expand
B compromise **D** die

The parallel construction of the sentence—"let the nation *survive*/rather than let it *perish*"—combined with the use of "rather," which means to the *contrary*, or *instead*, suggests that *perish* means the opposite of *survive*. *D* is the correct answer.

Writing Lesson

Diary Entry

It is the eve of the dedication of the cemetery at Gettysburg. As Lincoln, write a diary entry describing the message you will strive to deliver. Using the Gettysburg Address as your model, imagine Lincoln's feelings and note the main points he wanted to stress.

Prewriting Take notes on what you consider the three or four main points of the Gettysburg Address. Rank them in order of importance and summarize them in plain language. Spend a few minutes freewriting about each point. Use this as the basis of your draft.

Drafting From your notes, begin writing the diary entry. Use personal reflections and opinions as Lincoln would have in drafting the address. Emphasize your main points with persuasive language.

Revising Reread your draft to make sure it captures Lincoln's feelings with persuasive language. Add details to strengthen your argument.

Model: Revising to Add Persuasive Language

I know our country was born on the principle of freedom because our forefathers believed all men to be equal. Now ~~I want~~ *we must fight* to stop a terrible evil. ~~We can't have slavery.~~ *Slavery is wrong.* We must ensure freedom and equality for all.

Statements such as *we must fight* and *slavery is wrong* make the writing powerful and persuasive.

WG Prentice Hall Writing and Grammar Connection: Chapter 7, Section 3

Extend Your Learning

Speaking and Listening With a group, stage a **mock Supreme Court hearing** and argue for or against a state's rights to secede from the Union. After hearing arguments from "lawyers," each "judge" should render an opinion. As you plan, consider the following tips.

- Lawyers should point out fallacies and inconsistencies in their opponents' arguments.
- Judges should provide feedback on the arguments when rendering a decision.

Stage the hearing in class. **[Group Activity]**

Research and Technology Develop a plan for a **Web site** that provides information and images related to the Civil War. Create a flow chart that illustrates the links you plan to include in your site. If possible, use HTML software to develop an offline version of your site.

For: An additional research activity
Visit: www.PHSchool.com
Web Code: erd-7405

❸ Writing Lesson

- To guide students in writing this diary entry, give them the **Support for Writing Lesson** page p. 83 in ***Unit 4 Resources.***
- Students' diary entries should include all the main points in Lincoln's Gettysburg Address, reflect a strong organization, and employ slightly less formal diction than does the finished speech.
- Encourage students to reread the speech several times in order to identify Lincoln's main points and several crucial details that might be mentioned in the diary entry.
- Remind students to include interesting ideas or images in the diary entry that Lincoln might later have omitted.
- Use the Response to Literature rubrics in ***General Resources*** pp. 65–66, to evaluate students' diary entries.

❹ Listening and Speaking

- Encourage groups to spend more time preparing their arguments than they will delivering them. You might suggest a ratio such as 3:1 or 4:1 as a guideline.
- As they prepare, students should develop arguments for both sides of the issue in order to anticipate and answer opponents' arguments.
- Use the Speaking: Presenting Pros and Cons rubric in ***General Resources,*** p. 92, to evaluate students' presentations.
- The **Support for Extend Your Learning** page (***Unit 4 Resources,*** p. 84) provides guided note-taking opportunities to help students complete the Extend Your Learning activities.

Go Online Research — Have students type in the Web Code for another research activity.

Assessment Resources

Unit 4 Resources
- **Selection Test A,** pp. 86–88
- **Selection Test B,** pp. 89–91

General Resources
- **Rubrics for Response to Literature,** pp. 65–66
- **Rubric for Speaking: Presenting Pros and Cons,** p. 92

Go Online Assessment — Students may use the **Self-test** to prepare for **Selection Test A** or **Selection Test B.**

Meeting Your Standards

Students will

1. **understand and explain the language used in public documents.**
2. **read the Emancipation Proclamation.**

*See **Teacher Express™/Lesson View** for a detailed lesson plan for Reading Informational Materials.*

About Public Documents

- Have students read "About Public Documents." **Ask** students to identify and describe any such documents that they have encountered. **Answers** may include the Declaration of Independence, laws about driving, and statements of liability in hotels and other establishments.
- Ask students how public documents affect people's lives. Offer laws as an example. Help students recognize that laws are documents that affect their everyday behavior.

Reading Strategy
Analyzing an Author's Beliefs

- Have students read the information about analyzing an author's beliefs.
- Call students' attention to the Identifying the Author's Beliefs chart. Review the chart with the class, emphasizing that explicit statements usually reflect implicit beliefs. Ask students to apply this concept to the selection.
- Explain to students that public documents often contain highly formal and legal language that must be read and decoded carefully.

Reading Informational Materials

Public Documents

About Public Documents

What do the text of a law, the deed to a house, and the minutes from a legislative meeting have in common? They are all examples of **public documents,** official government papers that affect everyone living in a given part of a state or in the entire nation. These documents are referred to as public because they concern laws and issues in which all citizens have a stake. For this reason, these documents are made available for average citizens to read, analyze, and discuss.

The public document that you are about to read is one of the most important in United States history. It is the text of a formal announcement that President Abraham Lincoln signed on January 1, 1863, calling for the freeing of "all persons held as slaves" within the rebellious Southern states. Many historians believe that this public document, called the Emancipation Proclamation, altered the nature of the Civil War.

Reading Strategy

Analyzing an Author's Beliefs

Some public documents, such as census reports, are almost completely **objective**. They merely record factual information without seeking to support a particular point of view. Sometimes, however, public documents are **subjective**. They contain opinions and beliefs in addition to facts and express a specific point of view.

- Opinions may be hinted at indirectly through the author's choice of words or the decision to emphasize certain details.
- In contrast, the author's beliefs may be stated outright, making them explicit.
- Beliefs and opinions about a specific issue depend on assumptions—underlying claims that must be true if the opinion or belief is true. Writers may state their assumptions directly, making them explicit. Often, though, writers' assumptions are simply implied in the arguments they make. You can tell that they are making these implicit, or implied, assumptions by noting what general ideas or beliefs must be true for their stated arguments to be true.

To identify an author's beliefs, follow the steps outlined in the chart shown.

As you read the Emancipation Proclamation, consider the implicit and explicit beliefs it represents.

Identifying an Author's Beliefs

Step One

Look for opinion words such as *think, I believe,* or *in my opinion,* which signal explicit beliefs.

Step Two

Look for other words that sugg opinion. These words may be adjectives that have clear oppos For example, a writer might say that a course of action is *just;* another might say that it is *unfa*

Step Three

Look for details that suggest a specific point of view. Read the document sentence by sentenc Consider whether each detail is factual or whether someone co make an argument against it.

Differentiated Instruction Solutions for All Learners

Reading Support
Give students reading support with the appropriate version of the ***Reader's Notebooks:***

Reader's Notebook [**L2, L3**]

Reader's Notebook [**L1, L2**]

Reader's Notebook: English Learner's Version [**EL**]

By the President of the United States of America:

A Proclamation.

The source and type of public document should always be clear

Whereas, on the twenty-second day of September, in the year of our Lord one thousand eight hundred and sixty-two, a proclamation was issued by the President of the United States, containing, among other things, the following, to wit:

"That on the first day of January, in the year of our Lord one thousand eight hundred and sixty-three, all persons held as slaves within any State or designated part of a State, the people whereof shall then be in rebellion against the United States, shall be then, thenceforward, and forever free; and the Executive Government of the United States, including the military and naval authority thereof, will recognize and maintain the freedom of such persons, and will do no act or acts to repress such persons, or any of them, in any efforts they may make for their actual freedom."

"That the Executive will, on the first day of January aforesaid, by proclamation, designate the States and parts of States, if any, in which the people thereof, respectively, shall then be in rebellion against the United States; and the fact that any State, or the people thereof, shall on that day be, in good faith, represented in the Congress of the United States by members chosen thereto at elections wherein a majority of the qualified voters of such State shall have participated, shall, in the absence of strong countervailing testimony, be deemed conclusive evidence that such State, and the people thereof, are not then in rebellion against the United States."

Many public documents go into a great amount of detail. The details may slow down your reading of the document, but they are very important.

Now, therefore I, Abraham Lincoln, President of the United States, by virtue of the power in me vested as Commander-in-Chief, of the Army and Navy of the United States in time of actual armed rebellion against the authority and government of the United States, and as a fit and necessary war measure for suppressing said rebellion, do, on this first day of January, in the year of our Lord one thousand eight hundred and sixty-three, and in accordance with my purpose so to do publicly proclaimed for the full period of one hundred days, from the day first above mentioned, order and designate as the States and parts of States wherein the people thereof respectively, are this day in rebellion against the United States, the following, to wit:

Arkansas, Texas, Louisiana, (except the Parishes of St. Bernard, Plaquemines, Jefferson, St. John, St. Charles, St. James Ascension, Assumption, Terrebonne, Lafourche, St. Mary, St. Martin, and Orleans, including the City of New Orleans) Mississippi, Alabama, Florida, Georgia, South Carolina, North Carolina, and Virginia, (except the forty-eight counties designated as West Virginia, and also the counties of Berkley, Accomac, Northampton, Elizabeth City, York, Princess Ann, and Norfolk, including the cities of Norfolk and Portsmouth[)], and which excepted parts, are for the present, left precisely as if this proclamation were not issued.

The point of this language is to show that the proclamation applies only to states that have seceded from the Union. It does not end slavery in the border states or in parts of the Confederacy that had already come under Union control.

And by virtue of the power, and for the purpose aforesaid, I do order and declare that all persons held as slaves within said designated States, and parts of States, are, and henceforward shall be free; and that the Executive government of the United States, including the military and naval authorities thereof, will recognize and maintain the freedom of said persons.

Legal and formal language is common in proclamations.

Reading Public Documents

- Ask students to share their background knowledge about the Emancipation Proclamation. Point out that this document signed into law a proclamation first made public about 100 days earlier.
- Have students read the Proclamation and the notes that identify the elements of this document.
- Work with the notes to explicate the text. Call students' attention to the second note before they read the second paragraph. As students read, ask them to record in their notebooks the main points and the details that support the main points.
- If students are confused by the legal and formal language in the proclamation, have them read the last note. **Ask** students why they think such language is used.
  Answer: The language emphasizes the seriousness of this and other legal documents; it also ensures that the law is clear.

Differentiated Instruction

Solutions for All Learners

Support for English Learners

These students may find the language in the Emancipation Proclamation difficult to understand. Help them identify the main points of each paragraph. Then, have them read the paragraphs through once for an overview of meaning. Students can then use this context to determine the meanings of unfamiliar words. Have them check these meanings in the dictionary.

Strategy for Advanced Readers

These students may find that the Emancipation Proclamation is less than clear. Challenge these students to rewrite the document in a simple, clear style. Suggest that their revisions encompass diction and organization. You may wish to have students work in small groups to exchange ideas and then to share their new versions with the class. Revising the document will assure that they understand its main points.

ASSESS

Answers

Reading: Analyzing an Author's Beliefs

1. D

Reading: Comprehension and Interpretation

2. (a) Lincoln believes in the power that the Constitution vests in the President. He also implies that the emancipation of slaves is warranted by the Constitution. (b) He has decided to use that authority because it is a way to stop the rebellion against the United States.
3. (a) Lincoln calls on the freed slaves to work faithfully for legal wages and to be nonviolent, except when they need to defend themselves. (b) He will use the army and navy to defend the freedom of the former slaves.

Timed Writing

- Review the text notes to help students recall that public documents include a source note, use many details, and employ formal and often difficult language.
- Suggest that students plan their time to give 5 minutes to planning, 15 minutes to writing, and 5 minutes to reviewing and revising.

And I hereby enjoin upon the people so declared to be free to abstain from all violence, unless in necessary self-defence; and I recommend to them that, in all cases when allowed, they labor faithfully for reasonable wages.

And I further declare and make known, that such persons of suitable condition, will be received into the armed service of the United States to garrison forts, positions, stations, and other places, and to man vessels of all sorts in said service.

And upon this act, sincerely believed to be an act of justice, warranted by the Constitution, upon military necessity, I invoke the considerate judgment of mankind, and the gracious favor of Almighty God.

In witness whereof, I have hereunto set my hand and caused the seal of the United States to be affixed.

Done at the City of Washington, this first day of January, in the year of our Lord one thousand eight hundred and sixty three, and of the Independence of the United States of America the eighty-seventh.

Considering their legal and, at times, historic effects, place and date are key elements of public documents.

By the President: Abraham Lincoln

Secretary of State. William H. Seward

Monitor Your Progress

Assessment Practice

Reading: Analyzing an Author's Beliefs

Directions: *Choose the letter of the best answer to each question about the proclamation.*

1. Which of these beliefs is implicit but not directly stated in this document?
   - **A** The emancipation of slaves is an act of justice.
   - **B** The emancipation of slaves is warranted by military necessity.
   - **C** The Constitution states that slavery is unjust.
   - **D** The Constitution vests power in the president.

Reading: Comprehension and Interpretation

Directions: *Write your answers on a separate sheet of paper.*

2. **(a)** According to Lincoln, why does he have the authority to issue this proclamation? **(b)** According to the proclamation, why has he decided to use that authority?

Timed Writing: Exposition

Write your own public document to announce a new national tradition or holiday, such as a day commemorating an important event. **(25 *minutes*)**

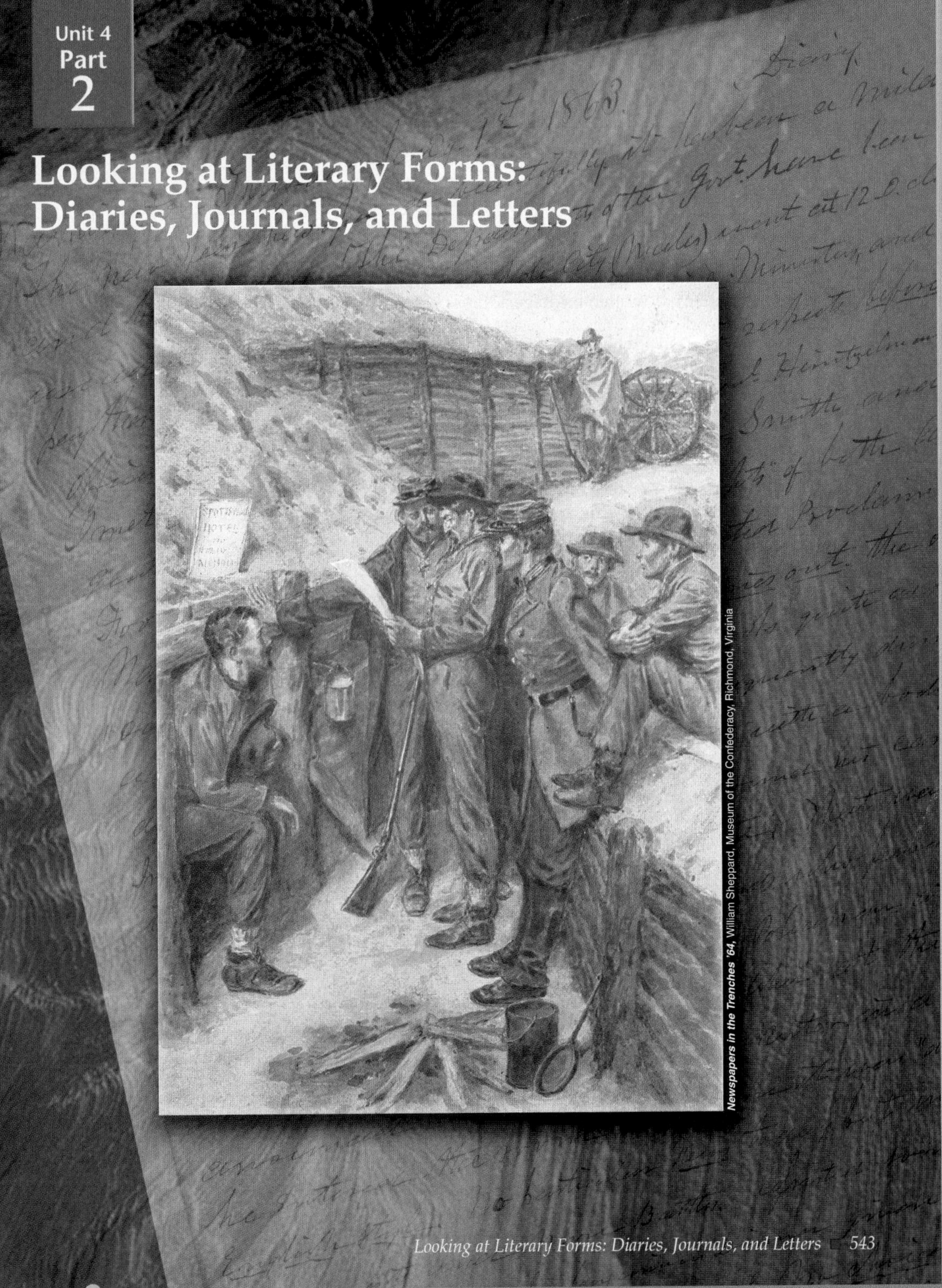

Unit 4
Part
2

Looking at Literary Forms: Diaries, Journals, and Letters

Newspapers in the Trenches '64, William Sheppard, Museum of the Confederacy, Richmond, Virginia

Selection Planning Guide

The firsthand accounts in Part 2 tell the story of the Civil War and its aftermath in the words of those who experienced it, both on and off the battlefield. In her journal, southern gentlewoman Mary Chesnut describes the attack on Fort Sumter. The accounts of Warren Lee Goss, Randolph McKim, and Stonewall Jackson provide three perspectives on the war from the soldiers who fought it. "Reaction to the Emancipation Proclamation" shows how the African American community responded to Lincoln's momentous proclamation, while Sojourner Truth's account demonstrates how much was still to be done in the fight for equality.

Humanities

Newspapers in the Trenches '64, William Ludwell Sheppard

This work shows another side of the war—the human faces of the men who, between battles, turned from soldiers into letter writers, journal keepers, and sharers of news.

Use these questions for discussion:

1. How does the artist communicate the fact that reading a newspaper is a special event for the soldiers?
   Possible response: They are gathered attentively around the single soldier who is holding a newspaper and they appear eager to hear the latest news.
2. Why might letters, journals, diaries, and newspapers have been so important to Civil War soldiers?
   Possible response: Besides being a diversion, reading and writing were a means of contact with the world outside the trenches; writing also helped them preserve a sense of their own individuality and humanity and gave them some hope of living on in some form, even if they died in battle.

Differentiated Instruction Solutions for All Learners

Accessibility at a Glance

More Accessible
An Account of the Battle of Bull Run
Reaction to the Emancipation Proclamation
An Account of an Experience With Discrimination

Average
from Mary Chesnut's Civil War
Recollections of a Private
A Confederate Account of The Battle of Gettysburg

Students will

1. recognize and appreciate features and perspectives of diaries, journals, and letters.
2. apply strategies for reading diaries, journals, and letters.

❶ Features of Diaries, Journals, and Letters

- **Ask** students why many people find diaries, journals, and letters interesting.
  Possible answer: Students may indicate that these forms offer insights into a person's thoughts and information about a person's private life.
- Review the distinctions among these types of writing and their value to readers and researchers. Diaries are meant for the personal use of the writer: to record daily events, emotions, and observations. Journals are similar to diaries but may record a specific event such as a journey. They are often meant to be read by others. Letters are written for a specific reader or readers, but collections of correspondence can provide insights to relationships between historical figures. Direct students' attention to the chart for examples of each.

❷ Flexible Forms

- After students have read these pages, **ask** how letters they write might differ from e-mails.
- **Answer:** Students may mention that e-mails are transmitted instantly to the reader. Because of their immediacy, they resemble conversations as much as they do written correspondence, which takes more time to exchange.
  Ask students to speculate on how people one hundred years from now might view our writing habits and styles.
  Answer: Students may speculate that our writing will appear odd or old-fashioned to people in the future, just as historical writing seems quaint to us.

Defining Diaries, Journals, and Letters

A **diary** is an autobiographical record of daily events, personal thoughts, and observations. Like a diary, a **journal** is also a record of daily events and the writer's personal responses, but it is usually less intimate than a diary. A **letter** is a written message addressed to a specific reader or readers. As works of nonfiction, diaries, journals, and letters are often written for small audiences to record the writer's ideas and reflections.

❶ **Features of Diaries, Journals, and Letters**
Diaries, journals, and letters often share certain characteristics.

Primary Sources Diaries, journals, and letters are all considered **primary source documents:** firsthand accounts of specific historical periods or events, written by eyewitnesses or participants. As a result, these three forms of writing often provide fascinating glimpses of real life during notable historical times—and are therefore valuable to historians.

A CONSCIENTIOUS JOURNAL KEEPER IS REALLY THE NATURAL HISTORIAN OF HIS OWN LIFE. —*Verlyn Klinkenborg*

Original Limited Audiences Diaries, letters, and journals are usually private forms of writing that are not intended for publication. Sometimes, however, interesting diaries and journals, or those written by famous people, are published after their death.

- A **private letter,** also called a **personal letter,** is not intended for publication but may end up being published anyway: for example, in a biography, history, or collection of letters by a famous person.
- A **public letter,** also called a **literary letter** or **epistle,** is a literary work written in the form of a personal letter but intended for publication.

❷ **Flexible Forms** Diaries, journals, and letters are usually written in **prose,** but there is virtually no limit to the flexibility of these forms. Diary and journal entries may include lines of poetry, fragmentary thoughts, anecdotes, drawings, and quotations that the writer finds inspiring or memorable. Similarly, a letter writer may use any style of writing, including poetry. Today, an e-mail, an instant message, or even a bulletin board posting on the Internet may be considered a type of letter, while a Web log, or **blog,** has become a popular type of diary for both ordinary people and journalists.

Extend the Lesson

Activity

- Have students skim the letter Abigail Adams wrote to her daughter, p. 216.
- **Ask** students the following questions:
  1. What unique perspective did Abigail Adams have on the White House?
     Answer: She was the first First Lady to live in the White House.
  2. What evidence in the letter suggests that Adams does not expect this letter to be published?
     Answer: Adams compares Georgetown unfavorably to Milton and asks her daughter not to share some of Adams's feelings about the White House and Washington with others.
- Have students evaluate a paragraph of the letter, noting which sentences are facts and which are opinions.

Perspective and Credibility

Diaries, journals, and letters have a certain honesty and credibility because the writer usually has no reason to try to influence a particular audience. On the other hand, the writer's reactions may be intensely personal and subjective. These personal forms are often a mix of fact and opinion. A **fact** is a statement that can be proved true. In contrast, an **opinion** is a viewpoint that cannot be proved, although it can by supported by facts and arguments. As you read, keep the following distinctions in mind:

- An **objective account** presents facts rather than opinions. The writer describes or explains something without interjecting opinions, commentary, or interpretation.
- A **subjective account** may include facts, but it also presents the writer's opinions, feelings, and judgments. Because diaries, journals, and letters are inherently personal forms of writing, we can assume that they are usually subjective accounts—and we value the opinions and insights they present. Keep in mind, however, that they may vary in their degree of subjectivity. Some examples may even be **biased**, reflecting a one-sided perspective or "slant" that obscures the facts.

Strategies for Reading Diaries, Journals, and Letters

Use these strategies as you read these literary forms.

Identify the Writer's Relationship to Events Determine whether the writer is an active participant in events, like Warren Lee Goss in "Recollections of a Private," p. 554, or an interested observer, like Mary Chesnut in her diary entries about the Civil War, p. 550. Consider how this relationship affects the writer's perspective and credibility.

Make Inferences About the Writer's Point of View As you read, look for details that reveal the writer's level of objectivity, subjectivity, or even bias. Consider what insights the writer reveals that might not appear in more formal writing aimed at a wider audience.

Compare and Contrast You can gain insight about a historical period or event by analyzing how different writers approach a similar subject or theme. For example, compare and contrast Stonewall Jackson's letter about the Battle of Bull Run, p. 558, with Randolph McKim's diary entry about the Battle of Gettysburg, p. 556, to understand two perspectives on the war.

- Review differences between facts and opinions with students.
- **Ask** students why journals and diaries may be better sources for the writer's true opinions than letters might be.
  Answer: Journals and diaries are usually not meant for publication; therefore, the writers would not have any reason to hide their true feelings. Letters are meant for other people to read, so the writing in letters might not reveal the writer's real thoughts.
- Have students clarify differences between objective and subjective accounts.
  Answer: Objective accounts contain facts and verifiable observations; subjective accounts include personal reactions and emotions in addition to facts.

4 Strategies for Reading Diaries, Journals, and Letters

- Tell students that the personal nature of diaries, journals, and letters makes it necessary for readers to use special strategies when reading them. Students need to keep in mind as they read these personal documents that the author intended them for specific readers, not for the public.
- Remind students that when they read these types of writing, they must take into account the influence of the writer's personal feelings and point of view.
- Emphasize that personal opinions and details can make history come alive for readers. Encourage students to look for reactions and personal connections to historical events as they read diaries, journals, and letters.

Differentiated Instruction Solutions for All Learners

Strategy for English Learners
Help students understand that the informality of diaries, journals, and letters is often evident in a writer's use of sentence fragments. For practice, have students write a fragment and then revise it as a complete sentence. Then, have students write a complete sentence and reduce it to a fragment. Discuss the different effects produced by fragments and complete sentences. Fragments may at times give a clearer picture of emotions than complete sentences will. They may also leave out information that that the original recipient of the writing would have understood yet cannot be reconstructed in later years, research.

Strategy for Advanced Readers
As they read selections in this grouping, guide students to "read between the lines" by looking for evidence of each writer's emotions, such as fear, passion, and anger. Have students work in pairs to determine whether both partners see the same emotions or whether the literature can be interpreted in more than one way. Encourage students to examine the relationship between the various emotions and each writer's personal circumstances and biases.

Meeting Your Standards

Students will

1. **analyze and respond to literary elements.**
   - Literary Analysis: Diaries, Journals, and Letters
2. **read, comprehend, analyze, and critique nonfiction.**
   - Reading Strategy: Distinguishing Fact From Opinion
   - Reading Check questions
   - Apply the Skills questions
   - Assessment Practice (ATE)
3. **develop vocabulary.**
   - Vocabulary Lesson: Latin Prefix: *ob-*
4. **understand and apply written and oral language conventions.**
   - Spelling Strategy
   - Grammar and Style Lesson: Capitalization of Proper Nouns
5. **develop writing proficiency.**
   - Writing Lesson: Problem-and-Solution Essay
6. **develop appropriate research strategies.**
   - Extend Your Learning: Model/Map
7. **understand and apply listening and speaking strategies.**
   - Extend Your Learning: Dramatic Reading

Block Scheduling: Use one 90-minute class period to preteach the skills and have students read the selection. Use a second 90-minute class period to assess students' mastery of skills, extend their learning, and monitor their progress.

Homework Suggestions

Following are possibilities for homework assignments.

- Support pages from *Unit 4 Resources:*
  Literary Analysis
  Reading Strategy
  Vocabulary Builder
  Grammar and Style
- An Extend Your Learning project and the Writing Lesson for this selection group may be completed over several days.

Step-by-Step Teaching Guide	Pacing Guide
PRETEACH	
• Administer Vocabulary and Reading Warm-ups as necessary.	5 min.
• Engage students' interest with the motivation activity.	5 min.
• Read and discuss author, background, and From the Scholar's Desk features. **FT**	10 min.
• Introduce the Literary Analysis Skill: Diaries, Journals, and Letters. **FT**	5 min.
• Introduce the Reading Strategy: Distinguishing Fact From Opinion. **FT**	10 min.
• Prepare students to read by teaching the selection vocabulary. **FT**	
TEACH	
• Informally monitor comprehension while students read independently or in groups. **FT**	30 min.
• Monitor students' comprehension with the Reading Check notes.	as students read
• Reinforce vocabulary with Vocabulary Builder notes.	as students read
• Develop students' understanding of diaries, journals, and letters with the Literary Analysis annotations. **FT**	5 min.
• Develop students' ability to distinguish fact from opinion with the Reading Strategy annotations. **FT**	5 min.
ASSESS/EXTEND	
• Assess students' comprehension and mastery of the Literary Analysis and Reading Strategy by having them answer the Apply the Skills questions. **FT**	15 min.
• Have students complete the Vocabulary Lesson and the Grammar and Style Lesson. **FT**	15 min.
• Apply students' ability to gather details by using the Writing Lesson. **FT**	45 min. or homework
• Apply students' understanding by using one or more of the Extend Your Learning activities.	20–90 min. or homework
• Administer Selection Test A or Selection Test B. **FT**	15 min.

Resources

PRINT

Unit 4 Resources

- From the Scholar's Desk .... p. 92
- Listening and Viewing .... p. 93
- Vocabulary Warm-up Word Lists **[L1, L2, EL]** .... p. 94
- Vocabulary Warm-up Practice **[L1, L2, EL]** .... p. 95
- Reading Warm-up A **[L1, L2, EL]** .... p. 96
- Reading Warm-up B **[L1, L2, L3]** .... p. 97

TRANSPARENCY

Graphic Organizer Transparencies

- Literary Analysis Graphic Organizer A **[L3]** .... p. 112
- Literary Analysis Graphic Organizer B **[L1, L2, EL]** .... p. 113
- Reading Strategy Graphic Organizer A **[L3]** .... p. 114
- Reading Strategy Graphic Organizer B **[L1, L2, EL]** .... p. 115

TECHNOLOGY

- From the Scholar's Desk DVD — Nell Irvin Painter, Segment 2

PRINT

Reader's Notebook [L2]

Reader's Notebook: Adapted Version [L1]

Reader's Notebook: English Learner's Version [EL]

Unit 4 Resources

- Literary Analysis **[L3]** .... p. 98
- Reading Strategy **[L3]** .... p. 99
- Vocabulary Builder **[L3]** .... p. 100

TECHNOLOGY

Listening to Literature Audio CDs [L2, EL]

Reader's Notebook: Adapted Version Audio CD [L1, L2]

PRINT

Unit 4 Resources

- Grammar and Style **[L3]** .... p. 101
- Support for Writing Lesson **[L3]** .... p. 102
- Support for Extend Your Learning **[L3]** .... p. 103
- Enrichment **[L4]** .... p. 104
- Selection Test A **[L1, L2, EL]** .... pp. 105–107
- Selection Test B **[L3, L4]** .... pp. 108–110

General Resources

- Rubrics for Problem-Solution Essay **[L3]** .... pp. 59–60
- Rubric for Peer Assessment: Oral Interpretation **[L3]** .... p. 130

TECHNOLOGY

Go Online: Research **[L3]**

Go Online: Self-test **[L3]**

***ExamView®*, Test Bank [L3]**

Choosing Resources for Differentiated Instruction

[L1] Special Needs Students

[L2] Below-Level Students

[L3] All Students

[L4] Advanced Students

[EL] English Learners

FT Fast Track Instruction: To move the lesson more quickly, use the strategies and activities identified with **FT**.

Scaffolding for Less Proficient and Advanced Students

The leveled Critical Thinking questions after selections progress in the levels of thinking required to answer them. To address the needs of your different students, you may use the (a) level questions for your less proficient students and the (b) level questions with your on-level and advanced students. The occasional (c) level questions are appropriate for your advanced students.

PRENTICE HALL **TeacherEXPRESS™** Plan · Teach · Assess Use this complete suite of powerful teaching tools to make lesson planning and testing quicker and easier.

Use the interactive textbook (online and on CD-ROM) to make selections and activities come alive with audio and video support and interactive questions.

From the Author's Desk

Nell Irvin Painter

- Nell Irvin Painter, a well-known historian, writes about Sojourner Truth's 1865 account of being discriminated against on a streetcar in Washington, D.C. (page 561). Have students review Painter's comments in **Setting the Scene** on pages 470–471.
- Have students read the introductory paragraph about Nell Irvin Painter. Then, show Segment 2 on Nell Irvin Painter on the ***From the Author's Desk*** DVD to provide insight into Painter's writing about Sojourner Truth. After the students have watched the segment, **ask:** How does Nell Irvin Painter dispel some misconceptions about Sojourner Truth?
Answer: She offers a personal description of Sojourner Truth and mentions some surprising details about her life.

Two American Histories

- Painter explains that Sojourner Truth's experience of discrimination arises in part because the nation's capital, Washington, D.C., began as a southern city. She notes that various modes of public transportation were common sites for discrimination against African Americans. Both the local incident and the national pattern it illustrates were not dealt with by the law until the mid-twentieth century. **Ask:** What point does Painter make by connecting Sojourner Truth's individual experience of discrimination with a larger national pattern?
Answer: Linking Truth's account with national pattern of discrimination enables Painter to show in specific terms how the discrimination hurt ordinary people and famous people alike. It also provides a reminder that this discrimination lasted long past the Civil War because it was embedded in America's early history.

From the Scholar's Desk

NELL IRVIN PAINTER INTRODUCES

"An Account of an Experience with Discrimination" by Sojourner Truth

Nell Irvin Painter

Nell Irvin Painter is an award-winning historian and professor. Her book *Sojourner Truth: A Life, A Symbol* was a choice of both the Book of the Month Club and the History Book Club.

A Public Figure Encounters Discrimination

Sojourner Truth, an African American abolitionist born in upstate New York in 1797, belonged to a group of antislavery women volunteering with the ex-slave refugees in Washington, D. C., during the Civil War. Poor people from the battlefields of Virginia and from slaveholding Maryland sought protection and jobs in the nation's capital. Volunteers like Truth and her comrades, Josephine Griffing and Laura Haviland, helped them cope with their situation. Although Truth did not read or write, she dictated this account for publication in the antislavery press. In this way, people who cared about human rights would know that one Washington, D. C., streetcar conductor had not stopped for her and another had tried to push her from the platform of the car, even though she was a well-known public figure.

Two American Histories

Truth's experience of discrimination in public transportation belongs to two American histories, both beginning in the early nineteenth century and both ending with the passage and enforcement of federal legislation against discrimination in public services in the 1950s and 1960s. The first history is that of Washington, D. C., a Southern city. The second history is that of discrimination against African Americans throughout the United States.

In 1791, President George Washington chose land on the border of Maryland and Virginia near his own home to serve as the nation's capital. In the 1790s, slavery existed in virtually the whole country. But during the early nineteenth century the Northern states abolished slavery, while the institution grew stronger in the South, of which Washington, D. C., was a part. The Washington slave market sat near the capitol building, and slavery flourished in the District until abolition in 1862. The discrimination Sojourner Truth experienced belonged partly to

Teaching Resources

The following resources can be used to enrich or extend the instruction for From the Scholar's Desk.

Unit 4 Resources
From the Scholar's Desk, p. 92
Listening and Viewing, p. 93

From the Author's Desk DVD
Nell Irvin Painter, Segment 2

Washington's Southern traditions. However, even after the abolition of slavery, racial discrimination in transportation remained a national problem. The war between black people and American railroads was national in scope, because racial discrimination was national in scope.

Truth's Experience Was Not Unique

Sojourner Truth's painful experience caused her psychic and physical pain—she was in her sixties at the time. However, the insult she suffered was one she shared with many other black people trying to get from one place to another before the middle of the twentieth century.

Before the Civil War, the black abolitionists Frederick Douglass and David Ruggles had traded blows with conductors pushing them out of their seats. During the war, Harriet Tubman, who had guided Union troops during the Civil War, suffered shoulder injuries in New Jersey, when a conductor and three other men dragged her out of her seat and threw her into the baggage car. After the war, Frances Ellen Watkins Harper, the most prominent black woman writer of the era, experienced humiliating and bruising conflicts on railroads and streetcars. George T. Downing, an African American businessman, encountered difficulties in railroad transportation during Reconstruction. The Civil War and Reconstruction ended slavery but not discrimination and exclusion.

◀ **Critical Viewing** Compare and contrast this photograph of Sojourner Truth with the painting of her on page 561. Which portrait seems more like the "public figure" that Painter describes in this essay? Why?. **[Compare and Contrast]**

Thinking About the Commentary

1. **(a) Recall:** Who was Sojourner Truth? **(b) Recall:** What was she doing in Washington, D. C., during and after the Civil War? **(c) Connect:** Was the act of making public her own experience with discrimination related in any way to her purpose for being in Washington? Explain.
2. **(a) Recall:** To what two American histories does Truth's experience of discrimination belong? **(b) Speculate:** Why do you think discrimination persisted in both the North and South even after slavery ended?

As You Read "An Account of an Experience with Discrimination" . . .

3. Identify two ways in which Painter's commentary helps you better understand Sojourner Truth's experiences and reactions.
4. Decide what an individual who experiences or witnesses discrimination in transportation should do.

ASSESS

Answers

1. (a) She was an African American who worked for the abolition of slavery. (b) She helped ex-slave refugees as they sought sanctuary in Washington, D.C. (c) By making her experience of discrimination public, Truth helped white people realize how such discrimination injured innocent individuals; she also helped prevent future incidents.
2. (a) Truth's experience of discrimination belongs to both the local history of Washington, D.C., which began as a Southern city in which slaveholding was legal, and the national history of discrimination throughout the United States.
(b) **Possible answer:** Discrimination persisted because it was deeply embedded in American traditions and because slavery had to be ended forcibly rather than voluntarily. It is also part of the negative side of human nature for groups of people to set themselves above other groups.
3. Possible answer: Painter's commentary shows how the incidents Truth relates reach forward into our own time. By mentioning other examples, the commentary also shows how innocent people suffer the effects of racial prejudice.
4. **Possible answer:** Individuals experiencing or witnessing discrimination in transportation should record the name of the person doing the discriminating and report the incident as soon as possible. Witnesses should also do their best to take care of the victims if there is physical injury. They should also make it clear that they saw what happened and that it will be reported.

PRETEACH

Motivation

The words of actual witnesses to history are often more powerful than those of any secondhand account. Ask students to bring to class any firsthand accounts of historic events that may be in their family's possession, such as a letter from a grandfather who fought in World War II, or a diary entry recounting President Kennedy's assassination. To help students better appreciate the power of firsthand accounts, show an excerpt from *The Civil War series,* or display the companion book. Then, explain that the diaries, journals, and letters they are about to read were written by people from different walks of life, each of whom offers a unique perspective on the events surrounding the Civil War.

❶ Background
More About the Authors

Mary Chesnut's circle of friends included Jefferson Davis and others in the highest ranks of the Confederacy.

Along with several generals and other officers, Warren Lee Goss was one of 230 contributors to *Battles and Leaders of the Civil War,* a four-volume compilation of essays published in the 1880s.

During the war, Randolph McKim became the chaplain for a Virginia cavalry regiment.

Thomas J. Jackson left his teaching position at the Virginia Military Institute to join the Confederate Army. He was killed at Chancellorsville just a few months before the Battle of Gettysburg.

Henry M. Turner was one the leaders of the post-war African American community.

Sojourner Truth was born Isabella Baumfree. According to Frederick Douglass, she had a "strange compound of wit and wisdom, of wild enthusiasm, and flint-like common sense . . ."

Build Skills *Primary Sources*

❶ Civil War Diaries, Journals, and Letters

Civil War Voices

The Civil War was one of the most painful chapters in American history, tearing families apart and scarring the lives of millions of soldiers and civilians. The following diaries, journals, and letters tell the story of the war through the eyes of just a few of those whose lives were affected by it.

A Daughter of the South No one was hurt when the opening shots of the war were fired on Fort Sumter on April 12, 1860, but **Mary Boykin Chesnut** (1823–1886) seems to have sensed the carnage to come. The daughter of a cotton plantation owner and United States senator, Mary Boykin was raised in an aristocratic family in Charleston, South Carolina. At the age of seventeen, she married James Chesnut, Jr., a wealthy lawyer and future senator. Her journal entries convey the Southern aristocracy's mingled optimism and dread that marked the opening days of the Civil War.

On the Front Lines Men hurried to enlist in what most believed would be a swift and glorious conflict. Some young men saw the military as an opportunity for respect and advancement as we learn from the account of Union soldier **Warren Lee Goss.** The harsh realities of the training camp and battlefield soon taught soldiers on both sides that lives and limbs were the price of glory. The cost was especially high at the Battle of Gettysburg—a stunning defeat for Confederate general Robert E. Lee. In his diary, Confederate soldier **Randolph McKim** recounts the bravery of his companions, many of whom were among the 51,000 killed or wounded at Gettysburg after Confederate troops advanced on Culp's Hill, led by McKim.

A Master Strategist Confederate general and military strategist **Thomas Jonathan "Stonewall" Jackson** (1824–1863) earned his nickname early in the war for his steadiness and determination during the Battle of Bull Run in 1861. Jackson, who recounted the battle in a letter to his wife, died two years after his great victory; he was accidentally shot by his own troops and died of complications.

Freedom's Cry The war raged on, but the Emancipation Proclamation, issued by President Lincoln on September 22, 1862, changed the purpose of the war. By declaring that all slaves would be freed on January 1, 1863, the Proclamation transformed the conflict into a war to end slavery, as well as a war to restore the Union. **Reverend Henry M. Turner,** a freeborn African American who lived in Washington, D.C., recounts his community's joyous reaction to the news of Lincoln's proclamation.

The Enduring Battle When the war ended in 1865, abolitionist **Sojourner Truth** (1797–1883) had only begun to battle discrimination. A preacher and former slave, Truth also earned fame as an advocate of women's rights, temperance, and workplace and prison reform.

Born into slavery in Ulster County, New York, Truth was freed when the state emancipated slaves in 1827. In 1843, she began preaching along the east coast. During the Civil War, Truth gathered contributions of food and clothing for the African American regiments. She met with President Abraham Lincoln in the White House in 1864. Truth was a powerful speaker whose passion and charisma often drew large crowds to her informal lectures.

Preview

Connecting to the Literature

Today, you can learn about events almost immediately through instant access news sources. The Civil War took place before news networks were invented, however, so the best way to learn about the war and share the experiences of those involved is through their letters, journals, diaries, and photographs.

Literary Analysis

Diaries, Journals, and Letters

Diaries, journals, and **letters** are personal records of events, thoughts, feelings, and observations. These literary forms allow people to record immediate responses to their day-to-day experiences.

- Diaries and journals are generally for personal use. Usually written in an informal style, they capture the writers' ideas and emotions.
- Personal letters are not written for general publication, but because they are addressed to another person, the writing is not entirely private.

As you read these selections, use a chart like the one shown to analyze the information each selection provides and to determine what those details reveal about the writer.

Statement From Writer

What It Reveals

Comparing Literary Works

The selections presented here reflect a wide spectrum of opinions and experiences related to the Civil War. As firsthand accounts of the period, these are valuable examples of **historical narratives.** In this kind of writing, people living through historic events describe their personal experiences and reactions, providing historians an intimate perspective on history. As you read, compare the different perspectives these selections offer of the Civil War.

Reading Strategy

Distinguishing Fact From Opinion

A *fact* is a statement that can be proved true; an *opinion* is a judgment that cannot be proved, though it can be supported by arguments. As you read, **distinguish fact from opinion** by determining whether a statement can be proved or merely supported.

Vocabulary Builder

capitulate (kə pich′ ə lāt′) *v.* surrender conditionally (p. 551)

audaciously (ô dā′ shəs lē) *adv.* boldly or daringly (p. 551)

foreboding (fôr bōd′ iŋ) *n.* presentiment (p. 551)

obstinate (äb′ stə nit) *adj.* stubborn (p. 552)

imprecations (im′ pri kā′ shənz) *n.* curses (p. 552)

serenity (sə ren′ ə tē) *n.* calmness (p. 553)

❷ Literary Analysis

Diaries, Journals, and Letters

- Give students a copy of **Literary Analysis Graphic Organizer A** from ***Graphic Organizer Transparencies***, p. 112, to use as they read these selections.
- Explain that students will focus on diaries, journals, and letters as they read the six selections in this lesson.
- Read the instruction about diaries, journals, and letters aloud as students read silently. Draw students' attention to the description of how these literary forms allow people to record their immediate responses to people, events, and other experiences.
- As they read each selection, have students look for elements of informality that indicate the private nature of the writing. Point out that letters—and especially diaries and journals—are likely to contain passages that reveal the writer's true emotions and ideas.

❸ Reading Strategy

Distinguishing Fact from Opinion

- Invite a student volunteer to suggest an example of a provable fact. Have the student share the fact and identify the sources one could use to verify it. Then, encourage other students to state whether or not they agree that the statement is a fact rather than an opinion.
- You might wish to engage students in a discussion of the "gray areas" between fact and opinion, such as human emotions. For example, if a person says, "I feel sad," is that a fact or is it an opinion? How might one verify such a statement?
- As they read the selections in this grouping, urge students to remain aware of the differences between facts and opinions.

Vocabulary Builder

- Pronounce each vocabulary word for students, and read the definitions as a class. Have students identify any words with which they are already familiar.

Differentiated Instruction Solutions for All Learners

Support for Special Needs Students
Have students complete the **Preview** and **Build Skills** pages for these selections in the ***Reader's Notebook: Adapted Version.*** These pages provide a selection summary, an abbreviated presentation of the reading and literary skills, and the graphic organizer on the **Build Skills** page in the student book.

Support for Less Proficient Readers
Have students complete the **Preview** and **Build Skills** pages for these selections in the ***Reader's Notebook.*** These pages provide a selection summary, an abbreviated presentation of the reading and literary skills, and the graphic organizer on the **Build Skills** page in the student book.

Support for English Learners
Have students complete the **Preview** and **Build Skills** pages for these selections in the ***Reader's Notebook: English Learner's Version.*** These pages provide a selection summary, an abbreviated presentation of the skills, additional contextual vocabulary, and the graphic organizer on the **Build Skills** page in the student book.

TEACH

Learning Modalities for Intrapersonal Learners To help these students appreciate the value of journals, use the Enrichment Activity in *Unit 4 Resources*, p. 104.

❶ About the Selection

Mary Chesnut, who was both on the scene and privy to the actions and reactions of higher-ups in the Confederacy, started keeping a diary as the tension mounted in Charleston. In these entries, she provides readers with a vivid picture of the chaos and excitement accompanying the dizzying events during the days leading up to the bombardment of Fort Sumter.

❷ Literary Analysis

Diaries, Journals, and Letters

- Read aloud for students the first four paragraphs of Chesnut's account.
- **Ask** students the Literary Analysis question: What details of style and context tell you that you are reading a diary or journal entry?
  Answer: The inclusion of the date and the reflective recounting of daily events indicate that this is a diary or journal entry.

❶ from Mary Chesnut's Civil War

Mary Chesnut

Background In the early days of April 1861, the nation held its collective breath as the tension between North and South mounted. On April 12, the opening shots of the Civil War were fired on Fort Sumter, a Union military post in Charleston, South Carolina, as the city's citizens watched from their rooftops.

Filmmaker and historian Ken Burns, who produced the 1990 television documentary *The Civil War*, noted that during the war "Soldiers at the front and civilians at home left an astonishingly rich and moving record of what they saw and felt . . . hundreds of voices from across the spectrum of American experience, men and women whose lives were touched or destroyed or permanently changed by the war." Here, Mary Chesnut's diary is a memorable chapter in that record.

April 7, 1861. Today things seem to have settled down a little.

❷ One can but hope still. Lincoln or Seward[1] have made such silly advances and then far sillier drawings back. There may be a chance for peace, after all.

Things are happening so fast.

My husband has been made an aide-de-camp[2] of General Beauregard.

Three hours ago we were quietly packing to go home. The convention has adjourned.

Now he tells me the attack upon Fort Sumter[3] may begin tonight. Depends upon Anderson and the fleet outside. The *Herald* says that this show of war outside of the bar is intended for Texas.

John Manning came in with his sword and red sash. Pleased as a boy to be on Beauregard's staff while the row goes on. He has gone with Wigfall to Captain Hartstene with instructions.

Mr. Chesnut is finishing a report he had to make to the convention.

Mrs. Hayne called. She had, she said, "but one feeling, pity for those who are not here."

Literary Analysis
Diaries, Journals, and Letters What details of style and context tell you that you are reading a diary or journal entry?

1. **Seward** William Henry Seward (1801–1872), U.S. Secretary of State from 1861 through 1869.
2. **aide-de-camp** (ād′ də kamp′) *n.* officer serving as assistant and confidential secretary to a superior.
3. **Fort Sumter** fort in Charleston Harbor, South Carolina. At the time, the fort was occupied by Union troops commanded by Major Robert Anderson.

Differentiated Instruction Solutions for All Learners

Accessibility at a Glance

	from Mary Chesnut's Civil War	Recollections of a Private	Confederate Account of Gettysburg	Bull Run	Reaction to Emancipation	Experience with Discrimination
Context	Civil War Period	Civil War Period	Civil War Period	Civil War Period	Civil War Period	Post Civil War
Language	Accessible	Formal	Vocabulary footnotes	Long Sentences	Long Sentences	Accessible
Concept Level	Moderate (war diary)	Moderate (war diary)	Moderate (war diary)	Accessible (letter)	Accessible (historic account)	Accessible (letter)
Literary Merit	Factual account	Personal saga	Historical	Historical	Historical	Personal saga
Lexile	700	1080	1310	1020	1300	1130
Overall Rating	Average	Average	Average	More accessible	More accessible	More accessible

Jack Preston, Willie Alston—"the take-life-easys," as they are called—with John Green, "the big brave," have gone down to the island—volunteered as privates.

Seven hundred men were sent over. Ammunition wagons rumbling along the streets all night. Anderson burning blue lights—signs and signals for the fleet outside, I suppose.

Today at dinner there was no allusion to things as they stand in Charleston Harbor. There was an undercurrent of intense excitement. There could not have been a more brilliant circle. In addition to our usual quartet (Judge Withers, Langdon Cheves, and Trescot) our two governors dined with us, Means and Manning.

These men all talked so delightfully. For once in my life I listened.

That over, business began. In earnest, Governor Means rummaged a sword and red sash from somewhere and brought it for Colonel Chesnut, who has gone to demand the surrender of Fort Sumter.

And now, patience—we must wait.

Why did that green goose Anderson go into Fort Sumter? Then everything began to go wrong.

Now they have intercepted a letter from him, urging them to let him surrender. He paints the horrors likely to ensue if they will not.

He ought to have thought of all that before he put his head in the hole.

April 12, 1861. Anderson will not capitulate.

Yesterday was the merriest, maddest dinner we have had yet. Men were more audaciously wise and witty. We had an unspoken foreboding it was to be our last pleasant meeting. Mr. Miles dined with us today. Mrs. Henry King rushed in: "The news, I come for the latest news—all of the men of the King family are on the island"—of which fact she seemed proud.

While she was here, our peace negotiator—or envoy—came in. That is, Mr. Chesnut returned—his interview with Colonel Anderson had been deeply interesting—but was not inclined to be communicative, wanted his dinner. Felt for Anderson. Had telegraphed to President Davis[4] for instructions.

What answer to give Anderson, etc., etc. He has gone back to Fort Sumter with additional instructions.

4. **President Davis** Jefferson Davis (1808–1889), president of the Confederacy (1861–1865).

Bombardment of Sumter, Harper's Weekly, 1861

3

4 **▲ Critical Viewing**
Describe the people's reaction to the bombing of Fort Sumter as depicted in this illustration. **[Analyze]**

Vocabulary Builder

capitulate (kə pich′ ə lāt′) *v.* surrender conditionally

audaciously (ô dā′ shəs lē) *adv.* boldly or daringly

foreboding (fôr bōd′ iŋ) *n.* presentiment

5 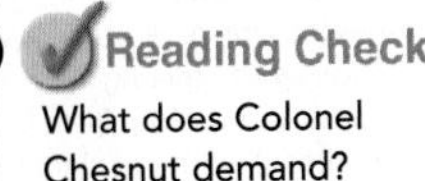

Reading Check
What does Colonel Chesnut demand?

3 Humanities

Bombardment of Fort Sumter, 1861

This wood engraving was done by an unknown artist for the May 4, 1861 edition of *Harper's Weekly,* one of two major illustrated Northern newspapers that provided on-the-spot coverage of the Civil War. Correspondents and artists were dispatched by the paper to war zones in order to provide a steady flow of written and pictorial information for publication. Although photography had recently been invented, there was as yet no method for reproducing photographs in a newspaper. On-the-scene drawings were the means by which events of the war were visually recorded for the public. These drawings were sent to the newspaper, where a skilled artisan engraved the image into a block of wood that was then inked and pressed onto paper.

Use these questions for discussion:

1. What details correspond to those in Chesnut's account?
   Possible response: Chesnut describes the women as being "wild" as they watched from the rooftops.
2. Do you think a photograph of the same scene would have been more or less effective than the drawing? Why?
   Answer: Students might note that a photograph captures only a single moment, whereas an artist is free to document two or more events that may have happened over a period of time.

4 Critical Viewing

Answer: Most of the women seem to be quite upset by the shelling and are trying to console one another. A number of them appear to be in a state of collapse.

5 Reading Check

Answer: He demands "the surrender of Fort Sumter."

Differentiated Instruction Solutions for All Learners

Enrichment for Gifted/Talented Students

Encourage these students to study the details of the artwork, which is closely related to Chesnut's text. Have them consider these questions:

- What does the artwork reveal about the battle for Fort Sumter?
- What does it reveal about the city of Charleston at the time of the battle?
- What does it reveal about the attitude of those living in Charleston toward the events that were taking place?

The fact that Fort Sumter is burning suggests that the Southerners are in the process of winning a decisive victory. The buildings in the illustration and the clothing worn by the people suggest that Charleston is a thriving, cosmopolitan city. The number of people on the rooftops and their body language indicate that the people of Charleston are engrossed by the conflict and are concerned about where the fighting might lead.

❻ Literary Analysis
Diaries, Journals, and Letters

- Invite students to read this passage silently. Then, read the passage aloud to them once again. Encourage students to discuss briefly why Chesnut is so distracted and anxious.
- **Ask** students the first Literary Analysis question: What characteristics of a diary or journal do these sentences have?
  Answer: These sentences feature a first-person narrator, use informal language, and express fragmented thoughts and feelings.

❼ Literary Analysis
Diaries, Journals, and Letters

- Have students scan earlier sections of Chesnut's journal and locate descriptions of her dinner guests. Then, have a student volunteer read the bracketed passage aloud for the class.
- **Ask** students the second Literary Analysis question: What do you learn about Mary Chesnut's life based on her dinner guests?
  Answer: She is one of Charleston's elite citizens.

When they were about to leave the wharf, A. H. Boykin sprang into the boat, in great excitement; thought himself ill-used. A likelihood of fighting—and he to be left behind!

❻ I do not pretend to go to sleep. How can I? If Anderson does not accept terms—at four—the orders are—he shall be fired upon.

I count four—St. Michael chimes. I begin to hope. At half-past four, the heavy booming of a cannon.

I sprang out of bed. And on my knees—prostrate—I prayed as I never prayed before.

There was a sound of stir all over the house—pattering of feet in the corridor—all seemed hurrying one way. I put on my double gown and a shawl and went, too. It was to the housetop.

The shells were bursting. In the dark I heard a man say "waste of ammunition."

I knew my husband was rowing about in a boat somewhere in that dark bay. And that the shells were roofing it over—bursting toward the fort. If Anderson was obstinate—he was to order the forts on our side to open fire. Certainly fire had begun. The regular roar of the cannon—there it was. And who could tell what each volley accomplished of death and destruction.

The women were wild, there on the housetop. Prayers from the women and imprecations from the men, and then a shell would light up the scene. Tonight, they say, the forces are to attempt to land.

The *Harriet Lane*[5] had her wheelhouse[6] smashed and put back to sea.

We watched up there—everybody wondered. Fort Sumter did not fire a shot.

❼ Today Miles and Manning, colonels now—aides to Beauregard—dined with us. The latter hoped I would keep the peace. I give him only good words, for he was to be under fire all day and night, in the bay carrying orders, etc.

Last night—or this morning truly—up on the housetop I was so weak and weary I sat down on something that looked like a black stool.

"Get up, you foolish woman—your dress is on fire," cried a man. And he put me out.

It was a chimney, and the sparks caught my clothes. Susan Preston and Mr. Venable then came up. But my fire had been extinguished before it broke out into a regular blaze.

Do you know, after all that noise and our tears and prayers, nobody has been hurt. Sound and fury, signifying nothing.[7] A delusion and a snare. . . .

Literary Analysis
Diaries, Journals, and Letters What characteristics of a diary or journal do these sentences have?

Vocabulary Builder
obstinate (äb′ stə nət) *adj.* stubborn

Vocabulary Builder
imprecations (im′ pri kā′ shən) *n.* curses

Literary Analysis
Diaries, Journals, and Letters What do you learn about Mary Chesnut's life based on her dinner guests?

5. **The *Harriet Lane*** federal steamer that had brought provisions to Fort Sumter.
6. **wheelhouse** *n.* enclosed place on the upper deck of a ship, in which the helmsman stands while steering.
7. **Sound . . . nothing** from Shakespeare's *Macbeth*, Act V, Scene v, lines 27–28. Macbeth is contemplating the significance of life and death after learning of his wife's death.

Enrichment

Fort Sumter

South Carolina had seceded from the Union on December 20, 1860, and demanded all the Federal property within the state. Federal Major Robert Anderson refused to surrender Fort Sumter, a fortification on an island in Charleston Harbor. On April 6, President Lincoln notified the governor of South Carolina that a ship would be bringing provisions to the fort. In response, the Confederacy decided to attack before relief arrived. After 34 hours of fighting, the Union surrendered the fort to the Confederates. Although there were no casualties during the actual bombardment, one Union soldier was killed and three were wounded during the evacuation. The fort became a national monument in 1948.

Coincidentally, while an artillery instructor at West Point, Major Anderson taught Pierre Gustave Toutant Beauregard, the Confederate brigadier general in charge of the batteries that fired on Fort Sumter.

Somebody came in just now and reported Colonel Chesnut asleep on the sofa in General Beauregard's room. After two such nights he must be so tired as to be able to sleep anywhere. . . .

April 13, 1861. Nobody hurt, after all. How gay we were last night.

Reaction after the dread of all the slaughter we thought those dreadful cannons were making such a noise in doing.

Not even a battery[8] the worse for wear.

Fort Sumter has been on fire. He has not yet silenced any of our guns. So the aides—still with swords and red sashes by way of uniform—tell us.

But the sound of those guns makes regular meals impossible. None of us go to table. But tea trays pervade the corridors, going everywhere.

Some of the anxious hearts lie on their beds and moan in solitary misery. Mrs. Wigfall and I solace ourselves with tea in my room.

These women have all a satisfying faith.

April 15, 1861. I did not know that one could live such days of excitement.

They called, "Come out—there is a crowd coming."

A mob indeed, but it was headed by Colonels Chesnut and Manning.

The crowd was shouting and showing these two as messengers of good news. They were escorted to Beauregard's headquarters. Fort Sumter had surrendered.

Those up on the housetop shouted to us, "The fort is on fire." That had been the story once or twice before.

When we had calmed down, Colonel Chesnut, who had taken it all quietly enough—if anything, more unruffled than usual in his serenity—told us how the surrender came about.

Wigfall was with them on Morris Island when he saw the fire in the fort, jumped in a little boat and, with his handkerchief as a white flag, rowed over to Fort Sumter. Wigfall went in through a porthole.

When Colonel Chesnut arrived shortly after and was received by the regular entrance, Colonel Anderson told him he had need to pick his way warily, for it was all mined.

As far as I can make out, the fort surrendered to Wigfall.

But it is all confusion. Our flag is flying there. Fire engines have been sent to put out the fire.

Everybody tells you half of something and then rushes off to tell something else or to hear the last news. . . .

8. **battery** *n.* artillery unit.

8 ***The Angel of the Battlefield***

Like Mary Chesnut, many women were on the scene during the Civil War. Clara Barton is known for her brave assistance to wounded soldiers. Barton spent from 1862 to 1864 at the front, delivering bandages, socks, and other goods to wounded soldiers. In so doing, she earned the name "Angel of the Battlefield." In 1864, Barton was appointed superintendent of Union nurses. After the Civil War, she engaged in a search for missing soldiers and lectured about her war experiences.

In 1881, the American Red Cross was formed, and Barton served as its first president. This organization still provides relief around the world in times of war or disaster.

Connect to the Literature

How might the tone of Mary Chesnut's diary be different if she had been a nurse during the Civil War?

Vocabulary Builder

serenity (sə ren′ ə tē) *n.* calmness

9 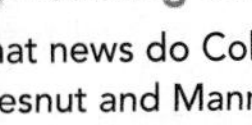 **Reading Check**

What news do Colonels Chesnut and Manning bring back to camp?

8 Background
The Angel of the Battle field

Several years after the American Red Cross was established, Clara Barton amended the organization's mission statement to clarify that the group would offer assistance during peacetime as well as during wartime. While Barton served the American Red Cross, she directed the relief work that followed countless famines, floods, pestilence outbreaks, and earthquakes.

Connect to the Literature

Encourage students to explain at least two ways that Clara Barton's involvement in the war out made her daily life different from Mary Chesnut's life.

Her tone would have been grave and dismal.

9 Reading Check

Answer: They bring news that Fort Sumter has surrendered to the Confederate forces.

Differentiated Instruction
Solutions for All Learners

Strategy for Less Proficient Readers

To help students through these diary and journal entries and letters, suggest that partners paraphrase complex passages. Have them focus in particular on passages filled with terminology peculiar to the Civil War era or on passages that contain military terms that might present difficulties.

Enrichment for Gifted/Talented Students

Explain to students that, in past eras, it was not uncommon for women's skirts to catch fire. Long, flowing skirts and open hearths were a deadly combination that left thousands of women badly—even fatally—injured. Encourage students to conduct research on the clothes worn by women during the Civil War period in the United States. Interested students may also research the dress reform movement, led by such figures as Amelia Bloomer, that emerged in the United States shortly after the Civil War.

⑩ About the Selection

In this journal entry, a recent Union recruit describes the reality of the drudgery of camp life for enlisted men—mud, drill, and more drill. His observations contrast sharply with the expectations that he and many other recruits had prior to enlisting.

⑪ Literary Analysis

Diaries, Journals, and Letters

- Have students listen to an oral reading of the passage on **Listening to Literature Audio CDs** before they reread it silently. Then, **ask** students the Literary Analysis question: What details of Goss's writing style indicate that this is part of a diary or journal entry?
  Answer: Goss's use of first-person pronouns, his stringing together a series of clauses with semicolons, and his inclusion of incomplete thoughts indicates that this is a diary or journal entry.

⑫ Reading Strategy

Distinguishing Fact from Opinion

- Have two student volunteers read the passage aloud—the first using a flat, impersonal tone, the second using an animated tone.
- Then, **ask** students the Reading Strategy question: Identify one opinion in this description of enlisting.
  Answer: Students might mention the passage's first, second, third, and final sentences.

⑩

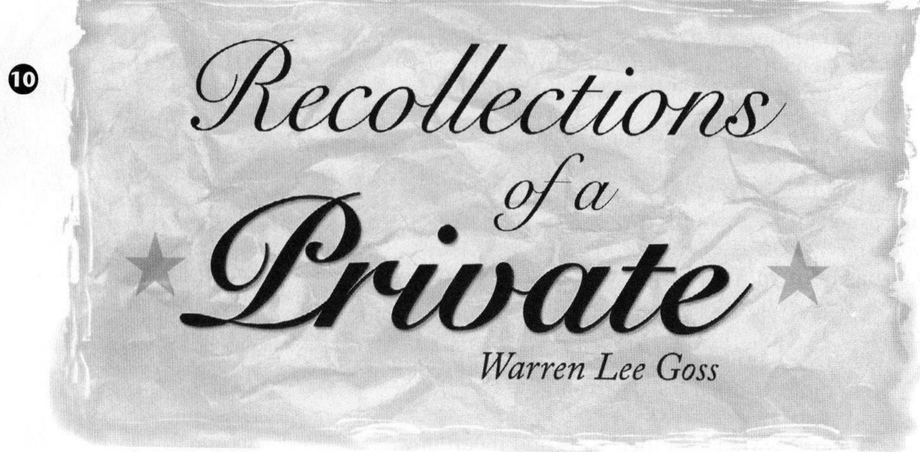

Recollections of a Private

Warren Lee Goss

In the weeks that followed the attack on Fort Sumter, thousands of men on both sides volunteered to fight. Among the early enlistees was Warren Lee Goss of Massachusetts.

"Cold chills" ran up and down my back as I got out of bed after the sleepless night, and shaved preparatory to other desperate deeds of valor. I was twenty years of age, and when anything unusual was to be done, like fighting or courting, I shaved.

With a nervous tremor convulsing my system, and my heart thumping like muffled drumbeats, I stood before the door of the recruiting office, and before turning the knob to enter read and reread the advertisement for recruits posted thereon, until I knew all its peculiarities. The promised chances for "travel and promotion" seemed good, and I thought I might have made a mistake in considering war so serious after all. "Chances for travel!" I must confess now, after four years of soldiering, that the "chances for travel" were no myth; but "promotion" was a little uncertain and slow.

I was in no hurry to open the door. Though determined to enlist, I was half inclined to put it off awhile; I had a fluctuation of desires; I was fainthearted and brave; I wanted to enlist, and yet—Here I turned the knob, and was relieved. . . .

⑪ My first uniform was a bad fit: My trousers were too long by three or four inches; the flannel shirt was coarse and unpleasant, too large at the neck and too short elsewhere. The forage cap[1] was an ungainly bag with pasteboard top and leather visor; the blouse was the only part

Literary Analysis
Diaries, Journals, and Letters What details of Goss's writing style indicate that this is part of a diary or journal entry?

1. **forage cap** cap worn by infantry soldiers.

Enrichment

Women in the Civil War

While men fought the Civil War on the battlefield, women participated at home in several crucial ways. Many women single-handedly ran family businesses, farms, and plantations while their husbands and sons were away. Women from both the North and South worked in factories, hospitals, and in relief efforts. Some sewed uniforms at home; others functioned as spies. Hundreds even disguised themselves as men and joined the ranks.

Invite students to find out more about the role of women during the war. For instance, they can research the work of Dorothea Dix and of Clara Barton. They can find out about Sally Tompkins and the hospital she ran in Richmond, Virginia, and of organizations such as the Women's Central Association of Relief. Some students might find it interesting to look into the espionage work of Belle Boyd, Elizabeth Van Lew, or Rose Greenhow. Encourage students to share their findings with the class.

which seemed decent; while the overcoat made me feel like a little nubbin of corn in a large preponderance of husk. Nothing except "Virginia mud" ever took down my ideas of military pomp quite so low.

After enlisting I did not seem of so much consequence as I had expected. There was not so much excitement on account of my military appearance as I deemed justly my due. I was taught my facings, and at the time I thought the drillmaster needlessly fussy about shouldering, ordering, and presenting arms. At this time men were often drilled in company and regimental evolutions long before they learned the manual of arms, because of the difficulty of obtaining muskets. These we obtained at an early day, but we would willingly have resigned them after carrying them a few hours. The musket, after an hour's drill, seemed heavier and less ornamental than it had looked to be.

The first day I went out to drill, getting tired of doing the same things over and over, I said to the drill sergeant: "Let's stop this fooling and go over to the grocery." His only reply was addressed to a corporal: "Corporal, take this man out and drill him"; and the corporal did! I found that suggestions were not so well appreciated in the army as in private life, and that no wisdom was equal to a drillmaster's "Right face," "Left wheel," and "Right, oblique, march." It takes a raw recruit some time to learn that he is not to think or suggest, but obey. Some never do learn. I acquired it at last, in humility and mud, but it was tough. Yet I doubt if my patriotism, during my first three weeks' drill, was quite knee high. Drilling looks easy to a spectator, but it isn't. After a time I had cut down my uniform so that I could see out of it, and had conquered the drill sufficiently to see through it. Then the word came: on to Washington! . . .

Reading Strategy
Distinguishing Fact from Opinion Identify one opinion in this description of enlisting.

Critical Reading

1. **Respond:** Would you have volunteered to fight during the early days of the Civil War? Why or why not?
2. **(a) Recall:** What events does Mary Chesnut describe in her diary entries? **(b) Interpret:** What does her diary reveal about her attitude toward the war?
3. **(a) Summarize:** Describe Warren Lee Goss's feelings on the day he was to enlist in the army. **(b) Analyze:** How did Private Goss's attitudes and expectations change after he enlisted?
4. **(a) Recall:** According to Goss, what takes a long time for a recruit to learn? **(b) Infer:** What do you think happened to cause him to say, "I acquired it at last, in humility and mud, but it was tough"?
5. **Apply:** How might Chesnut's diary have been different if she had been from the North?

For: More about Mary Boykin Chesnut and Warren Lee Goss
Visit: www.PHSchool.com
Web Code: ere-9407

13 Vocabulary Builder
Latin Prefix: *ob-*

- Read the passage aloud and ask students to identify words that contains the prefix *ob-*.
- Point out that the word *obtaining* contains the Latin prefix *ob-*. What word in the next paragraph also contains the prefix?
  Answer: The words *obtain* and *oblique* contains the prefix *ob-*.
- Tell students that the Latin prefix *ob-* has several meanings, including *"to or toward", "against", "over",* and "completely."
- Define the words *oblique* and *obtain,* and an explanation of the meanings of their roots. (The root of the word *oblique,* which means "slanted," derives from the Latin *liqu,* meaning "bent." The root of the word *obtain,* which means "to gain a hold of," derives from the Latin *tenere,* meaning "to hold").
- Then, **ask** students to explain which meaning of the prefix *ob-* is at work in each word.
  Answer: In *oblique,* means "to" or "toward." In *obtain,* the means *"completely."*

ASSESS

Answers

1. Students should explain the reasoning behind their responses.
2. (a) She describes the events surrounding the firing on Fort Sumter by Confederate troops. (b) She thinks the South has no choice but to fight, but she is afraid of the war's consquences.
3. (a) He is nervous and excited and feels "a fluctuation of desires." (b) Before enlisting, he imagines himself looking impressive and exciting in uniform; after enlisting, he develops a more realistic and humble image of himself.
4. (a) It takes a long time for a recruit to learn to obey without thinking or making suggestions. (b) Students may say that Goss was "drilled," or vigorously trained, until he responded instinctively with obedience.

Answers continued

5. **Possible response:** She probably would have dreaded the shelling even more, and would have seen the Union soldiers who defended Fort Sumter as heroes.

Go Online Author Link For additional information about Mary Boykin Chesnut or Warren Lee Goss, have students type in the Web Code, then select C or G from the alphabet, and then select Chesnut or Goss.

⓮ About the Selection

In this diary entry, Confederate soldier Randolph McKim describes the futile and bloody attempts of his and others' regiments to capture Culp's Hill, the extreme right of the Federal position.

⓮ A Confederate Account of the Battle of Gettysburg

Randolph McKim

From July 1 to July 3, 1863, Union and Confederate troops fought near the small town of Gettysburg, Pennsylvania. After Union troops gained control of the hills surrounding the town, the Confederate troops commanded by Robert E. Lee launched a risky attack on the strongest Union position. When the attack failed, the Confederate troops were forced to retreat at a great cost of lives. The battle, the first in which troops commanded by Lee were defeated, marked a turning point in the war. In a diary entry, Confederate soldier Randolph McKim described the final day of the battle.

Enrichment

Civil War Music

In 1862, abolitionist and suffragist Julia Ward Howe wrote "The Battle Hymn of the Republic" and sold it to the *Atlantic Monthly.* Reportedly, Union soldiers sang this song over and over. In fact, music was ever-present during the American Civil War. Robert E. Lee said that he didn't believe there could be an army without music. Drumbeats spurred soldiers into battle, and regimental bands raised the spirits of marching soldiers and entertained at reviews and parades. During the lengthy and lonely encampments, soldiers sang both patriotic and sentimental songs.

Today one can identify a wide selection of music that was composed around the time of (or became associated with) the Civil War. Have students research the songs the Federal and Confederate armies sang and listened to, and have students listen to the music themselves. Invite them to learn more about the origins of some songs and to present their findings to the class.

Then came General Ewell's order to assume the offensive and assail the crest of Culp's Hill, on our right. . . . The works to be stormed ran almost at right angles to those we occupied. Moreover, there was a double line of entrenchments, one above the other, and each filled with troops. In moving to the attack we were exposed to enfilading fire[1] from the woods on our left flank, besides the double line of fire which we had to face in front, and a battery of artillery posted on a hill to our left rear opened upon us at short range. . . .

On swept the gallant little brigade, the Third North Carolina on the right of the line, next the Second Maryland, then the three Virginia regiments (10th, 23d, and 37th), with the First North Carolina on the extreme left. Its ranks had been sadly thinned, and its energies greatly depleted by those six fearful hours of battle that morning; but its nerve and spirit were undiminished. Soon, however, the left and center were checked and then repulsed, probably by the severe flank fire from the woods; and the small remnant of the Third North Carolina, with the stronger Second Maryland (I do not recall the banners of any other regiment), were far in advance of the rest of the line. On they pressed to within about twenty or thirty paces of the works—a small but gallant band of heroes daring to attempt what could not be done by flesh and blood.

The end soon came. We were beaten back to the line from which we had advanced with terrible loss, and in much confusion, but the enemy did not make a countercharge. By the strenuous efforts of the officers of the line and of the staff, order was restored, and we re-formed in the breastworks[2] from which we had emerged, there to be again exposed to an artillery fire exceeding in violence that of the early morning. It remains only to say that, like Pickett's men[3] later in the day, this single brigade was hurled unsupported against the enemy's works. Daniel's brigade remained in the breastworks during and after the charge, and neither from that command nor from any other had we any support. Of course it is to be presumed that General Daniel acted in obedience to orders. We remained in this breastwork after the charge about an hour before we finally abandoned the Federal entrenchments and retired to the foot of the hill.

16

Reading Strategy
Distinguishing Fact From Opinion What is Randolph McKim describing in the sentence beginning "On they pressed"? Is he stating the facts or giving his opinion?

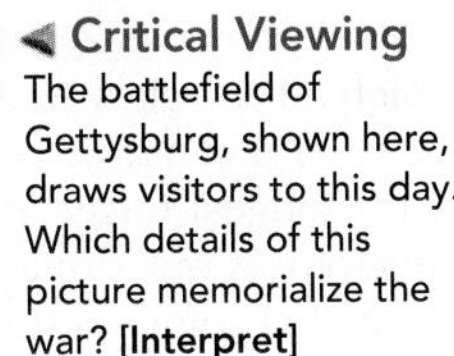

17 **Critical Viewing** The battlefield of Gettysburg, shown here, draws visitors to this day. Which details of this picture memorialize the war? **[Interpret]**

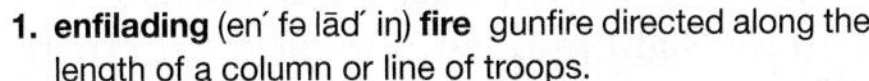

1. **enfilading** (en′ fə lād′ iŋ) **fire** gunfire directed along the length of a column or line of troops.
2. **breastworks** low walls put up quickly as a defense in battle.
3. **Pickett's men** General George Pickett was a Confederate officer who led the unsuccessful attack on the Union position.

18 **Reading Check**
What happens at the end of the battle?

15 Reading Strategy
Distinguishing Fact from Opinion

- Have one or two student volunteers provide concise, one-sentence definitions that clarify the essential difference between a fact and an opinion.
- Then, read aloud the bracketed passage slowly for the class. **Ask** students the Reading Strategy question: What is Randolph McKim describing in the sentence beginning "On they pressed"? Is he stating the facts or giving his opinion?
Answer: He is describing the Confederate soldiers engaged in battle at Culp's Hill. The first half of the sentence is factual, while the second half states an opinion gained from firsthand experience.

16 Background

McKim correctly observes that, like Pickett's disastrous charge, the attack in which he participated was not sufficiently supported by artillery—nor were its flanks, or sides, protected from enfilading fire.

17 Critical Viewing

Answer: Numerous stone markers memorialize the war's fallen soldiers.

18 Reading Check

Answer: At the end of the battle, the Confederate troops retreat to the foot of Culp's Hill.

19 About the Selection

Stonewall Jackson writes to his wife to inform her that he has been in a great battle. He credits God with providing for his own safety and the achievements of his troops. The letter reveals Jackson's bravery, modesty, and religious devotion.

20 Humanities

Stonewall Jackson at Bull Run, c. 1900, by H. A. Ogden

Henry Alexander Ogden was an illustrator who specialized in military subjects. This image was created approximately forty years after the Battle of Bull Run actually took place.

Use the following questions for discussion:

1. Based on both this illustration and his letter, what can you infer about Jackson's personality?
   Answer: He seems calm and controlled, even in battle.
2. Reread Jackson's description of the battle, and explain how it differs from the illustration.
   Answer: Students should note that Jackson mentions his horse, suggesting that he commanded from horseback. He also speaks of having led troops into battle, though he appears to be removed from the fighting in the illustration.

21 Critical Viewing

Answer: Jackson's confident, composed posture, his full officer's dress, and his flamboyant hat mark him as the officer in charge.

22 Reading Strategy

Distinguishing Fact from Opinion

- Have a student volunteer read the passage aloud. Draw students' attention to phrases—such as *hardest that I have ever been in*—that show that Jackson participated in the events he describes.
- **Ask** students the Reading Strategy question: Is the general being factual or stating his opinion in describing the nature of the victory and indicating to whom the glory belongs?
  Answer: He is offering his opinion about the nature and cause of the victory.

19 An Account of the Battle of Bull Run

20

Stonewall Jackson

In this letter to his wife, Confederate General Thomas "Stonewall" Jackson recounts the first southern victory of the war: a battle fought in July 1861, outside Washington, D.C., near a small stream named Bull Run.

My precious pet,

Yesterday we fought a great battle and gained a great victory, for which all the glory is due to God alone. Although under a heavy fire for several continuous hours, I received only one wound, the breaking of the longest finger of my left hand; but the doctor says the finger can be saved. It was broken about midway between the hand and knuckle, the ball passing on the side next [to] the forefinger. Had it struck the center, I should have lost the finger.

22 My horse was wounded, but not killed. Your coat got an ugly wound near the hip, but my servant, who is very handy, has so far repaired it that it doesn't show very much. My preservation was entirely due, as was the glorious victory, to our God, to whom be all the honor, praise and glory. The battle was the hardest that I have ever been in, but not near so hot in its fire. I commanded the center more particularly, though one of my regiments extended to the right for some distance. There were other commanders on my right and left. Whilst great credit is due to other parts of our gallant army, God made my brigade more instrumental than any other in repulsing the main attack. This is for your information only—say nothing about it. Let others speak praise, not myself.

21 **▲Critical Viewing** How does this depiction of Jackson enable the viewer to distinguish the general from his officers and soldiers? **[Analyze]**

Reading Strategy
Distinguishing Fact From Opinion Is the general being factual or stating his opinion in describing the nature of the victory and indicating to whom the glory belongs? Explain.

Enrichment

Stonewall Jackson

Jackson's stand at Bull Run is the reason for his nickname, Stonewall. He held his line against overwhelming odds, bringing about an unexpected Confederate victory. His repeated references to God's hand in the victory reflect his religious fervor, which his detractors mocked with another nickname, Deacon Jackson.

Ironically, Jackson, a master tactician, died as an indirect result of a careless error. Returning at dusk after a daring and successful maneuver, he was shot accidentally by his own men. His arm was amputated, complications resulted, and he died two weeks later on May 10, 1863.

From August 1851 until the beginning of the Civil War in April 1861, Jackson had served on the faculty of the Virginia Military Institute (VMI) as professor of natural and experimental philosophy and instructor of artillery. After Jackson's death, the school honored his memory with gun salutes every half-hour from sunrise to sunset and draped his lecture hall in mourning black for six months.

23 Reaction to the Emancipation Proclamation

Reverend Henry M. Turner

On September 22, 1862, President Lincoln issued the Emancipation Proclamation, declaring that all slaves in states still in rebellion would be free as of January 1, 1863. Because those states were not under Union control at the time, no slaves were actually set free that day. The Proclamation, however, was a powerful symbol of hope for those still in slavery and inspired a wave of Union support from free African Americans. In this account, Reverend Henry M. Turner, a freeborn African American living in Washington, D.C., describes his people's reaction to the news of the Proclamation.

Seeing such a multitude of people in and around my church, I hurriedly sent up to the office of the first paper in which the proclamation of freedom could be printed, known as the *Evening Star,* and squeezed myself through the dense crowd that was waiting for the paper. The first sheet run off with the proclamation in it was grabbed for by three of us, but some active young man got possession of it and fled. The next sheet was grabbed for by several, and was torn into tatters. The third sheet from the press was grabbed for by several, but I succeeded in procuring so much of it as contained the proclamation, and off I went for life and death. Down Pennsylvania Avenue I ran as for my life, and when the people saw me coming with the paper in my hand they raised a shouting cheer that was almost deafening. As many as could get around me lifted me to a great platform, and I started to read the proclamation. I had run the best end of a mile,

Literary Analysis
Diaries, Journals, and Letters How would you describe the tone of Reverend Turner's description?

25  **Reading Check**
What do people do when they see the reverend running down the street?

23 About the Selection

Reverend Henry M. Turner uses an effusive tone to describe the exciting experience of being among the exhilarated crowd clamoring to read the Emancipation Proclamation when it is still hot off the presses.

24 Literary Analysis

Diaries, Journals, and Letters

- As you read the bracketed passage aloud, encourage students to listen for words and phrases, such as *hurriedly, squeezed, grabbed for, went for life and death, a shouting cheer, a great platform, great force and clearness,* that indicate Reverend Turner's attitude toward his subject.

➤ **Monitor Progress: Ask** students the Literary Analysis question: How would you describe the tone of Reverend Turner's description?
Answer: Students might describe Turner's tone as excited, anxious, joyous, or wondrous.

25 Reading Check

Answer: They cheer.

Differentiated Instruction Solutions for All Learners

Strategy for Special Needs Students
Help students summarize what they learn about Confederate General Thomas "Stonewall" Jackson from this letter to his wife. Through discussion and oral rereading of the text, guide students to perceive Jackson's pride and confidence, which he conveys without boastfulness, as well as his strong religious beliefs.

Strategy for Less Proficient Readers
You might wish to discuss some of the ways in which the distinctions between fact and opinion can be blurred. For instance, a firsthand observer of an event sometimes expresses an opinion so fervently and eloquently that a reader or listener believes these observations are factual. For this reason, students may need help recognizing that Reverend Turner's euphoric conclusion, however forceful, is pure opinion.

26 Background
History
Point out that during this period in American history, African Americans were commonly referred to as "colored people."

27 Humanities
Reading the Emancipation Proclamation, 1865, Anonymous

This lithograph is a dramatization of an event that must have occurred countless times in the South in 1863, the year the Emancipation Proclamation was issued. Created by an artist whose name is lost to history, the lithograph shows a Union soldier reading the proclamation to African Americans living in a cabin in the South. Although the artist may have been overly sentimental in this depiction, the proclamation must have inspired an intense emotional reaction.

Use these questions for discussion:

1. How does the artist create a sense of drama?
   Answer: Students may note how a burning torch is held over the soldier, lighting both the proclamation and the dramatic figure of the kneeling woman, who is dressed in white.
2. What emotions do the people in the picture exhibit?
   Answer: The soldier has the undivided attention of the listeners. Their faces, gestures, and body language appear to express relief, amazement, awe, and excitement.

28 Critical Viewing
Answer: Students may respond that the rapt attention the readers and listeners display bears similarities to the scene described by Reverend Turner.

I was out of breath, and could not read. Mr. Hinton, to whom I handed the paper, read it with great force and clearness. While he was reading every kind of demonstration and gesticulation was going on. Men 26 squealed, women fainted, dogs barked, white and colored people shook hands, songs were sung, and by this time cannons began to fire at the navy yard, and follow in the wake of the roar that had for some time been going on behind the White House. . . . Great processions of colored and white men marched to and fro and passed in front of the White House and congratulated President Lincoln on his proclamation. The President came to the window and made responsive bows, and thousands told him, if he would come out of that palace, they would hug him to death. . . . It was indeed a time of times, and nothing like it will ever be seen again in this life.

27

28 ▲ **Critical Viewing** In what way does this illustration relate to Reverend Turner's account? **[Connect]**

29 An Account of an *Experience with Discrimination*

Sojourner Truth

Although the Civil War brought an end to slavery, the struggle against racial discrimination was just beginning. Before the war, Sojourner Truth worked tirelessly to free slaves. After the war, she fought for a number of causes, including the woman's suffrage movement and the desegregation of public transportation. Once, when a driver of a streetcar refused her passage, she brought a local street to a standstill. With the support of a crowd behind her, the driver was forced to allow her on board. In the following letter, written on October 1, 1865, Sojourner Truth describes other encounters with racism.

30 ▲ **Critical Viewing** In what ways does this image compare with your impression of Sojourner Truth based on her account? Explain. **[Compare and Contrast]**

A few weeks ago I was in company with my friend Josephine S. Griffing, when the conductor of a streetcar refused to stop his car for me, although [I was] closely following Josephine and holding on to the iron rail. They dragged me a number of yards before she succeeded in 31 stopping them. She reported the conductor to the president of the City Railway, who dismissed him at once, and told me to take the number of the car whenever I was mistreated by a conductor or driver.

Reading Check
What does Josephine S. Griffing do to help her friend?

29 About the Selection

Sojourner Truth describes her proactive responses to acts of racial discrimination on a streetcar.

30 Critical Viewing

Answer: Students should support their responses with clear reasoning and with detailed references to the image and to the text.

31 Reading Check

Answer: Griffing stopped the streetcar that was dragging Truth, reported the conductor to the city railway, and advised Truth to take the number of the streetcar whenever she was mistreated by a conductor or driver.

Differentiated Instruction Solutions for All Learners

Support for English Learners
When reading Reverend Turner's account, students may need your help understanding the reasons for capitalization of the word *president.* Tell them that the word *President* is capitalized in the first instance because it is a title, and in the second instance because it refers to a particular chief executive of the United States, Abraham Lincoln.

Enrichment for Advanced Readers
To gain a richer appreciation of the common soldier's experience in the Civil War, historians rely heavily on regimental histories and individual memoirs. Students interested in pursuing further reading of such firsthand accounts may enjoy the published histories of the First Minnesota or of the Iron Brigade. Or they may enjoy *All for the Union: The Civil War Diary* and *Letters of Elisha Hunt Rhodes.*

On the 13th I had occasion to go for necessities for the patients in the Freedmen's Hospital where I have been doing and advising for a number of months. I thought now I would get a ride without trouble as I was in company with another friend, Laura S. Haviland of Michigan. As I ascended the platform of the car, the conductor pushed me, saying "Go back—get off here." I told him I was not going off, then "I'll put you off" said he furiously, clenching my right arm with both hands, using such
32 violence that he seemed about to succeed, when Mrs. Haviland told him he was not going to put me off. "Does she belong to you?" said he in a hurried angry tone. She replied, "She does not belong to me, but she belongs to humanity." The number of the car was noted, and conductor dismissed at once upon the report to the president, who advised his arrest for assault and battery as my shoulder was sprained by his effort to put me off. Accordingly I had him arrested and the case tried before Justice Thompson. My shoulder was very lame and swollen, but is better. It is hard for the old slaveholding spirit to die. But die it must. . . .

Nell Irvin Painter
Scholar's Insight
The African American journalist Ida B. Wells went to court in 1884 after being denied first-class passage despite having purchased a first-class ticket. (She won her case, then lost on appeal.)

Critical Reading

1. **Respond:** In what ways have these accounts added to your understanding of the Civil War? Explain.
2. **(a) Recall:** Explain the events described in the accounts of Randolph McKim and Stonewall Jackson. **(b) Compare:** How are they similar? **(c) Contrast:** How do they differ?
3. **(a) Recall:** What is the reaction to the Emancipation Proclamation among the members of Reverend Turner's audience? **(b) Speculate:** Why do you think the Emancipation Proclamation had such an emotional effect?
4. **(a) Recall:** What does the streetcar conductor say to Laura Haviland about Sojourner Truth? **(b) Infer:** What does his question reveal about the "old slaveholding spirit"?
5. **(a) Recall:** What happens to the conductor who wanted to refuse service to Truth? **(b) Connect:** What details of these events of 1865 have in common with the Civil Rights Movement of the 1960s?
6. **(a) Compare and Contrast:** In what ways do the tones or attitudes of Sojourner Truth and Henry Turner differ? **(b) Speculate:** Why do you think their feelings are different?
7. **Take a Position:** If you were alive during the Civil War, which position might you have taken—the North's or South's? Explain.

For: More about Randolph McKim, Thomas Jonathan "Stonewall" Jackson, Reverend Henry M. Turner, and Sojourner Truth
Visit: www.PHSchool.com
Web Code: ere-9409

32 Scholar's Insight

- Have a student read the bracketed passage. Then, draw students' attention to Painter's note about Ida B. Wells. Ask students how this note further exemplifies Truth's remarks in the passage.
  Possible response: It is another example of the how the "slaveholding spirit" is hard to kill.

ASSESS

Answers

1. Students' responses should reflect a new awareness of the impact of the war on the lives of individuals.
2. (a) McKim describes how Confederate forces retreated from Union forces at Culp's Hill; Jackson describes a Confederate victory at Bull Run. (b) The accounts are similar in that both provide detailed descriptions of specific battles and were written by actual participants. (c) McKim's account contains more details, and is written from the perspective of an enlisted soldier. Jackson's account provides an overview of the battle, as seen by a strategist and leader. In addition, Jackson's account is marked by repeated references to his subservience to God's power.
3. (a) The proclamation is received with jubilation, relief, and gratitude. (b) **Possible response:** It represented an official recognition of the rights of African Americans to live in freedom and symbolized the beginning of a new era in United States history.
4. (a) He says, "Does she belong to you?" (b) It reveals that the slaveholding spirit is still alive in the streetcar conductor.
5. (a) He is dismissed from his job, arrested, and tried for assault and battery. (b) Both demostrate the struggles involved in ending segregation in stores, public places, schools, on public transportation, and in other areas of American society.
6. (a) Reverend Turner's tone is one of excitement and hope, whereas Sojourner Truth's tone reflects the pain of discrimination. (b) Students may note that Turner's attitude reflects the newness of emancipation, while Truth's feelings reflect

continued

Answers continued

her bitterness and disappointment that the struggle must continue.

7. Students should support their responses with clear reasoning.

Go Online Author Link For additional information about Randolph McKim, Stonewall Jackson, Reverend Henry M. Turner, and Sojourner Truth, have students type in the Web Code, then select the first letter of the author's last name from the alphabet, and then select the authors' name.

Apply the Skills

Civil War Diaries, Journals, and Letters

Literary Analysis

Diaries, Journals, and Letters

1. Note at least two examples from Mary Chesnut's **diaries** that indicate her dislike of the war.
2. Find three details or ideas that Jackson probably would have omitted from his **letter** if it were intended for publication.
3. What does Sojourner Truth's letter reveal about her personality?

Comparing Literary Works

4. What details about the Civil War can you learn from Mary Chesnut's diary that you might not learn from a history book?
5. What facts or details can you learn from two of the other selections?
6. **(a)** What makes these **historical narratives** valuable to students of the Civil War? **(b)** What might make them unreliable?
7. Which selection would you say is most valuable to historians? Why?

Reading Strategy

Distinguishing Fact From Opinion

8. **Distinguish the facts from opinions** in the following passage from Goss's account:

   The forage cap was an ungainly bag with pasteboard top and leather visor; the blouse was the only part which seemed decent; while the overcoat made me feel like a little nubbin of corn in a large preponderance of husk.
9. Identify two facts and two opinions from Jackson's account. Record them in a chart like the one shown.

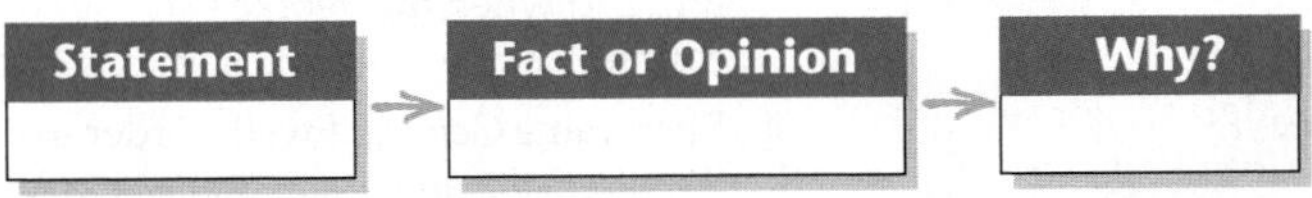

10. In the accounts by Reverend Turner and Sojourner Truth, which contains more facts and which contains more opinions? Explain your answer.

Extend Understanding

11. **Social Studies Connection:** More than a century later, the Civil War continues to engage the interest of Americans. Why do you think this is so?

QuickReview

Diaries and journals are personal records of daily events, usually written in prose. A **personal letter** is one that is written without the intention of publication.

Historical narratives are personal accounts of significant historical events.

To **distinguish fact from opinion,** determine whether or not a statement can be proved conclusively true.

For: Self-test
Visit: www.PHSchool.com
Web Code: era-6406

Answers

1. **Possible answers include:** She writes, "I begin to hope [that there will be no fighting]." She is so distracted by the prospect of war that she accidentally sets herself on fire.
2. **Possible answer:** He would have omitted the salutation to his wife, the details about the wound to his finger, and the information about his brigade being central to the Confederate victory.
3. It reveals that she is a strong, determined woman who will not allow herself to be intimidated.
4. One can learn about the ways in which ordinary citizens responded to the war, details about the social atmosphere of the South, and even details about the makeshift uniforms worn by Confederate leaders.
5. **Possible answer:** Private Goss—details about how it felt for an ordinary citizen to enlist; McKim—details about Confederate maneuvers.
6. (a) These narratives provide intimate, firsthand looks at historic events. (b) They may be unreliable because each presents the potentially biased view of an individual.
7. Students may point to Jackson's letter, which provides insights into the thoughts of a Confederate general, McKim's diary, which offers a soldier's view of battle, or Chesnut's journal, which gives a "backstage" view of Confederate leaders.
8. **Facts:** The forage cap had a pasteboard top and leather visor. **Opinions:** The cap was an "ungainly bag"; the blouse was "decent"; and the coat made him feel like a small ear of corn lost in its husk.
9. **Sample answer—Facts:** Jackson's coat was damaged; his servant repaired it. **Opinions:** The word *ugly* and the statement that the repair "doesn't show very much."

   Another sample answer can be found on **Reading Strategy Graphic Organizer B,** p. 115 in ***Graphic Organizer Transparencies.***
10. Both accounts contain presumably factual observations; at the

Answers continued

conclusion of each account, the writer offers an opinion.

11. Responses should reflect a new awareness of the impact of the war on the nation.

Go Online Assessment — Students may use the **Self-test** to prepare for **Selection Test A** or **Selection Test B.**

EXTEND/ASSESS

Answers

1 Vocabulary Lesson

Word Analysis

1. c
2. a
3. b

Spelling Strategy

1. celebration
2. litigation
3. speculation

Vocabulary Builder

1. imprecations
2. serenity
3. foreboding
4. capitulate
5. obstinate
6. audaciously

2 Grammar and Style Lesson

1. *Herald;* Texas
2. Third North Carolina; Second Maryland; Virginia
3. Avenue; people
4. Culp's
5. President; proclamation

Writing Application

Students' paragraphs should reflect correct capitalization.

Writing and Grammar, Ruby Level

Students will find further instruction and practice on capitalization of proper nouns in Chapter 26.

Build Language Skills

1 Vocabulary Lesson

Word Analysis: Latin Prefix *ob-*

The word *obstinate* comes from a combination of the Latin prefix *ob-*, meaning "against," and a form of the Latin root *-stare-*, meaning "stand." Use your understanding of the meaning of *ob-* to match each word to the numbered item that most closely relates to it.

a. obstruction **b.** obscure **c.** object

1. voice opposition in the courtroom
2. a fallen tree blocking the road
3. cloud an issue with confusing arguments

Spelling Strategy

Verbs that end in *-ate* have noun forms ending in *-ion.* Drop the final *e* before adding the suffix, as in *imprecate/imprecation* and *capitulate/capitulation.* Spell the noun forms of the following words:

1. celebrate **2.** litigate **3.** speculate

Vocabulary Builder: Sentence Completion

Complete these sentences with the correct word from the vocabulary list on page 549.

1. When the rifle jammed, the soldier muttered __?__ at his bad luck.
2. There was no __?__ to be found in the troubled hearts and minds of soldiers and civilians.
3. As enemy shells exploded in the distance, a sense of __?__ hung over the camp like fog.
4. Despite the overwhelming odds facing his brigade, the general refused to __?__.
5. What one person would call __?__, another might call courageous.
6. After midnight, the spies crept __?__ close to the enemy's encampment.

2 Grammar and Style Lesson

Capitalization of Proper Nouns

The name of a person, street, road, town, city, county, or state is considered a **proper noun** and should begin with a **capital letter.** Directional words (*east, west,* and so on) that are part of the name of a place should also begin with a capital, as in *West Virginia.*

Proper Nouns: Why did that green goose *Anderson* go into *Fort Sumter*?

Practice Rewrite each of the following sentences in your notebook, correcting any errors in capitalization.

1. The *Herald* says that this show of war outside of the bar is intended for texas.
2. On swept the gallant little brigade, the third north Carolina on the right of the line, next the second maryland, and then the three virginia regiments.
3. Down Pennsylvania avenue I ran as for my life, and when the People saw me coming . . . they raised a shouting cheer.
4. Then came General Ewell's order to assume the offensive and assail the crest of culp's Hill.
5. They passed the White House and congratulated President lincoln on his proclamation.

Writing Application Write a paragraph about a recent trip you took. Be sure to name places and use capital letters when necessary.

Prentice Hall Writing and Grammar Connection: Chapter 26

Assessment Practice

Context **(For more practice, see *Standardized Test Preparation Workbook*, p. 31.)**

Many tests require students to use context clues to determine the meaning of unfamiliar words. Use this sample test item to give students practice in this skill.

With a nervous tremor convulsing my system, and my heart thumping like muffled drumbeats, I stood before the door of the recruiting office.

In this passage, the word convulsing most nearly means—

A shaking
B settling
C straightening
D deadening

There is no contextual support for the last three answers. A "tremor" is a trembling motion. The overall context—the nervousness, the thumping heart—suggests agitation. *A* is correct.

3 Writing Lesson

Timed Writing: Problem-and-Solution Essay

Today, few take the time to write letters or keep a journal. In what way might this be a loss? In an essay, explore the personal benefits and historical value of engaging in this type of private writing. Use examples and insights from these selections to illustrate your point. ***(40 minutes)***

Prewriting *(10 minutes)* Brainstorm for a list of the benefits of journal writing and the disadvantages that could occur when historical events are not documented in this way. Use a chart like the one shown to gather your ideas.

Model: Gathering Details

Personal Benefits	Historical Value	Loss From No Journal
Journals can be passed down through family.	History is documented for society at large.	Valuable information could be lost forever.

Drafting *(20 minutes)* Begin with an introduction of the topic. Then, write one paragraph on three of your ideas, connecting them with personal experiences to provide insight. Tie your thoughts together in the conclusion.

Revising *(10 minutes)* Compare your draft with your list to be sure you have included the essential points you want to make. Make sure that your personal reflections clearly connect with your main ideas.

WG Prentice Hall Writing and Grammar Connection: Chapter 4, Section 2

Extend Your Learning

Listening and Speaking Rev. Turner recounts the emotional impact of the Emancipation Proclamation. Deliver a **dramatic reading** of the document, accompanied by music that conveys the tone of your interpretation. Consider the following:

- Read main points with emotion for emphasis.
- Make eye contact or use hand gestures that convey power or determination.

After practicing, present the reading to your class.

Research and Technology With a group, research the Battle of Gettysburg. Create a **model** or **map** of the battlefield, identify the locations of key events, and provide explanatory captions. Integrate Internet graphics and word-processed text. **[Group Activity]**

For: An additional research activity
Visit: www.PHSchool.com
Web Code: erd-7406

Assessment Resources

Unit 4 Resources
- **Selection Test A,** pp. 105–107
- **Selection Test B,** pp. 108–110

General Resources
- **Rubric for Problem–and–Solution Essay,** pp. 59–60
- **Rubric for Peer Assessment: Oral Interpretation,** p. 130

Go Online Assessment Students may use the **Self-test** to prepare for **Selection Test A** or **Selection Test B.**

3 Writing Lesson

You may use this Writing Lesson as timed-writing practice, or you may allow students to develop the essay as a writing assignment over several days.

- To guide students in writing this problem and solution essay, give them the **Support for Writing Lesson** page (***Unit 4 Resources,*** p. 102).
- Students' problem-and-solution essays should clearly articulate the ways in which a modern inattention to journal writing might present a loss, both to individuals and to society. They should also suggest some solutions to this loss.
- Students might benefit from brainstorming for two lists—one noting the value of documenting their own daily lives in the 21st century, and another noting the value of documenting more obviously dramatic or historic events.
- Use the Problem-Solution Essay rubrics in ***General Resources*** pp. 59–60, to evaluate students' problem-and-solution essays.

4 Listening and Speaking

- Encourage students to reread Lincoln's text many times and "score" it by noting passages requiring emphasis, shifts in tone, and emotional intensity.
- Students should rehearse the speech in front of one or more trusted peers or family members. Some students may find it helpful to record themselves on videotape or audiotape, in order to learn where adjustments might be made to strengthen their presentations.
- The **Support for Extend Your Learning** page (***Unit 4 Resources,*** p. 103) provides guided note-taking opportunities to help students complete the Extend Your Learning activities.
- Use the rubric for Peer Assessment: Oral Interpretation, p. 130 in ***General Resources,*** to evaluate students' readings.

Go Online Research Have students type in the Web code for another research activity.

Meeting Your Standards

Students will

1. understand the connections between views of war in literature from different eras.
2. gain insights about human nature from writers' observations of war.

Connections

Literature Around the World

Students might reread the Civil War diaries of Mary Chesnut, Warren Lee Goss, and Randolph McKim to gain perspective on the presentation of war in literature. Pirandello's views of war are from a different century and continent, yet students may find similarities between his thoughts and those of the American writers.

The Prism of War

- Have students discuss contradictory views of war as a noble mission and as a brutal exercise in inhumanity.
- Brainstorm with students to name works of literature set during a war. Have them identify the writer's view of war.
- Read aloud "A Different Perspective on War" to introduce the Pirandello story. **Ask** why fiction can reveal truths that may not be apparent in nonfiction.
  Answer: Nonfiction is about real life, and the nonfiction writer might not gather many opinions as research for his or her writing. An author of fiction can create characters who voice a range of opinions that will enrich the view of a topic.

CONNECTIONS

Literature Around the World

Italy

The Prism of War

Few events in human experience evoke such startlingly diverse emotions as war does. Throughout history, armed conflict has been fed by idealism, patriotism, sacrifice, heroism, and visions of glory. Among war's less noble motivations have been jealousy, greed, fear, religious hatred, and imperialism. The twentieth century has offered several horrifying examples of how war may join with genocide in the attempt to wipe out entire peoples.

War is a prism through which we can catch glimpses of some of the best and worst in human nature. Perhaps this is one reason that war—aside from its inherent conflict and suspense—has been the setting for some of the greatest works in world literature, ranging from Homer's *Iliad* through Leo Tolstoy's *War and Peace* and Stephen Crane's *Red Badge of Courage.*

A Different Perspective on War The collection of diaries, journals, and letters in this unit (pages 548–565) presents first-person accounts of the Civil War, written by participants as well as observers. As some of these selections show, war can have a powerful effect on the soldiers who experience combat, but it also affects the families who worry about their loved ones on the front lines—and mourn for them when they die.

Set in Italy during World War I, Luigi Pirandello's story "War," presented here, focuses on the parents that soldiers leave behind. During World War I, which broke out in 1914, Italy fought on the side of Great Britain, France, Russia, and the United States and suffered devastating casualties. Approximately 650,000 Italians died—nearly two percent of the country's population—and almost 950,000 were wounded.

The Civil War diaries are works of nonfiction, written to present real events as accurately as possible. In contrast, Pirandello's story is a work of fiction. Nevertheless, you may find that it reveals essential truths about war.

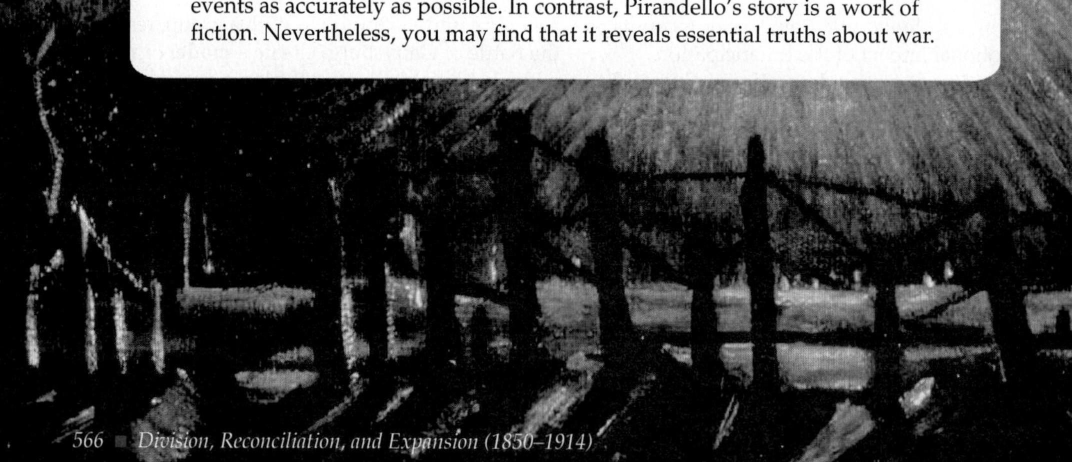

Enrichment

History

In the late nineteenth and early twentieth centuries, political tensions in Europe led to alliances among several major powers. Germany, Austria-Hungary, and Italy formed the Triple Alliance; Great Britain, France, and Russia formed the Triple Entente. When World War I broke out in 1914, however, Italy did not join in on the side of its allies. Instead, Italian officials made a secret treaty with the Triple Entente, promising Italy's military help in return for land gains at the war's end. Italy then declared war on its former allies. In the years of fighting that followed, approximately 650,000 Italians died—nearly 2 percent of the country's population—and almost 950,000 more were wounded. It is against this bitter cultural landscape that Pirandello's story unfolds.

CONNECTIONS

War

Luigi Pirandello *translated by* Samuel Putnam

The passengers who had left Rome by the night express had had to stop until dawn at the small station of Fabriano[1] in order to continue their journey by the small old-fashioned "local" joining the main line with Sulmona.[2]

▼ **Critical Viewing**
Do you think this painting of a World War I battlefield suggests hope or terror? **[Explain]**

At dawn, in a stuffy and smoky second-class carriage in which five people had already spent the night, a bulky woman in deep mourning was hoisted in—almost like a shapeless bundle. Behind her—puffing and moaning, followed her husband—a tiny man, thin and weakly, his face death-white, his eyes small and bright and looking shy and uneasy.

Having at last taken a seat he politely thanked the passengers who had helped his wife and who had made room for her; then he turned round to the woman trying to pull down the collar of her coat and politely enquired:

"Are you all right, dear?"

The wife, instead of answering, pulled up her collar again to her eyes, so as to hide her face.

"Nasty world," muttered the husband with a sad smile.

And he felt it his duty to explain to his travelling companions that the poor woman was to be pitied for the war was taking away from her her only son, a

A Star Shell, exh. 1916, Christopher R.W. Nevinson, Tate Gallery, London

1. **Fabriano** (fa′ brē a′ nō) city in eastern Italy, approximately 100 miles from Rome.
2. **Sulmona** (so͞ol mō′ na) city in eastern Italy, approximately 75 miles from Rome.

Humanities

A Star Shell by Christopher R. W. Nevinson

British artist Christopher R. W. Nevinson (1889–1946) experienced the horrors of World War I firsthand as a Red Cross ambulance driver in France. Because of illness, he left active service in 1916, but in 1917, he became an Official War Artist and returned to the front. Like Nevinson's other depictions of war, *A Star Shell* captures the stark and disturbing realities of battle.

Use the following question for discussion:

- Nevinson chose not to show a human presence in this painting. How does his painting contrast with Pirandello's story?
  Answer: The absence of humans and the striking image of an explosion depict destruction and loss. The image could be considered ironically beautiful; Pirandello's "War" conveys the emotional and personal costs of war.

Critical Viewing

Answer: The painting suggests terror. The land, which has been dug up for the trenches, has been decimated. A fiery shell, not a star, provides light. The scene provides little reason for hope.

Differentiated Instruction Solutions for All Learners

Strategy for Less Proficient Readers

Point out to these students that the first two paragraphs of the story introduce the setting and two characters. Organize students into pairs, and have them read the first two paragraphs aloud. Then, review the details of the paragraphs, and ask students to write a brief summary to make sure that they understand who the characters are and what is happening. Create a story timeline on the board, and encourage students to offer information from their summaries to complete the chronology with events and the introduction of characters. Ask students to revise their summaries as needed after the class has completed the timeline.

Enrichment for Advanced Readers

In his journal, Pirandello wrote, "There is somebody who is living my life and I know nothing about him." In this statement, the author expresses a theme that he revisits in his plays and fiction. People, he contends, wear social "masks," or facades, and may not be aware of doing so. Discuss with students the "masks" they find in "War." Use these questions for discussion: Who in the story is wearing a "mask"? Are these characters aware that they are wearing "masks"? Develop a list on the board from student's reflections on the idea of character masks.

Humanities

Italian Soldiers by Karl Fahringer

This drawing appears in the Heeresgeschichtliches Museum of Military History in Vienna, Austria. The museum is the oldest museum in Vienna and houses a collection of war-related items.

Use these questions for discussion:

1. How does the style of this drawing reflect the realities of war?
   Possible response: The jumbled and vigorous lines reflect the chaos and tension of battle. The lines almost appear to tie the soldiers together, illustrating their camaraderie.
2. How is this drawing an appropriate illustration for Pirandello's story?
   Possible responses: It depicts the realities of war that worry Pirandello's characters.

Critical Viewing

Answer: The drawing, with its energetic lines, emphasizes the violence and chaos of combat.

Thematic Connection

Possible response: The man's view is convincing because he is looking not just at losing a child to war, but also at life after the war. Or, the man's view is unreasonable because he thinks that his own situation is worst, while not taking others into consideration.

boy of twenty to whom both had devoted their entire life, even breaking up their home at Sulmona to follow him to Rome where he had to go as a student, then allowing him to volunteer for war with an assurance, however, that at least for six months he would not be sent to the front and now, all of a sudden, receiving a wire saying that he was due to leave in three days' time and asking them to go and see him off.

The woman under the big coat was twisting and wriggling, at times growling like a wild animal, feeling certain that all those explanations would not have aroused even a shadow of sympathy from those people who—most likely—were in the same plight as herself. One of them, who had been listening with particular attention, said:

"You should thank God that your son is only leaving now for the front. Mine has been sent there the first day of the war. He has already come back twice wounded and been sent back again to the front."

"What about me? I have two sons and three nephews at the front," said another passenger.

"Maybe, but in our case it is our *only* son," ventured the husband.

"What difference can it make? You may spoil your only son with excessive attentions, but you cannot love him more than you would all your other children if you had any. Paternal love is not like bread that can be broken into pieces and spilt amongst the children in equal shares. A father gives all his love to each one of his children without discrimination, whether it be one or ten, and if I am suffering now for my two sons, I am not suffering half for each of them but double. . . ."

"True . . . true . . ." sighed the embarrassed husband, "but suppose (of course we all hope it will never be your case) a father has two sons at the front and he loses one of them, there is still one left to console him . . . while . . ."

"Yes," answered the other, getting cross, "a son left to console him but also a son left for whom he must survive, while in the case of the father of an only son if the son dies the father can die too and put an end to his distress. Which of the two positions is the worse? Don't you see how my case would be worse than yours?"

"Nonsense," interrupted another traveller, a fat, red-faced man with bloodshot eyes of the palest grey.

He was panting. From his bulging eyes seemed to spurt inner violence of an uncontrolled vitality which his weakened body could hardly contain.

▲ Critical Viewing
Which aspect of war does this drawing exphasize **[Interpret]**

Vocabulary Builder

plight (plīt) *n.* sad or difficult situation

paternal (pə tʉr′ nəl) *adj.* like a father

discrimination (di skrim′ inā′ shən) *n.* show of partiality or prejudice

Thematic Connection
Do you think the man's argument is convincing? Why or why not?

Enrichment

The Nobel Prize

In 1934, Luigi Pirandello won the Nobel Prize for Literature, which is awarded to recognize the most distinguished body of literary work. The Nobel Prize has been beneficial in bringing otherwise little-known writers and their countries into the public light as contributors to world literature.

At the same time, however, the Nobel Prize for Literature has had its share of controversy. The Nobel committee for literature is composed of four or five members, primarily from Sweden. Some critics suspect a small bias, citing the fact that Scandinavian countries have received the prize most often, collecting 17.4 percent of the prizes. Recently, however, the awards have spanned the globe, honoring writers from Guatemala, Czechoslovakia, and Iceland.

Pirandello was an Italian patriot and supported Mussolini's government, yet his writing offered insights into the damage war does to society. Pirandello's dramatic work, including *Six Characters in Search of an Author,* was considered groundbreaking, and influenced the Surrealists and the Absurdists.

"Nonsense," he repeated, trying to cover his mouth with his hand so as to hide the two missing front teeth. "Nonsense. Do we give life to our children for our own benefit?"

The other travellers stared at him in distress. The one who had had his son at the front since the first day of the war sighed: "You are right. Our children do not belong to us, they belong to the Country. . . ."

"Bosh," retorted the fat traveller. "Do we think of the Country when we give life to our children? Our sons are born because . . . well, because they must be born and when they come to life they take our own life with them. This is the truth. We belong to them but they never belong to us. And when they reach twenty they are exactly what we were at their age. We too had a father and mother, but there were so many other things as well . . . girls, cigarettes, illusions, new ties . . . and the Country, of course, whose call we would have answered—when we were twenty—even if father and mother had said no. Now, at our age, the love of our Country is still great, of course, but stronger than it is the love for our children. Is there any one of us here who wouldn't gladly take his son's place at the front if he could?"

There was a silence all round, everybody nodding as to approve.

"Why then," continued the fat man, "shouldn't we consider the feelings of our children when they are twenty? Isn't it natural that at their age they should consider the love for their Country (I am speaking of decent boys, of course) even greater than the love for us? Isn't it natural that it should be so, as after all they must look upon us as upon old boys who cannot move any more and must stay at home? If Country exists, if Country is a natural necessity like bread, of which each of us must eat in order not to die of hunger, somebody must go to defend it. And our sons go, when they are twenty, and they don't want tears, because if they die, they die inflamed and happy (I am speaking, of course, of decent boys). Now, if one dies young and happy, without having the ugly sides of life, the boredom of it, the pettiness, the bitterness of disillusion . . . what more can we ask for him? Everyone should stop crying: everyone should laugh, as I do . . . or at least thank God—as I do—because my son, before dying, sent me a message saying that he was dying satisfied at having ended his life in the best way he could have wished. That is why, as you see, I do not even wear mourning. . . ."

He shook his light fawn[3] coat as to show it; his livid[4] lip over his missing teeth was trembling, his eyes were watery and motionless and soon after he ended with a shrill laugh which might well have been a sob.

"Quite so . . . quite so . . . " agreed the others.

3. fawn (fôn) pale, yellowish brown.
4. livid (liv´ id) discolored, as from a bruise; black-and-blue.

CONNECTIONS

Thematic Connection
Does the fat traveller's description of the young men's emotions on this page seem realistic? Why or why not?

▼ Critical Viewing
In what ways do you think the couple in this drawing are similar to and different from the couple in this story? **[Compare and Contrast]**

Reading Check
According to the fat man, why should everyone stop crying?

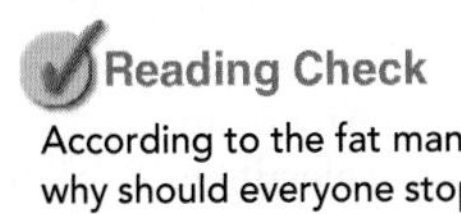

Thematic Connection

Possible response:
Some students may think that the description seems realistic because young men have always been moved by patriotism to fight in wars. However, more students probably will think it does not seem realistic because love of country seems less instinctive than love of one's parents. It is unrealistic to believe that young men do not die inflamed and happy in battle. In addition, the man's reasoning is not a reliable because he is trying to rationalize his own grief.

Humanities

Old Couple by Käthe Kollwitz

Born in Königsberg, Prussia, Käthe Kollwitz (1867–1945) was known for her dramatic etchings, wood-cuts, lithographs, and sculptures.

Use these questions for discussion:

1. How does the lack of color contribute to the mood of the piece?
   Possible response: Because the piece and the emotions exhibited by its subjects are not "colored" by connotation, both remain raw and pure.
2. How do the many layers of lines contribute to the emotion of the sketch?
   Possible response: The repeated lines enhance the darkness of the sketch, emphasizing the couple's isolation and dependence on one another.

Critical Viewing

Possible response: The man appears small, and the woman appears shapeless as Pirandello describes. However, the woman in the story is described as bulky, whereas this woman appears small.

Reading Check

Answer: The fat man says that his son sent a message saying that he was satisfied about the way he was dying.

Differentiated Instruction Solutions for All Learners

Support for English Learners

Draw students' attention to the word *livid* at the bottom of this page, and read the corresponding footnote. Tell students that people sometimes use the word *livid* to mean "enraged." Explain how this particular use of the word relates to the definition provided in the footnote. Offer an example of the word used in a sentence, such as: He was livid with rage about his son's death.

Enrichment for Gifted/Talented Students

In "War," Pirandello offers several physical descriptions of the fat man, including those on pp. 567 and 568. Ask students to use these descriptions to create an illustration of the character. Then, have students consider how these physical, external descriptions contrast with the man's emotions. Ask students to create another illustration—this time depicting the man's internal state. Have students share their illustrations and discuss how the conflict between the external and the internal add meaning to Pirandello's story.

Thematic Connection

Answer: It seems that the father is speaking boldly because he does not realize that his son is actually dead. His reaction to her question takes away illusions about war because the fact of the son's death makes him weep, which undercuts his brave earlier statements.

ASSESS

Answers

1. The perspective in the Pirandello story is that of family members who wait and wonder about a war. It is similar to the perspective in Mary Chesnut's diary, yet Chesnut is close enough to the war so that she is not waiting and wondering from a distance. Pirandello's perspective is different from that of Goss, who is joining the service, going though training, and viewing life as a soldier, not as an elderly parent. Goss also sees humor in his situation, which Pirandello does not see. Pirandello's perspective also is different from McKim's reports from inside the battle, telling about troop movements and the futility of losses.
2. Students may respond that the Civil War divided families, and battles were fought within U.S. borders. This made the Civil War more destructive to the United States than World War I. World War I was fought mostly in Europe and unified the United States against a common foe. This context may make World War I seem like a less negative experience for the country than the Civil War.

The woman who, bundled in a corner under her coat, had been sitting and listening had—for the last three months—tried to find in the words of her husband and her friends something to console her in her deep sorrow, something that might show her how a mother should resign herself to send her son not even to death but to a probable danger of life. Yet not a word had she found amongst the many which had been said . . . and her grief had been greater in seeing that nobody—as she thought—could share her feelings.

But now the words of the traveller amazed and almost stunned her. She suddenly realized that it wasn't the others who were wrong and could not understand her but herself who could not rise up to the same height of those fathers and mothers willing to resign themselves, without crying, not only to the departure of their sons but even to their death.

She lifted her head, she bent over from her corner trying to listen with great attention to the details which the fat man was giving to his companions about the way his son had fallen as a hero, for his King and his Country, happy and without regrets. It seemed to her that she had stumbled into a world she had never dreamt of, a world so far unknown to her and she was so pleased to hear everyone joining in congratulating that brave father who could so stoically speak of his child's death.

Then suddenly, just as if she had heard nothing of what had been said and almost as if waking up from a dream, she turned to the old man, asking him:

"Then . . . is your son really dead?"

Everybody stared at her. The old man, too, turned to look at her, fixing his great, bulging, horribly watery light grey eyes, deep in her face. For some little time he tried to answer, but words failed him. He looked and looked at her, almost as if only then—at that silly, incongruous question—he had suddenly realized at last that his son was really dead . . . gone for ever . . . for ever. His face contracted, became horribly distorted, then he snatched in haste a handkerchief from his pocket and, to the amazement of everyone, broke into harrowing, heart-rending, uncontrollable sobs.

Vocabulary Builder

stoically (stō´ i klē) *adv.* done with indifference to pain or pleasure

incongruous (in käŋ´ groo əs) *adv.* inappropriate

harrowing (har´ ō iŋ) *adj.* disturbing; frightening

Thematic Connection

Explain how the story's ending strips away some people's illusions about war?

Luig Pirandello (1867–1936)

Luigi Pirandello is best remembered for his pioneering plays *Six Characters in Search of an Author* (1921) and *Henry IV* (1922). In both his fiction and drama, Pirandello probed the uncertainties of modern life. Perhaps he summed up his work best when he wrote, "Life is full of infinite absurdities, which, strangely enough, do not even need to appear plausible, since they are true." Pirandello won the Nobel Prize for Literature in 1934.

Connecting Literature Around the World

1. Compare and contrast the perspective on war in Pirandello's "War" with those offered by Mary Chesnut, Warren Lee Goss, and Randolph McKim in their Civil War diaries.
2. In what ways, if any, do the different historical contexts of the American Civil War and World War I affect your reactions to these selections? Explain your response.

Unit 4 Part 3

Forging New Frontiers

Selection Planning Guide

The selections in this section capture the flavor of frontier life in the Old West, a unique time and place in American history. The hilarious narrative of "The Notorious Jumping Frog of Calaveras County" takes students deep into the American frontier. "The Outcasts of Poker Flat" presents an entirely different aspect of frontier life—its singular system of justice. "Heading West" is an excerpt from a diary of a woman who, along with her husband, leaves the comfortable East to move to a community in the Kansas frontier. "I Will Fight No More Forever" is Native American Chief Joseph's poignant surrender speech in which he relates the tragic plight of his people, who are scattered, dead, or starving because of battles with the United States Army. The classic story "To Build a Fire" pits the brutal cold of the Yukon against a foolish traveler.

Humanities

The Home Ranch, by Thomas Eakins

Thomas Eakins (1844–1916) was an American realist painter. Eakins studied at the Pennsylvania Academy of Fine Arts and the École des Beaux-Arts (School of Fine Arts) in Paris. He chiefly painted portraits of sports scenes and his friends. Eakin's contemporaries rejected his piece entitled "The Gross Clinic," which was later considered his masterpiece. The painting was of a group of medical students watching a physician perform surgery.

Eakins taught at the Pennsylvania Academy of Arts from the late 1870s until 1886. He also taught at the National Academy of Design in New York City and the Art Students League. Use the following question for discussion:

- What themes in literature do you expect to read given the title of the part and the painting?
  Possible response: Students may suggest stories about the pioneers heading west. Themes may include adventure, conflict, and hardship.

Differentiated Instruction — Solutions for All Learners

Accessibility at a Glance

More Accessible	Average	More Challenging
Heading West	The Boy's Ambition *from* Life on the Mississippi	The Notorious Jumping Frog of Calaveras County
I Will Fight No More Forever	The Outcasts of Poker Flat	
	To Build a Fire	

Students will

1. **understand the role of Mark Twain in American literature.**
2. **communicate effectively with others in a cooperative situation to assess American humor today.**

Background

American Literature

Huckleberry Finn has been described as the quintessential American novel. It employs themes of escape from civilization, racism, and human relationships against a setting of a raft trip on the Mississippi River. Twain picks up Huck's story where he left it at the end of *Tom Sawyer;* the orphaned Huck has been adopted by a rich widow who plans to "civilize" her new son. Civilization does not suit Huck, however, and soon he is running away across country with Jim, the widow's African slave. At first, Huck condescends to Jim because he is black and a slave, but he eventually learns to appreciate and respect him. Huck narrates his own story in the colorful dialect Twain excelled at reproducing in print.

Critical Viewing

Answer: Being captain of a riverboat would probably be exciting and challenging.

Mark Twain: The American Bard

In the late 1800s, readers might have known him as Thomas Jefferson Snodgrass, W. Epaminandos Adrastus Blab, or simply Josh. Today, we know Samuel Langhorne Clemens as Mark Twain, his most famous literary pseudonym. Whichever name he used, Twain pulled off a rare literary feat—he created stories, novels, and essays that were both wildly popular in his own day and models of wit and skill more than a century later. Twain was so influential that fifty years after his death, Ernest Hemingway said that "all American literature begins" with Twain's novel *The Adventures of Huckleberry Finn.*

> *"At a time when most American writers were copying European movelists, Twain wrote about American themes."*

Life on the Mississippi Born in 1835, Samuel Clemens grew up in the small river town of Hannibal, Missouri. Steamboat men, religious revivalists, circus performers, minstrel companies, showboat actors, and every other kind of traveler imaginable made appearances in Hannibal. As a boy, Clemens met many of the characters that he would later write about.

After his father's death in 1847, Clemens was forced to leave school and take a job as a printer's apprentice. During the 1850s, he wrote a few stories, some of which were published under pseudonyms. Twain also traveled the country. A boat trip down the Mississippi brought back childhood memories, and he decided to become a riverboat pilot. He served as a pilot until 1861, when the Civil War closed the Mississippi to boat traffic.

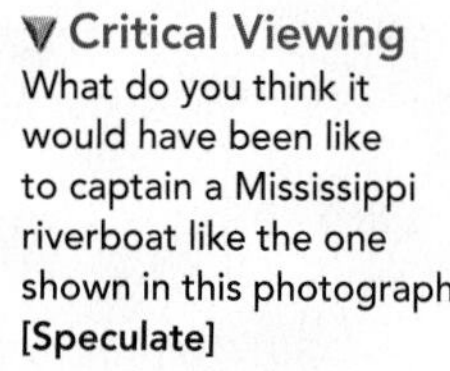

▼ **Critical Viewing**
What do you think it would have been like to captain a Mississippi riverboat like the one shown in this photograph? **[Speculate]**

Mark Twain Is Born In 1862, Clemens took a job as a reporter on a Virginia City newspaper, where he found his calling as a humorist under the byline Mark Twain. The new name, which is actually a signal yelled out by riverboat pilots, freed him to develop a new style. Before becoming "Twain," his work was typical of the low humor of the time, filled with bad puns and intentional misspellings. But in 1865, Twain published a short story entitled "The Notorious Jumping Frog of Calaveras County" (page 581). The story won the author fame and financial success, and it marked the first appearance of his distinctive comic style.

Enrichment

"Mark Twain!"

Twain borrowed his pen name from his days as a riverboat pilot. "Mark twain" is a call indicating that the boat is sailing on water two fathoms deep. In his book *Life on the Mississippi,* Twain recounts his days as an apprentice or "cub" pilot on the Mississippi, including a hard lesson he learned the first time he was allowed to pilot the boat without supervision. As a joke, the crew told the young pilot that he was in shallow water; panicking, Twain begged the engineer to reverse the great paddlewheels. As the crew began laughing at him, the pilot, Mr. Bixby, appeared and warned him never to be tricked again. "Didn't you *know* there's no bottom in that crossing? . . . Then you shouldn't have allowed me or anyone else to shake your confidence in that knowledge." Twain never forgot this lesson.

Tom Sawyer's feigned interest in his chores will fool his friend into doing the work for him.

Ordinary American Speech The targets of Twain's jokes were not new. He distrusted technology and railed against political figures, calling them swindlers and con men. What was new was Twain's feel for ordinary American people and their language. He wrote using the American English that people actually spoke. In that unlikely source, he found rich and comic poetry.

Twain's novels, such as *Tom Sawyer* (1876) and *Huckleberry Finn* (1884), were unlike any books the world had ever seen. At a time when most American writers were copying European novelists, Twain wrote about American themes. His heroes were dirt-poor and plain-spoken, but in Twain's hands, their moral choices had as much drama as those of any tormented aristocrat in a European novel.

Not everyone appreciated Twain's humor. The author fled Virginia City when a rival journalist, offended by a story, challenged him to a pistol duel. He was chased out of San Francisco by policemen angered by critical articles. Even as his fame grew, some critics dismissed him as little more than a jokester.

Yet the American public loved Twain. He made a fortune from his writings, settling with his family into a Hartford, Connecticut, mansion that was elaborately decorated to look like the inside of a steamboat.

The Old Man in a White Suit In the late 1800s, the deaths of Twain's wife and daughters left the writer bitter and cynical. Twain became so reclusive that a newspaper reported he was dead. Twain immediately wired the editors: "Reports of my death have been greatly exaggerated."

History has not exaggerated Twain's legacy. He was the first, and possibly the greatest, authentically American writer.

▲ **Critical Viewing**
In what ways does this illustration for an early edition of *The Adventures of Tom Sawyer* convey the wit that marks Twain's writing? **[Connect]**

Activity

American Humor

Mark Twain's nineteenth-century humor is considered quintessentially American. Contemporary comic writers and comedians also find humor in ordinary Americans and American life.

With a group, share your thoughts about what constitutes American humor today. Use these questions to guide your discussion:

- Think about the humor in television shows, movies, and other media, including current books and magazines. Which topics and styles of comedy are presented most often?
- Has American humor changed since Twain's time? If so, how?

Choose a point person to share your ideas with the class.

Critical Thinking

1. What does the popularity of Twain's stories suggest about the American reading public?
   Answer: Because Twain wrote about ordinary working people, his popularity suggests that similar people bought and enjoyed his books. This in turn suggests that America was a highly literate country in which people of all social classes and income levels liked to read for entertainment.
2. How do you think Twain's travels and varied experiences helped his writing?
   Answer: Wherever he traveled, he could find new people and things to write about. His different job experiences helped him write knowledgeably about people who had those jobs. He saw a great deal of life by traveling and working. He was able to write about actual experiences rather than about things he had only read or heard about.

Activity

Form students into groups. Suggest that one student record the group's ideas to share them with the class. Encourage students to give specific examples of their favorite aspects of American humor today. Define the amount of time that groups will have to work together.

Meeting Your Standards

Students will

1. **analyze and respond to literary elements.**
   - Literary Analysis: Humor
2. **read, comprehend, analyze, and critique nonfiction and a short story.**
   - Reading Strategy: Understanding Regional Dialect
   - Reading Check questions
   - Apply the Skills questions
   - Assessment Practice (ATE)
3. **develop vocabulary.**
   - Vocabulary Lesson: Greek Prefix: *mono-*
4. **understand and apply written and oral language conventions.**
   - Spelling Strategy
   - Grammar and Style Lesson: Double Negatives
5. **develop writing proficiency.**
   - Writing Lesson: Analytic Essay
6. **develop appropriate research strategies.**
   - Extend Your Learning: Multimedia Report
7. **understand and apply listening and speaking strategies.**
   - Extend Your Learning: Interview

Block Scheduling: Use one 90-minute class period to preteach the skills and have students read the selection. Use a second 90-minute class period to assess students' mastery of skills, extend their learning, and monitor their progress.

Homework Suggestions

Following are possibilities for homework assignments:

- Support pages from *Unit 4 Resources:*
  Literary Analysis
  Reading Strategy
  Vocabulary Builder
  Grammar and Style
- An Extend Your Learning project and the Writing Lesson for this selection group may be completed over several days.

Step-by-Step Teaching Guide	Pacing Guide
PRETEACH	
• Administer Vocabulary and Reading Warm-ups as necessary.	5 min.
• Engage students' interest with the motivation activity.	5 min.
• Read and discuss author and background features. **FT**	10 min.
• Introduce the Literary Analysis Skill: Humor **FT**	5 min.
• Introduce the Reading Strategy: Understanding Regional Dialect **FT**	10 min.
• Prepare students to read by teaching the selection vocabulary. **FT**	
TEACH	
• Informally monitor comprehension while students read independently or in groups. **FT**	30 min.
• Monitor students' comprehension with the Reading Check notes.	as students read
• Reinforce vocabulary with Vocabulary Builder notes.	as students read
• Develop students' understanding of humor with the Literary Analysis annotations. **FT**	5 minutes
• Develop students' ability to understand regional dialect with the Reading Strategy annotations. **FT**	5 minutes
ASSESS/EXTEND	
• Assess students' comprehension and mastery of the Literary Analysis and Reading Strategy by having them answer the Apply the Skills questions. **FT**	15 min.
• Have students complete the Vocabulary Lesson and the Grammar and Style Lesson. **FT**	15 min.
• Apply students' ability to organize to show comparison by using the Writing Lesson. **FT**	45 min. or homework
• Apply students' understanding using one or more of the Extend Your Learning activities.	20–90 min. or homework
• Administer Selection Test A or Selection Test B. **FT**	15 min.

Resources

PRINT

Unit 4 Resources

Vocabulary Warm-up Word Lists **[L1, L2, EL]** .p. 120
Vocabulary Warm-up Practice **[L1, L2, EL]** . . . . .p. 121
Reading Warm-up A **[L1, L2, EL]** . . . . .p. 122
Reading Warm-up B **[L1, L2, L3]** . . . . .p. 123

TRANSPARENCY

Graphic Organizer Transparencies

Reading Strategy Graphic Organizer A **[L3]** . . . . .pp. 116, 118
Reading Strategy Graphic Organizer B **[L1, L2, EL]** . . . . .pp. 117, 119

PRINT

Reader's Notebook [L2]
Reader's Notebook: Adapted Version [L1]
Reader's Notebook: English Learner's Version [EL]

Unit 4 Resources

Literary Analysis **[L3]** . . . . .p. 124
Reading Strategy **[L3]** . . . . .p. 125
Vocabulary Builder **[L3]** . . . . .p. 126

TECHNOLOGY

Listening to Literature Audio CDs [L2, EL]
Reader's Notebook: Adapted Version Audio CD [L1, L2]

PRINT

Unit 4 Resources

Grammar and Style **[L3]** . . . . .p. 127
Support for Writing Lesson **[L3]** . . . . .p. 128
Support for Extend Your Learning **[L3]** . . . . .p. 129
Enrichment **[L4]** . . . . .p. 130
Selection Test A **[L1, L2, EL]** . . . . .pp. 131–133
Selection Test B **[L3, L4]** . . . . .pp. 134–136

General Resources

Rubrics for Response to Literature **[L3]** . . . . .pp. 65–66
Rubrics for Multimedia Presentation **[L3]** . . . . .pp. 51–52

TECHNOLOGY

Go Online: Research **[L3]**
Go Online: Self-test **[L3]**
***ExamView®*, Test Bank [L3]**

Choosing Resources for Differentiated Instruction

[L1] Special Needs Students
[L2] Below-Level Students
[L3] All Students
[L4] Advanced Students
[EL] English Learners

FT Fast Track Instruction: To move the lesson more quickly, use the strategies and activities identified with **FT**.

Scaffolding for Less Proficient and Advanced Students

The leveled Critical Thinking questions after selections progress in the levels of thinking required to answer them. To address the needs of your different students, you may use the (a) level questions for your less proficient students and the (b) level questions with your on-level and advanced students. The occasional (c) level questions are appropriate for your advanced students.

PRENTICE HALL **TeacherEXPRESS™** Plan · Teach · Assess Use this complete suite of powerful teaching tools to make lesson planning and testing quicker and easier.

Use the interactive textbook (online and on CD-ROM) to make selections and activities come alive with audio and video support and interactive questions.

PRETEACH

Motivation

Tell students that Mark Twain was a writer who used exaggeration, embellishment, regional dialect, and boyhood recollections to make his stories humorous. Then ask students to brainstorm for a list of different kinds of humor that they enjoy—such as humorous stories, jokes, or riddles—and invite students to name examples for each category. Ask them to distinguish between spoken humor and humor meant to be read, and have them describe what it is about written humor that makes them laugh. Then invite them to enjoy two selections by an eminent American writer and humorist, Mark Twain.

1 Background

More About the Author

The critic Maurice LeBreton said of Mark Twain's accomplishments: "[His] work is a panorama of the West in all its vitality. He has observed everything: landscapes, environments, ways of life, customs, beliefs, superstitions. Through him we know the little Missouri town . . . He has described for us the Mississippi . . . We follow him into the isolated Arkansas farm . . . The entire West files past us in a succession of precise, faithful images."

Poet T. S. Eliot wrote that Twain had "discovered a new way of writing . . . a literary language based on American colloquial speech."

1 Build Skills | *Nonfiction • Short Story*

The Boys' Ambition *from* Life on the Mississippi • The Notorious Jumping Frog of Calaveras County

Mark Twain (1835–1910)

Although Mark Twain is widely regarded as one of the greatest American writers, the world-renowned author once indicated that he would have preferred to spend his life as a Mississippi riverboat pilot. The comment was probably not entirely serious, but Twain so loved life on the river that as a young man, he did in fact work as a riverboat pilot for several years. His childhood on the banks of the Mississippi fostered more than a love of riverboats—it also became the basis for many of his most famous works, including *The Adventures of Tom Sawyer* (1876) and *The Adventures of Huckleberry Finn* (1884).

Life on the River Twain, whose given name was Samuel Langhorne Clemens, felt so closely tied to the Mississippi River that he even took his pen name, Mark Twain, from a river man's call meaning "two fathoms deep," indicating that the river is deep enough for a boat to pass safely. He grew up in the Mississippi River town of Hannibal, Missouri. His father died when he was eleven, and he left school to become a printer's apprentice. He worked as a printer in a number of different cities before deciding at age twenty-one to pursue a career as a riverboat pilot.

A Traveling Man When the Civil War closed traffic on the Mississippi, Twain went west to Nevada. There, he supported himself as a journalist and lecturer, developing the entertaining writing style that made him famous. In 1865, Twain published "The Notorious Jumping Frog of Calaveras County," his version of a tall tale he had heard in a mining camp in California while he was working as a gold prospector. The story made him an international celebrity.

Following the publication of *The Innocents Abroad* (1869), a successful book of humorous travel letters, Twain moved to Hartford, Connecticut, where he was to make his home for the rest of his life. There, Twain began using his past experiences as raw material for his books. He drew on his travels in the western mining region for *Roughing It* (1872). He turned to his childhood experiences on the Mississippi for *The Adventures of Tom Sawyer, Life on the Mississippi,* and his masterpiece, *The Adventures of Huckleberry Finn.*

A Restless Soul Twain traveled widely throughout his life, including residential stints in such major American cities as St. Louis, New York, Philadelphia, Cincinnati, and San Francisco. He made extended visits to England, Germany, Switzerland, Italy, and Palestine. His adventures, both at home and abroad, were fuel for a number of books. After living in Europe for several years, he returned home with his family. Following the death of his wife and three of their four children, Twain was unable to reproduce the balance between pessimism and humor that he had captured so brilliantly in *Huckleberry Finn.* In his later works, such as *A Connecticut Yankee in King Arthur's Court* (1889), *Pudd'nhead Wilson* (1894), and *The Man That Corrupted Hadleyburg* (1900), Twain's writing depicted an increasingly pessimistic view of society and human nature. However, he continued to display the same masterful command of language that had already established him as one of America's finest fiction writers.

Background Mark Twain was an eyewitness to the nineteenth-century expansion of the western frontier. He was a young man when wagon trains left his home state of Missouri to cross the prairies, and he later saw the transcontinental railroad built. He traveled throughout the growing nation, working first on the Mississippi and then in the West, before settling in Connecticut. The rich variety of people and places he observed is reflected in the setting, characters, and dialogue of his uniquely American literature.

The Boys' Ambition

When I was a boy, there was but one permanent ambition among my comrades in our village[1] on the west bank of the Mississippi River. That was, to be a steamboatman. We had transient ambitions of other sorts, but they were only transient.

When a circus came and went, it left us all burning to become clowns; the first Negro minstrel show that came to our section left us all suffering to try that kind of life; now and then we had a hope that if we lived and were good, God would permit us to be pirates. These ambitions faded out, each in its turn; but the ambition to be a steamboatman always remained.

Once a day a cheap, gaudy packet[2] arrived upward from St. Louis, and another downward from Keokuk.[3] Before these events, the day was glorious with expectancy; after them, the day was a dead and empty thing. Not only the boys, but the whole village, felt this. After all these years I can picture that old time to myself now, just as it was then: the white town drowsing in the sunshine of a summer's morning; the streets empty, or pretty nearly so; one or two clerks sitting in front of the Water Street stores, with their splint-bottomed chairs tilted back against the wall, chins on breasts, hats slouched over their faces, asleep—with shingle shavings enough around to show what broke them down; a sow and a litter of pigs loafing along the sidewalk, doing a good business in watermelon rinds and seeds; two or three lonely little freight piles scattered about the levee;[4] a pile of skids[5] on the slope of the stone-paved wharf, and the fragrant town drunkard asleep in the shadow of them; two or three wood flats[6] at the head of the wharf, but nobody to listen to the peaceful lapping of the wavelets against them; the great Mississippi, the majestic, the magnificent Mississippi, rolling its mile-wide tide along, shining in

Vocabulary Builder
transient (tran′ zē ənt) *adj.* not permanent

1. **our village** Hannibal, Missouri.
2. **packet** *n.* boat that travels a regular route, carrying passengers, freight, and mail.
3. **Keokuk** (kē′ ə kuk′) town in southeastern Iowa.
4. **levee** (lev′ ē) *n.* landing place along the bank of a river.
5. **skids** *n.* low, movable wooden platforms.
6. **flats** *n.* small, flat-bottomed boats.

5  **Reading Check**
In what way did the boys' ambitions change with each new visitor to their town?

4 Background
Emphasize to students the importance of riverboat trade to the economy around the river. In an age without television or radio, the boats were also an important link between river communities and the rest of the world.

5 Reading Check
Answer: The boys want (for a short while) to try the kind of life lived by each glamorous visitor to their town.

Differentiated Instruction
Solutions for All Learners

Background for Special Needs Students
Encourage students to obtain and examine a map showing the Mississippi River and the states of Missouri, Indiana, Nebraska, and Iowa. You might need to help students get more specific bearings by locating Hannibal, Keokuk, and St. Louis for them.Have students use the Internet to identify which of these towns have museums or festivals that celebrate the days of riverboats.

Enrichment for Gifted/Talented Students
Have students jot notes and create storyboards or sketches to demonstrate how they would capture the mood of Twain's opening lines in the opening scene of a video. Encourage students to suggest sound effects and camera effects as well as the actual images to be filmed. Have students research the role of river traffic in the lives of river dwellers of the 19th century to support their storyboards or sketches.

6 Critical Thinking
Draw Conclusions

- Point out that "husbanded grandeur" refers to a deliberately created effect. Tell students that pitch pine is wood from the heart of a pine tree, and that it is heavily saturated with pitch, burns quickly, and emits large amounts of black smoke.
- Then **ask** students this question: Why would the crew want to create a special effect with black smoke?
  Answer: Clouds of smoke made the boat's entrance very dramatic. It suggested that the crew was performing extremely difficult, dangerous or important work.

7 Critical Viewing

Answer: Students may suggest that the Mississippi River served as a highway, a wide thoroughfare for shipping goods, such as tobacco and cotton, that the plantations produced. Products shipped downriver to the port of New Orleans could go from there to the East Coast and to Europe, as could the goods shipped to the river (and railroad) cities of Memphis, Vicksburg, and St. Louis. Land near the Mississippi riverbank was extremely fertile.

the sun; the dense forest away on the other side; the point above the town, and the point below, bounding the river-glimpse and turning it into a sort of sea, and withal a very still and brilliant and lonely one. Presently a film of dark smoke appears above one of those remote points; instantly a Negro drayman,[7] famous for his quick eye and prodigious voice, lifts up the cry, "S-t-e-a-m-boat a-comin'!" and the scene changes! The town drunkard stirs, the clerks wake up, a furious clatter of drays follows, every house and store pours out a human contribution, and all in a twinkling the dead town is alive and moving. Drays, carts, men, boys, all go hurrying from many quarters to a common center, the wharf. Assembled there, the people fasten their eyes upon the coming boat as upon a wonder they are seeing for the first time. And the boat is rather a handsome sight, too. She is long and sharp and trim and pretty; she has two tall, fancy-topped chimneys, with a gilded device of some kind swung between them; a fanciful pilothouse, all glass and gingerbread, perched on top of the texas deck[8] behind them; the paddleboxes are gorgeous with a picture or with gilded rays above the boat's name; the boiler deck, the hurricane deck, and the texas deck are fenced and ornamented with clean white railings; there is a flag gallantly flying from the jackstaff;[9] the furnace doors are open and the fires glaring bravely; the upper decks are black with passengers; the captain stands by the big bell, calm, imposing, the envy of all; great volumes of the 6 blackest smoke are rolling and tumbling out of the chimneys—a husbanded grandeur created with a bit of pitch pine just before arriving at a town; the crew are grouped on the forecastle;[10] the broad stage is run far out over the port bow, and an envied deckhand stands picturesquely on the end of it with a coil of rope in his hand; the pent steam is screaming through the gauge cocks; the captain lifts his hand, a bell rings, the wheels stop; then they turn back, churning the water to foam, and the steamer is at rest. Then such a scramble as there is to get aboard, and to get ashore, and to take in freight and to discharge freight, all at one and the same time; and such a yelling and cursing as the mates facilitate it all with! Ten minutes later the steamer is under way again, with no flag on the jackstaff and no black smoke issuing from the chimneys. After ten more minutes the town is dead again, and the town drunkard asleep by the skids once more.

Vocabulary Builder
prodigious (prə dij′ əs) *adj.* of great power or size

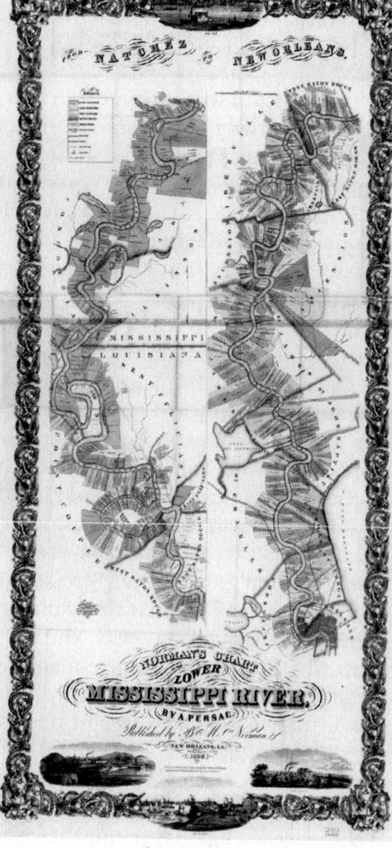

7 ▲ **Critical Viewing** This map shows the location of plantation lands on the banks of the Mississippi. Why might the river have been a desirable location for plantations, as well as for towns? **[Infer]**

7. **drayman** (drā′ mən) *n.* driver of a dray, a low cart with detachable sides.
8. **texas deck** deck adjoining the officers' cabins, the largest cabins on the ship.
9. **jackstaff** (jak′ staf) *n.* small staff at the bow of a ship for flying flags.
10. **forecastle** (fōk′ səl) *n.* front part of the upper deck.

Enrichment

Life on the Mississippi

Life on the Mississippi was published in 1883. Loved and admired second only to *Huckleberry Finn* (1884), the book grew out of a series of articles about Mississippi River piloting that Twain wrote for the *Atlantic Monthly* in 1875. The first half of the book tells how Twain became a pilot and relates his experiences learning about the river. The second half tells about the author's 1882 trip down the river and his visit to his home in Hannibal, Missouri.

Life on the Mississippi offers an outstanding depiction of the profession of steamboat piloting. The steamboat and the job of pilot are seen through the eyes of a boy who romanticizes and glamorizes whatever is foreign to his limited experience. At the same time, however, the reader gets a second point of view: the older narrator looks back on his boyhood, and gently mocks his own innocence.

My father was a justice of the peace, and I supposed he possessed the power of life and death over all men and could hang anybody that offended him. This was distinction enough for me as a general thing; but the desire to be a steamboatman kept intruding, nevertheless. I first wanted to be a cabin boy, so that I could come out with a white apron on and shake a tablecloth over the side, where all my old comrades could see me; later I thought I would rather be the deckhand who stood on the end of the stage plank with the coil of rope in his hand, because he was particularly conspicuous. But these were only daydreams—they were too heavenly to be contemplated as real possibilities. By and by one of our boys went away. He was not heard of for a long time. At last he turned up as apprentice engineer or striker on a steamboat. This thing shook the bottom out of all my Sunday school teachings. That boy had been notoriously worldly, and I just the reverse; yet he was exalted to this eminence, and I left in obscurity and misery. There was nothing generous about this fellow in his greatness. He would always manage to have a rusty bolt to scrub while his boat tarried at our town, and he would sit on the inside guard and scrub it, where we could all see him and envy him and loathe him. And whenever his boat was laid up he would come home and swell around the town in his blackest and greasiest clothes, so that nobody could help remembering that he was a steamboatman; and he used all sorts of steamboat technicalities in his talk, as if he were so used to them that he forgot common people could not understand them. He would speak of the labboard[11] side of a horse in an easy, natural way that would make one wish he was dead. And he was always talking about "St. Looey" like an old citizen; he would refer casually to occasions when he "was coming down Fourth Street," or when he was "passing by the Planter's House," or when there was a fire and he took a turn on the brakes of "the old Big Missouri"; and then he would go on and lie about how many towns the size of ours were burned down there that day. Two or three of the boys had long been persons of consideration among us because they had been to St. Louis once and had a vague general knowledge of its wonders, but the day of their glory was over now. They lapsed into a humble silence, and learned to disappear when the ruthless cub engineer approached. This fellow had money, too, and hair oil. Also an ignorant silver watch and a showy brass watch chain. He wore a leather belt and used no suspenders. If ever a youth was cordially admired and hated by his comrades, this one was. No girl could withstand his charms. He cut out every boy in the village. When his boat blew up at last, it diffused a tranquil contentment among us such as we had not known for months. But when he came home the next week, alive, renowned, and appeared in church all battered up and bandaged, a shining hero, stared at and wondered over by everybody, it seemed to us that the partiality of Providence for an undeserving reptile had reached a point where it was open to criticism. 9

11. **labboard** (lab′ ərd) larboard, the left-hand side of a ship.

Vocabulary Builder
eminence (em′ i nəns) *n.* greatness; celebrity

Reading Strategy
Understanding Regional Dialect What does the apprentice engineer's use of riverboat jargon reveal about him?

Reading Check
What activities and actions of the boy who worked on a steamship inspired envy?

8 Reading Strategy
Understanding Regional Dialect

- Read the passage aloud for students and urge them to note any examples of jargon or other terms that indicate a familiarity with the world of riverboats. If necessary, draw students' attention to terms such as *labboard, St. Looey, Fourth Street, Planter's House,* and *the old Big Missouri.*
- **Ask** students the Reading Strategy question: What does the apprentice engineer's use of riverboat jargon reveal about him?
  Answer: Some students may say that the apprentice uses jargon to enhance the celebrity of his position before his envious former peers. Others might say that it reveals that he is little different from young Twain and his friends—they plan to do the same if they get the chance.

9 Reading Check

Answer: The boy inspires envy merely by scrubbing a rusty bolt, walking around town in his dirty work clothes, or by using riverboat jargon.

Differentiated Instruction
Solutions for All Learners

Vocabulary for Special Needs Students
Point out the jargon in the selection. Encourage students to identify other pursuits that require the use of specialized terms, or jargon. Examples might include medicine, law, or their own science or social studies classes. Help students see that such terms help people communicate effectively about specialized topics.

Enrichment for Advanced Readers
Inform students that Twain actually did become a riverboat pilot. Suggest that they read and compare other excerpts from *Life on the Mississippi* with this one in order to learn more about that phase of the writer's life. Ask students to speculate about what Twain as a young pilot might have thought about his younger, envious self.

ASSESS

Answers

1. Students' responses should be supported by details from the selection.
2. (a) All want to be steamboat men. (b) Twain's ambition to travel to different places as captain of a steamboat reflects the American desire for expansion and adventure.
3. (a) They hurry to greet the boat as it arrives, and watch the boat's operations with fascination. (b) Twain's description of the town suggests that it is a sleepy place where not much happens: the arrival of the steamboat causes great excitement.
4. (a) His boat blows up. (b) The other boys are at once resentful and envious of him.
5. (a) Most students will probably say that Twain's firsthand experience as a pilot was crucial to his writing so convincingly about riverboat life. (b) **Possible response:** Twain's love for the Mississippi River led him to describe the river, its towns, and its people eloquently. His love for the river also led him to use regional dialect that brings the people of the area vividly to life.
6. Students should support their responses with clear reasoning.

Go Online Author Link For additional information about Mark Twain, have students type in the Web Code, then select T from the alphabet, and then select Mark Twain.

This creature's career could produce but one result, and it speedily followed. Boy after boy managed to get on the river. The minister's son became an engineer. The doctor's and the postmaster's sons became mud clerks; the wholesale liquor dealer's son became a barkeeper on a boat; four sons of the chief merchant, and two sons of the county judge, became pilots. Pilot was the grandest position of all. The pilot, even in those days of trivial wages, had a princely salary—from a hundred and fifty to two hundred and fifty dollars a month, and no board to pay. Two months of his wages would pay a preacher's salary for a year. Now some of us were left disconsolate. We could not get on the river—at least our parents would not let us.

So by and by I ran away. I said I never would come home again till I was a pilot and could come in glory. But somehow I could not manage it. I went meekly aboard a few of the boats that lay packed together like sardines at the long St. Louis wharf, and very humbly inquired for the pilots, but got only a cold shoulder and short words from mates and clerks. I had to make the best of this sort of treatment for the time being, but I had comforting daydreams of a future when I should be a great and honored pilot, with plenty of money, and could kill some of these mates and clerks and pay for them.

Critical Reading

1. **Respond:** Would working on a riverboat appeal to you? Explain why or why not.
2. **(a) Recall:** What is the one permanent ambition of the narrator and his boyhood friends? **(b) Connect:** How does this childhood ambition reflect the American spirit that gave rise to the settlement of new frontiers?
3. **(a) Recall:** How do the people of Hannibal respond to the arrival of the steamboat? **(b) Interpret:** What impression does Twain convey of this town by this response?
4. **(a) Recall:** What happens to the young apprentice engineer? **(b) Infer:** How would you describe the attitude of the other boys toward the apprentice engineer?
5. **(a) Hypothesize:** Do you think Twain could have written so well about riverboat life had he not become a pilot himself? Explain. **(b) Apply:** In what ways do you think Twain's love for the Mississippi River contributed to his success as a writer?
6. **Evaluate:** The last paragraph suggests that the narrator was driven by a desire for glory. Is a desire for glory a reasonable motivation in life? Explain.

Go Online Author Link
For: More about Mark Twain
Visit: www.PHSchool.com
Web Code: ere-9413

Enrichment

Steamboats

By the early nineteenth century, steamboats were regularly carrying cargo upstream on the Mississippi and Ohio rivers. The boats were essential to the economy of towns along these rivers, linking them to each other and to the rest of the world. Until the 1850s, when railroad development grew rapidly in the West, steamboats carried more freight than trains did.

Have students do research to find out about life on the great riverboats. Among other things, they can research routes, available jobs, and on-board entertainment. Have them look into how large the boats were, how fast they traveled, and what cargo they carried. Students can also learn about tours and trips, such as Civil War excursions, that can be enjoyed today in modern riverboats.

10 # *The* Notorious Jumping Frog *of* Calaveras County

Mark Twain

11 

Mark Twain (Samuel L. Clemens) Riding the Celebrated Jumping Frog—an English caricature, 1872, Frederic Waddy

In compliance with the request of a friend of mine, who wrote me from the East, I called on good-natured, garrulous old Simon Wheeler, and inquired after my friend's friend, Leonidas W. Smiley, as requested to do, and I hereunto append the result. I have a lurking suspicion that *Leonidas W.* Smiley is a myth; that my friend never knew such a personage: and that he only conjectured that if I asked old Wheeler about him, it would remind him of his infamous *Jim* Smiley, and he would go to work and bore me to death with some exasperating reminiscence of him as long and as tedious as it should be useless to me. If that was the design, it succeeded.

I found Simon Wheeler dozing comfortably by the barroom stove of the dilapidated tavern in the decayed mining camp of Angel's, and I noticed that he was fat and baldheaded, and had an expression of winning gentleness and simplicity upon his tranquil countenance. He roused up, and gave me good day. I told him a friend of mine had commissioned me to make some inquiries about a cherished companion of his boyhood named *Leonidas W.* Smiley—*Rev. Leonidas W.* Smiley, a young minister of the Gospel, who he had heard was at one time a resident of Angel's Camp. I added that if Mr. Wheeler could tell me anything about this Rev. Leonidas W. Smiley, I would feel under many obligations to him.

Simon Wheeler backed me into a corner and blockaded me there with his chair, and then sat down and reeled off the monotonous narrative which follows this paragraph. He never smiled, he never frowned, he never changed his voice from the gentle-flowing key to which he tuned his initial sentence, he never betrayed the slightest suspicion of enthusiasm; but all through the interminable narrative there ran a vein of impressive earnestness and sincerity, which showed me plainly that, so far from his imagining that there was anything ridiculous or funny about his story, he regarded it as a really

12 ▲ Critical Viewing
Would Twain have been amused or offended by this caricature of himself? Explain. **[Make a Judgment]**

Vocabulary Builder
garrulous (gar′ ə ləs) *adj.* talking too much

conjectured (kən jek′ chərd) *v.* guessed

13 **Vocabulary Builder**
monotonous (mə nät′ ən əs) *adj.* tiresome because unvarying

interminable (in tʉr′ mi nə bəl) *adj.* seeming to last forever

14 ✓ Reading Check
What does the narrator suspect about Leonidas W. Smiley?

10 About the Selection

According to one of Mark Twain's biographers, Twain first heard the story that was the inspiration for this one while in the bar of a rundown tavern in Angel's Camp, California. Like the storyteller in that bar, Twain's narrator, Simon Wheeler, spins a funny, improbable yarn about the exploits of a betting man.

11 Humanities

Mark Twain Riding the Celebrated Jumping Frog, [1872] by Frederick Waddy

A caricature is a drawing made to satirize or poke fun at someone by exaggerating certain features so that the person looks ridiculous, yet recognizable. Waddy was an English caricaturist, whose drawings were reproduced as wood engravings in the *Illustrated London News.*

Use this question for discussion:

- At what aspects of Twain does Waddy poke fun in this drawing?
  Possible response: Students may say that the artist lampoons the idea that Twain's fame could ride on something as silly as a jumping frog.

12 Critical Viewing

Answer: Students may say that Twain, as a writer who knew the effectiveness of exaggeration, would have enjoyed the humor in this caricature—particularly the deadpan expression on his face.

13 Vocabulary Builder

The Greek Prefix *mono-*

- Explain that one of the meanings of the prefix *mono-* is "single." Invite students to look for context clues (such as *reeled off* and *never changed his voice*) that will help them determine the meaning of *monotonous.*
- Have students **brainstorm** a list of other English words containing *mono-*.
  Answer: Students might mention words such as *monogamy, monopoly,* or *monorail.*

14 Reading Check

Answer: The narrator suspects that he does not exist.

Differentiated Instruction
Solutions for All Learners

Strategy for Less Proficient Readers

Help students understand the premise of the story as set forth in the opening paragraph. Point out that Twain knows that he might be the target of his friend's prank. As needed, have students refer back to this opening passage when they have finished reading the story. As they read, have students locate moments in the story when the reader is given clues that indicate that Simon Wheeler's garrulousness is intended to make the reader laugh and appreciate the narrator's plight all the more. Such moments include the extended description of Smiley's mare, or the careful pause in which Wheeler makes sure the narrator knows the bull pup's name—Andrew Jackson—even though the information is completely irrelevant. Have students record these junctures in a chart.

15 Reading Strategy
Understanding Regional Dialect

- Invite a student volunteer to read aloud the first several sentences of Wheeler's narrative. Then have students go back and read the same sentences silently once more.
- **Ask** students the Reading Strategy question: What examples of dialect can you find as Wheeler's tale begins?
  Answer: Examples include *feller, by the name of, recollect, warn't, when he first come, curiousest, you ever see, he'd,* and *so's.*

16 Literary Analysis
Humor

- Review with students some of the techniques writers use to create humor, such as exaggerating and embellishing incidents and personal characteristics.
- Then, read aloud the last paragraph as students listen for examples of Twain's use of these techniques.
- **Ask** students the Literary Analysis question: What is humorous about this description of the mare?
  Answer: Students might mention the nickname "the fifteen-minute nag," the idea of betting on such a slow horse, or the host of medical conditions from which the mare is said to suffer.

important matter, and admired its two heroes as men of transcendent genius in *finesse*. I let him go on in his own way, and never interrupted him once.

15 "Rev. Leonidas W. H'm, Reverend Le—well, there was a feller here once by the name of *Jim* Smiley, in the winter of '49—or maybe it was the spring of '50—I don't recollect exactly, somehow, though what makes me think it was one or the other is because I remember the big flume[1] warn't finished when he first come to the camp; but anyway, he was the curiousest man about always betting on anything that turned up you ever see, if he could get anybody to bet on the other side; and if he couldn't he'd change sides. Any way that suited the other man would suit *him*—any way just so's he got a bet, *he* was satisfied. But still he was lucky, uncommon lucky; he most always come out winner. He was always ready and laying for a chance; there couldn't be no solit'ry thing mentioned but that feller'd offer to bet on it, and take ary side you please, as I was just telling you. If there was a horse race, you'd find him flush or you'd find him busted at the end of it; if there was a dogfight, he'd bet on it; if there was a cat fight, he'd bet on it; if there was a chicken fight, he'd bet on it; why, if there was two birds setting on a fence, he would bet you which one would fly first; or if there was a camp meeting,[2] he would be there reg'lar to bet on Parson Walker, which he judged to be the best exhorter about here and so he was too, and a good man. If he even see a straddle bug[3] start to go anywheres, he would bet you how long it would take him to get to—to wherever he was going to, and if you took him up, he would foller that straddle bug to Mexico but what he would find out where he was bound for and how long he was on the road. Lots of the boys here has seen that Smiley, and can tell you about him. Why, it never made no difference to *him*—he'd bet on *any* thing—the dangdest feller. Parson Walker's wife laid very sick once, for a good while, and it seemed as if they warn't going to save her; but one morning he come in, and Smiley up and asked him how she was, and he said she was considable better—thank the Lord for his inf'nite mercy—and coming on so smart that with the blessing of Prov'dence she'd get well yet; and Smiley, before he thought, says, 'Well, I'll resk two-and-a-half she don't anyway.'

Thish-yer Smiley had a mare—the boys called her the fifteen-minute nag, but that was only in fun, you know, because of course she was faster than that—and he used to win money on that horse, for all she was so slow and always had the asthma, or the distemper, or the consumption, or something of that kind. They used to give her two or three hundred yards start, and then pass her under way; but always at the fag end[4] of the race she'd get excited and desperate like,

Reading Strategy
Understanding Regional Dialect What examples of dialect do you notice as Wheeler's tale begins?

Literary Analysis
Humor What is humorous about this description of the mare?

1. **flume** (flo͞om) *n.* artificial channel for carrying water to provide power and transport objects.
2. **camp meeting** religious gathering at the mining camp.
3. **straddle bug** insect with long legs.
4. **fag end** last part.

Enrichment

Calaveras County

Inform students that Calaveras County is a real place located in central California, southeast of Sacramento and northeast of Modesto. It borders Tuolomne County to the east, home of Yosemite National Park. Every spring, on the Calaveras Fairgrounds in Angel's Camp, California, there is a fair and a re-enactment of Twain's celebrated contest. The contest annually attracts people from all over the world who bring more than 3,000 frogs.

Invite students to find out more about the history of—and records associated with—this "Olympics" of frog jumping. Students can find out how to enter the contest and what kind of jump it would take to win. They can get information by writing to the 39th District Agricultural Association, Box 489, S. Highway 49, Angels Camp, CA 95222, or by visiting the Internet website www.visitcalaveras.org.

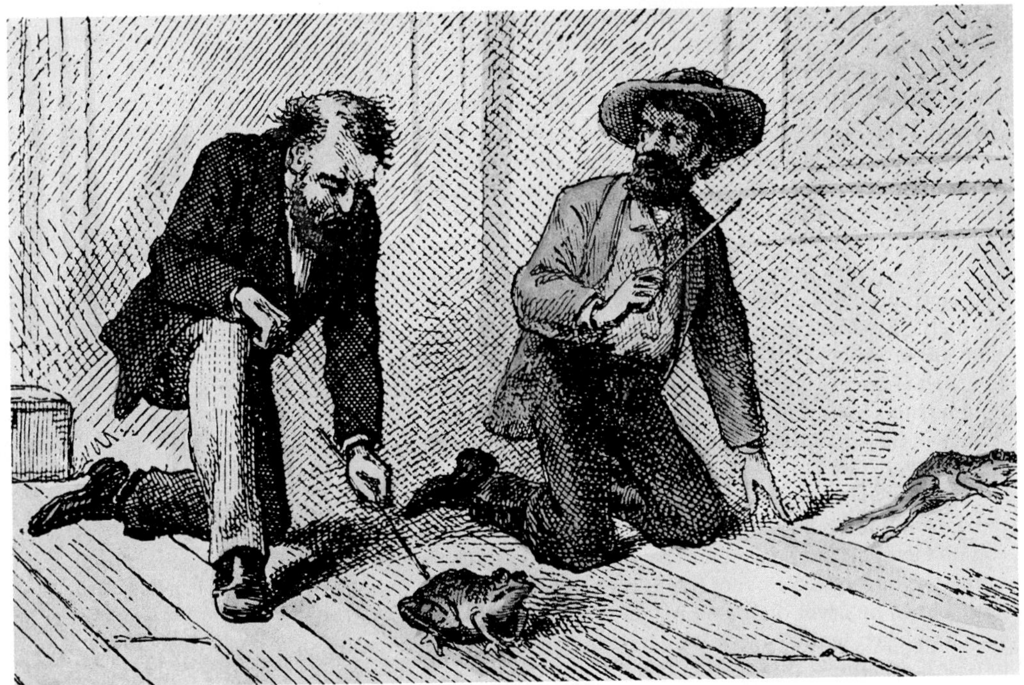

and come cavorting and straddling up, and scattering her legs around limber, sometimes in the air, and sometimes out to one side among the fences, and kicking up m-o-r-e dust and raising m-o-r-e racket with her coughing and sneezing and blowing her nose—and *always* fetch up at the stand just about a neck ahead, as near as you could cipher it down.

And he had a little small bull-pup, that to look at him you'd think he warn't worth a cent but to set around and look ornery and lay for a chance to steal something. But as soon as money was up on him he was a different dog; his under-jaw'd begin to stick out like the fo' castle[5] of a steamboat, and his teeth would uncover and shine like the furnaces. And a dog might tackle him and bullyrag him, and bite him, and throw him over his shoulder two or three times, and Andrew Jackson—which was the name of the pup—Andrew Jackson would never let on but what *he* was satisfied, and hadn't expected nothing else—and the bets being doubled and doubled on the other side all the time, till the money was all up; and then all of a sudden he would grab that other dog jest by the j'int of his hind leg and freeze to it—not chaw, you understand, but only just grip and hang on till they throwed up the sponge, if it was a year. Smiley always come out winner on that pup, till

5. **fo'castle** (fōk′ səl) *n.* forecastle; the forward part of the upper deck.

17 ▲ Critical Viewing
Which moment of the story is depicted in this illustration? **[Connect]**

Reading Strategy
Understanding Regional Dialect How would you rephrase the sentence beginning "And he had . . . " in Standard English?

Vocabulary Builder
ornery (ôr′ nər ē) *adj.* having a mean disposition

19 Reading Check
What was most unusual about Smiley and his betting habits?

17 Critical Viewing

Answer: Students may say that the illustration shows the defeat of Dan'l by the stranger's frog.

18 Reading Strategy
Understanding Regional Dialect

- Have two or three student volunteers read this sentence aloud slowly for their classmates. Point out potentially challenging examples of dialect, such as *warn't* ("wasn't").
- **Ask** students the Reading Strategy question: How would you rephrase the sentence beginning "And he had . . ." in Standard English?
  Answer: Smiley's bulldog puppy looked as though it did nothing but look bad-tempered and try to sneak food.

19 Reading Check

Possible response: He would wager on anything, but often won unlikely bets, such as the ones on the mare and the dog named Andrew Jackson.

Differentiated Instruction Solutions for All Learners

Enrichment for Less Proficient Readers

Humor can be the driving force of a story. It can also be subtle and coy, teasing the reader just enough to lighten the mood of the story or to break up a long narrative paragraph. Either way, humor provides added enjoyment when reading. Help students recognize the humorous elements in Twain's writing, from his creation of unique characters to his deadpan delivery of absurd statements. Reading to be entertained is a valid purpose for reading, and many books are written primarily for entertainment. Encourage students to read to be entertained, looking for the humorous elements in Twain's writing. Suggest that students try their hands at writing or telling their own "shaggydog" stories. Do they know of any comical events that would lend themselves to such humorous exaggeration?

20 Literary Analysis
Humor

- Invite a student volunteer to read the passage aloud as other students jot down Twain's humorous embellishments.
- **Ask** students the Literary Analysis question: What embellishments in this passage make the description humorous?
Answer: Students might mention details such as *nothing for three months, give him a little punch behind, whirling in the air like a doughnut, turn one summerset, come down flatfooted, nail a fly,* and *all a frog wanted was education.*

he harnessed a dog once that didn't have no hind legs, because they'd been sawed off in a circular saw, and when the thing had gone along far enough, and the money was all up, and he come to make a snatch for his pet holt,[6] he see in a minute how he'd been imposed on, and how the other dog had him in the door, so to speak, and he 'peared surprised, and then he looked sorter discouraged-like, and didn't try no more to win the fight, and so he got shucked out bad. He give Smiley a look, as much as to say his heart was broke, and it was his fault, for putting up a dog that hadn't no hind legs for him to take holt of, which was his main dependence in a fight, and then he limped off a piece and laid down and died. It was a good pup, was that Andrew Jackson, and would have made a name for hisself if he'd lived, for the stuff was in him and he had genius—I know it, because he hadn't no opportunities to speak of, and it don't stand to reason that a dog could make such a fight as he could under them circumstances if he hadn't no talent. It always makes me feel sorry when I think of that last fight of his'n, and the way it turned out.

Well, thish-yer Smiley had rat terriers,[7] and chicken cocks,[8] and tomcats and all them kind of things, till you couldn't rest, and you couldn't fetch nothing for him to bet on but he'd match you. He ketched a frog one day, and took him home, and said he cal'lated to educate him; and so he never done nothing for three months but set in his back yard and learn that frog to jump. And you bet you he *did* learn him, too. He'd give him a little punch behind, and the next minute you'd
20 see that frog whirling in the air like a doughnut—see him turn one summerset, or maybe a couple, if he got a good start, and come down flatfooted and all right, like a cat. He got him up so in the matter of ketching flies, and kep' him in practice so constant, that he'd nail a fly every time as fur as he could see him. Smiley said all a frog wanted was education, and he could do 'most anything—and I believe him. Why, I've seen him set Dan'l Webster down here on this floor—Dan'l Webster was the name of the frog—and sing out, "Flies, Dan'l, flies!" and quicker'n you could wink he'd spring straight up and snake a fly off'n the counter there, and flop down on the floor ag'in as solid as a gob of mud, and fall to scratching the side of his head with his hind foot as indifferent as if he hadn't no idea he'd been doin' any more'n any frog might do. You never see a frog so modest and straightfor'ard as he was, for all he was so gifted. And when it come to fair and square jumping on a dead level, he could get over more ground at one straddle than any animal of his breed you ever see. Jumping on a dead level was his strong suit, you understand; and when it come to that, Smiley would ante up money on him as long as he had a red.[9] Smiley was monstrous proud of his frog, and well he

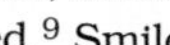

Literary Analysis
Humor What embellishments in this passage make the description humorous?

6. **holt** hold.
7. **rat terriers** dogs skilled in catching rats.
8. **chicken cocks** roosters trained to fight.
9. **a red** red cent; colloquial expression for "any money at all."

Differentiated Instruction
Solutions for All Learners

Enrichment for Advanced Readers
Suggest that students read additional works by Mark Twain. You may *also* wish to use **Authors In Depth, The American Experience,** which contains the following selections:
- "Perplexing Lessons" from *Life on the Mississippi* (nonfiction p. 91)
- "An Encounter With an Interviewer" (fiction, p. 97)
- "A General Reply" (nonfiction, p. 101)
- "The Boss" and "The Yankee Fights With the Knights" from *A Connecticut Yankee in King Arthur's Court*

After students have read these or other works by Twain, have them form discussion groups in which they compare and contrast the selections they have read. Suggest criteria for comparison, such as author's perspective or implied readership. To extend the activity, have volunteers present brief reports on Twain's status as a celebrity during his lifetime.

might be, for fellers that had traveled and been everywheres all said he laid over any frog that ever *they* see.

Well, Smiley kep' the beast in a little lattice box, and he used to fetch him downtown sometimes and lay for a bet. One day a feller—a stranger in the camp, he was—come acrost him with his box, and says:

'What might it be that you've got in the box?'

And Smiley says, sorter indifferent-like, 'It might be a parrot, or it might be a canary, maybe, but it ain't—it's only just a frog.'

And the feller took it, and looked at it careful, and turned it round this way and that, and says, 'H'm—so 'tis. Well, what's *he* good for?'

'Well,' Smiley says, easy and careless, 'he's good enough for *one* thing, I should judge—he can outjump any frog in Calaveras county.'

The feller took the box again, and took another long, particular look, and give it back to Smiley, and says, very deliberate, 'Well,' he says, 'I don't see no p'ints about that frog that's any better'n any other frog.'

'Maybe you don't,' Smiley says. 'Maybe you understand frogs and maybe you don't understand 'em; maybe you've had experience, and maybe you ain't only a amature, as it were. Anyways, I've got *my* opinion, and I'll resk forty dollars that he can outjump any frog in Calaveras county.'

And the feller studied a minute, and then says, kinder sad like, 'Well, I'm only a stranger here, and I ain't got no frog; but if I had a frog, I'd bet you.'

And then Smiley says, 'That's all right—that's all right—if you'll hold my box a minute, I'll go and get you a frog.' And so the feller took the box, and put up his forty dollars along with Smiley's, and set down to wait.

So he set there a good while thinking and thinking to hisself, and then he got the frog out and prized his mouth open and took a teaspoon and filled him full of quailshot[10]—filled him pretty near up to his chin—and set him on the floor. Smiley he went to the swamp and slopped around in the mud for a long time, and finally he ketched a frog, and fetched him in, and give him to this feller, and says:

'Now, if you're ready, set him alongside of Dan'l, with his forepaws just even with Dan'l's, and I'll give the word.' Then he says, 'One—two—three—*git*!' and him and the feller touched up the frogs from behind, and the new frog hopped off lively, but Dan'l give a heave, and hysted up his shoulders—so—like a Frenchman, but it warn't no use—he couldn't budge; he was planted as solid as a church, and he couldn't no more stir than if he was anchored out. Smiley was a good deal surprised, and he was disgusted too, but he didn't have no idea what the matter was, of course.

The feller took the money and started away; and when he was going out at the door, he sorter jerked his thumb over his shoulder—so—at Dan'l, and says again, very deliberate, 'Well,' he says, 'I don't see no p'ints about that frog that's any better'n any other frog.' 22

10. **quailshot** small lead pellets used for shooting quail.

Literary Analysis
Humor How does the use of dialect add to the humor of this passage?

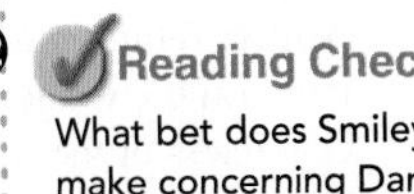

Reading Check
What bet does Smiley make concerning Dan'l Webster?

21 Literary Analysis
Humor

- As you read this passage aloud, have students identify examples of Twain's use of dialect. If students need help focusing on the dialect, point out examples such as *git, hopped off lively, give a heave, hysted up his shoulders, warn't no use,* or *couldn't no more stir.*
- **Ask** students the Literary Analysis question: How does the use of dialect add to the humor of this passage?
  Answer: It both grounds the characters—the stranger, the frog, and especially Smiley—in time and place, as well as exaggerating certain aspects of their personalities or behaviors.

22 Reading Check

Answer: He bets a stranger that the frog, Dan'l Webster, can out-jump any other frog in Calaveras County.

Differentiated Instruction
Solutions for All Learners

Strategy for Special Needs Students
Have students recall favorite funny stories, involving exaggeration and embellishment, that are retold by family members. Invite these students to explain the accounts and to compare and contrast their knowledge of what actually happened with how it is rendered in those amusing tales.

Enrichment for Gifted/Talented Students
Explain to students that forty dollars was a great deal of money—perhaps equal to a month's wages—at the time of this story. Have these students do research to learn what basic necessities cost in 1865, as well as how much people were paid for various jobs, in this country around the middle of the nineteenth century.

ASSESS

Answers

1. You may wish to have students listen to Hal Holbrook's *Mark Twain Tonight* to appreciate the kind of verbal humor that was characteristic of Twain.
2. (a) The narrator's friend suggests that he ask about a friend with the same last name. (b) The narrator now suspects that his friend knew that Wheeler would tell the story of Jim Smiley.
3. (a) He would bet on anything and everything. (b) **Sample response:** He is a comic, exaggerated character.
4. (a) He was proud because he had taught the frog to be a champion jumper. (b) Students may say that it is important because he expects the frog to earn him a lot of money.
5. (a) **Possible response:** The story does succeed in conveying the character of Simon Wheeler. Twain's depiction of Wheeler's mannerisms and dialect gives us a portrait of Wheeler as a garrulous bore greatly given to hyperbole. (b) Twain probably chose to have Wheeler (instead of the narrator) tell the tale because it allowed him to relate the story in regional dialect, thereby making it more humorous.
6. The tale suggests that entertainment was hard to come by and people were often eccentric on the frontier.

Smiley he stood scratching his head and looking down at Dan'l a long time, and at last he says, 'I do wonder what in the nation that frog throw'd off for—I wonder if there ain't something the matter with him—he 'pears to look mighty baggy, somehow.' And he ketched Dan'l by the nap of the neck, and hefted him, and says, 'Why blame my cats if he don't weigh five pound!' and turned him upside down and he belched out a double handful of shot. And then he see how it was, and he was the maddest man—he set the frog down and took out after that feller, but he never ketched him. And—"

Here Simon Wheeler heard his name called from the front yard, and got up to see what was wanted. And turning to me as he moved away, he said: "Just set where you are, stranger, and rest easy—I ain't going to be gone a second."

But, by your leave, I did not think that a continuation of the history of the enterprising vagabond *Jim* Smiley would be likely to afford me much information concerning the Rev. *Leonidas W.* Smiley, and so I started away.

At the door I met the sociable Wheeler returning, and he buttonholed me and recommenced:

"Well, thish-yer Smiley had a yaller one-eyed cow that didn't have no tail, only just a short stump like a bannanner, and—"

However, lacking both time and inclination, I did not wait to hear about the afflicted cow, but took my leave.

Critical Reading

1. **Respond:** If Mark Twain were a stand-up comic today, would you want to see him perform? Explain why or why not.
2. **(a) Recall:** What prompts Simon Wheeler to tell the story of Jim Smiley? **(b) Infer:** Why had the narrator's friend suggested that he ask Wheeler about Leonidas Smiley?
3. **(a) Recall:** What was Jim Smiley's response to any event? **(b) Infer:** Based on this behavior, what can you infer about his character?
4. **(a) Recall:** Why was Smiley so proud of his frog? **(b) Draw Conclusions:** Why is the frog important to Smiley?
5. **(a) Evaluate:** Does this story convey the character of Simon Wheeler as effectively as it does the character of Jim Smiley, the subject of the tale? **(b) Hypothesize:** Why might Twain have chosen to develop the story this way?
6. **Apply:** Telling tall tales like this one was a common form of entertainment on the western frontier. What does such a tale suggest about the characters of the developing West?

Go Online
Author Link
For: More about Mark Twain
Visit: www.PHSchool.com
Web Code: ere-9413

Go Online **Author Link** For additional information about Mark Twain, have students type in the Web Code, then select T from the alphabet, and then select Mark Twain.

Apply the Skills

The Boys' Ambition* from *Life on the Mississippi* • *The Notorious Jumping Frog of Calaveras County

Literary Analysis

Humor

1. In "The Boys' Ambition," what does Twain's use of the word "heavenly" to describe ordinary steamboat activities, such as shaking out a tablecloth or holding a rope, add to the **humor** of his narrative?
2. Find two examples of exaggeration in "The Notorious Jumping Frog of Calaveras County," and explain why each is amusing.
3. **(a)** How does the use of **dialect** in "The Notorious Jumping Frog" add to the story's humor? **(b)** Why would the story be less effective if Wheeler spoke in Standard English?

Comparing Literary Works

4. **(a)** What is Twain's main purpose in "The Boys' Ambition"? **(b)** In what ways does humor help him achieve this purpose?
5. **(a)** What is Twain's main purpose in telling the story of the notorious jumping frog? **(b)** How does humor help him achieve this purpose?
6. In which selection does Twain seem to view the characters with more respect? Explain your choice.

Reading Strategy

Understanding Regional Dialect

7. Interpret the following passage in your own words:

   > . . . he 'peared surprised, and then he looked sorter discouraged-like, and didn't try no more to win the fight, and so he got shucked out bad.

8. Interpret the given examples of **dialect** in Standard English by completing a chart like the one shown.

Regional Dialect	St. Looey	chaw	yaller	bannanner	thish-yer
Standard English					

Extend Understanding

9. **Career Connection:** Why do you think young people dream of romantic or adventurous careers, like Twain's riverboat pilot or its modern equivalent, the astronaut?

QuickReview

Humor is writing meant to evoke laughter.

To **understand regional dialect**, sound out words so that you may recognize their Standard English counterparts.

For: Self-test
Visit: www.PHSchool.com
Web Code: era-6407

Answers

1. Twain's description adds humor by showing through contrast how foolish some of his childhood ambitions were.
2. One example of exaggeration is the frog whirling in the air, doing one or two somersaults, and landing like a cat. Another example is the frog leaping upward on command to catch flies. Each example is amusing because it attributes abilities to the frog like those of dogs or cats.
3. (a) The use of dialect underscores the exaggerated qualities Twain gives to characters and situations. (b) The story would be less effective because the dialect adds humor, particularly to those moments when Wheeler is trying to be serious and straightforward.
4. (a) His main purpose is to portray life in a small river town—with special attention to the hopes and dreams of young males there. (b) Humor helps Twain avoid sentimentality as he shows the sleepy town and the eager, impressionable boys.
5. (a) His main purpose is to entertain the reader. (b) Humor makes the story immediately entertaining.
6. Students may say that Twain views the characters with more respect in "The Boys' Ambition," since that story involves people involved in honest, interesting work, such as piloting riverboats, whereas the latter story involves primarily loafers and rascals.
7. He appeared surprised and discouraged. He gave up the fight and was badly fooled.
8. *St Louis; chew; yellow; banana; this here*
   Another sample answer can be found on **Reading Strategy Graphic Organizer B,** p. 119 in ***Graphic Organizer Transparencies.***
9. Students should support their responses with clear reasoning.

Go Online Assessment Students may use the **Self-test** to prepare for **Selection Test A** or **Selection Test B.**

EXTEND/ASSESS

Answers

❶ Vocabulary Lesson

Word Analysis

1. monotheism = belief in one god
2. monologue = speech given by one person
3. monolith = a single giant stone
4. monochrome = something of one color

Spelling Strategy

a. hard c. hard
b. soft

Vocabulary Builder

1. d 5. f
2. b 6. a
3. g 7. h
4. c 8. e

❷ Grammar and Style Lesson

1. Why, it never made any difference to him. . . .
2. . . . you couldn't fetch anything for him to bet on but he'd match you.
3. . . . maybe you've had experience and maybe you are only an amateur.
4. . . . it wasn't any use—he couldn't budge.
5. a yellow, one-eyed cow that had no tail . . .

Looking at Style

Wheeler's use of double negatives shows him to be a rugged frontiersman, and it adds to the humor by adding extra flair to the story.

Writing and Grammar, Ruby Level

Students will find further instruction and practice on double negatives in Chapter 25, Section 1.

Build Language Skills

❶ Vocabulary Lesson

Word Analysis: Greek Prefix *mono-*

The Greek prefix *mono-* means "alone," "one," or "single." A monotonous storyteller uses a single tone, without varying voice quality or pace.

Use your understanding of the prefix *mono-* and the definition of the roots given below to tell the meaning of the new word formed by adding the prefix *mono-*.

1. *theism* = belief in god
2. *logue* = speaking
3. *lith* = stone
4. *chrome* = color

Spelling Strategy

The vowels *a, o,* and *u* after the letter *g* indicate the "hard" sound of *g*, as in *garrulous, gob,* and *guide.* The vowels *i* and *e* after *g* often indicate the "soft" *g* sound, as in *prodigious* and *generous.* Identify whether the *g* sound in each of these words is hard or soft:

1. vagabond 2. managed 3. obligation

Vocabulary Builder: Antonyms

Antonyms are words with opposite meanings. Review the words in the vocabulary list on page 575. Then, select the letter of the word in the right column that is the best antonym for each vocabulary word in the left column.

1. transient	a. varied
2. prodigious	b. meager
3. eminence	c. quiet
4. garrulous	d. permanent
5. conjectured	e. kind
6. monotonous	f. verified
7. interminable	g. obscurity
8. ornery	h. brief

❷ Grammar and Style Lesson

Double Negatives

Double negatives are created by using two negative words in a sentence where only one is needed. In effect, two negatives cancel each other out, thereby changing the intended meaning of a sentence. Double negatives are not accepted in Standard English, but they do appear in some regional dialects. Here, Simon Wheeler speaks with a double negative:

Examples: ". . . he had*n't no* opportunities to speak of . . ."
"there could*n't* be *no* solit'ry thing mentioned but that feller'd offer to bet on it . . ."

Practice Rewrite the following sentences from the story, revising them to eliminate double negatives.

1. Why, it never made no difference to him . . .
2. . . . you couldn't fetch nothing for him to bet on but he'd match you.
3. . . . I don't see no p'ints about that frog . . .
4. . . . it warn't no use—he couldn't budge.
5. . . . a yaller one-eyed cow that didn't have no tail . . .

Looking at Style Explain how Simon Wheeler's frequent use of double negatives fits his character and contributes to the story's humor.

Prentice Hall Writing and Grammar Connection: Chapter 25, Section 1

Assessment Practice

Context **(For more practice, see *Standardized Test Preparation Workbook*, p. 32.)**

Many tests require students to use contextual analysis to determine the meaning of figurative expressions. Use the following sample test item to demonstrate.

I went meekly aboard a few of the boats that lay packed together like sardines at the long St. Louis wharf, and very humbly inquired for the pilots, but got only a cold shoulder and short words from mates and clerks.

In this passage, the expression packed together like sardines means—

A The boats were docked close together.
B The boats had been fishing for sardines.
C The boats were made of metal like tins for sardines.
D The boats were packed with passengers.

A is the correct answer.

Writing Lesson

Timed Writing: Analytical Essay

Mark Twain wrote, "The humorous story may be spun out to great length, and may wander around as much as it pleases, and arrive nowhere in particular . . . [It] is told gravely; the teller does his best to conceal the fact that he even dimly suspects there is anything funny about it." Write an essay discussing Twain's use of these techniques in "Jumping Frog." *(40 minutes)*

Prewriting *(10 minutes)* Select several humorous passages to assess according to the main ideas in Twain's comment. Create a chart like the one shown to organize your thoughts.

Model: Organizing to Show Comparison

spins out at length	arrives nowhere	is told gravely	conceals humor

Drafting *(20 minutes)* Organize your essay point by point, connecting Twain's comment to passages from the story. Make sure you clearly explain the connection in each case.

Revising *(10 minutes)* Review your essay to find places where you could elaborate by providing examples, details, or quotations to support your ideas. Return to your notes or to the story to find needed support.

WG *Prentice Hall Writing and Grammar Connection: Chapter 14, Section 3*

Extend Your Learning

Listening and Speaking In "The Boys' Ambition," Twain wrote about one of his career dreams. Prepare a list of questions about a career that interests you. Then, conduct an **interview** with someone in that field. Be sure to include the following questions:

- Why did you choose this career?
- How did you prepare for it?
- What are its responsibilities and rewards?
- What advice would you give about this career?

Share your findings with the class.

Research and Technology With a group, create a **multimedia report** on Mississippi riverboats. Draw information from a variety of sources, such as audio and video clips, newspapers, magazines, CD-ROMs, and the Internet to convey the sights and sounds of nineteenth-century riverboat life. **[Group Activity]**

For: An additional research activity
Visit: www.PHSchool.com
Web Code: erd-7407

❸ Writing Lesson

You may use this Writing Lesson as timed-writing practice, or you may allow students to develop the essay as a writing assignment over several days.

- To guide students in writing this analytical essay, give them the **Support for Writing Lesson** page (***Unit 4 Resources,*** p. 128).
- You might suggest that students begin by writing down their impressions of Twain's humor in the story after a single reading. Then have students reread the story at least once, taking notes about Twain's humor and his use of the techniques mentioned in his quoted comment.
- Remind students to consider why Twain frames the comic tale involving Jim Smiley with brief scenes between an unnamed narrator and Simon Wheeler.
- Use the rubrics for Response to Literature, pp. 65–66 in ***General Resources,*** to evaluate students' essays.

❹ Research and Technology

- Group members might divide research tasks according to sources. One person might be responsible for researching printed reference and history books, another for newspaper and periodicals, a third for Internet sites, and a fourth for CD-ROMs.
- Students might consider including an annotated map of the Mississippi River as a part of their report.
- The **Support for Extend Your Learning** page (***Unit 4 Resources,*** p. 129) provides guided note-taking opportunities to help students complete the Extend Your Learning activities.
- Use the rubrics for Multimedia Presentation, pp. 51–52 in ***General Resources,*** to evaluate students' reports.

Go Online Research — Have students type in the Web Code for another research activity.

Assessment Resources

The following resources can be used to assess students' knowledge and skills.

Unit 4 Resources
- **Selection Test A,** pp. 131–133
- **Selection Test B,** pp. 134–136

General Resources
- **Rubrics for Response to Literature,** pp. 65–66
- **Rubrics for Multimedia Presentation,** pp. 51–52

Go Online Assessment — Students may use the **Self-test** to prepare for **Selection Test A** or **Selection Test B.**

Meeting Your Standards

Students will

1. **analyze and respond to literary elements.**
   - Literary Analysis: Regionalism
2. **read, comprehend, analyze, and critique a short story.**
   - Reading Strategy: Questioning the Text
   - Reading Check questions
   - Apply the Skills questions
   - Assessment Practice (ATE)
3. **develop vocabulary.**
   - Vocabulary Lesson: Latin Word Part: *-bel-*
4. **understand and apply written and oral language conventions.**
   - Spelling Strategy
   - Grammar and Style Lesson: Coordinating Conjunctions in Compound Sentences
5. **develop writing proficiency.**
   - Writing Lesson: Critical Review
6. **develop appropriate research strategies.**
   - Extend Your Learning: Prospecting and Mining Report
7. **understand and apply listening and speaking strategies.**
   - Extend Your Learning: Eulogy

Block Scheduling: Use one 90-minute class period to preteach the skills and have students read the selection. Use a second 90-minute class period to assess students' mastery of skills, extend their learning, and monitor their progress.

Homework Suggestions

Following are possibilities for homework assignments.

- Support pages from *Unit 4 Resources:*
  Literary Analysis
  Reading Strategy
  Vocabulary Builder
  Grammar and Style
- An Extend Your Learning project and the Writing Lesson for this selection may be completed over several days.

Step-by-Step Teaching Guide	Pacing Guide
PRETEACH	
• Administer Vocabulary and Reading Warm-ups as necessary.	5 min.
• Engage students' interest with the motivation activity.	5 min.
• Read and discuss author and background features. **FT**	10 min.
• Introduce the Literary Analysis Skill: Regionalism. **FT**	5 min.
• Introduce the Reading Strategy: Questioning the Text **FT**	10 min.
• Prepare students to read by teaching the selection vocabulary. **FT**	
TEACH	
• Informally monitor comprehension while students read independently or in groups. **FT**	30 min.
• Monitor students' comprehension with the Reading Check notes.	as students read
• Reinforce vocabulary with Vocabulary Builder notes.	as students read
• Develop students' understanding of Regionalism with the Literary Analysis annotations. **FT**	5 min.
• Develop students' ability to question the text with the Reading Strategy annotations. **FT**	5 min.
ASSESS/EXTEND	
• Assess students' comprehension and mastery of the Literary Analysis and Reading Strategy by having them answer the Apply the Skills questions. **FT**	15 min.
• Have students complete the Vocabulary Lesson and the Grammar and Style Lesson. **FT**	15 min.
• Apply students' ability to use evaluative modifiers by using the Writing Lesson. **FT**	45 min. or homework
• Apply students' understanding by using one or more of the Extend Your Learning activities.	20–90 min. or homework
• Administer Selection Test A or Selection Test B. **FT**	15 min.

Resources

PRINT

Unit 4 Resources

TRANSPARENCY

Graphic Organizer Transparencies

PRINT

Reader's Notebook [L2]
Reader's Notebook: Adapted Version [L1]
Reader's Notebook: English Learner's Version [EL]

Unit 4 Resources

TECHNOLOGY

Listening to Literature Audio CDs [L2, EL]

PRINT

Unit 4 Resources

General Resources

TECHNOLOGY

Go Online: Research **[L3]**
Go Online: Self-test **[L3]**
***ExamView*® Test Bank [L3]**

Choosing Resources for Differentiated Instruction

[L1] Special Needs Students
[L2] Below-Level Students
[L3] All Students
[L4] Advanced Students
[EL] English Learners

FT Fast Track Instruction: To move the lesson more quickly, use the strategies and activities identified with **FT**.

Scaffolding for Less Proficient and Advanced Students

The leveled Critical Thinking questions after selections progress in the levels of thinking required to answer them. To address the needs of your different students, you may use the (a) level questions for your less proficient students and the (b) level with your on-level and advanced students. The occasional (c) level questions are appropriate for your advanced students.

PRENTICE HALL **TeacherEXPRESS™** Plan · Teach · Assess — Use this complete suite of powerful teaching tools to make lesson planning and testing quicker and easier.

PRENTICE HALL **StudentEXPRESS™** Learn · Study · Succeed — Use the interactive textbook (online and on CD-ROM) to make selections and activities come alive with audio and video support and interactive questions.

PRETEACH

Motivation

Discuss the idea that in both life and literature, people may not be as they appear at first impression. Point out, for example, that students may know seemingly tough characters who inevitably reveal a heart of gold—or weak ones who show an unexpected inner strength during a crisis. Have students think about and suggest a list of fictional characters from short stories, books, movies, and television who turn out to be different than their initial impressions suggest. Guide students to notice how their views of the different characters in this story change as they read.

❶ Background

More About the Author

When he was eleven years old, Bret Harte published his first poem, "Autumn Musings," in the *Sunday Morning Atlas.* His family members criticized the poem for being too emotional. Harte later said, "I sometimes wonder that I ever wrote another line of verse." But he did, and eventually won the respect of many writers.

Build Skills | *Short Story*

❶ The Outcasts of Poker Flat

Bret Harte (1836–1902)

A literary pioneer, Bret Harte played a key role in creating a vivid, lasting portrait of the Old West. His stories, filled with picturesque, intriguing characters and colorful dialogue, provided much of post-Civil War America with its first glimpse of western life and established the Old West as a popular literary setting. In their locations, plots, characters, and uses of both humor and violence, the roots of the Hollywood western can be traced back to Harte's tales.

Heading West Harte was born and raised in Albany, New York. In 1854, when he was eighteen, he traveled across the country to California, a land undergoing a turbulent period of rapid growth due to the discovery of gold in 1848. During his first few years in California, Harte worked as a schoolteacher, tutor, messenger, clerk, and prospector. While Harte's life seemed to have little direction at the time, his observations of the rugged, often violent, life in the mining camps and the towns and cities of the new frontier provided him with the inspiration for his most successful short stories.

A Career of Ups and Downs After working as a typesetter and writer for two California periodicals and publishing two books of verse, *Outcroppings* (1865) and *The Lost Galleon* (1867), Harte became the editor in 1868 of the *Overland Monthly,* a new literary magazine. At that time, the country's population and geographical area were both expanding at a rapid pace. Yet, there were few ways for people to learn about life in regions other than their own.

The American public was eager to learn about life in the new frontier. Harte's writing addressed this need. When he published his story "The Luck of Roaring Camp," in *Overland Monthly's* second issue, he immediately became famous. Over the next two years, he published "The Outcasts of Poker Flat" and several other stories for the magazine about life on the frontier. His popularity continued to climb.

Following the publication of *The Luck of Roaring Camp and Other Sketches* in 1870, Harte's popularity reached its peak. In 1871, *The Atlantic Monthly,* a distinguished literary magazine, contracted to pay Harte the large sum of $10,000 for any twelve sketches or stories he contributed over the next year. Harte returned to the East to fulfill his contract, but the stories he wrote were flat and disappointing compared with his earlier work. His celebrity waned almost as quickly as it had grown.

A Political Appointment Harte continued to publish stories, short novels, and plays during the next twenty years, but most of his later work was unsuccessful. Some friends helped him land a diplomatic post, however, and from 1878 to 1885 Harte served as a United States consul in Germany and Scotland. He retired to London for the remainder of his life.

Recognition by His Peers Richard O'Conner, a biographer of Harte, summarized Harte's legacy this way:

> "Kipling said he owed 'many things' to the storyteller's art he learned from reading Harte . . . [and] H. L. Mencken believed he was entitled to a 'sort of immortality' . . . and the even tougher critic Ambrose Bierce granted Harte a place 'very close to the head' of all American writers."

Preview

Connecting to the Literature

The "outcasts" in Bret Harte's story are tested by circumstances. Think about a situation in which you, or someone that you know, described an event as, "a real test of character." What qualities did the situation bring out in the people involved?

2 Literary Analysis

Regionalism

Regionalism is a literary movement in which writers attempt to depict and analyze the distinctive and unique qualities of a geographical area and its people. Stories like "The Outcasts of Poker Flat" paint vivid and engaging portraits of what life was like in the far reaches of the country. As you read, notice how Harte captures the characteristics of the region and its inhabitants.

Connecting Literary Elements

The unique characters in this story are an essential part of the **local color** of a rough mining town in the Sierra Nevadas, a mountain range in northern California. An aspect of regionalism, local color highlights characteristics and details unique to a specific area. Local color captures the physical environment, as well as the mood of a time and a place, and includes the ways in which people talk and how they think. Use a chart like the one shown to record the elements of local color in the story.

Language

Setting In Town | Setting Outside Town

Local Color

Attitude Toward Vices | Attitude Toward Religion

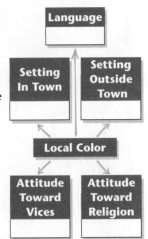

3 Reading Strategy

Questioning the Text

When you read any literature, **question the text** to improve your involvement and understanding. Ask yourself questions like these:

- What is happening?
- What is the author's purpose?
- What are the motives for the characters' actions?

Look for answers to questions like these as you read.

Vocabulary Builder

expatriated (eks pā´ trē āt id) *adj.* deported; driven from one's native land (p. 594)

anathema (ə nath´ ə mə) *n.* curse (p. 594)

bellicose (bel ə kōs) *adj.* quarrelsome (p. 595)

recumbent (ri kum´ bənt) *adj.* resting (p. 595)

equanimity (ek´ wə nim ə tē) *n.* composure (p. 595)

vociferation (vō sif ər ā shən) *n.* loud or vehement shouting (p. 599)

vituperative (vī to͞o´ pər ə tiv) *adj.* spoken abusively (p. 600)

querulous (kwer´ ə ləs) *adj.* inclined to find fault (p. 600)

2 Literary Analysis

Regionalism

- Explain to students that as they read this story they will focus on the literary movement known as regionalism.
- Read the instruction about regionalism aloud. Point out that writers of regional literature are especially interested in conveying what is unique about a particular place and its people.
- Explain that regionalism was especially popular in the United States during the mid- to late-1800s, when the nation's population and geographical area were expanding at a rapid pace. At that time, there were few ways for people to learn about life in regions other than their own.
- Invite students to look for descriptions, dialogue, and attitudes in this story that are characteristic of the Old West.
- Give students a copy of **Literary Analysis Graphic Organizer A,** p. 120 in ***Graphic Organizer Transparencies***, to use as they read The Outcasts of Poker Flat.

3 Reading Strategy

Questioning the Text

- Point out to students that, with practice, their ability to question the text will become almost second nature. Encourage them to see the important link between reading a text and writing notes about it. In short, encourage students to cultivate the habit of reading with a pencil in hand.
- Remind students that questioning the text can involve clarifying seemingly irrelevant details that might also create confusion. It can also involve clarifying a literary work's central ideas.

Vocabulary Builder

- Pronounce each vocabulary word for students, and read the definitions as a class. Have students identify any words with which they are already familiar.

Differentiated Instruction Solutions for All Learners

Support for Special Needs Students
Have students complete the **Preview** and **Build Skills** pages for the selection in the ***Reader's Notebook: Adapted Version***. These pages provide a selection summary, an abbreviated presentation of the reading and literary skills, and the graphic organizer on the **Build Skills** page in the student book.

Support for Less Proficient Readers
Have students complete the **Preview** and **Build Skills** pages for the selection in the ***Reader's Notebook***. These pages provide a selection summary, an abbreviated presentation of the reading and literary skills, and the graphic organizer on the **Build Skills** page in the student book.

Support for English Learners
Have students complete the **Preview** and **Build Skills** pages for the selection in the ***Reader's Notebook: English Learner's Version***. These pages provide a selection summary, an abbreviated presentation of the skills, additional contextual vocabulary, and the graphic organizer on the **Build Skills** page in the student book.

TEACH

Learning Modalities
Interpersonal Learners Guide students to notice the composition of characters in the group of outcasts, and how each contributes to the group's dynamics. Compare this combination of individuals with those depicted in typical contemporary disaster movies. Explain how these groups routinely include an intrepid male leader, a young innocent, a corrupt old man, a tough, worldly woman, and an untrustworthy young drifter.

❶ About the Selection

In a regenerative effort, the mining town of Poker Flat has been ridding itself of unsavory characters. The gambler John Oakhurst and three other outcasts attempt to make their way to the more hospitable camp of Sandy Bar. A snowstorm stops their travel and links them with two "innocents" heading in the opposite direction. As the story of survival unfolds, readers come to understand each of the characters in a new light.

❷ Humanities

Edge of Town, by Charles Burchfield

Charles Burchfield (1893–1967) studied at the Cleveland Art Institute, where he developed his poetic and introspective painting style. This work, the last of Burchfield's "main street" paintings, provides a view of a small-town street on a bleak winter day.

Use these questions for discussion.

1. How does the artist create a scene filled with mystery?
   Answer: The buildings glow with a dull light that is in eerie contrast to the stormy sky. The static figures are more like elements of the landscape than people.
2. Why is this painting an appropriate image for this story?
   Answer: The painting is appropriate because it depicts a small western town with an ominous undercurrent.

❶ THE OUTCASTS OF POKER FLAT

BRET HARTE

❷

❸ ▲ Critical Viewing Does the mood of this painting echo the mood of the story's opening paragraphs? Explain. **[Compare]**

Differentiated Instruction Solutions for All Learners

Accessibility at a Glance

	The Outcasts of Poker Flat
Context	American West
Language	Vocabulary footnotes
Concept Level	Accessible (survival)
Literary Merit	Noted author
Lexile	1160
Overall Rating	Average

Background

Mr. Oakhurst, a gambler and the main character of "The Outcasts of Poker Flat," is a generous, genial man who is seemingly nonchalant in the face of danger. As you read the story, you may find yourself wondering how true-to-life Mr. Oakhurst is. Harte's biographer, Henry Childs Merwin, described a real-life character named Lucky Bill, a gambler who demonstrated traits similar to Mr. Oakhurst's. According to Merwin, Lucky Bill was known for his generosity, and, although he was hanged by a vigilance committee, he was also known to have advised his own son to avoid bad company, keep out of saloons, and lead an industrious and honest life.

As Mr. John Oakhurst, gambler, stepped into the main street of Poker Flat on the morning of the twenty-third of November, 1850, he was conscious of a change in its moral atmosphere since the preceding night. Two or three men, conversing earnestly together, ceased as he approached, and exchanged significant glances. There was a Sabbath lull in the air which, in a settlement unused to Sabbath influences, looked ominous.

Mr. Oakhurst's calm, handsome face betrayed small concern in these indications. Whether he was conscious of any predisposing cause was another question. "I reckon they're after somebody," he reflected; "likely it's me." He returned to his pocket the handkerchief with which he had been whipping away the red dust of Poker Flat from his neat boots, and quietly discharged his mind of any further conjecture.

In point of fact, Poker Flat was "after somebody." It had lately suffered the loss of several thousand dollars, two valuable horses, and a prominent citizen. It was experiencing a spasm of virtuous reaction, quite as lawless and ungovernable as any of the acts that had provoked it. A secret committee had determined to rid the town of all improper persons. This was done permanently in regard of two men who were then hanging from the boughs of a sycamore in the gulch, and temporarily in the banishment of certain other objectionable characters. I regret to say that some of these were ladies. It is but due to the sex, however, to state that their impropriety was professional, and it was only in such easily established standards of evil that Poker Flat ventured to sit in judgment.

Mr. Oakhurst was right in supposing that he was included in this category. A few of the committee had urged hanging him as a possible example, and a sure method of reimbursing themselves from his pockets of the sums he had won from them. "It's agin justice," said Jim Wheeler, "to let this yer young man from Roaring Camp—an entire stranger—carry away our money." But a crude sentiment of equity residing in the breasts of those who had been fortunate enough to win from Mr. Oakhurst overruled this narrower local prejudice.

Mr. Oakhurst received his sentence with philosophic calmness, none the less coolly that he was aware of the hesitation of his judges. He was

Literary Analysis
Regionalism What does this passage reveal about some of the inhabitants of Poker Flat?

5 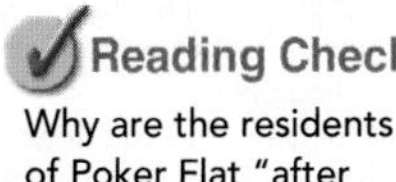
Why are the residents of Poker Flat "after somebody"?

Differentiated Instruction Solutions for All Learners

Strategy for Special Needs Students
To launch students into their reading of "The Outcasts of Poker Flat," pick a strong reader to read aloud the first several paragraphs while students follow in their texts. Afterward, answer any questions that students might have. Then, have students read the rest of the selection aloud in pairs or small groups. Suggest that they note any difficult lines or passages for later discussion.

Support for Less Proficient Readers
This story contains an abundance of lengthy and potentially confusing compound sentences. To help students better understand these sentences, suggest that they break them down into discrete sections as they read. Have students identify the core of each sentence—its main subject and verb—and state the action each sentence describes. Guide students to use coordinating conjunctions to clarify the connections between pairs of ideas.

3 Critical Viewing

Answer: The mood of the painting accurately echoes the mood of the opening paragraphs. The painting shows a small western town that is quite still except for the few people milling about in the street. The daylight upon the buildings is eerie, and the dark clouds are ominous. The scene evokes not only a calm similar to the "Sabbath lull" Harte describes, but also a sense of foreboding.

4 Literary Analysis
Regionalism

- Have a student volunteer read the third and fourth paragraphs of the story aloud, and encourage listeners to distinguish two groups of Poker Flat "committee members."
- **Ask** students the Literary Analysis question: What does this passage reveal about some of the inhabitants of Poker Flat?
  Answer: Students may say that some of the inhabitants are hypocritical, and motivated by revenge and greed—if they have lost money, they would hang a gambler; if they have won money, they would not.

▶ **Monitor Progress:** Have students use a graphic organizer to track the regional qualities reflected in the story. To do so, create two charts on the chalkboard and ask students to copy them in their notebooks. Label the first chart *Physical Environment,* then list the following categories: *weather, climate, vegetation,* and *landscape.* Label the second chart *Cultural Environment,* then list the following categories: *political attitudes, religious beliefs, social attitudes, language/dialect, art,* and *traditions.* Have students fill in both charts as they read the story.

5 Reading Check

Answer: The town had lately "suffered the loss of several thousand dollars, two valuable horses, and a prominent citizen."

❻ Literature in Context

Sierra Nevada It was in the Sierra Nevadas that a group of some eighty immigrants led by George and Jacob Donner became trapped by snowstorms during the winter of 1846–47. More than half of "the Donner Party" eventually died in what came to be known as the Donner Pass on the route between Reno and San Francisco.

Connect to the Literature
Encourage students to issue at least two possible challenges and then explain their predictions.
Possible response: The mountain range will force the characters to deal with extreme weather conditions, unpredictable terrain, and isolation.

too much of a gambler not to accept Fate. With him life was at best an uncertain game, and he recognized the usual percentage in favor of the dealer.

A body of armed men accompanied the deported wickedness of Poker Flat to the outskirts of the settlement. Besides Mr. Oakhurst, who was known to be a coolly desperate man, and for whose intimidation the armed escort was intended, the expatriated party consisted of a young woman familiarly known as the "Duchess"; another, who had won the title of "Mother Shipton";[1] and "Uncle Billy," a suspected sluice robber[2] and confirmed drunkard. The cavalcade provoked no comments from the spectators, nor was any word uttered by the escort. Only when the gulch which marked the uttermost limit of Poker Flat was reached, the leader spoke briefly and to the point. The exiles were forbidden to return at the peril of their lives.

As the escort disappeared, their pent-up feelings found vent in a few hysterical tears from the Duchess, some bad language from Mother Shipton, and a Parthian volley of expletives[3] from Uncle Billy. The philosophic Oakhurst alone remained silent. He listened calmly to Mother Shipton's desire to cut somebody's heart out, to the repeated statements of the Duchess that she would die in the road, and to the alarming oaths that seemed to be bumped out of Uncle Billy as he rode forward. With the easy good humor characteristic of his class, he insisted upon exchanging his own riding horse, "Five Spot," for the sorry mule which the Duchess rode. But even this act did not draw the party into any closer sympathy. The young woman readjusted her somewhat draggled plumes with a feeble, faded coquetry; Mother Shipton eyed the possessor of "Five Spot" with malevolence, and Uncle Billy included the whole party in one sweeping anathema.

The road to Sandy Bar—a camp that, not having as yet experienced the regenerating influences of Poker Flat, consequently seemed to offer some invitation to the emigrants—lay over a steep mountain range. It was distant a day's severe travel. In that advanced season, the party soon passed out of the moist, temperate regions of the foothills into the dry, cold, bracing air of the Sierras.♦ The trail was narrow and difficult. At noon the Duchess, rolling out of her saddle upon the ground, declared her intention of going no farther, and the party halted.

1. **"Mother Shipton"** English woman who lived in the sixteenth century and was suspected of being a witch.
2. **sluice robber** person who steals gold from sluices—long troughs used for sifting gold.
3. **Parthian . . . expletives** hostile remarks made while leaving. The Parthians were an ancient society whose cavalrymen usually shot at the enemy while retreating or pretending to retreat.

Literature in Context

❻ Geography Connection

♦ ***The Sierra Nevadas***

The outcasts find shelter in the Sierra Nevadas, a majestic mountain range in northern California. The Sierra Nevada range is about 450 miles long and 60 to 80 miles wide. The craggy granite peaks include the national parks of Yosemite, Sequoia, and Kings Canyon, as well as the giant sequoia forests. Five hundred peaks in the Sierras exceed 12,000 feet; Mount Whitney, at 14,494 feet, is the tallest mountain in the continental United States, excluding Alaska.

Connect to the Literature

What challenges do you predict this mountain range, despite its beauty, will present to the characters in Harte's story?

Vocabulary Builder

expatriated (eks pā´ trē āt´ id) *adj.* deported; driven from one's native land

anathema (ə nath´ ə mə) *n.* curse

Enrichment

Mining Towns

Visitors to any of several western states can see vestiges of what was once for a brief time a booming mining industry. Not only the discovery of gold, but silver and copper strikes brought fortune seekers by the thousands to sites in the mountains of Nevada, Arizona, Colorado, and other states and territories. Today, some of these towns are gone completely, while others are "ghost towns" whose remains might include a dilapidated building or two and an abandoned mine shaft. Still others have transformed themselves into artist communities or tourist destinations.

Have students choose a specific mining town and research its boom and bust. One such town is Virginia City, Nevada. Students can gather information about life there in its heyday and learn about its current status. Invite students to share any interesting findings about the place or the people who lived there.

The spot was singularly wild and impressive. A wooded amphitheater, surrounded on three sides by precipitous cliffs of naked granite, sloped gently toward the crest of another precipice that overlooked the valley. It was, undoubtedly, the most suitable spot for a camp, had camping been advisable. But Mr. Oakhurst knew that scarcely half the journey to Sandy Bar was accomplished, and the party were not equipped or provisioned for delay. This fact he pointed out to his companions curtly, with a philosophic commentary on the folly of "throwing up their hand before the game was played out." But they were furnished with liquor, which in this emergency stood them in place of food, fuel, rest, and prescience. In spite of his remonstrances, it was not long before they were more or less under its influence. Uncle Billy passed rapidly from a bellicose state into one of stupor, the Duchess became maudlin, and Mother Shipton snored. Mr. Oakhurst alone remained erect, leaning against a rock calmly surveying them.

Mr. Oakhurst did not drink. It interfered with a profession which required coolness, impassiveness, and presence of mind, and, in his own language, he "couldn't afford it." As he gazed at his recumbent fellow exiles, the loneliness begotten of his pariah trade, his habits of life, his very vices, for the first time seriously oppressed him. He bestirred himself in dusting his black clothes, washing his hands and face, and other acts characteristic of his studiously neat habits, and for a moment forgot his annoyance. The thought of deserting his weaker and more pitiable companions never perhaps occurred to him. Yet he could not help feeling the want of that excitement which singularly enough, was most conducive to that calm equanimity for which he was notorious. He looked at the gloomy walls that rose a thousand feet sheer above the circling pines around him; at the sky, ominously clouded; at the valley below, already deepening into shadow. And, doing so, suddenly he heard his own name called.

A horseman slowly ascended the trail. In the fresh, open face of the newcomer Mr. Oakhurst recognized Tom Simson, otherwise known as the "Innocent" of Sandy Bar. He had met him some months before over a "little game," and had, with perfect equanimity, won the entire fortune—amounting to some forty dollars—of that guileless youth. After the game was finished, Mr. Oakhurst drew the youthful speculator behind the door and thus addressed him: "Tommy, you're a good little man, but you can't gamble worth a cent. Don't try it over again." He then handed him his money back, pushed him gently from the room, and so made a devoted slave of Tom Simson.

There was a remembrance of this in his boyish and enthusiastic greeting of Mr. Oakhurst. He had started, he said, to go to Poker Flat to seek his fortune. "Alone?" No, not exactly alone; in fact (a giggle), he had run away with Piney Woods. Didn't Mr. Oakhurst remember Piney? She that used to wait on the table at the Temperance House? They had been engaged a long time, but old Jake Woods had objected, and so they had run away, and were going to Poker Flat to be married, and here they were. And they were tired out, and how lucky it

Vocabulary Builder
bellicose (bel′ ə kōs) *adj.* quarrelsome

Vocabulary Builder
recumbent (ri kum′ bənt) *adj.* resting

Vocabulary Builder
equanimity (ek′ wə nim ə tē) *n.* composure

9 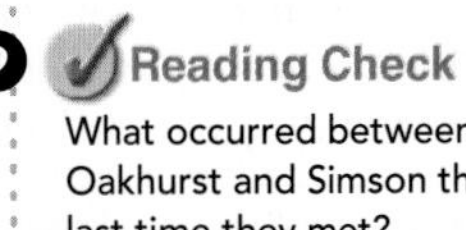

Reading Check
What occurred between Oakhurst and Simson the last time they met?

7 Vocabulary Builder
Latin Word Part *-bel-*

- Point out the word *bellicose* and read its definition.
- Tell students that the word derives its meaning from the Latin word *bellum,* which means war.
- Then, give students the meaning of the prefix *ante-,* which means "before," and **ask** them what the word *antebellum* might mean.
  Answer: *Antebellum* means "before the war."
- After they have correctly answered the question, inform students that references to the antebellum period in the United States usually indicate the years before the Civil War.

8 Critical Thinking
Analyze

- Have students read the two bracketed paragraphs and think about their assessment of Mr. Oakhurst.
- In particular, encourage students to **identify** any paradoxes Mr. Oakhurst's personality and to speculate on why he became a gambler in the first place.
  Answer: Students may say that although he thrives on the excitement he finds in card games, Oakhurst has the bearing of someone who relies on cool, dispassionate reason, and who likes to be in control. They may say that his composure and calm personality, combined with his belief in the significance of luck and the inevitability of fate, ideally suit him to his chosen profession.

9 Reading Check

Answer: Oakhurst won forty dollars from Simson and subsequently returned it to him along with the advice not to gamble again.

Differentiated Instruction
Solutions for All Learners

Background for Special Needs Students
Students may be confused by the reference to "the usual percentage in favor of the dealer" at the end of the first paragraph on the previous page. Explain the principle that in games of chance, the gambling institution, known as the "house," usually has the mathematical advantage, and therefore the greater probability of winning. Although the odds usually favor the house the degree to which they do so may differ from game to game. A professional gambler like Oakhurst must know the precise advantage held by the dealer.

Strategy for Gifted/Talented Students
Ask students to describe Oakhurst's view of life. Students may say that he believes that luck determines the direction one's life will take. They may guess that, as a gambler, Oakhurst plays the odds, calculates the probability of events, and responds in a way that will give him the best chance of success. Students may note that when Oakhurst says that he "recognized the usual percentage . . . ," he means that he knows when to accept defeat. Students might also note that the "dealer" Oakhurst refers to is God, or fate.

⓾ The American Experience

The Western Even before the makers of motion pictures and radio and television programs took advantage of Americans' thirst for stories about white settlement of the Old West, authors such as James Fenimore Cooper (*The Prairie,* 1827), Stephen Crane ("The Bride Comes to Yellow Sky," 1898), and Zane Grey (*Riders of the Purple Sage,* 1912) had great success with westerns. The ancestor of Hollywood westerns is Edwin S. Porter's *The Great Train Robbery* (1903). During the 1930s Americans went to local cinemas to see *Cimarron* and *Stagecoach* (starring John Wayne). In the next decade, films such as *Red River, The Ox-Bow Incident,* and *Duel in the Sun* were released.

Connect to the Literature
Encourage students to name at least three character types that Harte presents, and then give explanations for their choices.
Possible response: Mr. Oakhurst represents the confident, fearless gambler who mirrors his life with his gambling habits. Uncle Billy is the stereotypical drunk and thief, and Piney is the uneducated, sweet innocent.

⓫ Literary Analysis
Regionalism and Local Color

- Read the bracketed passage aloud, inviting students to jot down notes about details suggesting local color. Make sure students listen for details describing both the physical place and time and the cultural norms.
- Invite volunteers to share their notes with the class as you write their responses on the chalkboard.

▶ **Monitor Progress: Ask** the Literary Analysis question: In what ways does this description of both the physical environment and the characters reflect qualities unique to the region?
Answer: Elements suggesting distinctive qualities of local color in the physical environment include Uncle Billy's retiring "up the canyon" to laugh among the "tall pine trees"; the strange chill in the air and the tethered animals. Local color in the characters is revealed by Uncle Billy's finding comedy in the idea of the Duchess being "Mrs. Oakhurst"; Uncle Billy's use of dialect, his body language and his use of profanity.

was they had found a place to camp and company. All this the Innocent delivered rapidly, while Piney, a stout, comely damsel of fifteen, emerged from behind the pine tree, where she had been blushing unseen, and rode to the side of her lover.

Mr. Oakhurst seldom troubled himself with sentiment, still less with propriety; but he had a vague idea that the situation was not fortunate. He retained, however, his presence of mind sufficiently to kick Uncle Billy, who was about to say something, and Uncle Billy was sober enough to recognize in Mr. Oakhurst's kick a superior power that would not bear trifling. He then endeavored to dissuade Tom Simson from delaying further, but in vain. He even pointed out the fact that there was no provision, nor means of making a camp. But, unluckily, the Innocent met this objection by assuring the party that he was provided with an extra mule loaded with provisions and by the discovery of a rude attempt at a log house near the trail. "Piney can stay with Mrs. Oakhurst," said the Innocent, pointing to the Duchess, "and I can shift for myself."

⓫ Nothing but Mr. Oakhurst's admonishing foot saved Uncle Billy from bursting into a roar of laughter. As it was, he felt compelled to retire up the canyon until he could recover his gravity. There he confided the joke to the tall pine trees, with many slaps of his leg, contortions of his face, and the usual profanity. But when he returned to the party, he found them seated by a fire—for the air had grown strangely chill and the sky overcast—in apparently amicable conversation. Piney was actually talking in an impulsive, girlish fashion to the Duchess, who was listening with an interest and animation she had not shown for many days. The Innocent was holding forth, apparently with equal effect, to Mr. Oakhurst and Mother Shipton, who was actually relaxing into amiability. "Is this yer a d——d picnic?" said Uncle Billy with inward scorn as he surveyed the sylvan[4] group, the glancing firelight, and the tethered animals in the foreground. Suddenly an idea mingled with the alcoholic fumes that disturbed his brain. It was apparently of a jocular nature, for he felt impelled to slap his leg again and cram his fist into his mouth.

As the shadows crept slowly up the mountain, a slight breeze rocked the tops of the pine trees, and moaned through their long and gloomy aisles. The ruined cabin, patched and covered with pine boughs, was set apart for the ladies. As the lovers parted, they unaffectedly exchanged a kiss, so honest and sincere that it might have been heard above the swaying pines. The frail Duchess and the malevolent Mother Shipton were probably too stunned to remark upon this last evidence of simplicity, and so turned without a word to the hut. The fire was replenished, the men lay down before the door, and in a few minutes were asleep.

4. **sylvan** (sil′ vən) *adj.* characteristic of the forest.

⓾ ***The Western***

The American West was settled from the middle to late 1800s. As settlers moved west on the Santa Fe and Oregon trails, they developed thriving businesses in livestock. Cow towns grew up around railroad stations, and immense cattle drives moved across the plains. This period in American life provided the material for the American western—a literary and film genre that has been a staple of popular culture ever since.

Both legendary and real-life characters such as Jesse James, Wild Bill Hickok, Kit Carson, and Buffalo Bill Cody, were featured in stagecoach dramas and books. Soon, filmmakers produced minute-long "Cowboys and Indians" flicks. By 1939, Hollywood was churning out westerns. The biggest box office returns went to villains such as Jesse James and Billy the Kid—outlaws whose brawling and gun fighting provided hours of diversion for American filmgoers.

Connect to the Literature
What familiar western character types does Harte present?

Literary Analysis
Regionalism and Local Color In what ways does this description of both the setting and the characters reflect qualities unique to the region?

Enrichment

Outcasts
Ever since the beginning of civilization, individuals have been rejected from societies for a wide range of reasons. Outcasts may have been seen as antisocial, or their religious beliefs may have challenged popularly accepted views. About five hundred years ago, Jews were forced to leave Spain unless they converted to Catholicism. Until the American Revolution, Great Britain shipped criminals to America, and continued to send them to Australia well into the nineteenth century. Until 1950, India's rigid caste system forced an entire class of people, called Untouchables, to live a life of poverty.

Have students research a group of people who have been considered outcasts of society. Students' research should attempt to uncover the reasons the people were viewed as outcasts, descriptions of their daily lives, and—in the cases in which the outcasts were not criminals—explanations of why the exclusion was allowed to occur. Invite students to report their findings to the class.

Mr. Oakhurst was a light sleeper. Toward morning he awoke benumbed and cold. As he stirred the dying fire, the wind, which was now blowing strongly, brought to his cheek that which caused the blood to leave it—snow!

He started to his feet with the intention of awakening the sleepers, for there was no time to lose. But turning to where Uncle Billy had been lying, he found him gone. A suspicion leaped to his brain and a curse to his lips. He ran to the spot where the mules had been tethered; they were no longer there. The tracks were already rapidly disappearing in the snow.

Reading Strategy
Questioning the Text What question can you ask about Oakhurst's discovery that Uncle Billy is missing?

The momentary excitement brought Mr. Oakhurst back to the fire with his usual calm. He did not waken the sleepers. The Innocent slumbered peacefully, with a smile on his good-humored, freckled face; the virgin Piney slept beside her frailer sisters as sweetly as though attended by celestial guardians; and Mr. Oakhurst, drawing his blanket over his shoulders, stroked his mustaches and waited for the dawn. It came slowly in a whirling mist of snowflakes that dazzled and confused the eye. What could be seen of the landscape appeared magically changed. He looked over the valley, and summed up the present and future in two words—"snowed in!"

A careful inventory of the provisions, which, fortunately for the party, had been stored within the hut and so escaped the felonious fingers of Uncle Billy, disclosed the fact that with care and prudence they might last ten days longer. "That is," said Mr. Oakhurst, sotto voce[5] to the Innocent, "if you're willing to board us. If you ain't—and perhaps you'd better not—you can wait till Uncle Billy gets back with provisions." For some occult reason, Mr. Oakhurst could not bring himself to disclose Uncle Billy's rascality, and so offered the hypothesis that he had wandered from the camp and had accidentally stampeded the animals. He dropped a warning to the Duchess and Mother Shipton, who of course knew the facts of their associate's defection. "They'll find out the truth about us *all* when they find out anything," he added, significantly, "and there's no good frightening them now."

Tom Simson not only put all his worldly store at the disposal of Mr. Oakhurst, but seemed to enjoy the prospect of their enforced seclusion. "We'll have a good camp for a week, and then the snow'll melt, and we'll all go back together." The cheerful gaiety of the young man, and Mr. Oakhurst's calm, infected the others. The Innocent with the aid of pine boughs extemporized a thatch for the roofless cabin, and the Duchess directed Piney in the rearrangement of the interior with a taste and tact that opened the blue eyes of that provincial maiden to their fullest extent. "I reckon now you're used to fine things at Poker Flat," said Piney. The Duchess turned away sharply to conceal something that reddened her cheek through its professional tint, and Mother Shipton requested Piney not to "chatter." But when Mr. Oakhurst returned from a weary search for the trail, he heard

13

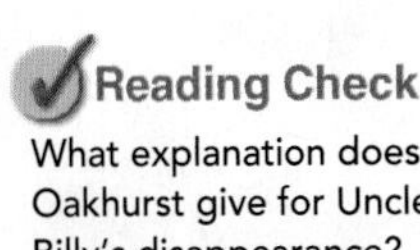

Reading Check
What explanation does Oakhurst give for Uncle Billy's disappearance?

5. **sotto voce** (sät′ ō vō′ chē) in an undertone.

12 Reading Strategy
Questioning the Text

- Invite students to listen as you read the bracketed passage aloud. Ask students to think about what they have just heard and to identify the discovery that Mr. Oakhurst has just made.
- Then, **ask** students the Reading Strategy question: What question can you ask about Oakhurst's discovery that Uncle Billy is missing? **Possible response:** "What is the meaning behind Uncle Billy's disappearance?"

13 Reading Check

Answer: He says that Uncle Billy wandered from the camp in search of more provisions.

Differentiated Instruction
Solutions for All Learners

Enrichment for Advanced Readers

This story was made into a movie in the late 1930s. Here is a review of the film from *Time* magazine.

"Though skimpily produced, it invokes with a fidelity unusual in a double-biller the wild land and rugged times in which its scene is laid, and the nostalgic charm of the Harte stories. Its worst fault is the failure of explicitness in the last sequence, leaving the audience completely fuddled."

Use these questions for discussion:

1. Do you agree with the reviewer that there is a nostalgic charm to Harte's story? Why or why not?
   Answer: Students may say yes because of regional descriptions of an earlier era in the West.
2. The reviewer considers the last scenes to be confusing. Do you think that the end of the original story is believable and logical? Why or why not?
   Answer: Students might say that the ending of the story is a believable resolution of the conflict.

14 Critical Viewing

Answer: The photograph illustrates enormous mountains like those that surround the group of outcasts. The snow in the photograph also indicates a wintry scene. However, the image does not illustrate snow of considerable depth, and it does not present the hopelessly snowbound condition that has stranded the group in Harte's tale.

the sound of happy laughter echoed from the rocks. He stopped in some alarm, and his thoughts first naturally reverted to the whisky, which he had prudently cached.[6] "And yet it don't somehow sound like whisky," said the gambler. It was not until he caught sight of the blazing fire through the still-blinding storm and the group around it that he settled to the conviction that it was "square fun."

Whether Mr. Oakhurst had cached his cards with the whisky as something debarred the free access of the community, I cannot say.

6. **cached** (kasht) *v.* hidden.

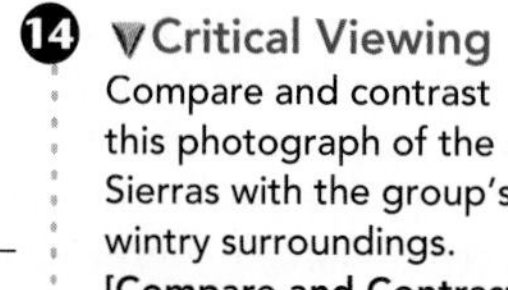

14 ▼**Critical Viewing** Compare and contrast this photograph of the Sierras with the group's wintry surroundings. **[Compare and Contrast]**

Enrichment

Personal Space

In "The Outcasts of Poker Flat," several strangers or near-strangers are forced to camp together for a while. The challenges people face in living with others in cramped conditions for long periods of time is an issue that NASA and astronauts must address when planning and executing space missions. Scientists designing vehicles for space travel usually place technical and research needs above human comfort. Ask students to imagine, for example, what it would be like to live in a spaceship on a mission to Mars. The trip would take many months and would require that a group of people live and work together in very tight quarters.

Ask students to discuss what they think would be easy, difficult, or impossible about that experience or one like it. Have them talk about what kind of person might survive best in tight quarters. Ask them if they would be willing to try such an adventure themselves.

It was certain that, in Mother Shipton's words, he "didn't say cards once" during that evening. Haply the time was beguiled by an accordion, produced somewhat ostentatiously by Tom Simson from his pack. Notwithstanding some difficulties attending the manipulation of this instrument, Piney Woods managed to pluck several reluctant melodies from its keys, to an accompaniment by the Innocent on a pair of bone castanets. But the crowning festivity of the evening was reached in a rude camp-meeting hymn, which the lovers, joining hands, sang with great earnestness and vociferation. I fear that a certain defiant tone and Covenanter's[7] swing to its chorus, rather than any devotional quality, caused it speedily to infect the others, who at last joined in the refrain:

"I'm proud to live in the service of the Lord,
And I'm bound to die in His army."[8]

The pines rocked, the storm eddied and whirled above the miserable group, and the flames of their altar leaped heavenward as if in token of the vow.

At midnight the storm abated, the rolling clouds parted, and the stars glittered keenly above the sleeping camp. Mr. Oakhurst, whose professional habits had enabled him to live on the smallest possible amount of sleep, in dividing the watch with Tom Simson somehow managed to take upon himself the greater part of that duty. He excused himself to the Innocent by saying that he had "often been a week without sleep." "Doing what?" asked Tom. "Poker!" replied Oakhurst, sententiously; "when a man gets a streak of luck, he don't get tired. The luck gives in first. Luck," continued the gambler, reflectively, "is a mighty queer thing. All you know about it for certain is that it's bound to change. And it's finding out when it's going to change that makes you. We've had a streak of bad luck since we left Poker Flat—you come along, and slap you get into it, too. If you can hold your cards right along you're all right. For," added the gambler, with cheerful irrelevance,

" 'I'm proud to live in the service of the Lord,
And I'm bound to die in His army.' "

The third day came, and the sun, looking through the white-curtained valley, saw the outcasts divide their slowly decreasing store of provisions for the morning meal. It was one of the peculiarities of that mountain climate that its rays diffused a kindly warmth over the wintry landscape, as if in regretful commiseration of the past. But it revealed drift on drift of snow piled high around the hut—a hopeless,

7. **Covenanter's** (kuv′ ə nan′ tərz) seventeenth-century Scottish Presbyterians who resisted the rule of the Church of England.
8. **"I'm . . . army"** lines from the early American spiritual "Service of the Lord."

Literary Analysis
Regionalism and Local Color What aspects of local color does this description of the evening's music convey?

Vocabulary Builder
vociferation (vō sif′ ər ā′ shən) *n.* loud or vehement shouting

What does the group do in the evening before going to sleep?

15 Literary Analysis
Regionalism and Local Color

- Review with students the definition of local color. Encourage students to think about how authors use details and descriptive language to convey information about a particular place and time.
- Then, read the passage aloud and **ask** students the Literary Analysis question: What aspects of local color does this description of the evening's music convey?
  Answer: Students may say that the outcasts unite in singing hymns. Students may know that in the nineteenth century many Americans had strong religious beliefs, and that even for people living in the wildest parts of the country, religion was often a unifying force.

16 Reading Check

Answer: They play music and sing together.

Differentiated Instruction
Solutions for All Learners

Strategy for Less Proficient Readers
Students may benefit from pausing occasionally during their reading of the story in order to predict what will happen next. One likely place for students to ask themselves such questions is after the outcasts become snowbound. Invite students to offer their predictions about how the plot will unfold. Have them identify the outcasts' major challenges, and predict ways in which the characters will—or will not—successfully meet those challenges.

Support for English Learners
Help students understand difficult passages by paraphrasing them using simpler language. For instance, the sentence on the previous page that begins "Whether Mr. Oakhurst had cached . . ." can be paraphrased as *I don't know whether he hid his cards with the whiskey so that the others couldn't get at them.*

17 Reading Strategy
Questioning the Text

- **Ask** students to describe in their own words what Mother Shipton has done. Ask them to explain why she did it and what this action reveals about her.
Answer: Mrs. Shipton has been starving herself while stockpiling her food for Piney to eat later. She has sacrificed herself so that the younger woman might survive. Students may surmise that underneath her coarse, hard-hearted exterior, the old woman has a loving heart—and that she has been taken by Piney's purity and innocence.
- Have students **discuss** why Harte included this event in the story.
Answer: Mother Shipton's death underscores the severity of the group's situation.

uncharted, trackless sea of white lying below the rocky shores to which the castaways still clung. Through the marvelously clear air the smoke of the pastoral village of Poker Flat rose miles away. Mother Shipton saw it, and from a remote pinnacle of her rocky fastness hurled in that direction a final malediction. It was her last vituperative attempt, and perhaps for that reason was invested with a certain degree of sublimity. It did her good, she privately informed the Duchess. "Just you go out there and cuss, and see." She then set herself to the task of amusing "the child," as she and the Duchess were pleased to call Piney. Piney was no chicken, but it was a soothing and original theory of the pair thus to account for the fact that she didn't swear and wasn't improper.

Vocabulary Builder
vituperative (vī to͞o′ pər ə tiv) *adj.* spoken abusively

When night crept up again through the gorges, the reedy notes of the accordion rose and fell in fitful spasms and long-drawn gasps by the flickering campfire. But music failed to fill entirely the aching void left by insufficient food, and a new diversion was proposed by Piney—storytelling. Neither Mr. Oakhurst nor his female companions caring to relate their personal experiences, this plan would have failed too but for the Innocent. Some months before he had chanced upon a stray copy of Mr. Pope's[9] ingenious translation of the *Iliad.*[10] He now proposed to narrate the principal incidents of that poem—having thoroughly mastered the argument and fairly forgotten the words—in the current vernacular of Sandy Bar. And so for the rest of that night the Homeric demigods again walked the earth. Trojan bully and wily Greek wrestled in the winds, and the great pines in the canyon seemed to bow to the wrath of the son of Peleus.[11] Mr. Oakhurst listened with quiet satisfaction. Most especially was he interested in the fate of "Ash-heels," as the Innocent persisted in denominating the "swift-footed Achilles."

So with small food and much of Homer and the accordion, a week passed over the heads of the outcasts. The sun again forsook them, and again from leaden skies the snowflakes were sifted over the land. Day by day closer around them drew the snowy circle, until at last they looked from their prison over drifted walls of dazzling white that towered twenty feet above their heads. It became more and more difficult to replenish their fires, even from the fallen trees beside them, now half-hidden in the drifts. And yet no one complained. The lovers turned from the dreary prospect and looked into each other's eyes, and were happy. Mr. Oakhurst settled himself coolly to the losing game before him. The Duchess, more cheerful than she had been, assumed the care of Piney. Only Mother Shipton—once the strongest of the party—seemed to sicken and fade. At midnight on the tenth

day she called Oakhurst to her side. "I'm going," she said, in a voice of querulous weakness, "but don't say anything about it. Don't waken the kids. Take the bundle from under my head and open it."

Vocabulary Builder
querulous (kwer′ ə ləs) *adj.* inclined to find fault

9. **Mr. Pope** English poet Alexander Pope (1688–1744).
10. ***Iliad*** (il′ ē əd) Greek epic poem written by Homer that tells the story of the Trojan War.
11. **son of Peleus** (pē′ lē əs) Achilles (ə kil′ ēz), the Greek warrior hero in the *Iliad*.

Mr. Oakhurst did so. It contained Mother Shipton's rations for the last week, untouched. "Give 'em to the child," she said, pointing to the sleeping Piney. "You've starved yourself," said the gambler. "That's what they call it," said the woman, querulously, as she lay down again and, turning her face to the wall, passed quietly away.

The accordion and the bones were put aside that day, and Homer was forgotten. When the body of Mother Shipton had been committed to the snow, Mr. Oakhurst took the Innocent aside, and showed him a pair of snowshoes, which he had fashioned from the old pack saddle. "There's one chance in a hundred to save her yet," he said, pointing to Piney; "but it's there," he added, pointing toward Poker Flat. "If you can reach there in two days she's safe." "And you?" asked Tom Simson. "I'll stay here," was the curt reply.

The lovers parted with a long embrace. "You are not going, too?" said the Duchess as she saw Mr. Oakhurst apparently waiting to accompany him. "As far as the canyon," he replied. He turned suddenly, and kissed the Duchess, leaving her pallid face aflame and her trembling limbs rigid with amazement.

Night came, but not Mr. Oakhurst. It brought the storm again and the whirling snow. Then the Duchess, feeding the fire, found that someone had quietly piled beside the hut enough fuel to last a few days longer. The tears rose to her eyes, but she hid them from Piney.

The women slept but little. In the morning, looking into each other's faces, they read their fate. Neither spoke; but Piney, accepting the position of the stronger, drew near and placed her arm around the Duchess's waist. They kept this attitude for the rest of the day. That night the storm reached its greatest fury, and, rending asunder the protecting pines, invaded the very hut.

Toward morning they found themselves unable to feed the fire, which gradually died away. As the embers slowly blackened, the Duchess crept closer to Piney, and broke the silence of many hours: "Piney, can you pray?" "No, dear," said Piney, simply. The Duchess, without knowing exactly why, felt relieved, and, putting her head upon Piney's shoulder, spoke no more. And so reclining, the younger and purer pillowing the head of her soiled sister upon her virgin breast, they fell asleep.

The wind lulled as if it feared to waken them. Feathery drifts of snow, shaken from the long pine boughs, flew like white-winged birds, and settled about them as they slept. The moon through the rifted clouds looked down upon what had been the camp. But all human stain, all trace of earthly travail, was hidden beneath the spotless mantle mercifully flung from above.

They slept all that day and the next, nor did they waken when voices and footsteps broke the silence of the camp. And when pitying fingers brushed the snow from their wan faces, you could scarcely have told from the equal peace that dwelt upon them which was she that had sinned. Even the law of Poker Flat recognized this, and turned away, leaving them still locked in each other's arms.

Reading Strategy
Questioning the Text Why did the gambler make only one pair of shoes?

Reading Strategy
Questioning the Text What question might you ask about Mr. Oakhurst's decision to stay?

20 

What happens to Mother Shipton?

18 Reading Strategy
Questioning the Text

- Reread the passage aloud, and **ask** students if they have noticed anything odd about the description of the snowshoes. Make sure they understand the significance of the snowshoes as a way to increase the possibility of survival.
- Then, **ask** students the first Reading Strategy question on: Why did the gambler make only one pair of shoes?
  Answer: Students might say that Oakhurst had enough material for only a single pair.

19 Reading Strategy
Questioning the Text

- Read the passage aloud for students. **Ask** them to explain what Mr. Oakhurst has done for Tom.
  Answer: Mr. Oakhurst has fashioned a single pair of snowshoes, which he gives to Tom instead of keeping them for himself. This allows Tom to escape the camp, and will maximize his chances of reaching Poker Flat.

▶ **Monitor Progress** **Ask** the second Reading Strategy question: What question might you ask about Mr. Oakhurst's decision to stay?
Possible answer: Does Mr. Oakhurst really intend to remain?

20 Reading Check

Answer: After starving herself and giving her accumulated rations to Piney, Mother Shipton dies.

Differentiated Instruction Solutions for All Learners

Support for Special Needs Students
Help these students make sense of the language Harte uses to describe the fate of the two woman left at the camp (*. . . all human stain, all trace of earthly travail, was hidden beneath the spotless mantle mercifully flung from above*). Discuss the symbolism of the "spotless mantle" that covers the outcasts. Guide students to understand that beneath that layer of snow, both the innocent and the sinner reach the same peaceful state.

Enrichment for Advanced Readers
Invite students to compare and contrast the views of fate and death expressed in this story with those expressed in other selections they may have read, such as stories and poems by Irving, Hawthorne, Melville, Dickinson, Bierce, and Poe. Which characters are stoic and accepting in the face of death? Which characters find new strength in dire circumstances? Which sink to new lows? Which complain or become bitter? Which become heroic?

But at the head of the gulch, on one of the largest pine trees, they found the deuce of clubs pinned to the bark with a bowie knife. It bore the following, written in pencil, in a firm hand:

BENEATH THIS TREE
LIES THE BODY
OF
JOHN OAKHURST,
WHO STRUCK A STREAK OF BAD LUCK
ON THE 23D OF NOVEMBER, 1850
AND
HANDED IN HIS CHECKS
ON THE 7TH DECEMBER, 1850.

And pulseless and cold, with a Derringer[12] by his side and a bullet in his heart, though still calm as in life, beneath the snow lay he who was at once the strongest and yet the weakest of the outcasts of Poker Flat.

---

12. **Derringer** small pistol.

Critical Reading

1. **Respond:** Which character did you admire the most? Why?
2. **(a) Recall:** At the opening of the story, what has the secret committee of Poker Flat decided? **(b) Infer:** What motivates the committee to take action against Mr. Oakhurst?
3. **(a) Recall:** Who joins the outcasts at their camp? **(b) Analyze:** What effect do the newcomers have on the outcasts?
4. **(a) Recall:** What does Mr. Oakhurst discover when he awakens after his first night at the camp? **(b) Draw Conclusions:** What do you think happened to Uncle Billy?
5. **(a) Recall:** What does Mother Shipton do with her rations? **(b) Analyze:** Why do you think she does this?
6. **(a) Recall:** What explanation does Oakhurst give for his ability to go without sleep? **(b) Infer:** Do you think Oakhurst knew their "luck" was about to run out? Explain.
7. **(a) Recall:** What does the rescue party discover? **(b) Interpret:** What theme or message might their discovery—and this story—convey?
8. **Apply:** Although the characters in the story have little in common, they band together. For what reasons do people tend to draw together in life? Explain.

Go Online
Author Link
For: More about Bret Harte
Visit: www.PHSchool.com
Web Code: ere-9414

ASSESS

Answers

1. Many students are likely to name Mr. Oakhurst, because he proves to be coolheaded and compassionate. Some might name Mother Shipton, because she sacrifices her own life to save Piney's.
2. (a) They have decided to rid the town of unwanted people by hanging two and banishing several others. (b) Some of the secret committee's members are angry that they lost money while gambling against Mr. Oakhurst.
3. (a) Tom Simson and Piney Woods, who are running away in order to get married, join the outcasts. (b) They evoke the outcasts' feelings of protectiveness, and they also lift everyone's spirits. Tom and Piney are young, open-hearted, and naïve; these qualities bring out tenderness in the others.
4. (a) He discovers that Uncle Billy has disappeared, along with the mules. (b) Students' responses will vary. Accept all logical answers.
5. (a) She stops eating and stores her rations for Piney's later use. (b) She may believe that only a few of those snowbound will survive—and that a young woman's life is more valuable than her own.
6. (a) He indicates that his "professional habits" as a gambler have trained him to function on little sleep. (b) Students may say that Oakhurst clearly knows their chances for survival are low at best, and so he leaves the camp and takes his own life.
7. (a) They find the frozen bodies of Piney and the Duchess, the farewell note, and the body of Mr. Oakhurst. (b) Sample response: Regardless of one's "good" or "bad" deeds during life, in the end death spares no person.
8. Students may cite natural disasters, such as hurricanes and floods, and situations in which people unite in the name of a social, political, or environmental cause.

Go Online
Author Link
For additional information about Bret Harte, have students type in the Web Code, then select H from the alphabet, and then select Harte.

Apply the Skills

The Outcasts of Poker Flat

Literary Analysis

Regionalism

1. Find three details that establish the **regionalism** of the story.
2. **(a)** Find a passage in which Harte describes the physical environment. **(b)** What details help you picture the California landscape?
3. What point about the culture of the West does Harte convey? Explain.

Connecting Literary Elements

4. What inferences about the **local color** of Poker Flat can you make from the following passage?

   A few of the committee had urged hanging him as a possible example, and a sure method of reimbursing themselves from his pocket of the sums he had won from them.

5. Explain why the story would not be as effective if the setting were changed—for example—to New England.

Reading Strategy

Questioning the Text

6. What is meant by the following passage?

   There was a Sabbath lull in the air which, in a settlement unused to Sabbath influences, looked ominous.

7. What does Harte mean when he writes that Oakhurst "was at once the strongest and yet the weakest of the outcasts of Poker Flat"?
8. Find three complex passages in the text. Use a chart like the one shown to record your questions and answers.

Passage From Text	Question	Answer

Extend Understanding

9. **Social Studies Connection:** What conclusions can you draw about law in the settlements that emerged during the Gold Rush?

QuickReview

Regionalism is a literary movement that depicts and analyzes the distinctive qualities of a geographical area and its people.

Details of **local color** capture the attitudes and customs of a geographical area.

To **question the text,** analyze important statements, plot developments, and the author's purpose.

For: Self-test
Visit: www.PHSchool.com
Web Code: era-6408

Go Online Assessment Students may use the **Self-test** to prepare for **Selection Test A** or **Selection Test B.**

Answers

1. Examples that appear early in the story include: *the main street of Poker Flat, a settlement unused to Sabbath influences, "I reckon . . .", red dust, neat boots, hanging from the boughs of a sycamore in the gulch, "agin justice to let this yer young man from Roaring Camp,"* and so on.
2. (a) Students might cite the paragraph on p. 582 beginning "The road to Sandy Bar . . ."
   (b) Details include "steep mountain range," "day's severe travel," "moist, temperate regions," "cold, bracing air," and "narrow and difficult."
3. Harte notes that the challenging terrain shapes people's attitudes, perhaps making them tougher, and less sympathetic.
4. The inhabitants of Poker Flat have a distorted conception of justice and try to use this idea to serve their own needs.
5. The story's effectiveness depends on the frigid and changeable mountain landscape of the Sierra Nevadas, as well as on the sense of "law and order" and "justice" at work in the newly established communities of the Old West.
6. Given that people in Poker Flat did not observe the Sabbath in any significant way, a sober and serene atmosphere, such as one might find on Sunday in a town of churchgoers, seemed unnatural and of ill omen.
7. He is the strongest in that he squarely faces the hopelessness of the group's situation; he is also the only one who actively takes measures to secure their survival. He is the weakest in that he "hand[s] in his checks" rather than see the "losing game" through to the end.
8. Students' responses should contain entries for each section of the chart. Their questions should concern important matters of the story.

   Another sample answer can be found on **Reading Strategy Graphic Organizer B,** p. 123 in ***Graphic Organizer Transparencies.***

9. Justice was not blind. Law was a convenience of those in the majority, and could be bent to suit their personal wills or to enact vendettas.

EXTEND/ASSESS

Answers

1 Vocabulary Lesson

Word Analysis

1. b
2. a

Spelling Strategy

1. quarreled
2. queasy
3. quest

Vocabulary Builder

1. c
2. a
3. b
4. b
5. c
6. b
7. a
8. c

2 Grammar and Style Lesson

Practice

1. He wasn't joking, yet she continued.
2. He raced to the gate, for the plane was about to depart.
3. Vitamins can be good supplements, but they are no substitute for a healthy diet.
4. The cat jumped up onto the table, and spilled the milk.
5. I am very tired, so I will take a nap.

Writing Application

Students' editorials should contain at least two compound sentences.

WG Writing and Grammar, Ruby Level

Students will find further instruction and practice on coordinating conjunctions in compound sentences in Chapter 17, Section 4.

Build Language Skills

1 Vocabulary Lesson

Word Analysis: Latin Word Part *-bel-*

The word *bellicose,* like *belligerent,* uses the Latin word part *-bel-* from the word *bellum,* meaning "war." Both *bellicose* and *belligerent* mean "warlike" or "ready to fight or quarrel."

Choose the letter of the item that best defines the italicized word in each sentence.

a. quarrelsome **b.** act of resistance

1. The *rebellion* was the result of opposition to the government.
2. He must control his rage and not be so *bellicose.*

Spelling Strategy

In English words, the letter *q* is almost always followed by the letter *u,* as in *querulous.* Find a synonym that begins with *qu* for each of the following words.

1. argued 2. nauseated 3. mission

Vocabulary Builder: Synonyms

Select the letter of the word that is closest in meaning to the first word.

1. expatriated: **(a)** honored, **(b)** ignored, **(c)** expelled
2. anathema: **(a)** curse, **(b)** riddle, **(c)** chant
3. bellicose: **(a)** strong, **(b)** quarrelsome, **(c)** beautiful
4. recumbent: **(a)** full, **(b)** reclining, **(c)** unnecessary
5. equanimity: **(a)** fairness, **(b)** precision, **(c)** serenity
6. vociferation: **(a)** uncertainty, **(b)** loudness, **(c)** cleverness
7. vituperative: **(a)** scolding, **(b)** healthful, **(c)** complex
8. querulous: **(a)** trustworthy, **(b)** mysterious, **(c)** disagreeable

2 Grammar and Style Lesson

Coordinating Conjunctions in Compound Sentences

Coordinating conjunctions connect words or groups of words. These conjunctions include *and, but, for, nor, or, so,* and *yet.* Place a comma before a coordinating conjunction that joins the independent clauses in a compound sentence.

They slept all day, *and* they did not awaken . . .

Practice Use the coordinating conjunction provided to form compound sentences.

1. He wasn't joking. She continued. (*yet*)
2. He raced to the gate. The plane was about to depart. (for)
3. Vitamins can be good supplements. They are no substitute for a healthy diet. (*but*)
4. The cat jumped up onto the table. It spilled the milk. (*and*)
5. I am very tired. I will take a nap. (*so*)

Writing Application As a newspaper editor serving mining towns, write a brief editorial about the outcasts and their fate. Use at least two compound sentences.

WG Prentice Hall Writing and Grammar Connection: Chapter 17, Section 4

Assessment Practice

Context **(For more practice, see *Standardized Test Preparation Workbook,* p.33.)**

Many tests require students to use context to determine the meaning of unfamiliar words. Use the following sample test item to give students practice in this skill.

> But even this act did not draw the group into any closer sympathy. . . . Mother Shipton eyed the possessor of "Five Spot" with malevolence, and Uncle Billy included the whole party in one sweeping anathema.

In this passage, malevolence means—

A sympathy **C** hatred
B contentment **D** mellowness

The *but* at the beginning of the passage indicates that sympathy is in contrast to malevolence. The *and* before Uncle Billy's reaction indicates that *anathema* is similar to *malevolence.* These context clues should lead students to discover that the correct response is C.

Writing Lesson

Timed Writing: Critical Review

Write a critical review of "The Outcasts of Poker Flat" to appear in a magazine targeted at fans of westerns. Support your opinion of the story while analyzing its plot, main ideas, and effect on the reader. ***(40 minutes)***

Prewriting *(10 minutes)* Select passages describing the characters, conflicts, main ideas, or setting that move you to respond. Jot down your thoughts on each of these passages.

Drafting *(20 minutes)* Begin with an introduction that summarizes your opinions about the story. Then, analyze each passage you have selected, and explain what it reveals about the story.

Revising *(10 minutes)* The evaluative words you use to convey praise or judgment about the story should be precise. Review your conclusion to be sure it incorporates language that conveys a strong evaluation.

Model: Revising to Include Evaluative Modifiers

These examples reinforce my belief that this story is ~~interesting and good.~~ *well-crafted and entertaining*. People who like westerns will find Harte's setting and the characters *engaging and* realistic.

Specific modifiers such as *well-crafted, entertaining,* and *engaging* convey the writer's attitude toward the work.

WG Prentice Hall Writing and Grammar Connection: Chapter 14, Section 4

Extend Your Learning

Listening and Speaking As Tom Simson, the only survivor of the stranded group, prepare and deliver a **eulogy**—a speech in honor of someone who has died—for Mr. Oakhurst. Speaking candidly but respectfully, be sure to include these details:

- colorful, informal "western" language
- personal experiences you have had with Mr. Oakhurst

After rehearsing, deliver the eulogy to classmates.

Research and Technology With a group, use library databases or the Internet to research the techniques used during a gold rush. Then, develop a **prospecting and mining report** that outlines the main steps in each process. Include photographs, flow-charts, or other visuals to present your findings. **[Group Activity]**

For: An additional research activity
Visit: www.PHSchool.com
Web Code: erd-7408

Assessment Resources

The following resources can be used to assess students' knowledge and skills.

Unit 4 Resources
- **Selection Test A,** pp. 148–150
- **Selection Test B,** pp. 151–153

General Resources
- **Rubrics for Response to Literature,** pp. 65–66
- **Rubric for Peer Assessment: Speech,** p. 129

Go Online Assessment: Students may use the **Self-test** to prepare for **Selection Test A** or **Selection Test B.**

3 Writing Lesson

- To guide students in writing this critical review, give them the **Support for Writing Lesson** page (***Unit 4 Resources,*** p. 145).
- Students' critical reviews should contain clear opinions about the story as well as careful, insightful analysis of the story's content, themes, and effect on the reader.
- Remind students that the spring-board for each of their critical reviews is his or her own authentic response to the story. In other words, there is no single "correct" response. Each reader must find the best possible ways to support his or her own view of Harte's work.
- Use the rubrics for Response to Literature, pp. 65–66 in ***General Resources,*** to evaluate students' work.

4 Listening and Speaking

- Encourage students to reread all passages from "The Outcasts of Poker Flat" that contain information about Simson. After they have reviewed Harte's descriptions of the "innocent" and his relationship with Oakhurst, encourage students to write a few sentences that concisely summarize the younger man.
- Point out that eulogies usually contain remarks about the deceased person's positive qualities, as well as anecdotes that illustrate the personality of the individual.
- As they work, remind students to view Mr. Oakhurst through Simson's eyes.
- The **Support for Extend Your Learning** page (**Unit 4 Resources,** p. 146) provides guided note-taking opportunities to help students complete the Extend Your Learning activities.
- Use the rubric for Peer Assessment: Speech, p. 129, ***General Resources,*** to evaluate students' eulogies.

Go Online Research: Have students type in the Web Code for another research activity.

Meeting Your Standards

Students will

1. **analyze and respond to literary elements.**
   - Literary Analysis: Tone
2. **read, comprehend, analyze, and critique nonfiction and a speech.**
   - Reading Strategy: Responding
   - Reading Check questions
   - Apply the Skills questions
   - Assessment Practice (ATE)
3. **develop vocabulary.**
   - Vocabulary Lesson: Latin Term: *terra firma*
4. **understand and apply written and oral language conventions.**
   - Spelling Strategy
   - Grammar and Style Lesson: Sentence Fragments
5. **develop writing proficiency.**
   - Writing Lesson: Position Paper on Development
6. **develop appropriate research strategies.**
   - Extend Your Learning: Marketing Brochure
7. **understand and apply listening and speaking strategies.**
   - Extend Your Learning: Oral Interpretation

Block Scheduling: Use one 90-minute class period to preteach the skills and have students read the selection. Use a second 90-minute class period to assess students' mastery of skills, extend their learning, and monitor their progress.

Homework Suggestions

Following are possibilities for homework assignments.

- Support pages from *Unit 4 Resources:*
  Literary Analysis
  Reading Strategy
  Vocabulary Builder
  Grammar and Style
- An Extend Your Learning project and the Writing Lesson for this selection group may be completed over several days.

Step-by-Step Teaching Guide	Pacing Guide
PRETEACH	
• Administer Vocabulary and Reading Warm-ups as necessary.	5 min.
• Engage students' interest with the motivation activity.	5 min.
• Read and discuss author, and background, features. **FT**	10 min.
• Introduce the Literary Analysis Skill: Tone. **FT**	5 min.
• Introduce the Reading Strategy: Responding. **FT**	10 min.
• Prepare students to read by teaching the selection vocabulary. **FT**	
TEACH	
• Informally monitor comprehension while students read independently or in groups. **FT**	30 min.
• Monitor students' comprehension with the Reading Check notes.	as students read
• Reinforce vocabulary with Vocabulary Builder notes.	as students read
• Develop students' understanding of tone with the Literary Analysis annotations. **FT**	5 min.
• Develop students' ability to respond with the Reading Strategy annotations. **FT**	5 min.
ASSESS/EXTEND	
• Assess students' comprehension and mastery of the Literary Analysis and Reading Strategy by having them answer the Apply the Skills questions. **FT**	15 min.
• Have students complete the Vocabulary Lesson and the Grammar and Style Lesson. **FT**	15 min.
• Apply students' understanding of coherence in writing by using the Writing Lesson. **FT**	45 min. or homework
• Apply students' understanding by using one or more of the Extend Your Learning activities.	20–90 min. or homework
• Administer Selection Test A or Selection Test B. **FT**	15 min.

Resources

PRINT

Unit 4 Resources

TRANSPARENCY

Graphic Organizer Transparencies

PRINT

Reader's Notebook [L2]

Reader's Notebook: Adapted Version [L1]

Reader's Notebook: English Learner's Version [EL]

Unit 4 Resources

TECHNOLOGY

Listening to Literature Audio CDs [L2, EL]

PRINT

Unit 4 Resources

General Resources

TECHNOLOGY

Go Online: Research [**L3**]

Go Online: Self-test [**L3**]

***ExamView®*, Test Bank [L3]**

Choosing Resources for Differentiated Instruction

[**L1**] Special Needs Students

[**L2**] Below-Level Students

[**L3**] All Students

[**L4**] Advanced Students

[**EL**] English Learners

FT Fast Track Instruction: To move the lesson more quickly, use the strategies and activities identified with **FT**.

Scaffolding for Less Proficient and Advanced Students

The leveled Critical Thinking questions after selections progress in the levels of thinking required to answer them. To address the needs of your different students, you may use the (a) level questions for your less proficient students and the (b) level questions with your on-level and advanced students. The occasional (c) level questions are appropriate for your advanced students.

PRENTICE HALL **TeacherEXPRESS™** Plan · Teach · Assess Use this complete suite of powerful teaching tools to make lesson planning and testing quicker and easier.

PRENTICE HALL **StudentEXPRESS™** Learn · Study · Succeed Use the interactive textbook (online and on CD-ROM) to make selections and activities come alive with audio and video support and interactive questions.

PREETEACH

Motivation

Ask students to imagine that they must leave America to relocate elsewhere. Have them form groups to discuss how they will respond. Where will they go? How and with whom will they travel? How will they bid goodbye to friends and family? Then tell students they will read about two people who left home for very different reasons: Miriam Davis Colt's family left their upstate New York home by choice to live in a prairie settlement, while Chief Joseph and his people were forced off their land.

❶ Background

More About the Authors

"The earth is the mother of all people, and all people should have equal rights upon it." Chief Joseph's words express the point of view of Native Americans, who saw themselves as using land but never owning it. Because they were a culture of hunters, the Nez Percé ranged over a vast territory. Settlers like Miriam Davis Colt, however, were farmers, and they had a very different view of the land. They wanted individual plots to cultivate, and they considered the land they settled as their own. These opposing viewpoints were a source of ongoing strife in frontier America.

❶ Build Skills *Primary Source • Speech*

Heading West • I Will Fight No More Forever

Miriam Davis Colt (1815–c.1900)

Miriam Davis Colt was one of a quarter of a million Americans who traveled across the United States in the mid-1800s to forge a new frontier. These pioneers knew they were making history, and hundreds of them kept diaries to send to relatives back east or to pass down to their children.

The Women's Perspective Usually, the pioneer men, filled with a sense of destiny and excitement, made the decision to sell their homes and move their families west. The women's diaries, however, reveal a different point of view. Many women describe their anguish at leaving home, their struggle to maintain some domestic comforts in harsh conditions, and their fear of the dangers ahead.

A Vision of the Future The women, nevertheless, did share their husbands' belief that they were building a better future for their children. The path to that future might be hard, but it was also filled with moments of sudden beauty, like the "crab-apple trees . . . blooming in sheets of whiteness" that Colt saw by the side of a Kansas road as she and her family traveled to a new life in a "city" established by a group of vegetarians. Her family was one of many that invested money to create this new settlement, where they hoped to live with people "whose tastes and habits" would coincide with their own.

The Extending Frontier In 1856, when Colt and her family set out from upstate New York on their journey, they were heading for Kansas. At the time, Kansas was considered the far "West," the destination for many eastern emigrants. It was not until later in the nineteenth century that settlers sought the even farther reaches of California and Oregon, journeys that required the treacherous crossings of the plains and mountains, and presented even more spectacular hardships than those suffered by the Colts.

Chief Joseph (1840–1904)

Chief Joseph was born in the Wallowa Valley in what is now Oregon. In 1871, he succeeded his father as leader of the Nez Percé (nez′ purs′ or pər sā′) tribe. At that time, the United States government was trying to force the tribe to relocate to Idaho. The Nez Percé had signed a treaty in 1863 giving the government control of the tribe's land, but Chief Joseph felt that the treaty was illegal and refused to recognize it.

A Reluctant Warrior In 1877, the dispute between the Nez Percé and the United States government erupted into war. Chief Joseph, hoping to join forces with the Sioux, led his people on a long march through Idaho and Montana, during which the outnumbered Nez Percé frequently clashed with federal troops. Under Chief Joseph's astute and able military leadership, they won several battles.

The Bitter End By the fall, however, the Nez Percé were cold, starving, and scattered. On October 5, after defeat in a battle in the Bear Paw Mountains of Montana, Chief Joseph finally surrendered. The Nez Percé were sent to live in a barren Oklahoma territory. There, many of them became ill and died.

The speech in which Chief Joseph finally accepted defeat contains some of the most achingly sad and beautiful words ever spoken. Because of the attention his words received, Chief Joseph became for many a symbol of the Nez Percé and their tragic plight.

Preview

Connecting to the Literature

Both Chief Joseph and Miriam Davis Colt had to say goodbye to the places they called home. Think about how you would feel if you suddenly had to leave everything that you loved, with no possibility of ever returning.

2 Literary Analysis

Tone

Tone is a quality of language you encounter every day in speech. Two people might say the exact same words, but differences in tone reveal their distinct emotions. In much the same way, a writer's attitude emerges in his or her tone. Consider the optimistic tone in this passage from Colt's diary:

> Full of hope, as we leave the smoking embers of our camp-fire this morning. Expect tonight to arrive at our new home.

The tone of a literary work is established by the writer's choice of descriptions and details. Use a chart like the one shown to interpret the tone of these selections.

Excerpt
No escort is seen! No salute is heard! We move slowly and drippingly into town . . . .

Tone
Angry, even sarcastic

Comparing Literary Works

These selections put a human face on two different aspects of the western expansion of the United States. Fueled by hope, Colt journeyed in search of a new life. In contrast, Chief Joseph lost the battle to save his people and their ancient way of life. These opposing circumstances are reflected in each piece's **mood**—the feeling created in the reader. As you read, compare the conflicts that motivated each writer. Note the circumstances and emotions each experienced, and identify the mood that each evokes.

3 Reading Strategy

Responding

The selections you are about to read describe life-changing events, the kind that are sure to evoke responses that will affect your appreciation of the works. As you read, take time to **respond** to the literature. Note the emotions you feel, and the images each work prompts in your imagination.

Vocabulary Builder

genial (jēn′ yəl) *adj.* promoting life and growth (p. 609)

pervading (pər vād′ iŋ) *adj.* spreading throughout (p. 609)

terra firma (ter′ ə fʉr′ mə) *n.* firm earth; solid ground (Latin) (p. 609)

emigrants (em′ i grəntz) *n.* people who leave one area to move to another (p. 610)

profusion (prō fyōō′ zhən) *n.* abundance; rich supply (p. 610)

depredations (dep′ rə dā′ shənz) *n.* acts of robbing (p. 610)

nonplused (nän′ plüsd′) *adj.* bewildered; perplexed (p. 612)

2 Literary Analysis

Tone

- Explain that an author's choice of details reveals how he or she feels about a subject. As they read "Heading West" and "I Will Fight No More Forever," have students pay special attention to tone.
- Tell students they can determine tone from the way an author describes events and details. A text's historical context can also affect tone.
- Use the instruction for Comparing Literary Works to point out that Miriam Davis Colt and Chief Joseph had very different relationships with land. Have students consider how this might affect the tone of their writings.
- Give students a copy of **Literary Analysis Graphic Organizer A,** p. 124 in ***Graphic Organizer Transparencies,*** to use as they read the selections.

3 Reading Strategy

Responding

- Explain that responding to a text involves carefully considering the emotions you feel as you read.
- To help students appreciate their responses to texts, suggest that they pause after reading powerful passages and write down their responses.

Vocabulary Builder

- Pronounce each vocabulary word for students, and read the definitions as a class. Have students identify any words with which they are already familiar.

Differentiated Instruction

Solutions for All Learners

Support for Special Needs Students
Have students complete the **Preview** and **Build Skills** pages for these selections in the **Reader's Notebook: Adapted Version.** These pages provide a selection summary, an abbreviated presentation of the reading and literary skills, and the graphic organizer on the **Build Skills** page in the student book.

Support for Less Proficient Readers
Have students complete the **Preview** and **Build Skills** pages for these selections in the **Reader's Notebook.** These pages provide a selection summary, an abbreviated presentation of the reading and literary skills, and the graphic organizer on the **Build Skills** page in the student book.

Support for English Learners
Have students complete the **Preview** and **Build Skills** pages for these selections in the **Reader's Notebook: English Learner's Version.** These pages provide a selection summary, an abbreviated presentation of the skills, additional contextual vocabulary, and the graphic organizer on the **Build Skills** page in the student book.

TEACH

Visual/Spatial Learners
Learning Modalities

Have students locate Potsdam and Antwerp on a map of New York State. Suggest that they follow the Colt family's route west by locating the other places the author mentions, such as Kansas City, Westport, and the Little Osage River.

❶ About the Selection

Miriam Davis Colt and her family are among a group of families making the trip to join a commune of vegetarians in the Kansas territory. Her journal entries describe what she saw, felt, and experienced en route and upon arrival.

❷ Critical Viewing

Possible response: Students may say that it is surprising that despite being in the wilderness, the family still eats lunch graciously on a white tablecloth.

❸ Literary Analysis
Tone

- Have students read the entry for January 5th. **Ask** them to pay special attention to the details of the plans that Colt describes.
- **Ask** students the Literary Analysis question: What is the tone of this description of Colt's experiences on January 5th?
  Possible response: Students should recognize the hopeful, optimistic tone of this passage. They may guess that the author is trying to convince herself of the strengths of her family's plans.

❶ HEADING WEST

Miriam Davis Colt

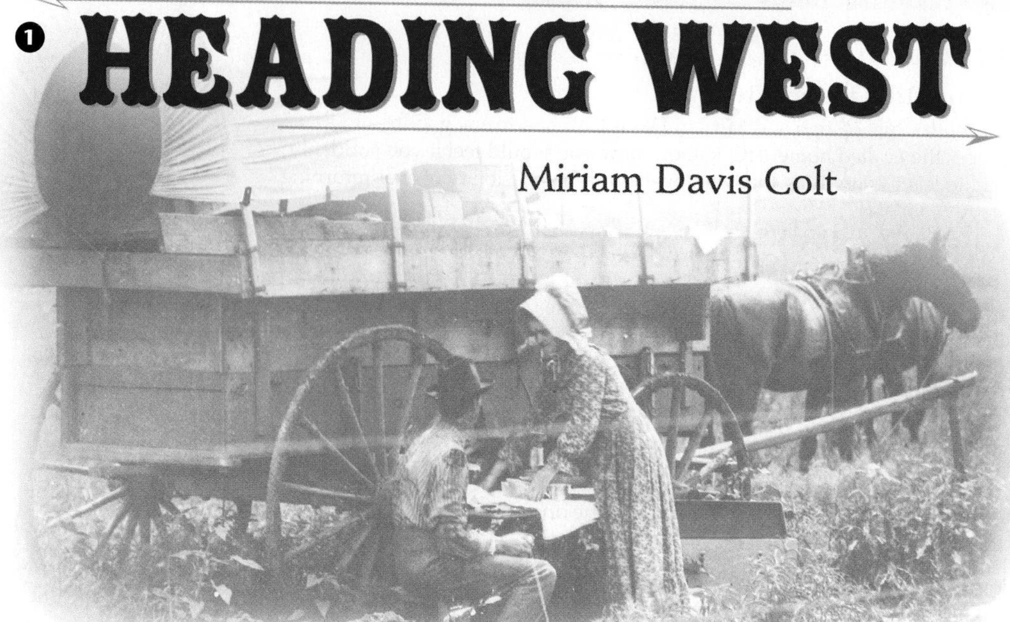

Emigrants stopping to lunch on a white tablecloth in

❷ **▲ Critical Viewing** Which details in this photograph of pioneers stopping for lunch seem surprising or out of place? **[Analyze]**

Background Most of the settlers of the American West, like Miriam Davis Colt and her family, were farmers who sought a better life for themselves and their children. A better life meant fertile land that they could own, cultivate, and pass on to their children. For Native Americans, however, the land was a gift that belonged to no one individual. "The earth is the mother of all people, and all people should have equal rights upon it," Chief Joseph once said. These opposing views were a source of ongoing strife in frontier America.

❸ **JANUARY 5TH, 1856.** We are going to Kansas. The Vegetarian Company that has been forming for many months, has finally organized, formed its constitution, elected its directors, and is making all necessary preparations for the spring settlement. . . . We can have, I think, good faith to believe, that our directors will fulfill on their part; and we, as settlers of a new country, by going in a company will escape the hardships attendant on families going in singly, and at once find ourselves surrounded by improving society in a young and flourishing city. It will be better for ourselves pecuniarily,[1] and better in the future for our children.

Literary Analysis
Tone What is the tone of this description of Colt's experiences on January 5?

1. **pecuniarily** (pi kyōō′ nē er′ i lē) *adv.* financially.

Differentiated Instruction Solutions for All Learners

Accessibility at a Glance

	Heading West	I Will Fight No More Forever
Context	Journal entries	Famous speech
Language	Vocabulary footnotes	Short sentences
Concept Level	Accessible (frontier)	Accessible (Native Amer.)
Literary Merit	Historical	Historical
Lexile	1200	360
Overall Rating	More accessible	More accessible

My husband has long been a practical vegetarian, and we expect much from living in such a genial clime, where fruit is so quickly grown, and with people whose tastes and habits will coincide with our own.

JANUARY 15TH. We are making every necessary preparation for our journey, and our home in Kansas. My husband has sold his farm, purchased shares in the company, sent his money as directed by H.S. Clubb . . . . I am very busy in repairing all of our clothing, looking over bags of pieces, tearing off and reducing down, bringing everything into as small a compass as possible, so that we shall have no unnecessary baggage.

APRIL 15TH. Have been here in West Stockholm, at my brother's, since Friday last. Have visited Mother very hard, for, in all probability, it is the last visit we shall have until we meet where parting never comes—believe we have said everything we can think of to say.

APRIL 16TH. Antwerp, N.Y. Bade our friends good bye, in Potsdam, this morning, at the early hour of two o'clock.

APRIL 22ND. Have been on the cars[2] again since yesterday morning. Last night was a lovely moonlit night, a night of thought, as we sped almost with lightning speed, along in the moonlight, past the rail fences.

Found ourselves in this miserable hotel before we knew it. Miserable fare—herring boiled with cabbage—miserable, dirty beds, and an odor pervading the house that is not at all agreeable. Mistress gone.

APRIL 23RD. On board steamer "Cataract," bound for Kansas City.

APRIL 24TH. A hot summer day. The men in our company are out in the city, purchasing wagons and farming implements, to take along on the steamer up to Kansas City.

APRIL 28TH. The steamer struck a "snag" last night; gave us a terrible jar; tore off a part of the kitchen; ladies much frightened. Willie is not very well; the water is bad; it affects all strangers.

APRIL 30TH. Here we are, at Kansas City, all safely again on terra firma. Hasten to the hotel—find it very much crowded. Go up, up, up, and upstairs to our lodging rooms.

MAY 1ST. Take a walk out onto the levee—view the city, and see that it takes but a few buildings in this western world to make a city. The houses and shops stand along on the levee, extending back into the hillsides. The narrow street is literally filled with huge merchandise wagons bound for Santa Fe. The power attached to these wagons

2. **cars** train cars.

Vocabulary Builder
genial (jēn′ yəl) *adj.* promoting life and growth

Reading Strategy
Responding How would you feel if you were allowed to keep only a few items out of all the things you own?

Vocabulary Builder
pervading (pər vād iŋ) *adj.* spreading throughout

Vocabulary Builder
terra firma (ter′ ə fur′ mə) *n.* firm earth; solid ground (Latin)

6 **Reading Check**
Why do the Colts decide to travel to Kansas?

4 Reading Strategy
Responding

- Have students read the entry for January 15th. **Ask** students what possessions they think the Colt family might have brought with them.
  Possible response: Students may think the Colts brought only necessities—clothing, tools, supplies—and left behind anything unnecessary.
- Then, **ask** students the Reading Strategy question: How would they feel if they were allowed to keep only a few of the things they own?
  Possible response: Students may feel strong attachments to their possessions and be daunted by the prospect of choosing only a few items to keep.
- Encourage students to apply their responses by imagining how Colt felt about leaving behind most of the things her family owned.

5 Vocabulary Builder
The Latin Term *terra firma*

- Call students' attention to the phrase *terra firma* and its definition: "firm earth" or "solid ground."
- Explain to students that Latin phrases such as *terra firma* are often used in literature. They can often find the definitions of such Latin phrases in the dictionary.
- **Ask** students what tone Miriam Davis Colt creates by using the phrase *terra firma.*
  Possible response: The phrase creates a relieved tone; Colt was very happy to be off of the steamboat.

6 Reading Check

Answer: The Colts have decided to move to Kansas in order to live in a commune organized by the Vegetarian Company, where they expect to improve their lives and their children's futures.

Differentiated Instruction
Solutions for All Learners

Strategy for Less Proficient Readers
Have these students list the events of Colt's trip thus far and construct a chain-of-events chart. This strategy can help students comprehend the events related in "Heading West."

Support for English Learners
The many sentence fragments in "Heading West" may confuse students. Help them to identify the missing subjects or verbs. You may guide them to restate the fragments as complete sentences. The description of the hotel in the April 22nd entry, is an example of sentence fragments.

Strategy for Advanced Readers
Encourage students to compare and contrast Miriam Davis Colt's journal entries with any others they have read. Also, guide them to look for the ways in which the entries written by women are different from and similar to those written by men.

❼ Literary Analysis
Tone

- Have students copy the bracketed passage in the *Passage* circle. **Ask** them to explain what Colt is writing about.
  Answer: On her eleventh wedding anniversary, Colt is looking back on her past and worrying about her future.
- **Ask** students the Literary Analysis question: What is Colt's tone as she looks back on her life? Have them write their answers in the **Literary Analysis Graphic Organizer A.**
  Possible response: Colt writes fondly of the years of her marriage. But as she thinks of the future her tone becomes anxious and uncertain.

❽ Critical Thinking
Compare and Contrast

- **Ask** students to consider what it would be like to travel long distances in a wagon drawn by oxen.
- Read aloud the bracketed passage. **Ask** students: What are some of the difficulties nineteenth-century pioneer travelers faced that made traveling more difficult than today?
  Possible Response: The pioneers had to depend upon oxen and other animals for power. Such animals had to be fed and cared for. Wagons traveled slowly and often needed repairs. Roads in some areas were little more than dirt trails.

is seven or eight and sometimes nine pair of long-eared mules, or as many pair of oxen, with a Mexican driver who wields a whip long enough to reach the foremost pair, and who does not hesitate to use it with severity, and a noise, too.

Large droves of cattle are driven into town to be sold to emigrants, who like us, are going into the Territory. Our husbands are all out today buying oxen, provisions and cooking utensils for our ox-wagon journey into the Territory.

❼ This is the anniversary of my wedding-day, and as I review the past pleasant years as they have passed, one after another, until they now number eleven, a shadow comes over me, as I try to look away into the future and ask, "What is my destiny?"

Ah! away with all these shadowings. We shall be very busy this year in making our home comfortable, so that no time can be spared for that dreaded disease, "home—sickness," to take hold of us, and we mean to obey physical laws,[3] thereby securing to ourselves strength of body and vigor of mind.

MAY 2ND. A lovely day. Our husbands are loading the ox-wagons. . . . Women and children walk along up the hill out of this "Great City," wait under a tree—what a beautiful country is spread out before us! Will our Kansas scenery equal this . . .?

❽ One mile from the city, and Dr. Thorn has broke his wagon tongue;[4] it must be sent back to Kansas City to be mended. Fires kindled—women cooking—supper eaten sitting round on logs, stones and wagon tongues. This I am sure is a "pic-nic." We expect "pic-nic" now all the time. We are shaded by the horse-chestnut, sweet walnut, and spreading oak; flowers blooming at our feet, and grasshoppers in profusion hopping in every direction. This is summer time.

MAY 3RD. The women and children, who slept in their wagons last night, got a good drenching from the heavy shower. It was fortunate for mother, sister, myself and children, that lodgings were found for us in a house. My husband said not a rain drop found him; he had the whole wagon to himself, besides all of our Indian blankets. Father, it seems, fell back a little and found a place to camp in a tavern (not a hotel), where he fell in with the scores of Georgians who loaded a steamer and came up the river the same time that we did. He said he had to be very shrewd indeed not to have them find out that he was a "Free States"[5] man. These Bandits have been sent in here, and will commit all sorts of depredations on the Free State settlers, and no doubt commit many a bloody murder.

Have passed Westport, the foothold for Border-Ruffianism. The town looks new, but the hue is dingy. Our drivers used their goads

Vocabulary Builder
emigrants (em′ i grənts) *n.* people who leave one area to move to another

Literary Analysis
Tone What is Colt's tone as she looks back on her life?

Vocabulary Builder
profusion (prō fyo͞o′ zhən) *n.* abundance; rich supply

Vocabulary Builder
depredations (dep′ rə dā′ shənz) *n.* acts of robbing

3. **physical laws** community's by-laws that dictated members abstain from alcohol and meat.
4. **wagon tongue** harnessing pole attached to the front axle of a horse-drawn vehicle.
5. **"Free States"** Free Soil movement; a group whose goal was to keep slavery out of the western territories.

Enrichment
Troubles on the Western Frontier

When students think of a pioneer excursion westward, they may imagine a long and treacherous one across the heartland, the plains, and the mountains to reach California or Oregon. Remind students that in 1856, Kansas was the western frontier. The then territories of Kansas, Nebraska, and the Dakotas often were final destinations for intrepid settlers in search of the frontier.

According to the Kansas-Nebraska Act of 1854, settlers in these two territories were to determine for themselves whether the territories would be slave or free territories. Hostilities between bands of pro-slavery and anti-slavery settlers erupted. Pro-slavery southerners known as "border ruffians" sacked the anti-slavery town of Lawrence, Kansas. In response, John Brown and his sons slaughtered five pro-slavery settlers along Pottawatomie Creek. The violence in "bleeding Kansas" continued into 1861. Miriam Davis Colt's family entered Kansas during this time of bloodshed and chaos.

to hurry up the oxen's heavy tread, for we felt somewhat afraid, for we learned the Georgians had centered here. Here, too, came in the Santa Fe and Indian trade—so here may be seen the huge Mexican wagon, stubborn mule, swarthy driver with his goad-like whip, and the red man of the prairie on his fleet Indian pony, laden with dried meat, furs, and buffalo robes.

"What! fast in the mud, and with our wagon tongue broke?" "Why yes, to be sure." So a long time is spent before my husband and Dr. House can put our vehicle in moving order again. Meanwhile, we women folks and children must sit quietly in the wagon to keep out of the rain—lunch on soda biscuit, look at the deep, black mud in which our wagon is set, and inhale the sweet odor that comes from the blossoms of the crab-apple trees that are blooming in sheets of whiteness along the roadside. . . .

MAY 6TH. Dined on the prairie, and gathered flowers, while our tired beasts filled themselves with the fresh, green grass. . . . Have driven 18 miles to-day . . . so here we are, all huddled into this little house 12 by 16—cook supper over the fire . . . fill the one bed lengthwise and crosswise; the family of the house take to the trundle-bed,[6] while the floor is covered . . . with men, women and children, rolled in Indian blankets like silk worms in cocoons.

MAY 11TH. "Made" but a few miles yesterday. Forded the Little Osage; the last river, they say, we have to ford . . . our "noble lords" complained of the great weight of the wagons. . . . That our wagon is heavily loaded, have only to make a minute of what we have stowed away in it—eight trunks, one valise, three carpet bags, a box of soda crackers, 200 lbs. flour, 100 lbs. corn meal, a few lbs. of sugar, rice, dried apple, one washtub of little trees, utensils for cooking, and two provision boxes—say nothing of mother, a good fat sister, self, and two children, who ride through the rivers. . . .

At nightfall came to a log-cabin at the edge of the wood, and inquired of the "Lord of the Castle" if some of the women and children could take shelter under his roof for the night; the masculine number and whichever of the women that chose, couching in the wagons and under them. He said we could. His lady, who was away, presently came, with bare feet, and a white sack twisted up and thrown over her shoulder, with a few quarts of corn meal in the end that hung down her back. I said to myself—"Is that what I have got to come to?" She seemed pleased to have company—allowed us the first chance of the broad, Dutch-backed fireplace with its earthy hearth, and without pot hooks or trammels,[7] to make ready our simple evening repast. . . . 11

6. **trundle-bed** low, portable bed that can be stored beneath a larger bed.
7. **trammels** (tram′ əlz) *n.* devices for hanging several pothooks in a fireplace.

10 ***Moving West***

The search for "greener pastures" has been a constant factor in our nation's history. The phrase "The Great Migration" describes a steady westward shift of the American population. It includes the westward movement of the Puritans from Europe to the New World in the 1630s, of the coastal colonists to inland farms and towns, and of pioneer families headed west over the plains and prairies throughout the nineteenth century. Transience was fundamental to pioneer life, as "movers" continually searched for the next open space. Of course, some pioneers—the "stickers"—had strong urges to put down roots and develop communities. The Great American Migration blends tales of how both the movers and the stickers endured physical, financial, political, and spiritual challenges in hopes of establishing better lives for themselves and for their families.

Connect to the Literature

The Colts were heading to Kansas to join a vegetarian community. Do you think they will find "greener pastures"?

Reading Check

What methods of travel do the Colts use in their journey?

Differentiated Instruction Solutions for All Learners

Support for Special Needs Students
These students may have difficulty reading Miriam Davis Colt's diary entries because of their relatively informal nature. To help them, have them read the selection along with **Listening to Literature Audio CD.** Make sure students pay equal attention to the text and to the recorded selection.

Strategy for Advanced Readers
Discuss the style that Miriam Colt uses in her diary. This is a first-person narrative, arranged chronologically, and it contains sentence fragments as well as complete sentences. Students should also notice that Colt's writing style changes, from providing facts to describing her surroundings to personal reflections. Have students identify these elements in Colt's writings and in other journals they have read.

9 Reading Strategy
Responding

- Have students read the bracketed passage. **Ask** them how Miriam Davis Colt tries to put a positive spin on this latest disaster.
  Answer: She focuses on the sweetness of the crabapple blossoms.
- **Ask** students how they think they themselves would cope under such trying circumstances.
  Possible Response: Students may hope that they would have Miriam Davis Colt's patience, but many will admit that they would be angry and frustrated.

Monitor Progress: Ask students to write descriptive paragraphs about what traveling in Colt's day would have been like.

Answer: Student paragraphs should respond on a personal level to the details in Colt's diary.

10 The American Experience

Moving West *Manifest Destiny* was a phrase used by politicians and leaders to explain territorial expansion of U.S. boundaries westward to the Pacific Ocean. The idea of Manifest Destiny encompassed the belief that it was the mission of the United States not only to extend its borders territorially, but to spread the democratic ideals upon which the nation was built.

Practically, Manifest Destiny allowed for individuals and families to seek new opportunities on the frontier. Land was cheap and natural resources were plentiful. Politically, it allowed the government the necessary justification needed to claim new territories.

Connect to the Literature
Encourage students to utilize knowledge from history classes to answer this question.
Possible response: The Colts' new life will be disappointing. They probably will find many hardships. Despite the troubles they will face, however, they will successfully cultivate a garden for their new home.

11 Reading Check

Answer: The Colts travel by train, by steamboat, and by ox-wagon.

12 Literary Analysis
Tone and Mood

- Have students read the bracketed passage. **Ask** them to pay special attention to the details of the Colts' final approach to their new home.

Monitor Progress: Ask students the Literary Analysis question: What contrasting moods does Colt seem to feel as the settlers near their new home?
Possible Response: Students should notice that the heavy rain creates a somber mood. Despite the rain, the ordeals of the journey, and the many disappointments, Colt's mood is optimistic—she still has great hopes for her new home.

13 Critical Viewing

Possible Response: Students may conclude that in these frontier towns, travelers such as the Colts might get to sleep under a roof, or join groups heading back east. They could get supplies and medical help, get their wagons fixed, and learn what they would face in the miles ahead.

Are now [May 11th] crossing the 20 mile prairie, no roads—Think Mrs. Voorhees will get walking enough crossing this prairie. She is quite a pedestrian, surely, for she has walked every bit of the way in, so far, from Kansas City, almost 100 miles.

Arrive at Elm Creek—no house to lodge in tonight—campfire kindled—supper cooked, and partaken of with a keen relish, sitting in family groups around the "great big" fire. Some will sleep in wagons, others under the canopy of the blue vault of Heaven. The young men have built some shady little bowers of the green boughs; they are looking very cosily under them, wrapped in their white Indian blankets.

We ladies, or rather, "emigrant women," are having a chat around the camp-fire—the bright stars are looking down upon us—we wonder if we shall be neighbors to each other in the great "Octagon City. . . ."

12 **MAY 12TH.** Full of hope, as we leave the smoking embers of our camp-fire this morning. Expect tonight to arrive at our new home.

It begins to rain, rain, rain, like a shower; we move slowly on, from high prairie, around the deep ravine—are in sight of the timber that skirts the Neosho river. Have sent three men in advance to announce our coming; are looking for our Secretary, (Henry S. Clubb) with an escort to welcome us into the embryo city. If the booming of cannon is not heard at our approach, shall expect a salute from the firing of Sharp's rifles, certainly.

No escort is seen! no salute is heard! We move slowly and drippingly into town just at nightfall—feeling not a little nonplused on learning that our worthy, or unworthy Secretary was out walking in the rain with his *dear* wife. We leave our wagons and make our way to the large camp-fire. It is surrounded by men and women cooking their suppers—while others are busy close by, grinding their hominy[8] in hand mills.

8. **hominy** (häm′ ə nē) *n.* dry corn, usually ground and boiled for food.

Literary Analysis
Tone and Mood What contrasting moods does Colt seem to feel as the settlers near their new home?

Vocabulary Builder
nonplused (nän′ plüsd′) *adj.* bewildered; perplexed

13 ▼Critical Viewing
This 1866 photograph shows covered wagons on Main Street in Ottawa, Kansas. What does Colt's diary suggest about the importance of towns like this one to the wagon trains of settlers traveling westward? **[Draw Conclusions]**

Covered wagons on Main Street in Ottawa, Kansas, 1866, Kansas State Historical Society

DRUGS

Differentiated Instruction
Solutions for All Learners

Support for Less Proficient Readers
If students are having difficulty understanding what is happening to the Colt family towards the end of Miriam Davis Colt's journal, have them pair up with more advanced readers to help them draw conclusions based on the tone in the selection.

Enrichment for Gifted/Talented Students
Ask students to consider what might happen to Miriam Davis Colt and her family after May 13, 1856. Would the family remain at the settlement, despite their disappointment? Would they begin to build a home? Would they move on to parts further west? Have students write a new final entry for Miriam Colt's journal. They can present their entries to the class.

Look around, and see the grounds all around the camp-fire are covered with tents, in which the families are staying. Not a house is to be seen. In the large tent here is a cook stove—they have supper prepared for us; it consists of hominy, soft Johnny cake (or corn bread, as it is called here), stewed apple, and tea. We eat what is set before us, "asking no questions for conscience' sake."

The ladies tell us they are sorry to see us come to this place; which shows us that all is not right. Are too weary to question, but with hope depressed go to our lodgings, which we find around in the tents, and in our wagons.

MAY 13TH. Can anyone imagine our disappointment this morning, on learning from this and that member, that no mills have been built; that the directors, after receiving our money to build mills, have not fulfilled the trust reposed in them, and that in consequence, some families have already left the settlement . . .?

As it is, we find the families, some living in tents of cloth, some of cloth and green bark just peeled from the trees, and some wholly of green barn, stuck up on the damp ground, without floors or fires. Only two stoves in the company. . . .

We see that the city grounds, which have been surveyed . . . contain only one log cabin, 16 by 16, muddled between the logs on the inside, instead of on the outside; neither door nor window; the roof covered with "shakes" (western shingles), split out of oak I should think, 3½ feet in length, and about as wide as a sheet of fools cap paper.[9]

Reading Strategy
Responding Do you share the surprise and disappointment Colt describes when she arrives at her new home? Explain.

9. **fools cap paper** writing paper usually measuring 13 by 16 inches.

Critical Reading

1. **Respond:** Would you have had the courage and determination to leave your home and family to become a pioneer? Explain.
2. **(a) Recall:** What financial arrangements did the Colts make as part of their preparations for heading west? **(b) Evaluate:** Do you think they were too naive and trusting? Explain.
3. **(a) Recall:** What is the appearance of the settler woman whom Colt describes meeting in her entry of May 11? **(b) Analyze:** What does this settler woman suggest to Colt about her own future?
4. **Compare and Contrast:** How do Colt's expectations about life at Octagon City compare with reality?
5. **Synthesize:** Based on Colt's experiences, explain which character traits you feel were necessary to being a successful pioneer.

For: More about Miriam Davis Colt
Visit: www.PHSchool.com
Web Code: ere-9415

Go Online Author Link For additional information about Miriam Davis Colt, have students type in the Web Code, then select C from the alphabet, and then Miriam Davis Colt.

14 Reading Strategy
Responding

- Have students read the bracketed passage. Then, tell them to pause and consider Colt's reaction to what she sees.
- **Ask** students to describe Colt's reaction to the settlement.
  Possible Response: Students should recognize that Colt is very disappointed by the lack of buildings and the poor quality of the food.
- **Ask** students the Reading Strategy question: Do you share the surprise and disappointment Colt describes when she arrives at her new home? Explain.
  Possible Response: Students may note that the dismal conditions are consistent with the conditions of the journey; therefore, however disappointing, they should have come as no surprise.

ASSESS
Answers

1. **Possible Response:** Students should discuss the requirements of pioneer life.
2. (a) Colt's husband sold their farm, invested in the Vegetarian Company, and sent money for the settlement at a company director's direction.
   (b) **Possible Response:** Being aware that the directors failed to fill their obligations, most students will think that the Colts were too naïve and trusting.
3. (a) The woman has bare feet and carries a white sack of corn meal slung over her shoulder.
   (b) Colt fears that she will become just as unkempt.
4. Colt expected a better life for herself and her family; the reality is very disappointing.
5. **Possible Response:** Successful pioneers had to be courageous, flexible, adaptable, and dedicated, even in the face of enormous disappointment.

⓯ About the Selection

In this speech, a weary and demoralized Chief Joseph, speaking for a people in desperate straits, decides to stop his losing fight with the pursuing United States Army.

ASSESS

Answers

1. **Possible response:** Students should describe in terms of their own experience the difference between knowing something intellectually and knowing something emotionally or intuitively.
2. (a) The other chiefs have been killed. (b) The young men have been left to carry on the fight. (c) **Possible response:** He directs part of his speech to the chiefs because he needs to explain his surrender to them.
3. (a) He is tired of fighting, the chiefs have been killed, and his people are cold and hungry. (b) **Possible response:** Many students will feel that the stark and spare details of the speech are deeply moving and thus effective.
4. (a) He wants to find his children, some of whom may be dead. (b) He is like a father to his people; he cannot bear to see them suffering and dying.
5. His purpose was to build awareness of his people's plight.
6. **Possible response:** Some students may say that surrendering was the only choice Chief Joseph had because it was winter, his people were starving and defeat was certain.

⓯ I Will Fight No More Forever

Chief Joseph

Tell General Howard I know his heart. What he told me before, I have in my heart. I am tired of fighting. Our chiefs are killed. Looking Glass is dead. Toohoolhoolzote is dead. The old men are all dead. It is the young men who say yes and no. He who led on the young men is dead. It is cold and we have no blankets. The little children are freezing to death. My people, some of them, have run away to the hills and have no blankets, no food; no one knows where they are—perhaps freezing to death. I want to have time to look for my children and see how many I can find. Maybe I shall find them among the dead. Hear me, my chiefs. I am tired; my heart is sick and sad. From where the sun now stands I will fight no more forever.

Critical Reading

1. **Respond:** Chief Joseph says that he knows his enemy's heart. Have you ever felt that you knew something with your heart rather than with your head? What is the difference?
2. **(a) Recall:** What has happened to the other Nez Percé chiefs? **(b) Infer:** Who has been left to carry on the fight? **(c) Speculate:** Why do you think Chief Joseph directs part of his speech to his chiefs?
3. **(a) Recall:** What reasons does Chief Joseph give for his surrender? **(b) Evaluate:** Would Chief Joseph's speech have been more or less effective had it contained more detailed explanations of his reasons for surrender? Explain.
4. **(a) Recall:** What does Chief Joseph want to do now that the battle is lost? **(b) Infer:** Based on this speech, how would you describe Chief Joseph's relationship to his people? Explain.
5. **Synthesize:** Although Chief Joseph delivered his speech to confirm his tribe's surrender, the speech had another, equally important purpose. What was that purpose?
6. **Take a Position:** Do you think surrender was the right choice? Why or why not?

Go Online
Author Link
For: More about Chief Joseph
Visit: www.PHSchool.com
Web Code: ere-9416

Go Online Author Link For additional information about Chief Joseph, have students type in the Web Code, then select *J* from the alphabet, and then select Chief Joseph.

Apply the Skills

Heading West* • *I Will Fight No More Forever

Literary Analysis

Tone

1. Find two examples of an upbeat, positive **tone** in Miriam Davis Colt's diary.
2. Find two examples of a negative, downcast tone in Colt's diary.
3. A military leader might adopt many tones when admitting defeat. **(a)** What is the overall tone of Chief Joseph's surrender? **(b)** What details contribute to this tone?

Comparing Literary Works

4. Chief Joseph's speech generates a single **mood,** while Colt's journal entries inspire varying moods. Identify a passage in Colt's work that most closely echoes the mood of Chief Joseph's speech.
5. Both Colt and Chief Joseph face struggles and disappointments as they work for what they feel is right, yet their conflicts differ greatly. Identify the conflict each writer faces. Then, compare and contrast these conflicts.
6. Using a Venn diagram like the one shown, compare the future Chief Joseph faces with the one Colt faces. **(a)** How are their hopes for the future different? **(b)** How are their hopes similar?

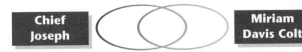

Reading Strategy

Responding

7. **(a)** Cite a passage from Colt's journal that affected you strongly, and describe your **response. (b)** Cite a passage from Chief's Joseph's speech that affected you deeply, and describe your response.
8. Did the way in which you responded to each of these selections affect your appreciation of it? Explain.

Extend Understanding

9. **Social Studies Connection:** Moving west was a risky and difficult endeavor for pioneers. Why were so many of them willing to emigrate west despite the dangers?

QuickReview

Tone is a writer's attitude toward his or her subject.

Mood, or atmosphere, is the feeling created in the reader by a literary work or passage.

To **respond** to literature, recognize your personal reactions to the work and notice how the writing affects you.

For: Self-test
Visit: www.PHSchool.com
Web Code: era-6409

Answers

1. **Possible response:** Examples include Colt's first entry, describing her family's goals and the May 2 description of the "pic-nic."
2. **Possible response:** Examples include her April 22 description of the "miserable hotel," and her subdued reaction when she actually arrives in "Octagon City."
3. (a) The overall tone of Chief Joseph's surrender is one of weary resignation to his fate. (b) He describes his own exhaustion and his people's desperate plight, and conveys his understanding of the enemy's position.
4. **Possible response:** The dark and disappointed mood of Colt's descriptions of the "Octagon City" settlement closely echoes the mood of Chief Joseph's speech.
5. **Possible response:** Both Colt and Chief Joseph face overwhelming disappointment. Colt's struggles are undertaken voluntarily in the hopes of a better life, however, while Chief Joseph has lost his final struggle and is resigned to his fate.
6. **Possible response:**

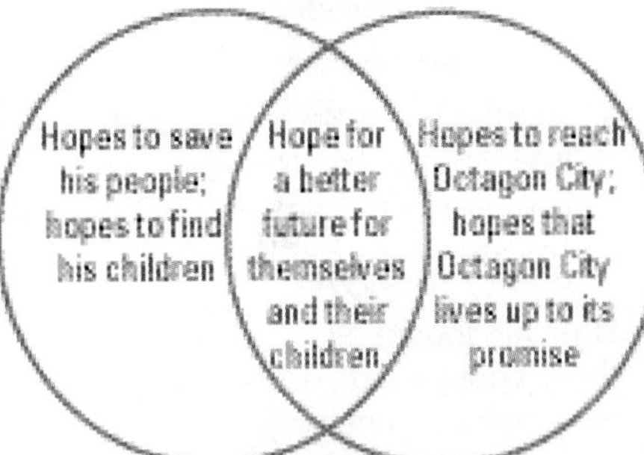

7. (a) **Possible response:** Students may cite Colt's May 11 description of an encounter with a settler woman, which could make students wonder about their own futures.
(b) **Possible response:** Students may cite a personal response to his description of his people and their children freezing without blankets.
8. **Possible response:** Students' appreciation of the selections may have increased when they were able to form personal responses and connect to the authors.

Answers continued

9. **Possible response:** People moved west in search of free land, opportunities, and a better life.

Go Online Assessment Students may use the **Self-test** to prepare for **Selection Test A** or **Selection Test B.**

EXTEND/ASSESS

Answers

1 Vocabulary Lesson

Word Analysis

1. **Possible response:** After their voyage, the Pilgrims were glad to be on *terra firma.*
2. **Possible response:** The balloon's basket jolted violently as it struck *terra firma.*

Spelling Strategy

1. bragged
2. stopped
3. flitted

Vocabulary Builder

1. emigrants
2. depredations
3. genial
4. pervading
5. profusion
6. nonplused
7. Ah, *terra firma!*

2 Grammar and Style Lesson

1. fragment; sample sentence: It was a hot summer day.
2. fragment; sample sentence: I have been here in West Stockholm, at my brother's, since Friday last.
3. fragment; sample sentence: We hasten to the hotel and find it very much crowded.
4. complete sentence
5. fragment; sample sentence: That evening, we dined on the prairie and gathered flowers.

Looking at Style

Students should recognize that Colt's short, choppy style evokes her demanding journey.

WG **Writing and Grammar, Ruby Level**

Students will find further instruction and practice on sentence fragments in Chapter 20, Section 4.

Build Language Skills

1 Vocabulary Lesson

Word Analysis: Latin Term *terra firma*

Miriam Davis Colt uses the Latin term *terra firma,* which means "firm earth" or "solid ground." If you encounter an unfamiliar Latin word or phrase when reading, you can often find its meaning in a dictionary.

Follow the directions for each item below by writing sentences including the term *terra firma.*

1. Describe the Pilgrims landing on Plymouth Rock after months at sea in a tiny boat.
2. Describe a hot-air balloon safely touching down after a rough flight.

Spelling Strategy

When adding *-ed* to a one-syllable word that ends in a single consonant preceded by a vowel, double the final consonant. For example, *rub* becomes *rubbed.* Add *-ed* to each of the following words.

1. brag **2.** stop **3.** flit

Vocabulary Builder: Word Choice

Select the word from the vocabulary list on page 607 that best describes or relates to each description below.

1. People who left America to live in another country
2. Acts committed by hostile invading troops against civilians
3. The personality of a pleasant host
4. The scents in a perfume shop
5. A buffet of more than fifty sumptuous and inviting desserts
6. An auto mechanic perplexed by a car he cannot fix despite six days of problem solving
7. A phrase said when stepping off a roller coaster

2 Grammar and Style Lesson

Sentence Fragments

Sentence fragments are incomplete sentences that may lack either a subject or a verb.

Although they may lend a sense of urgency to a piece of writing, sentence fragments are not acceptable in formal English.

Fragment: "Made" but a few miles yesterday. (*no subject*)

Fragment: Even if we traveled for five more days. (*not a complete thought*)

Practice Identify which of the following sentences are incomplete. Then, rewrite each sentence fragment as a complete sentence.

1. A hot summer day.
2. Have been here in West Stockholm, at my brother's, since Friday last.
3. Hasten to the hotel—find it very much crowded.
4. We are going to Kansas.
5. Dined on the prairie and gathered flowers.

Looking at Style Write an evaluation in which you explain how Colt's use of sentence fragments affects your understanding of her experiences.

WG *Prentice Hall Writing and Grammar Connection: Chapter 20, Section 4*

Assessment Practice

Context **(For more practice, see *Standardized Test Preparation Workbook,* p.34.)**

The reading sections of many tests require students to use context clues such as definitions and explanations to determine the meanings of unfamiliar words and phrases. Write the following passage from p. 601 on the chalkboard. Then use the following exercise to help them use context clues to identify the correct definition.

In the large tent here is a cook stove—they have supper prepared for us; it consists of hominy, soft Johnny cake (or corn bread, as it is called here), stewed apple, and tea.

According to information found in this passage, what is "Johnny cake"?

A apple cake
B corn bread
C hominy
D tea cake

B is the correct answer, because it contains the explanation found in the parenthetical phrase: "Johnny cake (or corn bread, as it is called here)."

Writing Lesson

Timed Writing: Position Paper on Development

The vast stretches of land where both Chief Joseph and Miriam Davis Colt lived have almost disappeared. Imagine that you live in a town where the last open piece of land is about to be turned into a mall. Support or oppose the development in a position paper—a formal piece of writing that argues one side of a controversial issue. ***(40 minutes)***

Prewriting *(10 minutes)* List the reasons you support or oppose the project, along with facts to back up your reasons.

Drafting *(20 minutes)* Start with a clear statement of your position. Provide reasons and specific details to support your case. End with a persuasive conclusion.

Revising *(10 minutes)* Make sure your argument flows smoothly from one paragraph to the next. Check this coherence by highlighting and evaluating the transitions you have used.

Model: Revising for Coherence

The mall will not create jobs, as some believe. Instead of new jobs, we will get traffic and pollution. ^In addition, ^The mall will steal business from locally owned shops.

Using transition words and phrases builds coherence in a piece of writing.

WG *Prentice Hall Writing and Grammar Connection: Chapter 7, Section 4*

Extend Your Learning

Listening and Speaking Chief Joseph's speech so moved the officers who heard it that they were unable to speak. Recite the speech for the class in an **oral interpretation.** Use these tips to prepare:

- Identify the tone of Chief Joseph's voice as he gave his speech.
- Think about his posture and bearing—how he held his body.

Visualize Chief Joseph as you re-create his speech. Then, ask classmates to evaluate your presentation. **[Group Activity]**

Research and Technology The history of the West is full of stories like that of the Colts, who sought an ideal—or utopian—way of life. Using a variety of resources, research these communities and their effect on the development of the American frontier. Then, produce a **marketing brochure** to draw new settlers to such a community.

For: An additional research activity
Visit: www.PHSchool.com
Web Code: erd-7409

Assessment Resources

The following resources can be used to assess students' knowledge and skills.

Unit 4 Resources
- **Selection Test A,** pp. 165–167
- **Selection Test B,** pp. 168–170

General Resources
- **Rubrics for Persuasion: Persuasive Essay,** pp. 45–46
- **Rubric for Peer Assessment: Oral Interpretation,** p. 130

Go Online Assessment — Students may use the **Self-test** to prepare for **Selection Test A** or **Selection Test B.**

3 Writing Lesson

You may use this Writing Lesson as timed-writing practice, or you may allow students to develop the essay as a writing assignment over several days.

- To guide students in writing this position paper, give them the **Support for Writing Lesson** page (***Unit 4 Resources,*** p. 162).
- Remind students that a position paper must persuade readers by stating its position as clearly as possible and supporting that position with compelling details.
- Urge students to write coherently by choosing an organizational method (for example, chronological order, comparison and contrast, or cause and effect) and using it consistently; using specific rather than vague terminology; and by repeating words to emphasize important points.
- Use the rubrics for Persuasion: Persuasive Essay, pp. 45–46 in **General Resources,** to evaluate students' work.

4 Listening and Speaking

- Remind students that to recite a speech is not just to say the words aloud but to say them with feeling and with regard for the audience.
- Have groups of students find out more about the tragic experience of the Nez Percé. Groups can discuss how to best capture Chief Joseph's passion and resignation, and select a member to deliver the speech.
- Have one member of a group introduce the speech by providing background information on the Nez Percé. Then, have the speaker give the dramatic presentation of Chief Joseph's words.
- The **Support for Extend Your Learning** page (**Unit 4 Resources,** p. 163) provides guided note-taking opportunities to help students complete the Extend Your Learning activities.
- Use the rubric for Peer Assessment: Oral Interpretation, p.130 in ***General Resources,*** to evaluate students' interpretations.

Go Online Research — Have students type in the Web Code for another research activity.

Meeting Your Standards

Students will

1. **analyze and respond to literary elements.**
   - Literary Analysis: Conflict
2. **read, comprehend, analyze, and critique a short story.**
   - Reading Strategy: Predicting
   - Reading Check questions
   - Apply the Skills questions
   - Assessment Practice (ATE)
3. **develop vocabulary.**
   - Vocabulary Lesson: Latin Word Root: *-ject-*
4. **understand and apply written and oral language conventions.**
   - Spelling Strategy
   - Grammar and Style Lesson: Adverb Clauses
5. **develop writing proficiency.**
   - Writing Lesson: Literary Analysis
6. **develop appropriate research strategies.**
   - Extend Your Learning: Booklet
7. **understand and apply listening and speaking strategies.**
   - Extend Your Learning: Enactment

Block Scheduling: Use one 90-minute class period to preteach the skills and have students read the selection. Use a second 90-minute class period to assess students' mastery of skills, extend their learning, and monitor their progress.

Homework Suggestions

Following are possibilities for homework assignments.

- Support pages from ***Unit 4 Resources:***
  Literary Analysis
  Reading Strategy
  Vocabulary Builder
  Grammar and Style
- An Extend Your Learning project and the Writing Lesson for this selection group may be completed over several days.

Step-by-Step Teaching Guide	Pacing Guide
PRETEACH	
• Administer Vocabulary and Reading Warm-ups as necessary.	5 min.
• Engage students' interest with the motivation activity.	5 min.
• Read and discuss author and background features. **FT**	10 min.
• Introduce the Literary Analysis Skill: Conflict. **FT**	5 min.
• Introduce the Reading Strategy: Predicting. **FT**	10 min.
• Prepare students to read by teaching the selection vocabulary. **FT**	
TEACH	
• Informally monitor comprehension while students read independently or in groups. **FT**	30 min.
• Monitor students' comprehension with the Reading Check notes.	as students read
• Reinforce vocabulary with Vocabulary Builder notes.	as students read
• Develop students' understanding of conflict with the Literary Analysis annotations. **FT**	5 min.
• Develop students' ability to predict with the Reading Strategy annotations. **FT**	5 min.
ASSESS/EXTEND	
• Assess students' comprehension and mastery of the Literary Analysis and Reading Strategy by having them answer the Apply the Skills questions. **FT**	15 min.
• Have students complete the Vocabulary Lesson and the Grammar and Style Lesson. **FT**	15 min.
• Apply students' ability to elaborate to support an argument by using the Writing Lesson. **FT**	45 min. or homework
• Apply students' understanding by using one or more of the Extend Your Learning activities.	20–90 min. or homework
• Administer Selection Test A or Selection Test B. **FT**	15 min.

Resources

PRINT

Unit 4 Resources

- Vocabulary Warm-up Word Lists [**L1, L2, EL**] .... p. 171
- Vocabulary Warm-up Practice [**L1, L2, EL**] .... p. 172
- Reading Warm-up A [**L1, L2, EL**] .... p. 173
- Reading Warm-up B [**L1, L2, L3**] .... p. 174

TRANSPARENCY

Graphic Organizer Transparencies

- Literary Analysis Graphic Organizer A [**L3**] .... p. 130
- Literary Analysis Graphic Organizer B [**L1, L2, EL**] .... p. 131
- Reading Strategy Graphic Organizer A [**L3**] .... p. 128
- Reading Strategy Graphic Organizer B [**L1, L2, EL**] .... p. 129

PRINT

Reader's Notebook [L2]
Reader's Notebook: Adapted Version [L1]
Reader's Notebook: English Learner's Version [EL]

Unit 4 Resources

- Literary Analysis [**L3**] .... p. 175
- Reading Strategy [**L3**] .... p. 176
- Vocabulary Builder [**L3**] .... p. 177

TECHNOLOGY

Listening to Literature Audio CDs [L2, EL]

PRINT

Unit 4 Resources

- Grammar and Style [**L3**] .... p. 178
- Support for Writing Lesson [**L3**] .... p. 179
- Support for Extend Your Learning [**L3**] .... p. 180
- Enrichment [**L4**] .... p. 181
- Selection Test A [**L1, L2, EL**] .... pp. 182–184
- Selection Test B [**L3, L4**] .... pp. 185–187

General Resources

- Rubrics for Response to Literature [**L3**] .... p. 65

TECHNOLOGY

Go Online: Research [**L3**]
Go Online: Self-test [**L3**]
***ExamView®*, Test Bank [L3]**

Choosing Resources for Differentiated Instruction

[**L1**] Special Needs Students
[**L2**] Below-Level Students
[**L3**] All Students
[**L4**] Advanced Students
[**EL**] English Learners

FT Fast Track Instruction: To move the lesson more quickly, use the strategies and activities identified with **FT**.

Scaffolding for Less Proficient and Advanced Students

The leveled Critical Thinking questions after selections progress in the levels of thinking required to answer them. To address the needs of your different students, you may use the (a) level questions for your less proficient students and the (b) level questions with your on-level and advanced students. The occasional (c) level questions are appropriate for your advanced students.

PRENTICE HALL
TeacherEXPRESS™
Plan · Teach · Assess

Use this complete suite of powerful teaching tools to make lesson planning and testing quicker and easier.

Use the interactive textbook (online and on CD-ROM) to make selections and activities come alive with audio and video support and interactive questions.

PRE   TEACH

Motivation

Draw students into the story by using the following description:

"Day had broken, cold and gray. . . There was no sun nor hint of sun. . . The Yukon lay a mile wide and hidden under three feet of ice. On top of this ice was as many feet of snow. North and South, as far as he could see, it was unbroken white. . . Undoubtedly it was colder than fifty degrees below zero. . . ."

Encourage students to speculate about what might happen to a person who sets out on a day-long journey on foot in such conditions.

❶ Background

More About the Author

Arthur Calder-Marshall, in his introduction to a collection of Jack London's works, commented: "Jack London's stories still compel the reader to read on. He learned to tell a tale, he says, when he was bumming across the United States . . . He tells his stories like a tramp. At the end you are left with no distillation of truth, no new vision of life. But you have experienced something vicariously. . . ."

Build Skills *Short Story*

❶ To Build a Fire

Jack London (1876–1916)

Jack London had endured more hardships by the age of twenty-one than most people experience in a lifetime. His struggles gave him a sympathy for the working class and a lasting dislike of drudgery. They also provided inspiration for novels and short stories, and became the foundation of his success as a writer.

Difficult Beginnings London grew up in San Francisco in extreme poverty. At the age of eleven, he left school and supported himself through a succession of unskilled jobs—working as a paper boy, in bowling alleys, on ice wagons, and in canneries and mills. Despite the long hours spent toiling at these jobs, London was able to read constantly, borrowing travel and adventure books from the library.

The books London read inspired him to travel, and his job experiences led him to become active in fighting for the rights of workers. He sailed to Japan on a sealing expedition and joined a cross-country protest march with a group of unemployed workers. After being arrested for vagrancy near Buffalo, New York, London decided to educate himself and reshape his life. He completed high school in a single year and then enrolled at the University of California.

After only one semester, however, the lure of fortune and adventure proved irresistible. In 1897, London abandoned his studies and traveled to the Alaskan Yukon in search of gold. Although he was unsuccessful as a miner, London's experiences in Alaska taught him about the human desire for wealth and power and about humankind's inability to control the forces of nature. While in Alaska, London also absorbed memories and stories that would make him a household name.

A Writing Life Once back in California, London became determined to earn a living as a writer. He rented a typewriter and worked up to fifteen hours a day, spinning his Alaskan adventures into short stories and novels.

According to legend, London's stack of rejection slips from publishers grew to five feet in height. Even so, London persevered. He wrote diligently every morning, setting himself a 1,000-word minimum.

In 1903, he earned national fame when he published the popular novel *The Call of the Wild.* He soon became the highest-paid and most-industrious writer in the country. During his career, London produced more than fifty books, including both fiction and nonfiction, and earned more than a million dollars—the first American writer to earn such a staggering sum. Several of his novels, including *The Call of the Wild* (1903), *The Sea-Wolf* (1904), and *White Fang* (1906), have become American classics. His best works depict an individual's struggle for survival against the powerful forces of nature. "To Build a Fire," for example, tells the story of an unnamed man's fight to survive the bitter cold of the Alaskan wilderness.

Recognition by His Peers The well-known writer Upton Sinclair wrote that Jack London "was the true king of our storytellers." London's friend Oliver Madox Hueffer agreed. He recalled that London "was the ideal yarnster—his spoken stories were even better than his written—and one reason why I think him likely to be numbered as among the writers of real mark was that he was perfectly unconscious of it. Like Peter Pan, he never grew up, and he lived in his own stories with such intensity that he ended by believing them himself."

Preview

Connecting to the Literature

Some people enjoy pushing themselves to their limits through sports such as rock climbing and sky diving. In some cases, as in this story, people push themselves to such extremes that they place their lives in jeopardy.

2 Literary Analysis

Conflict

Conflict, the struggle between two opposing forces, can take two forms:

- **internal,** occurring within the mind of a character
- **external,** occurring between a character and society, nature, another person, God, or fate.

A character's efforts to resolve conflict form the basis for the plot of a literary work. In "To Build a Fire," a man is in the throes of a deadly external conflict, struggling to survive in the bitter cold of the Alaskan wilderness.

Connecting Literary Elements

Irony involves a discrepancy between what is stated and what is meant, or between what is expected to happen and what actually happens. In **dramatic irony,** there is a contradiction between what a character thinks and what the reader knows to be true. Dramatic irony often serves to heighten the sense of conflict. For example, in "To Build a Fire," the reader knows that the temperature is far lower than the man realizes:

> He pulled the mitten on hurriedly and stood up. He was a bit frightened. He stamped up and down until the stinging returned into the feet. It certainly was cold, was his thought.

As you read, notice those passages where it is clear that the reader understands more than the man does.

3 Reading Strategy

Predicting

The main character in this story fails to recognize the depth of the conflict he faces until it is too late. A more alert person might have interpreted the signs of danger, anticipated their outcome, and taken action. As a reader, you too can anticipate, or **predict,** what will happen by noting clues that hint at later events. Use a chart like the one shown to identify clues and record your predictions.

Clues
repeated references to the cold

↓

Prediction

Vocabulary Builder

conjectural (kən jek′ chər əl) *adj.* based on guesswork (p. 621)

unwonted (un wän′ tid) *adj.* unusual; unfamiliar (p. 622)

conflagration (kän′ flə grā′ shən) *n.* big, destructive fire (p. 627)

peremptorily (pər emp′ tə rə lē) *adj.* decisively; commandingly (p. 631)

2 Literary Analysis

Conflict

- Tell students that *conflict* drives literary works. Works of literature are about characters struggling to resolve the conflicts that they face.
- Explain that conflicts may also be internal—that is, a character may face a conflict within him- or herself.

3 Reading Strategy

Predicting

- Explain to students that they can often predict what will happen in a literary work by paying close attention to the details in the text.
- Have students read the passage in the instruction for Connecting Literary Elements. Then, direct them to the graphic organizer on the student page. Point out that "Repeated references to the cold" is written in the box labeled "Clues."
- **Ask** students to consider what predictions they might make based on this clue. Give students a copy of **Reading Strategy Graphic Organizer A,** p. 128 in ***Graphic Organizer Transparencies,*** to use as they read the selection.

Vocabulary Builder

- Pronounce each vocabulary word for students, and read the definitions as a class. Have students identify any words with which they are already familiar.

Differentiated Instruction Solutions for All Learners

Support for Special Needs Students
Have students complete the **Preview** and **Build Skills** pages for "To Build a Fire" in the ***Reader's Notebook: Adapted Version.*** These pages provide a selection summary, an abbreviated presentation of the reading and literary skills, and the graphic organizer on the **Build Skills** page in the student book.

Support for Less Proficient Readers
Have students complete the **Preview** and **Build Skills** pages for "To Build a Fire" in the ***Reader's Notebook.*** These pages provide a selection summary, an abbreviated presentation of the reading and literary skills, and the graphic organizer on the **Build Skills** page in the student book.

Support for English Learners
Have students complete the **Preview** and **Build Skills** pages for "To Build a Fire" in the ***Reader's Notebook: English Learner's Version.*** These pages provide a selection summary, an abbreviated presentation of the skills, additional contextual vocabulary, and the graphic organizer on the **Build Skills** page in the student book.

Learning Modalities
Visual/ Spatial Learners
It would be helpful to provide these students with a map of Alaska and of the Yukon Territory so that they can orient themselves as to the main character's locations. They can see how far north the man was and note the remoteness of the region.

❶ About the Selection

Along the Yukon River in the frozen northern wilderness, an inexperienced but confident prospector and his work dog make a long and dangerous journey on foot toward a camp. The temperature is far colder than the man thinks, too cold for a solitary journey. That is his first mistake. His second mistake—building a fire in the wrong spot—proves fatal. Though nature is the antagonist of this tale, the man's own overconfidence contributes to his downfall. The dog, sensing the danger of their predicament from the start, still stays with the man until the very end. Then its instincts direct it on toward the camp, where other food and fire providers are to be found.

❷ Critical Viewing

Possible response: When students have read the story, they may choose several descriptive words or passages from the story to describe the scenes, including "intangible pall over the face of things," "subtle gloom," "gentle undulations," "spruce-covered island," "silent creek," and "arctic winter."

❶ To Build a Fire

Jack London

Background The United States Secretary of State William Seward purchased Alaska from Russia in 1867 for two cents an acre. Many Americans, believing it to be nothing but a frozen, barren wasteland, called the purchase "Seward's Folly." In 1896, the discovery of a rich lode of gold in the Yukon, part of the Arctic wilderness, led to the Klondike Gold Rush of 1897–1898 (named for the river where the gold was found). Thousands of prospectors headed for the frozen north, lured by the promise of quick riches. Jack London was among the first of these prospectors. He may have searched for more than gold, however. London once commented, "True, the new territory was mostly barren; but its several hundred thousand square miles of frigidity at least gave breathing space to those who else would have suffocated at home."

❷ ▲ **Critical Viewing**
Which words or passages from the story could be used to describe this scene? **[Analyze]**

Differentiated Instruction Solutions for All Learners

Accessibility at a Glance

	To Build a Fire
Context	Yukon setting
Language	No dialogue, much description
Concept Level	Accessible (survival)
Literary Merit	Noted author, widely anthologized
Lexile	970
Overall Rating	Average

Day had broken cold and gray, exceedingly cold and gray, when the man turned aside from the main Yukon[1] trail and climbed the high earth-bank, where a dim and little-traveled trail led eastward through the fat spruce timberland. It was a steep bank, and he paused for breath at the top, excusing the act to himself by looking at his watch. It was nine o'clock. There was no sun nor hint of sun, though there was not a cloud in the sky. It was a clear day, and yet there seemed an intangible pall over the face of things, a subtle gloom that made the day dark, and that was due to the absence of sun. This fact did not worry the man. He was used to the lack of sun. It had been days since he had seen the sun, and he knew that a few more days must pass before that cheerful orb, due south, would just peep above the skyline and dip immediately from view.

The man flung a look back along the way he had come. The Yukon lay a mile wide and hidden under three feet of ice. On top of this ice were as many feet of snow. It was all pure white, rolling in gentle undulations where the ice jams of the freeze-up had formed. North and south, as far as his eye could see, it was unbroken white, save for a dark hairline that curved and twisted from around the spruce-covered island to the south, and that curved and twisted away into the north, where it disappeared behind another spruce-covered island. This dark hairline was the trail—the main trail—that led south five hundred miles to the Chilcoot Pass, Dyea,[2] and salt water; and that led north seventy miles to Dawson, and still on to the north a thousand miles to Nulato,[3] and finally to St. Michael on Bering Sea, a thousand miles and half a thousand more.

But all this—the mysterious, far-reaching hairline trail, the absence of sun from the sky, the tremendous cold, and the strangeness and weirdness of it all—made no impression on the man. It was not because he was long used to it. He was a newcomer in the land, a *chechaquo*,[4] and this was his first winter. The trouble with him was that he was without imagination. He was quick and alert in the things of life, but only in the things, and not in the significances. Fifty degrees below zero meant eighty-odd degrees of frost. Such fact impressed him as being cold and uncomfortable, and that was all. It did not lead him to meditate upon his frailty as a creature of temperature, and upon man's frailty in general, able only to live within certain narrow limits of heat and cold; and from there on it did not lead him to the conjectural field of immortality and man's place in the universe. Fifty degrees below zero stood for a bite of frost that hurt and that must be guarded against by the use of mittens, earflaps, warm moccasins, and thick socks. Fifty degrees below zero was to him just precisely fifty degrees below zero. That there should be anything more to it than that was a thought that never entered his head.

Reading Strategy
Predicting What do you predict will happen to the "newcomer" in the "tremendous cold and the strangeness and weirdness"? Why?

Vocabulary Builder
conjectural (kən jekʹ chər əl) *adj.* based on guesswork

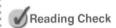

5 **Reading Check**
Where is the man, and what weather conditions is he experiencing?

1. **Yukon** (yo͞oʹ kän) territory in northwestern Canada, east of Alaska; also, a river.
2. **Dyea** (dīʹ ā) former town in Alaska at the start of the Yukon trail.
3. **Dawson . . . Nulato** former gold-mining villages in the Yukon.
4. ***chechaquo*** (chē chäʹ kwō) slang for newcomer.

3 Reading Strategy
Predicting

- Have students read the bracketed passage. **Ask** them to identify any details that might hint at events to come.
  Possible response: Students may notice that the passage refers to the mysteriousness of the trail, the extreme cold, the strange landscape, and the man's failure to respond to any of this.
- Point out that London presents a picture of the man and his limitations, and also of a dangerous environment.
- **Ask** students the Reading Strategy question: What do you predict will happen to the "newcomer" in the "tremendous cold and the strangeness and weirdness"? Why?
  Possible response: Students may predict that the unimaginative man will be challenged by the cold in ways that he does not foresee. His lack of foresight is due to his newness to the land and to his lack of imagination—his inability to perceive the meaning in his experiences and observations.

4 Vocabulary Builder
The Latin Root *-ject-*

- Call students' attention to the word *conjectural* and its definition. Explain that the Latin word root *-ject-* means "to throw."
- Have students suggest words and phrases that contain this root, and list them on the chalkboard.
  Possibilities include: *object, reject, project, interject, inject,* and *object.*
- Next, have students look up the meanings of these words in a dictionary.

5 Reading Check

Answer: The man is in the frozen wilderness along the Yukon River, far from any settlement, and he is experiencing the extreme cold of the Arctic winter.

Differentiated Instruction Solutions for All Learners

Strategy for Less Proficient Readers
These students will be challenged by the fact that London's story contains no dialogue and consists mostly of long passages filled with detailed descriptions. To help students overcome these obstacles, encourage them to pause at the end of each paragraph to jot down the key descriptive details that it contains.

Strategy for English Learners
This story's long and detailed descriptive passages often contain language specific to the time and place in which it is set and may be especially challenging. Encourage students to pause at the end of each setting and jot down key descriptive terms. Then, have them define difficult words and paraphrase descriptive passages.

Strategy for Advanced Readers
Challenge these students to place this selection in an appropriate historical and literary context by identifying how it illustrates the key characteristics of Naturalism—a late nineteenth century literary movement that stressed the idea that people's lives are shaped by forces of society and nature beyond their control.

6 Literary Analysis
Conflict

- Instruct students to create a chart identifying conflicts the man faces. Have them begin by drawing a box and writing "The Man" in its center.
- Have them read the bracketed passage. Point out that London elaborates extensively on the cold.
- Suggest that these details point out the story's central conflict. Then, **ask** students the Literary Analysis question: With what or whom is the man in conflict?
  Possible response: The man is in conflict with the forces of extreme weather conditions. Students may say that he is also in conflict with the limits of his own perceptions.
- Have students place their answers in a circle drawn on to their charts and connect the circles to "The Man."

7 Literary Analysis
Conflict and Irony

- Remind students that dramatic irony is created when what the reader knows about a character's circumstances contradicts what a character believes to be true.
- Have students read the bracketed passage. Encourage them to pay special attention to the dog's instincts.
- Point out to students that the dog's basic instincts tell it what the man has yet to conclude: that it is too dangerously cold to be traveling.
- **Ask** students the Literary Analysis question: In what ways does the description of the dog's instinct create a sense of dramatic irony?
  Possible response: The dog's instincts let the reader know just how dangerous the situation is, which ironically emphasizes how poorly the man understands his environment.

As he turned to go on, he spat speculatively. There was a sharp, explosive crackle that startled him. He spat again. And again, in the air, before it could fall to the snow, the spittle crackled. He knew that at fifty below spittle crackled on the snow, but this spittle had crackled in the air. Undoubtedly it was colder than fifty below—how much colder he did not know. But the temperature did not matter. He was bound for the old claim on the left fork of Henderson Creek, where the boys were already. They had come over across the divide from the Indian Creek country, while he had come the roundabout way to take a look at the possibilities of getting out logs in the spring from the islands in the Yukon. He would be in to camp by six o'clock; a bit after dark, it was true, but the boys would be there, a fire would be going, and a hot supper would be ready. As for lunch, he pressed his hand against the protruding bundle under his jacket. It was also under his shirt, wrapped up in a handkerchief and lying against the naked skin. It was the only way to keep the biscuits from freezing. He smiled agreeably to himself as he thought of those biscuits, each cut open and sopped in bacon grease, and each enclosing a generous slice of fried bacon.

He plunged in among the big spruce trees. The trail was faint. A foot of snow had fallen since the last sled had passed over, and he was glad he was without a sled, traveling light. In fact, he carried nothing but the lunch wrapped in the handkerchief. He was surprised, however, at the cold. It certainly was cold, he concluded, as he rubbed his numb nose and cheekbones with his mittened hand. He was a warm-whiskered man, but the hair on his face did not protect the high cheekbones and the eager nose that thrust itself aggressively into the frosty air.

At the man's heels trotted a dog, a big native husky, the proper wolf dog, gray-coated and without any visible or temperamental difference from its brother, the wild wolf. The animal was depressed by the tremendous cold. It knew that it was no time for traveling. Its instinct told it a truer tale than was told to the man by the man's judgment. In reality, it was not merely colder than fifty below zero; it was colder than sixty below, than seventy below. It was seventy-five below zero. Since the freezing point is thirty-two above zero, it meant that one hundred and seven degrees of frost obtained. The dog did not know anything about thermometers. Possibly in its brain there was no sharp consciousness of a condition of very cold such as was in the man's brain. But the brute had its instinct. It experienced a vague but menacing apprehension that subdued it and made it slink along at the man's heels, and that made it question eagerly every unwonted movement of the man as if expecting him to go into camp or to seek shelter somewhere and build a fire. The dog had learned fire, and it wanted fire, or else to burrow under the snow and cuddle its warmth away from the air.

The frozen moisture of its breathing had settled on its fur in a fine powder of frost, and especially were its jowls, muzzle, and eyelashes whitened by its crystalled breath. The man's red beard and mustache

Literary Analysis
Conflict The great elaboration on the cold in this description points out the central conflict in this story. With what or whom is the man in conflict?

Literary Analysis
Conflict and Irony In what ways does the description of the dog's instinct create a sense of dramatic irony?

Vocabulary Builder
unwonted (un wän′ tid) *adj.* unusual; unfamiliar

Enrichment
Dangers of Cold Weather

Discuss with students how the rising popularity of winter outdoor activities has led to a rise in cold-weather accidents. Frostbite is one result of prolonged exposure to extremely cold temperatures, and so is hypothermia, or subnormal body temperature. The most obvious signs of frostbite are progressive, painful loss of feeling (usually beginning in vulnerable areas, such as the hands, feet, and face) leading to numbness, skin discoloration, and then loss of function. Students can find out about the effects of hypothermia by following what happens to the man in this story. They can notice his difficulty moving, his confusion, his drowsiness, and his eventual death.

Interested students can research the precautions that people who plan to spend time in sub-freezing temperatures can take to prevent these severe problems, and what first-aid steps to follow if frostbite or hypothermia occurs.

were likewise frosted, but more solidly, the deposit taking the form of ice and increasing with every warm, moist breath he exhaled. Also, the man was chewing tobacco, and the muzzle of ice held his lips so rigidly that he was unable to clear his chin when he expelled the juice. The result was that a crystal beard of the color and solidity of amber was increasing its length on his chin. If he fell down it would shatter itself, like glass, into brittle fragments. But he did not mind the appendage. It was the penalty all tobacco-chewers paid in that country, and he had been out before in two cold snaps. They had not been so cold as this, he knew, but by the spirit thermometer[5] at Sixty Mile he knew they had been registered at fifty below and at fifty-five.

He held on through the level stretch of woods for several miles, crossed a wide flat, and dropped down a bank to the frozen bed of a small stream. This was Henderson Creek, and he knew he was ten miles from the forks. He looked at his watch. It was ten o'clock. He was making four miles an hour, and he calculated that he would arrive at the forks at half past twelve. He decided to celebrate that event by eating his lunch there.

The dog dropped in again at his heels, with a tail drooping discouragement, as the man swung along the creek bed. The furrow of the old sled trail was plainly visible, but a dozen inches of snow covered the marks of the last runners. In a month no man had come up or down that silent creek. The man held steadily on. He was not much given to thinking, and just then particularly he had nothing to think about save that he would eat lunch at the forks and that at six o'clock he would be in camp with the boys. There was nobody to talk to; and, had there been, speech would have been impossible because of the ice-muzzle on his mouth. So he continued monotonously to chew tobacco and to increase the length of his amber beard.

Once in a while the thought reiterated itself that it was very cold and that he had never experienced such cold. As he walked along he rubbed his cheekbones and nose with the back of his mittened hand. He did this automatically, now and again changing hands. But rub as he would, the instant he stopped his cheekbones went numb, and the following instant the end of his nose went numb. He was sure to frost his cheeks; he knew that, and experienced a pang of regret that he had not devised a nose strap of the sort Bud wore in cold snaps. Such a strap passed across the cheeks, as well, and saved them. 11

5. **spirit thermometer** thermometer containing alcohol; used in extreme cold.

Literature in Context

10 History Connection

Dogs and the Yukon

Dogs like the one in "To Build a Fire" have long played a key role in the Yukon. For centuries, native people in Alaska have bred dogs for a variety of purposes, including transportation. When the Klondike Gold Rush brought thousands of miners to the Yukon, the problem of transportation became acute. In 1910, the federal government constructed a trail more than 1,000 miles long for use by dog sled teams. That trail became known as the Iditarod.

Sled dogs are among the most powerful draft animals on earth. A team of twenty dogs can pull a ton or more. Though the man in London's story does not treat his dog with affection, for many dog sled drivers these valiant dogs provided warmth and companionship on the long, cold trail.

Connect to the Literature

Why do you think London chooses to portray the dog's thoughts and feelings?

Reading Check

Is the man aware of how cold it truly is? How do you know?

8 Critical Thinking
Evaluate

- Have students read the bracketed passage. **Ask** them to pay close attention to man's plan.
- **Ask** students: Does the man's plan make sense? Why or why not?
Possible response: Students may point out that four miles an hour is a very quick walking pace, and one that he is unlikely to be able to keep up for very long in the snow.

9 Reading Strategy
Predicting

- Point out that the path has not been used for a long time, as the snow indicates.
- **Ask** students to tell whether they believe the man will reach camp as he plans, now that he is traveling on an unused trail.
Possible response: Unlike the man, students may recognize that the trail has been unused for a reason; perhaps it is too dangerous to travel on now. They may predict he won't arrive as planned.

Monitor Progress **Ask** students to support their predictions.

Possible response: Students may cite the dog's discouragement and the fact that the man "was not given much to thinking."

10 Literature in Context
Dogs and the Yukon The exact blood line of the Alaskan husky is often debated. Some experts believe the it to be a cross-breed between wolves, Siberian huskies—the genetic source of the blue eyes in many Alaskan huskies—Irish setters, or any other breed known for speed and endurance.

Connect to Literature Encourage students to give two reasons for their responses.
Possible response: The dog's thoughts and feelings tell the reader the severity of the situation. It also helps to show how the man has underestimated the temperature.

11 Reading Check
Answer: The man is not aware of how cold it truly is; we know because the dog does understand.

Differentiated Instruction
Solutions for All Learners

Support for Special Needs Students
Students may have difficulty understanding the narrator's detailed explanation of the temperature in the bracketed passage 7. Guide them through this passage. Then, ask them why London points out that the freezing point is thirty-two above zero—even though they almost certainly know this. Explain that London uses the freezing point to provide the reader with perspective to understand the true severity of the cold.

Enrichment for Advanced Readers
After students read the bracketed passage 7, ask them to ponder Jack London's attitude toward animal instinct. Encourage them to discuss what the dog represents in this story. Help students recognize that London places high value on natural instinct as a survival mechanism and model for humans. London clearly shows that the man fails to learn from the cues in his environment, such as the dog's behavior.

12 Reading Strategy
Predicting

- Instruct students to construct a chart with two columns. Have them write "Clues in Passage" on the left and "You Can Predict" on the right.
- Have students read the bracketed passage. **Ask** them to write clues they find in the left columns of their charts.
  Possible response: Students may include such details as "the changes in the creek," the springs that never freeze, the word "traps," and the fact that a person could "wet himself to the waist."
- **Ask** students the Reading Strategy question: Based on the passage describing the hidden creek, what do you predict might happen? Have them write their answers on the right side of their charts.
  Possible response: Students will probably predict that the man might step into a spring and get soaking wet.

13 Literary Analysis
Conflict

- Remind students that the major external conflict the man has faced up to this point has been the cold.
- Have students read the bracketed passage. Encourage them to look for new dangers the man faces in the world around him.
- **Ask** students the Literary Analysis question: What other element of conflict is introduced in the passages describing the creek?
  Answer: Students can recognize that now the man faces the danger of hidden traps in the landscape, such as hidden pockets of water. These hidden traps place him at an even greater disadvantage in his struggle against the harsh environment.

But it didn't matter much, after all. What were frosted cheeks? A bit painful, that was all: they were never serious.

12 Empty as the man's mind was of thoughts, he was keenly observant, and he noticed the changes in the creek, the curves and bends and timber jams, and always he sharply noted where he placed his feet. Once, coming around a bend, he shied abruptly, like a startled horse, curved away from the place where he had been walking, and retreated several paces back along the trail. The creek he knew was frozen clear to the bottom—no creek could contain water in that arctic winter—but he knew also that there were springs that bubbled out from the hillsides and ran along under the snow and on top the ice of the creek. He knew that the coldest snaps never froze these springs, and he knew likewise their danger. They were traps. They hid pools of water under the snow that might be three inches deep, or three feet. Sometimes a skin of ice half an inch thick covered them, and in turn was covered by the snow. Sometimes there were alternate layers of water and ice skin, so that when one broke through he kept on breaking through for a while, sometimes wetting himself to the waist.

That was why he had shied in such panic. He had felt the give under his feet and heard the crackle of a snow-hidden ice skin. And to get his feet wet in such a temperature meant trouble and danger. At the very least it meant delay, for he would be forced to stop and build a fire, and under its protection to bare his feet while he dried his socks and moccasins. He stood and studied the creek bed and its banks, and decided that the flow of water came from the right. He reflected awhile, rubbing his nose and cheeks, then skirted to the left, stepping gingerly and testing the footing for each step. Once clear of the danger, he took a fresh chew of tobacco and swung along at his four-mile gait.

In the course of the next two hours he came upon several similar traps. Usually the snow above the hidden pools had a sunken, candied appearance that advertised the danger. Once again, however, he had a close call; and once, suspecting danger, he compelled the dog to go on in front. The dog did not want to go. It hung back until the man shoved it forward, and then it went quickly across the white, unbroken surface. 13 Suddenly it broke through, floundered to one side, and got away to firmer footing. It had wet its forefeet and legs, and almost immediately the water that clung to it turned to ice. It made quick efforts to lick the ice off its legs, then dropped down in the snow and began to bite out the ice that had formed between the toes. This was a matter of instinct. To permit the ice to remain would mean sore feet. It did not know this. It merely obeyed the mysterious prompting that arose from the deep crypts of its being. But the man knew, having achieved a judgment on the subject, and he removed the mitten from his right hand and helped tear out the ice particles. He did not expose his fingers more than a minute, and was astonished at the swift numbness that smote them. It certainly was cold. He pulled on the mitten hastily, and beat the hand savagely across his chest.

Reading Strategy
Predicting Based on this passage describing the hidden creek, what do you predict might happen?

Literary Analysis
Conflict Until now, the man has struggled with the cold. What other element of conflict is introduced in the passages describing the creek?

Enrichment

The Race to the South Pole

Inform students that the deadly situation presented in "To Build a Fire" has many parallels in real-life explorations of the Arctic regions. Relate the story of the race to the South Pole, in which British explorer Robert Falcon Scott and Norwegian explorer Roald Amundsen competed to see who would be the first to lead an exploration party to the newly-charted pole. Their goal: to reach the South Pole in 1910. When Amundsen and his party finally arrived in December 1911, they were the first to set foot on the fabled South Pole. Traveling by sled, Scott and four others reached the spot in January 1912, only to find that Amundsen's party had beaten them to their goal. By March, Scott and his party were dead, victims of illness, extreme weather conditions, and a shortage of supplies.

Encourage interested students to research the details of the race and to share their findings with the class.

At twelve o'clock the day was at its brightest. Yet the sun was too far south on its winter journey to clear the horizon. The bulge of the earth intervened between it and Henderson Creek, where the man walked under a clear sky at noon and cast no shadow. At half-past twelve, to the minute, he arrived at the forks of the creek. He was pleased at the speed he had made. If he kept it up, he would certainly be with the boys by six. He unbuttoned his jacket and shirt and drew forth his lunch. The action consumed no more than a quarter of a minute, yet in that brief moment the numbness laid hold of the exposed fingers. He did not put the mitten on, but, instead, struck the fingers a dozen sharp smashes against his leg. Then he sat down on a snow-covered log to eat. The sting that followed upon the striking of his fingers against his leg ceased so quickly that he was startled. He had had no chance to take a bite of biscuit. He struck the fingers repeatedly and returned them to the mitten, baring the other hand for the purpose of eating. He tried to take a mouthful, but the ice muzzle prevented. He had forgotten to build a fire and thaw out. He chuckled at his foolishness, and as he chuckled he noted the numbness creeping into the exposed fingers. Also, he noted that the stinging which had first come to his toes when he sat down was already passing away. He wondered whether the toes were warm or numb. He moved them inside the moccasins and decided that they were numb.

He pulled the mitten on hurriedly and stood up. He was a bit frightened. He stamped up and down until the stinging returned into the feet. It certainly was cold, was his thought. That man from Sulphur Creek had spoken the truth when telling how cold it sometimes got in the country. And he had laughed at him at the time! That showed one must not be too sure of things. There was no mistake about it, it was cold. He strode up and down, stamping his feet and threshing his arms, until reassured by the returning warmth. Then he got out matches and proceeded to make a fire. From the undergrowth, where high water of the previous spring had lodged a supply of seasoned twigs, he got his firewood. Working carefully from a small beginning, he soon had a roaring fire, over which he thawed the ice from his face and in the protection of which he ate his biscuits. For the moment the cold of space was outwitted. The dog took satisfaction in the fire, stretching out close enough for warmth and far enough away to escape being singed.

When the man had finished, he filled his pipe and took his comfortable time over a smoke. Then he pulled on his mittens, settled the earflaps of his cap firmly about his ears, and took the creek trail up the left fork. The dog was disappointed and yearned back toward the fire. This man did not know cold. Possibly all the generations of his ancestry had been ignorant of cold, of real cold, of cold one hundred and seven degrees below freezing point. But the dog knew; all its ancestry knew, and it had inherited the knowledge. And it knew that it was not good to walk abroad in such fearful cold. It was the time to **16** lie snug in a hole in the snow and wait for a curtain of cloud to be drawn across the face of outer space whence this cold came. On the

Literary Analysis
Conflict and Irony In what ways is the man's thought that "one must not be too sure of things" ironic?

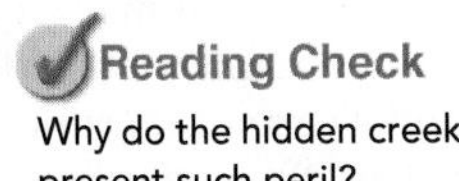

Why do the hidden creeks present such peril?

14 Critical Thinking
Analyze

- Explain to students that in literary works, a seemingly trivial detail can symbolize or represent an important truth.
- Have students read the bracketed passage. Call their attention to the point that at noon, the man casts no shadow.
- **Ask** students what the idea that the man casts no shadow might symbolize.
  Possible response: Students may understand it to suggest that he has no presence there and shouldn't be there at all, or that he is marked for death and, like one already dead, no longer exists in the physical world.

15 Literary Analysis
Conflict and Irony

- Remind students that irony involves a contrast between what a character expects to happen and what actually happens.
- Have students read the bracketed passage. Encourage them to reflect on what the man has done to arrive here.
- **Ask** students the Literary Analysis question: In what ways is the man's thought that "one must not be too sure of things" ironic?
  Possible response: His thought is ironic because he has gotten himself into this very dangerous and frightening situation by being too sure that he knew what he was doing.

16 Reading Check

Answer: The creek is so perilous because it hides springs, pockets of water that can soak the man's clothing and freeze solid in a matter of seconds.

Differentiated Instruction
Solutions for All Learners

Support for Special Needs Students
These students may have difficulty with London's dense text. You can have them read along with the recording of this selection on **Listening to Literature Audio CDs.** Encourage students to keep pace with the recording.

Strategy for English Learners
Students might be confused by London's dispassionate description of the dog in the bracketed passage 12. Guide students through the passage. Emphasize that dogs are not regarded as pets in this environment. Help students recognize the boundaries between the man and the dog; it is his worker and he uses it as a tool.

Enrichment for Gifted/Talented Students
Encourage these students to create an illustration of the forks of Henderson Creek, where the man stops to have lunch and builds a fire. Students may use any materials they choose, but should try to capture both the comfort of the fire and the danger of the landscape.

17 Critical Thinking
Analyze

- Before students read the bracketed passage, have them pause and consider the man's situation. Remind them that the man is traveling on an unused trail that conceals dangerous pools of unfrozen water.
- Have students read the bracketed passage. Then, **ask** them: How has the narrator prepared us for this possibility and what it might mean?
  Possible response: Students should respond that the narrator has already detailed the great danger presented by water in such an environment. He has also explained that stepping in water would require a traveler to stop and build a fire, or risk freezing to death.

18 Literary Analysis
Conflict and Irony

- Have students read the bracketed passage. Then **ask** them this question: What are the man's biggest concerns when he falls into the creek?
  Answer: He is angry because making a fire and drying his footgear will delay his return to the camp by an hour.
- **Ask** students this follow-up question: Given his situation, how are his concerns ironic?
  Answer: His concerns are ironic because London has made it very clear that the man is in very grave danger and may not make it back to the camp at all.

19 Critical Viewing

Possible response: The landscape is spare and severe; there seems to be no sources of food or warmth for miles. Nevertheless, the dog appears to be moving with great speed and energy.

other hand, there was no keen intimacy between the dog and the man. The one was the toil slave of the other, and the only caresses it had ever received were the caresses of the whiplash and of harsh and menacing throat sounds that threatened the whiplash. So the dog made no effort to communicate its apprehension to the man. It was not concerned in the welfare of the man; it was for its own sake that it yearned back toward the fire. But the man whistled, and spoke to it with the sound of whiplashes, and the dog swung in at the man's heels and followed after.

The man took a chew of tobacco and proceeded to start a new amber beard. Also, his moist breath quickly powdered with white his mustache, eyebrows, and lashes. There did not seem to be so many springs on the left fork of the Henderson, and for half an hour the man saw no signs of any. And then it happened. 17 At a place where there were no signs, where the soft, unbroken snow seemed to advertise solidity beneath, the man broke through. It was not deep. He wet himself halfway to the knees before he floundered out to the firm crust.

18 He was angry, and cursed his luck aloud. He had hoped to get into camp with the boys at six o'clock, and this would delay him an hour, for he would have to build a fire and dry out his footgear. This was imperative at that low temperature—he knew that much; and he turned aside to the bank, which he climbed. On top, tangled in the underbrush about the trunks of several small spruce trees, was a high-water deposit of dry firewood—sticks and twigs, principally, but also larger portions of seasoned branches and fine, dry, last year's grasses. He threw down several large pieces on top of the snow. This served for a foundation and prevented the young flame from drowning itself in the snow it otherwise would melt. The flame he got by touching a match to a small shred of birch bark that he took from his pocket. This burned even more readily than paper. Placing it on the foundation, he fed the young flame with wisps of dry grass and with the tiniest dry twigs.

He worked slowly and carefully, keenly aware of his danger. Gradually, as the flame grew stronger, he increased the size of the twigs with which he fed it. He squatted in the snow, pulling the twigs out from their entanglement in the brush and feeding directly to the flame.  He knew there must be no failure. When it is seventy-five below zero, a man must not fail in his first attempt to build a fire—that is, if his feet are wet. If his feet are dry, and he fails, he can run along the trail for half a mile and restore his circulation. But the circulation of wet and freezing feet cannot be restored by running when it is seventy-five below. No matter how fast he runs, the wet feet will freeze the harder.

19 ▲ Critical Viewing In what ways does this image convey both the starkness of the Yukon wilderness and the dog's comfort in that landscape? **[Assess]**

Reading Strategy
Predicting Now that he is wet, what do you predict will happen to the man?

20 All this the man knew. The old-timer on Sulphur Creek had told him about it the previous fall, and now he was appreciating the advice. Already all sensation had gone out of his feet. To build the fire he had been forced to remove his mittens, and the fingers had quickly gone numb. His pace of four miles an hour had kept his heart pumping blood to the surface of his body and to all the extremities. But the instant he stopped, the action of the pump eased down. The cold of space smote the unprotected tip of the planet, and he, being on that unprotected tip, received the full force of the blow. The blood of his body recoiled before it. The blood was alive, like the dog, and like the dog it wanted to hide away and cover itself up from the fearful cold. So long as he walked four miles an hour, he pumped that blood, willy-nilly, to the surface; but now it ebbed away and sank down into the recesses of his body. The extremities were the first to feel its absence. His wet feet froze the faster, and his exposed fingers numbed the faster, though they had not yet begun to freeze. Nose and cheeks were already freezing, while the skin of all his body chilled as it lost its blood.

But he was safe. Toes and nose and cheeks would be only touched by the frost, for the fire was beginning to burn with strength. He was feeding it with twigs the size of his finger. In another minute he would be able to feed it with branches the size of his wrist, and then he could remove his wet foot-gear, and, while it dried, he could keep his naked feet warm by the fire, rubbing them at first, of course, with snow. The fire was a success. He was safe. He remembered the advice of the old-timer on Sulphur Creek, and smiled. The old-timer had been very serious in laying down the law that no man must travel alone in the Klondike after fifty below. Well, here he was; he had had the accident; he was alone; and he had saved himself. Those old-timers were rather womanish, some of them, he thought. All a man had to do was to keep his head, and he was all right. Any man who was a man could travel alone. But it was surprising, the rapidity with which his cheeks and nose were freezing. And he had not thought his fingers could go lifeless in so short a time. Lifeless they were, for he could scarcely make them move together to grip a twig, and they seemed remote from his body and from him. When he touched a twig, he had to look and see whether or not he had hold of it. The wires were pretty well down between him and his finger ends.

All of which counted for little. There was the fire, snapping and crackling and promising life with every dancing flame. He started to untie his moccasins. They were coated with ice; the thick German socks were like sheaths of iron halfway to the knees; and the moccasin strings were like rods of steel all twisted and knotted as by some conflagration. For a moment he tugged with his numb fingers, then, realizing the folly of it, he drew his sheath-knife.

But before he could cut the strings, it happened. It was his own fault or, rather, his mistake. He should not have built the fire under the spruce tree. He should have built it in the open. But it had been

Literary Analysis
Conflict and Irony Has the man saved himself, as he believes? What does the reader understand about the old-timer's advice that the man does not?

Vocabulary Builder
conflagration (kän′ flə grā′ shən) *n.* big, destructive fire

Reading Check
What does the man do after he falls into the creek?

20 Reading Strategy
Conflict

- Have students read the bracketed passage. **Ask** them to identify clues in the text that suggest what will happen.
  Answer: Students should answer that "a man must not fail in his first attempt to build a fire—that is, if his feet are wet," because his feet will freeze.
- **Ask** students the Reading Strategy question on the previous page: Now that he is wet, what do you predict will happen to the man?
  Possible response: Students will probably predict that he will fail to build a fire, and his feet will freeze.

21 Literary Analysis
Conflict and Irony

- Have students read the bracketed passage. Then, **ask** them the first part of the Literary Analysis question: Has the man saved himself, as he believes?
  Possible response: Students will suspect that he has not saved himself, because his hands are too frozen to build the fire.
- Point out to students that the man still faces a major conflict—he is still struggling against nature, and he is still at a great disadvantage.
- **Ask** students the second part of the Literary Analysis question: What does the reader understand about the old-timer's advice that the man does not?
  Possible response: The reader understands that it is much colder than fifty below zero, weather that is more than anyone can face alone. The man still does not understand this, and his ignorance creates dramatic irony.

22 Reading Check

Answer: He struggles to build a fire to dry out his footgear before his feet freeze.

Differentiated Instruction
Solutions for All Learners

Strategy for Less Proficient Readers
If students are excessively surprised by the bracketed passage 17 or have difficulty with the Step-by-Step activity 17, they may need to review the story up to this point. Guide students to understand how the narrator has prepared readers for this crisis; then, have them reread the passage.

Strategy for Advanced Readers
Encourage students to discuss the man's reaction to having saved himself at the end of the page. Then, ask them to analyze the man's thoughts and actions. Some may respond that he is being cocky, but others might suggest that he is a man who is all alone, deep in a harsh wilderness, and simply talks to himself to keep his spirits up, as anyone might do in similar circumstances.

23 Reading Strategy
Predicting

- Before they read the bracketed passage, **ask** students to pause and consider the man's progress up to this point. Have his efforts been successful?
Possible response: Students may observe that he remains calm after falling into the water and successfully builds a fire. Others may feel that getting wet in the first place indicates that the man is failing in his effort to get to the camp.
- Have students read the bracketed passage. Then, **ask** them to tell whether they were able to predict this accident. Have them provide details to back up their predictions.
Possible response: Most students will have been caught by surprise, but they are likely to have expected some type of disaster to occur. Details are likely to include the man's dismissive memory of the old-timer's warning, which suggests that the man is much too confident.

24 Literary Analysis
Conflict

- Remind students that the main conflict in this story comes from the man's struggle against natural forces. **Ask** them to consider what the man has done so far to resolve this conflict.
- Have students read the bracketed passage. Then, **ask** them the Literary Analysis question: In what ways does the conflict intensify as the man begins to build another fire?
Possible response: The situation becomes far more dangerous; the man feels as if "he had just heard his own sentence of death," and realizes that if he survives, he will at least lose some toes.

Monitor Progress: Encourage students to **discuss** the ways in which the story has built conflict. To what climax do they think the conflict will build?
Possible response: At this point, students may have concluded that the man is going to freeze to death.

23 easier to pull the twigs from the brush and drop them directly on the fire. Now the tree under which he had done this carried a weight of snow on its boughs. No wind had blown for weeks, and each bough was fully freighted. Each time he had pulled a twig he had communicated a slight agitation to the tree—an imperceptible agitation, so far as he was concerned, but an agitation sufficient to bring about the disaster. High up in the tree one bough capsized its load of snow. This fell on the boughs beneath, capsizing them. This process continued, spreading out and involving the whole tree. It grew like an avalanche, and it descended without warning upon the man and the fire, and the fire was blotted out! Where it had burned was a mantle of fresh and disordered snow.

24 The man was shocked. It was as though he had just heard his own sentence of death. For a moment he sat and stared at the spot where the fire had been. Then he grew very calm. Perhaps the old-timer on Sulphur Creek was right. If he had only had a trail mate he would have been in no danger now. The trail mate could have built the fire. Well, it was up to him to build the fire over again, and this second time there must be no failure. Even if he succeeded, he would most likely lose some toes. His feet must be badly frozen by now, and there would be some time before the second fire was ready.

Literary Analysis
Conflict In what ways does the conflict intensify as the man begins to build another fire?

Such were his thoughts, but he did not sit and think them. He was busy all the time they were passing through his mind. He made a new foundation for a fire, this time in the open, where no treacherous tree could blot it out. Next, he gathered dry grasses and tiny twigs from the high-water flotsam. He could not bring his fingers together to pull them out, but he was able to gather them by the handful. In this way he got many rotten twigs and bits of green moss that were undesirable, but it was the best he could do. He worked methodically, even collecting an armful of the larger branches to be used later when the fire gathered strength. And all the while the dog sat and watched him, a certain yearning wistfulness in its eyes, for it looked upon him as the fire provider, and the fire was slow in coming.

When all was ready, the man reached in his pocket for a second piece of birch bark. He knew the bark was there, and, though he could not feel it with his fingers, he could hear its crisp rustling as he fumbled for it. Try as he would, he could not clutch hold of it. And all the time, in his consciousness, was the knowledge that each instant his feet were freezing. This thought tended to put him in a panic, but he fought against it and kept calm. He pulled on his mittens with his teeth, and threshed his arms back and forth, beating his hands with all his might against his sides. He did this sitting down, and he stood up to do it; and all the while the dog sat in the snow, its wolf brush of a tail curled around warmly over its forefeet, its sharp wolf ears pricked forward intently as it watched the man. And the man, as he beat and threshed with his arms and hands, felt a great surge of envy as he regarded the creature that was warm and secure in its natural covering.

After a time he was aware of the first faraway signals of sensation in his beaten fingers. The faint tingling grew stronger till it evolved into a

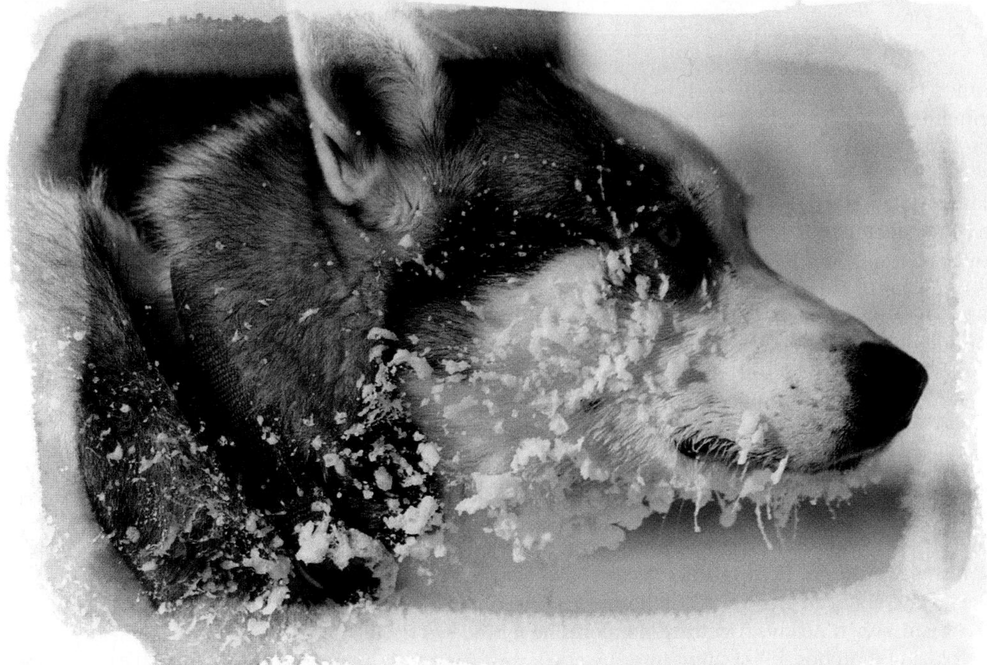

stinging ache that was excruciating, but which the man hailed with satisfaction. He stripped the mitten from his right hand and fetched forth the birch bark. The exposed fingers were quickly going numb again. Next he brought out his bunch of sulphur matches. But the tremendous cold had already driven the life out of his fingers. In his effort to separate one match from the others, the whole bunch fell in the snow. He tried to pick it out of the snow, but failed. The dead
26 fingers could neither touch nor clutch. He was very careful. He drove the thought of his freezing feet, and nose, and cheeks, out of his mind, devoting his whole soul to the matches. He watched, using the sense of vision in place of that of touch, and when he saw his fingers on each side the bunch, he closed them—that is, he willed to close them, for the wires were down, and the fingers did not obey. He pulled the mitten on the right hand, and beat it fiercely against his knee. Then, with both mittened hands, he scooped the bunch of matches, along with much snow, into his lap. Yet he was no better off.

After some manipulation he managed to get the bunch between the heels of his mittened hands. In this fashion he carried it to his mouth. The ice crackled and snapped when by a violent effort he opened his mouth. He drew the lower jaw in, curled the upper lip out of the way, and scraped the bunch with his upper teeth in order to separate a match. He succeeded in getting one, which he dropped on his lap. He was no better off. He could not pick it up. Then he devised a way. He picked it up in his teeth and scratched it on his leg. Twenty times he scratched before he succeeded in lighting it. As it

25 **▲ Critical Viewing**
Study the eyes of this husky. What human characteristics would you attribute to its eyes? Which, if any, of those characteristics apply to the dog in the story? **[Infer; Relate]**

Reading Strategy
Predicting As the man struggles to light the matches, what do you predict about his success? Why?

27 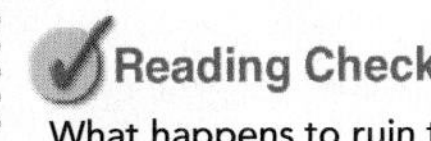
Reading Check
What happens to ruin the man's fire?

25 Critical Viewing

Possible response: Students may say that the husky's eyes indicate an intense focus or alertness, one that is unfettered by any sense of imagination or other distraction. Some may detect intelligence, wisdom, or signs of the survival instinct that guides the actions of the husky in the story.

26 Literary Analysis
Conflict

- Point out that the man is attempting to build a second fire. **Ask** students to explain what happens to his efforts in this passage.
  Answer: He has to struggle to regain feeling in his hands, which he loses immediately; his numbed fingers make him drop the matches; he cannot pick one match up, so he scoops the bunch into his lap.
- After reviewing these details, **ask** students how this passage builds the conflict between the man and nature.
  Possible response: Students may note that the man now feels the initial pangs of panic; with each mishap, his attitude has changed. Overconfident at first, he begins to laugh at his errors, then to appreciate his limitations, and, now, to experience real concern.

▶ Monitor Progress: After discussing external conflict, **ask** if this passage also reveals a new internal conflict.
Answer: The passage reveals an internal conflict between the man and his frozen and failing body.

27 Reading Check

Answer: The snow piled on the branches of a tree falls on the fire and puts it out.

Differentiated Instruction
Solutions for All Learners

Strategy for Special Needs Students
Students who own dogs might be encouraged to respond to London's description of the dog's reactions. Help these students connect to the text by asking them to read passages about the dog closely and tell whether they think London's descriptions are accurate.

Enrichment for Gifted/Talented Students
Ask students to imagine the man's frustration as all of his painstaking efforts begin to come to nothing. Have students write and perform short monologues on situations from their own lives when circumstances beyond their control foiled their best efforts.

Enrichment for Advanced Readers
Ask these students to write character analyses of the main character. Have them organize their analyses around this question: In what ways does the character change in response to his developing conflict with nature?

28 Reading Strategy
Predicting

- **Ask** students to read the bracketed passage, looking closely at the details. Then, **ask** them what clues in the passage might help them predict what is going to happen next.
  Possible response: Students should notice that the man's frozen hands and face make it difficult for him to light a match. They may also notice the repeated clause "He was no better off."
- **Ask** students the Reading Strategy question: As the man struggles to light the matches, what do you predict about his success? Why?
  Possible response: Most students will predict that the man will fail to light a match and start another fire because he is so incapacitated by the extreme cold.

Monitor Progress: Invite students to discuss the reasons behind their predictions. Be sure that they use details from the text to support their arguments.

29 Literary Analysis
Conflict

- Instruct students to construct or add to previously constructed charts identifying conflicts in the story.
- Have students read the bracketed passage. Point out that the man's fear and pain show that he is now fully aware of how cold it actually is.
- **Ask** students the Literary Analysis question: What is the new conflict with which he now struggles desperately?
  Possible response: He must now struggle with his freezing, nearly useless hands and shivering body.
- Have students add a new circle to their charts for this new conflict.

30 Critical Viewing

Possible response: The landscape pictured seems less dense with trees and less cold. In the photograph, the river is not fully iced over; stretches of unfrozen water are clearly visible.

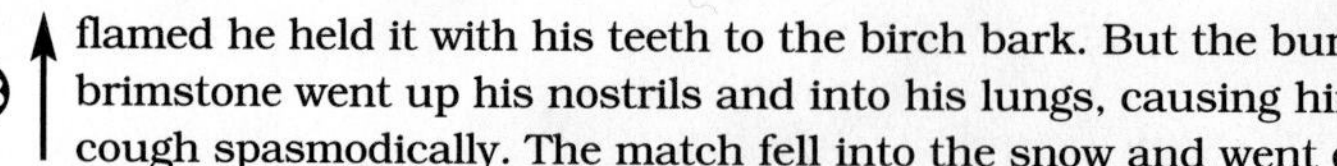

28 flamed he held it with his teeth to the birch bark. But the burning brimstone went up his nostrils and into his lungs, causing him to cough spasmodically. The match fell into the snow and went out.

The old-timer on Sulphur Creek was right, he thought in the moment of controlled despair that ensued: after fifty below, a man should travel with a partner. He beat his hands, but failed in exciting any sensation. Suddenly he bared both hands, removing the mittens with his teeth. He caught the whole bunch between the heels of his hands. His arm muscles not being frozen enabled him to press the hand heels tightly against the matches. Then he scratched the bunch along his leg. It flared into flame, seventy sulphur matches at once! There was no wind to blow them out. He kept his head to one side to escape the strangling fumes, and held the blazing bunch to the birch bark. As he so held it, he became aware of sensation in his hand. His flesh was burning. He could smell it. Deep down below the surface he could feel it. The sensation developed into pain that grew acute. And still he endured it, holding the flame of the matches clumsily to the bark that would not light readily because his own burning hands were in the way, absorbing most of the flame.

29 At last, when he could endure no more, he jerked his hands apart. The blazing matches fell sizzling into the snow, but the birch bark was alight. He began laying dry grasses and the tiniest twigs on the flame. He could not pick and choose, for he had to lift the fuel between the heels of his hands. Small pieces of rotten wood and green moss clung to the twigs, and he bit them off as well as he could with his teeth. He cherished the flame carefully and awkwardly. It meant life, and it must not perish. The withdrawal of blood from the surface of his body now made him begin to shiver, and he grew more awkward. A large piece of green moss fell squarely on the little fire. He tried to poke it out with his fingers, but his shivering frame made him poke too far, and he disrupted the nucleus of the little fire, the burning grasses and tiny twigs separating and scattering. He tried to poke them together again, but in spite of the tenseness of the effort, his shivering got away with him, and the

Literary Analysis
Conflict The man is now fully aware of how cold it actually is. What is the conflict with which he now struggles desperately?

30 **▼Critical Viewing**
Compare and contrast this landscape with the one in London's story. **[Compare and Contrast]**

Enrichment

Eco-Tourism

There are few people who would want to venture into the Arctic wilderness by themselves like the man in this story. However, there is a growing tourist industry that fulfills people's desire to travel into areas of unspoiled wilderness in all parts of the world, from Alaska to the Antarctic and from the rainforests of Central America to the African savannah. This industry is called eco-tourism. Explain to students that there are many career opportunities in eco-tourism. Cooks, naturalists, pilots, and booking agents are just a few of the people employed by eco-tourism companies. Encourage students to conduct research to learn about this growing industry and the opportunities it provides, and to share their findings with their classmates.

twigs were hopelessly scattered. Each twig gushed a puff of smoke and went out. The fire provider had failed. As he looked apathetically about him, his eyes chanced on the dog, sitting across the ruins of the fire from him, in the snow, making restless, hunching movements, slightly lifting one forefoot and then the other, shifting its weight back and forth on them with wistful eagerness.

The sight of the dog put a wild idea into his head. He remembered the tale of the man, caught in a blizzard, who killed a steer and crawled inside the carcass, and so was saved. He would kill the dog and bury his hands in the warm body until the numbness went out of them. Then he could build another fire. He spoke to the dog, calling it to him; but in his voice was a strange note of fear that frightened the animal, who had never known the man to speak in such way before. Something was the matter, and its suspicious nature sensed danger—it knew not what danger, but somewhere, somehow, in its brain arose an apprehension of the man. It flattened its ears down at the sound of the man's voice, and its restless, hunching movements and the liftings and shiftings of its forefeet became more pronounced; but it would not come to the man. He got on his hands and knees and crawled toward the dog. This unusual posture again excited suspicion, and the animal sidled mincingly away.

The man sat up in the snow for a moment and struggled for calmness. Then he pulled on his mittens, by means of his teeth, and got upon his feet. He glanced down at first in order to assure himself that he was really standing up, for the absence of sensation in his feet left him unrelated to the earth. His erect position in itself started to drive the webs of suspicion from the dog's mind; and when he spoke peremptorily, with the sound of whiplashes in his voice, the dog rendered its customary allegiance and came to him. As it came within reaching distance, the man lost his control. His arms flashed out to the dog, and he experienced genuine surprise when he discovered that his hands could not clutch, that there was neither bend nor feeling in the fingers. He had forgotten for the moment that they were

Literary Analysis
Conflict What conflict is intensified in the passage beginning "the sight of the dog . . ."?

Vocabulary Builder
peremptorily (pər emp′ tə rə lē) *adj.* decisively; commandingly

32  **Reading Check**
What happens to the man's second attempt to build a fire?

31 Literary Analysis
Conflict

- **Ask** students to consider how the man's conflict with nature has developed up to this point in the story. Point out that his struggles with his environment have become steadily more difficult.
- Have students read the bracketed passage. If any students find this passage upsetting, encourage them to consider how their discomfort builds their sense of the story's conflict.
- **Ask** students the Literary Analysis question: What conflict is intensified in this passage?
  Possible response: The conflict between the man and the extreme cold is intensified when killing the dog becomes his last chance to escape the cold.

➤ **Monitor Progress: Ask** students what details add to the intensity of the conflict.
Possible response: Students may cite such details as "put a wild idea into his head," the "strange note of fear" in the man's voice, the dog's building suspicions of the man, and the dog's "restless, hunching movements."

32 Reading Check

Answer: Shivering uncontrollably, he drops a large piece of moss on the fire; when he tries to poke the moss out, he extinguishes the fire.

Differentiated Instruction Solutions for All Learners

Strategy for Less Proficient Readers
Have students summarize what is happening between the man and the dog. Guide them to understand that the man is making an awkward, desperate attempt to capture the dog, kill it, and use its body warmth to undo his numbness, and that his movements and sounds make the dog apprehensive. Encourage students to reread if necessary.

Strategy for English Learners
These students may have difficulty decoding the passage describing the man's second attempt to start a fire. Ask students to write down and look up words they do not understand. Guide them to recognize that the man drops his first match, burns his hands with the rest but lights his kindling, and finally puts out the fire himself with his frozen and useless hands.

㉝ Critical Viewing

Possible answer: The landscape appears desolate and harsh; difficult to travel. No signs of active outdoor life might indicate intolerable weather conditions.

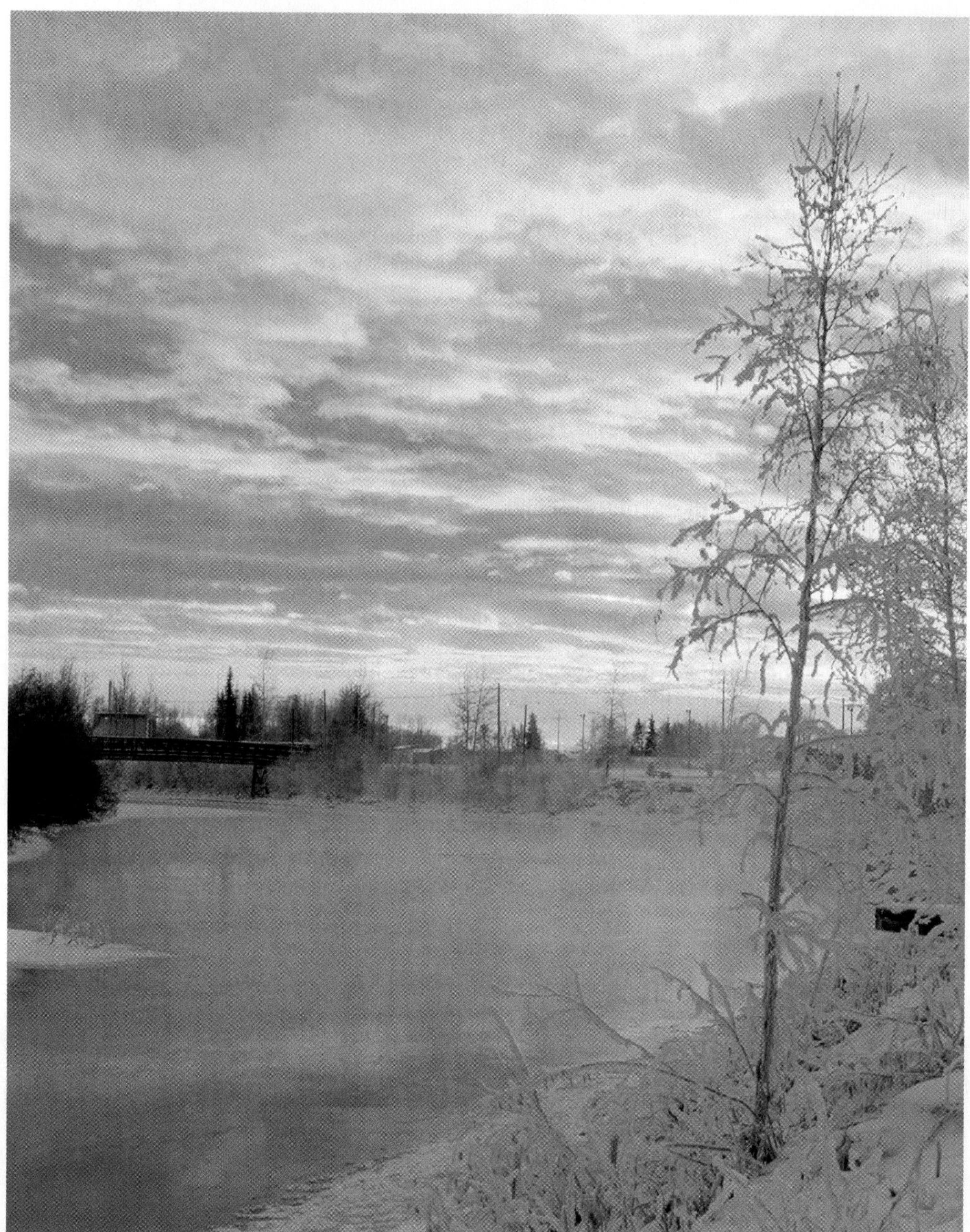

㉝ ▲ **Critical Viewing** What aspects of this Alaskan landscape suggest that it is a dangerous place, despite its beauty?

frozen and that they were freezing more and more. All this happened quickly, and before the animal could get away, he encircled its body with his arms. He sat down in the snow, and in this fashion held the dog, while it snarled and whined and struggled.

But it was all he could do, hold its body encircled in his arms and sit there. He realized that he could not kill the dog. There was no way to do it. With his helpless hands he could neither draw nor hold his sheath-knife nor throttle the animal. He released it, and it plunged wildly away, with tail between its legs, and still snarling. It halted forty feet away and surveyed him curiously, with ears sharply pricked forward. The man looked down at his hands in order to locate them, and found them hanging on the ends of his arms. It struck him as curious that one should have to use his eyes in order to find out where his hands were. He began threshing his arms back and forth, beating the mittened hands against his sides. He did this for five minutes, violently, and his heart pumped enough blood up to the surface to put a stop to his shivering. But no sensation was aroused in the hands. He had an impression that they hung like weights on the ends of his arms, but when he tried to run the impression down, he could not find it.

A certain fear of death, dull and oppressive, came to him. This fear quickly became poignant as he realized that it was no longer a mere matter of freezing his fingers and toes, or of losing his hands and feet, but that it was a matter of life and death with the chances against him. This threw him into a panic, and he turned and ran up the creek-bed along the old, dim trail. The dog joined in behind and kept up with him. He ran blindly, without intention, in fear such as he had never known in his life. Slowly, as he plowed and floundered through the snow, he began to see things again—the banks of the creek, the old timber jams, the leafless aspens, and the sky. The running made him feel better. He did not shiver. Maybe, if he ran on, his feet would thaw out; and, anyway, if he ran far enough, he would reach camp and the boys. Without doubt he would lose some fingers and toes and some of his face; but the boys would take care of him, and save the rest of him when he got there. And at the same time there was another thought in his mind that said he would never get to the camp and the boys; that it was too many miles away, that the freezing had too great a start on him, and that he would soon be stiff and dead. This thought he kept in the background and refused to consider. Sometimes it pushed itself forward and demanded to be heard, but he thrust it back and strove to think of other things.

It struck him as curious that he could run at all on feet so frozen that he could not feel them when they struck the earth and took the weight of his body. He seemed to himself to skim along above the surface, and to have no connection with the earth. Somewhere he had once seen a winged Mercury,[6] and he wondered if Mercury felt as he felt when skimming over the earth. 36

6. **Mercury** from Roman mythology, the wing-footed messenger of the gods.

Reading Strategy
Predicting Does the man still have a chance for survival? Explain why or why not.

Reading Check
What thought does the man refuse to consider?

Differentiated Instruction Solutions for All Learners

Strategy for Less Proficient Readers

If students need help understanding the concept of conflict in this story, have them use the following graphic organizer. Remind them that conflict is a common ingredient in fictional plots, and that it follows a pattern. Show students the organizer and suggest that they copy it. On the left side, have them list the events that lead up to the turning point, or climax, of the main character's conflict. On the right side, have them list the events that follow this turning point.

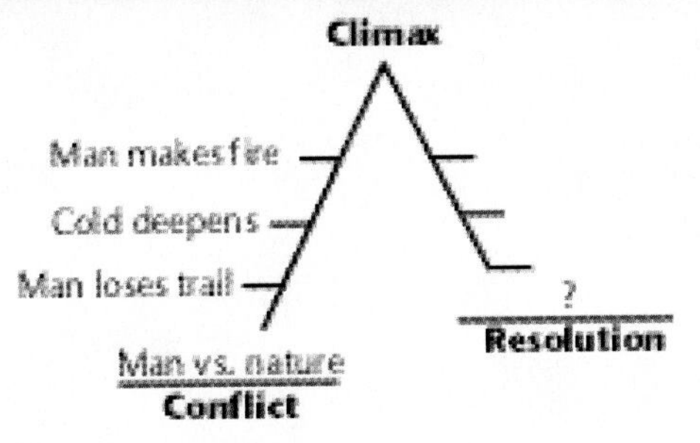

34 Reading Strategy
Predicting

- Before they read the bracketed passage, **ask** students to compare the man's survival skills with the dog's. Remind them that the narrator indicates that the dog's instincts give it a better grasp of the cold than the man has.
- Have students read the bracketed passage. Then, **ask** them to predict whether the man will survive and whether the dog will survive. Students should support their answers with details.
  Possible response: Based on the fact that the man has no means by which to start a fire, it is unlikely he will survive. The dog, on the other hand, is likely to survive because of its protective coat and strong instincts for survival.

35 Reading Strategy
Predicting

- Instruct students to construct or add to previously constructed Predicting charts, with two columns.
- Have students read the bracketed passage. **Ask** them to write clues from the passage in the left-hand column of their charts.
  Possible response: Students may note the man's growing "fear of death" and panic, as well as his new hope that he might run all the way to the camp.
- **Ask** students the Reading Strategy question: Does the man still have a chance for survival? Explain why or why not.
  Possible response: Students might say that the man will die because his hypothermia is too severe and the camp is too far away. Others might feel there's still a hope that someone will catch up to him on the trail and save him.
- Have students write their responses in the right-hand columns on their charts.

36 Reading Check

Possible response: He refuses to consider that the camp is too far away and that he may die from the cold.

37 **Literary Analysis**

Conflict and Irony

- Use the Enrichment: Science Connection note at the bottom of p. 622 in this Teacher's Edition to inform students about the symptoms of hypothermia.
- **Ask** students the Literary Analysis question: As the man begins to feel "quite warm and comfortable," what does the reader know that the man does not?
  Answer: The reader knows that the feeling of comfortable warmth is a sign that the man is dying of hypothermia.
- Point out to students that this situation is ironic because the man believes he is now all right while the reader knows that he is about to die.

38 **Literary Analysis**

Conflict

- Remind students that in literary works, conflict builds up to a *climax*—a crisis or turning point in the story's plot. From the climax, the story moves to a resolution, where the conflict comes to an end.
- Have students read the bracketed passage. Point out that the man undergoes an important change here; for the first time, he accepts the inevitability of his death.
- **Ask** students: How does this passage suggest the story's conflict—man versus nature—will be resolved?
  Possible response: Students should recognize that the man is dying and answer that he has lost in his struggle with the extreme weather conditions, and thus will lose his life.

His theory of running until he reached camp and the boys had one flaw in it: he lacked the endurance. Several times he stumbled, and finally he tottered, crumpled up, and fell. When he tried to rise, he failed. He must sit and rest, he decided, and next time he would merely walk and keep on going. As he sat and regained his breath, he noted that he was feeling quite warm and comfortable. He was 37 not shivering, and it even seemed that a warm glow had come to his chest and trunk. And yet, when he touched his nose or cheeks, there was no sensation. Running would not thaw them out. Nor would it thaw out his hands and feet. Then the thought came to him that the frozen portions of his body must be extending. He tried to keep this thought down, to forget it, to think of something else; he was aware of the panicky feeling that it caused, and he was afraid of the panic. But the thought asserted itself, and persisted, until it produced a vision of his body totally frozen. This was too much, and he made another wild run along the trail. Once he slowed down to a walk, but the thought of the freezing extending itself made him run again.

Literary Analysis
Conflict and Irony As the man begins to feel "quite warm and comfortable" what does the reader know that the man does not?

And all the time the dog ran with him, at his heels. When he fell down a second time, it curled its tail over its forefeet and sat in front of him, facing him, curiously eager and intent. The warmth and security of the animal angered him, and he cursed it till it flattened down its ears appeasingly. This time the shivering came more quickly upon the man. He was losing in his battle with the frost. It was creeping into his body from all sides. The thought of it drove him on, but he ran no more than a hundred feet, when he staggered and pitched headlong. It was his last panic. When he had recovered his breath and control, he sat up and entertained in his mind the conception of meeting death with dignity. However, the conception did not come to him in such terms. His idea of it was that he had been making a fool of himself, running around like a chicken with its head 38 cut off—such was the simile that occurred to him. Well, he was bound to freeze anyway, and he might as well take it decently. With this new-found peace of mind came the first glimmerings of drowsiness. A good idea, he thought, to sleep off to death. It was like taking an anaesthetic. Freezing was not so bad as people thought. There were lots worse ways to die.

He pictured the boys finding his body next day. Suddenly he found himself with them, coming along the trail and looking for himself. And, still with them, he came around a turn in the trail and found himself lying in the snow. He did not belong with himself any more, for even then he was out of himself; standing with the boys and looking at himself in the snow. It certainly was cold, was his thought. When he got back to the States he could tell the folks what real cold was. He drifted on from this to a vision of the old-timer on Sulphur Creek. He could see him quite clearly, warm and comfortable, and smoking a pipe.

"You were right, old hoss; you were right," the man mumbled to the old-timer of Sulphur Creek.

Then the man drowsed off into what seemed to him the most comfortable and satisfying sleep he had ever known. The dog sat facing him and waiting. The brief day drew to a close in a long, slow twilight. There were no signs of a fire to be made, and, besides, never in the dog's experience had it known a man to sit like that in the snow and make no fire. As the twilight drew on, its eager yearning for the fire mastered it, and with a great lifting and shifting of forefeet, it whined softly, then flattened its ears down in anticipation of being chidden[7] by the man. But the man remained silent. Later, the dog whined loudly. And still later it crept close to the man and caught the scent of death. This made the animal bristle and back away. A little longer it delayed, howling under the stars that leaped and danced and shone brightly in the cold sky. Then it turned and trotted up the trail in the direction of the camp it knew, where were the other food providers and fire providers.

7. **chidden** scolded.

Critical Reading

1. **Respond:** Could you imagine yourself falling into the same circumstances as the man? How could you avoid them?
2. **(a) Recall:** What advice from an old-timer does the man choose to ignore? **(b) Infer:** What does this decision suggest about the man's character?
3. **(a) Recall:** What do the dog's instincts tell it about the cold? **(b) Compare and Contrast:** By contrast, why does the extreme cold "make no impression" on the man? **(c) Make a Judgment:** Who is better equipped to survive in the cold, the dog or the man? Explain.
4. **(a) Recall:** What trap does the man try—unsuccessfully—to avoid? **(b) Analyze Cause and Effect:** What deadly chain of events is started by his inability to avoid the trap?
5. **(a) Recall:** When the man breaks through the snow into the icy water, he becomes angry and curses. What is it that he curses? **(b) Evaluate:** Is the outcome of the story due to fate, to the man's character, or to some other cause? Explain.
6. **(a) Assess:** Why do you think London did not give the man a name? **(b) Speculate:** How might the effect of this story be different if the man had a name?
7. **(a) Draw Conclusions:** What does the story suggest about human strength in the face of nature's power? **(b) Take a Position:** Is London's message true? Explain.

For: More about Jack London
Visit: www.PHSchool.com
Web Code: ere-9418

Go Online Author Link For additional information about Jack London, have students type in the Web Code, then select L from the alphabet, and then select Jack London.

ASSESS

Answers

1. **Possible response:** Students may respond that they would never have set out alone or chosen to travel in such harsh weather.
2. (a) No one should travel alone in the Klondike if the temperature is colder than fifty below zero. (b) **Possible response:** It suggests that he is thoughtless and overly self-confident.
3. **Possible response:** (a) The dog's instincts tell it not to travel, but to stay where there is fire. (b) The man does not have the imagination to understand the significance of the cold or the possible consequences of traveling in such weather. (c) The dog is better equipped to survive.
4. (a) The man tries to avoid the hidden pools of water. (b) His feet get wet, requiring him to build a fire; he builds his fire by a tree, which dumps snow on it; his hands are too frozen to build a second fire; he freezes to death.
5. (a) He curses his luck. (b) **Possible response:** Students may respond that the man's own character flaws—lack of imagination and overconfidence — contribute to his downfall.
6. **Possible response:** (a) Perhaps because the man serves as a symbol for the human desire to control or disregard the power of nature. (b) Students may recognize that they would have greater sympathy with the man, despite his flaws.
7. **Possible response:** (a) It suggests that human strength cannot control nature. Nature is a much more powerful force than humanity, and must be respected. (b) Students may agree with London's message because today ecological problems persist despite our efforts to solve them.

Answers

1. (a) The conflict is between man and nature. (b) **Possible response:** The central conflict is man vs. nature. Students' charts should list appropriate details from the story.

   Another sample answer can be found on **Literary Analysis Graphic Organizer B**, p. 131 in ***Graphic Organizer Transparencies.***
2. **Possible response:** The forces of nature affect the man more and more as the story progresses; gradually, the man becomes aware of how dangerous his situation has become.
3. Falling snow puts out the man's fire; he is unable to start a second fire. He freezes to death.
4. The man's lack of judgment and overconfidence conflict with his genuine fear for his own safety as he battles to stay calm in the face of rising panic.
5. It is ironic because he has been keeping a careful eye out for exactly the trap he falls into.
6. It is ironic because in his overconfidence, he builds it beneath a snow-laden tree.
7. By describing the dog's feelings and instincts, London lets the reader know what the man does not: that he is walking into deadly danger.
8. (a) One should never travel alone in the Klondike when the temperature is less than fifty degrees below zero.
   (b) **Possible response:** Each time the man remembers the advice and laughs, it is a reminder of the fatal danger he faces.
9. **Possible response:** (a) and (b) Student answers will vary, but should be supported with details from the text.
10. **Possible response:** Student responses should accurately summarize the basic information in the story and perhaps use the man's death as a warning to others.

Go Online Assessment Students may use the **Self-test** to prepare for **Selection Test A** or **Selection Test B.**

Apply the Skills

To Build a Fire

Literary Analysis

Conflict

1. **(a)** What **external conflict** is central to the plot of "To Build a Fire"? **(b)** Use a chart like the one shown to examine the details London uses to portray the central conflict.

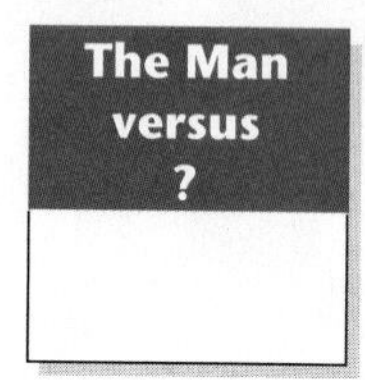

Details

1. ____
2. ____
3. ____

2. Does the man's awareness of the conflict intensify as the story unfolds? Explain.
3. What events finally resolve the conflict?
4. What is the **internal conflict** that develops as the story progresses?

Connecting Literary Elements

5. What is **ironic** about the fact that the man breaks through the snow and steps in the spring?
6. What is ironic about the location in which he builds his fire?
7. In what way do London's descriptions of the dog's feelings and its instincts about survival increase the story's **dramatic irony**?

Reading Strategy

Predicting

8. **(a)** What information do the man's recollections of his conversation with the old-timer provide? **(b)** In what ways does this information help you **predict** the end of the story?
9. **(a)** At what point did you first predict that the man would not survive his journey? **(b)** On what clues did you base your prediction?

Extend Understanding

10. **Social Studies Connection:** Suppose that you were the editor of a newspaper in Alaska during the time of the Klondike Gold Rush. If you learned of this man's sad tale, what might you have written in an editorial about the event?

QuickReview

A **conflict** is a struggle between two opposing forces. An **external conflict** occurs between a character and an outside force or another character. An **internal conflict** occurs within a character's own mind.

Irony is a discrepancy between what is stated and what is meant, or between what is expected and what happens. **Dramatic irony** occurs when the reader knows more than the character does.

To **predict** what will happen in a story, look for clues that hint at later events.

For: Self-test
Visit: www.PHSchool.com
Web Code: era-6411

Build Language Skills

1 Vocabulary Lesson

Word Analysis: Latin Root *-ject-*

The Latin root *-ject-* means "to throw." If you *reject* an idea, you throw it back. Each word below contains the root *-ject-*. Use the clues to match each word with the situation to which it applies.

1. object (*ob* = toward; over; against)
2. conjecture (*con* = with; *ure* = act; process)
3. abject (*ab* = away from)
4. eject (*e* = out; away)

a. you throw an idea together
b. you speak out against something
c. you remove someone from the premises
d. you feel this way when your friends shun you

Vocabulary Builder: Sentence Completions

Fill in the blanks with the appropriate words from the vocabulary list on page 619.

A lightning storm in the parched woodland sparked a __?__. The shy fire chief acted with __?__ authority, __?__ ordering all firefighters to work round the clock, though his estimates of how long it would take to overcome the fire were __?__ at best.

Spelling Strategy

To add a suffix to a word ending in a *y* preceded by a consonant, change the *y* to *i* (*peremptory* + *ly* = *peremptorily*). For each of the following sentences, write the correct form of the word in italics.

1. My parents *accompany* me to Alaska.
2. We *happy* watched as the run scored.

2 Grammar and Style Lesson

Adverb Clauses

An **adverb clause** is a group of words that modifies a verb, an adjective, or another adverb by explaining *how, where, when, why, to what extent,* or *under what circumstances.* An adverb clause has a subject and verb but cannot stand by itself as a sentence.

> Day had broken cold and gray, exceedingly cold and gray, *when the man turned aside from the main Yukon trail* . . . . (tells *when*)

Practice Identify the adverb clause and the word it modifies in each item below.

1. North and south, as far as the eye could see, it was unbroken white . . . .
2. A foot of snow had fallen since the last sled had passed over.
3. He made a new foundation for a fire, where no treacherous tree could blot it out.
4. If he kept it up, he would certainly be with the boys by six.
5. At last, when he could endure no more, he jerked his hands apart.

Writing Application Write four sentences describing a frightening encounter with nature. Use at least one adverb clause in each sentence. Identify the function of each adverb clause in your draft.

WG *Prentice Hall Writing and Grammar Connection: Chapter 19, Section 3*

EXTEND/ASSESS

Answers

1 Vocabulary Lesson

Word Analysis

1. b
2. a
3. d
4. c

Vocabulary Builder

conflagration; unwonted; peremptorily; conjectural

Spelling Strategy

1. accompanied
2. happily

2 Grammar and Style Lesson

1. as far as the eye could see; modifies *was*
2. since the last sled had passed over; modifies *had fallen*
3. where no treacherous tree could blot it out; modifies *made*
4. If he kept it up; modifies *would be*
5. When he could endure no more; modifies *jerked*

Writing Application

Each of the four sentences should contain an adverb clause—always a dependent clause that functions as an adverb. All four sentences should relate to a frightening encounter with nature.

WG **Writing and Grammar, Ruby Level**

Students will find further instruction and practice adverb clauses in Chapter 19, Section 3.

Assessment Practice

Context **(For more practice, see *Standardized Test Preparation Workbook*, p. 35.)**

Many tests require students to use contextual analysis to determine the meanings of words and phrases. Use the following to demonstrate.

> Fifty degrees below zero meant eighty-odd degrees of frost. Such fact. . . did not lead him to meditate upon his *frailty as a creature of temperature,* and upon man's frailty in general, able only to live within certain narrow limits of heat and cold.

In this passage, the phrase *frailty as a creature of temperature* means—

A Humans can be killed by heat and cold.
B Humans are frail when they have a temperature.
C Humans can survive in the cold.
D Even frail humans can withstand extreme temperatures.

The last part of the sentence gives context clues that show *A* is the correct answer.

❸ Writing Lesson

You may use this Writing Lesson as timed-writing practice, or you may allow students to develop the essay as a writing assignment over several days.

- To guide students in writing this literary analysis, give them the **Support for Writing Lesson** page (***Unit 4 Resources,*** p. 179).
- Explain to students that unlike a book report that simply restates the story, a literary analysis digs beneath the surface to present an interpretation of the work. This interpretation forms the thesis, or main point, of the analysis.
- Using the Writing Lesson, guide students to begin prewriting. Emphasize that each point in the essay will need to be supported with details from the story.
- Literary Analyses should present convincing interpretations supported by appropriate details from the story.
- Use the rubrics for Response to Literature, pp. 65–66 in ***General Resources,*** to evaluate students' work.

❹ Research and Technology

- Explain that booklets will present general information. Because they offer condensed information, booklets should give readers only the most important or useful facts, guidelines, or details.
- Have students work in pairs to research the causes, symptoms, and recommended treatment for hypothermia.
- Partners can combine the most important points, guidelines, and tips for avoiding, detecting, and treating hypothermia. Help students to print and assemble their booklets.
- Assess students' booklets based on the completeness and effective presentation of the information.
- The **Support for Extend Your Learning** page (***Unit 4 Resources,*** p. 180) provides guided note-taking opportunities to help students complete the Extend Your Learning activities.

Go Online Research Have students type in the Web Code for another research activity.

SAT PREP ACT

❸ Writing Lesson

Timed Writing: Literary Analysis

A literary analysis explores how the elements of a piece of literature, such as plot, setting, characters, and point of view, work together to convey a message. Write a literary analysis in which you explain the message of "To Build a Fire," and discuss how the various elements of the story contribute to its meaning. ***(40 minutes)***

Prewriting *(10 minutes)* Review the story to identify London's message about the relationship between humanity and nature. Gather details that support your interpretation.

Drafting *(20 minutes)* In your introduction, state your thesis and outline your main points. Focus each body paragraph on one main point. Cite supporting details from the story.

Model: Elaborating to Support an Argument

The dog, equipped by centuries of evolution for life in the bitter cold, serves as a symbolic foil to the man. Unlike the man, who disregards plain evidence, ". . . the dog knew; all its ancestry knew, and it had inherited the knowledge. And it knew that it was not good to walk abroad in such fearful cold."

Providing details from the work helps to elaborate on the main point, underlined here.

Revising *(10 minutes)* Review your draft, making sure your thesis is clear and your support is convincing. Look for opportunities to elaborate on your key points.

WG Prentice Hall Writing and Grammar Connection: Chapter 14, Section 4

❹ Extend Your Learning

Listening and Speaking If the dog could voice its thoughts about the man, what would it say? Write and present an **enactment** of the dog's thoughts and feelings as a scene of this story unfolds. Keep these tips in mind as you work:

- Refer to the text of the story for accuracy.
- Include details that reflect the dog's highly developed senses of smell and hearing.

Work to create a specific sense of character, so that your dog has an individual voice and expresses a clear point of view.

Research and Technology The man in the story dies of hypothermia, or subnormal body temperature. With a partner, research this condition, using a variety of sources, including the Internet. Then, create a word-processed **booklet** of guidelines for avoiding hypothermia. **[Group Activity]**

Go Online Research **For:** An additional research activity
Visit: www.PHSchool.com
Web Code: erd-7410

Assessment Resources

The following resources can be used to assess students' knowledge and skills.

Unit 4 Resources
- **Selection Test A,** pp. 182–184
- **Selection Test B,** pp. 185–186

General Resources
- **Rubrics for Response to Literature,** pp. 65–66

Go Online Assessment Students may use the **Self-test** to prepare for **Selection Test A** or **Selection Test B.**

Unit 4
Part
4

Living in a Changing World

Channel to the Mills, 1913, Edwin M. Dawes. Minneapolis Institute of Arts

Selection Planning Guide

These works examine the effects of the societal changes taking place at the turn of the twentieth century. Students will be interested to learn that Kate Chopin's dark tale, "The Story of an Hour," was considered scandalous because it suggested that a woman might be happier without her husband. African Americans' struggle for acceptance and equality is reflected in the poems of Paul Laurence Dunbar. Edwin Arlington Robinson and Edgar Lee Masters paint memorable verbal portraits of four uniquely American characters who reflect the changing values of their day. Willa Cather contrasts the rigors of American frontier life with the cultural centers of the East in "A Wagner Matinée."

Humanities

Channel to the Mills, 1913, Edwin M. Dawes

Encourage students to contrast this artwork with pieces like *Early Morning at Cold Spring* (page 383). Help them see that the natural landscape had dominated earlier paintings. In contrast, Dawes chooses a group of mills to dominate the landscape of this painting.

1. What changes in the American environment does this artwork suggest?
   Possible response: The artwork focuses on the change from a rural to an industrial society.
2. What attitude toward these changes does the artist communicate, and how?
   Possible responses: The soft, shimmering colors of the artwork suggest that the artist's attitude is positive. A negative attitude is suggested by the title, which draws attention to the water that the mills are polluting, and by the way the buildings loom so large and blot out the horizon.

Differentiated Instruction Solutions for All Learners

Accessibility at a Glance

Average
The Story of an Hour
Douglass
We Wear the Mask
Luke Havergal
Richard Cory
Lucinda Matlock
Richard Bone

More Challenging
A Wagner Matinée

Meeting Your Standards

Students will

1. **analyze and respond to literary elements.**
    - Literary Analysis: Irony
2. **read, comprehend, analyze, and critique a short story.**
    - Reading Strategy: Recognizing Ironic Details
    - Reading Check questions
    - Apply the Skills questions
    - Assessment Practice (ATE)
3. **develop vocabulary.**
    - Vocabulary Lesson: Anglo-Saxon Prefix: *fore-*
4. **understand and apply written and oral language conventions.**
    - Spelling Strategy
    - Grammar and Style Lesson: Appositives and Appositive Phrases
5. **develop writing proficiency.**
    - Writing Lesson: Reflective Essay
6. **develop appropriate research strategies.**
    - Extend Your Learning: Oral Report
7. **understand and apply listening and speaking strategies.**
    - Extend Your Learning: Soliloquy

Block Scheduling: Use one 90-minute class period to preteach the skills and have students read the selection. Use a second 90-minute class period to assess students' mastery of skills, extend their learning, and monitor their progress.

Homework Suggestions

Following are possibilities for homework assignments.

- Support pages from ***Unit 4 Resources:***
    Literary Analysis
    Reading Strategy
    Vocabulary Builder
    Grammar and Style
- An Extend Your Learning project and the Writing Lesson for this selection may be completed over several days.

Step-by-Step Teaching Guide	Pacing Guide
PRETEACH	
• Administer Vocabulary and Reading Warm-ups as necessary.	5 min.
• Engage students' interest with the motivation activity.	5 min.
• Read and discuss author and background features. **FT**	10 min.
• Introduce the Literary Analysis Skill: Irony. **FT**	5 min.
• Introduce the Reading Strategy: Recognizing Ironic Details. **FT**	10 min.
• Prepare students to read by teaching the selection vocabulary. **FT**	
TEACH	
• Informally monitor comprehension while students read independently or in groups. **FT**	30 min.
• Monitor students' comprehension with the Reading Check notes.	as students read
• Reinforce vocabulary with Vocabulary Builder notes.	as students read
• Develop students' understanding of irony with the Literary Analysis annotations. **FT**	5 min.
• Develop students' ability to recognize ironic details with the Reading Strategy annotations. **FT**	5 min.
ASSESS/EXTEND	
• Assess students' comprehension and mastery of the Literary Analysis and Reading Strategy by having them answer the Apply the Skills questions. **FT**	15 min.
• Have students complete the Vocabulary Lesson and the Grammar and Style Lesson. **FT**	15 min.
• Apply students' ability to gather details by using the Writing Lesson. **FT**	45 min. or homework
• Apply students' understanding by using one or more of the Extend Your Learning activities.	20–90 min. or homework
• Administer Selection Test A or Selection Test B. **FT**	15 min.

Resources

PRINT

Unit 4 Resources

- Vocabulary Warm-up Word Lists [**L1, L2, EL**] .... p. 188
- Vocabulary Warm-up Practice [**L1, L2, EL**] .... p. 189
- Reading Warm-up A [**L1, L2, EL**] .... p. 190
- Reading Warm-up B [**L1, L2, L3**] .... p. 191

TRANSPARENCY

Graphic Organizer Transparencies

- Literary Analysis Graphic Organizer A [**L3**] .... p. 134
- Literary Analysis Graphic Organizer B [**L1, L2, EL**] .... p. 135
- Reading Strategy Graphic Organizer A [**L3**] .... p. 132
- Reading Strategy Graphic Organizer B [**L1, L2, EL**] .... p. 133

PRINT

Reader's Notebook [**L2**]
Reader's Notebook: Adapted Version [**L1**]
Reader's Notebook: English Learner's Version [**EL**]

Unit 4 Resources

- Literary Analysis [**L3**] .... p. 192
- Reading Strategy [**L3**] .... p. 193
- Vocabulary Builder [**L3**] .... p. 194

TECHNOLOGY

Listening to Literature Audio CDs [**L2, EL**]
Reader's Notebook: Adapted Version Audio CD [**L1, L2**]

PRINT

Unit 4 Resources

- Grammar and Style [**L3**] .... p. 195
- Support for Writing Lesson [**L3**] .... p. 196
- Support for Extend Your Learning [**L3**] .... p. 197
- Enrichment [**L4**] .... p. 198
- Selection Test A [**L1, L2, EL**] .... pp. 199–201
- Selection Test B [**L3, L4**] .... pp. 202–204

General Resources

- Rubrics for Reflective Essay [**L3**] .... pp. 47–48
- Rubric for Peer Assessment: Dramatic Performance [**L3**] .... p. 131

TECHNOLOGY

Go Online: Research [**L3**]
Go Online: Self-test [**L3**]
***ExamView®*, Test Bank** [**L3**]

Choosing Resources for Differentiated Instruction

[**L1**] Special Needs Students
[**L2**] Below-Level Students
[**L3**] All Students
[**L4**] Advanced Students
[**EL**] English Learners

FT Fast Track Instruction: To move the lesson more quickly, use the strategies and activities identified with **FT**.

Scaffolding for Less Proficient and Advanced Students

The leveled Critical Thinking questions after selections progress in the levels of thinking required to answer them. To address the needs of your different students, you may use the (a) level questions for your less proficient students and the (b) level questions with your on-level and advanced students. The occasional (c) level questions are appropriate for your advanced students.

PRENTICE HALL **TeacherEXPRESS™** Plan · Teach · Assess

Use this complete suite of powerful teaching tools to make lesson planning and testing quicker and easier.

Use the interactive textbook (online and on CD-ROM) to make selections and activities come alive with audio and video support and interactive questions.

tudents gener-
nes" that would
example, you
g the lottery,
the death of a loved one, or early admission to college.

Then, tell students that in the story they are about to read, a character has unexpected reactions to unanticipated news. Discuss the idea that in life, things are not always as they appear, that there's often more than one way to look at them.

❶ Background

Chopin's story addresses issues of women's liberation in a time when these issues were not frequently raised. Activists were just beginning to stir the national conscience. Women and minorities were seeking to expand their civil rights. In addition, psychologists such as William James were debating free will, the ability of individuals to control their own destiny. These developments began a social revolution whose effects are still being felt today.

❶ The Story of an Hour

Kate Chopin (1850–1904)

Despite her conservative, aristocratic upbringing, Kate O'Flaherty Chopin (shō´ pan) became one of the most powerful and controversial writers of her time. In her stories, sketches, and novels, she not only captured the local color of Louisiana but also boldly explored the role of women in society.

Family Life Kate O'Flaherty was born in St. Louis, Missouri, the daughter of a wealthy businessman. When Kate was five years old, her father died in a railroad accident. The young Kate was taken out of school and educated at home for the next two years by her mother, grandmother, and great-grandmother. When she was twenty, Kate married Oscar Chopin, a Louisiana cotton trader. The couple settled in New Orleans, where they lived for ten years before moving to a plantation in rural northwestern Louisiana.

Tragedy Strikes In 1882, Chopin's husband died, leaving her to raise their six children on her own. Chopin carried on the work of the plantation alone for more than a year, using her knowledge of finance and developing skills as a businesswoman. However, in 1884 she yielded to her mother's urgings, sold most of her holdings, and returned to St. Louis with her children. Her mother's sudden death in 1885 left Chopin in deep sorrow. It was at the suggestion of her family doctor, who was concerned about her emotional health, that she began to write fiction. Chopin kept St. Louis as her home for the rest of her life and devoted much of her energy to writing.

Chopin the Writer and Rebel Influenced by American Regionalists such as Sarah Orne Jewett, and fascinated by the mixture of cultures in Louisiana, Chopin focused on capturing the essence of life in Louisiana in her writing. Like most of her other works, Chopin's first novel, *At Fault* (1890), was set in a small Louisiana town inhabited by Creoles, descendants of the original French and Spanish settlers, and Cajuns, descendants of French Canadian settlers who arrived later. Through her vivid descriptions and use of dialect, Chopin captured the local color of the region. In her stories, published in *Bayou Folk* (1894) and *A Night In Acadie* (1897), she exhibited her deep understanding of the different attitudes and concerns of the Louisiana natives.

Her charming portraits of Louisiana life often obscured the fact that she explored themes considered radical at the time: the nature of marriage, racial prejudice, and women's desire for social, economic, and political equality. Chopin understood the risk she took in challenging social boundaries, but felt that true art required bravery. She once wrote, "The artist must possess the courageous soul that dares and defies."

The Awakening Chopin's finest novel, *The Awakening* (1899), is a psychological account of a woman's search for independence and fulfillment. Because the novel explored the issue of infidelity, it aroused a storm of protest. The book was severely attacked by critics and eventually banned. As a result, Chopin's reputation was badly damaged. Then, in the 1950s, *The Awakening* was resurrected. Today, the book is among the five most-read American novels in colleges and universities. Chopin is now considered an early practitioner of American Realism—a literary style that seeks to avoid sentimental depictions of life. She is widely respected for her portrayal of the psychology of women and her ability to capture local color.

Preview

Connecting to the Literature

Often, life-changing events—a chance encounter with someone who becomes important in our lives, the loss of a loved one, a sudden move to a new place—sneak up on us unexpectedly. The story you are about to read focuses on a woman's surprising reaction to a shocking piece of news.

2 Literary Analysis

Irony

Irony is a contradiction between appearance and reality, between expectation and outcome, or between meaning and intention. In literature, readers frequently encounter three types of irony:

- **Verbal irony** occurs when someone says something that deliberately contradicts what that person actually means.
- **Situational irony** occurs when something happens that contradicts our expectations.
- **Dramatic irony** occurs when the reader or audience is aware of something that a character does not know.

As you read, decide which type of irony best describes the events in this story.

Connecting Literary Elements

The **climax** is the high point of interest or suspense in a story—the moment when the conflict reaches its greatest intensity. As in many other works of fiction or drama, the climax of "The Story of an Hour" involves a keen sense of irony.

3 Reading Strategy

Recognizing Ironic Details

The details of a story often lead readers to have certain expectations. When events are not resolved as details have led us to expect, we recognize a sense of irony. While reading "The Story of an Hour," use a chart like the one shown to note how specific details imply certain feelings, circumstances, or events that may not, in fact, be what they appear. After reading the story, note whether or not your expectations were met.

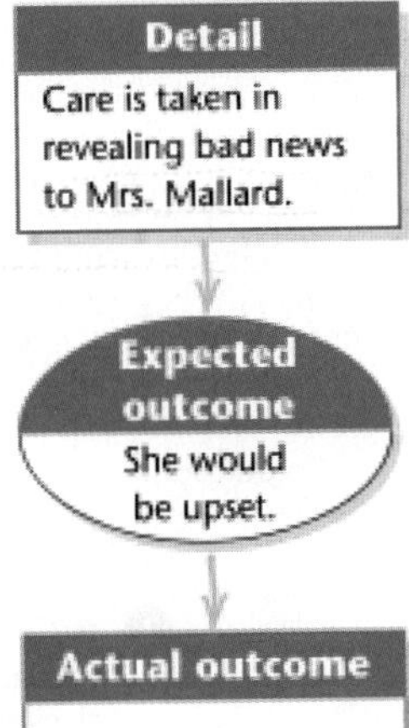

Detail
Care is taken in revealing bad news to Mrs. Mallard.
Expected outcome
She would be upset.
Actual outcome

Vocabulary Builder

forestall (fôr stôl´) *v.* prevent by acting ahead of time (p. 644)

repression (ri presh´ ən) *n.* restraint (p. 645)

elusive (ē lo͞o´ siv) *adj.* hard to grasp (p. 645)

tumultuously (to͞o mul´ cho͞o wəs lē) *adv.* in an agitated way (p. 645)

importunities (im´ pôr to͞on´ ə tēz) *n.* persistent requests or demands (p. 646)

2 Literary Analysis

Irony

- Tell students that as they read "The Story of an Hour," they will notice that Mrs. Mallard's reactions to the news she receives are the opposite of what everyone around her expects. Explain that this contrast is *irony.*
- Review the instruction for Irony. Make sure students understand that there are three major categories of irony: *verbal irony, dramatic irony,* and *situational irony.*
- Suggest that students keep notes on the story's ironic events, identifying each type of irony as it occurs.

3 Reading Strategy

Recognizing Ironic Details

- Give students a copy of **Reading Strategy Graphic Organizer A,** p. 132 in ***Graphic Organizer Transparencies*** to use as they read the selection.
- Remind students that the details of a story can create *irony.* If the details suggest one outcome but the actual outcome is different, irony can result.

Vocabulary Builder

- Pronounce each vocabulary word for students, and read the definitions as a class. Have students identify any words with which they are already familiar.

Differentiated Instruction Solutions for All Learners

Support for Special Needs Students
Have students read the adapted version of "The Story of an Hour" in the ***Reader's Notebook: Adapted Version.*** This version provides basic-level instruction in an interactive format with questions and write-on lines. Completing these pages will prepare students to read the selection in the Student Edition.

Support for Less Proficient Readers
Have students read "The Story of an Hour" in the ***Reader's Notebook.*** This version provides basic-level instruction in an interactive format with questions and write-on lines. After students finish the selection in the ***Reader's Notebook,*** have them complete the questions and activities in the Student Edition.

Support for English Learners
Have students read "The Story of an Hour" in the ***Reader's Notebook: English Learner's Version.*** This version provides basic-level instruction in an interactive format with questions and write-on lines. Completing these pages will prepare students to read the selection in the Student Edition.

TEACH

Learning Modalities
Visual/Spatial Learners

After they have read "The Story of an Hour," show students Art Transparency 6 in **Fine Art Transparencies, Volume 1**. Encourage students to draw connections between the woman in Cassatt's painting and Mrs. Mallard. Have students create their own art projects, using whatever materials they'd like, to represent the contrast between Mrs. Mallard's domestic life and the deep unhappiness and desire for escape that she actually felt. Students should explain how their projects represent the story's themes.

❶ About the Selection

Chopin's story presents its heroine with one unexpected shock and its readers with another.

Mrs. Mallard gets the unexpected news that her husband has been killed in an accident. She quickly recovers from the shock to discover that what she really feels is relief. Though she mourns his passing, she delights in the freedom that is now hers. She shuts herself in her room and relishes the opportunities ahead of her. When Mr. Mallard returns as unexpectedly as he supposedly died, Mrs. Mallard suffers a fatal heart attack caused by the sudden loss of independence. The doctors, mistakenly assuming that she had been grieving, attribute the death to "joy that kills."

❶

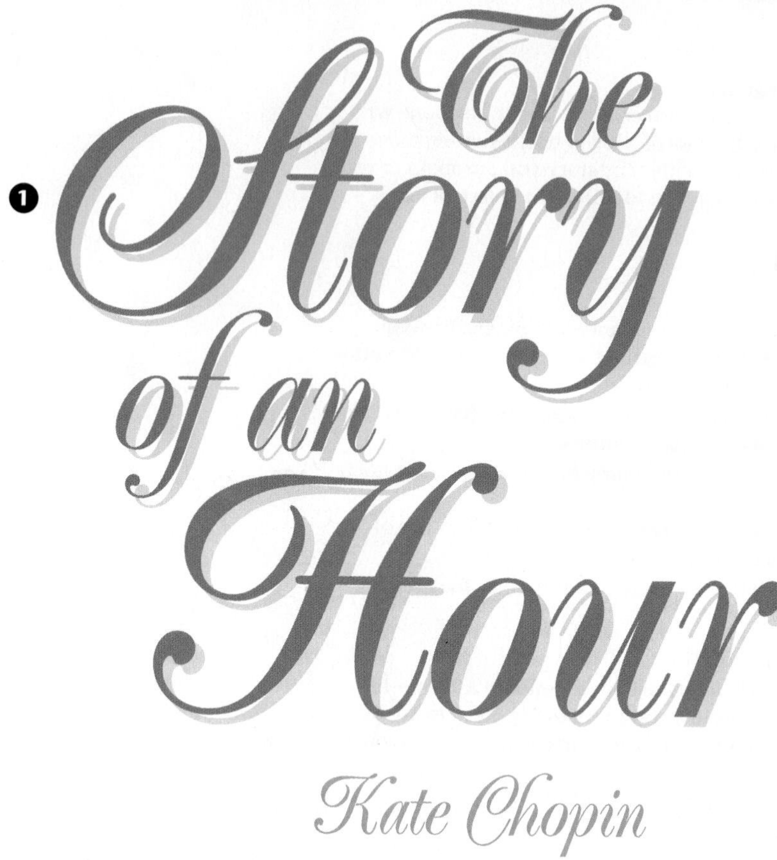

The Story of an Hour

Kate Chopin

Background "The Story of an Hour" was considered daring in the nineteenth century. The editors of at least two magazines refused the story because they thought it was immoral. They wanted Chopin to soften her female character, to make her less independent and unhappy in her marriage. Undaunted, Chopin continued to deal with issues of women's growth and emancipation in her writing, advancing ideas that are widely accepted today.

❸ ▶ **Critical Viewing** This story presents a "subtle and elusive" revelation. What connection do you see between the light shining through the uncovered portion of the window and such a discovery? **[Connect]**

Afternoon in Piedmont (Elsie at the Window), c. 1911, Xavier Martinez, Collection of The Oakland Museum of California

Differentiated Instruction Solutions for All Learners

Accessibility at a Glance

	The Story of an Hour
Context	Gender roles
Language	Formal
Concept Level	Accessible (irony of woman's death)
Literary Merit	Important statement on the status of women
Lexile	970
Overall Rating	Average

2

❷ Humanities

Afternoon in Piedmont, by Xavier Martinez

Xavier Martinez was born in Guadalajara, Mexico, in 1869. He eventually moved to San Francisco, where he later taught at the California School of Fine Arts. Martinez's work has been described as poetic. His *Afternoon at Piedmont* used as its inspiration James Whistler's famous painting of his mother. In his work, Martinez moved the scene to his house and used his wife as the model.

After students have read the selection, return to this painting and use these questions for discussion:

1. How would you describe the mood of this painting?
   Possible response: Students may see the yellow light entering the dark interior as the coming of dawn, bringing with it a comforting awakening.
2. What scene in the story does the painting best represent?
   Possible response: Students may say that it describes the scene in which Mrs. Mallard is looking out at the signs of early spring and is herself awakening to her true feelings and a new approach to life.

❸ Critical Viewing

Possible response: Students may say that the light shows Mrs. Mallard's calm contentment upon recognizing the first stages of her newly found freedom. They may suggest that the light is symbolic of the new beginning of her life.

Differentiated Instruction

Solutions for All Learners

Strategy for Less Proficient Readers

To help students get the most from this story, have them read it twice, once to follow the plot and once more to notice the ironic details. You may use the **Reader's Notebook** to provide further guidance for these students.

Background for English Learners

Students may come from cultures in which gender roles are strictly defined. Discuss the role of women and marriage in late nineteenth century America, making clear the contrast between life then and now. Help students recognize the radical ideas Chopin presents.

Background for Advanced Readers

Point out that the idea of an emancipated woman was a radical notion in the 1890s. Then, guide students to look for further examples of ideas in this story that were ahead of their time.

❹ Vocabulary Builder

The Anglo-Saxon Prefix *fore-*

- Call students' attention to the word *forestall* and its definition. Tell students that the Anglo-Saxon prefix *fore-* means "before"—in time, place, or condition.
- Have students suggest words and phrases that begin with this prefix, and list them on the chalkboard. Possibilities include *foretell, forethought, foreman, foremost,* and *forefathers.*
- Next, have students look up the meanings of these words in a dictionary.
- Finally, direct students to reread the story, looking for places where they can replace an existing word or phrase with a word beginning with the Anglo-Saxon prefix *fore-*. Call on volunteers to read their new sentences aloud.

❺ Reading Strategy

Recognizing Ironic Details

- Remind students that a story's details can create irony by failing to meet a reader's expectations or by encouraging false expectations.
- Have students read the bracketed passage. Encourage them to note its details in a chart such as the one on p. 641.
- **Ask** students the Reading Strategy question: Considering the news she has just received, what is ironic about the details Mrs. Mallard notices through her window?
  Answer: It is ironic that Mrs. Mallard, newly widowed, should see signs of the new life of spring and breaks in the clouds, and hear the sounds and songs of life.
- Encourage students to add their responses to their charts.

➤ **Monitor Progress** Make sure students can explain why each detail on their charts is ironic.

Knowing that Mrs. Mallard was afflicted with a heart trouble, great care was taken to break to her as gently as possible the news of her husband's death.

It was her sister Josephine who told her, in broken sentences; veiled hints that revealed in half concealing. Her husband's friend Richards was there, too, near her. It was he who had been in the newspaper office when intelligence of the railroad disaster was received, with Brently Mallard's name leading the list of "killed." He had only taken the time to assure himself

❹ of its truth by a second telegram, and had hastened to forestall any less careful, less tender friend in bearing the sad message.

She did not hear the story as many women have heard the same, with a paralyzed inability to accept its significance. She wept at once, with sudden, wild abandonment, in her sister's arms. When the storm of grief had spent itself she went away to her room alone. She would have no one follow her.

There stood, facing the open window, a comfortable, roomy armchair. Into this she sank, pressed down by a physical exhaustion that haunted her body and seemed to reach into her soul.

She could see in the open square before her house the tops of trees that were all aquiver with the new spring life. The delicious breath of rain was in the air. In the street below a peddler was crying his wares. The

❺ notes of a distant song which someone was singing reached her faintly, and countless sparrows were twittering in the eaves.

There were patches of blue sky showing here and there through the clouds that had met and piled one above the other in the west facing her window.

She sat with her head thrown back upon the cushion of the chair, quite motionless, except when a sob came up into her throat and shook her, as a child who has cried itself to sleep continues to sob in its dreams.

Vocabulary Builder
forestall (fôr stôl′) *v.* prevent by acting ahead of time

Reading Strategy
Recognizing Ironic Details Considering the news she has just received, what is ironic about the details Mrs. Mallard notices through her window?

Enrichment

Communication Technology

Point out that the failure of long-distance communication in this story leads to a fatal misunderstanding. While the telegram was a major method of long-distance communication in Chopin's time, newer, faster modes have since made the telegram obsolete.

By 1887, the telephone was becoming widely available and U.S. telephone companies served more than 150,000 customers. One hundred years later, fax machines became a popular mode of communication, allowing people to send reproductions of documents through telephone lines. In the early 1990s, the Internet was introduced to the general public with the highly designed World Wide Web. Personal Internet access allowed people to send and receive e-mail from the comfort of their homes.

She was young, with a fair, calm face, whose lines bespoke repression and even a certain strength. But now there was a dull stare in her eyes, whose gaze was fixed away off yonder on one of those patches of blue sky. It was not a glance of reflection, but rather indicated a suspension of intelligent thought.

There was something coming to her and she was waiting for it, fearfully. What was it? She did not know; it was too subtle and elusive to name. But she felt it, creeping out of the sky, reaching toward her through the sounds, the scents, the color that filled the air.

Now her bosom rose and fell tumultuously. She was beginning to recognize this thing that was approaching to possess her, and she was striving to beat it back with her will—as powerless as her two white slender hands would have been.

When she abandoned herself, a little whispered word escaped her slightly parted lips. She said it over and over under her breath: "free, free, free!" The vacant stare and the look of terror that had followed it went from her eyes. They stayed keen and bright. Her pulses beat fast, and the coursing blood warmed and relaxed every inch of her body.

She did not stop to ask if it were or were not a monstrous joy that held her. A clear and exalted perception enabled her to dismiss the suggestion as trivial.

She knew that she would weep again when she saw the kind, tender hands folded in death; the face that had never looked save with love upon her, fixed and gray and dead. But she saw beyond that bitter moment a long procession of years to come that would belong to her absolutely. And she opened and spread her arms out to them in welcome.

There would be no one to live for her during those coming years; she would live for herself. There would be no powerful will bending hers in that blind persistence with which men and women believe they have a right to impose a private will upon a fellow creature. A kind intention or a cruel intention made the act seem no less a crime as she looked upon it in that brief moment of illumination.

And yet she had loved him—sometimes. Often she had not. What did it matter! What could love, the unsolved mystery, count for in face of this possession of self-assertion which she suddenly recognized as the strongest impulse of her being!

"Free! Body and soul free!" she kept whispering.

Josephine was kneeling before the closed door with her lips to the keyhole, imploring for admission. "Louise, open the door! I beg; open the door—you will make yourself ill. What are you doing, Louise? For heaven's sake open the door."

"Go away. I am not making myself ill." No; she was drinking in a very elixir of life[1] through that open window.

1. **elixir of life** (i liks′ ər) imaginary substance believed in medieval times to prolong life indefinitely.

Vocabulary Builder
repression (ri presh′ ən) *n.* restraint

Vocabulary Builder
elusive (ē lōō′ siv) *adj.* hard to grasp

tumultuously (tōō mul′ chōō əs lē) *adv.* in an agitated way

Literary Analysis
Irony Why are Mrs. Mallard's whispered words ironic?

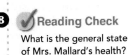

8 **Reading Check**
What is the general state of Mrs. Mallard's health?

6 Reading Strategy
Recognizing Ironic Details

- Remind students that the story includes ironic details. Point out that ironic details can lead readers to expect an outcome very different from the one the author has planned.
- Have students read the bracketed passage. Encourage them to write the details in charts such as the one on p. 641.
- Discuss with students what outcomes could render these details ironic. Encourage them to complete their charts when they learn the outcome.

7 Literary Analysis
Irony

- Remind students that there are three major kinds of irony: *verbal irony, situational irony,* and *dramatic irony.* Explain that dramatic irony occurs when readers have information that a character in a story does not have.
- **Ask** students the Literary Analysis question: Why are Mrs. Mallard's whispered words ironic?
  Possible Answer: They are ironic because the expected reaction would be grief at the loss of her husband, not relief and a sense of freedom.
- Have students read the bracketed passage. Then, **ask** why Josephine's reaction is an example of dramatic irony.
  Answer: Josephine is very worried that her sister is suffering from intense grief, but the reader knows that Louise feels a sense of relief.

➤ **Monitor Progress** Have students discuss how Chopin has built the story's irony to this point, and speculate on how the story will be resolved.

8 Reading Check

Answer: Mrs. Mallard has a weak heart.

Differentiated Instruction Solutions for All Learners

Strategy for Special Needs Students
This story is filled with irony. To help students recognize and appreciate the irony, have them use a chart like the one shown. Begin by pointing out some examples, and then have students continue reading to record the different examples they find.

Detail	"There was something coming to her and she was waiting for it, fearfully."
Expected Outcome	grief, even death
Actual Outcome	signs of spring coming through the window
Type of Irony	situational

Her fancy was running riot along those days ahead of her. Spring days, and summer days, and all sorts of days that would be her own. She breathed a quick prayer that life might be long. It was only yesterday she had thought with a shudder that life might be long.

She arose at length and opened the door to her sister's importunities. There was a feverish triumph in her eyes, and she carried herself unwittingly like a goddess of Victory. She clasped her sister's waist, and together they descended the stairs. Richards stood waiting for them at the bottom.

Someone was opening the front door with a latchkey. It was Brently Mallard who entered, a little travel-stained, composedly carrying his gripsack[2] and umbrella. He had been far from the scene of accident, and did not know there had been one. He stood amazed at Josephine's piercing cry; at Richards's quick motion to screen him from the view of his wife.

But Richards was too late.

When the doctors came they said she had died of heart disease—of joy that kills.

2. **gripsack** (grip′ sak) *n.* small bag for holding clothes.

Vocabulary Builder

importunities (im′ pôr tōōn′ i tēz) *n.* persistent requests or demands

Critical Reading

1. **Respond:** Were you surprised by the end of the story? Explain why or why not.
2. **(a) Recall:** At the beginning of the story, what does the narrator call the ailment that afflicts Mrs. Mallard? **(b) Interpret:** What, in addition to a medical condition, might the narrator mean by this phrase?
3. **(a) Recall:** What does Mrs. Mallard see as she gazes out the window of her room? **(b) Connect:** In what ways does the scene outside Mrs. Mallard's window foreshadow the feelings that sweep over her as she sits in her chair?
4. **(a) Recall:** What word does Mrs. Mallard whisper to herself repeatedly? **(b) Infer:** What has Mrs. Mallard apparently resented about her marriage?
5. **(a) Recall:** According to the doctors, what is the cause of Mrs. Mallard's sudden death? **(b) Draw Conclusions:** What do you believe is the actual reason for Mrs. Mallard's death?
6. **(a) Speculate:** Why do you think Chopin does not elaborate more about Mrs. Mallard's death? **(b) Evaluate:** Is this choice effective? Explain.
7. **Evaluate:** Would "The Story of an Hour" seem believable as a modern tale? Explain.

Go Online
Author Link

For: More about Kate Chopin
Visit: www.PHSchool.com
Web Code: ere-9419

ASSESS

Answers

1. **Possible response:** Students may respond that they were surprised; they should support their opinions with details from the story. Invite students who disagree to defend their positions.
2. (a) The author writes that Mrs. Mallard was afflicted with "a heart trouble." (b) **Possible response:** It might refer to her lack of love for her husband and her unenthusiastic outlook on life.
3. (a) She sees green trees, sparrows, and patches of blue sky—all signs of the new life of spring. (b) The spring scene conveys a sense of rebirth.
4. (a) She whispers "free, free, free!" (b) **Possible response:** Mrs. Mallard resented the limits placed upon her freedom.
5. (a) They say she died "of heart disease—of joy that kills." (b) **Possible response:** Her death is caused by the feelings of shock and disappointment that result from the return of her husband.
6. (a) **Possible response:** Chopin does not elaborate more about Mrs. Mallard's death because she wants to focus on the irony of it, not on the physical details. (b) Students will probably say that the lack of details draws their attention to the irony of the situation as a whole.
7. **Possible responses:** Many students will feel it would not be believable because women's roles in marriage have changed a great deal since Chopin's time. Students should support their responses.

Go Online **Author Link** For additional information about Kate Chopin, have students type in the Web Code, then select C from the alphabet, and then select Kate Chopin.

Apply the Skills

The Story of an Hour

Literary Analysis

Irony

1. **(a)** In what ways is Mrs. Mallard's reaction to her husband's death an example of **situational irony?** **(b)** Do you think Mrs. Mallard is as surprised by her reaction as the reader is? Explain.
2. **(a)** In what ways is Mrs. Mallard's death an example of situational irony? **(b)** Note two details from earlier in the story that add to the poignancy of this ironic ending.
3. In what way is the diagnosis of Mrs. Mallard's cause of death an example of **dramatic irony?**
4. Use a chart like the one shown to examine elements of irony evident in the story's descriptive passages.

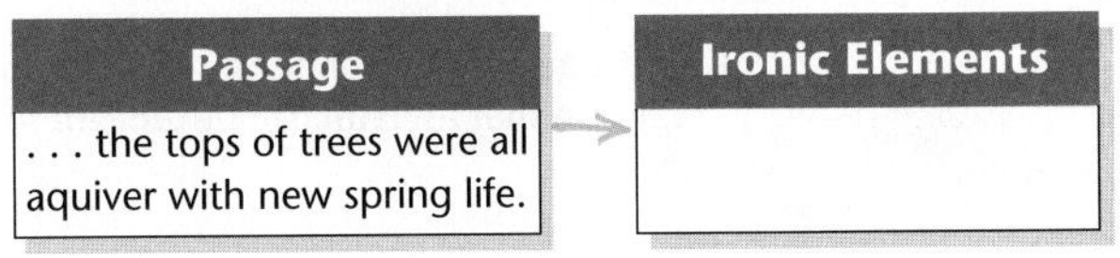

Connecting Literary Elements

5. Review the story to identify the moment of **climax.**
6. What is ironic about the story's climax?

Reading Strategy

Recognizing Ironic Details

7. What **ironic details** lead you to believe that Mrs. Mallard will be truly grieved by her husband's death?
8. Which detail in the second paragraph makes Mr. Mallard's arrival at the end all the more ironic?

Extend Understanding

9. **Sociology Connection:** With her husband dead, Mrs. Mallard notes:

   > There would be no powerful will bending hers in that blind persistence with which men and women believe they have a right to impose a private will upon a fellow creature.

   Do you think this statement accurately reflects interactions between people in close relationships? Explain.

QuickReview

Irony is a contradiction between appearance and reality, expectation and outcome, or meaning and intention. **Verbal irony** occurs when someone says something that contradicts what that person actually means. **Situational irony** occurs when something happens that contradicts our expectations. **Dramatic irony** occurs when the reader knows something a character does not.

The **climax** is the point at which the conflict reaches its greatest intensity or suspense.

To **recognize ironic details,** look for elements that imply specific feelings or circumstances that may not be what they appear.

For: Self-test
Visit: www.PHSchool.com
Web Code: era-6412

Answers

1. **Possible responses:** (a) Neither the reader nor Mrs. Mallard knows that Mr. Mallard is actually alive. (b) Most students will believe she is as surprised as they are by her response, because she expects only to grieve.
2. (a) Mrs. Mallard has just begun to look forward to leading a long life. (b) **Possible response:** Details include the beauty of the spring world outside Mrs. Mallard's window and her prayer for a long life.
3. It is dramatic irony because the reader knows that the diagnosis is wrong.
4. **Possible response:**
   Passage:
   . . . the tops of trees were all aquiver with new spring life.
   Ironic Elements:
   We expect her thoughts to be of death.
   Passage:
   . . . she was drinking the very elixir of life through that open window.
   Ironic Elements:
   Within minutes, her heart fails and she dies.

   Another sample answer can be found on **Literary Analysis Graphic Organizer B,** p. 135 in ***Graphic Organizer Transparencies.***
5. The climax comes when Mr. Mallard returns home and Mrs. Mallard dies.
6. It is ironic because Mrs. Mallard was relieved that her husband was dead, and dies, in part, of her disappointment.
7. **Possible response:** Her family is careful to break the news gently; her husband's friend is in attendance.
8. Two sources confirm Mr. Mallard's death.
9. **Possible response:** Many students will see Mrs. Mallard's thought as a very negative view of close relationships; students may believe that people in such relationships make compromises for each other.

Go Online Assessment Students may use the **Self-test** to prepare for **Selection Test A** or **Selection Test B.**

EXTEND/ASSESS

Answers

1 Vocabulary Lesson

Word Analysis

1. to tell or announce beforehand
2. a person in charge of a group of workers
3. to prevent ahead of time
4. ancestors

Spelling Strategy

1. agencies
2. attorneys
3. penalties

Vocabulary Builder

1. importunities
2. forestall
3. repression
4. tumultuously
5. elusive

2 Grammar and Style Lesson

1. Mrs. Mallard, *an unconventional woman,* was not grieved by her husband's death.
2. She sank gratefully into the chair, *a comfortable, roomy armchair.*
3. She felt like a new woman, *the goddess of Victory,* as she left her room.
4. Her friend *Richards* tried to shield the visitor from Mrs. Mallard's sight.
5. Though "travel-stained," the person at the door, *Brently Mallard,* was very much alive.

Writing Application

Students' paragraphs should use appositive phrases correctly and contain both *nonessential* and *essential* appositives.

WG Writing and Grammar, Ruby Level

Students will find further instruction and practice on appositives and appositive phrases in Chapter 19, Section 1.

Build Language Skills

1 Vocabulary Lesson

Word Analysis: Anglo-Saxon Prefix *fore-*

The Anglo-Saxon prefix *fore-* means "before," in the sense of time, place, or condition. Using this knowledge, write a definition for each of the following words.

1. foretell
2. foreman
3. forestall
4. forefathers

Spelling Strategy

To form the plural of a word that ends in a consonant plus *y,* change the *y* to *i* and add *es*—for example, *importunity* becomes *importunities.* For words that end in a vowel plus *y,* add *s* to form the plural, as in *days* or *monkeys.* Write the plurals of the following words.

1. agency
2. attorney
3. penalty

Vocabulary Builder: Word Choice

Replace the italicized words or phrases in the following sentences with the appropriate vocabulary word from the list on page 641.

1. Chopin gave in to her mother's *insistent pleas* and returned to St. Louis.
2. A doctor thought that writing would *head off* a slide into depression.
3. Chopin exposed the conventions of her time that kept women in a state of near constant *restraint.*
4. Her characters often lived *in a state of agitation.*
5. Outrage over one of her novels taught Chopin that acclaim can be *difficult to hold on to.*

2 Grammar and Style Lesson

Appositives and Appositive Phrases

An **appositive** is a noun or pronoun placed near another noun or pronoun to provide more information about it. When an appositive is accompanied by its own modifiers, it forms an **appositive phrase.**

If an appositive can be omitted from a sentence without altering its basic meaning, it must be set off by commas. If the appositive is essential to the sentence's meaning, commas are not used. Appositive phrases are always set off by commas or dashes.

Nonessential: Richards, her husband's friend, was also present.

Essential: The long novel *Moby-Dick* has a tragic ending.

Practice Rewrite each sentence below, incorporating the information given as an appositive.

1. Mrs. Mallard was not grieved by her husband's death. (*unconventional woman*)
2. She sank gratefully into the chair. (*comfortable, roomy armchair*)
3. She felt like a new woman as she left her room. (*the goddess of Victory*)
4. Her friend tried to shield the visitor from Mrs. Mallard's sight. (*Richards*)
5. Though "travel-stained," the person at the door was very much alive. (*Brently Mallard*)

Writing Application Write a paragraph in which you use at least three appositives or appositive phrases to describe three people.

WG *Prentice Hall Writing and Grammar Connection: Chapter 19, Section 1*

Assessment Practice

Context (For more practice, see *Standardized Test Preparation Workbook*, p. 37.)

The reading sections of many tests specify that students use the context of a targeted word or phrase to determine its meaning. Because figurative expressions are not literally true, students must try to infer the meaning of the expression from the surrounding context. Use the following sample test item to demonstrate.

Her fancy was running riot along those days ahead of her. Spring days, and summer days, and all sorts of days that would be her own.

In this passage, the words running riot most nearly mean—

A quietly contemplating
B causing a public disturbance
C becoming overactive
D going numb

The excitement communicated in the second sentence should lead students to recognize that *C* is correct.

3 Writing Lesson

Reflective Essay

In a reflective essay, a writer describes personal experiences and conveys his or her feelings about them. Draw upon your memory and observations to write your own "Story of an Hour" about a moment when your life dramatically changed. As you write your essay, strive for a personal tone.

Prewriting To gather details for your essay, use a diagram like the one shown. Write your topic in the center circle and then write your observations and feelings about the topic on spokes radiating from the circle.

Model: Gathering Details

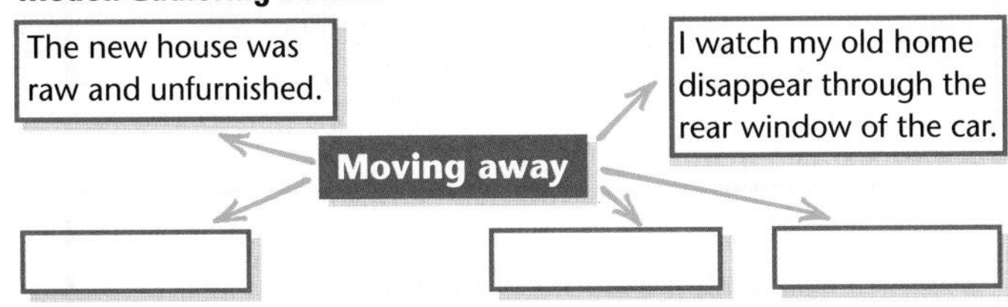

The new house was raw and unfurnished.
I watch my old home disappear through the rear window of the car.
Moving away

Drafting Organize the details in either chronological order or order of importance. Use words and phrases that come naturally, and write honestly about your subject.

Revising Read your essay, focusing on sections that could be made clearer. Add or eliminate details to strengthen the overall impression.

WG Prentice Hall Writing and Grammar Connection: Chapter 4, Section 2

Extend Your Learning

Listening and Speaking What might Mrs. Mallard have made of her life if her husband had not returned? Present a **soliloquy** in which she reflects on her life ten years later. As you work, address these questions:

- Has Mrs. Mallard's heart trouble improved, or not?
- What has it meant to "live for herself"?

Create an authentic voice for Mrs. Mallard, so that she is a believable extension of Chopin's character.

Research and Technology Research the status of women in another culture, and present an **oral report** comparing their lives with women's lives in the United States. Use a variety of research tools, including the Internet. After your report, lead your class in a discussion of the issues you have raised. **[Group Activity]**

Go Online
Research

For: An additional research activity
Visit: www.PHSchool.com
Web Code: erd-7411

Assessment Resources

The following resources can be used to assess students' knowledge and skills.

Unit 4 Resources
- **Selection Test A,** pp. 199–201
- **Selection Test B,** pp. 202–204

General Resources
- **Rubrics for Reflective Essay,** pp. 47–48
- **Rubric for Peer Assessment: Dramatic Performance,** p. 131

Go Online Assessment: Students may use the **Self-test** to prepare for **Selection Test A** or **Selection Test B.**

3 Writing Lesson

- To guide students in writing this reflective essay, give them the **Support for Writing Lesson** page (*Unit 4 Resources,* p. 196).
- Be sure students understand that a reflective essay describes a personal experience and explains how the author feels about it. Reflective essays also explain the experience's significance.
- When they have selected subjects for their essays, direct students to use in their prewriting the Gathering Details organizer modeled on this page.
- Encourage students to use a personal tone in their essays by writing in the first person, using an informal conversational style, and including personal opinions and feelings.
- Use the Reflective Essay rubric in *General Resources,* pp. 47–48, to evaluate students' essays.

4 Listening and Speaking

- Divide the class into pairs to work on developing and writing soliloquies. Make sure students understand that their soliloquies should present an authentic voice for Mrs. Mallard, based on her character in the story.
- Pairs should begin by answering the bulleted questions. Then, instruct students to imagine Mrs. Mallard's first ten years as a widow.
- When soliloquies are ready, pairs should decide who will make the speech. Have partners introduce each soliloquy.
- Use the rubric for Peer Assessment: Dramatic Performance in *General Resources,* p. 131, to assess students' work.
- The **Support for Extend Your Learning** page (*Unit 4 Resources,* p. 197) provides guided note-taking opportunities to help students complete the Extend Your Learning activities.

Go Online Research: Have students type in the Web code for another research activity.

Meeting Your Standards

Students will

1. **analyze and respond to literary elements.**
   - Literary Analysis: Rhyme
2. **read, comprehend, analyze, and critique poetry.**
   - Reading Strategy: Interpreting
   - Reading Check questions
   - Apply the Skills questions
   - Assessment Practice (ATE)
3. **develop vocabulary.**
   - Vocabulary Lesson: Related Words: Forms of *guile*
4. **understand and apply written and oral language conventions.**
   - Spelling Strategy
   - Grammar and Style Lesson: Punctuation of Interjections
5. **develop writing proficiency.**
   - Writing Lesson: Poem to Honor a Hero
6. **develop appropriate research strategies.**
   - Extend Your Learning: Research Report
7. **understand and apply listening and speaking strategies.**
   - Extend Your Learning: Oral Interpretation

Block Scheduling: Use one 90-minute class period to preteach the skills and have students read the selection. Use a second 90-minute class period to assess students' mastery of skills, extend their learning, and monitor their progress.

Homework Suggestions

Following are possibilities for homework assignments.

- Support pages from ***Unit 4 Resources:***
  Literary Analysis
  Reading Strategy
  Vocabulary Builder
  Grammar and Style
- An Extend Your Learning project and the Writing Lesson for this selection group may be completed over several days.

Step-by-Step Teaching Guide	Pacing Guide
PRETEACH	
• Administer Vocabulary and Reading Warm-ups as necessary.	5 min.
• Engage students' interest with the motivation activity.	5 min.
• Read and discuss author and background features. **FT**	10 min.
• Introduce the Literary Analysis Skill: Rhyme. **FT**	5 min.
• Introduce the Reading Strategy: Interpreting. **FT**	10 min.
• Prepare students to read by teaching the selection vocabulary. **FT**	
TEACH	
• Informally monitor comprehension while students read independently or in groups. **FT**	30 min.
• Monitor students' comprehension with the Reading Check notes.	as students read
• Reinforce vocabulary with Vocabulary Builder notes.	as students read
• Develop students' understanding of rhyme with the Literary Analysis annotations. **FT**	5 min.
• Develop students' ability to interpret with the Reading Strategy annotations. **FT**	5 min.
ASSESS/EXTEND	
• Assess students' comprehension and mastery of the Literary Analysis and Reading Strategy by having them answer the Apply the Skills questions. **FT**	15 min.
• Have students complete the Vocabulary Lesson and the Grammar and Style Lesson. **FT**	15 min.
• Apply students' ability to create a main impression by using the Writing Lesson. **FT**	45 min. or homework
• Apply students' understanding by using one or more of the Extend Your Learning activities.	20–90 min. or homework
• Administer Selection Test A or Selection Test B. **FT**	15 min.

Resources

PRINT

Unit 4 Resources

- Vocabulary Warm-up Word Lists **[L1, L2, EL]** . . . . . p. 205
- Vocabulary Warm-up Practice **[L1, L2, EL]** . . . . . p. 206
- Reading Warm-up A **[L1, L2, EL]** . . . . . p. 207
- Reading Warm-up B **[L1, L2, L3]** . . . . . p. 208

TRANSPARENCY

Graphic Organizer Transparencies

- Reading Strategy Graphic Organizer A **[L3]** . . . . . pp. 136, 138
- Reading Strategy Graphic Organizer B **[L1, L2, EL]** . . . . . pp. 137, 139

PRINT

Reader's Notebook [L2]
Reader's Notebook: Adapted Version [L1]
Reader's Notebook: English Learner's Version [EL]

Unit 4 Resources

- Literary Analysis **[L3]** . . . . . p. 209
- Reading Strategy **[L3]** . . . . . p. 210
- Vocabulary Builder **[L3]** . . . . . p. 211

TECHNOLOGY

Listening to Literature Audio CDs [L2, EL]

PRINT

Unit 4 Resources

- Grammar and Style **[L3]** . . . . . p. 212
- Support for Writing Lesson **[L3]** . . . . . p. 213
- Support for Extend Your Learning **[L3]** . . . . . p. 214
- Enrichment **[L4]** . . . . . p. 215
- Selection Test A **[L1, L2, EL]** . . . . . pp. 216–218
- Selection Test B **[L3, L4]** . . . . . pp. 219–221

General Resources

- Rubrics for Poem (Rhyming) **[L3]** . . . . . pp. 73–74
- Rubric for Peer Assessment: Oral Interpretation **[L3]** . . . . . p. 130

TECHNOLOGY

Go Online: Research **[L3]**
Go Online: Self-test **[L3]**
***ExamView®*, Test Bank [L3]**

Choosing Resources for Differentiated Instruction

[L1] Special Needs Students
[L2] Below-Level Students
[L3] All Students
[L4] Advanced Students
[EL] English Learners

FT Fast Track Instruction: To move the lesson more quickly, use the strategies and activities identified with **FT**.

Scaffolding for Less Proficient and Advanced Students

The leveled Critical Thinking questions after selections progress in the levels of thinking required to answer them. To address the needs of your different students, you may use the (a) level questions for your less proficient students and the (b) level questions with your on-level and advanced students. The occasional (c) level questions are appropriate for your advanced students.

PRENTICE HALL **TeacherEXPRESS™** Plan · Teach · Assess

Use this complete suite of powerful teaching tools to make lesson planning and testing quicker and easier.

Use the interactive textbook (online and on CD-ROM) to make selections and activities come alive with audio and video support and interactive questions.

PRETEACH

Motivation

Prepare students for reading and interpreting these poems by asking them to wear a mask to class. Students' masks might range from simple eye coverings to surgical face masks to homemade masks of paper or fabric. Have groups discuss what it is like for two or more people to communicate when wearing a mask. Guide students to notice that masks can fool, hide, frighten, or amuse, but seldom do they encourage honesty or frankness. Then have students remove the physical masks but assume mask-like facial expressions—joy, fear, boredom, and so on. How convincing can they be in maintaining the mask of an emotion when talking with friends? With strangers?

❶ Background

More About the Author

Dunbar long idolized Frederick Douglass, and on one occasion the two men met. The young poet appeared with Douglass in Chicago at the 1893 World's Columbian Exposition, where he recited the poem "Colored Americans," which he had written for the occasion.

Writing at a time when prejudice against African Americans was mounting in both the northern and southern regions of the United States, Dunbar created poetry that disputed the unflattering image of his people found in magazines and newspapers. He gained national prominence as a poet by the turn of the century.

❶ Douglass • We Wear the Mask

Paul Laurence Dunbar (1872–1906)

Paul Laurence Dunbar was the first African American to attain national recognition and support himself entirely with his writing. Throughout his short career, he displayed great versatility in his literary work. Dunbar wrote poems in both a formal, elegant style and in regional dialect. He also wrote four novels and four volumes of short stories.

A Literary Child Dunbar was born in Dayton, Ohio, the son of former slaves. Encouraged by his mother, he began writing poetry at an early age. During high school, Dunbar, who was the only African American student in his class, frequently recited his poetry during school assemblies. He also served as president of the literary society, class poet, and editor of the school newspaper.

Dunbar Attains Recognition Following his graduation, Dunbar sought work in a legal office or a newspaper, but he found it difficult because of his race. He finally took a job as an elevator operator, earning four dollars a week and supporting himself while continuing to write. He first earned recognition among writers and critics in 1892, when he gave a poetry reading during a meeting of the Western Association of Writers. A year later, he took out a loan and published his first collection of poetry, *Oak and Ivy*. In 1895, he published a second collection, *Majors and Minors*, which was received with great enthusiasm by critics. In fact, William Dean Howells, the leading critic of the day, was so impressed with the book that he wrote an introduction for Dunbar's next collection, *Lyrics of a Lowly Life* (1896). That book sold over twelve thousand copies and established Dunbar's reputation and audience.

Characters, Themes, and Forms Dunbar's fiction often focuses on daily life in the vanished world of the southern plantation. Sometimes, however, his writing revolves around social problems facing African Americans in Midwestern towns and urban ghettoes at the turn of the century. His characters include farmers, politicians, preachers, traders, entertainers, and professional people.

Popularity at a Price Dunbar composed poems in two styles—one formal and elegant, the other informal, using a rural dialect, which he called "jingles in a broken tongue." His gift for re-creating dialect and using it to create believable characters was profound. However, it also drew criticism. Called the "Poet Laureate of the Negro Race" by Booker T. Washington, Dunbar was criticized by other African Americans who believed that his dialect poems pandered to white readers' desire for sentimental stereotypes of prewar African Americans. In poems such as "Douglass" and "We Wear the Mask," however, Dunbar demonstrates a command of the English language that was often overlooked, capturing the struggles of African Americans in a dignified, graceful manner.

Despite his success as a poet, Dunbar was disillusioned by the critics' tendency to focus on the poetry he wrote in dialect, while virtually ignoring the poetry he wrote in more formal verse.

An Untimely Death By his late twenties, Dunbar was a nationally prominent poet. Unfortunately, his life was cut short by tuberculosis in 1906. By the end of his life, his poetry was so popular that he was able to write from Florida, "Down here one finds my poems recited everywhere."

Preview

Connecting to the Literature

The rules of courtesy often dictate that people smile even when they feel sad or disappointed. Paul Laurence Dunbar describes such a reaction in his poems as he explores the struggle for identity and truth.

2 Literary Analysis

Rhyme

Rhyme, which along with rhythm gives poetry its musical quality, is the repetition of sounds in the accented syllables of two or more words appearing close together. Poets use rhyme in different ways:

- **Exact rhyme** occurs when the vowel sounds and any consonants appearing after them are exactly the same, as in *days* and *ways.*
- **Slant rhyme** occurs when words sound alike but don't rhyme exactly, as in *prove* and *love.*
- **End rhymes** occur at the ends of two or more poetic lines.
- **Internal rhymes** appear within a single line.

As you read the following poems, take note of Dunbar's use of rhyme.

Comparing Literary Works

Each of the following poems addresses African American struggles for racial identity, but they express different emotions. While "Douglass" expresses indignation for the injustices suffered by African Americans, "We Wear the Mask" conveys a profound sorrow. As you read these two poems, compare Dunbar's varying attitudes and identify the emotions each one evokes in you.

3 Reading Strategy

Interpreting

Poets often mean much more than the surface of their poems might initially convey. For example, to **interpret** "We Wear the Mask," consider who *we* refers to and the time and historical context in which the poem was written. Then, consider what the image of a mask suggests—what it reveals and what it hides. Use a chart like the one shown to help interpret and understand these poems.

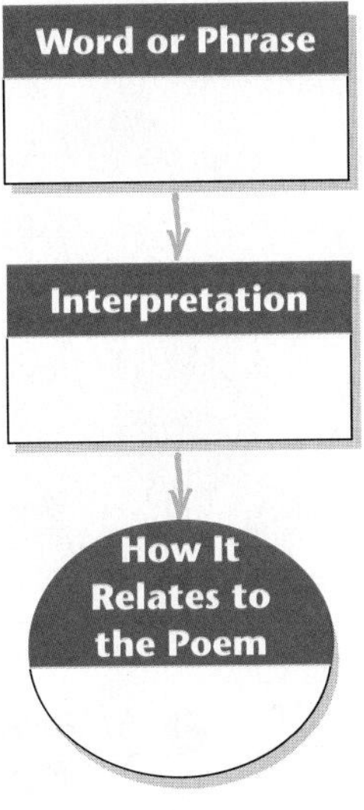

Vocabulary Builder

salient (sāl′ yənt) *adj.* standing out from the rest (p. 653)

tempest (tem′ pist) *n.* violent storm (p. 653)

stark (stärk) *adj.* stiff; rigid (p. 653)

guile (gīl) *n.* craftiness (p. 654)

myriad (mir′ ē əd) *adj.* countless (p. 654)

2 Literary Analysis

Rhyme

- Tell students that as they read the two poems in this grouping, they will focus on several variations of the sound device called rhyme.
- Read the instruction about rhyme aloud with students. Draw their attention to the four different ways in which poets use rhyme—two of which relate to the actual sounds of a rhyme, and two of which relate to where rhymes fall in a poetic line.
- Invite students as they read not only to enjoy the musical quality of rhyming words, but also to note how Dunbar uses sound repetitions differently in the two poems.

3 Reading Strategy

Interpreting

- Give students a copy of **Reading Strategy Graphic Organizer A,** p. 136 in ***Graphic Organizer Transparencies*** to use as they read the selection.
- Point out that interpreting is the process of finding meaning in a literary work. Especially as it relates to poetry, interpreting usually involves reading between and beyond the lines to discover what the poet really means.
- As they read the following two poems, urge students to read each work once aloud before returning to the first line and starting to interpret Dunbar's meanings.

Vocabulary Builder

- Pronounce each vocabulary word for students, and read the definitions as a class. Have students identify any words with which they are already familiar.

Differentiated Instruction — Solutions for All Learners

Support for Special Needs Students
Have students complete the **Preview** and **Build Skills** pages for these selections in the ***Reader's Notebook: Adapted Version.*** These pages provide a selection summary, an abbreviated presentation of the reading and literary skills, and the graphic organizer on the **Build Skills** page in the student book.

Support for Less Proficient Readers
Have students complete the **Preview** and **Build Skills** pages for these selections in the ***Reader's Notebook.*** These pages provide a selection summary, an abbreviated presentation of the reading and literary skills, and the graphic organizer on the **Build Skills** page in the student book.

Support for English Learners
Have students complete the **Preview** and **Build Skills** pages for these selections in the ***Reader's Notebook: English Learner's Version.*** These pages provide a selection summary, an abbreviated presentation of the skills, additional contextual vocabulary, and the graphic organizer on the **Build Skills** page in the student book.

TEACH

Learning Modalities
Interpersonal Learners
Invite students to imagine that they are the speaker of "We Wear the Mask." Have them write diary entries describing a day in the life of the speaker. Encourage students to focus on imaginary encounters in which they are required to "wear the mask."

1 Humanities

Frederick Douglass, artist unknown

This portrait of the abolitionist Frederick Douglass (1817–1895) appeared in the November 24, 1883, issue of *Harper's Weekly.*

Use this question for discussion:

- What qualities of Douglass does the artist capture in this portrait?
  Answer: Students might cite the powerful face, intense stare, and expression of determination.

2 Critical Viewing

Answer: Douglass was an abolitionist who helped to bring about great change in the lives of African Americans.

1

2 ▲ Critical Viewing Why is a civil rights activist like Frederick Douglass an appropriate inspiration for Dunbar? **[Speculate]**

Differentiated Instruction Solutions for All Learners

Accessibility at a Glance

	Douglass	We Wear the Mask
Context	Social Issues	Racial discrimination
Language	Poetic diction	Poetic diction
Concept Level	Accessible (African-American struggle for equality)	Accessible (hidden despair)
Literary Merit	Noted author	Noted author
Lexile	NP	NP
Overall Rating	Average	Average

❸ # Douglass

Paul Laurence Dunbar

Background Paul Laurence Dunbar was among the last generation to have an ongoing contact with former African American slaves. As a child, Dunbar heard many stories from his father, who had escaped captivity and joined the Civil War cause. In these poems, Dunbar speaks of the social issues faced by those struggling to rebuild the country after the Civil War. He expresses the pain of racial injustice and conveys the ongoing struggles of African Americans to achieve equality.

Ah, Douglass,[1] we have fall'n on evil days,
    Such days as thou, not even thou didst know,
    When thee, the eyes of that harsh long ago
Saw, salient, at the cross of devious ways,
And all the country heard thee with amaze.
    Not ended then, the passionate ebb and flow.
    The awful tide that battled to and fro;
We ride amid a tempest of dispraise.

Now, when the waves of swift dissension swarm,
    And Honor, the strong pilot, lieth[2] stark,
Oh, for thy voice high-sounding o'er the storm,
    For thy strong arm to guide the shivering bark,[3]
The blast-defying power of thy form,
    To give us comfort through the lonely dark.

Vocabulary Builder

salient (sāl′ yənt) *adj.* standing out from the rest

tempest (tem′ pist) *n.* violent storm

stark (stärk) *adj.* stiff; rigid

❹ 
Reading Check
What does the speaker say is the difference between the current time and the time in which Douglass lived?

1. **Douglass** Frederick Douglass, an African American abolitionist (1818–1895).
2. **lieth** (lī′ eth) *v.* lies.
3. **bark** boat.

❸ About the Selections

In both of the poems in this lesson, the writer addresses the struggles of African Americans. In "Douglass," the speaker cries out to a hero of an earlier age. In "We Wear the Mask," the speaker describes how African Americans hide their despair from the eyes of white America.

❹ Reading Check

Answer: The speaker says that the current time is harsher even than Douglass's time was.

Differentiated Instruction Solutions for All Learners

Strategy for Special Needs Students

Give students who are having difficulty interpreting "We Wear the Mask" some strategies for reading between the lines to determine the poet's meaning. Point out the words *we* and *mask* in the title.

Tell students to ask themselves three questions as they read: What's the purpose of the mask? What is the mask hiding? Who is the "we" the speaker mentions? Draw the following chart on the chalkboard to get students started. Have students fill in more information as they read the poem.

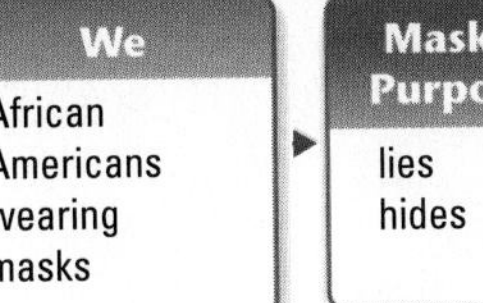

5 Literary Analysis

Rhyme

- Have students identify the rhyme scheme in this poem, in which most lines are either true or slant rhymes. If necessary, help students see that the rhyme scheme is *aabba, aabc, aabbac.*
- **Ask** students the Literary Analysis question: Where does the poet use exact rhyme? Which lines do not rhyme?
  Answer: Lines 1, 2, 6, 7, 10, 11, and 14, and lines 3, 4, 8, 12, and 13 are exact rhymes. Lines 9 and 15 are non-rhyming. Students may observe that these lines stand out. Perhaps Dunbar isolated the lines to reflect the speaker's feelings of isolation from his surroundings.

ASSESS

Answers

1. Students may say that they feel awkward or angry.
2. (a) Dunbar refers to the abolitionist Frederick Douglass. (b) He thinks that Douglass could help African Americans out of their current difficulties.
3. (a) It was heard "long ago" in a harsher time. (b) According to the speaker, the present day needs Douglass's singleness of purpose to counter criticism and dissent.
4. (a) Dunbar speaks for African Americans. (b) They struggle against prejudice and injustice. (c) Students might say that "the lonely dark" refers to a time of injustice and unenlightenment about racial issues.
5. (a) The mask hides pain and torment. (b) The speaker implies that showing the world their "tears and sighs" would weaken African Americans' position in society.
6. (a) Students might say that Dunbar would like to see greater honesty and equality in the world. (b) **Possible response:** Students may differ over whether relations between African Americans and other races have improved greatly.

Go Online Author Link For additional information about Paul Laurence Dunbar, have students type in the Web Code, then select *D* from the alphabet, and then select Paul Laurence Dunbar.

3 We Wear the Mask

Paul Laurence Dunbar

We wear the mask that grins and lies,
It hides our cheeks and shades our eyes—
This debt we pay to human guile;
With torn and bleeding hearts we smile,
And mouth with myriad subtleties.

Why should the world be overwise,
In counting all our tears and sighs?
5 Nay, let them only see us, while
We wear the mask.

We smile, but, O great Christ, our cries
To thee from tortured souls arise.
We sing, but oh the clay is vile
Beneath our feet, and long the mile;
But let the world dream otherwise,
We wear the mask!

Vocabulary Builder

guile (gīl) *n.* craftiness

myriad (mir′ ē əd) *adj.* countless

Literary Analysis

Rhyme Where does the poet use exact rhyme? Which lines do not rhyme?

Critical Reading

1. **Respond:** How do you feel when you must appear or behave as others expect?
2. **(a) Recall:** Who is the Douglass to whom Dunbar refers?
   (b) Draw Conclusions: Why do you think the speaker addresses Douglass?
3. **(a) Infer:** When was Douglass's voice heard by the nation?
   (b) Compare: How does Douglass's message relate to what the speaker of "Douglass" describes?
4. **(a) Infer:** Who is the "we" in this poem? **(b) Analyze:** What struggles do they face? **(c) Interpret:** What is the "lonely dark"?
5. **(a) Recall:** In "We Wear the Mask," what emotions does the mask hide? **(b) Draw Conclusions:** Why do you think they wear the mask?
6. **(a) Extend:** How might Dunbar like to see the world change?
   (b) Apply: If Dunbar were alive today, do you think he would still have the views he expresses in this poem? Why or why not?

Go Online Author Link

For: More about Paul Laurence Dunbar
Visit: www.PHSchool.com
Web Code: ere-9420

Apply the Skills

Douglass • We Wear the Mask

Literary Analysis

Rhyme

1. List all the words in "We Wear the Mask" that are **exact rhymes** with the word *lies.*
2. What **slant rhyme** does Dunbar use in this poem?
3. The rhyme scheme, or pattern, in the first stanza of "Douglass" can be expressed as *abbaabba.* (The letter *a* stands for words rhyming with *days* and the letter *b* stands for words rhyming with *know.*) What is the rhyme scheme in the second stanza?
4. In your opinion, what is the effect of rhyme in these poems?

Comparing Literary Works

5. **(a)** Note three emotions Dunbar addresses in "Douglass."
   (b) Note three emotions he expresses in "We Wear the Mask."
   (c) In what ways is the emotional content of these poems similar?
   (d) In what ways is it different?
6. **(a)** In what ways are the tones or attitudes of these poems similar?
   (b) In what ways do they differ?
7. Which poem do you think is more personal—related most directly to Dunbar's daily experience? Explain.

Reading Strategy

Interpreting

8. What situation might Dunbar's speaker be describing for African Americans in general in "We Wear the Mask"?
9. Poets use symbolic language—words and images that represent larger ideas. In a chart like the one shown, list and **interpret** the symbolic language you find in both poems.

	Symbolic Language	Interpretation
"Douglass"		
"We Wear the Mask"		

Extend Understanding

10. **Social Studies Connection:** How might Dunbar have characterized the situation of African Americans in the past decade? Explain.

QuickReview

Rhyme occurs when two or more words have identical or similar vowel and final consonant sounds in their accented syllables. **Exact rhyme** occurs when these vowel sounds are identical. **Slant rhyme** occurs when words sound alike but don't rhyme perfectly. **End rhymes** occur at the ends of lines, while **internal rhymes** appear within lines.

To **interpret** a poem, consider the poet's word choice, symbolism, and historical context to discover the poet's deeper meaning.

For: Self-test
Visit: www.PHSchool.com
Web Code: era-6413

Answers

1. *eyes, overwise, sighs, cries, arise, otherwise*
2. *lies/subtleties*
3. The rhyme scheme is *cdcdcd.*
4. Students may say that rhyme makes the poems more musical, coherent, and engaging.
5. (a) Students may mention emotions such as amazement and loneliness, as well as characteristics such as leadership, honor, strength, and power. (b) Students might use words such as desperate, miserable, valiant, sad, and angry in their responses. (c) In both poems, the speakers convey an attitude of determination and inner strength in the face of terrible conflict. (d) The speaker of "We Wear the Mask" is resolute and defiant, whereas the speaker of "Douglass" seems vulnerable.
6. (a) Both poems address the pain and frustration of living in a bigoted society. (b) "We Wear the Mask" conveys anger, "Douglass" addresses the situation in measured tones.
7. Students should support their answers.
8. **Possible response:** He might be describing the situation of emancipated African Americans trying to overcome the effects of slavery.
9. "Douglass"—*that harsh long ago* and *the cross of devious ways* (the era of slavery), *passionate ebb and flow, awful tide, tempest of dispraise, waves of swift dissension, storm, lonely dark* (stormy race relations), *pilot* (Douglass, a leader of the African American cause), *shivering bark* (the effort to gain true freedom for African Americans); "Mask" —*mask* (behavior that conceals true feelings), *debt* (the consequence for hiding truth), *torn and bleeding hearts* (hopelessness, despair), *tears and sighs* (sorrow, exhaustion), *clay* (living conditions for African Americans), *mile* (the effort to gain true freedom for African Americans).
10. **Possible response:** He would see great improvements but also see the continuing need for true equality.

Go Online Assessment Students may use the **Self-test** to prepare for **Selection Test A** or **Selection Test B.**

EXTEND/ASSESS

Answers

❶ Vocabulary Lesson

Word Analysis

1. guileful (*adj.*)
2. guilefully (*adv.*)
3. guilefulness (*n.*)
4. guileless (*adj.*)
5. guilelessly (*adv.*)
6. guilelessness (*n.*)

Vocabulary Builder

1. e
2. a
3. d
4. c
5. b

Spelling Strategy

1. pyre
2. type
3. myriad

❷ Grammar and Style Lesson

1. Hey! We need you to guide us!
2. Ah, we long to be comforted by your wisdom!
3. No, I'm afraid I can't reveal my authentic feelings.
4. Oh! Is that what you think?
5. Yes, one must remain as strong as possible in the face of a great challenge.

Writing Application

Students' paragraphs should focus on a topic with special meaning for them and should contain three correctly-used interjections.

WG Writing and Grammar, Ruby Level

Students will find further instruction and practice on punctuation of interjections in Chapter 17, Section 4.

Build Language Skills

❶ Vocabulary Lesson

Word Analysis: Forms of *guile*

The word *guile* is a noun meaning "craftiness." By adding prefixes or suffixes to *guile*, you can form related words such as the adjective *guileless* ("innocent" or "naïve") and the verb *beguile* ("mislead" or "trick").

Combine *guile* with the suffixes below to create six words. Label each word's part of speech.

1. *-ful*
2. *-fully*
3. *-fulness*
4. *-less*
5. *-lessly*
6. *-lessness*

Vocabulary Builder: Antonyms

An antonym is a word meaning the opposite of another. Match each word in the left column with its antonym in the right column.

1. guile	**a.** tranquility; stillness
2. tempest	**b.** not many
3. salient	**c.** elastic; flexible
4. stark	**d.** inconspicuous
5. myriad	**e.** honesty

Spelling Strategy

There is no spelling rule governing the use of *y* as a vowel; you will need to memorize the spelling of such words. For each of these pairs of words, choose the correct spelling.

1. pyre/pire **2.** tipe/type **3.** myriad/miriad

❷ Grammar and Style Lesson

Punctuation of Interjections

An **interjection,** a word used to express emotion, has no grammatical relation to other words in a sentence. An interjection can express a variety of sentiments, such as happiness, fear, anger, pain, surprise, sorrow, exhaustion, or hesitation. Use a comma to punctuate an interjection that expresses mild emotion. Use an exclamation point to punctuate an interjection that expresses strong emotion. Consider the following examples:

Mild Emotion: *Ah,* Douglass, we have fall'n on evil days, . . .

Strong Emotion: *Oh!* If you could only help!

Practice Add a comma or an exclamation point to correct the punctuation of the interjections in each of the following sentences. Capitalize the resulting sentences as necessary.

1. Hey we need you to guide us!
2. Ah we long to be comforted by your wisdom!
3. No I'm afraid I can't reveal my authentic feelings.
4. Oh is that what you think?
5. Yes one must remain as strong as possible in the face of a great challenge.

Writing Application Write a paragraph on a topic that has special meaning for you. Use at least three examples of interjections.

WG Prentice Hall Writing and Grammar Connection: Chapter 17, Section 4

Assessment Practice

Context **(For more practice, see *Standardized Test Preparation Workbook*, p. 38.)**

Some tests require students to use context to determine the meanings of unfamiliar words. Write the following passage from p. 653 on the chalkboard. Then have students answer the question that follows.

We ride amid a tempest of dispraise,/Now, when the waves of swift dissension swarm,/And Honor, the strong pilot, lieth stark,/Oh, for thy voice high-sounding o'er the storm.

In this passage, tempest means—

A storm
B sinking boat
C discussion
D voice

The first part of the passage says the speaker rides amid a tempest. *Amid,* in combination with the references to waves and a storm, should provide the context that helps students choose *A* as the correct answer.

❸ Writing Lesson

Poem to Honor a Hero

Think of another historical figure who, if alive today, might help inspire people to solve some of society's problems. Compose a poem in which you address this hero as Dunbar addresses Douglass.

Prewriting First, list the accomplishments and character traits that contribute to your subject's heroism. Then, brainstorm for sensory details and descriptions of behavior that illustrate this person's ability to tackle challenging aspects of today's world. Consider using figurative or symbolic language to convey your ideas.

Drafting Choose a form for your poem, such as a regular rhythm and rhyme scheme or free verse. Use images and sound devices that convey a vivid main impression of your subject.

Model: Creating a Main Impression

Oh, Martin Luther King, like an oak in a storm,
Your life was not in vain.
Through all the blustering wind and rain,
Your strength was our gain.

The images comparing the subject to an oak convey the sense of the subject as a powerful figure.

Revising Reread your poem. Consider adding or eliminating details to sharpen the main impression of your subject. If necessary, use images and descriptive language to convey your ideas more effectively.

WG Prentice Hall Writing and Grammar Connection: Chapter 7, Section 3

Extend Your Learning

Listening and Speaking Prepare an **oral interpretation** of one of the two Dunbar poems. Begin by analyzing the meaning and form of each line. The following tips will help you:

- Consider which words and phrases to emphasize so that your reading is expressive.
- Read the poem aloud several times to practice your pacing and phrasing.

Present your oral interpretation to the class, inviting feedback. **[Group Activity]**

Research and Technology Dunbar's work received mixed reviews from critics. Using library and Internet resources, conduct research to find examples of both positive and negative responses. In a **report,** summarize your findings and then take a position about Dunbar's legacy as a poet.

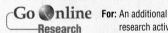

For: An additional research activity
Visit: www.PHSchool.com
Web Code: erd-7412

Assessment Resources

The following resources can be used to assess students' knowledge and skills.

Unit 4 Resources
- **Selection Test A,** pp. 216–218
- **Selection Test B,** pp. 219–221

General Resources
- **Rubrics for Poem (Rhyming),** pp. 73–74
- **Rubric for Peer Assessment: Oral Interpretation,** p. 130

Go Online Assessment Students may use the **Self-test** to prepare for **Selection Test A** or **Selection Test B.**

❸ Writing Lesson

- To guide students in writing this Poem, give them the **Support for Writing Lesson** page (*Unit 4 Resources,* p. 213).
- Students' poems to honor a hero should convey a vivid main impression of their subjects, as well as containing effective imagery and sound devices.
- Point out to students that the choice of subject matter is crucial to their poems' success. Moreover, they must make every effort to link particular hereos with specific societal problems in a way that makes sense.
- Encourage them to spend time in groups brainstorming for lists of accomplishments and character traits of their chosen heroes.
- Use the Poem (Rhyming) rubrics in *General Resources,* pp. 73–74 to evaluate students' poems.

❹ Listening and Speaking

- Encourage students to paraphrase every line (in its entirety) for a listener as part of the preparation process. Any line that they cannot paraphrase—or that the listener fails to comprehend—indicates a passage that needs further study.
- Point out the effectiveness of a natural speaking style and urge students to avoid a stagy, presentational delivery. You might suggest that students choose a single (unnamed, and not necessarily present) person to whom they will imagine they are addressing their poems. This device can help foster true, specific expressions of ideas.
- Use the Peer Assessment: Oral Interpretation rubric in *General Resources,* p. 130, to evaluate students' poems.
- The **Support for Extend Your Learning** page (*Unit 4 Resources,* p. 214) provides guided note-taking opportunities to help students complete the Extend Your Learning activities.

Go Online Research Have students type in the Web code for another research activity.

Meeting Your Standards

Students will

1. **analyze and respond to literary elements.**
   - Literary Analysis: Speaker
2. **read, comprehend, analyze, and critique poetry.**
   - Reading Strategy: Recognizing Attitudes
   - Reading Check questions
   - Apply the Skills questions
   - Assessment Practice (ATE)
3. **develop vocabulary.**
   - Vocabulary Lesson: Word Analysis: Latin Root: *-pose-*
4. **understand and apply written and oral language conventions.**
   - Spelling Strategy
   - Grammar and Style Lesson: Noun Clauses
5. **develop writing proficiency.**
   - Writing Lesson: Firsthand Biography
6. **develop appropriate research strategies.**
   - Extend Your Learning: Illustrated Booklet
7. **understand and apply listening and speaking strategies.**
   - Extend Your Learning: Class Discussion

Block Scheduling: Use one 90-minute class period to preteach the skills and have students read the selection. Use a second 90-minute class period to assess students' mastery of skills, extend their learning, and monitor their progress.

Homework Suggestions

Following are possibilities for homework assignments.

- Support pages from *Unit 4 Resources:*
  Literary Analysis
  Reading Strategy
  Vocabulary Builder
  Grammar and Style
- An Extend Your Learning project and the Writing Lesson for this selection group may be completed over several days.

Step-by-Step Teaching Guide	Pacing Guide
PRETEACH	
• Administer Vocabulary and Reading Warm-ups as necessary.	5 min.
• Engage students' interest with the motivation activity.	5 min.
• Read and discuss author and background features. **FT**	10 min.
• Introduce the Literary Analysis Skill: Speaker. **FT**	5 min.
• Introduce the Reading Strategy: Recognizing Attitudes. **FT**	10 min.
• Prepare students to read by teaching the selection vocabulary. **FT**	
TEACH	
• Informally monitor comprehension while students read independently or in groups. **FT**	30 min.
• Monitor students' comprehension with the Reading Check notes.	as students read
• Reinforce vocabulary with Vocabulary Builder notes.	as students read
• Develop students' understanding of speaker with the Literary Analysis annotations. **FT**	5 min.
• Develop students' ability to recognize attitudes with the Reading Strategy annotations. **FT**	5 min.
ASSESS/EXTEND	
• Assess students' comprehension and mastery of the Literary Analysis and Reading Strategy by having them answer the Apply the Skills questions. **FT**	15 min.
• Have students complete the Vocabulary Lesson and the Grammar and Style Lesson. **FT**	15 min.
• Apply students' ability to use transitions to show order of importance by using the Writing Lesson. **FT**	45 min. or homework
• Apply students' understanding by using one or more of the Extend Your Learning activities.	20–90 min. or homework
• Administer Selection Test A or Selection Test B. **FT**	15 min.

Resources

PRINT

Unit 4 Resources

- Vocabulary Warm-up Word Lists [**L1, L2, EL**] .... p. 231
- Vocabulary Warm-up Practice [**L1, L2, EL**] .... p. 232
- Reading Warm-up A [**L1, L2, EL**] .... p. 233
- Reading Warm-up B [**L1, L2, L3**] .... p. 234

TRANSPARENCY

Graphic Organizer Transparencies

- Reading Strategy Graphic Organizer A [**L3**] .... pp. 140, 142
- Reading Strategy Graphic Organizer B [**L1, L2, EL**] .... pp. 141, 143

PRINT

Reader's Notebook [L2]

Reader's Notebook: Adapted Version [L1]

Reader's Notebook: English Learner's Version [EL]

Unit 4 Resources

- Literary Analysis [**L3**] .... p. 235
- Reading Strategy [**L3**] .... p. 236
- Vocabulary Builder [**L3**] .... p. 237

TECHNOLOGY

Listening to Literature Audio CDs [L2, EL]

PRINT

Unit 4 Resources

- Grammar and Style [**L3**] .... p. 238
- Support for Writing Lesson [**L3**] .... p. 239
- Support for Extend Your Learning [**L3**] .... p. 240
- Enrichment [**L4**] .... p. 241
- Selection Test A [**L1, L2, EL**] .... pp. 242–244
- Selection Test B [**L3, L4**] .... pp. 245–247

General Resources

- Rubrics for Biography [**L3**] .... pp. 77–78

TECHNOLOGY

Go Online: Research [**L3**]

Go Online: Self-test [**L3**]

***ExamView®*, Test Bank** [**L3**]

Choosing Resources for Differentiated Instruction

[**L1**] Special Needs Students

[**L2**] Below-Level Students

[**L3**] All Students

[**L4**] Advanced Students

[**EL**] English Learners

FT Fast Track Instruction: To move the lesson more quickly, use the strategies and activities identified with **FT**.

Scaffolding for Less Proficient and Advanced Students

The leveled Critical Thinking questions after selections progress in the levels of thinking required to answer them. To address the needs of your different students, you may use the (a) level questions for your less proficient students and the (b) level questions with your on-level and advanced students. The occasional (c) level questions are appropriate for your advanced students.

PRENTICE HALL **TeacherEXPRESS™** Plan · Teach · Assess — Use this complete suite of powerful teaching tools to make lesson planning and testing quicker and easier.

Use the interactive textbook (online and on CD-ROM) to make selections and activities come alive with audio and video support and interactive questions.

PREFEACH

Motivation

Bring in several obituary notices from newspapers or news magazines. (You might duplicate them for students, or you might prefer to read them aloud.) Alternately, have students visit a local cemetery to see the kinds of messages inscribed on gravestones there. Then, challenge students to write their own obituary notice or gravestone epitaph in the style of the ones they have read or seen. Allow ten to fifteen minutes for this task, and then invite volunteers to share the obituaries or epitaphs. Finally, tell students that all four poems in this grouping concern people who have died, though the texts are neither typical obituaries nor epitaphs.

1 Background

More About the Authors

Among the later works of Edwin Arlington Robinson are several long, blank-verse narrative poems—such as *Merlin* (1917), *Lancelot* (1920), and *Tristram* (1927)—based on the King Arthur legends.

In commenting on Edgar Lee Masters's *Spoon River Anthology,* poet May Swenson wrote that Masters gave "outlet to all his grudges, beliefs, indignations, insights, prophesies, discoveries of glaring injustice, revelations of life's mysteries and paradoxes—and his own eccentric philosophy. Miraculously he also created . . . a world in microcosm, new in form, timeless in space."

Build Skills *Poems*

1 Luke Havergal • Richard Cory • Lucinda Matlock • Richard Bone

Edwin Arlington Robinson (1869–1935)

In his mid-thirties, Edwin Arlington Robinson earned twenty cents per hour as a New York City subway inspector. Yet, friends helped him arrange the private printing of three books of his poetry during these lean times, allowing Robinson to become the most successful American poet of the 1920s.

Robinson grew up in Gardiner, Maine, a small town that was the model for Tilbury Town, the fictional setting of many of his poems. He attended college for two years, but he was forced to return to Gardiner after his father's death. Upon his return, Robinson began writing poetry, depending on friends and patrons for financial support. Four years later, he returned to New York City, hoping to improve his financial situation. When President Theodore Roosevelt appointed him to a post at the New York Customhouse, Robinson was set free from his financial worries.

The Inner Struggle Robinson continued to write poems and established his poetic voice. His best poems focus on people's inner struggles. They paint portraits of desperate characters who view their lives as trivial and meaningless or who long to live in another place or time. Despite his characters' pessimistic outlook, Robinson's poems possess a certain dignity that results from his traditional style, command of language, and imagination and wit.

Robinson found success when his fourth volume of verse, *The Town Down the River* (1910), sold well and received much critical acclaim. He went on to publish many acclaimed books and receive three Pulitzer Prizes.

Edgar Lee Masters (1868–1950)

For years, Edgar Lee Masters practiced criminal law by day in a successful Chicago firm and wrote poems, plays, and essays by night. In 1914, however, Masters' direction as a writer changed dramatically when a friend gave him a copy of *Selected Epitaphs from the Greek Anthology.* This collection included many concise, interconnected epitaphs that captured the essence of people's personal lives.

Spoon River Anthology Using the structure suggested by that anthology, and abandoning conventional rhyme and meter, Masters wrote a series of poems about the lives of people in rural southern Illinois. Published as *Spoon River Anthology* in 1915, the book provoked strong reactions among critics and became a bestseller. The volume was so successful that Masters quit his law career and moved to New York to earn a living as a writer.

The anthology consists of 244 epitaphs for characters buried in the mythical Spoon River cemetery. The dead themselves serve as the speakers of the poems, often revealing secrets they kept hidden during their lifetimes. Many types of people are represented, including storekeepers, housewives, and murderers. Some had happy lives, but many more had lives filled with frustration and despair. Presented together, the epitaphs paint a vivid portrait of the loneliness and isolation confronting people in small Midwestern towns around the turn of the century.

Masters went on to produce other volumes of poetry, novels, biographies, and his autobiography, *Across Spoon River.* However, he is still remembered almost exclusively for *Spoon River Anthology.*

Preview

Connecting to the Literature

Have you ever wondered how you will be remembered a century from now? The following poems create a memorable impression of four characters from small-town America one hundred years ago. Compare them with the impression you would like to leave behind.

2 Literary Analysis

Speaker

The **speaker** is the voice that is speaking in a poem. Although the speaker may be the poet, it can also be a fictional character or a nonhuman entity. For example, the speakers of the poems in Masters' *Spoon River Anthology* are characters buried in a cemetery in the fictional town of Spoon River, as these lines from "Lucinda Matlock" demonstrate:

> At ninety-six I had lived enough, that is all,
> And passed to a sweet repose.

Instead of using a neutral speaker, Masters allows characters to speak candidly for themselves. In this way, the poet can delve deeply into the minds and hearts of Spoon River's former citizens.

Comparing Literary Works

All of these poems share the common themes of life and death. The speakers—some of whose voices come from the grave—examine the quality of the lives they have lived. Lucinda Matlock, whose life was long and satisfying, says "It takes life to love Life." By contrast, Richard Cory appears to have lived with terrible secrets. As you read these poems, compare the speakers and the message each expresses about how we spend our days.

3 Reading Strategy

Recognizing Attitudes

The **attitudes** and beliefs of a poem's speaker color the depiction of the characters, settings, and events. As you read a poem, determine who the speaker is, and look for clues to the speaker's attitudes or outlook on life. For example, in "Lucinda Matlock," the speaker believes that the younger generation is not as tough and hard-working as her generation was. Use a chart like the one shown to help you recognize the speaker's attitudes in these poems.

Speaker's Attitude	Evidence

Vocabulary Builder

imperially (im pir′ ē əl ē) *adv.* majestically (p. 662)

repose (ri pōz′) *n.* state of being at rest (p. 663)

degenerate (dē jen′ ər it) *adj.* morally corrupt (p. 663)

epitaph (ep′ ə taf′) *n.* inscription on a tombstone or grave marker (p. 664)

2 Literary Analysis

Speaker

- Tell students that as they read the four poems in this grouping, they will focus on each poem's speaker.
- Read the instruction about speaker together as a class. Explain that the speaker can take the form of a character, or it can take a more "neutral" form as the poet him- or herself.
- Invite students as they read to think about the identity of the speaker, and to reflect on how the speaker's sensibility affects the poem's look, sound, and meaning.

3 Reading Strategy

Recognizing Attitudes

- Point out that identifying a poem's speaker and recognizing how his or her attitudes and beliefs affect the details of the poem is akin to analyzing the point of view of a prose story.
- Explain to students that recognizing a speaker's attitudes involves analyzing how the poet uses language to express the thoughts, feelings, and behavior of the speaker. Of course, sometimes readers may need to look *between* the lines to recognize attitudes that are implied but not stated directly.
- Provide students with a copy of **Reading Strategy Graphic Organizer A,** p. 140 in ***Graphic Organizer Transparencies,*** to use as they read the selections.

Vocabulary Builder

- Pronounce each vocabulary word for students, and read the definitions as a class. Have students identify any words with which they are already familiar.

Differentiated Instruction

Solutions for All Learners

Support for Special Needs Students

Have students complete the **Preview** and **Build Skills** pages for these selections in the ***Reader's Notebook: Adapted Version.*** These pages provide a selection summary, an abbreviated presentation of the reading and literary skills, and the graphic organizer on the **Build Skills** page in the student book.

Support for Less Proficient Readers

Have students complete the **Preview** and **Build Skills** pages for these selections in the ***Reader's Notebook.*** These pages provide a selection summary, an abbreviated presentation of the reading and literary skills, and the graphic organizer on the **Build Skills** page in the student book.

Support for English Learners

Have students complete the **Preview** and **Build Skills** pages for these selections in the ***Reader's Notebook: English Learner's Version.*** These pages provide a selection summary, an abbreviated presentation of the skills, additional contextual vocabulary, and the graphic organizer on the **Build Skills** page in the student book.

Learning Modalities
Verbal/Linguistic Learners
Students may notice repetition in the last two lines of each stanza of "Luke Havergal"—as well as in the western gate image that is introduced in the first stanza and echoed in the last. Have students discuss the soothing and hypnotic effects of repetition in this poem.

❶ About the Selections

These two poems by Robinson address the pain of loss. Luke Havergal grieves for his beloved and questions whether he can go on living. The speaker seems to suggest that Havergal can commune with her spirit until it is his rightful time to die and his beloved meet again in the next life. In contrast, "Richard Cory" reveals a whole town in shock and grief. Because ordinary townsfolk idealized the life of a wealthy, elegant man, they are unprepared for his sudden suicide.

❶ Luke Havergal

Edwin Arlington Robinson

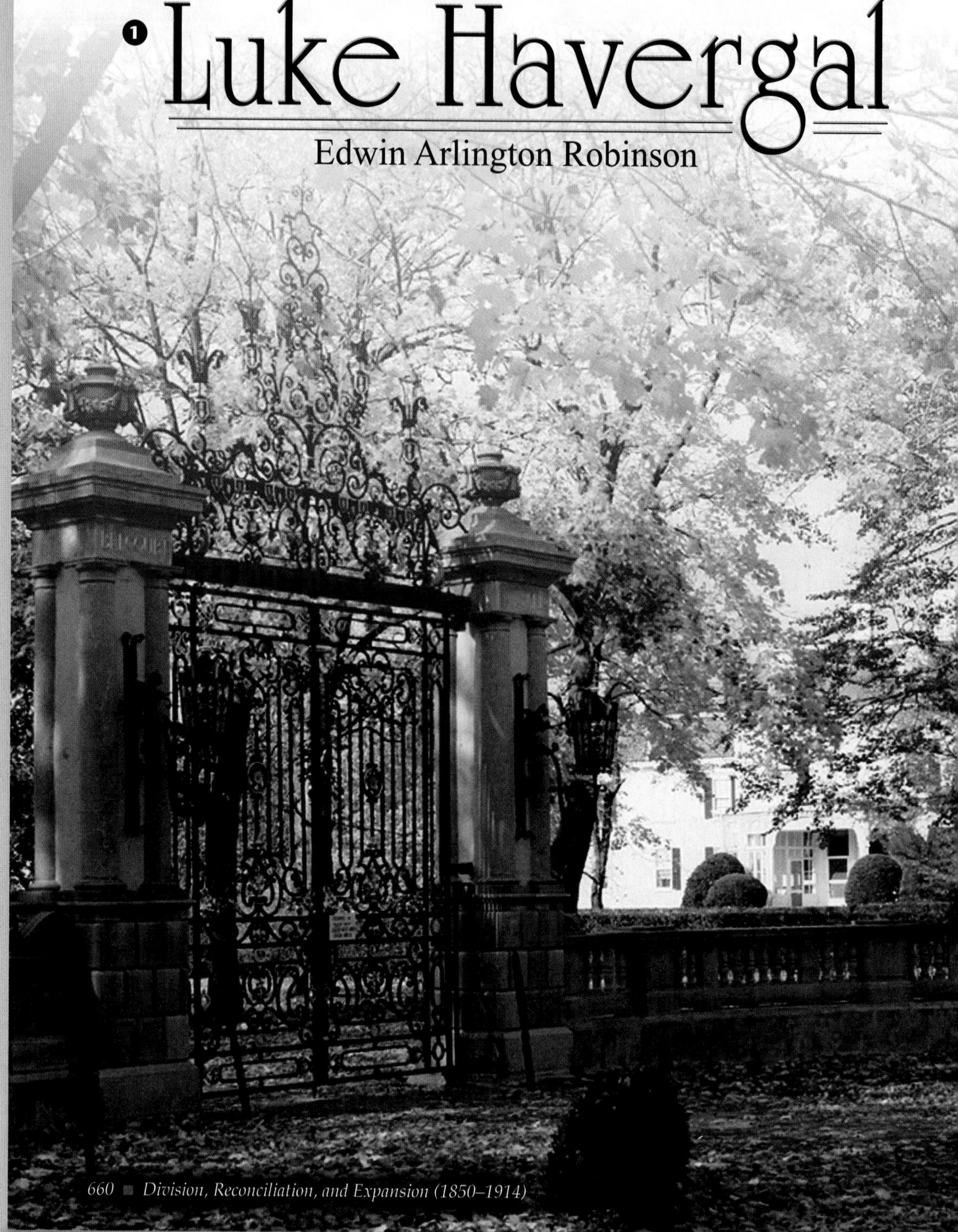

Differentiated Instruction Solutions for All Learners

Accessibility at a Glance

	Luke Haveral	Richard Cory	Lucinda Matlock	Richard Bone
Context	Grief for loved one	Perceptions of townspeople	Speaking from the grave	Carver of epitaphs
Language	Repetition	Rhyme Scheme	Vocabulary footnotes	Simple language
Concept Level	Accessible (loss)	Accessible (suicide)	Accessible (life)	Accessible (death)
Literary Merit	Classic	Classic	Classic	Classic
Lexile	NP	NP	NP	NP
Overall Rating	Average	Average	Average	Average

Background Two years into Edwin Arlington Robinson's college career at Harvard, he was forced to leave school to support his family, which had suffered devastating financial losses. Both of Robinson's brothers died young after lives marred by failure. Robinson himself endured years of poverty. Success finally arrived, but the years of struggle had shaped Robinson's world view. He filled his poems with the voices and stories of the lost and the sorrowful, exploring the themes of personal defeat and unfulfilled longing. Luke Havergal, who suffers the loss of a loved one, and Richard Cory, who suffers with hidden pain, are typical of his work.

Go to the western gate, Luke Havergal,
There where the vines cling crimson on the wall,
And in the twilight wait for what will come.
The leaves will whisper there of her, and some,
Like flying words, will strike you as they fall;
But go, and if you listen she will call.
Go to the western gate, Luke Havergal—
Luke Havergal.

No, there is not a dawn in eastern skies
To rift the fiery night that's in your eyes;
But there, where western glooms are gathering,
The dark will end the dark, if anything:
God slays Himself with every leaf that flies,
And hell is more than half of paradise.
No, there is not a dawn in eastern skies—
In eastern skies.

❷ Out of a grave I come to tell you this,
Out of a grave I come to quench the kiss
That flames upon your forehead with a glow
That blinds you to the way that you must go.
Yes, there is yet one way to where she is,
Bitter, but one that faith may never miss.
Out of a grave I come to tell you this—
To tell you this.

There is the western gate, Luke Havergal,
There are the crimson leaves upon the wall.
Go, for the winds are tearing them away,—
Nor think to riddle the dead words they say,
Nor any more to feel them as they fall;
But go, and if you trust her she will call.
There is the western gate, Luke Havergal—
Luke Havergal.

Literary Analysis
Speaker Who is the "I" who speaks in this poem? Is there more than one possible interpretation?

❸ 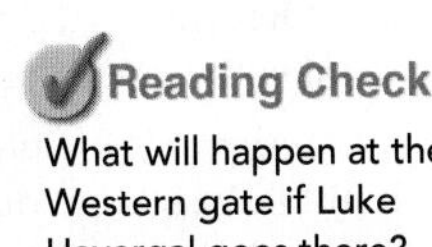
Reading Check
What will happen at the Western gate if Luke Havergal goes there?

❷ Literary Analysis
Speaker

- Have a student volunteer read the poem aloud clearly and slowly. **Ask** students to offer comments about their overall impressions of the setting, characters, and sound devices of the poem.
- Then, **ask** students the Literary Analysis question: Who is the speaker in this poem?
  Answer: Students might suggest that the speaker is a supreme being, the spirit of Havergal's lost love, or part of Havergal's inner self.

❸ Reading Check

Answer: Luke Havergal will hear his love calling.

Differentiated Instruction Solutions for All Learners

Strategy for Special Needs Students
Help these students recognize and interpret key symbols in these poems. For instance, in "Luke Havergal," the western gate can represent not only an actual cemetery gate, but also (because it is where the sun descends) death itself.

Strategy for Less Proficient Readers
It may help students to paraphrase some lines to uncover Robinson's meaning. For instance, students might paraphrase lines 9 and 10 as "This is not just a bad dream that you can wake up from."

❹ Humanities

***The Thinker* (Portrait of Louis N. Kenton),** 1900, by Thomas Eakins

Thomas Eakins (1844–1916) was an American portrait and genre painter from Philadelphia. He studied art in Paris and at the Pennsylvania Academy of Fine Arts. Eakins grew interested in using photography to record human and animal locomotion. Some of his photographic studies served as a basis for paintings. His later work reveals deep psychological insights, especially in representing contemplative moods. *The Thinker* is a fine example of Eakins's presentation of a state of mind. The intense and haunting image of a man embodies sadness, frustration, and resignation.

Use the following questions for discussion:

1. What might the man in the portrait be thinking?
   Answer: Responses should reflect the serious and somber expression on the man's face.
2. How does the artist's use of color affect the message of the portrait?
   Answer: Students may say that the black suit and the brown walls suggest depression, dark thoughts, and a lack of hope.

❺ Critical Viewing

Answer: Students may say that the demeanor of the man, his fine clothes, and the quiet, sober expression on his face suggest Richard Cory more than they do the envious speaker.

ASSESS

Answers

1. Students should support their responses with clear reasons and examples.
2. (a) He should go there if he wishes to hear his beloved calling. (b) The gate symbolizes death.
3. (a) He has come from "out of a grave." (b) **Possible response:** The message urges Luke Havergal to visit the cemetery to commune with the spirit of his beloved until it is his rightful time to die.
4. (a) He was envied for his wealth, grace, and social position. (b) In contrast to Cory's fine qualities,

❶

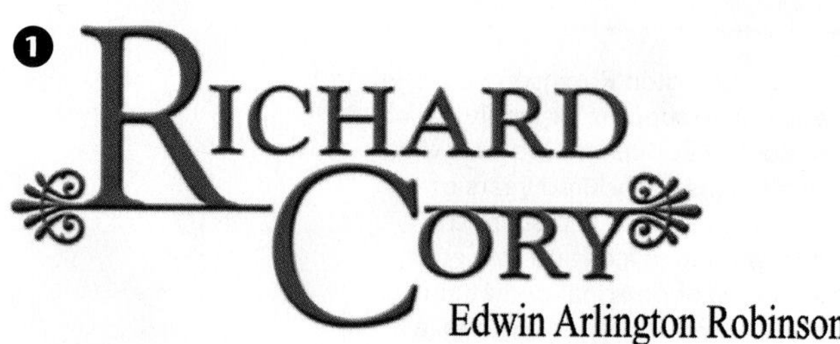

Edwin Arlington Robinson

❹

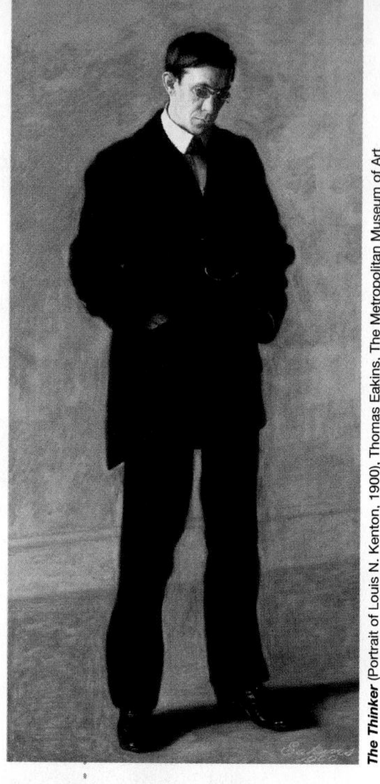

The Thinker (Portrait of Louis N. Kenton, 1900), Thomas Eakins, The Metropolitan Museum of Art

Whenever Richard Cory went down town,
We people on the pavement looked at him:
He was a gentleman from sole to crown,
Clean favored, and imperially slim.

And he was always quietly arrayed,
And he was always human when he talked;
But still he fluttered pulses when he said,
"Good-morning," and he glittered when he walked.

And he was rich—yes, richer than a king—
And admirably schooled in every grace:
In fine, we thought that he was everything
To make us wish that we were in his place.

So on we worked, and waited for the light,
And went without the meat, and cursed the bread;
And Richard Cory, one calm summer night,
Went home and put a bullet through his head.

❺ **▲ Critical Viewing**
Do you think this painting suggests Richard Cory or the poem's speaker? Explain. **[Connect]**

Vocabulary Builder
imperially (im pir´ ē əl ē) *adv.* majestically

Critical Reading

1. **Respond:** Were you surprised by the last line of "Richard Cory"? Explain.
2. **(a) Recall:** Why should Luke Havergal go to the gate? **(b) Speculate:** What might the gate symbolize?
3. **(a) Recall:** In "Luke Havergal," from where has the speaker come? **(b) Interpret:** What is the speaker's message?
4. **(a) Recall:** Why was Richard Cory envied? **(b) Contrast:** In what ways does Richard Cory differ from the other townspeople?
5. **(a) Recall:** What does Cory do one night? **(b) Infer:** Do you think the town was surprised by his action? Explain.
6. **(a) Apply:** Why might Richard Cory have been miserable? **(b) Relate:** What do you think are the keys to individual happiness?

For: More about Edwin Arlington Robinson
Visit: www.PHSchool.com
Web Code: ere-9421

Answers continued

the townspeople are ordinary working people who struggle to make ends meet.

5. (a) He shoots himself. (b) Since they imagined Cory had everything, they wouldn't expect him to take his life.
6. (a) **Possible response:** Cory might not have had close, gratifying personal relationships; he may have achieved material success and still have felt empty.
   (b) Students should support their responses with clear reasoning.

Go Online — Author Link For additional information about Edwin Arlington Robinson, have students type in the Web Code, then select *R* from the alphabet, and then select Edwin Arlington Robinson.

6 Lucinda Matlock

Edgar Lee Masters

I went to the dances at Chandlerville,
And played snap-out[1] at Winchester.
One time we changed partners,
Driving home in the moonlight of middle June,
And then I found Davis.
We were married and lived together for seventy years,
Enjoying, working, raising the twelve children,
Eight of whom we lost
Ere I had reached the age of sixty.
I spun, I wove, I kept the house, I nursed the sick,
I made the garden, and for holiday
Rambled over the fields where sang the larks,
And by Spoon River gathering many a shell,
And many a flower and medicinal weed—
Shouting to the wooded hills, singing to the green valleys.
At ninety-six I had lived enough, that is all,
And passed to a sweet repose.
What is this I hear of sorrow and weariness,
Anger, discontent and drooping hopes?
Degenerate sons and daughters,
Life is too strong for you—
It takes life to love Life.

1. **snap-out** game in which a long line of players who are holding hands spin around in a circle, causing the players on the ends to be flung off by centrifugal force.

Vocabulary Builder

repose (ri pōz′) *n.* state of being at rest

degenerate (dē jen′ ər it) *adj.* morally corrupt

Critical Reading

1. **Respond:** What is your opinion of Lucinda Matlock? Is she someone you would strive to emulate? Why or why not?
2. **(a) Recall:** Summarize Lucinda Matlock's domestic life. **(b) Analyze:** What is her attitude about her life?
3. **(a) Recall:** How old was Lucinda Matlock when she died? **(b) Infer:** Why might she have thought she "lived enough"?
4. **(a) Recall:** Whom does she address at the end of the poem? **(b) Interpret:** What is the meaning of Matlock's message to those she addresses?
5. **(a) Apply:** How might Matlock respond to the complaint that life today is too complex? **(b) Connect:** Do you agree? Explain.

For: More about Edgar Lee Masters
Visit: www.PHSchool.com
Web Code: ere-9422

6 About the Selections

The two poems by Masters demonstrate two characters' abilities to face life in a changing world. From the detached distance of the grave, both characters speak frankly about their lives. Matlock died when she was ninety-six after a hard but fulfilling life. She dismisses the complaints she hears from the younger generation, whom she feels never developed the power to embrace life and survive its many troubles.

As a carver of tombstones, Bone came to know the people in Spoon River and to learn how closeness and affection caused relatives to ask him to carve "false chronicles" into the stone.

ASSESS

Answers

1. Whether students like or dislike Matlock, they should support their opinions with evidence from the poem.
2. (a) She had a marriage that produced twelve children (although eight had died before she turned sixty), and she was charitable and hard-working. (b) She seems to think that she lived well.
3. (a) She died at ninety-six. (b) Being a pragmatic woman, she may have felt that she had accomplished everything she wanted or needed to do.
4. (a) She addresses younger generations, who complain of hopelessness. (b) They must live and experience the joys and stand up to the sorrows.
5. (a) Matlock would probably disagree and point out that her life was equally complex. (b) Students should support their responses with clear reasoning and examples from the text.

Go Online Author Link For additional information about Edgar Lee Masters, have students type in the Web Code, then select *M* from the alphabet, and then select Edgar Lee Masters.

Differentiated Instruction Solutions for All Learners

Strategy for Gifted/Talented Students

Have students complete a graphic organizer like the one shown to analyze the personality of the speakers in "Lucinda Matlock" and "Richard Bone." Then, have students compare and contrast the speakers. Suggest that students explore the fact that, even though both poems are written in the first person, the voices of the speakers are distinct.

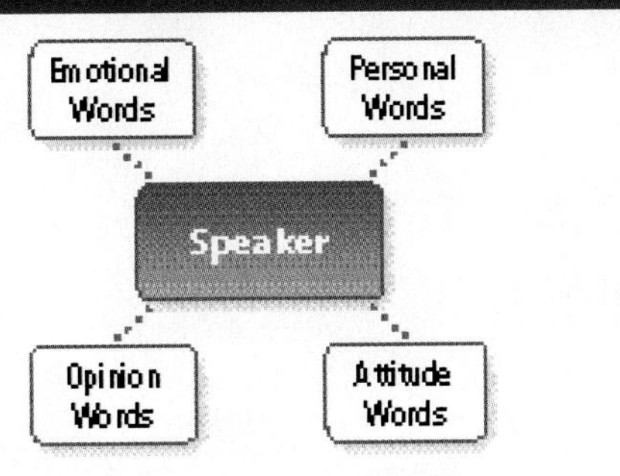

ASSESS

Answers

1. Students should support their responses with clear reasoning and examples from the text.
2. (a) He is a tombstone carver. (b) He becomes familiar with the townspeople and can determine whether their epitaphs are true. (c) He continues to make his living carving gravestones, though the work implicates him in the hypocrisy of the epitaphs.
3. (a) He is familiar with the true natures of the deceased persons. (b) **Possible responses:** The townspeople believe them; they want to show their love for the deceased.
4. Both provide a written record of lives in the past.
5. **Possible answers:** Yes, Bone played an important role because he gave the townspeople a way to honor their loved ones.

Go Online Author Link For additional information about Edgar Lee Masters, have students type in the Web Code, then select *M* from the alphabet, and then select Edgar Lee Masters.

6 Richard Bone

Edgar Lee Masters

When I first came to Spoon River
I did not know whether what they told me
Was true or false.
They would bring me the epitaph
And stand around the shop while I worked
And say "He was so kind," "He was wonderful,"
"She was the sweetest woman," "He was a consistent Christian."
And I chiseled for them whatever they wished,
All in ignorance of its truth.
But later, as I lived among the people here,
I knew how near to the life
Were the epitaphs that were ordered for them as they died.

But still I chiseled whatever they paid me to chisel
and made myself party to the false chronicles
Of the stones,
Even as the historian does who writes
Without knowing the truth,
Or because he is influenced to hide it.

Vocabulary Builder
epitaph (ep′ ə taf′) *n.* inscription on a tombstone or grave marker

Critical Reading

1. **Respond:** What is your opinion of Richard Bone after reading this poem? Explain.
2. **(a) Recall:** What is Richard Bone's occupation? **(b) Infer:** What does he learn after years in Spoon River? **(c) Speculate:** Does his attitude change? If so, how?
3. **(a) Interpret:** Why does Bone think the epitaphs are "false chronicles"? **(b) Speculate:** Why do you think the townspeople compose such epitaphs for their loved ones?
4. **Analyze:** Explain why Bone might compare a tombstone carver to a historian.
5. **Apply:** Do you think Bone played an important role in Spoon River? Support your answer.

Go Online Author Link
For: More about Edgar Lee Masters
Visit: www.PHSchool.com
Web Code: ere-9422

Apply the Skills

Luke Havergal • Richard Cory • Lucinda Matlock • Richard Bone

Literary Analysis

Speaker

1. What details suggest that the **speaker** of "Richard Cory" is speaking for the entire town?
2. In what ways does the speaker's admiration for Richard Cory add to the power of the poem?
3. **(a)** In what ways might "Lucinda Matlock" be different if Masters had used a different speaker? **(b)** If "Richard Cory" spoke for himself, how might the poem be different?
4. The speakers in Master's *Spoon River Anthology* are dead. Why might this allow them to discuss their lives more openly?

Comparing Literary Works

5. In both "Luke Havergal" and "Lucinda Matlock," voices speak from the grave. Compare and contrast the messages they deliver.
6. If Richard Bone were asked to carve epitaphs for Luke Havergal, Richard Cory, and Lucinda Matlock, what would he write? Explain each response.

Reading Strategy

Recognizing Attitudes

7. In what way does the speaker's **attitude** toward Richard Cory differ from Cory's attitude toward himself? Support your answer.
8. Identify and explain the attitude of the speaker in "Richard Bone."
9. Use a chart like this to describe Lucinda Matlock's outlook on life.

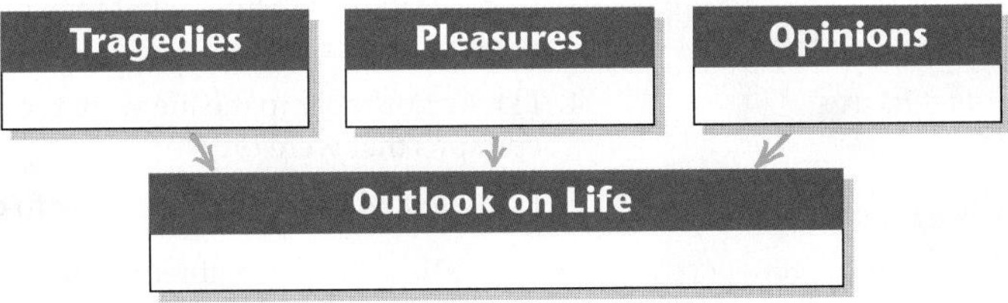

Extend Understanding

10. **Psychology Connection:** Consider the ways in which these characters deal with change and explain other, healthier options.

QuickReview

The **speaker** is the voice that is speaking in a poem.

To **recognize the attitudes** of a poem's speaker, look for details that suggest how a speaker feels about a subject.

For: Self-test
Visit: www.PHSchool.com
Web Code: era-6414

Answers

1. The speaker uses the words *We people* in line 2.
2. The speaker's admiration prepares the reader to believe that Cory is destined for a great, long life.
3. (a) Another speaker might convey different attitudes about the details—and overall significance—of Matlock's life. (b) Cory might have explained his true feelings and why he committed suicide.
4. Speakers who are "dead" are detached from the world and thus have nothing to gain or lose from their honesty.
5. In "Luke Havergal," an anguished man is drawn toward death by the promise of reunion with his lost love. In "Lucinda Matlock," the speaker celebrates a life well lived and a peaceful, contented death.
6. The epitaphs might aim to idealize the lives of the dead.
7. Cory does not believe that he has everything to live for; the speaker thinks Cory does.
8. The speaker seems disdainful of the people he serves.
9. Tragedies such as outliving eight children, pleasures such as singing and gathering shells, and opinions such as disapproving of the younger generation's moral weakness contribute to her belief that one must live with gusto and strength.

   Another sample answer can be found on **Reading Strategy Graphic Organizer B**, p. 143 in ***Graphic Organizer Transparencies.***
10. Matlock seems almost to ignore change as she proceeds vigorously through life; Bone grows more bitter and cynical as his relationships with the townspeople develop. Students might describe ways in which people can deal with change without isolating themselves from others.

Go Online Assessment Students may use the **Self-test** to prepare for **Selection Test A** or **Selection Test B.**

Answers

❶ Vocabulary Lesson

Word Analysis

1. b
2. c
3. a

Vocabulary Builder

1. a
2. c
3. a
4. a

Spelling Strategy

1. symphonic
2. sinful
3. decipher
4. catastrophe

❷ Grammar and Style Lesson

1. *where she is:* object of a preposition
2. *whatever they wished:* direct object
3. *whether what they told me was true or false:* direct object
4. *the epitaphs that were ordered:* predicate noun
5. *whatever they paid me to chisel:* direct object

Writing Application

Each student's sentences should include at least three noun clauses and should describe various aspects of a familiar person or place.

WG Writing and Grammar, Ruby Level

Students will find further instruction and practice on noun clauses in Chapter 19, Section 3.

Build Language Skills

❶ Vocabulary Lesson

Word Analysis: Latin Root *-pose-*

The word *repose* combines the Latin root *-pose-* ("place" or "rest") with the prefix *re-* ("back"). Using this word analysis, *repose* can be defined as "the state of being at rest."

Use each of the words below to complete the sentences.

a. depose **b.** impose **c.** interpose

1. He hated to __?__ on his friends, but he was unable to find a hotel room.
2. Each time audience members __?__ comments, the speaker loses his train of thought.
3. When we __?__ the prime minister, we will set this nation on a course toward true freedom.

Vocabulary Builder: Synonyms

Write the letter of the best synonym for the first word.

1. imperially: **(a)** grandly, **(b)** scornfully, **(c)** strongly
2. repose: **(a)** model, **(b)** silence, **(c)** ease
3. degenerate: **(a)** evil, **(b)** degraded, **(c)** slow
4. epitaph: **(a)** inscription, **(b)** homily, **(c)** graph

Spelling Strategy

In many English words of Greek origin, *ph* is used to spell the *f* sound, as in *epitaph, trophy,* and *physique.* For each of the following pairs, choose the correct spelling.

1. symfonic/symphonic
2. sinful/sinphul
3. decifer/decipher
4. catastrofe/catastrophe

❷ Grammar and Style Lesson

Noun Clauses

A **noun clause** is a subordinate clause used as a noun. It can be used as a subject, a predicate nominative, a direct object, an indirect object, or the object of a preposition. Noun clauses are commonly introduced by words such as *that, which, where, what, who, whatever, whoever,* and *why.*

Subject: *Whoever knows about life* will tell you.

Direct Object: We thought *that he was everything.*

Predicate Nominative: He is *whatever we admire.*

Object of a Preposition: He tells his story to *whoever will listen.*

Practice Copy the following sentences and underline the noun clause in each. Explain the function of each noun clause.

1. There is yet one way to where she is.
2. I chiseled for them whatever they wished.
3. I did not know whether what they told me was true or false.
4. I knew how near to the life were the epitaphs that were ordered.
5. I chiseled whatever they paid me to chisel.

Writing Application Write three or four sentences to describe different aspects of a familiar person or place. In your writing, include at least three noun clauses.

WG Prentice Hall Writing and Grammar Connection: Chapter 19, Section 3

Assessment Practice

Context **(For more practice, see *Standardized Test Preparation Workbook*, p. 39.)**

The reading sections of many tests require students to use context clues to identify the appropriate meaning of a multiple-meaning word in a given passage. Use the following sample test item to demonstrate.

Whenever Richard Cory went to town,
We people on the pavement looked at him:
He was a gentleman from sole to crown.
Clean favored, and imperially slim.

In this passage, the word crown most nearly means—

A symbol of royalty
B hit on the head
C top of head
D royal government

The juxtaposition of *sole* and *crown,* and the general context of describing a gentleman's appearance should lead students to recognize that *C* is the most appropriate choice.

Writing Lesson

Firsthand Biography

Poems like those by Robinson and Masters are one way to create vivid portraits of people. Another way to present a portrait is through a firsthand biography—a story about events in the life of a person with whom the writer has a personal relationship. Write a firsthand biography in which you share your impressions of a person.

Prewriting After you have selected and interviewed your subject, list his or her key personality traits and the events that reveal them. Then, arrange these details in their order of importance.

Drafting Focus your draft on a single event or a series of events that illustrate the person's most important personality traits. Use transitional words like the ones shown.

Model: Choosing Transitions

Sequence	Causality	Comparison/ Contrast	Example/ Definition
first	because	on the other hand	for instance
next	as a result	similarly	for example
then	consequently	contrary to	in other words
afterward	due to	likewise	significantly
finally	since	in contrast	specifically

Revising Review your biography and add more details to make sure that it conveys the impression of your subject that you intended.

WG Prentice Hall Writing and Grammar Connection: Chapter 4, Connected Assignment

Extend Your Learning

Speaking and Listening Find a copy of folk duo Simon and Garfunkel's adaptation of "Richard Cory" and compare it with the poem, addressing the following issues:

- Is the song effective?
- Does it capture the message of the poem?
- In what ways, if any, does the song alter Robinson's meaning?

Lead a **class discussion** in which you compare the poem to the song. **[Group Activity]**

Research and Technology Review *Spoon River Anthology* to find several poems that convey a similar theme, such as jealousy, honesty, or love. Prepare an **illustrated booklet** of these poems. In addition to providing images that enhance the meaning of the poems, write an introduction explaining the connection among the poems.

For: An additional research activity
Visit: www.PHSchool.com
Web Code: erd-7413

3 Writing Lesson

- To guide students in writing this firsthand biography, give them the **Support for Writing Lesson** page (***Unit 4 Resources,*** p. 239).
- Students' firsthand biographies should use detailed descriptions of events and character traits to convey a clear impression of a person they know well.
- Encourage students to be specific about the aspects of the subject's personality they wish to evoke. They might focus on an experience or an occasion that conveys the subject's personality.
- Use the rubrics for Biography, pp. 77–78 in ***General Resources,*** to evaluate students' work.

4 Listening and Speaking

- Encourage students to listen to Simon's song (and to reread Robinson's poem) several times before the class discussion. Students might benefit from taking the time to transcribe the song's lyrics for close comparison with the poem.
- Invite students to explore questions in writing or with partners to prepare for leading the class discussion.
- The **Support for Extend Your Learning** page (***Unit 4 Resources,*** p. 240) provides guided note-taking opportunities to help students complete the Extend Your Learning activities.

Go Online Research Have students type in the Web code for another research activity.

Assessment Resources

The following resources can be used to assess students' knowledge and skills.

Unit 4 Resources
- **Selection Test A,** pp. 242–244
- **Selection Test B,** pp. 245–247

General Resources
- **Rubrics for Biography,** pp. 77–78

Go Online Assessment Students may use the **Self-test** to prepare for **Selection Test A** or **Selection Test B.**

Meeting Your Standards

Students will

1. **analyze and respond to literary elements.**
   - Literary Analysis: Characterization
2. **read, comprehend, analyze, and critique a short story.**
   - Reading Strategy: Clarifying
   - Reading Check questions
   - Apply the Skills questions
   - Assessment Practice (ATE)
3. **develop vocabulary.**
   - Vocabulary Lesson: Words From Music
4. **understand and apply written and oral language conventions.**
   - Spelling Strategy
   - Grammar and Style Lesson: Reflexive and Intensive Pronouns
5. **develop writing proficiency.**
   - Writing Lesson: Editorial
6. **develop appropriate research strategies.**
   - Extend Your Learning: Musical Presentation
7. **understand and apply listening and speaking strategies.**
   - Extend Your Learning: Monologues

Block Scheduling: Use one 90-minute class period to preteach the skills and have students read the selection. Use a second 90-minute class period to assess students' mastery of skills, extend their learning, and monitor their progress.

Homework Suggestions

Following are possibilities for homework assignments.

- Support pages from *Unit 4 Resources:*
  Literary Analysis
  Reading Strategy
  Vocabulary Builder
  Grammar and Style
- An Extend Your Learning project and the Writing Lesson for this selection may be completed over several days.

Step-by-Step Teaching Guide	Pacing Guide
PRETEACH	
• Administer Vocabulary and Reading Warm-ups as necessary.	5 min.
• Engage students' interest with the motivation activity.	5 min.
• Read and discuss author and background features. **FT**	10 min.
• Introduce the Literary Analysis Skill: Characterization. **FT**	5 min.
• Introduce the Reading Strategy: Clarifying. **FT**	10 min.
• Prepare students to read by teaching the selection vocabulary. **FT**	
TEACH	
• Informally monitor comprehension while students read independently or in groups. **FT**	30 min.
• Monitor students' comprehension with the Reading Check notes.	as students read
• Reinforce vocabulary with Vocabulary Builder notes.	as students read
• Develop students' understanding of characterization with the Literary Analysis annotations. **FT**	5 min.
• Develop students' ability to clarify with the Reading Strategy annotations. **FT**	5 min.
ASSESS/EXTEND	
• Assess students' comprehension and mastery of the Literary Analysis and Reading Strategy by having them answer the Apply the Skills questions. **FT**	15 min.
• Have students complete the Vocabulary Lesson and the Grammar and Style Lesson. **FT**	15 min.
• Apply students' ability to use specific language in writing by using the Writing Lesson. **FT**	45 min. or homework
• Apply students' understanding by using one or more of the Extend Your Learning activities.	20–90 min. or homework
• Administer Selection Test A or Selection Test B. **FT**	15 min.

Resources

PRINT

Unit 4 Resources

- Vocabulary Warm-up Word Lists [**L1, L2, EL**] .... p. 248
- Vocabulary Warm-up Practice [**L1, L2, EL**] .... p. 249
- Reading Warm-up A [**L1, L2, EL**] .... p. 250
- Reading Warm-up B [**L1, L2, L3**] .... p. 251

TRANSPARENCY

Graphic Organizer Transparencies

- Literary Analysis Graphic Organizer A [**L3**] .... p. 146
- Literary Analysis Graphic Organizer B [**L1, L2, EL**] .... p. 147
- Reading Strategy Graphic Organizer A [**L3**] .... p. 144
- Reading Strategy Graphic Organizer B [**L1, L2, EL**] .... p. 145

PRINT

Reader's Notebook [L2]
Reader's Notebook: Adapted Version [L1]
Reader's Notebook: English Learner's Version [EL]

Unit 4 Resources

- Literary Analysis [**L3**] .... p. 252
- Reading Strategy [**L3**] .... p. 253
- Vocabulary Builder [**L3**] .... p. 254

TECHNOLOGY

Listening to Literature Audio CDs [L2, EL]

PRINT

Unit 4 Resources

- Grammar and Style [**L3**] .... p. 255
- Support for Writing Lesson [**L3**] .... p. 256
- Support for Extend Your Learning [**L3**] .... p. 257
- Enrichment [**L4**] .... p. 258
- Selection Test A [**L1, L2, EL**] .... pp. 259–261
- Selection Test B [**L3, L4**] .... pp. 262–264

General Resources

- Rubrics for Persuasion: Persuasive Essay [**L3**] .... pp. 45–46
- Rubric for Peer Assessment: Dramatic Performance [**L3**] .... p. 131

TECHNOLOGY

Go Online: Research [**L3**]
Go Online: Self-test [**L3**]
***ExamView®*, Test Bank [L3]**

Choosing Resources for Differentiated Instruction

[**L1**] Special Needs Students
[**L2**] Below-Level Students
[**L3**] All Students
[**L4**] Advanced Students
[**EL**] English Learners

FT Fast Track Instruction: To move the lesson more quickly, use the strategies and activities identified with **FT**.

Scaffolding for Less Proficient and Advanced Students

The leveled Critical Thinking questions after selections progress in the levels of thinking required to answer them. To address the needs of your different students, you may use the (a) level questions for your less proficient students and the (b) level questions with your on-level and advanced students. The occasional (c) level questions are appropriate for your advanced students.

PRENTICE HALL
TeacherEXPRESS™ Plan · Teach · Assess

Use this complete suite of powerful teaching tools to make lesson planning and testing quicker and easier.

PRENTICE HALL

Use the interactive textbook (online and on CD-ROM) to make selections and activities come alive with audio and video support and interactive questions.

PREFEACH

Motivation

Before class, write "Wagner Matinée" on the chalkboard, as if to announce a concert, and give the composer's full name and dates (1813–1883). Prepare a list of the pieces mentioned in the story: Overture from *Tannhäuser,* Prelude to *Tristan and Isolde,* selections from *The Flying Dutchman, The Ring (The Rheingold, The Valkyrie, Siegfried, and Dusk of the Gods),* Forest Music from *Siegfried,* and Siegfried's funeral march. As students enter the room, pass out the "program" and dim the lights, as if in a concert hall. Play one or more excerpts from these pieces, all of which are readily available. Invite students to respond to the emotion of the music. Then let students know that an afternoon concert featuring the composer whose work they have just heard is a key event in the story they are about to read.

1 Background

More About the Author

In 1944, Willa Cather received the Gold Medal of the National Institute of the American Academy of Arts and Letters in recognition of the entire body of her work. Cather wrote fiction with a contemporary setting, as well as stories and novels that explored the traditional values of the pioneer era. Although she continued to live in New York after leaving *McClure's Magazine,* Cather visited her home town of Red Cloud, Nebraska, twice a year and maintained close ties with her family.

Build Skills Short Story

1 A Wagner Matinée

Willa Cather (1873–1947)

Although Willa Cather lived more than half her life in New York City, she turned again and again to the Nebraska prairie of her youth—at the time, a recently settled area of the American frontier—for inspiration and material for her writing. Cather captured with unflinching honesty the difficulties of life on the expanding frontier.

A Prairie Childhood Born in a small town in western Virginia, Cather moved to the Nebraska frontier when she was nine. Many of her new neighbors were immigrants struggling to build new lives while preserving their native cultures. Commenting on the diversity that surrounded her during her childhood, Cather once wrote, "On Sundays we could drive to a Norwegian church and listen to a sermon in that language, or to a Danish or Swedish church. We could go to a French Catholic settlement or into a Bohemian township and hear one in Czech, or we could go to the church with the German Lutherans."

In addition to all that she learned from observing the diverse group of people who surrounded her, Cather received a rich formal education, studying foreign languages, history, classical music, and opera. In 1891, Cather left home to study at the University of Nebraska, becoming one of the first women to receive a college education.

The Making of a Literary Giant After graduating from the University of Nebraska in 1895, Cather worked as an editor at a Pittsburgh newspaper while she wrote poems and short stories in her spare time. Her first collection of stories, *The Troll Garden,* was published in 1905. In 1906, she moved to New York and joined the editorial staff of *McClure's Magazine.* After her first novel, *Alexander's Bridge,* was published in 1912, Cather left *McClure's* to devote herself to writing. She remained in New York for the rest of her life, but her memories of the prairie inspired her greatest work.

Over the next 35 years, Cather produced ten novels, two short-story collections, and two collections of essays. Among her outstanding works are *O Pioneers!* (1913), *My Ántonia* (1918), and *One of Ours* (1922), all of which capture the flavor of life on the Midwestern prairie. *One of Ours* won Cather the Pulitzer Prize in 1923. Cather then shifted her attention from the Midwest to New Mexico in *Death Comes for the Archbishop* (1927) and to seventeenth-century Canada in *Shadows on the Rock* (1931).

Portraits of Prairie Life Although Cather's fiction was by no means limited to "prairie stories"—her fictional settings ranged from contemporary New York City to the American Southwest to Quebec—it was her stories about Nebraskan immigrants that most appealed to readers and critics. In these stories, she displayed her admiration for the courage and spirit of the immigrants and other settlers of the frontier. At the same time, she conveyed an intense awareness of the loss felt by the pioneers and the loneliness and isolation from which they suffered. In "A Wagner Matinée," for example, Cather captures this sense of loneliness and isolation by contrasting the stark realities of frontier life with the possibilities of life in a more cultured world.

Preview

Connecting to the Literature

Music can exert a powerful tug on our feelings, memories, and fantasies. In this story, a woman experiences a flood of long-buried emotions when she attends a special concert.

2 Literary Analysis

Characterization

A writer uses **characterization** to reveal a character's personality. Characterization is generally developed through one of the following methods:

- Direct statements about the character
- Descriptions of the character's appearance
- The character's actions, thoughts, or comments
- Comments about the character made by other characters.

As you read, note how these methods of characterization are used to develop the personality of Aunt Georgiana.

Connecting Literary Elements

When a story is told by a character involved in the action, the writer is using the **first-person point of view.** In such a story, all impressions of events, places, and characters are filtered through the narrator. In "A Wagner Matinée," Aunt Georgiana is presented to the reader exactly as she is perceived by the narrator—her nephew, Clark.

3 Reading Strategy

Clarifying

Cather's story is packed with details about its main character. To fully understand the character's actions, **clarify** the details that are provided. This may involve reading a footnote or looking up a word in a dictionary. You may also need to reread a passage to refresh your memory about previous details or even read ahead to find details that clarify meaning. Use a chart like the one shown to clarify difficult passages from the text.

Detail	Clarifying Strategy
"Howard followed her."	*Reread to find out who Howard is.*
inexplicable	*Look the word up in the dictionary.*
"took a homestead in Red Willow County"	*Find out where Red Willow County is.*

Vocabulary Builder

reverential (rev′ ə ren′ shəl) *adj.* caused by a feeling of deep respect and love (p. 673)

tremulously (trem′ yo͞o ləs lē) *adv.* fearfully; timidly (p. 673)

semi-somnambulant (sem′ i säm nam′ byo͞o lənt) *adj.* half-sleepwalking (p. 673)

inert (in urt′) *adj.* motionless (p. 674)

prelude (prel′ yo͞od′) *n.* introductory section or movement of a work of music (p. 676)

jocularity (jäk′ yo͞o lar′ ə tē) *n.* joking good humor (p. 677)

Differentiated Instruction Solutions for All Learners

Support for Special Needs Students
Have students complete the **Preview** and **Build Skills** pages for the selection in the ***Reader's Notebook: Adapted Version.*** These pages provide a selection summary, an abbreviated presentation of the reading and literary skills, and the graphic organizer on the **Build Skills** page in the student book.

Support for Less Proficient Readers
Have students complete the **Preview** and **Build Skills** pages for the selection in the ***Reader's Notebook***. These pages provide a selection summary, an abbreviated presentation of the reading and literary skills, and the graphic organizer on the **Build Skills** page in the student book.

Support for English Learners
Have students complete the **Preview** and **Build Skills** pages for the selection in the ***Reader's Notebook: English Learners's Version.*** These pages provide a selection summary, an abbreviated presentation of the skills, additional contextual vocabulary, and the graphic organizer on the **Build Skills** page in the student book.

2 Literary Analysis

Characterization

- Read the instruction about characterization as a class. Encourage student volunteers to create an example to illustrate each of the four bulleted methods of characterization.
- Discuss how point of view relates to characterization. Point out that a third-person omniscient narrator can provide detailed information about the actions, feelings, and thoughts of every character in a story, whereas a first-person narrator can only speculate about the feelings and thoughts of other characters.

3 Reading Strategy

Clarifying

- Point out that even the most experienced and skillful readers must clarify details as they read by rereading a text or previewing later passages.
- Guide students to see the importance of monitoring their own understanding as they read. Most readers know the sensation of suddenly realizing that they have been reading for several seconds with no awareness of what they are reading. Tell students that it is vital at such times to go back and pick up where they stopped making sense of the text.
- Encourage students to see how leaving the narrative momentarily to clarify details is a sign of respect for oneself as a learner. It is a skill that students can use over and over as they encounter various types of texts.
- Provide students with a copy of **Reading Strategy Graphic Organizer A,** p. 144 in ***Graphic Organizer Transparencies,*** to use as they read the selection.

Vocabulary Builder

- Pronounce each vocabulary word for students, and read the definitions as a class. Have students identify any words with which they are already familiar.

Learning Modalities
Musical/Rhythmic Learners
Have these students listen to the musical pieces mentioned in the story and comment on their emotional impact. Also have them identify terms, used here and elsewhere, that have general meanings as well as specific definitions as musical terms. Examples include *motif, crescendo, development,* and *counterpoint.*

1 About the Selection

The story explores the contrast between cultured city life and the rugged life that nineteenth-century settlers led after moving to the frontier. The narrator's Aunt Georgiana returns to Boston for a visit years after moving to Nebraska with her husband. A former music teacher, Georgiana has been outwardly toughened by frontier life. Yet when her nephew takes her to the opera, she has a deep emotional response: she cries with joy at the music and with grief at the cultural opportunities she has forfeited to live with her husband. Through his aunt's pain, the narrator learns that the soul never really dies, but "withers to the outward eye only" as it waits to be reawakened.

2

From Arkansas, 1939, George Schreiber, Sheldon Swope Art Museum, Terre Haute, Indiana

3 ▲ Critical Viewing In what ways does the woman in the painting seem like Aunt Georgiana? **[Connect; Interpret]**

Differentiated Instruction Solutions for All Learners

Accessibility at a Glance

	A Wagner Matinée
Context	First person narrator
Language	Vocabulary footnotes
Concept Level	Challenging (the soul)
Literary Merit	Noted author
Lexile	1410
Overall Rating	More challenging

A Wagner Matinée ❶

Willa Cather

Background When "A Wagner Matinée" first appeared in 1904, Cather's readers would have been as familiar with Richard Wagner (Väg nər) as people are today with the Beatles. Wagner, who was German, was one of the nineteenth century's greatest composers. His operas are characterized by their adventurous harmonic language and their innovative intermarriage of music and drama. Although many critics judged Wagner's music unfavorably during his lifetime, his operas became enormously popular after his death in 1883.

I received one morning a letter written in pale ink, on glassy, blue-lined notepaper, and bearing the postmark of a little Nebraska village. This communication, worn and rubbed, looking as though it had been carried for some days in a coat pocket that was none too clean, was from my Uncle Howard. It informed me that his wife had been left a small legacy by a bachelor relative who had recently died, and that it had become necessary for her to come to Boston to attend to the settling of the estate. He requested me to meet her at the station, and render her whatever services might prove necessary. On examining the date indicated as that of her arrival, I found it no later than tomorrow. He had characteristically delayed writing until, had I been away from home for a day, I must have missed the good woman altogether.

The name of my Aunt Georgiana called up not alone her own figure, at once pathetic and grotesque, but opened before my feet a gulf of recollections so wide and deep that, as the letter dropped from my hand, I felt suddenly a stranger to all the present conditions of my existence, wholly ill at ease and out of place amid the surroundings

❹ **Reading Check**
Why is Aunt Georgiana going to Boston?

❷ Humanities

From Arkansas, 1939, by George Schreiber

Belgian-born George Schreiber came to the United States in the 1920s. Like many artists during the Great Depression, Schreiber turned his focus to the great Midwestern farmlands. Although Schreiber was not a major figure in the Regionalist art movement, this painting demonstrates his talent and interest in recording the spirit of rural America during one of its most trying times. He portrays the woman with stark realism: her face, ragged apron, and stance reflect the hardships she has endured and the strength with which she has met them.

Use these questions for discussion:

1. What can you infer about the woman's feelings from the way she holds her arms?
   Answer: Students may say that she is weary, resigned to a difficult life, or frustrated.
2. What details of the setting reflect the description of Aunt Georgiana's homestead?
   Answer: The flat, barren land, bare tree branches, and dilapidated building are similar to those described in the story.

❸ Critical Viewing

Answer: Students may say that both women look bent, weary, and worn from suffering and hard work.

❹ Reading Check

Answer: She needs to be present for the settling of the estate of one of her recently deceased relatives.

Differentiated Instruction — Solutions for All Learners

Strategy for Special Needs Students
Students may benefit from spending time rereading and discussing the first two paragraphs of the story. Help them identify and understand Clark's reaction to thinking about his aunt. He is shocked at how quickly her name transports him to his modest past as "the gangling farmer boy" his aunt had once known, yet he recalls with affection the influence she had upon him when he was young.

Enrichment for Gifted/Talented Students
One of Cather's long-held, deeply-felt concerns was the conflict between the artist and the workaday world. "A Wagner Matinée" explores the conflict between a woman's love for music and the withering effects of the harsh farming life that leaves neither time nor energy for the pursuit of fine arts. Invite students to read one or more additional stories from *The Troll Garden,* the collection from which this story comes, and discuss how each story explores the theme of the artist in—or against—society.

5 Literary Analysis
Characterization

- Read this paragraph aloud for students and ask them to listen for details about Georgiana's early life in Boston and about her subsequent life in Nebraska. Encourage them to be alert, also, for indications of how much time has elapsed since she left Boston.
- **Ask** students the Literary Analysis question: What do the contrasting details of Aunt Georgiana's life in Boston and Nebraska reveal about her character?
  Answer: They reveal that she was once a refined and cultured woman who, for the sake of romantic passion, exchanged life in Boston for a life that transformed her into a figure "at once pathetic and grotesque."

of my study. I became, in short, the gangling farmer boy my aunt had known, scourged with chilblains and bashfulness, my hands cracked and raw from the corn husking. I felt the knuckles of my thumb tentatively, as though they were raw again. I sat again before her parlor organ, thumbing the scales with my stiff, red hands, while she beside me made canvas mittens for the huskers.

The next morning, after preparing my landlady somewhat, I set out for the station. When the train arrived I had some difficulty in finding my aunt. She was the last of the passengers to alight, and when I got her into the carriage she looked not unlike one of those charred, smoked bodies that firemen lift from the *débris* of a burned building. She had come all the way in a day coach; her linen duster[1] had become black with soot and her black bonnet gray with dust during the journey. When we arrived at my boardinghouse the landlady put her to bed at once, and I did not see her again until the next morning.

Whatever shock Mrs. Springer experienced at my aunt's appearance she considerately concealed. Myself, I saw my aunt's misshapen figure with that feeling of awe and respect with which we behold explorers who have left their ears and fingers north of Franz Josef Land,[2] or their health somewhere along the upper Congo.[3] My Aunt Georgiana had been a music teacher at the Boston Conservatory, somewhere back in the latter sixties. One summer, which she had spent in the little village in the Green Mountains[4] where her ancestors had dwelt for generations, she had kindled the callow[5] fancy of the most idle and shiftless of all the village lads, and had conceived for this Howard Carpenter one of those absurd and extravagant passions which a handsome country boy of twenty-one sometimes inspires in a plain, angular, spectacled woman of thirty. When she returned to her duties in Boston, Howard followed her; and the upshot of this inexplicable infatuation was that she eloped with him, eluding the reproaches of her family and the criticism of her friends by going with him to the Nebraska frontier. Carpenter, who of course had no money, took a homestead in Red Willow County,[6] fifty miles from the railroad. There they measured off their eighty acres by driving across the prairie in a wagon, to the wheel of which they had tied a red cotton handkerchief, and counting its revolutions. They built a dugout in the red hillside, one of those cave dwellings whose inmates usually reverted to the conditions of primitive savagery. Their water they got from the lagoons where the buffalo drank, and their slender stock of provisions was always at the mercy of bands of roving Indians. For thirty years my aunt had not been farther than fifty miles from the homestead.

Literary Analysis
Characterization What do the contrasting details of Aunt Georgiana's life in Boston and Nebraska reveal about her character?

1. **duster** *n.* short, loose smock worn to protect clothing from dust.
2. **Franz Josef Land** group of islands in the Arctic Ocean.
3. **Congo** river in central Africa.
4. **Green Mountains** mountains in Vermont.
5. **callow** (kal′ ō) *adj.* immature; inexperienced.
6. **Red Willow County** county in southwestern Nebraska that borders on Kansas.

Enrichment

Reaction to Cather's Story

When this story appeared, it created a hue and cry among some of Willa Cather's fellow-Nebraskans, who claimed it was unfair to the state in which she had been raised. The story also offended Cather's family, because her uncle and aunt were obviously the models for the fictional Uncle Howard and Aunt Georgiana. (Cather's Aunt Franc, who had attended Smith College and Mount Holyoke College, later married George Cather and went to live in a sod house in Nebraska.) Cather defended her story, saying that it paid tribute to the brave women who endured the desolation and loneliness of life on the frontier.

But Mrs. Springer knew nothing of all this, and must have been considerably shocked at what was left of my kinswoman. Beneath the soiled linen duster, which on her arrival was the most conspicuous feature of her costume, she wore a black stuff dress whose ornamentation showed that she had surrendered herself unquestioningly into the hands of a country dressmaker. My poor aunt's figure, however, would
6 have presented astonishing difficulties to any dressmaker. Her skin was yellow from constant exposure to a pitiless wind, and to the alkaline water which transforms the most transparent cuticle into a sort of flexible leather. She wore ill-fitting false teeth. The most striking thing about her physiognomy, however, was an incessant twitching of the mouth and eyebrows, a form of nervous disorder resulting from isolation and monotony, and from frequent physical suffering.

In my boyhood this affliction had possessed a sort of horrible fascination for me, of which I was secretly very much ashamed, for in those days I owed to this woman most of the good that ever came my way, and had a reverential affection for her. During the three winters when I was riding herd for my uncle, my aunt, after cooking three meals for half a dozen farmhands, and putting the six children to bed, would often stand until midnight at her ironing board, hearing me at the kitchen table beside her recite Latin declensions and conjugations, and gently shaking me when my drowsy head sank down over a page of irregular verbs. It was to her, at her ironing or mending, that I read my first Shakespeare; and her old textbook of mythology was the first that ever came into my empty hands. She taught me my scales and exercises, too, on the little parlor organ which her husband had bought her after fifteen years, during which she had not so much as seen any
7 instrument except an accordion, that belonged to one of the Norwegian farmhands. She would sit beside me by the hour, darning and counting, while I struggled with the "Harmonious Blacksmith"; but she seldom talked to me about music, and I understood why. She was a pious woman; she had the consolation of religion; and to her at least her martyrdom was not wholly sordid. Once when I had been doggedly beating out some passages from an old score of "Euryanthe" I had found among her music books, she came up to me and, putting her hands over my eyes, gently drew my head back upon her shoulder, saying tremulously, "Don't love it so well, Clark, or it may be taken from you. Oh! dear boy, pray that whatever your sacrifice be it is not that."

When my aunt appeared on the morning after her arrival, she was still in a semi-somnambulant state. She seemed not to realize that she was in the city where she had spent her youth, the place longed for hungrily for half a lifetime. She had been so wretchedly trainsick throughout the journey that she had no recollection of anything but her discomfort, and, to all intents and purposes, there were but a few hours 8
of nightmare between the farm in Red Willow County and my study on Newbury Street. I had planned a little pleasure for her that afternoon, to repay her for some of the glorious moments she had given me when

Literary Analysis
Characterization and First-Person Point-of-View Which details of this paragraph show who is narrating this story?

Vocabulary Builder
reverential (rev′ ə ren′ shəl) *adj.* caused by a feeling of deep respect and love

Vocabulary Builder
tremulously (trem′ yo͞o ləs lē) *adv.* fearfully; timidly

semi-somnambulant (sem′ i säm nam′ byo͞o lənt) *adj.* half-sleepwalking

Reading Check
When Clark was a boy, what subjects did he learn from his aunt?

6 Literary Analysis
Characterization and First-Person Narrator

- **Ask** a student volunteer to summarize the characteristics of first-person narration. Then invite students to identify the narrator of this story and to state the relationship between him and the main characters.
- **Ask** students the Literary Analysis question: Which details of this paragraph show who is narrating the story?
  Answer: Students might mention details such as *my kinswoman* and *My poor aunt's figure.*

7 Critical Thinking
Connect; Analyze

- Explain to students that in *Euryanthe,* the opera by Carl Maria von Weber (1786–1826), Euryanthe is falsely accused and then led by the man she loves into the desert to die. If necessary, point out how Euryanthe's story echoes the theme of martyrdom in the wilderness to which Cather alludes in this passage.
- Invite students to discuss Aunt Georgiana's martyrdom, and its relation to the strong feelings she has for music. **Ask** students how these things influence her warning to Clark.
  Possible response: Students may say that Aunt Georgiana is a martyr because she left something she loved deeply in order to be with her husband. Recognizing the pain of her decision, she advises Clark to moderate his love for music, lest he lose it and feel pain, as she did.

8 Reading Check
Answer: He studied Latin, Shakespeare, mythology, and music.

Differentiated Instruction
Solutions for All Learners

Strategy for Less Proficient Readers
Slowly read aloud—and then have students reread—the first paragraph on this page. Then, guide students to notice how this passage presents physical descriptions of Georgiana that provide further insight into her character. What can students infer about Georgiana's temperament from this description of the effects of life on the prairie? What does the narrator's description tell the reader about *his* character?

Enrichment for Advanced Readers
Encourage students to do research in order to report on the effect of the Homestead Act, which allowed Georgiana's husband to get land without paying for it. In 1862, Congress passed the Homestead Act to advance settlement of the prairie lands of the American West. The Act offered 160 acres of free land to anyone over twenty-one years of age who was an American citizen. Permanent ownership of the land came after five years of residence or after six months and payment of $1.25 an acre.

9 Literature in Context

Wagner's Operas Wagner's tragic opera *Tristan* and *Isolde* (the prelude of which Clark and his aunt hear toward the end of the story) is an example of a tragic ending brought on by love. Isolde has been promised to the King, and Tristan must deliver her to him. As Tristan and Isolde declare their love for one another, one of the King's knights surprises them in the King's garden. Tristan is mortally wounded and Isolde breathes her last breath over his body.

Connect to the Literature

Encourage students to think about a time when they had to give something up that they loved.

Possible response: Aunt Georgiana's response is not the result of a specific note or lyric; her response comes from an awakening in her soul of something she had lost.

10 Vocabulary Builder

Word Origins

- Read aloud this passage for students and draw their attention to the capitalized word *Conservatory.* Invite a student volunteer to explain why the word is capitalized here. (It refers to a particular institution, the Boston Conservatory, first mentioned on p. 678.)
- Have students look up the origins of the word *conservatory* as a strategy for understanding its meaning. **Ask** them to trace the changes in the word's usage.
- Invite some students to **explain** to the rest of the class how the origins of *conservatory* relate to its use in the story.
  Answer: The word derives from the Latin word *servare* ("to keep, preserve"), which in turn comes from the Indo-European stem *ser* ("to watch over"). A conservatory is a school devoted to the preservation and teaching of an art form such as music, as well as to the nurture of developing artists.

we used to milk together in the straw-thatched cowshed, and she, because I was more than usually tired, or because her husband had spoken sharply to me, would tell me of the splendid performance of Meyerbeer's *Les Huguenots*[7] she had seen in Paris in her youth. At two o'clock the Boston Symphony Orchestra was to give a Wagner♦ program, and I intended to take my aunt, though as I conversed with her I grew doubtful about her enjoyment of it. Indeed, for her own

10 sake, I could only wish her taste for such things quite dead, and the long struggle mercifully ended at last. I suggested our visiting the Conservatory and the Common[8] before lunch, but she seemed altogether too timid to wish to venture out. She questioned me absently about various changes in the city, but she was chiefly concerned that she had forgotten to leave instructions about feeding half-skimmed milk to a certain weakling calf, "Old Maggie's calf, you know, Clark," she explained, evidently having forgotten how long I had been away. She was further troubled because she had neglected to tell her daughter about the freshly opened kit of mackerel in the cellar, that would spoil if it were not used directly.

I asked her whether she had ever heard any of the Wagnerian operas, and found that she had not, though she was perfectly familiar with their respective situations and had once possessed the piano score of *The Flying Dutchman.* I began to think it would have been best to get her back to Red Willow County without waking her, and regretted having suggested the concert.

From the time we entered the concert hall, however, she was a trifle less passive and inert, and seemed to begin to perceive her surroundings. I had felt some trepidation[9] lest one might become aware of the absurdities of her attire, or might experience some painful embarrassment at stepping suddenly into the world to which she had been dead for a quarter of a century. But again I found how superficially I had judged her. She sat looking about her with eyes as impersonal, almost as stony, as those with which the granite Ramses[10] in a museum watches the froth and fret that ebbs and flows about his pedestal, separated from it by the lonely stretch of centuries. I have seen this same aloofness in old miners who drift into the Brown Hotel at Denver, their pockets full of bullion, their linen soiled, their haggard faces unshorn, and who stand in the thronged corridors as solitary as though

7. ***Les Huguenots*** (lāz hyo͞o′ gə nät′) opera written in 1836 by Giacomo Meyerbeer (1791–1864).
8. **Common** Boston Common, a small park in Boston.
9. **trepidation** (trep′ ə dā′ shən) *n.* fearful anxiety; apprehension.
10. **Ramses** (ram′ sēz) one of the eleven Egyptian kings by that name who ruled from c. 1292 to c. 1075 B.C.

Literature in Context

9 Music Connection

♦ ***Wagner Operas***

Aunt Georgiana has a strong reaction to the music of Richard Wagner, the composer of *The Flying Dutchman* (1843). Wagner rejected some of the traditions of opera. He usually avoided lengthy musical speeches and instead originated the *leitmotif*, a recurring musical theme used to symbolize an emotion or event. Wagner also wrote what he called "music dramas." An entire series of these works, called *The Ring of the Nibelung*, consumed twenty-six years of his life. In "A Wagner Matinée," the audience hears excerpts from the *Ring* and *Siegfried*, an opera based on the adventures of a legendary German hero.

Connect to the Literature

Does the reader need to be familiar with Wagner's operas to understand Aunt Georgiana's response? Explain.

Vocabulary Builder

inert (in ʉrt′) *adj.* motionless

Enrichment

Opera

Opera is as rich culturally as it is musically. Richard Wagner's opera brought German mythology to life with stirring music and drama. Earlier opera composers, such as Claudio Monteverdi and Christoph Gluck, relied on classical stories of ancient Greece and Rome for their subjects. Nationalism burst onto the musical scene in Czechoslovakia and Russia in the operas of Antonin Dvorák and Modest Mussorgsky, who incorporated their cultures' rich folk music into their operas. English composer Gustav Holst's opera *Savitri* is based on an episode from the Hindu epic *Mahabharata,* and George Gershwin dramatized African American life in *Porgy and Bess.* Today, opera is truly an international art form: singers perform in many languages in opera houses around the world. Have students listen to some or all of an opera or watch a video of an operatic performance. Ask them to analyze how the music conveys the characters' feelings and thoughts, and reaches audiences in ways that differ from non-musical theatrical productions.

they were still in a frozen camp on the Yukon, or in the yellow blaze of the Arizona desert, conscious that certain experiences have isolated them from their fellows by a gulf no haberdasher could conceal.

The audience was made up chiefly of women. One lost the contour of faces and figures, indeed any effect of line whatever, and there was only the color contrast of bodices past counting, the shimmer and shading of fabrics soft and firm, silky and sheer, resisting and yielding: red, mauve, pink, blue, lilac, purple, ecru, rose, yellow, cream, and white, all the colors that an impressionist finds in a sunlit landscape, with here and there the dead black shadow of a frock coat. My Aunt Georgiana regarded them as though they had been so many daubs of tube paint on a palette.

When the musicians came out and took their places, she gave a little stir of anticipation, and looked with quickening interest down over
11 the rail at that invariable grouping; perhaps the first wholly familiar thing that had greeted her eye since she had left old Maggie and her weakling calf. I could feel how all those details sank into her soul, for I had not forgotten how they had sunk into mine when I came fresh from plowing forever and forever between green aisles of corn, where, as in a treadmill, one might walk from daybreak to dusk without perceiving a shadow of change in one's environment. I reminded myself of the impression made on me by the clean profiles of the musicians, the gloss of their linen; the dull black of their coats, the beloved shapes of the instruments, the patches of yellow light thrown by the green-shaded stand-lamps on the smooth, varnished bellies of the cellos and the bass viols in the rear, the restless, wind-tossed forest of fiddle necks and bows; I recalled how, in the first orchestra I had ever heard, those long bow strokes seemed to draw the soul out of me, as a conjuror's stick reels out paper ribbon from a hat.

The first number was the Tannhäuser overture. When the violins drew out the first strain of the Pilgrims' chorus, my Aunt Georgiana clutched my coat sleeve. Then it was that I first realized that for her this singing of basses and stinging frenzy of lighter strings broke a silence of thirty years, the inconceivable silence of the plains. With the battle between the two motifs, with the bitter frenzy of the Venusberg[11] theme and its ripping of strings, came to me an overwhelming sense of the waste and wear we are so powerless to combat. I saw again the tall, naked house on the prairie, black and grim as a wooden fortress; the black pond where I had learned to swim, the rain-gullied clay about the naked house; the four dwarf ash seedlings on which the dishcloths were always hung to dry before the kitchen door. The world there is the flat world of the ancients; to the east, a cornfield that stretched to daybreak; to the west, a corral that stretched to sunset; between, the sordid conquests of peace, more merciless than those of war.

11. **Venusberg** (vē′ nəs burg′) legendary mountain in Germany where Venus, the Roman goddess of love, held court.

Literary Analysis
Characterization What does Aunt Georgiana's excitement about the upcoming performance reveal about her?

Reading Strategy
Clarifying What details and references in this paragraph are unfamiliar to you?

12 **Reading Check**
What is Clark's initial feeling about being in public with Aunt Georgiana? How does that attitude change?

11 Literary Analysis
Characterization

- Encourage students to summarize how Aunt Georgiana has behaved up until this point in the story.
- Then **ask** students the Literary Analysis question: What does Aunt Georgiana's excitement about the upcoming performance reveal about her?
  Answer: It reveals that her love for music is reawakening; her suffering has not numbed her soul completely.

Reading Strategy
Clarifying

- Encourage students to summarize in their own words the details in the paragraph.
- Then **ask** the students the Reading Strategy question: What details and references in this paragraph are unfamiliar to you?
  Answer: The details of some of the instruments, the green-shaded lamps, the movements of the fiddle players, and the layout of the orchestra are unfamiliar.
- Invite students who have seen an orchestra to provide insights from their experiences.

12 Reading Check

Answer: At first he feels anxious and embarrassed about how out of place and ill at ease his aunt seems. When he sees that she is absorbing details of the musicians' appearances, however, his mind wanders to memories of his own first passionate responses to the sights and sounds of an orchestra in a concert hall.

Differentiated Instruction Solutions for All Learners

Support for Less Proficient Readers
Encourage students to reread the two paragraphs beginning at the bottom of the previous page to appreciate them. Help them notice that Clark was at first embarrassed by being seen with Aunt Georgiana because she looked so out of place, yet it was his idea to bring her to the concert in the first place. Clark still thinks of her as a haggard pioneer, a confused stranger in her own land. His appreciation for her grows as he realizes how much her isolation has provided her with an austere dignity.

Strategy for Advanced Readers
Explain that students can dig deeper into Cather's meaning by understanding more about her references to Wagner and his operas. For example, *The Flying Dutchman,* a milestone in Wagner's career, is about a Dutch sea captain who is doomed forever to roam the seas until a curse he rashly uttered can be broken by the love of a faithful woman. Discuss how Aunt Georgiana's rash decision to marry and live out her life on the prarie has doomed her to live without her greatest joy.

13 Reading Strategy
Clarifying

- Have a student volunteer read this passage aloud. Encourage students to listen for a word that today has a meaning relating to the visual arts—but which here has a different meaning.
- **Ask** students: What does the author mean by "films"?
- To help students clarify, remind them to consider when Willa Cather wrote this short story.
Answer: Students should realize that, in this context, films are probably thin layers of grime or thin membranes that grow over aging eyes, separating Aunt Georgiana from the sights of the concert hall and the world she once knew. When this story was written, the word *film* did not mean "moving picture," as it does today.

13 The overture closed. My aunt released my coat sleeve, but she said nothing. She sat staring at the orchestra through a dullness of thirty years, through the films made, little by little, by each of the three hundred and sixty-five days in every one of them. What, I wondered, did she get from it? She had been a good pianist in her day, I knew, and her musical education had been broader than that of most music teachers of a quarter of a century ago. She had often told me of Mozart's operas and Meyerbeer's, and I could remember hearing her sing, years ago, certain melodies of Verdi. When I had fallen ill with a fever she used to sit by my cot in the evening, while the cool night wind blew in through the faded mosquito netting tacked over the window, and I lay watching a bright star that burned red above the cornfield, and sing "Home to our mountains, oh, let us return!" in a way fit to break the heart of a Vermont boy near dead of homesickness already.

I watched her closely through the prelude to *Tristan and Isolde,* trying vainly to conjecture what that warfare of motifs, that seething turmoil of strings and winds, might mean to her. Had this music any message for her? Did or did not a new planet swim into her ken? Wagner had been a sealed book to Americans before the sixties. Had she anything left with which to comprehend this glory that had flashed around the world since she had gone from it? I was in a fever of curiosity, but Aunt Georgiana sat silent upon her peak in Darien.[12] She preserved this utter immobility throughout the numbers from the *Flying Dutchman,* though her fingers worked mechanically upon her black dress, as though of themselves they were recalling the piano score they had once played. Poor old hands! They were stretched and pulled and twisted into mere tentacles to hold, and lift, and knead with; the palms unduly

Vocabulary Builder
prelude (prel′ yo͞od) *n.* introductory section of a work of music

12. **peak in Darien** (der′ ē ən′) mountain on the Isthmus of Panama; from "On First Looking at Chapman's Homer" by English poet John Keats (1795–1821).

Differentiated Instruction
Solutions for All Learners

Enrichment for Advanced Readers

Suggest that students read additional works by Willa Cather. Provide students with copies of *O Pioneers!, My Antonia,* and *Death Comes for the Archbishop.* You may also wish to use ***Authors In Depth: The American Experience,*** which contains the following selections:

- From *My Ántonia* (fiction, p. 123)
- "Prairie Spring" (poem, p. 131)
- "The Sentimentality of William Taverner" (fiction, p. 133)

After students have read these or other works by Cather, have them form discussion groups in which they compare and contrast the selections they have read. Suggest criteria for comparison, such as historical context or sense of place. To extend the activity, have volunteers present brief reports on Cather's influence on later writers, such as Truman Capote.

⓮ Reading Check

Answer: After a quickly-drawn breath, she begins to weep as she listens to the melody played by the musicians.

swollen, the fingers bent and knotted, on one of them a thin worn band that had once been a wedding ring. As I pressed and gently quieted one of those groping hands, I remembered, with quivering eyelids, their services for me in other days.

Soon after the tenor began the "Prize Song," I heard a quick-drawn breath, and turned to my aunt. Her eyes were closed, but the tears were glistening on her cheeks, and I think in a moment more they were in my eyes as well. It never really dies, then, the soul? It withers to the outward eye only, like that strange moss which can lie on a dusty shelf half a century and yet, if placed in water, grows green again. My aunt wept gently throughout the development and elaboration of the melody.

During the intermission before the second half of the concert, I questioned my aunt and found that the "Prize Song" was not new to her. Some years before there had drifted to the farm in Red Willow County a young German, a tramp cow puncher who had sung in the chorus at Bayreuth,[13] when he was a boy, along with the other peasant boys and girls. On a Sunday morning he used to sit on his blue gingham-sheeted bed in the hands' bedroom, which opened off the kitchen, cleaning the leather of his boots and saddle, and singing the "Prize Song," while my aunt went about her work in the kitchen. She had hovered about him until she had prevailed upon him to join the country church, though his sole fitness for this step, so far as I could gather, lay in his boyish face and his possession of this divine melody. Shortly afterward he had gone to town on the Fourth of July, lost his money at a faro[14] table, ridden a saddled Texas steer on a bet, and disappeared with a fractured collarbone.

"Well, we have come to better things than the old *Trovatore* at any rate, Aunt Georgie?" I queried, with well-meant jocularity.

Vocabulary Builder
jocularity (jäk′ yōō lar′ ə tē) *n.* joking good humor

Her lip quivered and she hastily put her handkerchief up to her mouth. From behind it she murmured, "And you've been hearing this ever since you left me, Clark?" Her question was the gentlest and saddest of reproaches.

"But do you get it, Aunt Georgiana, the astonishing structure of it all?" I persisted.

"Who could?" she said, absently; "why should one?"

The second half of the program consisted of four numbers from the *Ring*. This was followed by the forest music from *Siegfried*[15] and the program closed with Siegfried's funeral march. My aunt wept quietly, but almost continuously. I was perplexed as to what measure of musical comprehension was left to her, to her who had heard nothing for so many years but the singing of gospel hymns in Methodist services at the square frame schoolhouse on Section Thirteen. I was unable to

13. **Bayreuth** (bī roit′) city in Germany known for its annual Wagnerian music festivals.
14. **faro** (fer′ ō) gambling game in which players bet on the cards to be turned up from the top of the dealer's deck.
15. ***Siegfried*** (sēg′ frēd) opera based on the adventures of Siegfried, a legendary hero in medieval German literature.

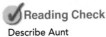

Reading Check
Describe Aunt Georgiana's reaction during the "Prize Song."

Differentiated Instruction Solutions for All Learners

Support for Less Proficient Readers
Help students understand the meaning of the end of this story. For instance, help students clarify that the phrase *just outside the door* at the beginning of the story's last paragraph is intended to be taken both literally and symbolically. The concert hall represents an oasis in Aunt Georgiana's life; once she leaves it, she must return to a life of deprivation on the prairie. Clark recognizes that Georgiana might as well step directly from the hall into her bleak yard in Nebraska.

Vocabulary for Gifted/Talented Students
The passage beginning at the bottom of p. 675 contains many technical words from music, including *overture, violins, strain, chorus, basses,* and *motifs,* as well as descriptions of the way the violin passages sound: *singing, lighter strings, ripping of strings.* Invite students to use a musical dictionary or other resource to explore the meaning of all of these terms.

ASSESS

Answers

1. Students should be prepared to explain their answers.
2. (a) She taught music at the Boston Conservatory. (b) Life in Red Willow County is physically and psychologically brutal: the climate is harsh; the work never-ending and back-breaking; there are few people with whom to socialize; and there is no music or sophisticated culture. By contrast, life amid Boston's cultural opportunities, people, and society seems stimulating and enjoyable.
3. (a) He practiced musical scales, exercises, the "Harmonious Blacksmith," and some passages from "Euryanthe." (b) She means that when one loves something deeply, that person can become vulnerable to a profound sense of loss if that thing disappears. (c) Her own deep engagement with music was lost when she moved to the Nebraska prairie.
4. (a) She stirs in her seat, breathes quickly, and weeps. (b) She hasn't heard such music in decades, and it awakens her long-dormant passion for music.
5. (a) It evokes memories of "a young German, a tramp cow puncher" who sang the song while she worked in the kitchen. (b) She doesn't get up, and she cries out that she doesn't want to leave.
6. Some may agree that it would be better if she had not come, because her visit is a cruel reminder of all that she lost when she moved to Nebraska.

Go Online Author Link For additional information about Willa Cather, have students type in the Web Code, then select C from the alphabet, and then select Willa Cather.

gauge how much of it had been dissolved in soapsuds, or worked into bread, or milked into the bottom of a pail.

The deluge of sound poured on and on; I never knew what she found in the shining current of it; I never knew how far it bore her, or past what happy islands, or under what skies. From the trembling of her face I could well believe that the *Siegfried* march, at least, carried her out where the myriad graves are, out into the gray, burying grounds of the sea; or into some world of death vaster yet, where, from the beginning of the world, hope has lain down with hope, and dream with dream and, renouncing, slept.

The concert was over; the people filed out of the hall chattering and laughing, glad to relax and find the living level again, but my kinswoman made no effort to rise. I spoke gently to her. She burst into tears and sobbed pleadingly, "I don't want to go, Clark, I don't want to go!"

I understood. For her, just outside the door of the concert hall, lay the black pond with the cattle-tracked bluffs, the tall, unpainted house, naked as a tower, with weather-curled boards; the crookbacked ash seedlings where the dishcloths hung to dry, the gaunt, moulting turkeys picking up refuse about the kitchen door.

Critical Reading

1. **Respond:** Do you feel sorry for Aunt Georgiana? Why or why not?
2. **(a) Recall:** What part did Boston play in Aunt Georgiana's earlier life? **(b) Compare and Contrast:** In what ways would you compare and contrast life in Boston and life in Red Willow County?
3. **(a) Recall:** As a boy, what did the narrator practice on the "parlor organ" in the Nebraska farmhouse? **(b) Interpret:** What does Aunt Georgiana mean when she says, "Don't love it so well, Clark, or it may be taken from you"? **(c) Connect:** Do the events of the story reinforce her statement? Explain.
4. **(a) Recall:** What physical reactions indicate that Aunt Georgiana is affected powerfully by the concert? **(b) Analyze:** Why does the music have this effect on her?
5. **(a) Recall:** What memories does the "Prize Song" evoke in Aunt Georgiana? **(b) Connect:** How does Aunt Georgiana react at the end of the concert?
6. **Take a Position:** Would it have been better for Aunt Georgiana if she had not come to Boston? Explain.

For: More about Willa Cather
Visit: www.PHSchool.com
Web Code: ere-9423

Apply the Skills

A Wagner Matinée

Literary Analysis

Characterization

1. What is revealed about Aunt Georgiana's **character** through descriptions of her appearance or comments by her and other characters? Record your findings in a chart like the one shown.

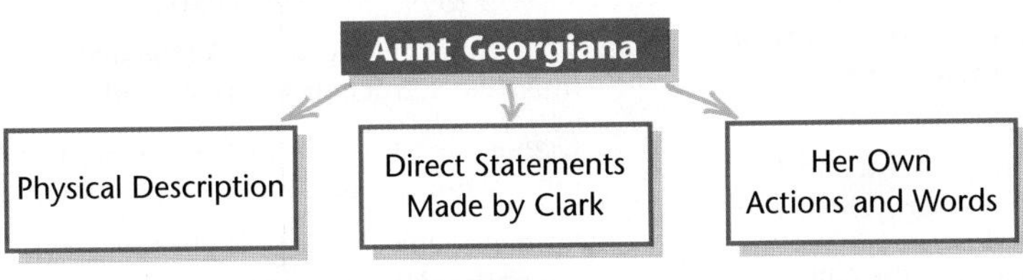

2. What does Aunt Georgiana's reaction to the opera reveal about her personality?
3. What do his thoughts and feelings about his aunt reveal about Clark's personality?

Connecting Literary Elements

4. What effect does Clark's **first-person point of view** have on your perception of Aunt Georgiana?
5. **(a)** Find two examples of events Clark recalls from living with Aunt Georgiana. **(b)** How do these events help to shape your impression of her?
6. **(a)** How do Clark's feelings toward his aunt change during the course of the story? **(b)** How do his feelings affect your response to her?
7. If the story were told by Aunt Georgiana, how would it change?

Reading Strategy

Clarifying

8. Which details about the harshness of life in Nebraska help to **clarify** your understanding of Aunt Georgiana's background?
9. Which details about Aunt Georgiana's life in Nebraska help you understand her timid behavior upon arriving in Boston?
10. Explain the significance of the fact that Aunt Georgiana's husband bought her "a little parlor organ" after fifteen years in Nebraska.

Extend Understanding

11. **Cultural Connection:** How are people's personalities shaped by the environment in which they live? Support your answer.

QuickReview

Characterization is the variety of techniques a writer uses to reveal a character's personality.

When a story is told from the **first-person point of view,** a character involved in the action is the narrator.

To **clarify** the meaning of something you do not understand, reread a passage, read a footnote, look up a word, or read ahead.

For: Self-test
Visit: www.PHSchool.com
Web Code: era-6415

Answers

1. Physical description—roughened and aged, twitches nervously
Clark's statements—"with that feeling of awe and respect with which we behold explorers . . .", "She was a pious woman. . . .";
Her actions/words "Don't love it so well, Clark, or it may be taken from you."
2. Her passionate love for music is still alive; her harsh life has not deadened her spirit.
3. He is grateful and affectionate toward his aunt for all she has done for him. Yet, as a cultured Bostonian, he is embarrassed by his aunt's appearance.
4. Because we learn from him about the type of person she once was and all that she has done for Clark, we come to view Aunt Georgiana with respect and sympathy.
5. (a) Students might mention events such as her listening to him practice Latin and musical scales, or exhorting him not to love music too much.
(b) Despite the harshness of her life and her physical oddities, Georgiana feels a deep, constant passion for music and for a cultured life.
6. (a) At the beginning of the story he feels embarrassed about her, since he sees her as a pathetic figure; by the story's end, he recognizes that her soul, as revealed in her love of music, is intact.
(b) His feelings encourage the reader to see her first as merely a victim, but later as a fascinating, deeply conflicted person of great imagination and feeling.
7. **Possible response:** The reader would see Clark's role in in her past and present life more clearly.
8. Students might mention details such as the dugout likened to a "cave dwelling," "cooking three meals a day for half a dozen farmhands . . .", or her concern about the weak calf and about the uneaten mackerel.
9. After decades of isolation from the elegance and culture of Boston, Georgiana feels and acts as though she is walking through a dream world.

Answers continued

10. **Possible response:** The well-meaning gesture merely accentuates the enormity of her sacrifice.
11. Students' responses should reflect their understanding of how Georgiana was changed by her years on the farm.

Go Online Assessment Students may use the **Self-test** to prepare for **Selection Test A** or **Selection Test B.**

EXTEND/ASSESS

Answers

1 Vocabulary Lesson

Concept Development

1. b 2. b

Spelling Strategy

1. potential 2. exponential

Vocabulary Builder

1. They respect her.
2. A child is more likely to speak fearfully or timidly. Students may also respond that Georgiana is a musician, and speaks tremulously.
3. dazed—A half-sleep walking person is dazed.
4. motionless—Students may point out that an inert substance does not react with other elements, while an inert object does not move.
5. seriousness—An introduction to bad news is most often serious.
6. Talk-show hosts often display joking good humor.

2 Grammar and Style Lesson

1. *herself,* reflexive
2. *herself,* reflexive
3. *itself,* intensive
4. *themselves,* reflexive
5. *herself,* intensive

Writing Application

Students' descriptions of conversations among three or more people should contain at least one reflexive and one intensive pronoun.

WG Writing and Grammar, Ruby Level

Students will find further instruction and practice on reflexive and intensive pronouns in Chapter 17, Section 1.

Build Language Skills

1 Vocabulary Lesson

Concept Development: Words From Music

Musical vocabulary can have two meanings. A *prelude* is a musical introduction, but it also refers to preparation for any important matter. Select the best definition for each sentence.

overture: (a) an introductory movement to an extended musical work, **(b)** any first movement

concert: (a) a performance of several short compositions, **(b)** working together

1. We put a *concerted* effort into the game.
2. He made an *overture* to pay my bill.

Spelling Strategy

When adding the suffix *-ial* to words ending in two consonants, keep the spelling of the base word. For example, *reverent* becomes *reverential.* Fill in the blanks with *-ial* words.

1. A talented person has great *p__ial.*
2. Our speed grew at an *ex__ial* rate.

Vocabulary Builder: Word Meanings

Review the words in the vocabulary list on p. 669. Then, answer the following questions. Explain your responses.

1. If students are *reverential* toward a teacher, do they ignore or respect her?
2. Who is most likely to speak *tremulously*—a musician, a truck driver, or a child?
3. Does *semi-somnambulant* describe someone who is angry, dazed, or busy?
4. Is an *inert* substance motionless or weightless?
5. As a *prelude* to bad news, would you expect sarcasm or seriousness?
6. Is *jocularity* likely to be the trademark of a funeral director or a talk-show host?

2 Grammar and Style Lesson

Reflexive and Intensive Pronouns

Both reflexive and intensive pronouns end in *-self* or *-selves,* but they function differently. **Reflexive pronouns** refer to the subject and are necessary to the meaning of a sentence. **Intensive pronouns** emphasize a word in a sentence, but can be omitted without changing the meaning of a sentence. Consider the following examples:

Reflexive: He took *himself* to the box office.
Intensive: *Myself,* I saw her approaching.

Practice Identify the reflexive and intensive pronouns in these sentences.

1. Cather devoted herself to writing.
2. She quit her job to give herself time.
3. For Cather, writing itself was a full-time job.
4. Books don't write themselves.
5. Cather herself said writing was challenging.

Writing Application Write a description of a conversation among three or more people. Use reflexive and intensive pronouns.

WG *Prentice Hall Writing and Grammar Connection: Chapter 17, Section 1*

Assessment Practice

Context **(For more practice, see *Standardized Test Preparation Workbook*, p. 40.)**

Many tests require students to use context clues to choose the appropriate definition of multiple-meaning words. Use the following sample test item:

When the train arrived I had some difficulty in finding my aunt. She was the last of the passengers to alight, and when I got her into the carriage she looked not unlike one of those charred, smoked bodies that firemen lift from the débris of a burned building.

In this passage, the word alight means—

A light a fire on the platform
B descend from the train
C turn on the light
D enter her compartment

The narrator is waiting for his aunt and has trouble finding her because she is the last passenger to get off the train. *B* is the correct answer.

Writing Lesson

Timed Writing: Editorial

"A Wagner Matinée" provoked an outcry among Nebraskans who felt Cather had portrayed the state unfairly. Cather responded that the story was a tribute to pioneer strength and endurance. As the editor of a Nebraska newspaper, take a position and write an editorial stating and defending your view. ***(40 minutes)***

Prewriting *(10 minutes)* Reread the story. Analyze the details Cather gives to portray both Nebraska and Boston, and decide whether or not you agree with her views. Jot down your thoughts that support or rebut Cather.

Drafting *(20 minutes)* Arrange your views in order of priority. Provide both factual evidence and emotional appeals to support your statements.

Revising *(10 minutes)* Reread your editorial to make sure that your language is specific and persuasive and that you have defended your views. Replace vague words to make your writing stronger and add more support as needed.

Model: Using Specific Language

Cather implies that Boston offers more than Nebraska. While it may be true that Boston is a center for art, Nebraska offers many ~~things~~ cultural resources without the ~~trouble~~ pollution and congestion of a major city.

Specific references such as *cultural resources* and *pollution and congestion* make the editorial clear and persuasive.

Prentice Hall Writing and Grammar Connection: Chapter 15, Section 2

Extend Your Learning

Listening and Speaking With a classmate, take on the roles of Aunt Georgiana and Clark. Create **monologues** that give contrasting interpretations of the effect of the opera on Aunt Georgiana. Consider the following details:

- What memories are drawn out?
- What are their physical reactions?

Present both monologues to the class. **[Group Activity]**

Research and Technology Listen to a recording of one of Wagner's operas, and research the opera's story. Give a **musical presentation** of one of the passages from the opera, playing the recorded passage and explaining its significance in the opera.

Go Online Research **For:** An additional research activity
Visit: www.PHSchool.com
Web Code: erd-7414

Assessment Resources

The following resources can be used to assess students' knowledge and skills.

Unit 4 Resources
Selection Test A, pp. 259–261
Selection Test B, pp. 262–264

General Resources
Rubrics for Persuasion: Persuasive Essay, pp. 45–46
Rubric for Peer Assessment: Dramatic Performance, p. 131

Go Online Assessment Students may use the **Self-test** to prepare for **Selection Test A** or **Selection Test B.**

3 Writing Lesson

You may use this Writing Lesson as timed-writing practice, or you may allow students to develop the essay as a writing assignment over several days.

- To guide students in writing this editorial, give them the **Support for Writing Lesson** page (***Unit 4 Resources,*** p. 256).
- Students' editorials should clearly express and support an opinion about Cather's portrayal of Nebraska in "A Wagner Matinée."
- If students have trouble identifying with Cather's fellow-Nebraskans, as a prewriting activity you might wish to have students reflect on how an author such as Willa Cather might portray the area in which you live. Encourage students to identify and discuss any aspects of your community or region that might be portrayed in what some might consider an "unfavorable light."
- Use the rubrics for Persuasion: Persuasive Essay, pp. 45–46 in ***General Resources,*** to evaluate students' work.

4 Listening and Speaking

- Encourage students to reread several times the paragraphs concerning Clark's and Georgiana's time in the concert hall.
- You might have each group divide itself into Aunt Georgianas and Clarks and urge them to discuss their contrasting interpretations while they are "in character." One student might write down especially convincing details to be used in each character's monologue.
- The **Support for Extend Your Learning** page (***Unit 4 Resources,*** p. 257) provides guided note-taking opportunities to help students complete the Extend Your Learning activities.
- Use the rubric for Peer Assessment: Dramatic Performance, p. 131 in ***General Resources,*** to evaluate students' monologues.

Go Online Research Have students type in the Web Code for another research activity.

Meeting Your Standards

Students will

1. write an analytical essay comparing and contrasting literary themes.
2. analyze three or more selections from Unit 4 and determine the writers' views toward their enemies.
3. construct a thesis statement summing up the similarities and differences and support it with examples.
4. use writing strategies to generate ideas, plan, organize, evaluate, and revise writing.

Prewriting

- Explain to students that they should begin prewriting by carefully considering their impressions of the works in Unit 4.
- Instruct students to reread any selections from Unit 4 that made strong impressions on them. As they read, students should ask themselves the Review the Material questions and write the answers in their notes.
- Have students review their notes and choose several works that offer the most striking similarities and contrasts. Then, ask them to create charts like the one on this page to analyze the similarities and differences among the works.
Possible responses: The Gettysburg Address: enemy is not mentioned explicitly; enemy is fighting *against* a just and noble cause; **An Account of the Battle of Bull Run:** enemy is not mentioned explicitly; no mention of either side's cause for fighting

Tips for Test Taking

A writing prompt on the SAT or ACT test may assess students' ability to analyze a topic, state a point of view regarding a topic, and support the point of view with evidence. When writing under timed circumstances, students will need to quickly clarify a point of view (their thesis statement) and the evidence that supports it. Since they won't be able to refer to a text, their evidence must be based on their own experiences, readings, or observations.

Writing About Literature

Compare and Contrast Literary Themes

Many of the selections in this unit address the American experience in the years just before and during the Civil War. Unlike other wars, in which the enemy was a separate and distant power, the Civil War pitted neighbor against neighbor, friend against friend, son against father. The enemy, as both an idea and a reality, had never before posed so painful or complex a problem.

Explore this issue in greater depth by completing the assignment given in the yellow box at right.

Assignment: Attitudes Toward the Enemy

Write an analytical essay that compares and contrasts the way three or more writers viewed the enemy during or directly preceding the American Civil War.

Criteria:

- Include a clear thesis statement that sums up the similarities or differences among the writers' attitudes toward the enemy.
- Support your thesis with details from at least three selections.
- Approximate length: 700 words.

Prewriting

Review the material. After reading the selections in this unit, make notes exploring your impressions about each writer's attitude toward the enemy. Use the following questions to organize your thinking:

- Does each writer seem sure of the rightness of his or her cause?
- Does each writer seem eager for armed conflict?
- Does any writer express fear that the enemy might be victorious?
- Does any writer express sympathy for or understanding of the enemy?
- Does any writer seem to lack strong feeling toward the enemy?

As you address these and other questions, write brief statements identifying the selections that show the strongest connections or present the starkest contrasts.

Reread the selections, paying careful attention to the attitudes behind the words.

Select works to compare and contrast. To create an engaging essay, the works you select should present marked differences or similarities. Use a chart like the one shown to develop your analysis.

Model: Charting to Analyze Similarities and Differences

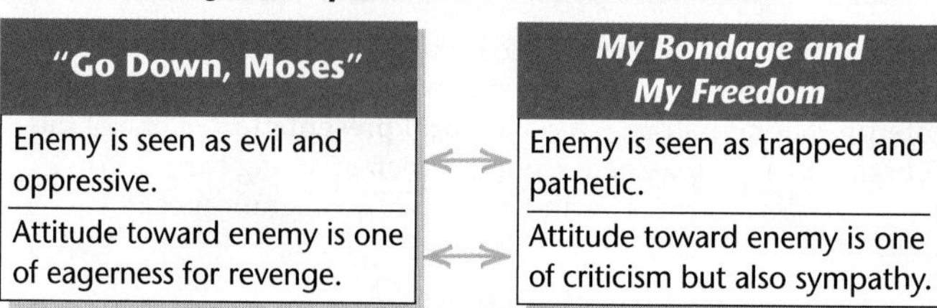

"Go Down, Moses"
Enemy is seen as evil and oppressive.
Attitude toward enemy is one of eagerness for revenge.
My Bondage and My Freedom
Enemy is seen as trapped and pathetic.
Attitude toward enemy is one of criticism but also sympathy.

After completing your analysis, identify the points of comparison and contrast that you find most interesting and important. Determine an initial approach to organizing your essay. You may either compare three selections in depth, or discuss a larger number of selections more briefly.

Teaching Resources

The following resources can be used to extend or enrich the instruction for Writing About Literature.

General Resources

Rubrics for Exposition: Comparison-and-Contrast Essay, pp. 69–70

Graphic Organizer Transparencies

Two-column Chart, p. 315

Drafting

Organize examples. Make some organizational decisions before you begin to write. For example, consider using either one of the following strategies:

- **Grouping Ideas:** With this type of organization you discuss all the similarities between selections, and then discuss all of the differences.
- **Grouping Selections:** With this type of organization, you break your discussion down selection by selection, analyzing both similarities and differences for each one.

Draw conclusions. As you draft, draw conclusions about the writers' attitudes toward the enemy based on the specific selections you have chosen to analyze. Make sure that you offer clear supporting evidence for every point you make.

Write to Learn
The writers whose works you are exploring cared deeply about their subjects. By writing about them, you, too, can develop your own ideas about moral and political conflict.

Revising and Editing

Review content: Check for completeness and accuracy. Once you have decided to discuss a particular selection, you have a responsibility to analyze it thoroughly and accurately. You may not merely skim it for the details that support your thesis. Instead, you must account for each aspect of the selection that is relevant to your subject.

Write to Explain
Because you will be making subtle distinctions about attitudes and emotions, make sure that your language is especially precise. Your reader must always know exactly what you are talking about.

Model: Revising for Thoroughness

In "Go Down, Moses," the attitude of the slave toward the slaveowner is one of moral condemnation and rage. In *My Bondage and My Freedom,* however, Frederick Douglass ~~expresses sympathy for his master's wife.~~ ^condemns his owner's wife, arguing that she is morally corrupt because she is a slaveowner. Surprisingly, he also expresses some sympathy for her position.

Review style: Correctly punctuate and capitalize titles. Make sure you have correctly formatted and capitalized titles. The titles of full-length books are generally capitalized and italicized or underlined, while those of shorter works usually appear capitalized in quotation marks.

Publishing and Presenting

Generate a poster. Use the ideas developed in your essay to create a poster about attitudes toward the enemy during the Civil War. Emphasize main ideas with headlines. Then, note your primary supporting evidence.

WG *Prentice Hall Writing and Grammar Connection: Chapter 9*

Drafting

- Be sure students understand the two major strategies for organizing compare and contrast essays: organizing by points of similarity or difference, and organizing by literary works.
- Remind students that they must draw conclusions about the writers' views of their enemies, and then clearly state and support those conclusions.

Revising and Editing

- Remind students to treat their literary works completely and accurately. If they find their treatment of a work to be incomplete or inaccurate, instruct them to reread the work, making new notes to use in revising.

Presenting

- Be sure students understand that the major focus of their posters should be their analysis of the literary works they are comparing. Each poster should clearly state—in writing—its thesis and major points.
- Tell students that posters may also include illustrations.

WG Writing and Grammar, Ruby Level

Students will find further instruction and practice on writing a comparison-and-contrast essay in Chapter 9.

Writing and Grammar Interactive Textbook CD-ROM

Students can use the following tools as they complete their comparison-and-contrast essays:

- Organizer
- Customizable Outliner
- Unity and Coherence

Six Traits Focus

✓	Ideas		Word Choice
✓	Organization		Sentence Fluency
	Voice		Conventions

Assessing the Essay

To evaluate students' essays use the Rubrics for Comparison-and-Contrast Essay, pp. 69–70 in ***General Resources.***

Differentiated Instruction

Solutions for All Learners

Strategy for Less Proficient Writers
To help these students with prewriting, instruct them to copy the Review the Material questions into their notes. For each work, have these students write a clear answer to each question. Answers should be in full sentences. Then, students can sort their answers to look for patterns.

Strategy for English Learners
Answering the Review the Material questions may prove challenging for students. For each selection, ask students to find sentences that they feel support their answers to these questions. Then, have them look up any unfamiliar words in the sentences they cite. Do the sentences still support students' interpretations?

Strategy for Advanced Writers
It is not likely that these students will have difficulty reviewing the selections. You can place them into small groups with less proficient writers and English learners to review key works. Students can help guide their classmates through the Review the Material questions.

Meeting Your Standards

Students will

1. write a research paper.
2. use writing strategies to generate ideas and to plan, organize, evaluate, and revise the composition.
3. apply grammar skills

 **From the Scholar's Desk**

Nell Irvin Painter

Show students Segment 3 on Nell Irvin Painter on ***From the Author's Desk DVD.*** Discuss Painter's comments about the benefits of doing intensive research.

Writing Genres

Using the Form Point out to students that researched information often appears in other types of writing. Mention these examples:

- Biographical narratives are based on research into the subject's life and activities.
- Various forms of expository writing such as cause-and-effect essays and problem-solution essays often require research into specific questions that the author needs to answer.
- Even creative writing can involve research. A short story or play set in another time period might require the author to investigate specific details about that period.

 **Online Essay Scorer**

A writing prompt for this mode of writing can be found on the ***PH Online Essay Scorer*** at PHSuccessNet.com.

Writing Workshop

Research: Research Paper

In the past, you have probably read scientific articles, nonfiction investigations, and political essays that made a firm statement and offered solid factual proof. Such writing is similar to a **research paper,** which gathers information on a single topic from various sources and presents it in a formal, written document. Follow the steps in this workshop to write your own research paper.

Assignment Write a research paper that presents your findings on a subject of interest to you.

What to Include Your research paper should feature the following elements:

- a clear thesis statement
- factual support from a variety of outside sources, including direct quotations whose sources are credited
- consideration of how sources can vary, without some being less accurate than others
- logical organization that includes an introduction, a body, and a conclusion
- a bibliography or works-cited list

To preview the criteria on which your research paper may be assessed, see the rubric on page 693.

Using the Form

You may use elements of research in these writing situations:

- lab reports
- documented essays
- persuasive essays

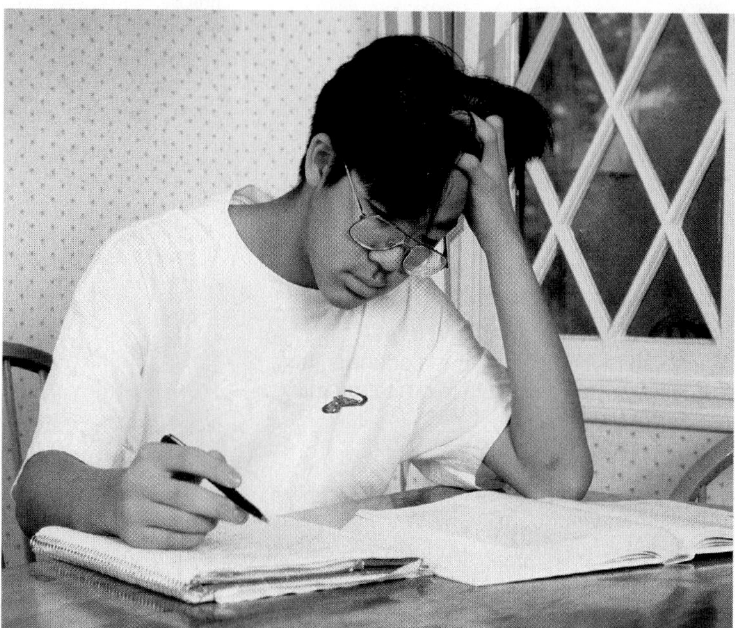

To see how research information can be presented, read "Mark Twain: The American Bard" on page 572.

Teaching Resources

The following resources can be used to enrich or extend the instruction for the Writing Workshop.

Unit 4 Resources
Writing Workshop, pp. 267 and 268

General Resources
Rubrics for Research: Research Report, pp. 49 and 50

Graphic Organizer Transparencies
Cluster Diagram, p. 307
Outline, p. 309
Analyze Conclude Diagram, p. 303

From the Author's Desk DVD
Nell Irvin Painter, Segments 3 and 4

Prewriting

Choosing Your Topic

To choose a topic suitable for the research sources that are available to you, use one of the following strategies:

- **Notebook and Textbook Review** As you flip through school notebooks, textbooks, and writing journals, make a list of topics that have caught your interest or subjects you would like to know more about. Go over your list, and choose a topic on which to focus.
- **Self-Interview** Ask yourself questions about your own interests:
  - Which subjects, like the environment, politics, sports, music, technology, or literature, interest you?
  - Which people in history or current events would you like to understand better?

Review your answers to choose a topic.

Narrowing Your Topic

After you have found an area of interest to explore, limit your topic to one that is appropriate for a short research paper. As you research your broad topic by browsing through encyclopedias, the Internet, or your library's reference section, look for ways to narrow your topic into a more focused subject, as this flow chart demonstrates.

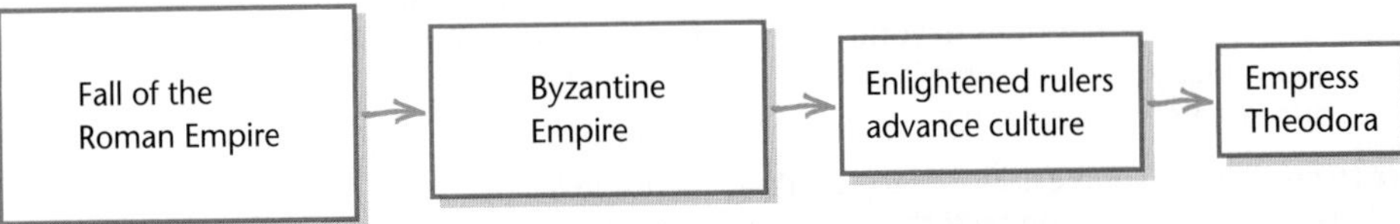

Gathering Information

Take accurate notes. Use an index card to record each relevant fact or scholarly opinion that you find. Record the author's name, title, publisher, city, and date of publication for each source you consult.

Determine your audience. As you conduct research, determine the appropriate level of information to include in your paper. Match your audience to the type of specialized references that require a definition and an explanation.

- Novices, who are not familiar with your topic, will need basic, general information.
- General audiences may have some basic knowledge, but you will need to define specialized vocabulary.
- Experts can understand the more complex issues of your topic.

Note the references that you will need to define for your audience.

TEACH

Prewriting

- Have students generate topics by using the strategies outlined in the text.
- Use pp. 267 and 268 from ***Unit 4 Resources*** for lesson support.
- Have students explore ideas they find interesting, curious, enjoyable, exciting, or even suspicious.
- Suggest students use the Cluster Diagram, p. 307 in ***Graphic Organizer Transparencies*** to visually track and relate their ideas.
- Emphasize the importance of crafting a well-defined, focused topic. Use general-to-specific examples for the class such as: *Pollution is a problem* versus *Indoor air pollution is a problem* versus *Indoor air contaminants pose a greater health risk than outdoor air pollution.* Point out that additional details and accurate word choice not only create focus but generate greater interest and attention for the writer and audience.
- Remind students to keep accurate, detailed records of sources and data during research. Suggest that students use index cards, and remind students to document the author, title, publication information, referenced page numbers, direct and indirect quotations, and paraphrases for each source used.
- Emphasize to students that research may uncover facts that change their minds about their topic. Tell them such discoveries are normal. Suggest they let the research aid in shaping a new focus for them.

Six Traits Focus

✗	Ideas	✗	Word Choice
✗	Organization		Sentence Fluency
	Voice		Conventions

Writing and Grammar, Ruby Level

Students will find additional instruction on prewriting for a research paper in Chapter 13, Section 2.

Writing and Grammar Interactive Textbook CD-ROM

Students can use the following tools as they complete their research papers:

- Cluster Diagram
- Outline
- Unity and Coherence Revising Tool
- Language Variety Revising Tool

Tips for Using Rubrics

- Before students begin work on this assignment, have them preview the Rubric for Self-Assessment, (p. 693), to know what is expected.
- Review the Assessment criteria in class. Before students use the Rubric for Self-Assessment, work with them to rate the student model by applying one or more criteria to it.
- If you wish to assess students' research papers with a 4-, 5-, or 6-point scoring rubric, see ***General Resources***, pp. 49 and 50.

Drafting

- Explain to students that their thesis statements should express the conclusions they have reached as a result of their research; these statements should not be taken directly from a source. Sources should supply a variety of supporting evidence.
- Review the Selecting an Organizational Approach chart. For each approach, ask students to identify an appropriate research topic. **Possible responses:** *Chronological:* A paper arguing that Lincoln's youth made him a great president. *Order of Importance:* A paper discussing the most important impact of the railroads. *Comparison and Contrast:* A paper contrasting Jack London's and Bret Harte's portrayals of nature in "To Build a Fire" and "The Outcasts of Poker Flat."
- Model formal outlines for students using the Outline transparency on p. 309 in ***Graphic Organizer Transparencies.***
- Have students consider organizing their research notes under an outline format that corresponds to the headings and subheadings of their formal outlines. This strategy aligns notes, quotations, and statistics with the relevant text.
- Remind students during drafting to incorporate their source material into passages and paraphrases, weaving the information in with their own words.
- Have students adhere to a single format or style for citing source material.

Drafting

Shaping Your Writing

Propose a thesis statement. An effective thesis statement expresses a position that can be supported by research. Review your notes and develop a statement that reflects a general tendency in the data you collected. Incorporate this statement into your draft.

Choose a type of organization. There are many effective methods for organizing your information and ideas. Depending on the main purpose of your paper, you may want to present events either in the order in which they occurred or in their order of importance. You may instead prefer to compare and contrast events or trends, or you might choose to relate elements of a single event or topic to the whole. Use a chart like the one shown to select an organizational strategy that best suits your topic, audience, and purpose.

Write a formal outline. After you have selected an organizational strategy, prepare a formal outline.

Organizational Approaches

Purpose of Paper: Examine Wheatley's style and argue her importance in American literature	
Approach	**Benefit/Drawback**
Chronological	Does not establish her significance
Order of importance	Possible
Comparison and contrast	Not as useful
Parts to whole	Since I am exploring elements of her life and work, this makes best sense.

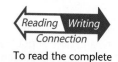

Providing Elaboration

Include a variety of outside sources. As you draft, frequently review your research notes. Use direct quotations, paraphrases, and visuals to provide a variety of information that goes beyond your own observations. You might even conduct your own surveys or field studies to expand the scope of your research and sources.

Prepare to credit your sources. During the drafting stage, circle any ideas from others, direct quotes, and facts that are available from only a single source. Also include in parentheses the author's last name and the page numbers on which the information was found. Later, this information will allow you to create formal citations in your research paper.

To read the complete student model, see page 690.

Student Model: Preparing to Credit Sources

Although many have ventured to say that Wheatley's "unquestioning embrace of New England and white cultures" prompted her to neglect the issue of slavery (Smith, Baechler, Litz 476), a closer examination of her poetry reveals that she was quite "race conscious" (Davis 192).

Circle direct quotes and note source material.

Six Traits Focus

✗	Ideas	✗	Word Choice
✗	Organization		Sentence Fluency
	Voice		Conventions

Writing and Grammar, Ruby Level

Students will find additional instruction on drafting a research paper in Chapter 13, Section 3.

From the Scholar's Desk
Nell Irvin Painter on Using Research

Nell Irvin Painter

These words come from the introduction to my history of the United States between 1877 and 1919. I wanted to break down gross generalizations about Americans based on race (black/white) and ethnicity (Irish, German, Jewish) by talking about socio-economic class. Men and women experience class in different ways. In order to speak broadly, I had to research the incomes and lifestyles of many kinds of Americans, not just middle-class white people.

"The broader your research, the more appealing your writing."

——— *Nell Irvin Painter*

Professional Model:

from *Standing at Armageddon, 1877–1919*

In both 1877 and 1919 native-born white Protestant Americans were presumed to belong to the middle (or upper) classes, even though in the South, West, and Midwest large numbers of such people belonged to the agricultural and industrial working classes. The standing of descendants of immigrants changed over time because the arrival of new groups of immigrants altered assumptions about relative class status. The Irish, who had seemed in 1877 to constitute a permanent class of casual laborers and domestic servants, had by 1919 become skilled workers and foremen, while many Irishwomen had become the teachers of the eastern and southern European immigrants who early in the twentieth century formed a new industrial working class. Similarly, German Jews, many of whom in the mid-nineteenth century had been itinerant peddlers, were largely middle- and upper-class by the time of heavy Russian Jewish immigration after 1905. And the process continued. By 1920 the children of Europeans who had immigrated in the late nineteenth century had become the teachers and foremen of southern black migrants in the North and Midwest.

I purposefully included the words white and Protestant to break up an equation that many readers take for granted: that middle-class is the same as white and Protestant. I also did research in sources that discussed the lives of many kinds of people.

I specifically mentioned Irish immigrants, because many readers forget the history of Irish Americans as immigrants. I wanted this section to convey the sense of change over time in the status of Irish Americans in relation to later immigrants.

I used these two particular vocations because one, teachers, is associated with women, and the other, foremen, is associated with men.

From the Author's Desk

- Show students Segment 4 on Nell Irvin Painter on ***From the Author's Desk DVD.*** Discuss her comments about the importance of doing a wide range of research within your subject.
- Point out that Painter recognizes the importance of grounding her assertions about ethnicity in careful research about economic classes. Just as Painter discovered relationships between ethnicity and class, other scholars were discovering new truths as they carefully questioned old assumptions.
- Review Painter's comments about her findings regarding the shifts in class among ethnic groups from 1877 to 1919. Ask students to explain how Painter's research changes their perceptions of social hierarchies and class mobility in America.

Differentiated Instruction
Solutions for All Learners

Support for English Learners
Help students work carefully in wording their thesis statements because these statements will guide their research and writing. Make sure they understand each word or phrase in their thesis statements. Tell them that if discovered information makes it necessary to change their thesis statements, they should do so, but very carefully. Assist them in rewording the statements.

Strategy for Advanced Writers
Point out to students that preliminary research can lead to additional perspectives on the subject and more effective thesis statements. Encourage students to learn more about their topics by reading encyclopedia entries and general reference sources. Then, encourage them to compose several thesis statements, each based on differing source material related to their topic. Finally, have them analyze each option to determine which has the most potential for development.

Revising

Revising Your Paragraphs

Add transitions to improve the flow of ideas. As you introduce blocks of information, help the reader follow your train of thought. Transitional words and phrases like *because, as a result, if, therefore, in addition, despite,* and *recently* encourage a flow and clarify the connections you want to stress. To select appropriate transitions, follow these steps:

1. Identify the relationship between the two paragraphs you are linking.
2. Determine whether the link is clear without a transition.
3. Add a transition if the relationship needs clarifying. Try various possibilities to see which best serves as a bridge between ideas.

Student Model: Add Transitions to Improve the Flow of Ideas

In addition to the key role of Christian religious messages in Wheatley's work,
^Many of her writings also exhibit a subtle presence of African traditions.
For example,
^Wheatley uses solar imagery throughout her poems.

These transitions link earlier ideas to statements made in these sentences.

Revising Your Word Choice

Define specialized vocabulary. Your readers may not understand the specialized terms you have encountered in your research. Other words may be familiar only to experts in the field. You may need to identify or define jargon that is specific to a topic. Review your work, and add clarifications to increase your readers' understanding of your ideas.

Consider defining essential terms and eliminating specialized vocabulary and jargon that can be replaced with simpler language.

To read the complete student model, see page 690.

Term	Definition
Neoclassical	Neoclassicism, a widespread movement in the visual and literary arts, began in the 1760s and lasted until the 1850s. Classical history and mythology were important Neoclassical subjects. Alexander Pope is an example of a poet from this movement.

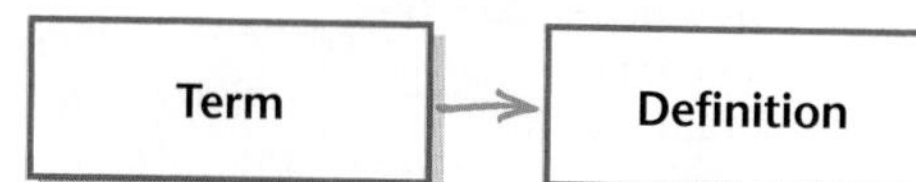

Peer Review: Ask a classmate to review your draft and identify specialized vocabulary that needs further definition.

Revising

Revising Your Paragraphs

- Supply students with flags (page markers) and instruct them to mark each use of source material in their drafts, including paraphrased or indirectly quoted material. Have them confirm the documentation and its accuracy. Documentation is particularly important when the fact is directly linked to support of the thesis. An undocumented fact *cannot* be used.
- Remind students that widely known facts (sometimes referred to as *common knowledge*), such as the date of Abraham Lincoln's assassination, require no documentation.
- Provide examples of effective transitions. Model these for the class. Then provide examples of text with poor or no transitions and have the class provide them.
- Explain that a transition must provide the reader with a logical bridge from one related idea to another. Tell students that transitions are somewhat like a writer's version of turn signals or road signs in writing: they make the trip smoother and clearer and help avoid mishaps.

Revising Your Word Choice

- Explain that word choice depends, in part, on the audience. Specialized words, such as *sampling* (from contem porary music), may need explanation for a general audience.
  Ask students to give other examples of terms used in contemporary music or technology that would be familiar to them but possibly not to their parents or grandparents.

Six Traits Focus

✔	Ideas	✔	Word Choice
✔	Organization	✔	Sentence Fluency
	Voice		Conventions

WG Writing and Grammar, Ruby Level

Students will find additional instruction on revising a research paper in Chapter 13, Section 4.

Tips for Using Technology in Writing

If students have access to word processors, encourage them to use the Insert mode, rather than the Type-over mode, for making corrections. By using the Insert mode in revising, students can insert proper citations and any additional information or words as needed. In addition, many word processing programs have features for creating Works Cited pages. Students can also use the organizing tools and revision checkers on **Writing and Grammar / Text.** Remind them that source materials can be found or possibly verified online.

Developing Your Style

Quotations and Source Materials

Integrating Quotations and Source Materials Just as you write an introduction and a conclusion to frame the body of your draft, you need to provide context for the direct quotations that you include in your research paper. You also need to avoid plagiarism, using someone else's words or ideas as though they were your own.

For each quotation, follow a simple strategy. First, introduce the quotation by naming the writer or by linking the quotation to the material it follows. Then, present the quoted material. Finally, explain the quotation by showing how it supports the point you are presenting.

Reading Writing Connection

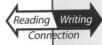

To read the complete student model, see page 690.

Student Model: Framing Source Material

Sample Sentence: Almost every one of Wheatley's poems develops around a central theme of religious morality and sometimes has an "air of message from the pulpit" (Mason 15–17). One theme, Christian salvation, underlies nearly everything she wrote (Redding 10).

The writer integrates direct quotations into the argument, including the exact source of each one.

Find It in Your Reading Read or review the student model on page 690.

1. Identify three sentences in the student model that provide seamless integration of quotes or source materials. For each sentence, note the transitions or other devices the writer uses.
2. Identify three examples in the student model that show proper quoting from sources. Notice the techniques the writer uses to avoid plagiarism.

Apply It to Your Writing Go back and review what you have written so far in this workshop.

1. Circle sentences that could use improvement by smoothing out quotations.
2. Review your notes, and compare the original source with the one you used in your work. Make sure you have properly quoted and credited the source.
3. Underline the parts of your writing where you have reformulated and combined the ideas of others. Make sure you have not committed plagiarism by presenting the writing or ideas of someone else as though they were your own.

WG *Prentice Hall Writing and Grammar Connection: Chapter 13, Section 2*

Developing Your Style

Integrating Quotations and Source Material

- Model methods of linking a quotation to the related text. For example: "It is possible that Shakespeare's mysterious family life was to some extent reflected in his plays. Scholar Stephen Greenblatt points out in his discussion of Shakespeare's later years, 'If *King Lear* is any indication, he shared with his contemporaries a fear of retirement and dread of dependence on children.' (Greenblatt, 361)"
- Remind students that another way to integrate source material into text is by using interpretations and indirect quotations. Have students compare the following reference to Greenblatt's ideas about Shakespeare to the preceding example: "It is possible that Shakespeare's mysterious family life was to some extent reflected in his plays. For instance, Greenblatt points out that Shakespeare wrote *King Lear,* his great play about parents and children, when he was an aging man with several grown daughters, like Lear. (Greenblatt, 356-61)."
- Review possible responses to the **Find It in your Writing** questions with the class.
- Have students review what they have written so far. Ask them to work with partners and to focus on word choice and sentence fluency, in particular on sentences into which source material has been integrated. Have students use the Unity and Coherence tool in the ***Writing and Grammar Interactive Textbook CD ROM.***

Tips for Test-Taking

Some writing tests direct students to read articles, synthesize the information, and then write an essay based on this information. Students can approach these tests as research assignments for which a topic has already been chosen and sources already gathered. The prompt will provide a research question. Students should note how each given article addresses that question. The thesis statement should answer the prompt directly, and the essay should support the thesis with evidence from the articles.

Student Model

- Explain that the student model is a sample and that many research papers are longer.
- Have students read the first paragraph. **Ask** them to identify the essay's topic and its thesis statement.
  Answer: The topic is the significance of Wheatley's poetry. Lauren's thesis is, "Although many do not consider her to be a important writer judged by today's values of originality, she persevered through the challenges of her social status to become not only a celebrated poet but the starting point for the study of African-American literature."
- Call students' attention to Lauren's second paragraph and the note that accompanies it.
  Ask students to identify the sources she uses to support her opinions.
  Answer: She cites Miller, de Dwyer, Wood, Misson, and Redding.
- Point out the subheadings that Lauren uses and explain that these make her essay more organized and easier to follow.
- Point out that in her fourth paragraph, Lauren combines factual evidence from sources and interpretation of Wheatley's poetry, giving her opinions strong support.

Writing Genres
Research Papers in the Workplace

Tell students that research writing is not limited to school. Many useful and important documents are based on the same methods of research that students are using to create their papers. Government reports, medical findings, scientific discoveries, business studies all involve research and crediting sources. Much journalism can also be considered research writing because journalists investigate a topic and, wherever possible, cite their sources.

Student Model: Lauren Shepherd, Tupelo, Mississippi

The Writing Style of Phillis Wheatley

In an era when African Americans were struggling to carve an identity for themselves, Phillis Wheatley emerged as the first truly significant black poet in American literature. Although many do not consider her to be an important writer judged by today's values of originality, she persevered through the challenges of her social status to become not only a celebrated poet but the starting point for the study of African American literature. In this paper, I will discuss her work as a whole, and present a detailed analysis of one of her most famous poems, "To His Excellency General Washington."

> Lauren clearly states her thesis in the opening paragraph.

Religious Message Wheatley was highly educated for her time, and had read the classics as well as the best English Poets (Miller, de Dwyer, Wood 48). She was deeply influenced by the work of the great English poet John Milton (1608–1674), who saw himself as a writer in the service of God. Like Milton, Wheatley expressed a constant awareness of "God, His Son, His beneficence and His Power." Almost every one of Wheatley's poems develops around a central theme of religious morality and sometimes has an "air of message from the pulpit" (Mason 15–17). One theme, Christian salvation, underlies nearly everything she wrote (Redding 10).

> Lauren provides thorough support for all the opinions expressed in this passage.

Wheatley's religious messages are often conveyed through embellished Bible stories. In fact, a tradition within African American literature of augmenting biblical accounts with creative license and poetic flair can be traced directly to Wheatley. Both her poems "Goliath and Gath" and "Isaiah LXIII" add creative information to a foundation of biblical narrative.

African Influences In addition to the key role of Christian religious messages in Wheatley's work, many of her writings also exhibit a subtle presence of African traditions. For example, Wheatley uses solar imagery throughout her body of poems. Her frequent use of sun imagery in such poems as "A Hymn to the Morning," and "A Hymn to the Evening," suggest that her early religious training in Africa may have consisted of some kind of hierophantic—or sun—worship (Smith, Baechler, Litz 474). Wheatley usually uses such sun imagery as a metaphor for Christian revelation, thus connecting the two essential elements of her religious life.

> Subheads add to the orderliness of her essay.

> Lauren provides factual support for an interesting literary analysis.

Also reminiscent of Wheatley's childhood in Africa is her constant interest in panegyric—or praise—poetry. In many of the cultures of Africa, poets were instructed that political praise constituted the very core of their responsibility as writers (Smith, Baechler, Litz 476). In keeping with that tradition, the majority of Wheatley's works are directed towards politically and socially prominent individuals, such as George Whitehead, a famous English clergyman, and George Washington (Johnson 29).

Racial Consciousness Although many have ventured to say that Wheatley's "unquestioning embrace of New England and white cultures" prompted her to neglect the issue of slavery (Smith, Baechler, Litz 476), a closer examination of her poetry reveals that she was quite "race conscious" (Davis 192). She refers to herself on several occasions as "Africa's muse," and even uses her skin color and presumed low social status as a reference point for her religious message of salvation (Davis 192–193).

The essay provides a variety of interpretations of the material.

Neoclassical Style The majority of Wheatley's poems adhere to the established patterns of the neoclassical style. Neoclassicism was a widespread movement in the visual and literary arts that began in the 1760s and lasted until the 1840s and 1850s. Classical history and mythology provided much of the subject matter of Neoclassical works. The poetry of Homer, Virgil, and Ovid, and the plays of Aeschylus, Sophocles, and Euripides provided the bulk of classical sources. Neoclassical writers, such as Alexander Pope (1688–1744) stressed order, harmony, and restraint.

Necessary background information is essential to the readers' understanding.

Like the Neoclassicists she admired, Wheatley's work was noted for an unfaltering preoccupation with regular rhyme and rhythm (Mason 14). Breaking out of her usual form on only six occasions Wheatley most frequently wrote using the heroic couplet—two-line stanzas written in iambic pentameter—that Alexander Pope made so effective (Mason 20). Considering that she is labeled as a spontaneous poet who would write during bouts of inspiration, the general regularity of her meter is remarkable. The influence of the Neoclassical writers also shows in Wheatley's use of elevated language (Mason 16), and in her numerous classical and mythological allusions.

Lauren refers to other points of view regarding Wheatley's work.

"To His Excellency General Washington" The poem "To His Excellency General Washington" serves as a good example of Wheatley's style. Troubled by poor health since her arrival in America in 1761, when she was only eight years old (Perkins et al. 272), Wheatley traveled from Boston to London in 1773 in hope that the sea air would improve her well-being. Upon her return to the rebellious colonies in 1774, she found the fighting in the Boston vicinity had escalated. Wheatley composed her poem to George Washington and crossed the battle lines to deliver it in person. Two years later, Wheatley received a letter from the General himself thanking her for her adulation but insisting that she had placed him on too high a pedestal. In April 1776, Thomas Paine published her poem, its accompanying note, and Washington's reply in *Pennsylvania Magazine or American Monthly Museum* (Sheeler 8–10).

The essay makes use of a variety of historical documents, including this primary source.

Although Washington's response to Wheatley's poem was modest, Wheatley gives the reader clear insight as to her opinions of the man. The entire poem is devoted to the veneration of the Continental Army and the leadership of General Washington. Wheatley adheres to her favorite poetic form of heroic couplets. She does not merely revere Washington, she portrays him as a royal figure, referring to him as "Your Excellency," and ascribing to him "a crown, a mansion and a throne that shine."

Student Model (cont.)

- Note that Lauren offers a variety of interpretations of Wheatley's poetry (for example, her discussion of Wheatley's "Racial Consciousness" in paragraph 6), making her essay richer and more complex.
- Remind students of Lauren's definition of neoclassicism in paragraph 7. **Ask** what earlier term Lauren defined for her readers.
  Answer: *Hierophantic* in paragraph 4, is defined as "sun worship"
- Point out other valuable types of evidence that Lauren uses, for example, her reference to Thomas Paine's publication of Wheatley's poem. **Ask** students to explain how this information enhances the essay.
  Answer: It provides strong evidence that Wheatley's poetry was recognized as important even during her lifetime, despite her social status.

Differentiated Instruction Solutions for All Learners

Strategy for Special Needs Students

Students may find the independent reading involved in doing research especially challenging. Instruct students to keep track of what they read by making notecards for each source. Monitor the students' work, periodically reviewing their cards with them to make sure that they have taken relevant notes and recorded the source information correctly. To check comprehension, have students explain the points in their own words.

Strategy for Gifted/Talented Students

Students may use visual materials among their sources. For example, reproductions of photographs and artwork, charts, graphs, or tables might be useful and interesting additions to a research paper. Explain that visual sources are intended to complement, not replace, written sources. Tell students that when they include visual materials, they should identify and refer to these items in the text as they write, using a system such as "Figure 1 (etc.)."

Student Model (cont.)

- Call special attention to the first sentence of the final paragraph. Explain that Lauren has restated her thesis, in simpler terms, with the paragraph explaining her argument.
- Call attention to Lauren's "Works Cited" list. Point out that each entry provides information about one of her sources, including the author's name, the title of the source, and the place and date of publication.

Wheatley resorts to a striking use of personification in the poem. In the opening lines, she mentions the sorrow of "mother earth" at the bloodshed ravaging the land. In line 15, she personifies heaven as a maiden with a "fair face." Her use of alliteration in that image adds to its effect. Wheatley also gives life to the "nations" in line 33, and describes Brittania as a defeated being who "droops the pensive head" (line 35).

Perhaps Wheatley's most notable use of personification lies in her image of the American colonies as the Goddess Columbia (line 9) who is a "native of the skies" (line 11). Wheatley created this new goddess in honor of Christopher Columbus. Later popularized by Revolutionary War poets such as Philip Freneau, the image of Columbia has its first appearance in Wheatley's poem (Jensen).

Wheatley also weaves various allusions into her poem. For example, the European countries in conflict with America are said to be "Gallic powers" (line 30). This allusion refers to the Gallic Wars at the time of Julius Caesar when France was called Gaul. Further evidence of her classical knowledge appears in the reference to "Aeolus," the God of the wind (line 15). Aeolus appeared in Homer's *Odyssey* (Tripp 24), which Wheatley read in Alexander Pope's famous translation. Wheatley scholars generally agree that Pope's translation of Homer greatly affected her poetry (Mason 16).

Although Phillis Wheatley never achieved a truly original poetic style, she is undoubtedly an important figure in American literature. She transcended racial and language barriers to occupy a significant position in the social and intellectual scene of both Boston and London. If one judges her work based on the impact of her poetry on her contemporaries, she is an important pioneer in the development of American literature.

Lauren concludes by reiterating her thesis.

Works Cited

Davis, Arthur P. "Personal Elements in the Poetry of Phillis Wheatley." Phylon: *The Atlanta University Review of Race and Culture.* 13 vols. June 1953, pp. 191–198.

Johnson, James Weldon., ed. *The Book of American Negro Poetry.* New York: Harcourt Brace Jovanovich Inc., 1922.

Mason, Julian D., Jr., ed. *The Poems of Phillis Wheatley.* North Carolina: The University of North Carolina Press, 1989.

Miller, James E., Jr., Carlota Cárdenas de Dwyer, and Kerry M. Wood. *The United States in Literature.* Illinois: Scott, Foresman, and Company, 1985.

Perkins, George, et al., eds. *The American Tradition in Literature.* 1 vol. New York: McGraw-Hill Publishing Company, 1990.

Redding, J. Saunders. *To Make a Poet Black.* New York: Cornell University Press, 1988.

Sheeler, Karissa L. *Phillis Wheatley.* 11 February 2000. <http://www.kutztown.edu/faculty/reagan/wheat1.html>

Smith, Valerie, Lea Baechler, and A. Walton Litz, eds. *African American Writers.* New York: Charles Scribner's Sons, 1991.

Tripp, Edward. *Cromwell's Handbook of Classical Mythology.* New York: Thomas Y. Cromwell Company, 1970.

A complete works-cited list provides information on the sources Lauren references in the essay.

Editing and Proofreading

Review your research paper to eliminate errors in grammar, punctuation, and spelling.

Focus on Accuracy: Consult your notecards to be sure you have quoted material exactly. Confirm all spellings and check all dates and statistics.

Publishing and Presenting

Create a reference list. Your research paper should include a works-cited list that provides full bibliographic information on each source you cite. Standards for documentation are set by several organizations, such as the MLA and APA. Follow the format your teacher prefers. (For more information, see Writing Criticism and Citing Sources, pages R27–R29).

Consider one of the following ways to share your research paper:

Present an oral report. Summarize your research paper in an oral report. Provide classmates with a handout outlining key points and sources.

Submit your paper for publication. Submit your paper to a magazine that publishes student writing or that covers your research topic.

Reflecting on Your Writing

Writer's Journal Jot down your thoughts on the experience of writing a research paper. Begin by answering these questions:

- Which strategies would you use again?
- Which aspect of researching a topic in depth most surprised you?

 *Prentice Hall Writing and Grammar Connection: Chapter 13*

Rubric for Self-Assessment

Evaluate your research paper *using the following criteria and rating scale, or, with your classmates, determine your own reasonable evaluation criteria.*

Criteria	Rating Scale (not very – very)
Focus: How clearly worded is your thesis statement?	1 2 3 4 5
Organization: How clear and logical is the organization?	1 2 3 4 5
Support/Elaboration: How well do you use facts from a variety of sources to support your thesis?	1 2 3 4 5
Style: How well do you explain differences among the sources?	1 2 3 4 5
Conventions: According to an accepted format, how complete and accurate are your citations?	1 2 3 4 5

Editing and Proofreading

- Have students read their research papers carefully, marking them for for line to line edits, including changes in word choice and corrections in grammar, spelling, and punctuation.
- Ask students to exchange papers for peer assessment. Have students produce their final draft.

Six Traits Focus

✗	Ideas	✗	Word Choice
✗	Organization	✗	Sentence Fluency
	Voice	✗	Conventions

ASSESS

Publishing and Presenting

- Remind students to verify that their "works cited" page is accurate and complies with the chosen format.
- Ask students to think about the audience they had in mind when they started. Did they write for the appropriate audience?
- Remind students that their teacher is a part of that audience and that they must meet requirements and expectations for the assignment.
- Review the self-assessment criteria with the students.
- Ask students to evaluate the Student Model, using these assessment criteria. Discuss how well the Model meets these standards.
- Encourage students to organize and outline an oral presentation of their research findings for their classmates.

Reflecting on Your Writing

- Ask students to discuss what they learned from researching a subject. Do the results alter the perspective that the student once had of the subject?
- Ask the students to compare writing this research paper to other research papers. What did they do differently this time?

WG Writing and Grammar, Ruby Level

Students will find additional instruction on editing and proofreading, publishing, and presenting, and reflecting on a research paper in Chapter 13, Section 13.5.

Tips for Test-Taking

Help students improve their timed-writing performance by practicing the writing stages they will have time for during an actual test: creating a thesis statement, drafting (including supporting evidence), and proofreading Create test-like conditions when practicing in class.

Meeting Your Standards

Students will

1. **learn the terms *apply, demonstrate,* and *Illustrate.***
2. **apply knowledge of these terms in standardized-test situations.**

Know Your Terms: Demonstrating Understanding

Explain that students will respond to the terms listed under Terms to Learn when asked to recall and use information from a reading passage in standardized-test situations.

Terms to Learn

- Review *apply.* Tell students that to apply information is to use given knowledge to produce new information, such as an answer to a question. For example, tell students that if a chart shows that a region's industries grew rapidly during a specific time period, students can apply this information to explain why the region's population density grew.
- Review *demonstrate.* Explain to students that to demonstrate is show what they know about a subject.
- Review *illustrate.* Tell students that to illustrate means to explain by giving examples. To illustrate Twain's use of humorous dialogue, students would give examples that provide a clear "picture" of humorous conversation.

Vocabulary Workshop

High-Frequency Academic Words

High-frequency academic words are words that appear often in textbooks and on standardized tests. Though you may already know the meaning of many of these words, they usually have a more specific meaning when they are used in textbooks and on tests.

Know Your Terms: Analyzing Information

Each of the words listed is a verb that tells you to show that you recognize the significance of text details and the relationships among them. The words indicate the kinds of information you should provide in your answer.

Terms to Learn

Differentiate Identify and explain the qualities that distinguish two items or ideas.

Sample test item: ***Differentiate*** between symbol and motif.

Analyze Break down a topic or an issue into parts and explain them.

Sample test item: ***Analyze*** the story's main character.

Infer Show that you have used text details to figure out what is not stated.

Sample test item: Based on the setting of "The Outcasts of Poker Flats," what can you ***infer*** about the story's mood?

Practice

Directions: *Read the following passage from Jack London's short story "To Build a Fire." Then, on a separate piece of paper, answer questions 1–3.*

But all this—the mysterious, far-reaching hairline trail, the absence of sun from the sky, the tremendous cold, and the strangeness and weirdness of it all—made no impression on the man. It was not because he was long used to it. He was a newcomer in the land, a *chechaquo,* and this was his first winter. The trouble with him was that he was without imagination. He was quick and alert in the things of life, but only in the things, and not in the significances. Fifty degrees below zero meant eighty-odd degrees of frost. Such fact impressed him as being cold and uncomfortable, and that was all. It did not lead him to meditate upon his frailty as a creature of temperature, and upon man's frailty in general, able only to live within certain narrow limits of heat and cold; and from there on it did not lead him to the conjectural field of immortality and man's place in the universe. . . .

1. *Analyze* the character described in this passage. In your analysis, explain how his characteristics influence his view of his situation.
2. What can you *infer* about the narrator's attitude toward the weather?
3. *Differentiate* between the writer's and the character's perspectives.

ASSESS

Answers

1. **Possible response:** Students may suggest the first line of the passage.
2. **Possible answer:** Answers should contain an example of how the person was misunderstood and how he or she was great.
3. **Possible answer:** Answers should reflect students' applications of Emerson's comments.

Tips for Test Taking

Students are often asked in testing situations to demonstrate understanding of what they know about a topic by explaining it to other people. Remind students that teaching an idea reinforces their own learning process. Students can think of the verbs *apply, demonstrate,* and *illustrate* as different ways of teaching others what they have learned about a piece of literature.

Assessment Workshop

Critical Reading: Context Clues

The reading sections of some tests require you to use context to determine the meaning of unfamiliar or uncommon words and figurative expressions. The following strategies will help you answer such test questions:

- Remember that context is defined as the words and phrases that surround a word or figurative expression and provide clues to its meaning.
- Infer the meaning of certain words and figurative expressions by determining what the expression is being used to describe or illustrate. Then, restate the passage in your own words.
- Read the passage, leaving out the unfamiliar word, and then substitute a word or meaning you infer. See whether your substitution makes sense.

Practice

Directions: *Read the passages, and then answer questions 1–3:*

Passage A. The practice of celebrating Thanksgiving dates back to the year 1621, when the Pilgrims of Plymouth, Massachusetts, joined with local Wampanoag Indians to give thanks for the bountiful harvest. The feast included ducks, geese, corn, potatoes, lobsters, bass, clams, and dried fruit. For the Pilgrims, the food was like manna to the Israelites.

Passage B. Amy and Jane listened closely to the weather forecast as they packed their bags. For nearly a year, they had eagerly anticipated taking a ski trip to Colorado. As they listened to the ominous predictions of freezing rain, sleet, and snow, their hearts sank like lead. Such dangerous weather conditions would surely ground their plane and force them to cancel their plans.

1. In Passage A, judging from the context, what might you determine the meaning of the word *bountiful* to be?

   A lacking
   B spoiled
   C abundant
   D tasty

2. In Passage B, judging from the context in which it is used, which of these words best defines the word *ominous*?

   A optimistic
   B troubling
   C incorrect
   D long-range

3. Judging from the context, which of these sentences best defines the idiom *their hearts sank like lead*?

   A Their spirits rose.
   B They changed their minds.
   C They experienced sudden despair.
   D They felt balanced.

Test-Taking Strategies

- Restate the passage in your own words to clarify the author's message.
- Familiar words sometimes have multiple meanings, some of which may be unfamiliar. Use phrases and sentences surrounding a word to help determine its specific meaning in the passage.

Tips for Test Taking

Explain to students that they can use prior background knowledge—especially knowledge they already have about context—to help determine the meanings of unfamiliar words. Students should apply any relevant prior knowledge to the context before answering test questions.

Meeting Your Standards

Students will

1. **use context in order to determine the meanings of unfamiliar words in a test situation.**
2. **use background knowledge to determine the meanings of unfamiliar words.**

Critical Reading

- Have students read the sample test item. Then, **ask** them to identify and explain what the passage describes.
  Answer: The passage describes the first Thanksgiving, celebrated by Pilgrims and Native Americans in Massachusetts.
- Next, **ask** students to describe any prior knowledge they can apply to this passage.
  Possible response: Most students will say that Thanksgiving is a celebration of plentiful food.
- Have students read the Practice passage and **answer** the questions.
- Point out that in question 1, A is the opposite of the mood established in the context. Answers C and D have no connection to the context at all. B is correct because the context of ominous includes a description of "dangerous weather conditions" and Amy and Jane's disappointment.
- Point out that in question 2, A, B, and D describe mental states that do not match the mood produced by such bad news. C is correct because the context indicates that Amy and Jane's mood is a negative one.
- Point out that in question 3, A, B, and D are not supported by the context. C is correct because the context indicates that their mood sank.

ASSESS

Answers

1. B
2. C
3. C

Meeting Your Standards

Students will

1. critically evaluate and respond to persuasive arguments.
2. recognize logical fallacies and avoid being persuaded by them.
3. critique the reasoning in an argument, identifying faulty reasoning.
4. critique the reliability of the information used to support an argument.

Critique Reasoning

- Explain to students that faulty reasoning makes an argument less persuasive. Suggest that they maintain a Feedback Form for logical fallacies, based on the model on this page.
- Review the major fallacies of reasoning with students. Be sure that students understand and can identify each fallacy; they should recognize "But my friends get to stay out late!" as an example of *bandwagon effect*. Have students discuss how these fallacies undermine the persuasiveness of an argument.

Critique Information

- Explain that logical fallacies can undermine the information a speaker uses to support an argument, as well as the speaker's reasoning.
- Review the informational fallacies with the class. Be sure students understand and can identify the fallacies; for example, they should recognize "Something at the arena makes people sick because I went there and afterwards I got sick" as an example of *false causality*.
- Once again, encourage students to fill out Feedback Forms to help them spot logical fallacies when they evaluate persuasive arguments.

Assess the Activity

To evaluate students persuasive arguments, use the Evaluating a Persuasive Presentation rubric, p. 83 in ***General Resources.***

Critique Persuasive Arguments

Speakers employ many kinds of arguments to convince listeners of the soundness of their positions. These arguments sometimes contain logical fallacies and even propaganda techniques that can influence listeners' responses. The listening strategies outlined below will help you critically review persuasive speeches and recognize faulty reasoning and misleading information. Use the form on this page to record your reactions.

Critique Reasoning

To be persuasive, arguments must be logical. Use these strategies to critique persuasive arguments:

- **Challenge generalizations.** Make sure the speaker supports general claims with facts. Listen for over-generalizations and stereotypes drawn from samples that may be too small to represent broad truths.
- **Identify circular reasoning.** Listen for arguments in which the support merely restates the claim—for example, "Teenagers should not be hired because they lack experience." To check for circular reasoning, study the proof and make sure it offers new information.
- **Spot bandwagon effect.** A speaker may urge listeners to agree because "everyone else" does, or may cite a celebrity's support. Avoid accepting a bandwagon appeal that urges you to join the crowd.

Feedback Form for Persuasive Arguments

Rating System: Logical Fallacies
+ = Not Present
✓ = Sometimes Present
– = Present Often

Reasoning
Weak generalizations ______
Circular reasoning ______
Bandwagon effect ______

Information
Attack *ad hominum* ______
Red herring ______
False causality ______

Answer the following questions:
Was the speaker's argument built on any faulty reasoning or information?
Without that faulty reasoning or information, does the speaker's argument remain convincing?

Critique Information

Speakers may also build arguments on faulty or misleading information. Listen for the following kinds of illogical or manipulative techniques:

- **Attack *ad hominem*** In this type of argument, named for the Latin phrase meaning "to the man," a speaker attacks an opponent personally, rather than responding to his or her arguments.
- **Red Herring** Named for the odorous fish once used to distract hunting dogs, the red herring argument presents dramatic but irrelevant information designed to confuse and distract listeners.
- **False Causality** When speakers suggest that events or facts have a cause-and-effect relationship, determine whether the events are actually causally linked or merely sequential or coincidental.

Activity *Oral Address and Feedback* Choose a topic about which you feel strongly and deliver a persuasive oral address stating your position and urging listeners' agreement. Take turns with classmates delivering addresses and respectfully critiquing arguments.

Differentiated Instruction Solutions for All Learners

Strategy for Special Needs Students
Students may find identifying logical fallacies in persuasive presentations challenging. Encourage them to practice in pairs or small groups with written texts. Review their responses before students begin to evaluate spoken arguments.

Support for Less Proficient Readers
Be sure students understand how logical fallacies undermine arguments. Explain that to be persuasive, arguments must be supported by evidence, rather than logical fallacies. Students should notice how speakers support arguments and determine whether credible evidence or logical fallacies have been used.

Strategy for English Learners
Spotting logical fallacies in an argument may be challenging for English learners. Encourage them to note the main points that a speaker makes. Under each point, these students should sum up the support the speaker provides. If evidence does not support a point, students should look for a logical fallacy.

Suggestions for Further Reading

Featured Titles:

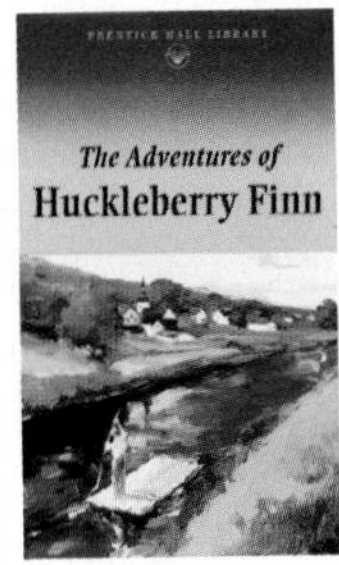

The Adventures of Huckleberry Finn
Mark Twain *Pearson Prentice Hall, 2000*

Novel Ernest Hemingway once wrote that "all modern American literature comes from one book by Mark Twain called *Huckleberry Finn*." This influential novel concerns the adventures of two "runaways" on the Mississippi River. One is Huck Finn, the hero of the novel, who is escaping from his abusive father. The other is Jim, an enslaved African trying to gain his freedom. Twain's novel has earned its place of honor in American literature through its vivid depiction of American life and its compassionate analysis of race relations.

My Ántonia
Willa Cather *Pearson Prentice Hall, 2000*

Novel Willa Cather drew on her girlhood experiences to write *My Ántonia*. The book's heroine, Ántonia, is a self-reliant and spirited young woman growing up on the Nebraska frontier. The narrator, Jim Burden, has lost both his parents and travels to Nebraska to live with his grandparents. Cather chronicles the friendship between Jim and Ántonia as they grow, experience pain and joy, lose sight of each other for twenty years, and renew their relationship. This novel celebrates the pioneer spirit and realistically portrays both the beauty and hardship of frontier life.

The Sea-Wolf and Selected Stories
Jack London *Signet Classic, 1964*

Short stories Jack London wrote about the conflict between wildness and civilization in many novels and tales. In *The Sea-Wolf*, this conflict takes the form of a struggle between the captain of a seal-hunting ship and a reluctant crewman. This volume also contains four other stories.

Works Presented in Unit Four

If sampling a portion of the following texts has built your interest, treat yourself to the full works.

Narrative of the Life of Frederick Douglass
Frederick Douglass *Signet Classic, 1997*

Spoon River Anthology
Edgar Lee Masters *Signet Classic, 1992*

Many of these titles are available in the Prentice Hall/Penguin Literature Library. Consult your teacher before choosing one.

Planning Students' Further Reading

Discussions of literature can raise sensitive and often controversial issues. Before you recommend further reading to your students, consider the values and sensitivities of your community as well as the age, ability, and sophistication of your students. It is also good policy to preview literature before you recommend it to students. The notes below offer some guidance on specific titles.

***The Adventures of Huckleberry Finn* by Mark Twain**

Adapted: Although Twain uses dialect to give his novel a vivid sense of realism, some readers may consider the dialects of Huck and Jim to be offensive stereotypes. They may also find Jim's simplicity and superstitious beliefs offensive, although Huck and Jim emerge as the novel's only truly admirable, heroic characters. Other sensitive issues might include Pap's drunkenness and child abuse, the murder of Pap, and Twain's satire of religious revivalists.

In addition to depicting slavery and racism, the book contains negative racial stereotypes and offensive language, including frequent, casual use of the word *nigger.* Child abuse and alcoholism are also depicted.

Lexile: 990

***My Antonia* by Willa Cather**

Racism, prejudice against immigrants, insensitivity toward the mentally retarded and developmentally disabled, and other biased attitudes are expressed in the novel.

Lexile: 1010

***The Sea-Wolf and Selected Stories* by Jack London**

This volume includes scenes of violence and cruelty. Explain that these scenes provide an unsentimental look at the "darker" or "less civilized" side of human beings. Point out that London uses such scenes to provide insights about good and evil.

Lexile: 1020

***Narrative of the Life of Frederick Douglass* by Frederick Douglass**

Some students may feel angry and frustrated by the injustices of slavery and the countless cruel acts that went unpunished. The narratives contain many disturbing images of slaves being brutally beaten and whipped. References are made to

Continued from right column

adultery in the form of the rape of slave women by their masters. In one instance, a female slave is purchased for the purpose of breeding. The word *nigger* is used occasionally.

Lexile: 1080

***Spoon River Anthology* by Edgar Lee Masters**

The poems touch on adultery, sex without marriage, unwed motherhood, homosexuality, prostitution, venereal disease, abortion, rape, arson, murder, suicide, religious doubt, patriotic doubt, crooked business practices, dishonest.

Lexile: RL 6

INDEX OF AUTHORS AND TITLES

Note: Nonfiction selections and informational text appear in red. Page numbers in italic text refer to background or biographical information.

L

M

N

O

P

Q

R

S

T

U

W

INDEX OF SKILLS

Note: Page numbers in **boldface** refer to pages where terms are defined.

Literary Analysis

Reading Strategies

Grammar and Style

Vocabulary

Critical Reading

Critical Viewing

Writing

Listening and Speaking

Research and Technology

INDEX OF FEATURES

Note: Page numbers in **boldface** refer to pages where terms are defined.

ACKNOWLEDGMENTS

Grateful acknowledgment is made to the following for copyrighted material:

Harvard University Press "Because I could not stop for Death (#712)" by Emily Dickinson from The *Poems Of Emily Dickinson,* Thomas H. Johnson, ed., Cambridge, Mass.: The Belknap Press of Harvard University Press, Copyright (c) 1951, 1955, 1979 by the Presidents and Fellows of Harvard College. Reprinted by permission of the publishers and the Trustees of Amherst College. "There's a certain Slant of light (#258)" by Emily Dickinson from *The Poems of Emily Dickinson,* Thomas H. Johnson, ed., Cambridge, Mass.: The Belknap Press of Harvard University Press, Copyright (c) 1951, 1955, 1979 by the Presidents and Fellows of Harvard College. Reprinted by permission of the publishers and the Trustees of Amherst College. "I heard a Fly buzz—when I died (#465)" by Emily Dickinson from *The Poems Of Emily Dickinson,* Thomas H. Johnson, ed., Cambridge, Mass.: The Belknap Press of Harvard University Press, Copyright (c) 1951, 1955, 1979 by the Presidents and Fellows of Harvard College. Reprinted by permission of the publishers and the Trustees of Amherst College. "My life closed twice before its close (#1732)" by Emily Dickinson from *The Poems of Emily Dickinson,* Thomas H. Johnson, ed., Cambridge, Mass.: The Belknap Press of Harvard University Press, Copyright (c) 1951, 1955, 1979 by the Presidents and Fellows of Harvard College. Reprinted by permission of the publishers and the Trustees of Amherst College. "There is a solitude of space (#1695)" by Emily Dickinson from *The Poems of Emily Dickinson,* Thomas H. Johnson, ed., Cambridge, Mass.: The Belknap Press of Harvard University Press, Copyright (c) 1951, 1955, 1979 by the Presidents and Fellows of Harvard College. Reprinted by permission of the publishers and the Trustees of Amherst College. "The Soul selects her own Society (#303)" by Emily Dickinson from *The Poems of Emily Dickinson,* Thomas H. Johnson, ed., Cambridge, Mass.: The Belknap Press of Harvard University Press, Copyright (c) 1951, 1955, 1979 by the Presidents and Fellows of Harvard College. Reprinted by permission of the publishers and the Trustees of Amherst College.

Diana Chang Herrmann from "Most Satisfied by Snow" by Diana Chang. Copyright by Diana Chang.

Houghton Mifflin Company "Ambush" from *The Things They Carried* by Tim O'Brien. Copyright © 1990 by Tim O'Brien. Reprinted by permission of Houghton Mifflin Company. All rights reserved. "Loneliness...An American Malady", from The Mortgaged Heart by Carson McCullers. Copyright 1940, 1941, 1942, 1945, 1948, 1949, 1953, © 1956, 1959, 1963, 1971 by Floria V. Lasky, Executrix of the Estate of Carson McCullers. Used by permission of Houghton Mifflin Company. All rights reserved.

International African Institute "African Proverbs: Liberia: The Jabo: "Children are the wisdom . . ."" by Anonymous from *Jabo Proverbs From Liberia: Maxims In The Life Of A Native Tribe*. Published from the International Institute of African Languages & Cultures by Oxford University Press, London: Humphrey Milford, 1936. "African Proverbs: Liberia: The Jabo: "One who cannot pick up an ant . . ."" by Anonymous from *Jabo Proverbs From Liberia: Maxims In The Life Of A Native Tribe*. Published from the International Institute of African Languages & Cultures by Oxford University Press, London: Humphrey Milford, 1936. "African Proverbs: Liberia: The Jabo: "Daring talk . . ."" by Anonymous from *Jabo Proverbs From Liberia: Maxims In The Life Of A Native Tribe*. Published from the International Institute of African Languages & Cultures by Oxford University Press, London: Humphrey Milford, 1936. "African Proverbs: Liberia: The Jabo: "A man's ways are good . . ."" by Anonymous from *Jabo Proverbs From Liberia: Maxims In The Life Of A Native Tribe*. Published from the International Institute of African Languages & Cultures by Oxford University Press, London: Humphrey Milford, 1936. "African Proverbs: Liberia: The Jabo: "The one who listens . . ."" by Anonymous from *Jabo Proverbs From Liberia: Maxims In The Life Of A Native Tribe*. Published from the International Institute of African Languages & Cultures by Oxford University Press, London: Humphrey Milford, 1936. "African Proverbs: Liberia: The Jabo: "The butterfly that flies among . . ."" by Anonymous from *Jabo Proverbs From Liberia: Maxims In The Life Of A Native Tribe*. Published from the International Institute of African Languages & Cultures by Oxford University Press, London: Humphrey Milford, 1936.

Estate of Martin Luther King, Jr. c/o Writers House as agent for the proprietor "Letter from Birmingham City Jail (Why We Can't Wait)" by Martin Luther King, Jr. Reprinted by arrangement with The Heirs to the Estate of Martin Luther King, Jr. c/o Writers House as agent for the proprietor. Copyright 1963 Martin Luther King, Jr. renewed 1991 by Coretta Scott King.

Alfred A. Knopf, Inc. "A Noiseless Flash" from *Hiroshima* by John Hersey, copyright 1946 and renewed 1974 by John Hersey. Used by permission of Alfred A. Knopf, a division of Random House, Inc. "I, Too" from *The Selected Poems of Langston Hughes* by Langston Hughes, copyright © 1994 by the Estate of Langston Hughes. Used by permission of Alfred A. Knopf, a division of Random House, Inc. From "The Woman Warrior" by Maxine Hong Kingston, copyright © 1975, 1976 by Maxine Hong Kingston. Used by permission of Alfred A. Knopf, a division of Random House, Inc.

Little, Brown and Company, Inc. "Aliceville" by Tony Earley from *Here We Are In Paradise*. Copyright © 1994 by Tony Earley. All rights reserved.

Liveright Publishing Corporation "Runagate Runagate" by Robert Hayden Copyright © 1966 by Robert Hayden, from *Collected Poems of Rober Hayden by Robert Hayden,* edited by Frederick Glaysher. Used by permission of Liveright Publishing Corporation. "Frederick Douglass". Copyright © 1966 by Robert Hayden, from *Collected Poems of Rober Hayden,* edited by Frederick Glaysher. Used by permission of Liveright Publishing Corporation.

Milkweed Editions "Museum Indians" by Susan Power from *Roofwalker*. © 2002, Text by Susan Power. All rights reserved.

Navarre Scott Momaday "from The Names" by N. Scott Momaday from *The Names*.

William Morris Agency "Gold Glade" by Robert Penn Warren from *Selected Poems*.

Jonathan Musere "African Proverbs: Uganda: The Bagada: "A small deed out of friendship . . ."" by Anonymous from *African Proverbs And Proverbial Names*. Copyright © 1999 by Ariko Publications. "African Proverbs: Uganda: The Bagada: "One who loves you, warns you . . ."" by Anonymous from *African Proverbs And Proverbial Names*. Copyright © 1999 by Ariko Publications. "African Proverbs: Uganda: The Bagada: "Words are easy, but friendship is difficult . . ."" by Anonymous from *African Proverbs And Proverbial Names*. Copyright © 1999 by Ariko Publications. "African Proverbs: Uganda: The Bagada: "Where there are no dogs . . ."" by Anonymous *from African Proverbs And Proverbial Names*. Copyright © 1999 by Ariko Publications. "African Proverbs: Uganda: The Bagada: "The one who has not made the journey . . ."" by Anonymous from *African Proverbs And Proverbial Names*. Copyright © 1999 by Ariko Publications.

New Directions Publishing Corporation "Fern Hill" by Dylan Thomas, from *The Poems of Dylan Thomas*. Copyright © 1945 by The Trustees for the Copyrights of Dylan Thomas. Reprinted by permission of New Directions Publishing Corp. "from A Few Don'ts (A Retrospect)" by Ezra Pound, from *The Literary Essays of Ezra Pound*. Copyright © 1935 by Ezra Pound. Reprinted by permission of New Directions Publishing Corp.

The New York Times Agency "Onomatopoeia" by William Safire from *You Could Look It Up*. Copyright © 1964 by Eve Merriam.

Newsweek Magazine "One Day, Now Broken in Two" by Anna Quindlen from *Newsweek*.

W.W. Norton & Company, Inc. "Who Burns for the Perfection of Paper" by Martin Espada from *City Of Coughing And Dead Radiators.* "In a Classroom" by Adrienne Rich from *Time's Power: Poems, 1985-1988.* "from Civil Disobedience" by Henry David Thoreau from *Walden And Civil Disobedience.* Copyright © 1966 by W.W. Norton & Company, Inc.

Naomi Shihab Nye "Mint Snowball" by Naomi Shihab Nye from. Reprinted by permission of the author.

Simon Ortiz "Hunger in New York City" by Simon Ortiz from *Going For The Rain.* Published by Harper & Row 1976.© 1976 by Simon J. Ortiz.

Penguin Books Ltd., London "from The Rig Veda: Creation Hymn" by Wendy Doniger O'Flaherty, translated by Wendy Doniger O'Flaherty from *The Rig Veda: An Anthology.* Copyright © 1981 Wendy Doniger O'Flaherty. "from The Rig Veda: Night" by Wendy Doniger O'Flaherty, translated by Wendy Doniger O'Flaherty from *The Rig Veda: An Anthology.* Copyright © 1981. Wendy Doniger O'Flaherty.

Peter Pauper Press, Inc. "African Proverbs: Ghana: The Ashanti: "If you are in hiding . . ."" by Anonymous from *African Proverbs.* Copyright © 1962 by the Peter Pauper Press, Inc. "African Proverbs: Ghana: The Ashanti: "No one tests the depth of a river . . ."" by Anonymous from *African Proverbs.* Copyright © 1962 by the Peter Pauper Press, Inc. "African Proverbs: Nigeria: The Yoruba: "The day on which one starts out . . ."" by Anonymous from *African Proverbs.* Copyright © 1962 by the Peter Pauper Press, Inc. "African Proverbs: Nigeria: The Yoruba: "He who is being carried does not realize . . ."" by Anonymous from *African Proverbs.* Copyright © 1962 by the Peter Pauper Press, Inc. "African Proverbs: Nigeria: The Yoruba: "Little is better than nothing."" by Anonymous from *African Proverbs.* Copyright © 1962 by the Peter Pauper Press, Inc. "African Proverbs: Ghana: The Ashanti: "Rain beats a leopard skin . . ."" by Anonymous from *African Proverbs.* Copyright © 1962 by the Peter Pauper Press, Inc. "African Proverbs: Tanzania and Kenya: The Masai: "Do not say the first thing . . ."" by Anonymous from *African Proverbs.* Copyright © 1962 by the Peter Pauper Press, Inc. "African Proverbs: Nigeria: The Yoruba: "Time destroys all things."" by Anonymous from *African Proverbs.* Copyright © 1962 by the Peter Pauper Press, Inc. "African Proverbs: Ghana: The Ashanti: "One falsehood . . ."" by Anonymous from *African Proverbs.* Copyright © 1962 by the Peter Pauper Press, Inc.

Plimoth Plantation "Plimoth Plantation" by Staff from *www.plimoth.org/index.html.*

Princeton University Press "From Walden" by Henry David Thoreau. Copyright © 1971 by Princeton University Press. All rights reserved. Used by permission of Princeton University Press.

Random House, Inc. "A Rose for Emily" by William Faulkner from *Collected Stories Of William Faulkner.* Copyright © 1934, 1950 by Random House, Inc. Copyright © 1039 through 1948 by William Faulkner. All rights reserved. "From Lives of the Poets" by E.L. Doctorow, copyright © 1984 by E.L. Doctorow. Used by permission of Random House, Inc.

Russell & Volkening, Inc. "Average Waves in Unprotected Waters" by Anne Tyler from *The New Yorker.* Copyright © 1977 by Anne Tyler. This story originally appeared in The New Yorker, February 28th, 1977. Reproduced by permission of Russell & Volkening as agents for the author.

Scribner "The Far and the Near" is reprinted with the permission of Scribner, a division of Simon & Schuster from *Death to Morning* by Thomas Wolfe. Copyright 1935 by Charles Scribner's Sons; copyright renewed © 1963 by Paul Gitlin. Audio permission from McIntosh & Otis.

Sterling Lord Literistic, Inc. "The Crisis, Number 1" by Thomas Paine from *CITIZEN TOM PAINE.* Copyright by Howard Fast. Used by permission of Sterling Lord Literistic, Inc.

Syracuse University Press "The Iroquois Constitution" from *Parker on the Iroquois: Iroquois Uses of Maize and Other Food Plants; The Code of Handsome Lake; The Seneca Prophet; The Constitution of the Five Nations* by Arthur C. Parker, edited by William N. Fenton (Syracuse University Press, Syracuse, NY, 1981). Copyright © 1968 by Syracuse University Press.

University of Nebraska Press " Crossing the Great Divide" by Meriweather Lewis. Reprinted from *The Journals of the Lewis and Clark Expedition, volume 5,* edited by Gary E. Moulton by permission of the University of Nebraska Press. Copyright © 1988 by the University of Nebraska Press.

University of North Carolina Press "To His Excellency, General Washington" by Phillis Wheatley from *The Poems Of Phillis Wheatley.* "An Hymn to the Evening" by Phillis Wheatley from *The Poems Of Phillis Wheatley.*

University of Texas Press "Sonnet 71" by Pablo Neruda translated by Stephen Tapscott from *100 Love Sonnets: Cien Sonetos De Amor.* Copyright © Pablo Neruda, 1959. Copyright © 1986 by the University of Texas Press. All rights reserved. Originally published as Cien sonetos de amor © Editorial Losada, S.A., Buenos Aires, 1960. "Sonnet 49" by Pablo Neruda translated by Stephen Tapscott from *100 Love Sonnets: Cien Sonetos De Amor.* Copyright © Pablo Neruda, 1959. Copyright © 1986 by the University of Texas Press. All rights reserved. Originally published as Cien sonetos de amor © Editorial Losada, S.A., Buenos Aires, 1960.

Viking Penguin, Inc. "From The Crucible" by Arthur Miller, copyright 1952, 1953, 1954, renewed © 1980, 1981, 1982 by Arthur Miller. Used by permission of Viking Penguin, a division of Penguin Putnam, Inc.

Wesleyan University Press "What For" by Garrett Kaoru Hongo from *Yellow Light.* Used by permission of Wesleyan University Press. "Camouflaging the Chimera" by Yusef Komunyakaa from *Neon Vernacular.* Used by permission of Wesleyan University Press. "For My Children" by Colleen McElroy from *What Madness Brought Me Here.* Used by permission of Wesleyan University Press. Copyright © 1990 by Colleen J. McElroy.

Witwatersrand University Press "African Proverbs: South Africa: The Zulu: "Do not speak of rhinoceros . . ."" by Anonymous from *Zulu Proverbs.* "African Proverbs: South Africa: The Zulu: "Eyes do not see all."" by Anonymous from *Zulu Proverbs.* "African Proverbs: South Africa: The Zulu: "No dew ever competed . . ."" by Anonymous from *Zulu Proverbs.* "African Proverbs: South Africa: The Zulu: "What has happened before . . ."" by Anonymous from *Zulu Proverbs.* "African Proverbs: South Africa: The Zulu: "It never dawns in the same way."" by Anonymous from *Zulu Proverbs.* "African Proverbs: South Africa: The Zulu: "The one offended never forgets . . ."" by Anonymous from *Zulu Proverbs.* "African Proverbs: South Africa: The Zulu: "You cannot chase two gazelles."" by Anonymous from *Zulu Proverbs.* "African Proverbs: South Africa: The Zulu: "There is no foot . . ."" by Anonymous from *Zulu Proverbs.* "African Proverbs: South Africa: The Zulu: "Look as you fell a tree."" by Anonymous from *Zulu Proverbs.* Copyright © 1954 by Witwatersrand University Press.

Yale University Press Excerpt from "Sinners in the Hands of an Angry God" *from The Sermons of Jonathan Edwards: A Reader* published by Yale University Press. Copyright © 1999 by Yale University Press.

Yale University Press "from Mary Chesnut's Civil War, edited by C. Vann Woodward. Copyright © 1981 by C. Vann Woodward, Sally Bland Metts, Barbara G. Carpenter, Sally Bland Johnson, and Katherine W. Herbert. All rights reserved. Reproduced by permission of the publisher, Yale University Press.

Note: Every effort has been made to locate the copyright owner of material reproduced on this audio component. Omissions brought to our attention will be corrected in subsequent editions.

CREDITS

Cover: *Flag on Orange Field,* 1957, oil on canvas, Johns, Jasper (b:1930)/Ludwig Museum, Cologne, Germany, Lauros/ Giraudon;/ www.bridgeman.co.uk/Cover art © Jasper Johns/Licensed by VAGA, New York, NY **1:** *World Map,* 1630, Jan Jansson, The Huntington Library, Art Collections and Botanical Gardens, San Marino, CA;
2: (t.): Astrolabe, Museum fur Kunst und Gewerbe, Hamburg; **(m.):** Photo by Rebecca Dallinger; Courtesy of Susan Power; **(b.):** Marilyn "Angel" Wynn/Nativestock.com; **4: (t.):** Astrolabe, Museum fur Kunst und Gewerbe, Hamburg; **(m.l.):** CORBIS–Bettmann; **(m.m.):** John Smith (detail), National Portrait Gallery, Smithsonian Institution, Washington, D.C./Art Resource, NY; **(m.r.):** The Granger Collection, New York; **(b.):** Victoria & Albert Museum, London/Art Resource, NY;
5: (t.l.): North Wind Picture Archives; **(t.r.):** The Granger Collection, New York; **(b.):** Corel Professional Photos CD–ROM™; **6:** Astrolabe, Museum fur Kunst und Gewerbe, Hamburg; **7:** North Wind Picture Archives; **8: (t.):** Astrolabe, Museum fur Kunst und Gewerbe, Hamburg; **(b.):** Colonial Williamsburg Foundation; **10: (t.):** Astrolabe, Museum fur Kunst und Gewerbe, Hamburg; **(b.):** The Granger Collection, New York; **11:** The Bettmann Archive; **12: (t.):** Astrolabe, Museum fur Kunst und Gewerbe, Hamburg; **(b.):** Corel Professional Photos CD–ROM™;
13: North Wind Picture Archives; **15:** *Oneida Chieftain Shikellamy,* Unknown American, c.1820, 45 1/2" x 32", oil on canvas, Philadelphia Museum of Ar**(t.):** The Collection of Edgar William and Bernice Chrysler Garbisch; **16:** Silver Burdett Ginn;
18: Nicole Galeazzi/Omni–Photo Communications, Inc.;
22: *Dreamwalker,* Nancy Wood Taber, colored pencil, Courtesy of the artist; **27:** *Red Jacket,* George Catlin, From the Collection of Gilcrease Museum, Tulsa; **32: (t.):** Photo by Rebecca Dallinger; Courtesy of Susan Power; **(b.):** Viviane Moos/CORBIS; **34:** Marilyn "Angel" Wynn/Nativestock.com; **35:** inset Courtesy of the Library of Congress; **36:** Joseph Sohm; Visions of America/CORBIS; **37:** *The Old Guitarist,* 1903, Pablo Picasso, Spanish, 1881–1973, oil on panel 122.9 x 82.6 cm, Helen Birch Bartlett Memorial Collection, 1926.253. Reproduction, The Art Institute of Chicago, ©2004Estate of Pablo Picasso/Artists Rights Society (ARS), New York; **38:** Buffalo Bill Historical Center; Cody, Wyoming; Gift of Hon. and Mrs. William Henry Harrison; NA. 202.70; **42–43:** Corel Professional Photos CD–ROM™; **44:** Painting of Cabeza de Vaca, Esteban and their companions among various Texas Indian tribes, Tom Mirrat, The Institute of Texan Cultures, San Antonio, Texas; **47:** Jeff Greenberg/Photo Researchers, Inc.; **52–53:** © Matthias Kulka/CORBIS; **54:** © Otto Rogge/Stock Photos/CORBIS; **55:** The Bridgeman Art Library, London/New York; **56:** John Chase/Dorling Kindersley. © Museum of London; **58:** Erich Lessing/Art Resource, NY; **60:** Astrolabe, Museum fur Kunst und Gewerbe, Hamburg; **61:** CORBIS–Bettmann; **66: (t.):** Astrolabe, Museum fur Kunst und Gewerbe, Hamburg; **(b.):** Peabody Museum of Archaeology and Ethnology, Harvard University; **67:** The Rosenbach Museum & Library; **68: (l.):** *John Smith* (detail), National Portrait Gallery, Smithsonian Institution, Washington, D.C./Art Resource, NY; **(r.):** CORBIS–Bettmann; **70:** *The First Day at Jamestown, 14th May 1607,* from "The Romance and Tragedy of Pioneer Life" by Augustus L. Mason, 1883, William Ludlow Sheppard/Bridgeman Art Library, London/New York; **72:** Print Collection, Miriam and Ira D. Wallach Division of Art, Prints and Photographs, The New York Public Library, Astor, Lenox and Tilden Foundations; **74:** Architect of the Capitol;
77: *The Coming of the Mayflower,* N.C. Wyeth, from the Collection of Metropolitan Life Insurance Company, New York City, photograph by Malcolm Varon; **78:** *The Mayflower in Plymouth Harbor,* William Halsall, Burstein Collection/CORBIS; **81:** Cary Wolinsky/Stock, Boston;
82: The Granger Collection, New York; **91:** *Pilgrims Going to Church,* George Henry Boughton, Collection of The New-York Historical Society; **92:** Anne Bradstreet, *The Tenth Muse Lately Sprung Up in America,* Ladonna Gulley Warrick, Courtesy of the artist; **94:** Crewel Work Chair Seat Cover, Gift of Samuel Bradstreet, Courtesy, Museum of Fine Arts, Boston. Reproduced with permission. ©2002 Museum of Fine Arts, Boston. All Rights Reserved. 19.602; **100:** CORBIS–Bettmann; **103:** *The Puritan,* c. 1898, Frank E. Schoonover, Oil on canvas, Collection of The Brandywine River Museum, Gift of Mr. and Mrs. Jacob J. Foster, 1981. ©2002 Brandywine Conservancy; **112:** istockphoto.com;
124–125: *Washington Crossing the Delaware* (copy after the Emmanuel Leutze painting), Eastman Johnson, Private Collection/Art Resource, NY; **126: (t.):** Astrolabe, Museum fur Kunst und Gewerbe, Hamburg; **(b.):** Prentice Hall; **127:** Bettmann/CORBIS; **128: (t.):** Astrolabe, Museum fur Kunst und Gewerbe, Hamburg; **(m.l.):** The Granger Collection, New York; **(m.m.):** The Granger Collection, New York; **(m.r.):** The Granger Collection, New York; **(b.):** Independence National Historical Park; **129:** all The Granger Collection, New York;
131: Courtesy, American Antiquarian Society; **132: (t.):** Astrolabe, Museum fur Kunst und Gewerbe, Hamburg; **(b.):** Corel Professional Photos CD–ROM™; **133:** ©Archive Photos; **134: (t.):** Astrolabe, Museum fur Kunst und Gewerbe, Hamburg; **(b.):** Corel Professional Photos CD–ROM™; **135:** Courtesy of the Library of Congress;
136: Astrolabe, Museum fur Kunst und Gewerbe, Hamburg; **137: (t.):** Corel Professional Photos CD–ROM™; **(b.):** *George Washington* (Vaughan portrait), Gilbert Stuart, Photograph ©Board of Trustees, National Gallery of Art, Washington, Andrew Mellon Collection;
138: ©Archive Photos; **139: (m.):** *Miss Liberty,* Abby Aldrich Rockefeller Folk Art Center, Williamsburg, VA; **140:** *Benjamin Franklin* (detail), c.1790, Pierre Michel Alix, National Portrait Gallery, Smithsonian Institution, Washington, D.C./Art Resource, New York; **142:** *Quaker Meeting,* Unidentified Artist, Courtesy, Museum of Fine Arts, Boston. Reproduced with permission. ©2002 Museum of Fine Arts, Boston. All Rights Reserved. 64.456; **144:** ©British Museum; **146 & 148:** The Granger Collection, New York; **154: (t.):** Astrolabe, Museum fur Kunst und Gewerbe, Hamburg; **(b.):** ©Bettmann/CORBIS; **156:** Prentice Hall; **157:** The Art Archive/Maritime Museum Kronborg Castle Denmark/Dagli Orti; **158:** Royal Albert Memorial Museum, Exeter, Devon, UK/The Bridgeman Art Library, London/New York;
160: National Maritime Museum, London; **162:** Courtesy of the Library of Congress; **168: (l.):** The Granger Collection, New York; **(r.):** The Granger Collection, New York; **170:** Corel Professional Photos CD–ROM™; **171:** Yale University Art Gallery; **172: (l.):** Corel Professional Photos CD–ROM™; **(r.):** Ron Watts/CORBIS;
174: *Recruiting for the Continental Army,* William **(t.):** Ranney, Munson–Williams–Proctor Institute Museum of Art, Utica, New York;
180: Bettmann/CORBIS; **180–181:** © Matthias Kulka/CORBIS;
182–183: Corel Professional Photos CD–ROM™; **194:** Werner Forman/Art Resource, NY; **200: (l.):** *Patrick Henry* (detail), c.1835, James Barton Longacre after Lawrence Sully, The National Portrait Gallery, Smithsonian Institution, Washington, D.C./Art Resource, New York; **(r.):** Bettmann/CORBIS; **202:** *Patrick Henry Before the Virginia House of Burgesses 1851,* Peter F. Rothermel, Red Hill, The Patrick Henry National Memorial, Brookneal, Virginia; **205:** Courtesy of the Library of Congress; **207:** The American Philosophical Society; **208:** *Benjamin Franklin* (1706–90) – Overseeing the Printing of Poor Richard's Almanack, Norman Rockwell, Lawrence Steigrad Fine Arts, New York/The Bridgeman Art Library, London/New York; **212:** *George Washington, standing on the platform, Penn State Capitol, Harrisburg,* Photo: Brian K. Foster. Courtesy Senate Communications; **213:** 18th c. New England needlework, Colonial Williamsburg Foundation;
214: (l.): The Granger Collection, New York; **(r.):** The Granger Collection, New York; **216:** *Building the First White House,* 1930, N.C. Wyeth, Copyrighted © by the White House Historical Association, photo by the National Geographical Society; **220:** Independence (Squire Jack Porter), 1858, Frank Blackwell Mayer, National Museum of American Art, Smithsonian Institution, Bequest of Harriet Lane Johnson, Art Resource, New York; **228:** Cleve Bryant/PhotoEdit Inc.;
231: Prentice Hall; **244: (t.):** Astrolabe, Museum fur Kunst und Gewerbe, Hamburg; **(m.l.):** Seltzer, Lewis' First Glimpse of the Rockies, The Thomas Gilcrease Institute of Art Tulsa, Oklahoma; **(m.m.):** The Granger Collection, New York; **(m.r.):** Samuel S. Spaulding Collection, Buffalo and Erie County Historcal Society; **(b.l.):** Giraudon/Art Resource, NY; **(b.r.):** Adam Woolfit/CORBIS; **245: (t.):** Image Select/Art Resource, NY; **(m.):** The Granger Collection, New York; **(b.):** Christie's Images/SuperStock; **248:** The Granger Collection, New York; **250:** The National Portrait Gallery, Smithsonian Institution/Art Resource, NY; **253:** American Steel Foundries; **254:** Copyrighted by the White House Historical Association; Photograph by the National Geographic Society; **256:** *Washington Irving* (detail): Daniel Huntington, National Portrait Gallery, Smithsonian Institution, Washington, D.C./Art Resource, New York; **261:** John Quidor, American, 1801–1881, *The Devil and Tom Walker,* 1856. Oil on canvas, 68.8cm x 86.6cm. © The Cleveland

Museum of Art, 2002. Mr. and Mrs. William H. Marlatt Fund, 1967.18; **262:** Walking stick, King Georges County, Virginia, 1846, carved wood with ink decoration, 37 x 2 inches in diameter, Abby Aldrich Rockefeller Folk Art Center, Williamsburg VA; **263:** Yale University Art Gallery, New Haven. The Mabel Brady Garvan Collection; 264: Leonard Lee Rue III/Stock, Boston; **266:** Index Stock Photography, Inc.; **267: (l.):** Corel Professional Photos CD–ROM™; **(r.):** Ron Watts/CORBIS; **272: (t.l.):** *Henry Wadsworth Longfellow* (detail), Thomas B. Read, The National Portrait Gallery, Smithsonian Institution, Washington, D.C./Art Resource, New York; **(t.r.):** *Samuel F.B. Morse,* William Cullen Bryant, 1828–1829 Oil on Canvas, 29 1/2 x 34 3/4 in. National Academy Museum, New York (892–P); **(b.):** The Granger Collection, New York; **273: (t.):** *John Greenleaf Whittier* (detail), 1881, William Notman, The National Portrait Gallery, Smithsonian Institution, Washington, D.C./Art Resource, New York; **(b.):** The Granger Collection, New York; **275:** *Seashore in Normandy,* 1893, Maximilien Luce, Erich Lessing/Art Resource, NY; **276:** *Seashore in Normandy,* 1893, Maximilien Luce, Erich Lessing/Art Resource, NY; **277:** *Kindred Spirits,* Asher B. Durand, New York Public Library, Astor, Lenox and Tilden Foundations; **280:** Charles Krups/AP/Wide World Photos; **282–283:** *Old Holley House, Cos Cob,* John Henry Twachtman, Cincinnati Art Museum, John J. Emery Endowment; **296: (l.):** The Granger Collection, New York; **(r.):** *John Wesley Powell* (detail), Edmund Clarence Messer, National Portrait Gallery, Smithsonian Institution, Washington, D.C./Art Resource, NY; **298: (l.):** *Lewis and Clark with Sacajawea at the Great Falls of the Missouri,* Olaf Seltzer, #0137.871. The Thomas Gilcrease Institute of Art, Tulsa, Oklahoma; **(r.):**. *Draught of the Falls and Portage of the Missouri River (Clark's map of the Missouri River),* Missouri Historical Society, Clark Papers, Voorhis #1, 2 July 1805, ink on paper, L/A 464b.; **299:** *White Salmon Trout,* ink on paper (Clark's drawing of salmon from his journal) Missouri Historical Society MHS Archives, entry before 17 March 1806. L/A #407b; **301:** Corel Professional Photos CD–ROM™; **303:** *Grand Canyon with Rainbow,* 1912, Thomas Moran, oil on canvas, 25x30" (63.5 x 76.3cm) Collection of the Fine Arts Museums of San Francisco, Gift of Mr. and Mrs. Robert Gill through the Patrons of Art and Music, (1981.89); **310:** CORBIS–Bettmann; **313:** "I at length...," Edgar Allen Poe's Tales of Mystery and Imagination (London: George G. Harrap, 1935), Arthur Rackham, Print Collection, Miriam and Ira D. Wallach Division of Art, Prints and Photographs, The New York Public Library; Astor, Lenox and Tilden Foundations; **316: (l.):** Corel Professional Photos CD–ROM™; **(r.):** Ron Watts/CORBIS; **320–321:** Steve Mohlenkamp/ Index Stock Photography, Inc.; **327:** ©2000 The Munch Museum/The Munch–Ellingsen Group/Artists Rights Society (ARS), New York; **332:** *The Raven,* 1845, Edmund Dulac, The Granger Collection, New York; **338:** *Nathaniel Hawthorne* (detail), 1862, Emanuel Gottlieb Leutze, The National Portrait Gallery, Smithsonian Institution, Washington, D.C./Art Resource, New York; **341:** New York State Historical Association, Cooperstown, New York; **344: (l.):** Corel Professional Photos CD–ROM™; **(r.):** Ron Watts/CORBIS; **348:** *Cemetery,* Peter McIntyre, Courtesy of the artist; **356:** The Granger Collection, New York; **360:** *Captain Ahab on the deck of the Pequod,* 1930, pen and ink drawing, The Granger Collection, New York; **361:** Stock Newport, Inc.; **363:** CORBIS; **365:** *Moby–Dick,* 1930, pen and ink drawing, The Granger Collection, New York; **366:** The Whaling Museum; **368:** *Moby–Dick,* 1930, pen and ink drawing, The Granger Collection, New York; **373:** Culver Pictures, Inc.; **388:** *Ralph Waldo Emerson* (detail), Frederick Gutekunst/National Portrait Gallery, Smithsonian Institution, Washington ,D.C./Art Resource, NY; **390–391:** *Sunset,* Frederick Edwin Church, Munson–Williams–Proctor Institute Museum of Art, Utica, New York; **393:** Tom Bean/CORBIS; **395:** Leonard Harris/Stock, Boston; **396–397:** Frank Whitney/The Image Bank; **404:** Getty Images; **406:** Owen Franken/PNI; **411:** Burstein Collection/CORBIS; **412–413:** ©The Stock Market/Dan McCoy; **414:** ©Lee Snider; Lee Snider/CORBIS; **424:** Amherst College Archives and Special Collections, by permission of the Trustees of Amherst College; **426:** *Waiting Outside No. 12,* Anonymous, Crane Kalman Gallery; **428:** Room With a Balcony, Adolph von Menzel, Staatliche Museen Preubischer Kulturbesitz, Nationgalerie, Berlin; **430:** eStock Photography, LLC; **432:** Frederic Edwin Church, American, 1826–1900. *Twilight in the Wilderness,* 1860. Oil on canvas, 101.6 x 162.6 cm. © The Cleveland Museum of Art, 2002, Mr. and Mrs. William H. Marlett Fund, 1965.233; 438: The Granger Collection, New York; **442:** Courtesy of the Library of Congress; **446:** *The Lawrence Tree,* 1929, Georgia O'Keeffe, Wadsworth Atheneum, Hartford, C **(t.):** The Ella Gallup Sumner and Mary Catlin Sumner Collection, ©1998 The Georgia O'Keeffe Foundation/Artists Rights Society (ARS), New York; **449:** *The Reaper,* c.1881, Louis C. Tiffany, oil on canvas, National Academy of Design, New York City; **456:** Cleve Bryant/PhotoEdit Inc.; **459:** Prentice Hall; **472: (t.):** Astrolabe, Museum fur Kunst und Gewerbe, Hamburg; **(b.l.):** The Granger Collection, New York; **(b.m.):** The Granger Collection, New York; **(b.r.):** The Granger Collection, New York; **473: (t.l.):** The Granger Collection, New York; **(t.r.):** The Granger Collection, New York; **(m.):** The Granger Collection, New York; **(b.):** CORBIS–Bettmann; **474:** CORBIS–Bettmann; **475: (l.):** Courtesy of the Library of Congress; **(r.):** Courtesy of the Library of Congress; **477:** Nebraska State Historical Society; **481:** *Six O'Clock, Winter,* 1912, John Sloan, The Phillips Collection **482:** *Samuel Longhorne Clemens (Mark Twain),* (detail), 1935, Frank Edwin Larson, National Portrait Gallery, Smithsonian Institution, Washington, D.C./Art Resource, New York; **484: (l.):** CORBIS–Bettmann; **(r.):** Center for American Music. Stephen Foster Memorial, University of Pittsburgh; **486:** Courtesy of the Library of Congress; **489:** Courtesy National Archives; **490:** Museum of the Confederacy, Richmond, Virginia; **491:** *Young Soldier: Separate Study of a Soldier Giving Water to a Wounded Companion,* (detail) 1861, Winslow Homer, Oil, gouache, black crayon on canvas, 36x17.5 cm., United States, 1836–1910, Cooper–Hewitt, National Museum of Design, Smithsonian Institution, Gift of Charles Savage Homer, Jr., 1912–12–110, Photo by Ken Pelka, Courtesy of Art Resource, New York; **498:** Courtesy of the Library of Congress; **504**: *Frederick Douglass* (detail), c.1844, Attributed to Elisha Hammond, The National Portrait Gallery, Smithsonian Institution, Washington, D.C./Art Resource, New York; **506:** *The Chimney Corner,* 1863, Eastman Johnson, oil on cardboard, 15 1/2 x 13 in., Munson–Williams– Proctor Institute Museum of Art, Utica, New York; Gift of Edmund G. Munson, Jr.; **508:** *A Home on the Mississippi,* 1871, Currier & Ives, The Museum of the City of New York, Harry T Peters Collection; **510: (l.):** Corel Professional Photos CD–ROM™; **(r.):** Ron Watts/CORBIS; **516:** CORBIS–Bettmann; **518:** Superstock; **519:** The Kobal Collection; **530: (l.):** *Portrait of Abraham Lincoln* (detail), William Willard, National Portrait Gallery, Smithsonian Institution, Washington, D.C./Art Resource, New York; r. *Robert E. Lee* (detail), 1864–1865, Edward Caledon Bruce, The National Portrait Gallery, Smithsonian Institution, Washington, D.C./Art Resource, New York; **533:** CORBIS; **535:** Buddy Mays/CORBIS; **548 & 551:** Courtesy of the Library of Congress; **553: (l.):** Corel Professional Photos CD–ROM™; **(r.):** Ron Watts/CORBIS; **556:** Andre Jenny/Focus Group/PictureQuest; **558 & 559:** The Granger Collection, New York; **561:** Bettmann/ CORBIS; **574:** *Samuel Longhorne Clemens (Mark Twain),* (detail), 1935, Frank Edwin Larson, National Portrait Gallery, Smithsonian Institution, Washington, D.C./Art Resource, New York; **576:** *Paddle Steamboat Mississippi,* Shelburne Museum, Shelburne, Vermont, Photo by Ken Burris; **578:** Courtesy of the Library of Congress **581:** *Mark Twain (Samuel L. Clemens) Riding the Celebrated Jumping Frog* – an English caricature, 1872, Frederic Waddy, The Granger Collection, New York; **583:** The Granger Collection, New York; **584:** ©Craig K. Lorenz/ Photo Researchers, Inc.; **590:** The Granger Collection, New York; **592:** *Edge of Town,* Charles Ephraim Burchfield, The Nelson–Atkins Museum of Art, Kansas City, Missouri; **594:** Corel Professional Photos CD–ROM™; **596:** Ron Watts/CORBIS; **598:** Esbin/Anderson/ Omni–Photo Communications, Inc.; **606:** *Chief Joseph* (detail), 1878, Cyrenius Hall, National Portrait Gallery, Smithsonian Institution, Washington, D.C./Art Resource, New York; **608 & 612:** Kansas State Historical Society; **614:** National Museum of American History, Smithsonian Institution; **618:** CORBIS–Bettmann; **620:** Wayne Lynch/DRK Photo; **623 & 626:** Corel Professional Photos CD–ROM™; **629:** Annie Griffiths/DRK Photo; **630–631:** CORBIS; **632:** Niebrugge Images; **640:** Photograph courtesy Newberry Library, Chicago; **642–643:** *Afternoon in Piedmont,* (Elsie at the Window), c.1911, Xavier Martínez, Collection of The Oakland Museum of California, Gift of Dr. William S. Porter; **644:** Corel Professional Photos CD–ROM™; **650:** The Granger Collection, New York; **652:** Stock Montage, Inc.; **658: (l.):** *Edwin Arlington Robinson* (detail), 1933, Thomas Richard Hood, National Portrait Gallery, Smithsonian Institution, Washington, D.C./Art Resource, New York; **(r.):** *Edgar Lee Masters* (detail), 1946, Francis J.

Quirk, National Portrait Gallery, Smithsonian Institution, Washington, D.C./Art Resource, New York; **660:** Horst Oesterwinter/International Stock Photography, Ltd.; **662:** *THE THINKER (Portrait of Louis N. Kenton, 1900),* Thomas Eakins, The Metropolitan Museum of Art, John Stewart Kennedy Fund, 1917. (17.172) Photograph © 2001 The Metropolitan Museum of Art; **664:** Joel Greenstein/Omni–Photo Communications, Inc.; **668:** CORBIS–Bettmann; **670:** George Schreiber (1904–1977), *From Arkansas,* 1939, oil on canvas, Sheldon Swope Art Museum, Terre Haute, Indiana; **674:** Robbie Jack/CORBIS; **676:** The Granger Collection, New York; 684: Jonathan Nourok/PhotoEdit Inc.; **687:** Prentice Hall; **714:** *T. S. Elliot* (detail), 1888–1965, Sir Gerald Kelly, National Portrait Gallery, Smithsonian Institution, Art Resource, New York; **718:** Corel Professional Photos CD–ROM™; **724: (l.):** The Granger Collection, New York; **(r.):** *William Carlos Williams* (detail), The National Portrait Gallery, Smithsonian Institution, Washington, D.C./Art Resource, NY; **725:** CORBIS–Bettmann; **728:** The Granger Collection, New York; **731:** Zha Shibiao, Chinese, 1615–1698, Qing dynasty. Shibiao Waiting for the Moon from Landscape Album in Various Styles, 1684. Album of twelve leaves, ink or ink and color on paper; each 29.9 x 39.4 cm. © The Cleveland Museum of Art, 2002, Gift of Mr. and Mrs. Severance A. Millikin, 1955.37; **733:** *The Figure 5 in Gold,* 1928, Charles Demuth, oil on composition board. H. 36 in. W. 29–3/4 in. (91.4 x 75.6 cm) Signed (lower left): C.D. Inscribed (bottom center): W.C.W. (William Carlos Williams), The Metropolitan Museum of Art, Alfred Steiglitz Collection, 1949. (49.59.1). Photograph © 1986 The Metropolitan Museum of Art; **735:** Adam Jones/Photo Researchers, Inc.; **736:** *Overhanging Cloud in July,* Charles Burchfield, Collection of Whitney Museum of American Art. Purchase, with funds from the Friends of the Whitney Museum of American Art (60.23). Photography Copyright © 2000: Whitney Museum of American Art; **740:** F. Scott Fitzgerald (detail), David Silvette, The National Portrait Gallery, Smithsonian Institution, Washington, D.C./Art Resource, New York; **742:** Corel Professional Photos CD–ROM™; **746–747:** *Golf Course– California,* 1917, George Wesley Bellows, Oil on canvas, 30 x38 inches, Collection Cincinnati Art Museum, The Edwin and Virginia Irwin Memorial, 1966.6; **748:** Digital Imagery ©Copyright 2001 PhotoDisc, Inc.; **752:** *The Morning Sun,* c. 1920, o/c, 50 x 40 ins., Pauline Palmer, Collection Rockford Art Museum, Gift of the Friends of American Art, 1922; **754:** Bettmann/CORBIS; **756:** Digital Imagery ©Copyright 2001 PhotoDisc, Inc.; **758: (l.):** Corel Professional Photos CD–ROM™; **(r.):** Ron Watts/CORBIS; **764:** UPI/CORBIS–Bettmann; **766:** ©The Stock Market/Milt/Patti Putnam; **772:** Bettmann/CORBIS; **774:** *Remember Now the Days of Thy Youth,* 1950, Paul Starrett Sample, Oil on canvas, 34 x 48 inches, Hood Museum of Art, Dartmouth College, Hanover, NH; Gift of Frank L. Harrington, class of 1954; **777:** *The Turret Lathe Operator* (J.G. Cherry series), 1925, Grant Wood, oil on canvas 18" x 24" Cedar Rapids Museum of Art, Cedar Rapids, Iowa, Gift of the Cherry Burrell Charitable Foundation Collection. 75.5.8, ©Estate of Grant Wood/Licensed by VAGA, New York, NY; **782:** Bettmann/CORBIS; **784:** *Stone City, Iowa,* 1930, Grant Wood, Joslyn Art Museum, Omaha, Nebraska, ©Estate of Grant Wood/ Licensed by VAGA, New York, NY; **787: (l.):** Corel Professional Photos CD–ROM™; **(r.):** Ron Watts/CORBIS; **792: (t.l.):** The Granger Collection, New York; **(t.r.):** Corbis–Bettman; **(b.):** AP/Wide World Photos; 795: Silver Burdett Ginn; **796 & 797:** Index Stock Photography, Inc.; **798:** *Untitled,* 1964, Alexander Calder, (one of seven lithographs in series), 19 1/2 x 25 1/2" Solomon R. Guggenheim Museum, New York, Gift of the artist, 1965, Photo by David Heald, © The Solomon R. Guggenheim Foundation, New York, ©1998 Estate of Alexander Calder/Artists Rights Society (ARS), New York; **806: (l.):** Larry Burrows/Life Magazine © Time Warner Inc.; **(r.):** Bettmann/ CORBIS; **807:** Thomas Victor; **809:** American Red Cross; **811:** Verlog Suddeutscher–Bilderdienst; **812:** ©FPG International LLC; **813:** American Red Cross; **816:** © Ryan Beyer/Stone; **820:** *Miz Emily,* Joseph Holston, 24" x16", Courtesy of Joseph Holston (www.holstonar**(t.):**com); **824–825:** *Georgia Red Clay,* 1946, Nell Choate Jones, oil on canvas, 25 x 30 inches, 1989.01.094, Morris Museum of Art, Augusta, Georgia; **834–835:** P.J. Griffiths/Magnum Photos, Inc.; **838:** Time Life Pictures/ Getty Images ; **840:** Stock Montage, Inc.; **842:** Corel Professional Photos CD–ROM™; **846:** Getty Images; **849:** *Garden of Memories,* 1917, Charles Burchfield, The Museum of Modern Art, New York. Gift of Abby Aldrich Rockefeller (by exchange). Digital Image © The Museum of Modern Art/Licensed by SCALA/Art Resource, NY; **850:** ©Bettmann/ CORBIS; **854:** ©1993 J. Fishkin. All Rights Reserved; **860:** Time Life Pictures/Getty Images ; **864:** Collection of the Prentice and Paul Sack Photographic Trust of the San Francisco Museum of Modern Art; **865: (l.):** Corel Professional Photos CD–ROM™; **(r.):** Ron Watts/ CORBIS; **867:** *Woman by a Window,* Gustav Vermehren Snark/Art Resource, NY; **868:** 66.1522 Thomas Eakins, *Mrs. Thomas Eakins,* ca. 1899. Oil on Canvas, 20 1/8 x 16 1/8 Hirshhorn Museum/Smithsonian Institution; **871:** Elizabeth A. Whiting; Elizabeth Whiting & Associates/ CORBIS; **872:** Markus Amon/Getty Images; **873:** Elizabeth Barakah Hodges/SuperStock; **880:** CORBIS; **882–883:** Corel Professional Photos CD–ROM™; **885:** Corel Professional Photos CD–ROM™; **886:** Dewitt Jones/Woodfin Camp & Associates; **888:** Corel Professional Photos CD–ROM™; **892:** Ellis Herwig/PNI; **896: (l.):** CORBIS–Bettmann; **(r.):** AP/Wide World Photos; **898–901:** My Life and Hard Times Copyright ©1933 by James Thurber. Copyright © renewed 1961 by James Thurber. Reprinted by arrangement with Rosemary A. Thurber and The Barbara Hogenson Agency; **903:** Culver Pictures, Inc.; **912:** Courtesy of the Estate of Carl Van Vechten, Joseph Solomon, EXECUTOR, The National Portrait Gallery, Smithsonian Institution, Washington, D.C./Art Resource, New York; **914:** ©Hulton Getty/Archive Photos; **917:** *School Bell Time,* 1978 From the Profile/ Part I: The Twenties series (Mecklenburg County), Romare Bearden, 29 1/4 x 41" Collection: Kingsborough Community College, The City University of New York; ©Romare Bearden Foundation/Licensed by VAGA, New York, NY; **919: (l.):** Corel Professional Photos CD–ROM™; **(r.):** Ron Watts/CORBIS; **924: (l.):** *Langston Hughes* (detail), c.1925, Winold Reiss, The National Portrait Gallery, Smithsonian Institution, Washington, D.C./Art Resource, New York; **(r.):** The Granger Collection, New York; **927:** Aaron Douglas, *Into Bondage,* 1936, 60 3/8 x 60 1/2, oil on canvas. In the collection of the Corcoran Gallery of Art, Washington, DC. Museum Purchase and Partial Gift of Thurlow Tibbs Jr., The Evans–Tibbs Collection. 1996.9; **928:** *Nobody Around Here* Calls Me Citizen, 1943, Robert Gwathmey, oil on canvas, H. 14–1/4" x W. 17" Collection Frederick R. Weisman Art Museum at the University of Minnesota, Minneapolis, Bequest of Hudson Walker from the Ione and Hudson Walker Collection. ©Estate of Robert Gwathmey/Licensed by VAGA, New York, NY; **930:** *Girls Skipping,* 1949, Hale Woodruff, oil on canvas, 24" x 32 , Private Collection. Courtesy of Michael Rosenfeld Gallery, New York; **932:** Michael Skott/Getty Images; **936: (t.):** *Countee Cullen* (detail), c.1925, Winold Reiss, The National Portrait Gallery, Smithsonian Institution, Washington, D.C./Art Resource, New York; **(m.):** *Jean Toomer* (detail), c.1925, Winold Reiss, Gift of Laurence A. Fleischman and Howard Garfinkle with a matching grant from the National Endowment of the Arts, National Portrait Gallery, Smithsonian Institution, Washington, D.C./Art Resource, New York; **(b.):** UPI/CORBIS–Bettmann; **939:** *Hoeing,* 1934, Robert Gwathmey, Oil on canvas, 40 by 60 1/4 (101.6 by 153), Carnegie Institute Museum of Art, Pittsburgh, Pennsylvania, Patrons Art Fund, 44.3. Photograph by Richard Stoner, ©Estate of Robert Gwathmey/Licensed by VAGA, New York, NY; **940:** Corel Professional Photos CD–ROM™; **952:** David Young–Wolff/PhotoEdit Inc.; **968: (t.l.):** Nancy Crampton; **(t.r.):** The Granger Collection, New York; **(m.l.):** Jay Leviton/Black Star; **(m.r.):** Peter Garfield/Folio, Inc; **(b.):** UPI/CORBIS–Bettmann; **969: (l.):** ©1985 Peter Marlow/ Magnum Photots, Inc.; **(m.):** ©Larry Downing/Woodfin Camp & Associates; **(r.):** ©Dan Groshong/CORBIS Sygma; **970:** The Granger Collection, New York; **975:** *Down 18th Street,* 1980, Wayne Thiebaud, Hirshorn Museum and Sculpture Garden, Smithsonian Institution, Museum Purchase with Funds Donated by Edward R. Downe, Jr., 1980. Photography by Ricardo Blanc; **977:** ©Mark Bolster/International Stock Photography, Ltd.; **978:** Digital Imagery ©Copyright 2001 PhotoDisc, Inc.; **980:** Flannery O'Connor Collection, Ina Dillard Russel Library, Georgia College; **982:** *Deep Fork Overlook,* Joan Marron–LaRue, Courtesy of the artist; **987:** Black Walnuts, Joseph Pollet, Collection of Whitney Museum of American Ar**(t.):** Purchase and gift of Gertrude Vanderbilt Whitney, by exchange (52.30). Photograph Copyright © 2000: Whitney Museum of American Art; **991: (l.):** Corel Professional Photos CD–ROM™; **(r.):**. Ron Watts/CORBIS; **996:** Nancy Crampton; **998:** Culver Pictures, Inc.; **1002: (l.):** Corel Professional Photos CD–ROM™; **(r.):**. Ron Watts/ CORBIS; **1004:** ©The Stock

Market/Shiki; **1010:** Andrea Renault/ Globe Photos; **1013:** *Laurence Typing,* 1952, Fairfield Porter, oil on canvas 40 x 30 1/8 inches, The Parrish Art Museum, Southampton, New York, Gift of the Estate of Fairfield Porter; **1015:** Digital Imagery ©Copyright 2001 PhotoDisc, Inc.; **1016:** Courtesy of Rebecca Graziano; **1018:** *Letters and Postcards,* Reid Christman, 24" x 18" (61cm x 45.7cm) Fredrix linen canvas; **1022–1023:** Courtesy of General Motors; **1028:** Miriam Berkley; **1030:** *Sunrise. Pinkfeet against the Cumbrian Hills,* 1994, Julian Novrol/Private Collection/The Bridgeman Art Library, London/New York; **1032–1033:** The State Russian Museum/CORBIS; 1037: Courtesy of the Library of Congress; **1038–1039:** CORBIS; **1040–1041:** Private Collection, David Findlay, Jr. Fine Art, NYC/The Bridgeman Art Library, London/New York; **1043:** Pinkfooted Geese Over the Roost, 2000, Julian Novrol/Private Collection/The Bridgeman Art Library, London/New York; **1044:** Sunrise. Pinkfeet against the Cumbrian Hills, 1994, Julian Novrol/Private Collection/The Bridgeman Art Library, London/New York; **1048: (t.):** Robert Penn Warren (detail), 1935, Conrad A. Albrizio, The National Portrait Gallery, Smithsonian Institution, Washington, D.C./Art Resource, New York; **(m.):** Kit Stafford; **(b.):** AP/Wide World Photos; **1050 & 1052:** Corel Professional Photos CD–ROM™; **1053:** Tim Lynch/Stock, Boston; **1060:** Diana Walker; **1062:** © Fred Charles/ Stone; **1069:** *Girl Looking at Landscape,* 1957, Richard Diebenkorn, oil on canvas, 59 x 60 3/8 inches, (149.9 x 153.4 cm), Gift of Mr. and Mrs. Alan H. Temple, 61.49, Collection of Whitney Museum of American Art, photograph by Geoffrey Clements, N.Y., Photograph copyright (c) 1997: Whitney Museum of American Art; **1074: (t.):** Thomas Victor; **(m.):** Photo by Paul Abdoo; **(b.):** Photo by Michael Nye; **1077:** *Passion of Paints,* Bob Peters, Exclusively represented by Applejack Licensing International; **1079:** Museo de Santa Cruz/Bridgeman Art Library, London/New York **1081:** Culver Pictures, Inc.; **1083:** *Getting Down,* Joseph Holston, 14" x 14", Courtesy of Joseph Holston (www.holstonar**(t.)**:com); **1088:** Thomas Victor; **1090:** Jeff Greenberg/ Omni–Photo Communications, Inc.; **1095:** Museum of English Rural Life/© Dorling Kindersley; **1096:** Lee Russell/CORBIS; **1097:** Jeff Greenberg/Omni–Photo Communications, Inc.; **1102:** ©Anthony Barboza/Life Magazine; **1104:** AP/Wide World Photos; **1107: (l.):** Corel Professional Photos CD–ROM™; **(r.):** Ron Watts/CORBIS; **1108–1109:** © Matt Lambert/Stone; **1114:** Prentice Hall; **1116:** *Fruit Vendor,* 1951, Olga Costa, Museo de Arte Moderno, Mexico. © Olga Costa – SOMAAP, Mexico, 1999; **1121:** Richard Bickel/CORBIS; **1124:** Andre Jenny/Focus Group/PictureQuest; **1130: (t.l.):** Shelley Rotner/Omni–Photo Communications, Inc.; **(t.r.):** Marlene Fostor; **(b.l.):** Rollie McKenna; **(b.r.):**Photo courtesy of Garrett Gongo; **1132:** Arlene Collins; **1135:** Animals Animals/©John Lemker; **1144: (t.l.):** AP/Wide World Photos; **(t.r.):** The Granger Collection, New York; **(b.l.):** © 1996 Sigrid Estrada; **(b.):**r. John Barrett/Globe Photos; **1146:** Blam, 1962,© Roy Lichtenstein, oil on canvas, 68 x 80 in.; **1149 & 1150:** Warner Bros./Photofest; **1153:** © Paul Edmondson/Stone; **1157:** Reuters/CORBIS; **1162: (t.):** AP/Wide World Photos; m. Robert Foothorap; **(b.):** Robert Severi/Getty Images; **1165:** *Biography,* 1988, Marina Gutierrez, Courtesy of the artist; **1169:** Digital Imagery ©Copyright 2001 PhotoDisc, Inc.; **1172:** Jim McHugh; **1175:** Gary Gay/The Image Bank; **1182:** Thomas Victor; **1184:** *Push to Walk,* collage 48" x 48"Phoebe Beasley; **1189:** ©Telegraph Colour Library 1998/FPG International LLC; **1196: (l.):** AP/Wide World Photos; **(r.):** Rollie McKenna; **1198:** FPG International Corp.; **1200:** ©CORBIS; **1202:** FPG International Corp.; **1204–1205:** Courtesy National Archives; **1206: (l.):** Corel Professional Photos CD–ROM™; **(r.):** Ron Watts/CORBIS; **1209 & 1210:** Stock Montage, Inc.; **1214: (t.l.):** AP/Wide World Photos; **(t.r.):** ©Nancy Crampton; **(b.l.):** Thomas Victor; **(b.r.):** Pach/Corbis– Bettmann; **1216:** *Mirror II,* George Tooker, (1920–1938), Egg tempera on gesso panel, 20x20 in., 1968.4, Gift of R. H. Donnelley Erdman (PA 1956), ©Addison Gallery of American Art, Phillips Academy, Andover, Massachusetts. All Rights Reserved.; **1219:** *Part II, The Free Man,* No. 30, *The Frederick Douglass Series,* Jacob Lawrence, Hampton University Museum, Hampton, Virginia, ©Gwendolyn Knight Lawrence, courtesy of the Jacob and Gwendolyn Lawrence Foundation; **1221:** © Pekka Parviainen/Science Photo Library/Photo Researchers, Inc.; **1226: (l.):** AP/Wide World Photos; **(r.):** UPI/CORBIS–Bettmann; **1230:** *Retroactive I,* Robert Rauschenberg, 1964, Wadsworth Atheneum, Hartford, CT, Gift of Susan Morse Hilles, ©Robert Rauschenberg/Licensed by VAGA, New York, NY; **1231: (l.):** Corel Professional Photos CD–ROM™; **(r.):** Ron Watts/CORBIS; **1233:** UPI/CORBIS–Bettmann; **1238: (t.):** Nihad Becirovic; **(m.):** Photo by Mandy Sayer; **(b.):** Thomas Victor **1240:** *The Madonna And Child,* 1990, Momodou Ceesay, Dialogue Systems, Inc.; **1243:** *Winter,* Ozz Franca , Oil, 24 x 18", Edition of 1999 s/n, Courtesy of The Hadley Companies; **1245:** Brian Parker/Tom Stack & Associates; **1254:** AP/Wide World Photos; **1255:** *The Trial of Two "Witches" at Salem, Massachusetts, in 1662,* Howard Pyle, The Granger Collection, New York; **1258:** © James Cotier/Stone; **1260:** *The Execution of the Reverend Stephen Burroughs for Witchcraft at Salem Massachusetts, in 1692,* 19th century engraving, The Granger Collection, New York; **1264:** AP/Wide World Photos; **1266–1272:** Photofest; **1277:** Musee Conde, Chantilly, France/ Bridgeman Art Library, London/New York; **1278:** Digital Imagery ©Copyright 2001 PhotoDisc, Inc.; **1283:** Photofest; **1291:** © James Cotier/Stone; **1294:** Photofest; **1296: (l.):** Corel Professional Photos CD–ROM™; **(r.):** Ron Watts/CORBIS; **1304:** Pocumtuck Valley Memorial Association, Memorial Hall Museum, Deerfield, Massachusetts; 1308: Photofest; **1315:** © James Cotier/Stone; **1319:** © Joe Sohm/Stone; **1326–1332:** Photofest; **1333:** Corel Professional Photos CD–ROM™; **1334:** Mitchell Funk/The Image Bank; **1334:** Playbill, is a registered trademark of Playbill, Inc. All rights reserved. Used by permission.; **1336:** Penguin USA; **1343:** © James Cotier/Stone; **1347 & 1350:** Photofest; **1352:** ©Reuters/Brad Rickerby/Archive Photos; **1357:** Photofest; **1368:** IT Stock/PictureQuest

Map and Art Credits: All graphic organizers: In-House Pros; All maps by Mapping Specialist, except where noted

Staff Credits: Ernie Albanese, Diane Alimena, **Rosalyn Arcilla,** Jasjit Arneja, Penny Baker, **Nancy Barker, Amy Baron,** Rachel Beckman, Betsy Bostwick, **Ellen Bowler,** Jennifer Brady, Evonne Burgess, Pradeep Byram, Rui Camarinha, **Pam Carey,** Lisa Carrillo, Jaime Cohen, Allison Cook, **Irene Ehrmann,** Leanne Esterly, Steve Frankel, Philip Fried, **Maggie Fritz,** Michael Ginsberg, **Elaine Goldman,** Patricia Hade, **Monduane Harris, Martha Heller,** Beth Hyslip, Vicki A. Kane, **Kate Krimsky,** Mary Sue Langan, Monica Lehmann, **Mary Luthi, George Lychock,** Gregory Lynch, Daniela Mastria, John McClure, Jim McDonough, Kathleen Mercandetti, Kerrie Miller, Karyl Murray, Ken Myett, Kim Ortell, Carolyn Pallof, Sal Pisano, Jackie Regan, Erin Rehill-Seker, Bruce Rolff, **Laura Ross,** Carolyn Sapontzis, Donna Schindler, Mildred Schulte, **Melissa Shustyk, Robert Siek, Rita Sullivan, Cynthia Summers,** Patrice Titterington, Elizabeth Torjussen, Jane S. Traulsen

Additional Credits: Susan C. Ball, William Bingham, Andrea Brescia, Donna Chappelle, Jennifer Ciccone, Jason Cuoco, Florrie Gadson, Judith Gaelick, Phillip Gagler, James Garratt, Allen Gold, Kristan Hoskins, Lisa Iozzia, Mohamed Kaptan, Barbara Kehr, Terry Kim, Stuart Kirschenbaum, Linda Latino, Julian Liby, Karen Mancinelli, Ginidir Marshall, Bill McAllister, Patrick J. McCarthy, Caroline McDonnell, Michael McLaughlin, Meg Montgomery, Gita Nadas, Lesley Pierson, Maureen Raymond, Rachel Ross, Lloyd Sabin, James Savakis, Donna Schindler, Debi Taffet, Elizabeth Torjussen, Ryan Vaarsi, Alfred Voto, Gina M. Wangrycht, Lindsay White

Zlata Filipovic
Cornelius Eady
Pat Mora
John Phillip Santos
Joao Magueijo
Anita Desai
Frank Kermode
Gary Soto
Walter Dean Myers
Julius Lester
Coleman Barks
Patricia McKissack
William L. Andrews
Jean Craighead George
Richard Rodriguez
Laurence Yep
Judith Ortiz Cofer
Pat Mora
Susan Power
Gretel Ehrlich
David Mamet
Jane Yolen
Richard Peck
Jon Scieszka
Jamaica Kincaid
Burton Raffel
Royall Tyler
Susan Vreeland
Jacqueline Woodson
Wayson Choy
Charles Johnson
Andrew Mishkin
Cherie Bennett
David Henry Hwang
Nell Irvin Painter
Walter Dean Myers
Chinua Achebe
Elizabeth McCracken
Frank Kermode
Anita Desai
C.J. Cherryh
Patricia McKissack
Gary Blackwood
Zlata Filipovic
Elizabeth McCracken
Jean Craighead George
Jon Scieszka
Julius Lester
Walter Dean Myers
Dean Smith
Richard Mühlberger
Pat Mora
Jamaica Kincaid
Gretel Ehrlich
Arthur Miller
Rebecca Walker
James Berry
Seamus Heaney
Joseph Bruchac
Lan Samantha Chang
Tim O'Brien
Wendy Doniger
Gretel Ehrlich
James Berry
Cornelius Eady
Arthur Miller